PETERSON'S 440 GREAT COLLEGES FOR TOP STUDENTS

2009

PETERSON'S

A **nelnet** COMPANY

PETERSON'S

A (n)elnet COMPANY

About Peterson's, a Nelnet company

Peterson's (www.petersons.com) is a leading provider of education information and advice, with books and online resources focusing on education search, test preparation, and financial aid. Its Web site offers searchable databases and interactive tools for contacting educational institutions, online practice tests and instruction, and planning tools for securing financial aid. Peterson's serves 110 million education consumers annually.

For more information, contact Peterson's, 2000 Lenox Drive, Lawrenceville, NJ 08648; 800-338-3282; or find us on the World Wide Web at www.petersons.com/about.

Editor: Fern A. Oram; Production Editor: Mark D. Snider; Copy Editor: Michael Haines; Research Project Manager: Daniel Margolin; Research Associate: Cathleen Fee; Programmer: Phyllis Johnson; Manufacturing Manager: Ray Golaszewski; Composition Manager: Linda M. Williams; Client Relations Representatives: Janet Garwo, Mimi Kaufman, Danielle Vreeland

ISSN 0887-0152
ISBN-13: 978-0-7689-2542-5
ISBN-10: 0-7689-2542-8

Printed in the United States

10 9 8 7 6 5 4 3 2 1   10 09 08

Twenty-eighth Edition

CONTENTS

A NOTE FROM THE PETERSON'S EDITORS

WHY SHOULD YOU CONSIDER A COMPETITIVE COLLEGE?

Excellent colleges typically take great care in admitting students. For them, selecting the entering class is, as Bill Fitzsimmons, Dean of Admissions and Financial Aid at Harvard University, describes it: a process of "sculpting" the best possible class from the pool of qualified applicants. The goal of an admission committee is to bring together a community of students who can learn from one another, each one bringing their own particular talents, skills, and experiences that will contribute to the development of all the others.

Students who have excelled in high school want to go on excelling. They need an educational environment that will push them, test them, help them go beyond their past accomplishments. They require a college that "fits," one that will help them develop into what they can uniquely become.

At the start, you'll likely find that everyone's list of "best" colleges is very much alike. Except for adding the most popular regional schools or schools serving an unusual interest or a family's traditional alma mater, your initial list probably will include the Ivy League schools and one or more of up to a dozen other similarly prestigious colleges and universities. The one quality shared by these schools is prestige. It certainly can be argued that it helps to graduate from a prestigious college. But prestige is a limited and very expensive factor upon which to base one's college choice. There are truly excellent college choices beyond the eight Ivy League schools and a newsstand magazine's designated top schools. One of these "other" college choices could very well be the best fit for your particular requirements and goals.

We make only one assumption in this guide. This is that the most influential factor in determining your experience on campus is the other students you will find there. In selecting colleges for inclusion in this book, we measure the competitiveness of the admission environment at colleges. This is measured over a meaningful period of time by entering-class statistics, such as GPA, class rank, and test scores. The 440 colleges selected for inclusion in this book routinely attract and admit an above-average share of the nation's high-achieving students.

Peterson's publishes a full line of resources to help guide you and your family through the college admission process. Peterson's publications can be found at your local bookstore, library, and high school guidance office, and you can access us online at **www. petersons.com/colleges**.

We welcome any comments or suggestions you may have about this publication and invite you to complete our online survey at **www.petersons.com/ booksurvey**. Or you can fill out the survey at the back of this book, tear it out, and mail it to us at:

> Publishing Department
> Peterson's, a Nelnet company
> 2000 Lenox Drive
> Lawrenceville, NJ 08648

Your feedback will help us to make your educational dreams possible.

Selecting a college is a great adventure, and colleges will be pleased to know that Peterson's helped you in your selection. Admissions staff members are more than happy to answer questions, address specific problems, and help in any way they can. The editors at Peterson's wish you great success in your college search!

GETTING INTO A COMPETITIVE COLLEGE

UNDERSTANDING THE COLLEGE ADMISSION PROCESS

TED SPENCER
Associate Vice Provost and Executive Director of Undergraduate Admissions at the University of Michigan

The process you are about to begin, that of choosing a college, can be very challenging, sometimes frustrating, but most often rewarding. As Executive Director of Undergraduate Admissions at a large, selective university, I would like to provide some basic information about the admission process that should help you get into the college of your choice. Although each competitive college or university has its own distinctive qualities and goals, the process of applying to them is strikingly similar. The following will give you the basic information you need to help you plan and apply to college.

GATHERING INFORMATION

How do you get the information you need to choose a college? Although colleges publish volumes of information about themselves that they are willing to mail or give out in person, another way to find out about them is through a guide such as this one.

The major difference between the college-published materials and this guide is that the colleges present only the most appealing picture of themselves and are perhaps, then, somewhat less objective. As a student seeking information about college, you should review both the information provided in guides like this one and the information sent by the colleges. Your goal should be to use all of the available literature to assist you in developing your list of the top five or ten colleges in which you are interested.

Chances are that if you are a top student and you have taken the PSAT, SAT, SAT Subject Tests, ACT, or AP (Advanced Placement) tests, you will receive a great deal of material directly from many colleges and universities. Colleges purchase lists of names of students taking these exams and then screen the list for students they think will be most successful at their institutions. Some colleges will also automatically mail course catalogs, posters, departmental brochures, and pamphlets, as well as DVDs. If you do not receive this information but would like a sample, write or call that particular college.

My advice is to take a look at the materials you receive and then use them to help you decide (if you don't already know) about the type of college you would like to attend. Allow the materials to help you narrow your list of top schools by comparing key facts and characteristics.

OTHER HELPFUL SOURCES

Published information about colleges, printed by the colleges, is certainly an important way to narrow your choices. But there are other means of learning more about colleges and universities:

- *High School Counselors.* Most high school counselors have established positive relationships with the college representatives in your state as well as with out-of-state universities where large numbers of their students apply. As you attempt to gain more information while narrowing your choice of colleges, the high school counselor can give you a fairly accurate assessment of colleges to which you will have the best chance of gaining admission.

- *Parents.* Because most prospective students and their parents are at that stage in life in which they view issues in different ways, students tend to be reluctant to ask parents' opinions about college choices. However, you may find that parents are very helpful because they often are actively gathering information about the colleges that they feel are best suited for you. And not only do they gather information—you can be sure that they have thoroughly read the piles of literature that colleges have mailed to you. Ask your parents questions about what they have read and also about the colleges from which they graduated. As alumni of schools on your list, parents can be a very valuable resource.

- *College Day/Night/Fairs Visitation.* One of the best ways to help narrow your college choices is to meet with a person representing a college while they are visiting your area or high school. In fact, most admission staff members spend a good portion of the late spring and fall visiting high schools and attending college fairs. In some cases, college fairs feature students, faculty members, and alumni. Before attending one of these sessions, you should prepare a list of questions you would like to ask the representatives. Most students want to know about five major areas:

1. Academic preparation
2. The admission process
3. Financial aid
4. Social life
5. Job preparation

Most college representatives can be extremely helpful in addressing these questions as well as the many others that you may have. It is then up to you to decide if their answers fit your criteria of the college you are seeking.

- *Alumni.* For many schools, alumni are a very important part of the admission process. In some cases, alumni conduct interviews and even serve as surrogate admission officers, particularly when admission office staff cannot travel. As recent graduates, alumni can talk about their own experience and can give balance to the materials you have received from the college or university.

- *Campus Visits.* Finally, try to schedule a campus visit as part of your information-gathering process in an effort to make sure that the reality lives up to whatever material you've read. Most colleges and universities provide daily campus tours to both prospective and admitted students. The tours for prospective students are generally set up to help you answer questions about the following: class size and student-to-teacher ratio; size of the library, residence halls, and computer centers; registration and faculty advising; and retention, graduation rates, and career placement planning. Since the tours may not cover

everything you came prepared to ask about, be sure to ask questions of as many staff, students, and faculty members as possible before leaving the campus.

THE ADMISSION PROCESS

ADMISSION CRITERIA

After you go through the process of selecting a college or narrowing your choices to a few schools, the admission process now focuses on you—your academic record and skills—and judgment will be passed on these pieces of information for admission to a particular school. The first four things you should find out about each college on your priority list are the admission criteria—what it takes to get in:

1. Does the college or university require standardized tests—the ACT or SAT? Do they prefer one or the other, or will they accept either?

2. Do they require SAT Subject Tests and, if so, which ones?

3. Are Advanced Placement scores accepted and, if so, what are the minimums needed?

4. In terms of grades and class rank, what is the profile of a typical entering student?

It is also important to find out which type of admission notification system the college uses—rolling or deferred admission. On a rolling system, you find out your status within several weeks of applying; with the deferred system, notification is generally made in the spring. For the most part, public universities and colleges use rolling admission and private colleges generally use deferred admission.

THE APPLICATION

The application is the primary vehicle used to introduce yourself to the admission office. As with any introduction, you want to make a good first impression. The first thing you should do in presenting your application is to find out what the college or university wants from you. This means you should read the application carefully to learn the following:

- Is there an application fee and, if so, how much is it?

- Is there a deadline and, if so, when is it?

- What standardized tests are required?
- Is an essay required?
- Is an interview required?
- Should you send letters of recommendation?
- How long will it take to find out the admission decision?
- What other things can you do to improve your chances for admission?

My advice is to submit your application early. It does not guarantee admission, but it is much better than submitting it late or near the deadline. Also, don't assume that colleges using rolling admission will always have openings close to their deadlines. Regardless of when you submit it, make sure that the application has all the information that is requested.

TRANSCRIPTS

While all of the components of the application are extremely important in the admission process, perhaps the single most important item is your transcript because it tells what courses you took, which courses were college-preparatory and challenging, class rank, and grades and test scores.

- *Required Course Work.* Generally speaking, most colleges look at the high school transcript to see if the applicant followed a college-preparatory track while in high school. So, if you have taken four years of English, math, natural science, social sciences, and foreign language, you are on the right track. Many selective colleges require four years of English; three years each of math, natural science, and social science; and two years of a foreign language. It is also true that some selective colleges believe students who are interested in majoring in math and science need more than the minimum requirements in those areas.
- *Challenging Courses.* As college admission staff members continue to evaluate your transcript, they also look to see how demanding your course load has been during high school. If the high school offered Advanced Placement or Honors courses, the expectation of most selective colleges is that students will have taken seven or more honors classes or four or more AP courses during their four years in high school. However, if you

do elect to take challenging courses, it is also important that you make good grades in those courses. Quite often, students ask, "If I take Honors and AP courses and get a 'C,' does that count more than getting a 'B' or higher in a strictly college-prep course?" It's a difficult question to answer, because too many C's and B's can outweigh mostly A's. On the other hand, students who take the more challenging courses will be better prepared to take the more rigorous courses in college. Consequently, many colleges will give extra consideration when making their selections to the students who take the more demanding courses.

- *Transcript Trends.* Because the courses you take in high school are such a critical part of the college decision-making process, your performance in those courses indicates to colleges whether you are following an upward or downward trend. Beginning with the ninth grade, admission staff look at your transcript to see if you have started to develop good academic habits. In general, when colleges review your performance in the ninth grade, they are looking to see if you are in the college-preparatory track.

By sophomore year, students should begin choosing more demanding courses and become more involved in extracurricular activities. This will show that you are beginning to learn how to balance your academic and extracurricular commitments. Many admission officers consider the sophomore year to be the most critical and telling year for a student's future success.

The junior year is perhaps the second-most-important year in high school. The grades you earn and the courses you take will help to reinforce the trend you began in your sophomore year. At the end of your junior year, many colleges will know enough about the type of student you are to make their admission decision.

The upward and positive trend must continue, however, during your senior year. Many selective schools do not use senior grades in making their admission decisions. However, almost all review the final transcript, so your last year needs to show a strong performance to the end. The research shows that students who finish their senior year with strong grades will start their freshman year in college with strong grades.

THE APPLICATION REVIEW PROCESS

WHAT'S NEXT?

At this point, you have done all you can do. So you might as well sit back and relax, if that's possible, and wait for the letters to come in the mail. Hopefully, if you've evaluated all the college materials you were sent earlier and you prepared your application carefully and sent it to several colleges, you will be admitted to either your first, second, or third choice. It may help your peace of mind, however, to know what happens to your application after the materials have been submitted.

Once your application is received by the admission office, it is reviewed, in most cases by noncounseling staff, to determine if you have completed the application properly. If items are missing, you will receive a letter of notification identifying additional information that must be provided. Be sure to send any additional or missing information the college requests back to them as soon as possible. Once your application is complete, it is then ready for the decision process.

READER REVIEW

The process by which the decision is finalized varies from school to school. Most private colleges and universities use a system in which each application is read by two or more admission staff members. In some cases, faculty members are also readers. If all of the readers agree on the decision, a letter is sent. Under this system, if the readers do not agree, the application will be reviewed by a committee or may be forwarded to an associate dean, dean, or director of admission for the final decision. One advantage to this process is that each applicant is reviewed by several people, thereby eliminating bias.

COMMITTEE REVIEW

At some universities, a committee reviews every application. Under that system, a committee member is assigned a number of applications to present. It is that member's responsibility to prepare background information on each applicant and then present the file to the committee for discussion and a vote. In this process, every applicant is voted on.

COUNSELOR REVIEW

The review process that many selective public institutions use is one in which the counselor responsible for a particular school or geographical territory makes the final decision. In this case, the counselor who makes the admission decision is also the one who identified and recruited the student, thereby lending a more personal tone to the process.

COMPUTER-GENERATED REVIEW

Many large state universities that process nearly 20,000 applications a year have developed computer-generated guidelines to admit their applicants. If applicants meet the required GPA and test scores, they are immediately notified of the decision.

A WORD OF ADVICE

When you start the admission process, do so with the idea of exploring as many college opportunities as you can. From the very beginning, avoid focusing on just one college or, for that matter, one type of college. Look at private, public, large, small, highly selective, selective—in short, a variety of colleges and universities. Take advantage of every available resource, including students, parents, counselors, and college materials, in order to help identify the colleges that will be a great fit for you.

Finally, the most important thing you can do is to build a checklist of what you want out of the college experience and then match your list with one of the many wonderful colleges and universities just waiting for you to enroll.

CRAFTING A COMPETITIVE COLLEGE APPLICATION OR WHAT CAN I DO TO GET IN?

Not to discourage you about applying to competitive colleges, but the number of students who are over-the-top qualified to get into these schools versus the number of available slots is mind-boggling! Recently, the University of Southern California had 34,000 applications for 2,700 freshman seats, while the eight Ivy League schools' admission rate is just below 10 percent. (Thirty percent is considered competitive—get the picture?)

Mickey Gilbert, Guidance Counselor at Passaic High School in New Jersey, throws out a few figures to his students to help them understand the competition: There are about 32,000 high schools in the United States and roughly 4,000 high schools outside the country with students who apply to U.S. colleges. Take the top ten students from each class—those who are the academically gifted and who have done everything, been everything, and won everything. Multiply those ten students from each class by the 36,000 worldwide high schools and you get 360,000 students who are in the pool of well-qualified applicants. Granted, all high schools are not alike, but this gives you an idea of what you face if you are applying to a competitive school.

WHY SO MUCH COMPETITION?

THE SHEER NUMBER OF WELL-QUALIFIED APPLICANTS

"Twenty years ago it was a student's market," notes Kathy Cleaver, Co-Director of College Counseling at Durham Academy, a private high school in North Carolina. Back then, students could pretty much pick and choose. Not anymore. Today, more exceptional students are applying to more competitive colleges.

However, colleges haven't fully increased the size of their freshman classes to meet the demand, nor do they want to. Like other competitive schools, the University of Denver is committed to keeping classes small so that teachers can be involved with their students, instead of lecturing to thousands. The University of Southern California also faces the same dilemma—whether or not to increase the number of classes and faculty members.

"If we're already going 8 a.m. to 6 p.m., Monday through Friday, and are busy on weekends, there are finite limitations to how many people a professor can teach, how many sections we can offer," comments Dr. Katharine Harrington, Dean of Admissions and Financial Aid at USC.

THE PRESTIGE FACTOR

"Competition has increased for spaces because more students think that certain schools are their only road to success," observes Doris Davis, Cornell University's Associate Provost for Admissions and Enrollment. Many top students have a short list of possibilities and won't consider schools they think aren't up to their expectations. Their list is based only on the name of the university.

JUST HOW BRILLIANT ARE YOU?

Once the "most" brilliant applicants are chosen, admitting committees are faced with choosing from the "less" brilliant applicants. You could have done exceptionally well in your high school, but you're up against many others who are more brilliant than you.

"The worst part of this job is that we have to say 'no' to three out of four applicants because we can't accept all the students who can do the work," says Harrington. "The hard choices come at the margin."

GETTING ADMITTED ISN'T ALL ABOUT GRADES OR ACTIVITIES

Don't assume that if you have achieved great grades and test scores, done all the activities that admissions officers like to see, and written a dazzling essay, but you still weren't admitted, there's something wrong with you. There are other factors besides GPAs that count. Some admission officers say they "sculpt" or "shape" each freshman class. Schools don't just plug in grade averages and take the top students to fill their quota.

"Schools want to build racial, socioeconomic, religious, and geographic diversity into each class," says Cleaver. For instance, a prestigious school on the east coast might choose a student from Montana over someone with a higher GPA who lives in Massachusetts.

Those deciding whether you should or shouldn't be admitted are looking at the big picture of college life—not just what you'll learn in the classroom but also what you'll learn outside the classroom.

"A healthy community is one that is integrated along a number of points. We want to shape a class by identifying students who, together, will build a strong community," says Davis. "Students learn from each other. That's why it's so important to us."

Being exposed to people who look different, think differently, and act differently creates a "fabric or a stew," observes Cleaver, who uses the illustration to show that a greater variety of students becomes a flavorful and rich class. Admissions are looking for the mix of students from all kinds of backgrounds to give each incoming class the experience of studying, living, and playing with people who aren't all the same.

SO, HOW DO YOU GIVE YOURSELF THE EDGE?

Granted, the talk so far has been somewhat negative and it might sound like your chances are out of your control. That is not so. You do have control over a great deal of the process of getting into a competitive college.

HAVE YOU TAKEN CHALLENGING CLASSES?

Not all GPA's are equal to the people deciding to admit you. Admitting committees look at overall trends in your grades. Maybe you had a 3.5 GPA your first two years of high school, but in your junior and senior years, you have a 3.9 GPA.

"That's an upward trend that can help you if you're competing for those last spots in a freshman class at a competitive college," observes Todd Rinehart, Assistant Vice Chancellor/Director of Admission at the University of Denver.

ARE YOU LETTING OTHERS DECIDE WHICH COLLEGE IS BEST FOR YOU?

This includes your parents, your best friend who is applying to "The Best University," and your uncle who went to an Ivy League school, not to mention your own expectations that demand only one institution or else. When Harrington visits high schools to talk about the college application process, she makes sure parents know they can help facilitate their children getting into college, but the college choice is not about parents' bragging rights to their co-workers.

ARE YOU ONLY CONSIDERING THE NAME?

The schools heading the latest magazine list comprise a small percentage of colleges in the United States. Many outstanding students don't take full advantage of the tremendous range of schools but instead set their sights on only a few names. Do you assume smart, talented students only attend certain schools? Broaden your horizons and you'll find dozens of schools that match your needs.

"Look at your passion and what a school can offer you," advises Gilbert. He recalls one student who loved Civil War history and wanted to apply only to a competitive school that offered little to do with his fascination. Gilbert directed him to a small college that wasn't a brand name but was located in Gettysburg, right in the middle of his favorite period of history! He'll point another student who is leaning toward architecture to a school that isn't super competitive but has a terrific architecture program. "It's what you want to do, not its name," he says.

When counseling her high school students, Cleaver tells them that each college has a personality. Some get their identity from sports; others are more academically competitive, with a constant focus on grades. Some revolve around Greek life or religion or are known for their politically charged environment and student activism. Target a school because it matches your personality.

"If you bring a wonderful set of skills or a mindset that would strengthen a program, it will more easily help the admission office see why you would be a strong student at their institution," says Cleaver. Admitting committees want to find the best fit between your goals and their institution.

"We want students to find the best place for them," says Davis. "My goal is to make sure students are a good match with us."

DOES YOUR APPLICATION TELL WHO YOU ARE?

If your application speaks clearly about you, the admission people around the table (who have read hundreds of applications) will see you as a whole person, including your academic capabilities, what interests you, and what makes you unique. An application is the culmination of all the pieces that make up who you are.

"We're looking at your essay, your letters of recommendation, your responses to the questions on the application, your academics. If it all comes together, we know you're on to something," says Davis.

DOES YOUR ESSAY REVEAL WHAT MAKES YOU TICK?

Cleaver compares the essay to a hologram that stands on the table in front of the admitting committee to show you as a real person. Your essay can make you stand out from the student whose application they read half an hour ago. She offers an example of two essays. The first starts out, "I've done rock climbing 20 hours a week for the last three years." The second begins with, "I'm standing on a ledge, looking down hundreds of feet and wondering how I got there."

"Think about what you want someone to know about you," she advises. "Rather than repeat your grades or activities, show how you are a hard worker, overcame adversity, learned from failure, or faced your fears."

DO YOUR ACTIVITIES JUMP OFF THE PAGE?

Authenticity is what admitting committees look for when reading about your extracurricular activities. Just listing them doesn't tell who you are. Sure, you might have joined ten different clubs, volunteered at a soup kitchen for one semester and a hospital the next, and collected cans to save the environment, but that doesn't show your commitment. This is the time to brag about yourself, to bring out times when

you were responsible, whether it was as chairman of the clean-up committee or when you took care of a 4-year-old cousin for a summer.

DID YOU CHOOSE THE RIGHT TEACHER TO WRITE YOUR LETTER OF RECOMMENDATION?

The "right" teacher isn't necessarily the teacher who gave you the highest grades. Choose someone who understands what motivates you. Maybe you got a B in math because you were overcoming a tremendous challenge at the time and that teacher saw you persevere. Maybe it was someone who helped you develop leadership qualities and can write about how you will be an asset to a college.

"Ask a teacher who can write about both your academic interests and your skills," advises Cleaver.

AND HOW DO YOU LOSE THAT EDGE?

NOT HITTING THE SEND BUTTON

It can happen to the best students. You're rushing to get out those six applications to meet the deadline. You've made sure your information is correct, filled in the checklist, done the spell-check, and when everything was done, you sat back and relaxed. Sorry to say, you forgot to actually submit it! With more than 80 percent of applications submitted online, it's an easy mistake to make. So, call a week after you (think you) submitted your application to verify its receipt with the admission office.

HIRING SOMEONE TO WRITE YOUR APPLICATION ESSAY

Too bad the same person didn't write your SAT essay! Admission departments compare the essay you wrote for them and your SAT essay and can easily tell if the two match. It's okay to have your essay proofed by someone, but you should be the only author.

ALL MY LIFE I'VE WANTED TO GO TO (FILL IN THE BLANK)

Except the school you're applying to doesn't have that name! You can start with a standard application because much of the information is applicable to multiple schools, but make sure to customize each application—and then double-check everything to make sure all the school name references are correct. This is a more common mistake than you think.

Fancy Folders and Colored Paper Don't Impress

In fact, by the time your application gets to the people who will read it, they have probably already put it in a standard folder. The presentation of your application should concentrate on content, spelling, and grammar, not the packaging.

Forget Clever and Cute

The applicant who had a chair delivered to the admissions office with the attached note, "Hope this reserves a chair for me," was creative, but no one was impressed. Same with the shoe another student sent saying, "Now that I have one foot in the door." Then there was the essay someone wrote on a football. Every admission office has stories of the crazy things applicants do to try to stand out. It isn't effective. Show your creativity and resourcefulness in presenting a detailed application and well-written essay.

Applying to Professional Colleges for Art and Music

Theresa Bedoya
Vice President and Dean of Admissions and Financial Aid, Maryland Institute, College of Art

The term "competitive" will have a different meaning if you are applying to a professional college specializing in art or music. The goal of selective art and music colleges is to admit students of extraordinary talent. Since you are using this resource as part of your college search, you most likely have distinguished yourself academically. But to gain admission to the music and art colleges listed in this guide, you will also need to be competitive in your achievements in the arts.

ADMISSION CRITERIA

In order to choose the most talented students from those who apply, most professional art and music colleges require evidence of talent, skill, ability, experience, and desire as demonstrated in an audition or by a portfolio of artwork. Each art and music college has expectations and academic requirements particular to the program of study you choose.

Admission will be based upon the review of traditional criteria such as your grade point average, level of course work, test scores, essays, and interviews. However, for most professional colleges, the evaluation of your portfolio or your audition will supersede the review of all other criteria for admission. (Many visual arts colleges even prescreen potential applicants through review of the portfolio prior to application in order to determine eligibility for admission. This process, which occurs early in the senior year, allows students the opportunity to gain valuable guidance early in the admission process. It also creates a more "acceptable" pool of applicants and is the reason that acceptance rates at many visual arts colleges appear to be higher than other selective

institutions.) In some cases, the evaluation of your talent and academic achievement will be given equal weight.

In contrast, most comprehensive colleges and universities offering majors in art and music will rely on academic criteria to make an admission decision. The portfolio or audition, if required, will play a secondary role. You should take these factors into account when deciding whether to apply to art and music schools or to colleges and universities that offer art and music programs.

PREPARING FOR YOUR PORTFOLIO REVIEW OR AUDITION

If you are interested in the visual arts, you should gain as much studio experience as possible in order to develop a strong portfolio. Take full advantage of your high school art program and enroll in Saturday or summer classes or seek private tutoring. Exhibit your artwork when the opportunity is provided. Become better informed as an artist by studying art history and the works of contemporary artists.

If you plan to study music, remember that experience and confidence need to be clearly evident in your audition. Therefore, become involved as much as possible in your own high school music activities as well as local, district, and state youth orchestras, choirs, and performance ensembles. The more you perform and study, the more confident you will be on stage.

Contact the schools to which you are applying early in the process to learn how and when they will receive your portfolio or conduct your audition.

PAYING FOR COLLEGE

DON BETTERTON
Former Director of Financial Aid at Princeton University

Regardless of which college a student chooses, higher education requires a major investment of time, energy, and money. By taking advantage of a variety of available resources, most students can bring the education that is right for them within reach.

A NOTE OF ENCOURAGEMENT

While there is no denying that the cost of an education at some competitive colleges can be high, it is important to recognize that, although the rate of increase in costs in recent years has outpaced gains in family income, there are more options available to pay for college than ever before.

Many families find it is economically wise to spread costs out over a number of years by borrowing money for college. A significant amount of government money, both federal and state, is available to students. Moreover, colleges themselves have expanded their own student aid efforts considerably. In spite of rapidly increasing costs, most competitive colleges are still able to provide financial aid to all admitted students with demonstrated need.

In addition, many colleges have developed ways to assist families who are not eligible for need-based assistance. These include an increasing number of merit scholarships as well as various forms of parental loans. There also are a number of organizations that give merit awards based on a student's academic record, talent, or special characteristics. Thus, regardless of your family's income, if you are academically qualified and knowledgeable about the many different sources of aid, you should be able to attend the college of your choice.

ESTIMATING COSTS

If you have not yet settled on specific colleges and you would like to begin early financial planning, estimate a budget. As reported in *Trends in College Pricing 2007* (College Board) the average New England region private college costs for 2007–08

include tuition and fees of $30,154, room and board $10,232, and other costs of $2623, for total expenses of $43,009. Yet in the southwest, private school total costs are just under $30,200. Nationally, 2007–08 total costs at private school averaged about $35,300. Given this rather wide variation, it is best to check with each school you are considering. You can assume a 5 percent cost increase each year.

IDENTIFYING RESOURCES

There are essentially four sources of funds you can use to pay for college:

1 Money from your parents

2 Need-based scholarships or grants from federal and/or state programs, a college, or outside organization

3 Your own contribution from savings, loans, and jobs

4 Other forms of assistance unrelated to demonstrated financial need

All of these are considered by the financial aid office, and the aid "package" given to a student after the parental contribution has been determined usually consists of a combination of scholarships, loans, and campus work.

THE PARENTAL CONTRIBUTION

The financial aid policies of most colleges are based on the assumption that parents should contribute as much as they reasonably can to the education expenses of their children. The amount of this contribution varies greatly, according to a family's current financial situation.

Because there is no limit on aid eligibility based solely on income, the best rule of thumb is *apply for financial aid if there is any reasonable doubt about your ability to meet college costs*. Since it is generally true that applying for financial aid does not affect a student's chances of being admitted (known as "need-blind" admission), any candidate for admission should apply for aid if his or her family feels they will be unable to pay the entire cost of attendance. (In spite of considerable publicity on the subject, there are still only a handful of competitive colleges that practice need-sensitive admissions.)

Application for aid is made by completing the Free Application for Federal Student Aid (FAFSA). In addition, many competitive colleges will require you to also file a separate application called PROFILE®, since they need more detailed information to award their own funds. The financial aid section of a college's admission information booklet will tell you which financial aid application is required, when it should be filed, and whether a separate aid form of the college's own design is also necessary.

All colleges use the same government formula (the Federal Methodology) to determine eligibility for federal and state student aid. This process of coming up with an expected contribution from you (the student) and your parents is called "need analysis." The information on the FAFSA—parental and student income and assets, the number of family members, and the number attending college as well as other variables—is analyzed to derive the Expected Family Contribution (EFC).

You can estimate how much your parents might be asked to contribute for college by consulting the "Approximate Expected Family Contribution Chart" at the end of this article. Keep in mind that the actual parental contribution is determined on campus by a financial aid officer, using the government formula as a guideline.

Competitive colleges that also require the PROFILE will have at their disposal information they will analyze in addition to what is reported on the FAFSA. The net result of this further examination (for example, adding the value of the family home to the equation) will usually increase the expected parental contribution compared to the Federal Methodology.

Parental Borrowing
Some families who are judged to have sufficient resources to be able to finance their children's college costs find that lack of cash at any moment prevents

them from paying college bills without difficulty. Other families prefer to use less current income by extending their payments over more than four years. In both instances, these families rely on borrowing to assist with college payments. Each year parental loans become a more important form of college financing.

The Federal PLUS Program (PLUS), part of the Federal Family Education Loan Program and the Direct Loan Program, is designed to help both aid and non-aid families. It allows parents to pay their share of education costs by borrowing at a reasonable interest rate, with the backing of the federal government. These loans are available through both the Direct Loan (DL) program, administered at the college or university, and the Federal Family Education Loan Program (FFELP), administered through banks and financial institutions. For 2007–08, the interest rate for Federal PLUS loans is fixed at 8.5 percent and for Direct PLUS Loans it is fixed at 7.9 percent. Interest is charged on the loan from the date of the first disbursement until the loan is paid. Many competitive colleges, state governments, and commercial lenders also have their own parental loan programs patterned along the lines of PLUS. For more information about parent loans for students, contact a college financial aid office or your state higher education department.

NEED-BASED SCHOLARSHIP OR GRANT ASSISTANCE
Need-based aid is primarily available from federal and state governments and from colleges themselves. It is not necessary for a student to apply directly for a particular scholarship at a college; the financial aid office will match an eligible applicant with the appropriate fund.

The Federal Pell Grant is by far the largest single form of federal student assistance; an estimated 5.3 million students receive awards annually. Families with incomes of up to $45,000 (often higher when other family members are in college or family assets are relatively low) may be eligible for grants up to $4310 for the 2007–08 award year. By filing the FAFSA, you automatically apply for the Federal Pell Grant and the Federal Supplemental Educational Opportunity Grant. Students eligible for a Federal Pell Grant who complete a rigorous high school program (as defined by their state) may be eligible for an Academic Competitiveness Grant ($750 first year; $1300 second year). Federal Pell Grant students who major in science, math, and certain foreign languages and maintain a 3.0 GPA may be eligible for a SMART Grant ($4000 a year for up to 2 years). Further information is available from the financial aid office.

Most state-administered financial aid programs use the FAFSA as their application form. In general, state aid programs are usually not portable, meaning that they cannot be used out-of-state. Check with your state higher education department for additional information on application procedures and restrictions.

THE STUDENT'S OWN CONTRIBUTION

All undergraduates, not only those who apply for financial aid, can assume responsibility for meeting a portion of their college expenses by borrowing, working during the academic year and the summer, and contributing a portion of their savings. Many private colleges require aid recipients to provide a "self-help" contribution before awarding grant and scholarship money because they believe students should pay a reasonable share of their own education costs.

Student Loans

Virtually every student will be able to borrow to help pay for college. Colleges administer three types of loans (all backed by the federal government):

1. The Direct Stafford Loan
2. The Federal Family Education Loan (FFEL) Stafford Loan
3. The Federal Perkins Loan

Students must demonstrate financial need to be eligible for the Federal Perkins Loan. While every student is eligible for the Stafford Loan programs, financial need must be demonstrated to have the interest on the loan subsidized by the federal government.

Note: Rather than providing FFEL Stafford Loans, some colleges have made arrangements to participate in the Direct Stafford Loan program. Under the Direct Loan program, the U.S. Department of Education serves as the lender, while under the FFELP, students and parents deal with a private lender, usually a bank or credit union. As far as the student is concerned, the loan terms are essentially the same. Once you have selected your college, the financial aid office will guide you through the process.

Summer Employment

All students, whether or not they are receiving financial aid, should plan to work during the summer months. Students may be expected to save from $800 to $1850 before their freshman year and $1500 to $2550 each summer while enrolled in college. It is worthwhile for a student to begin working while in high school to increase the chance of finding summer employment during college vacations.

Term-Time Employment

Colleges have student employment offices that find jobs for students during the school year. Aid recipients on the Federal Work-Study Program receive priority in placement, but once they have been assisted, non-aid students are helped as well. Some jobs relate closely to academic interests; others should be viewed as a source of income rather than intellectual stimulation. A standard 8- to 15-hour-per-week job does not normally interfere with academic work or extracurricular activities and results in approximately $1500 to $2500 in earnings during the academic year.

Student Savings

Student assets accumulated prior to starting college are available to help pay college bills. The need-analysis system expects 20 percent of each year's student savings to go toward college expenses. This source can often be quite substantial, particularly when families have accumulated large sums in the student's name (or in a trust fund with the student as the beneficiary). If you have a choice whether to keep college savings in the parents' name or the student's name, you should realize that the contribution rate on parental assets can never be more than 5.6 percent, compared to 20 percent for the student's savings.

AID NOT REQUIRING NEED AS AN ELIGIBILITY CRITERION

There are scholarships available to students whether or not they are eligible for need-based financial aid. Awards based on merit are given by certain state scholarship programs, and National Merit Scholarship winners usually receive a $2500 stipend regardless of family financial circumstances. Scholarships and prizes are also awarded by community organizations and other local groups. In addition, some parents receive tuition payments for their children as employment benefits. Most colleges offer merit scholarships to a limited group of highly qualified applicants. The selection of recipients for such awards depends on unusual talent in a specific area or on overall academic excellence.

The Reserve Officers' Training Corps sponsors an extensive scholarship program that pays for tuition and books and provides an expense allowance of $300 a month for the first school year and increasing each subsequent year. The Army, Air Force, and Navy/Marine Corps have ROTC units at many colleges.

High school guidance offices have brochures describing ROTC application procedures. Since each branch of the service has a number of incentive programs, check with your ROTC recruiter for more information.

Students are encouraged to aggressively seek out private sources of financial aid. Many books are available, including *Peterson's Scholarships, Grants & Prizes*. Peterson's Web site, www.petersons.com, has scholarship search features and links to other financial aid-related topics.

Aid recipients are required to notify the college financial aid office about outside awards, as colleges take into consideration grants from all sources in developing the financial aid package for their students.

A SIMPLE METHOD FOR ESTIMATING EXPECTED FAMILY CONTRIBUTION

The chart that follows will enable you to make an approximation of the yearly amount the federal financial aid need-analysis system will expect you to pay for college.

To use the chart, you need to work with your family's income, assets, and size of your family. Read the instructions below and enter the proper amounts in the spaces provided.

1. Parents' total income before taxes

   A. Adjusted gross income (equivalent to tax return entry; use actual or estimated) _____A

   B. Nontaxable income (Social Security benefits, child support, welfare, etc.) _____B

   Total Income: A + B _____ ①

2. Parents' total assets

   C. Total of cash, savings, and checking accounts _____C

   D. Total value of investments (stocks, bonds, real estate other than home, etc.) _____D

   Total Assets: C + D _____ ②

3. Family size (include student, parents, other dependent children, and other dependents) _____③

Now find the figures on the "Approximate Expected Family Contribution Chart" that correspond to your entries in ①, ②, and ③ to determine the approximate expected parental contribution, interpolating as necessary.

4. Estimated parental contribution from chart _____④

If there will be more than one family member in college half-time or more, divide the figure above by the number in college.

5. Estimated parental contribution for each person in college _____⑤

6. Student's savings _____ × .20 =_____ ⑥

7. Finally, add the estimated parent contribution in ⑤ and the estimated student contribution in ⑥ to arrive at the total Expected Family Contribution _____⑦

This number can be compared to college costs to determine an approximate level of need.

APPROXIMATE EXPECTED FAMILY CONTRIBUTION CHART

		Income Before Taxes								
Assets		$20,000	30,000	40,000	50,000	60,000	70,000	80,000	90,000	100,000
$20,000										
FAMILY SIZE	3	$0	160	1,800	3,500	5,800	9,100	12,600	14,100	17,400
	4	0	0	850	2,500	4,400	7,100	10,600	12,000	15,300
	5	0	0	0	1,600	3,300	5,500	8,600	10,100	13,400
	6	0	0	0	600	2,200	4,100	6,600	7,900	11,200
$30,000										
FAMILY SIZE	3	$0	160	1,800	3,500	5,800	9,100	12,600	14,100	17,400
	4	0	0	850	2,500	4,400	7,100	10,600	12,000	15,300
	5	0	0	0	1,600	3,300	5,500	8,600	10,100	13,400
	6	0	0	0	600	2,200	4,100	6,600	7,900	11,200
$40,000										
FAMILY SIZE	3	$0	160	1,800	3,500	5,800	9,100	12,600	14,100	17,400
	4	0	0	850	2,500	4,400	7,100	10,600	12,000	15,300
	5	0	0	0	1,600	3,300	5,500	8,600	10,100	13,400
	6	0	0	0	600	2,200	4,100	6,600	7,900	11,200
$50,000										
FAMILY SIZE	3	$0	340	2,000	3,800	6,200	9,500	13,000	14,500	17,800
	4	0	0	1,100	2,700	4,700	7,400	11,000	12,400	15,700
	5	0	0	0	1,800	3,500	5,800	9,000	10,400	13,750
	6	0	0	0	800	2,400	4,300	6,900	8,300	11,600
$60,000										
FAMILY SIZE	3	$0	600	2,300	4,100	6,600	10,000	13,600	15,000	18,300
	4	0	0	1,300	3,000	5,000	8,000	11,500	13,000	16,300
	5	0	0	400	2,050	3,800	6,200	9,600	11,000	14,300
	6	0	0	0	1,000	2,700	4,600	7,400	8,800	12,150

Paying for College

Assets		Income Before Taxes								
		$20,000	30,000	40,000	50,000	60,000	70,000	80,000	90,000	100,000
$80,000										
FAMILY SIZE	3	$0	1,130	2,800	4,800	7,600	11,200	14,700	16,150	19,500
	4	0	170	1,800	3,600	5,900	9,100	9,600	14,100	17,400
	5	0	0	900	2,600	4,500	7,200	10,700	12,100	15,450
	6	0	0	0	1,600	3,200	5,400	8,500	10,000	13,300
$100,000										
FAMILY SIZE	3	$0	1,660	3,400	5,600	8,800	12,300	15,900	17,300	20,600
	4	0	700	2,400	4,200	6,800	10,250	13,800	15,200	18,500
	5	0	0	1,400	3,100	5,300	8,300	11,800	13,300	16,600
	6	0	0	400	2,100	3,900	6,300	9,700	11,100	14,400
$120,000										
FAMILY SIZE	3	$0	2,190	4,000	6,500	9,900	13,400	17,000	18,400	21,700
	4	0	1,220	3,000	4,900	7,800	11,400	14,900	16,350	19,650
	5	0	310	2,000	3,700	6,100	9,500	13,000	14,400	17,700
	6	0	0	1,000	2,600	4,600	7,300	10,800	12,200	15,550
$140,000										
FAMILY SIZE	3	$0	2,700	4,700	7,500	11,000	13,400	18,100	19,500	22,850
	4	0	1,750	3,500	5,700	9,000	12,500	16,000	17,750	20,800
	5	0	850	2,500	4,400	7,100	10,500	14,100	15,500	18,850
	6	0	0	1,500	3,200	5,300	8,400	11,900	13,350	16,650

This chart makes the following assumptions:
• Two parent family where age of older parent is 45
• Lower income families will file the 1040A or 1040EZ tax form
• Student income is less than $2300
• There are no student assets
• There is only one family member in college

All figures are estimates and may vary when the complete FAFSA or PROFILE application is submitted.

SPONSOR LIST

These sponsors arranged for copies of this guide to reach outstanding students—students eager to learn more about top schools. This icon appears in each sponsor's profile:

SPONSOR

Agnes Scott College
Albany College of Pharmacy of
    Union University
Alfred University
Alma College
American University
Amherst College
Augustana College (IL)
Bard College at Simon's Rock
Barnard College
Belmont University
Beloit College
Berry College
Bethel University
Birmingham-Southern College
Boston College
Boston University
Bradley University
Brown University
Bucknell University
Butler University
Calvin College
Canisius College
Carnegie Mellon University
Chapman University
Clarkson University
Clemson University
College of Charleston
The College of New Jersey
College of Saint Benedict
College of the Atlantic
College of the Holy Cross
The College of Wooster
Colorado State University
Cornell College
Cornell University
Denison University
Dominican University
Drake University

Elizabethtown College
Emerson College
Eugene Lang College The New
    School for Liberal Arts
Florida Institute of Technology
Fordham University
Georgia State University
Gettysburg College
Goshen College
Goucher College
Grove City College
Hamilton College (NY)
Hamline University
Harding University
Haverford College
Hendrix College
Hillsdale College
Hobart and William Smith Colleges
Illinois Institute of Technology
Ithaca College
Juniata College
Kettering University
Lafayette College
Lawrence Technological University
Lebanon Valley College
Linfield College
List College, The Jewish
    Theological Seminary
Loyola College in Maryland
Loyola University New Orleans
Marietta College
Marlboro College
Maryville College
Messiah College
Michigan State University
Middlebury College
Mills College
Mount Holyoke College
Muhlenberg College

New College of Florida
New Jersey Institute of Technology
New York School of Interior Design
North Central College
Oberlin College
Oglethorpe University
Ohio Northern University
Ohio Wesleyan University
Pitzer College
Presbyterian College
Princeton University
Providence College
Quincy University
Quinnipiac University
Randolph College
Reed College
Regis University
Rensselaer Polytechnic Institute
Rice University
Ripon College
Rochester Institute of Technology
Saint Francis University
St. John's College (MD)
St. John's College (NM)
Saint John's University (MN)
Saint Joseph's University
St. Lawrence University
Saint Louis University
Saint Mary's College
St. Mary's College of Maryland
St. Norbert College
Samford University
Sarah Lawrence College
Seattle University
Siena College
Simpson College
Skidmore College
Smith College
Southern Methodist University

Sponsor List

Southwestern University
State University of New York College of Environmental Science and Forestry
Stevens Institute of Technology
Susquehanna University
Sweet Briar College
Syracuse University
Texas Christian University
Transylvania University
Union College (NY)
Union University
United States Air Force Academy
United States Coast Guard Academy
United States Merchant Marine Academy

United States Military Academy
University at Buffalo, the State University of New York
University of Arkansas
University of Central Florida
University of Dayton
University of Denver
University of Nebraska–Lincoln
University of Redlands
University of Rhode Island
University of Rochester
University of St. Thomas (MN)
University of San Diego
The University of Scranton
University of South Carolina
University of the Sciences in Philadelphia

Valparaiso University
Villanova University
Virginia Military Institute
Wabash College
Washington College
Wellesley College
Wells College
Wesleyan College
Wesleyan University
Western Washington University
Westminster College (UT)
Williams College
Wisconsin Lutheran College
Worcester Polytechnic Institute

How to Use This Guide

PROFILES OF COMPETITIVE COLLEGES

This section presents pertinent factual and statistical data for each college in a standard format for easy comparison. All college information presented was supplied to Peterson's by the colleges themselves. Any item that does not apply to a particular college or for which no information was supplied is omitted from that college's profile.

GENERAL INFORMATION

The first paragraph gives a brief introduction to the college, covering the following elements.

Campus setting: This indicates the size of the campus in acres or hectares and its location.

Institutional control: A *public* college receives its funding wholly or primarily from the federal, state, and/or local government. The term *private* indicates an independent, nonprofit institution, that is, one whose funding comes primarily from private sources and tuition. This category includes independent, religious colleges, which may also specify a particular religious denomination or church affiliation. Profit-making institutions are designated as *proprietary*.

Type of student body: The categories are *men's* (100 percent of the student body), *primarily men's*, *women's* (100 percent of the student body), *primarily women's*, and *coed*. A few schools are designated as *undergraduate: women only, graduate: coed* or *undergraduate: men only, graduate: coed*. A college may also be designated as coordinate with another institution, indicating that there are separate colleges or campuses for men and women, but facilities, courses, and institutional governance are shared.

Contact information: Along with the school's location and Web address, the name, title, mailing address, telephone, fax, and e-mail address of the person to contact for more information on application and admission procedures are given here.

ACADEMICS

This paragraph contains information on the following items.

Degree levels: An *associate* degree program may consist of either a college-transfer program, equivalent to the first two years of a bachelor's degree, or a one- to three-year terminal program that provides training for a specific occupation. A *bachelor's* degree program represents a three- to five-year liberal arts, science, professional, or preprofessional program. A *master's* degree is the first graduate degree in the liberal arts and sciences and certain professional fields and usually requires one to two years of full-time study. A *doctoral* degree is the highest degree awarded in research-oriented academic disciplines and usually requires from three to six years of full-time graduate study; the *first professional* degrees in such fields as law and medicine are also at the doctoral level. For colleges that award degrees in one field only, such as art or music, the field of specialization is indicated.

Challenging opportunities: *Advanced placement* gives credit for acceptable scores on College Board Advanced Placement tests. *Accelerated degree programs* allow students to earn a bachelor's degree in three academic years. *Self-designed major* is a program of study based on individual interests, designed by the student with the assistance of an adviser. *Freshmen honors college* is a separate academic program for talented freshmen. *Honors programs* are any special programs for very able students, offering the opportunity for educational enrichment, independent study, acceleration, or some combination of these. *Double major* consists of a program of study in which a student concurrently completes the requirements of two majors. *Independent study* consists of academic work, usually undertaken outside the regular classroom structure, chosen or designed by the student with departmental approval and instructor supervision. *Senior project* indicates a special advanced program is required for students.

Most frequently chosen baccalaureate fields: The most popular field or fields of study at the college, in terms of the number of undergraduate degrees conferred in 2007, are listed.

Faculty: The number of full-time and part-time faculty members as of fall 2007 is given, followed by the percentage of the full-time faculty members who hold doctoral, first professional, or terminal degrees and the student-faculty ratio. (Not all colleges calculate the student-faculty ratio in the same way; Peterson's prints the ratio as provided by the college.)

STUDENTS OF THE COLLEGE
The total number of students and undergraduates enrolled in degree programs as of fall 2007 are given. With reference to the undergraduate enrollment for fall 2007, the percentages of women and men and the number of states and countries from which students hail are listed. The following percentages are also provided: in-state, international, American Indian, African American, Hispanic American, and Asian American or Pacific Islander students, and the percentage of students who returned for their sophomore year.

FACILITIES AND RESOURCES

Computers/terminals: This paragraph includes information on the numbers of computers/terminals and ports available on campus for general student use and what computer technology is accessible to students. Information is also given on the availability of a campuswide network, the percentage of college-owned or -operated housing units wired for high-speed Internet access, and the availability of a wireless campus network.

Libraries: The numbers of books, serials, and audiovisual materials in the college's collections are listed.

CAMPUS LIFE
How many active organizations are represented on campus including information on drama-theater groups, student-run campus newspapers, student-run radio stations, student-run television stations, choral groups, and marching bands. National sorority and national fraternity representation is also provided.

Membership in one or more of the following athletic associations is indicated:

NCAA: National Collegiate Athletic Association

NAIA: National Association of Intercollegiate Athletics

NCCAA: National Christian College Athletic Association

NSCAA: National Small College Athletic Association

NJCAA: National Junior College Athletic Association

CIS: Canadian Interuniversity Sports

The overall NCAA division in which all or most intercollegiate teams compete may be designated by a roman numeral I, II, or III. All teams that do not compete in this division are listed as exceptions.

Intercollegiate sports offered by the college are designated as (m) or (w) following the name of each sport indicating that it is offered for men or women.

CAMPUS SAFETY
Campus safety measures including 24-hour emergency response devices (telephones and alarms) and patrols by trained security personnel, student patrols, late-night transport-escort service, and controlled dormitory access (key, security card, etc.).

APPLYING
The supporting data that a student must submit when applying for freshman admission are grouped into these categories: required for all, recommended, and required for some. They may include an essay, a high school transcript, high school course requirements (e.g., three years of math), letters of recommendation, an interview on campus or with local alumni, standardized test scores, and, for certain types of schools or programs, special requirements such as a musical audition or an art portfolio.

The most commonly required standardized tests are the ACT and the College Board's SAT and SAT Subject Tests. TOEFL (Test of English as a Foreign Language) is for international students whose native language is not English.

The application deadline for admission is given as either a specific date or *rolling*. Rolling means that applications are processed as they are received, and qualified students are accepted as long as there are openings. The application deadline for out-of-state students is indicated if it differs from the date for state residents. *Early decision* and *early action* deadlines are also given when applicable. Early decision is a program whereby students may apply early, are notified of acceptance or rejection well in advance of the usual notification date, and agree to accept an offer of admission, the assumption being that only one early application has been made. Early action is the same as early decision except that applicants are not obligated to accept an offer of admission. *Deferred admission* refers to the perogative of a student to defer admission to a future semester.

Financial aid application deadline: This deadline may be given as a specific date, as continuous processing up to a specific date or until all available aid has been awarded, or as a priority date rather than a strict deadline, meaning that students are encouraged to apply by that date in order to have the best chance of obtaining aid.

GETTING ACCEPTED
Figures are given for the number of students who applied for fall admission, the percentage of those who were accepted, and the number who enrolled. Freshman statistics include the percentage of students graduating in the top tenth of their high school class; average high school GPA; mean SAT critical reading score; mean SAT math score; mean SAT writing score; mean ACT score; the percentage of freshmen who took the SAT and received critical reading, math, and writing scores above 600, and above 700; the percentage who took the ACT and received scores above 24, and above 30; and the numbers of class presidents and valedictorians.

Graduation and after: Percentages are given for those graduating in four, five, or six years; pursuing further study (and most popular fields, if provided); and with job offers within six months. The number of organizations recruiting on campus is also detailed.

Financial matters: Annual expenses are expressed as a comprehensive fee (includes full-time tuition and mandatory fees) and as a separate figure for room and board. For public institutions where tuition differs according to residence, separate figures are given for area and/or state residents and for nonresidents.

The tuition structure at some institutions is complex in that freshmen and sophomores may be charged a different rate from that for juniors and seniors or a professional or vocational division may have a different fee structure from the liberal arts division of the same institution. For colleges that report that room and board costs vary according to the type of accommodation and meal plan, the average costs are given. The phrase *no college housing* indicates that the college does not own or operate any housing facilities for its undergraduate students.

Also provided is the dollar amount of the average financial aid package, including scholarships, grants, loans, and part-time jobs, received by such undergraduates.

SPONSOR MESSAGE TO STUDENTS
These messages have been written by those sponsoring colleges that wished to supplement their profile data with additional information.

INDEXES
Specialized Indexes: Indexes are provided covering the following criteria: Twenty-Five Largest Colleges (by total enrollment), Twenty-Five Smallest Colleges (by total enrollment), Single-Sex Colleges: Men Only, Single-Sex Colleges: Women Only, Colleges with Religious Affiliation, Public Colleges, and Hispanic-Serving Institutions.

Majors by College: Listed here are the majors offered at the 440 profiled schools. The schools are listed alphabetically. Although the term "major" is used in this guide, some colleges may use other terms, such as "concentration," "program of study," or "field."

Geographical Listing of Colleges: This index gives the page locations of the colleges and universities included in this book.

DATA COLLECTION PROCEDURES
The data contained in the Profiles and Indexes were researched during the fall and winter of 2007–08 through *Peterson's Annual Survey of Undergraduate Institutions.* All data included in this edition have been submitted by officials (usually admissions and

financial aid officers, registrars, or institutional research personnel) at the colleges. In addition, many of the institutions that submitted data were contacted directly by the Peterson's research staff to verify unusual figures, resolve discrepancies, or obtain additional data. All usable information received in time for publication has been included. The omission of any particular item from an index or profile listing signifies that the information is either not applicable to that institution or not available. Because of Peterson's comprehensive editorial review and because all material comes directly from college officials, we believe that the information presented in this guide is accurate. You should check with a specific college or university at the time of application to verify such figures as tuition and fees, which may have changed since the publication of this volume.

PROFILES OF COMPETITIVE COLLEGES AND UNIVERSITIES

Agnes Scott College educates women to think deeply, live honorably, and to engage the intellectual and social challenges of their times through a twenty-first-century curriculum that emphasizes academic excellence in the liberal arts and sciences. Programs such as the First-Year Seminars, Global Awareness, and Global Connections enrich the Agnes Scott experience. In the last ten years, students have been awarded Gilman, Goldwater, and Fulbright Scholarships and the College has had an NCAA finalist. It ranks in the top 6 percent of 1,325 baccalaureate-degree granting institutions in the percentage of graduates who earn Ph.D.'s. Atlanta provides opportunities for internships, community service, and cultural events. Agnes Scott is an excellent value in terms of academic quality, personalized attention, and a residential community with a student-governed honor system.

Getting Accepted
1,595 applied
45% were accepted
218 enrolled (30% of accepted)
41% from top tenth of their h.s. class
3.65 average high school GPA
Mean SAT critical reading score: 615
Mean SAT math score: 570
Mean SAT writing score: 610
Mean ACT score: 25
57% had SAT critical reading scores over 600
33% had SAT math scores over 600
57% had SAT writing scores over 600
66% had ACT scores over 24
21% had SAT critical reading scores over 700
9% had SAT math scores over 700
16% had SAT writing scores over 700
18% had ACT scores over 30
9 National Merit Scholars
4 class presidents
2 valedictorians

Graduation and After
64% graduated in 4 years
5% graduated in 5 years
26% pursued further study (9% arts and sciences, 5% law, 3% education)
50% had job offers within 6 months
30 organizations recruited on campus

Financial Matters
$28,200 tuition and fees (2008–09)
$9850 room and board
94% average percent of need met
$24,823 average financial aid amount received per undergraduate (2006–07 estimated)

AGNES SCOTT COLLEGE
URBAN SETTING ■ PRIVATE ■ INDEPENDENT RELIGIOUS
■ UNDERGRADUATE: WOMEN ONLY; GRADUATE: COED
DECATUR, GEORGIA

Web site: www.agnesscott.edu
Contact: Ms. Stephanie Balmer, Dean of Admission, 141 East College Avenue, Decatur, GA 30030-3797
Telephone: 404-471-6285 or toll-free 800-868-8602
Fax: 404-471-6414
E-mail: admission@agnesscott.edu

Academics
Agnes Scott awards bachelor's and master's **degrees** and post-bachelor's certificates. **Challenging opportunities** include advanced placement credit, accelerated degree programs, student-designed majors, double majors, independent study, and a senior project. Special programs include internships, summer session for credit, off-campus study, study-abroad, and Army and Air Force ROTC.

The most frequently chosen **baccalaureate** fields are social sciences, English, and psychology. A complete listing of majors at Agnes Scott appears in the Majors by College index beginning on page 471.

The **faculty** at Agnes Scott has 84 full-time members, 100% with terminal degrees. The student-faculty ratio is 9:1.

Students of Agnes Scott
The student body totals 892, of whom 885 are undergraduates. 99.7% are women and 0.3% are men. Students come from 43 states and territories and 23 other countries. 54% are from Georgia. 5.2% are international students. 21.2% are African American, 0.2% American Indian, 5% Asian American, and 3.5% Hispanic American. 80% returned for their sophomore year.

Facilities and Resources
429 **computers/terminals** and 3,819 ports are available on campus for general student use. Students can access the following: campus intranet, computer help desk, free student e-mail accounts, online (class) grades, online (class) registration, online (class) schedules. Campuswide network is available. 100% of college-owned or -operated housing units are wired for high-speed Internet access. Wireless service is available via entire campus. The **library** has 218,046 books and 1,842 subscriptions.

Campus Life
There are 80 active organizations on campus, including a drama/theater group, newspaper, television station, and choral group. No national or local **sororities**.

Agnes Scott is a member of the NCAA (Division III). **Intercollegiate sports** include basketball, cross-country running, soccer, softball, swimming and diving, tennis, volleyball.

Campus Safety
Student safety services include security systems in apartments, public safety facility, surveillance equipment, key required for residence hall entry, late-night transport/escort service, 24-hour emergency telephone alarm devices, 24-hour patrols by trained security personnel, and electronically operated dormitory entrances.

Applying
Agnes Scott requires an essay, SAT or ACT, a high school transcript, and 2 recommendations, and in some cases SAT and SAT Subject Tests or ACT. It recommends an interview and a minimum high school GPA of 3.0. Application deadline: 3/1; 5/1 for financial aid, with a 2/15 priority date. Early and deferred admission are possible.

ALBANY COLLEGE OF PHARMACY OF UNION UNIVERSITY

URBAN SETTING ■ PRIVATE ■ INDEPENDENT ■ COED
ALBANY, NEW YORK

SPONSOR

Web site: www.acp.edu
Contact: Ms. Carly Connors, Director of Admissions, 106 New Scotland Avenue, Albany, NY 12208-3492
Telephone: 518-694-7221 or toll-free 888-203-8010
Fax: 518-694-7322
E-mail: admissions@acp.edu

Academics

Albany College of Pharmacy awards bachelor's and first-professional **degrees**. **Challenging opportunities** include advanced placement credit and accelerated degree programs. Special programs include internships, summer session for credit, off-campus study, and Army, Navy, and Air Force ROTC.

The most frequently chosen **baccalaureate** field is health professions and related sciences. A complete listing of majors at Albany College of Pharmacy appears in the Majors by College index beginning on page 471.

The **faculty** at Albany College of Pharmacy has 82 full-time members. The student-faculty ratio is 16:1.

Students of Albany College of Pharmacy

The student body totals 1,423, of whom 1,016 are undergraduates. 58.1% are women and 41.9% are men. 90% are from New York. 8.4% are international students. 2.4% are African American, 0.1% American Indian, 12.8% Asian American, and 1% Hispanic American. 79% returned for their sophomore year.

Facilities and Resources

30 **computers/terminals** are available on campus for general student use. Students can access the following: computer help desk, free student e-mail accounts, online (class) grades, online (class) registration, online (class) schedules. Campuswide network is available. 100% of college-owned or -operated housing units are wired for high-speed Internet access. Wireless service is available via entire campus. The **library** has 16,124 books and 3,576 subscriptions.

Campus Life

There are 26 active organizations on campus, including a newspaper and choral group. 6% of eligible men and 5% of eligible women are members of national **fraternities** and national **sororities**.

Intercollegiate sports include basketball, soccer.

Campus Safety

Student safety services include 24-hour emergency telephone alarm devices, 24-hour patrols by trained security personnel, and electronically operated dormitory entrances.

Applying

Albany College of Pharmacy requires an essay, SAT or ACT, a high school transcript, and 2 recommendations, and in some cases an interview. It recommends ACT and a minimum high school GPA of 3.0. Application deadline: 2/1; 2/1 priority date for financial aid. Deferred admission is possible.

Getting Accepted
1,050 applied
54% were accepted
264 enrolled (47% of accepted)
47% from top tenth of their h.s. class
3.7 average high school GPA
Mean SAT critical reading score: 570
Mean SAT math score: 610
Mean SAT writing score: 560
Mean ACT score: 26
38% had SAT critical reading scores over 600
57% had SAT math scores over 600
28% had SAT writing scores over 600
78% had ACT scores over 24
4% had SAT critical reading scores over 700
6% had SAT math scores over 700
4% had SAT writing scores over 700
14% had ACT scores over 30

Graduation and After
56% graduated in 4 years
100% had job offers within 6 months
45 organizations recruited on campus

Financial Matters
$21,150 tuition and fees (2007–08)
$7300 room and board

Getting Accepted
2,243 applied
81% were accepted
503 enrolled (28% of accepted)
27% from top tenth of their h.s. class
3.52 average high school GPA
Mean SAT critical reading score: 565
Mean SAT math score: 583
Mean SAT writing score: 560
Mean ACT score: 24
42% had SAT critical reading scores over 600
46% had SAT math scores over 600
63% had ACT scores over 24
6% had SAT critical reading scores over 700
8% had SAT math scores over 700
11% had ACT scores over 30
2 National Merit Scholars
26 class presidents
20 valedictorians

Graduation and After
61% graduated in 4 years
9% graduated in 5 years
1% graduated in 6 years
83% had job offers within 6 months
186 organizations recruited on campus

Financial Matters
$27,530 tuition and fees (2007–08)
$7806 room and board
92% average percent of need met
$20,965 average financial aid amount received
    per undergraduate (2006–07 estimated)

ALBION COLLEGE
SMALL-TOWN SETTING ■ PRIVATE ■ INDEPENDENT RELIGIOUS ■ COED
ALBION, MICHIGAN

Web site: www.albion.edu
Contact: Mr. Doug Kellar, Associate Vice President for Enrollment, 611 East
    Porter Street, Albion, MI 49224
Telephone: 517-629-0600 or toll-free 800-858-6770
Fax: 517-629-0569
E-mail: admissions@albion.edu

Academics
Albion awards bachelor's **degrees**. **Challenging opportunities** include advanced placement credit, student-designed majors, an honors program, double majors, independent
study, and a senior project. Special programs include internships, summer session for
credit, off-campus study, and study-abroad.

    The most frequently chosen **baccalaureate** fields are business/marketing, biological/
life sciences, and social sciences. A complete listing of majors at Albion appears in the
Majors by College index beginning on page 471.

    The **faculty** at Albion has 132 full-time members, 93% with terminal degrees. The
student-faculty ratio is 14:1.

Students of Albion
The student body is made up of 1,938 undergraduates. 54.8% are women and 45.2% are
men. Students come from 29 states and territories and 14 other countries. 90% are from
Michigan. 1% are international students. 3.4% are African American, 0.3% American
Indian, 2.2% Asian American, and 0.5% Hispanic American. 84% returned for their
sophomore year.

Facilities and Resources
435 **computers/terminals** and 25 ports are available on campus for general student use.
Students can access the following: campus intranet, computer help desk, free student
e-mail accounts, online (class) grades, online (class) registration, online (class) schedules,
online student account and financial aid. Campuswide network is available. 100% of college-owned or -operated housing units are wired for high-speed Internet access. Wireless service is available via classrooms, computer centers, computer labs, dorm rooms,
learning centers, libraries, student centers. The **library** has 363,000 books and 2,016
subscriptions.

Campus Life
There are 122 active organizations on campus, including a drama/theater group,
newspaper, radio station, choral group, and marching band. 32% of eligible men and
32% of eligible women are members of national **fraternities** and national **sororities**.

    Albion is a member of the NCAA (Division III). **Intercollegiate sports** include
baseball (m), basketball, cheerleading, cross-country running, equestrian sports, football
(m), golf, soccer, softball (w), swimming and diving, tennis, track and field, volleyball (w).

Campus Safety
Student safety services include late-night transport/escort service, 24-hour emergency
telephone alarm devices, 24-hour patrols by trained security personnel, student patrols,
and electronically operated dormitory entrances.

Applying
Albion requires an essay, SAT or ACT, a high school transcript, and 1 recommendation,
and in some cases an interview. It recommends SAT and SAT Subject Tests or ACT and
a minimum high school GPA of 3.2. Application deadline: 3/1; 3/1 priority date for
financial aid. Early and deferred admission are possible.

ALBRIGHT COLLEGE

Suburban setting ■ Private ■ Independent Religious ■ Coed
Reading, Pennsylvania

Web site: www.albright.edu
Contact: Mr. Gregory Eichhorn, Vice President for Enrollment Management,
PO Box 15234, 13th and Bern Streets, Reading, PA 19612-5234
Telephone: 610-921-7260 or toll-free 800-252-1856
Fax: 610-921-7294
E-mail: admission@albright.edu

Academics

Albright awards bachelor's and master's **degrees**. **Challenging opportunities** include advanced placement credit, accelerated degree programs, student-designed majors, an honors program, independent study, and a senior project. Special programs include internships, summer session for credit, off-campus study, and study-abroad.

The most frequently chosen **baccalaureate** fields are business/marketing, social sciences, and psychology. A complete listing of majors at Albright appears in the Majors by College index beginning on page 471.

The **faculty** at Albright has 108 full-time members, 77% with terminal degrees. The student-faculty ratio is 13:1.

Students of Albright

The student body totals 2,233, of whom 2,176 are undergraduates. 58.7% are women and 41.3% are men. Students come from 24 states and territories and 21 other countries. 68% are from Pennsylvania. 1.2% are international students. 8.4% are African American, 0.4% American Indian, 1.7% Asian American, and 4.8% Hispanic American. 74% returned for their sophomore year.

Facilities and Resources

800 **computers/terminals** and 1,600 ports are available on campus for general student use. Students can access the following: campus intranet, computer help desk, free student e-mail accounts, online (class) grades, online (class) registration, online (class) schedules. Campuswide network is available. 100% of college-owned or -operated housing units are wired for high-speed Internet access. Wireless service is available via entire campus. The 2 **libraries** have 229,725 books and 14,126 subscriptions.

Campus Life

There are 72 active organizations on campus, including a drama/theater group, newspaper, radio station, television station, and choral group. 16% of eligible men and 23% of eligible women are members of national **fraternities** and national **sororities**.

Albright is a member of the NCAA (Division III). **Intercollegiate sports** include badminton (w), baseball (m), basketball, cheerleading, cross-country running, field hockey (w), football (m), golf (m), soccer, softball (w), swimming and diving, tennis, track and field, volleyball (w).

Campus Safety

Student safety services include late-night transport/escort service, 24-hour emergency telephone alarm devices, 24-hour patrols by trained security personnel, student patrols, and electronically operated dormitory entrances.

Applying

Albright requires an essay, SAT or ACT, a high school transcript, 1 recommendation, and secondary school report (guidance department). It recommends an interview. Application deadline: rolling admissions. Early and deferred admission are possible.

Getting Accepted

3,353 applied
77% were accepted
512 enrolled (20% of accepted)
23% from top tenth of their h.s. class
3.3 average high school GPA
15% had SAT critical reading scores over 600
14% had SAT math scores over 600
2% had SAT critical reading scores over 700
2% had SAT math scores over 700
1 class president
2 valedictorians

Graduation and After

53% graduated in 4 years
6% graduated in 5 years
32% pursued further study (12% arts and sciences, 9% law, 5% business)
98% had job offers within 6 months
51 organizations recruited on campus

Financial Matters

$28,884 tuition and fees (2007–08)
$8484 room and board
$18,291 average financial aid amount received per undergraduate (2005–06)

SPONSOR

Alfred University is a selective, nondenominational, residential university nestled at the foothills of the Allegheny Mountains in Alfred, New York. With more than sixty majors and concentrations to choose from, students can combine majors or minors, complete a second degree, or even design their own major through the College of Business, the College of Liberal Arts and Sciences, the School of Art and Design, and the Inamori School of Engineering. Students enjoy an interactive education with professors who know their names, challenge them to excel, and care deeply about their success.

Getting Accepted
2,355 applied
74% were accepted
518 enrolled (30% of accepted)
18% from top tenth of their h.s. class
3.13 average high school GPA
Mean SAT critical reading score: 552
Mean SAT math score: 561
Mean SAT writing score: 529
Mean ACT score: 24
30% had SAT critical reading scores over 600
33% had SAT math scores over 600
21% had SAT writing scores over 600
57% had ACT scores over 24
4% had SAT critical reading scores over 700
2% had SAT math scores over 700
3% had SAT writing scores over 700
9% had ACT scores over 30
3 valedictorians

Graduation and After
47% graduated in 4 years
15% graduated in 5 years
2% graduated in 6 years
24% pursued further study
54 organizations recruited on campus

Financial Matters
$24,278 tuition and fees (2008–09)
$10,796 room and board
86% average percent of need met
$19,697 average financial aid amount received per undergraduate (2006–07 estimated)

ALFRED UNIVERSITY
RURAL SETTING ■ PRIVATE ■ INDEPENDENT ■ COED
ALFRED, NEW YORK

Web site: www.alfred.edu
Contact: Mr. Jeremy Spencer, Director of Admissions, Alumni Hall, Alfred, NY 14802-1205
Telephone: 607-871-2115 or toll-free 800-541-9229
Fax: 607-871-2198
E-mail: admissions@alfred.edu

Academics
Alfred awards bachelor's, master's, and doctoral **degrees** and post-master's certificates. **Challenging opportunities** include advanced placement credit, accelerated degree programs, student-designed majors, an honors program, double majors, independent study, and a senior project. Special programs include cooperative education, internships, summer session for credit, off-campus study, study-abroad, and Army ROTC.

The most frequently chosen **baccalaureate** fields are visual and performing arts, engineering, and business/marketing. A complete listing of majors at Alfred appears in the Majors by College index beginning on page 471.

The **faculty** at Alfred has 172 full-time members. The student-faculty ratio is 12:1.

Students of Alfred
The student body totals 2,436, of whom 2,030 are undergraduates. 50.7% are women and 49.3% are men. Students come from 45 states and territories. 69% are from New York. 1.3% are international students. 3.7% are African American, 0.4% American Indian, 2.2% Asian American, and 2.5% Hispanic American. 79% returned for their sophomore year.

Facilities and Resources
450 **computers/terminals** are available on campus for general student use. Students can access the following: computer help desk, free student e-mail accounts, online (class) grades, online (class) registration, online (class) schedules. Campuswide network is available. 100% of college-owned or -operated housing units are wired for high-speed Internet access. Wireless service is available via classrooms, computer labs, libraries, student centers. The 2 **libraries** have 288,667 books and 1,478 subscriptions.

Campus Life
There are 90 active organizations on campus, including a drama/theater group, newspaper, radio station, television station, and choral group. No national or local **fraternities** or **sororities**.

Alfred is a member of the NCAA (Division III). **Intercollegiate sports** include basketball, cross-country running, equestrian sports, football (m), lacrosse, skiing (downhill), soccer, softball (w), swimming and diving, tennis, track and field, volleyball (w).

Campus Safety
Student safety services include late-night transport/escort service, 24-hour emergency telephone alarm devices, and student patrols.

Applying
Alfred requires an essay, SAT or ACT, a high school transcript, and 1 recommendation, and in some cases an interview and portfolio. It recommends an interview. Application deadline: 2/1; 3/15 for financial aid. Early and deferred admission are possible.

ALLEGHENY COLLEGE

SMALL-TOWN SETTING ■ PRIVATE ■ INDEPENDENT ■ COED
MEADVILLE, PENNSYLVANIA

Web site: www.allegheny.edu
Contact: Ms. Jennifer Winge, Director of Admissions, 520 North Main Street, Box 5, Meadville, PA 16335
Telephone: 814-332-4351 or toll-free 800-521-5293
Fax: 814-337-0431
E-mail: admissions@allegheny.edu

Academics

Allegheny awards bachelor's **degrees**. **Challenging opportunities** include advanced placement credit, student-designed majors, double majors, independent study, and a senior project. Special programs include internships, off-campus study, and study-abroad.

The most frequently chosen **baccalaureate** fields are social sciences, psychology, and biological/life sciences. A complete listing of majors at Allegheny appears in the Majors by College index beginning on page 471.

The **faculty** at Allegheny has 145 full-time members, 91% with terminal degrees. The student-faculty ratio is 14:1.

Students of Allegheny

The student body is made up of 2,193 undergraduates. 55.5% are women and 44.5% are men. Students come from 40 states and territories and 32 other countries. 63% are from Pennsylvania. 1.2% are international students. 2.2% are African American, 0.2% American Indian, 2.8% Asian American, and 1.5% Hispanic American. 87% returned for their sophomore year.

Facilities and Resources

311 **computers/terminals** and 200 ports are available on campus for general student use. Students can access the following: campus intranet, computer help desk, free student e-mail accounts, online (class) registration, online (class) schedules, online room selection, placement testing, course catalog, class lists, wireless computing, book buy, repair service, transcript review and ordering. Campuswide network is available. 100% of college-owned or -operated housing units are wired for high-speed Internet access. Wireless service is available via computer centers, computer labs, learning centers, libraries, student centers. The **library** has 294,646 books and 4,542 subscriptions.

Campus Life

There are 116 active organizations on campus, including a drama/theater group, newspaper, radio station, television station, and choral group. 20% of eligible men and 28% of eligible women are members of national **fraternities** and national **sororities**.

Allegheny is a member of the NCAA (Division III). **Intercollegiate sports** include baseball (m), basketball, cross-country running, football (m), golf, lacrosse (w), soccer, softball (w), swimming and diving, tennis, track and field, volleyball (w).

Campus Safety

Student safety services include local police patrol, late-night transport/escort service, 24-hour emergency telephone alarm devices, 24-hour patrols by trained security personnel, student patrols, and electronically operated dormitory entrances.

Applying

Allegheny requires an essay, SAT or ACT, a high school transcript, and 2 recommendations. It recommends an interview. Application deadline: 2/15; 2/15 priority date for financial aid. Early and deferred admission are possible.

Getting Accepted
4,354 applied
57% were accepted
584 enrolled (23% of accepted)
46% from top tenth of their h.s. class
3.8 average high school GPA
Mean SAT critical reading score: 610
Mean SAT math score: 604
Mean ACT score: 26
60% had SAT critical reading scores over 600
57% had SAT math scores over 600
78% had ACT scores over 24
14% had SAT critical reading scores over 700
9% had SAT math scores over 700
16% had ACT scores over 30
18 National Merit Scholars
21 valedictorians

Graduation and After
64% graduated in 4 years
6% graduated in 5 years
1% graduated in 6 years
48% pursued further study (21% arts and sciences, 14% medicine, 4% education)
67% had job offers within 6 months
40 organizations recruited on campus

Financial Matters
$32,000 tuition and fees (2008–09)
$8000 room and board
91% average percent of need met
$22,400 average financial aid amount received per undergraduate (2006–07 estimated)

ALLEN COLLEGE

SUBURBAN SETTING ■ PRIVATE ■ INDEPENDENT ■ COED, PRIMARILY WOMEN
WATERLOO, IOWA

Web site: www.allencollege.edu
Contact: Dina Dowden, Education Secretary-Student Services, Barrett Forum,
    1825 Logan Avenue, Waterloo, IA 50703
Telephone: 319-226-2000
Fax: 319-226-2051
E-mail: allencollegeadmissions@ihs.org

Getting Accepted
88 applied
76% were accepted
45 enrolled (67% of accepted)
27% from top tenth of their h.s. class
3.62 average high school GPA
Mean ACT score: 21
27% had ACT scores over 24

Graduation and After
35% graduated in 4 years
20% graduated in 5 years
100% had job offers within 6 months
40 organizations recruited on campus

Financial Matters
$14,895 tuition and fees (2008–09)
$6178 room and board
80% average percent of need met
$14,428 average financial aid amount received
  per undergraduate (2005–06)

Academics
Allen awards associate, bachelor's, and master's **degrees** (liberal arts and general education courses offered at either University of North Iowa or Wartburg College). **Challenging opportunities** include advanced placement credit, independent study, and a senior project. Special programs include internships, off-campus study, and Army ROTC.

The most frequently chosen **baccalaureate** field is health professions and related sciences. A complete listing of majors at Allen appears in the Majors by College index beginning on page 471.

The **faculty** at Allen has 27 full-time members, 22% with terminal degrees. The student-faculty ratio is 14:1.

Students of Allen
The student body totals 462, of whom 382 are undergraduates. 95.8% are women and 4.2% are men. Students come from 9 states and territories. 94% are from Iowa. 1% are African American, 0.8% American Indian, 0.3% Asian American, and 0.5% Hispanic American. 94% returned for their sophomore year.

Facilities and Resources
26 **computers/terminals** are available on campus for general student use. Campuswide network is available. Wireless service is available via entire campus. The **library** has 2,797 books and 199 subscriptions.

Campus Life
There are 4 active organizations on campus, including a newspaper. No national or local **fraternities** or **sororities**.

This institution has no intercollegiate sports.

Campus Safety
Student safety services include 24-hour patrols by trained security personnel and electronically operated dormitory entrances.

Applying
Allen requires an essay, ACT, a high school transcript, and 1 recommendation, and in some cases an interview. It recommends rank in upper 50% of high school class, minimum ACT score of 20 and a minimum high school GPA of 2.7. Application deadline: 7/1.

ALMA COLLEGE

SMALL-TOWN SETTING ■ PRIVATE ■ INDEPENDENT RELIGIOUS ■ COED
ALMA, MICHIGAN

SPONSOR

Web site: www.alma.edu
Contact: Mr. Evan Montague, Director of Admissions, Admissions Office,
  Alma, MI 48801-1599
Telephone: 800-321-ALMA
Fax: 989-463-7057
E-mail: admissions@alma.edu

Academics

Alma awards bachelor's **degrees**. **Challenging opportunities** include advanced placement credit, student-designed majors, an honors program, double majors, independent
study, and a senior project. Special programs include internships, summer session for
credit, off-campus study, study-abroad, and Army ROTC.

The most frequently chosen **baccalaureate** fields are business/marketing, social sciences, and biological/life sciences. A complete listing of majors at Alma appears in the
Majors by College index beginning on page 471.

The **faculty** at Alma has 81 full-time members, 88% with terminal degrees. The student-faculty ratio is 13:1.

Students of Alma

The student body is made up of 1,355 undergraduates. 56.5% are women and 43.5% are
men. Students come from 26 states and territories and 9 other countries. 96% are from
Michigan. 1% are international students. 1.3% are African American, 0.4% American
Indian, 1.5% Asian American, and 2.1% Hispanic American. 83% returned for their
sophomore year.

Facilities and Resources

292 **computers/terminals** are available on campus for general student use. Students can
access the following: campus intranet, computer help desk, free student e-mail accounts,
online (class) grades, online (class) registration, online (class) schedules. Campuswide
network is available. 100% of college-owned or -operated housing units are wired for
high-speed Internet access. Wireless service is available via classrooms, dorm rooms,
libraries, student centers. The **library** has 271,614 books and 1,562 subscriptions.

Campus Life

There are 75 active organizations on campus, including a drama/theater group,
newspaper, radio station, choral group, and marching band. 19% of eligible men and
27% of eligible women are members of national **fraternities**, national **sororities**, local
fraternities, and local sororities.

Alma is a member of the NCAA (Division III). **Intercollegiate sports** include
baseball (m), basketball, cross-country running, football (m), golf, soccer, softball (w),
swimming and diving, tennis, track and field, volleyball (w).

Campus Safety

Student safety services include 24-hour emergency telephone alarm devices and 24-hour
patrols by trained security personnel.

Applying

Alma requires SAT or ACT, a high school transcript, minimum SAT score of 1030 or
ACT score of 22, and a minimum high school GPA of 3.0, and in some cases an essay
and recommendations. It recommends an interview. Application deadline: rolling admissions; 3/1 priority date for financial aid. Deferred admission is possible.

Getting Accepted
2,044 applied
78% were accepted
423 enrolled (26% of accepted)
25% from top tenth of their h.s. class
3.49 average high school GPA
Mean SAT critical reading score: 582
Mean SAT math score: 595
Mean SAT writing score: 559
Mean ACT score: 24
43% had SAT critical reading scores over 600
47% had SAT math scores over 600
40% had SAT writing scores over 600
51% had ACT scores over 24
11% had SAT critical reading scores over 700
18% had SAT math scores over 700
4% had SAT writing scores over 700
8% had ACT scores over 30
7 National Merit Scholars
25 valedictorians

Graduation and After
52% graduated in 4 years
18% graduated in 5 years
3% graduated in 6 years
30% pursued further study

Financial Matters
$23,688 tuition and fees (2007–08)
$7774 room and board
84% average percent of need met
$19,393 average financial aid amount received
  per undergraduate (2006–07 estimated)

Getting Accepted
15,847 applied
53% were accepted
1,286 enrolled (15% of accepted)
50% from top tenth of their h.s. class
3.53 average high school GPA
Mean SAT critical reading score: 640
Mean SAT math score: 620
Mean SAT writing score: 640
Mean ACT score: 28
74% had SAT critical reading scores over 600
63% had SAT math scores over 600
68% had SAT writing scores over 600
91% had ACT scores over 24
24% had SAT critical reading scores over 700
14% had SAT math scores over 700
20% had SAT writing scores over 700
28% had ACT scores over 30

Graduation and After
85% had job offers within 6 months
200 organizations recruited on campus

Financial Matters
$33,283 tuition and fees (2008–09)
$12,418 room and board
75% average percent of need met
$26,453 average financial aid amount received per undergraduate (2005–06 estimated)

AMERICAN UNIVERSITY
SUBURBAN SETTING ■ PRIVATE ■ INDEPENDENT RELIGIOUS ■ COED
WASHINGTON, DISTRICT OF COLUMBIA

Web site: www.american.edu
Contact: Director of Admissions, 4400 Massachusetts Avenue, NW, Washington, DC 20016-8001
Telephone: 202-885-6000
Fax: 202-885-6014
E-mail: admissions@american.edu

Academics
American awards bachelor's, master's, doctoral, and first-professional **degrees** and post-bachelor's certificates. **Challenging opportunities** include advanced placement credit, accelerated degree programs, student-designed majors, an honors program, double majors, independent study, and a senior project. Special programs include cooperative education, internships, summer session for credit, off-campus study, study-abroad, and Army and Air Force ROTC.

The most frequently chosen **baccalaureate** fields are social sciences, business/marketing, and communications/journalism. A complete listing of majors at American appears in the Majors by College index beginning on page 471.

The **faculty** at American has 559 full-time members, 94% with terminal degrees. The student-faculty ratio is 14:1.

Students of American
The student body totals 11,450, of whom 6,042 are undergraduates. 62.5% are women and 37.5% are men. Students come from 54 states and territories and 137 other countries. 21% are from District of Columbia. 6.3% are international students. 4.8% are African American, 0.5% American Indian, 4.9% Asian American, and 4.6% Hispanic American. 86% returned for their sophomore year.

Facilities and Resources
690 **computers/terminals** are available on campus for general student use. Students can access the following: campus intranet, computer help desk, free student e-mail accounts, online (class) grades, online (class) registration, online (class) schedules, printers, scanners, online course support. Campuswide network is available. Wireless service is available via entire campus. The 2 **libraries** have 1,037,900 books and 23,955 subscriptions.

Campus Life
There are 180 active organizations on campus, including a drama/theater group, newspaper, radio station, television station, and choral group. 14% of eligible men and 16% of eligible women are members of national **fraternities** and national **sororities**.

American is a member of the NCAA (Division I). **Intercollegiate sports** (some offering scholarships) include basketball, cross-country running, field hockey (w), lacrosse (w), soccer, swimming and diving, tennis, track and field, volleyball (w), wrestling (m).

Campus Safety
Student safety services include late-night transport/escort service, 24-hour emergency telephone alarm devices, 24-hour patrols by trained security personnel, and electronically operated dormitory entrances.

Applying
American requires an essay, SAT or ACT, a high school transcript, 2 recommendations, and a minimum high school GPA of 2.0. It recommends SAT Subject Tests and a minimum high school GPA of 3.0. Application deadline: 1/15; 2/15 for financial aid. Deferred admission is possible.

AMHERST COLLEGE

SMALL-TOWN SETTING ■ PRIVATE ■ INDEPENDENT ■ COED
AMHERST, MASSACHUSETTS

Web site: www.amherst.edu
Contact: Mr. Thomas H. Parker, Dean of Admission and Financial Aid, PO
   Box 5000, Amherst, MA 01002
Telephone: 413-542-2328
Fax: 413-542-2040
E-mail: admission@amherst.edu

SPONSOR

Academics

Amherst awards bachelor's **degrees**. **Challenging opportunities** include student-designed majors, an honors program, double majors, independent study, and a senior project. Special programs include off-campus study and study-abroad.

The most frequently chosen **baccalaureate** fields are public administration and social services, foreign languages and literature, and psychology. A complete listing of majors at Amherst appears in the Majors by College index beginning on page 471.

The **faculty** at Amherst has 194 full-time members, 93% with terminal degrees. The student-faculty ratio is 8:1.

Students of Amherst

The student body is made up of 1,686 undergraduates. 49.6% are women and 50.4% are men. Students come from 48 states and territories and 41 other countries. 12% are from Massachusetts. 7.1% are international students. 9.5% are African American, 0.4% American Indian, 11.6% Asian American, and 9% Hispanic American. 96% returned for their sophomore year.

Facilities and Resources

182 **computers/terminals** are available on campus for general student use. Students can access the following: campus intranet, computer help desk, free student e-mail accounts, online (class) grades, online (class) schedules. Campuswide network is available. 100% of college-owned or -operated housing units are wired for high-speed Internet access. Wireless service is available via entire campus. The 6 **libraries** have 1,023,085 books and 12,190 subscriptions.

Campus Life

There are 100 active organizations on campus, including a drama/theater group, newspaper, radio station, and choral group. No national or local **fraternities** or **sororities**.

Amherst is a member of the NCAA (Division III). **Intercollegiate sports** include baseball (m), basketball, cross-country running, field hockey (w), football (m), golf, ice hockey, lacrosse, soccer, softball (w), squash, swimming and diving, tennis, track and field, volleyball (w).

Campus Safety

Student safety services include late-night transport/escort service, 24-hour emergency telephone alarm devices, 24-hour patrols by trained security personnel, student patrols, and electronically operated dormitory entrances.

Applying

Amherst requires an essay, SAT and SAT Subject Tests or ACT, a high school transcript, and 3 recommendations. Application deadline: 1/1; 2/15 priority date for financial aid. Early and deferred admission are possible.

Getting Accepted

6,680 applied
18% were accepted
474 enrolled (40% of accepted)
85% from top tenth of their h.s. class
Mean SAT critical reading score: 714
Mean SAT math score: 706
Mean ACT score: 31
95% had SAT critical reading scores over 600
92% had SAT math scores over 600
94% had SAT writing scores over 600
99% had ACT scores over 24
66% had SAT critical reading scores over 700
60% had SAT math scores over 700
62% had SAT writing scores over 700
70% had ACT scores over 30
85 National Merit Scholars
54 valedictorians

Graduation and After

84% graduated in 4 years
11% graduated in 5 years
1% graduated in 6 years
35% pursued further study
63% had job offers within 6 months
59 organizations recruited on campus

Financial Matters

$36,232 tuition and fees (2007–08)
$9420 room and board
100% average percent of need met
$32,041 average financial aid amount received
   per undergraduate (2006–07 estimated)

ASBURY COLLEGE

SMALL-TOWN SETTING ■ PRIVATE ■ INDEPENDENT RELIGIOUS ■ COED
WILMORE, KENTUCKY

Getting Accepted

1,354 applied
63% were accepted
312 enrolled (37% of accepted)
31% from top tenth of their h.s. class
3.57 average high school GPA
Mean SAT critical reading score: 597
Mean SAT math score: 597
Mean ACT score: 25
50% had SAT critical reading scores over 600
36% had SAT math scores over 600
56% had ACT scores over 24
13% had SAT critical reading scores over 700
7% had SAT math scores over 700
14% had ACT scores over 30

Graduation and After

54% graduated in 4 years
9% graduated in 5 years
2% graduated in 6 years
45 organizations recruited on campus

Financial Matters

$22,413 tuition and fees (2008–09)
$5414 room and board
79% average percent of need met
$14,794 average financial aid amount received
   per undergraduate (2006–07 estimated)

Web site: www.asbury.edu
Contact: Ronald Anderson, Director of Enrollment Management, 1 Macklem
   Drive, Wilmore, KY 40390
Telephone: 859-858-3511 Ext. 2142 or toll-free 800-888-1818
Fax: 859-858-3921
E-mail: admissions@asbury.edu

Academics

Asbury awards bachelor's and master's **degrees. Challenging opportunities** include
advanced placement credit, double majors, and a senior project. Special programs
include internships, summer session for credit, study-abroad, and Army and Air Force
ROTC.

The most frequently chosen **baccalaureate** fields are English, communication
technologies, and theology and religious vocations. A complete listing of majors at
Asbury appears in the Majors by College index beginning on page 471.

The **faculty** at Asbury has 79 full-time members, 76% with terminal degrees. The
student-faculty ratio is 11:1.

Students of Asbury

The student body totals 1,391, of whom 1,325 are undergraduates. 57% are women and
43% are men. Students come from 44 states and territories and 13 other countries. 34%
are from Kentucky. 1% are international students. 2.2% are African American, 0.4%
American Indian, 1.2% Asian American, and 1.6% Hispanic American. 87% returned for
their sophomore year.

Facilities and Resources

200 **computers/terminals** are available on campus for general student use. Students can
access the following: computer help desk, free student e-mail accounts, online (class)
registration, online (class) schedules. Campuswide network is available. 100% of college-
owned or -operated housing units are wired for high-speed Internet access. Wireless
service is available via libraries, student centers. The **library** has 146,708 books and 511
subscriptions.

Campus Life

There are 35 active organizations on campus, including a drama/theater group,
newspaper, radio station, television station, and choral group. No national or local
fraternities or **sororities**.

Asbury is a member of the NAIA and NCCAA. **Intercollegiate sports** (some offering scholarships) include baseball (m), basketball, cross-country running, soccer, swimming and diving, tennis, volleyball (w).

Campus Safety

Student safety services include late night security personnel, late-night transport/escort
service, 24-hour emergency telephone alarm devices, and electronically operated dormitory entrances.

Applying

Asbury requires an essay, SAT or ACT, a high school transcript, 2 recommendations, and
a minimum high school GPA of 2.5, and in some cases an interview. Application
deadline: rolling admissions; 3/1 priority date for financial aid. Early and deferred admission are possible.

AUBURN UNIVERSITY

SMALL-TOWN SETTING ■ PUBLIC ■ STATE-SUPPORTED ■ COED
AUBURN UNIVERSITY, ALABAMA

Web site: www.auburn.edu
Contact: Mr. Michael M. Waldrop, Associate Director, Marketing and
Recruitment, 202 Mary Martin Hall, Auburn, AL 36849-5145
Telephone: 334-844-6446 or toll-free 800-AUBURN9 (in-state)
E-mail: admissions@auburn.edu

Academics

Auburn awards bachelor's, master's, doctoral, and first-professional **degrees** and post-master's certificates. **Challenging opportunities** include advanced placement credit, accelerated degree programs, an honors program, double majors, independent study, and a senior project. Special programs include cooperative education, internships, summer session for credit, study-abroad, and Army, Navy, and Air Force ROTC.

The most frequently chosen **baccalaureate** fields are business/marketing, engineering, and education. A complete listing of majors at Auburn appears in the Majors by College index beginning on page 471.

The **faculty** at Auburn has 1,132 full-time members. The student-faculty ratio is 18:1.

Students of Auburn

The student body totals 24,137, of whom 19,812 are undergraduates. 48.9% are women and 51.1% are men. Students come from 52 states and territories and 48 other countries. 69% are from Alabama. 0.6% are international students. 8.9% are African American, 0.7% American Indian, 1.7% Asian American, and 2% Hispanic American. 86% returned for their sophomore year.

Facilities and Resources

1,722 **computers/terminals** are available on campus for general student use. Students can access the following: computer help desk, free student e-mail accounts, online (class) grades, online (class) registration, pay Bursar online, course materials available online. Campuswide network is available. 100% of college-owned or -operated housing units are wired for high-speed Internet access. Wireless service is available via entire campus. The 3 **libraries** have 3,697,283 books and 29,355 subscriptions.

Campus Life

There are 300 active organizations on campus, including a drama/theater group, newspaper, radio station, television station, choral group, and marching band. 22% of eligible men and 31% of eligible women are members of national **fraternities** and national **sororities**.

Auburn is a member of the NCAA (Division I). **Intercollegiate sports** (some offering scholarships) include baseball (m), basketball, cross-country running, equestrian sports (w), football (m), golf, gymnastics (w), soccer (w), softball (w), swimming and diving, tennis, track and field, volleyball (w).

Campus Safety

Student safety services include late-night transport/escort service, 24-hour emergency telephone alarm devices, 24-hour patrols by trained security personnel, and electronically operated dormitory entrances.

Applying

Auburn requires SAT or ACT, a high school transcript, and a minimum high school GPA of 2.0, and in some cases a minimum high school GPA of 3.0. Application deadline: rolling admissions; 3/1 priority date for financial aid. Early and deferred admission are possible.

Getting Accepted

17,798 applied
69% were accepted
4,191 enrolled (34% of accepted)
27% from top tenth of their h.s. class
3.6 average high school GPA
Mean SAT critical reading score: 561
Mean SAT math score: 577
Mean ACT score: 25
30% had SAT critical reading scores over 600
40% had SAT math scores over 600
63% had ACT scores over 24
5% had SAT critical reading scores over 700
6% had SAT math scores over 700
20% had ACT scores over 30
27 National Merit Scholars

Graduation and After

34% graduated in 4 years
24% graduated in 5 years
5% graduated in 6 years
35% pursued further study (9% business, 6% medicine, 5% arts and sciences)
75% had job offers within 6 months
650 organizations recruited on campus

Financial Matters

$5834 resident tuition and fees (2007–08)
$16,334 nonresident tuition and fees (2007–08)
$3200 room only
47% average percent of need met
$7917 average financial aid amount received per undergraduate (2005–06)

At Augustana College, students find an array of opportunities in a rich liberal arts environment to challenge and prepare them for meaningful work in a complex world. Important features of the academic program include an interdisciplinary general education sequence for all students; intensive global learning experiences; a liberal arts background fostering skills in creative and critical thinking, combined with depth of study in the major field(s); programs that focus on one's purpose or path in life; and domestic and international internships. Close connections with faculty mentors and a dynamic culture of inquiry foster collaboration in research, the arts, and social service. Fifth in the nation for the number of Academic All-Americans, the College offers a wide variety of extracurricular and cocurricular activities, campus ministries, and residential life programs to engage students beyond the classroom.

Getting Accepted
3,080 applied
73% were accepted
712 enrolled (32% of accepted)
34% from top tenth of their h.s. class
Mean ACT score: 26
69% had ACT scores over 24
13% had ACT scores over 30

Graduation and After
71% graduated in 4 years
4% graduated in 5 years
1% graduated in 6 years
42% pursued further study (22% arts and sciences, 7% business, 4% medicine)
59% had job offers within 6 months
162 organizations recruited on campus

Financial Matters
$26,484 tuition and fees (2007–08)
$7233 room and board
84% average percent of need met
$17,924 average financial aid amount received per undergraduate (2006–07 estimated)

AUGUSTANA COLLEGE

SUBURBAN SETTING ■ PRIVATE ■ INDEPENDENT RELIGIOUS ■ COED
ROCK ISLAND, ILLINOIS

Web site: www.augustana.edu
Contact: Megan Cooley, Director of Admissions, 639 38th Street, Rock Island, IL 61201-2296
Telephone: 309-794-7341 or toll-free 800-798-8100
Fax: 309-794-7422
E-mail: admissions@augustana.edu

Academics
Augustana awards bachelor's **degrees**. **Challenging opportunities** include advanced placement credit, accelerated degree programs, an honors program, double majors, independent study, and a senior project. Special programs include internships, summer session for credit, and study-abroad.

The most frequently chosen **baccalaureate** fields are business/marketing, biological/life sciences, and social sciences. A complete listing of majors at Augustana appears in the Majors by College index beginning on page 471.

The **faculty** at Augustana has 173 full-time members, 91% with terminal degrees. The student-faculty ratio is 12:1.

Students of Augustana
The student body is made up of 2,537 undergraduates. 56.6% are women and 43.4% are men. Students come from 26 states and territories and 18 other countries. 88% are from Illinois. 0.8% are international students. 2% are African American, 0.5% American Indian, 2.1% Asian American, and 3.8% Hispanic American. 87% returned for their sophomore year.

Facilities and Resources
600 **computers/terminals** and 1,800 ports are available on campus for general student use. Students can access the following: campus intranet, computer help desk, free student e-mail accounts, online (class) grades, online (class) registration, online (class) schedules. Campuswide network is available. 100% of college-owned or -operated housing units are wired for high-speed Internet access. The 4 **libraries** have 190,641 books and 1,705 subscriptions.

Campus Life
There are 116 active organizations on campus, including a drama/theater group, newspaper, radio station, and choral group. 19% of eligible men and 26% of eligible women are members of local **fraternities** and local **sororities**.

Augustana is a member of the NCAA (Division III). **Intercollegiate sports** include baseball (m), basketball, cross-country running, football (m), golf, soccer, softball (w), swimming and diving, tennis, track and field, volleyball (w), wrestling (m).

Campus Safety
Student safety services include late-night transport/escort service, 24-hour emergency telephone alarm devices, 24-hour patrols by trained security personnel, and electronically operated dormitory entrances.

Applying
Augustana requires a high school transcript, and in some cases an essay and an interview. It recommends SAT or ACT. Application deadline: rolling admissions; 3/15 priority date for financial aid. Deferred admission is possible.

AUGUSTANA COLLEGE

URBAN SETTING ■ PRIVATE ■ INDEPENDENT RELIGIOUS ■ COED
SIOUX FALLS, SOUTH DAKOTA

Web site: www.augie.edu
Contact: Ms. Nancy Davidson, Vice President for Enrollment, 2001 S.
   Summit Avenue, Sioux Falls, SD 57197
Telephone: 605-274-5516 or toll-free 800-727-2844 Ext. 5516 (in-state),
   800-727-2844 (out-of-state)
Fax: 605-274-5518
E-mail: admission@augie.edu

Academics

Augustana awards bachelor's and master's **degrees**. **Challenging opportunities** include advanced placement credit, accelerated degree programs, student-designed majors, freshman honors college, an honors program, double majors, independent study, and a senior project. Special programs include cooperative education, internships, summer session for credit, off-campus study, and study-abroad.

The most frequently chosen **baccalaureate** fields are education, business/marketing, and health professions and related sciences. A complete listing of majors at Augustana appears in the Majors by College index beginning on page 471.

The **faculty** at Augustana has 118 full-time members, 77% with terminal degrees. The student-faculty ratio is 12:1.

Students of Augustana

The student body totals 1,745, of whom 1,718 are undergraduates. 61.9% are women and 38.1% are men. Students come from 28 states and territories and 11 other countries. 46% are from South Dakota. 1.2% are international students. 1.6% are African American, 0.5% American Indian, 1.6% Asian American, and 0.4% Hispanic American. 78% returned for their sophomore year.

Facilities and Resources

275 **computers/terminals** are available on campus for general student use. Students can access the following: computer help desk, free student e-mail accounts, online (class) grades, online (class) registration, online (class) schedules. Campuswide network is available. 100% of college-owned or -operated housing units are wired for high-speed Internet access. Wireless service is available via learning centers, libraries, student centers. The 2 **libraries** have 279,918 books and 595 subscriptions.

Campus Life

There are 60 active organizations on campus, including a drama/theater group, newspaper, radio station, and choral group. No national or local **fraternities** or **sororities**.

Augustana is a member of the NCAA (Division II). **Intercollegiate sports** (some offering scholarships) include baseball (m), basketball, cheerleading (w), cross-country running, football (m), golf, soccer (w), softball (w), tennis, track and field, volleyball (w), wrestling (m).

Campus Safety

Student safety services include late-night transport/escort service, 24-hour emergency telephone alarm devices, 24-hour patrols by trained security personnel, and electronically operated dormitory entrances.

Applying

Augustana requires an essay, SAT or ACT, a high school transcript, 1 recommendation, minimum ACT score of 20, and a minimum high school GPA of 2.75. It recommends an interview. Application deadline: 8/1; 3/1 priority date for financial aid. Deferred admission is possible.

Getting Accepted

1,353 applied
82% were accepted
432 enrolled (39% of accepted)
30% from top tenth of their h.s. class
3.6 average high school GPA
Mean SAT critical reading score: 568
Mean SAT math score: 567
Mean ACT score: 25
47% had SAT critical reading scores over 600
31% had SAT math scores over 600
56% had ACT scores over 24
5% had SAT critical reading scores over 700
5% had SAT math scores over 700
7% had ACT scores over 30
32 valedictorians

Graduation and After

50% graduated in 4 years
13% graduated in 5 years
2% graduated in 6 years
28% pursued further study
99% had job offers within 6 months
49 organizations recruited on campus

Financial Matters

$21,182 tuition and fees (2007–08)
$5640 room and board
89% average percent of need met
$15,938 average financial aid amount received
   per undergraduate (2006–07 estimated)

AUSTIN COLLEGE

SUBURBAN SETTING ■ PRIVATE ■ INDEPENDENT RELIGIOUS ■ COED
SHERMAN, TEXAS

Web site: www.austincollege.edu
Contact: Ms. Nan Davis, Vice President for Institutional Enrollment, 900
    North Grand Avenue, Suite 6N, Sherman, TX 75090-4400
Telephone: 903-813-3000 or toll-free 800-442-5363
Fax: 903-813-3198
E-mail: admission@austincollege.edu

Getting Accepted
1,678 applied
71% were accepted
334 enrolled (28% of accepted)
38% from top tenth of their h.s. class
3.46 average high school GPA
Mean SAT critical reading score: 615
Mean SAT math score: 609
Mean ACT score: 25
61% had SAT critical reading scores over 600
55% had SAT math scores over 600
51% had SAT writing scores over 600
67% had ACT scores over 24
16% had SAT critical reading scores over 700
12% had SAT math scores over 700
13% had SAT writing scores over 700
14% had ACT scores over 30
8 National Merit Scholars
6 valedictorians

Graduation and After
75% graduated in 4 years
2% graduated in 5 years
1% graduated in 6 years
**32% pursued further study (11% arts and
    sciences, 7% medicine, 7% education)**
38% had job offers within 6 months
34 organizations recruited on campus

Financial Matters
$26,530 tuition and fees (2008–09)
$8304 room and board
99% average percent of need met
**$22,532 average financial aid amount received
    per undergraduate (2006–07 estimated)**

Academics
Austin awards bachelor's and master's **degrees. Challenging opportunities** include advanced placement credit, student-designed majors, an honors program, double majors, independent study, and a senior project. Special programs include internships, summer session for credit, off-campus study, and study-abroad.

The most frequently chosen **baccalaureate** fields are social sciences, psychology, and business/marketing. A complete listing of majors at Austin appears in the Majors by College index beginning on page 471.

The **faculty** at Austin has 95 full-time members, 96% with terminal degrees. The student-faculty ratio is 12:1.

Students of Austin
The student body totals 1,339, of whom 1,320 are undergraduates. 52.3% are women and 47.7% are men. Students come from 34 states and territories and 28 other countries. 93% are from Texas. 1.4% are international students. 2.8% are African American, 0.8% American Indian, 14.5% Asian American, and 8% Hispanic American. 82% returned for their sophomore year.

Facilities and Resources
165 **computers/terminals** are available on campus for general student use. Students can access the following: campus intranet, computer help desk, free student e-mail accounts, online (class) grades, online (class) schedules. Campuswide network is available. 100% of college-owned or -operated housing units are wired for high-speed Internet access. Wireless service is available via entire campus. The **library** has 240,944 books and 2,181 subscriptions.

Campus Life
There are 50 active organizations on campus, including a drama/theater group, newspaper, and choral group. 22% of eligible men and 28% of eligible women are members of local **fraternities** and local **sororities**.

Austin is a member of the NCAA (Division III). **Intercollegiate sports** include baseball (m), basketball, cheerleading, football (m), soccer, softball (w), swimming and diving, tennis, volleyball (w).

Campus Safety
Student safety services include late-night transport/escort service, 24-hour emergency telephone alarm devices, 24-hour patrols by trained security personnel, and electronically operated dormitory entrances.

Applying
Austin requires an essay, SAT or ACT, a high school transcript, and 2 recommendations, and in some cases an interview. It recommends an interview and a minimum high school GPA of 3.0. Application deadline: 5/1; 4/1 priority date for financial aid. Early and deferred admission are possible.

Azusa Pacific University

Small-town setting ■ Private ■ Independent Religious ■ Coed
Azusa, California

Web site: www.apu.edu
Contact: Ms. Lynette Barnes, Processing Coordinator, 901 East Alosta Avenue, PO Box 7000, Azusa, CA 91702-7000
Telephone: 626-812-3016 or toll-free 800-TALK-APU
E-mail: admissions@apu.edu

Academics

Azusa Pacific awards bachelor's, master's, doctoral, and first-professional **degrees**. **Challenging opportunities** include advanced placement credit, accelerated degree programs, freshman honors college, an honors program, double majors, independent study, and a senior project. Special programs include cooperative education, internships, summer session for credit, off-campus study, study-abroad, and Army ROTC.

The most frequently chosen **baccalaureate** fields are business/marketing, liberal arts/general studies, and communications/journalism. A complete listing of majors at Azusa Pacific appears in the Majors by College index beginning on page 471.

The **faculty** at Azusa Pacific has 319 full-time members, 70% with terminal degrees.

Students of Azusa Pacific

The student body totals 8,084, of whom 4,615 are undergraduates. 63.5% are women and 36.5% are men. Students come from 48 states and territories and 47 other countries. 81% are from California. 2.7% are international students. 4.7% are African American, 0.5% American Indian, 7.2% Asian American, and 14.4% Hispanic American. 80% returned for their sophomore year.

Facilities and Resources

300 **computers/terminals** are available on campus for general student use. Students can access the following: campus intranet, computer help desk, free student e-mail accounts, online (class) grades, online (class) registration. Campuswide network is available. Wireless service is available via entire campus. The 3 **libraries** have 185,708 books and 14,031 subscriptions.

Campus Life

There are 32 active organizations on campus, including a drama/theater group, newspaper, radio station, television station, choral group, and marching band. No national or local **fraternities** or **sororities**.

Azusa Pacific is a member of the NAIA. **Intercollegiate sports** (some offering scholarships) include baseball (m), basketball, cross-country running, football (m), golf (m), soccer, softball (w), tennis (m), track and field, volleyball.

Campus Safety

Student safety services include late-night transport/escort service, 24-hour emergency telephone alarm devices, 24-hour patrols by trained security personnel, student patrols, and electronically operated dormitory entrances.

Applying

Azusa Pacific requires an essay, SAT or ACT, a high school transcript, 2 recommendations, and a minimum high school GPA of 2.8, and in some cases an interview. Application deadline: 6/1; 7/1 for financial aid, with a 3/2 priority date. Early and deferred admission are possible.

Getting Accepted

3,229 applied
73% were accepted
855 enrolled (36% of accepted)
27% from top tenth of their h.s. class
3.59 average high school GPA
Mean SAT critical reading score: 546
Mean SAT math score: 543
Mean ACT score: 23
25% had SAT critical reading scores over 600
24% had SAT math scores over 600
45% had ACT scores over 24
2% had SAT critical reading scores over 700
5% had SAT math scores over 700
6% had ACT scores over 30

Graduation and After

51% graduated in 4 years
14% graduated in 5 years
1% graduated in 6 years
23 organizations recruited on campus

Financial Matters

$25,130 tuition and fees (2007–08)
$7518 room and board
61% average percent of need met
$19,785 average financial aid amount received per undergraduate (2005–06)

Getting Accepted
3,530 applied
38% were accepted
453 enrolled (34% of accepted)
22% from top tenth of their h.s. class
Mean SAT critical reading score: 601
Mean SAT math score: 640
54% had SAT critical reading scores over 600
74% had SAT math scores over 600
63% had SAT writing scores over 600
78% had ACT scores over 24
8% had SAT critical reading scores over 700
20% had SAT math scores over 700
10% had SAT writing scores over 700
12% had ACT scores over 30

Graduation and After
85% graduated in 4 years
4% graduated in 5 years
2% pursued further study (2% law)
97% had job offers within 6 months
537 organizations recruited on campus

Financial Matters
$34,112 tuition and fees (2007–08)
$11,670 room and board
97% average percent of need met
$27,453 average financial aid amount received
   per undergraduate (2006–07 estimated)

BABSON COLLEGE
SUBURBAN SETTING ■ PRIVATE ■ INDEPENDENT ■ COED
BABSON PARK, MASSACHUSETTS

Web site: www.babson.edu
Contact: Ms. Adrienne Fowkes, Assistant Director of Undergraduate
   Admission, Lunder Undergraduate Admission Center, Babson Park, MA
   02457-0310
Telephone: 781-239-5522 or toll-free 800-488-3696
Fax: 781-239-4135
E-mail: ugradadmission@babson.edu

Academics
Babson awards bachelor's and master's **degrees** and post-master's certificates. **Challenging opportunities** include advanced placement credit, accelerated degree programs, student-designed majors, freshman honors college, an honors program, independent study, and a senior project. Special programs include internships, summer session for credit, off-campus study, study-abroad, and Army, Navy, and Air Force ROTC.

The most frequently chosen **baccalaureate** field is business/marketing. A complete listing of majors at Babson appears in the Majors by College index beginning on page 471.

The **faculty** at Babson has 150 full-time members, 90% with terminal degrees. The student-faculty ratio is 16:1.

Students of Babson
The student body totals 3,434, of whom 1,799 are undergraduates. 40.6% are women and 59.4% are men. Students come from 47 states and territories and 69 other countries. 30% are from Massachusetts. 17.8% are international students. 4.4% are African American, 0.2% American Indian, 10.7% Asian American, and 7.9% Hispanic American. 93% returned for their sophomore year.

Facilities and Resources
290 **computers/terminals** are available on campus for general student use. Students can access the following: campus intranet, computer help desk, free student e-mail accounts, online (class) grades, online (class) registration, online (class) schedules, network drives and folders. Campuswide network is available. The 2 **libraries** have 131,436 books and 626 subscriptions.

Campus Life
There are 74 active organizations on campus, including a drama/theater group, newspaper, radio station, and choral group. 13% of eligible men and 15% of eligible women are members of national **fraternities** and national **sororities**.

Babson is a member of the NCAA (Division III). **Intercollegiate sports** include baseball (m), basketball, cross-country running, field hockey (w), golf (m), ice hockey (m), lacrosse, skiing (downhill), soccer, softball (w), swimming and diving, tennis, track and field, volleyball (w).

Campus Safety
Student safety services include late-night transport/escort service, 24-hour emergency telephone alarm devices, 24-hour patrols by trained security personnel, and electronically operated dormitory entrances.

Applying
Babson requires an essay, SAT or ACT, a high school transcript, and 2 recommendations. It recommends an interview. Application deadline: 1/15; 2/15 for financial aid, with a 2/15 priority date. Deferred admission is possible.

BALDWIN-WALLACE COLLEGE

SUBURBAN SETTING ■ PRIVATE ■ INDEPENDENT RELIGIOUS ■ COED
BEREA, OHIO

Web site: www.bw.edu
Contact: Ms. Grace B. Chalker, Interim Associate Director of Admissions, 275 Eastland Road, Berea, OH 44017-2088
Telephone: 440-826-2222 or toll-free 877-BWAPPLY (in-state)
Fax: 440-826-3830
E-mail: admission@baldwinw.edu

Academics

B-W awards bachelor's and master's **degrees. Challenging opportunities** include advanced placement credit, accelerated degree programs, student-designed majors, an honors program, double majors, independent study, and a senior project. Special programs include internships, summer session for credit, off-campus study, study-abroad, and Air Force ROTC.

The most frequently chosen **baccalaureate** fields are business/marketing, education, and visual and performing arts. A complete listing of majors at B-W appears in the Majors by College index beginning on page 471.

The **faculty** at B-W has 167 full-time members, 81% with terminal degrees. The student-faculty ratio is 15:1.

Students of B-W

The student body totals 4,394, of whom 3,638 are undergraduates. 57.2% are women and 42.8% are men. Students come from 35 states and territories and 15 other countries. 89% are from Ohio. 1.3% are international students. 6.7% are African American, 0.1% American Indian, 1.3% Asian American, and 1.9% Hispanic American. 83% returned for their sophomore year.

Facilities and Resources

465 **computers/terminals** and 100 ports are available on campus for general student use. Students can access the following: campus intranet, computer help desk, free student e-mail accounts, online (class) grades, online (class) registration, online (class) schedules. Campuswide network is available. 100% of college-owned or -operated housing units are wired for high-speed Internet access. Wireless service is available via entire campus. The 3 **libraries** have 200,000 books and 22,000 subscriptions.

Campus Life

There are 136 active organizations on campus, including a drama/theater group, newspaper, radio station, television station, choral group, and marching band. 11% of eligible men and 17% of eligible women are members of national **fraternities** and national **sororities.**

B-W is a member of the NCAA (Division III). **Intercollegiate sports** include baseball (m), basketball, cross-country running, football (m), golf, soccer, softball (w), swimming and diving, tennis, track and field, volleyball (w), wrestling (m).

Campus Safety

Student safety services include late-night transport/escort service, 24-hour emergency telephone alarm devices, 24-hour patrols by trained security personnel, student patrols, and electronically operated dormitory entrances.

Applying

B-W requires an essay, SAT or ACT, a high school transcript, 1 recommendation, and a minimum high school GPA of 2.75. It recommends an interview and a minimum high school GPA of 3.2. Application deadline: rolling admissions; 9/1 for financial aid, with a 5/1 priority date. Deferred admission is possible.

Getting Accepted

3,126 applied
66% were accepted
740 enrolled (36% of accepted)
27% from top tenth of their h.s. class
3.5 average high school GPA
Mean SAT critical reading score: 555
Mean SAT math score: 545
Mean SAT writing score: 530
Mean ACT score: 24
32% had SAT critical reading scores over 600
27% had SAT math scores over 600
21% had SAT writing scores over 600
52% had ACT scores over 24
5% had SAT critical reading scores over 700
2% had SAT math scores over 700
2% had SAT writing scores over 700
7% had ACT scores over 30
12 National Merit Scholars
20 valedictorians

Graduation and After

48% graduated in 4 years
17% graduated in 5 years
2% graduated in 6 years
28% pursued further study (6% arts and sciences, 5% medicine, 4% business)
39% had job offers within 6 months
60 organizations recruited on campus

Financial Matters

$23,524 tuition and fees (2008–09)
$7728 room and board
90% average percent of need met
$16,700 average financial aid amount received per undergraduate (2006–07 estimated)

BARD COLLEGE

RURAL SETTING ■ PRIVATE ■ INDEPENDENT ■ COED
ANNANDALE-ON-HUDSON, NEW YORK

Web site: www.bard.edu
Contact: Ms. Mary Backlund, Director of Admissions, PO Box 5000, 51
    Ravine Road, Annandale-on-Hudson, NY 12504-5000
Telephone: 845-758-7472
Fax: 845-758-5208
E-mail: admission@bard.edu

Getting Accepted
4,980 applied
27% were accepted
491 enrolled (36% of accepted)
63% from top tenth of their h.s. class
3.5 average high school GPA
Mean SAT critical reading score: 680
Mean SAT math score: 650
73% had SAT math scores over 600
83% had SAT writing scores over 600
22% had SAT math scores over 700
36% had SAT writing scores over 700

Graduation and After
67% graduated in 4 years
8% graduated in 5 years
2% graduated in 6 years

Financial Matters
$36,534 tuition and fees (2007–08)
$10,346 room and board
88% average percent of need met
$25,147 average financial aid amount received
    per undergraduate (2006–07 estimated)

Academics
Bard awards associate, bachelor's, master's, and doctoral **degrees. Challenging opportunities** include advanced placement credit, student-designed majors, double majors, independent study, and a senior project. Special programs include internships, off-campus study, and study-abroad.

The most frequently chosen **baccalaureate** fields are visual and performing arts, social sciences, and English. A complete listing of majors at Bard appears in the Majors by College index beginning on page 471.

The **faculty** at Bard has 140 full-time members, 96% with terminal degrees. The student-faculty ratio is 9:1.

Students of Bard
The student body totals 2,062, of whom 1,801 are undergraduates. 56.4% are women and 43.6% are men. Students come from 48 states and territories and 46 other countries. 30% are from New York. 10.3% are international students. 2.3% are African American, 0.6% American Indian, 2.8% Asian American, and 3.1% Hispanic American. 88% returned for their sophomore year.

Facilities and Resources
425 **computers/terminals** are available on campus for general student use. Students can access the following: campus intranet, computer help desk, free student e-mail accounts, online (class) grades, online (class) registration, online (class) schedules. Campuswide network is available. 100% of college-owned or -operated housing units are wired for high-speed Internet access. Wireless service is available via classrooms, computer centers, dorm rooms, libraries, student centers. The 4 **libraries** have 402,000 books and 15,450 subscriptions.

Campus Life
There are 100 active organizations on campus, including a drama/theater group, newspaper, radio station, and choral group. No national or local **fraternities** or **sororities**.

Bard is a member of the NCAA (Division III) and NAIA. **Intercollegiate sports** include basketball, cross-country running, soccer, squash (m), tennis, track and field, volleyball.

Campus Safety
Student safety services include late-night transport/escort service, 24-hour emergency telephone alarm devices, 24-hour patrols by trained security personnel, student patrols, and electronically operated dormitory entrances.

Applying
Bard requires an essay, a high school transcript, 3 recommendations, and a minimum high school GPA of 3.0, and in some cases an interview. It recommends an interview. Application deadline: 1/15; 2/15 for financial aid, with a 2/1 priority date. Early and deferred admission are possible.

BARD COLLEGE AT SIMON'S ROCK

RURAL SETTING ■ PRIVATE ■ INDEPENDENT ■ COED
GREAT BARRINGTON, MASSACHUSETTS

Web site: simons-rock.edu
Contact: Barbara Shultis, Assistant to the Director of Admissions, 84 Alford Road, Great Barrington, MA 01230
Telephone: 413-528-7312 or toll-free 800-235-7186
Fax: 413-528-7334
E-mail: admit@simons-rock.edu

Academics

Simon's Rock awards associate and bachelor's **degrees. Challenging opportunities** include student-designed majors, double majors, independent study, and a senior project. Special programs include internships, off-campus study, and study-abroad.

The most frequently chosen **baccalaureate** fields are area and ethnic studies, visual and performing arts, and English. A complete listing of majors at Simon's Rock appears in the Majors by College index beginning on page 471.

The **faculty** at Simon's Rock has 37 full-time members, 95% with terminal degrees. The student-faculty ratio is 8:1.

Students of Simon's Rock

The student body is made up of 408 undergraduates. 57.6% are women and 42.4% are men. Students come from 41 states and territories and 11 other countries. 18% are from Massachusetts. 4.3% are international students. 6.7% are African American, 0.8% American Indian, 4.3% Asian American, and 5.9% Hispanic American. 82% returned for their sophomore year.

Facilities and Resources

50 **computers/terminals** are available on campus for general student use. Students can access the following: campus intranet, computer help desk, free student e-mail accounts. Campuswide network is available. 100% of college-owned or -operated housing units are wired for high-speed Internet access. Wireless service is available via classrooms, computer centers, computer labs, dorm rooms, learning centers, libraries, student centers. The **library** has 73,514 books and 417 subscriptions.

Campus Life

There are 21 active organizations on campus, including a drama/theater group, newspaper, radio station, and choral group. No national or local **fraternities** or **sororities**.

Intercollegiate sports include basketball, cheerleading, cross-country running, fencing, racquetball, soccer, swimming and diving.

Campus Safety

Student safety services include 24-hour weekend patrols by trained security personnel, late-night transport/escort service, 24-hour emergency telephone alarm devices, and electronically operated dormitory entrances.

Applying

Simon's Rock requires an essay, a high school transcript, an interview, 2 recommendations, parent application, and a minimum high school GPA of 2.0, and in some cases SAT or ACT and PSAT. It recommends a minimum high school GPA of 3.0. Application deadline: 5/31; 4/15 priority date for financial aid. Deferred admission is possible.

Simon's Rock is the only four-year college of the liberal arts and sciences specifically designed to provide bright, highly motivated students with the opportunity to begin college in a residential setting after the tenth or eleventh grade. Students who successfully complete the requirements receive the Associate of Arts (A.A.) degree after two years of study and the Bachelor of Arts (B.A.) degree after four. Successful Simon's Rock students have in common a genuine love of learning, a readiness to accept more independence and responsibility, and the motivation to work hard when they're inspired by their studies.

Getting Accepted

236 applied
84% were accepted
182 enrolled (91% of accepted)
60% from top tenth of their h.s. class
Mean SAT critical reading score: 663
Mean SAT math score: 614
Mean SAT writing score: 630
Mean ACT score: 27
61% had SAT critical reading scores over 600
43% had SAT math scores over 600
88% had ACT scores over 24
20% had SAT critical reading scores over 700
13% had SAT math scores over 700
25% had ACT scores over 30

Graduation and After

69% graduated in 4 years
17% graduated in 5 years
2% graduated in 6 years

Financial Matters

$37,130 tuition and fees (2008–09)
$9730 room and board
68% average percent of need met
$18,892 average financial aid amount received per undergraduate (2004–05 estimated)

Barnard is a small, selective liberal arts college for women, located in New York City. Its superb faculty is composed of leading scholars who serve as dedicated, accessible teachers. Barnard's unique partnership with Columbia University, situated just across the street, provides students a vast selection of additional course offerings, extracurricular activities, NCAA Division I Ivy League athletic competition, and a fully coeducational social life. Barnard's metropolitan location grants students access to thousands of internships in addition to excellent cultural, intellectual, and social resources.

Getting Accepted
4,574 applied
29% were accepted
559 enrolled (43% of accepted)
75% from top tenth of their h.s. class
3.91 average high school GPA
Mean SAT critical reading score: 688
Mean SAT math score: 658
Mean SAT writing score: 688
Mean ACT score: 29
91% had SAT critical reading scores over 600
84% had SAT math scores over 600
91% had SAT writing scores over 600
96% had ACT scores over 24
49% had SAT critical reading scores over 700
28% had SAT math scores over 700
51% had SAT writing scores over 700
55% had ACT scores over 30
4 National Merit Scholars
44 class presidents
78 valedictorians

Graduation and After
82% graduated in 4 years
6% graduated in 5 years
1% graduated in 6 years
22% pursued further study (6% arts and sciences, 4% law, 3% education)
64% had job offers within 6 months
45 organizations recruited on campus

Financial Matters
$35,190 tuition and fees (2007–08)
$11,546 room and board
100% average percent of need met
$30,664 average financial aid amount received per undergraduate (2006–07 estimated)

BARNARD COLLEGE
URBAN SETTING ■ PRIVATE ■ INDEPENDENT ■ WOMEN ONLY
NEW YORK, NEW YORK

Web site: www.barnard.edu
Contact: Ms. Jennifer Gill Fondiller, Dean of Admissions, 3009 Broadway, New York, NY 10027
Telephone: 212-854-2014
Fax: 212-854-6220
E-mail: admissions@barnard.edu

Academics
Barnard awards bachelor's **degrees**. **Challenging opportunities** include advanced placement credit, accelerated degree programs, student-designed majors, double majors, independent study, and a senior project. Special programs include internships, off-campus study, and study-abroad.

The most frequently chosen **baccalaureate** fields are social sciences, psychology, and area and ethnic studies. A complete listing of majors at Barnard appears in the Majors by College index beginning on page 471.

The **faculty** at Barnard has 198 full-time members, 92% with terminal degrees. The student-faculty ratio is 10:1.

Students of Barnard
The student body is made up of 2,346 undergraduates. Students come from 48 states and territories and 40 other countries. 32% are from New York. 3.7% are international students. 4.9% are African American, 0.3% American Indian, 16.1% Asian American, and 8.6% Hispanic American. 95% returned for their sophomore year.

Facilities and Resources
210 **computers/terminals** are available on campus for general student use. Students can access the following: campus intranet, computer help desk, free student e-mail accounts, online (class) grades, online (class) registration, online (class) schedules. Campuswide network is available. 100% of college-owned or -operated housing units are wired for high-speed Internet access. Wireless service is available via computer centers, computer labs, dorm rooms, libraries, student centers. The **library** has 205,912 books and 463 subscriptions.

Campus Life
There are 100 active organizations on campus, including a drama/theater group, newspaper, radio station, television station, choral group, and marching band. No national or local **sororities**.

Barnard is a member of the NCAA (Division I). **Intercollegiate sports** include archery, basketball, crew, cross-country running, fencing, field hockey, golf, lacrosse, soccer, softball, swimming and diving, tennis, track and field, volleyball.

Campus Safety
Student safety services include gated campus with permanent security posts, late-night transport/escort service, 24-hour emergency telephone alarm devices, and 24-hour patrols by trained security personnel.

Applying
Barnard requires an essay, SAT with writing and two subject tests or ACT with writing, a high school transcript, 3 recommendations, and Common Application with Barnard supplement. It recommends an interview. Application deadline: 1/1; 2/1 for financial aid. Early and deferred admission are possible.

BATES COLLEGE
SMALL-TOWN SETTING ■ PRIVATE ■ INDEPENDENT ■ COED
LEWISTON, MAINE

Web site: www.bates.edu
Contact: Mr. Wylie Mitchell, Dean of Admissions, 23 Campus Avenue,
    Lewiston, ME 04240-6028
Telephone: 207-786-6000
Fax: 207-786-6025
E-mail: admissions@bates.edu

Academics
Bates awards bachelor's **degrees**. **Challenging opportunities** include advanced placement credit, accelerated degree programs, student-designed majors, an honors program,
double majors, independent study, and a senior project. Special programs include
cooperative education, internships, off-campus study, and study-abroad.

The most frequently chosen **baccalaureate** fields are social sciences, biological/life
sciences, and English. A complete listing of majors at Bates appears in the Majors by
College index beginning on page 471.

The **faculty** at Bates has 162 full-time members, 93% with terminal degrees. The
student-faculty ratio is 10:1.

Students of Bates
The student body is made up of 1,660 undergraduates. 51.6% are women and 48.4% are
men. Students come from 45 states and territories and 78 other countries. 11% are from
Maine. 5.3% are international students. 2.8% are African American, 0.5% American
Indian, 5.6% Asian American, and 2.4% Hispanic American. 93% returned for their
sophomore year.

Facilities and Resources
1,150 **computers/terminals** are available on campus for general student use. Students
can access the following: online (class) registration, course web pages, course evaluation,
financial records. Campuswide network is available. The 2 **libraries** have 588,211 books
and 25,674 subscriptions.

Campus Life
There are 91 active organizations on campus, including a drama/theater group,
newspaper, radio station, and choral group. No national or local **fraternities** or **sororities**.

Bates is a member of the NCAA (Division III). **Intercollegiate sports** include
baseball (m), basketball, crew, cross-country running, field hockey (w), football (m), golf,
lacrosse, skiing (cross-country), skiing (downhill), soccer, softball (w), squash, swimming
and diving, tennis, track and field, volleyball (w).

Campus Safety
Student safety services include late-night transport/escort service, 24-hour emergency
telephone alarm devices, 24-hour patrols by trained security personnel, student patrols,
and electronically operated dormitory entrances.

Applying
Bates requires an essay, a high school transcript, and 3 recommendations. It recommends
an interview. Application deadline: 1/1; 2/1 for financial aid. Early and deferred admission are possible.

Getting Accepted
4,434 applied
30% were accepted
442 enrolled (34% of accepted)
55% from top tenth of their h.s. class
91% had SAT critical reading scores over 600
90% had SAT math scores over 600
32% had SAT critical reading scores over 700
28% had SAT math scores over 700

Graduation and After
83% graduated in 4 years
4% graduated in 5 years
1% graduated in 6 years
64 organizations recruited on campus

Financial Matters
$46,800 comprehensive fee (2007–08)
100% average percent of need met
$27,428 average financial aid amount received
    per undergraduate (2005–06 estimated)

BAYLOR UNIVERSITY

URBAN SETTING ■ PRIVATE ■ INDEPENDENT RELIGIOUS ■ COED
WACO, TEXAS

Web site: www.baylor.edu
Contact: Ms. Jennifer Carron, Director of Admissions, PO Box 97056, Waco, TX 76798
Telephone: 254-710-3435 or toll-free 800-BAYLORU
Fax: 254-710-3436
E-mail: admissions@baylor.edu

Getting Accepted

26,514 applied
44% were accepted
2,732 enrolled (23% of accepted)
45% from top tenth of their h.s. class
Mean SAT critical reading score: 602
Mean SAT math score: 617
Mean SAT writing score: 587
Mean ACT score: 26
52% had SAT critical reading scores over 600
60% had SAT math scores over 600
44% had SAT writing scores over 600
67% had ACT scores over 24
12% had SAT critical reading scores over 700
14% had SAT math scores over 700
9% had SAT writing scores over 700
11% had ACT scores over 30
82 National Merit Scholars

Graduation and After

48% graduated in 4 years
21% graduated in 5 years
3% graduated in 6 years
329 organizations recruited on campus

Financial Matters

$26,234 tuition and fees (2008–09)
$7608 room and board
63% average percent of need met
$15,882 average financial aid amount received per undergraduate (2006–07 estimated)

Academics

Baylor awards bachelor's, master's, doctoral, and first-professional **degrees** and post-master's certificates. **Challenging opportunities** include advanced placement credit, accelerated degree programs, student-designed majors, an honors program, double majors, and a senior project. Special programs include internships, summer session for credit, study-abroad, and Air Force ROTC.

The most frequently chosen **baccalaureate** fields are business/marketing, communications/journalism, and health professions and related sciences. A complete listing of majors at Baylor appears in the Majors by College index beginning on page 471.

The **faculty** at Baylor has 813 full-time members, 81% with terminal degrees. The student-faculty ratio is 15:1.

Students of Baylor

The student body totals 14,174, of whom 11,902 are undergraduates. 58.5% are women and 41.5% are men. Students come from 51 states and territories and 71 other countries. 83% are from Texas. 1.8% are international students. 7.5% are African American, 0.6% American Indian, 7% Asian American, and 10.3% Hispanic American. 86% returned for their sophomore year.

Facilities and Resources

1,500 **computers/terminals** are available on campus for general student use. Students can access the following: campus intranet, computer help desk, free student e-mail accounts, online (class) grades, online (class) registration, online (class) schedules. Campuswide network is available. 99% of college-owned or -operated housing units are wired for high-speed Internet access. Wireless service is available via entire campus. The 9 **libraries** have 2,252,780 books and 8,429 subscriptions.

Campus Life

There are 289 active organizations on campus, including a drama/theater group, newspaper, radio station, television station, choral group, and marching band. 13% of eligible men and 17% of eligible women are members of national **fraternities**, national **sororities**, local fraternities, and local sororities.

Baylor is a member of the NCAA (Division I). **Intercollegiate sports** (some offering scholarships) include baseball (m), basketball, cross-country running, equestrian sports (w), football (m), golf, soccer (w), softball (w), tennis, track and field, volleyball (w).

Campus Safety

Student safety services include bicycle patrols, late-night transport/escort service, 24-hour emergency telephone alarm devices, 24-hour patrols by trained security personnel, and electronically operated dormitory entrances.

Applying

Baylor requires SAT or ACT, ACT essay, and a high school transcript, and in some cases an essay, recommendations, and a minimum high school GPA of 2.5. It recommends an interview. Application deadline: 2/1; 2/15 priority date for financial aid. Early admission is possible.

BELMONT UNIVERSITY

URBAN SETTING ■ PRIVATE ■ INDEPENDENT RELIGIOUS ■ COED
NASHVILLE, TENNESSEE

SPONSOR

Web site: www.belmont.edu
Contact: Dr. Kathryn Baugher, Dean of Enrollment Services, 1900 Belmont
Boulevard, Nashville, TN 37212-3757
Telephone: 615-460-6785 or toll-free 800-56E-NROL
Fax: 615-460-5434
E-mail: buadmission@mail.belmont.edu

Academics

Belmont awards bachelor's, master's, and doctoral **degrees** and post-master's
certificates. **Challenging opportunities** include advanced placement credit, accelerated
degree programs, student-designed majors, an honors program, double majors,
independent study, and a senior project. Special programs include cooperative education,
internships, summer session for credit, off-campus study, study-abroad, and Army and
Navy ROTC.

The most frequently chosen **baccalaureate** fields are visual and performing arts,
business/marketing, and health professions and related sciences. A complete listing of
majors at Belmont appears in the Majors by College index beginning on page 471.

The **faculty** at Belmont has 239 full-time members, 81% with terminal degrees. The
student-faculty ratio is 12:1.

Students of Belmont

The student body totals 4,756, of whom 4,028 are undergraduates. 59.2% are women
and 40.8% are men. Students come from 48 states and territories and 29 other countries.
44% are from Tennessee. 1.2% are international students. 3.9% are African American,
0.4% American Indian, 1.7% Asian American, and 2.2% Hispanic American. 80%
returned for their sophomore year.

Facilities and Resources

400 **computers/terminals** are available on campus for general student use. Students can
access the following: campus intranet, free student e-mail accounts, online (class) grades,
online (class) registration, online (class) schedules, individual student information via
BANNER Web. Campuswide network is available. 100% of college-owned or -operated
housing units are wired for high-speed Internet access. Wireless service is available via
entire campus. The **library** has 200,630 books and 1,415 subscriptions.

Campus Life

There are 69 active organizations on campus, including a drama/theater group,
newspaper, radio station, television station, choral group, and marching band. 3% of
eligible men and 4% of eligible women are members of national **fraternities** and
national **sororities**.

Belmont is a member of the NCAA (Division I). **Intercollegiate sports** (some offering scholarships) include baseball (m), basketball, cross-country running, golf, soccer,
softball (w), tennis, track and field, volleyball (w).

Campus Safety

Student safety services include bicycle patrol, late-night transport/escort service, 24-hour
emergency telephone alarm devices, 24-hour patrols by trained security personnel, and
electronically operated dormitory entrances.

Applying

Belmont requires an essay, SAT or ACT, a high school transcript, recommendations,
resume of activities, and a minimum high school GPA of 3.0, and in some cases an
interview. Application deadline: 8/1; 3/1 priority date for financial aid. Early and deferred
admission are possible.

Getting Accepted
2,766 applied
62% were accepted
804 enrolled (47% of accepted)
31% from top tenth of their h.s. class
3.5 average high school GPA
Mean SAT critical reading score: 587
Mean SAT math score: 582
Mean ACT score: 26
37% had SAT critical reading scores over 600
38% had SAT math scores over 600
71% had ACT scores over 24
5% had SAT critical reading scores over 700
6% had SAT math scores over 700
13% had ACT scores over 30
43 valedictorians

Graduation and After
57% graduated in 4 years
8% graduated in 5 years
1% graduated in 6 years
25% pursued further study (10% arts and
sciences, 10% business, 8% education)
80% had job offers within 6 months
180 organizations recruited on campus

Financial Matters
$19,780 tuition and fees (2007–08)
$9529 room and board
84% average percent of need met
$10,159 average financial aid amount received
per undergraduate (2005–06)

SPONSOR

Beloit College offers students the potential to put their education into action. With extensive opportunities to study abroad, engage in internships and field terms, study broadly and creatively, collaborate with professors, start businesses, form clubs, and play sports, students plunge into campus life and emerge with the experiences and global knowledge to live meaningfully in the twenty-first century. Beloit's 1,250 students—from nearly every state and more than forty other countries—are at home in a world of ideas and leave the College able to make critical connections between thought and action.

Getting Accepted
2,157 applied
60% were accepted
325 enrolled (25% of accepted)
31% from top tenth of their h.s. class
3.4 average high school GPA
Mean SAT critical reading score: 650
Mean SAT math score: 630
Mean ACT score: 27
82% had SAT critical reading scores over 600
71% had SAT math scores over 600
84% had ACT scores over 24
34% had SAT critical reading scores over 700
13% had SAT math scores over 700
24% had ACT scores over 30
6 National Merit Scholars
11 valedictorians

Graduation and After
74% graduated in 4 years
5% graduated in 5 years
1% graduated in 6 years
33% pursued further study (24% arts and sciences, 3% medicine, 2% business)
72% had job offers within 6 months

Financial Matters
$29,908 tuition and fees (2007–08)
$6408 room and board
100% average percent of need met
$22,781 average financial aid amount received per undergraduate (2006–07 estimated)

BELOIT COLLEGE
SMALL-TOWN SETTING ■ PRIVATE ■ INDEPENDENT ■ COED
BELOIT, WISCONSIN
Web site: www.beloit.edu
Contact: Mr. James S. Zielinski, Director of Admissions, 700 College Street, Beloit, WI 53511-5596
Telephone: 608-363-2500 or toll-free 800-9-BELOIT
Fax: 608-363-2075
E-mail: admiss@beloit.edu

Academics
Beloit awards bachelor's **degrees**. **Challenging opportunities** include advanced placement credit, student-designed majors, double majors, independent study, and a senior project. Special programs include internships, summer session for credit, off-campus study, and study-abroad.

The most frequently chosen **baccalaureate** fields are social sciences, visual and performing arts, and foreign languages and literature. A complete listing of majors at Beloit appears in the Majors by College index beginning on page 471.

The **faculty** at Beloit has 120 full-time members, 94% with terminal degrees. The student-faculty ratio is 11:1.

Students of Beloit
The student body is made up of 1,352 undergraduates. 57.7% are women and 42.3% are men. Students come from 47 states and territories and 43 other countries. 23% are from Wisconsin. 6.1% are international students. 3.4% are African American, 0.5% American Indian, 3.8% Asian American, and 2.9% Hispanic American. 89% returned for their sophomore year.

Facilities and Resources
270 **computers/terminals** are available on campus for general student use. Students can access the following: campus intranet, computer help desk, free student e-mail accounts, online (class) schedules. Campuswide network is available. 100% of college-owned or -operated housing units are wired for high-speed Internet access. Wireless service is available via classrooms, computer centers, computer labs, dorm rooms, libraries, student centers. The **library** has 183,736 books and 946 subscriptions.

Campus Life
There are 85 active organizations on campus, including a drama/theater group, newspaper, radio station, television station, and choral group. 15% of eligible men and 5% of eligible women are members of national **fraternities**, national **sororities**, local fraternities, and local sororities.

Beloit is a member of the NCAA (Division III). **Intercollegiate sports** include baseball (m), basketball, cross-country running, football (m), golf, soccer, softball (w), swimming and diving, tennis, track and field, volleyball (w).

Campus Safety
Student safety services include late-night transport/escort service, 24-hour emergency telephone alarm devices, 24-hour patrols by trained security personnel, and electronically operated dormitory entrances.

Applying
Beloit requires an essay, SAT or ACT, a high school transcript, and 1 recommendation, and in some cases an interview. It recommends an interview. Application deadline: 1/15; 3/1 priority date for financial aid. Early and deferred admission are possible.

BENEDICTINE UNIVERSITY

SUBURBAN SETTING ■ PRIVATE ■ INDEPENDENT RELIGIOUS ■ COED
LISLE, ILLINOIS

Web site: www.ben.edu
Contact: Ms. Kari Gibbons, Dean of Enrollment, 5700 College Road, Lisle, IL 60532-0900
Telephone: 630-829-6300 or toll-free 888-829-6363 (out-of-state)
Fax: 630-829-6301
E-mail: admissions@ben.edu

Academics

Benedictine awards associate, bachelor's, master's, and doctoral **degrees** and post-bachelor's certificates. **Challenging opportunities** include advanced placement credit, accelerated degree programs, an honors program, double majors, independent study, and a senior project. Special programs include internships, summer session for credit, off-campus study, study-abroad, and Army ROTC.

The most frequently chosen **baccalaureate** fields are business/marketing, health professions and related sciences, and psychology. A complete listing of majors at Benedictine appears in the Majors by College index beginning on page 471.

The **faculty** at Benedictine has 87 full-time members, 91% with terminal degrees. The student-faculty ratio is 13:1.

Students of Benedictine

The student body totals 3,900, of whom 2,657 are undergraduates. 57.3% are women and 42.7% are men. Students come from 41 states and territories and 9 other countries. 97% are from Illinois. 0.8% are international students. 10% are African American, 0.2% American Indian, 12.9% Asian American, and 5.7% Hispanic American. 71% returned for their sophomore year.

Facilities and Resources

Campuswide network is available. The **library** has 201,190 books and 14,177 subscriptions.

Campus Life

There are 38 active organizations on campus, including a newspaper, television station, and choral group. No national or local **fraternities** or **sororities**.

Benedictine is a member of the NCAA (Division III). **Intercollegiate sports** include baseball (m), basketball, cross-country running, football (m), golf (m), soccer, softball (w), swimming and diving, tennis (w), track and field, volleyball (w).

Campus Safety

Student safety services include late-night transport/escort service, 24-hour emergency telephone alarm devices, 24-hour patrols by trained security personnel, and electronically operated dormitory entrances.

Applying

Benedictine requires an essay, ACT, a high school transcript, and recommendations, and in some cases an interview. It recommends rank in upper 50% of high school class, minimum ACT score of 21. Application deadline: rolling admissions. Deferred admission is possible.

Getting Accepted
1,321 applied
81% were accepted
379 enrolled (35% of accepted)
19% from top tenth of their h.s. class
3.35 average high school GPA
Mean ACT score: 23
37% had ACT scores over 24
4% had ACT scores over 30
4 valedictorians

Graduation and After
31% graduated in 4 years
15% graduated in 5 years
5% graduated in 6 years

Financial Matters
$21,310 tuition and fees (2007–08)
$6955 room and board
85% average percent of need met
$11,980 average financial aid amount received per undergraduate (2005–06)

BENNINGTON COLLEGE

SMALL-TOWN SETTING ■ PRIVATE ■ INDEPENDENT ■ COED
BENNINGTON, VERMONT

Web site: www.bennington.edu
Contact: Mr. Ken Himmelman, Dean of Admissions and Financial Aid, One
   College Drive, Bennington, VT 05201-6003
Telephone: 802-440-4312 or toll-free 800-833-6845
Fax: 802-440-4320
E-mail: admissions@bennington.edu

Getting Accepted
1,011 applied
63% were accepted
204 enrolled (32% of accepted)
28% from top tenth of their h.s. class
3.4 average high school GPA
Mean SAT critical reading score: 642
Mean SAT math score: 574
Mean SAT writing score: 629
Mean ACT score: 26

Graduation and After
50% graduated in 4 years
6% graduated in 5 years
1% graduated in 6 years

Financial Matters
$36,800 tuition and fees (2007–08)
$9380 room and board
78% average percent of need met
$26,894 average financial aid amount received
   per undergraduate (2006–07 estimated)

Academics

Bennington awards bachelor's and master's **degrees** and post-bachelor's certificates.
Challenging opportunities include accelerated degree programs, student-designed
majors, double majors, independent study, and a senior project. Special programs include
internships and study-abroad.

The most frequently chosen **baccalaureate** fields are visual and performing arts,
English, and foreign languages and literature. A complete listing of majors at Bennington
appears in the Majors by College index beginning on page 471.

The **faculty** at Bennington has 60 full-time members, 73% with terminal degrees.
The student-faculty ratio is 8:1.

Students of Bennington

The student body totals 723, of whom 583 are undergraduates. 67.6% are women and
32.4% are men. Students come from 43 states and territories and 13 other countries. 4%
are from Vermont. 3.1% are international students. 2.1% are African American, 0.2%
American Indian, 2.1% Asian American, and 2.1% Hispanic American. 81% returned for
their sophomore year.

Facilities and Resources

90 **computers/terminals** and 25 ports are available on campus for general student use.
Students can access the following: campus intranet, computer help desk, free student
e-mail accounts, online (class) schedules. Campuswide network is available. 100% of college-owned or -operated housing units are wired for high-speed Internet access. Wireless service is available via classrooms, computer centers, computer labs, libraries, student
centers. The 2 **libraries** have 121,500 books and 13,500 subscriptions.

Campus Life

There are 18 active organizations on campus, including a drama/theater group,
newspaper, and choral group. No national or local **fraternities** or **sororities**.

This institution has no intercollegiate sports.

Campus Safety

Student safety services include prevention/awareness program, late-night transport/
escort service, 24-hour emergency telephone alarm devices, and 24-hour patrols by
trained security personnel.

Applying

Bennington requires an essay, a high school transcript, 2 recommendations, and graded
analytic paper, and in some cases TOEFL (minimum score—577 paper-based ; 233 com-
puter-based; 90-91 internet-based). It recommends an interview. Application deadline:
1/3; 3/1 priority date for financial aid. Early and deferred admission are possible.

BENTLEY COLLEGE

SUBURBAN SETTING ■ PRIVATE ■ INDEPENDENT ■ COED
WALTHAM, MASSACHUSETTS

Web site: www.bentley.edu
Contact: 175 Forest Street, Waltham, MA 02452
Telephone: 781-891-2244 or toll-free 800-523-2354
Fax: 781-891-3414
E-mail: ugadmission@bentley.edu

Academics

Bentley awards associate, bachelor's, and master's **degrees** and post-bachelor's and post-master's certificates. **Challenging opportunities** include advanced placement credit, accelerated degree programs, student-designed majors, an honors program, double majors, independent study, and a senior project. Special programs include internships, summer session for credit, off-campus study, study-abroad, and Army and Air Force ROTC.

The most frequently chosen **baccalaureate** fields are business/marketing, computer and information sciences, and interdisciplinary studies. A complete listing of majors at Bentley appears in the Majors by College index beginning on page 471.

The **faculty** at Bentley has 267 full-time members, 84% with terminal degrees. The student-faculty ratio is 12:1.

Students of Bentley

The student body totals 5,593, of whom 4,200 are undergraduates. 40.2% are women and 59.8% are men. Students come from 42 states and territories and 81 other countries. 50% are from Massachusetts. 7.5% are international students. 2.7% are African American, 8.1% Asian American, and 4.4% Hispanic American. 92% returned for their sophomore year.

Facilities and Resources

4,620 **computers/terminals** and 13,336 ports are available on campus for general student use. Students can access the following: campus intranet, computer help desk, free student e-mail accounts, online (class) grades, online (class) registration, online (class) schedules, grade checking, online admission, Blackboard, resume review, student employment, interlibrary loan. Campuswide network is available. 100% of college-owned or -operated housing units are wired for high-speed Internet access. Wireless service is available via entire campus. The **library** has 146,104 books and 30,800 subscriptions.

Campus Life

There are 90 active organizations on campus, including a drama/theater group, newspaper, radio station, television station, and choral group. 9% of eligible men and 12% of eligible women are members of national **fraternities**, national **sororities**, and local fraternities.

Bentley is a member of the NCAA (Division II). **Intercollegiate sports** (some offering scholarships) include baseball (m), basketball, cross-country running, field hockey (w), football (m), golf (w), ice hockey (m), lacrosse, soccer, softball (w), swimming and diving, tennis, track and field, volleyball (w).

Campus Safety

Student safety services include security cameras, late-night transport/escort service, 24-hour emergency telephone alarm devices, 24-hour patrols by trained security personnel, and electronically operated dormitory entrances.

Applying

Bentley requires an essay, SAT or ACT, a high school transcript, and 2 recommendations. It recommends an interview. Application deadline: 1/15, 1/15 for nonresidents; 2/1 for financial aid. Early and deferred admission are possible.

Getting Accepted

6,689 applied
38% were accepted
934 enrolled (37% of accepted)
42% from top tenth of their h.s. class
Mean SAT critical reading score: 590
Mean SAT math score: 640
Mean SAT writing score: 600
Mean ACT score: 26
47% had SAT critical reading scores over 600
77% had SAT math scores over 600
52% had SAT writing scores over 600
80% had ACT scores over 24
5% had SAT critical reading scores over 700
18% had SAT math scores over 700
7% had SAT writing scores over 700
16% had ACT scores over 30

Graduation and After

78% graduated in 4 years
7% graduated in 5 years
2% graduated in 6 years
17% pursued further study (12% business, 1% law)

Financial Matters

$32,896 tuition and fees (2007–08)
$10,940 room and board
91% average percent of need met
$23,305 average financial aid amount received per undergraduate (2005–06)

Getting Accepted

2,083 applied
29% were accepted
421 enrolled (71% of accepted)
26% from top tenth of their h.s. class
3.42 average high school GPA
Mean SAT critical reading score: 539
Mean SAT math score: 543
Mean SAT writing score: 528
Mean ACT score: 23
25% had SAT critical reading scores over 600
29% had SAT math scores over 600
17% had SAT writing scores over 600
46% had ACT scores over 24
4% had SAT critical reading scores over 700
4% had SAT math scores over 700
4% had SAT writing scores over 700
4% had ACT scores over 30

Graduation and After

45% graduated in 4 years
17% graduated in 5 years
1% graduated in 6 years
125 organizations recruited on campus

Financial Matters

$790 tuition and fees (2007–08)
$5492 room and board
92% average percent of need met
$28,059 average financial aid amount received per undergraduate (2006–07 estimated)

BEREA COLLEGE

SMALL-TOWN SETTING ■ PRIVATE ■ INDEPENDENT ■ COED
BEREA, KENTUCKY

Web site: www.berea.edu
Contact: Ms. Erika Smith, Director of Admissions, CPO 2220, Berea, KY 40404
Telephone: 859-985-3500 or toll-free 800-326-5948
Fax: 859-985-3512
E-mail: admissions@berea.edu

Academics

Berea awards bachelor's **degrees**. **Challenging opportunities** include advanced placement credit, student-designed majors, an honors program, double majors, independent study, and a senior project. Special programs include internships, summer session for credit, off-campus study, and study-abroad.

The most frequently chosen **baccalaureate** fields are business/marketing, engineering technologies, and social sciences. A complete listing of majors at Berea appears in the Majors by College index beginning on page 471.

The **faculty** at Berea has 128 full-time members, 89% with terminal degrees. The student-faculty ratio is 11:1.

Students of Berea

The student body is made up of 1,582 undergraduates. 59.7% are women and 40.3% are men. Students come from 40 states and territories and 51 other countries. 43% are from Kentucky. 7% are international students. 17.3% are African American, 0.8% American Indian, 1.6% Asian American, and 2% Hispanic American. 83% returned for their sophomore year.

Facilities and Resources

20 **computers/terminals** and 850 ports are available on campus for general student use. Students can access the following: campus intranet, computer help desk, free student e-mail accounts, online (class) grades, online (class) registration, online (class) schedules. Campuswide network is available. 100% of college-owned or -operated housing units are wired for high-speed Internet access. Wireless service is available via libraries, student centers. The 2 **libraries** have 366,926 books and 1,067 subscriptions.

Campus Life

There are 50 active organizations on campus, including a drama/theater group, newspaper, and choral group. No national or local **fraternities** or **sororities**.

Berea is a member of the NAIA. **Intercollegiate sports** include baseball (m), basketball, cross-country running, golf (m), soccer, softball (w), swimming and diving, tennis, track and field, volleyball (w).

Campus Safety

Student safety services include crime prevention programs, late-night transport/escort service, 24-hour emergency telephone alarm devices, 24-hour patrols by trained security personnel, and electronically operated dormitory entrances.

Applying

Berea requires an essay, SAT or ACT, a high school transcript, an interview, and financial aid application. It recommends 2 recommendations. Application deadline: 4/30; 8/1 for financial aid, with a 4/15 priority date.

BERNARD M. BARUCH COLLEGE OF THE CITY UNIVERSITY OF NEW YORK

URBAN SETTING ■ PUBLIC ■ STATE AND LOCALLY SUPPORTED ■ COED
NEW YORK, NEW YORK

Web site: www.baruch.cuny.edu
Contact: Ms. Marybeth Murphy, Assistant Vice President for Undergraduate Admissions and Financial Aid, Box H-0720, New York, NY 10010-5585
Telephone: 646-312-1400
E-mail: marybeth_murphy@baruch.cuny.edu

Academics

Baruch College awards bachelor's and master's **degrees** and post-master's certificates. **Challenging opportunities** include advanced placement credit, accelerated degree programs, student-designed majors, an honors program, double majors, independent study, and a senior project. Special programs include internships, summer session for credit, and study-abroad.

The most frequently chosen **baccalaureate** fields are business/marketing, communications/journalism, and psychology. A complete listing of majors at Baruch College appears in the Majors by College index beginning on page 471.

The **faculty** at Baruch College has 501 full-time members, 91% with terminal degrees. The student-faculty ratio is 19:1.

Students of Baruch College

The student body totals 16,097, of whom 12,863 are undergraduates. 52.1% are women and 47.9% are men. 97% are from New York. 12.6% are international students. 11.1% are African American, 0.1% American Indian, 29.8% Asian American, and 16.5% Hispanic American. 88% returned for their sophomore year.

Facilities and Resources

1,300 **computers/terminals** are available on campus for general student use. Students can access the following: campus intranet, computer help desk, free student e-mail accounts, online (class) grades, online (class) registration, online (class) schedules. Campuswide network is available. Wireless service is available via classrooms, computer centers, computer labs, libraries, student centers. The 2 **libraries** have 456,132 books and 35,000 subscriptions.

Campus Life

There are 172 active organizations on campus, including a drama/theater group, newspaper, radio station, and choral group. Baruch College has national **fraternities**, national **sororities**, local fraternities, and local sororities.

Baruch College is a member of the NCAA (Division III). **Intercollegiate sports** include baseball (m), basketball, cheerleading (w), cross-country running, soccer (m), softball (w), swimming and diving, tennis, volleyball.

Campus Safety

Student safety services include controlled access by ID card, late-night transport/escort service, 24-hour emergency telephone alarm devices, and 24-hour patrols by trained security personnel.

Applying

Baruch College requires SAT or ACT, a high school transcript, 16 academic units, and a minimum high school GPA of 2.5, and in some cases an interview and recommendations. Application deadline: 2/1; 4/30 for financial aid, with a 3/15 priority date. Early admission is possible.

Getting Accepted

17,114 applied
26% were accepted
1,479 enrolled (34% of accepted)
3.0 average high school GPA
Mean SAT critical reading score: 530
Mean SAT math score: 590
20% had SAT critical reading scores over 600
47% had SAT math scores over 600
2% had SAT critical reading scores over 700
11% had SAT math scores over 700

Graduation and After

33% graduated in 4 years
22% graduated in 5 years
5% graduated in 6 years
75% had job offers within 6 months
300 organizations recruited on campus

Financial Matters

$4320 resident tuition and fees (2008–09)
$8960 nonresident tuition and fees (2008–09)
63% average percent of need met
$4800 average financial aid amount received per undergraduate (2005–06 estimated)

Getting Accepted
1,813 applied
70% were accepted
537 enrolled (42% of accepted)
34% from top tenth of their h.s. class
3.61 average high school GPA
Mean SAT critical reading score: 573
Mean SAT math score: 562
Mean ACT score: 26
35% had SAT critical reading scores over 600
30% had SAT math scores over 600
75% had ACT scores over 24
7% had SAT critical reading scores over 700
2% had SAT math scores over 700
16% had ACT scores over 30
8 valedictorians

Graduation and After
51% graduated in 4 years
9% graduated in 5 years
1% graduated in 6 years
70% had job offers within 6 months
139 organizations recruited on campus

Financial Matters
$20,570 tuition and fees (2007–08)
$7626 room and board
81% average percent of need met
$15,575 average financial aid amount received per undergraduate (2006–07 estimated)

BERRY COLLEGE
SUBURBAN SETTING ■ PRIVATE ■ INDEPENDENT RELIGIOUS ■ COED
MOUNT BERRY, GEORGIA

Web site: www.berry.edu
Contact: Mr. Timothy Tarpley, Associate Director of Admissions and Financial Aid, PO Box 490159, 2277 Martha Berry Highway, NW, Mount Berry, GA 30149-0159
Telephone: 706-236-2215 or toll-free 800-237-7942
Fax: 706-290-2178
E-mail: admissions@berry.edu

Academics
Berry awards bachelor's and master's **degrees** and post-master's certificates. **Challenging opportunities** include advanced placement credit, accelerated degree programs, student-designed majors, an honors program, double majors, independent study, and a senior project. Special programs include cooperative education, internships, summer session for credit, and study-abroad.

The most frequently chosen **baccalaureate** fields are business/marketing, education, and social sciences. A complete listing of majors at Berry appears in the Majors by College index beginning on page 471.

The **faculty** at Berry has 145 full-time members, 83% with terminal degrees. The student-faculty ratio is 12:1.

Students of Berry
The student body totals 1,858, of whom 1,737 are undergraduates. 66% are women and 34% are men. Students come from 39 states and territories and 20 other countries. 83% are from Georgia. 2.2% are international students. 3.3% are African American, 0.2% American Indian, 1.6% Asian American, and 2.3% Hispanic American. 76% returned for their sophomore year.

Facilities and Resources
140 **computers/terminals** and 80 ports are available on campus for general student use. Students can access the following: campus intranet, computer help desk, free student e-mail accounts, online (class) grades, online (class) registration, online (class) schedules. Campuswide network is available. 100% of college-owned or -operated housing units are wired for high-speed Internet access. Wireless service is available via classrooms, computer centers, computer labs, learning centers, libraries, student centers. The 2 **libraries** have 203,522 books and 2,082 subscriptions.

Campus Life
There are 80 active organizations on campus, including a drama/theater group, newspaper, television station, and choral group. No national or local **fraternities** or **sororities**.

Berry is a member of the NAIA. **Intercollegiate sports** (some offering scholarships) include baseball (m), basketball, cheerleading, cross-country running, golf, soccer, tennis, track and field.

Campus Safety
Student safety services include lighted pathways, 24-hour emergency telephone alarm devices, 24-hour patrols by trained security personnel, and electronically operated dormitory entrances.

Applying
Berry requires SAT or ACT, a high school transcript, and recommendations. Application deadline: 7/25; 4/1 priority date for financial aid. Early and deferred admission are possible.

Bethel University

Suburban setting ■ Private ■ Independent Religious ■ Coed
St. Paul, Minnesota

Web site: www.bethel.edu
Contact: Mr. Jay Fedje, Director of Admissions, 3900 Bethel Drive, St. Paul,
  MN 55112
Telephone: 651-638-6242 or toll-free 800-255-8706 Ext. 6242
Fax: 651-635-1490
E-mail: buadmissions-cas@bethel.edu

SPONSOR

> Bethel University provides academic excellence in a dynamic Christian environment. *U.S. News & World Report* has recognized Bethel as one of the top Midwestern universities. Outstanding faculty members, numerous extracurricular activities, service-learning experiences, and off-campus study opportunities make Bethel a great place to live and learn. Bethel is committed to providing a high-quality education that equips men and women for culturally sensitive leadership, scholarship, and service around the world.

Academics

Bethel awards associate, bachelor's, master's, doctoral, and first-professional **degrees** and post-bachelor's and post-master's certificates. **Challenging opportunities** include advanced placement credit, accelerated degree programs, student-designed majors, an honors program, double majors, independent study, and a senior project. Special programs include internships, summer session for credit, off-campus study, study-abroad, and Army and Air Force ROTC.

The most frequently chosen **baccalaureate** fields are business/marketing, health professions and related sciences, and education. A complete listing of majors at Bethel appears in the Majors by College index beginning on page 471.

The **faculty** at Bethel has 177 full-time members, 80% with terminal degrees. The student-faculty ratio is 14:1.

Students of Bethel

The student body totals 4,162, of whom 3,327 are undergraduates. 62.5% are women and 37.5% are men. Students come from 40 states and territories and 18 other countries. 74% are from Minnesota. 0.3% are international students. 3% are African American, 0.3% American Indian, 2.7% Asian American, and 1.5% Hispanic American. 86% returned for their sophomore year.

Facilities and Resources

375 **computers/terminals** are available on campus for general student use. Students can access the following: campus intranet, computer help desk, free student e-mail accounts, online (class) grades, online (class) registration, online (class) schedules. Campuswide network is available. 100% of college-owned or -operated housing units are wired for high-speed Internet access. Wireless service is available via classrooms, computer centers, computer labs, dorm rooms, learning centers, libraries, student centers. The 2 **libraries** have 184,000 books and 21,343 subscriptions.

Campus Life

There are 74 active organizations on campus, including a drama/theater group, newspaper, radio station, and choral group. No national or local **fraternities** or **sororities**.

Bethel is a member of the NCAA (Division III). **Intercollegiate sports** include baseball (m), basketball, cross-country running, football (m), golf (m), ice hockey, soccer, softball (w), tennis, track and field, volleyball (w).

Campus Safety

Student safety services include late-night transport/escort service, 24-hour emergency telephone alarm devices, 24-hour patrols by trained security personnel, student patrols, and electronically operated dormitory entrances.

Applying

Bethel requires an essay, SAT or ACT, 2 recommendations, and rank in upper 50% of high school class, minimum ACT score of 21 or SAT score of 920. It recommends an interview. Application deadline: 4/15 priority date for financial aid. Early and deferred admission are possible.

Getting Accepted
1,643 applied
88% were accepted
572 enrolled (40% of accepted)
30% from top tenth of their h.s. class
3.52 average high school GPA
Mean SAT critical reading score: 579
Mean SAT math score: 574
Mean ACT score: 25
48% had SAT critical reading scores over 600
46% had SAT math scores over 600
58% had ACT scores over 24
11% had SAT critical reading scores over 700
9% had SAT math scores over 700
15% had ACT scores over 30
4 National Merit Scholars
32 valedictorians

Graduation and After
69% graduated in 4 years
7% graduated in 5 years
1% graduated in 6 years
70% had job offers within 6 months
160 organizations recruited on campus

Financial Matters
$24,510 tuition and fees (2007–08)
$7380 room and board
80% average percent of need met
$16,609 average financial aid amount received
  per undergraduate (2006–07 estimated)

BIOLA UNIVERSITY

SUBURBAN SETTING ■ PRIVATE ■ INDEPENDENT RELIGIOUS ■ COED
LA MIRADA, CALIFORNIA

Web site: www.biola.edu
Contact: Mr. Andre Stephens, Director of Enrollment Management, 13800
    Biola Avenue, La Mirada, CA 90639
Telephone: 562-903-4752 or toll-free 800-652-4652
Fax: 562-903-4709
E-mail: admissions@biola.edu

Getting Accepted
2,315 applied
82% were accepted
3.51 average high school GPA
Mean SAT critical reading score: 560
Mean SAT math score: 550
Mean SAT writing score: 560
Mean ACT score: 24

Graduation and After
30% had job offers within 6 months
1241 organizations recruited on campus

Financial Matters
$26,424 tuition and fees (2008–09)
70% average percent of need met
$15,200 average financial aid amount received
    per undergraduate (2004–05)

Academics
Biola awards bachelor's, master's, doctoral, and first-professional **degrees**. **Challenging opportunities** include advanced placement credit, accelerated degree programs, an honors program, double majors, independent study, and a senior project. Special programs include cooperative education, internships, summer session for credit, off-campus study, study-abroad, and Army and Air Force ROTC.

The most frequently chosen **baccalaureate** fields are business/marketing, communications/journalism, and theology and religious vocations. A complete listing of majors at Biola appears in the Majors by College index beginning on page 471.

The **faculty** at Biola has 213 full-time members, 75% with terminal degrees. The student-faculty ratio is 17:1.

Students of Biola
The student body totals 5,858, of whom 3,989 are undergraduates. Students come from 49 states and territories and 42 other countries. 75% are from California. 3.7% are international students. 4% are African American, 1% American Indian, 10.2% Asian American, and 11.6% Hispanic American. 83% returned for their sophomore year.

Facilities and Resources
165 **computers/terminals** are available on campus for general student use. Students can access the following: campus intranet, computer help desk, free student e-mail accounts, online (class) grades, online (class) registration, online (class) schedules. Campuswide network is available. 100% of college-owned or -operated housing units are wired for high-speed Internet access. Wireless service is available via computer centers, computer labs, dorm rooms, libraries, student centers. The **library** has 301,956 books and 17,876 subscriptions.

Campus Life
There are 33 active organizations on campus, including a drama/theater group, newspaper, radio station, television station, and choral group. No national or local **fraternities** or **sororities**.

Biola is a member of the NAIA. **Intercollegiate sports** (some offering scholarships) include baseball (m), basketball, cheerleading (w), cross-country running, golf, soccer, softball (w), swimming and diving, tennis, track and field, volleyball (w).

Campus Safety
Student safety services include access gates to roads through the middle of campus, late-night transport/escort service, 24-hour emergency telephone alarm devices, 24-hour patrols by trained security personnel, student patrols, and electronically operated dormitory entrances.

Applying
Biola requires an essay, SAT or ACT, a high school transcript, and 2 recommendations, and in some cases an interview. It recommends an interview and a minimum high school GPA of 3.0. Application deadline: 3/1. Early and deferred admission are possible.

BIRMINGHAM-SOUTHERN COLLEGE

URBAN SETTING ■ PRIVATE ■ INDEPENDENT RELIGIOUS ■ COED
BIRMINGHAM, ALABAMA

Web site: www.bsc.edu
Contact: Ms. Sheri E. Salmon, Associate Vice President for Admission, Box 549008, Birmingham, AL 35254
Telephone: 205-226-4696 or toll-free 800-523-5793
Fax: 205-226-3074
E-mail: admitme@bsc.edu

SPONSOR

Academics

Birmingham-Southern awards bachelor's and master's **degrees**. **Challenging opportunities** include advanced placement credit, student-designed majors, an honors program, double majors, independent study, and a senior project. Special programs include internships, summer session for credit, off-campus study, study-abroad, and Army and Air Force ROTC.

The most frequently chosen **baccalaureate** fields are business/marketing, English, and visual and performing arts. A complete listing of majors at Birmingham-Southern appears in the Majors by College index beginning on page 471.

The **faculty** at Birmingham-Southern has 103 full-time members, 96% with terminal degrees. The student-faculty ratio is 11:1.

Students of Birmingham-Southern

The student body totals 1,256, of whom 1,207 are undergraduates. 59% are women and 41% are men. Students come from 33 states and territories and 23 other countries. 73% are from Alabama. 0.2% are international students. 8% are African American, 0.4% American Indian, 3.1% Asian American, and 1.3% Hispanic American.

Facilities and Resources

156 **computers/terminals** are available on campus for general student use. Campuswide network is available. The **library** has 232,330 books and 949 subscriptions.

Campus Life

There are 70 active organizations on campus, including a drama/theater group, newspaper, radio station, and choral group. 44% of eligible men and 51% of eligible women are members of national **fraternities** and national **sororities**.

Birmingham-Southern is a member of the NCAA (Division I). **Intercollegiate sports** (some offering scholarships) include baseball (m), basketball, cross-country running, golf, riflery (w), soccer, softball (w), tennis, volleyball (w).

Campus Safety

Student safety services include vehicle safety inspection, late-night transport/escort service, 24-hour emergency telephone alarm devices, 24-hour patrols by trained security personnel, and electronically operated dormitory entrances.

Applying

Birmingham-Southern requires an essay, SAT or ACT, a high school transcript, 1 recommendation, and a minimum high school GPA of 2.0, and in some cases an interview. It recommends an interview. Application deadline: rolling admissions; 3/1 priority date for financial aid. Early and deferred admission are possible.

Getting Accepted
2,198 applied
57% were accepted
292 enrolled (23% of accepted)
34% from top tenth of their h.s. class
3.34 average high school GPA
Mean SAT critical reading score: 576
Mean SAT math score: 592
Mean ACT score: 25
51% had SAT critical reading scores over 600
38% had SAT math scores over 600
69% had ACT scores over 24
14% had SAT critical reading scores over 700
6% had SAT math scores over 700
20% had ACT scores over 30
7 National Merit Scholars
28 valedictorians

Graduation and After
62% graduated in 4 years
6% graduated in 5 years
3% graduated in 6 years
38% pursued further study (8% arts and sciences, 6% medicine, 4% law)
24 organizations recruited on campus

Financial Matters
$24,300 tuition and fees (2007–08)
$8062 room and board
87% average percent of need met
$22,166 average financial aid amount received per undergraduate (2006–07 estimated)

Boston College is a university with international stature strengthened by the more than 450-year tradition of Jesuit education, which emphasizes rigorous academic development grounded in the arts and sciences and a commitment to the development of the whole person. Through opportunities to participate in honors programs, research with faculty members, independent study, study abroad, and service learning, students are challenged to fulfill their potential as scholars. With artistic, cultural, service, social, religious, and athletic opportunities that abound on campus and throughout the city of Boston, students are challenged to fulfill their potential as caring, thoughtful individuals and future leaders in society.

Getting Accepted
28,850 applied
27% were accepted
2,291 enrolled (29% of accepted)
80% from top tenth of their h.s. class
Mean SAT critical reading score: 660
Mean SAT math score: 675
Mean SAT writing score: 665
Mean ACT score: 30
82% had SAT critical reading scores over 600
87% had SAT math scores over 600
84% had SAT writing scores over 600
95% had ACT scores over 24
31% had SAT critical reading scores over 700
41% had SAT math scores over 700
35% had SAT writing scores over 700
58% had ACT scores over 30
17 National Merit Scholars

Graduation and After
88% graduated in 4 years
2% graduated in 5 years
25% pursued further study (6% arts and sciences, 5% education, 5% law)
64% had job offers within 6 months

Financial Matters
$35,674 tuition and fees (2007–08)
$12,053 room and board
100% average percent of need met
$25,967 average financial aid amount received per undergraduate (2006–07 estimated)

BOSTON COLLEGE
SUBURBAN SETTING ■ PRIVATE ■ INDEPENDENT RELIGIOUS ■ COED
CHESTNUT HILL, MASSACHUSETTS

Web site: www.bc.edu
Contact: Office of Undergraduate Admissions, 140 Commonwealth Avenue, Devlin 208, Chestnut Hill, MA 02467-3809
Telephone: 617-552-3100 or toll-free 800-360-2522
Fax: 617-552-0798
E-mail: ugadmis@bc.edu

Academics
BC awards bachelor's, master's, doctoral, and first-professional **degrees** and post-master's certificates (also offers continuing education program with significant enrollment not reflected in profile). **Challenging opportunities** include advanced placement credit, accelerated degree programs, student-designed majors, freshman honors college, an honors program, double majors, independent study, and a senior project. Special programs include internships, summer session for credit, off-campus study, study-abroad, and Army, Navy, and Air Force ROTC.

The most frequently chosen **baccalaureate** fields are business/marketing, social sciences, and communications/journalism. A complete listing of majors at BC appears in the Majors by College index beginning on page 471.

The **faculty** at BC has 675 full-time members, 98% with terminal degrees. The student-faculty ratio is 13:1.

Students of BC
The student body totals 13,723, of whom 9,081 are undergraduates. 51.8% are women and 48.2% are men. Students come from 54 states and territories and 55 other countries. 29% are from Massachusetts. 2.1% are international students. 5.6% are African American, 0.4% American Indian, 9.5% Asian American, and 8.1% Hispanic American. 95% returned for their sophomore year.

Facilities and Resources
1,000 **computers/terminals** are available on campus for general student use. Students can access the following: campus intranet, computer help desk, free student e-mail accounts, online (class) grades, online (class) registration, online (class) schedules. Campuswide network is available. Wireless service is available via entire campus. The 7 **libraries** have 2,124,242 books and 52,338 subscriptions.

Campus Life
There are 215 active organizations on campus, including a drama/theater group, newspaper, radio station, television station, choral group, and marching band. No national or local **fraternities** or **sororities**.

BC is a member of the NCAA (Division I). **Intercollegiate sports** (some offering scholarships) include baseball (m), basketball, crew (w), cross-country running, fencing, field hockey (w), football (m), golf, ice hockey, lacrosse (w), sailing, skiing (downhill), soccer, softball (w), swimming and diving, tennis, track and field, volleyball (w), wrestling (m).

Campus Safety
Student safety services include late-night transport/escort service, 24-hour emergency telephone alarm devices, 24-hour patrols by trained security personnel, and electronically operated dormitory entrances.

Applying
BC requires an essay, SAT and SAT Subject Tests or ACT, a high school transcript, and 2 recommendations. Application deadline: 1/1; 2/1 priority date for financial aid. Early and deferred admission are possible.

BOSTON UNIVERSITY

URBAN SETTING ■ PRIVATE ■ INDEPENDENT ■ COED
BOSTON, MASSACHUSETTS

Web site: www.bu.edu
Contact: Ms. Kelly Walter, Director of Undergraduate Admissions, 121 Bay
State Road, Boston, MA 02215
Telephone: 617-353-2300
Fax: 617-353-9695
E-mail: admissions@bu.edu

SPONSOR

> Boston University (BU) has ten undergraduate schools and colleges, with more than 250 programs of study in areas as diverse as biochemistry, theater arts, physical therapy, elementary education, and broadcast journalism. Students can major in more than one area of interest through the Boston University Collaborative Degree Program. BU has an international student body, with students representing every state and 100 different countries. In addition, opportunities to excel exist in all areas of study through research, internships, directed study, and honors programs.

Academics

BU awards bachelor's, master's, doctoral, and first-professional **degrees** and post-bachelor's, post-master's, and first-professional certificates. **Challenging opportunities** include advanced placement credit, accelerated degree programs, student-designed majors, an honors program, double majors, independent study, and a senior project. Special programs include cooperative education, internships, summer session for credit, off-campus study, study-abroad, and Army, Navy, and Air Force ROTC.

The most frequently chosen **baccalaureate** fields are communications/journalism, social sciences, and business/marketing. A complete listing of majors at BU appears in the Majors by College index beginning on page 471.

The **faculty** at BU has 1,481 full-time members, 76% with terminal degrees. The student-faculty ratio is 16:1.

Students of BU

The student body totals 31,574, of whom 18,521 are undergraduates. 59.1% are women and 40.9% are men. Students come from 54 states and territories and 100 other countries. 23% are from Massachusetts. 6% are international students. 2.8% are African American, 0.4% American Indian, 12.8% Asian American, and 6.4% Hispanic American. 91% returned for their sophomore year.

Facilities and Resources

750 **computers/terminals** are available on campus for general student use. Students can access the following: online (class) registration, research and educational networks. Campuswide network is available. The 19 **libraries** have 2,427,253 books and 33,983 subscriptions.

Campus Life

There are 380 active organizations on campus, including a drama/theater group, newspaper, radio station, television station, choral group, and marching band. 3% of eligible men and 5% of eligible women are members of national **fraternities** and national **sororities**.

BU is a member of the NCAA (Division I). **Intercollegiate sports** (some offering scholarships) include basketball, crew, cross-country running, field hockey (w), golf, ice hockey, lacrosse (w), soccer, softball (w), swimming and diving, tennis, track and field, wrestling (m).

Campus Safety

Student safety services include security personnel at residence hall entrances, self-defense education, well-lit sidewalks, late-night transport/escort service, 24-hour emergency telephone alarm devices, 24-hour patrols by trained security personnel, and electronically operated dormitory entrances.

Applying

BU requires an essay, SAT and SAT Subject Tests or ACT, a high school transcript, and 2 recommendations, and in some cases an interview and audition, portfolio. It recommends a minimum high school GPA of 3.0. Application deadline: 1/1; 2/15 priority date for financial aid. Early and deferred admission are possible.

Getting Accepted
31,851 applied
58% were accepted
4,124 enrolled (22% of accepted)
53% from top tenth of their h.s. class
3.46 average high school GPA
Mean SAT critical reading score: 628
Mean SAT math score: 644
Mean SAT writing score: 632
Mean ACT score: 27
68% had SAT critical reading scores over 600
76% had SAT math scores over 600
71% had SAT writing scores over 600
91% had ACT scores over 24
16% had SAT critical reading scores over 700
22% had SAT math scores over 700
18% had SAT writing scores over 700
24% had ACT scores over 30
108 valedictorians

Graduation and After
65% graduated in 4 years
10% graduated in 5 years
2% graduated in 6 years
25% pursued further study
70% had job offers within 6 months
400 organizations recruited on campus

Financial Matters
$35,418 tuition and fees (2007–08)
$10,950 room and board
90% average percent of need met
$27,633 average financial aid amount received per undergraduate (2005–06)

BOWDOIN COLLEGE
SMALL-TOWN SETTING ■ PRIVATE ■ INDEPENDENT ■ COED
BRUNSWICK, MAINE

Web site: www.bowdoin.edu
Contact: Peter T. Wiley, Associate Dean of Admissions, 5000 College Station, Brunswick, ME 04011-8411
Telephone: 207-725-3190
Fax: 207-725-3101
E-mail: admissions@bowdoin.edu

Getting Accepted
5,961 applied
19% were accepted
476 enrolled (42% of accepted)
89% from top tenth of their h.s. class
Mean SAT critical reading score: 690
Mean SAT math score: 690
Mean SAT writing score: 700
Mean ACT score: 31
89% had SAT critical reading scores over 600
86% had SAT math scores over 600
89% had SAT writing scores over 600
97% had ACT scores over 24
49% had SAT critical reading scores over 700
45% had SAT math scores over 700
51% had SAT writing scores over 700
70% had ACT scores over 30
30 National Merit Scholars
49 valedictorians

Graduation and After
83% graduated in 4 years
5% graduated in 5 years
2% graduated in 6 years
15% pursued further study (4% arts and sciences, 4% medicine, 3% law)
80% had job offers within 6 months
65 organizations recruited on campus

Financial Matters
$36,370 tuition and fees (2007–08)
$9890 room and board
100% average percent of need met
$29,641 average financial aid amount received per undergraduate (2006–07 estimated)

Academics
Bowdoin awards bachelor's **degrees** (SAT or ACT considered if submitted. Test scores are required for home-schooled applicants). **Challenging opportunities** include advanced placement credit, accelerated degree programs, student-designed majors, double majors, and independent study. Special programs include off-campus study and study-abroad.

The most frequently chosen **baccalaureate** fields are social sciences, foreign languages and literature, and visual and performing arts. A complete listing of majors at Bowdoin appears in the Majors by College index beginning on page 471.

The **faculty** at Bowdoin has 166 full-time members, 96% with terminal degrees. The student-faculty ratio is 10:1.

Students of Bowdoin
The student body is made up of 1,716 undergraduates. 51.9% are women and 48.1% are men. Students come from 52 states and territories and 30 other countries. 12% are from Maine. 3% are international students. 6% are African American, 0.9% American Indian, 12.6% Asian American, and 7.4% Hispanic American. 99% returned for their sophomore year.

Facilities and Resources
450 **computers/terminals** and 5,500 ports are available on campus for general student use. Students can access the following: campus intranet, computer help desk, free student e-mail accounts, online (class) grades, online (class) schedules, training classes on variety of desktop and academic software. Campuswide network is available. 100% of college-owned or -operated housing units are wired for high-speed Internet access. Wireless service is available via entire campus. The 7 **libraries** have 1,009,122 books and 9,121 subscriptions.

Campus Life
There are 109 active organizations on campus, including a drama/theater group, newspaper, radio station, television station, and choral group. No national or local **fraternities** or **sororities**.

Bowdoin is a member of the NCAA (Division III). **Intercollegiate sports** include baseball (m), basketball, cross-country running, field hockey (w), football (m), golf, ice hockey, lacrosse, rugby (w), sailing, skiing (cross-country), soccer, softball (w), squash, swimming and diving, tennis, track and field, volleyball (w).

Campus Safety
Student safety services include self-defense education, whistle program, safe ride service (daytime), late-night transport/escort service, 24-hour emergency telephone alarm devices, 24-hour patrols by trained security personnel, and electronically operated dormitory entrances.

Applying
Bowdoin requires an essay, a high school transcript, and 3 recommendations. It recommends an interview. Application deadline: 1/1; 2/15 for financial aid. Early and deferred admission are possible.

Bradley University

Suburban setting ■ Private ■ Independent ■ Coed
Peoria, Illinois

Web site: www.bradley.edu
Contact: Mr. Rodney San Jose, Director of Admissions, 1501 West Bradley
  Avenue, 100 Swords Hall, Peoria, IL 61625-0002
Telephone: 309-677-1000 or toll-free 800-447-6460
Fax: 309-677-2797
E-mail: admissions@bradley.edu

SPONSOR

Academics

Bradley awards bachelor's, master's, and first-professional **degrees**. **Challenging opportunities** include advanced placement credit, accelerated degree programs, student-designed majors, an honors program, double majors, independent study, and a senior project. Special programs include cooperative education, internships, summer session for credit, off-campus study, study-abroad, and Army ROTC.

The most frequently chosen **baccalaureate** fields are business/marketing, engineering, and education. A complete listing of majors at Bradley appears in the Majors by College index beginning on page 471.

The **faculty** at Bradley has 335 full-time members, 82% with terminal degrees. The student-faculty ratio is 14:1.

Students of Bradley

The student body totals 6,053, of whom 5,215 are undergraduates. 54.6% are women and 45.4% are men. Students come from 40 states and territories and 21 other countries. 89% are from Illinois. 0.7% are international students. 6.2% are African American, 0.4% American Indian, 3.7% Asian American, and 3.1% Hispanic American. 89% returned for their sophomore year.

Facilities and Resources

2,000 **computers/terminals** are available on campus for general student use. Students can access the following: computer help desk, free student e-mail accounts, online (class) grades, online (class) registration, online (class) schedules. Campuswide network is available. 100% of college-owned or -operated housing units are wired for high-speed Internet access. Wireless service is available via entire campus. The **library** has 518,000 books and 3,529 subscriptions.

Campus Life

There are 220 active organizations on campus, including a drama/theater group, newspaper, radio station, television station, and choral group. 28% of eligible men and 31% of eligible women are members of national **fraternities** and national **sororities**.

Bradley is a member of the NCAA (Division I). **Intercollegiate sports** (some offering scholarships) include baseball (m), basketball, cheerleading, cross-country running, golf, soccer (m), softball (w), tennis, track and field (w), volleyball (w).

Campus Safety

Student safety services include bicycle patrol, late-night transport/escort service, 24-hour emergency telephone alarm devices, 24-hour patrols by trained security personnel, and electronically operated dormitory entrances.

Applying

Bradley requires an essay, SAT or ACT, a high school transcript, and recommendations. It recommends an interview and a minimum high school GPA of 3.0. Application deadline: rolling admissions; 3/1 priority date for financial aid. Early and deferred admission are possible.

Bradley is a private university in Peoria, Illinois, offering more than 100 academic programs to 6,000 students. Students enjoy extensive resources not available at most small colleges and personal attention not commonly found at large universities. In addition to liberal arts and sciences, academic programs include business, communications, education, engineering, fine and performing arts, and health sciences. Unique programs include entrepreneurship, multimedia, and physical therapy. Faculty members teach classes that average 23 students, and students participate in a diverse residential campus life that includes more than 240 student organizations.

Getting Accepted
4,612 applied
83% were accepted
1,080 enrolled (28% of accepted)
28% from top tenth of their h.s. class
3.6 average high school GPA
Mean SAT critical reading score: 561
Mean SAT math score: 574
Mean SAT writing score: 544
Mean ACT score: 25
32% had SAT critical reading scores over 600
45% had SAT math scores over 600
67% had ACT scores over 24
5% had SAT critical reading scores over 700
7% had SAT math scores over 700
10% had ACT scores over 30
2 National Merit Scholars
37 valedictorians

Graduation and After
52% graduated in 4 years
19% graduated in 5 years
2% graduated in 6 years
17% pursued further study
77% had job offers within 6 months
400 organizations recruited on campus

Financial Matters
$21,360 tuition and fees (2007–08)
$7050 room and board
80% average percent of need met
$13,037 average financial aid amount received
  per undergraduate (2005–06)

Brandeis University

Suburban setting ■ Private ■ Independent ■ Coed
Waltham, Massachusetts

Getting Accepted
7,562 applied
34% were accepted
701 enrolled (27% of accepted)
71% from top tenth of their h.s. class
3.8 average high school GPA
86% had SAT critical reading scores over 600
89% had SAT math scores over 600
95% had ACT scores over 24
42% had SAT critical reading scores over 700
45% had SAT math scores over 700
61% had ACT scores over 30
32 National Merit Scholars

Graduation and After
85% graduated in 4 years
3% graduated in 5 years
28% pursued further study

Financial Matters
$35,702 tuition and fees (2007–08)
$9908 room and board
85% average percent of need met
$25,928 average financial aid amount received per undergraduate (2006–07 estimated)

Web site: www.brandeis.edu
Contact: Mr. Gil J. Villanueva, Dean of Admissions, 415 South Street, Waltham, MA 02254-9110
Telephone: 781-736-3500 or toll-free 800-622-0622 (out-of-state)
Fax: 781-736-3536
E-mail: admissions@brandeis.edu

Academics
Brandeis awards bachelor's, master's, and doctoral **degrees** and post-bachelor's certificates. **Challenging opportunities** include advanced placement credit, student-designed majors, an honors program, double majors, independent study, and a senior project. Special programs include internships, summer session for credit, off-campus study, study-abroad, and Army and Air Force ROTC.

The most frequently chosen **baccalaureate** fields are social sciences, area and ethnic studies, and biological/life sciences. A complete listing of majors at Brandeis appears in the Majors by College index beginning on page 471.

The **faculty** at Brandeis has 351 full-time members, 96% with terminal degrees. The student-faculty ratio is 8:1.

Students of Brandeis
The student body totals 5,333, of whom 3,233 are undergraduates. 55.9% are women and 44.1% are men. Students come from 48 states and territories and 52 other countries. 25% are from Massachusetts. 7.4% are international students. 3.7% are African American, 0.2% American Indian, 9.1% Asian American, and 4.3% Hispanic American. 94% returned for their sophomore year.

Facilities and Resources
104 **computers/terminals** are available on campus for general student use. Students can access the following: computer help desk, free student e-mail accounts, online (class) grades, online (class) registration, online (class) schedules, educational software. Campuswide network is available. Wireless service is available via entire campus. The 3 **libraries** have 1,191,645 books.

Campus Life
There are 200 active organizations on campus, including a drama/theater group, newspaper, radio station, television station, and choral group. No national or local **fraternities** or **sororities**.

Brandeis is a member of the NCAA (Division III). **Intercollegiate sports** include baseball (m), basketball, cross-country running, fencing, golf (m), sailing, soccer (w), softball (w), swimming and diving, tennis, track and field, volleyball (w).

Campus Safety
Student safety services include late-night transport/escort service, 24-hour emergency telephone alarm devices, 24-hour patrols by trained security personnel, and electronically operated dormitory entrances.

Applying
Brandeis requires an essay, SAT and SAT Subject Tests or ACT, a high school transcript, and 2 recommendations. It recommends an interview. Application deadline: 1/15; 1/15 priority date for financial aid. Deferred admission is possible.

BRIGHAM YOUNG UNIVERSITY

SUBURBAN SETTING ■ PRIVATE ■ INDEPENDENT RELIGIOUS ■ COED
PROVO, UTAH

Web site: www.byu.edu
Contact: Mr. Tom Gourley, Dean of Admissions and Records, A-153 Abraham
    Smoot Building, Provo, UT 84602
Telephone: 801-422-2507
Fax: 801-422-0005
E-mail: admissions@byu.edu

Academics

BYU awards bachelor's, master's, doctoral, and first-professional **degrees**. **Challenging opportunities** include advanced placement credit, accelerated degree programs, freshman honors college, an honors program, double majors, independent study, and a senior project. Special programs include cooperative education, internships, summer session for credit, off-campus study, study-abroad, and Army and Air Force ROTC.

The most frequently chosen **baccalaureate** fields are business/marketing, education, and social sciences. A complete listing of majors at BYU appears in the Majors by College index beginning on page 471.

The **faculty** at BYU has 1,305 full-time members, 81% with terminal degrees. The student-faculty ratio is 21:1.

Students of BYU

The student body totals 34,174, of whom 30,873 are undergraduates. 49.2% are women and 50.8% are men. Students come from 56 states and territories and 125 other countries. 39% are from Utah. 4.1% are international students. 0.4% are African American, 0.7% American Indian, 3.4% Asian American, and 3.4% Hispanic American. 84% returned for their sophomore year.

Facilities and Resources

2,000 **computers/terminals** are available on campus for general student use. Students can access the following: campus intranet, online (class) registration. Campuswide network is available. The 3 **libraries** have 3,539,032 books and 27,161 subscriptions.

Campus Life

There are 390 active organizations on campus, including a drama/theater group, newspaper, radio station, television station, choral group, and marching band. No national or local **fraternities** or **sororities**.

BYU is a member of the NCAA (Division I). **Intercollegiate sports** (some offering scholarships) include baseball (m), basketball, cheerleading, cross-country running, football (m), golf, gymnastics (w), racquetball, soccer (w), softball (w), swimming and diving, tennis, track and field, volleyball.

Campus Safety

Student safety services include late-night transport/escort service, 24-hour emergency telephone alarm devices, 24-hour patrols by trained security personnel, and electronically operated dormitory entrances.

Applying

BYU requires an essay, ACT, a high school transcript, an interview, and 1 recommendation. Application deadline: 2/1; 4/20 priority date for financial aid. Early and deferred admission are possible.

Getting Accepted

9,979 applied
74% were accepted
4,784 enrolled (65% of accepted)
3.76 average high school GPA
59% had SAT critical reading scores over 600
65% had SAT math scores over 600
89% had ACT scores over 24
16% had SAT critical reading scores over 700
18% had SAT math scores over 700
29% had ACT scores over 30

Graduation and After

32% graduated in 4 years
22% graduated in 5 years
25% graduated in 6 years
75% had job offers within 6 months
450 organizations recruited on campus

Financial Matters

$7680 tuition and fees (2007–08)
$6460 room and board
31% average percent of need met
$4067 average financial aid amount received
    per undergraduate (2005–06)

BROWN UNIVERSITY

URBAN SETTING ■ PRIVATE ■ INDEPENDENT ■ COED
PROVIDENCE, RHODE ISLAND

Web site: www.brown.edu
Contact: Mr. James Miller, Dean of Admission, Box 1876, Providence, RI
02912
Telephone: 401-863-2378
Fax: 401-863-9300
E-mail: admission_undergraduate@brown.edu

Brown is a university/college with renowned faculty members who teach students in the undergraduate college, the graduate school, and the medical school. The unique, nonrestrictive curriculum allows students freedom in selecting their courses, and they may choose their concentration from eighty-three areas, complete a double major, or pursue an independent concentration. The 140-acre campus is set in a residential neighborhood (National Historic District) and features state-of-the-art computing facilities and an athletic complex. A real sense of community exists on campus, as every student has an academic adviser, and there are several peer counselors in the residence halls.

Getting Accepted
19,097 applied
14% were accepted
1,479 enrolled (55% of accepted)
92% from top tenth of their h.s. class
Mean SAT critical reading score: 705
Mean SAT math score: 713
Mean SAT writing score: 703
Mean ACT score: 30
90% had SAT critical reading scores over 600
94% had SAT math scores over 600
90% had SAT writing scores over 600
96% had ACT scores over 24
61% had SAT critical reading scores over 700
66% had SAT math scores over 700
62% had SAT writing scores over 700
63% had ACT scores over 30
141 valedictorians

Graduation and After
35% pursued further study (10% arts and
    sciences, 10% law, 9% medicine)
60% had job offers within 6 months
400 organizations recruited on campus

Financial Matters
$36,342 tuition and fees (2007–08)
$9606 room and board
100% average percent of need met
$26,477 average financial aid amount received
    per undergraduate (2004–05)

Academics
Brown awards bachelor's, master's, doctoral, and first-professional **degrees**. **Challenging opportunities** include advanced placement credit, accelerated degree programs, student-designed majors, an honors program, double majors, independent study, and a senior project. Special programs include internships, summer session for credit, off-campus study, study-abroad, and Army ROTC.

The most frequently chosen **baccalaureate** fields are social sciences, biological/life sciences, and physical sciences. A complete listing of majors at Brown appears in the Majors by College index beginning on page 471.

The **faculty** at Brown has 661 full-time members, 95% with terminal degrees. The student-faculty ratio is 9:1.

Students of Brown
The student body totals 8,167, of whom 6,008 are undergraduates. 52.4% are women and 47.6% are men. Students come from 52 states and territories and 81 other countries. 4% are from Rhode Island. 7% are international students. 6.8% are African American, 0.7% American Indian, 15.3% Asian American, and 8.4% Hispanic American. 98% returned for their sophomore year.

Facilities and Resources
500 **computers/terminals** are available on campus for general student use. Students can access the following: computer help desk, free student e-mail accounts, online (class) registration, online (class) schedules. Campuswide network is available. 100% of college-owned or -operated housing units are wired for high-speed Internet access. Wireless service is available via entire campus. The 6 **libraries** have 3,000,000 books and 17,000 subscriptions.

Campus Life
There are 240 active organizations on campus, including a drama/theater group, newspaper, radio station, television station, choral group, and marching band. 12% of eligible men and 2% of eligible women are members of national **fraternities** and national **sororities**.

Brown is a member of the NCAA (Division I). **Intercollegiate sports** include baseball (m), basketball, crew, cross-country running, equestrian sports (w), fencing, field hockey (w), football (m), golf, gymnastics (w), ice hockey, lacrosse, skiing (downhill) (w), soccer, softball (w), squash, swimming and diving, tennis, track and field, volleyball (w), water polo, wrestling (m).

Campus Safety
Student safety services include late-night transport/escort service, 24-hour emergency telephone alarm devices, 24-hour patrols by trained security personnel, and electronically operated dormitory entrances.

Applying
Brown requires an essay, SAT and SAT Subject Tests or ACT, a high school transcript, and 2 recommendations, and in some cases 3 recommendations. Application deadline: 1/1; 2/1 for financial aid. Early and deferred admission are possible.

BRYAN COLLEGE

SMALL-TOWN SETTING ■ PRIVATE ■ INDEPENDENT RELIGIOUS ■ COED
DAYTON, TENNESSEE

Web site: www.bryan.edu
Contact: Michael Sapienza, Director of Admissions, PO Box 7000, Dayton,
   TN 37321-7000
Telephone: 423-775-2041 or toll-free 800-277-9522
Fax: 423-775-7199
E-mail: admissions@bryan.edu

Academics

Bryan awards associate, bachelor's, and master's **degrees**. **Challenging opportunities**
include advanced placement credit, an honors program, double majors, independent
study, and a senior project. Special programs include internships, summer session for
credit, and study-abroad.

The most frequently chosen **baccalaureate** fields are business/marketing, com-
munications/journalism, and education. A complete listing of majors at Bryan appears in
the Majors by College index beginning on page 471.

The **faculty** at Bryan has 35 full-time members, 80% with terminal degrees. The
student-faculty ratio is 13:1.

Students of Bryan

The student body totals 1,044, of whom 1,020 are undergraduates. Students come from
33 states and territories and 7 other countries. 39% are from Tennessee. 1% are international students. 4.3% are African American, 0.3% American Indian, 0.7% Asian
American, and 1.2% Hispanic American. 74% returned for their sophomore year.

Facilities and Resources

74 **computers/terminals** are available on campus for general student use. Students can
access the following: campus intranet, computer help desk, free student e-mail accounts,
online (class) grades, online (class) schedules. Campuswide network is available. The
library has 98,413 books and 4,212 subscriptions.

Campus Life

There are 7 active organizations on campus, including a drama/theater group,
newspaper, and choral group. No national or local **fraternities** or **sororities**.
Bryan is a member of the NAIA and NCCAA. **Intercollegiate sports** (some offering
scholarships) include baseball (m), basketball, cross-country running, soccer, volleyball
(w).

Campus Safety

Student safety services include police patrols, late-night transport/escort service, student
patrols, and electronically operated dormitory entrances.

Applying

Bryan requires an essay, SAT or ACT, a high school transcript, 3 recommendations, and
a minimum high school GPA of 2.0, and in some cases an interview. Application
deadline: rolling admissions; 2/15 priority date for financial aid. Early and deferred
admission are possible.

Getting Accepted
542 applied
71% were accepted
234 enrolled (60% of accepted)
3.6 average high school GPA

Graduation and After
75% had job offers within 6 months
18 organizations recruited on campus

Financial Matters
$17,020 tuition and fees (2008–09)
$5095 room and board
67% average percent of need met
$12,203 average financial aid amount received
   per undergraduate (2006–07 estimated)

Getting Accepted

2,106 applied
45% were accepted
352 enrolled (37% of accepted)
62% from top tenth of their h.s. class
Mean SAT critical reading score: 670
Mean SAT math score: 627
Mean SAT writing score: 668
Mean ACT score: 27
85% had SAT critical reading scores over 600
69% had SAT math scores over 600
82% had SAT writing scores over 600
92% had ACT scores over 24
42% had SAT critical reading scores over 700
20% had SAT math scores over 700
36% had SAT writing scores over 700
38% had ACT scores over 30
5 National Merit Scholars
10 valedictorians

Graduation and After

80% graduated in 4 years
3% graduated in 5 years
1% graduated in 6 years
20% pursued further study
52% had job offers within 6 months
100 organizations recruited on campus

Financial Matters

$34,650 tuition and fees (2007–08)
$11,024 room and board
100% average percent of need met
$29,169 average financial aid amount received
  per undergraduate (2006–07 estimated)

BRYN MAWR COLLEGE

SUBURBAN SETTING ■ PRIVATE ■ INDEPENDENT
■ UNDERGRADUATE: WOMEN ONLY; GRADUATE: COED
BRYN MAWR, PENNSYLVANIA

Web site: www.brynmawr.edu
Contact: Ms. Jody Sanford Sweeney, Director of Admissions, 101 North
  Merion Avenue, Bryn Mawr, PA 19010
Telephone: 610-526-5152 or toll-free 800-BMC-1885 (out-of-state)
Fax: 610-526-7471
E-mail: admissions@brynmawr.edu

Academics

Bryn Mawr awards bachelor's, master's, and doctoral **degrees** and post-bachelor's
certificates. **Challenging opportunities** include advanced placement credit, accelerated
degree programs, student-designed majors, double majors, independent study, and a
senior project. Special programs include internships, summer session for credit, off-
campus study, study-abroad, and Air Force ROTC.

The most frequently chosen **baccalaureate** fields are social sciences, foreign
languages and literature, and English. A complete listing of majors at Bryn Mawr appears
in the Majors by College index beginning on page 471.

The **faculty** at Bryn Mawr has 153 full-time members, 97% with terminal degrees.
The student-faculty ratio is 8:1.

Students of Bryn Mawr

The student body totals 1,790, of whom 1,287 are undergraduates. 99.8% are women
and 0.2% are men. Students come from 49 states and territories and 42 other countries.
18% are from Pennsylvania. 7.1% are international students. 6.1% are African
American, 0.1% American Indian, 11.7% Asian American, and 3.4% Hispanic American.
94% returned for their sophomore year.

Facilities and Resources

200 **computers/terminals** and 1,500 ports are available on campus for general student
use. Students can access the following: campus intranet, computer help desk, free student
e-mail accounts, online (class) grades, online (class) registration, online (class) schedules.
Campuswide network is available. 100% of college-owned or -operated housing units are
wired for high-speed Internet access. Wireless service is available via classrooms,
computer centers, computer labs, dorm rooms, learning centers, libraries, student
centers. The 3 **libraries** have 1,135,493 books and 4,400 subscriptions.

Campus Life

There are 100 active organizations on campus, including a drama/theater group,
newspaper, and choral group. No national or local **sororities**.

Bryn Mawr is a member of the NCAA (Division III).

Campus Safety

Student safety services include shuttle bus service, awareness programs, bicycle registration, security Website, late-night transport/escort service, 24-hour emergency telephone
alarm devices, 24-hour patrols by trained security personnel, and electronically operated
dormitory entrances.

Applying

Bryn Mawr requires an essay, SAT and SAT Subject Tests or ACT, a high school
transcript, and 3 recommendations. It recommends an interview. Application deadline:
1/15; 3/1 for financial aid. Early and deferred admission are possible.

Bucknell University

SMALL-TOWN SETTING ■ PRIVATE ■ INDEPENDENT ■ COED
LEWISBURG, PENNSYLVANIA

Web site: www.bucknell.edu
Contact: Mr. Kurt M. Thiede, Vice President, Enrollment Management and Dean of Admissions, Lewisburg, PA 17837
Telephone: 570-577-1101
Fax: 570-577-3538
E-mail: admissions@bucknell.edu

SPONSOR

Academics

Bucknell awards bachelor's and master's **degrees**. **Challenging opportunities** include advanced placement credit, student-designed majors, an honors program, double majors, independent study, and a senior project. Special programs include internships, summer session for credit, off-campus study, study-abroad, and Army ROTC.

The most frequently chosen **baccalaureate** fields are social sciences, engineering, and business/marketing. A complete listing of majors at Bucknell appears in the Majors by College index beginning on page 471.

The **faculty** at Bucknell has 317 full-time members, 97% with terminal degrees. The student-faculty ratio is 11:1.

Students of Bucknell

The student body totals 3,677, of whom 3,520 are undergraduates. 51% are women and 49% are men. Students come from 47 states and territories and 41 other countries. 27% are from Pennsylvania. 2.7% are international students. 3.2% are African American, 0.5% American Indian, 6.6% Asian American, and 3.2% Hispanic American. 94% returned for their sophomore year.

Facilities and Resources

940 **computers/terminals** are available on campus for general student use. Students can access the following: campus intranet, computer help desk, free student e-mail accounts, online (class) grades, online (class) registration, online (class) schedules. Campuswide network is available. 100% of college-owned or -operated housing units are wired for high-speed Internet access. Wireless service is available via entire campus. The 3 **libraries** have 804,890 books.

Campus Life

There are 135 active organizations on campus, including a drama/theater group, newspaper, radio station, and choral group. 54% of eligible men and 53% of eligible women are members of national **fraternities** and national **sororities**.

Bucknell is a member of the NCAA (Division I). **Intercollegiate sports** (some offering scholarships) include baseball (m), basketball (m), crew (w), cross-country running, field hockey (w), football (m), golf, lacrosse, soccer, softball (w), swimming and diving, tennis, track and field, volleyball (w), water polo, wrestling (m).

Campus Safety

Student safety services include well-lit pathways, self-defense education, safety/security orientation, late-night transport/escort service, 24-hour emergency telephone alarm devices, 24-hour patrols by trained security personnel, and student patrols.

Applying

Bucknell requires an essay, SAT or ACT, a high school transcript, and 1 recommendation, and in some cases SAT Subject Tests. Application deadline: 1/1; 1/1 for financial aid. Deferred admission is possible.

Among the fifty or so top liberal arts institutions in the nation, Bucknell stands alone with the largest enrollment in the group and the broadest curricular offerings. With 3,450 undergraduates and 150 graduate students, Bucknell offers an intimate college experience combined with the extensive choices offered by a distinguished university, giving students opportunities they are not likely to find elsewhere. With the help of committed professors who provide sound advice, students find many ways to add breadth, depth, and imagination to their program of study.

Getting Accepted

8,943 applied
30% were accepted
887 enrolled (33% of accepted)
72% from top tenth of their h.s. class
Mean SAT critical reading score: 647
Mean SAT math score: 669
Mean SAT writing score: 643
Mean ACT score: 28
80% had SAT critical reading scores over 600
89% had SAT math scores over 600
94% had ACT scores over 24
23% had SAT critical reading scores over 700
34% had SAT math scores over 700
39% had ACT scores over 30
22 valedictorians

Graduation and After

86% graduated in 4 years
3% graduated in 5 years
22% pursued further study (6% arts and sciences, 5% law, 3% engineering)
69% had job offers within 6 months
567 organizations recruited on campus

Financial Matters

$39,652 tuition and fees (2008–09)
$8728 room and board
100% average percent of need met
$23,400 average financial aid amount received per undergraduate (2006–07 estimated)

SPONSOR

At Butler University, students are actively engaged in the learning experience from the minute they step on campus. With small class sizes, students receive direct access to faculty members, personalized attention, and hands-on learning opportunities. Participation in research is an opportunity rarely offered to undergraduates; at Butler, students not only have the chance to participate in research with faculty members, they also originate research projects and develop them into professional presentations and publications. Butler students receive research grants through the Butler Summer Institute and present their projects at the Undergraduate Research Conference, hosted by Butler every April.

Getting Accepted
5,265 applied
76% were accepted
988 enrolled (25% of accepted)
48% from top tenth of their h.s. class
3.7 average high school GPA
Mean SAT critical reading score: 577
Mean SAT math score: 591
Mean SAT writing score: 565
Mean ACT score: 27
41% had SAT critical reading scores over 600
49% had SAT math scores over 600
35% had SAT writing scores over 600
82% had ACT scores over 24
7% had SAT critical reading scores over 700
7% had SAT math scores over 700
4% had SAT writing scores over 700
23% had ACT scores over 30
7 National Merit Scholars
53 valedictorians

Graduation and After
55% graduated in 4 years
9% graduated in 5 years
10% graduated in 6 years
25% pursued further study (13% arts and sciences, 3% law, 3% medicine)
72% had job offers within 6 months
213 organizations recruited on campus

Financial Matters
$26,806 tuition and fees (2007–08)
$8960 room and board
$18,743 average financial aid amount received per undergraduate (2006–07 estimated)

BUTLER UNIVERSITY
URBAN SETTING ■ PRIVATE ■ INDEPENDENT ■ COED
INDIANAPOLIS, INDIANA

Web site: www.butler.edu
Contact: Mr. Scott McIntyre, Director of Admissions, 4600 Sunset Avenue, Indianapolis, IN 46208-3485
Telephone: 317-940-8100 or toll-free 888-940-8100
Fax: 317-940-8150
E-mail: admission@butler.edu

Academics
Butler awards associate, bachelor's, master's, and first-professional **degrees**. **Challenging opportunities** include advanced placement credit, student-designed majors, an honors program, double majors, independent study, and a senior project. Special programs include cooperative education, internships, summer session for credit, off-campus study, study-abroad, and Army and Air Force ROTC.

The most frequently chosen **baccalaureate** fields are health professions and related sciences, business/marketing, and education. A complete listing of majors at Butler appears in the Majors by College index beginning on page 471.

The **faculty** at Butler has 302 full-time members, 82% with terminal degrees. The student-faculty ratio is 11:1.

Students of Butler
The student body totals 4,479, of whom 3,617 are undergraduates. 61.1% are women and 38.9% are men. Students come from 47 states and territories and 51 other countries. 60% are from Indiana. 2.9% are international students. 3.3% are African American, 0.3% American Indian, 2.2% Asian American, and 1.8% Hispanic American. 86% returned for their sophomore year.

Facilities and Resources
430 **computers/terminals** are available on campus for general student use. Students can access the following: campus intranet, computer help desk, free student e-mail accounts, online (class) grades, online (class) registration, online (class) schedules. Campuswide network is available. 100% of college-owned or -operated housing units are wired for high-speed Internet access. Wireless service is available via entire campus. The 2 **libraries** have 346,805 books and 13,441 subscriptions.

Campus Life
There are 100 active organizations on campus, including a drama/theater group, newspaper, television station, choral group, and marching band. 23% of eligible men and 27% of eligible women are members of national **fraternities** and national **sororities**.

Butler is a member of the NCAA (Division I). **Intercollegiate sports** (some offering scholarships) include baseball (m), basketball, cross-country running, football (m), golf, soccer, softball (w), swimming and diving (w), tennis, track and field, volleyball (w).

Campus Safety
Student safety services include late-night transport/escort service, 24-hour emergency telephone alarm devices, 24-hour patrols by trained security personnel, and electronically operated dormitory entrances.

Applying
Butler requires an essay, SAT or ACT, and a high school transcript, and in some cases an interview and audition. Application deadline: rolling admissions; 3/1 priority date for financial aid. Deferred admission is possible.

California Institute of Technology

Suburban setting ■ Private ■ Independent ■ Coed
Pasadena, California

Web site: www.caltech.edu
Contact: Mr. Rick T. Bischoff, Director of Admissions, 1200 East California Boulevard, Pasadena, CA 91125-0001
Telephone: 626-395-6341
Fax: 626-683-3026
E-mail: ugadmissions@caltech.edu

Academics

Caltech awards bachelor's, master's, and doctoral **degrees. Challenging opportunities** include student-designed majors, double majors, and independent study. Special programs include cooperative education, off-campus study, study-abroad, and Army and Air Force ROTC. A complete listing of majors at Caltech appears in the Majors by College index beginning on page 471.

The **faculty** at Caltech has 291 full-time members, 98% with terminal degrees. The student-faculty ratio is 3:1.

Students of Caltech

The student body totals 2,086, of whom 864 are undergraduates. 28.8% are women and 71.2% are men. Students come from 46 states and territories and 28 other countries. 31% are from California. 8% are international students. 0.6% are African American, 0.1% American Indian, 37.4% Asian American, and 5.6% Hispanic American. 97% returned for their sophomore year.

Facilities and Resources

600 **computers/terminals** are available on campus for general student use. Campuswide network is available. The 11 **libraries** have 3,165,000 books and 3,500 subscriptions.

Campus Life

There are 85 active organizations on campus, including a drama/theater group, newspaper, and choral group. No national or local **fraternities** or **sororities**.

Caltech is a member of the NCAA (Division III). **Intercollegiate sports** include baseball (m), basketball, cross-country running, fencing, golf (m), soccer (m), swimming and diving, tennis, track and field, volleyball (w), water polo.

Campus Safety

Student safety services include late-night transport/escort service, 24-hour emergency telephone alarm devices, and 24-hour patrols by trained security personnel.

Applying

Caltech requires an essay, SAT or ACT, SAT Subject Test in Math Level II C and either physics, chemistry, or biology, a high school transcript, and 2 recommendations. Application deadline: 1/1; 1/15 priority date for financial aid. Early and deferred admission are possible.

Getting Accepted

3,330 applied
17% were accepted
214 enrolled (37% of accepted)
88% from top tenth of their h.s. class
95% had SAT critical reading scores over 600
100% had SAT math scores over 600
100% had ACT scores over 24
72% had SAT critical reading scores over 700
100% had SAT math scores over 700
100% had ACT scores over 30
56 National Merit Scholars
76 valedictorians

Graduation and After

79% graduated in 4 years
8% graduated in 5 years
2% graduated in 6 years
Graduates pursuing further study: 26% arts and sciences, 20% engineering, 3% medicine
109 organizations recruited on campus

Financial Matters

$32,835 tuition and fees (2007–08)
$9540 room and board
100% average percent of need met
$25,923 average financial aid amount received per undergraduate (2006–07 estimated)

Getting Accepted
30,176 applied
45% were accepted
4,369 enrolled (32% of accepted)
42% from top tenth of their h.s. class
3.7 average high school GPA
Mean SAT critical reading score: 570
Mean SAT math score: 613
Mean ACT score: 25
37% had SAT critical reading scores over 600
60% had SAT math scores over 600
72% had ACT scores over 24
5% had SAT critical reading scores over 700
14% had SAT math scores over 700
12% had ACT scores over 30

Graduation and After
23% graduated in 4 years
36% graduated in 5 years
9% graduated in 6 years
15% pursued further study
90% had job offers within 6 months
630 organizations recruited on campus

Financial Matters
$4689 resident tuition and fees (2007–08)
$19,548 nonresident tuition and fees (2007–08)
$8817 room and board
64% average percent of need met
$7456 average financial aid amount received per undergraduate (2005–06)

CALIFORNIA POLYTECHNIC STATE UNIVERSITY, SAN LUIS OBISPO
SMALL-TOWN SETTING ■ PUBLIC ■ STATE-SUPPORTED ■ COED
SAN LUIS OBISPO, CALIFORNIA

Web site: www.calpoly.edu
Contact: Mr. James Maraviglia, Director of Admissions and Evaluations, 1 Grand Avenue, San Luis Obispo, CA 93407
Telephone: 805-756-2311
Fax: 805-756-5400
E-mail: admissions@calpoly.edu

Academics
Cal Poly awards bachelor's and master's **degrees**. **Challenging opportunities** include advanced placement credit, an honors program, double majors, independent study, and a senior project. Special programs include cooperative education, internships, summer session for credit, off-campus study, study-abroad, and Army ROTC.

The most frequently chosen **baccalaureate** fields are engineering, business/marketing, and agriculture. A complete listing of majors at Cal Poly appears in the Majors by College index beginning on page 471.

The **faculty** at Cal Poly has 786 full-time members, 79% with terminal degrees. The student-faculty ratio is 20:1.

Students of Cal Poly
The student body totals 19,777, of whom 18,842 are undergraduates. 43.1% are women and 56.9% are men. Students come from 46 states and territories and 39 other countries. 97% are from California. 0.7% are international students. 1.2% are African American, 0.8% American Indian, 11.4% Asian American, and 10.9% Hispanic American. 90% returned for their sophomore year.

Facilities and Resources
Students can access the following: campus intranet, free student e-mail accounts, online (class) grades, online (class) registration, online (class) schedules. Campuswide network is available. Wireless service is available via classrooms, computer centers, computer labs, learning centers, libraries, student centers. The 2 **libraries** have 763,651 books and 5,529 subscriptions.

Campus Life
There are 400 active organizations on campus, including a drama/theater group, newspaper, radio station, television station, choral group, and marching band. 11% of eligible men and 12% of eligible women are members of national **fraternities**, national **sororities**, local fraternities, and local sororities.

Cal Poly is a member of the NCAA (Division I). **Intercollegiate sports** (some offering scholarships) include baseball (m), basketball, cross-country running, football (m), golf, soccer, softball (w), swimming and diving, tennis, track and field, volleyball (w), wrestling (m).

Campus Safety
Student safety services include late-night transport/escort service, 24-hour emergency telephone alarm devices, 24-hour patrols by trained security personnel, student patrols, and electronically operated dormitory entrances.

Applying
Cal Poly requires SAT or ACT and a high school transcript. Application deadline: 11/30; 6/30 for financial aid, with a 3/1 priority date. Early admission is possible.

CALVIN COLLEGE

SUBURBAN SETTING ■ PRIVATE ■ INDEPENDENT RELIGIOUS ■ COED
GRAND RAPIDS, MICHIGAN

Web site: www.calvin.edu
Contact: Mr. Dale D. Kuiper, Director of Admissions, 3201 Burton Street, SE, Grand Rapids, MI 49546
Telephone: 616-526-6106 or toll-free 800-688-0122
Fax: 616-526-6777
E-mail: admissions@calvin.edu

Academics
Calvin awards bachelor's and master's **degrees** and post-bachelor's certificates. **Challenging opportunities** include advanced placement credit, accelerated degree programs, student-designed majors, an honors program, double majors, independent study, and a senior project. Special programs include internships, summer session for credit, off-campus study, study-abroad, and Army ROTC.

The most frequently chosen **baccalaureate** fields are business/marketing, social sciences, and health professions and related sciences. A complete listing of majors at Calvin appears in the Majors by College index beginning on page 471.

The **faculty** at Calvin has 322 full-time members, 83% with terminal degrees. The student-faculty ratio is 12:1.

Students of Calvin
The student body totals 4,224, of whom 4,169 are undergraduates. 53.8% are women and 46.2% are men. Students come from 49 states and territories and 45 other countries. 56% are from Michigan. 6.8% are international students. 1.4% are African American, 0.1% American Indian, 3.1% Asian American, and 1.6% Hispanic American. 89% returned for their sophomore year.

Facilities and Resources
800 **computers/terminals** are available on campus for general student use. Students can access the following: computer help desk, free student e-mail accounts, online (class) grades, online (class) registration, online (class) schedules. Campuswide network is available. 100% of college-owned or -operated housing units are wired for high-speed Internet access. Wireless service is available via classrooms, computer centers, computer labs, dorm rooms, libraries, student centers. The 2 **libraries** have 824,806 books and 14,464 subscriptions.

Campus Life
There are 65 active organizations on campus, including a drama/theater group, newspaper, television station, and choral group. No national or local **fraternities** or **sororities**.

Calvin is a member of the NCAA (Division III). **Intercollegiate sports** include baseball (m), basketball, cross-country running, golf, soccer, softball (w), swimming and diving, tennis, track and field, volleyball (w).

Campus Safety
Student safety services include crime prevention programs, crime alert bulletins, late-night transport/escort service, 24-hour emergency telephone alarm devices, 24-hour patrols by trained security personnel, student patrols, and electronically operated dormitory entrances.

Applying
Calvin requires an essay, SAT or ACT, a high school transcript, 1 recommendation, and a minimum high school GPA of 2.5. It recommends an interview. Application deadline: 8/15; 2/15 priority date for financial aid. Deferred admission is possible.

Getting Accepted
2,277 applied
95% were accepted
1,039 enrolled (48% of accepted)
26% from top tenth of their h.s. class
3.59 average high school GPA
47% had SAT critical reading scores over 600
47% had SAT math scores over 600
72% had ACT scores over 24
14% had SAT critical reading scores over 700
13% had SAT math scores over 700
17% had ACT scores over 30
23 National Merit Scholars
49 valedictorians

Graduation and After
56% graduated in 4 years
17% graduated in 5 years
1% graduated in 6 years
20% pursued further study (5% arts and sciences, 2% education, 2% medicine)
73% had job offers within 6 months
295 organizations recruited on campus

Financial Matters
$21,685 tuition and fees (2007–08)
$7460 room and board
80% average percent of need met
$14,200 average financial aid amount received per undergraduate (2006–07 estimated)

CANISIUS COLLEGE

URBAN SETTING ■ PRIVATE ■ INDEPENDENT RELIGIOUS ■ COED
BUFFALO, NEW YORK

Web site: www.canisius.edu
Contact: Ms. Ann Marie Moscovic, Director of Admissions, 2001 Main Street, Buffalo, NY 14208-1098
Telephone: 716-888-2200 or toll-free 800-843-1517
Fax: 716-888-3230
E-mail: admissions@canisius.edu

With more than seventy majors and special programs, small classes taught by caring faculty members, state-of-the-art living and learning facilities, and an unlimited range of learning opportunities outside the classroom, Canisius has everything a student could want in a challenging college experience. Thousands of Canisius graduates are leaders in their professions, including doctors, lawyers, scientists, business executives, and teachers. Canisius is all about giving students the best possible start to their careers and their future. It is how and where leaders are made.

Getting Accepted
3,695 applied
79% were accepted
846 enrolled (29% of accepted)
26% from top tenth of their h.s. class
3.44 average high school GPA
Mean SAT critical reading score: 541
Mean SAT math score: 556
Mean ACT score: 24
23% had SAT critical reading scores over 600
29% had SAT math scores over 600
57% had ACT scores over 24
4% had SAT critical reading scores over 700
3% had SAT math scores over 700
7% had ACT scores over 30

Graduation and After
54% graduated in 4 years
9% graduated in 5 years
2% graduated in 6 years
25% pursued further study (8% education, 6% arts and sciences, 3% medicine)
64.5% had job offers within 6 months
30 organizations recruited on campus

Financial Matters
$26,427 tuition and fees (2007–08)
$9770 room and board
79% average percent of need met
$19,698 average financial aid amount received per undergraduate (2006–07 estimated)

Academics

Canisius awards associate, bachelor's, and master's **degrees** and post-master's certificates. **Challenging opportunities** include advanced placement credit, an honors program, double majors, independent study, and a senior project. Special programs include internships, summer session for credit, off-campus study, study-abroad, and Army ROTC.

The most frequently chosen **baccalaureate** fields are business/marketing, education, and communications/journalism. A complete listing of majors at Canisius appears in the Majors by College index beginning on page 471.

The **faculty** at Canisius has 213 full-time members, 95% with terminal degrees. The student-faculty ratio is 13:1.

Students of Canisius

The student body totals 4,984, of whom 3,490 are undergraduates. 55.4% are women and 44.6% are men. Students come from 35 states and territories and 12 other countries. 93% are from New York. 3.7% are international students. 5.5% are African American, 0.3% American Indian, 1.5% Asian American, and 2.4% Hispanic American. 81% returned for their sophomore year.

Facilities and Resources

500 **computers/terminals** are available on campus for general student use. Students can access the following: computer help desk, free student e-mail accounts, online (class) grades, online (class) registration, online (class) schedules, online accounts. Campuswide network is available. 100% of college-owned or -operated housing units are wired for high-speed Internet access. Wireless service is available via entire campus. The 2 **libraries** have 379,498 books and 24,000 subscriptions.

Campus Life

There are 100 active organizations on campus, including a drama/theater group, newspaper, radio station, television station, and choral group. 1% of eligible men and 1% of eligible women are members of national **fraternities** and national **sororities**.

Canisius is a member of the NCAA (Division I). **Intercollegiate sports** (some offering scholarships) include baseball (m), basketball, cross-country running, golf (m), ice hockey (m), lacrosse, soccer, softball (w), swimming and diving, volleyball (w).

Campus Safety

Student safety services include crime prevention programs, closed-circuit television monitors, late-night transport/escort service, 24-hour emergency telephone alarm devices, 24-hour patrols by trained security personnel, and electronically operated dormitory entrances.

Applying

Canisius requires SAT or ACT, a high school transcript, and a minimum high school GPA of 2.5, and in some cases an interview. It recommends an essay, an interview, and recommendations. Application deadline: 5/1; 2/15 priority date for financial aid. Early and deferred admission are possible.

CARLETON COLLEGE

SMALL-TOWN SETTING ■ PRIVATE ■ INDEPENDENT ■ COED
NORTHFIELD, MINNESOTA

Web site: www.carleton.edu
Contact: Mr. Paul Thiboutot, Dean of Admissions, 100 South College Street, Northfield, MN 55057
Telephone: 507-646-4190 or toll-free 800-995-2275
Fax: 507-646-4526
E-mail: admissions@acs.carleton.edu

Academics

Carleton awards bachelor's **degrees**. **Challenging opportunities** include advanced placement credit, accelerated degree programs, student-designed majors, double majors, independent study, and a senior project. Special programs include internships, off-campus study, and study-abroad.

The most frequently chosen **baccalaureate** fields are social sciences, biological/life sciences, and visual and performing arts. A complete listing of majors at Carleton appears in the Majors by College index beginning on page 471.

The **faculty** at Carleton has 200 full-time members, 95% with terminal degrees. The student-faculty ratio is 9:1.

Students of Carleton

The student body is made up of 1,980 undergraduates. 53.2% are women and 46.8% are men. Students come from 51 states and territories and 30 other countries. 27% are from Minnesota. 5.1% are international students. 5.5% are African American, 0.7% American Indian, 10.1% Asian American, and 5% Hispanic American. 96% returned for their sophomore year.

Facilities and Resources

221 **computers/terminals** are available on campus for general student use. Students can access the following: online (class) registration. Campuswide network is available. The 2 **libraries** have 1,113,497 books and 10,964 subscriptions.

Campus Life

There are 132 active organizations on campus, including a drama/theater group, newspaper, radio station, and choral group. No national or local **fraternities** or **sororities**.

Carleton is a member of the NCAA (Division III). **Intercollegiate sports** include baseball (m), basketball, cross-country running, football (m), golf, soccer, softball (w), swimming and diving, tennis, track and field, volleyball (w).

Campus Safety

Student safety services include late-night transport/escort service, 24-hour emergency telephone alarm devices, 24-hour patrols by trained security personnel, student patrols, and electronically operated dormitory entrances.

Applying

Carleton requires an essay, SAT or ACT, a high school transcript, 2 recommendations, and common application supplement. It recommends SAT Subject Tests and an interview. Application deadline: 1/15; 2/15 for financial aid, with a 2/15 priority date. Early and deferred admission are possible.

Getting Accepted

4,450 applied
32% were accepted
504 enrolled (36% of accepted)
78% from top tenth of their h.s. class
92% had SAT critical reading scores over 600
94% had SAT math scores over 600
90% had SAT writing scores over 600
95% had ACT scores over 24
57% had SAT critical reading scores over 700
55% had SAT math scores over 700
48% had SAT writing scores over 700
69% had ACT scores over 30
78 National Merit Scholars
65 valedictorians

Graduation and After

81% graduated in 4 years
5% graduated in 5 years
1% graduated in 6 years
23% pursued further study (11% arts and sciences, 4% medicine, 3% law)
65% had job offers within 6 months
32 organizations recruited on campus

Financial Matters

$36,156 tuition and fees (2007–08)
$9489 room and board
100% average percent of need met
$29,116 average financial aid amount received per undergraduate (2005–06)

Carnegie Mellon University has rapidly evolved into a powerful internationally recognized institution, with top-ranked business and liberal arts programs that are equally matched by world-class fine arts, technology, sciences, and computer science programs. More than 8,000 undergraduate and graduate students receive an education characterized by its focus on creating and implementing solutions to solve real problems, interdisciplinary collaboration, and innovation. A small student-faculty ratio provides an opportunity for close interaction between students and professors. Carnegie Mellon students learn to view life through a wide variety of lenses and leave prepared to make an important and lasting impact on society.

Getting Accepted
18,864 applied
34% were accepted
1,428 enrolled (22% of accepted)
75% from top tenth of their h.s. class
3.61 average high school GPA
Mean SAT critical reading score: 657
Mean SAT math score: 728
Mean SAT writing score: 657
Mean ACT score: 30
81% had SAT critical reading scores over 600
98% had SAT math scores over 600
81% had SAT writing scores over 600
97% had ACT scores over 24
30% had SAT critical reading scores over 700
74% had SAT math scores over 700
29% had SAT writing scores over 700
61% had ACT scores over 30
63 valedictorians

Graduation and After
66% graduated in 4 years
16% graduated in 5 years
3% graduated in 6 years
32% pursued further study (14% arts and sciences, 6% business, 5% engineering)
68% had job offers within 6 months
856 organizations recruited on campus

Financial Matters
$37,354 tuition and fees (2007–08)
$9660 room and board
81% average percent of need met
$22,143 average financial aid amount received per undergraduate (2005–06 estimated)

Carnegie Mellon University
Urban setting ■ Private ■ Independent ■ Coed
Pittsburgh, Pennsylvania
Web site: www.cmu.edu
Contact: Mr. Michael Steidel, Director of Admissions, 5000 Forbes Avenue, Pittsburgh, PA 15213
Telephone: 412-268-2082
Fax: 412-268-7838
E-mail: undergraduate-admissions@andrew.cmu.edu

Academics
Carnegie Mellon awards bachelor's, master's, and doctoral **degrees** and post-master's certificates. **Challenging opportunities** include advanced placement credit, student-designed majors, freshman honors college, double majors, independent study, and a senior project. Special programs include cooperative education, internships, summer session for credit, off-campus study, study-abroad, and Army, Navy, and Air Force ROTC.

The most frequently chosen **baccalaureate** fields are engineering, business/marketing, and computer and information sciences. A complete listing of majors at Carnegie Mellon appears in the Majors by College index beginning on page 471.

The **faculty** at Carnegie Mellon has 838 full-time members, 98% with terminal degrees. The student-faculty ratio is 10:1.

Students of Carnegie Mellon
The student body totals 10,120, of whom 5,669 are undergraduates. 38.9% are women and 61.1% are men. Students come from 52 states and territories and 49 other countries. 24% are from Pennsylvania. 13.5% are international students. 5.3% are African American, 0.5% American Indian, 23.9% Asian American, and 5% Hispanic American. 95% returned for their sophomore year.

Facilities and Resources
402 **computers/terminals** are available on campus for general student use. Students can access the following: online (class) registration. Campuswide network is available. The 3 **libraries** have 1,084,013 books and 28,769 subscriptions.

Campus Life
There are 100 active organizations on campus, including a drama/theater group, newspaper, radio station, television station, choral group, and marching band. 13% of eligible men and 13% of eligible women are members of national **fraternities**, national **sororities**, and local sororities.

Carnegie Mellon is a member of the NCAA (Division III). **Intercollegiate sports** include basketball, cheerleading, cross-country running, football (m), golf (m), soccer, swimming and diving, tennis, track and field, volleyball (w).

Campus Safety
Student safety services include late-night transport/escort service, 24-hour emergency telephone alarm devices, 24-hour patrols by trained security personnel, and electronically operated dormitory entrances.

Applying
Carnegie Mellon requires an essay, SAT or ACT, a high school transcript, and 1 recommendation, and in some cases SAT and SAT Subject Tests or ACT and portfolio, audition. It recommends an interview. Application deadline: 1/1; 5/1 for financial aid, with a 2/15 priority date. Early and deferred admission are possible.

CARROLL COLLEGE

SMALL-TOWN SETTING ■ PRIVATE ■ INDEPENDENT RELIGIOUS ■ COED
HELENA, MONTANA

Web site: www.carroll.edu
Contact: Ms. Cynthia Thornquist, Director of Admissions and Enrollment,
   1601 North Benton Avenue, Helena, MT 59625-0002
Telephone: 406-447-4384 or toll-free 800-992-3648
Fax: 406-447-4533
E-mail: enroll@carroll.edu

Academics

Carroll awards associate and bachelor's **degrees**. **Challenging opportunities** include advanced placement credit, accelerated degree programs, student-designed majors, freshman honors college, an honors program, double majors, independent study, and a senior project. Special programs include cooperative education, internships, summer session for credit, study-abroad, and Army ROTC.

The most frequently chosen **baccalaureate** fields are business/marketing, education, and biological/life sciences. A complete listing of majors at Carroll appears in the Majors by College index beginning on page 471.

The **faculty** at Carroll has 80 full-time members, 70% with terminal degrees. The student-faculty ratio is 13:1.

Students of Carroll

The student body is made up of 1,452 undergraduates. 57.1% are women and 42.9% are men. Students come from 33 states and territories and 14 other countries. 65% are from Montana. 0.8% are international students. 0.3% are African American, 1.1% American Indian, 0.8% Asian American, and 1.4% Hispanic American. 79% returned for their sophomore year.

Facilities and Resources

91 **computers/terminals** are available on campus for general student use. Students can access the following: online book order. Campuswide network is available. The 2 **libraries** have 89,003 books and 2,721 subscriptions.

Campus Life

There are 35 active organizations on campus, including a drama/theater group, newspaper, radio station, and choral group. No national or local **fraternities** or **sororities**.

Carroll is a member of the NAIA. **Intercollegiate sports** (some offering scholarships) include basketball, cheerleading, football (m), golf (w), soccer (w), swimming and diving, volleyball (w).

Campus Safety

Student safety services include late-night transport/escort service and electronically operated dormitory entrances.

Applying

Carroll requires an essay, SAT or ACT, a high school transcript, 1 recommendation, and a minimum high school GPA of 2.0, and in some cases SAT Subject Tests and an interview. It recommends an interview and a minimum high school GPA of 3.0. Application deadline: 6/1. Deferred admission is possible.

Getting Accepted
1,048 applied
79% were accepted
304 enrolled (37% of accepted)
22% from top tenth of their h.s. class
3.39 average high school GPA
Mean SAT critical reading score: 534
Mean SAT math score: 539
Mean ACT score: 23
24% had SAT critical reading scores over 600
27% had SAT math scores over 600
50% had ACT scores over 24
2% had SAT critical reading scores over 700
1% had SAT math scores over 700
3% had ACT scores over 30
27 valedictorians

Graduation and After
42% graduated in 4 years
17% graduated in 5 years
1% graduated in 6 years
22% pursued further study (4% arts and sciences, 3% medicine, 2% business)
55% had job offers within 6 months
100 organizations recruited on campus

Financial Matters
$19,590 tuition and fees (2007–08)
$6608 room and board
80% average percent of need met
$15,113 average financial aid amount received per undergraduate (2005–06 estimated)

CARROLL COLLEGE

SUBURBAN SETTING ■ PRIVATE ■ INDEPENDENT RELIGIOUS ■ COED
WAUKESHA, WISCONSIN

Web site: www.cc.edu
Contact: Mr. James Wiseman, Vice President of Enrollment, 100 North East Avenue, Waukesha, WI 53186-5593
Telephone: 262-524-7221 or toll-free 800-CARROLL
Fax: 262-524-7139
E-mail: cc.info@ccadmin.cc.edu

Getting Accepted
2,728 applied
72% were accepted
657 enrolled (33% of accepted)
21% from top tenth of their h.s. class
3.3 average high school GPA
Mean ACT score: 23
44% had ACT scores over 24
3% had ACT scores over 30

Graduation and After
41% graduated in 4 years
11% graduated in 5 years
2% graduated in 6 years
3 organizations recruited on campus

Financial Matters
$20,830 tuition and fees (2008–09)
$6350 room and board
100% average percent of need met
$14,979 average financial aid amount received per undergraduate (2006–07 estimated)

Academics

Carroll awards bachelor's, master's, and doctoral **degrees**. **Challenging opportunities** include advanced placement credit, student-designed majors, an honors program, double majors, independent study, and a senior project. Special programs include internships, summer session for credit, study-abroad, and Army and Air Force ROTC.

The most frequently chosen **baccalaureate** fields are business/marketing, health professions and related sciences, and education. A complete listing of majors at Carroll appears in the Majors by College index beginning on page 471.

The **faculty** at Carroll has 121 full-time members, 63% with terminal degrees. The student-faculty ratio is 16:1.

Students of Carroll

The student body totals 3,325, of whom 3,060 are undergraduates. 67.8% are women and 32.2% are men. Students come from 23 states and territories and 25 other countries. 80% are from Wisconsin. 1.7% are international students. 2.1% are African American, 0.4% American Indian, 1.5% Asian American, and 3% Hispanic American. 74% returned for their sophomore year.

Facilities and Resources

250 **computers/terminals** are available on campus for general student use. Students can access the following: online (class) registration. Campuswide network is available. 95% of college-owned or -operated housing units are wired for high-speed Internet access. Wireless service is available via classrooms, computer centers, computer labs, libraries. The **library** has 150,000 books and 18,000 subscriptions.

Campus Life

There are 40 active organizations on campus, including a drama/theater group, newspaper, radio station, and choral group. 10% of eligible men and 11% of eligible women are members of national **sororities** and local **fraternities**.

Carroll is a member of the NCAA (Division III). **Intercollegiate sports** include baseball (m), basketball, cross-country running, football (m), golf, soccer, swimming and diving, track and field, volleyball (w).

Campus Safety

Student safety services include late-night transport/escort service, 24-hour emergency telephone alarm devices, 24-hour patrols by trained security personnel, student patrols, and electronically operated dormitory entrances.

Applying

Carroll requires SAT or ACT, a high school transcript, 1 recommendation, and a minimum high school GPA of 2.0, and in some cases an essay. It recommends ACT and an interview. Application deadline: rolling admissions. Deferred admission is possible.

CARSON-NEWMAN COLLEGE

SMALL-TOWN SETTING ■ PRIVATE ■ INDEPENDENT RELIGIOUS ■ COED
JEFFERSON CITY, TENNESSEE

Web site: www.cn.edu
Contact: Mr. Tom Huebner, Dean of Admissions, PO Box 72025, Jefferson
City, TN 37760
Telephone: 865-471-3223 or toll-free 800-678-9061
Fax: 865-471-3502
E-mail: cnadmiss@cn.edu

Academics

Carson-Newman awards associate, bachelor's, and master's **degrees**. **Challenging opportunities** include advanced placement credit, accelerated degree programs, student-designed majors, an honors program, and a senior project. Special programs include internships, summer session for credit, off-campus study, study-abroad, and Army and Air Force ROTC.

The most frequently chosen **baccalaureate** fields are health professions and related sciences, education, and business/marketing. A complete listing of majors at Carson-Newman appears in the Majors by College index beginning on page 471.

The **faculty** at Carson-Newman has 126 full-time members, 55% with terminal degrees. The student-faculty ratio is 13:1.

Students of Carson-Newman

The student body totals 2,012, of whom 1,834 are undergraduates. 57.5% are women and 42.5% are men. Students come from 37 states and territories and 22 other countries. 69% are from Tennessee. 2.9% are international students. 8.6% are African American, 0.5% American Indian, 0.7% Asian American, and 1.1% Hispanic American. 69% returned for their sophomore year.

Facilities and Resources

200 **computers/terminals** are available on campus for general student use. Campuswide network is available. The 2 **libraries** have 218,371 books and 3,966 subscriptions.

Campus Life

There are 63 active organizations on campus, including a drama/theater group, newspaper, choral group, and marching band. 5% of eligible men and 5% of eligible women are members of national **fraternities**, national **sororities**, local fraternities, and local sororities.

Carson-Newman is a member of the NCAA (Division II). **Intercollegiate sports** (some offering scholarships) include baseball (m), basketball, cross-country running, football (m), golf (m), soccer, softball (w), tennis, track and field, volleyball (w), wrestling (m).

Campus Safety

Student safety services include late-night transport/escort service, 24-hour emergency telephone alarm devices, 24-hour patrols by trained security personnel, and electronically operated dormitory entrances.

Applying

Carson-Newman requires SAT or ACT, a high school transcript, medical history, and a minimum high school GPA of 2.25, and in some cases an essay, an interview, and recommendations. It recommends an interview. Application deadline: 8/1; 4/1 priority date for financial aid. Deferred admission is possible.

Getting Accepted

3,298 applied
62% were accepted
436 enrolled (21% of accepted)
27% from top tenth of their h.s. class
3.35 average high school GPA
36% had ACT scores over 24
6% had ACT scores over 30

Graduation and After

37% graduated in 4 years
12% graduated in 5 years
2% graduated in 6 years
27% pursued further study
24 organizations recruited on campus

Financial Matters

$16,980 tuition and fees (2007–08)
$5360 room and board
78% average percent of need met
$13,645 average financial aid amount received
per undergraduate (2006–07 estimated)

CASE WESTERN RESERVE UNIVERSITY

URBAN SETTING ■ PRIVATE ■ INDEPENDENT ■ COED
CLEVELAND, OHIO

Getting Accepted
7,297 applied
75% were accepted
1,133 enrolled (21% of accepted)
66% from top tenth of their h.s. class
Mean SAT critical reading score: 637
Mean SAT math score: 665
Mean SAT writing score: 627
Mean ACT score: 29
70% had SAT critical reading scores over 600
82% had SAT math scores over 600
67% had SAT writing scores over 600
90% had ACT scores over 24
25% had SAT critical reading scores over 700
38% had SAT math scores over 700
21% had SAT writing scores over 700
46% had ACT scores over 30
48 National Merit Scholars
78 valedictorians

Graduation and After
59% graduated in 4 years
20% graduated in 5 years
2% graduated in 6 years
43% pursued further study (11% engineering, 11% medicine, 7% arts and sciences)
85% had job offers within 6 months
191 organizations recruited on campus

Financial Matters
$33,538 tuition and fees (2007–08)
$9938 room and board
94% average percent of need met
$32,131 average financial aid amount received per undergraduate (2006–07 estimated)

Web site: www.case.edu
Contact: Ms. Elizabeth Woyczynski, Director of Undergraduate Admission, 10900 Euclid Avenue, Cleveland, OH 44106
Telephone: 216-368-4450
Fax: 216-368-5111
E-mail: admission@case.edu

Academics
Case awards bachelor's, master's, doctoral, and first-professional **degrees** and post-bachelor's certificates. **Challenging opportunities** include advanced placement credit, accelerated degree programs, student-designed majors, an honors program, double majors, independent study, and a senior project. Special programs include cooperative education, internships, summer session for credit, off-campus study, study-abroad, and Army and Air Force ROTC.

The most frequently chosen **baccalaureate** fields are engineering, social sciences, and biological/life sciences. A complete listing of majors at Case appears in the Majors by College index beginning on page 471.

The **faculty** at Case has 727 full-time members, 90% with terminal degrees. The student-faculty ratio is 9:1.

Students of Case
The student body totals 9,844, of whom 4,207 are undergraduates. 42.3% are women and 57.7% are men. Students come from 52 states and territories and 26 other countries. 55% are from Ohio. 3.2% are international students. 5.5% are African American, 0.2% American Indian, 16.1% Asian American, and 2.3% Hispanic American. 91% returned for their sophomore year.

Facilities and Resources
415 **computers/terminals** and 1,000 ports are available on campus for general student use. Students can access the following: campus intranet, computer help desk, free student e-mail accounts, online (class) grades, online (class) registration, online (class) schedules, software library, online reference databases, electronic books and journals. Campuswide network is available. 100% of college-owned or -operated housing units are wired for high-speed Internet access. Wireless service is available via entire campus. The 7 **libraries** have 2,471,504 books and 20,265 subscriptions.

Campus Life
There are 190 active organizations on campus, including a drama/theater group, newspaper, radio station, choral group, and marching band. 27% of eligible men and 23% of eligible women are members of national **fraternities**, national **sororities**, and local sororities.

Case is a member of the NCAA (Division III). **Intercollegiate sports** include baseball (m), basketball, cross-country running, football (m), soccer, softball (w), swimming and diving, tennis, track and field, volleyball (w), wrestling (m).

Campus Safety
Student safety services include crime prevention programs, late-night transport/escort service, 24-hour emergency telephone alarm devices, 24-hour patrols by trained security personnel, student patrols, and electronically operated dormitory entrances.

Applying
Case requires an essay, SAT or ACT, a high school transcript, and 1 recommendation. It recommends an interview. Application deadline: 1/15; 2/15 priority date for financial aid. Early and deferred admission are possible.

CEDARVILLE UNIVERSITY
RURAL SETTING ■ PRIVATE ■ INDEPENDENT RELIGIOUS ■ COED
CEDARVILLE, OHIO

Web site: www.cedarville.edu
Contact: Mr. Roscoe Smith, Director of Admissions, 251 North Main Street, Cedarville, OH 45314-0601
Telephone: 937-766-7700 or toll-free 800-CEDARVILLE
Fax: 937-766-7575
E-mail: admiss@cedarville.edu

Academics
Cedarville awards bachelor's and master's **degrees**. **Challenging opportunities** include advanced placement credit, accelerated degree programs, an honors program, double majors, independent study, and a senior project. Special programs include internships, summer session for credit, off-campus study, study-abroad, and Army and Air Force ROTC.

The most frequently chosen **baccalaureate** fields are education, business/marketing, and health professions and related sciences. A complete listing of majors at Cedarville appears in the Majors by College index beginning on page 471.

The **faculty** at Cedarville has 185 full-time members, 61% with terminal degrees. The student-faculty ratio is 16:1.

Students of Cedarville
The student body totals 3,055, of whom 3,006 are undergraduates. 55.3% are women and 44.7% are men. Students come from 49 states and territories and 14 other countries. 36% are from Ohio. 0.5% are international students. 1.3% are African American, 0.3% American Indian, 1.2% Asian American, and 2% Hispanic American. 85% returned for their sophomore year.

Facilities and Resources
2,600 **computers/terminals** are available on campus for general student use. Students can access the following: campus intranet, computer help desk, free student e-mail accounts, online (class) registration, online (class) schedules, over 150 software packages. Campuswide network is available. 100% of college-owned or -operated housing units are wired for high-speed Internet access. Wireless service is available via classrooms, computer centers, computer labs, dorm rooms, learning centers, libraries, student centers. The **library** has 170,561 books and 6,400 subscriptions.

Campus Life
There are 61 active organizations on campus, including a drama/theater group, newspaper, radio station, and choral group. No national or local **fraternities** or **sororities**.

Cedarville is a member of the NAIA and NCCAA. **Intercollegiate sports** (some offering scholarships) include baseball (m), basketball, cross-country running, golf (m), soccer, softball (w), tennis, track and field, volleyball (w).

Campus Safety
Student safety services include late-night transport/escort service, 24-hour emergency telephone alarm devices, 24-hour patrols by trained security personnel, student patrols, and electronically operated dormitory entrances.

Applying
Cedarville requires an essay, SAT or ACT, a high school transcript, 2 recommendations, clear testimony of faith in Jesus Christ and evidence of consistent Christian lifestyle, and a minimum high school GPA of 3.0, and in some cases an interview. It recommends SAT and SAT Subject Tests or ACT. Application deadline: rolling admissions; 3/1 priority date for financial aid. Early and deferred admission are possible.

Getting Accepted
2,654 applied
76% were accepted
762 enrolled (38% of accepted)
37% from top tenth of their h.s. class
3.62 average high school GPA
Mean SAT critical reading score: 604
Mean SAT math score: 587
Mean SAT writing score: 582
Mean ACT score: 26
52% had SAT critical reading scores over 600
48% had SAT math scores over 600
42% had SAT writing scores over 600
72% had ACT scores over 24
15% had SAT critical reading scores over 700
8% had SAT math scores over 700
8% had SAT writing scores over 700
23% had ACT scores over 30
4 National Merit Scholars
51 valedictorians

Graduation and After
54% graduated in 4 years
12% graduated in 5 years
2% graduated in 6 years
10% pursued further study (3% theology, 2% arts and sciences, 2% business)
91% had job offers within 6 months
272 organizations recruited on campus

Financial Matters
$21,130 tuition and fees (2007–08)
$5010 room and board
35% average percent of need met
$16,048 average financial aid amount received per undergraduate (2006–07 estimated)

CENTRAL COLLEGE

SMALL-TOWN SETTING ■ PRIVATE ■ INDEPENDENT RELIGIOUS ■ COED
PELLA, IOWA

Web site: www.central.edu
Contact: Ms. Carol Williamson, Dean of Admission and Student Enrollment Services, 812 University Street, Pella, IA 50219-1999
Telephone: 641-628-7600 or toll-free 877-462-3687 (in-state), 877-462-3689 (out-of-state)
Fax: 641-628-5316
E-mail: admissions@central.edu

Getting Accepted

1,919 applied
79% were accepted
424 enrolled (28% of accepted)
23% from top tenth of their h.s. class
3.46 average high school GPA
Mean SAT critical reading score: 519
Mean SAT math score: 538
Mean ACT score: 24
18% had SAT critical reading scores over 600
20% had SAT math scores over 600
53% had ACT scores over 24
1% had SAT critical reading scores over 700
1% had SAT math scores over 700
7% had ACT scores over 30
25 valedictorians

Graduation and After

67% graduated in 4 years
5% graduated in 5 years
15% pursued further study (9% arts and sciences, 4% medicine, 1% business)
95% had job offers within 6 months
70 organizations recruited on campus

Financial Matters

$23,944 tuition and fees (2008–09)
$8006 room and board
84% average percent of need met
$18,016 average financial aid amount received per undergraduate (2006–07 estimated)

Academics

Central awards bachelor's **degrees**. **Challenging opportunities** include student-designed majors, an honors program, double majors, independent study, and a senior project. Special programs include internships, summer session for credit, off-campus study, and study-abroad.

The most frequently chosen **baccalaureate** fields are business/marketing, parks and recreation, and education. A complete listing of majors at Central appears in the Majors by College index beginning on page 471.

The **faculty** at Central has 89 full-time members, 92% with terminal degrees. The student-faculty ratio is 13:1.

Students of Central

The student body is made up of 1,605 undergraduates. 54% are women and 46% are men. Students come from 38 states and territories and 15 other countries. 79% are from Iowa. 1.8% are international students. 1.2% are African American, 0.2% American Indian, 0.9% Asian American, and 1.7% Hispanic American. 82% returned for their sophomore year.

Facilities and Resources

400 **computers/terminals** and 1,600 ports are available on campus for general student use. Students can access the following: campus intranet, computer help desk, free student e-mail accounts, online (class) grades, online (class) registration, online (class) schedules, student academic records and data. Campuswide network is available. 100% of college-owned or -operated housing units are wired for high-speed Internet access. Wireless service is available via classrooms, learning centers, libraries, student centers. The 4 **libraries** have 220,526 books and 1,161 subscriptions.

Campus Life

There are 72 active organizations on campus, including a drama/theater group, newspaper, radio station, and choral group. 15% of eligible men and 7% of eligible women are members of local **fraternities** and local **sororities**.

Central is a member of the NCAA (Division III). **Intercollegiate sports** include baseball (m), basketball, cross-country running, football (m), golf, soccer, softball (w), tennis, track and field, volleyball (w), wrestling (m).

Campus Safety

Student safety services include late-night transport/escort service, 24-hour emergency telephone alarm devices, student patrols, and electronically operated dormitory entrances.

Applying

Central requires SAT or ACT and a high school transcript, and in some cases an essay, an interview, and 3 recommendations. It recommends an interview and a minimum high school GPA of 2.5. Application deadline: rolling admissions; 3/15 priority date for financial aid. Deferred admission is possible.

CENTRE COLLEGE

SMALL-TOWN SETTING ■ PRIVATE ■ INDEPENDENT RELIGIOUS ■ COED
DANVILLE, KENTUCKY

Web site: www.centre.edu
Contact: Mr. Bob Nesmith, Director of Admission, 600 West Walnut Street, Danville, KY 40422-1394
Telephone: 859-238-5350 or toll-free 800-423-6236
Fax: 859-238-5373
E-mail: admission@centre.edu

Academics

Centre awards bachelor's **degrees**. **Challenging opportunities** include advanced placement credit, student-designed majors, double majors, independent study, and a senior project. Special programs include internships, off-campus study, study-abroad, and Army and Air Force ROTC.

The most frequently chosen **baccalaureate** fields are social sciences, foreign languages and literature, and English. A complete listing of majors at Centre appears in the Majors by College index beginning on page 471.

The **faculty** at Centre has 102 full-time members, 97% with terminal degrees. The student-faculty ratio is 11:1.

Students of Centre

The student body is made up of 1,189 undergraduates. 54.6% are women and 45.4% are men. Students come from 37 states and territories and 16 other countries. 64% are from Kentucky. 1.9% are international students. 2.8% are African American, 0.3% American Indian, 2.3% Asian American, and 1.8% Hispanic American. 94% returned for their sophomore year.

Facilities and Resources

150 **computers/terminals** are available on campus for general student use. Students can access the following: campus intranet, computer help desk, free student e-mail accounts, online (class) grades, online (class) registration, online (class) schedules. Campuswide network is available. 100% of college-owned or -operated housing units are wired for high-speed Internet access. Wireless service is available via classrooms, computer centers, computer labs, dorm rooms, learning centers, libraries, student centers. The 2 **libraries** have 217,751 books and 750 subscriptions.

Campus Life

There are 76 active organizations on campus, including a drama/theater group, newspaper, and choral group. 37% of eligible men and 38% of eligible women are members of national **fraternities** and national **sororities**.

Centre is a member of the NCAA (Division III). **Intercollegiate sports** include baseball (m), basketball, cheerleading (w), cross-country running, field hockey (w), football (m), golf, soccer, softball (w), swimming and diving, tennis, track and field, volleyball (w).

Campus Safety

Student safety services include late-night transport/escort service, 24-hour emergency telephone alarm devices, 24-hour patrols by trained security personnel, and electronically operated dormitory entrances.

Applying

Centre requires an essay, SAT or ACT, a high school transcript, and 1 recommendation. It recommends an interview. Application deadline: 2/1; 3/1 for financial aid. Early and deferred admission are possible.

Getting Accepted

2,159 applied
61% were accepted
316 enrolled (24% of accepted)
58% from top tenth of their h.s. class
3.6 average high school GPA
63% had SAT critical reading scores over 600
66% had SAT math scores over 600
92% had ACT scores over 24
25% had SAT critical reading scores over 700
10% had SAT math scores over 700
32% had ACT scores over 30
30 valedictorians

Graduation and After

71% graduated in 4 years
2% graduated in 5 years
1% graduated in 6 years
40% pursued further study (15% law, 11% medicine, 10% arts and sciences)
70% had job offers within 6 months
25 organizations recruited on campus

Financial Matters

$35,000 comprehensive fee (2007–08)
88% average percent of need met
$20,235 average financial aid amount received per undergraduate (2006–07 estimated)

CHAPMAN UNIVERSITY

SUBURBAN SETTING ■ PRIVATE ■ INDEPENDENT RELIGIOUS ■ COED
ORANGE, CALIFORNIA

Web site: www.chapman.edu
Contact: Mr. Michael Drummy, Assistant Vice President of Enrollment Services and Chief Admission Officer, One University Drive, Orange, CA 92866
Telephone: 714-997-6711 or toll-free 888-CUAPPLY
Fax: 714-997-6713
E-mail: admit@chapman.edu

Academics

Chapman awards bachelor's, master's, doctoral, and first-professional **degrees** and post-bachelor's certificates. **Challenging opportunities** include advanced placement credit, student-designed majors, an honors program, double majors, independent study, and a senior project. Special programs include internships, summer session for credit, study-abroad, and Army and Air Force ROTC.

The most frequently chosen **baccalaureate** fields are business/marketing, visual and performing arts, and communications/journalism. A complete listing of majors at Chapman appears in the Majors by College index beginning on page 471.

The **faculty** at Chapman has 309 full-time members, 90% with terminal degrees. The student-faculty ratio is 14:1.

Students of Chapman

The student body totals 6,022, of whom 4,193 are undergraduates. 59.2% are women and 40.8% are men. Students come from 47 states and territories and 32 other countries. 75% are from California. 2.3% are international students. 2.3% are African American, 0.8% American Indian, 7.8% Asian American, and 10.4% Hispanic American. 87% returned for their sophomore year.

Facilities and Resources

453 **computers/terminals** are available on campus for general student use. Students can access the following: campus intranet, computer help desk, free student e-mail accounts, online (class) grades, online (class) registration, online (class) schedules. Campuswide network is available. 100% of college-owned or -operated housing units are wired for high-speed Internet access. Wireless service is available via entire campus. The 2 **libraries** have 220,759 books and 1,731 subscriptions.

Campus Life

There are 64 active organizations on campus, including a drama/theater group, newspaper, radio station, and choral group. 26% of eligible men and 30% of eligible women are members of national **fraternities** and national **sororities**.

Chapman is a member of the NCAA (Division III). **Intercollegiate sports** include baseball (m), basketball, crew (w), cross-country running, football (m), golf (m), soccer, softball (w), swimming and diving (w), tennis, track and field (w), volleyball (w), water polo.

Campus Safety

Student safety services include full safety education program, late-night transport/escort service, 24-hour emergency telephone alarm devices, 24-hour patrols by trained security personnel, and electronically operated dormitory entrances.

Applying

Chapman requires an essay, SAT or ACT, a high school transcript, and 1 recommendation. It recommends SAT Subject Tests and an interview. Application deadline: 1/15; 3/2 priority date for financial aid.

In addition to the traditional type of academic advising and counseling available at most universities, all Chapman freshmen are assigned an executive-style personal coach to help them improve their motivation and effectiveness and achieve their goals. Thirty-minute weekly coaching sessions are focused on providing personal development, assistance with planning and organization, and, most importantly, motivation and encouragement. Coaches work with students to develop and review long-term and short-term goals; evaluate current academic performance and connect with their goals; clearly identify reasons for success, or lack of success, during the prior week; share positive feedback for successful activities; directly address ineffective activities; and create strategies, define action plans, and set deadlines for the coming week. This type of personal coaching in the university context provides an invaluable safety net, helping to improve academic preparedness and performance as well as maximize utilization of all of Chapman's services and programs, resulting in a "win-win" situation for everyone.

Getting Accepted
4,861 applied
49% were accepted
937 enrolled (39% of accepted)
55% from top tenth of their h.s. class
3.67 average high school GPA
Mean SAT critical reading score: 608
Mean SAT math score: 611
Mean SAT writing score: 611
Mean ACT score: 27
55% had SAT critical reading scores over 600
55% had SAT math scores over 600
56% had SAT writing scores over 600
80% had ACT scores over 24
9% had SAT critical reading scores over 700
11% had SAT math scores over 700
9% had SAT writing scores over 700
16% had ACT scores over 30
10 class presidents

Graduation and After
50% graduated in 4 years
13% graduated in 5 years
5% graduated in 6 years

Financial Matters
$34,700 tuition and fees (2008–09)
$11,315 room and board
100% average percent of need met
$20,421 average financial aid amount received per undergraduate (2005–06)

CHRISTENDOM COLLEGE

RURAL SETTING ■ PRIVATE ■ INDEPENDENT RELIGIOUS ■ COED
FRONT ROYAL, VIRGINIA

Web site: www.christendom.edu
Contact: Mr. Tom McFadden, Director of Admissions, 134 Christendom
   Drive, Front Royal, VA 22630-5103
Telephone: 540-636-2900 or toll-free 800-877-5456 Ext. 290
Fax: 540-636-1655
E-mail: tmcfadden@christendom.edu

Academics

Christendom awards associate, bachelor's, and master's **degrees**. **Challenging oppor-tunities** include advanced placement credit, accelerated degree programs, double majors, independent study, and a senior project. Special programs include cooperative education, internships, summer session for credit, and study-abroad.

The most frequently chosen **baccalaureate** fields are history, theology and religious vocations, and English. A complete listing of majors at Christendom appears in the Majors by College index beginning on page 471.

The **faculty** at Christendom has 20 full-time members, 65% with terminal degrees. The student-faculty ratio is 14:1.

Students of Christendom

The student body totals 465, of whom 397 are undergraduates. 53.7% are women and 46.3% are men. Students come from 13 states and territories and 2 other countries. 25% are from Virginia. 2.5% are international students. 0.3% are American Indian, 2% Asian American, and 2.8% Hispanic American. 88% returned for their sophomore year.

Facilities and Resources

60 **computers/terminals** are available on campus for general student use. Students can access the following: computer help desk, free student e-mail accounts. Wireless service is available via student centers. The **library** has 64,265 books and 262 subscriptions.

Campus Life

There are 15 active organizations on campus, including a drama/theater group, newspaper, and choral group. No national or local **fraternities** or **sororities**.

Christendom is a member of the NCCAA. **Intercollegiate sports** include baseball (m), basketball, soccer, volleyball (w).

Campus Safety

Student safety services include night patrols by trained security personnel, late-night transport/escort service, and 24-hour emergency telephone alarm devices.

Applying

Christendom requires an essay, SAT or ACT, a high school transcript, and 2 recom-mendations. It recommends an interview and a minimum high school GPA of 3.0. Ap-plication deadline: 3/1; 4/1 priority date for financial aid. Early admission is possible.

Getting Accepted
254 applied
81% were accepted
93 enrolled (45% of accepted)
40% from top tenth of their h.s. class
3.6 average high school GPA
Mean SAT critical reading score: 618
Mean SAT math score: 566
Mean SAT writing score: 606
Mean ACT score: 25
60% had SAT critical reading scores over 600
43% had SAT math scores over 600
53% had SAT writing scores over 600
25% had SAT critical reading scores over 700
6% had SAT math scores over 700
16% had SAT writing scores over 700
2 National Merit Scholars
2 class presidents
2 valedictorians

Graduation and After
18% pursued further study (6% law, 4% arts and sciences, 4% education)
76% had job offers within 6 months
6 organizations recruited on campus

Financial Matters
$18,756 tuition and fees (2008–09)
$6688 room and board
90% average percent of need met
$12,785 average financial aid amount received per undergraduate (2006–07 estimated)

Christian Brothers University

URBAN SETTING ■ PRIVATE ■ INDEPENDENT RELIGIOUS ■ COED
MEMPHIS, TENNESSEE

Web site: www.cbu.edu
Contact: Ms. Tracey Dysart-Ford, Dean of Admissions, 650 East Parkway South, Memphis, TN 38104
Telephone: 901-321-3205 or toll-free 800-288-7576
Fax: 901-321-3202
E-mail: admissions@cbu.edu

Getting Accepted

1,360 applied
69% were accepted
321 enrolled (34% of accepted)
29% from top tenth of their h.s. class
3.34 average high school GPA
Mean SAT critical reading score: 553
Mean SAT math score: 550
Mean ACT score: 24
30% had SAT critical reading scores over 600
36% had SAT math scores over 600
47% had ACT scores over 24
6% had SAT critical reading scores over 700
4% had SAT math scores over 700
7% had ACT scores over 30
9 valedictorians

Graduation and After

46% graduated in 4 years
13% graduated in 5 years
2% graduated in 6 years
15% pursued further study
93% had job offers within 6 months
234 organizations recruited on campus

Financial Matters

$22,600 tuition and fees (2008–09)
$5880 room and board
82% average percent of need met
$15,808 average financial aid amount received per undergraduate (2006–07 estimated)

Academics

CBU awards bachelor's and master's **degrees**. **Challenging opportunities** include advanced placement credit, accelerated degree programs, an honors program, double majors, independent study, and a senior project. Special programs include internships, summer session for credit, off-campus study, study-abroad, and Army, Navy, and Air Force ROTC.

The most frequently chosen **baccalaureate** fields are business/marketing, psychology, and engineering. A complete listing of majors at CBU appears in the Majors by College index beginning on page 471.

The **faculty** at CBU has 94 full-time members, 91% with terminal degrees. The student-faculty ratio is 14:1.

Students of CBU

The student body totals 1,874, of whom 1,462 are undergraduates. 55.1% are women and 44.9% are men. Students come from 27 states and territories and 15 other countries. 80% are from Tennessee. 1.9% are international students. 32.6% are African American, 4.8% Asian American, and 2.3% Hispanic American. 80% returned for their sophomore year.

Facilities and Resources

300 **computers/terminals** are available on campus for general student use. Students can access the following: online (class) registration, online class listings, e-mail, course assignments. Campuswide network is available. Wireless service is available via classrooms, computer centers, computer labs, libraries. The **library** has 107,000 books and 437 subscriptions.

Campus Life

There are 37 active organizations on campus, including a drama/theater group and choral group. 24% of eligible men and 22% of eligible women are members of national **fraternities**, national **sororities**, and local sororities.

CBU is a member of the NCAA (Division II). **Intercollegiate sports** (some offering scholarships) include baseball (m), basketball, cross-country running, golf, soccer, softball (w), tennis, volleyball (w).

Campus Safety

Student safety services include late-night transport/escort service, 24-hour emergency telephone alarm devices, 24-hour patrols by trained security personnel, student patrols, and electronically operated dormitory entrances.

Applying

CBU requires an essay, SAT or ACT, a high school transcript, and a minimum high school GPA of 2.5, and in some cases recommendations. It recommends an interview. Application deadline: 8/1; 2/15 priority date for financial aid. Early and deferred admission are possible.

CLAREMONT MCKENNA COLLEGE

SMALL-TOWN SETTING ■ PRIVATE ■ INDEPENDENT ■ COED
CLAREMONT, CALIFORNIA

Web site: www.claremontmckenna.edu
Contact: Mr. Richard C. Vos, Vice President/Dean of Admission and
Financial Aid, 890 Columbia Avenue, Claremont, CA 91711
Telephone: 909-621-8088
Fax: 909-621-8516
E-mail: admission@claremontmckenna.edu

Academics

CMC awards bachelor's degrees. **Challenging opportunities** include advanced placement credit, accelerated degree programs, student-designed majors, an honors program, double majors, independent study, and a senior project. Special programs include internships, off-campus study, study-abroad, and Army and Air Force ROTC.

The most frequently chosen **baccalaureate** fields are social sciences, psychology, and interdisciplinary studies. A complete listing of majors at CMC appears in the Majors by College index beginning on page 471.

The **faculty** at CMC has 112 full-time members, 100% with terminal degrees. The student-faculty ratio is 9:1.

Students of CMC

The student body is made up of 1,135 undergraduates. 45.6% are women and 54.4% are men. Students come from 47 states and territories and 23 other countries. 45% are from California. 4.9% are international students. 4.5% are African American, 0.2% American Indian, 13.3% Asian American, and 12.7% Hispanic American. 97% returned for their sophomore year.

Facilities and Resources

125 **computers/terminals** are available on campus for general student use. Students can access the following: campus intranet, computer help desk, free student e-mail accounts, online (class) grades, online (class) schedules. Campuswide network is available. 100% of college-owned or -operated housing units are wired for high-speed Internet access. The 4 **libraries** have 2,028,793 books and 6,028 subscriptions.

Campus Life

There are 280 active organizations on campus, including a drama/theater group, newspaper, radio station, and choral group. No national or local **fraternities** or **sororities**.
CMC is a member of the NCAA (Division III). **Intercollegiate sports** include baseball (m), basketball, cross-country running, football (m), golf (m), lacrosse (w), soccer, softball (w), swimming and diving, tennis, track and field, volleyball (w), water polo.

Campus Safety

Student safety services include late-night transport/escort service, 24-hour emergency telephone alarm devices, 24-hour patrols by trained security personnel, student patrols, and electronically operated dormitory entrances.

Applying

CMC requires an essay, SAT or ACT, a high school transcript, 3 recommendations, and a minimum high school GPA of 3.0, and in some cases SAT Subject Tests. It recommends an interview. Application deadline: 1/2. Early and deferred admission are possible.

Getting Accepted

3,778 applied
18% were accepted
268 enrolled (40% of accepted)
84% from top tenth of their h.s. class
Mean SAT critical reading score: 700
Mean SAT math score: 700
Mean ACT score: 31
90% had SAT critical reading scores over 600
90% had SAT math scores over 600
52% had SAT critical reading scores over 700
53% had SAT math scores over 700
13 National Merit Scholars
23 class presidents
22 valedictorians

Graduation and After

85% graduated in 4 years
4% graduated in 5 years
20% pursued further study
62% had job offers within 6 months
120 organizations recruited on campus

Financial Matters

$34,980 tuition and fees (2007–08)
$10,536 room and board
100% average percent of need met
$28,191 average financial aid amount received
per undergraduate (2006–07 estimated)

CLARKE COLLEGE

URBAN SETTING ■ PRIVATE ■ INDEPENDENT RELIGIOUS ■ COED
DUBUQUE, IOWA

Web site: www.clarke.edu
Contact: Mr. Andy Shroeder, Director of Admissions, 1550 Clarke Drive,
    Dubuque, IA 52001-3198
Telephone: 563-588-6316 or toll-free 800-383-2345
Fax: 563-588-6789
E-mail: admissions@clarke.edu

Getting Accepted
1,020 applied
62% were accepted
188 enrolled (30% of accepted)
17% from top tenth of their h.s. class
3.73 average high school GPA
Mean SAT critical reading score: 518
Mean SAT math score: 552
Mean SAT writing score: 540
Mean ACT score: 22
20% had SAT critical reading scores over 600
10% had SAT math scores over 600
20% had SAT writing scores over 600
42% had ACT scores over 24
16% had ACT scores over 30

Graduation and After
58% graduated in 4 years
10% graduated in 5 years
2% graduated in 6 years
14% pursued further study (11% arts and
    sciences, 2% education, 1% law)
70% had job offers within 6 months
78 organizations recruited on campus

Financial Matters
$21,312 tuition and fees (2007–08)
$6574 room and board
85% average percent of need met
$17,276 average financial aid amount received
    per undergraduate (2006–07 estimated)

Academics

Clarke awards associate, bachelor's, and master's **degrees. Challenging opportunities**
include advanced placement credit, accelerated degree programs, student-designed
majors, an honors program, double majors, independent study, and a senior project.
Special programs include cooperative education, internships, summer session for credit,
off-campus study, study-abroad, and Army ROTC.

The most frequently chosen **baccalaureate** fields are health professions and related
sciences, business/marketing, and education. A complete listing of majors at Clarke appears in the Majors by College index beginning on page 471.

The **faculty** at Clarke has 74 full-time members, 57% with terminal degrees. The
student-faculty ratio is 11:1.

Students of Clarke

Students come from 23 states and territories and 5 other countries. 62% are from Iowa.
0.7% are international students. 1.8% are African American, 0.2% American Indian,
0.5% Asian American, and 2% Hispanic American. 70% returned for their sophomore
year.

Facilities and Resources

237 **computers/terminals** are available on campus for general student use. Students can
access the following: campus intranet, free student e-mail accounts, online (class) grades,
online (class) registration, online (class) schedules. Campuswide network is available.
Wireless service is available via learning centers, libraries, student centers. The **library**
has 182,649 books and 508 subscriptions.

Campus Life

There are 63 active organizations on campus, including a drama/theater group,
newspaper, radio station, and choral group. No national or local **fraternities** or **sororities.**

Clarke is a member of the NAIA. **Intercollegiate sports** include baseball (m),
basketball, cross-country running, golf, soccer, softball (w), tennis, volleyball.

Campus Safety

Student safety services include late-night transport/escort service, 24-hour emergency
telephone alarm devices, 24-hour patrols by trained security personnel, and electronically operated dormitory entrances.

Applying

Clarke requires SAT or ACT, a high school transcript, rank in upper 50% of high school
class, minimum ACT score of 21 or SAT score of 1000, and a minimum high school
GPA of 2.0, and in some cases an interview. Application deadline: rolling admissions;
4/15 priority date for financial aid. Deferred admission is possible.

CLARKSON UNIVERSITY

SMALL-TOWN SETTING ■ PRIVATE ■ INDEPENDENT ■ COED
POTSDAM, NEW YORK

SPONSOR

Web site: www.clarkson.edu
Contact: Mr. Brian Grant, Director of Admission, Holcroft House, Potsdam, NY 13699-5605
Telephone: 315-268-6480 or toll-free 800-527-6577
Fax: 315-268-7647
E-mail: admission@clarkson.edu

Academics

Clarkson awards bachelor's, master's, doctoral, and first-professional **degrees**. **Challenging opportunities** include advanced placement credit, accelerated degree programs, student-designed majors, an honors program, double majors, independent study, and a senior project. Special programs include cooperative education, internships, summer session for credit, off-campus study, study-abroad, and Army and Air Force ROTC. A complete listing of majors at Clarkson appears in the Majors by College index beginning on page 471.

The **faculty** at Clarkson has 183 full-time members, 86% with terminal degrees. The student-faculty ratio is 15:1.

Students of Clarkson

The student body totals 2,949, of whom 2,540 are undergraduates. 25.9% are women and 74.1% are men. Students come from 41 states and territories and 25 other countries. 72% are from New York. 2.9% are international students. 2.6% are African American, 0.3% American Indian, 2.7% Asian American, and 2.2% Hispanic American. 85% returned for their sophomore year.

Facilities and Resources

400 **computers/terminals** and 10,000 ports are available on campus for general student use. Students can access the following: campus intranet, computer help desk, free student e-mail accounts, online (class) grades, online (class) registration, online (class) schedules. Campuswide network is available. 100% of college-owned or -operated housing units are wired for high-speed Internet access. Wireless service is available via classrooms, computer centers, computer labs, learning centers, libraries, student centers. The 2 **libraries** have 269,059 books and 1,778 subscriptions.

Campus Life

There are 55 active organizations on campus, including a drama/theater group, newspaper, radio station, television station, and choral group. 14% of eligible men and 13% of eligible women are members of national **fraternities**, national **sororities**, and local fraternities.

Clarkson is a member of the NCAA (Division III). **Intercollegiate sports** (some offering scholarships) include baseball (m), basketball, cross-country running, golf (m), ice hockey, lacrosse, skiing (cross-country), skiing (downhill), soccer, swimming and diving, volleyball (w).

Campus Safety

Student safety services include late-night transport/escort service, 24-hour emergency telephone alarm devices, 24-hour patrols by trained security personnel, and electronically operated dormitory entrances.

Applying

Clarkson requires SAT or ACT, a high school transcript, and 2 recommendations. It recommends SAT Subject Tests and an interview. Application deadline: 1/15; 2/15 priority date for financial aid. Early and deferred admission are possible.

Clarkson is New York State's highest-ranked small research institution, with majors in business, engineering, health sciences, liberal arts, and science. Located in upstate New York's Northern Adirondack region near the St. Lawrence River Valley, the 3,100-student campus combines high-powered academics with a friendly, personal atmosphere. Students enjoy easy access to Clarkson's faculty members, state-of-the-art learning facilities, and outstanding outdoor recreational opportunities. Rigorous academic programs emphasize interactive learning and a collaborative approach in project-based problem solving. Students develop technical expertise; skills in innovation, communication, and teamwork; and versatility vital in today's knowledge-based economy.

Getting Accepted
2,943 applied
82% were accepted
682 enrolled (28% of accepted)
40% from top tenth of their h.s. class
3.52 average high school GPA
Mean SAT critical reading score: 572
Mean SAT math score: 608
Mean SAT writing score: 557
Mean ACT score: 25
32% had SAT critical reading scores over 600
57% had SAT math scores over 600
64% had ACT scores over 24
4% had SAT critical reading scores over 700
13% had SAT math scores over 700
11% had ACT scores over 30
13 valedictorians

Graduation and After
58% graduated in 4 years
15% graduated in 5 years
1% graduated in 6 years
25% pursued further study (6% engineering, 5% arts and sciences, 5% business)
49% had job offers within 6 months
96 organizations recruited on campus

Financial Matters
$29,160 tuition and fees (2007–08)
$10,130 room and board
86% average percent of need met
$19,993 average financial aid amount received per undergraduate (2006–07 estimated)

CLARK UNIVERSITY

Urban setting ■ Private ■ Independent ■ Coed
Worcester, Massachusetts

Web site: www.clarku.edu
Contact: Mr. Harold Wingood, Dean of Admissions, Admissions House, 950 Main Street, Worcester, MA 01610
Telephone: 508-793-7431 or toll-free 800-GO-CLARK
Fax: 508-793-8821
E-mail: admissions@clarku.edu

Getting Accepted
5,201 applied
56% were accepted
574 enrolled (20% of accepted)
32% from top tenth of their h.s. class
3.47 average high school GPA
Mean SAT critical reading score: 609
Mean SAT math score: 594
Mean ACT score: 26
57% had SAT critical reading scores over 600
47% had SAT math scores over 600
78% had ACT scores over 24
15% had SAT critical reading scores over 700
7% had SAT math scores over 700
10% had ACT scores over 30

Graduation and After
69% graduated in 4 years
6% graduated in 5 years
1% graduated in 6 years
30% pursued further study (16% arts and sciences, 4% business, 3% education)
100 organizations recruited on campus

Financial Matters
$32,865 tuition and fees (2007–08)
$6300 room and board
94% average percent of need met
$24,072 average financial aid amount received per undergraduate (2006–07 estimated)

Academics

Clark awards bachelor's, master's, and doctoral **degrees** and post-bachelor's and post-master's certificates. **Challenging opportunities** include advanced placement credit, accelerated degree programs, student-designed majors, an honors program, double majors, independent study, and a senior project. Special programs include internships, summer session for credit, off-campus study, study-abroad, and Army, Navy, and Air Force ROTC.

The most frequently chosen **baccalaureate** fields are social sciences, psychology, and visual and performing arts. A complete listing of majors at Clark appears in the Majors by College index beginning on page 471.

The **faculty** at Clark has 173 full-time members, 97% with terminal degrees. The student-faculty ratio is 10:1.

Students of Clark

The student body totals 3,210, of whom 2,320 are undergraduates. 60.2% are women and 39.8% are men. Students come from 44 states and territories and 62 other countries. 36% are from Massachusetts. 8.2% are international students. 2.3% are African American, 0.3% American Indian, 3.8% Asian American, and 1.9% Hispanic American. 88% returned for their sophomore year.

Facilities and Resources

58 **computers/terminals** and 4,000 ports are available on campus for general student use. Students can access the following: campus intranet, computer help desk, free student e-mail accounts, online (class) grades, online (class) registration, online (class) schedules, online course support. Campuswide network is available. 100% of college-owned or -operated housing units are wired for high-speed Internet access. Wireless service is available via classrooms, computer centers, computer labs, learning centers, libraries, student centers. The 5 **libraries** have 289,658 books and 1,383 subscriptions.

Campus Life

There are 80 active organizations on campus, including a drama/theater group, newspaper, radio station, television station, choral group, and marching band. No national or local **fraternities** or **sororities**.

Clark is a member of the NCAA (Division III). **Intercollegiate sports** include baseball (m), basketball, crew, cross-country running, field hockey (w), lacrosse (m), soccer, softball (w), swimming and diving, tennis, volleyball (w).

Campus Safety

Student safety services include late-night transport/escort service, 24-hour emergency telephone alarm devices, 24-hour patrols by trained security personnel, student patrols, and electronically operated dormitory entrances.

Applying

Clark requires an essay, SAT or ACT, a high school transcript, and 2 recommendations. It recommends an interview. Application deadline: 1/15; 2/1 for financial aid, with a 2/1 priority date. Early and deferred admission are possible.

CLEMSON UNIVERSITY
SMALL-TOWN SETTING ■ PUBLIC ■ STATE-SUPPORTED ■ COED
CLEMSON, SOUTH CAROLINA

SPONSOR

Web site: www.clemson.edu
Contact: Mr. Timothy R. Galbreath, Assistant Director of Admissions, PO Box 345124, 105 Sikes Hall, Clemson, SC 29634
Telephone: 864-656-2287
Fax: 864-656-2464
E-mail: cuadmissions@clemson.edu

Academics
Clemson awards bachelor's, master's, and doctoral **degrees**. **Challenging opportunities** include advanced placement credit, accelerated degree programs, an honors program, double majors, and a senior project. Special programs include cooperative education, internships, summer session for credit, study-abroad, and Army and Air Force ROTC.

The most frequently chosen **baccalaureate** fields are business/marketing, engineering, and education. A complete listing of majors at Clemson appears in the Majors by College index beginning on page 471.

The **faculty** at Clemson has 1,015 full-time members, 86% with terminal degrees. The student-faculty ratio is 15:1.

Students of Clemson
The student body totals 17,165, of whom 14,096 are undergraduates. 45.6% are women and 54.4% are men. Students come from 53 states and territories and 84 other countries. 68% are from South Carolina. 0.8% are international students. 6.9% are African American, 0.4% American Indian, 1.6% Asian American, and 1% Hispanic American. 89% returned for their sophomore year.

Facilities and Resources
1,250 **computers/terminals** are available on campus for general student use. Students can access the following: online (class) registration, wireless network. Campuswide network is available. The 2 **libraries** have 1,233,478 books and 5,587 subscriptions.

Campus Life
There are 250 active organizations on campus, including a drama/theater group, newspaper, radio station, television station, choral group, and marching band. 15% of eligible men and 22% of eligible women are members of national **fraternities** and national **sororities**.

Clemson is a member of the NCAA (Division I). **Intercollegiate sports** (some offering scholarships) include baseball (m), basketball, cheerleading, crew (w), cross-country running, football (m), golf (m), soccer, swimming and diving, tennis, track and field, volleyball (w).

Campus Safety
Student safety services include late-night transport/escort service, 24-hour emergency telephone alarm devices, 24-hour patrols by trained security personnel, and electronically operated dormitory entrances.

Applying
Clemson requires SAT or ACT and a high school transcript. It recommends an essay and recommendations. Application deadline: 5/1; 4/1 priority date for financial aid.

Getting Accepted
12,463 applied
57% were accepted
2,903 enrolled (41% of accepted)
45% from top tenth of their h.s. class
3.9 average high school GPA
Mean SAT critical reading score: 600
Mean SAT math score: 625
Mean ACT score: 26
54% had SAT critical reading scores over 600
69% had SAT math scores over 600
81% had ACT scores over 24
9% had SAT critical reading scores over 700
15% had SAT math scores over 700
20% had ACT scores over 30
23 National Merit Scholars
88 valedictorians

Graduation and After
44% graduated in 4 years
27% graduated in 5 years
4% graduated in 6 years
45% had job offers within 6 months
212 organizations recruited on campus

Financial Matters
$10,370 resident tuition and fees (2007–08)
$22,300 nonresident tuition and fees (2007–08)
$6170 room and board
62% average percent of need met
$9743 average financial aid amount received per undergraduate (2006–07 estimated)

COE COLLEGE

URBAN SETTING ■ PRIVATE ■ INDEPENDENT RELIGIOUS ■ COED
CEDAR RAPIDS, IOWA

Web site: www.coe.edu
Contact: Mr. John Grundig, Dean of Admission, 1220 1st Avenue, NE, Cedar Rapids, IA 52402-5070
Telephone: 319-399-8500 or toll-free 877-225-5263
Fax: 319-399-8816
E-mail: admission@coe.edu

Getting Accepted

1,647 applied
68% were accepted
276 enrolled (25% of accepted)
34% from top tenth of their h.s. class
3.68 average high school GPA
Mean SAT critical reading score: 607
Mean SAT math score: 598
Mean ACT score: 25
70% had SAT critical reading scores over 600
78% had SAT math scores over 600
67% had ACT scores over 24
23% had SAT critical reading scores over 700
22% had SAT math scores over 700
13% had ACT scores over 30
8 valedictorians

Graduation and After

66% graduated in 4 years
6% graduated in 5 years
26% pursued further study (17% arts and sciences, 2% business, 2% law)
98% had job offers within 6 months
83 organizations recruited on campus

Financial Matters

$26,390 tuition and fees (2007–08)
$6600 room and board
94% average percent of need met
$21,859 average financial aid amount received per undergraduate (2006–07 estimated)

Academics

Coe awards bachelor's and master's **degrees**. **Challenging opportunities** include advanced placement credit, accelerated degree programs, student-designed majors, an honors program, double majors, independent study, and a senior project. Special programs include internships, summer session for credit, off-campus study, study-abroad, and Army and Air Force ROTC.

The most frequently chosen **baccalaureate** fields are social sciences, business/marketing, and psychology. A complete listing of majors at Coe appears in the Majors by College index beginning on page 471.

The **faculty** at Coe has 77 full-time members, 94% with terminal degrees. The student-faculty ratio is 10:1.

Students of Coe

The student body totals 1,300, of whom 1,275 are undergraduates. 54.4% are women and 45.6% are men. Students come from 43 states and territories and 18 other countries. 64% are from Iowa. 4.4% are international students. 2.4% are African American, 0.5% American Indian, 1% Asian American, and 1.8% Hispanic American. 82% returned for their sophomore year.

Facilities and Resources

275 **computers/terminals** are available on campus for general student use. Students can access the following: online (class) registration. Campuswide network is available. The 2 **libraries** have 218,881 books and 1,576 subscriptions.

Campus Life

There are 60 active organizations on campus, including a drama/theater group, newspaper, radio station, and choral group. 26% of eligible men and 19% of eligible women are members of national **fraternities** and national **sororities**.

Coe is a member of the NCAA (Division III). **Intercollegiate sports** include baseball (m), basketball, cheerleading (w), cross-country running, football (m), golf, soccer, softball (w), swimming and diving, tennis, track and field, volleyball (w), wrestling (m).

Campus Safety

Student safety services include late-night transport/escort service, 24-hour emergency telephone alarm devices, 24-hour patrols by trained security personnel, and electronically operated dormitory entrances.

Applying

Coe requires an essay, SAT or ACT, a high school transcript, and 1 recommendation. It recommends an interview and a minimum high school GPA of 3.0. Application deadline: 3/1; 3/1 priority date for financial aid. Early and deferred admission are possible.

COLBY COLLEGE

SMALL-TOWN SETTING ■ PRIVATE ■ INDEPENDENT ■ COED
WATERVILLE, MAINE

Web site: www.colby.edu
Contact: Mr. Steve Thomas, Director of Admissions, Office of Admissions and Financial Aid, 4800 Mayflower Hill, Waterville, ME 04901-8848
Telephone: 207-859-4800 or toll-free 800-723-3032
Fax: 207-859-4828
E-mail: admissions@colby.edu

Academics

Colby awards bachelor's **degrees**. **Challenging opportunities** include advanced placement credit, student-designed majors, an honors program, double majors, independent study, and a senior project. Special programs include internships, off-campus study, study-abroad, and Army ROTC.

The most frequently chosen **baccalaureate** fields are social sciences, English, and area and ethnic studies. A complete listing of majors at Colby appears in the Majors by College index beginning on page 471.

The **faculty** at Colby has 159 full-time members, 96% with terminal degrees. The student-faculty ratio is 10:1.

Students of Colby

The student body is made up of 1,867 undergraduates. 54.8% are women and 45.2% are men. Students come from 50 states and territories and 62 other countries. 10% are from Maine. 6.3% are international students. 2.4% are African American, 0.5% American Indian, 7.7% Asian American, and 2.9% Hispanic American. 93% returned for their sophomore year.

Facilities and Resources

350 **computers/terminals** are available on campus for general student use. Students can access the following: campus intranet, computer help desk, free student e-mail accounts, online (class) grades, online (class) registration, online (class) schedules, Portal. Campuswide network is available. 100% of college-owned or -operated housing units are wired for high-speed Internet access. Wireless service is available via dorm rooms, learning centers, libraries, student centers. The 3 **libraries** have 350,000 books and 1,850 subscriptions.

Campus Life

There are 98 active organizations on campus, including a drama/theater group, newspaper, radio station, and choral group. No national or local **fraternities** or **sororities**.

Colby is a member of the NCAA (Division III). **Intercollegiate sports** include baseball (m), basketball, crew, cross-country running, field hockey (w), football (m), golf, ice hockey, lacrosse, skiing (cross-country), skiing (downhill), soccer, softball (w), squash, swimming and diving, tennis, track and field, volleyball (w).

Campus Safety

Student safety services include campus lighting, student emergency response team, self-defense class, property id program, party monitors, late-night transport/escort service, 24-hour emergency telephone alarm devices, 24-hour patrols by trained security personnel, and electronically operated dormitory entrances.

Applying

Colby requires an essay, SAT or ACT, a high school transcript, and 2 recommendations. It recommends an interview. Application deadline: 1/1; 2/1 for financial aid. Early and deferred admission are possible.

Getting Accepted
4,679 applied
32% were accepted
467 enrolled (31% of accepted)
60% from top tenth of their h.s. class
Mean SAT critical reading score: 670
Mean SAT math score: 679
Mean SAT writing score: 642
Mean ACT score: 29
91% had SAT critical reading scores over 600
91% had SAT math scores over 600
87% had SAT writing scores over 600
97% had ACT scores over 24
45% had SAT critical reading scores over 700
38% had SAT math scores over 700
34% had SAT writing scores over 700
47% had ACT scores over 30
19 valedictorians

Graduation and After
84% graduated in 4 years
3% graduated in 5 years
22% pursued further study (10% arts and sciences, 4% law, 2% business)
65% had job offers within 6 months
43 organizations recruited on campus

Financial Matters
$46,100 comprehensive fee (2007–08)
100% average percent of need met
$29,908 average financial aid amount received per undergraduate (2006–07 estimated)

COLGATE UNIVERSITY

RURAL SETTING ■ PRIVATE ■ INDEPENDENT ■ COED
HAMILTON, NEW YORK

Web site: www.colgate.edu
Contact: Mr. Gary L. Ross, Dean of Admission, 13 Oak Drive, Hamilton, NY 13346-1383
Telephone: 315-228-7401
Fax: 315-228-7544
E-mail: admission@mail.colgate.edu

Getting Accepted
8,759 applied
26% were accepted
694 enrolled (31% of accepted)
64% from top tenth of their h.s. class
3.7 average high school GPA
Mean SAT critical reading score: 667
Mean SAT math score: 669
Mean ACT score: 30
85% had SAT critical reading scores over 600
86% had SAT math scores over 600
98% had ACT scores over 24
38% had SAT critical reading scores over 700
36% had SAT math scores over 700
63% had ACT scores over 30
13 valedictorians

Graduation and After
85% graduated in 4 years
4% graduated in 5 years
1% graduated in 6 years
20% pursued further study (5% arts and sciences, 5% law, 4% medicine)
80% had job offers within 6 months
132 organizations recruited on campus

Financial Matters
$37,660 tuition and fees (2007–08)
$9170 room and board
100% average percent of need met
$31,355 average financial aid amount received per undergraduate (2006–07 estimated)

Academics

Colgate awards bachelor's and master's **degrees**. **Challenging opportunities** include advanced placement credit, student-designed majors, an honors program, double majors, independent study, and a senior project. Special programs include internships, off-campus study, study-abroad, and Army ROTC.

The most frequently chosen **baccalaureate** fields are social sciences, English, and biological/life sciences. A complete listing of majors at Colgate appears in the Majors by College index beginning on page 471.

The **faculty** at Colgate has 253 full-time members, 97% with terminal degrees. The student-faculty ratio is 10:1.

Students of Colgate

The student body totals 2,790, of whom 2,780 are undergraduates. 53.2% are women and 46.8% are men. Students come from 40 states and territories and 33 other countries. 29% are from New York. 94% returned for their sophomore year.

Facilities and Resources

Students can access the following: campus intranet, computer help desk, free student e-mail accounts, online (class) registration, online (class) schedules, software applications. Campuswide network is available. 100% of college-owned or -operated housing units are wired for high-speed Internet access. The 2 **libraries** have 1,172,551 books and 29,632 subscriptions.

Campus Life

There are 160 active organizations on campus, including a drama/theater group, newspaper, radio station, television station, and choral group. Colgate has national **fraternities**, national **sororities**, and local fraternities.

Colgate is a member of the NCAA (Division I). **Intercollegiate sports** (some offering scholarships) include basketball, crew, cross-country running, field hockey (w), football (m), golf (m), ice hockey, lacrosse, soccer, softball (w), swimming and diving, tennis, track and field, volleyball (w).

Campus Safety

Student safety services include late-night transport/escort service, 24-hour emergency telephone alarm devices, 24-hour patrols by trained security personnel, student patrols, and electronically operated dormitory entrances.

Applying

Colgate requires an essay, SAT or ACT, a high school transcript, and 3 recommendations. Application deadline: 1/15; 1/15 for financial aid. Deferred admission is possible.

COLLEGE OF CHARLESTON

URBAN SETTING ■ PUBLIC ■ STATE-SUPPORTED ■ COED
CHARLESTON, SOUTH CAROLINA

Web site: www.cofc.edu
Contact: Ms. Suzette Stille, Director of Undergraduate Admissions, 66 George Street, Charleston, SC 29424-0001
Telephone: 843-953-5670 or toll-free 843-953-5670 (in-state)
Fax: 843-953-6322
E-mail: admissions@cofc.edu

SPONSOR

Academics

C of C awards bachelor's and master's **degrees** (also offers graduate degree programs through University of Charleston, South Carolina). **Challenging opportunities** include advanced placement credit, accelerated degree programs, an honors program, double majors, independent study, and a senior project. Special programs include cooperative education, internships, summer session for credit, off-campus study, study-abroad, and Air Force ROTC.

The most frequently chosen **baccalaureate** fields are business/marketing, social sciences, and communications/journalism. A complete listing of majors at C of C appears in the Majors by College index beginning on page 471.

The **faculty** at C of C has 521 full-time members, 86% with terminal degrees. The student-faculty ratio is 13:1.

Students of C of C

The student body totals 11,316, of whom 9,923 are undergraduates. 63.9% are women and 36.1% are men. Students come from 51 states and territories and 69 other countries. 64% are from South Carolina. 1.6% are international students. 6.2% are African American, 0.3% American Indian, 1.7% Asian American, and 1.9% Hispanic American. 82% returned for their sophomore year.

Facilities and Resources

578 **computers/terminals** are available on campus for general student use. Students can access the following: online (class) registration. Campuswide network is available. The 2 **libraries** have 701,774 books and 4,099 subscriptions.

Campus Life

There are 144 active organizations on campus, including a drama/theater group, newspaper, radio station, and choral group. 15% of eligible men and 20% of eligible women are members of national **fraternities** and national **sororities**.

C of C is a member of the NCAA (Division I). **Intercollegiate sports** (some offering scholarships) include baseball (m), basketball, cross-country running, equestrian sports (w), golf, sailing, soccer, softball (w), swimming and diving, tennis, volleyball (w).

Campus Safety

Student safety services include late-night transport/escort service, 24-hour emergency telephone alarm devices, 24-hour patrols by trained security personnel, student patrols, and electronically operated dormitory entrances.

Applying

C of C requires an essay, SAT or ACT, and a high school transcript. It recommends an interview. Application deadline: 4/1; 3/15 priority date for financial aid. Deferred admission is possible.

The College of Charleston is a nationally preeminent, public liberal arts and sciences university located in historic Charleston, South Carolina. The College was founded in 1770; its distinctive combination of a beautiful historic campus, modern facilities, and innovative programs positions it among the nation's best universities for academics, student life, and affordability. Students choose the College of Charleston for its small-college feel blended with the advantages and diversity of an urban, midsized university. The College provides an intellectually stimulating environment where students are challenged by a dedicated faculty of distinguished teacher-scholars. The city of Charleston—world-renowned for its history, culture, architecture, and coastal environment—serves as a living and learning laboratory.

Getting Accepted

8,941 applied
65% were accepted
2,064 enrolled (36% of accepted)
27% from top tenth of their h.s. class
3.82 average high school GPA
Mean SAT critical reading score: 611
Mean SAT math score: 609
Mean ACT score: 24
48% had SAT critical reading scores over 600
57% had SAT math scores over 600
64% had ACT scores over 24
10% had SAT critical reading scores over 700
6% had SAT math scores over 700
3% had ACT scores over 30
34 valedictorians

Graduation and After

44% graduated in 4 years
13% graduated in 5 years
2% graduated in 6 years
93.9% had job offers within 6 months
261 organizations recruited on campus

Financial Matters

$7778 resident tuition and fees (2007–08)
$18,732 nonresident tuition and fees (2007–08)
$8495 room and board
65% average percent of need met
$10,379 average financial aid amount received per undergraduate (2006–07 estimated)

THE COLLEGE OF IDAHO

SUBURBAN SETTING ■ PRIVATE ■ INDEPENDENT ■ COED
CALDWELL, IDAHO

Getting Accepted

911 applied
81% were accepted
242 enrolled (33% of accepted)
33% from top tenth of their h.s. class
3.62 average high school GPA
Mean SAT critical reading score: 559
Mean SAT math score: 565
Mean SAT writing score: 541
Mean ACT score: 24
41% had SAT critical reading scores over 600
34% had SAT writing scores over 600
61% had ACT scores over 24
5% had SAT critical reading scores over 700
3% had SAT writing scores over 700
10% had ACT scores over 30

Graduation and After

55% graduated in 4 years
5% graduated in 5 years
5% graduated in 6 years
22% pursued further study
13 organizations recruited on campus

Financial Matters

$18,990 tuition and fees (2008–09)
$6567 room and board
90% average percent of need met
$14,850 average financial aid amount received
    per undergraduate (2006–07 estimated)

Web site: www.albertson.edu
Contact: Ms. Charlene Brown, Director of Admissions, 2112 Cleveland
    Boulevard, Caldwell, ID 83605-4494
Telephone: 208-459-5689 or toll-free 800-244-3246
Fax: 208-459-5151
E-mail: admission@collegeofidaho.edu

Academics

Albertson awards bachelor's and master's **degrees**. **Challenging opportunities** include advanced placement credit, student-designed majors, an honors program, double majors, independent study, and a senior project. Special programs include cooperative education, internships, off-campus study, study-abroad, and Army ROTC.

The most frequently chosen **baccalaureate** fields are business/marketing, visual and performing arts, and psychology. A complete listing of majors at Albertson appears in the Majors by College index beginning on page 471.

The **faculty** at Albertson has 75 full-time members, 71% with terminal degrees. The student-faculty ratio is 9:1.

Students of Albertson

The student body totals 840, of whom 826 are undergraduates. 60.7% are women and 39.3% are men. Students come from 17 states and territories and 11 other countries. 69% are from Idaho. 3.1% are international students. 0.7% are African American, 0.4% American Indian, 2.7% Asian American, and 6.7% Hispanic American. 82% returned for their sophomore year.

Facilities and Resources

242 **computers/terminals** are available on campus for general student use. Students can access the following: campus intranet, computer help desk, free student e-mail accounts, online (class) grades, online (class) registration, online (class) schedules, online course syllabi, course assignments, course discussion, online yearly catalog, College You_Tube. Campuswide network is available. 100% of college-owned or -operated housing units are wired for high-speed Internet access. Wireless service is available via entire campus. The **library** has 183,308 books and 703 subscriptions.

Campus Life

There are 55 active organizations on campus, including a drama/theater group, newspaper, radio station, and choral group. 25% of eligible men and 26% of eligible women are members of national **fraternities**, national **sororities**, local fraternities, and local sororities.

Albertson is a member of the NAIA. **Intercollegiate sports** (some offering scholarships) include baseball (m), basketball, cross-country running, golf, skiing (cross-country), skiing (downhill), soccer, softball (w), swimming and diving, tennis (w), track and field, volleyball (w).

Campus Safety

Student safety services include late-night transport/escort service, 24-hour emergency telephone alarm devices, 24-hour patrols by trained security personnel, student patrols, and electronically operated dormitory entrances.

Applying

Albertson requires an essay, SAT and SAT Subject Tests or ACT, a high school transcript, and 1 recommendation. It recommends an interview and extracurricular activities. Application deadline: 6/1; 2/15 priority date for financial aid. Early and deferred admission are possible.

THE COLLEGE OF NEW JERSEY

SUBURBAN SETTING ■ PUBLIC ■ STATE-SUPPORTED ■ COED
EWING, NEW JERSEY

Web site: www.tcnj.edu
Contact: Ms. Lisa Angeloni, Dean of Admissions, PO Box 7718, Ewing, NJ 08628
Telephone: 609-771-2131 or toll-free 800-624-0967
Fax: 609-637-5174
E-mail: admiss@tcnj.edu

Academics

TCNJ awards bachelor's and master's **degrees** and post-bachelor's and post-master's certificates. **Challenging opportunities** include advanced placement credit, student-designed majors, an honors program, double majors, independent study, and a senior project. Special programs include internships, summer session for credit, off-campus study, study-abroad, and Army and Air Force ROTC.

The most frequently chosen **baccalaureate** fields are education, business/marketing, and psychology. A complete listing of majors at TCNJ appears in the Majors by College index beginning on page 471.

The **faculty** at TCNJ has 335 full-time members, 88% with terminal degrees. The student-faculty ratio is 13:1.

Students of TCNJ

The student body totals 6,964, of whom 6,205 are undergraduates. 58.4% are women and 41.6% are men. Students come from 19 states and territories and 12 other countries. 95% are from New Jersey. 0.1% are international students. 6.2% are African American, 0.1% American Indian, 7.5% Asian American, and 8.4% Hispanic American. 95% returned for their sophomore year.

Facilities and Resources

800 **computers/terminals** are available on campus for general student use. Students can access the following: online (class) grades, online (class) registration, online (class) schedules. Campuswide network is available. 100% of college-owned or -operated housing units are wired for high-speed Internet access. Wireless service is available via classrooms, computer labs, learning centers, libraries, student centers. The **library** has 662,152 books and 429,632 subscriptions.

Campus Life

There are 196 active organizations on campus, including a drama/theater group, newspaper, radio station, television station, and choral group. 12% of eligible men and 11% of eligible women are members of national **fraternities**, national **sororities**, local fraternities, and local sororities.

TCNJ is a member of the NCAA (Division III). **Intercollegiate sports** include baseball (m), basketball, cross-country running, field hockey (w), football (m), golf (m), lacrosse (w), soccer, softball (w), swimming and diving, tennis, track and field, wrestling (m).

Campus Safety

Student safety services include late-night transport/escort service, 24-hour emergency telephone alarm devices, 24-hour patrols by trained security personnel, student patrols, and electronically operated dormitory entrances.

Applying

TCNJ requires an essay, SAT, and a high school transcript, and in some cases an interview and art portfolio or music audition. It recommends 3 recommendations and a minimum high school GPA of 3.5. Application deadline: 2/15; 10/1 for financial aid, with a 3/1 priority date. Early and deferred admission are possible.

The College of New Jersey (TCNJ) is the state's most competitive public college and attracts the highest-achieving students from throughout the region. The College has created a challenging and dynamic learning environment. On an elegant campus in small classes, students and faculty members collaborate in a transformative educational process. From undergraduate research to internships and study abroad, TCNJ students have opportunities to shape their education in exciting ways. From the first year on, students blur the boundaries between living and learning and between "student" and "life."

Getting Accepted
8,607 applied
47% were accepted
1,297 enrolled (32% of accepted)
61% from top tenth of their h.s. class
Mean SAT critical reading score: 606
Mean SAT math score: 627
Mean SAT writing score: 609
59% had SAT critical reading scores over 600
68% had SAT math scores over 600
59% had SAT writing scores over 600
12% had SAT critical reading scores over 700
17% had SAT math scores over 700
12% had SAT writing scores over 700
23 valedictorians

Graduation and After
65% graduated in 4 years
16% graduated in 5 years
2% graduated in 6 years
22% pursued further study (7% education, 3% arts and sciences, 3% law)
88% had job offers within 6 months
400 organizations recruited on campus

Financial Matters
$11,307 resident tuition and fees (2007–08)
$18,530 nonresident tuition and fees (2007–08)
$9242 room and board
55% average percent of need met
$9207 average financial aid amount received per undergraduate (2006–07 estimated)

COLLEGE OF SAINT BENEDICT
COORDINATE WITH SAINT JOHN'S UNIVERSITY

SMALL-TOWN SETTING ■ PRIVATE ■ INDEPENDENT RELIGIOUS ■ COED, PRIMARILY WOMEN
SAINT JOSEPH, MINNESOTA

Web site: www.csbsju.edu
Contact: Ms. Karen Backes, Associate Dean of Admissions, 37 South College Avenue, St. Joseph, MN 56374
Telephone: 320-363-2196 or toll-free 800-544-1489
Fax: 320-363-2750
E-mail: admissions@csbsju.edu

Getting Accepted
1,677 applied
76% were accepted
537 enrolled (42% of accepted)
43% from top tenth of their h.s. class
3.75 average high school GPA
Mean SAT critical reading score: 582
Mean SAT math score: 586
Mean ACT score: 25
35% had SAT critical reading scores over 600
38% had SAT math scores over 600
67% had ACT scores over 24
12% had SAT critical reading scores over 700
9% had SAT math scores over 700
11% had ACT scores over 30

Graduation and After
75% graduated in 4 years
4% graduated in 5 years
23% pursued further study (8% arts and sciences, 2% law, 2% medicine)
72% had job offers within 6 months
118 organizations recruited on campus

Financial Matters
$26,530 tuition and fees (2007–08)
$7430 room and board
86% average percent of need met
$18,940 average financial aid amount received per undergraduate (2006–07 estimated)

Academics
CSB awards bachelor's **degrees** (coordinate with Saint John's University for men). **Challenging opportunities** include advanced placement credit, accelerated degree programs, student-designed majors, an honors program, double majors, independent study, and a senior project. Special programs include internships, off-campus study, study-abroad, and Army ROTC.

The most frequently chosen **baccalaureate** fields are English, health professions and related sciences, and psychology. A complete listing of majors at CSB appears in the Majors by College index beginning on page 471.

The **faculty** at CSB has 160 full-time members, 83% with terminal degrees. The student-faculty ratio is 12:1.

Students of CSB
The student body is made up of 2,087 undergraduates. 100% are women. Students come from 34 states and territories and 20 other countries. 84% are from Minnesota. 4.7% are international students. 0.8% are African American, 0.3% American Indian, 2.8% Asian American, and 1.8% Hispanic American. 90% returned for their sophomore year.

Facilities and Resources
643 **computers/terminals** and 3,000 ports are available on campus for general student use. Students can access the following: computer help desk, free student e-mail accounts, online (class) grades, online (class) registration, online (class) schedules, online student accounts. Campuswide network is available. 100% of college-owned or -operated housing units are wired for high-speed Internet access. Wireless service is available via classrooms, computer centers, computer labs, dorm rooms, learning centers, libraries, student centers. The 4 **libraries** have 481,338 books and 5,315 subscriptions.

Campus Life
There are 90 active organizations on campus, including a drama/theater group, newspaper, radio station, and choral group. No national or local **fraternities** or **sororities**.

CSB is a member of the NCAA (Division III). **Intercollegiate sports** include basketball (w), cross-country running (w), golf (w), ice hockey (w), skiing (cross-country) (w), soccer (w), softball (w), swimming and diving (w), tennis (w), track and field (w), volleyball (w).

Campus Safety
Student safety services include well-lit pathways, late-night transport/escort service, 24-hour emergency telephone alarm devices, 24-hour patrols by trained security personnel, student patrols, and electronically operated dormitory entrances.

Applying
CSB requires an essay, SAT or ACT, a high school transcript, and 1 recommendation. It recommends an interview and a minimum high school GPA of 3.0. Application deadline: rolling admissions; 3/15 priority date for financial aid. Deferred admission is possible.

COLLEGE OF ST. CATHERINE

URBAN SETTING ■ PRIVATE ■ INDEPENDENT RELIGIOUS
■ UNDERGRADUATE: WOMEN ONLY; GRADUATE: COED
ST. PAUL, MINNESOTA

Web site: www.stkate.edu
Contact: Ms. Cory Piper-Hauswirth, Associate Director of Admission and
Financial Aid, 2004 Randolph Avenue, F-02, St. Paul, MN 55105
Telephone: 651-690-6047 or toll-free 800-656-5283 (in-state)
Fax: 651-690-8824
E-mail: stkate@stkate.edu

Academics

CSC awards associate, bachelor's, master's, and doctoral **degrees** and post-bachelor's
certificates. **Challenging opportunities** include advanced placement credit, student-
designed majors, an honors program, double majors, independent study, and a senior
project. Special programs include internships, summer session for credit, off-campus
study, study-abroad, and Army and Air Force ROTC.

The most frequently chosen **baccalaureate** fields are health professions and related
sciences, business/marketing, and education. A complete listing of majors at CSC appears in the Majors by College index beginning on page 471.

The **faculty** at CSC has 261 full-time members. The student-faculty ratio is 11:1.

Students of CSC

The student body totals 5,246, of whom 3,831 are undergraduates. 96.1% are women
and 3.9% are men. Students come from 37 states and territories and 16 other countries.
90% are from Minnesota. 1.6% are international students. 10.6% are African American,
0.5% American Indian, 7.3% Asian American, and 2.7% Hispanic American. 80%
returned for their sophomore year.

Facilities and Resources

350 **computers/terminals** are available on campus for general student use. Students can
access the following: transcript. Campuswide network is available. The 3 **libraries** have
263,495 books and 1,141 subscriptions.

Campus Life

There are 42 active organizations on campus, including a drama/theater group,
newspaper, and choral group. 8% of eligible undergraduates are members of local
sororities.

CSC is a member of the NCAA (Division III). **Intercollegiate sports** include
basketball, cross-country running, ice hockey, soccer, softball, swimming and diving, tennis, track and field, volleyball.

Campus Safety

Student safety services include late-night transport/escort service, 24-hour emergency
telephone alarm devices, 24-hour patrols by trained security personnel, student patrols,
and electronically operated dormitory entrances.

Applying

CSC requires SAT or ACT, a high school transcript, and 1 recommendation, and in
some cases an essay and an interview. It recommends an interview. Application deadline:
rolling admissions; 4/15 priority date for financial aid. Deferred admission is possible.

Getting Accepted
1,632 applied
81% were accepted
437 enrolled (33% of accepted)
34% from top tenth of their h.s. class
3.64 average high school GPA
Mean ACT score: 23
55% had ACT scores over 24
4% had ACT scores over 30
4 National Merit Scholars
8 valedictorians

Graduation and After
41% graduated in 4 years
14% graduated in 5 years
3% graduated in 6 years
14% pursued further study
82% had job offers within 6 months

Financial Matters
$25,922 tuition and fees (2007–08)
$6788 room and board
72% average percent of need met
$23,534 average financial aid amount received
per undergraduate (2006–07 estimated)

THE COLLEGE OF ST. SCHOLASTICA

SUBURBAN SETTING ■ PRIVATE ■ INDEPENDENT RELIGIOUS ■ COED
DULUTH, MINNESOTA

Web site: www.css.edu
Contact: Mr. Brian Dalton, Vice President for Enrollment Management, 1200
 Kenwood Avenue, Duluth, MN 55811-4199
Telephone: 218-723-6053 or toll-free 800-249-6412
Fax: 218-723-5991
E-mail: admissions@css.edu

Getting Accepted
1,461 applied
88% were accepted
448 enrolled (35% of accepted)
23% from top tenth of their h.s. class
3.49 average high school GPA
Mean SAT critical reading score: 584
Mean SAT math score: 591
Mean ACT score: 23
42% had SAT critical reading scores over 600
46% had SAT math scores over 600
45% had ACT scores over 24
8% had SAT critical reading scores over 700
21% had SAT math scores over 700
5% had ACT scores over 30
12 valedictorians

Graduation and After
57% graduated in 4 years
6% graduated in 5 years
1% graduated in 6 years
21% pursued further study
68% had job offers within 6 months
22 organizations recruited on campus

Financial Matters
$24,990 tuition and fees (2007–08)
$6684 room and board
87% average percent of need met
$17,801 average financial aid amount received
 per undergraduate (2006–07 estimated)

Academics
St. Scholastica awards bachelor's, master's, and first-professional **degrees** and post-bachelor's and post-master's certificates. **Challenging opportunities** include advanced placement credit, accelerated degree programs, student-designed majors, an honors program, double majors, independent study, and a senior project. Special programs include internships, summer session for credit, off-campus study, study-abroad, and Air Force ROTC.

The most frequently chosen **baccalaureate** fields are health professions and related sciences, business/marketing, and biological/life sciences. A complete listing of majors at St. Scholastica appears in the Majors by College index beginning on page 471.

The **faculty** at St. Scholastica has 152 full-time members, 59% with terminal degrees. The student-faculty ratio is 13:1.

Students of St. Scholastica
The student body totals 3,259, of whom 2,538 are undergraduates. 69.8% are women and 30.2% are men. Students come from 35 states and territories and 33 other countries. 85% are from Minnesota. 3.6% are international students. 1.6% are African American, 2.5% American Indian, 2.1% Asian American, and 1.2% Hispanic American. 79% returned for their sophomore year.

Facilities and Resources
205 **computers/terminals** are available on campus for general student use. Students can access the following: campus intranet, computer help desk, free student e-mail accounts, online (class) grades, online (class) registration, online (class) schedules, student account information and transcripts online. Campuswide network is available. 100% of college-owned or -operated housing units are wired for high-speed Internet access. Wireless service is available via classrooms, computer centers, computer labs, dorm rooms, learning centers, libraries, student centers. The **library** has 130,353 books and 21,656 subscriptions.

Campus Life
There are 70 active organizations on campus, including a drama/theater group, newspaper, television station, and choral group. No national or local **fraternities** or **sororities**.

St. Scholastica is a member of the NCAA (Division III) and NAIA. **Intercollegiate sports** include baseball (m), basketball, cross-country running, football (m), ice hockey (m), soccer, softball (w), tennis, track and field, volleyball (w).

Campus Safety
Student safety services include student door monitor at night, late-night transport/escort service, 24-hour emergency telephone alarm devices, 24-hour patrols by trained security personnel, and electronically operated dormitory entrances.

Applying
St. Scholastica requires SAT or ACT and a high school transcript, and in some cases an interview and a minimum high school GPA of 2.0. It recommends an interview. Application deadline: rolling admissions; 3/15 priority date for financial aid. Early and deferred admission are possible.

THE COLLEGE OF SAINT THOMAS MORE

URBAN SETTING ■ PRIVATE ■ INDEPENDENT RELIGIOUS ■ COED
FORT WORTH, TEXAS

Web site: www.cstm.edu
Contact: Dr. James A. Patrick, 3020 Lubbock Avenue, Fort Worth, TX
    76109-2323
Telephone: 817-928-8459 or toll-free 800-583-6489 (out-of-state)
Fax: 817-924-3206
E-mail: more-info@cstm.edu

Academics

CSTM awards associate and bachelor's **degrees**. Special programs include cooperative education, summer session for credit, study-abroad, and Army ROTC.

The most frequently chosen **baccalaureate** field is liberal arts/general studies. A complete listing of majors at CSTM appears in the Majors by College index beginning on page 471.

The **faculty** at CSTM has 3 full-time members, 67% with terminal degrees. The student-faculty ratio is 5:1.

Students of CSTM

The student body is made up of 53 undergraduates. 45.3% are women and 54.7% are men. Students come from 5 states and territories. 76% are from Texas. 2.6% are African American and 7.9% Hispanic American. 89% returned for their sophomore year.

Facilities and Resources

7 **computers/terminals** are available on campus for general student use. The **library** has 13,739 books and 50 subscriptions.

Campus Life

There are 3 active organizations on campus. No national or local **fraternities** or **sororities**.

This institution has no intercollegiate sports.

Campus Safety

Student safety services include late-night transport/escort service, 24-hour patrols by trained security personnel, and student patrols.

Applying

CSTM requires an essay, a high school transcript, 1 recommendation, and a minimum high school GPA of 2.0. It recommends an interview. Application deadline: rolling admissions; 4/15 priority date for financial aid. Early and deferred admission are possible.

Getting Accepted
12 applied
83% were accepted
4 enrolled (40% of accepted)
3.2 average high school GPA

Financial Matters
$12,150 tuition and fees (2007–08)
$3690 room only
85% average percent of need met
$8560 average financial aid amount received
    per undergraduate (2005–06)

COLLEGE OF THE ATLANTIC
SMALL-TOWN SETTING ■ PRIVATE ■ INDEPENDENT ■ COED
BAR HARBOR, MAINE

Web site: www.coa.edu
Contact: Ms. Sarah Baker, Director of Admission, 105 Eden Street, Bar
   Harbor, ME 04609-1198
Telephone: 207-288-5015 Ext. 233 or toll-free 800-528-0025
Fax: 207-288-4126
E-mail: inquiry@coa.edu

The College of the Atlantic (COA) is an intellectually challenging, resolutely different college located between the ocean and Acadia National Park on Mount Desert Island, Maine. COA is small, with no departments and no majors, and its courses are interdisciplinary and value centered. The College looks for students seeking a rigorous academic experience but a different kind of education than that offered by more traditionally structured colleges and universities. COA's mission is to foster independent thought, to challenge conventional wisdom, to deal with pressing environmental and social change, and to be passionately engaged in transforming the world into a better place.

Getting Accepted
305 applied
77% were accepted
84 enrolled (36% of accepted)
33% from top tenth of their h.s. class
3.51 average high school GPA
Mean SAT critical reading score: 637
Mean SAT math score: 592
Mean SAT writing score: 623
Mean ACT score: 28
81% had SAT critical reading scores over 600
43% had SAT math scores over 600
70% had SAT writing scores over 600
88% had ACT scores over 24
23% had SAT critical reading scores over 700
13% had SAT math scores over 700
10% had SAT writing scores over 700
38% had ACT scores over 30
1 valedictorian

Graduation and After
32% graduated in 4 years
19% graduated in 5 years
4% graduated in 6 years
3% pursued further study (2% arts and sciences)
80% had job offers within 6 months
10 organizations recruited on campus

Financial Matters
$29,970 tuition and fees (2007–08)
$8190 room and board
95% average percent of need met
$24,478 average financial aid amount received per undergraduate (2004–05 estimated)

Academics
COA awards bachelor's and master's **degrees**. **Challenging opportunities** include advanced placement credit, accelerated degree programs, student-designed majors, independent study, and a senior project. Special programs include cooperative education, internships, off-campus study, and study-abroad.

The most frequently chosen **baccalaureate** field is liberal arts/general studies. A complete listing of majors at COA appears in the Majors by College index beginning on page 471.

The **faculty** at COA has 26 full-time members, 85% with terminal degrees. The student-faculty ratio is 11:1.

Students of COA
The student body totals 349, of whom 341 are undergraduates. 63.9% are women and 36.1% are men. Students come from 36 states and territories and 36 other countries. 20% are from Maine. 13.5% are international students. 0.3% are African American, 0.6% Asian American, and 1.2% Hispanic American. 85% returned for their sophomore year.

Facilities and Resources
38 **computers/terminals** and 50 ports are available on campus for general student use. Students can access the following: computer help desk, free student e-mail accounts, on-line (class) schedules. Campuswide network is available. 100% of college-owned or -operated housing units are wired for high-speed Internet access. Wireless service is available via entire campus. The **library** has 50,000 books and 3,000 subscriptions.

Campus Life
There are 12 active organizations on campus, including a drama/theater group, newspaper, and choral group. No national or local **fraternities** or **sororities**.

This institution has no intercollegiate sports.

Campus Safety
Student safety services include late-night transport/escort service, 24-hour emergency telephone alarm devices, and 24-hour patrols by trained security personnel.

Applying
COA requires an essay, a high school transcript, and 3 recommendations, and in some cases an interview. It recommends SAT or ACT, an interview, and a minimum high school GPA of 3.0. Application deadline: 2/15; 2/15 priority date for financial aid. Early and deferred admission are possible.

COLLEGE OF THE HOLY CROSS

SUBURBAN SETTING ■ PRIVATE ■ INDEPENDENT RELIGIOUS ■ COED
WORCESTER, MASSACHUSETTS

SPONSOR

Web site: www.holycross.edu
Contact: Ms. Ann Bowe McDermott, Director of Admissions, 105 Fenwick
 Hall, 1 College Street, Worcester, MA 01610-2395
Telephone: 508-793-2443 or toll-free 800-442-2421
Fax: 508-793-3888
E-mail: admissions@holycross.edu

Academics

Holy Cross awards bachelor's **degrees** (standardized tests are optional for admission to
the College of Holy Cross). **Challenging opportunities** include advanced placement
credit, accelerated degree programs, student-designed majors, an honors program,
double majors, independent study, and a senior project. Special programs include internships, off-campus study, study-abroad, and Army, Navy, and Air Force ROTC.

 The most frequently chosen **baccalaureate** fields are social sciences, psychology, and
history. A complete listing of majors at Holy Cross appears in the Majors by College
index beginning on page 471.

 The **faculty** at Holy Cross has 240 full-time members, 94% with terminal degrees.
The student-faculty ratio is 11:1.

Students of Holy Cross

The student body is made up of 2,846 undergraduates. 55.7% are women and 44.3% are
men. Students come from 49 states and territories and 13 other countries. 39% are from
Massachusetts. 1% are international students. 4.4% are African American, 0.5%
American Indian, 5.4% Asian American, and 5.5% Hispanic American. 94% returned for
their sophomore year.

Facilities and Resources

485 **computers/terminals** are available on campus for general student use. Students can
access the following: computer help desk, free student e-mail accounts, online (class)
registration. Campuswide network is available. 100% of college-owned or -operated
housing units are wired for high-speed Internet access. Wireless service is available via
classrooms, computer centers, computer labs, dorm rooms, libraries, student centers.
The 6 **libraries** have 606,847 books and 1,570 subscriptions.

Campus Life

There are 106 active organizations on campus, including a drama/theater group,
newspaper, radio station, choral group, and marching band. No national or local
fraternities or **sororities.**

 Holy Cross is a member of the NCAA (Division I). **Intercollegiate sports** (some
offering scholarships) include baseball (m), basketball, crew, cross-country running, field
hockey (w), football (m), golf, ice hockey, lacrosse, soccer, softball (w), swimming and
diving, tennis, track and field, volleyball (w).

Campus Safety

Student safety services include late-night transport/escort service, 24-hour emergency
telephone alarm devices, 24-hour patrols by trained security personnel, and electronically operated dormitory entrances.

Applying

Holy Cross requires an essay, a high school transcript, and 2 recommendations. It
recommends an interview. Application deadline: 1/15; 2/1 for financial aid. Early and
deferred admission are possible.

Established in 1843, the College of
the Holy Cross is renowned for its
mentoring-based liberal arts education in the Jesuit tradition. With a
total enrollment of 2,700 and a student-faculty ratio of 10:1, students
are assured of highly personalized
instruction. Professors of the
exclusively undergraduate college
conduct all their own classes and
laboratories, and students have full
access to state-of-the-art equipment
and information technology. A storied
sports tradition and diverse extracurricular activities round out the Holy
Cross experience. Integrating faith
and knowledge with an emphasis on
public service, Holy Cross prepares its
students for success in all aspects of
life.

Getting Accepted
7,066 applied
33% were accepted
717 enrolled (31% of accepted)
65% from top tenth of their h.s. class
Mean SAT critical reading score: 645
Mean SAT math score: 633
76% had SAT critical reading scores over 600
79% had SAT math scores over 600
19% had SAT critical reading scores over 700
20% had SAT math scores over 700
5 National Merit Scholars
15 valedictorians

Graduation and After
88% graduated in 4 years
4% graduated in 5 years
22% pursued further study (8% arts and sciences, 6% law, 3% education)
68% had job offers within 6 months
54 organizations recruited on campus

Financial Matters
$37,242 tuition and fees (2008–09)
$10,260 room and board
100% average percent of need met
$25,264 average financial aid amount received
 per undergraduate (2006–07 estimated)

THE COLLEGE OF WILLIAM AND MARY

SMALL-TOWN SETTING ■ PUBLIC ■ STATE-SUPPORTED ■ COED
WILLIAMSBURG, VIRGINIA

Web site: www.wm.edu
Contact: Henry Broaddus, Dean of Admissions, PO Box 8795, Williamsburg, VA 23187-8795
Telephone: 757-221-4223
Fax: 757-221-1242
E-mail: admiss@wm.edu

Getting Accepted

10,853 applied
34% were accepted
1,346 enrolled (37% of accepted)
79% from top tenth of their h.s. class
4.0 average high school GPA
Mean SAT critical reading score: 677
Mean SAT math score: 662
Mean SAT writing score: 663
Mean ACT score: 29
85% had SAT critical reading scores over 600
84% had SAT math scores over 600
83% had SAT writing scores over 600
93% had ACT scores over 24
45% had SAT critical reading scores over 700
32% had SAT math scores over 700
36% had SAT writing scores over 700
46% had ACT scores over 30

Graduation and After

83% graduated in 4 years
7% graduated in 5 years
1% graduated in 6 years
33% pursued further study (13% arts and sciences, 6% law, 6% medicine)
47% had job offers within 6 months
230 organizations recruited on campus

Financial Matters

$9164 resident tuition and fees (2007–08)
$26,725 nonresident tuition and fees (2007–08)
$7385 room and board
84% average percent of need met
$12,252 average financial aid amount received per undergraduate (2006–07 estimated)

Academics

William and Mary awards bachelor's, master's, doctoral, and first-professional **degrees** and post-master's certificates. **Challenging opportunities** include advanced placement credit, accelerated degree programs, student-designed majors, an honors program, double majors, independent study, and a senior project. Special programs include summer session for credit, study-abroad, and Army ROTC.

The most frequently chosen **baccalaureate** fields are social sciences, business/marketing, and interdisciplinary studies. A complete listing of majors at William and Mary appears in the Majors by College index beginning on page 471.

The **faculty** at William and Mary has 619 full-time members, 89% with terminal degrees. The student-faculty ratio is 11:1.

Students of William and Mary

The student body totals 7,795, of whom 5,792 are undergraduates. 53.8% are women and 46.2% are men. Students come from 47 states and territories and 54 other countries. 69% are from Virginia. 2.4% are international students. 6.7% are African American, 0.7% American Indian, 7.4% Asian American, and 5.6% Hispanic American. 95% returned for their sophomore year.

Facilities and Resources

400 **computers/terminals** and 6,000 ports are available on campus for general student use. Students can access the following: campus intranet, computer help desk, free student e-mail accounts, online (class) grades, online (class) registration, online (class) schedules. Campuswide network is available. 100% of college-owned or -operated housing units are wired for high-speed Internet access. Wireless service is available via entire campus. The 10 **libraries** have 2,107,953 books and 36,877 subscriptions.

Campus Life

There are 300 active organizations on campus, including a drama/theater group, newspaper, radio station, television station, and choral group. 22% of eligible men and 27% of eligible women are members of national **fraternities** and national **sororities**.

William and Mary is a member of the NCAA (Division I). **Intercollegiate sports** (some offering scholarships) include baseball (m), basketball, cross-country running, field hockey (w), football (m), golf, gymnastics, lacrosse (w), soccer, swimming and diving, tennis, track and field, volleyball (w).

Campus Safety

Student safety services include late-night transport/escort service, 24-hour emergency telephone alarm devices, 24-hour patrols by trained security personnel, student patrols, and electronically operated dormitory entrances.

Applying

William and Mary requires an essay, SAT or ACT, and a high school transcript. It recommends SAT Subject Tests and 1 recommendation. Application deadline: 1/1; 2/15 priority date for financial aid. Early and deferred admission are possible.

THE COLLEGE OF WOOSTER

SMALL-TOWN SETTING ■ PRIVATE ■ INDEPENDENT RELIGIOUS ■ COED
WOOSTER, OHIO

Web site: www.wooster.edu
Contact: Mary Karen Vellines, Vice President for Enrollment, 847 College
   Avenue, Wooster, OH 44691
Telephone: 330-263-2270 Ext. 2118 or toll-free 800-877-9905
Fax: 330-263-2621
E-mail: admissions@wooster.edu

SPONSOR

Academics

Wooster awards bachelor's **degrees**. **Challenging opportunities** include advanced
placement credit, student-designed majors, double majors, independent study, and a
senior project. Special programs include cooperative education, internships, summer
session for credit, off-campus study, and study-abroad.

The most frequently chosen **baccalaureate** fields are social sciences, history, and
English. A complete listing of majors at Wooster appears in the Majors by College index
beginning on page 471.

The **faculty** at Wooster has 137 full-time members, 97% with terminal degrees. The
student-faculty ratio is 11:1.

Students of Wooster

The student body is made up of 1,819 undergraduates. 51% are women and 49% are
men. Students come from 46 states and territories and 37 other countries. 46% are from
Ohio. 4.7% are international students. 3.9% are African American, 0.3% American
Indian, 2.1% Asian American, and 1.8% Hispanic American. 87% returned for their
sophomore year.

Facilities and Resources

500 **computers/terminals** are available on campus for general student use. Campuswide
network is available. The 4 **libraries** have 581,518 books.

Campus Life

There are 102 active organizations on campus, including a drama/theater group,
newspaper, radio station, choral group, and marching band. 9% of eligible men and 10%
of eligible women are members of local **fraternities**, local **sororities**, and coed
fraternity.

Wooster is a member of the NCAA (Division III). **Intercollegiate sports** include
baseball (m), basketball, cross-country running, field hockey (w), football (m), golf (m),
lacrosse, soccer, softball (w), swimming and diving, tennis, track and field, volleyball (w).

Campus Safety

Student safety services include late-night transport/escort service, 24-hour emergency
telephone alarm devices, 24-hour patrols by trained security personnel, student patrols,
and electronically operated dormitory entrances.

Applying

Wooster requires an essay, SAT or ACT, a high school transcript, and 2 recommendations. It recommends an interview. Application deadline: 2/15; 9/1 for financial aid, with
a 2/15 priority date. Early and deferred admission are possible.

The College of Wooster acts on this conviction: everyone, not only "honors" students, can benefit from an honors education. At Wooster, that philosophy enhances the entire college experience. Small classes and an accessible faculty, which is committed to teaching, ensure individual attention for every student—from First-Year Seminar to senior year, when students work one-on-one with a faculty adviser on an Independent Study Project that pulls together everything they have learned in their first three years at Wooster.

Getting Accepted
2,504 applied
80% were accepted
493 enrolled (25% of accepted)
27% from top tenth of their h.s. class
3.5 average high school GPA
Mean SAT critical reading score: 609
Mean SAT math score: 608
Mean ACT score: 26
52% had SAT critical reading scores over 600
56% had SAT math scores over 600
56% had SAT writing scores over 600
69% had ACT scores over 24
16% had SAT critical reading scores over 700
8% had SAT math scores over 700
8% had SAT writing scores over 700
17% had ACT scores over 30

Graduation and After
68% graduated in 4 years
6% graduated in 5 years
1% graduated in 6 years
42% pursued further study
90% had job offers within 6 months
32 organizations recruited on campus

Financial Matters
$42,420 comprehensive fee (2008–09)
94% average percent of need met
$24,981 average financial aid amount received
   per undergraduate (2006–07 estimated)

COLORADO CHRISTIAN UNIVERSITY

SUBURBAN SETTING ■ PRIVATE ■ INDEPENDENT RELIGIOUS ■ COED
LAKEWOOD, COLORADO

Web site: www.ccu.edu
Contact: Mr. Jeff Cazer, Associate, 180 South Garrison Street, Lakewood, CO
  80226
Telephone: 303-963-3200 or toll-free 800-44-FAITH
Fax: 303-963-3201
E-mail: admission@ccu.edu

Getting Accepted

772 applied
65% were accepted
225 enrolled (45% of accepted)
25% from top tenth of their h.s. class
3.45 average high school GPA
Mean SAT critical reading score: 555
Mean SAT math score: 528
Mean ACT score: 23
27% had SAT critical reading scores over 600
24% had SAT math scores over 600
46% had ACT scores over 24
6% had SAT critical reading scores over 700
3% had SAT math scores over 700
9% had ACT scores over 30

Graduation and After

34% graduated in 4 years
9% graduated in 5 years
1% graduated in 6 years

Financial Matters

$18,350 tuition and fees (2007–08)
$7625 room and board
54% average percent of need met
$8931 average financial aid amount received
  per undergraduate (2004–05 estimated)

Academics

CCU awards associate, bachelor's, and master's **degrees. Challenging opportunities**
include advanced placement credit, accelerated degree programs, student-designed
majors, an honors program, double majors, independent study, and a senior project.
Special programs include cooperative education, internships, summer session for credit,
off-campus study, study-abroad, and Army ROTC.

The most frequently chosen **baccalaureate** fields are business/marketing, computer
and information sciences, and education. A complete listing of majors at CCU appears in
the Majors by College index beginning on page 471.

The **faculty** at CCU has 43 full-time members, 70% with terminal degrees. The student-faculty ratio is 21:1.

Students of CCU

The student body totals 2,221, of whom 1,897 are undergraduates. 60.7% are women
and 39.3% are men. Students come from 45 states and territories and 9 other countries.
44% are from Colorado. 0.5% are international students. 3.9% are African American,
1.1% American Indian, 1.3% Asian American, and 8.6% Hispanic American. 86%
returned for their sophomore year.

Facilities and Resources

141 **computers/terminals** are available on campus for general student use. Students can
access the following: online (class) registration. Campuswide network is available. The 2
libraries have 71,565 books and 1,192 subscriptions.

Campus Life

There are 26 active organizations on campus, including a drama/theater group,
newspaper, and choral group. No national or local **fraternities** or **sororities**.

CCU is a member of the NCAA (Division II). **Intercollegiate sports** (some offering
scholarships) include basketball, cross-country running, golf (m), soccer, tennis, volleyball (w).

Campus Safety

Student safety services include 24-hour emergency telephone alarm devices, 24-hour
patrols by trained security personnel, and student patrols.

Applying

CCU requires an essay, SAT or ACT, a high school transcript, an interview, and 2
recommendations, and in some cases an interview, 3 recommendations, and a minimum
high school GPA of 2.8. Application deadline: 8/21; 3/15 priority date for financial aid.
Deferred admission is possible.

THE COLORADO COLLEGE

URBAN SETTING ■ PRIVATE ■ INDEPENDENT ■ COED
COLORADO SPRINGS, COLORADO

Web site: www.coloradocollege.edu
Contact: Mr. Matt Bonser, Associate Director of Admission, 900 Block North
   Cascade, West, Colorado Springs, CO 80903-3294
Telephone: 719-389-6344 or toll-free 800-542-7214
Fax: 719-389-6816
E-mail: admission@coloradocollege.edu

Academics

CC awards bachelor's and master's **degrees** (master's degree in education only). **Challenging opportunities** include advanced placement credit, student-designed majors, double majors, independent study, and a senior project. Special programs include internships, summer session for credit, off-campus study, study-abroad, and Army ROTC.

The most frequently chosen **baccalaureate** fields are social sciences, biological/life sciences, and visual and performing arts. A complete listing of majors at CC appears in the Majors by College index beginning on page 471.

The **faculty** at CC has 160 full-time members, 94% with terminal degrees. The student-faculty ratio is 11:1.

Students of CC

The student body totals 2,075, of whom 2,053 are undergraduates. 53.7% are women and 46.3% are men. Students come from 49 states and territories and 25 other countries. 26% are from Colorado. 3.3% are international students. 1.9% are African American, 0.8% American Indian, 5% Asian American, and 6.7% Hispanic American. 96% returned for their sophomore year.

Facilities and Resources

208 **computers/terminals** are available on campus for general student use. Students can access the following: campus intranet, computer help desk, free student e-mail accounts, online (class) grades, online (class) registration, online (class) schedules. Campuswide network is available. 100% of college-owned or -operated housing units are wired for high-speed Internet access. Wireless service is available via entire campus. The 3 **libraries** have 532,793 books and 4,649 subscriptions.

Campus Life

There are 122 active organizations on campus, including a drama/theater group, newspaper, radio station, and choral group. 7% of eligible men and 11% of eligible women are members of national **fraternities** and national **sororities**.

CC is a member of the NCAA (Division III). **Intercollegiate sports** (some offering scholarships) include basketball, cross-country running, football (m), ice hockey (m), lacrosse, soccer, softball (w), swimming and diving, tennis, track and field, volleyball (w).

Campus Safety

Student safety services include whistle program, student escort service, good campus lighting, late-night transport/escort service, 24-hour emergency telephone alarm devices, 24-hour patrols by trained security personnel, and electronically operated dormitory entrances.

Applying

CC requires an essay, SAT or ACT, a high school transcript, and recommendations. It recommends an interview. Application deadline: 1/15, 1/15 for nonresidents; 2/15 for financial aid, with a 2/15 priority date. Deferred admission is possible.

Getting Accepted

4,826 applied
32% were accepted
524 enrolled (34% of accepted)
60% from top tenth of their h.s. class
Mean SAT critical reading score: 660
Mean SAT math score: 660
Mean SAT writing score: 660
Mean ACT score: 29
83% had SAT critical reading scores over 600
85% had SAT math scores over 600
75% had SAT writing scores over 600
93% had ACT scores over 24
30% had SAT critical reading scores over 700
22% had SAT math scores over 700
25% had SAT writing scores over 700
45% had ACT scores over 30
24 valedictorians

Graduation and After

74% graduated in 4 years
8% graduated in 5 years
1% graduated in 6 years
25% pursued further study (13% arts and sciences, 3% law, 3% education)
22 organizations recruited on campus

Financial Matters

$33,972 tuition and fees (2007–08)
$8498 room and board
91% average percent of need met
$29,982 average financial aid amount received per undergraduate (2006–07 estimated)

COLORADO SCHOOL OF MINES
SMALL-TOWN SETTING ■ PUBLIC ■ STATE-SUPPORTED ■ COED
GOLDEN, COLORADO

Web site: www.mines.edu
Contact: Ms. Heather Boyd, Associate Director of Enrollment Management, Student Center, 1600 Maple Street, Golden, CO 80401
Telephone: 303-273-3227 or toll-free 800-446-9488 Ext. 3220 (out-of-state)
Fax: 303-273-3509
E-mail: admit@mines.edu

Getting Accepted
4,188 applied
85% were accepted
787 enrolled (22% of accepted)
53% from top tenth of their h.s. class
3.7 average high school GPA
Mean SAT critical reading score: 595
Mean SAT math score: 655
Mean ACT score: 28
51% had SAT critical reading scores over 600
76% had SAT math scores over 600
87% had ACT scores over 24
11% had SAT critical reading scores over 700
24% had SAT math scores over 700
23% had ACT scores over 30
85 class presidents
90 valedictorians

Graduation and After
15% pursued further study (11% engineering, 1% arts and sciences, 1% business)
95% had job offers within 6 months
140 organizations recruited on campus

Financial Matters
$10,154 resident tuition and fees (2007–08)
$23,140 nonresident tuition and fees (2007–08)
$7350 room and board
93% average percent of need met
$14,800 average financial aid amount received per undergraduate (2006–07 estimated)

Academics
CSM awards bachelor's, master's, doctoral, and first-professional **degrees**. **Challenging opportunities** include advanced placement credit, accelerated degree programs, an honors program, double majors, independent study, and a senior project. Special programs include cooperative education, internships, summer session for credit, study-abroad, and Army ROTC.

The most frequently chosen **baccalaureate** fields are engineering, physical sciences, and computer and information sciences. A complete listing of majors at CSM appears in the Majors by College index beginning on page 471.

The **faculty** at CSM has 200 full-time members, 98% with terminal degrees. The student-faculty ratio is 15:1.

Students of CSM
The student body totals 4,268, of whom 3,310 are undergraduates. 21.8% are women and 78.2% are men. Students come from 44 states and territories and 52 other countries. 80% are from Colorado. 6.2% are international students. 1.6% are African American, 0.8% American Indian, 4.8% Asian American, and 6.3% Hispanic American. 86% returned for their sophomore year.

Facilities and Resources
400 **computers/terminals** are available on campus for general student use. Students can access the following: campus intranet, computer help desk, free student e-mail accounts, online (class) grades, online (class) registration, online (class) schedules. Campuswide network is available. 100% of college-owned or -operated housing units are wired for high-speed Internet access. Wireless service is available via classrooms, computer labs, student centers. The **library** has 150,000 books and 4,883 subscriptions.

Campus Life
There are 95 active organizations on campus, including a drama/theater group, newspaper, radio station, choral group, and marching band. 19% of eligible men and 19% of eligible women are members of national **fraternities** and national **sororities**.

CSM is a member of the NCAA (Division II). **Intercollegiate sports** (some offering scholarships) include baseball (m), basketball, cross-country running, football (m), golf, skiing (downhill) (m), soccer, softball (w), swimming and diving, tennis, track and field, volleyball (w), wrestling (m).

Campus Safety
Student safety services include late-night transport/escort service, 24-hour emergency telephone alarm devices, 24-hour patrols by trained security personnel, and electronically operated dormitory entrances.

Applying
CSM requires SAT or ACT and a high school transcript, and in some cases an essay, an interview, and recommendations. It recommends rank in upper one-third of high school class. Application deadline: 6/1; 3/1 priority date for financial aid. Deferred admission is possible.

COLORADO STATE UNIVERSITY

URBAN SETTING ■ PUBLIC ■ STATE-SUPPORTED ■ COED
FORT COLLINS, COLORADO

SPONSOR

Web site: www.colostate.edu
Contact: Ms. Mary Ontiveros, Associate Vice President for Enrollment and Access and Executive Director of Admissions, Spruce Hall, Fort Collins, CO 80523-0015
Telephone: 970-491-6909
Fax: 970-491-7799
E-mail: admissions@colostate.edu

Academics

Colorado State awards bachelor's, master's, doctoral, and first-professional **degrees**. **Challenging opportunities** include advanced placement credit, accelerated degree programs, an honors program, double majors, independent study, and a senior project. Special programs include cooperative education, internships, summer session for credit, off-campus study, study-abroad, and Army and Air Force ROTC.

The most frequently chosen **baccalaureate** fields are business/marketing, family and consumer sciences, and social sciences. A complete listing of majors at Colorado State appears in the Majors by College index beginning on page 471.

The **faculty** at Colorado State has 889 full-time members, 99% with terminal degrees. The student-faculty ratio is 17:1.

Students of Colorado State

The student body totals 27,569, of whom 21,679 are undergraduates. 51.8% are women and 48.2% are men. Students come from 53 states and territories and 44 other countries. 83% are from Colorado. 1.7% are international students. 2.2% are African American, 1.6% American Indian, 3.1% Asian American, and 6.5% Hispanic American. 81% returned for their sophomore year.

Facilities and Resources

2,700 **computers/terminals** and 3,200 ports are available on campus for general student use. Students can access the following: campus intranet, computer help desk, free student e-mail accounts, online (class) grades, online (class) registration, online (class) schedules, online course management, personalized portal services including transcripts and financials (billing, financial aid). Campuswide network is available. 100% of college-owned or -operated housing units are wired for high-speed Internet access. Wireless service is available via classrooms, computer centers, computer labs, libraries, student centers. The 4 **libraries** have 2,137,478 books and 31,372 subscriptions.

Campus Life

There are 255 active organizations on campus, including a drama/theater group, newspaper, radio station, television station, choral group, and marching band. 2% of eligible men and 4% of eligible women are members of national **fraternities**, national **sororities**, local fraternities, and local sororities.

Colorado State is a member of the NCAA (Division I). **Intercollegiate sports** (some offering scholarships) include basketball, cross-country running, football (m), golf, softball (w), swimming and diving (w), tennis (w), track and field, volleyball (w), water polo (w).

Campus Safety

Student safety services include late-night transport/escort service, 24-hour emergency telephone alarm devices, 24-hour patrols by trained security personnel, student patrols, and electronically operated dormitory entrances.

Applying

Colorado State requires an essay, SAT or ACT, a high school transcript, and recommendations. Application deadline: 7/1; 3/1 priority date for financial aid. Deferred admission is possible.

Colorado State University's scenic location at the base of the Rocky Mountain foothills offers the perfect setting for intellectual and personal growth. Committed to providing a distinctive, high-quality education, Colorado State offers more than 150 undergraduate programs of study. The University emphasizes learning beyond classroom walls, with opportunities for field experience, laboratory research, professional internships, study abroad, and community outreach. Students describe Colorado State as a friendly, comfortable place, where they can feel free to be themselves and are encouraged to develop their own unique talents. Colorado State is ranked in the top tier by *U.S. News & World Report* (2008).

Getting Accepted
11,727 applied
86% were accepted
4,392 enrolled (44% of accepted)
19% from top tenth of their h.s. class
3.5 average high school GPA
Mean SAT critical reading score: 540
Mean SAT math score: 566
Mean ACT score: 24
32% had SAT critical reading scores over 600
36% had SAT math scores over 600
25% had SAT writing scores over 600
55% had ACT scores over 24
6% had SAT critical reading scores over 700
5% had SAT math scores over 700
3% had SAT writing scores over 700
7% had ACT scores over 30
17 National Merit Scholars

Graduation and After
36% graduated in 4 years
24% graduated in 5 years
4% graduated in 6 years
590 organizations recruited on campus

Financial Matters
$5419 resident tuition and fees (2007–08)
$18,859 nonresident tuition and fees (2007–08)
$7382 room and board
82% average percent of need met
$8455 average financial aid amount received per undergraduate (2005–06)

COLUMBIA COLLEGE

URBAN SETTING ■ PRIVATE ■ INDEPENDENT ■ COED
NEW YORK, NEW YORK

Web site: www.college.columbia.edu
Contact: Ms. Jessica Marinaccio, Director of Undergraduate Admissions, 212
    Hamilton Hall MC 2807, 1130 Amsterdam Avenue, New York, NY 10027
Telephone: 212-854-2522
Fax: 212-854-1209
E-mail: ugrad-admiss@columbia.edu

Getting Accepted
17,151 applied
10% were accepted
1,022 enrolled (61% of accepted)
86% from top tenth of their h.s. class
3.8 average high school GPA
Mean SAT critical reading score: 707
Mean SAT math score: 704
92% had SAT critical reading scores over 600
94% had SAT math scores over 600
62% had SAT critical reading scores over 700
58% had SAT math scores over 700
303 National Merit Scholars

Graduation and After
86% graduated in 4 years
6% graduated in 5 years
2% graduated in 6 years
80% pursued further study
300 organizations recruited on campus

Financial Matters
$37,216 tuition and fees (2007–08)
$9937 room and board
100% average percent of need met
$27,749 average financial aid amount received
    per undergraduate (2004–05 estimated)

Academics

Columbia awards bachelor's **degrees**. **Challenging opportunities** include advanced
placement credit, student-designed majors, an honors program, double majors,
independent study, and a senior project. Special programs include internships, summer
session for credit, off-campus study, study-abroad, and Army, Navy, and Air Force
ROTC.

The most frequently chosen **baccalaureate** fields are social sciences, English, and
history. A complete listing of majors at Columbia appears in the Majors by College index
beginning on page 471.

The **faculty** at Columbia has 790 full-time members. The student-faculty ratio is 5:1.

Students of Columbia

The student body is made up of 4,184 undergraduates. 51.6% are women and 48.4% are
men. Students come from 54 states and territories and 72 other countries. 26% are from
New York. 6% are international students. 9.7% are African American, 0.7% American
Indian, 13.3% Asian American, and 10.3% Hispanic American. 97% returned for their
sophomore year.

Facilities and Resources

400 **computers/terminals** are available on campus for general student use. Students can
access the following: online (class) registration. Campuswide network is available. The 21
libraries have 7,200,000 books and 66,000 subscriptions.

Campus Life

There are 300 active organizations on campus, including a drama/theater group,
newspaper, radio station, television station, choral group, and marching band. 19% of
eligible men and 25% of eligible women are members of national **fraternities**, national
sororities, and coed fraternities.

Columbia is a member of the NCAA (Division I). **Intercollegiate sports** include
archery (w), baseball (m), basketball, crew, cross-country running, fencing, field hockey
(w), football (m), golf (m), lacrosse (w), softball (w), swimming and diving, track and field,
wrestling (m).

Campus Safety

Student safety services include 24-hour ID check at door, late-night transport/escort
service, 24-hour emergency telephone alarm devices, 24-hour patrols by trained security
personnel, and student patrols.

Applying

Columbia requires an essay, SAT and SAT Subject Tests or ACT, a high school
transcript, and 3 recommendations. Application deadline: 1/2; 2/10 for financial aid.
Early and deferred admission are possible.

COLUMBIA UNIVERSITY, THE FU FOUNDATION SCHOOL OF ENGINEERING AND APPLIED SCIENCE

URBAN SETTING ■ PRIVATE ■ INDEPENDENT ■ COED
NEW YORK, NEW YORK

Web site: www.engineering.columbia.edu
Contact: Ms. Jessica Marinaccio, Director of Undergraduate Admissions, 212 Hamilton Hall MC 2807, 1130 Amsterdam Avenue, New York, NY 10027
Telephone: 212-854-2522
Fax: 212-854-1209
E-mail: ugrad-admiss@columbia.edu

Academics

Columbia SEAS awards bachelor's, master's, and doctoral **degrees**. **Challenging opportunities** include advanced placement credit, an honors program, double majors, and independent study. Special programs include internships, summer session for credit, study-abroad, and Army, Navy, and Air Force ROTC.

The most frequently chosen **baccalaureate** fields are engineering, social sciences, and computer and information sciences. A complete listing of majors at Columbia SEAS appears in the Majors by College index beginning on page 471.

The **faculty** at Columbia SEAS has 137 full-time members. The student-faculty ratio is 10:1.

Students of Columbia SEAS

The student body is made up of 1,409 undergraduates. 29% are women and 71% are men. Students come from 44 states and territories and 59 other countries. 31% are from New York. 13.2% are international students. 2.9% are African American, 32.4% Asian American, and 7% Hispanic American. 98% returned for their sophomore year.

Facilities and Resources

400 **computers/terminals** are available on campus for general student use. Students can access the following: online (class) registration. Campuswide network is available. The 21 **libraries** have 7,200,000 books and 66,000 subscriptions.

Campus Life

There are 300 active organizations on campus, including a drama/theater group, newspaper, radio station, television station, choral group, and marching band. 19% of eligible men and 25% of eligible women are members of national **fraternities** and national **sororities**.

Columbia SEAS is a member of the NCAA (Division I). **Intercollegiate sports** include archery (w), baseball (m), basketball, crew, cross-country running, fencing, field hockey (w), football (m), golf (m), lacrosse (w), softball (w), swimming and diving, track and field, wrestling (m).

Campus Safety

Student safety services include 24-hour ID check at door, late-night transport/escort service, 24-hour emergency telephone alarm devices, and 24-hour patrols by trained security personnel.

Applying

Columbia SEAS requires an essay, SAT and SAT Subject Tests or ACT, a high school transcript, and 3 recommendations. It recommends an interview. Application deadline: 1/2; 2/10 for financial aid. Early and deferred admission are possible.

Getting Accepted

2,702 applied
24% were accepted
315 enrolled (49% of accepted)
91% from top tenth of their h.s. class
3.8 average high school GPA
Mean SAT critical reading score: 692
Mean SAT math score: 758
92% had SAT critical reading scores over 600
100% had SAT math scores over 600
51% had SAT critical reading scores over 700
90% had SAT math scores over 700
136 National Merit Scholars

Graduation and After

78% graduated in 4 years
7% graduated in 5 years
2% graduated in 6 years
300 organizations recruited on campus

Financial Matters

$37,216 tuition and fees (2007–08)
$9937 room and board
100% average percent of need met
$26,036 average financial aid amount received per undergraduate (2004–05 estimated)

CONCORDIA COLLEGE

SUBURBAN SETTING ■ PRIVATE ■ INDEPENDENT RELIGIOUS ■ COED
MOORHEAD, MINNESOTA

Getting Accepted
2,517 applied
85% were accepted
830 enrolled (39% of accepted)
32% from top tenth of their h.s. class
3.72 average high school GPA
Mean SAT critical reading score: 612
Mean SAT math score: 614
Mean ACT score: 24
49% had SAT critical reading scores over 600
50% had SAT math scores over 600
47% had SAT writing scores over 600
64% had ACT scores over 24
14% had SAT critical reading scores over 700
14% had SAT math scores over 700
10% had SAT writing scores over 700
12% had ACT scores over 30
7 National Merit Scholars

Graduation and After
63% graduated in 4 years
6% graduated in 5 years
23% pursued further study (12% arts and
    sciences, 3% law, 2% medicine)
75% had job offers within 6 months
75 organizations recruited on campus

Financial Matters
$24,120 tuition and fees (2008–09)
$6160 room and board
86% average percent of need met
$15,899 average financial aid amount received
    per undergraduate (2006–07 estimated)

Web site: www.concordiacollege.edu
Contact: Mr. Scott E. Ellingson, Director of Admissions, 901 8th Street
    South, Moorhead, MN 56562
Telephone: 218-299-3004 or toll-free 800-699-9897
Fax: 218-299-3947
E-mail: admissions@cord.edu

Academics
Concordia awards bachelor's and master's **degrees**. **Challenging opportunities** include advanced placement credit, an honors program, double majors, independent study, and a senior project. Special programs include cooperative education, internships, summer session for credit, off-campus study, study-abroad, and Army and Air Force ROTC.

The most frequently chosen **baccalaureate** fields are education, business/marketing, and social sciences. A complete listing of majors at Concordia appears in the Majors by College index beginning on page 471.

The **faculty** at Concordia has 189 full-time members, 75% with terminal degrees. The student-faculty ratio is 15:1.

Students of Concordia
The student body totals 2,815, of whom 2,805 are undergraduates. 61.2% are women and 38.8% are men. 3.5% are international students. 0.6% are African American, 0.3% American Indian, 1.5% Asian American, and 1% Hispanic American. 80% returned for their sophomore year.

Facilities and Resources
570 **computers/terminals** and 87 ports are available on campus for general student use. Students can access the following: computer help desk, free student e-mail accounts, on-line (class) grades, online (class) schedules, online degree audit. Campuswide network is available. 100% of college-owned or -operated housing units are wired for high-speed Internet access. Wireless service is available via computer centers. The **library** has 325,408 books and 3,528 subscriptions.

Campus Life
There are 80 active organizations on campus, including a drama/theater group, newspaper, radio station, television station, and choral group. Concordia has local **sororities** and local coed fraternity.

Concordia is a member of the NCAA (Division III). **Intercollegiate sports** include baseball (m), basketball, cross-country running, football (m), golf, ice hockey, soccer, softball (w), swimming and diving (w), tennis, track and field, volleyball (w), wrestling (m).

Campus Safety
Student safety services include well-lit campus, 24-hour locked wing doors, late-night transport/escort service, 24-hour emergency telephone alarm devices, 24-hour patrols by trained security personnel, and student patrols.

Applying
Concordia requires SAT or ACT, a high school transcript, 2 recommendations, and references. Application deadline: rolling admissions. Early and deferred admission are possible.

CONNECTICUT COLLEGE

SUBURBAN SETTING ■ PRIVATE ■ INDEPENDENT ■ COED
NEW LONDON, CONNECTICUT

Web site: www.conncoll.edu
Contact: Ms. Martha Merrill, Dean of Admissions and Financial Aid, 270 Mohegan Avenue, New London, CT 06320-4196
Telephone: 860-439-2200
Fax: 860-439-4301
E-mail: admission@conncoll.edu

Academics

Connecticut awards bachelor's and master's **degrees. Challenging opportunities** include advanced placement credit, student-designed majors, an honors program, double majors, independent study, and a senior project. Special programs include internships, summer session for credit, off-campus study, and study-abroad.

The most frequently chosen **baccalaureate** fields are social sciences, visual and performing arts, and biological/life sciences. A complete listing of majors at Connecticut appears in the Majors by College index beginning on page 471.

The **faculty** at Connecticut has 171 full-time members, 91% with terminal degrees. The student-faculty ratio is 9:1.

Students of Connecticut

The student body totals 1,869, of whom 1,857 are undergraduates. 59.5% are women and 40.5% are men. Students come from 46 states and territories and 74 other countries. 15% are from Connecticut. 4.6% are international students. 4.1% are African American, 0.1% American Indian, 3.8% Asian American, and 5.3% Hispanic American. 90% returned for their sophomore year.

Facilities and Resources

Students can access the following: campus intranet, computer help desk, free student e-mail accounts, online (class) grades, online (class) registration, online (class) schedules. Campuswide network is available. 100% of college-owned or -operated housing units are wired for high-speed Internet access. Wireless service is available via entire campus. The 2 **libraries** have 496,817 books and 2,279 subscriptions.

Campus Life

There are 60 active organizations on campus, including a drama/theater group, newspaper, radio station, and choral group. No national or local **fraternities** or **sororities.**

Connecticut is a member of the NCAA (Division III). **Intercollegiate sports** include basketball, crew, cross-country running, field hockey (w), ice hockey, lacrosse, sailing, soccer, squash, swimming and diving, tennis, track and field, volleyball, water polo.

Campus Safety

Student safety services include late-night transport/escort service, 24-hour emergency telephone alarm devices, 24-hour patrols by trained security personnel, and electronically operated dormitory entrances.

Applying

Connecticut requires an essay, ACT or any 2 SAT Subject Tests required, a high school transcript, recommendations, and a minimum high school GPA of 2.0. It recommends an interview. Application deadline: 1/1; 2/1 for financial aid. Deferred admission is possible.

Getting Accepted

4,742 applied
35% were accepted
492 enrolled (30% of accepted)
60% from top tenth of their h.s. class
Mean SAT critical reading score: 663
Mean SAT math score: 650
Mean SAT writing score: 672
86% had SAT critical reading scores over 600
83% had SAT math scores over 600
86% had SAT writing scores over 600
84% had ACT scores over 24
37% had SAT critical reading scores over 700
23% had SAT math scores over 700
41% had SAT writing scores over 700
22% had ACT scores over 30

Graduation and After

78% graduated in 4 years
3% graduated in 5 years

Financial Matters

$46,675 comprehensive fee (2007–08)
100% average percent of need met
$28,154 average financial aid amount received per undergraduate (2006–07 estimated)

CONVERSE COLLEGE

URBAN SETTING ■ PRIVATE ■ INDEPENDENT
■ UNDERGRADUATE: WOMEN ONLY; GRADUATE: COED
SPARTANBURG, SOUTH CAROLINA

Web site: www.converse.edu
Contact: Mr. Aaron Meis, Dean of Admission, 580 East Main Street,
Spartanburg, SC 29302
Telephone: 864-596-9040 Ext. 9746 or toll-free 800-766-1125
Fax: 864-596-9225
E-mail: admissions@converse.edu

Getting Accepted

1,361 applied
47% were accepted
162 enrolled (25% of accepted)
30% from top tenth of their h.s. class
3.85 average high school GPA
Mean SAT critical reading score: 560
Mean SAT math score: 540
Mean ACT score: 23
26% had SAT critical reading scores over 600
22% had SAT math scores over 600
19% had SAT writing scores over 600
40% had ACT scores over 24
6% had SAT critical reading scores over 700
1% had SAT math scores over 700
2% had ACT scores over 30

Graduation and After

55% graduated in 4 years
2% graduated in 5 years
80% had job offers within 6 months
100 organizations recruited on campus

Financial Matters

$23,334 tuition and fees (2007–08)
$7190 room and board
87% average percent of need met
$19,427 average financial aid amount received
  per undergraduate (2006–07 estimated)

Academics

Converse awards bachelor's and master's **degrees** and post-master's certificates. **Challenging opportunities** include advanced placement credit, student-designed majors, an honors program, double majors, independent study, and a senior project. Special programs include cooperative education, internships, summer session for credit, off-campus study, study-abroad, and Army ROTC.

The most frequently chosen **baccalaureate** fields are education, visual and performing arts, and social sciences. A complete listing of majors at Converse appears in the Majors by College index beginning on page 471.

The **faculty** at Converse has 84 full-time members, 89% with terminal degrees. The student-faculty ratio is 11:1.

Students of Converse

The student body totals 1,977, of whom 752 are undergraduates. 100% are women. Students come from 30 states and territories and 8 other countries. 77% are from South Carolina. 3.6% are international students. 11.6% are African American, 0.3% American Indian, 0.8% Asian American, and 1.7% Hispanic American. 73% returned for their sophomore year.

Facilities and Resources

72 **computers/terminals** are available on campus for general student use. Students can access the following: online (class) registration. Campuswide network is available. The **library** has 150,817 books and 19,808 subscriptions.

Campus Life

There are 30 active organizations on campus, including a drama/theater group, newspaper, and choral group. No national or local **sororities**.

Converse is a member of the NCAA (Division II). **Intercollegiate sports** (some offering scholarships) include basketball, cheerleading, cross-country running, soccer, tennis, volleyball.

Campus Safety

Student safety services include late-night transport/escort service, 24-hour emergency telephone alarm devices, 24-hour patrols by trained security personnel, and electronically operated dormitory entrances.

Applying

Converse requires SAT or ACT, a high school transcript, and 1 recommendation. It recommends an essay, an interview, and a minimum high school GPA of 3.0. Application deadline: 3/1 priority date for financial aid. Early and deferred admission are possible.

Cooper Union for the Advancement of Science and Art

URBAN SETTING ■ PRIVATE ■ INDEPENDENT ■ COED
NEW YORK, NEW YORK

Web site: www.cooper.edu
Contact: Mr. Mitchell L. Lipton, Dean of Admissions and Records and Registrar, 30 Cooper Square, New York, NY 10003
Telephone: 212-353-4120
Fax: 212-353-4342
E-mail: admissions@cooper.edu

Academics

Cooper Union awards bachelor's and master's **degrees** (also offers master's program primarily made up of currently-enrolled students). **Challenging opportunities** include advanced placement credit, student-designed majors, an honors program, independent study, and a senior project. Special programs include internships, summer session for credit, off-campus study, and study-abroad.

The most frequently chosen **baccalaureate** fields are education, visual and performing arts, and architecture. A complete listing of majors at Cooper Union appears in the Majors by College index beginning on page 471.

The **faculty** at Cooper Union has 50 full-time members, 90% with terminal degrees. The student-faculty ratio is 8:1.

Students of Cooper Union

The student body totals 957, of whom 906 are undergraduates. 37.4% are women and 62.6% are men. Students come from 44 states and territories and 25 other countries. 60% are from New York. 15.6% are international students. 5.2% are African American, 0.4% American Indian, 17.4% Asian American, and 8.4% Hispanic American. 95% returned for their sophomore year.

Facilities and Resources

400 **computers/terminals** are available on campus for general student use. Campuswide network is available. 100% of college-owned or -operated housing units are wired for high-speed Internet access. The **library** has 103,289 books and 4,254 subscriptions.

Campus Life

There are 85 active organizations on campus, including a drama/theater group, newspaper, and choral group. 15% of eligible men and 10% of eligible women are members of national **fraternities** and national **sororities**.

Intercollegiate sports include badminton, basketball (m), cross-country running, football (m), soccer (m), table tennis, tennis, volleyball.

Campus Safety

Student safety services include security guards, 24-hour emergency telephone alarm devices, 24-hour patrols by trained security personnel, and electronically operated dormitory entrances.

Applying

Cooper Union requires an essay, SAT or ACT, a high school transcript, 2 recommendations, and a minimum high school GPA of 2.0, and in some cases SAT and SAT Subject Tests or ACT, an interview, 3 recommendations, portfolio, home examination, and a minimum high school GPA of 3.5. It recommends a minimum high school GPA of 3.0. Application deadline: 1/1; 6/1 for financial aid, with a 4/15 priority date. Early and deferred admission are possible.

Getting Accepted

2,551 applied
11% were accepted
219 enrolled (80% of accepted)
93% from top tenth of their h.s. class
3.6 average high school GPA
Mean SAT critical reading score: 656
Mean SAT math score: 695
84% had SAT critical reading scores over 600
86% had SAT math scores over 600
29% had SAT critical reading scores over 700
56% had SAT math scores over 700

Graduation and After

72% graduated in 4 years
14% graduated in 5 years
3% graduated in 6 years
48% pursued further study (30% engineering, 5% business, 5% law)
98% had job offers within 6 months
100 organizations recruited on campus

Financial Matters

$1450 tuition and fees (2008–09)
$13,700 room and board
93% average percent of need met
$27,500 average financial aid amount received per undergraduate (2005–06)

CORNELL COLLEGE

SMALL-TOWN SETTING ■ PRIVATE ■ INDEPENDENT RELIGIOUS ■ COED
MOUNT VERNON, IOWA

Web site: www.cornellcollege.edu
Contact: Todd White, Director of Admissions, 600 First Street West, Mount Vernon, IA 52314-1098
Telephone: 319-895-4167 or toll-free 800-747-1112
Fax: 319-895-4451
E-mail: twhite@cornellcollege.edu

Few colleges are as truly distinctive as Cornell, recognized as one of the nation's finest colleges. Cornell offers students "one extraordinary opportunity after another—in the classroom, on campus, and in the world." During each of nine blocks, students immerse themselves in a single subject through the One-Course-At-A-Time (OCAAT) academic, or block, calendar. The flexibility of OCAAT creates numerous off-campus study opportunities. A standardized schedule enables Cornell students to pursue extracurricular interests with the same passion as they do their course work. This attractively diverse college community typically receives applicants from all fifty states and more than forty countries. The College's beautiful hilltop campus is listed in its entirety on the National Register of Historic Places.

Getting Accepted
2,659 applied
45% were accepted
316 enrolled (26% of accepted)
25% from top tenth of their h.s. class
3.44 average high school GPA
Mean SAT critical reading score: 605
Mean SAT math score: 592
Mean ACT score: 26
51% had SAT critical reading scores over 600
46% had SAT math scores over 600
77% had ACT scores over 24
18% had SAT critical reading scores over 700
10% had SAT math scores over 700
20% had ACT scores over 30
15 valedictorians

Graduation and After
61% graduated in 4 years
3% graduated in 5 years
52% had job offers within 6 months
5 organizations recruited on campus

Financial Matters
$26,280 tuition and fees (2007–08)
$6970 room and board
91% average percent of need met
$21,500 average financial aid amount received per undergraduate (2006–07 estimated)

Academics

Cornell College awards bachelor's **degrees**. **Challenging opportunities** include advanced placement credit, student-designed majors, double majors, independent study, and a senior project. Special programs include internships, off-campus study, and study-abroad.

The most frequently chosen **baccalaureate** fields are social sciences, biological/life sciences, and visual and performing arts. A complete listing of majors at Cornell College appears in the Majors by College index beginning on page 471.

The **faculty** at Cornell College has 83 full-time members, 95% with terminal degrees. The student-faculty ratio is 11:1.

Students of Cornell College

The student body is made up of 1,083 undergraduates. 50.8% are women and 49.2% are men. Students come from 46 states and territories and 20 other countries. 29% are from Iowa. 3.1% are international students. 3% are African American, 0.6% American Indian, 1.6% Asian American, and 2.8% Hispanic American. 85% returned for their sophomore year.

Facilities and Resources

176 **computers/terminals** are available on campus for general student use. Students can access the following: campus intranet, computer help desk, free student e-mail accounts, online (class) grades, online (class) schedules. Campuswide network is available. 100% of college-owned or -operated housing units are wired for high-speed Internet access. Wireless service is available via classrooms, computer centers, computer labs, learning centers, libraries, student centers. The 2 **libraries** have 194,131 books and 490 subscriptions.

Campus Life

There are 76 active organizations on campus, including a drama/theater group, newspaper, radio station, and choral group. 20% of eligible men and 21% of eligible women are members of local **fraternities** and local **sororities**.

Cornell College is a member of the NCAA (Division III). **Intercollegiate sports** include baseball (m), basketball, cross-country running, football (m), golf, soccer, softball (w), tennis, track and field, volleyball (w), wrestling (m).

Campus Safety

Student safety services include 24-hour emergency telephone alarm devices and 24-hour patrols by trained security personnel.

Applying

Cornell College requires an essay, SAT or ACT, a high school transcript, and 1 recommendation. It recommends SAT Subject Tests, an interview, and a minimum high school GPA of 2.80. Application deadline: 3/1; 3/1 for financial aid. Early and deferred admission are possible.

CORNELL UNIVERSITY

SMALL-TOWN SETTING ■ PRIVATE ■ INDEPENDENT ■ COED
ITHACA, NEW YORK

Web site: www.cornell.edu
Contact: Mr. Jason Locke, Director of Undergraduate Admissions, 410
    Thurston Avenue, Ithaca, NY 14850
Telephone: 607-255-1446
Fax: 607-255-0659
E-mail: admissions@cornell.edu

Academics

Cornell awards bachelor's, master's, doctoral, and first-professional **degrees**. **Challenging opportunities** include advanced placement credit, accelerated degree programs, student-designed majors, an honors program, double majors, independent study, and a senior project. Special programs include cooperative education, internships, summer session for credit, off-campus study, study-abroad, and Army and Air Force ROTC.

The most frequently chosen **baccalaureate** fields are engineering, agriculture, and business/marketing. A complete listing of majors at Cornell appears in the Majors by College index beginning on page 471.

The **faculty** at Cornell has 1,728 full-time members, 92% with terminal degrees. The student-faculty ratio is 9:1.

Students of Cornell

The student body totals 19,800, of whom 13,510 are undergraduates. 48.9% are women and 51.1% are men. Students come from 58 states and territories and 76 other countries. 38% are from New York. 7.6% are international students. 5.3% are African American, 0.5% American Indian, 16.3% Asian American, and 5.6% Hispanic American. 96% returned for their sophomore year.

Facilities and Resources

2,650 **computers/terminals** and 1,000 ports are available on campus for general student use. Students can access the following: campus intranet, computer help desk, free student e-mail accounts, online (class) grades, online (class) registration. Campuswide network is available. 100% of college-owned or -operated housing units are wired for high-speed Internet access. The 18 **libraries** have 7,200,000 books and 64,760 subscriptions.

Campus Life

There are 832 active organizations on campus, including a drama/theater group, newspaper, radio station, television station, choral group, and marching band. 28% of eligible men and 22% of eligible women are members of national **fraternities**, national **sororities**, and local fraternities.

Cornell is a member of the NCAA (Division I). **Intercollegiate sports** include baseball (m), basketball, crew, cross-country running, equestrian sports (w), fencing (w), field hockey (w), football (m), golf (m), gymnastics (w), ice hockey, lacrosse, soccer, softball (w), squash, swimming and diving, tennis, track and field, volleyball (w), wrestling (m).

Campus Safety

Student safety services include escort service, late-night transport/escort service, 24-hour emergency telephone alarm devices, 24-hour patrols by trained security personnel, and electronically operated dormitory entrances.

Applying

Cornell requires an essay, SAT or ACT, a high school transcript, and 2 recommendations, and in some cases SAT Subject Tests and an interview. Application deadline: 1/1; 2/11 for financial aid. Early and deferred admission are possible.

Cornell University, an Ivy League university and public land-grant institution located in the Finger Lakes region of New York State, is home to 13,500 undergraduates pursuing studies in more than ninety majors and interdisciplinary programs found in the University's seven small to midsized undergraduate colleges: Arts & Sciences; Agriculture & Life Sciences; Architecture, Art, & Planning; Engineering; Hotel Administration; Human Ecology; and Industrial & Labor Relations. Students come from all fifty states and more than 120 countries. Cornell's special features include a world-renowned faculty; an outstanding undergraduate research program; twenty libraries; superb research and teaching facilities; a large, diverse study-abroad program; more than 800 student organizations; thirty-six varsity sports; and a graduation rate of 92 percent.

Getting Accepted
30,383 applied
21% were accepted
3,010 enrolled (46% of accepted)
87% from top tenth of their h.s. class
87% had SAT critical reading scores over 600
92% had SAT math scores over 600
95% had ACT scores over 24
42% had SAT critical reading scores over 700
59% had SAT math scores over 700
57% had ACT scores over 30
64 National Merit Scholars

Graduation and After
84% graduated in 4 years
6% graduated in 5 years
1% graduated in 6 years
33% pursued further study (8% law, 7% engineering, 7% medicine)
52% had job offers within 6 months
756 organizations recruited on campus

Financial Matters
$34,781 tuition and fees (2007–08)
$11,190 room and board
100% average percent of need met
$28,682 average financial aid amount received per undergraduate (2006–07 estimated)

CORNERSTONE UNIVERSITY

SUBURBAN SETTING ■ PRIVATE ■ INDEPENDENT RELIGIOUS ■ COED
GRAND RAPIDS, MICHIGAN

Getting Accepted
981 applied
62% were accepted
292 enrolled (48% of accepted)
3.4 average high school GPA
Mean ACT score: 23
47% had ACT scores over 24
6% had ACT scores over 30

Graduation and After
28% graduated in 4 years
14% graduated in 5 years
3% graduated in 6 years
15% pursued further study
66% had job offers within 6 months
160 organizations recruited on campus

Financial Matters
$18,360 tuition and fees (2007–08)
$6300 room and board
85% average percent of need met
$13,320 average financial aid amount received
   per undergraduate (2004–05)

Web site: www.cornerstone.edu
Contact: Mr. Brent Rudin, Dean of Admissions, 1001 East Beltline Avenue,
   NE, Grand Rapids, MI 49525
Telephone: 616-222-1426 or toll-free 800-787-9778
Fax: 616-222-1400
E-mail: admissions@cornerstone.edu

Academics
Cornerstone awards associate, bachelor's, master's, and first-professional **degrees. Challenging opportunities** include advanced placement credit, accelerated degree programs, an honors program, double majors, and independent study. Special programs include internships, summer session for credit, off-campus study, study-abroad, and Army ROTC.

The most frequently chosen **baccalaureate** fields are business/marketing, education, and theology and religious vocations. A complete listing of majors at Cornerstone appears in the Majors by College index beginning on page 471.

The **faculty** at Cornerstone has 66 full-time members, 47% with terminal degrees. The student-faculty ratio is 13:1.

Students of Cornerstone
The student body totals 2,466, of whom 1,841 are undergraduates. 58.8% are women and 41.2% are men. Students come from 36 states and territories and 8 other countries. 81% are from Michigan. 1% are international students. 11.6% are African American, 0.5% American Indian, 0.9% Asian American, and 3.3% Hispanic American. 70% returned for their sophomore year.

Facilities and Resources
531 **computers/terminals** are available on campus for general student use. Students can access the following: campus intranet, computer help desk, free student e-mail accounts, online (class) grades, online (class) registration, online (class) schedules. Campuswide network is available. 100% of college-owned or -operated housing units are wired for high-speed Internet access. Wireless service is available via entire campus. The **library** has 109,376 books and 1,073 subscriptions.

Campus Life
There are 13 active organizations on campus, including a drama/theater group, newspaper, and choral group. No national or local **fraternities** or **sororities**.

Cornerstone is a member of the NAIA. **Intercollegiate sports** (some offering scholarships) include basketball, cross-country running, golf (m), soccer, softball (w), track and field, volleyball (w).

Campus Safety
Student safety services include late-night transport/escort service, 24-hour emergency telephone alarm devices, 24-hour patrols by trained security personnel, student patrols, and electronically operated dormitory entrances.

Applying
Cornerstone requires an essay, SAT or ACT, a high school transcript, 1 recommendation, pastoral letter, and a minimum high school GPA of 2.5. It recommends an interview. Application deadline: rolling admissions; 3/1 for financial aid. Deferred admission is possible.

COVENANT COLLEGE

SUBURBAN SETTING ■ PRIVATE ■ INDEPENDENT RELIGIOUS ■ COED
LOOKOUT MOUNTAIN, GEORGIA

Web site: www.covenant.edu
Contact: Mrs. Jan Weaver, Assistant Director of Admissions, 14049 Scenic
  Highway, Lookout Mountain, GA 30750
Telephone: 706-419-1148 or toll-free 888-451-2683
Fax: 706-419-2255
E-mail: admissions@covenant.edu

Academics

Covenant awards associate, bachelor's, and master's **degrees** (master's degree in education only). **Challenging opportunities** include advanced placement credit, student-
designed majors, double majors, independent study, and a senior project. Special
programs include internships, summer session for credit, off-campus study, and study-
abroad.

The most frequently chosen **baccalaureate** fields are social sciences, business/
marketing, and education. A complete listing of majors at Covenant appears in the
Majors by College index beginning on page 471.

The **faculty** at Covenant has 65 full-time members, 83% with terminal degrees. The
student-faculty ratio is 14:1.

Students of Covenant

The student body totals 1,063, of whom 1,007 are undergraduates. 56% are women and
44% are men. Students come from 49 states and territories and 18 other countries. 26%
are from Georgia. 1.4% are international students. 2.6% are African American, 0.2%
American Indian, 1.7% Asian American, and 1.3% Hispanic American. 80% returned for
their sophomore year.

Facilities and Resources

137 **computers/terminals** are available on campus for general student use. Students can
access the following: free student e-mail accounts, online (class) registration, online
student information system. Campuswide network is available. 100% of college-owned
or -operated housing units are wired for high-speed Internet access. Wireless service is
available via classrooms, computer labs, dorm rooms, libraries. The **library** has 85,000
books and 12,000 subscriptions.

Campus Life

There are 48 active organizations on campus, including a drama/theater group,
newspaper, radio station, and choral group. No national or local **fraternities** or **sororities**.

Covenant is a member of the NAIA. **Intercollegiate sports** (some offering scholarships) include baseball (m), basketball, cross-country running, golf (m), soccer, softball
(w), tennis (w), volleyball (w).

Campus Safety

Student safety services include night security guards.

Applying

Covenant requires an essay, SAT or ACT, a high school transcript, an interview, 2
recommendations, and a minimum high school GPA of 2.5. Application deadline: rolling
admissions; 3/31 priority date for financial aid. Early and deferred admission are possible.

Getting Accepted
939 applied
65% were accepted
291 enrolled (48% of accepted)
27% from top tenth of their h.s. class
3.6 average high school GPA
Mean SAT critical reading score: 588
Mean SAT math score: 555
Mean SAT writing score: 567
Mean ACT score: 24
52% had SAT critical reading scores over 600
37% had SAT math scores over 600
36% had SAT writing scores over 600
57% had ACT scores over 24
15% had SAT critical reading scores over 700
5% had SAT math scores over 700
9% had SAT writing scores over 700
16% had ACT scores over 30

Graduation and After
50% graduated in 4 years
8% graduated in 5 years
100 organizations recruited on campus

Financial Matters
$22,840 tuition and fees (2007–08)
$6490 room and board

CREIGHTON UNIVERSITY

URBAN SETTING ■ PRIVATE ■ INDEPENDENT RELIGIOUS ■ COED
OMAHA, NEBRASKA

Getting Accepted
4,274 applied
81% were accepted
950 enrolled (27% of accepted)
43% from top tenth of their h.s. class
3.78 average high school GPA
Mean SAT critical reading score: 587
Mean SAT math score: 602
Mean SAT writing score: 581
Mean ACT score: 27
47% had SAT critical reading scores over 600
52% had SAT math scores over 600
46% had SAT writing scores over 600
78% had ACT scores over 24
11% had SAT critical reading scores over 700
15% had SAT math scores over 700
7% had SAT writing scores over 700
25% had ACT scores over 30
14 National Merit Scholars
105 class presidents
125 valedictorians

Graduation and After
60% graduated in 4 years
14% graduated in 5 years
1% graduated in 6 years
40% pursued further study (12% medicine, 10% arts and sciences, 9% law)
95% had job offers within 6 months
200 organizations recruited on campus

Financial Matters
$26,634 tuition and fees (2007–08)
$8180 room and board
91% average percent of need met
$21,260 average financial aid amount received per undergraduate (2006–07 estimated)

Web site: www.creighton.edu
Contact: Ms. Mary Chase, Assistant Vice President for Enrollment Management and Director of Admissions and Scholarships, 2500 California Plaza, Omaha, NE 68178-0001
Telephone: 402-280-3105 or toll-free 800-282-5835
Fax: 402-280-2685
E-mail: admissions@creighton.edu

Academics
Creighton awards bachelor's, master's, doctoral, and first-professional **degrees** and post-bachelor's certificates. **Challenging opportunities** include advanced placement credit, accelerated degree programs, freshman honors college, an honors program, double majors, independent study, and a senior project. Special programs include internships, summer session for credit, off-campus study, study-abroad, and Army and Air Force ROTC.

The most frequently chosen **baccalaureate** fields are business/marketing, health professions and related sciences, and biological/life sciences. A complete listing of majors at Creighton appears in the Majors by College index beginning on page 471.

The **faculty** at Creighton has 501 full-time members, 87% with terminal degrees. The student-faculty ratio is 12:1.

Students of Creighton
The student body totals 6,992, of whom 4,104 are undergraduates. 59.9% are women and 40.1% are men. Students come from 52 states and territories and 33 other countries. 43% are from Nebraska. 1.1% are international students. 3.4% are African American, 1.1% American Indian, 8.4% Asian American, and 3.7% Hispanic American. 86% returned for their sophomore year.

Facilities and Resources
505 **computers/terminals** are available on campus for general student use. Students can access the following: campus intranet, computer help desk, free student e-mail accounts, online (class) grades, online (class) registration, online (class) schedules, financial aid information. Campuswide network is available. 100% of college-owned or -operated housing units are wired for high-speed Internet access. Wireless service is available via entire campus. The 3 **libraries** have 466,556 books and 27,144 subscriptions.

Campus Life
There are 160 active organizations on campus, including a drama/theater group, newspaper, radio station, and choral group. 23% of eligible men and 21% of eligible women are members of national **fraternities**, national **sororities**, local fraternities, and local sororities.

Creighton is a member of the NCAA (Division I). **Intercollegiate sports** (some offering scholarships) include baseball (m), basketball, crew (w), cross-country running, golf, soccer, softball (w), tennis, volleyball (w).

Campus Safety
Student safety services include late-night transport/escort service, 24-hour emergency telephone alarm devices, 24-hour patrols by trained security personnel, student patrols, and electronically operated dormitory entrances.

Applying
Creighton requires an essay, SAT or ACT, a high school transcript, 1 recommendation, and a minimum high school GPA of 2.75. Application deadline: 2/15; 5/15 priority date for financial aid. Deferred admission is possible.

DARTMOUTH COLLEGE

SMALL-TOWN SETTING ■ PRIVATE ■ INDEPENDENT ■ COED
HANOVER, NEW HAMPSHIRE

Web site: www.dartmouth.edu
Contact: Maria Laskaris, Dean of Admissions and Financial Aid, 6016
   McNutt Hall, Hanover, NH 03755
Telephone: 603-646-2875 or toll-free 603-646-2875 (in-state)
E-mail: admissions.office@dartmouth.edu

Academics

Dartmouth awards bachelor's, master's, doctoral, and first-professional **degrees. Challenging opportunities** include advanced placement credit, student-designed majors, an honors program, double majors, independent study, and a senior project. Special programs include internships, summer session for credit, off-campus study, study-abroad, and Army ROTC.

The most frequently chosen **baccalaureate** fields are social sciences, history, and psychology. A complete listing of majors at Dartmouth appears in the Majors by College index beginning on page 471.

The **faculty** at Dartmouth has 492 full-time members, 93% with terminal degrees. The student-faculty ratio is 8:1.

Students of Dartmouth

The student body totals 5,849, of whom 4,164 are undergraduates. 50.1% are women and 49.9% are men. Students come from 54 states and territories and 47 other countries. 4% are from New Hampshire. 6.4% are international students. 7.3% are African American, 3.6% American Indian, 13.7% Asian American, and 6.4% Hispanic American. 98% returned for their sophomore year.

Facilities and Resources

200 **computers/terminals** are available on campus for general student use. Students can access the following: campus intranet, computer help desk, free student e-mail accounts, online (class) grades, online (class) registration, online (class) schedules. Campuswide network is available. 100% of college-owned or -operated housing units are wired for high-speed Internet access. Wireless service is available via entire campus.

Campus Life

There are 250 active organizations on campus, including a drama/theater group, newspaper, radio station, television station, choral group, and marching band. 59% of eligible men and 55% of eligible women are members of national **fraternities**, national **sororities**, local fraternities, and local sororities.

Dartmouth is a member of the NCAA (Division I). **Intercollegiate sports** include baseball (m), basketball, crew, cross-country running, equestrian sports, field hockey (w), football (m), golf, ice hockey, lacrosse, sailing, skiing (cross-country), skiing (downhill), soccer, softball (w), squash, swimming and diving, tennis, track and field, volleyball (w).

Campus Safety

Student safety services include late-night transport/escort service, 24-hour emergency telephone alarm devices, 24-hour patrols by trained security personnel, student patrols, and electronically operated dormitory entrances.

Applying

Dartmouth requires an essay, SAT and SAT Subject Tests or ACT, a high school transcript, 2 recommendations, and peer evaluation. It recommends an interview. Application deadline: 1/1; 2/1 for financial aid. Early and deferred admission are possible.

Getting Accepted
14,176 applied
15% were accepted
1,119 enrolled (52% of accepted)
91% from top tenth of their h.s. class
Mean SAT critical reading score: 711
Mean SAT math score: 716
Mean SAT writing score: 707
Mean ACT score: 31
91% had SAT critical reading scores over 600
93% had SAT math scores over 600
91% had SAT writing scores over 600
94% had ACT scores over 24
65% had SAT critical reading scores over 700
65% had SAT math scores over 700
64% had SAT writing scores over 700
67% had ACT scores over 30
224 National Merit Scholars
78 class presidents
142 valedictorians

Graduation and After
87% graduated in 4 years
6% graduated in 5 years
1% graduated in 6 years
20% pursued further study
215 organizations recruited on campus

Financial Matters
$35,178 tuition and fees (2007–08)
$10,305 room and board
100% average percent of need met
$31,840 average financial aid amount received
   per undergraduate (2005–06)

DAVIDSON COLLEGE

SMALL-TOWN SETTING ■ PRIVATE ■ INDEPENDENT RELIGIOUS ■ COED
DAVIDSON, NORTH CAROLINA

Web site: www.davidson.edu
Contact: Mr. Christopher J. Gruber, Vice President and Dean of Admission and Financial Aid, Box 7156, Davidson, NC 28035-7156
Telephone: 704-894-2230 or toll-free 800-768-0380
Fax: 704-894-2016
E-mail: admission@davidson.edu

Getting Accepted
3,992 applied
28% were accepted
465 enrolled (41% of accepted)
83% from top tenth of their h.s. class
4.0 average high school GPA
Mean SAT critical reading score: 678
Mean SAT math score: 677
Mean ACT score: 30
87% had SAT critical reading scores over 600
88% had SAT math scores over 600
97% had ACT scores over 24
41% had SAT critical reading scores over 700
40% had SAT math scores over 700
56% had ACT scores over 30

Graduation and After
91% graduated in 4 years
62% had job offers within 6 months
500 organizations recruited on campus

Financial Matters
$31,794 tuition and fees (2007–08)
$9020 room and board
100% average percent of need met
$19,045 average financial aid amount received per undergraduate (2005–06)

Academics

Davidson awards bachelor's **degrees**. **Challenging opportunities** include advanced placement credit, student-designed majors, an honors program, double majors, independent study, and a senior project. Special programs include off-campus study, study-abroad, and Army and Air Force ROTC.

The most frequently chosen **baccalaureate** fields are social sciences, English, and biological/life sciences. A complete listing of majors at Davidson appears in the Majors by College index beginning on page 471.

The **faculty** at Davidson has 167 full-time members, 96% with terminal degrees. The student-faculty ratio is 10:1.

Students of Davidson

The student body is made up of 1,674 undergraduates. 50.6% are women and 49.4% are men. Students come from 49 states and territories and 36 other countries. 20% are from North Carolina. 3.8% are international students. 6.5% are African American, 0.6% American Indian, 3.2% Asian American, and 4.4% Hispanic American. 96% returned for their sophomore year.

Facilities and Resources

142 **computers/terminals** are available on campus for general student use. Students can access the following: campus intranet, computer help desk, free student e-mail accounts, online (class) registration, online (class) schedules. Campuswide network is available. 100% of college-owned or -operated housing units are wired for high-speed Internet access. Wireless service is available via entire campus. The 2 **libraries** have 422,035 books and 2,767 subscriptions.

Campus Life

There are 162 active organizations on campus, including a drama/theater group, newspaper, radio station, and choral group. 41% of eligible men are members of national **fraternities**.

Davidson is a member of the NCAA (Division I). **Intercollegiate sports** (some offering scholarships) include baseball (m), basketball, cross-country running, field hockey (w), football (m), golf (m), lacrosse (w), soccer, swimming and diving, tennis, track and field, volleyball (w), wrestling (m).

Campus Safety

Student safety services include late-night transport/escort service, 24-hour emergency telephone alarm devices, 24-hour patrols by trained security personnel, and electronically operated dormitory entrances.

Applying

Davidson requires an essay, SAT or ACT, a high school transcript, and 3 recommendations. It recommends SAT Subject Tests and an interview. Application deadline: 1/2; 2/15 priority date for financial aid. Early and deferred admission are possible.

DENISON UNIVERSITY

SMALL-TOWN SETTING ■ PRIVATE ■ INDEPENDENT ■ COED
GRANVILLE, OHIO

Web site: www.denison.edu
Contact: Mr. Perry Robinson, Director of Admissions, Box H, Granville, OH 43023
Telephone: 740-587-6276 or toll-free 800-DENISON
E-mail: admissions@denison.edu

SPONSOR

Academics

Denison awards bachelor's **degrees**. **Challenging opportunities** include advanced placement credit, student-designed majors, an honors program, double majors, independent study, and a senior project. Special programs include cooperative education, internships, off-campus study, study-abroad, and Army ROTC.

The most frequently chosen **baccalaureate** fields are social sciences, communications/journalism, and psychology. A complete listing of majors at Denison appears in the Majors by College index beginning on page 471.

The **faculty** at Denison has 193 full-time members, 98% with terminal degrees. The student-faculty ratio is 10:1.

Students of Denison

The student body is made up of 2,242 undergraduates. 56.9% are women and 43.1% are men. Students come from 50 states and territories and 27 other countries. 36% are from Ohio. 4.2% are international students. 5% are African American, 0.4% American Indian, 2.8% Asian American, and 2.4% Hispanic American. 93% returned for their sophomore year.

Facilities and Resources

587 **computers/terminals** are available on campus for general student use. Campuswide network is available. The **library** has 767,118 books and 6,616 subscriptions.

Campus Life

There are 147 active organizations on campus, including a drama/theater group, newspaper, radio station, television station, and choral group. 19% of eligible men and 26% of eligible women are members of national **fraternities** and national **sororities**.

Denison is a member of the NCAA (Division III). **Intercollegiate sports** include baseball (m), basketball, cross-country running, field hockey (w), football (m), golf (m), lacrosse, soccer, softball (w), swimming and diving, tennis, track and field, volleyball (w).

Campus Safety

Student safety services include security lighting, escort service, late-night transport/escort service, 24-hour emergency telephone alarm devices, 24-hour patrols by trained security personnel, student patrols, and electronically operated dormitory entrances.

Applying

Denison requires an essay, a high school transcript, and 2 recommendations, and in some cases SAT or ACT. It recommends an interview. Application deadline: 1/15; 2/15 priority date for financial aid. Early and deferred admission are possible.

Getting Accepted
5,196 applied
39% were accepted
586 enrolled (29% of accepted)
52% from top tenth of their h.s. class
3.6 average high school GPA
Mean SAT critical reading score: 636
Mean SAT math score: 625
Mean ACT score: 30
70% had SAT critical reading scores over 600
68% had SAT math scores over 600
92% had ACT scores over 24
23% had SAT critical reading scores over 700
16% had SAT math scores over 700
35% had ACT scores over 30
16 National Merit Scholars
27 class presidents
35 valedictorians

Graduation and After
74% graduated in 4 years
4% graduated in 5 years
1% graduated in 6 years
22% pursued further study (15% arts and sciences, 2% law, 2% medicine)
65% had job offers within 6 months
35 organizations recruited on campus

Financial Matters
$33,010 tuition and fees (2007–08)
$8570 room and board
94% average percent of need met
$26,424 average financial aid amount received per undergraduate (2006–07 estimated)

DePauw University

Small-town setting ■ Private ■ Independent Religious ■ Coed
Greencastle, Indiana

Web site: www.depauw.edu
Contact: Brett Kennedy, Senior Associate Director of Admission, 101 East Seminary Street, Greencastle, IN 46135-0037
Telephone: 765-658-4006 or toll-free 800-447-2495
Fax: 765-658-4007
E-mail: admission@depauw.edu

Getting Accepted

3,624 applied
69% were accepted
664 enrolled (27% of accepted)
50% from top tenth of their h.s. class
3.6 average high school GPA
57% had SAT critical reading scores over 600
63% had SAT math scores over 600
52% had SAT writing scores over 600
87% had ACT scores over 24
11% had SAT critical reading scores over 700
16% had SAT math scores over 700
12% had SAT writing scores over 700
25% had ACT scores over 30

Graduation and After

79% graduated in 4 years
2% graduated in 5 years
1% graduated in 6 years
23% pursued further study (8% law, 6% arts and sciences, 2% medicine)
90% had job offers within 6 months
35 organizations recruited on campus

Financial Matters

$29,700 tuition and fees (2007–08)
$8100 room and board
98% average percent of need met
$24,873 average financial aid amount received per undergraduate (2005–06 estimated)

Academics

DePauw awards bachelor's **degrees**. **Challenging opportunities** include advanced placement credit, student-designed majors, an honors program, double majors, independent study, and a senior project. Special programs include internships, off-campus study, study-abroad, and Army and Air Force ROTC.

The most frequently chosen **baccalaureate** fields are social sciences, biological/life sciences, and English. A complete listing of majors at DePauw appears in the Majors by College index beginning on page 471.

The **faculty** at DePauw has 231 full-time members, 88% with terminal degrees. The student-faculty ratio is 10:1.

Students of DePauw

The student body is made up of 2,398 undergraduates. 56.3% are women and 43.7% are men. Students come from 43 states and territories and 32 other countries. 46% are from Indiana. 2.4% are international students. 5.8% are African American, 0.3% American Indian, 2.6% Asian American, and 3.2% Hispanic American. 87% returned for their sophomore year.

Facilities and Resources

424 **computers/terminals** are available on campus for general student use. Students can access the following: online (class) registration. Campuswide network is available. The 4 **libraries** have 333,346 books and 2,030 subscriptions.

Campus Life

There are 90 active organizations on campus, including a drama/theater group, newspaper, radio station, television station, choral group, and marching band. 72% of eligible men and 68% of eligible women are members of national **fraternities** and national **sororities**.

DePauw is a member of the NCAA (Division III). **Intercollegiate sports** include baseball (m), basketball, cross-country running, field hockey (w), football (m), golf, soccer, softball (w), swimming and diving, tennis, track and field, volleyball (w).

Campus Safety

Student safety services include late-night transport/escort service, 24-hour emergency telephone alarm devices, 24-hour patrols by trained security personnel, student patrols, and electronically operated dormitory entrances.

Applying

DePauw requires an essay, SAT or ACT, a high school transcript, and 1 recommendation. It recommends an interview. Application deadline: 2/1; 2/15 for financial aid. Early and deferred admission are possible.

DICKINSON COLLEGE

SUBURBAN SETTING ■ PRIVATE ■ INDEPENDENT ■ COED
CARLISLE, PENNSYLVANIA

Web site: www.dickinson.edu
Contact: Catherine Davenport, Acting Dean of Admissions, PO Box 1773,
Carlisle, PA 17013-2896
Telephone: 800-644-1773
Fax: 717-245-1442
E-mail: admit@dickinson.edu

Academics

Dickinson awards bachelor's **degrees**. **Challenging opportunities** include advanced placement credit, accelerated degree programs, student-designed majors, double majors, independent study, and a senior project. Special programs include internships, summer session for credit, off-campus study, study-abroad, and Army ROTC.

The most frequently chosen **baccalaureate** fields are social sciences, foreign languages and literature, and English. A complete listing of majors at Dickinson appears in the Majors by College index beginning on page 471.

The **faculty** at Dickinson has 188 full-time members, 96% with terminal degrees. The student-faculty ratio is 11:1.

Students of Dickinson

The student body is made up of 2,381 undergraduates. 55.3% are women and 44.7% are men. Students come from 41 states and territories and 46 other countries. 25% are from Pennsylvania. 5.6% are international students. 4.4% are African American, 0.3% American Indian, 4.6% Asian American, and 4.7% Hispanic American. 91% returned for their sophomore year.

Facilities and Resources

600 **computers/terminals** and 5,000 ports are available on campus for general student use. Students can access the following: campus intranet, computer help desk, free student e-mail accounts, online (class) grades, online (class) registration, online (class) schedules. Campuswide network is available. 100% of college-owned or -operated housing units are wired for high-speed Internet access. Wireless service is available via classrooms, computer centers, computer labs, libraries, student centers. The 7 **libraries** have 517,000 books and 1,300 subscriptions.

Campus Life

There are 140 active organizations on campus, including a drama/theater group, newspaper, radio station, and choral group. 16% of eligible men and 28% of eligible women are members of national **fraternities**, national **sororities**, local fraternities, and local sororities.

Dickinson is a member of the NCAA (Division III). **Intercollegiate sports** include baseball (m), basketball, cross-country running, field hockey (w), football (m), golf, lacrosse, soccer, softball (w), swimming and diving, tennis, track and field, volleyball (w).

Campus Safety

Student safety services include late-night transport/escort service, 24-hour emergency telephone alarm devices, 24-hour patrols by trained security personnel, student patrols, and electronically operated dormitory entrances.

Applying

Dickinson requires an essay, a high school transcript, and 2 recommendations. It recommends SAT or ACT, an interview, and a minimum high school GPA of 3.0. Application deadline: 2/1, 2/1 for nonresidents; 2/1 for financial aid, with a 11/15 priority date. Deferred admission is possible.

Getting Accepted

5,844 applied
42% were accepted
621 enrolled (25% of accepted)
48% from top tenth of their h.s. class
Mean SAT critical reading score: 644
Mean SAT math score: 631
Mean ACT score: 28
78% had SAT critical reading scores over 600
71% had SAT math scores over 600
24% had SAT critical reading scores over 700
16% had SAT math scores over 700

Graduation and After

79% graduated in 4 years
3% graduated in 5 years
1% graduated in 6 years
28% pursued further study (14% arts and sciences, 5% law, 2% business)
75% had job offers within 6 months
34 organizations recruited on campus

Financial Matters

$38,234 tuition and fees (2008–09)
$9600 room and board
96% average percent of need met
$26,239 average financial aid amount received per undergraduate (2006–07 estimated)

Dominican University, located just 10 miles from downtown Chicago, offers a comprehensive liberal arts education with a dynamic curriculum and inspiring faculty members. Students choose from fifty majors and participate in a series of four interdisciplinary seminars with their classmates to explore such topics as "Diversity, Culture, and Community" or "Virtues and Values." As a Catholic institution, Dominican is known for its rigorous and engaging academics, its enduring commitment to social justice programs, and the diversity of its students, faculty, and staff. This relationship-centered community encourages students to achieve amazing things—personally and professionally.

Getting Accepted
1,265 applied
85% were accepted
367 enrolled (34% of accepted)
20% from top tenth of their h.s. class
3.37 average high school GPA
Mean ACT score: 23
33% had ACT scores over 24
3% had ACT scores over 30
4 valedictorians

Graduation and After
48% graduated in 4 years
12% graduated in 5 years
2% graduated in 6 years
15% pursued further study
95% had job offers within 6 months
13 organizations recruited on campus

Financial Matters
$22,450 tuition and fees (2007–08)
$7000 room and board
78% average percent of need met
$16,344 average financial aid amount received per undergraduate (2006–07 estimated)

DOMINICAN UNIVERSITY
SUBURBAN SETTING ■ PRIVATE ■ INDEPENDENT RELIGIOUS ■ COED
RIVER FOREST, ILLINOIS

Web site: www.dom.edu
Contact: Mr. Glenn Hamilton, Director of Freshman Admission, 7900 West Division Street, River Forest, IL 60305
Telephone: 708-524-6800 or toll-free 800-828-8475
Fax: 708-524-6864
E-mail: domadmis@dom.edu

Academics
Dominican awards bachelor's and master's **degrees** and post-bachelor's and post-master's certificates. **Challenging opportunities** include advanced placement credit, accelerated degree programs, student-designed majors, an honors program, double majors, independent study, and a senior project. Special programs include internships, summer session for credit, off-campus study, and study-abroad.

The most frequently chosen **baccalaureate** fields are business/marketing, social sciences, and psychology. A complete listing of majors at Dominican appears in the Majors by College index beginning on page 471.

The **faculty** at Dominican has 124 full-time members, 84% with terminal degrees. The student-faculty ratio is 12:1.

Students of Dominican
The student body totals 3,338, of whom 1,598 are undergraduates. 69.8% are women and 30.2% are men. Students come from 33 states and territories and 18 other countries. 91% are from Illinois. 2.1% are international students. 7% are African American, 3.3% Asian American, and 21.8% Hispanic American. 77% returned for their sophomore year.

Facilities and Resources
625 **computers/terminals** are available on campus for general student use. Students can access the following: campus intranet, computer help desk, free student e-mail accounts, online (class) grades, online (class) registration, online (class) schedules, online student account information, online financial aid information. Campuswide network is available. 100% of college-owned or -operated housing units are wired for high-speed Internet access. Wireless service is available via computer centers, learning centers, libraries, student centers. The **library** has 255,840 books and 14,089 subscriptions.

Campus Life
There are 30 active organizations on campus, including a drama/theater group, newspaper, and choral group. No national or local **fraternities** or **sororities**.

Dominican is a member of the NCAA (Division III). **Intercollegiate sports** include baseball (m), basketball, cross-country running, golf (m), soccer, softball (w), tennis, volleyball (w).

Campus Safety
Student safety services include door alarms, late-night transport/escort service, 24-hour emergency telephone alarm devices, 24-hour patrols by trained security personnel, student patrols, and electronically operated dormitory entrances.

Applying
Dominican requires an essay, SAT or ACT, a high school transcript, and a minimum high school GPA of 2.75, and in some cases an interview and 2 recommendations. It recommends an interview and recommendations. Application deadline: rolling admissions; 6/1 priority date for financial aid. Deferred admission is possible.

DRAKE UNIVERSITY
SUBURBAN SETTING ■ PRIVATE ■ INDEPENDENT ■ COED
DES MOINES, IOWA

SPONSOR

Web site: www.drake.edu
Contact: Ms. Laura Linn, Director of Admission, 2507 University Avenue, Des Moines, IA 50311
Telephone: 515-271-3181 Ext. 3182 or toll-free 800-44DRAKE Ext. 3181
Fax: 515-271-2831
E-mail: admission@drake.edu

Academics

Drake awards bachelor's, master's, doctoral, and first-professional **degrees** and post-master's certificates. **Challenging opportunities** include advanced placement credit, accelerated degree programs, student-designed majors, an honors program, double majors, independent study, and a senior project. Special programs include cooperative education, internships, summer session for credit, off-campus study, study-abroad, and Army and Air Force ROTC.

The most frequently chosen **baccalaureate** fields are business/marketing, communications/journalism, and social sciences. A complete listing of majors at Drake appears in the Majors by College index beginning on page 471.

The **faculty** at Drake has 246 full-time members, 95% with terminal degrees. The student-faculty ratio is 14:1.

Students of Drake

The student body totals 5,366, of whom 3,255 are undergraduates. 55.9% are women and 44.1% are men. 39% are from Iowa. 6.1% are international students. 2.9% are African American, 0.2% American Indian, 3.9% Asian American, and 1.6% Hispanic American. 88% returned for their sophomore year.

Facilities and Resources

1,000 **computers/terminals** are available on campus for general student use. Campuswide network is available. The 2 **libraries** have 511,168 books and 31,500 subscriptions.

Campus Life

There are 160 active organizations on campus, including a drama/theater group, newspaper, radio station, television station, choral group, and marching band. 28% of eligible men and 23% of eligible women are members of national **fraternities** and national **sororities**.

Drake is a member of the NCAA (Division I). **Intercollegiate sports** (some offering scholarships) include basketball, cheerleading, crew (w), cross-country running, football (m), golf, soccer, softball (w), tennis, track and field, volleyball (w).

Campus Safety

Student safety services include 24-hour desk attendants in residence halls, late-night transport/escort service, 24-hour emergency telephone alarm devices, and 24-hour patrols by trained security personnel.

Applying

Drake requires SAT or ACT, PCAT for pharmacy transfers, and a high school transcript. It recommends an essay and an interview. Application deadline: 3/1; 3/1 priority date for financial aid. Early and deferred admission are possible.

A Drake education offers a unique mix of advantages for future success. Drake is large enough to offer more than seventy undergraduate academic programs, 160 organizations, and a community of students from around the world. Yet Drake's exceptional faculty and academic and extracurricular options are highly accessible to students beginning their first year of college. Drake's location in Des Moines, Iowa's capital, offers numerous professional internships; more than 63 percent of Drake students graduate having had one or more internships. Drake is affordable; 98 percent of its students receive financial assistance. It is a great value, too—nearly all Drake graduates (92 percent in 2006) obtain career positions or enter graduate school within six months after receiving their degrees.

Getting Accepted
4,049 applied
80% were accepted
781 enrolled (24% of accepted)
40% from top tenth of their h.s. class
3.62 average high school GPA
Mean SAT critical reading score: 584
Mean SAT math score: 599
Mean ACT score: 26
43% had SAT critical reading scores over 600
48% had SAT math scores over 600
73% had ACT scores over 24
11% had SAT critical reading scores over 700
13% had SAT math scores over 700
17% had ACT scores over 30
6 National Merit Scholars

Graduation and After
55% graduated in 4 years
11% graduated in 5 years
1% graduated in 6 years
25% pursued further study (5% law, 2% medicine, 1% business)
50 organizations recruited on campus

Financial Matters
$23,692 tuition and fees (2007–08)
$6920 room and board
82% average percent of need met
$18,450 average financial aid amount received per undergraduate (2006–07 estimated)

DREW UNIVERSITY

SUBURBAN SETTING ■ PRIVATE ■ INDEPENDENT RELIGIOUS ■ COED
MADISON, NEW JERSEY

Web site: www.drew.edu
Contact: Ms. Mary Beth Carey, Dean of Admissions and Financial Assistance,
 36 Madison Avenue, Madison, NJ 07940-1493
Telephone: 973-408-3739
Fax: 973-408-3068
E-mail: cadm@drew.edu

Getting Accepted
3,816 applied
77% were accepted
456 enrolled (16% of accepted)
28% from top tenth of their h.s. class
3.35 average high school GPA
Mean SAT critical reading score: 585
Mean SAT math score: 570
Mean SAT writing score: 590
Mean ACT score: 23
46% had SAT critical reading scores over 600
36% had SAT math scores over 600
46% had SAT writing scores over 600
48% had ACT scores over 24
12% had SAT critical reading scores over 700
6% had SAT math scores over 700
10% had SAT writing scores over 700
9% had ACT scores over 30

Graduation and After
23% pursued further study (13% arts and
 sciences, 5% law, 1% business)
68.1% had job offers within 6 months
43 organizations recruited on campus

Financial Matters
$34,790 tuition and fees (2007–08)
$9476 room and board
82% average percent of need met
$23,242 average financial aid amount received
 per undergraduate (2005–06)

Academics
Drew awards bachelor's, master's, doctoral, and first-professional **degrees** and post-bachelor's certificates. **Challenging opportunities** include advanced placement credit, accelerated degree programs, student-designed majors, an honors program, double majors, independent study, and a senior project. Special programs include internships, summer session for credit, off-campus study, and study-abroad.

The most frequently chosen **baccalaureate** fields are social sciences, psychology, and visual and performing arts. A complete listing of majors at Drew appears in the Majors by College index beginning on page 471.

The **faculty** at Drew has 158 full-time members, 95% with terminal degrees. The student-faculty ratio is 11:1.

Students of Drew
The student body totals 2,640, of whom 1,676 are undergraduates. 60.7% are women and 39.3% are men. Students come from 45 states and territories and 16 other countries. 59% are from New Jersey. 2% are international students. 6.1% are African American, 0.3% American Indian, 4.8% Asian American, and 7.4% Hispanic American. 83% returned for their sophomore year.

Facilities and Resources
200 **computers/terminals** are available on campus for general student use. Students can access the following: online (class) registration. Campuswide network is available. The **library** has 581,734 books.

Campus Life
There are 80 active organizations on campus, including a drama/theater group, newspaper, radio station, television station, and choral group. No national or local **fraternities** or **sororities**.

Drew is a member of the NCAA (Division III). **Intercollegiate sports** include baseball (m), basketball, cross-country running, equestrian sports, fencing, field hockey (w), lacrosse, soccer, softball (w), swimming and diving, tennis.

Campus Safety
Student safety services include late-night transport/escort service, 24-hour emergency telephone alarm devices, 24-hour patrols by trained security personnel, and electronically operated dormitory entrances.

Applying
Drew requires an essay, a high school transcript, and 1 recommendation. It recommends an interview. Application deadline: 2/15; 2/15 for financial aid. Early and deferred admission are possible.

DREXEL UNIVERSITY

URBAN SETTING ■ PRIVATE ■ INDEPENDENT ■ COED
PHILADELPHIA, PENNSYLVANIA

Web site: www.drexel.edu
Contact: Ms. Joan MacDonald, Vice President of Enrollment Management,
  3141 Chestnut Street, Philadelphia, PA 19104-2875
Telephone: 215-895-2400 or toll-free 800-2-DREXEL
Fax: 215-895-5939
E-mail: enroll@drexel.edu

Academics

Drexel awards associate, bachelor's, master's, doctoral, and first-professional **degrees** and post-bachelor's, post-master's, and first-professional certificates. **Challenging opportunities** include advanced placement credit, accelerated degree programs, freshman honors college, an honors program, double majors, independent study, and a senior project. Special programs include cooperative education, internships, summer session for credit, study-abroad, and Army and Air Force ROTC.

The most frequently chosen **baccalaureate** fields are business/marketing, engineering, and health professions and related sciences. A complete listing of majors at Drexel appears in the Majors by College index beginning on page 471.

The student-faculty ratio is 10:1.

Students of Drexel

The student body totals 20,682, of whom 13,194 are undergraduates. 43.6% are women and 56.4% are men. Students come from 50 states and territories and 93 other countries. 52% are from Pennsylvania. 6.6% are international students. 8.4% are African American, 0.3% American Indian, 12.4% Asian American, and 3% Hispanic American.

Facilities and Resources

6,500 **computers/terminals** are available on campus for general student use. Students can access the following: online (class) registration. Campuswide network is available. Wireless service is available via entire campus. The **library** has 570,335 books and 8,321 subscriptions.

Campus Life

Active organizations on campus include a drama/theater group, newspaper, radio station, television station, and choral group. Drexel has national **fraternities**, national **sororities**, and local fraternities.

Drexel is a member of the NCAA (Division I). **Intercollegiate sports** (some offering scholarships) include basketball, crew, field hockey (w), golf (m), lacrosse, soccer, softball (w), swimming and diving, tennis, wrestling (m).

Campus Safety

Student safety services include late-night transport/escort service, 24-hour emergency telephone alarm devices, 24-hour patrols by trained security personnel, and electronically operated dormitory entrances.

Applying

Drexel requires SAT or ACT, a high school transcript, and a minimum high school GPA of 2.0, and in some cases an essay. It recommends SAT, an interview, and 2 recommendations. Application deadline: 3/1; 3/15 for financial aid. Deferred admission is possible.

Getting Accepted
16,867 applied
72% were accepted
2,396 enrolled (20% of accepted)
3.5 average high school GPA

Graduation and After
8% pursued further study
50% had job offers within 6 months
265 organizations recruited on campus

Financial Matters
$30,440 tuition and fees (2008–09)
$12,135 room and board
59% average percent of need met
$15,076 average financial aid amount received
  per undergraduate (2005–06 estimated)

DRURY UNIVERSITY

URBAN SETTING ■ PRIVATE ■ INDEPENDENT ■ COED
SPRINGFIELD, MISSOURI

Web site: www.drury.edu
Contact: Mr. Chip Parker, Director of Admission, 900 North Benton, Bay Hall, Springfield, MO 65802
Telephone: 417-873-7205 or toll-free 800-922-2274
Fax: 417-866-3873
E-mail: druryad@drury.edu

Getting Accepted
1,193 applied
76% were accepted
398 enrolled (44% of accepted)
33% from top tenth of their h.s. class
4.0 average high school GPA
Mean SAT critical reading score: 560
Mean SAT math score: 567
Mean SAT writing score: 562
Mean ACT score: 25
67% had ACT scores over 24
15% had ACT scores over 30
31 valedictorians

Graduation and After
52% graduated in 4 years
14% graduated in 5 years
2% graduated in 6 years
28% pursued further study
68.6% had job offers within 6 months
17 organizations recruited on campus

Financial Matters
$18,409 tuition and fees (2008–09)
$6384 room and board
84% average percent of need met
$7689 average financial aid amount received per undergraduate (2006–07 estimated)

Academics
Drury awards bachelor's and master's **degrees** (also offers evening program with significant enrollment not reflected in profile). **Challenging opportunities** include advanced placement credit, accelerated degree programs, student-designed majors, an honors program, double majors, independent study, and a senior project. Special programs include cooperative education, internships, summer session for credit, off-campus study, study-abroad, and Army ROTC.

The most frequently chosen **baccalaureate** fields are business/marketing, visual and performing arts, and communications/journalism. A complete listing of majors at Drury appears in the Majors by College index beginning on page 471.

The **faculty** at Drury has 125 full-time members, 95% with terminal degrees. The student-faculty ratio is 13:1.

Students of Drury
The student body totals 2,084, of whom 1,608 are undergraduates. 52.8% are women and 47.2% are men. Students come from 35 states and territories and 33 other countries. 83% are from Missouri. 5.3% are international students. 1.7% are African American, 0.9% American Indian, 1.7% Asian American, and 1.9% Hispanic American. 82% returned for their sophomore year.

Facilities and Resources
323 **computers/terminals** are available on campus for general student use. Students can access the following: campus intranet, computer help desk, free student e-mail accounts, online (class) grades, online (class) registration, online (class) schedules, digital imaging lab, online bill payment/student information. Campuswide network is available. 100% of college-owned or -operated housing units are wired for high-speed Internet access. Wireless service is available via entire campus. The 2 **libraries** have 168,600 books and 1,755 subscriptions.

Campus Life
There are 60 active organizations on campus, including a drama/theater group, newspaper, radio station, television station, and choral group. 37% of eligible men and 33% of eligible women are members of national **fraternities** and national **sororities**.

Drury is a member of the NCAA (Division II). **Intercollegiate sports** (some offering scholarships) include baseball (m), basketball, cheerleading, cross-country running, golf, soccer, softball (w), swimming and diving, tennis, volleyball (w).

Campus Safety
Student safety services include security cameras in parking areas, late-night transport/escort service, 24-hour emergency telephone alarm devices, 24-hour patrols by trained security personnel, student patrols, and electronically operated dormitory entrances.

Applying
Drury requires an essay, SAT or ACT, a high school transcript, 1 recommendation, minimum ACT score of 21, and a minimum high school GPA of 2.7. It recommends an interview. Application deadline: 8/1; 3/15 priority date for financial aid. Deferred admission is possible.

DUKE UNIVERSITY

SUBURBAN SETTING ■ PRIVATE ■ INDEPENDENT RELIGIOUS ■ COED
DURHAM, NORTH CAROLINA

Web site: www.duke.edu
Contact: Mr. Christoph Guttentag, Director of Admissions, 2138 Campus Drive, Durham, NC 27708
Telephone: 919-684-3214
Fax: 919-684-8941
E-mail: askduke@admiss.duke.edu

Academics

Duke awards bachelor's, master's, doctoral, and first-professional **degrees** and post-bachelor's and post-master's certificates. **Challenging opportunities** include advanced placement credit, accelerated degree programs, student-designed majors, an honors program, double majors, independent study, and a senior project. Special programs include internships, summer session for credit, off-campus study, study-abroad, and Army, Navy, and Air Force ROTC.

The most frequently chosen **baccalaureate** fields are social sciences, engineering, and psychology. A complete listing of majors at Duke appears in the Majors by College index beginning on page 471.

The **faculty** at Duke has 990 full-time members, 96% with terminal degrees. The student-faculty ratio is 8:1.

Students of Duke

The student body totals 13,598, of whom 6,394 are undergraduates. 49% are women and 51% are men. Students come from 53 states and territories and 89 other countries. 13% are from North Carolina. 5.8% are international students. 10% are African American, 0.2% American Indian, 19.5% Asian American, and 6.2% Hispanic American. 97% returned for their sophomore year.

Facilities and Resources

450 **computers/terminals** are available on campus for general student use. Students can access the following: campus intranet, computer help desk, free student e-mail accounts, online (class) registration. Campuswide network is available. 100% of college-owned or -operated housing units are wired for high-speed Internet access. Wireless service is available via entire campus. The 15 **libraries** have 5,560,966 books and 31,892 subscriptions.

Campus Life

There are 400 active organizations on campus, including a drama/theater group, newspaper, radio station, television station, choral group, and marching band. 29% of eligible men and 42% of eligible women are members of national **fraternities** and national **sororities**.

Duke is a member of the NCAA (Division I). **Intercollegiate sports** (some offering scholarships) include baseball (m), basketball, crew (w), cross-country running, fencing, field hockey (w), football (m), golf, lacrosse, soccer, swimming and diving, tennis, track and field, volleyball (w), wrestling (m).

Campus Safety

Student safety services include late-night transport/escort service, 24-hour emergency telephone alarm devices, 24-hour patrols by trained security personnel, and electronically operated dormitory entrances.

Applying

Duke requires an essay, SAT and SAT Subject Tests or ACT, a high school transcript, and recommendations, and in some cases audition tape for dance, drama, or music; slides of work for art. It recommends an interview. Application deadline: 1/2; 2/1 for financial aid. Early and deferred admission are possible.

Getting Accepted

17,748 applied
23% were accepted
1,700 enrolled (42% of accepted)
90% from top tenth of their h.s. class
92% had SAT critical reading scores over 600
94% had SAT math scores over 600
91% had SAT writing scores over 600
96% had ACT scores over 24
60% had SAT critical reading scores over 700
68% had SAT math scores over 700
57% had SAT writing scores over 700
72% had ACT scores over 30
197 valedictorians

Graduation and After

26% pursued further study
47% had job offers within 6 months
280 organizations recruited on campus

Financial Matters

$35,512 tuition and fees (2007–08)
$9609 room and board
100% average percent of need met
$29,449 average financial aid amount received per undergraduate (2006–07 estimated)

DUQUESNE UNIVERSITY

URBAN SETTING ■ PRIVATE ■ INDEPENDENT RELIGIOUS ■ COED
PITTSBURGH, PENNSYLVANIA

Web site: www.duq.edu
Contact: Mr. Paul-James Cukanna, Associate Vice President for Enrollment Management and Director of Admissions, 1st Floor Administration Building, 600 Forbes Avenue, Pittsburgh, PA 15282-0201
Telephone: 412-396-5002 or toll-free 800-456-0590
Fax: 412-396-5644
E-mail: admissions@duq.edu

Getting Accepted
5,374 applied
74% were accepted
1,361 enrolled (34% of accepted)
26% from top tenth of their h.s. class
3.65 average high school GPA
Mean SAT critical reading score: 556
Mean SAT math score: 564
Mean SAT writing score: 553
Mean ACT score: 24
26% had SAT critical reading scores over 600
33% had SAT math scores over 600
27% had SAT writing scores over 600
53% had ACT scores over 24
3% had SAT critical reading scores over 700
3% had SAT math scores over 700
2% had SAT writing scores over 700
6% had ACT scores over 30

Graduation and After
57% graduated in 4 years
11% graduated in 5 years
2% graduated in 6 years
35% pursued further study (10% arts and sciences, 10% law, 5% business)
75% had job offers within 6 months
70 organizations recruited on campus

Financial Matters
$23,950 tuition and fees (2007–08)
$8546 room and board
89% average percent of need met
$15,204 average financial aid amount received per undergraduate (2006–07 estimated)

Academics

Duquesne awards bachelor's, master's, doctoral, and first-professional **degrees** and post-bachelor's and post-master's certificates. **Challenging opportunities** include advanced placement credit, accelerated degree programs, student-designed majors, freshman honors college, an honors program, double majors, independent study, and a senior project. Special programs include internships, summer session for credit, off-campus study, study-abroad, and Army, Navy, and Air Force ROTC.

The most frequently chosen **baccalaureate** fields are business/marketing, health professions and related sciences, and education. A complete listing of majors at Duquesne appears in the Majors by College index beginning on page 471.

The **faculty** at Duquesne has 447 full-time members, 86% with terminal degrees. The student-faculty ratio is 15:1.

Students of Duquesne

The student body totals 10,296, of whom 5,837 are undergraduates. 57.6% are women and 42.4% are men. Students come from 49 states and territories and 48 other countries. 82% are from Pennsylvania. 2.2% are international students. 3.2% are African American, 0.1% American Indian, 1.5% Asian American, and 1.1% Hispanic American. 88% returned for their sophomore year.

Facilities and Resources

1,000 **computers/terminals** are available on campus for general student use. Students can access the following: campus intranet, computer help desk, free student e-mail accounts, online (class) grades, online (class) registration, online (class) schedules. Campuswide network is available. 100% of college-owned or -operated housing units are wired for high-speed Internet access. Wireless service is available via classrooms, computer centers, computer labs, learning centers, libraries, student centers. The 2 **libraries** have 703,981 books and 20,020 subscriptions.

Campus Life

There are 150 active organizations on campus, including a drama/theater group, newspaper, radio station, television station, and choral group. 14% of eligible men and 18% of eligible women are members of national **fraternities**, national **sororities**, local fraternities, and local sororities.

Duquesne is a member of the NCAA (Division I). **Intercollegiate sports** (some offering scholarships) include baseball (m), basketball, crew (w), cross-country running, football (m), golf (m), lacrosse (w), soccer, swimming and diving, tennis, track and field, volleyball (w), wrestling (m).

Campus Safety

Student safety services include 24-hour front desk personnel, 24-hour video monitors at residence hall entrances, surveillance cameras throughout the campus, late-night transport/escort service, 24-hour emergency telephone alarm devices, 24-hour patrols by trained security personnel, and electronically operated dormitory entrances.

Applying

Duquesne requires an essay, SAT or ACT, a high school transcript, and 1 recommendation. It recommends an interview and a minimum high school GPA of 3.0. Application deadline: 7/1; 5/1 for financial aid. Early and deferred admission are possible.

EARLHAM COLLEGE

SMALL-TOWN SETTING ■ PRIVATE ■ INDEPENDENT RELIGIOUS ■ COED
RICHMOND, INDIANA

Web site: www.earlham.edu
Contact: Mr. Jeff Rickey, Dean of Admissions and Financial Aid, 801 National Road West, Richmond, IN 47374
Telephone: 765-983-1600 or toll-free 800-327-5426
Fax: 765-983-1560
E-mail: admission@earlham.edu

Academics

Earlham awards bachelor's, master's, and first-professional **degrees**. **Challenging opportunities** include advanced placement credit, accelerated degree programs, student-designed majors, double majors, independent study, and a senior project. Special programs include internships, off-campus study, and study-abroad.

The most frequently chosen **baccalaureate** fields are social sciences, interdisciplinary studies, and visual and performing arts. A complete listing of majors at Earlham appears in the Majors by College index beginning on page 471.

The **faculty** at Earlham has 97 full-time members, 96% with terminal degrees. The student-faculty ratio is 12:1.

Students of Earlham

The student body totals 1,360, of whom 1,194 are undergraduates. 55.4% are women and 44.6% are men. Students come from 45 states and territories and 62 other countries. 22% are from Indiana. 11.1% are international students. 5.9% are African American, 0.3% American Indian, 1.9% Asian American, and 2.5% Hispanic American. 84% returned for their sophomore year.

Facilities and Resources

164 **computers/terminals** and 30 ports are available on campus for general student use. Students can access the following: campus intranet, computer help desk, free student e-mail accounts, online (class) grades, online (class) schedules. Campuswide network is available. 95% of college-owned or -operated housing units are wired for high-speed Internet access. Wireless service is available via classrooms, computer centers, computer labs, learning centers, libraries, student centers. The 2 **libraries** have 406,699 books and 22,571 subscriptions.

Campus Life

There are 70 active organizations on campus, including a drama/theater group, newspaper, radio station, and choral group. No national or local **fraternities** or **sororities**.

Earlham is a member of the NCAA (Division III). **Intercollegiate sports** include baseball (m), basketball, cross-country running, field hockey (w), football (m), soccer, tennis, track and field, volleyball (w).

Campus Safety

Student safety services include late-night transport/escort service, 24-hour emergency telephone alarm devices, 24-hour patrols by trained security personnel, student patrols, and electronically operated dormitory entrances.

Applying

Earlham requires an essay, SAT or ACT, a high school transcript, 2 recommendations, and a minimum high school GPA of 3.0. It recommends an interview. Application deadline: 2/15; 3/1 priority date for financial aid. Early and deferred admission are possible.

Getting Accepted

1,748 applied
69% were accepted
300 enrolled (25% of accepted)
31% from top tenth of their h.s. class
3.5 average high school GPA
Mean SAT critical reading score: 630
Mean SAT math score: 590
Mean SAT writing score: 610
Mean ACT score: 26
58% had SAT critical reading scores over 600
43% had SAT math scores over 600
52% had SAT writing scores over 600
75% had ACT scores over 24
16% had SAT critical reading scores over 700
8% had SAT math scores over 700
14% had SAT writing scores over 700
14% had ACT scores over 30
6 National Merit Scholars
16 class presidents
8 valedictorians

Graduation and After

64% graduated in 4 years
10% graduated in 5 years
2% graduated in 6 years
21% pursued further study (17% arts and sciences, 1% medicine)
15 organizations recruited on campus

Financial Matters

$31,514 tuition and fees (2007–08)
$6504 room and board
95% average percent of need met
$21,215 average financial aid amount received per undergraduate

ELIZABETHTOWN COLLEGE

SMALL-TOWN SETTING ■ PRIVATE ■ INDEPENDENT RELIGIOUS ■ COED
ELIZABETHTOWN, PENNSYLVANIA

Web site: www.etown.edu
Contact: Ms. Debra Murray, Director of Admissions, One Alpha Drive,
 Elizabethtown, PA 17022
Telephone: 717-361-1400
Fax: 717-361-1365
E-mail: admissions@etown.edu

Located in southeastern Pennsylvania, Elizabethtown College was named to President Bush's 2007 Higher Education Community Service Honor Roll. Elizabethtown offers liberal arts and professional studies to more than 1,950 students through fifty-three academic programs. Encouraged and supported by engaging faculty members, students enjoy experiential learning opportunities that include research, internships, and off-campus study. Rigorous academics, combined with an array of service and leadership opportunities available through student organizations and athletics, prepare Elizabethtown's graduates for lives of purpose. The James B. Hoover Center for Business opened in fall 2006, and the Masters Center for Science, Mathematics, and Engineering opened in fall 2007.

Getting Accepted
3,370 applied
58% were accepted
518 enrolled (26% of accepted)
34% from top tenth of their h.s. class
Mean SAT critical reading score: 560
Mean SAT math score: 560
Mean ACT score: 23
31% had SAT critical reading scores over 600
35% had SAT math scores over 600
74% had ACT scores over 24
5% had SAT critical reading scores over 700
5% had SAT math scores over 700
9% had ACT scores over 30
16 valedictorians

Graduation and After
64% graduated in 4 years
6% graduated in 5 years
26 organizations recruited on campus

Financial Matters
$30,650 tuition and fees (2008–09)
$7950 room and board
83% average percent of need met
$18,309 average financial aid amount received
 per undergraduate (2006–07 estimated)

Academics

E-town awards associate, bachelor's, and master's **degrees** and post-bachelor's certificates. **Challenging opportunities** include advanced placement credit, an honors program, double majors, independent study, and a senior project. Special programs include internships, summer session for credit, off-campus study, and study-abroad.

The most frequently chosen **baccalaureate** fields are business/marketing, education, and social sciences. A complete listing of majors at E-town appears in the Majors by College index beginning on page 471.

The **faculty** at E-town has 131 full-time members, 82% with terminal degrees. The student-faculty ratio is 12:1.

Students of E-town

The student body totals 2,360, of whom 2,322 are undergraduates. 64.8% are women and 35.2% are men. Students come from 28 states and territories and 26 other countries. 69% are from Pennsylvania. 1.3% are international students. 2.8% are African American, 0.2% American Indian, 1.9% Asian American, and 2% Hispanic American. 86% returned for their sophomore year.

Facilities and Resources

200 **computers/terminals** and 200 ports are available on campus for general student use. Students can access the following: campus intranet, computer help desk, free student e-mail accounts, online (class) grades, online (class) registration, online (class) schedules, file space, personal web page, financial aid, student billing. Campuswide network is available. 100% of college-owned or -operated housing units are wired for high-speed Internet access. Wireless service is available via classrooms, computer labs, learning centers, libraries, student centers. The **library** has 200,073 books and 17,206 subscriptions.

Campus Life

There are 80 active organizations on campus, including a drama/theater group, newspaper, radio station, television station, and choral group. No national or local **fraternities** or **sororities**.

E-town is a member of the NCAA (Division III). **Intercollegiate sports** include baseball (m), basketball, cross-country running, field hockey (w), golf (m), lacrosse, soccer, softball (w), swimming and diving, tennis, track and field, volleyball (w), wrestling (m).

Campus Safety

Student safety services include self-defense workshops, crime prevention program, late-night transport/escort service, 24-hour emergency telephone alarm devices, 24-hour patrols by trained security personnel, student patrols, and electronically operated dormitory entrances.

Applying

E-town requires an essay, SAT or ACT, a high school transcript, 2 recommendations, and a minimum high school GPA of 2.0, and in some cases an interview. It recommends an interview and a minimum high school GPA of 3.0. Application deadline: 3/1; 3/15 priority date for financial aid. Early and deferred admission are possible.

ELMIRA COLLEGE

SMALL-TOWN SETTING ■ PRIVATE ■ INDEPENDENT ■ COED
ELMIRA, NEW YORK

Web site: www.elmira.edu
Contact: Mr. Gary Fallis, Dean of Admissions, Office of Admissions, Elmira, NY 14901
Telephone: 607-735-1724 or toll-free 800-935-6472
Fax: 607-735-1718
E-mail: admissions@elmira.edu

Academics

Elmira awards bachelor's and master's **degrees**. **Challenging opportunities** include advanced placement credit, accelerated degree programs, student-designed majors, double majors, and independent study. Special programs include internships, summer session for credit, off-campus study, study-abroad, and Army and Air Force ROTC.

The most frequently chosen **baccalaureate** fields are education, business/marketing, and health professions and related sciences. A complete listing of majors at Elmira appears in the Majors by College index beginning on page 471.

The **faculty** at Elmira has 82 full-time members, 100% with terminal degrees. The student-faculty ratio is 12:1.

Students of Elmira

The student body totals 1,853, of whom 1,484 are undergraduates. 71% are women and 29% are men. Students come from 35 states and territories and 23 other countries. 49% are from New York. 4.2% are international students. 1.8% are African American, 0.1% American Indian, 0.8% Asian American, and 1.3% Hispanic American. 84% returned for their sophomore year.

Facilities and Resources

105 **computers/terminals** are available on campus for general student use. Campuswide network is available. The **library** has 391,038 books and 859 subscriptions.

Campus Life

There are 80 active organizations on campus, including a drama/theater group, newspaper, radio station, and choral group. No national or local **fraternities** or **sororities**.

Elmira is a member of the NCAA (Division III). **Intercollegiate sports** include basketball, cheerleading (w), field hockey (w), golf, ice hockey, lacrosse, soccer, softball (w), tennis, volleyball (w).

Campus Safety

Student safety services include 24-hour locked residence hall entrances, late-night transport/escort service, and 24-hour patrols by trained security personnel.

Applying

Elmira requires an essay, SAT or ACT, a high school transcript, 2 recommendations, and a minimum high school GPA of 2.0, and in some cases an interview. It recommends an interview. Application deadline: 4/15; 2/1 priority date for financial aid. Early and deferred admission are possible.

Getting Accepted

1,966 applied
64% were accepted
323 enrolled (26% of accepted)
28% from top tenth of their h.s. class
3.5 average high school GPA
26% had SAT critical reading scores over 600
24% had SAT math scores over 600
61% had ACT scores over 24
4% had SAT critical reading scores over 700
4% had SAT math scores over 700
4% had ACT scores over 30
33 class presidents
26 valedictorians

Graduation and After

55% graduated in 4 years
4% graduated in 5 years
1% graduated in 6 years
41% pursued further study (18% education, 12% arts and sciences, 6% business)
97% had job offers within 6 months
55 organizations recruited on campus

Financial Matters

$31,700 tuition and fees (2007–08)
$9500 room and board
81% average percent of need met
$23,500 average financial aid amount received per undergraduate (2006–07 estimated)

ELON UNIVERSITY

Suburban setting ■ Private ■ Independent Religious ■ Coed
Elon, North Carolina

Getting Accepted
9,380 applied
41% were accepted
1,286 enrolled (33% of accepted)
29% from top tenth of their h.s. class
3.9 average high school GPA
Mean SAT critical reading score: 607
Mean SAT math score: 613
Mean ACT score: 26
59% had SAT critical reading scores over 600
61% had SAT math scores over 600
58% had SAT writing scores over 600
83% had ACT scores over 24
9% had SAT critical reading scores over 700
11% had SAT math scores over 700
11% had SAT writing scores over 700
13% had ACT scores over 30

Graduation and After
66% graduated in 4 years
7% graduated in 5 years
16% pursued further study (7% arts and sciences, 4% education, 3% business)
95% had job offers within 6 months
150 organizations recruited on campus

Financial Matters
$22,166 tuition and fees (2007–08)
$7296 room and board
70% average percent of need met
$12,794 average financial aid amount received per undergraduate (2006–07 estimated)

Web site: www.elon.edu
Contact: Ms. Melinda Wood, Associate Director of Admissions and Director of Application Review, 100 Campus Box, Elon, NC 27244
Telephone: 336-278-3566 or toll-free 800-334-8448
Fax: 336-278-7699
E-mail: admissions@elon.edu

Academics
Elon awards bachelor's, master's, doctoral, and first-professional **degrees**. **Challenging opportunities** include advanced placement credit, accelerated degree programs, student-designed majors, an honors program, double majors, independent study, and a senior project. Special programs include internships, summer session for credit, off-campus study, study-abroad, and Army and Air Force ROTC. A complete listing of majors at Elon appears in the Majors by College index beginning on page 471.

The **faculty** at Elon has 311 full-time members, 85% with terminal degrees. The student-faculty ratio is 14:1.

Students of Elon
The student body totals 5,456, of whom 4,939 are undergraduates. 58.9% are women and 41.1% are men. Students come from 46 states and territories and 45 other countries. 28% are from North Carolina. 2.1% are international students. 6% are African American, 0.2% American Indian, 1.1% Asian American, and 2.2% Hispanic American. 90% returned for their sophomore year.

Facilities and Resources
540 **computers/terminals** are available on campus for general student use. Students can access the following: free student e-mail accounts, online (class) grades, online (class) registration, online (class) schedules. Campuswide network is available. Wireless service is available via entire campus. The **library** has 250,119 books and 4,955 subscriptions.

Campus Life
There are 150 active organizations on campus, including a drama/theater group, newspaper, radio station, television station, choral group, and marching band. 24% of eligible men and 42% of eligible women are members of national **fraternities** and national **sororities**.

Elon is a member of the NCAA (Division I). **Intercollegiate sports** (some offering scholarships) include baseball (m), basketball, cheerleading, cross-country running, football (m), golf, soccer, softball (w), tennis, track and field (w), volleyball (w).

Campus Safety
Student safety services include late-night transport/escort service, 24-hour emergency telephone alarm devices, 24-hour patrols by trained security personnel, and electronically operated dormitory entrances.

Applying
Elon requires an essay, SAT or ACT, a high school transcript, and a minimum high school GPA of 2.7, and in some cases an interview. Application deadline: 1/10; 3/15 priority date for financial aid. Early and deferred admission are possible.

EMBRY-RIDDLE AERONAUTICAL UNIVERSITY

SUBURBAN SETTING ■ PRIVATE ■ INDEPENDENT ■ COED
PRESCOTT, ARIZONA

Web site: www.embryriddle.edu
Contact: Mr. Bill Thompson, Director of Admissions, 3700 Willow Creek
   Road, Prescott, AZ 86301-3720
Telephone: 928-777-6600 or toll-free 800-888-3728
Fax: 928-777-6606
E-mail: pradmit@erau.edu

Academics
Embry-Riddle awards bachelor's and master's **degrees**. **Challenging opportunities**
include advanced placement credit, accelerated degree programs, student-designed
majors, an honors program, double majors, independent study, and a senior project.
Special programs include cooperative education, internships, summer session for credit,
study-abroad, and Army and Air Force ROTC.

The most frequently chosen **baccalaureate** fields are visual and performing arts,
engineering, and social sciences. A complete listing of majors at Embry-Riddle appears
in the Majors by College index beginning on page 471.

The **faculty** at Embry-Riddle has 102 full-time members, 69% with terminal
degrees. The student-faculty ratio is 14:1.

Students of Embry-Riddle
The student body totals 1,707, of whom 1,676 are undergraduates. 17.4% are women
and 82.6% are men. Students come from 52 states and territories and 29 other countries.
21% are from Arizona. 3.6% are international students. 2.7% are African American,
1.3% American Indian, 6.9% Asian American, and 8.2% Hispanic American. 76%
returned for their sophomore year.

Facilities and Resources
450 **computers/terminals** are available on campus for general student use. Students can
access the following: online (class) registration. Campuswide network is available. Wireless service is available via entire campus.

Campus Life
There are 91 active organizations on campus, including a newspaper, radio station, and
television station. 85% of eligible men and 93% of eligible women are members of
national **fraternities** and national **sororities**.

Embry-Riddle is a member of the NAIA. **Intercollegiate sports** (some offering
scholarships) include volleyball (w), wrestling (m).

Campus Safety
Student safety services include late-night transport/escort service, 24-hour emergency
telephone alarm devices, 24-hour patrols by trained security personnel, and student
patrols.

Applying
Embry-Riddle requires SAT or ACT, SAT and SAT Subject Tests or ACT, a high school
transcript, and a minimum high school GPA of 2.0, and in some cases medical examination for flight students and a minimum high school GPA of 3.0. It recommends an essay,
an interview, and recommendations. Application deadline: rolling admissions. Deferred
admission is possible.

Getting Accepted
1,288 applied
85% were accepted
400 enrolled (36% of accepted)
21% from top tenth of their h.s. class
3.47 average high school GPA
Mean SAT critical reading score: 534
Mean SAT math score: 561
Mean ACT score: 25
25% had SAT critical reading scores over 600
33% had SAT math scores over 600
66% had ACT scores over 24
3% had SAT critical reading scores over 700
5% had SAT math scores over 700
14% had ACT scores over 30

Graduation and After
25% graduated in 4 years
21% graduated in 5 years
3% graduated in 6 years
20% pursued further study

Financial Matters
$26,130 tuition and fees (2007–08)
$7214 room and board
$15,248 average financial aid amount received
   per undergraduate (2006–07 estimated)

Boston is one of the best-known college towns in the country, and Emerson College is located right on Boston Common in the heart of the city's theater district. The campus is home to WERS-FM, the historic 1,200-seat Cutler Majestic Theatre, and the award-winning literary journal, *Ploughshares*. Emerson's 3,000 students come from across the United States and more than forty countries. There are more than sixty student organizations and performance groups, fourteen NCAA intercollegiate teams, and several student publications and honor societies. The College also sponsors programs in Los Angeles, Kasteel Well (the Netherlands), Taipei, Taiwan, summer film study in Prague, and course cross-registration with the six-member Boston ProArts Consortium.

Getting Accepted
4,981 applied
45% were accepted
776 enrolled (35% of accepted)
42% from top tenth of their h.s. class
3.62 average high school GPA
Mean SAT critical reading score: 633
Mean SAT math score: 599
Mean SAT writing score: 624
Mean ACT score: 27
70% had SAT critical reading scores over 600
52% had SAT math scores over 600
66% had SAT writing scores over 600
84% had ACT scores over 24
19% had SAT critical reading scores over 700
7% had SAT math scores over 700
16% had SAT writing scores over 700
18% had ACT scores over 30

Graduation and After
69% graduated in 4 years
3% graduated in 5 years
13% pursued further study
80% had job offers within 6 months
100 organizations recruited on campus

Financial Matters
$26,880 tuition and fees (2007–08)
$11,376 room and board
67% average percent of need met
$13,777 average financial aid amount received per undergraduate (2005–06)

EMERSON COLLEGE
URBAN SETTING ■ PRIVATE ■ INDEPENDENT ■ COED
BOSTON, MASSACHUSETTS

Web site: www.emerson.edu
Contact: Ms. Sara Ramirez, Director of Undergraduate Admission, 120 Boylston Street, Boston, MA 02116-4624
Telephone: 617-824-8600
Fax: 617-824-8609
E-mail: admission@emerson.edu

Academics
Emerson awards bachelor's, master's, and doctoral **degrees**. **Challenging opportunities** include advanced placement credit, student-designed majors, an honors program, double majors, independent study, and a senior project. Special programs include internships, summer session for credit, off-campus study, and study-abroad.

The most frequently chosen **baccalaureate** fields are communications/journalism, visual and performing arts, and English. A complete listing of majors at Emerson appears in the Majors by College index beginning on page 471.

The **faculty** at Emerson has 159 full-time members, 72% with terminal degrees. The student-faculty ratio is 14:1.

Students of Emerson
The student body totals 4,380, of whom 3,476 are undergraduates. 56% are women and 44% are men. Students come from 45 states and territories and 50 other countries. 26% are from Massachusetts. 2.4% are international students. 2.6% are African American, 0.6% American Indian, 4.6% Asian American, and 7.1% Hispanic American. 88% returned for their sophomore year.

Facilities and Resources
466 **computers/terminals** are available on campus for general student use. Students can access the following: computer help desk, free student e-mail accounts, online (class) registration. Campuswide network is available. 100% of college-owned or -operated housing units are wired for high-speed Internet access. Wireless service is available via classrooms, computer centers, computer labs, dorm rooms, learning centers, libraries, student centers. The 2 **libraries** have 165,000 books and 10,700 subscriptions.

Campus Life
There are 60 active organizations on campus, including a drama/theater group, newspaper, radio station, television station, and choral group. 3% of eligible men and 3% of eligible women are members of national **fraternities**, national **sororities**, local fraternities, and local sororities.

Emerson is a member of the NCAA (Division III). **Intercollegiate sports** include baseball (m), basketball, cross-country running, lacrosse, soccer, softball (w), tennis, volleyball.

Campus Safety
Student safety services include late-night transport/escort service, 24-hour emergency telephone alarm devices, 24-hour patrols by trained security personnel, and electronically operated dormitory entrances.

Applying
Emerson requires an essay, SAT or ACT, a high school transcript, and recommendations, and in some cases an interview and Performing Arts candidates must submit a resume of theatre-related activities and either audition or interview, or submit a portfolio or an essay. Application deadline: 1/5; 3/1 priority date for financial aid. Early and deferred admission are possible.

EMORY UNIVERSITY

SUBURBAN SETTING ■ PRIVATE ■ INDEPENDENT RELIGIOUS ■ COED
ATLANTA, GEORGIA

Web site: www.emory.edu
Contact: Ms. Jean Jordan, Interim Dean of Admission, 200 Boisfeuillet Jones
Center, Atlanta, GA 30322-1100
Telephone: 404-727-6036 or toll-free 800-727-6036
E-mail: admiss@learnlink.emory.edu

Academics

Emory awards associate, bachelor's, master's, doctoral, and first-professional **degrees**
(enrollment figures include Emory University, Oxford College; application data for main
campus only). **Challenging opportunities** include advanced placement credit, accelerated degree programs, an honors program, double majors, independent study, and a
senior project. Special programs include cooperative education, internships, summer
session for credit, off-campus study, study-abroad, and Army, Navy, and Air Force
ROTC.

The most frequently chosen **baccalaureate** fields are social sciences, business/
marketing, and psychology. A complete listing of majors at Emory appears in the Majors
by College index beginning on page 471.

The **faculty** at Emory has 1,241 full-time members, 100% with terminal degrees.
The student-faculty ratio is 7:1.

Students of Emory

The student body totals 12,338, of whom 6,646 are undergraduates. 57.6% are women
and 42.4% are men. Students come from 52 states and territories and 57 other countries.
29% are from Georgia. 4.9% are international students. 9.3% are African American,
0.3% American Indian, 17.6% Asian American, and 3.4% Hispanic American. 94%
returned for their sophomore year.

Facilities and Resources

600 **computers/terminals** are available on campus for general student use. Students can
access the following: online (class) registration. Campuswide network is available. The 8
libraries have 3,246,000 books and 51,500 subscriptions.

Campus Life

There are 220 active organizations on campus, including a drama/theater group,
newspaper, radio station, television station, and choral group. 31% of eligible men and
33% of eligible women are members of national **fraternities** and national **sororities**.

Emory is a member of the NCAA (Division III). **Intercollegiate sports** include
baseball (m), basketball, cross-country running, golf (m), soccer, softball (w), swimming
and diving, tennis, track and field, volleyball (w).

Campus Safety

Student safety services include late-night transport/escort service, 24-hour emergency
telephone alarm devices, 24-hour patrols by trained security personnel, and student
patrols.

Applying

Emory requires an essay, SAT or ACT, a high school transcript, and 1 recommendation.
It recommends SAT Subject Tests and a minimum high school GPA of 3.0. Application
deadline: 1/15; 3/1 for financial aid, with a 2/15 priority date. Early and deferred admission are possible.

Getting Accepted

14,222 applied
32% were accepted
1,665 enrolled (37% of accepted)
85% from top tenth of their h.s. class
3.7 average high school GPA
Mean SAT critical reading score: 660
Mean SAT math score: 690
Mean ACT score: 29
83% had SAT critical reading scores over 600
92% had SAT math scores over 600
85% had SAT writing scores over 600
97% had ACT scores over 24
29% had SAT critical reading scores over 700
46% had SAT math scores over 700
31% had SAT writing scores over 700
46% had ACT scores over 30
67 National Merit Scholars

Graduation and After

84% graduated in 4 years
4% graduated in 5 years
1% graduated in 6 years
42% pursued further study
250 organizations recruited on campus

Financial Matters

$34,336 tuition and fees (2007–08)
$11,020 room and board
100% average percent of need met
$27,971 average financial aid amount received
per undergraduate (2006–07 estimated)

ERSKINE COLLEGE

RURAL SETTING ■ PRIVATE ■ INDEPENDENT RELIGIOUS ■ COED
DUE WEST, SOUTH CAROLINA

Web site: www.erskine.edu
Contact: Mr. Bart Walker, Director of Admissions, PO Box 176, Due West, SC 29639
Telephone: 864-379-8830 or toll-free 800-241-8721
Fax: 864-379-8759
E-mail: admissions@erskine.edu

Getting Accepted
874 applied
66% were accepted
165 enrolled (29% of accepted)
30% from top tenth of their h.s. class
3.28 average high school GPA
Mean SAT critical reading score: 545
Mean SAT math score: 546
Mean SAT writing score: 535
Mean ACT score: 23
29% had SAT critical reading scores over 600
25% had SAT math scores over 600
22% had SAT writing scores over 600
41% had ACT scores over 24
4% had SAT critical reading scores over 700
4% had SAT math scores over 700
3% had SAT writing scores over 700
6% had ACT scores over 30

Graduation and After
57% graduated in 4 years
4% graduated in 5 years
1% graduated in 6 years
24% pursued further study
70% had job offers within 6 months
46 organizations recruited on campus

Financial Matters
$21,680 tuition and fees (2007–08)
$7426 room and board
87% average percent of need met
$19,100 average financial aid amount received per undergraduate (2005–06)

Academics

Erskine awards bachelor's, master's, doctoral, and first-professional **degrees**. **Challenging opportunities** include advanced placement credit, double majors, independent study, and a senior project. Special programs include internships, summer session for credit, off-campus study, and study-abroad.

The most frequently chosen **baccalaureate** fields are business/marketing, biological/life sciences, and education. A complete listing of majors at Erskine appears in the Majors by College index beginning on page 471.

The **faculty** at Erskine has 40 full-time members, 85% with terminal degrees. The student-faculty ratio is 12:1.

Students of Erskine

The student body totals 892, of whom 571 are undergraduates. 55.9% are women and 44.1% are men. Students come from 15 states and territories and 4 other countries. 73% are from South Carolina. 0.9% are international students. 6.7% are African American, 0.5% Asian American, and 1.1% Hispanic American. 78% returned for their sophomore year.

Facilities and Resources

Campuswide network is available. Wireless service is available via classrooms, dorm rooms, libraries, student centers. The **library** has 264,053 books and 1,045 subscriptions.

Campus Life

There are 49 active organizations on campus, including a drama/theater group, newspaper, radio station, and choral group. No national or local **fraternities** or **sororities**.

Erskine is a member of the NCAA (Division II). **Intercollegiate sports** (some offering scholarships) include baseball (m), basketball, cross-country running, lacrosse (w), soccer, softball (w), tennis.

Campus Safety

Student safety services include late-night transport/escort service, 24-hour patrols by trained security personnel, and electronically operated dormitory entrances.

Applying

Erskine requires an essay, SAT or ACT, a high school transcript, and 1 recommendation, and in some cases an interview. It recommends an interview. Application deadline: rolling admissions; 4/1 priority date for financial aid.

EUGENE LANG COLLEGE THE NEW SCHOOL FOR LIBERAL ARTS

URBAN SETTING ■ PRIVATE ■ INDEPENDENT ■ COED
NEW YORK, NEW YORK

SPONSOR

Web site: www.lang.edu
Contact: Nicole Curvin, Director of Admissions, 65 West 11th Street, New York, NY 10011-8601
Telephone: 212-229-5665 or toll-free 877-528-3321
Fax: 212-229-5166
E-mail: lang@newschool.edu

Academics

Eugene Lang awards bachelor's **degrees**. **Challenging opportunities** include advanced placement credit, accelerated degree programs, student-designed majors, independent study, and a senior project. Special programs include internships, summer session for credit, off-campus study, and study-abroad.

The most frequently chosen **baccalaureate** field is liberal arts/general studies. A complete listing of majors at Eugene Lang appears in the Majors by College index beginning on page 471.

The **faculty** at Eugene Lang has 53 full-time members, 87% with terminal degrees. The student-faculty ratio is 15:1.

Students of Eugene Lang

The student body is made up of 1,294 undergraduates. 68.9% are women and 31.1% are men. Students come from 49 states and territories and 36 other countries. 32% are from New York. 3.5% are international students. 3.8% are African American, 0.6% American Indian, 5% Asian American, and 6.5% Hispanic American. 73% returned for their sophomore year.

Facilities and Resources

1,200 **computers/terminals** are available on campus for general student use. Students can access the following: computer help desk, free student e-mail accounts, online (class) grades, online (class) registration, online (class) schedules, online portal. Campuswide network is available. 94% of college-owned or -operated housing units are wired for high-speed Internet access. Wireless service is available via entire campus. The 3 **libraries** have 4,137,530 books and 22,150 subscriptions.

Campus Life

There are 25 active organizations on campus, including a drama/theater group, newspaper, and choral group. No national or local **fraternities** or **sororities**.

This institution has no intercollegiate sports.

Campus Safety

Student safety services include 24-hour desk attendants in residence halls, 24-hour emergency telephone alarm devices, and electronically operated dormitory entrances.

Applying

Eugene Lang requires an essay, SAT or ACT, a high school transcript, an interview, and 2 recommendations. It recommends a minimum high school GPA of 3.0. Application deadline: 2/1. Early and deferred admission are possible.

Eugene Lang College offers students of diverse backgrounds the opportunity to design their own paths of study within one of twelve interdisciplinary liberal arts concentrations in the social sciences, arts, and humanities. Students discuss and debate issues in small seminar courses that are never larger than 20 students. They enrich their programs with internships in a wide variety of areas, such as media and publishing, community service, and education. As part of a larger urban university, students can pursue a dual degree at one of The New School's five other divisions. The Greenwich Village location, with all of the intellectual and cultural treasures of New York City, provides a distinct resource for academics and campus life.

Getting Accepted
1,670 applied
63% were accepted
321 enrolled (30% of accepted)
3.19 average high school GPA
Mean SAT critical reading score: 607
Mean SAT math score: 547
Mean SAT writing score: 609
Mean ACT score: 26
61% had SAT critical reading scores over 600
30% had SAT math scores over 600
57% had SAT writing scores over 600
67% had ACT scores over 24
14% had SAT critical reading scores over 700
4% had SAT math scores over 700
15% had SAT writing scores over 700
11% had ACT scores over 30

Graduation and After
30% graduated in 4 years
15% graduated in 5 years
2% graduated in 6 years
82% had job offers within 6 months

Financial Matters
$31,310 tuition and fees (2007–08)
$11,750 room and board
80% average percent of need met
$19,478 average financial aid amount received per undergraduate (2006–07 estimated)

FAIRFIELD UNIVERSITY

SUBURBAN SETTING ■ PRIVATE ■ INDEPENDENT RELIGIOUS ■ COED
FAIRFIELD, CONNECTICUT

Getting Accepted
8,557 applied
55% were accepted
842 enrolled (18% of accepted)
36% from top tenth of their h.s. class
3.4 average high school GPA
41% had SAT critical reading scores over 600
46% had SAT math scores over 600
5% had SAT critical reading scores over 700
6% had SAT math scores over 700
14 National Merit Scholars
32 class presidents

Graduation and After
78% graduated in 4 years
2% graduated in 5 years
1% graduated in 6 years
18% pursued further study (5% arts and sciences, 5% medicine, 4% law)
85% had job offers within 6 months
111 organizations recruited on campus

Financial Matters
$33,905 tuition and fees (2007–08)
$10,430 room and board
66% average percent of need met
$19,101 average financial aid amount received per undergraduate (2006–07 estimated)

Web site: www.fairfield.edu
Contact: Ms. Karen Pellegrino, Director of Admission, 1073 North Benson Road, Fairfield, CT 06824-5195
Telephone: 203-254-4100
Fax: 203-254-4199
E-mail: admis@mail.fairfield.edu

Academics
Fairfield awards associate, bachelor's, and master's **degrees** and post-master's certificates. **Challenging opportunities** include advanced placement credit, student-designed majors, an honors program, double majors, independent study, and a senior project. Special programs include internships, summer session for credit, study-abroad, and Army and Air Force ROTC.

The most frequently chosen **baccalaureate** fields are business/marketing, social sciences, and communications/journalism. A complete listing of majors at Fairfield appears in the Majors by College index beginning on page 471.

The **faculty** at Fairfield has 239 full-time members, 95% with terminal degrees. The student-faculty ratio is 13:1.

Students of Fairfield
The student body totals 5,024, of whom 4,030 are undergraduates. 58.1% are women and 41.9% are men. Students come from 32 states and territories and 17 other countries. 23% are from Connecticut. 0.7% are international students. 2.8% are African American, 0.2% American Indian, 3.1% Asian American, and 5.9% Hispanic American. 82% returned for their sophomore year.

Facilities and Resources
200 **computers/terminals** and 400 ports are available on campus for general student use. Students can access the following: campus intranet, computer help desk, free student e-mail accounts, online (class) grades, online (class) registration, online (class) schedules. Campuswide network is available. 100% of college-owned or -operated housing units are wired for high-speed Internet access. Wireless service is available via classrooms, dorm rooms, libraries, student centers. The **library** has 347,244 books and 1,614 subscriptions.

Campus Life
There are 100 active organizations on campus, including a drama/theater group, newspaper, radio station, television station, and choral group. No national or local **fraternities** or **sororities**.

Fairfield is a member of the NCAA (Division I). **Intercollegiate sports** (some offering scholarships) include baseball (m), basketball, crew, cross-country running, field hockey (w), golf, lacrosse, soccer, softball (w), swimming and diving, tennis, volleyball (w).

Campus Safety
Student safety services include bicycle patrols, late-night transport/escort service, 24-hour emergency telephone alarm devices, 24-hour patrols by trained security personnel, and electronically operated dormitory entrances.

Applying
Fairfield requires an essay, SAT or ACT, a high school transcript, 1 recommendation, rank in upper 20% of high school class, and a minimum high school GPA of 3.0. It recommends an interview. Application deadline: 1/15; 2/15 for financial aid, with a 2/15 priority date. Early and deferred admission are possible.

Florida Institute of Technology

Small-town setting ■ Private ■ Independent ■ Coed
Melbourne, Florida

SPONSOR

Web site: www.fit.edu
Contact: Michael J. Perry, Director of Undergraduate Admission, 150 West University Boulevard, Melbourne, FL 32901-6975
Telephone: 321-674-8030 or toll-free 800-888-4348
Fax: 321-723-9468
E-mail: admission@fit.edu

Academics

Florida Tech awards bachelor's, master's, and doctoral **degrees** and post-master's certificates. **Challenging opportunities** include advanced placement credit, double majors, independent study, and a senior project. Special programs include cooperative education, internships, summer session for credit, study-abroad, and Army ROTC.

The most frequently chosen **baccalaureate** fields are engineering, transportation and materials moving, and biological/life sciences. A complete listing of majors at Florida Tech appears in the Majors by College index beginning on page 471.

The **faculty** at Florida Tech has 224 full-time members, 89% with terminal degrees. The student-faculty ratio is 13:1.

Students of Florida Tech

The student body totals 5,118, of whom 2,594 are undergraduates. 29.6% are women and 70.4% are men. Students come from 50 states and territories and 81 other countries. 54% are from Florida. 21.3% are international students. 3.2% are African American, 0.6% American Indian, 2.1% Asian American, and 5.5% Hispanic American. 75% returned for their sophomore year.

Facilities and Resources

400 **computers/terminals** and 50 ports are available on campus for general student use. Students can access the following: computer help desk, free student e-mail accounts, online (class) grades, online (class) registration, online (class) schedules. Campuswide network is available. 100% of college-owned or -operated housing units are wired for high-speed Internet access. Wireless service is available via classrooms, computer centers, computer labs, learning centers, libraries, student centers. The **library** has 290,582 books and 18,051 subscriptions.

Campus Life

There are 98 active organizations on campus, including a drama/theater group, newspaper, radio station, television station, and choral group. 15% of eligible men and 14% of eligible women are members of national **fraternities**, national **sororities**, and local sororities.

Florida Tech is a member of the NCAA (Division II). **Intercollegiate sports** (some offering scholarships) include baseball (m), basketball, crew, cross-country running, golf, soccer, softball (w), tennis, volleyball (w).

Campus Safety

Student safety services include self-defense education, late-night transport/escort service, 24-hour emergency telephone alarm devices, and 24-hour patrols by trained security personnel.

Applying

Florida Tech requires SAT or ACT, a high school transcript, and a minimum high school GPA of 2.5, and in some cases a minimum high school GPA of 3.0. It recommends a minimum high school GPA of 2.0. Application deadline: rolling admissions; 3/15 priority date for financial aid. Early and deferred admission are possible.

Florida Institute of Technology is a national, doctoral-degree-granting research university on the Atlantic coast with a special focus on undergraduate education in a technologically enriched environment. Florida Tech students describe themselves as determined, ambitious leaders and are provided the opportunity to engage in the academic life of the community early and often. Here, students take hands-on major courses as freshman, work one-on-one with faculty members on funded research, and complete extraordinary senior design projects. They also research autism, build rockets, engineer solar-powered cars and concrete canoes, fly planes, tag sharks, track storms, and program robots to solve Rubik's Cubes.

Getting Accepted
3,027 applied
81% were accepted
681 enrolled (28% of accepted)
27% from top tenth of their h.s. class
3.41 average high school GPA
Mean SAT critical reading score: 561
Mean SAT math score: 586
Mean ACT score: 25
33% had SAT critical reading scores over 600
45% had SAT math scores over 600
74% had ACT scores over 24
5% had SAT critical reading scores over 700
8% had SAT math scores over 700
17% had ACT scores over 30
6 valedictorians

Graduation and After
36% graduated in 4 years
15% graduated in 5 years
3% graduated in 6 years
23% pursued further study (10% arts and sciences, 8% engineering, 2% business)
98% had job offers within 6 months
125 organizations recruited on campus

Financial Matters
$28,920 tuition and fees (2007–08)
$7770 room and board
82% average percent of need met
$22,448 average financial aid amount received per undergraduate (2006–07 estimated)

FLORIDA INTERNATIONAL UNIVERSITY

URBAN SETTING ■ PUBLIC ■ STATE-SUPPORTED ■ COED
MIAMI, FLORIDA

Web site: www.fiu.edu
Contact: Ms. Carmen Brown, Director of Admissions, 11200 SW Eighth
   Street, PC 140, Miami, FL 33199
Telephone: 305-348-3675
Fax: 305-348-3648
E-mail: admiss@fiu.edu

Getting Accepted
14,917 applied
47% were accepted
3.66 average high school GPA
Mean SAT critical reading score: 550
Mean SAT math score: 548
Mean SAT writing score: 485
Mean ACT score: 23
26% had SAT critical reading scores over 600
24% had SAT math scores over 600
19% had SAT writing scores over 600
38% had ACT scores over 24
2% had SAT critical reading scores over 700
2% had SAT math scores over 700
1% had SAT writing scores over 700
2% had ACT scores over 30

Graduation and After
21% graduated in 4 years
19% graduated in 5 years
9% graduated in 6 years
70% had job offers within 6 months
600 organizations recruited on campus

Financial Matters
$3414 resident tuition and fees (2007–08)
$15,813 nonresident tuition and fees (2007–08)
$10,608 room and board

Academics
FIU awards bachelor's, master's, doctoral, and first-professional **degrees**. **Challenging opportunities** include advanced placement credit, accelerated degree programs, freshman honors college, an honors program, double majors, independent study, and a senior project. Special programs include cooperative education, internships, summer session for credit, off-campus study, study-abroad, and Army and Air Force ROTC.

The most frequently chosen **baccalaureate** fields are business/marketing, health professions and related sciences, and psychology. A complete listing of majors at FIU appears in the Majors by College index beginning on page 471.

The **faculty** at FIU has 852 full-time members, 82% with terminal degrees. The student-faculty ratio is 21:1.

Students of FIU
The student body totals 38,290, of whom 31,390 are undergraduates. Students come from 52 states and territories and 175 other countries. 97% are from Florida. 3.6% are international students. 12.6% are African American, 0.2% American Indian, 3.7% Asian American, and 63.9% Hispanic American. 87% returned for their sophomore year.

Facilities and Resources
Students can access the following: free student e-mail accounts, online (class) grades, online (class) registration, online (class) schedules, online financial aid and cashier's information. Campuswide network is available. 100% of college-owned or -operated housing units are wired for high-speed Internet access. Wireless service is available via classrooms, computer centers, computer labs, student centers. The 3 **libraries** have 1,973,612 books and 40,813 subscriptions.

Campus Life
There are 190 active organizations on campus, including a drama/theater group, newspaper, radio station, choral group, and marching band. FIU has national **fraternities** and national **sororities**.

FIU is a member of the NCAA (Division I). **Intercollegiate sports** (some offering scholarships) include baseball (m), basketball, cross-country running, football (m), golf (w), soccer, softball (w), tennis (w), track and field, volleyball (w).

Campus Safety
Student safety services include late-night transport/escort service, 24-hour emergency telephone alarm devices, 24-hour patrols by trained security personnel, and electronically operated dormitory entrances.

Applying
FIU requires SAT or ACT, a high school transcript, and a minimum high school GPA of 3.0, and in some cases 1 recommendation. Application deadline: rolling admissions; 3/1 priority date for financial aid. Early and deferred admission are possible.

FLORIDA STATE UNIVERSITY
SUBURBAN SETTING ■ PUBLIC ■ STATE-SUPPORTED ■ COED
TALLAHASSEE, FLORIDA

Web site: www.fsu.edu
Contact: Ms. Janice Finney, Director of Admissions, PO Box 3062400, Tallahassee, FL 32306-2400
Telephone: 850-644-6200
Fax: 850-644-0197
E-mail: admissions@admin.fsu.edu

Academics

Florida State awards associate, bachelor's, master's, doctoral, and first-professional **degrees** and post-bachelor's and post-master's certificates. **Challenging opportunities** include advanced placement credit, accelerated degree programs, an honors program, double majors, independent study, and a senior project. Special programs include cooperative education, internships, summer session for credit, off-campus study, study-abroad, and Army, Navy, and Air Force ROTC.

The most frequently chosen **baccalaureate** fields are business/marketing, social sciences, and family and consumer sciences. A complete listing of majors at Florida State appears in the Majors by College index beginning on page 471.

The **faculty** at Florida State has 1,353 full-time members, 92% with terminal degrees. The student-faculty ratio is 24:1.

Students of Florida State

The student body totals 40,555, of whom 31,595 are undergraduates. 55.5% are women and 44.5% are men. Students come from 51 states and territories and 118 other countries. 88% are from Florida. 0.4% are international students. 11.1% are African American, 0.6% American Indian, 3.3% Asian American, and 11.3% Hispanic American. 88% returned for their sophomore year.

Facilities and Resources

3,771 **computers/terminals** are available on campus for general student use. Students can access the following: campus intranet, computer help desk, free student e-mail accounts, online (class) grades, online (class) registration, online (class) schedules, course home pages, course search, online fee payment. Campuswide network is available. Wireless service is available via entire campus. The 9 **libraries** have 2,945,078 books and 58,093 subscriptions.

Campus Life

There are 266 active organizations on campus, including a drama/theater group, newspaper, radio station, television station, choral group, and marching band. 13% of eligible men and 15% of eligible women are members of national **fraternities**, national **sororities**, local fraternities, and local sororities.

Florida State is a member of the NCAA (Division I). **Intercollegiate sports** (some offering scholarships) include baseball (m), basketball, cheerleading, cross-country running, football (m), golf, soccer (w), softball (w), swimming and diving, tennis, track and field, volleyball (w).

Campus Safety

Student safety services include late-night transport/escort service, 24-hour emergency telephone alarm devices, 24-hour patrols by trained security personnel, and electronically operated dormitory entrances.

Applying

Florida State requires an essay, SAT or ACT, and a high school transcript, and in some cases audition. It recommends a minimum high school GPA of 3.0. Application deadline: 2/14. Early admission is possible.

Getting Accepted
24,343 applied
55% were accepted
6,124 enrolled (46% of accepted)
26% from top tenth of their h.s. class
3.63 average high school GPA
Mean SAT critical reading score: 589
Mean SAT math score: 595
Mean SAT writing score: 565
Mean ACT score: 26
44% had SAT critical reading scores over 600
48% had SAT math scores over 600
32% had SAT writing scores over 600
75% had ACT scores over 24
6% had SAT critical reading scores over 700
6% had SAT math scores over 700
4% had SAT writing scores over 700
8% had ACT scores over 30
15 National Merit Scholars

Graduation and After
21% pursued further study
78% had job offers within 6 months
1044 organizations recruited on campus

Financial Matters
$3355 resident tuition and fees (2007–08)
$16,487 nonresident tuition and fees (2007–08)
$8000 room and board
67% average percent of need met
$8890 average financial aid amount received per undergraduate (2006–07 estimated)

Fordham, the Jesuit University of New York, offers an exceptional education distinguished by the Jesuit tradition, located in the "capital of the world." Fordham offers three undergraduate colleges on two residential campuses—the historic Rose Hill campus in the Bronx and the cosmopolitan Lincoln Center campus in the cultural heart of Manhattan. The world-class faculty members are committed to both teaching and research, challenging each student to excel, and the low student-faculty ratio of 12:1 ensures individual attention. Fordham offers more than sixty-five majors, 130 extracurricular activities, and one of the nation's most successful internship programs in the world's most competitive market.

Getting Accepted
18,161 applied
47% were accepted
1,722 enrolled (20% of accepted)
41% from top tenth of their h.s. class
3.7 average high school GPA
Mean SAT critical reading score: 602
Mean SAT math score: 599
Mean SAT writing score: 587
Mean ACT score: 26
57% had SAT critical reading scores over 600
54% had SAT math scores over 600
47% had SAT writing scores over 600
76% had ACT scores over 24
11% had SAT critical reading scores over 700
8% had SAT math scores over 700
8% had SAT writing scores over 700
12% had ACT scores over 30

Graduation and After
72% graduated in 4 years
4% graduated in 5 years
1% graduated in 6 years
25% pursued further study (7% arts and sciences, 6% law, 5% business)

Financial Matters
$32,857 tuition and fees (2007–08)
$12,300 room and board
77% average percent of need met
$19,953 average financial aid amount received per undergraduate (2004–05)

FORDHAM UNIVERSITY
URBAN SETTING ■ PRIVATE ■ INDEPENDENT RELIGIOUS ■ COED
NEW YORK, NEW YORK

Web site: www.fordham.edu
Contact: Mr. John W. Buckley, Dean of Admission, Duane Library, 441 East Fordham Road, New York, NY 10458
Telephone: 718-817-4000 or toll-free 800-FORDHAM
Fax: 718-367-9404
E-mail: enroll@fordham.edu

Academics
Fordham awards bachelor's, master's, doctoral, and first-professional **degrees** and post-master's certificates (branch locations at Rose Hill and Lincoln Center). **Challenging opportunities** include advanced placement credit, accelerated degree programs, student-designed majors, an honors program, double majors, independent study, and a senior project. Special programs include internships, summer session for credit, off-campus study, study-abroad, and Army, Navy, and Air Force ROTC. A complete listing of majors at Fordham appears in the Majors by College index beginning on page 471.

The student-faculty ratio is 12:1.

Students of Fordham
The student body totals 14,732, of whom 7,701 are undergraduates. 58.4% are women and 41.6% are men. Students come from 53 states and territories and 48 other countries. 55% are from New York. 1.5% are international students. 5.5% are African American, 0.3% American Indian, 6.2% Asian American, and 12.3% Hispanic American. 90% returned for their sophomore year.

Facilities and Resources
1,400 **computers/terminals** are available on campus for general student use. Students can access the following: online (class) registration. Campuswide network is available. The 4 **libraries** have 2,421,980 books and 32,300 subscriptions.

Campus Life
There are 133 active organizations on campus, including a drama/theater group, newspaper, radio station, choral group, and marching band. No national or local **fraternities** or **sororities**.

Fordham is a member of the NCAA (Division I). **Intercollegiate sports** (some offering scholarships) include baseball (m), basketball, crew (w), cross-country running, football (m), golf (m), soccer, softball (w), squash (m), swimming and diving, tennis, track and field, volleyball (w), water polo (m).

Campus Safety
Student safety services include security at each campus entrance and at residence halls, late-night transport/escort service, 24-hour emergency telephone alarm devices, 24-hour patrols by trained security personnel, student patrols, and electronically operated dormitory entrances.

Applying
Fordham requires an essay, SAT or ACT, a high school transcript, and 1 recommendation, and in some cases an interview. It recommends SAT Subject Tests and a minimum high school GPA of 3.0. Application deadline: 1/15; 2/1 for financial aid, with a 2/1 priority date. Early and deferred admission are possible.

Franciscan University of Steubenville

Suburban setting ■ Private ■ Independent Religious ■ Coed
Steubenville, Ohio

Web site: www.franciscan.edu
Contact: Mrs. Margaret Weber, Director of Admissions, 1235 University Boulevard, Steubenville, OH 43952-1763
Telephone: 740-283-6226 or toll-free 800-783-6220
Fax: 740-284-5456
E-mail: admissions@franciscan.edu

Academics

Franciscan awards associate, bachelor's, and master's **degrees. Challenging opportunities** include advanced placement credit, accelerated degree programs, an honors program, double majors, independent study, and a senior project. Special programs include internships, summer session for credit, study-abroad, and Army ROTC.

The most frequently chosen **baccalaureate** fields are theology and religious vocations, health professions and related sciences, and business/marketing. A complete listing of majors at Franciscan appears in the Majors by College index beginning on page 471.

The **faculty** at Franciscan has 115 full-time members, 72% with terminal degrees. The student-faculty ratio is 15:1.

Students of Franciscan

The student body totals 2,434, of whom 2,033 are undergraduates. 59.8% are women and 40.2% are men. Students come from 51 states and territories and 13 other countries. 22% are from Ohio. 1.1% are international students. 0.5% are African American, 0.5% American Indian, 1.4% Asian American, and 1.3% Hispanic American. 88% returned for their sophomore year.

Facilities and Resources

126 **computers/terminals** are available on campus for general student use. Students can access the following: campus intranet, computer help desk, free student e-mail accounts, online (class) grades, online (class) registration, online (class) schedules. Campuswide network is available. The **library** has 236,689 books and 392 subscriptions.

Campus Life

There are 35 active organizations on campus, including a drama/theater group, newspaper, radio station, and choral group. 1% of eligible women are members of national **sororities**.

Franciscan is a member of the NCAA. **Intercollegiate sports** include baseball (m), basketball, cross-country running, rugby (m), soccer, softball (w), track and field, volleyball (w).

Campus Safety

Student safety services include late-night transport/escort service, 24-hour emergency telephone alarm devices, 24-hour patrols by trained security personnel, and student patrols.

Applying

Franciscan requires an essay, SAT or ACT, a high school transcript, SAT or ACT, and a minimum high school GPA of 2.4, and in some cases recommendations. It recommends an interview. Application deadline: rolling admissions; 4/15 priority date for financial aid. Early and deferred admission are possible.

Getting Accepted

1,273 applied
81% were accepted
442 enrolled (43% of accepted)
33% from top tenth of their h.s. class
3.60 average high school GPA
Mean SAT critical reading score: 602
Mean SAT math score: 577
Mean ACT score: 25
50% had SAT critical reading scores over 600
41% had SAT math scores over 600
54% had ACT scores over 24
14% had SAT critical reading scores over 700
6% had SAT math scores over 700
14% had ACT scores over 30
9 valedictorians

Graduation and After

55% graduated in 4 years
10% graduated in 5 years
3% graduated in 6 years
29% pursued further study (3% theology, 2% arts and sciences, 2% business)
84% had job offers within 6 months
158 organizations recruited on campus

Financial Matters

$18,180 tuition and fees (2007–08)
$6300 room and board
62% average percent of need met
$10,631 average financial aid amount received per undergraduate

FRANKLIN & MARSHALL COLLEGE

SUBURBAN SETTING ■ PRIVATE ■ INDEPENDENT ■ COED
LANCASTER, PENNSYLVANIA

Web site: www.fandm.edu
Contact: Sara Harberson, Vice President for Enrollment Management, PO Box 3003, Lancaster, PA 17604-3003
Telephone: 717-291-3953
Fax: 717-291-4389
E-mail: admission@fandm.edu

Getting Accepted

5,018 applied
37% were accepted
569 enrolled (30% of accepted)
57% from top tenth of their h.s. class
3.57 average high school GPA
Mean SAT critical reading score: 641
Mean SAT math score: 654
77% had SAT critical reading scores over 600
86% had SAT math scores over 600
22% had SAT critical reading scores over 700
23% had SAT math scores over 700

Graduation and After

79% graduated in 4 years
5% graduated in 5 years
25% pursued further study (8% medicine, 7% arts and sciences, 7% law)
50% had job offers within 6 months
27 organizations recruited on campus

Financial Matters

$36,480 tuition and fees (2007–08)
$9174 room and board
96% average percent of need met
$26,165 average financial aid amount received per undergraduate (2006–07 estimated)

Academics

F&M awards bachelor's **degrees**. **Challenging opportunities** include advanced placement credit, accelerated degree programs, student-designed majors, an honors program, double majors, independent study, and a senior project. Special programs include internships, summer session for credit, off-campus study, and study-abroad.

The most frequently chosen **baccalaureate** fields are social sciences, health professions and related sciences, and biological/life sciences. A complete listing of majors at F&M appears in the Majors by College index beginning on page 471.

The **faculty** at F&M has 184 full-time members, 97% with terminal degrees. The student-faculty ratio is 10:1.

Students of F&M

The student body is made up of 2,104 undergraduates. 49.4% are women and 50.6% are men. Students come from 40 states and territories and 47 other countries. 34% are from Pennsylvania. 7.7% are international students. 3.7% are African American, 0.3% American Indian, 4.3% Asian American, and 3.9% Hispanic American. 91% returned for their sophomore year.

Facilities and Resources

125 **computers/terminals** are available on campus for general student use. Students can access the following: campus intranet, computer help desk, free student e-mail accounts, online (class) grades, online (class) registration, online (class) schedules, online degree audit, unofficial transcripts, course material. Campuswide network is available. 100% of college-owned or -operated housing units are wired for high-speed Internet access. Wireless service is available via entire campus. The 2 **libraries** have 494,099 books and 2,088 subscriptions.

Campus Life

There are 120 active organizations on campus, including a drama/theater group, newspaper, radio station, television station, and choral group. 26% of eligible men and 12% of eligible women are members of national **fraternities** and national **sororities**.

F&M is a member of the NCAA (Division III). **Intercollegiate sports** include baseball (m), basketball, crew (w), cross-country running, field hockey (w), football (m), golf, lacrosse, soccer, softball (w), squash, swimming and diving, tennis, track and field, volleyball (w), wrestling (m).

Campus Safety

Student safety services include residence hall security, campus security connected to city police and fire company, late-night transport/escort service, 24-hour emergency telephone alarm devices, 24-hour patrols by trained security personnel, and electronically operated dormitory entrances.

Applying

F&M requires an essay, a high school transcript, and 2 recommendations. It recommends SAT or ACT and an interview. Application deadline: 2/1; 3/1 for financial aid, with a 2/1 priority date. Early and deferred admission are possible.

FURMAN UNIVERSITY

SUBURBAN SETTING ■ PRIVATE ■ INDEPENDENT ■ COED
GREENVILLE, SOUTH CAROLINA

Web site: www.furman.edu
Contact: Mr. David R. O'Cain, Director of Admissions, 3300 Poinsett
   Highway, Greenville, SC 29613
Telephone: 864-294-2034
Fax: 864-294-2018
E-mail: admissions@furman.edu

Academics

Furman awards bachelor's and master's **degrees** and post-bachelor's certificates. **Challenging opportunities** include advanced placement credit, accelerated degree programs, student-designed majors, double majors, independent study, and a senior project. Special programs include internships, summer session for credit, study-abroad, and Army ROTC.

   The most frequently chosen **baccalaureate** fields are social sciences, business/marketing, and history. A complete listing of majors at Furman appears in the Majors by College index beginning on page 471.

   The **faculty** at Furman has 236 full-time members, 96% with terminal degrees. The student-faculty ratio is 11:1.

Students of Furman

The student body totals 2,951, of whom 2,774 are undergraduates. 56.1% are women and 43.9% are men. Students come from 47 states and territories and 46 other countries. 30% are from South Carolina. 1.9% are international students. 6.8% are African American, 0.2% American Indian, 2.2% Asian American, and 1.4% Hispanic American. 90% returned for their sophomore year.

Facilities and Resources

340 **computers/terminals** and 3,000 ports are available on campus for general student use. Students can access the following: campus intranet, computer help desk, free student e-mail accounts, online (class) grades, online (class) registration, online (class) schedules. Campuswide network is available. 100% of college-owned or -operated housing units are wired for high-speed Internet access. Wireless service is available via classrooms, computer centers, computer labs, learning centers, libraries, student centers. The 3 **libraries** have 453,211 books and 2,052 subscriptions.

Campus Life

There are 130 active organizations on campus, including a drama/theater group, newspaper, radio station, television station, choral group, and marching band. 33% of eligible men and 44% of eligible women are members of national **fraternities** and national **sororities**.

   Furman is a member of the NCAA (Division I). **Intercollegiate sports** (some offering scholarships) include baseball (m), basketball, cheerleading, cross-country running, football (m), golf, soccer, softball (w), tennis, track and field, volleyball (w).

Campus Safety

Student safety services include late-night transport/escort service, 24-hour emergency telephone alarm devices, 24-hour patrols by trained security personnel, student patrols, and electronically operated dormitory entrances.

Applying

Furman requires an essay and a high school transcript, and in some cases an interview. It recommends SAT or ACT. Application deadline: 1/15; 1/15 for financial aid. Early admission is possible.

Getting Accepted

3,879 applied
56% were accepted
700 enrolled (32% of accepted)
63% from top tenth of their h.s. class
3.54 average high school GPA
67% had SAT critical reading scores over 600
67% had SAT math scores over 600
86% had ACT scores over 24
22% had SAT critical reading scores over 700
18% had SAT math scores over 700
29% had ACT scores over 30
27 National Merit Scholars
32 valedictorians

Graduation and After

79% graduated in 4 years
4% graduated in 5 years
41% pursued further study (11% arts and
   sciences, 9% law, 6% medicine)
54% had job offers within 6 months
69 organizations recruited on campus

Financial Matters

$31,560 tuition and fees (2007–08)
$8064 room and board
83% average percent of need met
$23,132 average financial aid amount received
   per undergraduate (2006–07 estimated)

GEORGE FOX UNIVERSITY

SMALL-TOWN SETTING ■ PRIVATE ■ INDEPENDENT RELIGIOUS ■ COED
NEWBERG, OREGON

Getting Accepted
1,264 applied
83% were accepted
435 enrolled (41% of accepted)
26% from top tenth of their h.s. class
3.51 average high school GPA
Mean SAT critical reading score: 541
Mean SAT math score: 534
Mean SAT writing score: 522
Mean ACT score: 22
25% had SAT critical reading scores over 600
23% had SAT math scores over 600
20% had SAT writing scores over 600
40% had ACT scores over 24
6% had SAT critical reading scores over 700
2% had SAT math scores over 700
2% had SAT writing scores over 700
6% had ACT scores over 30
5 National Merit Scholars
31 valedictorians

Graduation and After
58% graduated in 4 years
7% graduated in 5 years
24% pursued further study (11% education, 8% arts and sciences, 3% medicine)
200 organizations recruited on campus

Financial Matters
$23,790 tuition and fees (2007–08)
$7600 room and board
63% average percent of need met
$16,709 average financial aid amount received per undergraduate (2006–07 estimated)

Web site: www.georgefox.edu
Contact: Mr. Ryan Dougherty, Director of Undergraduate Admissions, 414 North Meridian Street, Newberg, OR 97132
Telephone: 503-554-2240 or toll-free 800-765-4369
Fax: 503-554-3110
E-mail: admissions@georgefox.edu

Academics
George Fox awards bachelor's, master's, doctoral, and first-professional **degrees** and post-bachelor's and post-master's certificates. **Challenging opportunities** include advanced placement credit, accelerated degree programs, student-designed majors, an honors program, double majors, independent study, and a senior project. Special programs include internships, summer session for credit, off-campus study, study-abroad, and Air Force ROTC.

The most frequently chosen **baccalaureate** fields are business/marketing, interdisciplinary studies, and visual and performing arts. A complete listing of majors at George Fox appears in the Majors by College index beginning on page 471.

The **faculty** at George Fox has 167 full-time members, 67% with terminal degrees. The student-faculty ratio is 11:1.

Students of George Fox
The student body totals 3,293, of whom 1,934 are undergraduates. 62.6% are women and 37.4% are men. Students come from 27 states and territories and 9 other countries. 72% are from Oregon. 2.3% are international students. 1.3% are African American, 1.7% American Indian, 5.1% Asian American, and 3.9% Hispanic American. 80% returned for their sophomore year.

Facilities and Resources
154 **computers/terminals** and 200 ports are available on campus for general student use. Students can access the following: campus intranet, computer help desk, free student e-mail accounts, online (class) grades, online (class) registration, online (class) schedules. Campuswide network is available. 100% of college-owned or -operated housing units are wired for high-speed Internet access. Wireless service is available via entire campus. The **library** has 208,048 books and 3,900 subscriptions.

Campus Life
There are 20 active organizations on campus, including a drama/theater group, newspaper, radio station, and choral group. No national or local **fraternities** or **sororities**.

George Fox is a member of the NCAA (Division III). **Intercollegiate sports** include baseball (m), basketball, cross-country running, golf, soccer, softball (w), tennis, track and field, volleyball (w).

Campus Safety
Student safety services include late-night transport/escort service, 24-hour emergency telephone alarm devices, 24-hour patrols by trained security personnel, and electronically operated dormitory entrances.

Applying
George Fox requires an essay, SAT or ACT, a high school transcript, and 2 recommendations, and in some cases an interview. It recommends an interview and a minimum high school GPA of 2.6. Application deadline: 2/1; 2/1 priority date for financial aid. Deferred admission is possible.

GEORGETOWN COLLEGE

SUBURBAN SETTING ■ PRIVATE ■ INDEPENDENT RELIGIOUS ■ COED
GEORGETOWN, KENTUCKY

Web site: www.georgetowncollege.edu
Contact: Mr. Johnnie Johnson, Director of Admissions, 400 East College Street, Georgetown, KY 40324
Telephone: 502-863-8009 or toll-free 800-788-9985
Fax: 502-868-7733
E-mail: admissions@georgetowncollege.edu

Academics

Georgetown College awards bachelor's and master's **degrees**. **Challenging opportunities** include advanced placement credit, student-designed majors, an honors program, double majors, independent study, and a senior project. Special programs include cooperative education, internships, summer session for credit, off-campus study, study-abroad, and Army and Air Force ROTC.

The most frequently chosen **baccalaureate** fields are business/marketing, psychology, and communications/journalism. A complete listing of majors at Georgetown College appears in the Majors by College index beginning on page 471.

The **faculty** at Georgetown College has 111 full-time members, 93% with terminal degrees. The student-faculty ratio is 12:1.

Students of Georgetown College

The student body totals 1,903, of whom 1,368 are undergraduates. 56.9% are women and 43.1% are men. Students come from 29 states and territories and 10 other countries. 86% are from Kentucky. 1.1% are international students. 4.3% are African American, 0.1% American Indian, 0.5% Asian American, and 0.7% Hispanic American. 79% returned for their sophomore year.

Facilities and Resources

175 **computers/terminals** are available on campus for general student use. Students can access the following: campus intranet, computer help desk, free student e-mail accounts, online (class) grades, online (class) registration, online (class) schedules. Campuswide network is available. 100% of college-owned or -operated housing units are wired for high-speed Internet access. Wireless service is available via classrooms, computer centers, computer labs, dorm rooms, learning centers, libraries. The 2 **libraries** have 167,547 books and 526 subscriptions.

Campus Life

There are 97 active organizations on campus, including a drama/theater group, newspaper, radio station, and choral group. 33% of eligible men and 48% of eligible women are members of national **fraternities**, national **sororities**, and local fraternities.

Georgetown College is a member of the NAIA. **Intercollegiate sports** (some offering scholarships) include baseball (m), basketball, cheerleading (w), cross-country running, football (m), golf, soccer, softball (w), tennis, track and field, volleyball (w).

Campus Safety

Student safety services include late-night transport/escort service and 24-hour patrols by trained security personnel.

Applying

Georgetown College requires SAT or ACT, a high school transcript, and a minimum high school GPA of 2.5, and in some cases an essay, an interview, and recommendations. It recommends ACT. Application deadline: 8/1; 2/15 priority date for financial aid. Deferred admission is possible.

Getting Accepted

1,452 applied
85% were accepted
368 enrolled (30% of accepted)
39% from top tenth of their h.s. class
3.50 average high school GPA
Mean SAT critical reading score: 559
Mean SAT math score: 554
Mean ACT score: 23
24% had SAT critical reading scores over 600
28% had SAT math scores over 600
43% had ACT scores over 24
8% had SAT critical reading scores over 700
7% had ACT scores over 30
14 valedictorians

Graduation and After

49% graduated in 4 years
11% graduated in 5 years
1% graduated in 6 years
53% pursued further study
83% had job offers within 6 months
45 organizations recruited on campus

Financial Matters

$22,360 tuition and fees (2007–08)
$6380 room and board
90% average percent of need met
$19,510 average financial aid amount received per undergraduate (2006–07 estimated)

GEORGETOWN UNIVERSITY

URBAN SETTING ■ PRIVATE ■ INDEPENDENT RELIGIOUS ■ COED
WASHINGTON, DISTRICT OF COLUMBIA

Web site: www.georgetown.edu
Contact: Mr. Charles A. Deacon, Dean of Undergraduate Admissions, 37th
and O Street, NW, Washington, DC 20057
Telephone: 202-687-3600
Fax: 202-687-5084

Getting Accepted
16,163 applied
21% were accepted
1,582 enrolled (47% of accepted)
90% from top tenth of their h.s. class
90% had SAT critical reading scores over 600
90% had SAT math scores over 600
50% had SAT critical reading scores over 700
43% had SAT math scores over 700

Graduation and After
29% pursued further study (7% arts and sciences, 7% law, 6% medicine)
65% had job offers within 6 months
277 organizations recruited on campus

Financial Matters
$35,568 tuition and fees (2007–08)
$12,146 room and board
100% average percent of need met
$27,317 average financial aid amount received per undergraduate (2006–07 estimated)

Academics
Georgetown awards bachelor's, master's, doctoral, and first-professional **degrees. Challenging opportunities** include advanced placement credit, student-designed majors, an honors program, double majors, independent study, and a senior project. Special programs include internships, summer session for credit, off-campus study, study-abroad, and Army, Navy, and Air Force ROTC.

The most frequently chosen **baccalaureate** fields are social sciences, business/marketing, and English. A complete listing of majors at Georgetown appears in the Majors by College index beginning on page 471.

The **faculty** at Georgetown has 824 full-time members, 89% with terminal degrees. The student-faculty ratio is 11:1.

Students of Georgetown
The student body totals 14,826, of whom 7,038 are undergraduates. 54.5% are women and 45.5% are men. Students come from 53 states and territories and 83 other countries. 2% are from District of Columbia. 5.5% are international students. 6.9% are African American, 0.1% American Indian, 9.1% Asian American, and 6.7% Hispanic American. 96% returned for their sophomore year.

Facilities and Resources
400 **computers/terminals** are available on campus for general student use. Students can access the following: online (class) registration, online grade reports. Campuswide network is available. The 7 **libraries** have 2,472,239 books and 31,099 subscriptions.

Campus Life
There are 138 active organizations on campus, including a drama/theater group, newspaper, radio station, television station, and choral group. No national or local **fraternities** or **sororities**.

Georgetown is a member of the NCAA (Division I). **Intercollegiate sports** (some offering scholarships) include baseball (m), basketball, crew, cross-country running, field hockey (w), football (m), golf (m), lacrosse, sailing, soccer, swimming and diving, tennis, track and field, volleyball (w).

Campus Safety
Student safety services include student guards at residence halls and academic facilities, late-night transport/escort service, 24-hour emergency telephone alarm devices, 24-hour patrols by trained security personnel, and electronically operated dormitory entrances.

Applying
Georgetown requires an essay, SAT or ACT, a high school transcript, an interview, and 2 recommendations. It recommends SAT Subject Tests. Application deadline: 1/10; 2/1 for financial aid. Deferred admission is possible.

THE GEORGE WASHINGTON UNIVERSITY

URBAN SETTING ■ PRIVATE ■ INDEPENDENT ■ COED
WASHINGTON, DISTRICT OF COLUMBIA

Web site: www.gwu.edu
Contact: Dr. Kathryn M. Napper, Director of Admission, Office of
   Undergraduate Admissions, Washington, DC 20052
Telephone: 202-994-6040
Fax: 202-994-0325
E-mail: gwadm@gwis2.circ.gwu.edu

Academics

GW awards associate, bachelor's, master's, doctoral, and first-professional **degrees** and post-bachelor's and post-master's certificates. **Challenging opportunities** include advanced placement credit, accelerated degree programs, student-designed majors, an honors program, double majors, independent study, and a senior project. Special programs include cooperative education, internships, summer session for credit, off-campus study, study-abroad, and Army, Navy, and Air Force ROTC.

The most frequently chosen **baccalaureate** fields are social sciences, business/marketing, and psychology. A complete listing of majors at GW appears in the Majors by College index beginning on page 471.

The **faculty** at GW has 824 full-time members, 94% with terminal degrees. The student-faculty ratio is 13:1.

Students of GW

The student body totals 24,531, of whom 10,813 are undergraduates. 55.4% are women and 44.6% are men. Students come from 55 states and territories and 101 other countries. 2% are from District of Columbia. 4.5% are international students. 5.9% are African American, 0.3% American Indian, 9.8% Asian American, and 5.4% Hispanic American. 92% returned for their sophomore year.

Facilities and Resources

550 **computers/terminals** are available on campus for general student use. Campuswide network is available. The 3 **libraries** have 1,984,094 books and 15,365 subscriptions.

Campus Life

There are 208 active organizations on campus, including a drama/theater group, newspaper, radio station, television station, choral group, and marching band. 16% of eligible men and 13% of eligible women are members of national **fraternities** and national **sororities**.

GW is a member of the NCAA (Division I). **Intercollegiate sports** (some offering scholarships) include baseball (m), basketball, crew, cross-country running, golf (m), gymnastics (w), soccer, swimming and diving, tennis, volleyball (w), water polo (m).

Campus Safety

Student safety services include late-night transport/escort service, 24-hour emergency telephone alarm devices, 24-hour patrols by trained security personnel, and electronically operated dormitory entrances.

Applying

GW requires an essay, SAT or ACT, a high school transcript, and 2 recommendations. It recommends an interview. Application deadline: 1/15; 2/1 for financial aid, with a 2/1 priority date. Early and deferred admission are possible.

Getting Accepted

19,426 applied
38% were accepted
2,454 enrolled (33% of accepted)
65% from top tenth of their h.s. class
Mean SAT critical reading score: 640
Mean SAT math score: 640
Mean ACT score: 28
74% had SAT critical reading scores over 600
75% had SAT math scores over 600
71% had SAT writing scores over 600
91% had ACT scores over 24
22% had SAT critical reading scores over 700
22% had SAT math scores over 700
18% had SAT writing scores over 700
28% had ACT scores over 30
36 National Merit Scholars

Graduation and After

72% graduated in 4 years
5% graduated in 5 years
1% graduated in 6 years
21% pursued further study
383 organizations recruited on campus

Financial Matters

$39,240 tuition and fees (2007–08)
$11,520 room and board
91% average percent of need met
$33,196 average financial aid amount received
   per undergraduate (2005–06)

GEORGIA INSTITUTE OF TECHNOLOGY

URBAN SETTING ■ PUBLIC ■ STATE-SUPPORTED ■ COED, PRIMARILY MEN
ATLANTA, GEORGIA

Web site: www.gatech.edu

Contact: Ms. Ingrid Hayes, Director of Admissions (Undergraduate), Georgia Institute of Technology, Office of Undergraduate Admission, Atlanta, GA 30332-0320

Telephone: 404-894-4154

Fax: 404-894-9511

E-mail: admission@gatech.edu

Getting Accepted

9,664 applied
63% were accepted
2,654 enrolled (43% of accepted)
60% from top tenth of their h.s. class
3.73 average high school GPA
Mean SAT critical reading score: 656
Mean SAT math score: 700
Mean SAT writing score: 629
Mean ACT score: 29
73% had SAT critical reading scores over 600
93% had SAT math scores over 600
67% had SAT writing scores over 600
96% had ACT scores over 24
21% had SAT critical reading scores over 700
45% had SAT math scores over 700
16% had SAT writing scores over 700
37% had ACT scores over 30
101 National Merit Scholars

Graduation and After

33% graduated in 4 years
36% graduated in 5 years
8% graduated in 6 years
33% pursued further study (14% engineering, 5% medicine, 3% arts and sciences)
85% had job offers within 6 months
550 organizations recruited on campus

Financial Matters

$5642 resident tuition and fees (2007–08)
$23,366 nonresident tuition and fees (2007–08)
$7328 room and board
51% average percent of need met
$9033 average financial aid amount received per undergraduate (2006–07 estimated)

Academics

Georgia Tech awards bachelor's, master's, and doctoral **degrees**. **Challenging opportunities** include advanced placement credit, accelerated degree programs, student-designed majors, an honors program, double majors, independent study, and a senior project. Special programs include cooperative education, internships, summer session for credit, off-campus study, study-abroad, and Army, Navy, and Air Force ROTC.

The most frequently chosen **baccalaureate** fields are engineering, business/marketing, and computer and information sciences. A complete listing of majors at Georgia Tech appears in the Majors by College index beginning on page 471.

The **faculty** at Georgia Tech has 863 full-time members, 98% with terminal degrees. The student-faculty ratio is 14:1.

Students of Georgia Tech

The student body totals 18,742, of whom 12,565 are undergraduates. 29.7% are women and 70.3% are men. Students come from 53 states and territories and 74 other countries. 71% are from Georgia. 4.7% are international students. 6.7% are African American, 0.3% American Indian, 16.2% Asian American, and 4.7% Hispanic American. 92% returned for their sophomore year.

Facilities and Resources

1,996 **computers/terminals** are available on campus for general student use. Students can access the following: campus intranet, computer help desk, free student e-mail accounts, online (class) grades, online (class) registration, online (class) schedules. Campuswide network is available. 100% of college-owned or -operated housing units are wired for high-speed Internet access. Wireless service is available via classrooms, computer centers, computer labs, dorm rooms, learning centers, libraries, student centers. The 2 **libraries** have 2,449,323 books and 34,576 subscriptions.

Campus Life

There are 311 active organizations on campus, including a drama/theater group, newspaper, radio station, television station, choral group, and marching band. 23% of eligible men and 31% of eligible women are members of national **fraternities**, national **sororities**, and local sororities.

Georgia Tech is a member of the NCAA (Division I). **Intercollegiate sports** (some offering scholarships) include baseball (m), basketball, cheerleading, cross-country running, football (m), golf (m), softball (w), swimming and diving, tennis, track and field, volleyball (w).

Campus Safety

Student safety services include self defense education, lighted pathways and walks, video cameras, late-night transport/escort service, 24-hour emergency telephone alarm devices, 24-hour patrols by trained security personnel, and electronically operated dormitory entrances.

Applying

Georgia Tech requires an essay, SAT or ACT, and a high school transcript. Application deadline: 1/15; 3/1 for financial aid, with a 3/1 priority date. Early admission is possible.

GEORGIA STATE UNIVERSITY

URBAN SETTING ■ PUBLIC ■ STATE-SUPPORTED ■ COED
ATLANTA, GEORGIA

Web site: www.gsu.edu
Contact: Daniel Niccum, Associate Director of Admissions, PO Box 4009, Atlanta, GA 30302-4009
Telephone: 404-651-4110
Fax: 404-651-4811
E-mail: dniccum@gsu.edu

Academics

Georgia State awards bachelor's, master's, doctoral, and first-professional **degrees** and post-bachelor's, post-master's, and first-professional certificates. **Challenging opportunities** include advanced placement credit, accelerated degree programs, an honors program, double majors, and independent study. Special programs include cooperative education, internships, summer session for credit, off-campus study, study-abroad, and Army, Navy, and Air Force ROTC.

The most frequently chosen **baccalaureate** fields are business/marketing, social sciences, and psychology. A complete listing of majors at Georgia State appears in the Majors by College index beginning on page 471.

The **faculty** at Georgia State has 1,086 full-time members, 84% with terminal degrees. The student-faculty ratio is 17:1.

Students of Georgia State

The student body totals 27,137, of whom 19,904 are undergraduates. 60.7% are women and 39.3% are men. Students come from 49 states and territories and 144 other countries. 94% are from Georgia. 2.7% are international students. 29.3% are African American, 0.3% American Indian, 10.5% Asian American, and 4.5% Hispanic American. 80% returned for their sophomore year.

Facilities and Resources

1,000 **computers/terminals** are available on campus for general student use. Students can access the following: computer help desk, free student e-mail accounts, online (class) registration, online (class) schedules. Campuswide network is available. 100% of college-owned or -operated housing units are wired for high-speed Internet access. Wireless service is available via classrooms, computer labs, learning centers, libraries, student centers. The 2 **libraries** have 1,482,306 books and 7,788 subscriptions.

Campus Life

There are 270 active organizations on campus, including a drama/theater group, newspaper, radio station, television station, and choral group. Georgia State has national **fraternities** and national **sororities**.

Georgia State is a member of the NCAA (Division I). **Intercollegiate sports** (some offering scholarships) include baseball (m), basketball, cross-country running, golf, soccer, softball (w), tennis, track and field, volleyball (w).

Campus Safety

Student safety services include late-night transport/escort service, 24-hour emergency telephone alarm devices, 24-hour patrols by trained security personnel, and electronically operated dormitory entrances.

Applying

Georgia State requires SAT or ACT, a high school transcript, college prep high school curriculum, and a minimum high school GPA of 2.8, and in some cases SAT Subject Tests and an interview. It recommends an essay. Application deadline: 3/1; 11/1 for financial aid, with a 4/1 priority date. Deferred admission is possible.

Undergraduate education is a strong focus at Georgia State, with small classes and opportunities for students to work with faculty members in a research setting. There are a total of 1,046 faculty members in more than 250 fields of study. Students can live in University housing and participate in over 200 different student organizations. Georgia State is located in the heart of Atlanta, an exciting metropolis that offers a variety of job and internship opportunities. Students can walk to such places as the State Capitol and CNN Center or take the rapid transit system to explore all that Atlanta has to offer.

Getting Accepted
9,775 applied
53% were accepted
2,552 enrolled (49% of accepted)
3.30 average high school GPA
Mean SAT critical reading score: 545
Mean SAT math score: 545
Mean ACT score: 23
23% had SAT critical reading scores over 600
24% had SAT math scores over 600
39% had ACT scores over 24
3% had SAT critical reading scores over 700
2% had SAT math scores over 700
2% had ACT scores over 30
1 National Merit Scholar

Graduation and After
16% graduated in 4 years
21% graduated in 5 years
9% graduated in 6 years
241 organizations recruited on campus

Financial Matters
$5485 resident tuition and fees (2008–09)
$18,973 nonresident tuition and fees (2008–09)
$9230 room and board
70% average percent of need met
$7780 average financial aid amount received per undergraduate

---

Gettysburg College is a highly motivated community of determined students, faculty members, and administrators who come together to build in each other a passion for the responsibility of citizenship and the opportunity of leadership. With a strong liberal arts and sciences philosophy at its core, the Gettysburg curriculum instills in students a capacity for integrative and critical thinking from a global perspective. Students expand upon their classroom experiences by conducting collaborative research with esteemed faculty members in the campus' state-of-the-art facilities, immersing themselves in foreign cultures through Gettysburg's extensive array of off-campus study programs, and pursuing internships with some of the nation's most influential corporations and organizations. Students' active involvement in clubs, athletics, and community service creates a vibrant atmosphere on Gettysburg's residential campus. Gettysburg College challenges students to do great work, thereby preparing them to lead energetic, engaged, and enlightened lives.

Getting Accepted
6,126 applied
36% were accepted
695 enrolled (32% of accepted)
66% from top tenth of their h.s. class
Mean SAT critical reading score: 648
Mean SAT math score: 647
82% had SAT critical reading scores over 600
75% had SAT math scores over 600
19% had SAT critical reading scores over 700
10% had SAT math scores over 700

Graduation and After
77% graduated in 4 years
4% graduated in 5 years
40% pursued further study
78% had job offers within 6 months
93 organizations recruited on campus

Financial Matters
$35,990 tuition and fees (2007–08)
$8630 room and board
100% average percent of need met
$26,108 average financial aid amount received per undergraduate (2006–07 estimated)

GETTYSBURG COLLEGE
SMALL-TOWN SETTING ■ PRIVATE ■ INDEPENDENT RELIGIOUS ■ COED
GETTYSBURG, PENNSYLVANIA

Web site: www.gettysburg.edu
Contact: Ms. Gail Sweezey, Director of Admissions, 300 North Washington Street, Gettysburg, PA 17325
Telephone: 717-337-6100 or toll-free 800-431-0803
Fax: 717-337-6145
E-mail: admiss@gettysburg.edu

Academics
Gettysburg awards bachelor's **degrees**. **Challenging opportunities** include advanced placement credit, student-designed majors, double majors, independent study, and a senior project. Special programs include internships, off-campus study, study-abroad, and Army ROTC.

The most frequently chosen **baccalaureate** fields are social sciences, business/marketing, and biological/life sciences. A complete listing of majors at Gettysburg appears in the Majors by College index beginning on page 471.

The **faculty** at Gettysburg has 199 full-time members, 84% with terminal degrees. The student-faculty ratio is 11:1.

Students of Gettysburg
The student body is made up of 2,497 undergraduates. 52.6% are women and 47.4% are men. Students come from 40 states and territories and 35 other countries. 26% are from Pennsylvania. 1.8% are international students. 4.4% are African American, 1.6% Asian American, and 2.4% Hispanic American. 90% returned for their sophomore year.

Facilities and Resources
Students can access the following: campus intranet, computer help desk, online (class) registration. Campuswide network is available. 100% of college-owned or -operated housing units are wired for high-speed Internet access. The **library** has 393,163 books and 4,778 subscriptions.

Campus Life
There are 120 active organizations on campus, including a drama/theater group, newspaper, radio station, television station, choral group, and marching band. 40% of eligible men and 26% of eligible women are members of national **fraternities** and national **sororities**.

Gettysburg is a member of the NCAA (Division III). **Intercollegiate sports** include baseball (m), basketball, cheerleading, cross-country running, field hockey (w), football (m), golf, lacrosse, soccer, softball (w), swimming and diving, tennis, track and field, volleyball (w), wrestling (m).

Campus Safety
Student safety services include late-night transport/escort service, 24-hour emergency telephone alarm devices, 24-hour patrols by trained security personnel, and electronically operated dormitory entrances.

Applying
Gettysburg requires an essay, SAT or ACT, a high school transcript, and 2 recommendations. It recommends SAT Subject Tests, an interview, extracurricular activities, and a minimum high school GPA of 3.0. Application deadline: 2/1; 2/15 for financial aid. Early and deferred admission are possible.

GONZAGA UNIVERSITY

URBAN SETTING ■ PRIVATE ■ INDEPENDENT RELIGIOUS ■ COED
SPOKANE, WASHINGTON

Web site: www.gonzaga.edu
Contact: Ms. Julie McCulloh, Dean of Admission, 502 East Boone Avenue,
    Spokane, WA 99258-0102
Telephone: 509-323-6591 or toll-free 800-322-2584 Ext. 6572
Fax: 509-323-5780
E-mail: admissions@gonzaga.edu

Academics

Gonzaga awards bachelor's, master's, doctoral, and first-professional **degrees** and post-master's certificates. **Challenging opportunities** include advanced placement credit, accelerated degree programs, an honors program, double majors, independent study, and a senior project. Special programs include internships, summer session for credit, off-campus study, study-abroad, and Army ROTC.

The most frequently chosen **baccalaureate** fields are business/marketing, social sciences, and communications/journalism. A complete listing of majors at Gonzaga appears in the Majors by College index beginning on page 471.

The **faculty** at Gonzaga has 352 full-time members, 85% with terminal degrees. The student-faculty ratio is 11:1.

Students of Gonzaga

The student body totals 6,873, of whom 4,385 are undergraduates. 53.4% are women and 46.6% are men. Students come from 53 states and territories and 40 other countries. 46% are from Washington. 1.9% are international students. 1.3% are African American, 1% American Indian, 5.4% Asian American, and 4.1% Hispanic American. 91% returned for their sophomore year.

Facilities and Resources

625 **computers/terminals** are available on campus for general student use. Students can access the following: computer help desk, free student e-mail accounts, online (class) grades, online (class) registration, online (class) schedules. Campuswide network is available. Wireless service is available via classrooms, computer centers, computer labs, dorm rooms, libraries, student centers. The 2 **libraries** have 305,517 books and 32,106 subscriptions.

Campus Life

There are 69 active organizations on campus, including a drama/theater group, newspaper, radio station, television station, and choral group. No national or local **fraternities** or **sororities**.

Gonzaga is a member of the NCAA (Division I). **Intercollegiate sports** (some offering scholarships) include baseball (m), basketball, cross-country running, golf, soccer, tennis, track and field, volleyball (w).

Campus Safety

Student safety services include late-night transport/escort service, 24-hour emergency telephone alarm devices, 24-hour patrols by trained security personnel, and electronically operated dormitory entrances.

Applying

Gonzaga requires an essay, SAT or ACT, a high school transcript, 1 recommendation, and a minimum high school GPA of 3.0. It recommends an interview. Application deadline: 2/1; 2/1 priority date for financial aid. Deferred admission is possible.

Getting Accepted

5,744 applied
69% were accepted
1,036 enrolled (26% of accepted)
42% from top tenth of their h.s. class
3.69 average high school GPA
44% had SAT critical reading scores over 600
50% had SAT math scores over 600
81% had ACT scores over 24
9% had SAT critical reading scores over 700
9% had SAT math scores over 700
19% had ACT scores over 30

Graduation and After

66% graduated in 4 years
12% graduated in 5 years
2% graduated in 6 years
37% had job offers within 6 months
137 organizations recruited on campus

Financial Matters

$28,262 tuition and fees (2008–09)
$7860 room and board
88% average percent of need met
$18,004 average financial aid amount received
    per undergraduate (2005–06)

Gordon College

Suburban setting ■ Private ■ Independent Religious ■ Coed
Wenham, Massachusetts

Getting Accepted
1,574 applied
71% were accepted
457 enrolled (41% of accepted)
21% from top tenth of their h.s. class
3.55 average high school GPA
Mean SAT critical reading score: 593
Mean SAT math score: 570
Mean SAT writing score: 586
Mean ACT score: 25
48% had SAT critical reading scores over 600
39% had SAT math scores over 600
45% had SAT writing scores over 600
10% had SAT critical reading scores over 700
4% had SAT math scores over 700
7% had SAT writing scores over 700
6 National Merit Scholars

Graduation and After
60% graduated in 4 years
8% graduated in 5 years
3% graduated in 6 years
20% pursued further study
73 organizations recruited on campus

Financial Matters
$27,294 tuition and fees (2008–09)
$7424 room and board
70% average percent of need met
$14,540 average financial aid amount received
per undergraduate (2005–06 estimated)

Web site: www.gordon.edu

Contact: Barbara Layne, Associate Vice President for Enrollment, 255 Grapevine Road, Wenham, MA 01984-1899

Telephone: 978-867-4218 or toll-free 866-464-6736

Fax: 978-867-4682

E-mail: admissions@gordon.edu

Academics

Gordon awards bachelor's and master's **degrees**. **Challenging opportunities** include advanced placement credit, student-designed majors, an honors program, double majors, independent study, and a senior project. Special programs include cooperative education, internships, off-campus study, study-abroad, and Army and Air Force ROTC.

The most frequently chosen **baccalaureate** fields are social sciences, English, and business/marketing. A complete listing of majors at Gordon appears in the Majors by College index beginning on page 471.

The **faculty** at Gordon has 93 full-time members, 86% with terminal degrees. The student-faculty ratio is 12:1.

Students of Gordon

The student body totals 1,645, of whom 1,530 are undergraduates. 63.1% are women and 36.9% are men. Students come from 44 states and territories and 22 other countries. 28% are from Massachusetts. 2.4% are international students. 1.5% are African American, 0.3% American Indian, 1.4% Asian American, and 3.3% Hispanic American. 85% returned for their sophomore year.

Facilities and Resources

141 **computers/terminals** are available on campus for general student use. Students can access the following: free student e-mail accounts, online (class) registration, online (class) schedules. Campuswide network is available. 100% of college-owned or -operated housing units are wired for high-speed Internet access. Wireless service is available via learning centers, libraries, student centers. The **library** has 142,688 books and 8,555 subscriptions.

Campus Life

There are 35 active organizations on campus, including a drama/theater group, newspaper, and choral group. No national or local **fraternities** or **sororities**.

Gordon is a member of the NCAA (Division III). **Intercollegiate sports** include baseball (m), basketball, cheerleading, cross-country running, field hockey (w), lacrosse, soccer, softball (w), swimming and diving, tennis, track and field, volleyball (w).

Campus Safety

Student safety services include late-night transport/escort service, 24-hour emergency telephone alarm devices, 24-hour patrols by trained security personnel, and electronically operated dormitory entrances.

Applying

Gordon requires an essay, SAT or ACT, a high school transcript, an interview, 2 recommendations, and pastoral recommendation, statement of Christian faith. It recommends SAT Subject Tests and a minimum high school GPA of 3.0. Application deadline: rolling admissions; 3/1 priority date for financial aid. Early and deferred admission are possible.

156   *www.petersons.com/colleges*   *Peterson's 440 Great Colleges for Top Students 2009*

GOSHEN COLLEGE

SMALL-TOWN SETTING ■ PRIVATE ■ INDEPENDENT RELIGIOUS ■ COED
GOSHEN, INDIANA

SPONSOR

Web site: www.goshen.edu
Contact: Lynn Jackson, Director of Enrollment, 1700 South Main Street, Goshen, IN 46526-4794
Telephone: 574-535-7535 or toll-free 800-348-7422
Fax: 574-535-7609
E-mail: lynnj@goshen.edu

Academics

Goshen awards bachelor's **degrees**. **Challenging opportunities** include advanced placement credit, accelerated degree programs, student-designed majors, freshman honors college, an honors program, double majors, independent study, and a senior project. Special programs include internships, summer session for credit, off-campus study, and study-abroad.

The most frequently chosen **baccalaureate** fields are business/marketing, health professions and related sciences, and computer and information sciences. A complete listing of majors at Goshen appears in the Majors by College index beginning on page 471.

The **faculty** at Goshen has 73 full-time members, 63% with terminal degrees. The student-faculty ratio is 10:1.

Students of Goshen

The student body is made up of 951 undergraduates. 59.6% are women and 40.4% are men. Students come from 32 states and territories and 28 other countries. 45% are from Indiana. 7.5% are international students. 3.2% are African American, 0.1% American Indian, 1.5% Asian American, and 5.3% Hispanic American. 84% returned for their sophomore year.

Facilities and Resources

160 **computers/terminals** are available on campus for general student use. Students can access the following: online services. Campuswide network is available. The 3 **libraries** have 136,550 books and 496 subscriptions.

Campus Life

There are 26 active organizations on campus, including a drama/theater group, newspaper, radio station, television station, and choral group. No national or local **fraternities** or **sororities**.

Goshen is a member of the NAIA. **Intercollegiate sports** (some offering scholarships) include baseball (m), basketball, cross-country running, golf (m), soccer, softball (w), tennis, track and field, volleyball (w).

Campus Safety

Student safety services include late-night transport/escort service, 24-hour emergency telephone alarm devices, and 24-hour patrols by trained security personnel.

Applying

Goshen requires an essay, SAT or ACT, a high school transcript, 2 recommendations, rank in upper 50% of high school class, minimum SAT score of 1000 or ACT score of 22, and a minimum high school GPA of 2.5. It recommends an interview. Application deadline: 8/15; 2/15 priority date for financial aid. Deferred admission is possible.

Getting Accepted

586 applied
76% were accepted
209 enrolled (47% of accepted)
30% from top tenth of their h.s. class
3.52 average high school GPA
Mean SAT critical reading score: 566
Mean SAT math score: 561
Mean SAT writing score: 534
Mean ACT score: 24
42% had SAT critical reading scores over 600
37% had SAT math scores over 600
26% had SAT writing scores over 600
62% had ACT scores over 24
8% had SAT critical reading scores over 700
9% had SAT math scores over 700
2% had SAT writing scores over 700
10% had ACT scores over 30
9 National Merit Scholars
6 valedictorians

Graduation and After

46% graduated in 4 years
12% graduated in 5 years
2% graduated in 6 years
36% pursued further study (15% arts and sciences, 5% business, 5% medicine)
35 organizations recruited on campus

Financial Matters

$21,300 tuition and fees (2007–08)
$7000 room and board
87% average percent of need met
$16,555 average financial aid amount received per undergraduate (2005–06 estimated)

GOUCHER COLLEGE

SUBURBAN SETTING ■ PRIVATE ■ INDEPENDENT ■ COED
BALTIMORE, MARYLAND

Web site: www.goucher.edu
Contact: Mr. Carlton Surbeck III, Director of Admissions, 1021 Dulaney Valley Road, Baltimore, MD 21204-2794
Telephone: 410-337-6100 or toll-free 800-468-2437
Fax: 410-337-6354
E-mail: admissions@goucher.edu

Goucher College is a small, private, coeducational liberal arts and sciences college in Baltimore, Maryland, with an international emphasis and an academic program that partners classroom learning with real, hands-on experience. Since it was founded in 1885, Goucher has provided a truly global kind of education that puts learning in perspective against the events and developments of the entire world, encouraging students to test what they have learned against experience in service-learning, study-abroad, and internship programs throughout the nation and around the globe. Goucher is a small college with a big view of the world—an educational community without boundaries.

Getting Accepted
3,563 applied
66% were accepted
399 enrolled (17% of accepted)
17% from top tenth of their h.s. class
3.2 average high school GPA
Mean SAT critical reading score: 605
Mean SAT math score: 565
Mean SAT writing score: 595
63% had SAT critical reading scores over 600
47% had SAT math scores over 600
52% had SAT writing scores over 600
20% had SAT critical reading scores over 700
9% had SAT math scores over 700
12% had SAT writing scores over 700

Graduation and After
57% graduated in 4 years
8% graduated in 5 years
1% graduated in 6 years
26% pursued further study
80% had job offers within 6 months

Financial Matters
$31,082 tuition and fees (2007–08)
$9840 room and board
82% average percent of need met
$19,917 average financial aid amount received per undergraduate (2005–06)

Academics

Goucher awards bachelor's and master's **degrees** and post-bachelor's certificates. **Challenging opportunities** include advanced placement credit, student-designed majors, double majors, independent study, and a senior project. Special programs include internships, off-campus study, study-abroad, and Army ROTC.

The most frequently chosen **baccalaureate** fields are psychology, visual and performing arts, and social sciences. A complete listing of majors at Goucher appears in the Majors by College index beginning on page 471.

The **faculty** at Goucher has 128 full-time members, 87% with terminal degrees. The student-faculty ratio is 9:1.

Students of Goucher

The student body totals 2,362, of whom 1,472 are undergraduates. 66.7% are women and 33.3% are men. Students come from 43 states and territories and 7 other countries. 29% are from Maryland. 0.5% are international students. 4.9% are African American, 0.4% American Indian, 2.9% Asian American, and 3.5% Hispanic American. 78% returned for their sophomore year.

Facilities and Resources

170 **computers/terminals** are available on campus for general student use. Students can access the following: campus intranet, computer help desk, free student e-mail accounts, online (class) grades, online (class) schedules, transcripts, financial aid information, billing, ePortfolios. Campuswide network is available. Wireless service is available via entire campus. The **library** has 305,486 books and 27,416 subscriptions.

Campus Life

There are 60 active organizations on campus, including a drama/theater group, newspaper, radio station, television station, and choral group. No national or local **fraternities** or **sororities**.

Goucher is a member of the NCAA (Division III). **Intercollegiate sports** include basketball, cross-country running, equestrian sports, field hockey (w), lacrosse, soccer, swimming and diving, tennis, track and field, volleyball (w).

Campus Safety

Student safety services include late-night transport/escort service, 24-hour emergency telephone alarm devices, 24-hour patrols by trained security personnel, and electronically operated dormitory entrances.

Applying

Goucher requires an essay, a high school transcript, and a minimum high school GPA of 2.0. It recommends an interview, 3 recommendations, and a minimum high school GPA of 2.8. Application deadline: 2/1; 2/15 priority date for financial aid. Early and deferred admission are possible.

Grinnell College

SMALL-TOWN SETTING ■ PRIVATE ■ INDEPENDENT ■ COED
GRINNELL, IOWA

Web site: www.grinnell.edu
Contact: Mr. Seth Allen, Dean for Admission and Financial Aid, 1103 Park Street, Grinnell, IA 50112
Telephone: 641-269-3600 or toll-free 800-247-0113
Fax: 641-269-4800
E-mail: askgrin@grinnell.edu

Academics

Grinnell awards bachelor's **degrees**. **Challenging opportunities** include advanced placement credit, accelerated degree programs, student-designed majors, double majors, and independent study. Special programs include internships, off-campus study, and study-abroad.

The most frequently chosen **baccalaureate** fields are social sciences, foreign languages and literature, and biological/life sciences. A complete listing of majors at Grinnell appears in the Majors by College index beginning on page 471.

The **faculty** at Grinnell has 165 full-time members, 94% with terminal degrees. The student-faculty ratio is 9:1.

Students of Grinnell

The student body is made up of 1,654 undergraduates. 53.2% are women and 46.8% are men. Students come from 51 states and territories and 51 other countries. 12% are from Iowa, 11.2% are international students. 4.7% are African American, 0.4% American Indian, 6.8% Asian American, and 4.9% Hispanic American. 94% returned for their sophomore year.

Facilities and Resources

212 **computers/terminals** and 116 ports are available on campus for general student use. Students can access the following: campus intranet, computer help desk, free student e-mail accounts, online (class) grades, online (class) schedules. Campuswide network is available. 100% of college-owned or -operated housing units are wired for high-speed Internet access. Wireless service is available via entire campus. The 3 **libraries** have 1,117,669 books and 20,186 subscriptions.

Campus Life

There are 240 active organizations on campus, including a drama/theater group, newspaper, radio station, and choral group. No national or local **fraternities** or **sororities**.

Grinnell is a member of the NCAA (Division III). **Intercollegiate sports** include baseball (m), basketball, cross-country running, football (m), golf, soccer, softball (w), swimming and diving, tennis, track and field, volleyball (w).

Campus Safety

Student safety services include late-night transport/escort service, 24-hour emergency telephone alarm devices, 24-hour patrols by trained security personnel, student patrols, and electronically operated dormitory entrances.

Applying

Grinnell requires an essay, SAT or ACT, a high school transcript, and 3 recommendations. It recommends an interview. Application deadline: 1/20; 2/1 for financial aid. Early and deferred admission are possible.

Getting Accepted

3,077 applied
50% were accepted
426 enrolled (28% of accepted)
66% from top tenth of their h.s. class
81% had SAT critical reading scores over 600
83% had SAT math scores over 600
95% had ACT scores over 24
46% had SAT critical reading scores over 700
37% had SAT math scores over 700
66% had ACT scores over 30
37 National Merit Scholars
7 class presidents
34 valedictorians

Graduation and After

81% graduated in 4 years
4% graduated in 5 years
1% graduated in 6 years
30% pursued further study (12% arts and sciences, 9% education, 3% law)
50% had job offers within 6 months
89 organizations recruited on campus

Financial Matters

$34,392 tuition and fees (2007–08)
$8030 room and board
100% average percent of need met
$25,972 average financial aid amount received per undergraduate (2006–07 estimated)

GROVE CITY COLLEGE
SMALL-TOWN SETTING ■ PRIVATE ■ INDEPENDENT RELIGIOUS ■ COED
GROVE CITY, PENNSYLVANIA

Web site: www.gcc.edu
Contact: Mr. Jeffrey Mincey, Director of Admissions, 100 Campus Drive,
   Grove City, PA 16127-2104
Telephone: 724-458-2100
Fax: 724-458-3395
E-mail: admissions@gcc.edu

> Grove City has professors who like to teach, students who welcome the idea of being stretched intellectually, and a spiritual vitality that drifts far beyond the Chapel walls, permeating classrooms and dorm life. Also, the annual cost, including tuition, room and board, and a Tablet PC computer and printer, is less than $18,000.

Getting Accepted
1,916 applied
55% were accepted
655 enrolled (62% of accepted)
52% from top tenth of their h.s. class
3.71 average high school GPA
Mean SAT critical reading score: 637
Mean SAT math score: 631
Mean SAT writing score: 616
Mean ACT score: 28
70% had SAT critical reading scores over 600
71% had SAT math scores over 600
88% had ACT scores over 24
26% had SAT critical reading scores over 700
18% had SAT math scores over 700
29% had ACT scores over 30
20 National Merit Scholars
13 class presidents
64 valedictorians

Graduation and After
78% graduated in 4 years
3% graduated in 5 years
1% graduated in 6 years
21% pursued further study (12% arts and
   sciences, 3% business, 2% education)
91% had job offers within 6 months
183 organizations recruited on campus

Financial Matters
$11,500 tuition and fees (2007–08)
$6134 room and board
51% average percent of need met
$5232 average financial aid amount received
   per undergraduate (2006–07 estimated)

Academics
Grove City awards bachelor's **degrees. Challenging opportunities** include advanced placement credit, student-designed majors, double majors, independent study, and a senior project. Special programs include internships, summer session for credit, study-abroad, and Army ROTC.

The most frequently chosen **baccalaureate** fields are business/marketing, education, and biological/life sciences. A complete listing of majors at Grove City appears in the Majors by College index beginning on page 471.

The **faculty** at Grove City has 140 full-time members, 81% with terminal degrees. The student-faculty ratio is 15:1.

Students of Grove City
The student body is made up of 2,504 undergraduates. 49.5% are women and 50.5% are men. Students come from 42 states and territories and 11 other countries. 47% are from Pennsylvania. 0.7% are international students. 0.6% are African American, 0.1% American Indian, 2.3% Asian American, and 1.1% Hispanic American. 90% returned for their sophomore year.

Facilities and Resources
50 **computers/terminals** are available on campus for general student use. Students can access the following: campus intranet, computer help desk, free student e-mail accounts, online (class) grades, online (class) registration, online (class) schedules. Campuswide network is available. 100% of college-owned or -operated housing units are wired for high-speed Internet access. Wireless service is available via learning centers, student centers. The **library** has 139,000 books and 550 subscriptions.

Campus Life
There are 123 active organizations on campus, including a drama/theater group, newspaper, radio station, television station, choral group, and marching band. 17% of eligible men and 28% of eligible women are members of local **fraternities** and local **sororities.**

Grove City is a member of the NCAA (Division III). **Intercollegiate sports** include baseball (m), basketball, cheerleading (w), cross-country running, football (m), golf, soccer, softball (w), swimming and diving, tennis, track and field, volleyball (w), water polo (w).

Campus Safety
Student safety services include monitored women's residence hall entrances, late-night transport/escort service, 24-hour emergency telephone alarm devices, 24-hour patrols by trained security personnel, student patrols, and electronically operated dormitory entrances.

Applying
Grove City requires an essay, SAT or ACT, a high school transcript, and 2 recommendations. It recommends an interview. Application deadline: 2/1; 4/15 for financial aid. Early and deferred admission are possible.

GUSTAVUS ADOLPHUS COLLEGE

SMALL-TOWN SETTING ■ PRIVATE ■ INDEPENDENT RELIGIOUS ■ COED
ST. PETER, MINNESOTA

Web site: www.gustavus.edu
Contact: Mr. Mark Anderson, Vice President for Admission and Student Financial Aid, 800 West College Ave., St. Peter, MN 56082-1498
Telephone: 507-933-7676 or toll-free 800-GUSTAVU(S)
Fax: 507-933-7474
E-mail: admission@gac.edu

Academics

Gustavus awards bachelor's **degrees**. **Challenging opportunities** include advanced placement credit, accelerated degree programs, student-designed majors, an honors program, double majors, independent study, and a senior project. Special programs include cooperative education, internships, summer session for credit, off-campus study, study-abroad, and Army ROTC.

The most frequently chosen **baccalaureate** fields are social sciences, business/marketing, and biological/life sciences. A complete listing of majors at Gustavus appears in the Majors by College index beginning on page 471.

The **faculty** at Gustavus has 180 full-time members, 89% with terminal degrees. The student-faculty ratio is 13:1.

Students of Gustavus

The student body is made up of 2,628 undergraduates. 57% are women and 43% are men. Students come from 38 states and territories and 17 other countries. 82% are from Minnesota. 1.3% are international students. 1.8% are African American, 0.2% American Indian, 4.5% Asian American, and 1.6% Hispanic American. 90% returned for their sophomore year.

Facilities and Resources

440 **computers/terminals** and 5,000 ports are available on campus for general student use. Students can access the following: computer help desk, free student e-mail accounts, online (class) grades, online (class) registration, online (class) schedules. Campuswide network is available. 100% of college-owned or -operated housing units are wired for high-speed Internet access. Wireless service is available via entire campus. The 3 **libraries** have 297,861 books and 17,078 subscriptions.

Campus Life

There are 92 active organizations on campus, including a drama/theater group, newspaper, radio station, television station, and choral group. 7% of eligible men and 5% of eligible women are members of national **fraternities**, national **sororities**, local fraternities, and local sororities.

Gustavus is a member of the NCAA (Division III). **Intercollegiate sports** include baseball (m), basketball, cross-country running, football (m), golf, gymnastics (w), ice hockey, skiing (cross-country), soccer, softball (w), swimming and diving, tennis, track and field, volleyball (w).

Campus Safety

Student safety services include late-night transport/escort service, 24-hour emergency telephone alarm devices, 24-hour patrols by trained security personnel, and electronically operated dormitory entrances.

Applying

Gustavus requires an essay, a high school transcript, and 2 recommendations. It recommends SAT or ACT and an interview. Application deadline: 4/1; 4/1 for financial aid, with a 2/15 priority date. Early and deferred admission are possible.

Getting Accepted

2,208 applied
80% were accepted
670 enrolled (38% of accepted)
36% from top tenth of their h.s. class
3.64 average high school GPA
Mean SAT critical reading score: 618
Mean SAT math score: 634
Mean ACT score: 26
70% had SAT math scores over 600
81% had ACT scores over 24
18% had SAT math scores over 700
18% had ACT scores over 30
7 National Merit Scholars

Graduation and After

79% graduated in 4 years
1% graduated in 5 years
36% pursued further study (13% arts and sciences, 7% business, 5% law)
92% had job offers within 6 months

Financial Matters

$28,515 tuition and fees (2007–08)
$6775 room and board
89% average percent of need met
$18,100 average financial aid amount received per undergraduate (2005–06)

Students come to Hamilton to find their voice. As a national leader for teaching students to write effectively, learn from each other, and think for themselves, Hamilton produces graduates who have the knowledge, skills, and confidence to make their voices heard on issues of importance to them and their communities. A key component of the Hamilton experience is the College's open yet rigorous liberal arts curriculum. In place of distribution requirements that are common at most colleges, Hamilton gives students the freedom to choose the courses that reflect their unique interests and plans. A distinguished faculty then helps students fulfill those plans.

Getting Accepted
4,962 applied
28% were accepted
468 enrolled (34% of accepted)
74% from top tenth of their h.s. class
Mean SAT critical reading score: 671
Mean SAT math score: 672
87% had SAT critical reading scores over 600
91% had SAT math scores over 600
49% had SAT critical reading scores over 700
39% had SAT math scores over 700
5 National Merit Scholars
12 valedictorians

Graduation and After
83% graduated in 4 years
4% graduated in 5 years
1% graduated in 6 years
30% pursued further study
40 organizations recruited on campus

Financial Matters
$36,860 tuition and fees (2007–08)
$9350 room and board
100% average percent of need met
$29,148 average financial aid amount received per undergraduate (2006–07 estimated)

HAMILTON COLLEGE
SMALL-TOWN SETTING ■ PRIVATE ■ INDEPENDENT ■ COED
CLINTON, NEW YORK

Web site: www.hamilton.edu
Contact: Ms. Monica Inzer, Dean of Admission and Financial Aid, 198 College Hill Road, Clinton, NY 13323
Telephone: 315-859-4421 or toll-free 800-843-2655
Fax: 315-859-4457
E-mail: admission@hamilton.edu

Academics
Hamilton awards bachelor's **degrees**. **Challenging opportunities** include advanced placement credit, accelerated degree programs, student-designed majors, double majors, independent study, and a senior project. Special programs include internships, off-campus study, study-abroad, and Army and Air Force ROTC.

The most frequently chosen **baccalaureate** fields are social sciences, foreign languages and literature, and visual and performing arts. A complete listing of majors at Hamilton appears in the Majors by College index beginning on page 471.

The **faculty** at Hamilton has 172 full-time members, 96% with terminal degrees. The student-faculty ratio is 10:1.

Students of Hamilton*
The student body is made up of 1,842 undergraduates. 51.8% are women and 48.2% are men. Students come from 20 states and territories and 46 other countries. 34% are from New York. 5.2% are international students. 3.7% are African American, 0.9% American Indian, 7.1% Asian American, and 4.9% Hispanic American. 93% returned for their sophomore year.

Facilities and Resources
625 **computers/terminals** and 6,000 ports are available on campus for general student use. Students can access the following: computer help desk, free student e-mail accounts, online (class) grades, online (class) registration. Campuswide network is available. 100% of college-owned or -operated housing units are wired for high-speed Internet access. Wireless service is available via entire campus. The 4 **libraries** have 538,377 books and 3,585 subscriptions.

Campus Life
There are 80 active organizations on campus, including a drama/theater group, newspaper, radio station, television station, and choral group. 29% of eligible men and 19% of eligible women are members of national **fraternities** and local **sororities**.

Hamilton is a member of the NCAA (Division III). **Intercollegiate sports** include baseball (m), basketball, crew (w), cross-country running, field hockey (w), football (m), golf (m), ice hockey, lacrosse, soccer, softball (w), squash, swimming and diving, tennis, track and field, volleyball (w).

Campus Safety
Student safety services include student safety program, late-night transport/escort service, 24-hour emergency telephone alarm devices, 24-hour patrols by trained security personnel, and electronically operated dormitory entrances.

Applying
Hamilton requires an essay, SAT and SAT Subject Tests or ACT, a high school transcript, 1 recommendation, and sample of expository prose. It recommends an interview. Application deadline: 1/1; 2/8 for financial aid, with a 1/1 priority date. Deferred admission is possible.

Hamline University

Urban setting ■ Private ■ Independent Religious ■ Coed
St. Paul, Minnesota

Web site: www.hamline.edu
Contact: Ms. Ann Kjorstad, Director of Undergraduate Admission, 1536
   Hewitt Avenue, C1930, St. Paul, MN 55104-2458
Telephone: 651-523-2207 or toll-free 800-753-9753
Fax: 651-523-2458
E-mail: cla-admis@hamline.edu

Academics

Hamline awards bachelor's, master's, doctoral, and first-professional **degrees** and post-bachelor's certificates. **Challenging opportunities** include advanced placement credit, student-designed majors, an honors program, double majors, independent study, and a senior project. Special programs include internships, summer session for credit, off-campus study, study-abroad, and Air Force ROTC.

The most frequently chosen **baccalaureate** fields are social sciences, psychology, and business/marketing. A complete listing of majors at Hamline appears in the Majors by College index beginning on page 471.

The **faculty** at Hamline has 173 full-time members, 87% with terminal degrees. The student-faculty ratio is 14:1.

Students of Hamline

The student body totals 4,803, of whom 2,100 are undergraduates. 58.9% are women and 41.1% are men. Students come from 31 states and territories and 41 other countries. 3.3% are international students. 4.6% are African American, 0.6% American Indian, 5.6% Asian American, and 2.3% Hispanic American. 82% returned for their sophomore year.

Facilities and Resources

150 **computers/terminals** are available on campus for general student use. Students can access the following: computer help desk, free student e-mail accounts, online (class) grades, online (class) registration, online (class) schedules. Campuswide network is available. 100% of college-owned or -operated housing units are wired for high-speed Internet access. The 2 libraries have 228,973 books and 1,681 subscriptions.

Campus Life

There are 88 active organizations on campus, including a drama/theater group, newspaper, radio station, television station, and choral group. 3% of eligible men and 3% of eligible women are members of national **fraternities**, national **sororities**, and international dining club.

Hamline is a member of the NCAA (Division III). **Intercollegiate sports** include baseball (m), basketball, cross-country running, football (m), gymnastics (w), ice hockey, soccer, softball (w), swimming and diving, tennis, track and field, volleyball (w).

Campus Safety

Student safety services include late-night transport/escort service, 24-hour emergency telephone alarm devices, 24-hour patrols by trained security personnel, student patrols, and electronically operated dormitory entrances.

Applying

Hamline requires an essay, SAT or ACT, a high school transcript, and 2 recommendations. It recommends an interview and activity resume. Application deadline: rolling admissions. Early and deferred admission are possible.

Hamline's top-ranked undergraduate programs have built their national reputation with an innovative curriculum, personal attention, and outstanding faculty members. Hamline offers students a liberal arts college experience in a small university setting in the dynamic Twin Cities of Saint Paul and Minneapolis. Hamline offers its 2,000 undergraduates more than forty majors and programs, learning connected to internships and careers, amazing study-abroad opportunities, student-faculty collaborative research, NCAA Division III athletics, and a diverse and talented student body. Hamline is Minnesota's oldest university. The emphasis on personal and professional preparation for careers, service, and global awareness has distinguished Hamline for more than 150 years.

Getting Accepted
2,018 applied
78% were accepted
458 enrolled (29% of accepted)
22% from top tenth of their h.s. class
3.4 average high school GPA
Mean SAT critical reading score: 586
Mean SAT math score: 585
Mean SAT writing score: 561
Mean ACT score: 24
48% had SAT critical reading scores over 600
56% had SAT math scores over 600
31% had SAT writing scores over 600
52% had ACT scores over 24
19% had SAT critical reading scores over 700
11% had SAT math scores over 700
10% had SAT writing scores over 700
10% had ACT scores over 30
3 National Merit Scholars
8 valedictorians

Graduation and After
61% graduated in 4 years
6% graduated in 5 years
1% graduated in 6 years
22% pursued further study (5% law, 3% arts and sciences, 2% education)
91% had job offers within 6 months
70 organizations recruited on campus

Financial Matters
$26,533 tuition and fees (2007–08)
$7392 room and board

Getting Accepted

2,571 applied
55% were accepted
392 enrolled (28% of accepted)
28% from top tenth of their h.s. class
3.45 average high school GPA
Mean SAT critical reading score: 660
Mean SAT math score: 601
Mean ACT score: 28
80% had SAT critical reading scores over 600
55% had SAT math scores over 600
74% had SAT writing scores over 600
79% had ACT scores over 24
35% had SAT critical reading scores over 700
10% had SAT math scores over 700
26% had SAT writing scores over 700
36% had ACT scores over 30
194 class presidents
5 valedictorians

Graduation and After

57% graduated in 4 years
11% graduated in 5 years
3% graduated in 6 years
10% pursued further study (6% arts and sciences, 2% law, 2% medicine)
65% had job offers within 6 months

Financial Matters

$36,545 tuition and fees (2007–08)
$9545 room and board
97% average percent of need met
$27,990 average financial aid amount received per undergraduate (2006–07 estimated)

HAMPSHIRE COLLEGE

SMALL-TOWN SETTING ■ PRIVATE ■ INDEPENDENT ■ COED
AMHERST, MASSACHUSETTS

Web site: www.hampshire.edu
Contact: Ms. Karen S. Parker, Director of Admissions, 893 West Street, Amherst, MA 01002
Telephone: 413-559-5471 or toll-free 877-937-4267 (out-of-state)
Fax: 413-559-5631
E-mail: admissions@hampshire.edu

Academics

Hampshire awards bachelor's **degrees**. **Challenging opportunities** include advanced placement credit, accelerated degree programs, student-designed majors, independent study, and a senior project. Special programs include internships, off-campus study, study-abroad, and Army ROTC.

The most frequently chosen **baccalaureate** fields are visual and performing arts, social sciences, and English. A complete listing of majors at Hampshire appears in the Majors by College index beginning on page 471.

The **faculty** at Hampshire has 94 full-time members, 86% with terminal degrees. The student-faculty ratio is 12:1.

Students of Hampshire

The student body is made up of 1,431 undergraduates. 57.4% are women and 42.6% are men. Students come from 49 states and territories and 27 other countries. 17% are from Massachusetts. 3.6% are international students. 4.3% are African American, 0.7% American Indian, 3.8% Asian American, and 5.7% Hispanic American. 78% returned for their sophomore year.

Facilities and Resources

215 **computers/terminals** are available on campus for general student use. Students can access the following: campus intranet, computer help desk, free student e-mail accounts, online (class) registration. Campuswide network is available. 100% of college-owned or -operated housing units are wired for high-speed Internet access. Wireless service is available via entire campus. The **library** has 129,350 books and 2,288 subscriptions.

Campus Life

There are 107 active organizations on campus, including a drama/theater group, newspaper, radio station, and choral group. No national or local **fraternities** or **sororities**.

This institution has no intercollegiate sports.

Campus Safety

Student safety services include late-night transport/escort service, 24-hour emergency telephone alarm devices, 24-hour patrols by trained security personnel, and student patrols.

Applying

Hampshire requires an essay, a high school transcript, and 2 recommendations. It recommends an interview. Application deadline: 1/15; 2/1 priority date for financial aid. Early and deferred admission are possible.

HANOVER COLLEGE

RURAL SETTING ■ PRIVATE ■ INDEPENDENT RELIGIOUS ■ COED
HANOVER, INDIANA

Web site: www.hanover.edu
Contact: Mr. Bill Preble, Dean of Admission and Financial Assistance, Box 108, Hanover, IN 47243-0108
Telephone: 812-866-7021 or toll-free 800-213-2178
Fax: 812-866-7098
E-mail: admission@hanover.edu

Academics

Hanover awards bachelor's **degrees**. **Challenging opportunities** include advanced placement credit, student-designed majors, double majors, independent study, and a senior project. Special programs include internships, off-campus study, and study-abroad.

The most frequently chosen **baccalaureate** fields are social sciences, business/marketing, and English. A complete listing of majors at Hanover appears in the Majors by College index beginning on page 471.

The **faculty** at Hanover has 97 full-time members, 99% with terminal degrees. The student-faculty ratio is 10:1.

Students of Hanover

The student body is made up of 929 undergraduates. 53.7% are women and 46.3% are men. Students come from 26 states and territories and 13 other countries. 64% are from Indiana. 3.4% are international students. 1.1% are African American, 0.7% American Indian, 2.4% Asian American, and 0.7% Hispanic American. 77% returned for their sophomore year.

Facilities and Resources

112 **computers/terminals** are available on campus for general student use. Students can access the following: campus intranet, computer help desk, free student e-mail accounts, online (class) grades, online (class) registration, online (class) schedules. Campuswide network is available. 75% of college-owned or -operated housing units are wired for high-speed Internet access. Wireless service is available via entire campus. The **library** has 224,478 books and 1,035 subscriptions.

Campus Life

There are 46 active organizations on campus, including a drama/theater group, newspaper, radio station, television station, choral group, and marching band. 43% of eligible men and 52% of eligible women are members of national **fraternities** and national **sororities**.

Hanover is a member of the NCAA (Division III). **Intercollegiate sports** include baseball (m), basketball, cross-country running, football (m), golf, soccer, softball (w), tennis, track and field, volleyball (w).

Campus Safety

Student safety services include late-night transport/escort service, 24-hour emergency telephone alarm devices, 24-hour patrols by trained security personnel, and electronically operated dormitory entrances.

Applying

Hanover requires an essay, SAT or ACT, a high school transcript, and 1 recommendation. It recommends an interview. Application deadline: 3/1; 3/1 priority date for financial aid. Early and deferred admission are possible.

Getting Accepted

1,894 applied
66% were accepted
231 enrolled (19% of accepted)
39% from top tenth of their h.s. class
3.72 average high school GPA
Mean SAT critical reading score: 576
Mean SAT math score: 573
Mean ACT score: 25
40% had SAT critical reading scores over 600
40% had SAT math scores over 600
31% had SAT writing scores over 600
67% had ACT scores over 24
10% had SAT critical reading scores over 700
5% had SAT math scores over 700
3% had SAT writing scores over 700
11% had ACT scores over 30
9 valedictorians

Graduation and After

55% graduated in 4 years
3% graduated in 5 years
1% graduated in 6 years
26% pursued further study (7% arts and sciences, 6% law, 3% medicine)
30 organizations recruited on campus

Financial Matters

$24,220 tuition and fees (2007–08)
$7150 room and board
73% average percent of need met
$17,526 average financial aid amount received per undergraduate (2005–06)

HARDING UNIVERSITY
SMALL-TOWN SETTING ■ PRIVATE ■ INDEPENDENT RELIGIOUS ■ COED
SEARCY, ARKANSAS

Web site: www.harding.edu
Contact: Mr. Glenn Dillard, Assistant Vice President for Enrollment
  Management, Box 12255, Searcy, AR 72149-2255
Telephone: 501-279-4407 or toll-free 800-477-4407
Fax: 501-279-4129
E-mail: admissions@harding.edu

Located in the beautiful foothills of the Ozark Mountains, Harding is one of America's more highly regarded private universities. At Harding, students build lifetime friendships and upon graduation, are highly recruited. Harding's Christian environment and challenging academic program develop students who can compete and succeed. Whether on the main campus or in the international studies program in Australia, Chile, England, France/Switzerland, Greece, Italy or Zambia, Africa, students find Harding to be a caring and serving family. From Missouri flood relief to working with orphans in Haiti or farmers in Kenya, hundreds of Harding students serve others worldwide each year.

Getting Accepted
1,768 applied
80% were accepted
965 enrolled (68% of accepted)
27% from top tenth of their h.s. class
3.46 average high school GPA
Mean SAT critical reading score: 550
Mean SAT math score: 545
Mean ACT score: 24
34% had SAT critical reading scores over 600
34% had SAT math scores over 600
56% had ACT scores over 24
11% had SAT critical reading scores over 700
6% had SAT math scores over 700
15% had ACT scores over 30
12 National Merit Scholars
42 valedictorians

Graduation and After
37% graduated in 4 years
20% graduated in 5 years
3% graduated in 6 years
25% pursued further study (9% education, 6% arts and sciences, 3% business)
92% had job offers within 6 months
211 organizations recruited on campus

Financial Matters
$12,360 tuition and fees (2007–08)
$5578 room and board
70% average percent of need met
$9418 average financial aid amount received per undergraduate (2006–07 estimated)

Academics
Harding awards bachelor's, master's, doctoral, and first-professional **degrees** and post-master's certificates. **Challenging opportunities** include advanced placement credit, accelerated degree programs, freshman honors college, an honors program, double majors, independent study, and a senior project. Special programs include cooperative education, internships, summer session for credit, study-abroad, and Army ROTC.

The most frequently chosen **baccalaureate** fields are business/marketing, education, and health professions and related sciences. A complete listing of majors at Harding appears in the Majors by College index beginning on page 471.

The **faculty** at Harding has 226 full-time members, 67% with terminal degrees. The student-faculty ratio is 17:1.

Students of Harding
The student body totals 6,139, of whom 4,125 are undergraduates. 55% are women and 45% are men. Students come from 49 states and territories and 49 other countries. 30% are from Arkansas. 5% are international students. 4.3% are African American, 0.8% American Indian, 0.8% Asian American, and 2% Hispanic American. 80% returned for their sophomore year.

Facilities and Resources
495 **computers/terminals** are available on campus for general student use. Students can access the following: campus intranet, computer help desk, free student e-mail accounts, online (class) grades, online (class) registration, online (class) schedules. Campuswide network is available. 100% of college-owned or -operated housing units are wired for high-speed Internet access. The 2 **libraries** have 230,499 books and 16,582 subscriptions.

Campus Life
There are 52 active organizations on campus, including a drama/theater group, newspaper, radio station, television station, choral group, and marching band. 42% of eligible men and 40% of eligible women are members of local **fraternities** and local **sororities**.

Harding is a member of the NCAA (Division II). **Intercollegiate sports** (some offering scholarships) include baseball (m), basketball, cheerleading (w), cross-country running, football (m), golf, soccer, tennis, track and field, ultimate Frisbee, volleyball (w).

Campus Safety
Student safety services include late-night transport/escort service, 24-hour emergency telephone alarm devices, 24-hour patrols by trained security personnel, and electronically operated dormitory entrances.

Applying
Harding requires SAT or ACT, a high school transcript, and 2 recommendations. Application deadline: 4/15 priority date for financial aid. Early and deferred admission are possible.

HARVARD UNIVERSITY
Urban setting ■ Private ■ Independent ■ Coed
Cambridge, Massachusetts

Web site: www.harvard.edu
Contact: Dr. William R. Fitzsimmons, Office of Admissions and Financial Aid, Byerly Hall, 8 Garden Street, Cambridge, MA 02138
Telephone: 617-495-1551
E-mail: college@harvard.edu

Academics
Harvard awards bachelor's, master's, doctoral, and first-professional **degrees**. **Challenging opportunities** include advanced placement credit, accelerated degree programs, student-designed majors, an honors program, double majors, independent study, and a senior project. Special programs include internships, summer session for credit, off-campus study, study-abroad, and Army, Navy, and Air Force ROTC.

The most frequently chosen **baccalaureate** fields are social sciences, biological/life sciences, and history. A complete listing of majors at Harvard appears in the Majors by College index beginning on page 471.

The **faculty** at Harvard has 1,622 full-time members, 99% with terminal degrees. The student-faculty ratio is 7:1.

Students of Harvard
The student body totals 19,257, of whom 6,648 are undergraduates. 50.1% are women and 49.9% are men. Students come from 55 states and territories and 97 other countries. 19% are from Massachusetts. 9.7% are international students. 7.8% are African American, 0.7% American Indian, 15.5% Asian American, and 7% Hispanic American. 96% returned for their sophomore year.

Facilities and Resources
405 **computers/terminals** are available on campus for general student use. Students can access the following: computer help desk, free student e-mail accounts, online (class) grades, online (class) registration, online (class) schedules. Campuswide network is available. 100% of college-owned or -operated housing units are wired for high-speed Internet access. Wireless service is available via entire campus.

Campus Life
There are 390 active organizations on campus, including a drama/theater group, newspaper, radio station, television station, choral group, and marching band. Harvard has "House" system.

Harvard is a member of the NCAA (Division I). **Intercollegiate sports** include baseball (m), basketball, crew, cross-country running, fencing, field hockey (w), football (m), golf, ice hockey, lacrosse, sailing, skiing (cross-country), skiing (downhill), soccer, softball (w), squash, swimming and diving, tennis, track and field, volleyball, water polo, wrestling (m).

Campus Safety
Student safety services include required and optional safety courses, late-night transport/escort service, 24-hour emergency telephone alarm devices, 24-hour patrols by trained security personnel, and electronically operated dormitory entrances.

Applying
Harvard requires an essay, SAT Subject Tests, SAT or ACT, a high school transcript, an interview, and 2 recommendations. Application deadline: 1/1; 2/1 priority date for financial aid. Deferred admission is possible.

Getting Accepted
22,955 applied
9% were accepted
1,668 enrolled (79% of accepted)
95% from top tenth of their h.s. class

Graduation and After
88% graduated in 4 years
8% graduated in 5 years
1% graduated in 6 years
261 organizations recruited on campus

Financial Matters
$34,998 tuition and fees (2007–08)
$10,622 room and board
100% average percent of need met
$33,625 average financial aid amount received per undergraduate (2006–07 estimated)

HARVEY MUDD COLLEGE

SUBURBAN SETTING ■ PRIVATE ■ INDEPENDENT ■ COED
CLAREMONT, CALIFORNIA

Web site: www.hmc.edu
Contact: Mr. Peter Osgood, Director of Admissions, 301 Platt Boulevard,
    Claremont, CA 91711
Telephone: 909-621-8011
Fax: 909-607-7046
E-mail: admission@hmc.edu

Getting Accepted

2,493 applied
28% were accepted
196 enrolled (28% of accepted)
93% from top tenth of their h.s. class
Mean SAT critical reading score: 730
Mean SAT math score: 710
Mean SAT writing score: 720
99% had SAT critical reading scores over 600
100% had SAT math scores over 600
98% had SAT writing scores over 600
74% had SAT critical reading scores over 700
95% had SAT math scores over 700
72% had SAT writing scores over 700
50 National Merit Scholars
34 valedictorians

Graduation and After

43% pursued further study (40% arts and
    sciences, 3% engineering)
77% had job offers within 6 months
75 organizations recruited on campus

Financial Matters

$34,891 tuition and fees (2007–08)
$11,415 room and board
100% average percent of need met
$27,752 average financial aid amount received
    per undergraduate (2006–07 estimated)

Academics

Harvey Mudd awards bachelor's **degrees**. **Challenging opportunities** include advanced placement credit, student-designed majors, double majors, and a senior project. Special programs include internships, off-campus study, study-abroad, and Army and Air Force ROTC.

The most frequently chosen **baccalaureate** fields are engineering, mathematics, and computer and information sciences. A complete listing of majors at Harvey Mudd appears in the Majors by College index beginning on page 471.

The **faculty** at Harvey Mudd has 74 full-time members, 100% with terminal degrees. The student-faculty ratio is 9:1.

Students of Harvey Mudd

The student body is made up of 735 undergraduates. 33.1% are women and 66.9% are men. Students come from 46 states and territories and 16 other countries. 50% are from California. 3.9% are international students. 1.5% are African American, 0.8% American Indian, 20.4% Asian American, and 7.6% Hispanic American. 96% returned for their sophomore year.

Facilities and Resources

360 **computers/terminals** and 1,500 ports are available on campus for general student use. Students can access the following: campus intranet, computer help desk, free student e-mail accounts, online (class) grades, online (class) registration, online (class) schedules. Campuswide network is available. 100% of college-owned or -operated housing units are wired for high-speed Internet access. Wireless service is available via entire campus. The 2 **libraries** have 3,203,500 books and 16,308 subscriptions.

Campus Life

There are 80 active organizations on campus, including a drama/theater group, newspaper, radio station, and choral group. No national or local **fraternities** or **sororities**.

Harvey Mudd is a member of the NCAA (Division III). **Intercollegiate sports** include baseball (m), basketball, cross-country running, football (m), golf (m), lacrosse (w), soccer, softball (w), swimming and diving, tennis, track and field, volleyball (w), water polo.

Campus Safety

Student safety services include late-night transport/escort service, 24-hour emergency telephone alarm devices, and 24-hour patrols by trained security personnel.

Applying

Harvey Mudd requires an essay, SAT or ACT, SAT Subject Test in Math 2C and second exam of choice (Math 1C is not accepted), a high school transcript, and 3 recommendations. It recommends an interview. Application deadline: 1/2; 2/1 for financial aid. Deferred admission is possible.

HAVERFORD COLLEGE

SUBURBAN SETTING ■ PRIVATE ■ INDEPENDENT ■ COED
HAVERFORD, PENNSYLVANIA

SPONSOR

Web site: www.haverford.edu
Contact: Mr. Jess Lord, Dean of Admissions and Financial Aid, 370 Lancaster Avenue, Haverford, PA 19041-1392
Telephone: 610-896-1350
Fax: 610-896-1338
E-mail: admitme@haverford.edu

Academics

Haverford awards bachelor's **degrees**. **Challenging opportunities** include advanced placement credit, student-designed majors, double majors, independent study, and a senior project. Special programs include internships, off-campus study, and study-abroad.

The most frequently chosen **baccalaureate** fields are social sciences, biological/life sciences, and physical sciences. A complete listing of majors at Haverford appears in the Majors by College index beginning on page 471.

The **faculty** at Haverford has 113 full-time members, 95% with terminal degrees. The student-faculty ratio is 8:1.

Students of Haverford

The student body is made up of 1,169 undergraduates. 54% are women and 46% are men. Students come from 48 states and territories and 44 other countries. 13% are from Pennsylvania. 3.5% are international students. 8.4% are African American, 0.7% American Indian, 10.9% Asian American, and 8.4% Hispanic American. 96% returned for their sophomore year.

Facilities and Resources

300 **computers/terminals** and 1,600 ports are available on campus for general student use. Students can access the following: campus intranet, computer help desk, free student e-mail accounts, online (class) grades, online (class) registration, online (class) schedules. Campuswide network is available. 100% of college-owned or -operated housing units are wired for high-speed Internet access. Wireless service is available via classrooms, computer centers, computer labs, dorm rooms, learning centers, libraries, student centers. The 5 **libraries** have 773,401 books.

Campus Life

There are 100 active organizations on campus, including a drama/theater group, newspaper, radio station, and choral group. No national or local **fraternities** or **sororities**.

Haverford is a member of the NCAA (Division III). **Intercollegiate sports** include baseball (m), basketball, cross-country running, fencing, field hockey (w), lacrosse, soccer, softball (w), squash, tennis, track and field, volleyball (w).

Campus Safety

Student safety services include late-night transport/escort service, 24-hour emergency telephone alarm devices, 24-hour patrols by trained security personnel, and electronically operated dormitory entrances.

Applying

Haverford requires an essay, SAT Reasoning Test or ACT and two SAT Subject Tests, and 2 recommendations. It recommends an interview. Application deadline: 1/15; 1/31 for financial aid. Early and deferred admission are possible.

Haverford is a liberal arts college of 1,200 students located 10 miles outside of Philadelphia. Academic and intellectual rigor, integrity, and concern for others form the foundation of Haverford's approach to education. Aspects such as a student-run Honor Code, a sense of Quaker heritage, and a cooperative program with Bryn Mawr College, Swarthmore College, and the University of Pennsylvania mark Haverford as unique. Students thrive in part because classes are small and extracurricular commitment is expected and because the community is passionate about learning, understanding, and making sound and thoughtful judgments.

Getting Accepted
3,492 applied
25% were accepted
315 enrolled (36% of accepted)
89% from top tenth of their h.s. class
92% had SAT critical reading scores over 600
88% had SAT math scores over 600
91% had SAT writing scores over 600
55% had SAT critical reading scores over 700
49% had SAT math scores over 700
52% had SAT writing scores over 700

Graduation and After
86% graduated in 4 years
4% graduated in 5 years
1% graduated in 6 years
18% pursued further study (10% arts and sciences, 3% law, 3% medicine)
61% had job offers within 6 months
255 organizations recruited on campus

Financial Matters
$35,380 tuition and fees (2007–08)
$10,880 room and board
100% average percent of need met
$28,881 average financial aid amount received per undergraduate (2006–07 estimated)

HENDRIX COLLEGE

SUBURBAN SETTING ■ PRIVATE ■ INDEPENDENT RELIGIOUS ■ COED
CONWAY, ARKANSAS

Web site: www.hendrix.edu
Contact: Ms. Laura E. Martin, Director of Admission, 1600 Washington
Avenue, Conway, AR 72032
Telephone: 501-450-1362 or toll-free 800-277-9017
Fax: 501-450-3843
E-mail: martinl@hendrix.edu

A private, liberal arts college, Hendrix prepares students for the finest postgraduate programs in the country by combining classroom knowledge with hands-on learning. Students receive transcript credit for experiences—such as undergraduate research, study abroad, or internships—and through the curricular initiative, *Your Hendrix Odyssey: Engaging in Active Learning.* The College typically enrolls 1,100 students who are taught by a faculty of 85 professors, all of whom have Ph.D.'s or appropriate terminal degrees. Eighty percent of Hendrix students live on campus, fostering an intimate community for students and faculty members to interact. Hendrix is located in Conway, a suburb of Little Rock.

Academics

Hendrix awards bachelor's and master's **degrees. Challenging opportunities** include advanced placement credit, student-designed majors, an honors program, double majors, independent study, and a senior project. Special programs include cooperative education, internships, off-campus study, study-abroad, and Army ROTC.

The most frequently chosen **baccalaureate** fields are social sciences, biological/life sciences, and psychology. A complete listing of majors at Hendrix appears in the Majors by College index beginning on page 471.

The **faculty** at Hendrix has 92 full-time members, 97% with terminal degrees. The student-faculty ratio is 11:1.

Students of Hendrix

The student body totals 1,195, of whom 1,191 are undergraduates. 54.6% are women and 45.4% are men. Students come from 37 states and territories and 9 other countries. 54% are from Arkansas. 1.3% are international students. 4.2% are African American, 0.8% American Indian, 3.4% Asian American, and 3.3% Hispanic American. 86% returned for their sophomore year.

Facilities and Resources

75 **computers/terminals** are available on campus for general student use. Students can access the following: campus intranet, computer help desk, free student e-mail accounts, online (class) grades, online (class) registration, online (class) schedules. Campuswide network is available. 100% of college-owned or -operated housing units are wired for high-speed Internet access. Wireless service is available via entire campus. The **library** has 219,843 books and 37,162 subscriptions.

Campus Life

There are 65 active organizations on campus, including a drama/theater group, newspaper, radio station, and choral group. No national or local **fraternities** or **sororities.**

Hendrix is a member of the NCAA (Division III). **Intercollegiate sports** include baseball (m), basketball, cross-country running, field hockey (w), golf, lacrosse (w), soccer, softball (w), swimming and diving, tennis, track and field, volleyball (w).

Campus Safety

Student safety services include late-night transport/escort service, 24-hour emergency telephone alarm devices, 24-hour patrols by trained security personnel, and electronically operated dormitory entrances.

Applying

Hendrix requires an essay, SAT or ACT, and a high school transcript, and in some cases an interview. It recommends 1 recommendation. Application deadline: 8/1; 2/15 priority date for financial aid. Early and deferred admission are possible.

Getting Accepted
1,323 applied
83% were accepted
371 enrolled (34% of accepted)
43% from top tenth of their h.s. class
3.7 average high school GPA
Mean SAT critical reading score: 639
Mean SAT math score: 601
Mean ACT score: 28
69% had SAT critical reading scores over 600
54% had SAT math scores over 600
88% had ACT scores over 24
24% had SAT critical reading scores over 700
12% had SAT math scores over 700
37% had ACT scores over 30
8 National Merit Scholars
18 valedictorians

Graduation and After
56% graduated in 4 years
7% graduated in 5 years
2% graduated in 6 years
56% pursued further study
59% had job offers within 6 months
69 organizations recruited on campus

Financial Matters
$24,498 tuition and fees (2007–08)
$7200 room and board
80% average percent of need met
$16,968 average financial aid amount received per undergraduate (2006–07 estimated)

HILLSDALE COLLEGE

SMALL-TOWN SETTING ■ PRIVATE ■ INDEPENDENT ■ COED
HILLSDALE, MICHIGAN

Web site: www.hillsdale.edu
Contact: Mr. Jeffrey S. Lantis, Director of Admissions, 33 East College
    Street, Hillsdale, MI 49242-1298
Telephone: 517-607-2327
Fax: 517-607-2223
E-mail: admissions@hillsdale.edu

SPONSOR

Academics

Hillsdale awards bachelor's **degrees**. **Challenging opportunities** include advanced placement credit, accelerated degree programs, an honors program, double majors, independent study, and a senior project. Special programs include internships, summer session for credit, and study-abroad.

The most frequently chosen **baccalaureate** fields are business/marketing, history, and social sciences. A complete listing of majors at Hillsdale appears in the Majors by College index beginning on page 471.

The **faculty** at Hillsdale has 110 full-time members, 83% with terminal degrees. The student-faculty ratio is 10:1.

Students of Hillsdale

The student body is made up of 1,326 undergraduates. 52.3% are women and 47.7% are men. Students come from 48 states and territories and 7 other countries. 38% are from Michigan. 1.4% are international students. 88% returned for their sophomore year.

Facilities and Resources

200 **computers/terminals** are available on campus for general student use. Students can access the following: computer help desk, free student e-mail accounts. Campuswide network is available. 100% of college-owned or -operated housing units are wired for high-speed Internet access. Wireless service is available via entire campus. The 4 **libraries** have 240,000 books and 1,650 subscriptions.

Campus Life

There are 45 active organizations on campus, including a drama/theater group, newspaper, and choral group. 35% of eligible men and 45% of eligible women are members of national **fraternities** and national **sororities**.

Hillsdale is a member of the NCAA (Division II). **Intercollegiate sports** (some offering scholarships) include baseball (m), basketball, equestrian sports (w), football (m), ice hockey (m), lacrosse (m), riflery, soccer (w), softball (w), swimming and diving (w), track and field, volleyball (w).

Campus Safety

Student safety services include late-night transport/escort service, 24-hour emergency telephone alarm devices, 24-hour patrols by trained security personnel, and electronically operated dormitory entrances.

Applying

Hillsdale requires an essay, SAT or ACT, a high school transcript, and 2 recommendations, and in some cases an interview. It recommends SAT Subject Tests, an interview, and a minimum high school GPA of 3.3. Application deadline: 2/15, 2/15 for nonresidents; 4/1 for financial aid, with a 2/1 priority date. Early and deferred admission are possible.

At Hillsdale College, the curriculum and daily campus life are guided by ideals basic to the American way of life. Hillsdale's history of independence has tangible consequences in shaping administrative policy and academic rigor. The Judeo-Christian/Greco-Roman heritage and the honored truths of Western civilization form the basis for the education at Hillsdale College.

Getting Accepted
1,401 applied
64% were accepted
346 enrolled (39% of accepted)
47% from top tenth of their h.s. class
3.72 average high school GPA
Mean SAT critical reading score: 680
Mean SAT math score: 620
Mean SAT writing score: 640
Mean ACT score: 28
87% had SAT critical reading scores over 600
69% had SAT math scores over 600
78% had SAT writing scores over 600
84% had ACT scores over 24
40% had SAT critical reading scores over 700
16% had SAT math scores over 700
26% had SAT writing scores over 700
29% had ACT scores over 30
13 National Merit Scholars
45 class presidents
35 valedictorians

Graduation and After
67% graduated in 4 years
7% graduated in 5 years
2% graduated in 6 years
26% pursued further study (8% arts and sciences, 6% business, 4% law)
100% had job offers within 6 months
48 organizations recruited on campus

Financial Matters
$19,090 tuition and fees (2007–08)
$7340 room and board
80% average percent of need met
$15,000 average financial aid amount received per undergraduate (2006–07 estimated)

HIRAM COLLEGE
RURAL SETTING ■ PRIVATE ■ INDEPENDENT RELIGIOUS ■ COED
HIRAM, OHIO

Web site: www.hiram.edu
Contact: Mr. Sherman C. Dean II, Director of Admission, PO Box 96, Hiram, OH 44234
Telephone: 330-569-5169 or toll-free 800-362-5280
Fax: 330-569-5944
E-mail: admission@hiram.edu

Getting Accepted
1,058 applied
88% were accepted
312 enrolled (34% of accepted)
23% from top tenth of their h.s. class
3.34 average high school GPA
Mean SAT critical reading score: 553
Mean SAT math score: 549
Mean ACT score: 24
31% had SAT critical reading scores over 600
28% had SAT math scores over 600
40% had ACT scores over 24
7% had SAT critical reading scores over 700
5% had SAT math scores over 700
5% had ACT scores over 30
11 valedictorians

Graduation and After
55% graduated in 4 years
8% graduated in 5 years
1% graduated in 6 years
61% had job offers within 6 months
70 organizations recruited on campus

Financial Matters
$24,885 tuition and fees (2007–08)
$7980 room and board

Academics
Hiram awards bachelor's and master's **degrees**. **Challenging opportunities** include advanced placement credit, student-designed majors, double majors, independent study, and a senior project. Special programs include internships, summer session for credit, off-campus study, and study-abroad.

The most frequently chosen **baccalaureate** fields are business/marketing, social sciences, and biological/life sciences. A complete listing of majors at Hiram appears in the Majors by College index beginning on page 471.

The **faculty** at Hiram has 64 full-time members, 100% with terminal degrees. The student-faculty ratio is 12:1.

Students of Hiram
The student body totals 1,239, of whom 1,205 are undergraduates. 55.6% are women and 44.4% are men. Students come from 29 states and territories and 19 other countries. 87% are from Ohio. 2.7% are international students. 9.4% are African American, 0.3% American Indian, 1.8% Asian American, and 1.1% Hispanic American. 78% returned for their sophomore year.

Facilities and Resources
Campuswide network is available. The **library** has 187,451 books and 3,993 subscriptions.

Campus Life
There are 60 active organizations on campus, including a drama/theater group, newspaper, radio station, and choral group. 8% of eligible men and 12% of eligible women are members of local **fraternities** and local **sororities**.

Hiram is a member of the NCAA (Division III). **Intercollegiate sports** include baseball (m), basketball, cross-country running, football (m), golf, soccer, softball (w), swimming and diving, tennis, track and field, volleyball (w).

Campus Safety
Student safety services include late-night transport/escort service, 24-hour emergency telephone alarm devices, 24-hour patrols by trained security personnel, and electronically operated dormitory entrances.

Applying
Hiram requires an essay, SAT or ACT, a high school transcript, and 2 recommendations, and in some cases an interview. It recommends an interview and 3 recommendations. Application deadline: 4/1; 2/15 priority date for financial aid. Early and deferred admission are possible.

Hobart and William Smith Colleges

Small-town setting ■ Private ■ Independent ■ Coed
Geneva, New York

Web site: www.hws.edu
Contact: Don W. Emmons, Dean of Admissions and Vice President of Enrollment, 629 South Main Street, Geneva, NY 14456-3397
Telephone: 315-781-3472 or toll-free 800-245-0100
Fax: 315-781-5471
E-mail: admissions@hws.edu

Academics

HWS awards bachelor's **degrees**. **Challenging opportunities** include advanced placement credit, accelerated degree programs, student-designed majors, an honors program, double majors, independent study, and a senior project. Special programs include internships, off-campus study, and study-abroad.

The most frequently chosen **baccalaureate** fields are social sciences, English, and history. A complete listing of majors at HWS appears in the Majors by College index beginning on page 471.

The **faculty** at HWS has 156 full-time members, 94% with terminal degrees. The student-faculty ratio is 11:1.

Students of HWS

The student body totals 1,883, of whom 1,868 are undergraduates. 53.9% are women and 46.1% are men. Students come from 44 states and territories and 10 other countries. 45% are from New York. 1.9% are international students. 3.5% are African American, 0.1% American Indian, 1.6% Asian American, and 4% Hispanic American. 85% returned for their sophomore year.

Facilities and Resources

250 **computers/terminals** are available on campus for general student use. Students can access the following: online (class) registration. Campuswide network is available. The 2 **libraries** have 380,419 books and 2,469 subscriptions.

Campus Life

There are 60 active organizations on campus, including a drama/theater group, newspaper, radio station, and choral group. 15% of eligible men are members of national **fraternities**.

HWS is a member of the NCAA (Division III). **Intercollegiate sports** include basketball, crew, cross-country running, field hockey (w), football (m), golf, ice hockey (m), lacrosse, sailing, soccer, squash, swimming and diving (w), tennis.

Campus Safety

Student safety services include late-night transport/escort service, 24-hour emergency telephone alarm devices, 24-hour patrols by trained security personnel, and electronically operated dormitory entrances.

Applying

HWS requires an essay, SAT or ACT, a high school transcript, and 1 recommendation. It recommends SAT Subject Tests and an interview. Application deadline: 2/1; 3/15 for financial aid, with a 2/15 priority date. Early and deferred admission are possible.

Hobart and William Smith Colleges (HWS) are dedicated to providing a liberal arts education that is not merely informative, but also transformative, by emphasizing ideals as well as knowledge. In other words, they are committed to nurturing the whole person, not just the academic student. To achieve this goal, HWS melds an interdisciplinary curriculum with a worldview of learning, the highlights of which are an extensive and vibrant study-abroad program; local, national, and global internships; and a strong community-service component.

Getting Accepted
3,410 applied
65% were accepted
545 enrolled (25% of accepted)
33% from top tenth of their h.s. class
3.22 average high school GPA
Mean SAT critical reading score: 589
Mean SAT math score: 591
45% had SAT critical reading scores over 600
50% had SAT math scores over 600
8% had SAT critical reading scores over 700
6% had SAT math scores over 700
5 National Merit Scholars
18 class presidents
3 valedictorians

Graduation and After
71% graduated in 4 years
6% graduated in 5 years
1% graduated in 6 years
30% pursued further study (14% arts and sciences, 5% medicine, 4% law)
90% had job offers within 6 months
35 organizations recruited on campus

Financial Matters
$36,718 tuition and fees (2007–08)
$9250 room and board
80% average percent of need met
$25,059 average financial aid amount received per undergraduate (2006–07 estimated)

HOPE COLLEGE

SUBURBAN SETTING ■ PRIVATE ■ INDEPENDENT RELIGIOUS ■ COED
HOLLAND, MICHIGAN

Web site: www.hope.edu
Contact: Hope College Admissions, 69 East 10th Street, P.O. Box 9000,
 Holland, MI 49422-9000
Telephone: 616-395-7850 or toll-free 800-968-7850
Fax: 616-395-7130
E-mail: admissions@hope.edu

Getting Accepted

2,748 applied
83% were accepted
819 enrolled (36% of accepted)
35% from top tenth of their h.s. class
3.74 average high school GPA
44% had SAT critical reading scores over 600
51% had SAT math scores over 600
73% had SAT writing scores over 600
73% had ACT scores over 24
10% had SAT critical reading scores over 700
14% had SAT math scores over 700
20% had SAT writing scores over 700
20% had ACT scores over 30
8 National Merit Scholars

Graduation and After

62% graduated in 4 years
14% graduated in 5 years
2% graduated in 6 years
28% pursued further study (3% arts and sciences, 2% law, 1% business)
45 organizations recruited on campus

Financial Matters

$23,800 tuition and fees (2007–08)
$7300 room and board
85% average percent of need met
$18,771 average financial aid amount received per undergraduate (2006–07 estimated)

Academics

Hope awards bachelor's **degrees**. **Challenging opportunities** include advanced placement credit, student-designed majors, double majors, independent study, and a senior project. Special programs include internships, summer session for credit, off-campus study, study-abroad, and Army ROTC.

The most frequently chosen **baccalaureate** fields are education, business/marketing, and psychology. A complete listing of majors at Hope appears in the Majors by College index beginning on page 471.

The **faculty** at Hope has 219 full-time members, 76% with terminal degrees. The student-faculty ratio is 12:1.

Students of Hope

The student body is made up of 3,226 undergraduates. 58.8% are women and 41.2% are men. Students come from 45 states and territories and 31 other countries. 70% are from Michigan. 1.3% are international students. 2.3% are African American, 0.4% American Indian, 2.4% Asian American, and 2.9% Hispanic American. 88% returned for their sophomore year.

Facilities and Resources

300 **computers/terminals** and 5,000 ports are available on campus for general student use. Students can access the following: campus intranet, computer help desk, free student e-mail accounts, online (class) grades, online (class) registration, online (class) schedules. Campuswide network is available. 100% of college-owned or -operated housing units are wired for high-speed Internet access. Wireless service is available via entire campus. The 2 **libraries** have 358,329 books and 2,878 subscriptions.

Campus Life

There are 67 active organizations on campus, including a drama/theater group, newspaper, radio station, television station, and choral group. 6% of eligible men and 15% of eligible women are members of national **fraternities**, national **sororities**, local fraternities, and local sororities.

Hope is a member of the NCAA (Division III). **Intercollegiate sports** include baseball (m), basketball, cheerleading, cross-country running, football (m), golf, soccer, softball (w), swimming and diving, tennis, track and field, volleyball (w).

Campus Safety

Student safety services include late-night transport/escort service, 24-hour emergency telephone alarm devices, 24-hour patrols by trained security personnel, and electronically operated dormitory entrances.

Applying

Hope requires an essay, SAT or ACT, and a high school transcript, and in some cases 1 recommendation. It recommends an interview. Application deadline: rolling admissions; 3/1 priority date for financial aid. Early and deferred admission are possible.

HOUGHTON COLLEGE

RURAL SETTING ■ PRIVATE ■ INDEPENDENT RELIGIOUS ■ COED
HOUGHTON, NEW YORK

Web site: www.houghton.edu
Contact: Mr. Wayne MacBeth, Vice President for Enrollment Management
and Market Relations, PO Box 128, Houghton, NY 14744
Telephone: 585-567-9353 or toll-free 800-777-2556
Fax: 585-567-9522
E-mail: admission@houghton.edu

Academics

Houghton awards associate, bachelor's, and master's **degrees. Challenging opportunities** include advanced placement credit, an honors program, double majors, independent study, and a senior project. Special programs include internships, summer session for credit, off-campus study, study-abroad, and Army ROTC.

The most frequently chosen **baccalaureate** fields are business/marketing, education, and theology and religious vocations. A complete listing of majors at Houghton appears in the Majors by College index beginning on page 471.

The **faculty** at Houghton has 87 full-time members, 80% with terminal degrees. The student-faculty ratio is 14:1.

Students of Houghton

The student body totals 1,382, of whom 1,368 are undergraduates. 64% are women and 36% are men. Students come from 32 states and territories and 17 other countries. 68% are from New York. 3.2% are international students. 2% are African American, 0.4% American Indian, 1.7% Asian American, and 0.7% Hispanic American. 82% returned for their sophomore year.

Facilities and Resources

25 **computers/terminals** and 820 ports are available on campus for general student use. Students can access the following: computer help desk, free student e-mail accounts, on-line (class) grades, online (class) registration, online (class) schedules. Campuswide network is available. 100% of college-owned or -operated housing units are wired for high-speed Internet access. Wireless service is available via entire campus. The 2 **libraries** have 265,000 books and 11,000 subscriptions.

Campus Life

There are 50 active organizations on campus, including a drama/theater group, newspaper, and choral group. No national or local **fraternities** or **sororities**.

Houghton is a member of the NAIA. **Intercollegiate sports** (some offering scholarships) include basketball, cross-country running, field hockey (w), soccer, track and field, volleyball (w).

Campus Safety

Student safety services include phone connection to security patrols, late-night transport/escort service, 24-hour patrols by trained security personnel, and electronically operated dormitory entrances.

Applying

Houghton requires an essay, SAT or ACT, a high school transcript, 1 recommendation, and Christian character recommendation. It recommends an interview and a minimum high school GPA of 2.5. Application deadline: rolling admissions; 3/1 priority date for financial aid. Deferred admission is possible.

Getting Accepted

1,005 applied
84% were accepted
265 enrolled (31% of accepted)
33% from top tenth of their h.s. class
3.5 average high school GPA
Mean SAT critical reading score: 584
Mean SAT math score: 565
Mean SAT writing score: 570
Mean ACT score: 26
41% had SAT critical reading scores over 600
34% had SAT math scores over 600
36% had SAT writing scores over 600
58% had ACT scores over 24
12% had SAT critical reading scores over 700
7% had SAT math scores over 700
7% had SAT writing scores over 700
15% had ACT scores over 30
1 National Merit Scholar
11 valedictorians

Graduation and After

62% graduated in 4 years
9% graduated in 5 years
1% graduated in 6 years
33% pursued further study (48% arts and sciences, 14% education, 13% medicine)
63% had job offers within 6 months
45 organizations recruited on campus

Financial Matters

$21,620 tuition and fees (2007–08)
$6860 room and board
70% average percent of need met
$15,808 average financial aid amount received per undergraduate (2006–07 estimated)

ILLINOIS COLLEGE

SMALL-TOWN SETTING ■ PRIVATE ■ INDEPENDENT RELIGIOUS ■ COED
JACKSONVILLE, ILLINOIS

Web site: www.ic.edu
Contact: Mr. Rick Bystry, Associate Director of Admission, 1101 West College, Jacksonville, IL 62650
Telephone: 217-245-3030 or toll-free 866-464-5265
Fax: 217-245-3034
E-mail: admissions@ic.edu

Getting Accepted
917 applied
91% were accepted
260 enrolled (31% of accepted)
21% from top tenth of their h.s. class
3.29 average high school GPA
Mean SAT critical reading score: 542
Mean SAT math score: 542
Mean SAT writing score: 544
Mean ACT score: 24
11% had SAT critical reading scores over 600
44% had SAT math scores over 600
50% had SAT writing scores over 600
47% had ACT scores over 24
11% had SAT critical reading scores over 700
7% had ACT scores over 30
13 valedictorians

Graduation and After
46% graduated in 4 years
15% graduated in 5 years
27% pursued further study (8% arts and sciences, 5% business, 5% education)
97% had job offers within 6 months

Financial Matters
$18,800 tuition and fees (2007–08)
$6970 room and board
91% average percent of need met
$13,570 average financial aid amount received per undergraduate (2006–07 estimated)

Academics
IC awards bachelor's **degrees**. **Challenging opportunities** include advanced placement credit, accelerated degree programs, double majors, independent study, and a senior project. Special programs include internships, summer session for credit, and study-abroad.

The most frequently chosen **baccalaureate** fields are education, biological/life sciences, and business/marketing. A complete listing of majors at IC appears in the Majors by College index beginning on page 471.

The **faculty** at IC has 72 full-time members, 81% with terminal degrees. The student-faculty ratio is 13:1.

Students of IC
The student body is made up of 1,014 undergraduates. 51.7% are women and 48.3% are men. Students come from 22 states and territories and 15 other countries. 89% are from Illinois. 2.4% are international students. 3.4% are African American, 0.7% American Indian, 0.7% Asian American, and 1.7% Hispanic American. 80% returned for their sophomore year.

Facilities and Resources
110 **computers/terminals** are available on campus for general student use. Students can access the following: computer help desk, free student e-mail accounts, online (class) grades, online (class) registration, online (class) schedules. Campuswide network is available. 30% of college-owned or -operated housing units are wired for high-speed Internet access. Wireless service is available via entire campus. The 2 **libraries** have 163,810 books and 10,234 subscriptions.

Campus Life
There are 81 active organizations on campus, including a drama/theater group, newspaper, television station, and choral group. 22% of eligible men and 18% of eligible women are members of local **fraternities** and local **sororities**.

IC is a member of the NCAA (Division III). **Intercollegiate sports** include baseball (m), cheerleading (w), cross-country running, football (m), golf, soccer, softball (w), swimming and diving, tennis, track and field, volleyball (w).

Campus Safety
Student safety services include late-night transport/escort service, 24-hour emergency telephone alarm devices, 24-hour patrols by trained security personnel, and electronically operated dormitory entrances.

Applying
IC requires SAT or ACT, a high school transcript, and 1 recommendation, and in some cases an essay. It recommends an essay, an interview, and a minimum high school GPA of 2.5. Application deadline: 7/1; 3/1 priority date for financial aid.

ILLINOIS INSTITUTE OF TECHNOLOGY

URBAN SETTING ■ PRIVATE ■ INDEPENDENT ■ COED
CHICAGO, ILLINOIS

SPONSOR

Web site: www.iit.edu
Contact: Mr. Gerald Doyle, Associate Vice President, Undergraduate Admissions, Office of Undergraduate Admission, Perlstein 101, 10 West 33rd Street, Chicago, IL 60616
Telephone: 312-567-3025 or toll-free 800-448-2329 (out-of-state)
Fax: 312-567-6939
E-mail: admission@iit.edu

Academics

IIT awards bachelor's, master's, doctoral, and first-professional **degrees**. **Challenging opportunities** include advanced placement credit, double majors, independent study, and a senior project. Special programs include cooperative education, internships, summer session for credit, study-abroad, and Army, Navy, and Air Force ROTC.

The most frequently chosen **baccalaureate** fields are engineering, architecture, and computer and information sciences. A complete listing of majors at IIT appears in the Majors by College index beginning on page 471.

The **faculty** at IIT has 359 full-time members, 90% with terminal degrees. The student-faculty ratio is 8:1.

Students of IIT

The student body totals 7,409, of whom 2,576 are undergraduates. 26.7% are women and 73.3% are men. Students come from 47 states and territories and 83 other countries. 66% are from Illinois. 15.6% are international students. 3.8% are African American, 0.4% American Indian, 14.2% Asian American, and 7.1% Hispanic American. 86% returned for their sophomore year.

Facilities and Resources

500 **computers/terminals** are available on campus for general student use. Students can access the following: campus intranet, computer help desk, free student e-mail accounts, online (class) grades, online (class) registration, online (class) schedules. Campuswide network is available. 75% of college-owned or -operated housing units are wired for high-speed Internet access. Wireless service is available via classrooms, computer centers, computer labs, dorm rooms, learning centers, libraries, student centers. The 6 **libraries** have 1,104,834 books and 21,498 subscriptions.

Campus Life

There are 75 active organizations on campus, including a drama/theater group, newspaper, radio station, and choral group. 13% of eligible men and 15% of eligible women are members of national **fraternities**, national **sororities**, and local sororities.

IIT is a member of the NAIA. **Intercollegiate sports** (some offering scholarships) include baseball (m), basketball, cross-country running, soccer, swimming and diving, volleyball (w).

Campus Safety

Student safety services include late-night transport/escort service, 24-hour emergency telephone alarm devices, 24-hour patrols by trained security personnel, and electronically operated dormitory entrances.

Applying

IIT requires an essay, a high school transcript, 1 recommendation, and ACT or SAT scores, except for international students coming from countries where the tests are not widely administered. It recommends an interview. Application deadline: 8/1, 8/1 for nonresidents; 4/15 priority date for financial aid. Deferred admission is possible.

A private, independent, Ph.D.-granting coeducational research university founded in 1890, Illinois Institute of Technology (IIT) offers students a superb education in engineering, business, architecture, the sciences, psychology, and the humanities in an environment geared toward the undergraduate student. Located 10 minutes from downtown Chicago, IIT provides small class sizes, hands-on projects, undergraduate research, co-op and internship opportunities, and distinguished faculty members. Special opportunities are available in medicine, law, pharmacy, optometry, and business. IIT offers substantial need-based and merit scholarships.

Getting Accepted
4,383 applied
56% were accepted
521 enrolled (21% of accepted)
43% from top tenth of their h.s. class
3.77 average high school GPA
Mean SAT critical reading score: 601
Mean SAT math score: 663
Mean SAT writing score: 584
Mean ACT score: 28
55% had SAT critical reading scores over 600
82% had SAT math scores over 600
45% had SAT writing scores over 600
88% had ACT scores over 24
14% had SAT critical reading scores over 700
33% had SAT math scores over 700
10% had SAT writing scores over 700
32% had ACT scores over 30
10 valedictorians

Graduation and After
40% graduated in 4 years
22% graduated in 5 years
5% graduated in 6 years
77% pursued further study
203 organizations recruited on campus

Financial Matters
$25,746 tuition and fees (2007–08)
$8618 room and board
85% average percent of need met
$21,490 average financial aid amount received per undergraduate (2005–06)

ILLINOIS WESLEYAN UNIVERSITY

SUBURBAN SETTING ■ PRIVATE ■ INDEPENDENT ■ COED
BLOOMINGTON, ILLINOIS

Getting Accepted
2,963 applied
57% were accepted
538 enrolled (32% of accepted)
45% from top tenth of their h.s. class
58% had SAT critical reading scores over 600
72% had SAT math scores over 600
93% had ACT scores over 24
18% had SAT critical reading scores over 700
22% had SAT math scores over 700
31% had ACT scores over 30
5 National Merit Scholars
23 valedictorians

Graduation and After
79% graduated in 4 years
3% graduated in 5 years
1% graduated in 6 years
32% pursued further study (15% arts and
  sciences, 5% medicine, 3% law)
62.3% had job offers within 6 months
97 organizations recruited on campus

Financial Matters
$30,750 tuition and fees (2007–08)
$7030 room and board
92% average percent of need met
$21,417 average financial aid amount received
  per undergraduate (2006–07 estimated)

Web site: www.iwu.edu
Contact: Mr. Tony Bankston, Dean of Admissions, PO Box 2900,
  Bloomington, IL 61702-2900
Telephone: 309-556-3031 or toll-free 800-332-2498
Fax: 309-556-3820
E-mail: iwuadmit@iwu.edu

Academics

IWU awards bachelor's **degrees**. **Challenging opportunities** include advanced placement credit, student-designed majors, an honors program, double majors, independent study, and a senior project. Special programs include internships, off-campus study, study-abroad, and Army ROTC.

The most frequently chosen **baccalaureate** fields are business/marketing, visual and performing arts, and biological/life sciences. A complete listing of majors at IWU appears in the Majors by College index beginning on page 471.

The **faculty** at IWU has 161 full-time members, 93% with terminal degrees. The student-faculty ratio is 11:1.

Students of IWU

The student body is made up of 2,094 undergraduates. 57.9% are women and 42.1% are men. Students come from 39 states and territories and 22 other countries. 87% are from Illinois. 2.5% are international students. 5.3% are African American, 0.4% American Indian, 4.1% Asian American, and 3% Hispanic American. 92% returned for their sophomore year.

Facilities and Resources

400 **computers/terminals** are available on campus for general student use. Students can access the following: campus intranet, computer help desk, free student e-mail accounts, online (class) registration. Campuswide network is available. Wireless service is available via classrooms, libraries, student centers. The **library** has 313,495 books and 12,238 subscriptions.

Campus Life

There are 160 active organizations on campus, including a drama/theater group, newspaper, radio station, television station, and choral group. 33% of eligible men and 25% of eligible women are members of national **fraternities**, national **sororities**, and local sororities.

IWU is a member of the NCAA (Division III). **Intercollegiate sports** include baseball (m), basketball, cross-country running, football (m), golf, soccer, softball (w), swimming and diving, tennis, track and field, volleyball (w).

Campus Safety

Student safety services include emergency response team, late-night transport/escort service, 24-hour emergency telephone alarm devices, 24-hour patrols by trained security personnel, and electronically operated dormitory entrances.

Applying

IWU requires an essay, SAT or ACT, a high school transcript, 1 recommendation, and a minimum high school GPA of 2.0. It recommends an interview, 2 recommendations, and a minimum high school GPA of 3.0. Application deadline: rolling admissions; 3/1 for financial aid, with a 3/1 priority date. Early and deferred admission are possible.

Iowa State University of Science and Technology

Suburban setting ■ Public ■ State-supported ■ Coed
Ames, Iowa

Web site: www.iastate.edu
Contact: Mr. Phil Caffrey, Associate Director for Freshman Admissions, 100 Alumni Hall, Ames, IA 50011-2010
Telephone: 515-294-5836 or toll-free 800-262-3810
Fax: 515-294-2592
E-mail: admissions@iastate.edu

Academics

Iowa State awards bachelor's, master's, doctoral, and first-professional **degrees** and post-master's certificates. **Challenging opportunities** include advanced placement credit, accelerated degree programs, student-designed majors, freshman honors college, an honors program, double majors, independent study, and a senior project. Special programs include cooperative education, internships, summer session for credit, off-campus study, study-abroad, and Army, Navy, and Air Force ROTC.

The most frequently chosen **baccalaureate** fields are business/marketing, engineering, and agriculture. A complete listing of majors at Iowa State appears in the Majors by College index beginning on page 471.

The **faculty** at Iowa State has 1,346 full-time members, 93% with terminal degrees. The student-faculty ratio is 16:1.

Students of Iowa State

The student body totals 26,160, of whom 21,004 are undergraduates. 43.1% are women and 56.9% are men. Students come from 58 states and territories and 106 other countries. 71% are from Iowa. 3.6% are international students. 2.8% are African American, 0.3% American Indian, 3.2% Asian American, and 2.6% Hispanic American. 85% returned for their sophomore year.

Facilities and Resources

2,400 **computers/terminals** are available on campus for general student use. Students can access the following: campus intranet, computer help desk, free student e-mail accounts, online (class) grades, online (class) registration, online (class) schedules, network services. Campuswide network is available. 100% of college-owned or -operated housing units are wired for high-speed Internet access. Wireless service is available via entire campus. The 2 **libraries** have 2,470,745 books and 52,533 subscriptions.

Campus Life

There are 515 active organizations on campus, including a drama/theater group, newspaper, radio station, television station, choral group, and marching band. 11% of eligible men and 11% of eligible women are members of national **fraternities**, national **sororities**, and local fraternities.

Iowa State is a member of the NCAA (Division I). **Intercollegiate sports** (some offering scholarships) include basketball, cross-country running, football (m), golf, gymnastics (w), soccer (w), softball (w), swimming and diving, tennis (w), track and field, volleyball (w), wrestling (m).

Campus Safety

Student safety services include crime prevention programs, threat assessment team, motor vehicle help van, late-night transport/escort service, 24-hour emergency telephone alarm devices, 24-hour patrols by trained security personnel, student patrols, and electronically operated dormitory entrances.

Applying

Iowa State requires SAT or ACT, a high school transcript, and rank in upper 50% of high school class. Application deadline: 7/1; 3/1 priority date for financial aid. Early and deferred admission are possible.

Getting Accepted
11,058 applied
89% were accepted
4,347 enrolled (44% of accepted)
26% from top tenth of their h.s. class
3.47 average high school GPA
Mean ACT score: 24
39% had SAT critical reading scores over 600
57% had SAT math scores over 600
59% had ACT scores over 24
12% had SAT critical reading scores over 700
18% had SAT math scores over 700
12% had ACT scores over 30
40 National Merit Scholars

Graduation and After
32% graduated in 4 years
29% graduated in 5 years
5% graduated in 6 years
19% pursued further study
76% had job offers within 6 months
1825 organizations recruited on campus

Financial Matters
$6360 resident tuition and fees (2008–09)
$17,350 nonresident tuition and fees (2008–09)
82% average percent of need met
$9448 average financial aid amount received per undergraduate (2006–07 estimated)

Located in the heart of New York State's Finger Lakes region, Ithaca College is a nationally recognized, private residential college of 6,400 students and 460 full-time faculty members. Ithaca offers the perfect blend of liberal arts and professional programs, and its intimate student-faculty ratio of 11:1 ensures a first-rate education on a first-name basis. More than 100 degree programs are found in the College's five schools—business, communications, health sciences and human performance, humanities and sciences, and music—and interdisciplinary division. An Ithaca education emphasizes hands-on learning, social responsibility, and close student-faculty relationships. The College's broad, flexible curriculum prepares students to follow their passions in life.

Getting Accepted
11,235 applied
74% were accepted
1,798 enrolled (22% of accepted)
30% from top tenth of their h.s. class
Mean SAT critical reading score: 584
Mean SAT math score: 587
43% had SAT critical reading scores over 600
44% had SAT math scores over 600
8% had SAT critical reading scores over 700
6% had SAT math scores over 700
1 National Merit Scholar
14 valedictorians

Graduation and After
70% graduated in 4 years
6% graduated in 5 years
1% graduated in 6 years
40% pursued further study (33% arts and sciences, 4% education, 2% business)
286 organizations recruited on campus

Financial Matters
$28,670 tuition and fees (2007–08)
$10,728 room and board
86% average percent of need met
$22,694 average financial aid amount received per undergraduate (2006–07 estimated)

ITHACA COLLEGE
SMALL-TOWN SETTING ■ PRIVATE ■ INDEPENDENT ■ COED
ITHACA, NEW YORK

Web site: www.ithaca.edu
Contact: Gerard Turbide, Director of Admission, 100 Job Hall, Ithaca, NY 14850-7020
Telephone: 607-274-3124 or toll-free 800-429-4274
Fax: 607-274-1900
E-mail: admission@ithaca.edu

Academics
Ithaca awards bachelor's, master's, and doctoral **degrees**. **Challenging opportunities** include advanced placement credit, accelerated degree programs, student-designed majors, freshman honors college, an honors program, double majors, independent study, and a senior project. Special programs include internships, summer session for credit, off-campus study, study-abroad, and Army and Air Force ROTC.

The most frequently chosen **baccalaureate** fields are communications/journalism, visual and performing arts, and health professions and related sciences. A complete listing of majors at Ithaca appears in the Majors by College index beginning on page 471.

The **faculty** at Ithaca has 461 full-time members, 92% with terminal degrees. The student-faculty ratio is 12:1.

Students of Ithaca
The student body totals 6,660, of whom 6,260 are undergraduates. 54.8% are women and 45.2% are men. Students come from 50 states and territories and 67 other countries. 46% are from New York. 2% are international students. 2.7% are African American, 0.5% American Indian, 3.7% Asian American, and 4% Hispanic American. 87% returned for their sophomore year.

Facilities and Resources
640 **computers/terminals** and 20 ports are available on campus for general student use. Students can access the following: campus intranet, computer help desk, free student e-mail accounts, online (class) grades, online (class) registration, online (class) schedules. Campuswide network is available. 100% of college-owned or -operated housing units are wired for high-speed Internet access. The **library** has 363,648 books and 44,327 subscriptions.

Campus Life
There are 172 active organizations on campus, including a drama/theater group, newspaper, radio station, television station, and choral group. 1% of eligible men and 1% of eligible women are members of national **fraternities** and national **sororities**.

Ithaca is a member of the NCAA (Division III). **Intercollegiate sports** include baseball (m), basketball, crew, cross-country running, field hockey (w), football (m), gymnastics (w), lacrosse, soccer, softball (w), swimming and diving, tennis, track and field, volleyball (w), wrestling (m).

Campus Safety
Student safety services include patrols by trained security personnel 11 p.m. to 7 a.m, late-night transport/escort service, 24-hour emergency telephone alarm devices, student patrols, and electronically operated dormitory entrances.

Applying
Ithaca requires an essay, SAT or ACT, a high school transcript, and 1 recommendation, and in some cases audition. It recommends a minimum high school GPA of 3.0. Application deadline: 2/1; 2/1 priority date for financial aid. Early and deferred admission are possible.

James Madison University

SMALL-TOWN SETTING ■ PUBLIC ■ STATE-SUPPORTED ■ COED
HARRISONBURG, VIRGINIA

Web site: www.jmu.edu
Contact: Mr. Michael D. Walsh, Director of Admission, Office of Admissions, Harrisonburg, VA 22807
Telephone: 540-568-5681
Fax: 540-568-3332
E-mail: admissions@jmu.edu

Academics

JMU awards bachelor's, master's, and doctoral **degrees** and post-master's certificates (also offers specialist in education degree). **Challenging opportunities** include advanced placement credit, accelerated degree programs, freshman honors college, an honors program, double majors, independent study, and a senior project. Special programs include internships, summer session for credit, study-abroad, and Army and Air Force ROTC.

The most frequently chosen **baccalaureate** fields are business/marketing, health professions and related sciences, and social sciences. A complete listing of majors at JMU appears in the Majors by College index beginning on page 471.

The **faculty** at JMU has 854 full-time members, 80% with terminal degrees. The student-faculty ratio is 16:1.

Students of JMU

The student body totals 17,918, of whom 16,414 are undergraduates. 60.3% are women and 39.7% are men. Students come from 45 states and territories and 50 other countries. 70% are from Virginia. 0.9% are international students. 3.8% are African American, 0.3% American Indian, 4.8% Asian American, and 2.3% Hispanic American. 91% returned for their sophomore year.

Facilities and Resources

600 **computers/terminals** and 7,000 ports are available on campus for general student use. Students can access the following: campus intranet, computer help desk, free student e-mail accounts, online (class) grades, online (class) registration, online (class) schedules. Campuswide network is available. 100% of college-owned or -operated housing units are wired for high-speed Internet access. Wireless service is available via classrooms, learning centers, libraries, student centers. The 3 **libraries** have 659,136 books and 15,909 subscriptions.

Campus Life

There are 328 active organizations on campus, including a drama/theater group, newspaper, radio station, choral group, and marching band. 10% of eligible men and 12% of eligible women are members of national **fraternities** and national **sororities**.

JMU is a member of the NCAA (Division I). **Intercollegiate sports** (some offering scholarships) include baseball (m), basketball, cheerleading, cross-country running (w), field hockey (w), football (m), golf, lacrosse (w), soccer, softball (w), swimming and diving (w), tennis, track and field (w), volleyball (w).

Campus Safety

Student safety services include lighted pathways, late-night transport/escort service, 24-hour emergency telephone alarm devices, 24-hour patrols by trained security personnel, student patrols, and electronically operated dormitory entrances.

Applying

JMU requires SAT or ACT and a high school transcript. It recommends a minimum high school GPA of 3.0. Application deadline: 1/15; 3/1 priority date for financial aid. Deferred admission is possible.

Getting Accepted
18,352 applied
64% were accepted
3,867 enrolled (33% of accepted)
29% from top tenth of their h.s. class
3.71 average high school GPA
Mean SAT critical reading score: 565
Mean SAT math score: 575
Mean ACT score: 24
27% had SAT critical reading scores over 600
33% had SAT math scores over 600
55% had ACT scores over 24
3% had SAT critical reading scores over 700
3% had SAT math scores over 700
3% had ACT scores over 30

Graduation and After
64% graduated in 4 years
15% graduated in 5 years
2% graduated in 6 years
25% pursued further study (6% education, 4% business, 3% law)
183 organizations recruited on campus

Financial Matters
$6666 resident tuition and fees (2007–08)
$17,386 nonresident tuition and fees (2007–08)
$7108 room and board
50% average percent of need met
$7683 average financial aid amount received per undergraduate (2006–07 estimated)

JOHN BROWN UNIVERSITY

SMALL-TOWN SETTING ■ PRIVATE ■ INDEPENDENT RELIGIOUS ■ COED
SILOAM SPRINGS, ARKANSAS

Web site: www.jbu.edu
Contact: Mr. Don Crandall, Vice President for Enrollment Management, 200
    West University Street, Siloam Springs, AR 72761-2121
Telephone: 479-524-7150 or toll-free 877-JBU-INFO
Fax: 479-524-4196
E-mail: dcrandal@jbu.edu

Getting Accepted
891 applied
76% were accepted
363 enrolled (53% of accepted)
32% from top tenth of their h.s. class
3.57 average high school GPA
Mean SAT critical reading score: 590
Mean SAT math score: 580
Mean ACT score: 25
39% had SAT critical reading scores over 600
37% had SAT math scores over 600
63% had ACT scores over 24
15% had SAT critical reading scores over 700
8% had SAT math scores over 700
16% had ACT scores over 30
2 National Merit Scholars
17 valedictorians

Graduation and After
26% pursued further study (4% business, 4%
    medicine, 1% arts and sciences)
97% had job offers within 6 months
52 organizations recruited on campus

Financial Matters
$18,066 tuition and fees (2008–09)
$6580 room and board
50% average percent of need met
$8195 average financial aid amount received
    per undergraduate (2005–06 estimated)

Academics
JBU awards bachelor's and master's **degrees**. **Challenging opportunities** include advanced placement credit, freshman honors college, an honors program, double majors, independent study, and a senior project. Special programs include internships, study-abroad, and Army and Air Force ROTC.

The most frequently chosen **baccalaureate** fields are business/marketing, education, and visual and performing arts. A complete listing of majors at JBU appears in the Majors by College index beginning on page 471.

The **faculty** at JBU has 84 full-time members, 70% with terminal degrees. The student-faculty ratio is 13:1.

Students of JBU
The student body totals 2,061, of whom 1,702 are undergraduates. 53% are women and 47% are men. Students come from 40 states and territories and 45 other countries. 26% are from Arkansas. 6.4% are international students. 2.9% are African American, 1.9% American Indian, 1.2% Asian American, and 3.2% Hispanic American. 80% returned for their sophomore year.

Facilities and Resources
100 **computers/terminals** are available on campus for general student use. Students can access the following: campus intranet, computer help desk, free student e-mail accounts, online (class) grades, online (class) registration, online (class) schedules. Campuswide network is available. 100% of college-owned or -operated housing units are wired for high-speed Internet access. Wireless service is available via classrooms, dorm rooms, learning centers, libraries, student centers. The 7 **libraries** have 102,031 books and 751 subscriptions.

Campus Life
There are 20 active organizations on campus, including a drama/theater group, newspaper, radio station, television station, and choral group. No national or local **fraternities** or **sororities**.

JBU is a member of the NAIA. **Intercollegiate sports** (some offering scholarships) include basketball, soccer, tennis, volleyball (w).

Campus Safety
Student safety services include late-night transport/escort service, 24-hour emergency telephone alarm devices, and 24-hour patrols by trained security personnel.

Applying
JBU requires an essay, SAT or ACT, a high school transcript, 2 recommendations, and a minimum high school GPA of 2.5. It recommends an interview. Application deadline: rolling admissions; 3/1 priority date for financial aid. Deferred admission is possible.

John Carroll University

Suburban setting ■ Private ■ Independent Religious ■ Coed
University Heights, Ohio

Web site: www.jcu.edu
Contact: Mr. Thomas P. Fanning, Director of Admission, 20700 North Park
   Blvd, University Heights, OH 44118
Telephone: 216-397-4246
Fax: 216-397-4981
E-mail: tfanning@jcu.edu

Academics

John Carroll awards bachelor's and master's **degrees**. **Challenging opportunities** include advanced placement credit, accelerated degree programs, student-designed majors, an honors program, double majors, independent study, and a senior project. Special programs include cooperative education, internships, summer session for credit, off-campus study, study-abroad, and Army ROTC.

The most frequently chosen **baccalaureate** fields are business/marketing, public administration and social services, and biological/life sciences. A complete listing of majors at John Carroll appears in the Majors by College index beginning on page 471.

The **faculty** at John Carroll has 204 full-time members, 92% with terminal degrees. The student-faculty ratio is 14:1.

Students of John Carroll

The student body totals 3,766, of whom 3,075 are undergraduates. 54.2% are women and 45.8% are men. Students come from 38 states and territories. 72% are from Ohio. 5.1% are African American, 0.3% American Indian, 2% Asian American, and 2.5% Hispanic American. 84% returned for their sophomore year.

Facilities and Resources

210 **computers/terminals** are available on campus for general student use. Students can access the following: campus intranet, computer help desk, free student e-mail accounts, online (class) grades, online (class) registration, online (class) schedules. Campuswide network is available. 100% of college-owned or -operated housing units are wired for high-speed Internet access. Wireless service is available via entire campus. The **library** has 620,000 books and 2,198 subscriptions.

Campus Life

There are 87 active organizations on campus, including a drama/theater group, newspaper, radio station, television station, and choral group. 9% of eligible men and 14% of eligible women are members of national **fraternities** and national **sororities**.

John Carroll is a member of the NCAA (Division III). **Intercollegiate sports** include baseball (m), basketball, cross-country running, football (m), golf, soccer, softball (w), swimming and diving, tennis, track and field, volleyball (w), wrestling (m).

Campus Safety

Student safety services include late-night transport/escort service, 24-hour emergency telephone alarm devices, and 24-hour patrols by trained security personnel.

Applying

John Carroll requires SAT or ACT, a high school transcript, and 1 recommendation, and in some cases an interview. It recommends an essay and an interview. Application deadline: 2/1; 3/1 priority date for financial aid. Deferred admission is possible.

Getting Accepted

3,309 applied
86% were accepted
720 enrolled (25% of accepted)
22% from top tenth of their h.s. class
3.36 average high school GPA
Mean SAT critical reading score: 543
Mean SAT math score: 544
Mean SAT writing score: 539
Mean ACT score: 24
26% had SAT critical reading scores over 600
29% had SAT math scores over 600
24% had SAT writing scores over 600
51% had ACT scores over 24
3% had SAT critical reading scores over 700
3% had SAT math scores over 700
4% had SAT writing scores over 700
6% had ACT scores over 30
8 valedictorians

Graduation and After

65% graduated in 4 years
7% graduated in 5 years
1% graduated in 6 years
22% pursued further study (12% arts and sciences, 4% law, 2% business)
64% had job offers within 6 months
332 organizations recruited on campus

Financial Matters

$28,090 tuition and fees (2008–09)
$7934 room and board

THE JOHNS HOPKINS UNIVERSITY

URBAN SETTING ■ PRIVATE ■ INDEPENDENT ■ COED
BALTIMORE, MARYLAND

Getting Accepted
14,848 applied
24% were accepted
1,206 enrolled (33% of accepted)
82% from top tenth of their h.s. class
3.7 average high school GPA
Mean SAT critical reading score: 678
Mean SAT math score: 706
Mean ACT score: 30
88% had SAT critical reading scores over 600
92% had SAT math scores over 600
86% had SAT writing scores over 600
98% had ACT scores over 24
42% had SAT critical reading scores over 700
59% had SAT math scores over 700
43% had SAT writing scores over 700
65% had ACT scores over 30

Graduation and After
84% graduated in 4 years
7% graduated in 5 years
1% graduated in 6 years
42% pursued further study
247 organizations recruited on campus

Financial Matters
$35,900 tuition and fees (2007–08)
$11,092 room and board
100% average percent of need met
$31,176 average financial aid amount received
   per undergraduate (2006–07 estimated)

Web site: www.jhu.edu
Contact: Dr. John Latting, Dean of Undergraduate Admissions, 140 Garland
   Hall, 3400 North Charles Street, Baltimore, MD 21218-2699
Telephone: 410-516-8341
Fax: 410-516-6025
E-mail: gotojhu@jhu.edu

Academics
Johns Hopkins awards bachelor's, master's, doctoral, and first-professional **degrees** and post-bachelor's and post-master's certificates. **Challenging opportunities** include advanced placement credit, accelerated degree programs, student-designed majors, an honors program, double majors, independent study, and a senior project. Special programs include internships, summer session for credit, off-campus study, study-abroad, and Army and Air Force ROTC.

The most frequently chosen **baccalaureate** fields are health professions and related sciences, engineering, and social sciences. A complete listing of majors at Johns Hopkins appears in the Majors by College index beginning on page 471.

Students of Johns Hopkins
The student body totals 6,257, of whom 4,591 are undergraduates. 47.4% are women and 52.6% are men. Students come from 52 states and territories and 58 other countries. 15% are from Maryland. 5.3% are international students. 6.4% are African American, 0.6% American Indian, 24.9% Asian American, and 6.5% Hispanic American. 97% returned for their sophomore year.

Facilities and Resources
140 **computers/terminals** and 1,000 ports are available on campus for general student use. Students can access the following: campus intranet, computer help desk, free student e-mail accounts, online (class) grades, online (class) registration, online (class) schedules. Campuswide network is available. 100% of college-owned or -operated housing units are wired for high-speed Internet access. Wireless service is available via entire campus. The 7 **libraries** have 3,509,413 books and 30,023 subscriptions.

Campus Life
There are 180 active organizations on campus, including a drama/theater group, newspaper, radio station, and choral group. 21% of eligible men and 17% of eligible women are members of national **fraternities** and national **sororities**.

Johns Hopkins is a member of the NCAA (Division III). **Intercollegiate sports** (some offering scholarships) include baseball (m), basketball, crew, cross-country running, fencing, field hockey (w), football (m), lacrosse, soccer, swimming and diving, tennis, track and field, volleyball (w), water polo (m), wrestling (m).

Campus Safety
Student safety services include late-night transport/escort service, 24-hour emergency telephone alarm devices, 24-hour patrols by trained security personnel, student patrols, and electronically operated dormitory entrances.

Applying
Johns Hopkins requires an essay, SAT or ACT, a high school transcript, and recommendations. It recommends SAT Subject Tests and an interview. Application deadline: 1/1; 3/1 for financial aid, with a 3/1 priority date. Early and deferred admission are possible.

JUNIATA COLLEGE

SMALL-TOWN SETTING ■ PRIVATE ■ INDEPENDENT RELIGIOUS ■ COED
HUNTINGDON, PENNSYLVANIA

SPONSOR

Web site: www.juniata.edu
Contact: Terry Bollman-Dalansky, Director of Admissions, 1700 Moore Street, Huntingdon, PA 16652
Telephone: 814-641-3424 or toll-free 877-JUNIATA
Fax: 814-641-3100
E-mail: admissions@juniata.edu

Academics

Juniata awards bachelor's **degrees**. **Challenging opportunities** include advanced placement credit, accelerated degree programs, student-designed majors, freshman honors college, an honors program, double majors, independent study, and a senior project. Special programs include internships, summer session for credit, off-campus study, and study-abroad.

The most frequently chosen **baccalaureate** fields are biological/life sciences, business/marketing, and social sciences. A complete listing of majors at Juniata appears in the Majors by College index beginning on page 471.

The **faculty** at Juniata has 97 full-time members, 92% with terminal degrees. The student-faculty ratio is 13:1.

Students of Juniata

The student body is made up of 1,506 undergraduates. 54.4% are women and 45.6% are men. Students come from 36 states and territories and 34 other countries. 68% are from Pennsylvania. 5.4% are international students. 1.1% are African American, 0.1% American Indian, 1.5% Asian American, and 1.3% Hispanic American. 84% returned for their sophomore year.

Facilities and Resources

360 **computers/terminals** are available on campus for general student use. Students can access the following: campus intranet, computer help desk, free student e-mail accounts, online (class) grades, online (class) registration, online (class) schedules. Campuswide network is available. 100% of college-owned or -operated housing units are wired for high-speed Internet access. Wireless service is available via entire campus. The **library** has 350,000 books and 1,000 subscriptions.

Campus Life

There are 94 active organizations on campus, including a drama/theater group, newspaper, radio station, and choral group. No national or local **fraternities** or **sororities**.

Juniata is a member of the NCAA (Division III). **Intercollegiate sports** include baseball (m), basketball, cross-country running, field hockey (w), football (m), soccer, softball (w), swimming and diving (w), tennis, track and field, volleyball.

Campus Safety

Student safety services include fire safety training, adopt-an-officer program, security website, weather/terror alerts, travel forecast, crime statistics, late-night transport/escort service, 24-hour emergency telephone alarm devices, 24-hour patrols by trained security personnel, and student patrols.

Applying

Juniata requires an essay, a high school transcript, 1 recommendation, and a minimum high school GPA of 3.0. It recommends SAT or ACT and an interview. Application deadline: 3/1; 3/1 for financial aid, with a 3/1 priority date. Early and deferred admission are possible.

Juniata College is a caring and supportive learning community that challenges its students to think and to question while discovering countless opportunities for engaged learning. Juniata's 1,460 students benefit from top-notch academics, state-of-the-art technological resources, and guidance from dedicated faculty advisers. From the new William J. von Liebig Center for Science, the Entrepreneurial-based Business Program, and the new Halbritter Center for the Performing Arts, Juniata offers groundbreaking educational opportunities. Juniata is a place where students are encouraged to design their academic program and contribute to their community. The campus, located in the mountains of central Pennsylvania, is a friendly environment where students develop into successful leaders.

Getting Accepted
1,958 applied
67% were accepted
377 enrolled (29% of accepted)
36% from top tenth of their h.s. class
3.78 average high school GPA
Mean SAT critical reading score: 581
Mean SAT math score: 584
38% had SAT critical reading scores over 600
42% had SAT math scores over 600
8% had SAT critical reading scores over 700
4% had SAT math scores over 700
4 National Merit Scholars
12 valedictorians

Graduation and After
71% graduated in 4 years
5% graduated in 5 years
1% graduated in 6 years
31% pursued further study (17% arts and sciences, 4% business, 3% medicine)
60% had job offers within 6 months
13 organizations recruited on campus

Financial Matters
$30,280 tuition and fees (2007–08)
$8420 room and board
86% average percent of need met
$21,974 average financial aid amount received per undergraduate (2006–07 estimated)

KALAMAZOO COLLEGE

SUBURBAN SETTING ■ PRIVATE ■ INDEPENDENT RELIGIOUS ■ COED
KALAMAZOO, MICHIGAN

Web site: www.kzoo.edu
Contact: Mrs. Linda Wirgau, Records Manager, Mandelle Hall, 1200
    Academy Street, Kalamazoo, MI 49006-3295
Telephone: 269-337-7166 or toll-free 800-253-3602
Fax: 269-337-7190
E-mail: admissions@kzoo.edu

Getting Accepted

2,092 applied
63% were accepted
363 enrolled (28% of accepted)
44% from top tenth of their h.s. class
3.63 average high school GPA
Mean SAT critical reading score: 654
Mean SAT math score: 636
Mean ACT score: 28
72% had SAT critical reading scores over 600
66% had SAT math scores over 600
91% had ACT scores over 24
25% had SAT critical reading scores over 700
19% had SAT math scores over 700
30% had ACT scores over 30
11 National Merit Scholars
13 class presidents
16 valedictorians

Graduation and After

73% graduated in 4 years
4% graduated in 5 years
1% graduated in 6 years
33% pursued further study
14 organizations recruited on campus

Financial Matters

$28,716 tuition and fees (2007–08)
$7122 room and board
$22,820 average financial aid amount received
    per undergraduate (2006–07 estimated)

Academics

Kalamazoo awards bachelor's **degrees**. **Challenging opportunities** include advanced placement credit, double majors, independent study, and a senior project. Special programs include internships, off-campus study, study-abroad, and Army ROTC.

The most frequently chosen **baccalaureate** fields are social sciences, biological/life sciences, and English. A complete listing of majors at Kalamazoo appears in the Majors by College index beginning on page 471.

The **faculty** at Kalamazoo has 101 full-time members, 84% with terminal degrees. The student-faculty ratio is 11:1.

Students of Kalamazoo

The student body is made up of 1,340 undergraduates. 57.9% are women and 42.1% are men. Students come from 38 states and territories and 13 other countries. 71% are from Michigan. 1.1% are international students. 4.1% are African American, 0.1% American Indian, 6.2% Asian American, and 3.5% Hispanic American. 91% returned for their sophomore year.

Facilities and Resources

130 **computers/terminals** are available on campus for general student use. Students can access the following: campus intranet, computer help desk, free student e-mail accounts, online (class) grades, online (class) registration, online (class) schedules. Campuswide network is available. 100% of college-owned or -operated housing units are wired for high-speed Internet access. Wireless service is available via classrooms, computer centers, computer labs, libraries, student centers. The 2 **libraries** have 342,939 books and 1,495 subscriptions.

Campus Life

There are 50 active organizations on campus, including a drama/theater group, newspaper, radio station, television station, and choral group. No national or local **fraternities** or **sororities**.

Kalamazoo is a member of the NCAA (Division III). **Intercollegiate sports** include baseball (m), basketball, cross-country running, football (m), golf, soccer, softball (w), swimming and diving, tennis, volleyball (w).

Campus Safety

Student safety services include late-night transport/escort service, 24-hour emergency telephone alarm devices, 24-hour patrols by trained security personnel, and electronically operated dormitory entrances.

Applying

Kalamazoo requires an essay, SAT or ACT, a high school transcript, and 2 recommendations. It recommends an interview and a minimum high school GPA of 3.0. Application deadline: 2/1; 2/15 priority date for financial aid. Deferred admission is possible.

KENYON COLLEGE
RURAL SETTING ■ PRIVATE ■ INDEPENDENT ■ COED
GAMBIER, OHIO

Web site: www.kenyon.edu
Contact: Ms. Jennifer Delahunty, Dean of Admissions, Ransom Hall, Gambier, OH 43022
Telephone: 740-427-5778 or toll-free 800-848-2468
Fax: 740-427-5770
E-mail: admissions@kenyon.edu

Academics
Kenyon awards bachelor's **degrees**. **Challenging opportunities** include advanced placement credit, accelerated degree programs, student-designed majors, an honors program, double majors, independent study, and a senior project. Special programs include internships, off-campus study, and study-abroad.

The most frequently chosen **baccalaureate** fields are social sciences, English, and visual and performing arts. A complete listing of majors at Kenyon appears in the Majors by College index beginning on page 471.

The **faculty** at Kenyon has 152 full-time members, 98% with terminal degrees. The student-faculty ratio is 10:1.

Students of Kenyon
The student body is made up of 1,663 undergraduates. 52.1% are women and 47.9% are men. Students come from 46 states and territories and 29 other countries. 20% are from Ohio. 3.2% are international students. 3.8% are African American, 0.5% American Indian, 4.6% Asian American, and 2.7% Hispanic American. 95% returned for their sophomore year.

Facilities and Resources
300 **computers/terminals** are available on campus for general student use. Students can access the following: campus intranet, computer help desk, free student e-mail accounts, online (class) grades, online (class) registration, online (class) schedules, commercial databases. Campuswide network is available. 99% of college-owned or -operated housing units are wired for high-speed Internet access. Wireless service is available via entire campus. The 2 **libraries** have 826,059 books and 8,574 subscriptions.

Campus Life
There are 135 active organizations on campus, including a drama/theater group, newspaper, radio station, and choral group. 25% of eligible men and 10% of eligible women are members of national **fraternities**, local fraternities, and local **sororities**.

Kenyon is a member of the NCAA (Division III). **Intercollegiate sports** include baseball (m), basketball, cross-country running, field hockey (w), football (m), golf (m), lacrosse, soccer, softball (w), swimming and diving, tennis, track and field, volleyball (w).

Campus Safety
Student safety services include late-night transport/escort service, 24-hour emergency telephone alarm devices, 24-hour patrols by trained security personnel, and student patrols.

Applying
Kenyon requires an essay, SAT or ACT, a high school transcript, 1 recommendation, and counselor recommendation. It recommends an interview, 2 recommendations, and a minimum high school GPA of 3.5. Application deadline: 1/15, 1/15 for nonresidents; 2/15 priority date for financial aid. Early and deferred admission are possible.

Getting Accepted
4,626 applied
29% were accepted
458 enrolled (34% of accepted)
73% from top tenth of their h.s. class
3.86 average high school GPA
Mean SAT critical reading score: 681
Mean SAT math score: 649
Mean SAT writing score: 669
Mean ACT score: 29
88% had SAT critical reading scores over 600
79% had SAT math scores over 600
87% had SAT writing scores over 600
95% had ACT scores over 24
44% had SAT critical reading scores over 700
22% had SAT math scores over 700
37% had SAT writing scores over 700
53% had ACT scores over 30
22 National Merit Scholars
26 valedictorians

Graduation and After
82% graduated in 4 years
2% graduated in 5 years
25% pursued further study
25 organizations recruited on campus

Financial Matters
$40,240 tuition and fees (2008–09)
$6590 room and board
98% average percent of need met
$27,275 average financial aid amount received per undergraduate (2006–07 estimated)

Kettering University is a highly acclaimed university with a modern cooperative education program located in Flint, Michigan. All students alternate between terms of on-campus study and terms of full-time work for their co-op employers. Students graduate with up to 2½ years of professional experience in their job field and up to $65,000 in overall co-op earnings. Ninety-eight percent of students graduate with job offers or grad school acceptances in hand. Kettering University offers eleven bachelor's degree programs in engineering, applied science, and business. Students should visit http://www.kettering.edu for more information or to apply.

Getting Accepted

1,817 applied
72% were accepted
385 enrolled (29% of accepted)
32% from top tenth of their h.s. class
3.55 average high school GPA
Mean SAT critical reading score: 567
Mean SAT math score: 626
Mean ACT score: 26
36% had SAT critical reading scores over 600
69% had SAT math scores over 600
86% had ACT scores over 24
9% had SAT critical reading scores over 700
18% had SAT math scores over 700
19% had ACT scores over 30
18 valedictorians

Graduation and After

6% graduated in 4 years
41% graduated in 5 years
9% graduated in 6 years
30% pursued further study (28% business, 28% engineering, 1% law)
97% had job offers within 6 months
113 organizations recruited on campus

Financial Matters

$25,658 tuition and fees (2007–08)
$5798 room and board
52% average percent of need met
$13,586 average financial aid amount received per undergraduate (2005–06)

KETTERING UNIVERSITY

URBAN SETTING ■ PRIVATE ■ INDEPENDENT ■ COED, PRIMARILY MEN
FLINT, MICHIGAN

Web site: www.kettering.edu
Contact: Ms. Barbara Sosin, Director of Admissions, 1700 West Third Avenue, Flint, MI 48504-4898
Telephone: 810-762-7865 or toll-free 800-955-4464 Ext. 7865 (in-state), 800-955-4464 (out-of-state)
Fax: 810-762-9837
E-mail: admissions@kettering.edu

Academics

Kettering awards bachelor's and master's **degrees**. **Challenging opportunities** include advanced placement credit, accelerated degree programs, double majors, independent study, and a senior project. Special programs include cooperative education, internships, and study-abroad.

The most frequently chosen **baccalaureate** fields are engineering, business/marketing, and physical sciences. A complete listing of majors at Kettering appears in the Majors by College index beginning on page 471.

The **faculty** at Kettering has 125 full-time members, 82% with terminal degrees. The student-faculty ratio is 9:1.

Students of Kettering

The student body totals 2,675, of whom 2,178 are undergraduates. 14.9% are women and 85.1% are men. Students come from 50 states and territories and 8 other countries. 68% are from Michigan. 1.5% are international students. 5% are African American, 0.4% American Indian, 5.1% Asian American, and 2.4% Hispanic American. 85% returned for their sophomore year.

Facilities and Resources

300 **computers/terminals** and 800 ports are available on campus for general student use. Students can access the following: campus intranet, computer help desk, free student e-mail accounts, online (class) grades, online (class) registration, online (class) schedules. Campuswide network is available. 100% of college-owned or -operated housing units are wired for high-speed Internet access. Wireless service is available via classrooms, computer centers, computer labs, learning centers, libraries, student centers. The 2 **libraries** have 122,360 books and 525 subscriptions.

Campus Life

There are 40 active organizations on campus, including a drama/theater group, newspaper, radio station, and choral group. 40% of eligible men and 33% of eligible women are members of national **fraternities** and national **sororities**.

This institution has no intercollegiate sports.

Campus Safety

Student safety services include late-night transport/escort service, 24-hour emergency telephone alarm devices, 24-hour patrols by trained security personnel, and electronically operated dormitory entrances.

Applying

Kettering requires SAT or ACT and a high school transcript, and in some cases an essay. It recommends an interview and a minimum high school GPA of 3.0. Application deadline: rolling admissions; 2/14 priority date for financial aid. Deferred admission is possible.

Knox College

SMALL-TOWN SETTING ■ PRIVATE ■ INDEPENDENT ■ COED
GALESBURG, ILLINOIS

Web site: www.knox.edu
Contact: Mr. Paul Steenis, Director of Admissions, Box K-148, Galesburg, IL
  61401
Telephone: 309-341-7100 or toll-free 800-678-KNOX
Fax: 309-341-7070
E-mail: admission@knox.edu

Academics

Knox awards bachelor's **degrees**. **Challenging opportunities** include advanced placement credit, student-designed majors, an honors program, double majors, independent
study, and a senior project. Special programs include internships, off-campus study, and
study-abroad.

The most frequently chosen **baccalaureate** fields are social sciences, English, and
education. A complete listing of majors at Knox appears in the Majors by College index
beginning on page 471.

The **faculty** at Knox has 98 full-time members, 92% with terminal degrees. The student-faculty ratio is 12:1.

Students of Knox

The student body is made up of 1,371 undergraduates. 57.5% are women and 42.5% are
men. Students come from 46 states and territories and 36 other countries. 52% are from
Illinois. 6% are international students. 4.3% are African American, 0.6% American
Indian, 6.5% Asian American, and 5.3% Hispanic American. 91% returned for their
sophomore year.

Facilities and Resources

338 **computers/terminals** are available on campus for general student use. Students can
access the following: campus intranet, computer help desk, free student e-mail accounts,
online (class) registration, online (class) schedules, software applications. Campuswide
network is available. The 3 **libraries** have 316,886 books and 519 subscriptions.

Campus Life

There are 102 active organizations on campus, including a drama/theater group,
newspaper, radio station, and choral group. 26% of eligible men and 15% of eligible
women are members of national **fraternities** and national **sororities**.

Knox is a member of the NCAA. **Intercollegiate sports** include baseball (m),
basketball, cross-country running, football (m), golf, soccer, softball (w), swimming and
diving, tennis, track and field, volleyball (w), wrestling (m).

Campus Safety

Student safety services include late-night transport/escort service, 24-hour emergency
telephone alarm devices, and 24-hour patrols by trained security personnel.

Applying

Knox requires an essay, a high school transcript, and 2 recommendations. It recommends
SAT or ACT and an interview. Application deadline: 2/1; 2/1 priority date for financial
aid. Early and deferred admission are possible.

Getting Accepted

2,419 applied
61% were accepted
307 enrolled (21% of accepted)
40% from top tenth of their h.s. class
Mean ACT score: 29
84% had SAT critical reading scores over 600
66% had SAT math scores over 600
72% had SAT writing scores over 600
95% had ACT scores over 24
31% had SAT critical reading scores over 700
18% had SAT math scores over 700
19% had SAT writing scores over 700
43% had ACT scores over 30

Graduation and After

65% graduated in 4 years
5% graduated in 5 years
1% graduated in 6 years
35% pursued further study (23% arts and
  sciences, 4% law, 2% medicine)
54% had job offers within 6 months
79 organizations recruited on campus

Financial Matters

$30,507 tuition and fees (2008–09)
$6726 room and board
94% average percent of need met
$22,477 average financial aid amount received
  per undergraduate (2006–07 estimated)

LAFAYETTE COLLEGE

SUBURBAN SETTING ■ PRIVATE ■ INDEPENDENT RELIGIOUS ■ COED
EASTON, PENNSYLVANIA

Web site: www.lafayette.edu
Contact: Ms. Carol Rowlands, Director of Admissions, Easton, PA
   18042-1798
Telephone: 610-330-5100
Fax: 610-330-5355
E-mail: admissions@lafayette.edu

> Lafayette has achieved a unique niche in American higher education: liberal arts, sciences, and engineering programs in a most academically competitive small-college setting. Lafayette offers small classes, interdisciplinary first-year seminars, and student-faculty collaborative research on a residential campus located in eastern Pennsylvania, close to New York and Philadelphia.

Getting Accepted
6,364 applied
35% were accepted
592 enrolled (27% of accepted)
66% from top tenth of their h.s. class
3.44 average high school GPA
Mean SAT critical reading score: 625
Mean SAT math score: 665
Mean SAT writing score: 625
Mean ACT score: 28
66% had SAT critical reading scores over 600
80% had SAT math scores over 600
88% had ACT scores over 24
12% had SAT critical reading scores over 700
24% had SAT math scores over 700
20% had ACT scores over 30
6 National Merit Scholars

Graduation and After
85% graduated in 4 years
4% graduated in 5 years
34% pursued further study (12% arts and
   sciences, 8% engineering, 6% law)
43% had job offers within 6 months
240 organizations recruited on campus

Financial Matters
$36,200 tuition and fees (2008–09)
$11,200 room and board
99% average percent of need met
$22,888 average financial aid amount received
   per undergraduate

Academics

Lafayette awards bachelor's **degrees**. **Challenging opportunities** include advanced placement credit, accelerated degree programs, student-designed majors, and an honors program. Special programs include internships, summer session for credit, off-campus study, study-abroad, and Army ROTC.

The most frequently chosen **baccalaureate** fields are social sciences, engineering, and English. A complete listing of majors at Lafayette appears in the Majors by College index beginning on page 471.

The **faculty** at Lafayette has 199 full-time members, 100% with terminal degrees. The student-faculty ratio is 11:1.

Students of Lafayette

The student body is made up of 2,403 undergraduates. 47.8% are women and 52.2% are men. Students come from 38 states and territories and 41 other countries. 30% are from Pennsylvania. 6.2% are international students. 4.9% are African American, 0.1% American Indian, 3.1% Asian American, and 4.8% Hispanic American. 95% returned for their sophomore year.

Facilities and Resources

600 **computers/terminals** and 600 ports are available on campus for general student use. Students can access the following: computer help desk, free student e-mail accounts, online (class) grades, online (class) registration, online (class) schedules. Campuswide network is available. 100% of college-owned or -operated housing units are wired for high-speed Internet access. The 2 **libraries** have 530,000 books and 3,500 subscriptions.

Campus Life

There are 250 active organizations on campus, including a drama/theater group, newspaper, radio station, and choral group. 25% of eligible men and 45% of eligible women are members of national **fraternities**, national **sororities**, and social dorms.

Lafayette is a member of the NCAA (Division I). **Intercollegiate sports** include baseball (m), basketball, cross-country running, fencing, field hockey (w), football (m), golf (m), lacrosse, soccer, softball (w), swimming and diving, tennis, track and field, volleyball (w).

Campus Safety

Student safety services include late-night transport/escort service, 24-hour emergency telephone alarm devices, 24-hour patrols by trained security personnel, student patrols, and electronically operated dormitory entrances.

Applying

Lafayette requires an essay, SAT or ACT, a high school transcript, and 1 recommendation. It recommends SAT Subject Tests and an interview. Application deadline: 1/1; 3/15 for financial aid, with a 2/1 priority date. Early and deferred admission are possible.

LAKE FOREST COLLEGE

SUBURBAN SETTING ■ PRIVATE ■ INDEPENDENT ■ COED
LAKE FOREST, ILLINOIS

Web site: www.lakeforest.edu
Contact: Mr. William Motzer, Vice President for Admissions and Career
  Services, 555 North Sheridan Road, Lake Forest, IL 60045-2399
Telephone: 847-735-5000 or toll-free 800-828-4751
Fax: 847-735-6271
E-mail: admissions@lakeforest.edu

Academics

Lake Forest awards bachelor's and master's **degrees**. **Challenging opportunities** include advanced placement credit, accelerated degree programs, student-designed majors, freshman honors college, an honors program, double majors, independent study, and a senior project. Special programs include internships, summer session for credit, off-campus study, and study-abroad.

The most frequently chosen **baccalaureate** fields are social sciences, communications/journalism, and business/marketing. A complete listing of majors at Lake Forest appears in the Majors by College index beginning on page 471.

The **faculty** at Lake Forest has 90 full-time members, 94% with terminal degrees. The student-faculty ratio is 13:1.

Students of Lake Forest

The student body totals 1,456, of whom 1,436 are undergraduates. 59.2% are women and 40.8% are men. Students come from 47 states and territories and 42 other countries. 48% are from Illinois. 7.8% are international students. 4% are African American, 0.3% American Indian, 4.8% Asian American, and 5.6% Hispanic American. 82% returned for their sophomore year.

Facilities and Resources

190 **computers/terminals** and 1,200 ports are available on campus for general student use. Students can access the following: campus intranet, computer help desk, free student e-mail accounts, online (class) grades, online (class) schedules, file storage. Campuswide network is available. 100% of college-owned or -operated housing units are wired for high-speed Internet access. Wireless service is available via classrooms, computer centers, computer labs, dorm rooms, learning centers, libraries, student centers. The **library** has 263,918 books and 1,798 subscriptions.

Campus Life

There are 82 active organizations on campus, including a drama/theater group, newspaper, radio station, and choral group. 3% of eligible men and 14% of eligible women are members of national **fraternities** and national **sororities**.

Lake Forest is a member of the NCAA (Division III). **Intercollegiate sports** include basketball, cross-country running, football (m), ice hockey, soccer, softball (w), swimming and diving, tennis, volleyball (w).

Campus Safety

Student safety services include late-night transport/escort service, 24-hour emergency telephone alarm devices, 24-hour patrols by trained security personnel, student patrols, and electronically operated dormitory entrances.

Applying

Lake Forest requires an essay, a high school transcript, 2 recommendations, and graded paper, and in some cases SAT or ACT. It recommends an interview. Application deadline: 2/15; 3/1 priority date for financial aid. Early and deferred admission are possible.

Getting Accepted

2,203 applied
61% were accepted
356 enrolled (26% of accepted)
35% from top tenth of their h.s. class
3.5 average high school GPA
Mean SAT critical reading score: 610
Mean SAT math score: 603
Mean SAT writing score: 595
Mean ACT score: 27
54% had SAT critical reading scores over 600
58% had SAT math scores over 600
48% had SAT writing scores over 600
82% had ACT scores over 24
13% had SAT critical reading scores over 700
13% had SAT math scores over 700
6% had SAT writing scores over 700
18% had ACT scores over 30
17 valedictorians

Graduation and After

65% graduated in 4 years
3% graduated in 5 years
40% pursued further study (21% arts and
  sciences, 7% medicine, 6% law)
74% had job offers within 6 months
30 organizations recruited on campus

Financial Matters

$30,964 tuition and fees (2007–08)
$7326 room and board
100% average percent of need met
$23,024 average financial aid amount received
  per undergraduate (2006–07 estimated)

LAWRENCE TECHNOLOGICAL UNIVERSITY

SUBURBAN SETTING ■ PRIVATE ■ INDEPENDENT ■ COED
SOUTHFIELD, MICHIGAN

Web site: www.ltu.edu
Contact: Ms. Jane Rohrback, Director of Admissions, 21000 West Ten Mile Road, Southfield, MI 48075
Telephone: 248-204-3160 or toll-free 800-225-5588
Fax: 248-204-3188
E-mail: admissions@ltu.edu

Getting Accepted
1,585 applied
60% were accepted
399 enrolled (42% of accepted)
16% from top tenth of their h.s. class
3.21 average high school GPA
Mean ACT score: 23
50% had ACT scores over 24
7% had ACT scores over 30

Graduation and After
24% graduated in 4 years
14% graduated in 5 years
7% graduated in 6 years
93% had job offers within 6 months
700 organizations recruited on campus

Financial Matters
$20,496 tuition and fees (2007–08)
$7872 room and board
69% average percent of need met
$14,891 average financial aid amount received per undergraduate (2005–06)

Academics

Lawrence Tech awards associate, bachelor's, master's, and doctoral **degrees** and post-bachelor's certificates. **Challenging opportunities** include advanced placement credit, double majors, independent study, and a senior project. Special programs include cooperative education, internships, summer session for credit, off-campus study, study-abroad, and Army, Navy, and Air Force ROTC.

The most frequently chosen **baccalaureate** fields are engineering, architecture, and engineering technologies. A complete listing of majors at Lawrence Tech appears in the Majors by College index beginning on page 471.

The **faculty** at Lawrence Tech has 114 full-time members, 75% with terminal degrees. The student-faculty ratio is 13:1.

Students of Lawrence Tech

The student body totals 4,609, of whom 3,008 are undergraduates. 20.1% are women and 79.9% are men. Students come from 28 states and territories and 13 other countries. 98% are from Michigan. 8.5% are international students. 9.7% are African American, 0.3% American Indian, 2.5% Asian American, and 1.9% Hispanic American. 67% returned for their sophomore year.

Facilities and Resources

60 **computers/terminals** are available on campus for general student use. Students can access the following: campus intranet, computer help desk, free student e-mail accounts, online (class) grades, online (class) registration, online (class) schedules, degree audit, black board, SCT Banner (student information). Campuswide network is available. 100% of college-owned or -operated housing units are wired for high-speed Internet access. Wireless service is available via entire campus. The 2 **libraries** have 128,000 books and 750 subscriptions.

Campus Life

There are 37 active organizations on campus, including a drama/theater group and newspaper. 5% of eligible men and 7% of eligible women are members of national **fraternities**, national **sororities**, local fraternities, and local sororities.

This institution has no intercollegiate sports.

Campus Safety

Student safety services include late-night transport/escort service, 24-hour emergency telephone alarm devices, 24-hour patrols by trained security personnel, and electronically operated dormitory entrances.

Applying

Lawrence Tech requires SAT or ACT, a high school transcript, and a minimum high school GPA of 2.5, and in some cases an essay, an interview, and recommendations. Application deadline: 8/15; 4/1 priority date for financial aid. Early and deferred admission are possible.

LAWRENCE UNIVERSITY

SMALL-TOWN SETTING ■ PRIVATE ■ INDEPENDENT ■ COED
APPLETON, WISCONSIN

Web site: www.lawrence.edu
Contact: Mr. Steven T. Syverson, Vice President for Enrollment Management,
PO Box 599, Appleton, WI 54912-0599
Telephone: 920-832-6500 or toll-free 800-227-0982
Fax: 920-832-6782
E-mail: excel@lawrence.edu

Academics

Lawrence awards bachelor's **degrees**. **Challenging opportunities** include advanced placement credit, student-designed majors, double majors, independent study, and a senior project. Special programs include internships, off-campus study, and study-abroad.

The most frequently chosen **baccalaureate** fields are visual and performing arts, social sciences, and biological/life sciences. A complete listing of majors at Lawrence appears in the Majors by College index beginning on page 471.

The **faculty** at Lawrence has 153 full-time members, 95% with terminal degrees. The student-faculty ratio is 9:1.

Students of Lawrence

The student body is made up of 1,451 undergraduates. 53.8% are women and 46.2% are men. Students come from 43 states and territories and 50 other countries. 39% are from Wisconsin. 7% are international students. 1.7% are African American, 0.2% American Indian, 2.8% Asian American, and 2.1% Hispanic American. 88% returned for their sophomore year.

Facilities and Resources

354 **computers/terminals** and 1,055 ports are available on campus for general student use. Students can access the following: campus intranet, computer help desk, free student e-mail accounts, online (class) grades, online (class) registration, online (class) schedules, online transcripts, financial aid, financial account information. Campuswide network is available. 100% of college-owned or -operated housing units are wired for high-speed Internet access. Wireless service is available via classrooms, computer labs, learning centers, libraries. The **library** has 395,000 books and 2,816 subscriptions.

Campus Life

There are 100 active organizations on campus, including a drama/theater group, newspaper, radio station, and choral group. 9% of eligible men and 5% of eligible women are members of national **fraternities** and national **sororities**.

Lawrence is a member of the NCAA (Division III). **Intercollegiate sports** include baseball (m), basketball, cross-country running, fencing, football (m), golf (m), ice hockey (m), soccer, softball (w), swimming and diving, tennis, track and field, volleyball (w), wrestling (m).

Campus Safety

Student safety services include evening patrols by trained security personnel, late-night transport/escort service, 24-hour emergency telephone alarm devices, student patrols, and electronically operated dormitory entrances.

Applying

Lawrence requires an essay, a high school transcript, 2 recommendations, and audition for music program. It recommends an interview and a minimum high school GPA of 3.0. Application deadline: 1/15; 3/15 priority date for financial aid. Early and deferred admission are possible.

Getting Accepted

2,599 applied
56% were accepted
353 enrolled (24% of accepted)
39% from top tenth of their h.s. class
3.59 average high school GPA
82% had SAT critical reading scores over 600
71% had SAT math scores over 600
76% had SAT writing scores over 600
96% had ACT scores over 24
35% had SAT critical reading scores over 700
30% had SAT math scores over 700
23% had SAT writing scores over 700
43% had ACT scores over 30
8 National Merit Scholars
11 valedictorians

Graduation and After

63% graduated in 4 years
14% graduated in 5 years
2% graduated in 6 years
22% pursued further study (18% arts and sciences, 2% law, 1% medicine)
48% had job offers within 6 months
16 organizations recruited on campus

Financial Matters

$31,080 tuition and fees (2007–08)
$6690 room and board
96% average percent of need met
$23,900 average financial aid amount received per undergraduate (2006–07 estimated)

SPONSOR

Lebanon Valley College (LVC) offers bachelor's degrees in thirty-five majors; master's degrees in business administration, music education, and science education; and a doctoral degree in physical therapy. Fourteen graduates have been named Fulbright scholars, and, in the latest numbers released by the National Science Foundation, LVC ranked among the top 15 percent in the nation for Ph. D.'s produced from "Private, Predominantly Undergraduate Institutions" for biology, biochemistry, and chemistry for the last ten years. More than 70 percent of entering freshmen rank in the top 30 percent of their high school class and receive scholarships of up to half tuition. Lebanon Valley College ranks among the top 5 percent for average graduation rate for the 558 schools in the *U.S. News & World Report* category.

Getting Accepted
2,131 applied
71% were accepted
451 enrolled (30% of accepted)
36% from top tenth of their h.s. class
Mean SAT critical reading score: 538
Mean SAT math score: 554
Mean SAT writing score: 535
14 class presidents
8 valedictorians

Graduation and After
64% graduated in 4 years
6% graduated in 5 years
1% graduated in 6 years
27% pursued further study (22% arts and sciences, 1% business, 1% education)
79% had job offers within 6 months
28 organizations recruited on campus

Financial Matters
$27,800 tuition and fees (2007–08)
$7430 room and board
87% average percent of need met
$19,056 average financial aid amount received per undergraduate (2006–07 estimated)

LEBANON VALLEY COLLEGE
SMALL-TOWN SETTING ■ PRIVATE ■ INDEPENDENT RELIGIOUS ■ COED
ANNVILLE, PENNSYLVANIA

Web site: www.lvc.edu
Contact: Ms. Susan Sarisky, Director of Admission, 101 North College Avenue, Annville, PA 17003
Telephone: 866-LVC-4ADM
Fax: 717-867-6026
E-mail: admission@lvc.edu

Academics
LVC awards associate, bachelor's, master's, and doctoral **degrees** and post-bachelor's certificates. **Challenging opportunities** include advanced placement credit, student-designed majors, double majors, and independent study. Special programs include internships, summer session for credit, off-campus study, and study-abroad.

The most frequently chosen **baccalaureate** fields are education, business/marketing, and psychology. A complete listing of majors at LVC appears in the Majors by College index beginning on page 471.

The **faculty** at LVC has 100 full-time members, 89% with terminal degrees. The student-faculty ratio is 13:1.

Students of LVC
The student body totals 1,936, of whom 1,793 are undergraduates. 55.2% are women and 44.8% are men. Students come from 22 states and territories and 5 other countries. 79% are from Pennsylvania. 0.6% are international students. 1.4% are African American, 0.3% American Indian, 2.2% Asian American, and 2.5% Hispanic American. 83% returned for their sophomore year.

Facilities and Resources
195 **computers/terminals** are available on campus for general student use. Students can access the following: campus intranet, computer help desk, free student e-mail accounts, online (class) grades, online (class) registration, online (class) schedules. Campuswide network is available. 100% of college-owned or -operated housing units are wired for high-speed Internet access. Wireless service is available via classrooms, computer centers, computer labs, learning centers, libraries, student centers. The **library** has 187,289 books and 820 subscriptions.

Campus Life
There are 73 active organizations on campus, including a drama/theater group, newspaper, radio station, choral group, and marching band. 19% of eligible men and 13% of eligible women are members of national **fraternities**, national **sororities**, local fraternities, and local sororities.

LVC is a member of the NCAA (Division III). **Intercollegiate sports** include baseball (m), basketball, cross-country running, field hockey (w), football (m), golf (m), ice hockey (m), soccer, softball (w), swimming and diving, tennis, track and field, volleyball (w).

Campus Safety
Student safety services include dormitory entrances locked at midnight, late-night transport/escort service, 24-hour emergency telephone alarm devices, 24-hour patrols by trained security personnel, and electronically operated dormitory entrances.

Applying
LVC requires a high school transcript, and in some cases an essay and audition for music majors. It recommends an interview and 2 recommendations. Application deadline: rolling admissions; 3/1 priority date for financial aid.

LEHIGH UNIVERSITY

SUBURBAN SETTING ■ PRIVATE ■ INDEPENDENT ■ COED
BETHLEHEM, PENNSYLVANIA

Web site: www.lehigh.edu
Contact: J. Bruce Gardiner, Director of Admissions, 27 Memorial Drive West, Bethlehem, PA 18015
Telephone: 610-758-3100
Fax: 610-758-4361
E-mail: admissions@lehigh.edu

Academics

Lehigh awards bachelor's, master's, and doctoral **degrees** and post-bachelor's and post-master's certificates. **Challenging opportunities** include advanced placement credit, accelerated degree programs, an honors program, double majors, independent study, and a senior project. Special programs include cooperative education, internships, summer session for credit, off-campus study, study-abroad, and Army ROTC.

The most frequently chosen **baccalaureate** fields are business/marketing, engineering, and social sciences. A complete listing of majors at Lehigh appears in the Majors by College index beginning on page 471.

The **faculty** at Lehigh has 440 full-time members, 99% with terminal degrees. The student-faculty ratio is 9:1.

Students of Lehigh

The student body totals 6,845, of whom 4,756 are undergraduates. 41.4% are women and 58.6% are men. Students come from 49 states and territories and 44 other countries. 24% are from Pennsylvania. 2.5% are international students. 3.2% are African American, 0.1% American Indian, 5.8% Asian American, and 4.3% Hispanic American. 93% returned for their sophomore year.

Facilities and Resources

629 **computers/terminals** are available on campus for general student use. Students can access the following: campus intranet, computer help desk, free student e-mail accounts, online (class) grades, online (class) registration, online (class) schedules. Campuswide network is available. 100% of college-owned or -operated housing units are wired for high-speed Internet access. Wireless service is available via classrooms, computer centers, computer labs, learning centers, libraries, student centers. The 2 **libraries** have 1,176,028 books and 6,271 subscriptions.

Campus Life

There are 140 active organizations on campus, including a drama/theater group, newspaper, radio station, choral group, and marching band. 35% of eligible men and 38% of eligible women are members of national **fraternities** and national **sororities**.

Lehigh is a member of the NCAA (Division I). **Intercollegiate sports** (some offering scholarships) include baseball (m), basketball, crew (w), cross-country running, field hockey (w), football (m), golf, lacrosse, soccer, softball (w), swimming and diving, tennis, track and field, volleyball (w), wrestling (m).

Campus Safety

Student safety services include late-night transport/escort service, 24-hour emergency telephone alarm devices, 24-hour patrols by trained security personnel, student patrols, and electronically operated dormitory entrances.

Applying

Lehigh requires an essay, SAT or ACT, a high school transcript, 1 recommendation, and graded writing sample. It recommends an interview. Application deadline: 1/1; 2/1 for financial aid. Early and deferred admission are possible.

Getting Accepted

12,155 applied
32% were accepted
1,166 enrolled (30% of accepted)
93% from top tenth of their h.s. class
Mean SAT critical reading score: 636
Mean SAT math score: 672
76% had SAT critical reading scores over 600
87% had SAT math scores over 600
18% had SAT critical reading scores over 700
34% had SAT math scores over 700

Graduation and After

72% graduated in 4 years
10% graduated in 5 years
1% graduated in 6 years
32% pursued further study
55% had job offers within 6 months
227 organizations recruited on campus

Financial Matters

$35,610 tuition and fees (2007–08)
$9340 room and board
96% average percent of need met
$26,584 average financial aid amount received per undergraduate (2006–07 estimated)

LeTourneau University

SUBURBAN SETTING ■ PRIVATE ■ INDEPENDENT RELIGIOUS ■ COED
LONGVIEW, TEXAS

Getting Accepted
938 applied
70% were accepted
323 enrolled (49% of accepted)
34% from top tenth of their h.s. class
3.56 average high school GPA
41% had SAT critical reading scores over 600
47% had SAT math scores over 600
31% had SAT writing scores over 600
60% had ACT scores over 24
11% had SAT critical reading scores over 700
11% had SAT math scores over 700
5% had SAT writing scores over 700
17% had ACT scores over 30

Graduation and After
31% graduated in 4 years
16% graduated in 5 years
5% graduated in 6 years
92% had job offers within 6 months

Financial Matters
$17,910 tuition and fees (2007–08)
$6950 room and board
69% average percent of need met
$11,386 average financial aid amount received
per undergraduate (2005–06)

Web site: www.letu.edu
Contact: Mr. James Townsend, Director of Admissions, PO Box 7001,
Longview, TX 75607-7001
Telephone: 903-233-3400 or toll-free 800-759-8811
Fax: 903-233-3411
E-mail: admissions@letu.edu

Academics
LeTourneau awards associate, bachelor's, and master's **degrees. Challenging opportunities** include advanced placement credit, accelerated degree programs, an honors
program, double majors, independent study, and a senior project. Special programs
include cooperative education, internships, summer session for credit, off-campus study,
and study-abroad.

The most frequently chosen **baccalaureate** fields are engineering, business/market-
ing, and education. A complete listing of majors at LeTourneau appears in the Majors by
College index beginning on page 471.

The **faculty** at LeTourneau has 74 full-time members, 73% with terminal degrees.
The student-faculty ratio is 19:1.

Students of LeTourneau
The student body totals 3,921, of whom 3,597 are undergraduates. 57.6% are women
and 42.4% are men. Students come from 50 states and territories and 27 other countries.
45% are from Texas. 0.8% are international students. 21.5% are African American, 0.4%
American Indian, 1.5% Asian American, and 8.4% Hispanic American. 78% returned for
their sophomore year.

Facilities and Resources
191 **computers/terminals** are available on campus for general student use. Students can
access the following: online (class) registration. Campuswide network is available. The
library has 84,779 books and 383 subscriptions.

Campus Life
There are 22 active organizations on campus, including a drama/theater group,
newspaper, and choral group. LeTourneau has 3 societies for men, 1 society for women.

LeTourneau is a member of the NCAA (Division III) and NCCAA. **Intercollegiate
sports** include baseball (m), basketball, cross-country running, golf, soccer, softball (w),
tennis, volleyball (w).

Campus Safety
Student safety services include late-night transport/escort service, 24-hour emergency
telephone alarm devices, 24-hour patrols by trained security personnel, and electronically operated dormitory entrances.

Applying
LeTourneau requires SAT or ACT. Application deadline: 8/1; 2/1 priority date for
financial aid. Deferred admission is possible.

Lewis & Clark College

Suburban setting ■ Private ■ Independent ■ Coed
Portland, Oregon

Web site: www.lclark.edu
Contact: Mr. Michael Sexton, Dean of Admissions, 0615 SW Palatine Hill Road, Portland, OR 97219-7899
Telephone: 503-768-7040 or toll-free 800-444-4111
Fax: 503-768-7055
E-mail: admissions@lclark.edu

Academics

L & C awards bachelor's, master's, doctoral, and first-professional **degrees** and post-master's certificates. **Challenging opportunities** include advanced placement credit, accelerated degree programs, student-designed majors, an honors program, double majors, independent study, and a senior project. Special programs include internships, summer session for credit, off-campus study, and study-abroad.

The most frequently chosen **baccalaureate** fields are social sciences, psychology, and visual and performing arts. A complete listing of majors at L & C appears in the Majors by College index beginning on page 471.

The **faculty** at L & C has 221 full-time members, 91% with terminal degrees. The student-faculty ratio is 12:1.

Students of L & C

The student body totals 3,562, of whom 1,964 are undergraduates. 60.9% are women and 39.1% are men. Students come from 45 states and territories and 53 other countries. 21% are from Oregon. 4.5% are international students. 1.6% are African American, 0.9% American Indian, 5.8% Asian American, and 4.6% Hispanic American. 88% returned for their sophomore year.

Facilities and Resources

158 **computers/terminals** are available on campus for general student use. Students can access the following: campus intranet, computer help desk, free student e-mail accounts, online (class) grades, online (class) registration, online (class) schedules. Campuswide network is available. Wireless service is available via entire campus. The 2 **libraries** have 227,609 books and 7,477 subscriptions.

Campus Life

There are 70 active organizations on campus, including a drama/theater group, newspaper, radio station, television station, and choral group. No national or local **fraternities** or **sororities**.

L & C is a member of the NCAA (Division III) and NAIA. **Intercollegiate sports** include baseball (m), basketball, crew, cross-country running, football (m), golf, soccer (w), softball (w), swimming and diving, tennis, track and field, volleyball (w).

Campus Safety

Student safety services include late-night transport/escort service, 24-hour emergency telephone alarm devices, 24-hour patrols by trained security personnel, student patrols, and electronically operated dormitory entrances.

Applying

L & C requires an essay, SAT, ACT, or academic portfolio, a high school transcript, 2 recommendations, and a minimum high school GPA of 2.0, and in some cases SAT or ACT, 4 recommendations, and portfolio applicants must submit samples of graded work. It recommends an interview and a minimum high school GPA of 3.0. Application deadline: 2/1; 3/1 priority date for financial aid. Deferred admission is possible.

Getting Accepted

5,351 applied
56% were accepted
507 enrolled (17% of accepted)
46% from top tenth of their h.s. class
3.69 average high school GPA
82% had SAT critical reading scores over 600
73% had SAT math scores over 600
73% had SAT writing scores over 600
93% had ACT scores over 24
27% had SAT critical reading scores over 700
16% had SAT math scores over 700
17% had SAT writing scores over 700
33% had ACT scores over 30
14 National Merit Scholars
26 valedictorians

Graduation and After

67% graduated in 4 years
3% graduated in 5 years
1% graduated in 6 years
19% pursued further study (12% arts and sciences, 2% medicine, 1% business)
46 organizations recruited on campus

Financial Matters

$31,840 tuition and fees (2007–08)
$8450 room and board
91% average percent of need met
$25,018 average financial aid amount received per undergraduate (2006–07 estimated)

LINCOLN MEMORIAL UNIVERSITY

SMALL-TOWN SETTING ■ PRIVATE ■ INDEPENDENT ■ COED
HARROGATE, TENNESSEE

Getting Accepted
795 applied
69% were accepted
227 enrolled (41% of accepted)
28% from top tenth of their h.s. class
3.4 average high school GPA
42% had ACT scores over 24
3% had ACT scores over 30

Graduation and After
20% graduated in 4 years
9% graduated in 5 years
36% graduated in 6 years

Financial Matters
$14,400 tuition and fees (2007–08)
90% average percent of need met
$9800 average financial aid amount received
per undergraduate

Web site: www.lmunet.edu
Contact: Mr. Conrad Daniels, Dean of Admissions and Recruitment, 6965
Cumberland Gap Parkway, Harrogate, TN 37752-1901
Telephone: 423-869-6280 or toll-free 800-325-0900
Fax: 423-869-6444
E-mail: admissions@lmunet.edu

Academics

LMU awards associate, bachelor's, and master's **degrees** and post-master's certificates.
Challenging opportunities include advanced placement credit, accelerated degree
programs, student-designed majors, an honors program, double majors, and independent
study. Summer session for credit is a special program.

The most frequently chosen **baccalaureate** fields are business/marketing, education,
and health professions and related sciences. A complete listing of majors at LMU appears
in the Majors by College index beginning on page 471.

The **faculty** at LMU has 111 full-time members, 72% with terminal degrees. The
student-faculty ratio is 14:1.

Students of LMU

The student body totals 2,981, of whom 1,394 are undergraduates. 71.2% are women
and 28.8% are men. Students come from 30 states and territories and 15 other countries.
65% are from Tennessee. 3.7% are international students. 2.5% are African American,
0.1% American Indian, 0.4% Asian American, and 0.9% Hispanic American. 54%
returned for their sophomore year.

Facilities and Resources

150 **computers/terminals** are available on campus for general student use. Campuswide
network is available. The 2 **libraries** have 174,737 books and 20,982 subscriptions.

Campus Life

There are 26 active organizations on campus, including a drama/theater group,
newspaper, radio station, television station, and choral group. 5% of eligible men and
10% of eligible women are members of local **fraternities** and local **sororities**.

LMU is a member of the NCAA (Division II). **Intercollegiate sports** (some offering
scholarships) include baseball (m), basketball, cross-country running, golf, soccer, softball
(w), tennis, volleyball (w).

Campus Safety

Student safety services include 24-hour emergency telephone alarm devices and 24-hour
patrols by trained security personnel.

Applying

LMU requires SAT or ACT, a high school transcript, and a minimum high school GPA
of 2.3, and in some cases an essay. It recommends an interview. Application deadline:
rolling admissions; 4/1 priority date for financial aid.

LINFIELD COLLEGE

SMALL-TOWN SETTING ■ PRIVATE ■ INDEPENDENT RELIGIOUS ■ COED
MCMINNVILLE, OREGON

SPONSOR

Web site: www.linfield.edu
Contact: Ms. Lisa Knodle-Bragiel, Director of Admission, 900 SE Baker
  Street, McMinnville, OR 97128
Telephone: 503-883-2213 or toll-free 800-640-2287
Fax: 503-883-2472
E-mail: admission@linfield.edu

Academics

Linfield awards bachelor's **degrees**. **Challenging opportunities** include advanced placement credit, student-designed majors, double majors, independent study, and a senior project. Special programs include internships, summer session for credit, off-campus study, study-abroad, and Air Force ROTC.

The most frequently chosen **baccalaureate** fields are business/marketing, social sciences, and parks and recreation. A complete listing of majors at Linfield appears in the Majors by College index beginning on page 471.

The **faculty** at Linfield has 110 full-time members, 95% with terminal degrees. The student-faculty ratio is 12:1.

Students of Linfield

The student body is made up of 1,693 undergraduates. 54.5% are women and 45.5% are men. Students come from 30 states and territories and 21 other countries. 59% are from Oregon. 2.5% are international students. 1.5% are African American, 0.9% American Indian, 7.5% Asian American, and 4.1% Hispanic American. 81% returned for their sophomore year.

Facilities and Resources

250 **computers/terminals** are available on campus for general student use. Students can access the following: computer help desk, free student e-mail accounts, online (class) grades, online (class) registration, online (class) schedules. Campuswide network is available. 95% of college-owned or -operated housing units are wired for high-speed Internet access. Wireless service is available via classrooms, computer centers, computer labs, learning centers, libraries, student centers. The **library** has 179,098 books and 1,268 subscriptions.

Campus Life

Active organizations on campus include a drama/theater group, newspaper, radio station, and choral group. 17% of eligible men and 23% of eligible women are members of national **fraternities**, national **sororities**, local fraternities, and local sororities.

Linfield is a member of the NCAA (Division III). **Intercollegiate sports** include baseball (m), basketball, cross-country running, football (m), golf, lacrosse (w), soccer, softball (w), swimming and diving, tennis, track and field, volleyball (w).

Campus Safety

Student safety services include late-night transport/escort service, 24-hour emergency telephone alarm devices, 24-hour patrols by trained security personnel, and electronically operated dormitory entrances.

Applying

Linfield requires an essay, SAT or ACT, a high school transcript, and 1 recommendation. It recommends an interview. Application deadline: 2/15; 2/1 priority date for financial aid. Deferred admission is possible.

Linfield College in McMinnville, Oregon, has been described as a "hidden jewel" among the nation's colleges and has been named one of the Best Western Colleges by the *Princeton Review* (2007). One of the few solely undergraduate institutions in the vibrant Pacific Northwest, Linfield offers a close-knit learning community of 1,750 students, with a 12:1 student-faculty ratio. Students also have unique experiential learning opportunities throughout the world with Linfield's outstanding internship and international programs. By the time students have graduated, more than 50 percent have been abroad for a year, a semester, or the January Term.

Getting Accepted
2,050 applied
80% were accepted
476 enrolled (29% of accepted)
33% from top tenth of their h.s. class
3.56 average high school GPA
Mean SAT critical reading score: 548
Mean SAT math score: 560
Mean SAT writing score: 527
Mean ACT score: 24
31% had SAT critical reading scores over 600
30% had SAT math scores over 600
20% had SAT writing scores over 600
54% had ACT scores over 24
5% had SAT critical reading scores over 700
6% had SAT math scores over 700
3% had SAT writing scores over 700
14% had ACT scores over 30
2 National Merit Scholars
20 class presidents
34 valedictorians

Graduation and After
58% graduated in 4 years
10% graduated in 5 years
1% graduated in 6 years
20% pursued further study
85% had job offers within 6 months
10 organizations recruited on campus

Financial Matters
$25,644 tuition and fees (2007–08)
$7400 room and board
85% average percent of need met
$18,300 average financial aid amount received
  per undergraduate (2006–07 estimated)

LIPSCOMB UNIVERSITY

SUBURBAN SETTING ■ PRIVATE ■ INDEPENDENT RELIGIOUS ■ COED
NASHVILLE, TENNESSEE

Getting Accepted
2,240 applied
57% were accepted
576 enrolled (45% of accepted)
25% from top tenth of their h.s. class
3.49 average high school GPA
Mean SAT critical reading score: 558
Mean SAT math score: 552
Mean SAT writing score: 541
Mean ACT score: 24
35% had SAT critical reading scores over 600
32% had SAT math scores over 600
25% had SAT writing scores over 600
54% had ACT scores over 24
5% had SAT critical reading scores over 700
4% had SAT math scores over 700
3% had SAT writing scores over 700
12% had ACT scores over 30

Graduation and After
36% graduated in 4 years
18% graduated in 5 years
2% graduated in 6 years
93% had job offers within 6 months

Financial Matters
$16,811 tuition and fees (2007–08)
$7070 room and board
67% average percent of need met
$12,752 average financial aid amount received per undergraduate (2006–07 estimated)

Web site: www.lipscomb.edu
Contact: Corey Patterson, Senior Director of Enrollment, 3901 Granny White Pike, Nashville, TN 37204-3951
Telephone: 615-966-1000 or toll-free 877-582-4766
Fax: 615-966-1804
E-mail: admissions@lipscomb.edu

Academics
Lipscomb awards bachelor's, master's, and first-professional **degrees** and post-bachelor's certificates. **Challenging opportunities** include advanced placement credit, accelerated degree programs, an honors program, double majors, independent study, and a senior project. Special programs include internships, summer session for credit, study-abroad, and Army and Air Force ROTC.

The most frequently chosen **baccalaureate** fields are business/marketing, education, and health professions and related sciences. A complete listing of majors at Lipscomb appears in the Majors by College index beginning on page 471.

The **faculty** at Lipscomb has 108 full-time members, 85% with terminal degrees. The student-faculty ratio is 15:1.

Students of Lipscomb
The student body totals 2,744, of whom 2,363 are undergraduates. 57.3% are women and 42.7% are men. Students come from 38 states and territories and 26 other countries. 69% are from Tennessee. 1.4% are international students. 5.1% are African American, 0.5% American Indian, 1.6% Asian American, and 2.1% Hispanic American. 76% returned for their sophomore year.

Facilities and Resources
245 **computers/terminals** are available on campus for general student use. Students can access the following: online (class) registration. Campuswide network is available. Wireless service is available via entire campus. The 2 **libraries** have 253,398 books and 850 subscriptions.

Campus Life
There are 60 active organizations on campus, including a drama/theater group, newspaper, radio station, and choral group. No national or local **fraternities** or **sororities**.

Lipscomb is a member of the NCAA (Division I). **Intercollegiate sports** (some offering scholarships) include baseball (m), basketball, cross-country running, golf, soccer, softball (w), tennis, volleyball (w).

Campus Safety
Student safety services include late-night transport/escort service, 24-hour emergency telephone alarm devices, 24-hour patrols by trained security personnel, and electronically operated dormitory entrances.

Applying
Lipscomb requires SAT or ACT, a high school transcript, 2 recommendations, TOEFL, and a minimum high school GPA of 2.25. It recommends an essay and an interview. Application deadline: rolling admissions; 3/1 priority date for financial aid. Early and deferred admission are possible.

List College, The Jewish Theological Seminary

Urban setting ■ Private ■ Independent Religious ■ Coed
New York, New York

Web site: www.jtsa.edu
Contact: Ms. Reina Cohen, Director List Collect Admissions, 3080 Broadway, New York, NY 10027
Telephone: 212-678-8820
Fax: 212-280-6022
E-mail: lcadmissions@jtsa.edu

> The Albert A. List College of Jewish Studies, the undergraduate school of the Jewish Theological Seminary, offers students a unique opportunity to pursue two bachelor's degrees simultaneously. Students earn a degree from List in one of a dozen areas of Jewish study and a second degree in the liberal arts field of their choice from Columbia University or Barnard College. This exciting four-year program enables students to experience an intimate and supportive Jewish community as well as a diverse and dynamic campus life.

Academics

List College awards bachelor's, master's, doctoral, and first-professional **degrees** (double bachelor's degree with Barnard College, Columbia University, joint bachelor's degree with Columbia University). **Challenging opportunities** include advanced placement credit, student-designed majors, freshman honors college, an honors program, double majors, and a senior project. Special programs include internships, summer session for credit, off-campus study, study-abroad, and Army, Navy, and Air Force ROTC. A complete listing of majors at List College appears in the Majors by College index beginning on page 471.

The **faculty** at List College has 63 full-time members, 94% with terminal degrees. The student-faculty ratio is 6:1.

Students of List College

The student body totals 580, of whom 182 are undergraduates. 61% are women and 39% are men. Students come from 25 states and territories and 3 other countries. 22% are from New York. 2.2% are Hispanic American. 92% returned for their sophomore year.

Facilities and Resources

50 **computers/terminals** are available on campus for general student use. Students can access the following: computer help desk, free student e-mail accounts, online (class) registration. Campuswide network is available. 100% of college-owned or -operated housing units are wired for high-speed Internet access. Wireless service is available via classrooms, computer labs, dorm rooms, learning centers, libraries, student centers. The **library** has 380,000 books and 720 subscriptions.

Campus Life

Active organizations on campus include a drama/theater group, newspaper, radio station, and choral group. No national or local **fraternities** or **sororities**.

This institution has no intercollegiate sports.

Campus Safety

Student safety services include late-night transport/escort service, 24-hour emergency telephone alarm devices, 24-hour patrols by trained security personnel, and electronically operated dormitory entrances.

Applying

List College requires an essay, SAT or ACT, a high school transcript, and 2 recommendations. It recommends an interview and a minimum high school GPA of 3.0. Application deadline: 2/15; 3/1 for financial aid. Early and deferred admission are possible.

Getting Accepted
102 applied
61% were accepted
40 enrolled (65% of accepted)
3.7 average high school GPA
Mean SAT critical reading score: 687
Mean SAT math score: 654
Mean SAT writing score: 687
Mean ACT score: 31
94% had SAT critical reading scores over 600
88% had SAT math scores over 600
91% had SAT writing scores over 600
100% had ACT scores over 24
44% had SAT critical reading scores over 700
22% had SAT math scores over 700
57% had SAT writing scores over 700
77% had ACT scores over 30

Graduation and After
26% pursued further study (12% theology, 6% law, 4% arts and sciences)
67% had job offers within 6 months

Financial Matters
$15,000 tuition and fees (2008–09)

LOUISIANA STATE UNIVERSITY AND AGRICULTURAL AND MECHANICAL COLLEGE

URBAN SETTING ■ PUBLIC ■ STATE-SUPPORTED ■ COED
BATON ROUGE, LOUISIANA

Web site: www.lsu.edu
Contact: 110 Thomas Boyd Hall, Baton Rouge, LA 70803
Telephone: 225-578-1175
Fax: 225-578-4433
E-mail: admissions@lsu.edu

Getting Accepted
11,452 applied
73% were accepted
4,596 enrolled (55% of accepted)
27% from top tenth of their h.s. class
3.52 average high school GPA
Mean SAT critical reading score: 583
Mean SAT math score: 603
Mean SAT writing score: 555
Mean ACT score: 25
43% had SAT critical reading scores over 600
55% had SAT math scores over 600
34% had SAT writing scores over 600
67% had ACT scores over 24
12% had SAT critical reading scores over 700
12% had SAT math scores over 700
6% had SAT writing scores over 700
12% had ACT scores over 30
39 National Merit Scholars
282 valedictorians

Graduation and After
26% graduated in 4 years
26% graduated in 5 years
7% graduated in 6 years
63% had job offers within 6 months
1505 organizations recruited on campus

Financial Matters
$4543 resident tuition and fees (2007–08)
$12,843 nonresident tuition and fees (2007–08)
$6852 room and board
58% average percent of need met
$8011 average financial aid amount received per undergraduate (2005–06)

Academics
LSU awards bachelor's, master's, doctoral, and first-professional **degrees** and post-master's certificates. **Challenging opportunities** include advanced placement credit, accelerated degree programs, student-designed majors, freshman honors college, an honors program, double majors, independent study, and a senior project. Special programs include cooperative education, internships, summer session for credit, off-campus study, study-abroad, and Army, Navy, and Air Force ROTC.

The most frequently chosen **baccalaureate** fields are business/marketing, education, and biological/life sciences. A complete listing of majors at LSU appears in the Majors by College index beginning on page 471.

The **faculty** at LSU has 1,267 full-time members, 85% with terminal degrees. The student-faculty ratio is 20:1.

Students of LSU
The student body totals 28,628, of whom 23,393 are undergraduates. 51.4% are women and 48.6% are men. Students come from 49 states and territories and 76 other countries. 86% are from Louisiana. 1.6% are international students. 8.9% are African American, 0.4% American Indian, 3.1% Asian American, and 3% Hispanic American. 85% returned for their sophomore year.

Facilities and Resources
7,000 **computers/terminals** and 8,500 ports are available on campus for general student use. Students can access the following: computer help desk, free student e-mail accounts, online (class) grades, online (class) registration, online (class) schedules, free software for download, personal Web sites, storage, discounts on hardware, virtual computer lab. Campuswide network is available. 100% of college-owned or -operated housing units are wired for high-speed Internet access. Wireless service is available via entire campus. The 8 **libraries** have 1,369,607 books and 58,918 subscriptions.

Campus Life
There are 300 active organizations on campus, including a drama/theater group, newspaper, radio station, television station, choral group, and marching band. 12% of eligible men and 18% of eligible women are members of national **fraternities** and national **sororities**.

LSU is a member of the NCAA (Division I). **Intercollegiate sports** (some offering scholarships) include baseball (m), basketball, cheerleading, cross-country running, football (m), golf, gymnastics (w), soccer (w), softball (w), swimming and diving, tennis, track and field, volleyball (w).

Campus Safety
Student safety services include self-defense education, crime prevention programs, late-night transport/escort service, 24-hour emergency telephone alarm devices, 24-hour patrols by trained security personnel, and electronically operated dormitory entrances.

Applying
LSU requires SAT or ACT, a high school transcript, minimum ACT score of 22 or SAT score of 1030, and a minimum high school GPA of 3.0, and in some cases an essay and an interview. Application deadline: 4/15; 3/1 priority date for financial aid. Early and deferred admission are possible.

Loyola College in Maryland

Urban setting ■ Private ■ Independent Religious ■ Coed
Baltimore, Maryland

Web site: www.loyola.edu
Contact: Ms. Elena Hicks, Director of Undergraduate Admissions, 4501 North Charles Street, Baltimore, MD 21210
Telephone: 410-617-5012 or toll-free 800-221-9107 Ext. 2252 (in-state)
Fax: 410-617-2176

SPONSOR

> Traditional academic standards are central to Jesuit education. Loyola's curriculum is rigorous, and the faculty's expectations for students are high. The aim is to challenge students and to try to develop their skills and abilities. Hard work is required for a good education, and Loyola is interested in admitting students who have been ambitious in their course selection in high school and who have shown that they can do well in academic work.

Academics

Loyola awards bachelor's, master's, and doctoral **degrees** and post-master's certificates. **Challenging opportunities** include advanced placement credit, accelerated degree programs, an honors program, double majors, independent study, and a senior project. Special programs include internships, summer session for credit, off-campus study, study-abroad, and Army and Air Force ROTC.

The most frequently chosen **baccalaureate** fields are business/marketing, communications/journalism, and social sciences. A complete listing of majors at Loyola appears in the Majors by College index beginning on page 471.

The **faculty** at Loyola has 321 full-time members, 82% with terminal degrees. The student-faculty ratio is 12:1.

Students of Loyola

The student body totals 6,028, of whom 3,580 are undergraduates. 58.5% are women and 41.5% are men. Students come from 38 states and territories and 19 other countries. 18% are from Maryland. 0.8% are international students. 5.1% are African American, 0.1% American Indian, 2.7% Asian American, and 3.4% Hispanic American. 91% returned for their sophomore year.

Facilities and Resources

1,667 **computers/terminals** are available on campus for general student use. Students can access the following: computer help desk, free student e-mail accounts, online (class) grades, online (class) registration, online (class) schedules. Campuswide network is available. 100% of college-owned or -operated housing units are wired for high-speed Internet access. Wireless service is available via classrooms, computer centers, computer labs, dorm rooms, learning centers, libraries, student centers. The **library** has 293,639 books and 2,126 subscriptions.

Campus Life

There are 115 active organizations on campus, including a drama/theater group, newspaper, radio station, and choral group. No national or local **fraternities** or **sororities**.

Loyola is a member of the NCAA (Division I). **Intercollegiate sports** include basketball, crew, cross-country running, golf (m), lacrosse, soccer, swimming and diving, tennis, volleyball (w).

Campus Safety

Student safety services include late-night transport/escort service, 24-hour emergency telephone alarm devices, 24-hour patrols by trained security personnel, and electronically operated dormitory entrances.

Applying

Loyola requires an essay, SAT or ACT, and a high school transcript. It recommends an interview. Application deadline: 2/1; 2/15 for financial aid. Early and deferred admission are possible.

Getting Accepted
8,594 applied
60% were accepted
983 enrolled (19% of accepted)
37% from top tenth of their h.s. class
3.5 average high school GPA
Mean SAT critical reading score: 599
Mean SAT math score: 605
Mean SAT writing score: 606
Mean ACT score: 26
52% had SAT critical reading scores over 600
56% had SAT math scores over 600
77% had ACT scores over 24
10% had SAT critical reading scores over 700
8% had SAT math scores over 700
12% had ACT scores over 30

Graduation and After
77% graduated in 4 years
5% graduated in 5 years
1% graduated in 6 years
62% had job offers within 6 months
150 organizations recruited on campus

Financial Matters
98% average percent of need met
$20,830 average financial aid amount received per undergraduate (2006–07 estimated)

LOYOLA MARYMOUNT UNIVERSITY

SUBURBAN SETTING ■ PRIVATE ■ INDEPENDENT RELIGIOUS ■ COED
LOS ANGELES, CALIFORNIA

Web site: www.lmu.edu
Contact: Mr. Matthew X. Fissinger, Director of Admissions, 1 LMU Drive
   Suite 100, Los Angeles, CA 90045-8350
Telephone: 310-338-2750 or toll-free 800-LMU-INFO
E-mail: admissions@lmu.edu

Getting Accepted
8,533 applied
52% were accepted
1,268 enrolled (28% of accepted)
3.64 average high school GPA
Mean SAT critical reading score: 575
Mean SAT math score: 588
Mean ACT score: 25
41% had SAT critical reading scores over 600
48% had SAT math scores over 600
72% had ACT scores over 24
6% had SAT critical reading scores over 700
7% had SAT math scores over 700
11% had ACT scores over 30

Graduation and After
63% graduated in 4 years
9% graduated in 5 years
2% graduated in 6 years
82% had job offers within 6 months
306 organizations recruited on campus

Financial Matters
$31,914 tuition and fees (2007–08)
$11,145 room and board
76% average percent of need met
$17,254 average financial aid amount received
   per undergraduate (2004–05 estimated)

Academics

Loyola Marymount awards bachelor's, master's, doctoral, and first-professional **degrees** and post-bachelor's certificates. **Challenging opportunities** include advanced placement credit, accelerated degree programs, student-designed majors, an honors program, double majors, independent study, and a senior project. Special programs include cooperative education, internships, summer session for credit, study-abroad, and Army and Air Force ROTC.

The most frequently chosen **baccalaureate** fields are business/marketing, visual and performing arts, and communications/journalism. A complete listing of majors at Loyola Marymount appears in the Majors by College index beginning on page 471.

The **faculty** at Loyola Marymount has 485 full-time members. The student-faculty ratio is 13:1.

Students of Loyola Marymount

The student body totals 8,977, of whom 5,766 are undergraduates. 57.6% are women and 42.4% are men. Students come from 51 states and territories and 38 other countries. 75% are from California. 1.8% are international students. 8.1% are African American, 0.6% American Indian, 13.4% Asian American, and 19.9% Hispanic American. 88% returned for their sophomore year.

Facilities and Resources

300 **computers/terminals** are available on campus for general student use. Campuswide network is available. The 2 **libraries** have 495,920 books and 10,057 subscriptions.

Campus Life

There are 120 active organizations on campus, including a drama/theater group, newspaper, radio station, television station, and choral group. 56% of eligible men and 48% of eligible women are members of national **fraternities** and national **sororities**.

Loyola Marymount is a member of the NCAA (Division I). **Intercollegiate sports** (some offering scholarships) include baseball (m), basketball, crew, cross-country running, golf (m), soccer, softball (w), swimming and diving (w), tennis, volleyball (w), water polo.

Campus Safety

Student safety services include late-night transport/escort service, 24-hour emergency telephone alarm devices, 24-hour patrols by trained security personnel, and electronically operated dormitory entrances.

Applying

Loyola Marymount requires an essay, SAT or ACT, a high school transcript, and 2 recommendations. It recommends an interview. Application deadline: 1/15; 7/30 for financial aid, with a 2/15 priority date. Early and deferred admission are possible.

LOYOLA UNIVERSITY CHICAGO

URBAN SETTING ▪ PRIVATE ▪ INDEPENDENT RELIGIOUS ▪ COED, PRIMARILY WOMEN
CHICAGO, ILLINOIS

Web site: www.luc.edu
Contact: Ms. April Hansen, Director of Admission, 820 North Michigan
    Avenue, Suite 613, Chicago, IL 60611-9810
Telephone: 773-508-3079 or toll-free 800-262-2373
Fax: 312-508-8926
E-mail: admission@luc.edu

Academics

Loyola Chicago awards bachelor's, master's, doctoral, and first-professional **degrees** and
post-bachelor's and post-master's certificates (also offers adult part-time program with
significant enrollment not reflected in profile). **Challenging opportunities** include
advanced placement credit, accelerated degree programs, an honors program, double
majors, independent study, and a senior project. Special programs include internships,
summer session for credit, off-campus study, study-abroad, and Army, Navy, and Air
Force ROTC.

The most frequently chosen **baccalaureate** fields are business/marketing, social sciences, and biological/life sciences. A complete listing of majors at Loyola Chicago appears in the Majors by College index beginning on page 471.

The **faculty** at Loyola Chicago has 582 full-time members. The student-faculty ratio
is 14:1.

Students of Loyola Chicago

The student body totals 15,545, of whom 9,950 are undergraduates. 65% are women and
35% are men. Students come from 50 states and territories and 82 other countries. 66%
are from Illinois. 1.2% are international students. 5.1% are African American, 0.3%
American Indian, 12.2% Asian American, and 9.8% Hispanic American. 84% returned
for their sophomore year.

Facilities and Resources

696 **computers/terminals** are available on campus for general student use. Students can
access the following: campus intranet, computer help desk, free student e-mail accounts,
online (class) grades, online (class) registration, online (class) schedules. Campuswide
network is available. 40% of college-owned or -operated housing units are wired for
high-speed Internet access. Wireless service is available via entire campus. The 3 **libraries** have 1,421,507 books and 136,663 subscriptions.

Campus Life

There are 154 active organizations on campus, including a drama/theater group,
newspaper, and radio station. 6% of eligible men and 5% of eligible women are members
of national **fraternities** and national **sororities**.

Loyola Chicago is a member of the NCAA (Division I). **Intercollegiate sports**
(some offering scholarships) include basketball, cross-country running, golf, soccer,
softball (w), track and field, volleyball.

Campus Safety

Student safety services include late-night transport/escort service, 24-hour emergency
telephone alarm devices, 24-hour patrols by trained security personnel, and electronically operated dormitory entrances.

Applying

Loyola Chicago requires an essay, SAT or ACT, and a high school transcript. It recommends an interview. Application deadline: 4/1.

Getting Accepted
17,357 applied
73% were accepted
2,035 enrolled (16% of accepted)
33% from top tenth of their h.s. class
3.54 average high school GPA
Mean SAT critical reading score: 591
Mean SAT math score: 577
Mean SAT writing score: 570
Mean ACT score: 26
47% had SAT critical reading scores over 600
40% had SAT math scores over 600
36% had SAT writing scores over 600
73% had ACT scores over 24
8% had SAT critical reading scores over 700
7% had SAT math scores over 700
4% had SAT writing scores over 700
16% had ACT scores over 30
18 National Merit Scholars
30 valedictorians

Graduation and After
57% graduated in 4 years
5% graduated in 5 years
3% graduated in 6 years

Financial Matters
$29,486 tuition and fees (2008–09)
$10,490 room and board
77% average percent of need met
$21,689 average financial aid amount received
    per undergraduate (2006–07 estimated)

Loyola's unique combination of high-quality academic programs and outstanding faculty members, an ideal size that fosters a positive learning environment and individual attention, and the centuries-old Jesuit tradition of educating the whole person distinguishes it from other institutions. Loyola provides big-school experiences with small-school relationships. The University consistently ranks among the top regional colleges and universities in the South and is one of the top sixty in the U.S. Loyola's students have been awarded British Marshall, Fulbright, Goldwater, Mellon, Mitchell, and Rhodes scholarships and have been included as *USA Today*'s top students. A unique and expanded service-learning program offers Loyola students the opportunity to become engaged in the creation of a city and a region while strengthening their professional skills at the same time. Loyola students are actively involved in restoring local and national businesses, researching environmental impacts along the Gulf Coast, documenting oral histories, and exploring the importance of musical origins. Now more than ever, Loyola's students are offered an education like no other in the United States.

Getting Accepted
3,021 applied
58% were accepted
520 enrolled (30% of accepted)
26% from top tenth of their h.s. class
3.65 average high school GPA
64% had SAT critical reading scores over 600
46% had SAT math scores over 600
67% had ACT scores over 24
20% had SAT critical reading scores over 700
7% had SAT math scores over 700
14% had ACT scores over 30
12 valedictorians

Graduation and After
62% pursued further study
69.9% had job offers within 6 months
420 organizations recruited on campus

Financial Matters
$26,508 tuition and fees (2007–08)
$9150 room and board
81% average percent of need met
$23,188 average financial aid amount received
per undergraduate (2006–07 estimated)

LOYOLA UNIVERSITY NEW ORLEANS
URBAN SETTING ■ PRIVATE ■ INDEPENDENT RELIGIOUS ■ COED
NEW ORLEANS, LOUISIANA

Web site: www.loyno.edu
Contact: Ms. Deborah C. Stieffel, Dean of Admission and Enrollment Management, 6363 Saint Charles Avenue, Box 18, New Orleans, LA 70118-6195
Telephone: 504-865-3240 or toll-free 800-4-LOYOLA
Fax: 504-865-3383
E-mail: admit@loyno.edu

Academics
Loyola New Orleans awards bachelor's, master's, and first-professional **degrees** and post-bachelor's and post-master's certificates. **Challenging opportunities** include advanced placement credit, accelerated degree programs, student-designed majors, an honors program, double majors, independent study, and a senior project. Special programs include internships, summer session for credit, off-campus study, study-abroad, and Army, Navy, and Air Force ROTC. A complete listing of majors at Loyola New Orleans appears in the Majors by College index beginning on page 471.

The **faculty** at Loyola New Orleans has 259 full-time members, 91% with terminal degrees. The student-faculty ratio is 11:1.

Students of Loyola New Orleans
The student body totals 4,604, of whom 2,991 are undergraduates. 58.6% are women and 41.4% are men. Students come from 48 states and territories and 38 other countries. 42% are from Louisiana. 2.4% are international students. 11.3% are African American, 0.5% American Indian, 4.2% Asian American, and 11.8% Hispanic American.

Facilities and Resources
458 **computers/terminals** are available on campus for general student use. Students can access the following: online (class) registration. Campuswide network is available. The 2 **libraries** have 409,782 books and 37,520 subscriptions.

Campus Life
There are 140 active organizations on campus, including a drama/theater group, newspaper, radio station, television station, and choral group. 17% of eligible men and 18% of eligible women are members of national **fraternities**, national **sororities**, and local fraternities.

Loyola New Orleans is a member of the NAIA. **Intercollegiate sports** (some offering scholarships) include baseball (m), basketball, cross-country running, soccer (w), track and field, volleyball (w).

Campus Safety
Student safety services include self-defense education, bicycle patrols, closed circuit TV monitors, door alarms, crime prevention programs, late-night transport/escort service, 24-hour emergency telephone alarm devices, 24-hour patrols by trained security personnel, and electronically operated dormitory entrances.

Applying
Loyola New Orleans requires an essay, a high school transcript, and 1 recommendation, and in some cases SAT or ACT, PAA, and an interview. It recommends an interview. Application deadline: 1/15; 6/1 for financial aid, with a 2/15 priority date. Early and deferred admission are possible.

LUTHER COLLEGE

SMALL-TOWN SETTING ■ PRIVATE ■ INDEPENDENT RELIGIOUS ■ COED
DECORAH, IOWA

Web site: www.luther.edu
Contact: Kirk Neubauer, Director of Recruiting Services, 700 College Drive,
    Decorah, IA 52101
Telephone: 563-387-1287 or toll-free 800-458-8437
Fax: 563-387-2159
E-mail: admissions@luther.edu

Academics

Luther awards bachelor's **degrees**. **Challenging opportunities** include advanced placement credit, student-designed majors, an honors program, double majors, independent study, and a senior project. Special programs include internships, summer session for credit, off-campus study, and study-abroad.

The most frequently chosen **baccalaureate** fields are business/marketing, visual and performing arts, and biological/life sciences. A complete listing of majors at Luther appears in the Majors by College index beginning on page 471.

The **faculty** at Luther has 177 full-time members, 90% with terminal degrees. The student-faculty ratio is 12:1.

Students of Luther

The student body is made up of 2,476 undergraduates. 57% are women and 43% are men. Students come from 38 states and territories and 43 other countries. 36% are from Iowa. 3.7% are international students. 0.9% are African American, 0.2% American Indian, 2% Asian American, and 1.8% Hispanic American. 86% returned for their sophomore year.

Facilities and Resources

500 **computers/terminals** are available on campus for general student use. Students can access the following: campus intranet, computer help desk, free student e-mail accounts, online (class) grades, online (class) registration, online (class) schedules. Campuswide network is available. 100% of college-owned or -operated housing units are wired for high-speed Internet access. Wireless service is available via entire campus. The **library** has 334,814 books and 831 subscriptions.

Campus Life

There are 139 active organizations on campus, including a drama/theater group, newspaper, radio station, and choral group. 3% of eligible men and 4% of eligible women are members of local **fraternities** and local **sororities**.

Luther is a member of the NCAA (Division III). **Intercollegiate sports** include baseball (m), basketball, cross-country running, football (m), golf, soccer, softball (w), swimming and diving, tennis, track and field, volleyball (w), wrestling (m).

Campus Safety

Student safety services include late-night transport/escort service, 24-hour emergency telephone alarm devices, 24-hour patrols by trained security personnel, and electronically operated dormitory entrances.

Applying

Luther requires an essay, SAT or ACT, a high school transcript, and 1 recommendation. It recommends an interview. Application deadline: 3/1 priority date for financial aid. Deferred admission is possible.

Getting Accepted

2,054 applied
83% were accepted
659 enrolled (39% of accepted)
29% from top tenth of their h.s. class
3.6 average high school GPA
Mean SAT critical reading score: 579
Mean SAT math score: 597
Mean SAT writing score: 574
Mean ACT score: 25
51% had SAT critical reading scores over 600
54% had SAT math scores over 600
43% had SAT writing scores over 600
66% had ACT scores over 24
17% had SAT critical reading scores over 700
13% had SAT math scores over 700
12% had SAT writing scores over 700
18% had ACT scores over 30
6 National Merit Scholars
32 valedictorians

Graduation and After

63% graduated in 4 years
11% graduated in 5 years
1% graduated in 6 years
23% pursued further study (9% arts and sciences, 6% medicine, 3% law)
98.7% had job offers within 6 months
211 organizations recruited on campus

Financial Matters

$28,840 tuition and fees (2007–08)
$4660 room and board
89% average percent of need met
$20,916 average financial aid amount received per undergraduate (2006–07 estimated)

Lycoming College

SMALL-TOWN SETTING ■ PRIVATE ■ INDEPENDENT RELIGIOUS ■ COED
WILLIAMSPORT, PENNSYLVANIA

Web site: www.lycoming.edu
Contact: Mr. James Spencer, Vice President of Admissions and Financial Aid, 700 College Place, Williamsport, PA 17701
Telephone: 570-321-4026 or toll-free 800-345-3920 Ext. 4026
Fax: 570-321-4317
E-mail: admissions@lycoming.edu

Getting Accepted
1,585 applied
78% were accepted
399 enrolled (32% of accepted)
19% from top tenth of their h.s. class
Mean SAT critical reading score: 521
Mean SAT math score: 523
Mean SAT writing score: 510
Mean ACT score: 23
17% had SAT critical reading scores over 600
18% had SAT math scores over 600
17% had SAT writing scores over 600
41% had ACT scores over 24
1% had SAT critical reading scores over 700
2% had SAT math scores over 700
1% had SAT writing scores over 700
1% had ACT scores over 30
12 class presidents
4 valedictorians

Graduation and After
59% graduated in 4 years
7% graduated in 6 years
20% pursued further study (10% arts and sciences, 5% medicine, 1% business)
98% had job offers within 6 months
40 organizations recruited on campus

Financial Matters
$27,129 tuition and fees (2007–08)
$7238 room and board
76% average percent of need met
$19,152 average financial aid amount received per undergraduate (2006–07 estimated)

Academics

Lycoming awards bachelor's **degrees**. **Challenging opportunities** include advanced placement credit, accelerated degree programs, student-designed majors, an honors program, double majors, independent study, and a senior project. Special programs include internships, summer session for credit, off-campus study, study-abroad, and Army ROTC.

The most frequently chosen **baccalaureate** fields are business/marketing, social sciences, and psychology. A complete listing of majors at Lycoming appears in the Majors by College index beginning on page 471.

The **faculty** at Lycoming has 84 full-time members, 92% with terminal degrees. The student-faculty ratio is 14:1.

Students of Lycoming

The student body is made up of 1,431 undergraduates. 54.9% are women and 45.1% are men. Students come from 29 states and territories and 13 other countries. 69% are from Pennsylvania. 0.9% are international students. 2.7% are African American, 0.5% American Indian, 1% Asian American, and 1.6% Hispanic American. 80% returned for their sophomore year.

Facilities and Resources

140 **computers/terminals** are available on campus for general student use. Students can access the following: campus intranet, computer help desk, free student e-mail accounts, online (class) grades, online (class) registration, online (class) schedules. Campuswide network is available. 100% of college-owned or -operated housing units are wired for high-speed Internet access. Wireless service is available via entire campus. The 2 **libraries** have 183,395 books and 1,821 subscriptions.

Campus Life

There are 76 active organizations on campus, including a drama/theater group, newspaper, radio station, and choral group. 14% of eligible men and 17% of eligible women are members of national **fraternities**, national **sororities**, and local sororities.

Lycoming is a member of the NCAA (Division III). **Intercollegiate sports** include basketball, cross-country running, football (m), golf (m), lacrosse, soccer, softball (w), swimming and diving, tennis, volleyball (w), wrestling (m).

Campus Safety

Student safety services include late-night transport/escort service, 24-hour emergency telephone alarm devices, 24-hour patrols by trained security personnel, student patrols, and electronically operated dormitory entrances.

Applying

Lycoming requires an essay, SAT or ACT, a high school transcript, and 2 recommendations. It recommends an interview and a minimum high school GPA of 2.3. Application deadline: 5/1; 3/1 priority date for financial aid. Deferred admission is possible.

LYON COLLEGE

SMALL-TOWN SETTING ■ PRIVATE ■ INDEPENDENT RELIGIOUS ■ COED
BATESVILLE, ARKANSAS

Web site: www.lyon.edu
Contact: PO Box 2317, Batesville, AR 72503-2317
Telephone: 870-307-7250 or toll-free 800-423-2542
Fax: 870-793-1791
E-mail: admissions@lyon.edu

Academics

Lyon awards bachelor's **degrees**. **Challenging opportunities** include advanced placement credit, accelerated degree programs, student-designed majors, double majors, independent study, and a senior project. Special programs include internships, summer session for credit, and study-abroad.

The most frequently chosen **baccalaureate** fields are business/marketing, biological/life sciences, and history. A complete listing of majors at Lyon appears in the Majors by College index beginning on page 471.

The **faculty** at Lyon has 44 full-time members, 89% with terminal degrees. The student-faculty ratio is 10:1.

Students of Lyon

The student body is made up of 495 undergraduates. 53.9% are women and 46.1% are men. Students come from 21 states and territories and 11 other countries. 75% are from Arkansas. 2.5% are international students. 2.7% are African American, 1.7% American Indian, 1.2% Asian American, and 2.1% Hispanic American. 64% returned for their sophomore year.

Facilities and Resources

101 **computers/terminals** are available on campus for general student use. Students can access the following: campus intranet, computer help desk, free student e-mail accounts, online (class) grades, online (class) registration, online (class) schedules. Campuswide network is available. 100% of college-owned or -operated housing units are wired for high-speed Internet access. Wireless service is available via entire campus. The **library** has 199,573 books and 491 subscriptions.

Campus Life

There are 48 active organizations on campus, including a drama/theater group, newspaper, and choral group. 10% of eligible men and 13% of eligible women are members of national **fraternities** and national **sororities**.

Lyon is a member of the NAIA. **Intercollegiate sports** (some offering scholarships) include baseball (m), basketball, cross-country running, golf, soccer, softball (w), tennis, volleyball (w).

Campus Safety

Student safety services include late-night transport/escort service and 24-hour patrols by trained security personnel.

Applying

Lyon requires SAT or ACT, a high school transcript, and a minimum high school GPA of 2.5, and in some cases an essay and 2 recommendations. Application deadline: rolling admissions; 3/15 priority date for financial aid. Early and deferred admission are possible.

Getting Accepted

856 applied
69% were accepted
142 enrolled (24% of accepted)
30% from top tenth of their h.s. class
3.65 average high school GPA
Mean SAT critical reading score: 544
Mean SAT math score: 562
Mean ACT score: 25
22% had SAT critical reading scores over 600
35% had SAT math scores over 600
57% had ACT scores over 24
4% had SAT critical reading scores over 700
9% had SAT math scores over 700
6% had ACT scores over 30
10 valedictorians

Graduation and After

53% graduated in 4 years
3% graduated in 5 years
16% pursued further study (9% arts and sciences, 4% business, 4% law)
50% had job offers within 6 months
23 organizations recruited on campus

Financial Matters

$15,960 tuition and fees (2007–08)
$6644 room and board
78% average percent of need met
$13,927 average financial aid amount received per undergraduate (2006–07 estimated)

MACALESTER COLLEGE

URBAN SETTING ■ PRIVATE ■ INDEPENDENT RELIGIOUS ■ COED
ST. PAUL, MINNESOTA

Web site: www.macalester.edu
Contact: Mr. Lorne T. Robinson, Dean of Admissions and Financial Aid,
    1600 Grand Avenue, St. Paul, MN 55105-1899
Telephone: 651-696-6357 or toll-free 800-231-7974
Fax: 651-696-6724
E-mail: admissions@macalester.edu

Getting Accepted

4,967 applied
41% were accepted
485 enrolled (24% of accepted)
68% from top tenth of their h.s. class
Mean SAT critical reading score: 681
Mean SAT math score: 662
Mean SAT writing score: 663
Mean ACT score: 30
87% had SAT critical reading scores over 600
85% had SAT math scores over 600
83% had SAT writing scores over 600
96% had ACT scores over 24
47% had SAT critical reading scores over 700
31% had SAT math scores over 700
37% had SAT writing scores over 700
55% had ACT scores over 30
39 National Merit Scholars
45 valedictorians

Graduation and After

83% graduated in 4 years
4% graduated in 5 years
28% pursued further study (17% arts and
    sciences, 3% education, 1% business)
64% had job offers within 6 months
100 organizations recruited on campus

Financial Matters

$34,704 tuition and fees (2008–09)
$8472 room and board
100% average percent of need met
$25,238 average financial aid amount received
    per undergraduate (2005–06 estimated)

Academics

Macalester awards bachelor's **degrees. Challenging opportunities** include student-designed majors, an honors program, double majors, independent study, and a senior project. Special programs include internships, off-campus study, study-abroad, and Navy and Air Force ROTC.

The most frequently chosen **baccalaureate** fields are social sciences, foreign languages and literature, and interdisciplinary studies. A complete listing of majors at Macalester appears in the Majors by College index beginning on page 471.

The **faculty** at Macalester has 157 full-time members, 94% with terminal degrees. The student-faculty ratio is 10:1.

Students of Macalester

The student body is made up of 1,920 undergraduates. 57.7% are women and 42.3% are men. Students come from 53 states and territories and 87 other countries. 22% are from Minnesota. 12.4% are international students. 4.6% are African American, 0.9% American Indian, 8.8% Asian American, and 3.8% Hispanic American. 94% returned for their sophomore year.

Facilities and Resources

400 **computers/terminals** and 2,500 ports are available on campus for general student use. Students can access the following: campus intranet, computer help desk, free student e-mail accounts, online (class) registration, online (class) schedules, Web space. Campuswide network is available. 100% of college-owned or -operated housing units are wired for high-speed Internet access. Wireless service is available via entire campus. The **library** has 448,968 books and 3,559 subscriptions.

Campus Life

There are 80 active organizations on campus, including a drama/theater group, newspaper, radio station, and choral group. No national or local **fraternities** or **sororities**.

Macalester is a member of the NCAA (Division III). **Intercollegiate sports** include baseball (m), basketball, cross-country running, football (m), golf, soccer, softball (w), swimming and diving, tennis, track and field, volleyball (w), water polo (w).

Campus Safety

Student safety services include late-night transport/escort service, 24-hour emergency telephone alarm devices, 24-hour patrols by trained security personnel, and electronically operated dormitory entrances.

Applying

Macalester requires an essay, SAT or ACT, a high school transcript, and 3 recommendations. It recommends an interview. Application deadline: 1/15; 2/8 priority date for financial aid. Early and deferred admission are possible.

MAHARISHI UNIVERSITY OF MANAGEMENT
SMALL-TOWN SETTING ■ PRIVATE ■ INDEPENDENT ■ COED
FAIRFIELD, IOWA

Web site: www.mum.edu
Contact: Ms. Barbara Rainbow, Associate Dean of Admissions, Office of Admissions, Fairfield, IA 52557
Telephone: 641-472-1110 or toll-free 800-369-6480
Fax: 641-472-1179
E-mail: admissions@mum.edu

Academics
MUM awards bachelor's, master's, and doctoral **degrees** and post-bachelor's certificates. **Challenging opportunities** include advanced placement credit, student-designed majors, an honors program, double majors, independent study, and a senior project. Special programs include cooperative education, internships, and study-abroad.

The most frequently chosen **baccalaureate** fields are liberal arts/general studies, natural resources/environmental science, and visual and performing arts. A complete listing of majors at MUM appears in the Majors by College index beginning on page 471.

The **faculty** at MUM has 49 full-time members, 100% with terminal degrees. The student-faculty ratio is 16:1.

Students of MUM
The student body totals 948, of whom 204 are undergraduates. 43.1% are women and 56.9% are men. Students come from 38 states and territories and 72 other countries. 47% are from Iowa. 17.1% are international students. 2% are African American, 3.5% Asian American, and 6.5% Hispanic American. 61% returned for their sophomore year.

Facilities and Resources
20 **computers/terminals** are available on campus for general student use. Students can access the following: campus intranet, computer help desk, free student e-mail accounts, online (class) grades, online (class) schedules. Campuswide network is available. 100% of college-owned or -operated housing units are wired for high-speed Internet access. The **library** has 137,775 books and 11,146 subscriptions.

Campus Life
There are 15 active organizations on campus, including a drama/theater group, newspaper, radio station, and choral group. No national or local **fraternities** or **sororities**.

This institution has no intercollegiate sports.

Campus Safety
Student safety services include late-night transport/escort service, 24-hour emergency telephone alarm devices, 24-hour patrols by trained security personnel, and electronically operated dormitory entrances.

Applying
MUM requires an essay, a high school transcript, 2 recommendations, and a minimum high school GPA of 2.5. It recommends SAT or ACT and an interview. Application deadline: 8/1. Early and deferred admission are possible.

Getting Accepted
126 applied
41% were accepted
45 enrolled (87% of accepted)
1 National Merit Scholar

Graduation and After
41% graduated in 4 years
4% graduated in 5 years
75% had job offers within 6 months
20 organizations recruited on campus

Financial Matters
$24,430 tuition and fees (2008–09)
$6000 room and board
89% average percent of need met
$23,963 average financial aid amount received per undergraduate (2006–07 estimated)

MARIETTA COLLEGE
SMALL-TOWN SETTING ■ PRIVATE ■ INDEPENDENT ■ COED
MARIETTA, OHIO

Web site: www.marietta.edu
Contact: Mr. Jason Turley, Director of Admission, 215 Fifth Street, Marietta, OH 45750
Telephone: 740-376-4600 or toll-free 800-331-7896
Fax: 740-376-8888
E-mail: admit@marietta.edu

Founded in 1788, Marietta, Ohio, has the distinction of being the first permanent settlement of America's Northwest Territory. The College traces its beginning to 1797. Both the city and the College are rich in history, with stately homes, brick-paved streets, and antique stores. In 1860, Marietta College became only the sixteenth college in America to be awarded a chapter of Phi Beta Kappa. Students' academic life is enriched by the McDonough Leadership Program, the most comprehensive program in leadership studies in the country, whereby students may earn a minor, be actively involved in volunteer work, and participate in internships throughout the world.

Getting Accepted
2,320 applied
75% were accepted
416 enrolled (24% of accepted)
22% from top tenth of their h.s. class
3.41 average high school GPA
Mean SAT critical reading score: 544
Mean SAT math score: 538
Mean ACT score: 23
26% had SAT critical reading scores over 600
28% had SAT math scores over 600
48% had ACT scores over 24
6% had SAT critical reading scores over 700
2% had SAT math scores over 700
6% had ACT scores over 30

Graduation and After
45% graduated in 4 years
9% graduated in 5 years
2% graduated in 6 years
30% pursued further study (20% arts and sciences, 3% medicine, 2% business)
75% had job offers within 6 months
41 organizations recruited on campus

Financial Matters
$24,842 tuition and fees (2007–08)
$7390 room and board
92% average percent of need met
$19,488 average financial aid amount received per undergraduate

Academics
Marietta awards associate, bachelor's, and master's **degrees**. **Challenging opportunities** include advanced placement credit, accelerated degree programs, student-designed majors, an honors program, double majors, independent study, and a senior project. Special programs include internships, summer session for credit, off-campus study, and study-abroad.

The most frequently chosen **baccalaureate** fields are business/marketing, communications/journalism, and visual and performing arts. A complete listing of majors at Marietta appears in the Majors by College index beginning on page 471.

The **faculty** at Marietta has 96 full-time members, 78% with terminal degrees. The student-faculty ratio is 12:1.

Students of Marietta
The student body totals 1,606, of whom 1,502 are undergraduates. 51.2% are women and 48.8% are men. Students come from 35 states and territories and 20 other countries. 58% are from Ohio. 6.2% are international students. 3.7% are African American, 0.3% American Indian, 1.5% Asian American, and 1.5% Hispanic American. 80% returned for their sophomore year.

Facilities and Resources
350 **computers/terminals** are available on campus for general student use. Students can access the following: campus intranet, computer help desk, free student e-mail accounts, online (class) grades, online (class) registration, online (class) schedules. Campuswide network is available. 100% of college-owned or -operated housing units are wired for high-speed Internet access. Wireless service is available via classrooms, computer centers, computer labs, dorm rooms, learning centers, libraries, student centers. The **library** has 246,706 books and 28,188 subscriptions.

Campus Life
There are 100 active organizations on campus, including a drama/theater group, newspaper, radio station, television station, and choral group. 17% of eligible men and 22% of eligible women are members of national **fraternities** and national **sororities**.

Marietta is a member of the NCAA (Division III). **Intercollegiate sports** include baseball (m), basketball, crew, cross-country running, football (m), soccer, softball (w), tennis, track and field, volleyball (w).

Campus Safety
Student safety services include late-night transport/escort service, 24-hour emergency telephone alarm devices, 24-hour patrols by trained security personnel, student patrols, and electronically operated dormitory entrances.

Applying
Marietta requires an essay, SAT or ACT, a high school transcript, 1 recommendation, and a minimum high school GPA of 2.0. It recommends SAT Subject Tests, an interview, and a minimum high school GPA of 3.0. Application deadline: 5/1; 3/1 priority date for financial aid. Early and deferred admission are possible.

MARIST COLLEGE

SMALL-TOWN SETTING ■ PRIVATE ■ INDEPENDENT ■ COED
POUGHKEEPSIE, NEW YORK

Web site: www.marist.edu
Contact: Mr. Kenton Rinehart, Dean of Undergraduate Admissions, 3399
    North Road, Poughkeepsie, NY 12601
Telephone: 845-575-3226 or toll-free 800-436-5483
Fax: 845-575-3215
E-mail: admission@marist.edu

Academics

Marist awards bachelor's and master's **degrees** and post-bachelor's certificates. **Challenging opportunities** include advanced placement credit, accelerated degree programs, an honors program, double majors, independent study, and a senior project. Special programs include cooperative education, internships, summer session for credit, off-campus study, study-abroad, and Army ROTC.

The most frequently chosen **baccalaureate** fields are business/marketing, communications/journalism, and education. A complete listing of majors at Marist appears in the Majors by College index beginning on page 471.

The **faculty** at Marist has 218 full-time members, 78% with terminal degrees. The student-faculty ratio is 15:1.

Students of Marist

The student body totals 5,727, of whom 4,851 are undergraduates. 57.3% are women and 42.7% are men. Students come from 39 states and territories and 9 other countries. 59% are from New York. 0.3% are international students. 3.3% are African American, 0.2% American Indian, 2.4% Asian American, and 5.3% Hispanic American. 91% returned for their sophomore year.

Facilities and Resources

646 **computers/terminals** and 1,000 ports are available on campus for general student use. Students can access the following: campus intranet, computer help desk, free student e-mail accounts, online (class) grades, online (class) registration, online (class) schedules, admissions application, billing, transcript, degree audit, online financial aid summary, online library database search. Campuswide network is available. 100% of college-owned or -operated housing units are wired for high-speed Internet access. Wireless service is available via entire campus. The **library** has 197,209 books and 22,755 subscriptions.

Campus Life

There are 84 active organizations on campus, including a drama/theater group, newspaper, radio station, television station, choral group, and marching band. 1% of eligible men and 3% of eligible women are members of national **fraternities** and local **sororities**.

Marist is a member of the NCAA (Division I). **Intercollegiate sports** (some offering scholarships) include baseball (m), basketball, crew, cross-country running, football (m), lacrosse, soccer, softball (w), swimming and diving, tennis, track and field, volleyball (w), water polo (w).

Campus Safety

Student safety services include night residence hall monitors, late-night transport/escort service, 24-hour emergency telephone alarm devices, 24-hour patrols by trained security personnel, student patrols, and electronically operated dormitory entrances.

Applying

Marist requires an essay, SAT or ACT, a high school transcript, and 2 recommendations. Application deadline: 2/15; 5/1 for financial aid, with a 2/15 priority date. Early and deferred admission are possible.

Getting Accepted

8,328 applied
42% were accepted
1,019 enrolled (29% of accepted)
29% from top tenth of their h.s. class
3.3 average high school GPA
Mean SAT critical reading score: 580
Mean SAT math score: 580
Mean SAT writing score: 570
Mean ACT score: 25
36% had SAT critical reading scores over 600
42% had SAT math scores over 600
36% had SAT writing scores over 600
60% had ACT scores over 24
2% had SAT critical reading scores over 700
5% had SAT math scores over 700
2% had SAT writing scores over 700
9% had ACT scores over 30
17 class presidents
4 valedictorians

Graduation and After

70% graduated in 4 years
9% graduated in 5 years
1% graduated in 6 years
25% pursued further study (7% education,
    5% arts and sciences, 2% business)
84% had job offers within 6 months
227 organizations recruited on campus

Financial Matters

$24,040 tuition and fees (2007–08)
$10,250 room and board
68% average percent of need met
$13,925 average financial aid amount received
    per undergraduate (2006–07 estimated)

"Student-centered education enables a student to take ownership of learning right away," says Felicity Ratte, dean of faculty at Marlboro College in the Green Mountains of Vermont. One of the smallest (330 students) liberal arts colleges in the nation, Marlboro offers an excellent opportunity for students with an academic passion who are also attracted to community engagement in a rural setting. Marlboro was founded sixty years ago by World War II veterans who wanted a rigorous education rooted in an ideal of student independence; its location serves to both inspire and inform the unique nature of the undergraduate experience.

Getting Accepted
420 applied
44% were accepted
65 enrolled (35% of accepted)
3.3 average high school GPA
Mean SAT critical reading score: 648
Mean SAT math score: 558
Mean SAT writing score: 680
Mean ACT score: 26
74% had SAT critical reading scores over 600
34% had SAT math scores over 600
62% had ACT scores over 24
32% had SAT critical reading scores over 700
8% had SAT math scores over 700
24% had ACT scores over 30

Financial Matters
$30,680 tuition and fees (2007–08)
$8860 room and board
80% average percent of need met

MARLBORO COLLEGE
RURAL SETTING ■ PRIVATE ■ INDEPENDENT ■ COED
MARLBORO, VERMONT

Web site: www.marlboro.edu
Contact: Ms. Amy VanTassel, Associate Director of Admission, PO Box A, South Road, Marlboro, VT 05344-0300
Telephone: 800-343-0049
Fax: 800-451-7555
E-mail: admissions@marlboro.edu

Academics
Marlboro awards bachelor's, master's, and first-professional **degrees**. **Challenging opportunities** include advanced placement credit, accelerated degree programs, student-designed majors, double majors, independent study, and a senior project. Special programs include internships, off-campus study, and study-abroad. A complete listing of majors at Marlboro appears in the Majors by College index beginning on page 471.

The **faculty** at Marlboro has 40 full-time members, 75% with terminal degrees. The student-faculty ratio is 8:1.

Students of Marlboro
The student body totals 338, of whom 323 are undergraduates. 51.1% are women and 48.9% are men. Students come from 36 states and territories and 5 other countries. 20% are from Vermont. 1.3% are international students. 1% are African American, 0.3% American Indian, 3.5% Asian American, and 3.2% Hispanic American.

Facilities and Resources
47 **computers/terminals** are available on campus for general student use. Students can access the following: campus intranet, computer help desk, free student e-mail accounts. Campuswide network is available. Wireless service is available via classrooms, computer centers, computer labs, learning centers, libraries, student centers. The **library** has 71,000 books and 275 subscriptions.

Campus Life
There are 25 active organizations on campus, including a drama/theater group, newspaper, radio station, and choral group. No national or local **fraternities** or **sororities**.

Intercollegiate sports include rock climbing, soccer.

Campus Safety
Student safety services include 24-hour emergency telephone alarm devices.

Applying
Marlboro requires an essay, SAT or ACT, a high school transcript, 2 recommendations, and expository essay, and in some cases an interview. It recommends an interview. Application deadline: 3/1; 3/1 for financial aid. Early and deferred admission are possible.

MARQUETTE UNIVERSITY
URBAN SETTING ■ PRIVATE ■ INDEPENDENT RELIGIOUS ■ COED
MILWAUKEE, WISCONSIN

Web site: www.marquette.edu
Contact: Mr. Robert Blust, Dean of Undergraduate Admissions, PO Box
1881, Milwaukee, WI 53201-1881
Telephone: 414-288-7004 or toll-free 800-222-6544
Fax: 414-288-3764
E-mail: admissions@marquette.edu

Academics
Marquette awards bachelor's, master's, doctoral, and first-professional **degrees** and post-master's certificates. **Challenging opportunities** include advanced placement credit, an honors program, double majors, and a senior project. Special programs include cooperative education, internships, summer session for credit, off-campus study, study-abroad, and Army, Navy, and Air Force ROTC.

The most frequently chosen **baccalaureate** fields are business/marketing, communications/journalism, and social sciences. A complete listing of majors at Marquette appears in the Majors by College index beginning on page 471.

The **faculty** at Marquette has 609 full-time members, 89% with terminal degrees. The student-faculty ratio is 15:1.

Students of Marquette
The student body totals 11,516, of whom 7,955 are undergraduates. 53.7% are women and 46.3% are men. Students come from 51 states and territories and 47 other countries. 47% are from Wisconsin. 1.7% are international students. 5% are African American, 0.3% American Indian, 4.6% Asian American, and 4.9% Hispanic American. 89% returned for their sophomore year.

Facilities and Resources
1,200 **computers/terminals** and 500 ports are available on campus for general student use. Students can access the following: campus intranet, computer help desk, free student e-mail accounts, online (class) grades, online (class) registration, online (class) schedules. Campuswide network is available. 100% of college-owned or -operated housing units are wired for high-speed Internet access. Wireless service is available via classrooms, computer centers, computer labs, dorm rooms, learning centers, libraries, student centers. The 2 **libraries** have 1,482,930 books and 23,039 subscriptions.

Campus Life
There are 180 active organizations on campus, including a drama/theater group, newspaper, radio station, television station, and choral group. 5% of eligible men and 7% of eligible women are members of national **fraternities** and national **sororities**.

Marquette is a member of the NCAA (Division I). **Intercollegiate sports** (some offering scholarships) include basketball, cheerleading, cross-country running, golf (m), soccer, tennis, track and field, volleyball (w).

Campus Safety
Student safety services include 24-hour desk attendants in residence halls, late-night transport/escort service, 24-hour emergency telephone alarm devices, 24-hour patrols by trained security personnel, and student patrols.

Applying
Marquette requires an essay, SAT or ACT, a high school transcript, 1 recommendation, and a minimum high school GPA of 2.5. It recommends a minimum high school GPA of 3.4. Application deadline: 12/1. Deferred admission is possible.

Getting Accepted
13,375 applied
67% were accepted
1,820 enrolled (20% of accepted)
34% from top tenth of their h.s. class
Mean SAT critical reading score: 588
Mean SAT math score: 609
Mean SAT writing score: 585
Mean ACT score: 26
44% had SAT critical reading scores over 600
60% had SAT math scores over 600
45% had SAT writing scores over 600
78% had ACT scores over 24
9% had SAT critical reading scores over 700
12% had SAT math scores over 700
8% had SAT writing scores over 700
20% had ACT scores over 30

Graduation and After
57% graduated in 4 years
17% graduated in 5 years
1% graduated in 6 years
31% pursued further study
226 organizations recruited on campus

Financial Matters
$28,128 tuition and fees (2008–09)
77% average percent of need met
$18,248 average financial aid amount received
per undergraduate (2006–07 estimated)

Maryville provides a rigorous and transformational experience for each student. Through the unique Maryville curriculum and active mentoring from faculty and staff members, students are taught the skills and given the opportunities to be successful and to make a difference in the world. Classroom studies are supported by a rich array of experiential learning opportunities, including one of the nation's leading undergraduate research programs, internships, study abroad, service learning, and the College's distinctive outdoor adventure program, Mountain Challenge. Affiliated with the Presbyterian Church (U.S.A.) through a voluntary covenant, Maryville is located in Tennessee, near Knoxville and the Great Smoky Mountains National Park.

Getting Accepted
1,584 applied
76% were accepted
317 enrolled (26% of accepted)
28% from top tenth of their h.s. class
3.51 average high school GPA
Mean SAT critical reading score: 552
Mean SAT math score: 547
Mean SAT writing score: 547
Mean ACT score: 24
32% had SAT critical reading scores over 600
25% had SAT math scores over 600
28% had SAT writing scores over 600
54% had ACT scores over 24
8% had SAT critical reading scores over 700
2% had SAT math scores over 700
4% had SAT writing scores over 700
10% had ACT scores over 30
9 valedictorians

Graduation and After
40% graduated in 4 years
10% graduated in 5 years
2% graduated in 6 years
29% pursued further study
73% had job offers within 6 months
19 organizations recruited on campus

Financial Matters
$25,350 tuition and fees (2007–08)
$7800 room and board
92% average percent of need met
$20,380 average financial aid amount received per undergraduate (2005–06 estimated)

MARYVILLE COLLEGE
SUBURBAN SETTING ■ PRIVATE ■ INDEPENDENT RELIGIOUS ■ COED
MARYVILLE, TENNESSEE

Web site: www.maryvillecollege.edu
Contact: Ms. Linda L. Moore, Administrative Assistant of Admissions, 502 East Lamar Alexander Parkway, Maryville, TN 37804-5907
Telephone: 865-981-8092 or toll-free 800-597-2687
Fax: 865-981-8005
E-mail: admissions@maryvillecollege.edu

Academics
MC awards bachelor's **degrees**. **Challenging opportunities** include advanced placement credit, student-designed majors, an honors program, double majors, independent study, and a senior project. Special programs include internships, summer session for credit, off-campus study, and study-abroad.

The most frequently chosen **baccalaureate** fields are business/marketing, education, and social sciences. A complete listing of majors at MC appears in the Majors by College index beginning on page 471.

The **faculty** at MC has 78 full-time members, 85% with terminal degrees. The student-faculty ratio is 12:1.

Students of MC
The student body is made up of 1,176 undergraduates. 55.3% are women and 44.7% are men. Students come from 32 states and territories and 20 other countries. 78% are from Tennessee. 3.7% are international students. 5.8% are African American, 0.5% American Indian, 1.3% Asian American, and 1.7% Hispanic American. 72% returned for their sophomore year.

Facilities and Resources
265 **computers/terminals** are available on campus for general student use. Students can access the following: campus intranet, computer help desk, free student e-mail accounts, online (class) registration. Campuswide network is available. 100% of college-owned or -operated housing units are wired for high-speed Internet access. Wireless service is available via classrooms, computer centers, computer labs, dorm rooms, learning centers, libraries, student centers. The 2 **libraries** have 131,838 books and 14,531 subscriptions.

Campus Life
There are 55 active organizations on campus, including a drama/theater group, newspaper, and choral group. No national or local **fraternities** or **sororities**.

MC is a member of the NCAA (Division III). **Intercollegiate sports** include baseball (m), basketball, cheerleading, cross-country running, equestrian sports, football (m), soccer, softball (w), tennis, volleyball (w), wrestling (m).

Campus Safety
Student safety services include late-night transport/escort service, 24-hour emergency telephone alarm devices, 24-hour patrols by trained security personnel, and electronically operated dormitory entrances.

Applying
MC requires SAT or ACT, a high school transcript, and a minimum high school GPA of 2.5, and in some cases an essay, an interview, and recommendations. It recommends a minimum high school GPA of 3.0. Application deadline: 3/1; 3/1 priority date for financial aid. Early and deferred admission are possible.

MARYVILLE UNIVERSITY OF SAINT LOUIS

SUBURBAN SETTING ■ PRIVATE ■ INDEPENDENT ■ COED
ST. LOUIS, MISSOURI

Web site: www.maryville.edu
Contact: Ms. Shani Lenore, Admissions Director, 650 Maryville University
   Drive, St. Louis, MO 63141-7299
Telephone: 314-529-9350 or toll-free 800-627-9855
Fax: 314-529-9927
E-mail: admissions@maryville.edu

Academics

Maryville awards bachelor's, master's, and doctoral **degrees**. **Challenging opportunities** include advanced placement credit, accelerated degree programs, student-designed majors, freshman honors college, an honors program, double majors, independent study, and a senior project. Special programs include cooperative education, internships, summer session for credit, off-campus study, study-abroad, and Army ROTC.

The most frequently chosen **baccalaureate** fields are business/marketing, health professions and related sciences, and psychology. A complete listing of majors at Maryville appears in the Majors by College index beginning on page 471.

The **faculty** at Maryville has 108 full-time members, 78% with terminal degrees. The student-faculty ratio is 12:1.

Students of Maryville

The student body totals 3,422, of whom 2,801 are undergraduates. 77.2% are women and 22.8% are men. Students come from 22 states and territories and 10 other countries. 83% are from Missouri. 0.4% are international students. 7.5% are African American, 0.6% American Indian, 1.6% Asian American, and 1.3% Hispanic American. 82% returned for their sophomore year.

Facilities and Resources

425 **computers/terminals** are available on campus for general student use. Students can access the following: campus intranet, computer help desk, free student e-mail accounts, online (class) grades, online (class) registration, online (class) schedules, specialized software, university catalog. Campuswide network is available. Wireless service is available via entire campus. The **library** has 213,053 books and 14,110 subscriptions.

Campus Life

There are 40 active organizations on campus, including a drama/theater group, newspaper, and choral group. No national or local **fraternities** or **sororities**.

Maryville is a member of the NCAA (Division III). **Intercollegiate sports** include baseball (m), basketball, cross-country running, golf, soccer, softball (w), tennis, track and field, volleyball (w).

Campus Safety

Student safety services include video security system in residence halls, self-defense and education programs, late-night transport/escort service, 24-hour emergency telephone alarm devices, 24-hour patrols by trained security personnel, and electronically operated dormitory entrances.

Applying

Maryville requires SAT or ACT, a high school transcript, and a minimum high school GPA of 2.5, and in some cases an essay, an interview, recommendations, and audition, portfolio. Application deadline: 8/15; 3/1 priority date for financial aid. Early and deferred admission are possible.

Getting Accepted

1,167 applied
65% were accepted
303 enrolled (40% of accepted)
28% from top tenth of their h.s. class
3.53 average high school GPA
Mean ACT score: 24
56% had ACT scores over 24
8% had ACT scores over 30
9 valedictorians

Graduation and After

58% graduated in 4 years
4% graduated in 5 years
2% graduated in 6 years
92% had job offers within 6 months
57 organizations recruited on campus

Financial Matters

$19,050 tuition and fees (2007–08)
$7500 room and board
65% average percent of need met
$13,522 average financial aid amount received
   per undergraduate (2006–07 estimated)

Massachusetts Institute of Technology

Urban setting ■ Private ■ Independent ■ Coed
Cambridge, Massachusetts

Getting Accepted
12,445 applied
12% were accepted
1,067 enrolled (69% of accepted)
97% from top tenth of their h.s. class
Mean SAT critical reading score: 705
Mean SAT math score: 753
Mean SAT writing score: 699
Mean ACT score: 32
94% had SAT critical reading scores over 600
99% had SAT math scores over 600
100% had ACT scores over 24
59% had SAT critical reading scores over 700
87% had SAT math scores over 700
87% had ACT scores over 30
252 valedictorians

Graduation and After
83% graduated in 4 years
7% graduated in 5 years
2% graduated in 6 years
48% pursued further study (22% engineering,
   13% arts and sciences, 5% medicine)
42% had job offers within 6 months
427 organizations recruited on campus

Financial Matters
$34,986 tuition and fees (2007–08)
$10,400 room and board
100% average percent of need met
$29,831 average financial aid amount received
   per undergraduate (2005–06)

Web site: web.mit.edu
Contact: , Admissions Counselors, Building 3-108, 77 Massachusetts Avenue,
   Cambridge, MA 02139-4307
Telephone: 617-253-3400
Fax: 617-258-8304
E-mail: admissions@mit.edu

Academics
MIT awards bachelor's, master's, and doctoral **degrees. Challenging opportunities** include advanced placement credit and a senior project. Special programs include cooperative education, internships, off-campus study, study-abroad, and Army, Navy, and Air Force ROTC.

The most frequently chosen **baccalaureate** fields are engineering, computer and information sciences, and physical sciences. A complete listing of majors at MIT appears in the Majors by College index beginning on page 471.

The **faculty** at MIT has 1,362 full-time members, 91% with terminal degrees. The student-faculty ratio is 6:1.

Students of MIT
The student body totals 10,220, of whom 4,172 are undergraduates. 44.5% are women and 55.5% are men. Students come from 55 states and territories and 89 other countries. 10% are from Massachusetts. 8.2% are international students. 7.1% are African American, 1.3% American Indian, 25.9% Asian American, and 11.8% Hispanic American. 98% returned for their sophomore year.

Facilities and Resources
1,100 **computers/terminals** are available on campus for general student use. Students can access the following: campus intranet, computer help desk, free student e-mail accounts, online (class) grades, online (class) registration, online (class) schedules. Campuswide network is available. 85% of college-owned or -operated housing units are wired for high-speed Internet access. Wireless service is available via entire campus. The 12 **libraries** have 964,656 books and 22,991 subscriptions.

Campus Life
There are 415 active organizations on campus, including a drama/theater group, newspaper, radio station, television station, choral group, and marching band. MIT has national **fraternities**, national **sororities**, and local fraternities.

MIT is a member of the NCAA (Division III). **Intercollegiate sports** include baseball (m), basketball, crew, cross-country running, fencing, field hockey (w), football (m), golf (m), gymnastics, ice hockey (w), lacrosse, riflery, sailing, skiing (cross-country), skiing (downhill), soccer, softball (w), squash (m), swimming and diving, tennis, track and field, volleyball, water polo (m), wrestling (m).

Campus Safety
Student safety services include late-night transport/escort service, 24-hour emergency telephone alarm devices, 24-hour patrols by trained security personnel, and electronically operated dormitory entrances.

Applying
MIT requires an essay, SAT Subject Tests, a high school transcript, and 2 recommendations, and in some cases SAT or ACT. It recommends an interview. Application deadline: 1/1; 2/15 for financial aid, with a 2/15 priority date. Deferred admission is possible.

The Master's College and Seminary

Suburban setting ■ Private ■ Independent Religious ■ Coed
Santa Clarita, California

Web site: www.masters.edu
Contact: Ms. Hollie Gorsh, Director of Admissions, 21726 Placerita Canyon Road, Santa Clarita, CA 91321
Telephone: 661-259-3540 Ext. 3369 or toll-free 800-568-6248
Fax: 661-288-1037
E-mail: admissions@masters.edu

Academics

Master's awards bachelor's, master's, doctoral, and first-professional **degrees** and first-professional certificates. **Challenging opportunities** include advanced placement credit, accelerated degree programs, double majors, independent study, and a senior project. Special programs include cooperative education, internships, summer session for credit, and study-abroad.

The most frequently chosen **baccalaureate** fields are business/marketing, liberal arts/general studies, and communications/journalism. A complete listing of majors at Master's appears in the Majors by College index beginning on page 471.

The **faculty** at Master's has 70 full-time members, 79% with terminal degrees. The student-faculty ratio is 16:1.

Students of Master's

The student body totals 1,516, of whom 1,114 are undergraduates. 50.6% are women and 49.4% are men. Students come from 41 states and territories and 39 other countries. 64% are from California. 4.1% are international students. 2.1% are African American, 1% American Indian, 4.8% Asian American, and 7% Hispanic American. 80% returned for their sophomore year.

Facilities and Resources

57 **computers/terminals** are available on campus for general student use. Students can access the following: free student e-mail accounts, online (class) grades, online (class) registration, online (class) schedules. Campuswide network is available. Wireless service is available via entire campus. The 2 **libraries** have 178,337 books and 12,867 subscriptions.

Campus Life

There are 15 active organizations on campus, including a drama/theater group and choral group. No national or local **fraternities** or **sororities**.

Master's is a member of the NAIA and NCCAA. **Intercollegiate sports** (some offering scholarships) include baseball (m), basketball, cross-country running, golf (m), soccer, softball (w), volleyball (w).

Campus Safety

Student safety services include 24-hour patrols by trained security personnel.

Applying

Master's requires an essay, SAT or ACT, a high school transcript, an interview, 2 recommendations, and a minimum high school GPA of 2.50. Application deadline: 3/2 priority date for financial aid. Early and deferred admission are possible.

Getting Accepted

485 applied
84% were accepted
210 enrolled (52% of accepted)
33% from top tenth of their h.s. class
3.6 average high school GPA
Mean SAT critical reading score: 568
Mean SAT math score: 553
Mean ACT score: 25
40% had SAT critical reading scores over 600
34% had SAT math scores over 600
55% had ACT scores over 24
8% had SAT critical reading scores over 700
5% had SAT math scores over 700
19% had ACT scores over 30

Graduation and After

34% graduated in 4 years
14% graduated in 5 years
2% graduated in 6 years
11% pursued further study (10% theology, 1% law)
30 organizations recruited on campus

Financial Matters

$23,120 tuition and fees (2008–09)
$7250 room and board
69% average percent of need met
$15,054 average financial aid amount received per undergraduate (2005–06 estimated)

McDaniel College

Suburban setting ▪ Private ▪ Independent ▪ Coed
Westminster, Maryland

Getting Accepted

2,742 applied
73% were accepted
431 enrolled (21% of accepted)
28% from top tenth of their h.s. class
3.50 average high school GPA
Mean SAT critical reading score: 564
Mean SAT math score: 567
Mean ACT score: 24
32% had SAT critical reading scores over 600
35% had SAT math scores over 600
46% had ACT scores over 24
6% had SAT critical reading scores over 700
7% had SAT math scores over 700
7% had ACT scores over 30
14 National Merit Scholars
8 valedictorians

Graduation and After

43% pursued further study (12% arts and sciences, 9% education, 4% law)
65% had job offers within 6 months
160 organizations recruited on campus

Financial Matters

$28,940 tuition and fees (2007–08)
$5900 room and board
95% average percent of need met
$21,474 average financial aid amount received per undergraduate (2006–07 estimated)

Web site: www.mcdaniel.edu
Contact: Ms. Florence Hines, Vice President for Enrollment Management and Dean of Admissions, 2 College Hill, Westminster, MD 21157-4390
Telephone: 410-857-2230 or toll-free 800-638-5005
Fax: 410-857-2757
E-mail: admissions@mcdaniel.edu

Academics

McDaniel awards bachelor's and master's **degrees** and post-bachelor's certificates. **Challenging opportunities** include advanced placement credit, student-designed majors, an honors program, double majors, independent study, and a senior project. Special programs include internships, summer session for credit, off-campus study, study-abroad, and Army ROTC.

The most frequently chosen **baccalaureate** fields are social sciences, psychology, and business/marketing. A complete listing of majors at McDaniel appears in the Majors by College index beginning on page 471.

The **faculty** at McDaniel has 139 full-time members, 83% with terminal degrees. The student-faculty ratio is 12:1.

Students of McDaniel

The student body totals 3,642, of whom 1,731 are undergraduates. 55.5% are women and 44.5% are men. Students come from 34 states and territories and 10 other countries. 70% are from Maryland. 0.1% are international students. 4.7% are African American, 0.5% American Indian, 2.6% Asian American, and 1.7% Hispanic American. 84% returned for their sophomore year.

Facilities and Resources

150 **computers/terminals** and 1,350 ports are available on campus for general student use. Students can access the following: campus intranet, computer help desk, free student e-mail accounts, online (class) grades, online (class) registration, online (class) schedules. Campuswide network is available. 100% of college-owned or -operated housing units are wired for high-speed Internet access. Wireless service is available via libraries, student centers. The **library** has 422,055 books and 19,356 subscriptions.

Campus Life

There are 132 active organizations on campus, including a drama/theater group, newspaper, radio station, television station, and choral group. 13% of eligible men and 12% of eligible women are members of national **fraternities**, national **sororities**, local fraternities, and local sororities.

McDaniel is a member of the NCAA (Division III). **Intercollegiate sports** include baseball (m), basketball, cross-country running, field hockey (w), football (m), golf, lacrosse, soccer, softball (w), swimming and diving, tennis, track and field, volleyball (w), wrestling (m).

Campus Safety

Student safety services include late-night transport/escort service, 24-hour emergency telephone alarm devices, 24-hour patrols by trained security personnel, and electronically operated dormitory entrances.

Applying

McDaniel requires an essay, a high school transcript, recommendations, and a minimum high school GPA of 2.5, and in some cases SAT or ACT and an interview. It recommends an interview. Application deadline: 2/1; 3/1 priority date for financial aid. Early and deferred admission are possible.

McGill University

Urban setting ■ Public ■ Coed
Montréal, Quebec

Web site: www.mcgill.ca
Contact: Enrollment Services, 845 Sherbrooke Street West, James
  Administration Building, Room 205, Montreal, QC H3A 2T5 Canada
Telephone: 514-398-3910
Fax: 514-398-4193
E-mail: admissions@mcgill.ca

Academics

McGill awards bachelor's, master's, doctoral, and first-professional **degrees** and post-bachelor's and post-master's certificates. **Challenging opportunities** include advanced placement credit, accelerated degree programs, an honors program, double majors, independent study, and a senior project. Special programs include cooperative education, internships, summer session for credit, off-campus study, and study-abroad.

The most frequently chosen **baccalaureate** fields are social sciences, biological/life sciences, and business/marketing. A complete listing of majors at McGill appears in the Majors by College index beginning on page 471.

The **faculty** at McGill has 1,680 full-time members, 95% with terminal degrees. The student-faculty ratio is 16:1.

Students of McGill

The student body totals 31,081, of whom 22,262 are undergraduates. 59.4% are women and 40.6% are men. Students come from 13 states and territories and 118 other countries. 64% are from Quebec. 17.3% are international students. 92% returned for their sophomore year.

Facilities and Resources

3,797 **computers/terminals** are available on campus for general student use. Students can access the following: campus intranet, computer help desk, free student e-mail accounts, online (class) grades, online (class) registration, online (class) schedules. Campuswide network is available. 100% of college-owned or -operated housing units are wired for high-speed Internet access. Wireless service is available via entire campus. The 14 **libraries** have 4,236,684 books and 49,433 subscriptions.

Campus Life

There are 250 active organizations on campus, including a drama/theater group, newspaper, radio station, and choral group. No national or local **fraternities** or **sororities**.

Intercollegiate sports include badminton, baseball (m), basketball, cheerleading, crew, cross-country running, fencing, field hockey (w), football (m), golf, ice hockey, lacrosse, rugby, sailing, skiing (cross-country), skiing (downhill), soccer, squash, swimming and diving, tennis, track and field, ultimate Frisbee, volleyball, wrestling.

Campus Safety

Student safety services include late-night transport/escort service, 24-hour emergency telephone alarm devices, 24-hour patrols by trained security personnel, student patrols, and electronically operated dormitory entrances.

Applying

McGill requires a high school transcript and a minimum high school GPA of 3.3, and in some cases SAT and SAT Subject Tests or ACT, an interview, recommendations, and audition for music program, portfolio for architecture program. Application deadline: 1/15; 6/1 priority date for financial aid. Deferred admission is possible.

Getting Accepted

20,391 applied
54% were accepted
4,977 enrolled (45% of accepted)
3.53 average high school GPA
Mean SAT critical reading score: 687
Mean SAT math score: 683
Mean SAT writing score: 684
Mean ACT score: 30
93% had SAT critical reading scores over 600
92% had SAT math scores over 600
93% had SAT writing scores over 600
100% had ACT scores over 24
48% had SAT critical reading scores over 700
41% had SAT math scores over 700
42% had SAT writing scores over 700
55% had ACT scores over 30

Graduation and After

68% graduated in 4 years
15% graduated in 5 years
3% graduated in 6 years
3000 organizations recruited on campus

Financial Matters

$3189 resident tuition and fees (2007–08)
$6561 nonresident tuition and fees (2007–08)
$10,400 room and board

McKendree University

SMALL-TOWN SETTING ■ PRIVATE ■ INDEPENDENT RELIGIOUS ■ COED
LEBANON, ILLINOIS

Getting Accepted
1,097 applied
71% were accepted
339 enrolled (44% of accepted)
22% from top tenth of their h.s. class
3.5 average high school GPA
Mean SAT critical reading score: 514
Mean SAT math score: 572
Mean ACT score: 25
13% had SAT critical reading scores over 600
27% had SAT math scores over 600
13% had SAT writing scores over 600
39% had ACT scores over 24
18% had SAT math scores over 700
7% had ACT scores over 30
4 valedictorians

Graduation and After
51% graduated in 4 years
8% graduated in 5 years
1% graduated in 6 years
22% pursued further study (4% business, 4% law, 1% medicine)
96% had job offers within 6 months
100 organizations recruited on campus

Financial Matters
$20,150 tuition and fees (2007–08)
$7660 room and board
82% average percent of need met
$15,361 average financial aid amount received per undergraduate (2006–07 estimated)

Web site: www.mckendree.edu
Contact: Chris Hall, Vice President for Admissions and Financial Aid, 701 College Road, Lebanon, IL 62254
Telephone: 618-537-6833 or toll-free 800-232-7228 Ext. 6831
Fax: 618-537-6496
E-mail: inquiry@mckendree.edu

Academics
McKendree awards bachelor's and master's **degrees**. **Challenging opportunities** include advanced placement credit, accelerated degree programs, student-designed majors, an honors program, double majors, independent study, and a senior project. Special programs include internships, summer session for credit, off-campus study, study-abroad, and Army and Air Force ROTC.

The most frequently chosen **baccalaureate** fields are business/marketing, education, and health professions and related sciences. A complete listing of majors at McKendree appears in the Majors by College index beginning on page 471.

The **faculty** at McKendree has 94 full-time members, 78% with terminal degrees. The student-faculty ratio is 13:1.

Students of McKendree
The student body totals 3,393, of whom 2,456 are undergraduates. 55.5% are women and 44.5% are men. Students come from 24 states and territories and 24 other countries. 68% are from Illinois. 2.4% are international students. 13.4% are African American, 0.3% American Indian, 1% Asian American, and 2.1% Hispanic American. 77% returned for their sophomore year.

Facilities and Resources
140 **computers/terminals** are available on campus for general student use. Students can access the following: campus intranet, computer help desk, free student e-mail accounts, online (class) grades, online (class) registration, online (class) schedules. Campuswide network is available. 100% of college-owned or -operated housing units are wired for high-speed Internet access. Wireless service is available via entire campus. The **library** has 109,000 books and 450 subscriptions.

Campus Life
There are 54 active organizations on campus, including a drama/theater group, newspaper, radio station, choral group, and marching band. 7% of eligible men and 10% of eligible women are members of national **fraternities**, local fraternities, and local **sororities**.

McKendree is a member of the NAIA. **Intercollegiate sports** (some offering scholarships) include baseball (m), basketball, bowling, cheerleading, cross-country running, football (m), golf, ice hockey (m), soccer, softball (w), tennis, track and field, volleyball (w), wrestling (m).

Campus Safety
Student safety services include late-night transport/escort service, 24-hour emergency telephone alarm devices, 24-hour patrols by trained security personnel, student patrols, and electronically operated dormitory entrances.

Applying
McKendree requires an essay, SAT or ACT, a high school transcript, 1 recommendation, rank in upper 50% of high school class, minimum ACT score of 20, and a minimum high school GPA of 2.5, and in some cases an interview. Application deadline: rolling admissions; 5/31 priority date for financial aid. Deferred admission is possible.

MERCER UNIVERSITY

SUBURBAN SETTING ■ PRIVATE ■ INDEPENDENT RELIGIOUS ■ COED
MACON, GEORGIA

Web site: www.mercer.edu
Contact: Mr. Terry Whittum, Senior Vice President, Enrollment
    Management, 1400 Coleman Avenue, Macon, GA 31207-0003
Telephone: 478-301-2650 or toll-free 800-840-8577
Fax: 478-301-2828
E-mail: admissions@mercer.edu

Academics

Mercer awards bachelor's, master's, doctoral, and first-professional **degrees** and post-bachelor's and post-master's certificates. **Challenging opportunities** include advanced placement credit, accelerated degree programs, student-designed majors, an honors program, double majors, independent study, and a senior project. Special programs include cooperative education, internships, summer session for credit, off-campus study, study-abroad, and Army ROTC.

The most frequently chosen **baccalaureate** fields are business/marketing, engineering, and psychology. A complete listing of majors at Mercer appears in the Majors by College index beginning on page 471.

The **faculty** at Mercer has 352 full-time members, 88% with terminal degrees. The student-faculty ratio is 13:1.

Students of Mercer

The student body totals 5,253, of whom 2,267 are undergraduates. 53% are women and 47% are men. 77% are from Georgia. 2% are international students. 16.8% are African American, 0.2% American Indian, 7.1% Asian American, and 2.7% Hispanic American. 81% returned for their sophomore year.

Facilities and Resources

500 **computers/terminals** and 2,500 ports are available on campus for general student use. Students can access the following: campus intranet, computer help desk, free student e-mail accounts, online (class) grades, online (class) registration, online (class) schedules. Campuswide network is available. 100% of college-owned or -operated housing units are wired for high-speed Internet access. Wireless service is available via classrooms, computer centers, computer labs, learning centers, libraries, student centers. The 4 **libraries** have 692,225 books and 28,163 subscriptions.

Campus Life

There are 104 active organizations on campus, including a drama/theater group, newspaper, radio station, television station, and choral group. 24% of eligible men and 28% of eligible women are members of national **fraternities**, national **sororities**, and local sororities.

Mercer is a member of the NCAA (Division I). **Intercollegiate sports** (some offering scholarships) include baseball (m), basketball, cross-country running, golf, riflery (m), soccer, softball (w), tennis, volleyball (w).

Campus Safety

Student safety services include patrols by police officers, late-night transport/escort service, 24-hour emergency telephone alarm devices, 24-hour patrols by trained security personnel, student patrols, and electronically operated dormitory entrances.

Applying

Mercer requires SAT or ACT, a high school transcript, and a minimum high school GPA of 3.0, and in some cases an interview and 2 recommendations. It recommends an interview and counselor's evaluation. Application deadline: 7/1; 4/1 priority date for financial aid. Early and deferred admission are possible.

Getting Accepted
4,588 applied
60% were accepted
583 enrolled (21% of accepted)
42% from top tenth of their h.s. class
3.6 average high school GPA
Mean SAT critical reading score: 582
Mean SAT math score: 587
Mean SAT writing score: 567
Mean ACT score: 26
40% had SAT critical reading scores over 600
42% had SAT math scores over 600
34% had SAT writing scores over 600
70% had ACT scores over 24
7% had SAT critical reading scores over 700
7% had SAT math scores over 700
6% had SAT writing scores over 700
15% had ACT scores over 30

Graduation and After
35% graduated in 4 years
15% graduated in 5 years
4% graduated in 6 years
35% pursued further study (8% arts and sciences, 8% law, 7% medicine)
67% had job offers within 6 months
226 organizations recruited on campus

Financial Matters
$26,960 tuition and fees (2007–08)
$8015 room and board
89% average percent of need met
$24,969 average financial aid amount received per undergraduate (2006–07 estimated)

Messiah College provides an education that is both rigorously academic and unapologetically Christian. The learning process is characterized by a lively student-faculty interaction that actively integrates academic content and faith issues. Messiah offers a strategically located campus, impressive academic and residence life facilities, and more than sixty majors and fifty minors in the applied and liberal arts and sciences. Students pursue extracurricular interests in twenty-two intercollegiate sports, ministries, service-learning areas, music ensembles, and scores of other activities. A multifaceted internship program provides career experience for students before they graduate. After graduation, 99 percent of graduates report employment/voluntary service or enrollment in graduate school within six months.

Getting Accepted
2,496 applied
79% were accepted
696 enrolled (35% of accepted)
32% from top tenth of their h.s. class
3.71 average high school GPA
Mean SAT critical reading score: 575
Mean SAT math score: 573
Mean SAT writing score: 565
Mean ACT score: 25
38% had SAT critical reading scores over 600
37% had SAT math scores over 600
35% had SAT writing scores over 600
57% had ACT scores over 24
8% had SAT critical reading scores over 700
6% had SAT math scores over 700
6% had SAT writing scores over 700
13% had ACT scores over 30
3 National Merit Scholars
19 valedictorians

Graduation and After
67% graduated in 4 years
5% graduated in 5 years
1% graduated in 6 years
21% pursued further study (9% arts and sciences, 2% education, 2% medicine)
95% had job offers within 6 months
466 organizations recruited on campus

Financial Matters
$24,420 tuition and fees (2007–08)
$7340 room and board
61% average percent of need met
$11,017 average financial aid amount received per undergraduate (2005–06)

MESSIAH COLLEGE
SMALL-TOWN SETTING ■ PRIVATE ■ INDEPENDENT RELIGIOUS ■ COED
GRANTHAM, PENNSYLVANIA

Web site: www.messiah.edu
Contact: Mr. John Chopka, Dean for Enrollment Management, PO Box 3005, One College Avenue, Grantham, PA 17027
Telephone: 717-691-6000 or toll-free 800-233-4220
Fax: 717-796-5374
E-mail: admiss@messiah.edu

Academics
Messiah awards bachelor's **degrees**. **Challenging opportunities** include advanced placement credit, accelerated degree programs, student-designed majors, an honors program, double majors, independent study, and a senior project. Special programs include internships, summer session for credit, off-campus study, and study-abroad.

The most frequently chosen **baccalaureate** fields are education, business/marketing, and health professions and related sciences. A complete listing of majors at Messiah appears in the Majors by College index beginning on page 471.

The **faculty** at Messiah has 172 full-time members, 81% with terminal degrees. The student-faculty ratio is 13:1.

Students of Messiah
The student body is made up of 2,837 undergraduates. 63.2% are women and 36.8% are men. Students come from 37 states and territories and 23 other countries. 54% are from Pennsylvania. 2.1% are international students. 1.8% are African American, 0.1% American Indian, 1.8% Asian American, and 1.4% Hispanic American. 86% returned for their sophomore year.

Facilities and Resources
571 **computers/terminals** are available on campus for general student use. Students can access the following: campus intranet, computer help desk, free student e-mail accounts, online (class) grades, online (class) registration, online (class) schedules, access to software. Campuswide network is available. 100% of college-owned or -operated housing units are wired for high-speed Internet access. Wireless service is available via entire campus. The **library** has 293,357 books and 20,219 subscriptions.

Campus Life
There are 63 active organizations on campus, including a drama/theater group, newspaper, radio station, and choral group. No national or local **fraternities** or **sororities**.

Messiah is a member of the NCAA (Division III). **Intercollegiate sports** include baseball (m), basketball, cross-country running, field hockey (w), golf (m), lacrosse, soccer, softball (w), tennis, track and field, volleyball (w), wrestling (m).

Campus Safety
Student safety services include bicycle patrols, security lighting, self-defense classes, prevention/awareness programs, late-night transport/escort service, 24-hour emergency telephone alarm devices, 24-hour patrols by trained security personnel, student patrols, and electronically operated dormitory entrances.

Applying
Messiah requires an essay, a high school transcript, and 2 recommendations, and in some cases SAT or ACT. It recommends an interview. Application deadline: rolling admissions; 4/1 priority date for financial aid. Deferred admission is possible.

Miami University

SMALL-TOWN SETTING ■ PUBLIC ■ STATE-RELATED ■ COED
OXFORD, OHIO

Web site: www.muohio.edu
Contact: Laurie Koehler, Interim Director of Undergraduate Admissions, 301 South Campus Avenue, Oxford, OH 45056
Telephone: 513-529-2531
Fax: 513-529-1550
E-mail: admissions@muohio.edu

Academics

Miami awards associate, bachelor's, master's, and doctoral **degrees** and post-master's certificates. **Challenging opportunities** include advanced placement credit, student-designed majors, an honors program, double majors, independent study, and a senior project. Special programs include cooperative education, internships, summer session for credit, off-campus study, study-abroad, and Army, Navy, and Air Force ROTC.

The most frequently chosen **baccalaureate** fields are business/marketing, education, and social sciences. A complete listing of majors at Miami appears in the Majors by College index beginning on page 471.

The **faculty** at Miami has 828 full-time members, 90% with terminal degrees. The student-faculty ratio is 15:1.

Students of Miami

The student body totals 15,922, of whom 14,555 are undergraduates. 53.7% are women and 46.3% are men. Students come from 50 states and territories and 38 other countries. 70% are from Ohio. 1.1% are international students. 3.2% are African American, 0.6% American Indian, 2.8% Asian American, and 1.9% Hispanic American. 89% returned for their sophomore year.

Facilities and Resources

1,000 **computers/terminals** are available on campus for general student use. Students can access the following: campus intranet, computer help desk, free student e-mail accounts, online (class) grades, online (class) registration. Campuswide network is available. Wireless service is available via entire campus. The 4 **libraries** have 2,697,078 books and 14,089 subscriptions.

Campus Life

There are 350 active organizations on campus, including a drama/theater group, newspaper, radio station, television station, choral group, and marching band. 21% of eligible men and 24% of eligible women are members of national **fraternities** and national **sororities**.

Miami is a member of the NCAA (Division I). **Intercollegiate sports** (some offering scholarships) include baseball (m), basketball, cross-country running, field hockey (w), football (m), golf (m), ice hockey (m), soccer (w), softball (w), swimming and diving, tennis (w), track and field, volleyball (w).

Campus Safety

Student safety services include late-night transport/escort service, 24-hour emergency telephone alarm devices, 24-hour patrols by trained security personnel, student patrols, and electronically operated dormitory entrances.

Applying

Miami requires SAT or ACT and a high school transcript. It recommends an essay and 1 recommendation. Application deadline: 1/31; 2/15 priority date for financial aid. Deferred admission is possible.

Getting Accepted

15,925 applied
75% were accepted
3,404 enrolled (28% of accepted)
35% from top tenth of their h.s. class
3.7 average high school GPA
Mean SAT critical reading score: 593
Mean SAT math score: 612
Mean ACT score: 26
49% had SAT critical reading scores over 600
61% had SAT math scores over 600
79% had ACT scores over 24
9% had SAT critical reading scores over 700
11% had SAT math scores over 700
15% had ACT scores over 30
70 National Merit Scholars

Graduation and After

67% graduated in 4 years
12% graduated in 5 years
1% graduated in 6 years
550 organizations recruited on campus

Financial Matters

$11,925 resident tuition and fees (2007–08)
$24,377 nonresident tuition and fees (2007–08)
$8600 room and board
74% average percent of need met
$17,573 average financial aid amount received per undergraduate (2006–07 estimated)

On a Big Ten campus known and loved for its beauty, Michigan State University's modern facilities, historic buildings, and parklike setting provide a unique environment of tradition and innovation. A diverse and talented student body, a dynamic faculty, and a dedicated staff all create a friendly and stimulating academic community that balances intellectual challenge and support for student success. Undergraduate education comes first at MSU, with 200 undergraduate majors, a nationally recognized Honors College, and other highly regarded living-learning programs. Michigan State has the top-ranked public study-abroad program in the nation, with more than 200 programs on all seven continents. An MSU education attracts students who are interested in combining a high-quality liberal arts education with extraordinary opportunities for hands-on experiences through internships, undergraduate research, outreach, and public service.

Getting Accepted
24,436 applied
74% were accepted
7,541 enrolled (42% of accepted)
29% from top tenth of their h.s. class
3.59 average high school GPA
Mean SAT critical reading score: 548
Mean SAT math score: 583
Mean SAT writing score: 538
Mean ACT score: 24
33% had SAT critical reading scores over 600
47% had SAT math scores over 600
27% had SAT writing scores over 600
66% had ACT scores over 24
8% had SAT critical reading scores over 700
11% had SAT math scores over 700
5% had SAT writing scores over 700
11% had ACT scores over 30
53 National Merit Scholars

Graduation and After
44% graduated in 4 years
26% graduated in 5 years
4% graduated in 6 years
600 organizations recruited on campus

Financial Matters
$9640 resident tuition and fees (2007–08)
$23,500 nonresident tuition and fees (2007–08)
$6676 room and board
75% average percent of need met
$9307 average financial aid amount received per undergraduate (2006–07 estimated)

MICHIGAN STATE UNIVERSITY
SUBURBAN SETTING ■ PUBLIC ■ STATE-SUPPORTED ■ COED
EAST LANSING, MICHIGAN

Web site: www.msu.edu
Contact: James Cotter, Acting Director of Admissions, 250 Administration Building, East Lansing, MI 48824
Telephone: 517-355-8332
Fax: 517-353-1647
E-mail: admis@msu.edu

Academics
Michigan State awards bachelor's, master's, doctoral, and first-professional **degrees** and post-master's certificates. **Challenging opportunities** include advanced placement credit, accelerated degree programs, student-designed majors, freshman honors college, an honors program, double majors, independent study, and a senior project. Special programs include cooperative education, internships, summer session for credit, off-campus study, study-abroad, and Army and Air Force ROTC.

The most frequently chosen **baccalaureate** fields are business/marketing, communications/journalism, and social sciences. A complete listing of majors at Michigan State appears in the Majors by College index beginning on page 471.

The **faculty** at Michigan State has 2,576 full-time members, 93% with terminal degrees. The student-faculty ratio is 17:1.

Students of Michigan State
The student body totals 46,045, of whom 36,072 are undergraduates. 53.2% are women and 46.8% are men. Students come from 55 states and territories and 89 other countries. 92% are from Michigan. 4.1% are international students. 8.1% are African American, 0.7% American Indian, 5.1% Asian American, and 2.9% Hispanic American. 91% returned for their sophomore year.

Facilities and Resources
2,100 **computers/terminals** are available on campus for general student use. Students can access the following: campus intranet, computer help desk, free student e-mail accounts, online (class) grades, online (class) registration, online (class) schedules. Campuswide network is available. 100% of college-owned or -operated housing units are wired for high-speed Internet access. Wireless service is available via classrooms, computer centers, computer labs, learning centers, libraries, student centers. The 15 **libraries** have 4,830,861 books and 37,832 subscriptions.

Campus Life
There are 500 active organizations on campus, including a drama/theater group, newspaper, radio station, television station, choral group, and marching band. 8% of eligible men and 7% of eligible women are members of national **fraternities** and national **sororities**.

Michigan State is a member of the NCAA (Division I). **Intercollegiate sports** (some offering scholarships) include baseball (m), basketball, cheerleading, crew (w), cross-country running, field hockey (w), football (m), golf, gymnastics (w), ice hockey (m), soccer, softball (w), swimming and diving, tennis, track and field, volleyball (w), wrestling (m).

Campus Safety
Student safety services include self-defense workshops, late-night transport/escort service, 24-hour emergency telephone alarm devices, and 24-hour patrols by trained security personnel.

Applying
Michigan State requires an essay, SAT or ACT, and a high school transcript. Application deadline: rolling admissions. Deferred admission is possible.

MICHIGAN TECHNOLOGICAL UNIVERSITY

SMALL-TOWN SETTING ■ PUBLIC ■ STATE-SUPPORTED ■ COED
HOUGHTON, MICHIGAN

Web site: www.mtu.edu
Contact: Ms. Allison Carter, Director of Admissions, 1400 Townsend Drive, Houghton, MI 49931-1295
Telephone: 906-487-2335 or toll-free 888-MTU-1885
Fax: 906-487-2125
E-mail: mtu4u@mtu.edu

Academics

Michigan Tech awards associate, bachelor's, master's, and doctoral **degrees** and post-bachelor's certificates. **Challenging opportunities** include advanced placement credit, student-designed majors, an honors program, double majors, and a senior project. Special programs include cooperative education, internships, summer session for credit, off-campus study, study-abroad, and Army and Air Force ROTC.

The most frequently chosen **baccalaureate** fields are engineering, business/marketing, and engineering technologies. A complete listing of majors at Michigan Tech appears in the Majors by College index beginning on page 471.

The **faculty** at Michigan Tech has 349 full-time members, 87% with terminal degrees. The student-faculty ratio is 12:1.

Students of Michigan Tech

The student body totals 6,550, of whom 5,634 are undergraduates. 22.6% are women and 77.4% are men. Students come from 47 states and territories and 73 other countries. 74% are from Michigan. 4% are international students. 1.9% are African American, 1% American Indian, 1.1% Asian American, and 1.2% Hispanic American. 81% returned for their sophomore year.

Facilities and Resources

1,555 **computers/terminals** are available on campus for general student use. Students can access the following: online (class) registration. Campuswide network is available. The **library** has 799,775 books and 2,777 subscriptions.

Campus Life

There are 145 active organizations on campus, including a drama/theater group, newspaper, radio station, and choral group. 9% of eligible men and 15% of eligible women are members of national **fraternities**, national **sororities**, local fraternities, and local sororities.

Michigan Tech is a member of the NCAA (Division II). **Intercollegiate sports** (some offering scholarships) include basketball, cross-country running, football (m), ice hockey (m), skiing (cross-country), tennis, track and field, volleyball (w).

Campus Safety

Student safety services include late-night transport/escort service, 24-hour emergency telephone alarm devices, 24-hour patrols by trained security personnel, and electronically operated dormitory entrances.

Applying

Michigan Tech requires SAT or ACT and a high school transcript. It recommends an interview and a minimum high school GPA of 2.75. Application deadline: rolling admissions; 2/16 priority date for financial aid. Deferred admission is possible.

Getting Accepted

3,802 applied
82% were accepted
1,169 enrolled (38% of accepted)
31% from top tenth of their h.s. class
3.52 average high school GPA
Mean SAT critical reading score: 567
Mean SAT math score: 614
Mean SAT writing score: 538
Mean ACT score: 25
41% had SAT critical reading scores over 600
60% had SAT math scores over 600
22% had SAT writing scores over 600
67% had ACT scores over 24
8% had SAT critical reading scores over 700
18% had SAT math scores over 700
2% had SAT writing scores over 700
13% had ACT scores over 30
6 National Merit Scholars
70 valedictorians

Graduation and After

23% graduated in 4 years
29% graduated in 5 years
6% graduated in 6 years
17% pursued further study
85% had job offers within 6 months
290 organizations recruited on campus

Financial Matters

$9829 resident tuition and fees (2007–08)
$21,589 nonresident tuition and fees (2007–08)
$7315 room and board
76% average percent of need met
$9065 average financial aid amount received per undergraduate (2006–07 estimated)

MIDDLEBURY COLLEGE

SMALL-TOWN SETTING ■ PRIVATE ■ INDEPENDENT ■ COED
MIDDLEBURY, VERMONT

Web site: www.middlebury.edu
Contact: Mr. Robert Clagett, Dean of Admissions, Emma Willard House,
Middlebury, VT 05753-6002
Telephone: 802-443-3000
Fax: 802-443-2056
E-mail: admissions@middlebury.edu

Literary study, global understanding based on language proficiency and cultural knowledge, environmental studies grounded in science, language study and pedagogy, instruction by leading faculty members and scholars, application of learning to the real world—these elements have formed the academic core of excellence at Middlebury College since its founding in 1800. The beautiful campus in the mountains of Vermont has a new state-of-the-art library and technology center, a nationally recognized interdisciplinary science facility, a contemporary arts center, sophisticated computer networks, multimedia workstations for language study, and outstanding athletic facilities. To attend Middlebury is to have a lifetime of opportunities, made possible by one of the world's foremost liberal arts colleges.

Getting Accepted
7,180 applied
21% were accepted
644 enrolled (44% of accepted)
82% from top tenth of their h.s. class

Graduation and After
50% had job offers within 6 months
70 organizations recruited on campus

Financial Matters
$46,910 comprehensive fee (2007–08)
100% average percent of need met
$28,413 average financial aid amount received per undergraduate (2005–06)

Academics

Middlebury awards bachelor's, master's, and doctoral **degrees**. **Challenging opportunities** include advanced placement credit, accelerated degree programs, student-designed majors, an honors program, double majors, and independent study. Special programs include internships, summer session for credit, off-campus study, study-abroad, and Army ROTC.

The most frequently chosen **baccalaureate** fields are social sciences, history, and English. A complete listing of majors at Middlebury appears in the Majors by College index beginning on page 471.

The **faculty** at Middlebury has 249 full-time members, 97% with terminal degrees. The student-faculty ratio is 9:1.

Students of Middlebury

The student body is made up of 2,500 undergraduates. 50.8% are women and 49.2% are men. Students come from 52 states and territories and 75 other countries. 7% are from Vermont. 10.4% are international students. 2.9% are African American, 0.5% American Indian, 8.4% Asian American, and 5.7% Hispanic American.

Facilities and Resources

494 **computers/terminals** are available on campus for general student use. Students can access the following: computer help desk, free student e-mail accounts, online (class) registration, online (class) schedules, help-line, personal web pages, file servers. Campuswide network is available. Wireless service is available via entire campus. The 4 **libraries** have 853,000 books and 2,908 subscriptions.

Campus Life

There are 95 active organizations on campus, including a drama/theater group, newspaper, radio station, and choral group. No national or local **fraternities** or **sororities**.

Middlebury is a member of the NCAA (Division III). **Intercollegiate sports** include baseball (m), basketball, cross-country running, field hockey (w), football (m), golf, ice hockey, lacrosse, skiing (cross-country), skiing (downhill), soccer, softball (w), squash (w), swimming and diving, tennis, track and field, volleyball (w).

Campus Safety

Student safety services include late-night transport/escort service, 24-hour patrols by trained security personnel, student patrols, and electronically operated dormitory entrances.

Applying

Middlebury requires an essay, three tests to include: a writing test, a quantitative test, and an area of the applicant's choice, a high school transcript, and 3 recommendations. It recommends an interview. Application deadline: 1/1; 1/1 for financial aid, with a 11/15 priority date. Early and deferred admission are possible.

MILLIGAN COLLEGE

SUBURBAN SETTING ■ PRIVATE ■ INDEPENDENT RELIGIOUS ■ COED
MILLIGAN COLLEGE, TENNESSEE

Web site: www.milligan.edu
Contact: Ms. Tracy Brinn, Director of Enrollment Management, PO Box 210, Milligan College, TN 37682
Telephone: 423-461-8730 or toll-free 800-262-8337 (in-state)
Fax: 423-461-8982
E-mail: admissions@milligan.edu

Academics

Milligan awards bachelor's and master's **degrees**. **Challenging opportunities** include advanced placement credit, double majors, independent study, and a senior project. Special programs include cooperative education, internships, summer session for credit, off-campus study, study-abroad, and Army ROTC.

The most frequently chosen **baccalaureate** fields are business/marketing, education, and health professions and related sciences. A complete listing of majors at Milligan appears in the Majors by College index beginning on page 471.

The **faculty** at Milligan has 71 full-time members, 73% with terminal degrees. The student-faculty ratio is 11:1.

Students of Milligan

The student body totals 1,006, of whom 775 are undergraduates. 61.2% are women and 38.8% are men. Students come from 37 states and territories and 13 other countries. 46% are from Tennessee. 2.6% are international students. 3.3% are African American, 0.3% American Indian, 1.2% Asian American, and 1.6% Hispanic American. 74% returned for their sophomore year.

Facilities and Resources

97 **computers/terminals** are available on campus for general student use. Students can access the following: campus intranet, computer help desk, free student e-mail accounts, online (class) grades, online (class) registration, online (class) schedules. Campuswide network is available. 100% of college-owned or -operated housing units are wired for high-speed Internet access. Wireless service is available via classrooms, computer centers, computer labs, dorm rooms, libraries, student centers. The **library** has 179,619 books and 10,861 subscriptions.

Campus Life

There are 31 active organizations on campus, including a drama/theater group, newspaper, radio station, and choral group. No national or local **fraternities** or **sororities**.

Milligan is a member of the NAIA. **Intercollegiate sports** (some offering scholarships) include baseball (m), basketball, cross-country running, golf (m), soccer, softball (w), swimming and diving, tennis, volleyball (w).

Campus Safety

Student safety services include late-night transport/escort service and 24-hour patrols by trained security personnel.

Applying

Milligan requires an essay, SAT or ACT, a high school transcript, 2 recommendations, and a minimum high school GPA of 2.0, and in some cases an interview. It recommends a minimum high school GPA of 3.0. Application deadline: 8/1; 3/1 priority date for financial aid. Deferred admission is possible.

Getting Accepted

552 applied
78% were accepted
197 enrolled (46% of accepted)
30% from top tenth of their h.s. class
3.49 average high school GPA
Mean SAT critical reading score: 540
Mean SAT math score: 540
Mean SAT writing score: 510
Mean ACT score: 24
29% had SAT critical reading scores over 600
28% had SAT math scores over 600
27% had SAT writing scores over 600
43% had ACT scores over 24
7% had SAT critical reading scores over 700
2% had SAT math scores over 700
3% had SAT writing scores over 700
5% had ACT scores over 30
10 valedictorians

Financial Matters

$19,510 tuition and fees (2007–08)
$5350 room and board
51% average percent of need met
$14,512 average financial aid amount received per undergraduate (2005–06)

MILLSAPS COLLEGE
URBAN SETTING ■ PRIVATE ■ INDEPENDENT RELIGIOUS ■ COED
JACKSON, MISSISSIPPI

Web site: www.millsaps.edu
Contact: Mr. Mathew Cox, Dean of Enrollment Management, 1701 North State Street, Jackson, MS 39210-0001
Telephone: 601-974-1050 or toll-free 800-352-1050
Fax: 601-974-1059
E-mail: admissions@millsaps.edu

Getting Accepted
1,253 applied
77% were accepted
296 enrolled (31% of accepted)
40% from top tenth of their h.s. class
3.5 average high school GPA
Mean SAT critical reading score: 609
Mean SAT math score: 596
Mean ACT score: 26
58% had SAT critical reading scores over 600
48% had SAT math scores over 600
74% had ACT scores over 24
16% had SAT critical reading scores over 700
11% had SAT math scores over 700
24% had ACT scores over 30
18 National Merit Scholars
11 valedictorians

Graduation and After
64% graduated in 4 years
3% graduated in 5 years
2% graduated in 6 years
50% pursued further study (11% business, 7% medicine, 4% law)
98% had job offers within 6 months
60 organizations recruited on campus

Financial Matters
$24,754 tuition and fees (2008–09)
$8800 room and board
83% average percent of need met
$18,892 average financial aid amount received per undergraduate (2006–07 estimated)

Academics
Millsaps awards bachelor's and master's **degrees**. **Challenging opportunities** include advanced placement credit, accelerated degree programs, student-designed majors, an honors program, double majors, independent study, and a senior project. Special programs include internships, summer session for credit, off-campus study, study-abroad, and Army ROTC.

The most frequently chosen **baccalaureate** fields are business/marketing, biological/life sciences, and psychology. A complete listing of majors at Millsaps appears in the Majors by College index beginning on page 471.

The **faculty** at Millsaps has 91 full-time members, 97% with terminal degrees. The student-faculty ratio is 11:1.

Students of Millsaps
The student body totals 1,151, of whom 1,043 are undergraduates. 50.9% are women and 49.1% are men. Students come from 32 states and territories and 16 other countries. 48% are from Mississippi. 1.2% are international students. 10.8% are African American, 0.1% American Indian, 3.9% Asian American, and 1.5% Hispanic American. 81% returned for their sophomore year.

Facilities and Resources
150 **computers/terminals** are available on campus for general student use. Students can access the following: campus intranet, computer help desk, free student e-mail accounts, online (class) grades, online (class) registration, online (class) schedules, online transcripts. Campuswide network is available. 100% of college-owned or -operated housing units are wired for high-speed Internet access. Wireless service is available via entire campus. The **library** has 194,797 books and 16,221 subscriptions.

Campus Life
There are 70 active organizations on campus, including a drama/theater group, newspaper, and choral group. 49% of eligible men and 51% of eligible women are members of national **fraternities** and national **sororities**.

Millsaps is a member of the NCAA (Division III). **Intercollegiate sports** include baseball (m), basketball, cheerleading, cross-country running, football (m), golf, soccer, softball (w), tennis, volleyball (w).

Campus Safety
Student safety services include self-defense education, lighted pathways, late-night transport/escort service, 24-hour emergency telephone alarm devices, 24-hour patrols by trained security personnel, student patrols, and electronically operated dormitory entrances.

Applying
Millsaps requires an essay, SAT or ACT, a high school transcript, recommendations, and a minimum high school GPA of 2.5, and in some cases an interview. Application deadline: rolling admissions, rolling admissions for nonresidents; 3/1 priority date for financial aid. Early and deferred admission are possible.

Mills College

Urban setting ■ Private ■ Independent
■ Undergraduate: Women Only; Graduate: Coed
Oakland, California

SPONSOR

Web site: www.mills.edu
Contact: Ms. Giulietta Aquino, Vice President of Enrollment Management,
   5000 MacArthur Boulevard, Oakland, CA 94613-1301
Telephone: 510-430-2135 or toll-free 800-87-MILLS
Fax: 510-430-3314
E-mail: admission@mills.edu

Academics

Mills awards bachelor's, master's, and doctoral **degrees** and post-bachelor's certificates. **Challenging opportunities** include advanced placement credit, student-designed majors, an honors program, double majors, independent study, and a senior project. Special programs include internships, off-campus study, and study-abroad.

The most frequently chosen **baccalaureate** fields are social sciences, English, and visual and performing arts. A complete listing of majors at Mills appears in the Majors by College index beginning on page 471.

The **faculty** at Mills has 90 full-time members, 91% with terminal degrees. The student-faculty ratio is 11:1.

Students of Mills

The student body totals 1,446, of whom 941 are undergraduates. 100% are women. Students come from 45 states and territories and 16 other countries. 80% are from California. 2.1% are international students. 9.6% are African American, 1% American Indian, 7.9% Asian American, and 14.6% Hispanic American. 74% returned for their sophomore year.

Facilities and Resources

307 **computers/terminals** are available on campus for general student use. Students can access the following: campus intranet, computer help desk, free student e-mail accounts, online (class) grades, online (class) registration, online (class) schedules, online degree. Campuswide network is available. 100% of college-owned or -operated housing units are wired for high-speed Internet access. Wireless service is available via entire campus. The 2 **libraries** have 254,351 books and 13,211 subscriptions.

Campus Life

There are 30 active organizations on campus, including a drama/theater group, newspaper, and choral group. No national or local **sororities**.

Mills is a member of the NCAA (Division III) and NAIA. **Intercollegiate sports** include crew, cross-country running, soccer, swimming and diving, tennis, volleyball.

Campus Safety

Student safety services include late-night transport/escort service, 24-hour emergency telephone alarm devices, 24-hour patrols by trained security personnel, and electronically operated dormitory entrances.

Applying

Mills requires SAT or ACT, a high school transcript, 2 recommendations, and essay or graded paper. It recommends SAT Subject Tests and an interview. Application deadline: 5/1; 2/15 for financial aid, with a 2/15 priority date. Deferred admission is possible.

Getting Accepted

1,098 applied
64% were accepted
197 enrolled (28% of accepted)
40% from top tenth of their h.s. class
3.61 average high school GPA
Mean SAT critical reading score: 582
Mean SAT math score: 546
Mean SAT writing score: 572
Mean ACT score: 25
47% had SAT critical reading scores over 600
31% had SAT math scores over 600
42% had SAT writing scores over 600
60% had ACT scores over 24
12% had SAT critical reading scores over 700
3% had SAT math scores over 700
5% had SAT writing scores over 700
14% had ACT scores over 30

Graduation and After

50% graduated in 4 years
6% graduated in 5 years
17 organizations recruited on campus

Financial Matters

$35,432 tuition and fees (2007–08)
$10,820 room and board
83% average percent of need met
$24,002 average financial aid amount received per undergraduate (2005–06)

MILWAUKEE SCHOOL OF ENGINEERING

URBAN SETTING ■ PRIVATE ■ INDEPENDENT ■ COED, PRIMARILY MEN
MILWAUKEE, WISCONSIN

Web site: www.msoe.edu
Contact: Paul Borens, Director of Admissions, 1025 North Broadway,
    Milwaukee, WI 53202-3109
Telephone: 414-277-6765 or toll-free 800-332-6763
Fax: 414-277-7475
E-mail: borens@msoe.edu

Getting Accepted
2,732 applied
65% were accepted
575 enrolled (33% of accepted)
3.5 average high school GPA
Mean SAT critical reading score: 560
Mean SAT math score: 610
Mean ACT score: 25
47% had SAT critical reading scores over 600
81% had SAT math scores over 600
39% had SAT writing scores over 600
70% had ACT scores over 24
2% had SAT critical reading scores over 700
26% had SAT math scores over 700
14% had SAT writing scores over 700
13% had ACT scores over 30

Graduation and After
36% graduated in 4 years
14% graduated in 5 years
2% graduated in 6 years
6% pursued further study (3% engineering,
    2% business)
98% had job offers within 6 months
14 organizations recruited on campus

Financial Matters
$25,980 tuition and fees (2007–08)
$6501 room and board
72% average percent of need met
$16,915 average financial aid amount received
    per undergraduate (2005–06)

Academics
MSOE awards bachelor's and master's **degrees. Challenging opportunities** include advanced placement credit, double majors, independent study, and a senior project. Special programs include internships, summer session for credit, study-abroad, and Army, Navy, and Air Force ROTC.

The most frequently chosen **baccalaureate** fields are engineering, business/marketing, and engineering technologies. A complete listing of majors at MSOE appears in the Majors by College index beginning on page 471.

The **faculty** at MSOE has 119 full-time members, 70% with terminal degrees. The student-faculty ratio is 14:1.

Students of MSOE
The student body totals 2,516, of whom 2,317 are undergraduates. 18.7% are women and 81.3% are men. Students come from 36 states and territories and 16 other countries. 66% are from Wisconsin. 2.1% are international students. 3.6% are African American, 0.6% American Indian, 2.9% Asian American, and 2.5% Hispanic American. 73% returned for their sophomore year.

Facilities and Resources
125 **computers/terminals** and 2,000 ports are available on campus for general student use. Students can access the following: campus intranet, computer help desk, free student e-mail accounts, online (class) grades, online (class) registration, online (class) schedules. Campuswide network is available. 100% of college-owned or -operated housing units are wired for high-speed Internet access. Wireless service is available via entire campus. The **library** has 72,192 books and 376 subscriptions.

Campus Life
There are 70 active organizations on campus, including a drama/theater group, radio station, and choral group. 43% of eligible men and 35% of eligible women are members of national **fraternities**, national **sororities**, local fraternities, and local sororities.

MSOE is a member of the NCAA (Division III). **Intercollegiate sports** include baseball (m), basketball, cheerleading, cross-country running, golf, ice hockey (m), soccer, softball (w), tennis, track and field, volleyball, wrestling (m).

Campus Safety
Student safety services include late-night transport/escort service, 24-hour emergency telephone alarm devices, 24-hour patrols by trained security personnel, and electronically operated dormitory entrances.

Applying
MSOE requires SAT or ACT, a high school transcript, and a minimum high school GPA of 2.5, and in some cases an essay and an interview. Application deadline: rolling admissions, rolling admissions for nonresidents; 3/15 priority date for financial aid. Deferred admission is possible.

MISSISSIPPI COLLEGE

SUBURBAN SETTING ■ PRIVATE ■ INDEPENDENT RELIGIOUS ■ COED
CLINTON, MISSISSIPPI

Web site: www.mc.edu
Contact: Mr. Chad Phillips, Director of Admissions, PO Box 4026, 200 South Capitol Street, Clinton, MS 39058
Telephone: 601-925-3800 or toll-free 800-738-1236
Fax: 601-925-3804
E-mail: enrollment-services@mc.edu

Academics

MC awards bachelor's, master's, doctoral, and first-professional **degrees** and post-bachelor's certificates. **Challenging opportunities** include advanced placement credit, accelerated degree programs, an honors program, double majors, independent study, and a senior project. Special programs include cooperative education, internships, summer session for credit, study-abroad, and Army ROTC.

The most frequently chosen **baccalaureate** fields are business/marketing, education, and health professions and related sciences. A complete listing of majors at MC appears in the Majors by College index beginning on page 471.

The **faculty** at MC has 165 full-time members, 79% with terminal degrees. The student-faculty ratio is 16:1.

Students of MC

The student body totals 4,467, of whom 2,921 are undergraduates. 59.9% are women and 40.1% are men. Students come from 28 states and territories and 18 other countries. 84% are from Mississippi. 3.7% are international students. 23.9% are African American, 0.4% American Indian, 1.1% Asian American, and 0.6% Hispanic American. 77% returned for their sophomore year.

Facilities and Resources

250 **computers/terminals** are available on campus for general student use. Students can access the following: campus intranet, computer help desk, free student e-mail accounts, online (class) grades, online (class) registration, online (class) schedules. Campuswide network is available. 60% of college-owned or -operated housing units are wired for high-speed Internet access. Wireless service is available via classrooms, dorm rooms, libraries, student centers. The 2 **libraries** have 370,404 books and 4,742 subscriptions.

Campus Life

There are 26 active organizations on campus, including a drama/theater group, newspaper, radio station, choral group, and marching band. MC has local **fraternities** and local **sororities**.

MC is a member of the NCAA (Division III). **Intercollegiate sports** include baseball (m), basketball, cheerleading (w), cross-country running, equestrian sports (w), football (m), golf (m), soccer, softball (w), tennis, track and field, volleyball (w), wrestling (m).

Campus Safety

Student safety services include late-night transport/escort service, 24-hour emergency telephone alarm devices, 24-hour patrols by trained security personnel, and electronically operated dormitory entrances.

Applying

MC requires SAT or ACT, a high school transcript, and 1 recommendation. It recommends an interview and a minimum high school GPA of 2.0. Application deadline: rolling admissions; 3/1 priority date for financial aid. Early and deferred admission are possible.

Getting Accepted

1,642 applied
65% were accepted
541 enrolled (51% of accepted)
25% from top tenth of their h.s. class
3.42 average high school GPA
Mean SAT critical reading score: 520
Mean SAT math score: 520
Mean ACT score: 23
24% had SAT critical reading scores over 600
20% had SAT math scores over 600
42% had ACT scores over 24
3% had SAT critical reading scores over 700
3% had SAT math scores over 700
7% had ACT scores over 30

Graduation and After

44% graduated in 4 years
16% graduated in 5 years
1% graduated in 6 years
23% pursued further study

Financial Matters

$12,800 tuition and fees (2008–09)
$5800 room and board
82% average percent of need met
$13,680 average financial aid amount received per undergraduate

MISSOURI STATE UNIVERSITY

SUBURBAN SETTING ■ PUBLIC ■ STATE-SUPPORTED ■ COED
SPRINGFIELD, MISSOURI

Web site: www.missouristate.edu
Contact: Ms. Jill Duncan, Associate Director of Admissions, 901 South
National, Springfield, MO 65804
Telephone: 417-836-5517 or toll-free 800-492-7900
Fax: 417-836-6334
E-mail: info@missouristate.edu

Getting Accepted
7,677 applied
75% were accepted
2,649 enrolled (46% of accepted)
21% from top tenth of their h.s. class
3.44 average high school GPA
49% had ACT scores over 24
8% had ACT scores over 30

Graduation and After
27% graduated in 4 years
22% graduated in 5 years
6% graduated in 6 years
20% pursued further study (6% business, 4% arts and sciences, 4% education)
72% had job offers within 6 months
475 organizations recruited on campus

Financial Matters
$6606 resident tuition and fees (2007–08)
$11,706 nonresident tuition and fees (2007–08)
$5312 room and board
58% average percent of need met
$6093 average financial aid amount received per undergraduate (2006–07 estimated)

Academics

Missouri State awards bachelor's, master's, and doctoral **degrees** and post-bachelor's and post-master's certificates. **Challenging opportunities** include advanced placement credit, accelerated degree programs, student-designed majors, freshman honors college, an honors program, double majors, independent study, and a senior project. Special programs include cooperative education, internships, summer session for credit, off-campus study, study-abroad, and Army ROTC.

The most frequently chosen **baccalaureate** fields are business/marketing, education, and social sciences. A complete listing of majors at Missouri State appears in the Majors by College index beginning on page 471.

The **faculty** at Missouri State has 718 full-time members, 79% with terminal degrees. The student-faculty ratio is 19:1.

Students of Missouri State

The student body totals 19,348, of whom 16,255 are undergraduates. 55.8% are women and 44.2% are men. Students come from 47 states and territories and 81 other countries. 94% are from Missouri. 1.9% are international students. 2.9% are African American, 0.9% American Indian, 1.6% Asian American, and 1.9% Hispanic American. 74% returned for their sophomore year.

Facilities and Resources

1,800 **computers/terminals** are available on campus for general student use. Students can access the following: online (class) registration. Campuswide network is available. The 4 **libraries** have 1,699,860 books and 4,238 subscriptions.

Campus Life

There are 260 active organizations on campus, including a drama/theater group, newspaper, radio station, television station, choral group, and marching band. Missouri State has national **fraternities** and national **sororities**.

Missouri State is a member of the NCAA (Division I). **Intercollegiate sports** (some offering scholarships) include baseball (m), basketball, cross-country running (w), field hockey (w), football (m), golf, soccer, softball (w), swimming and diving, track and field (w), volleyball (w).

Campus Safety

Student safety services include on-campus police substation, late-night transport/escort service, 24-hour emergency telephone alarm devices, 24-hour patrols by trained security personnel, and electronically operated dormitory entrances.

Applying

Missouri State requires SAT or ACT and a high school transcript, and in some cases an essay, an interview, and recommendations. Application deadline: 7/20; 3/30 priority date for financial aid. Deferred admission is possible.

MISSOURI UNIVERSITY OF SCIENCE AND TECHNOLOGY

SMALL-TOWN SETTING ■ PUBLIC ■ STATE-SUPPORTED ■ COED
ROLLA, MISSOURI

Web site: www.mst.edu
Contact: Ms. Lynn Stichnote, Director of Admissions, 106 Parker Hall, 1870 Minor Circle, Rolla, MO 65409
Telephone: 573-341-4164 or toll-free 800-522-0938
Fax: 573-341-4082
E-mail: umrolla@umr.edu

Academics

Missouri S&T awards bachelor's, master's, and doctoral **degrees** and post-bachelor's certificates. **Challenging opportunities** include advanced placement credit, accelerated degree programs, freshman honors college, an honors program, double majors, independent study, and a senior project. Special programs include cooperative education, internships, summer session for credit, off-campus study, study-abroad, and Army, Navy, and Air Force ROTC. A complete listing of majors at Missouri S&T appears in the Majors by College index beginning on page 471.

The **faculty** at Missouri S&T has 336 full-time members, 86% with terminal degrees. The student-faculty ratio is 14:1.

Students of Missouri S&T

The student body totals 5,858, of whom 4,515 are undergraduates. 22.5% are women and 77.5% are men. Students come from 47 states and territories and 25 other countries. 80% are from Missouri. 2.6% are international students. 4.5% are African American, 0.4% American Indian, 2.2% Asian American, and 2.3% Hispanic American. 87% returned for their sophomore year.

Facilities and Resources

800 **computers/terminals** are available on campus for general student use. Students can access the following: online (class) registration. Campuswide network is available. The **library** has 255,768 books and 1,495 subscriptions.

Campus Life

There are 197 active organizations on campus, including a drama/theater group, newspaper, radio station, choral group, and marching band. 27% of eligible men and 24% of eligible women are members of national **fraternities**, national **sororities**, and local sororities.

Missouri S&T is a member of the NCAA (Division II). **Intercollegiate sports** (some offering scholarships) include baseball (m), basketball, cross-country running, football (m), soccer, softball (w), swimming and diving (m), track and field.

Campus Safety

Student safety services include crime prevention programs, late-night transport/escort service, 24-hour emergency telephone alarm devices, 24-hour patrols by trained security personnel, student patrols, and electronically operated dormitory entrances.

Applying

Missouri S&T requires SAT or ACT and a high school transcript. Application deadline: 7/1; 3/1 priority date for financial aid. Early and deferred admission are possible.

Getting Accepted
2,257 applied
90% were accepted
962 enrolled (47% of accepted)
39% from top tenth of their h.s. class
3.59 average high school GPA
Mean ACT score: 27
74% had SAT math scores over 600
83% had ACT scores over 24
38% had SAT math scores over 700
31% had ACT scores over 30
44 National Merit Scholars
37 valedictorians

Graduation and After
15% graduated in 4 years
36% graduated in 5 years
9% graduated in 6 years
17% pursued further study
82% had job offers within 6 months
440 organizations recruited on campus

Financial Matters
$8172 resident tuition and fees (2007–08)
$18,428 nonresident tuition and fees (2007–08)
$6660 room and board
84% average percent of need met
$9550 average financial aid amount received per undergraduate

MORAVIAN COLLEGE

SUBURBAN SETTING ■ PRIVATE ■ INDEPENDENT RELIGIOUS ■ COED
BETHLEHEM, PENNSYLVANIA

Web site: www.moravian.edu
Contact: Mr. James Mackin, Director of Admission, 1200 Main Street,
    Bethlehem, PA 18018
Telephone: 610-861-1320 or toll-free 800-441-3191
Fax: 610-625-7930
E-mail: admissions@moravian.edu

Getting Accepted
2,189 applied
64% were accepted
401 enrolled (29% of accepted)
29% from top tenth of their h.s. class
Mean SAT critical reading score: 553
Mean SAT math score: 561
Mean SAT writing score: 545
26% had SAT critical reading scores over 600
31% had SAT math scores over 600
24% had SAT writing scores over 600
3% had SAT critical reading scores over 700
5% had SAT math scores over 700
4% had SAT writing scores over 700
2 class presidents
1 valedictorian

Graduation and After
70% graduated in 4 years
5% graduated in 5 years
23% pursued further study (18% arts and
    sciences, 2% business, 2% law)
61% had job offers within 6 months
30 organizations recruited on campus

Financial Matters
$28,388 tuition and fees (2007–08)
$7993 room and board
75% average percent of need met
$18,154 average financial aid amount received
    per undergraduate (2006–07 estimated)

Academics
Moravian awards bachelor's, master's, and first-professional **degrees** and post-bachelor's certificates. **Challenging opportunities** include advanced placement credit, student-designed majors, an honors program, double majors, independent study, and a senior project. Special programs include internships, summer session for credit, off-campus study, study-abroad, and Army ROTC.

The most frequently chosen **baccalaureate** fields are business/marketing, social sciences, and psychology. A complete listing of majors at Moravian appears in the Majors by College index beginning on page 471.

The **faculty** at Moravian has 118 full-time members, 92% with terminal degrees. The student-faculty ratio is 11:1.

Students of Moravian
The student body totals 1,917, of whom 1,784 are undergraduates. 58.2% are women and 41.8% are men. Students come from 20 states and territories and 15 other countries. 57% are from Pennsylvania. 1.1% are international students. 1.8% are African American, 0.2% American Indian, 1.8% Asian American, and 3.1% Hispanic American. 86% returned for their sophomore year.

Facilities and Resources
263 **computers/terminals** and 150 ports are available on campus for general student use. Students can access the following: campus intranet, computer help desk, free student e-mail accounts, online (class) grades, online (class) schedules. Campuswide network is available. 100% of college-owned or -operated housing units are wired for high-speed Internet access. Wireless service is available via classrooms, computer centers, computer labs, learning centers, libraries, student centers. The **library** has 260,363 books and 3,274 subscriptions.

Campus Life
There are 77 active organizations on campus, including a drama/theater group, newspaper, radio station, choral group, and marching band. 14% of eligible men and 22% of eligible women are members of national **fraternities** and national **sororities**.

Moravian is a member of the NCAA (Division III). **Intercollegiate sports** include baseball (m), basketball, cross-country running, field hockey (w), football (m), golf (m), lacrosse, soccer, softball (w), tennis, track and field, volleyball (w).

Campus Safety
Student safety services include late-night transport/escort service, 24-hour emergency telephone alarm devices, 24-hour patrols by trained security personnel, and electronically operated dormitory entrances.

Applying
Moravian requires an essay, SAT or ACT, a high school transcript, and 3 recommendations. It recommends an interview. Application deadline: 3/1; 2/14 priority date for financial aid. Early and deferred admission are possible.

MOREHOUSE COLLEGE

URBAN SETTING ■ PRIVATE ■ INDEPENDENT ■ MEN ONLY
ATLANTA, GEORGIA

Web site: www.morehouse.edu
Contact: Mr. Terrance Dixon, Associate Dean for Admissions and
   Recruitment, 830 Westview Drive, SW, Atlanta, GA 30314
Telephone: 404-215-2632 or toll-free 800-851-1254
Fax: 404-524-5635
E-mail: janderso@morehouse.edu

Academics

Morehouse awards bachelor's **degrees**. **Challenging opportunities** include advanced placement credit, an honors program, double majors, and a senior project. Special programs include cooperative education, internships, summer session for credit, off-campus study, study-abroad, and Army, Navy, and Air Force ROTC.

The most frequently chosen **baccalaureate** fields are business/marketing, social sciences, and biological/life sciences. A complete listing of majors at Morehouse appears in the Majors by College index beginning on page 471.

The **faculty** at Morehouse has 161 full-time members, 87% with terminal degrees. The student-faculty ratio is 15:1.

Students of Morehouse

The student body is made up of 2,810 undergraduates. Students come from 41 states and territories and 15 other countries. 31% are from Georgia. 2.6% are international students. 95.3% are African American and 0.3% Hispanic American. 83% returned for their sophomore year.

Facilities and Resources

355 **computers/terminals** are available on campus for general student use. Students can access the following: online (class) registration, online (class) schedules. Campuswide network is available. The 2 **libraries** have 280,022 books and 30,083 subscriptions.

Campus Life

There are 34 active organizations on campus, including a drama/theater group, newspaper, choral group, and marching band. 1% of eligible undergraduates are members of national **fraternities**.

Morehouse is a member of the NCAA (Division II). **Intercollegiate sports** (some offering scholarships) include basketball, cross-country running, football, tennis, track and field.

Campus Safety

Student safety services include late-night transport/escort service, 24-hour emergency telephone alarm devices, 24-hour patrols by trained security personnel, and electronically operated dormitory entrances.

Applying

Morehouse requires an essay, SAT Subject Tests, SAT or ACT, a high school transcript, recommendations, and a minimum high school GPA of 2.8. It recommends an interview and a minimum high school GPA of 3.0. Application deadline: 2/15; 4/1 priority date for financial aid. Early and deferred admission are possible.

Getting Accepted
2,369 applied
59% were accepted
677 enrolled (48% of accepted)
14% from top tenth of their h.s. class
3.2 average high school GPA
Mean SAT critical reading score: 520
Mean SAT math score: 521
Mean ACT score: 21
16% had SAT critical reading scores over 600
14% had SAT math scores over 600
30% had ACT scores over 24
1% had SAT critical reading scores over 700
1% had SAT math scores over 700
2% had ACT scores over 30

Graduation and After
29% pursued further study
55% had job offers within 6 months
60 organizations recruited on campus

Financial Matters
$17,982 tuition and fees (2007–08)
$9928 room and board
25% average percent of need met
$11,079 average financial aid amount received
   per undergraduate

Mount Allison University

SMALL-TOWN SETTING ■ PUBLIC ■ COED
SACKVILLE, NEW BRUNSWICK

Getting Accepted
1,591 applied
88% were accepted
696 enrolled (50% of accepted)
64% from top tenth of their h.s. class
3.36 average high school GPA

Graduation and After
60% graduated in 4 years
4% graduated in 5 years
1% graduated in 6 years
35% pursued further study (10% arts and sciences, 7% business, 5% education)
15% had job offers within 6 months

Financial Matters
$6977 resident tuition and fees (2007–08)
$6795 room and board

Web site: www.mta.ca
Contact: Mr. Matt Sheridan-Jonah, Manager of Admissions, 65 York Street, Sackville, NB Canada
Telephone: 506-364-3294
Fax: 506-364-2272
E-mail: admissions@mta.ca

Academics
Mount Allison awards bachelor's and master's **degrees**. **Challenging opportunities** include advanced placement credit, student-designed majors, an honors program, double majors, independent study, and a senior project. Special programs include internships, summer session for credit, off-campus study, and study-abroad.

The most frequently chosen **baccalaureate** fields are social sciences, business/marketing, and psychology. A complete listing of majors at Mount Allison appears in the Majors by College index beginning on page 471.

The **faculty** at Mount Allison has 133 full-time members, 80% with terminal degrees. The student-faculty ratio is 15:1.

Students of Mount Allison
The student body totals 2,170, of whom 2,163 are undergraduates. 58.3% are women and 41.7% are men. Students come from 15 states and territories and 38 other countries. 40% are from New Brunswick. 76% returned for their sophomore year.

Facilities and Resources
100 **computers/terminals** and 120 ports are available on campus for general student use. Students can access the following: computer help desk, free student e-mail accounts, online (class) registration, online (class) schedules, online student account/Websis. Campuswide network is available. 100% of college-owned or -operated housing units are wired for high-speed Internet access. Wireless service is available via entire campus. The 4 **libraries** have 400,000 books and 1,700 subscriptions.

Campus Life
There are 100 active organizations on campus, including a drama/theater group, newspaper, radio station, and choral group. No national or local **fraternities** or **sororities**.

Intercollegiate sports include basketball, football (m), ice hockey (w), rugby, soccer, swimming and diving.

Campus Safety
Student safety services include late-night transport/escort service and 24-hour emergency telephone alarm devices.

Applying
Mount Allison requires a high school transcript and a minimum high school GPA of 3.0, and in some cases an essay and an interview. It recommends 2 recommendations. Application deadline: rolling admissions. Deferred admission is possible.

MOUNT HOLYOKE COLLEGE

SMALL-TOWN SETTING ■ PRIVATE ■ INDEPENDENT ■ WOMEN ONLY
SOUTH HADLEY, MASSACHUSETTS

Web site: www.mtholyoke.edu
Contact: Ms. Diane Anci, Dean of Admission, 50 College Street, South
    Hadley, MA 01075
Telephone: 413-538-2023
Fax: 413-538-2409
E-mail: admission@mtholyoke.edu

Academics

Mount Holyoke awards bachelor's and master's **degrees** and post-bachelor's certificates. **Challenging opportunities** include advanced placement credit, student-designed majors, an honors program, double majors, independent study, and a senior project. Special programs include cooperative education, internships, off-campus study, study-abroad, and Army and Air Force ROTC.

The most frequently chosen **baccalaureate** fields are social sciences, English, and visual and performing arts. A complete listing of majors at Mount Holyoke appears in the Majors by College index beginning on page 471.

The **faculty** at Mount Holyoke has 208 full-time members, 94% with terminal degrees. The student-faculty ratio is 10:1.

Students of Mount Holyoke

The student body totals 2,204, of whom 2,201 are undergraduates. Students come from 50 states and territories and 64 other countries. 25% are from Massachusetts. 16.2% are international students. 4.8% are African American, 0.6% American Indian, 12.1% Asian American, and 5.3% Hispanic American. 94% returned for their sophomore year.

Facilities and Resources

592 **computers/terminals** and 500 ports are available on campus for general student use. Students can access the following: campus intranet, computer help desk, free student e-mail accounts, online (class) grades, online (class) registration, online (class) schedules, personal Web pages. Campuswide network is available. 100% of college-owned or -operated housing units are wired for high-speed Internet access. Wireless service is available via classrooms, computer centers, computer labs, dorm rooms, learning centers, libraries, student centers.

Campus Life

There are 140 active organizations on campus, including a drama/theater group, newspaper, radio station, and choral group. No national or local **sororities**.

Mount Holyoke is a member of the NCAA (Division III). **Intercollegiate sports** include basketball, crew, cross-country running, equestrian sports, field hockey, golf, lacrosse, soccer, squash, swimming and diving, tennis, track and field, volleyball.

Campus Safety

Student safety services include police officers on-campus, late-night transport/escort service, 24-hour emergency telephone alarm devices, 24-hour patrols by trained security personnel, student patrols, and electronically operated dormitory entrances.

Applying

Mount Holyoke requires an essay, a high school transcript, and 2 recommendations, and in some cases SAT Subject Tests. It recommends an interview. Application deadline: 1/15; 3/1 for financial aid, with a 2/15 priority date. Early and deferred admission are possible.

Mount Holyoke is a highly selective, nondenominational, residential liberal arts college for women located in South Hadley, Massachusetts. Founded in 1837 by revolutionary educator Mary Lyon, the College is recognized worldwide for its rigorous and innovative academic program, its global community, its legacy of women leaders, and its commitment to connecting the work of the academy to the concerns of the world. Students benefit from membership in the Five College Consortium with Amherst, Hampshire, and Smith Colleges and the University of Massachusetts.

Getting Accepted

3,194 applied
52% were accepted
512 enrolled (31% of accepted)
55% from top tenth of their h.s. class
3.67 average high school GPA
90% had SAT critical reading scores over 600
73% had SAT math scores over 600
90% had SAT writing scores over 600
93% had ACT scores over 24
44% had SAT critical reading scores over 700
25% had SAT math scores over 700
37% had SAT writing scores over 700
38% had ACT scores over 30
25 National Merit Scholars
17 valedictorians

Graduation and After

78% graduated in 4 years
3% graduated in 5 years
18% pursued further study (13% arts and
   sciences, 2% law, 1% medicine)
44 organizations recruited on campus

Financial Matters

$35,940 tuition and fees (2007–08)
$10,520 room and board
100% average percent of need met
$28,464 average financial aid amount received
   per undergraduate (2006–07 estimated)

MOUNT SAINT VINCENT UNIVERSITY

SUBURBAN SETTING ■ PUBLIC ■ COED, PRIMARILY WOMEN
HALIFAX, NOVA SCOTIA

Graduation and After
972 organizations recruited on campus

Financial Matters
$6293 nonresident tuition and fees (2007–08)
$6795 room and board

Web site: www.msvu.ca
Contact: Mr. Karl Turner, Assistant Registrar/Admissions, 166 Bedford
    Highway, Halifax, NS B3M2J6 Canada
Telephone: 902-457-6117
Fax: 902-457-6498
E-mail: admissions@msvu.ca

Academics

MSVU awards bachelor's, master's, and first-professional **degrees** and post-bachelor's certificates. **Challenging opportunities** include an honors program, double majors, independent study, and a senior project. Special programs include cooperative education, internships, summer session for credit, off-campus study, and study-abroad.

The most frequently chosen **baccalaureate** fields are education, business/marketing, and communications/journalism. A complete listing of majors at MSVU appears in the Majors by College index beginning on page 471.

The **faculty** at MSVU has 149 full-time members, 79% with terminal degrees. The student-faculty ratio is 13:1.

Students of MSVU

The student body totals 4,414, of whom 2,856 are undergraduates. Students come from 13 states and territories and 40 other countries. 90% are from Nova Scotia. 79% returned for their sophomore year.

Facilities and Resources

Students can access the following: online (class) registration. Campuswide network is available. The 4 **libraries** have 356,763 books and 3,570 subscriptions.

Campus Life

There are 18 active organizations on campus, including a newspaper and choral group. No national or local **fraternities** or **sororities**.

Intercollegiate sports include badminton, basketball, soccer, volleyball (w).

Campus Safety

Student safety services include late-night transport/escort service, 24-hour emergency telephone alarm devices, 24-hour patrols by trained security personnel, and electronically operated dormitory entrances.

Applying

MSVU requires a high school transcript and a minimum high school GPA of 2.0, and in some cases an essay, an interview, 2 recommendations, and a minimum high school GPA of 3.0. Application deadline: 3/15, 5/30 for nonresidents; 11/3 for financial aid. Deferred admission is possible.

MUHLENBERG COLLEGE

SUBURBAN SETTING ■ PRIVATE ■ INDEPENDENT RELIGIOUS ■ COED
ALLENTOWN, PENNSYLVANIA

Web site: www.muhlenberg.edu
Contact: Mr. Christopher Hooker-Haring, Director of Undergraduate
    Admissions, 2400 Chew Street, Allentown, PA 18104
Telephone: 484-664-3245
Fax: 484-664-3234
E-mail: adm@muhlenberg.edu

Academics

Muhlenberg awards associate and bachelor's **degrees. Challenging opportunities**
include advanced placement credit, accelerated degree programs, student-designed
majors, an honors program, double majors, independent study, and a senior project.
Special programs include internships, summer session for credit, off-campus study,
study-abroad, and Army ROTC.

The most frequently chosen **baccalaureate** fields are business/marketing, visual and
performing arts, and social sciences. A complete listing of majors at Muhlenberg appears
in the Majors by College index beginning on page 471.

The **faculty** at Muhlenberg has 161 full-time members, 89% with terminal degrees.
The student-faculty ratio is 12:1.

Students of Muhlenberg

The student body is made up of 2,457 undergraduates. 58.6% are women and 41.4% are
men. Students come from 24 states and territories and 5 other countries. 30% are from
Pennsylvania. 0.2% are international students. 2.2% are African American, 0.2%
American Indian, 2.3% Asian American, and 3.7% Hispanic American. 92% returned for
their sophomore year.

Facilities and Resources

486 **computers/terminals** and 100 ports are available on campus for general student
use. Students can access the following: campus intranet, computer help desk, free student
e-mail accounts, online (class) grades, online (class) registration, online (class) schedules.
Campuswide network is available. 100% of college-owned or -operated housing units are
wired for high-speed Internet access. Wireless service is available via classrooms, dorm
rooms, libraries, student centers. The **library** has 309,550 books and 18,363 subscriptions.

Campus Life

There are 109 active organizations on campus, including a drama/theater group,
newspaper, radio station, television station, and choral group. 14% of eligible men and
17% of eligible women are members of national **fraternities** and national **sororities**.

Muhlenberg is a member of the NCAA (Division III). **Intercollegiate sports** include
baseball (m), basketball, cheerleading, cross-country running, field hockey (w), football
(m), golf, lacrosse, soccer, softball (w), tennis, track and field, volleyball (w), wrestling
(m).

Campus Safety

Student safety services include late-night transport/escort service, 24-hour emergency
telephone alarm devices, 24-hour patrols by trained security personnel, and electronically operated dormitory entrances.

Applying

Muhlenberg requires an essay, a high school transcript, and 2 recommendations, and in
some cases SAT or ACT, an interview, and graded paper. It recommends an interview.
Application deadline: 2/15; 2/15 for financial aid. Early and deferred admission are possible.

Located in a beautiful campus setting on the outskirts of a small city, Muhlenberg offers its students an active, highly participatory educational experience within the context of a friendly and very supportive community. Local internships, field study, study abroad, and a Washington semester all supplement the traditional classroom experience. Every year, large numbers of Muhlenberg students go on to law and medical school as well as into a variety of competitive entry-level career positions. They take with them an ability to analyze and think critically as well as an ability to express themselves effectively in person and in writing. These are the most prized outcomes of a Muhlenberg education.

Getting Accepted

4,703 applied
37% were accepted
551 enrolled (31% of accepted)
47% from top tenth of their h.s. class
3.41 average high school GPA
Mean SAT critical reading score: 602
Mean SAT math score: 612
Mean ACT score: 26
55% had SAT critical reading scores over 600
61% had SAT math scores over 600
79% had ACT scores over 24
10% had SAT critical reading scores over 700
12% had SAT math scores over 700
16% had ACT scores over 30
26 class presidents
4 valedictorians

Graduation and After

78% graduated in 4 years
4% graduated in 5 years
1% graduated in 6 years
29% pursued further study (10% arts and
    sciences, 7% medicine, 5% law)
70% had job offers within 6 months
466 organizations recruited on campus

Financial Matters

$33,090 tuition and fees (2007–08)
$7790 room and board
95% average percent of need met
$16,847 average financial aid amount received
    per undergraduate

MURRAY STATE UNIVERSITY

SMALL-TOWN SETTING ■ PUBLIC ■ STATE-SUPPORTED ■ COED
MURRAY, KENTUCKY

Getting Accepted

3,108 applied
85% were accepted
1,415 enrolled (54% of accepted)
25% from top tenth of their h.s. class
3.51 average high school GPA
Mean ACT score: 23
43% had ACT scores over 24
3% had ACT scores over 30
39 valedictorians

Graduation and After

33% graduated in 4 years
15% graduated in 5 years
3% graduated in 6 years
337 organizations recruited on campus

Financial Matters

$5418 resident tuition and fees (2007–08)
$7496 nonresident tuition and fees (2007–08)
$5670 room and board
87% average percent of need met
$4615 average financial aid amount received per undergraduate (2006–07 estimated)

Web site: www.murraystate.edu
Contact: Ms. Stacy Bell, Undergraduate Admissions Specialist, 113 Sparks Hall, Murray, KY 42701-0009
Telephone: 270-809-3035 or toll-free 800-272-4678
Fax: 270-809-3050
E-mail: admissions@murraystate.edu

Academics

Murray State awards bachelor's and master's **degrees** and post-master's certificates. **Challenging opportunities** include advanced placement credit, accelerated degree programs, an honors program, double majors, independent study, and a senior project. Special programs include cooperative education, internships, summer session for credit, off-campus study, study-abroad, and Army ROTC.

The most frequently chosen **baccalaureate** fields are education, business/marketing, and health professions and related sciences. A complete listing of majors at Murray State appears in the Majors by College index beginning on page 471.

The **faculty** at Murray State has 395 full-time members, 77% with terminal degrees. The student-faculty ratio is 16:1.

Students of Murray State

The student body totals 10,149, of whom 8,354 are undergraduates. 57.6% are women and 42.4% are men. Students come from 42 states and territories and 46 other countries. 74% are from Kentucky. 1.8% are international students. 5.8% are African American, 0.4% American Indian, 1% Asian American, and 0.9% Hispanic American. 76% returned for their sophomore year.

Facilities and Resources

1,800 **computers/terminals** are available on campus for general student use. Students can access the following: campus intranet, computer help desk, free student e-mail accounts, online (class) grades, online (class) registration, online (class) schedules, billing accounts. Campuswide network is available. 100% of college-owned or -operated housing units are wired for high-speed Internet access. Wireless service is available via entire campus. The 2 **libraries** have 518,450 books and 1,381 subscriptions.

Campus Life

There are 175 active organizations on campus, including a drama/theater group, newspaper, radio station, television station, choral group, and marching band. 16% of eligible men and 12% of eligible women are members of national **fraternities**, national **sororities**, local fraternities, and local sororities.

Murray State is a member of the NCAA (Division I). **Intercollegiate sports** (some offering scholarships) include baseball (m), basketball, bowling, cheerleading, crew, cross-country running, equestrian sports, football (m), golf, riflery, skiing (downhill), soccer (w), tennis, track and field, volleyball (w).

Campus Safety

Student safety services include late-night transport/escort service, 24-hour emergency telephone alarm devices, 24-hour patrols by trained security personnel, student patrols, and electronically operated dormitory entrances.

Applying

Murray State requires ACT, a high school transcript, and a minimum high school GPA of 3.0. Application deadline: 4/1 priority date for financial aid.

Nebraska Wesleyan University

Suburban setting ■ Private ■ Independent Religious ■ Coed
Lincoln, Nebraska

Web site: www.nebrwesleyan.edu
Contact: 5000 Saint Paul Avenue, Lincoln, NE 68504
Telephone: 402-465-2218 or toll-free 800-541-3818
Fax: 402-465-2177
E-mail: admissions@nebrwesleyan.edu

Academics

Nebraska Wesleyan awards bachelor's and master's **degrees** and post-bachelor's and post-master's certificates. **Challenging opportunities** include advanced placement credit, double majors, independent study, and a senior project. Special programs include internships, summer session for credit, off-campus study, study-abroad, and Army and Air Force ROTC.

The most frequently chosen **baccalaureate** fields are business/marketing, health professions and related sciences, and parks and recreation. A complete listing of majors at Nebraska Wesleyan appears in the Majors by College index beginning on page 471.

The **faculty** at Nebraska Wesleyan has 102 full-time members, 82% with terminal degrees. The student-faculty ratio is 13:1.

Students of Nebraska Wesleyan

The student body totals 2,107, of whom 1,888 are undergraduates. 57.4% are women and 42.6% are men. Students come from 23 states and territories and 14 other countries. 91% are from Nebraska. 0.2% are international students. 1.6% are African American, 0.2% American Indian, 1.4% Asian American, and 1.5% Hispanic American. 82% returned for their sophomore year.

Facilities and Resources

360 **computers/terminals** are available on campus for general student use. Students can access the following: computer help desk, free student e-mail accounts, online (class) grades, online (class) registration, online (class) schedules. Campuswide network is available. 100% of college-owned or -operated housing units are wired for high-speed Internet access. Wireless service is available via classrooms, computer centers, computer labs, learning centers, libraries, student centers. The **library** has 178,531 books and 743 subscriptions.

Campus Life

There are 65 active organizations on campus, including a drama/theater group, newspaper, and choral group. 14% of eligible men and 21% of eligible women are members of national **fraternities**, national **sororities**, local fraternities, and local sororities.

Nebraska Wesleyan is a member of the NCAA (Division III) and NAIA. **Intercollegiate sports** include baseball (m), basketball, cheerleading (w), cross-country running, football (m), golf, soccer, softball (w), tennis, track and field, volleyball (w).

Campus Safety

Student safety services include late-night transport/escort service, 24-hour emergency telephone alarm devices, and electronically operated dormitory entrances.

Applying

Nebraska Wesleyan requires SAT or ACT, a high school transcript, and a minimum high school GPA of 2.0, and in some cases an essay and resume of activities. It recommends an interview. Application deadline: 8/15. Deferred admission is possible.

Getting Accepted

1,632 applied
80% were accepted
439 enrolled (34% of accepted)
27% from top tenth of their h.s. class
43% had ACT scores over 24
10% had ACT scores over 30
39 valedictorians

Graduation and After

56% graduated in 4 years
11% graduated in 5 years
2% graduated in 6 years
30% pursued further study
70 organizations recruited on campus

Financial Matters

$20,252 tuition and fees (2007–08)
$5340 room and board
68% average percent of need met
$13,419 average financial aid amount received per undergraduate (2006–07 estimated)

New College is the state of Florida's officially designated "honors college for the arts and sciences." Located on the beautiful Gulf of Mexico in Sarasota, New College offers an innovative and individualized approach to the liberal arts, with an emphasis on self-directed learning and close collaboration between students and faculty members. Students at New College choose classes through discussion with faculty sponsors, create individual courses of study through independent research projects and tutorials, and receive written narrative evaluations instead of grades. The College's distinctive academic program and challenging curriculum make it a college of choice for highly motivated students who can manage the freedom and responsibility of designing their own education. These same qualities also explain why New College is annually among the nation's top producers of Fulbright Scholars. New College alumni are notable and diverse, including such luminaries as a Rhodes Scholar in physics, a Fields Medal winner in mathematics, the executive producer of a hit television series, and a current member of the U.S. Congress.

Getting Accepted
1,029 applied
57% were accepted
202 enrolled (34% of accepted)
53% from top tenth of their h.s. class
3.94 average high school GPA
Mean SAT critical reading score: 693
Mean SAT math score: 628
Mean ACT score: 28
92% had SAT critical reading scores over 600
66% had SAT math scores over 600
97% had ACT scores over 24
51% had SAT critical reading scores over 700
15% had SAT math scores over 700
33% had ACT scores over 30
9 National Merit Scholars
7 valedictorians

Graduation and After
43% graduated in 4 years
11% graduated in 5 years
3% graduated in 6 years
47% pursued further study (7% law, 5% medicine, 3% business)
27% had job offers within 6 months
90 organizations recruited on campus

Financial Matters
$3772 resident tuition and fees (2007–08)
$21,625 nonresident tuition and fees (2007–08)
$7035 room and board
92% average percent of need met
$12,018 average financial aid amount received per undergraduate (2006–07 estimated)

New College of Florida
Suburban setting ■ Public ■ State-supported ■ Coed
Sarasota, Florida

Web site: www.ncf.edu
Contact: Office of Admissions, 5800 Bay Shore Road, Sarasota, FL 34243-2109
Telephone: 941-487-5000
Fax: 941-487-5010
E-mail: admissions@ncf.edu

Academics
New College awards bachelor's **degrees**. **Challenging opportunities** include student-designed majors, an honors program, double majors, independent study, and a senior project. Special programs include internships, off-campus study, and study-abroad.

The most frequently chosen **baccalaureate** fields are interdisciplinary studies, psychology, and area and ethnic studies. A complete listing of majors at New College appears in the Majors by College index beginning on page 471.

The **faculty** at New College has 69 full-time members, 99% with terminal degrees. The student-faculty ratio is 10:1.

Students of New College
The student body is made up of 767 undergraduates. 60.9% are women and 39.1% are men. Students come from 38 states and territories and 21 other countries. 77% are from Florida. 0.7% are international students. 2% are African American, 0.4% American Indian, 2.5% Asian American, and 9.4% Hispanic American. 87% returned for their sophomore year.

Facilities and Resources
41 **computers/terminals** are available on campus for general student use. Students can access the following: campus intranet, computer help desk, free student e-mail accounts, online (class) registration. Campuswide network is available. 100% of college-owned or -operated housing units are wired for high-speed Internet access. Wireless service is available via classrooms, libraries, student centers. The **library** has 268,305 books and 953 subscriptions.

Campus Life
There are 43 active organizations on campus, including a drama/theater group, newspaper, radio station, and choral group. No national or local **fraternities** or **sororities**.

This institution has no intercollegiate sports.

Campus Safety
Student safety services include late-night transport/escort service, 24-hour emergency telephone alarm devices, and 24-hour patrols by trained security personnel.

Applying
New College requires an essay, SAT or ACT, a high school transcript, and 1 recommendation. It recommends analytical paper and a minimum high school GPA of 3.0. Application deadline: 4/15; 2/15 priority date for financial aid. Early and deferred admission are possible.

NEW JERSEY INSTITUTE OF TECHNOLOGY

URBAN SETTING ■ PUBLIC ■ STATE-SUPPORTED ■ COED
NEWARK, NEW JERSEY

Web site: www.njit.edu
Contact: Ms. Kathy Kelly, Director of Admissions, University Heights,
  Newark, NJ 07102-1982
Telephone: 973-596-3300 or toll-free 800-925-NJIT
Fax: 973-596-3461
E-mail: admissions@njit.edu

SPONSOR

> Recognized by *U.S News & World Report* as a top-tier national research university offering bachelor's, master's, and doctoral degrees, New Jersey Institute of Technology (NJIT) has been a leader in the field of engineering education for almost ninety years. NJIT's Newark College of Engineering is one of the largest professional engineering schools in the United States; among its more than 40,000 alumni are pioneers and leaders in such fields as aerospace, telecommunications, plastics, electronics, and environmental engineering.

Academics

NJIT awards bachelor's, master's, and doctoral **degrees** and post-bachelor's certificates. **Challenging opportunities** include advanced placement credit, accelerated degree programs, freshman honors college, an honors program, double majors, independent study, and a senior project. Special programs include cooperative education, internships, summer session for credit, off-campus study, study-abroad, and Air Force ROTC.

The most frequently chosen **baccalaureate** fields are engineering, computer and information sciences, and engineering technologies. A complete listing of majors at NJIT appears in the Majors by College index beginning on page 471.

The **faculty** at NJIT has 391 full-time members. The student-faculty ratio is 12:1.

Students of NJIT

The student body totals 8,288, of whom 5,428 are undergraduates. 20.5% are women and 79.5% arc men. Students come from 14 states and territories and 98 other countries. 92% are from New Jersey. 5.2% are international students. 10% are African American, 0.6% American Indian, 19.9% Asian American, and 16.9% Hispanic American. 80% returned for their sophomore year.

Facilities and Resources

1,938 **computers/terminals** are available on campus for general student use. Students can access the following: online (class) registration. Campuswide network is available. Wireless service is available via entire campus. The 2 **libraries** have 160,000 books and 1,100 subscriptions.

Campus Life

There are 70 active organizations on campus, including a drama/theater group, newspaper, and radio station. 9% of eligible men and 4% of eligible women are members of national **fraternities**, national **sororities**, local fraternities, and local sororities.

NJIT is a member of the NCAA (Division I). **Intercollegiate sports** include baseball (m), basketball, cross-country running, fencing, golf (m), soccer, softball (w), swimming and diving (w), tennis, track and field (w).

Campus Safety

Student safety services include bicycle patrols, late-night transport/escort service, 24-hour emergency telephone alarm devices, 24-hour patrols by trained security personnel, and electronically operated dormitory entrances.

Applying

NJIT requires SAT or ACT and a high school transcript, and in some cases an essay, SAT Subject Tests, and an interview. It recommends 1 recommendation. Application deadline: 4/1; 5/15 for financial aid, with a 3/15 priority date. Deferred admission is possible.

Getting Accepted
3,027 applied
64% were accepted
783 enrolled (40% of accepted)
28% from top tenth of their h.s. class
Mean SAT critical reading score: 535
Mean SAT math score: 601
Mean SAT writing score: 526
23% had SAT critical reading scores over 600
52% had SAT math scores over 600
19% had SAT writing scores over 600
3% had SAT critical reading scores over 700
11% had SAT math scores over 700
3% had SAT writing scores over 700

Graduation and After
12% graduated in 4 years
26% graduated in 5 years
14% graduated in 6 years
22% pursued further study
80% had job offers within 6 months
400 organizations recruited on campus

Financial Matters
$11,350 resident tuition and fees (2007–08)
$20,082 nonresident tuition and fees (2007–08)
$9108 room and board
81% average percent of need met
$10,089 average financial aid amount received per undergraduate (2006–07 estimated)

Getting Accepted

763 applied
55% were accepted
240 enrolled (57% of accepted)
31% from top tenth of their h.s. class
3.6 average high school GPA
Mean SAT critical reading score: 593
Mean SAT math score: 615
Mean ACT score: 26
52% had SAT critical reading scores over 600
58% had SAT math scores over 600
70% had ACT scores over 24
15% had SAT critical reading scores over 700
17% had SAT math scores over 700
20% had ACT scores over 30

Graduation and After

16% graduated in 4 years
22% graduated in 5 years
5% graduated in 6 years
16% pursued further study (8% arts and sciences, 8% engineering)
75% had job offers within 6 months
22 organizations recruited on campus

Financial Matters

$4105 resident tuition and fees (2007–08)
$11,761 nonresident tuition and fees (2007–08)
$5300 room and board
94% average percent of need met
$7849 average financial aid amount received per undergraduate (2004–05 estimated)

NEW MEXICO INSTITUTE OF MINING AND TECHNOLOGY

SMALL-TOWN SETTING ■ PUBLIC ■ STATE-SUPPORTED ■ COED
SOCORRO, NEW MEXICO

Web site: www.nmt.edu
Contact: Mr. Mike Kloeppel, Director of Admissions, 801 Leroy Place, Socorro, NM 87801
Telephone: 575-835-5424 or toll-free 800-428-TECH
Fax: 575-835-5989
E-mail: admission@admin.nmt.edu

Academics

New Mexico Tech awards associate, bachelor's, master's, and doctoral **degrees**. **Challenging opportunities** include advanced placement credit, accelerated degree programs, student-designed majors, double majors, independent study, and a senior project. Special programs include cooperative education, internships, and summer session for credit.

The most frequently chosen **baccalaureate** fields are engineering, physical sciences, and computer and information sciences. A complete listing of majors at New Mexico Tech appears in the Majors by College index beginning on page 471.

The **faculty** at New Mexico Tech has 119 full-time members, 97% with terminal degrees. The student-faculty ratio is 11:1.

Students of New Mexico Tech

The student body totals 1,882, of whom 1,327 are undergraduates. 33% are women and 67% are men. Students come from 24 states and territories and 29 other countries. 87% are from New Mexico. 1.9% are international students. 1.1% are African American, 2.6% American Indian, 3% Asian American, and 24.8% Hispanic American. 73% returned for their sophomore year.

Facilities and Resources

225 **computers/terminals** are available on campus for general student use. Students can access the following: computer help desk, free student e-mail accounts, online (class) registration, online (class) schedules. Campuswide network is available. Wireless service is available via computer centers, learning centers, student centers. The 2 **libraries** have 321,829 books and 884 subscriptions.

Campus Life

There are 55 active organizations on campus, including a drama/theater group, newspaper, radio station, and choral group. No national or local **fraternities** or **sororities**.

This institution has no intercollegiate sports.

Campus Safety

Student safety services include late-night transport/escort service, 24-hour emergency telephone alarm devices, and 24-hour patrols by trained security personnel.

Applying

New Mexico Tech requires SAT or ACT, a high school transcript, and a minimum high school GPA of 2.5, and in some cases 2 recommendations. It recommends ACT and an interview. Application deadline: 8/1; 6/1 priority date for financial aid. Deferred admission is possible.

New York School of Interior Design

Urban setting ■ Private ■ Independent ■ Coed, Primarily Women
New York, New York

Web site: www.nysid.edu
Contact: Cassandra Ramirez, Admissions Associate, 170 East 70th Street, New York, NY 10021-5110
Telephone: 212-472-1500 Ext. 204 or toll-free 800-336-9743 Ext. 204
Fax: 212-472-1867
E-mail: admissions@nysid.edu

Academics

NYSID awards associate, bachelor's, and master's **degrees. Challenging opportunities** include advanced placement credit, independent study, and a senior project. Special programs include internships, summer session for credit, and study-abroad. A complete listing of majors at NYSID appears in the Majors by College index beginning on page 471.

The **faculty** at NYSID has 2 full-time members. The student-faculty ratio is 10:1.

Students of NYSID

The student body totals 703, of whom 685 are undergraduates. 91.5% are women and 8.5% are men. 68% are from New York. 3.6% are African American, 0.1% American Indian, 9.1% Asian American, and 7.9% Hispanic American. 20% returned for their sophomore year.

Facilities and Resources

135 **computers/terminals** are available on campus for general student use. Campuswide network is available. The **library** has 12,000 books and 110 subscriptions.

Campus Life

There is 1 active organization on campus. No national or local **fraternities** or **sororities**.

This institution has no intercollegiate sports.

Campus Safety

Student safety services include security during school hours.

Applying

NYSID requires an essay, a high school transcript, 2 recommendations, portfolio, and a minimum high school GPA of 2.8, and in some cases SAT or ACT. Application deadline: 3/1; 5/1 priority date for financial aid. Deferred admission is possible.

Manhattan, with its world-famous museums, showrooms, and architectural landmarks, is home to the New York School of Interior Design (NYSID). NYSID is a single-major college dedicated solely to the study of interior design. Facilities include a lighting lab, a computer-aided design (CAD) lab, and an extensive reference library. Many NYSID graduates have gone on to find work in the best design and architectural firms in New York City and around the world. The Bachelor of Fine Arts degree program is accredited by CIDA, the Council for Interior Design Accreditation (formerly FIDER).

Getting Accepted
122 applied
48% were accepted
24 enrolled (41% of accepted)
3.1 average high school GPA
4% had SAT math scores over 600

Graduation and After
5% pursued further study

Financial Matters
$19,790 tuition and fees (2008–09)
50% average percent of need met
$6500 average financial aid amount received per undergraduate (2006–07 estimated)

New York University

Urban setting ■ Private ■ Independent ■ Coed
New York, New York

Web site: www.nyu.edu
Contact: Ms. Barbara Hall, Associate Provost for Admissions and Financial
   Aid, 22 Washington Square North, New York, NY 10011
Telephone: 212-998-4500
Fax: 212-995-4902
E-mail: nyuadmit@uccvm.nyu.edu

Getting Accepted

34,389 applied
37% were accepted
4,927 enrolled (38% of accepted)
66% from top tenth of their h.s. class
3.6 average high school GPA
Mean SAT critical reading score: 661
Mean SAT math score: 667
Mean SAT writing score: 639
Mean ACT score: 29
84% had SAT critical reading scores over 600
84% had SAT math scores over 600
85% had SAT writing scores over 600
99% had ACT scores over 24
32% had SAT critical reading scores over 700
35% had SAT math scores over 700
33% had SAT writing scores over 700
45% had ACT scores over 30

Graduation and After

78% graduated in 4 years
5% graduated in 5 years
1% graduated in 6 years
26% pursued further study (7% law, 5% arts
   and sciences, 4% education)
95% had job offers within 6 months
695 organizations recruited on campus

Financial Matters

$35,290 tuition and fees (2007–08)
$12,200 room and board
66% average percent of need met
$20,707 average financial aid amount received
   per undergraduate (2006–07 estimated)

Academics

NYU awards associate, bachelor's, master's, doctoral, and first-professional **degrees** and post-bachelor's, post-master's, and first-professional certificates. **Challenging opportunities** include advanced placement credit, student-designed majors, an honors program, double majors, independent study, and a senior project. Special programs include cooperative education, internships, summer session for credit, off-campus study, study-abroad, and Army and Navy ROTC.

The most frequently chosen **baccalaureate** fields are visual and performing arts, social sciences, and business/marketing. A complete listing of majors at NYU appears in the Majors by College index beginning on page 471.

The **faculty** at NYU has 2,132 full-time members. The student-faculty ratio is 12:1.

Students of NYU

The student body totals 41,783, of whom 21,327 are undergraduates. 61.6% are women and 38.4% are men. Students come from 52 states and territories and 93 other countries. 36% are from New York. 5.5% are international students. 4.3% are African American, 0.2% American Indian, 18.7% Asian American, and 7.5% Hispanic American. 92% returned for their sophomore year.

Facilities and Resources

4,500 **computers/terminals** are available on campus for general student use. Students can access the following: computer help desk, free student e-mail accounts, online (class) registration, online (class) schedules. Campuswide network is available. 100% of college-owned or -operated housing units are wired for high-speed Internet access. Wireless service is available via computer labs, learning centers, libraries, student centers. The 12 **libraries** have 5,235,527 books and 48,958 subscriptions.

Campus Life

There are 407 active organizations on campus, including a drama/theater group, newspaper, radio station, television station, choral group, and marching band. 1% of eligible men and 2% of eligible women are members of national **fraternities**, national **sororities**, and local sororities.

NYU is a member of the NCAA (Division III). **Intercollegiate sports** include basketball, cheerleading, cross-country running, fencing, golf (m), soccer, swimming and diving, tennis, track and field, volleyball, wrestling (m).

Campus Safety

Student safety services include 24-hour security in residence halls, late-night transport/escort service, 24-hour emergency telephone alarm devices, 24-hour patrols by trained security personnel, student patrols, and electronically operated dormitory entrances.

Applying

NYU requires an essay, SAT Subject Tests, SAT or ACT, a high school transcript, and 2 recommendations, and in some cases audition, portfolio. Application deadline: 1/15; 2/15 priority date for financial aid. Deferred admission is possible.

North Carolina State University

URBAN SETTING ■ PUBLIC ■ STATE-SUPPORTED ■ COED
RALEIGH, NORTH CAROLINA

Web site: www.ncsu.edu
Contact: Mr. Thomas Griffin, Director of Undergraduate Admissions, Box 7103, Raleigh, NC 27695
Telephone: 919-515-2434
Fax: 919-515-5039
E-mail: undergrad_admissions@ncsu.edu

Academics

NC State awards associate, bachelor's, master's, doctoral, and first-professional **degrees** and post-bachelor's and first-professional certificates. **Challenging opportunities** include advanced placement credit, accelerated degree programs, student-designed majors, an honors program, double majors, independent study, and a senior project. Special programs include cooperative education, internships, summer session for credit, off-campus study, study-abroad, and Army, Navy, and Air Force ROTC.

The most frequently chosen **baccalaureate** fields are engineering, business/marketing, and biological/life sciences. A complete listing of majors at NC State appears in the Majors by College index beginning on page 471.

The **faculty** at NC State has 1,723 full-time members, 90% with terminal degrees. The student-faculty ratio is 16:1.

Students of NC State

The student body totals 31,802, of whom 24,145 are undergraduates. 43.6% are women and 56.4% are men. Students come from 52 states and territories and 64 other countries. 93% are from North Carolina. 1% are international students. 8.9% are African American, 0.6% American Indian, 5.1% Asian American, and 2.6% Hispanic American. 89% returned for their sophomore year.

Facilities and Resources

3,000 **computers/terminals** and 500 ports are available on campus for general student use. Students can access the following: campus intranet, computer help desk, free student e-mail accounts, online (class) grades, online (class) registration, online (class) schedules, course materials, online homework submission, online testing/quizzes, financial aid/cashier's office account balances, wiki space, blogging service, web space, online storage space, on-site OS and virus removal, online/hybrid courses. Campuswide network is available. 100% of college-owned or -operated housing units are wired for high-speed Internet access. Wireless service is available via classrooms, computer centers, computer labs, dorm rooms, learning centers, libraries, student centers. The 7 **libraries** have 3,687,733 books and 49,480 subscriptions.

Campus Life

There are 300 active organizations on campus, including a drama/theater group, newspaper, radio station, television station, choral group, and marching band. 8% of eligible men and 10% of eligible women are members of national **fraternities**, national **sororities**, and local sororities.

NC State is a member of the NCAA (Division I). **Intercollegiate sports** (some offering scholarships) include baseball (m), basketball, cheerleading, cross-country running, fencing, football (m), golf, gymnastics (w), riflery, soccer, softball (w), swimming and diving, tennis, track and field, volleyball (w), wrestling (m).

Campus Safety

Student safety services include late-night transport/escort service, 24-hour emergency telephone alarm devices, 24-hour patrols by trained security personnel, student patrols, and electronically operated dormitory entrances.

Applying

NC State requires SAT or ACT and a high school transcript, and in some cases an interview. It recommends an essay and SAT Subject Tests. Application deadline: 2/1; 3/1 priority date for financial aid. Deferred admission is possible.

Getting Accepted

16,437 applied
60% were accepted
4,907 enrolled (50% of accepted)
37% from top tenth of their h.s. class
4.0 average high school GPA
Mean SAT critical reading score: 568
Mean SAT math score: 603
Mean SAT writing score: 557
Mean ACT score: 25
35% had SAT critical reading scores over 600
55% had SAT math scores over 600
30% had SAT writing scores over 600
60% had ACT scores over 24
5% had SAT critical reading scores over 700
11% had SAT math scores over 700
3% had SAT writing scores over 700
9% had ACT scores over 30
2 National Merit Scholars
70 valedictorians

Graduation and After

37% graduated in 4 years
28% graduated in 5 years
5% graduated in 6 years
26% pursued further study (10% arts and sciences, 5% engineering, 4% business)
60% had job offers within 6 months
350 organizations recruited on campus

Financial Matters

$5117 resident tuition and fees (2007–08)
$17,315 nonresident tuition and fees (2007–08)
$7373 room and board
79% average percent of need met
$8925 average financial aid amount received per undergraduate (2006–07 estimated)

NORTH CENTRAL COLLEGE

SUBURBAN SETTING ■ PRIVATE ■ INDEPENDENT RELIGIOUS ■ COED
NAPERVILLE, ILLINOIS

Web site: www.noctrl.edu
Contact: Ms. Martha Stolze, Director of Freshman Admission, 30 North
  Brainard Street, PO Box 3063, Naperville, IL 60566-7063
Telephone: 630-637-5800 or toll-free 800-411-1861
Fax: 630-637-5819
E-mail: admissions@noctrl.edu

North Central College, nestled in the heart of Naperville, Illinois—*Money* magazine's "Second Best Place to Live" in the nation—is just 29 miles from downtown Chicago. The College is committed to undergraduate teaching and to sustaining its strong campus life tradition. The curriculum is grounded in a liberal arts foundation, with an emphasis on leadership, ethics, and values. North Central College offers more than fifty-five academic areas of concentration in business, communication, education, liberal arts, and science as well as preprofessional programs. Co-curricular opportunities include nationally recognized Division III intercollegiate athletics, a student radio station, a Model UN team, a community conflict-resolution program, forensics, and community service.

Getting Accepted
2,234 applied
69% were accepted
422 enrolled (27% of accepted)
3.56 average high school GPA
Mean ACT score: 25
58% had ACT scores over 24
11% had ACT scores over 30
2 National Merit Scholars
7 valedictorians

Graduation and After
54% graduated in 4 years
11% graduated in 5 years
1% graduated in 6 years
11% pursued further study
70% had job offers within 6 months
35 organizations recruited on campus

Financial Matters
$24,564 tuition and fees (2007–08)
$7677 room and board
77% average percent of need met
$17,034 average financial aid amount received
  per undergraduate (2006–07 estimated)

Academics

North Central awards bachelor's and master's **degrees** and post-bachelor's certificates. **Challenging opportunities** include advanced placement credit, accelerated degree programs, student-designed majors, an honors program, double majors, independent study, and a senior project. Special programs include internships, summer session for credit, off-campus study, study-abroad, and Army and Air Force ROTC.

The most frequently chosen **baccalaureate** fields are business/marketing, social sciences, and education. A complete listing of majors at North Central appears in the Majors by College index beginning on page 471.

The **faculty** at North Central has 113 full-time members, 88% with terminal degrees. The student-faculty ratio is 15:1.

Students of North Central

The student body totals 2,559, of whom 2,232 are undergraduates. 57.3% are women and 42.7% are men. Students come from 27 states and territories and 31 other countries. 92% are from Illinois. 1.1% are international students. 3.3% are African American, 0.4% American Indian, 3.2% Asian American, and 4.4% Hispanic American. 80% returned for their sophomore year.

Facilities and Resources

255 **computers/terminals** and 12 ports are available on campus for general student use. Students can access the following: campus intranet, computer help desk, free student e-mail accounts, online (class) grades, online (class) registration, online (class) schedules, software packages. Campuswide network is available. 100% of college-owned or -operated housing units are wired for high-speed Internet access. Wireless service is available via computer centers, dorm rooms, learning centers, libraries, student centers. The **library** has 145,918 books and 2,243 subscriptions.

Campus Life

There are 59 active organizations on campus, including a drama/theater group, newspaper, radio station, and choral group. No national or local **fraternities** or **sororities**.

North Central is a member of the NCAA (Division III). **Intercollegiate sports** include baseball (m), basketball, cheerleading (w), cross-country running, football (m), golf, lacrosse (w), soccer, softball (w), swimming and diving, tennis, track and field, volleyball (w), wrestling (m).

Campus Safety

Student safety services include late-night transport/escort service, 24-hour emergency telephone alarm devices, and 24-hour patrols by trained security personnel.

Applying

North Central requires SAT or ACT, a high school transcript, and a minimum high school GPA of 2.5, and in some cases an interview. It recommends an essay, ACT, and 1 recommendation. Application deadline: rolling admissions. Deferred admission is possible.

Northwestern College

RURAL SETTING ■ PRIVATE ■ INDEPENDENT RELIGIOUS ■ COED
ORANGE CITY, IOWA

Web site: www.nwciowa.edu
Contact: Mr. Mark Bloemendaal, Director of Admissions, 101 7th Street SW,
    Orange City, IA 51041-1996
Telephone: 712-737-7130 or toll-free 800-747-4757
Fax: 712-707-7164
E-mail: admissions@nwciowa.edu

Academics

Northwestern College awards bachelor's **degrees**. **Challenging opportunities** include advanced placement credit, student-designed majors, an honors program, double majors, independent study, and a senior project. Special programs include cooperative education, internships, summer session for credit, off-campus study, and study-abroad.

The most frequently chosen **baccalaureate** fields are business/marketing, education, and biological/life sciences. A complete listing of majors at Northwestern College appears in the Majors by College index beginning on page 471.

The **faculty** at Northwestern College has 82 full-time members, 79% with terminal degrees. The student-faculty ratio is 15:1.

Students of Northwestern College

The student body is made up of 1,315 undergraduates. 60.7% are women and 39.3% are men. Students come from 30 states and territories and 20 other countries. 54% are from Iowa. 2.6% are international students. 0.9% are African American, 0.2% American Indian, 0.9% Asian American, and 1.4% Hispanic American. 76% returned for their sophomore year.

Facilities and Resources

250 **computers/terminals** are available on campus for general student use. Students can access the following: campus intranet, computer help desk, free student e-mail accounts, online (class) grades, online (class) registration, online (class) schedules, online degree audits. Campuswide network is available. Wireless service is available via classrooms, computer centers, computer labs, learning centers, libraries, student centers. The 2 **libraries** have 125,000 books and 615 subscriptions.

Campus Life

There are 30 active organizations on campus, including a drama/theater group, newspaper, television station, and choral group. No national or local **fraternities** or **sororities**.

Northwestern College is a member of the NAIA. **Intercollegiate sports** (some offering scholarships) include baseball (m), basketball, cross-country running, football (m), golf, soccer, softball (w), track and field, volleyball (w), wrestling (m).

Campus Safety

Student safety services include 24-hour emergency telephone alarm devices and electronically operated dormitory entrances.

Applying

Northwestern College requires an essay, SAT or ACT, a high school transcript, 1 recommendation, and a minimum high school GPA of 2.0. It recommends an interview and a minimum high school GPA of 2.5. Application deadline: rolling admissions; 4/1 priority date for financial aid. Early and deferred admission are possible.

Getting Accepted

1,311 applied
79% were accepted
324 enrolled (31% of accepted)
31% from top tenth of their h.s. class
3.54 average high school GPA
Mean ACT score: 24
61% had ACT scores over 24
9% had ACT scores over 30
30 valedictorians

Graduation and After

53% graduated in 4 years
7% graduated in 5 years
1% graduated in 6 years
22% pursued further study
93% had job offers within 6 months
35 organizations recruited on campus

Financial Matters

$21,648 tuition and fees (2007–08)
$6302 room and board
96% average percent of need met
$15,040 average financial aid amount received
    per undergraduate (2006–07 estimated)

NORTHWESTERN COLLEGE

SUBURBAN SETTING ■ PRIVATE ■ INDEPENDENT RELIGIOUS ■ COED
ST. PAUL, MINNESOTA

Getting Accepted
1,109 applied
93% were accepted
502 enrolled (49% of accepted)
28% from top tenth of their h.s. class
3.57 average high school GPA
Mean SAT critical reading score: 565
Mean SAT math score: 560
Mean ACT score: 24
40% had SAT critical reading scores over 600
46% had SAT math scores over 600
58% had ACT scores over 24
17% had SAT critical reading scores over 700
14% had SAT math scores over 700
11% had ACT scores over 30
15 valedictorians

Graduation and After
47% graduated in 4 years
11% graduated in 5 years
3% graduated in 6 years
9% pursued further study (4% theology, 3% arts and sciences, 1% education)
65% had job offers within 6 months
90 organizations recruited on campus

Financial Matters
$22,420 tuition and fees (2008–09)
$7050 room and board
75% average percent of need met
$14,551 average financial aid amount received per undergraduate (2005–06)

Web site: www.nwc.edu
Contact: Mr. Kenneth K. Faffler, Director of Admissions, Officer of Admissions, 3003 Snelling Avenue North, 212 Nazareth Hall, St. Paul, MN 55113-1598
Telephone: 651-631-5111 or toll-free 800-827-6827
Fax: 651-631-5680
E-mail: admissions@nwc.edu

Academics
Northwestern College awards associate, bachelor's, and master's **degrees**. **Challenging opportunities** include advanced placement credit, student-designed majors, an honors program, double majors, independent study, and a senior project. Special programs include internships, summer session for credit, off-campus study, study-abroad, and Army and Air Force ROTC.

The most frequently chosen **baccalaureate** fields are education, theology and religious vocations, and communications/journalism. A complete listing of majors at Northwestern College appears in the Majors by College index beginning on page 471.

The **faculty** at Northwestern College has 96 full-time members, 61% with terminal degrees. The student-faculty ratio is 15:1.

Students of Northwestern College
The student body totals 1,925, of whom 1,845 are undergraduates. 58.8% are women and 41.2% are men. Students come from 35 states and territories and 21 other countries. 68% are from Minnesota. 0.3% are international students. 2.7% are African American, 0.6% American Indian, 4.4% Asian American, and 2% Hispanic American. 83% returned for their sophomore year.

Facilities and Resources
100 **computers/terminals** and 12 ports are available on campus for general student use. Students can access the following: campus intranet, computer help desk, free student e-mail accounts, online (class) grades, online (class) registration, online (class) schedules. Campuswide network is available. 100% of college-owned or -operated housing units are wired for high-speed Internet access. Wireless service is available via classrooms, computer labs, dorm rooms, learning centers, libraries, student centers. The **library** has 117,745 books and 1,131 subscriptions.

Campus Life
There are 25 active organizations on campus, including a drama/theater group, newspaper, radio station, and choral group. No national or local **fraternities** or **sororities**.

Northwestern College is a member of the NCAA (Division III) and NCCAA. **Intercollegiate sports** include baseball (m), basketball, cheerleading (w), cross-country running, football (m), golf (m), soccer, softball (w), tennis, track and field, volleyball (w).

Campus Safety
Student safety services include late-night transport/escort service, 24-hour patrols by trained security personnel, and electronically operated dormitory entrances.

Applying
Northwestern College requires an essay, SAT or ACT, a high school transcript, 2 recommendations, lifestyle agreement, statement of Christian faith, and a minimum high school GPA of 2.0, and in some cases an interview. It recommends a minimum high school GPA of 3.0. Application deadline: 8/1; 5/1 for financial aid, with a 3/1 priority date. Early and deferred admission are possible.

NORTHWESTERN UNIVERSITY

SUBURBAN SETTING ■ PRIVATE ■ INDEPENDENT ■ COED
EVANSTON, ILLINOIS

Web site: www.northwestern.edu
Contact: Ms. Carol Lunkenheimer, Dean of Undergraduate Admission, PO Box 3060, Evanston, IL 60204-3060
Telephone: 847-491-7271
E-mail: ug-admission@northwestern.edu

Academics

Northwestern awards bachelor's, master's, doctoral, and first-professional **degrees** and post-master's certificates. **Challenging opportunities** include advanced placement credit, accelerated degree programs, student-designed majors, an honors program, double majors, independent study, and a senior project. Special programs include cooperative education, internships, summer session for credit, study-abroad, and Army, Navy, and Air Force ROTC.

The most frequently chosen **baccalaureate** fields are communications/journalism, social sciences, and engineering. A complete listing of majors at Northwestern appears in the Majors by College index beginning on page 471.

The **faculty** at Northwestern has 998 full-time members, 100% with terminal degrees. The student-faculty ratio is 7:1.

Students of Northwestern

The student body totals 17,460, of whom 8,153 are undergraduates. 52.8% are women and 47.2% are men. Students come from 51 states and territories and 48 other countries. 25% are from Illinois. 5.1% are international students. 5.6% are African American, 0.1% American Indian, 16.5% Asian American, and 6.3% Hispanic American. 98% returned for their sophomore year.

Facilities and Resources

678 **computers/terminals** are available on campus for general student use. Students can access the following: online (class) registration. Campuswide network is available. The 7 **libraries** have 4,687,828 books and 45,259 subscriptions.

Campus Life

There are 415 active organizations on campus, including a drama/theater group, newspaper, radio station, television station, choral group, and marching band. 32% of eligible men and 38% of eligible women are members of national **fraternities** and national **sororities**.

Northwestern is a member of the NCAA (Division I). **Intercollegiate sports** (some offering scholarships) include baseball (m), basketball, cheerleading, cross-country running (w), fencing (w), field hockey (w), football (m), golf, lacrosse (w), soccer, softball (w), swimming and diving, tennis, volleyball (w), wrestling (m).

Campus Safety

Student safety services include late-night transport/escort service, 24-hour emergency telephone alarm devices, 24-hour patrols by trained security personnel, and electronically operated dormitory entrances.

Applying

Northwestern requires an essay, SAT or ACT, a high school transcript, and 1 recommendation, and in some cases SAT Subject Tests and audition for music program. It recommends SAT Subject Tests. Application deadline: 1/1; 2/1 for financial aid. Early and deferred admission are possible.

Getting Accepted

18,385 applied
30% were accepted
2,062 enrolled (38% of accepted)
81% from top tenth of their h.s. class
Mean SAT critical reading score: 690
Mean SAT math score: 710
Mean ACT score: 31
91% had SAT critical reading scores over 600
95% had SAT math scores over 600
96% had ACT scores over 24
50% had SAT critical reading scores over 700
63% had SAT math scores over 700
71% had ACT scores over 30
152 National Merit Scholars
158 valedictorians

Graduation and After

84% graduated in 4 years
8% graduated in 5 years
1% graduated in 6 years
24% pursued further study (11% arts and sciences, 6% medicine, 4% law)
624 organizations recruited on campus

Financial Matters

$35,064 tuition and fees (2007–08)
$10,776 room and board
100% average percent of need met
$26,573 average financial aid amount received per undergraduate (2006–07 estimated)

Oberlin is a four-year, highly selective liberal arts college and home to America's oldest continuously operating music conservatory. From its founding, Oberlin has been a community of thinkers, scholars, scientists, musicians, athletes, activists, and artists—all of whom seek to make the world a better place. Oberlin invented coeducation in 1837 and made interracial education central to its mission in 1835. More Oberlin graduates have gone on to earn Ph. D.'s than those at any other American college. Oberlin alumni, who include 3 Nobel laureates and 6 MacArthur genius award recipients, are leaders in law, scientific and scholarly research, medicine, the arts, theology, communication, business, and government.

Getting Accepted
7,014 applied
31% were accepted
742 enrolled (34% of accepted)
68% from top tenth of their h.s. class
3.6 average high school GPA
Mean SAT critical reading score: 697
Mean SAT math score: 667
Mean SAT writing score: 682
Mean ACT score: 30
87% had SAT critical reading scores over 600
81% had SAT math scores over 600
89% had ACT scores over 24
53% had SAT critical reading scores over 700
33% had SAT math scores over 700
46% had ACT scores over 30
55 National Merit Scholars
41 valedictorians

Graduation and After
66% graduated in 4 years
15% graduated in 5 years
1% graduated in 6 years
22% pursued further study
90% had job offers within 6 months
32 organizations recruited on campus

Financial Matters
$36,282 tuition and fees (2007–08)
$10,080 room and board
100% average percent of need met
$24,255 average financial aid amount received per undergraduate (2006–07 estimated)

OBERLIN COLLEGE
SMALL-TOWN SETTING ■ PRIVATE ■ INDEPENDENT ■ COED
OBERLIN, OHIO

Web site: www.oberlin.edu
Contact: Ms. Debra Chermonte, Dean of Admissions and Financial Aid, Admissions Office, Carnegie Building, Oberlin, OH 44074-1090
Telephone: 440-775-8411 or toll-free 800-622-OBIE
Fax: 440-775-6905
E-mail: college.admissions@oberlin.edu

Academics
Oberlin awards bachelor's and master's **degrees** and post-bachelor's certificates. **Challenging opportunities** include advanced placement credit, student-designed majors, an honors program, double majors, independent study, and a senior project. Special programs include internships, off-campus study, and study-abroad. A complete listing of majors at Oberlin appears in the Majors by College index beginning on page 471.

The **faculty** at Oberlin has 275 full-time members. The student-faculty ratio is 9:1.

Students of Oberlin
The student body totals 2,774, of whom 2,762 are undergraduates. 54.8% are women and 45.2% are men. Students come from 50 states and territories and 44 other countries. 9% are from Ohio. 6% are international students. 6% are African American, 0.6% American Indian, 8% Asian American, and 4.6% Hispanic American. 92% returned for their sophomore year.

Facilities and Resources
340 **computers/terminals** are available on campus for general student use. Students can access the following: campus intranet, computer help desk, free student e-mail accounts, online (class) registration, online (class) schedules. Campuswide network is available. 100% of college-owned or -operated housing units are wired for high-speed Internet access. Wireless service is available via classrooms, computer centers, computer labs, dorm rooms, learning centers, libraries, student centers. The 4 **libraries** have 1,541,260 books and 4,560 subscriptions.

Campus Life
There are 120 active organizations on campus, including a drama/theater group, newspaper, radio station, choral group, and marching band. No national or local **fraternities** or **sororities**.

Oberlin is a member of the NCAA (Division III). **Intercollegiate sports** include baseball (m), basketball, cross-country running, field hockey (w), football (m), golf, lacrosse, soccer, swimming and diving, tennis, track and field, volleyball (w).

Campus Safety
Student safety services include crime prevention programs, late-night transport/escort service, 24-hour emergency telephone alarm devices, 24-hour patrols by trained security personnel, student patrols, and electronically operated dormitory entrances.

Applying
Oberlin requires an essay, SAT or ACT, a high school transcript, and 2 recommendations, and in some cases an interview. It recommends SAT Subject Tests. Application deadline: 1/15; 1/15 priority date for financial aid. Early and deferred admission are possible.

OCCIDENTAL COLLEGE

URBAN SETTING ■ PRIVATE ■ INDEPENDENT ■ COED
LOS ANGELES, CALIFORNIA

Web site: www.oxy.edu
Contact: Mr. Vince Cuseo, Dean of Admission, 1600 Campus Road, Los
Angeles, CA 90041
Telephone: 323-259-2700 or toll-free 800-825-5262
Fax: 323-341-4875
E-mail: admission@oxy.edu

Academics

Occidental awards bachelor's and master's **degrees. Challenging opportunities** include advanced placement credit, student-designed majors, an honors program, double majors, independent study, and a senior project. Special programs include internships, summer session for credit, off-campus study, study-abroad, and Army and Air Force ROTC.

The most frequently chosen **baccalaureate** fields are social sciences, history, and visual and performing arts. A complete listing of majors at Occidental appears in the Majors by College index beginning on page 471.

The **faculty** at Occidental has 157 full-time members, 93% with terminal degrees. The student-faculty ratio is 10:1.

Students of Occidental

The student body totals 1,877, of whom 1,863 are undergraduates. 56.3% are women and 43.7% are men. Students come from 47 states and territories and 22 other countries. 49% are from California. 1.8% are international students. 6.1% are African American, 1.4% American Indian, 13.4% Asian American, and 15.1% Hispanic American. 92% returned for their sophomore year.

Facilities and Resources

300 **computers/terminals** are available on campus for general student use. Students can access the following: computer help desk, free student e-mail accounts, online (class) grades, online (class) registration, online (class) schedules. Campuswide network is available. Wireless service is available via classrooms, computer centers, computer labs, dorm rooms, libraries, student centers. The 3 **libraries** have 497,161 books and 903 subscriptions.

Campus Life

There are 112 active organizations on campus, including a drama/theater group, newspaper, radio station, and choral group. 6% of eligible men and 13% of eligible women are members of national **fraternities**, national **sororities**, and local sororities.

Occidental is a member of the NCAA (Division III). **Intercollegiate sports** include baseball (m), basketball, cross-country running, football (m), golf, soccer, softball (w), swimming and diving, tennis, track and field, volleyball (w), water polo.

Campus Safety

Student safety services include lighted pathways and sidewalks; whistle alert program, late-night transport/escort service, 24-hour emergency telephone alarm devices, 24-hour patrols by trained security personnel, and electronically operated dormitory entrances.

Applying

Occidental requires an essay, SAT or ACT, a high school transcript, and 2 recommendations. It recommends SAT Subject Tests and an interview. Application deadline: 1/10; 2/1 for financial aid, with a 2/1 priority date. Early and deferred admission are possible.

Getting Accepted

5,275 applied
44% were accepted
458 enrolled (20% of accepted)
57% from top tenth of their h.s. class
3.57 average high school GPA
Mean SAT critical reading score: 640
Mean SAT math score: 650
Mean SAT writing score: 650
Mean ACT score: 29
74% had SAT critical reading scores over 600
77% had SAT math scores over 600
71% had SAT writing scores over 600
87% had ACT scores over 24
26% had SAT critical reading scores over 700
20% had SAT math scores over 700
21% had SAT writing scores over 700
51% had ACT scores over 30
6 National Merit Scholars
21 valedictorians

Graduation and After

76% graduated in 4 years
5% graduated in 5 years
1% graduated in 6 years
30% pursued further study (23% arts and sciences, 3% law, 3% medicine)
34 organizations recruited on campus

Financial Matters

$37,093 tuition and fees (2008–09)
$10,270 room and board
100% average percent of need met
$29,089 average financial aid amount received per undergraduate (2005–06 estimated)

> It is not just the rigorous core curriculum, the small class discussions, and the motivating professors that make Oglethorpe different. It is the location—near the center of one of the country's most exciting, dynamic, and international cities, Atlanta. A distinctive honors program and the dynamic Rich Foundation Urban Leadership Program are gaining much recognition from city leaders as Oglethorpe helps connect students to the rich resources of Atlanta. Internships are available in every major and are very popular among the students.

Getting Accepted
1,155 applied
48% were accepted
179 enrolled (32% of accepted)
23% from top tenth of their h.s. class
3.43 average high school GPA
Mean SAT critical reading score: 575
Mean SAT math score: 555
Mean SAT writing score: 555
Mean ACT score: 25
37% had SAT critical reading scores over 600
30% had SAT math scores over 600
33% had SAT writing scores over 600
57% had ACT scores over 24
7% had SAT critical reading scores over 700
3% had SAT math scores over 700
4% had SAT writing scores over 700
9% had ACT scores over 30

Graduation and After
49% graduated in 4 years
5% graduated in 5 years
36% pursued further study (14% business, 11% arts and sciences, 4% medicine)
70% had job offers within 6 months

Financial Matters
$25,580 tuition and fees (2008–09)
$9500 room and board
72% average percent of need met
$20,753 average financial aid amount received per undergraduate (2005–06)

OGLETHORPE UNIVERSITY
SUBURBAN SETTING ■ PRIVATE ■ INDEPENDENT ■ COED
ATLANTA, GEORGIA

Web site: www.oglethorpe.edu
Contact: Ms. Lucy Leusch, Vice President for Enrollment and Financial Aid, 4484 Peachtree Road, NE, Atlanta, GA 30319
Telephone: 404-364-8307 or toll-free 800-428-4484
Fax: 404-364-8491
E-mail: admission@oglethorpe.edu

Academics
Oglethorpe awards bachelor's and master's **degrees**. **Challenging opportunities** include advanced placement credit, accelerated degree programs, student-designed majors, an honors program, double majors, independent study, and a senior project. Special programs include cooperative education, internships, summer session for credit, off-campus study, and study-abroad.

The most frequently chosen **baccalaureate** fields are English, business/marketing, and social sciences. A complete listing of majors at Oglethorpe appears in the Majors by College index beginning on page 471.

The **faculty** at Oglethorpe has 57 full-time members, 91% with terminal degrees. The student-faculty ratio is 13:1.

Students of Oglethorpe
The student body totals 1,020, of whom 958 are undergraduates. 60.6% are women and 39.4% are men. Students come from 35 states and territories and 20 other countries. 70% are from Georgia. 4.8% are international students. 22.6% are African American, 0.5% American Indian, 4.6% Asian American, and 2.7% Hispanic American. 81% returned for their sophomore year.

Facilities and Resources
100 **computers/terminals** are available on campus for general student use. Students can access the following: campus intranet, computer help desk, free student e-mail accounts, online (class) grades, online (class) registration, online (class) schedules. Campuswide network is available. 100% of college-owned or -operated housing units are wired for high-speed Internet access. Wireless service is available via classrooms, computer centers, computer labs, learning centers, libraries, student centers. The **library** has 150,000 books and 710 subscriptions.

Campus Life
There are 52 active organizations on campus, including a drama/theater group, newspaper, radio station, and choral group. 33% of eligible men and 28% of eligible women are members of national **fraternities** and national **sororities**.

Oglethorpe is a member of the NCAA (Division III). **Intercollegiate sports** include baseball (m), basketball, cross-country running, golf, soccer, tennis, track and field, volleyball (w).

Campus Safety
Student safety services include late-night transport/escort service, 24-hour emergency telephone alarm devices, 24-hour patrols by trained security personnel, and electronically operated dormitory entrances.

Applying
Oglethorpe requires an essay, SAT or ACT, a high school transcript, and 1 recommendation, and in some cases an interview. It recommends an interview and a minimum high school GPA of 2.5. Application deadline: rolling admissions; 3/1 priority date for financial aid. Deferred admission is possible.

OHIO NORTHERN UNIVERSITY

SMALL-TOWN SETTING ■ PRIVATE ■ INDEPENDENT RELIGIOUS ■ COED
ADA, OHIO

SPONSOR

Web site: www.onu.edu
Contact: Ms. Deborah Miller, Director of Admission, 525 South Main, Ada, OH 45810-1599
Telephone: 419-772-2260 or toll-free 888-408-4ONU
Fax: 419-772-2821
E-mail: admissions-ug@onu.edu

Academics

Ohio Northern awards bachelor's, master's, and first-professional **degrees** and post-bachelor's certificates. **Challenging opportunities** include advanced placement credit, an honors program, double majors, independent study, and a senior project. Special programs include cooperative education, internships, summer session for credit, off-campus study, study-abroad, and Army and Air Force ROTC.

The most frequently chosen **baccalaureate** fields are business/marketing, engineering, and biological/life sciences. A complete listing of majors at Ohio Northern appears in the Majors by College index beginning on page 471.

The **faculty** at Ohio Northern has 228 full-time members, 79% with terminal degrees. The student-faculty ratio is 13:1.

Students of Ohio Northern

The student body totals 3,603, of whom 2,605 are undergraduates. 46.3% are women and 53.7% are men. Students come from 47 states and territories and 16 other countries. 85% are from Ohio. 1.8% are international students. 2.9% are African American, 0.3% American Indian, 1.4% Asian American, and 1.3% Hispanic American. 81% returned for their sophomore year.

Facilities and Resources

533 **computers/terminals** and 3,000 ports are available on campus for general student use. Students can access the following: campus intranet, computer help desk, free student e-mail accounts, online (class) grades, online (class) registration, online (class) schedules. Campuswide network is available. 100% of college-owned or -operated housing units are wired for high-speed Internet access. Wireless service is available via classrooms, computer centers, computer labs, dorm rooms, libraries, student centers.

Campus Life

There are 150 active organizations on campus, including a drama/theater group, newspaper, radio station, television station, choral group, and marching band. 14% of eligible men and 21% of eligible women are members of national **fraternities** and national **sororities.**

Ohio Northern is a member of the NCAA (Division III). **Intercollegiate sports** include baseball (m), basketball, cross-country running, football (m), golf, soccer, softball (w), swimming and diving, tennis, track and field, volleyball (w), wrestling (m).

Campus Safety

Student safety services include late-night transport/escort service, 24-hour emergency telephone alarm devices, 24-hour patrols by trained security personnel, and electronically operated dormitory entrances.

Applying

Ohio Northern requires SAT or ACT and a high school transcript, and in some cases 2 recommendations. It recommends an essay, an interview, and a minimum high school GPA of 2.5. Application deadline: 8/15; 4/15 priority date for financial aid. Deferred admission is possible.

Student-focused, high-quality academic programs with national recognition; smaller classes; excellent facilities; and outstanding, supportive faculty members are just a few of the features that set Ohio Northern University (ONU) apart from other universities in the Midwest. ONU offers a unique blend of the arts and sciences along with professional programs rich in cross-learning opportunities. Students come to ONU as highly motivated scholars who reflect the values of service and leadership. They are supported by individual attention from a close-knit community where they are prepared to lead successful lives in a changing world.

Getting Accepted
3,308 applied
88% were accepted
722 enrolled (25% of accepted)
38% from top tenth of their h.s. class
3.64 average high school GPA
Mean SAT critical reading score: 570
Mean SAT math score: 605
Mean SAT writing score: 570
Mean ACT score: 26
40% had SAT critical reading scores over 600
57% had SAT math scores over 600
42% had SAT writing scores over 600
72% had ACT scores over 24
6% had SAT critical reading scores over 700
13% had SAT math scores over 700
8% had SAT writing scores over 700
20% had ACT scores over 30

Graduation and After
46% graduated in 4 years
13% graduated in 5 years
4% graduated in 6 years

Financial Matters
$30,765 tuition and fees (2008–09)
$7890 room and board
85% average percent of need met
$22,130 average financial aid amount received per undergraduate (2005–06 estimated)

THE OHIO STATE UNIVERSITY
URBAN SETTING ■ PUBLIC ■ STATE-SUPPORTED ■ COED
COLUMBUS, OHIO

Getting Accepted
18,286 applied
68% were accepted
6,280 enrolled (51% of accepted)
43% from top tenth of their h.s. class
Mean SAT critical reading score: 587
Mean SAT math score: 617
Mean SAT writing score: 577
Mean ACT score: 26
46% had SAT critical reading scores over 600
62% had SAT math scores over 600
40% had SAT writing scores over 600
82% had ACT scores over 24
8% had SAT critical reading scores over 700
17% had SAT math scores over 700
8% had SAT writing scores over 700
17% had ACT scores over 30
98 National Merit Scholars
223 valedictorians

Graduation and After
35% graduated in 4 years
28% graduated in 5 years
5% graduated in 6 years

Financial Matters
$8676 resident tuition and fees (2007–08)
$21,285 nonresident tuition and fees (2007–08)
$7365 room and board
67% average percent of need met
$10,149 average financial aid amount received per undergraduate (2006–07 estimated)

Web site: www.osu.edu
Contact: Dr. Mabel G. Freeman, Assistant Vice President for Undergraduate Admissions and First Year Experience, Enarson Hall, 154 West 12th Avenue, Columbus, OH 43210
Telephone: 614-247-6281
Fax: 614-292-4818
E-mail: askabuckeye@osu.edu

Academics
Ohio State awards associate, bachelor's, master's, doctoral, and first-professional **degrees** and post-bachelor's and post-master's certificates. **Challenging opportunities** include advanced placement credit, accelerated degree programs, student-designed majors, freshman honors college, an honors program, double majors, independent study, and a senior project. Special programs include cooperative education, internships, summer session for credit, off-campus study, study-abroad, and Army, Navy, and Air Force ROTC.

The most frequently chosen **baccalaureate** fields are business/marketing, social sciences, and family and consumer sciences. A complete listing of majors at Ohio State appears in the Majors by College index beginning on page 471.

The **faculty** at Ohio State has 3,012 full-time members, 99% with terminal degrees. The student-faculty ratio is 13:1.

Students of Ohio State
The student body totals 51,818, of whom 38,479 are undergraduates. 47% are women and 53% are men. Students come from 54 states and territories and 74 other countries. 90% are from Ohio. 2.5% are international students. 7.2% are African American, 0.4% American Indian, 5.3% Asian American, and 2.6% Hispanic American. 92% returned for their sophomore year.

Facilities and Resources
800 **computers/terminals** are available on campus for general student use. Students can access the following: online (class) registration. Campuswide network is available. The 13 **libraries** have 5,881,219 books and 43,086 subscriptions.

Campus Life
There are 750 active organizations on campus, including a drama/theater group, newspaper, radio station, television station, choral group, and marching band. 6% of eligible men and 6% of eligible women are members of national **fraternities**, national **sororities**, local fraternities, and local sororities.

Ohio State is a member of the NCAA (Division I). **Intercollegiate sports** (some offering scholarships) include baseball (m), basketball, cheerleading, cross-country running, fencing, field hockey (w), football (m), golf, gymnastics, ice hockey, lacrosse, riflery, soccer, softball (w), swimming and diving, tennis, track and field, volleyball, wrestling (m).

Campus Safety
Student safety services include dorm entrances locked after 9 p.m., lighted pathways and sidewalks, self-defense education, late-night transport/escort service, 24-hour emergency telephone alarm devices, 24-hour patrols by trained security personnel, student patrols, and electronically operated dormitory entrances.

Applying
Ohio State requires an essay, SAT or ACT, and a high school transcript. Application deadline: 2/1, 2/1 for nonresidents; 3/1 priority date for financial aid.

Ohio Wesleyan University

SMALL-TOWN SETTING ■ PRIVATE ■ INDEPENDENT RELIGIOUS ■ COED
DELAWARE, OHIO

SPONSOR

Web site: www.owu.edu
Contact: Ms. Carol DelPropost, Assistant Vice President of Admission and Financial Aid, 61 South Sandusky Street, Delaware, OH 43015
Telephone: 740-368-3059 or toll-free 800-922-8953
Fax: 740-368-3314
E-mail: cjdelpro@owu.edu

Academics

Ohio Wesleyan awards bachelor's **degrees**. **Challenging opportunities** include advanced placement credit, student-designed majors, freshman honors college, an honors program, double majors, independent study, and a senior project. Special programs include internships, summer session for credit, off-campus study, study-abroad, and Army and Air Force ROTC.

The most frequently chosen **baccalaureate** fields are social sciences, business/marketing, and biological/life sciences. A complete listing of majors at Ohio Wesleyan appears in the Majors by College index beginning on page 471.

The **faculty** at Ohio Wesleyan has 136 full-time members, 98% with terminal degrees. The student-faculty ratio is 12:1.

Students of Ohio Wesleyan

The student body is made up of 1,967 undergraduates. 52.2% are women and 47.8% are men. Students come from 45 states and territories and 45 other countries. 54% are from Ohio. 8.6% are international students. 4.8% are African American, 0.4% American Indian, 1.7% Asian American, and 1.2% Hispanic American. 84% returned for their sophomore year.

Facilities and Resources

320 **computers/terminals** are available on campus for general student use. Campuswide network is available. The 4 **libraries** have 441,912 books and 1,073 subscriptions.

Campus Life

There are 85 active organizations on campus, including a drama/theater group, newspaper, radio station, and choral group. 36% of eligible men and 26% of eligible women are members of national **fraternities** and national **sororities**.

Ohio Wesleyan is a member of the NCAA (Division III). **Intercollegiate sports** include baseball (m), basketball, cross-country running, field hockey (w), football (m), golf (m), lacrosse, soccer, softball (w), swimming and diving, tennis, track and field, volleyball (w).

Campus Safety

Student safety services include late-night transport/escort service, 24-hour emergency telephone alarm devices, 24-hour patrols by trained security personnel, and electronically operated dormitory entrances.

Applying

Ohio Wesleyan requires an essay, SAT or ACT, a high school transcript, 1 recommendation, and a minimum high school GPA of 2.5. It recommends an interview and 2 recommendations. Application deadline: 3/1; 5/1 for financial aid, with a 3/1 priority date. Early and deferred admission are possible.

Ohio Wesleyan is a liberal arts university that transforms lives. Students form lifelong relationships with each other and their professors as they pursue a rigorous academic program. Internships, research, service learning, and mission trips encourage students to push personal boundaries and develop a wider perspective. Ohio Wesleyan helps students discover and follow their passions and prepares them to change the world.

Getting Accepted
3,815 applied
66% were accepted
576 enrolled (23% of accepted)
26% from top tenth of their h.s. class
3.27 average high school GPA
Mean SAT critical reading score: 609
Mean SAT math score: 616
Mean ACT score: 27
51% had SAT critical reading scores over 600
52% had SAT math scores over 600
76% had ACT scores over 24
11% had SAT critical reading scores over 700
11% had SAT math scores over 700
20% had ACT scores over 30
17 National Merit Scholars
22 valedictorians

Graduation and After
60% graduated in 4 years
7% graduated in 5 years
41% pursued further study (18% arts and sciences, 4% education, 4% law)
95% had job offers within 6 months
37 organizations recruited on campus

Financial Matters
$31,930 tuition and fees (2007–08)
$8030 room and board
82% average percent of need met
$20,854 average financial aid amount received per undergraduate (2006–07 estimated)

OKLAHOMA BAPTIST UNIVERSITY

SMALL-TOWN SETTING ■ PRIVATE ■ INDEPENDENT RELIGIOUS ■ COED
SHAWNEE, OKLAHOMA

Web site: www.okbu.edu
Contact: Mr. Trent Argo, Dean of Enrollment Management, Box 61174,
 Shawnee, OK 74804
Telephone: 405-878-2033 or toll-free 800-654-3285
Fax: 405-878-2046
E-mail: admissions@mail.okbu.edu

Getting Accepted

1,098 applied
85% were accepted
411 enrolled (44% of accepted)
45% from top tenth of their h.s. class
3.65 average high school GPA
48% had SAT critical reading scores over 600
38% had SAT math scores over 600
55% had ACT scores over 24
12% had SAT critical reading scores over 700
9% had SAT math scores over 700
10% had ACT scores over 30
6 National Merit Scholars
42 valedictorians

Graduation and After

35% graduated in 4 years
14% graduated in 5 years
4% graduated in 6 years
Graduates pursuing further study: 16% theology, 12% arts and sciences, 5% business
45 organizations recruited on campus

Financial Matters

$15,994 tuition and fees (2007–08)
$5000 room and board
72% average percent of need met
$11,873 average financial aid amount received per undergraduate (2005–06)

Academics

OBU awards bachelor's and master's **degrees**. **Challenging opportunities** include advanced placement credit, student-designed majors, an honors program, double majors, independent study, and a senior project. Special programs include cooperative education, internships, summer session for credit, off-campus study, study-abroad, and Air Force ROTC. A complete listing of majors at OBU appears in the Majors by College index beginning on page 471.

 The **faculty** at OBU has 119 members. The student-faculty ratio is 15:1.

Students of OBU

The student body totals 1,883, of whom 1,866 are undergraduates. 55.6% are women and 44.4% are men. Students come from 42 states and territories and 17 other countries. 61% are from Oklahoma. 74% returned for their sophomore year.

Facilities and Resources

170 **computers/terminals** are available on campus for general student use. Campuswide network is available. The **library** has 230,000 books and 1,800 subscriptions.

Campus Life

There are 50 active organizations on campus, including a drama/theater group, newspaper, television station, and choral group. 10% of eligible men and 10% of eligible women are members of local **fraternities** and local **sororities**.

 OBU is a member of the NAIA. **Intercollegiate sports** (some offering scholarships) include baseball (m), basketball, cross-country running, golf, softball (w), tennis, track and field.

Campus Safety

Student safety services include late-night transport/escort service, 24-hour emergency telephone alarm devices, 24-hour patrols by trained security personnel, and electronically operated dormitory entrances.

Applying

OBU requires SAT or ACT, a high school transcript, and a minimum high school GPA of 2.5, and in some cases an essay, an interview, and recommendations. Application deadline: rolling admissions; 3/1 priority date for financial aid. Early and deferred admission are possible.

Oklahoma City University

Urban setting ■ Private ■ Independent Religious ■ Coed
Oklahoma City, Oklahoma

Web site: www.okcu.edu
Contact: Ms. Michelle Lockhart, Associate Director, Undergraduate Admissions, 2501 North Blackwelder, Oklahoma City, OK 73106
Telephone: 405-208-5340 or toll-free 800-633-7242
Fax: 405-208-5916
E-mail: mlockhart@okcu.edu

Academics

OCU awards bachelor's, master's, and first-professional **degrees**. **Challenging opportunities** include advanced placement credit, accelerated degree programs, student-designed majors, an honors program, double majors, independent study, and a senior project. Special programs include cooperative education, internships, summer session for credit, off-campus study, study-abroad, and Army and Air Force ROTC.

The most frequently chosen **baccalaureate** fields are liberal arts/general studies, visual and performing arts, and health professions and related sciences. A complete listing of majors at OCU appears in the Majors by College index beginning on page 471.

The **faculty** at OCU has 189 full-time members, 78% with terminal degrees. The student-faculty ratio is 11:1.

Students of OCU

The student body totals 3,865, of whom 2,146 are undergraduates. 62% are women and 38% are men. Students come from 47 states and territories and 58 other countries. 61% are from Oklahoma. 17.2% are international students. 7.9% are African American, 4.8% American Indian, 3.5% Asian American, and 5.4% Hispanic American. 81% returned for their sophomore year.

Facilities and Resources

257 **computers/terminals** are available on campus for general student use. Students can access the following: campus intranet, computer help desk, free student e-mail accounts, online (class) grades, online (class) registration, online (class) schedules. Campuswide network is available. 100% of college-owned or -operated housing units are wired for high-speed Internet access. Wireless service is available via entire campus. The 2 **libraries** have 520,953 books and 14,000 subscriptions.

Campus Life

There are 42 active organizations on campus, including a drama/theater group, newspaper, television station, and choral group. 15% of eligible men and 17% of eligible women are members of national **fraternities** and national **sororities**.

OCU is a member of the NAIA. **Intercollegiate sports** (some offering scholarships) include baseball (m), basketball, cheerleading, crew, golf, soccer, softball (w), wrestling.

Campus Safety

Student safety services include Operation ID, late-night transport/escort service, 24-hour emergency telephone alarm devices, 24-hour patrols by trained security personnel, and student patrols.

Applying

OCU requires an essay, SAT or ACT, a high school transcript, and a minimum high school GPA of 3.0, and in some cases an interview and audition for music and dance programs. It recommends an interview. Application deadline: 8/20; 3/1 priority date for financial aid. Deferred admission is possible.

Getting Accepted

998 applied
81% were accepted
400 enrolled (50% of accepted)
30% from top tenth of their h.s. class
3.52 average high school GPA
Mean SAT critical reading score: 575
Mean SAT math score: 567
Mean ACT score: 25
38% had SAT critical reading scores over 600
39% had SAT math scores over 600
62% had ACT scores over 24
13% had SAT critical reading scores over 700
6% had SAT math scores over 700
9% had ACT scores over 30
10 National Merit Scholars
17 valedictorians

Graduation and After

33% graduated in 4 years
12% graduated in 5 years
2% graduated in 6 years
16 organizations recruited on campus

Financial Matters

$21,000 tuition and fees (2007–08)
$8400 room and board
79% average percent of need met
$11,702 average financial aid amount received per undergraduate

OKLAHOMA STATE UNIVERSITY

SMALL-TOWN SETTING ■ PUBLIC ■ STATE-SUPPORTED ■ COED
STILLWATER, OKLAHOMA

Web site: osu.okstate.edu
Contact: 219 Student Union, Stillwater, OK 74078
Telephone: 405-744-5358 or toll-free 800-233-5019 Ext. 1 (in-state),
   800-852-1255 (out-of-state)
Fax: 405-744-7092
E-mail: admissions@okstate.edu

Getting Accepted

6,415 applied
88% were accepted
3,209 enrolled (57% of accepted)
27% from top tenth of their h.s. class
3.54 average high school GPA
Mean SAT critical reading score: 551
Mean SAT math score: 568
Mean ACT score: 25
31% had SAT critical reading scores over 600
38% had SAT math scores over 600
60% had ACT scores over 24
6% had SAT critical reading scores over 700
8% had SAT math scores over 700
12% had ACT scores over 30
28 National Merit Scholars
405 valedictorians

Graduation and After

27% graduated in 4 years
25% graduated in 5 years
6% graduated in 6 years

Financial Matters

$5491 resident tuition and fees (2007–08)
$14,916 nonresident tuition and fees (2007–08)
$6267 room and board
73% average percent of need met
$9296 average financial aid amount received per undergraduate (2006–07 estimated)

Academics

Oklahoma State awards bachelor's, master's, doctoral, and first-professional **degrees** and post-bachelor's and post-master's certificates. **Challenging opportunities** include advanced placement credit, accelerated degree programs, student-designed majors, freshman honors college, an honors program, double majors, independent study, and a senior project. Special programs include internships, summer session for credit, off-campus study, study-abroad, and Army and Air Force ROTC.

The most frequently chosen **baccalaureate** fields are business/marketing, agriculture, and education. A complete listing of majors at Oklahoma State appears in the Majors by College index beginning on page 471.

The **faculty** at Oklahoma State has 985 full-time members, 91% with terminal degrees. The student-faculty ratio is 19:1.

Students of Oklahoma State

The student body totals 23,005, of whom 18,368 are undergraduates. 48.9% are women and 51.1% are men. Students come from 49 states and territories and 81 other countries. 84% are from Oklahoma. 3% are international students. 4.2% are African American, 9.6% American Indian, 1.8% Asian American, and 2.4% Hispanic American. 80% returned for their sophomore year.

Facilities and Resources

Students can access the following: campus intranet, computer help desk, free student e-mail accounts, online (class) grades, online (class) registration, online (class) schedules. Campuswide network is available. 100% of college-owned or -operated housing units are wired for high-speed Internet access. Wireless service is available via computer centers, libraries, student centers. The 4 **libraries** have 2,611,072 books and 38,745 subscriptions.

Campus Life

There are 360 active organizations on campus, including a drama/theater group, newspaper, radio station, television station, choral group, and marching band. 15% of eligible men and 17% of eligible women are members of national **fraternities** and national **sororities**.

Oklahoma State is a member of the NCAA (Division I). **Intercollegiate sports** (some offering scholarships) include baseball (m), basketball, cross-country running, equestrian sports (w), football (m), golf, soccer (w), softball (w), tennis, track and field, wrestling (m).

Campus Safety

Student safety services include 24-hour emergency telephone alarm devices, 24-hour patrols by trained security personnel, student patrols, and electronically operated dormitory entrances.

Applying

Oklahoma State requires SAT or ACT, a high school transcript, class rank, and a minimum high school GPA of 3.0, and in some cases an interview. Application deadline: rolling admissions, rolling admissions for nonresidents.

Pacific Lutheran University

Suburban setting ■ Private ■ Independent Religious ■ Coed
Tacoma, Washington

Web site: www.plu.edu
Contact: Dr. Laura Majovski, Vice President for Admissions and Student Life, Tacoma, WA 98447
Telephone: 253-535-7151 or toll-free 800-274-6758
Fax: 253-536-5136
E-mail: admission@plu.edu

Academics

Pacific Lutheran awards bachelor's and master's **degrees** and post-bachelor's and post-master's certificates. **Challenging opportunities** include advanced placement credit, student-designed majors, double majors, independent study, and a senior project. Special programs include cooperative education, internships, summer session for credit, study-abroad, and Army ROTC.

The most frequently chosen **baccalaureate** fields are business/marketing, social sciences, and health professions and related sciences. A complete listing of majors at Pacific Lutheran appears in the Majors by College index beginning on page 471.

The **faculty** at Pacific Lutheran has 240 full-time members, 83% with terminal degrees. The student-faculty ratio is 14:1.

Students of Pacific Lutheran

The student body totals 3,661, of whom 3,349 are undergraduates. 63.2% are women and 36.8% are men. Students come from 40 states and territories and 21 other countries. 79% are from Washington. 5.8% are international students. 2.2% are African American, 1.3% American Indian, 6.6% Asian American, and 2.1% Hispanic American. 84% returned for their sophomore year.

Facilities and Resources

390 **computers/terminals** and 1,200 ports are available on campus for general student use. Students can access the following: campus intranet, computer help desk, free student e-mail accounts, online (class) grades, online (class) registration, online (class) schedules. Campuswide network is available. 100% of college-owned or -operated housing units are wired for high-speed Internet access. The **library** has 350,750 books and 3,433 subscriptions.

Campus Life

There are 64 active organizations on campus, including a drama/theater group, newspaper, radio station, television station, and choral group. No national or local **fraternities** or **sororities**.

Pacific Lutheran is a member of the NCAA (Division III). **Intercollegiate sports** include baseball (m), basketball, cheerleading, crew, cross-country running, football (m), golf, soccer, softball (w), swimming and diving, tennis, track and field, volleyball (w).

Campus Safety

Student safety services include late-night transport/escort service, 24-hour emergency telephone alarm devices, 24-hour patrols by trained security personnel, and student patrols.

Applying

Pacific Lutheran requires an essay, SAT or ACT, a high school transcript, and 1 recommendation, and in some cases an interview. It recommends a minimum high school GPA of 2.5. Application deadline: rolling admissions; 3/1 priority date for financial aid. Early and deferred admission are possible.

Getting Accepted
2,236 applied
76% were accepted
715 enrolled (42% of accepted)
36% from top tenth of their h.s. class
3.61 average high school GPA
Mean SAT critical reading score: 558
Mean SAT math score: 548
Mean SAT writing score: 539
Mean ACT score: 25
36% had SAT critical reading scores over 600
30% had SAT math scores over 600
26% had SAT writing scores over 600
62% had ACT scores over 24
6% had SAT critical reading scores over 700
4% had SAT math scores over 700
4% had SAT writing scores over 700
16% had ACT scores over 30

Graduation and After
50% graduated in 4 years
14% graduated in 5 years
2% graduated in 6 years
75% had job offers within 6 months
80 organizations recruited on campus

Financial Matters
$25,088 tuition and fees (2007–08)
$7712 room and board
89% average percent of need met
$23,185 average financial aid amount received per undergraduate (2006–07 estimated)

PACIFIC UNIVERSITY

SMALL-TOWN SETTING ■ PRIVATE ■ INDEPENDENT ■ COED
FOREST GROVE, OREGON

Web site: www.pacificu.edu
Contact: Ms. Karen Dunston, Director of Undergraduate Admission, 2043
College Way, Forest Grove, OR 97116-1797
Telephone: 503-352-2218 or toll-free 877-722-8648
Fax: 503-352-2975
E-mail: admissions@pacificu.edu

Getting Accepted
1,258 applied
83% were accepted
372 enrolled (35% of accepted)
34% from top tenth of their h.s. class
3.61 average high school GPA
Mean SAT critical reading score: 550
Mean SAT math score: 560
Mean ACT score: 24
28% had SAT critical reading scores over 600
27% had SAT math scores over 600
53% had ACT scores over 24
4% had SAT critical reading scores over 700
4% had SAT math scores over 700
7% had ACT scores over 30

Graduation and After
53% graduated in 4 years
9% graduated in 5 years
35% pursued further study (10% arts and
sciences, 10% education, 8% medicine)
50% had job offers within 6 months
300 organizations recruited on campus

Financial Matters
$26,670 tuition and fees (2007–08)
$7170 room and board
86% average percent of need met
$17,492 average financial aid amount received
per undergraduate (2005–06 estimated)

Academics

Pacific awards bachelor's, master's, doctoral, and first-professional **degrees. Challenging opportunities** include advanced placement credit, double majors, and independent study. Special programs include cooperative education, internships, summer session for credit, off-campus study, study-abroad, and Army and Air Force ROTC.

The most frequently chosen **baccalaureate** fields are social sciences, parks and recreation, and business/marketing. A complete listing of majors at Pacific appears in the Majors by College index beginning on page 471.

The **faculty** at Pacific has 92 full-time members, 89% with terminal degrees. The student-faculty ratio is 12:1.

Students of Pacific

The student body totals 2,976, of whom 1,452 are undergraduates. 62.7% are women and 37.3% are men. Students come from 36 states and territories and 11 other countries. 48% are from Oregon. 0.4% are international students. 1.2% are African American, 1.2% American Indian, 23.9% Asian American, and 4.5% Hispanic American. 80% returned for their sophomore year.

Facilities and Resources

315 **computers/terminals** and 5,900 ports are available on campus for general student use. Students can access the following: campus intranet, computer help desk, free student e-mail accounts, online (class) grades, online (class) schedules, Web space, printing, student and academic information, WebCT, computer peripherals. Campuswide network is available. 100% of college-owned or -operated housing units are wired for high-speed Internet access. Wireless service is available via entire campus. The **library** has 206,198 books and 20,908 subscriptions.

Campus Life

There are 59 active organizations on campus, including a drama/theater group, newspaper, radio station, and choral group. 11% of eligible men and 10% of eligible women are members of local **fraternities** and local **sororities**.

Pacific is a member of the NCAA (Division III) and NAIA. **Intercollegiate sports** include baseball (m), basketball, cross-country running, golf, lacrosse (w), soccer, softball (w), swimming and diving, tennis, track and field, volleyball (w), wrestling.

Campus Safety

Student safety services include late-night transport/escort service, 24-hour emergency telephone alarm devices, 24-hour patrols by trained security personnel, and electronically operated dormitory entrances.

Applying

Pacific requires an essay, SAT or ACT, a high school transcript, 1 recommendation, and a minimum high school GPA of 3.0. It recommends an interview. Application deadline: 8/15; 2/15 priority date for financial aid. Deferred admission is possible.

PEABODY CONSERVATORY OF MUSIC OF THE JOHNS HOPKINS UNIVERSITY

URBAN SETTING ■ PRIVATE ■ INDEPENDENT ■ COED
BALTIMORE, MARYLAND

Web site: www.peabody.jhu.edu
Contact: Mr. David Lane, Director of Admissions, Peabody Conservatory Admissions Office, One East Mount Vernon Place, Baltimore, MD 21202-2397
Telephone: 410-659-8110 or toll-free 800-368-2521 (out-of-state)

Academics

Peabody Conservatory awards bachelor's, master's, and doctoral **degrees** and post-bachelor's certificates. **Challenging opportunities** include advanced placement credit, accelerated degree programs, an honors program, double majors, and independent study. Special programs include internships and off-campus study.

The most frequently chosen **baccalaureate** fields are visual and performing arts and education. A complete listing of majors at Peabody Conservatory appears in the Majors by College index beginning on page 471.

The **faculty** at Peabody Conservatory has 165 members, 23% with terminal degrees. The student-faculty ratio is 4:1.

Students of Peabody Conservatory

The student body totals 675, of whom 335 are undergraduates. 47.8% are women and 52.2% are men. Students come from 36 states and territories and 15 other countries. 33% are from Maryland. 19.4% are international students. 5.1% are African American, 8.1% Asian American, and 4.5% Hispanic American. 91% returned for their sophomore year.

Facilities and Resources

40 **computers/terminals** are available on campus for general student use. Students can access the following: word processing, music processing. Campuswide network is available. The **library** has 92,000 books and 225 subscriptions.

Campus Life

There are 84 active organizations on campus, including a choral group. No national or local **fraternities** or **sororities**.

This institution has no intercollegiate sports.

Campus Safety

Student safety services include late-night transport/escort service, 24-hour emergency telephone alarm devices, 24-hour patrols by trained security personnel, and electronically operated dormitory entrances.

Applying

Peabody Conservatory requires an essay, a high school transcript, an interview, 3 recommendations, and audition, and in some cases SAT or ACT. It recommends a minimum high school GPA of 3.0. Application deadline: 12/1; 3/1 priority date for financial aid.

Getting Accepted

750 applied
55% were accepted
99 enrolled (24% of accepted)
57% had SAT math scores over 600
53% had SAT writing scores over 600
16% had SAT math scores over 700
11% had SAT writing scores over 700

Graduation and After

49% graduated in 4 years
8% graduated in 5 years
4% graduated in 6 years
20% had job offers within 6 months
13 organizations recruited on campus

Financial Matters

$31,760 tuition and fees (2007–08)
$9900 room and board
34% average percent of need met
$8999 average financial aid amount received per undergraduate (2005–06)

PENN STATE UNIVERSITY PARK

SMALL-TOWN SETTING ■ PUBLIC ■ STATE-RELATED ■ COED
UNIVERSITY PARK, PENNSYLVANIA

Web site: www.psu.edu
Contact: Anne L. Rohrbach, Director for Undergraduate Admissions, 201 Shields Building, Box 3000, University Park, PA 16804-3000
Telephone: 814-865-4700
Fax: 814-863-7590
E-mail: admissions@psu.edu

Getting Accepted
39,551 applied
51% were accepted
6,495 enrolled (32% of accepted)
45% from top tenth of their h.s. class
3.58 average high school GPA
Mean SAT critical reading score: 578
Mean SAT math score: 612
43% had SAT critical reading scores over 600
60% had SAT math scores over 600
7% had SAT critical reading scores over 700
14% had SAT math scores over 700

Graduation and After
56% graduated in 4 years
27% graduated in 5 years
3% graduated in 6 years
22% pursued further study
84% had job offers within 6 months
798 organizations recruited on campus

Financial Matters
$12,844 resident tuition and fees (2007–08)
$23,712 nonresident tuition and fees (2007–08)
$7180 room and board
70% average percent of need met
$15,295 average financial aid amount received per undergraduate (2005–06)

Academics

Penn State awards associate, bachelor's, master's, doctoral, and first-professional **degrees** and post-bachelor's certificates. **Challenging opportunities** include advanced placement credit, accelerated degree programs, student-designed majors, freshman honors college, an honors program, double majors, independent study, and a senior project. Special programs include cooperative education, internships, summer session for credit, off-campus study, study-abroad, and Army, Navy, and Air Force ROTC.

The most frequently chosen **baccalaureate** fields are business/marketing, engineering, and communications/journalism. A complete listing of majors at Penn State appears in the Majors by College index beginning on page 471.

The **faculty** at Penn State has 2,344 full-time members, 77% with terminal degrees. The student-faculty ratio is 17:1.

Students of Penn State

The student body totals 43,252, of whom 36,815 are undergraduates. 44.9% are women and 55.1% are men. Students come from 52 states and territories and 80 other countries. 76% are from Pennsylvania. 2.4% are international students. 4.1% are African American, 0.1% American Indian, 5.4% Asian American, and 3.5% Hispanic American. 94% returned for their sophomore year.

Facilities and Resources

3,800 **computers/terminals** and 1,000 ports are available on campus for general student use. Students can access the following: campus intranet, computer help desk, free student e-mail accounts, online (class) grades, online (class) registration, online (class) schedules. Campuswide network is available. The 15 **libraries** have 5,031,196 books and 68,445 subscriptions.

Campus Life

There are 400 active organizations on campus, including a drama/theater group, newspaper, radio station, television station, choral group, and marching band. 12% of eligible men and 11% of eligible women are members of national **fraternities** and national **sororities**.

Penn State is a member of the NCAA (Division I). **Intercollegiate sports** (some offering scholarships) include baseball (m), basketball, cheerleading, cross-country running, fencing, field hockey (w), football (m), golf, gymnastics, lacrosse, soccer, softball (w), swimming and diving, tennis, track and field, volleyball, wrestling (m).

Campus Safety

Student safety services include late-night transport/escort service, 24-hour emergency telephone alarm devices, 24-hour patrols by trained security personnel, student patrols, and electronically operated dormitory entrances.

Applying

Penn State requires SAT or ACT and a high school transcript, and in some cases an interview and recommendations. It recommends an essay. Application deadline: rolling admissions; 2/15 priority date for financial aid. Early and deferred admission are possible.

PEPPERDINE UNIVERSITY

SMALL-TOWN SETTING ■ PRIVATE ■ INDEPENDENT RELIGIOUS ■ COED
MALIBU, CALIFORNIA

Web site: www.pepperdine.edu
Contact: Mr. Paul A. Long, Dean of Admission and Enrollment Management,
24255 Pacific Coast Highway, Malibu, CA 90263-4392
Telephone: 310-506-4392
Fax: 310-506-4861
E-mail: admission-seaver@pepperdine.edu

Academics

Pepperdine awards bachelor's, master's, doctoral, and first-professional **degrees** and
post-master's certificates. **Challenging opportunities** include advanced placement
credit, student-designed majors, an honors program, double majors, independent study,
and a senior project. Special programs include internships, summer session for credit,
study-abroad, and Army and Air Force ROTC.

The most frequently chosen **baccalaureate** fields are business/marketing, com-
munications/journalism, and social sciences. A complete listing of majors at Pepperdine
appears in the Majors by College index beginning on page 471.

The **faculty** at Pepperdine has 388 full-time members, 93% with terminal degrees.
The student-faculty ratio is 13:1.

Students of Pepperdine

The student body totals 7,582, of whom 3,398 are undergraduates. 55.4% are women
and 44.6% are men. Students come from 50 states and territories and 64 other countries.
50% are from California. 6.5% are international students. 7.4% are African American,
1.4% American Indian, 10.4% Asian American, and 10.4% Hispanic American. 91%
returned for their sophomore year.

Facilities and Resources

292 **computers/terminals** are available on campus for general student use. Students can
access the following: computer help desk, online (class) grades, online (class) registration.
Campuswide network is available. 100% of college-owned or -operated housing units are
wired for high-speed Internet access. Wireless service is available via entire campus. The
3 **libraries** have 1,470,192 books and 103,654 subscriptions.

Campus Life

There are 68 active organizations on campus, including a drama/theater group,
newspaper, radio station, television station, and choral group. 18% of eligible men and
33% of eligible women are members of national **fraternities** and national **sororities**.

Pepperdine is a member of the NCAA (Division I). **Intercollegiate sports** (some
offering scholarships) include baseball (m), basketball, cheerleading, cross-country running, golf, soccer (w), swimming and diving (w), tennis, volleyball, water polo (m).

Campus Safety

Student safety services include front gate security, 24-hour security in residence halls,
controlled access, crime prevention programs, late-night transport/escort service, 24-
hour emergency telephone alarm devices, 24-hour patrols by trained security personnel,
and student patrols.

Applying

Pepperdine requires an essay, SAT or ACT, a high school transcript, and 2 recommendations. It recommends an interview. Application deadline: 1/15; 2/15 for financial aid,
with a 2/15 priority date.

Getting Accepted

6,661 applied
35% were accepted
752 enrolled (32% of accepted)
46% from top tenth of their h.s. class
3.67 average high school GPA
Mean SAT critical reading score: 601
Mean SAT math score: 617
Mean ACT score: 26
58% had SAT critical reading scores over 600
61% had SAT math scores over 600
58% had SAT writing scores over 600
78% had ACT scores over 24
15% had SAT critical reading scores over 700
19% had SAT math scores over 700
14% had SAT writing scores over 700
22% had ACT scores over 30

Graduation and After

73% graduated in 4 years
6% graduated in 5 years
63% pursued further study
40% had job offers within 6 months
65 organizations recruited on campus

Financial Matters

$34,700 tuition and fees (2007–08)
$9930 room and board
89% average percent of need met
$30,991 average financial aid amount received
per undergraduate (2005–06 estimated)

PITZER COLLEGE
SUBURBAN SETTING ■ PRIVATE ■ INDEPENDENT ■ COED
CLAREMONT, CALIFORNIA

Web site: www.pitzer.edu
Contact: Angel Perez, Director of Admission, 1050 North Mills Avenue, Claremont, CA 91711-6101
Telephone: 909-621-8129 or toll-free 800-748-9371
Fax: 909-621-8770
E-mail: admission@pitzer.edu

Pitzer College, a liberal arts and sciences college, offers students membership in a closely knit academic community and access to the resources of a midsized university through its partnership with The Claremont Colleges. Pitzer's distinctive curriculum encourages students to discover the relationship among different academic subjects (interdisciplinary learning), gives students a chance to see issues and events from different cultural perspectives (intercultural understanding), and shows students how to take responsibility for making the world a better place (social responsibility). Pitzer College believes that students should have the freedom and responsibility for selecting what courses to take. Therefore, required general education courses are few.

Getting Accepted
3,748 applied
26% were accepted
243 enrolled (25% of accepted)
32% from top tenth of their h.s. class
3.72 average high school GPA

Graduation and After
65% graduated in 4 years
5% graduated in 5 years
2% graduated in 6 years
24% pursued further study (16% law, 6% business)

Financial Matters
$35,912 tuition and fees (2007–08)
$10,212 room and board
100% average percent of need met
$30,802 average financial aid amount received per undergraduate (2006–07 estimated)

Academics
Pitzer awards bachelor's **degrees**. **Challenging opportunities** include advanced placement credit, student-designed majors, an honors program, double majors, independent study, and a senior project. Special programs include cooperative education, internships, summer session for credit, off-campus study, study-abroad, and Army and Air Force ROTC.

The most frequently chosen **baccalaureate** fields are social sciences, interdisciplinary studies, and psychology. A complete listing of majors at Pitzer appears in the Majors by College index beginning on page 471.

The **faculty** at Pitzer has 64 full-time members, 100% with terminal degrees. The student-faculty ratio is 12:1.

Students of Pitzer
The student body is made up of 999 undergraduates. 58.8% are women and 41.2% are men. Students come from 42 states and territories and 13 other countries. 59% are from California. 3.2% are international students. 6.1% are African American, 0.3% American Indian, 9.7% Asian American, and 13.8% Hispanic American. 94% returned for their sophomore year.

Facilities and Resources
100 **computers/terminals** are available on campus for general student use. Students can access the following: campus intranet, computer help desk, free student e-mail accounts. Campuswide network is available. 100% of college-owned or -operated housing units are wired for high-speed Internet access. Wireless service is available via entire campus. The 4 **libraries** have 2,500,000 books and 16,000 subscriptions.

Campus Life
There are 75 active organizations on campus, including a drama/theater group, radio station, and choral group. No national or local **fraternities** or **sororities**.

Pitzer is a member of the NCAA (Division III). **Intercollegiate sports** include baseball (m), basketball, cross-country running, football (m), golf (m), lacrosse (w), soccer, softball (w), swimming and diving, tennis, track and field, volleyball (w), water polo.

Campus Safety
Student safety services include late-night transport/escort service, 24-hour emergency telephone alarm devices, 24-hour patrols by trained security personnel, and electronically operated dormitory entrances.

Applying
Pitzer requires an essay, a high school transcript, 3 recommendations, and a minimum high school GPA of 2.0, and in some cases SAT or ACT. It recommends an interview. Application deadline: 1/1; 2/1 for financial aid. Deferred admission is possible.

POINT LOMA NAZARENE UNIVERSITY

SUBURBAN SETTING ■ PRIVATE ■ INDEPENDENT RELIGIOUS ■ COED
SAN DIEGO, CALIFORNIA

Web site: www.pointloma.edu
Contact: Mr. Chip Killingsworth, Director of Admissions, 3900 Lomaland
   Drive, San Diego, CA 92106
Telephone: 619-849-2273 or toll-free 800-733-7770
Fax: 619-849-2601
E-mail: admissions@pointloma.edu

Academics

Point Loma awards bachelor's and master's **degrees**. **Challenging opportunities** include advanced placement credit, an honors program, double majors, independent study, and a senior project. Special programs include internships, summer session for credit, off-campus study, study-abroad, and Army, Navy, and Air Force ROTC.

   The most frequently chosen **baccalaureate** fields are business/marketing, psychology, and health professions and related sciences. A complete listing of majors at Point Loma appears in the Majors by College index beginning on page 471.

   The **faculty** at Point Loma has 177 full-time members, 73% with terminal degrees. The student-faculty ratio is 16:1.

Students of Point Loma

The student body totals 3,404, of whom 2,346 are undergraduates. 61.3% are women and 38.7% are men. Students come from 37 states and territories and 10 other countries. 79% are from California. 0.5% are international students. 2.2% are African American, 0.9% American Indian, 5.7% Asian American, and 11% Hispanic American. 87% returned for their sophomore year.

Facilities and Resources

196 **computers/terminals** are available on campus for general student use. Students can access the following: free student e-mail accounts, online (class) grades, online (class) registration, online (class) schedules. Campuswide network is available. 100% of college-owned or -operated housing units are wired for high-speed Internet access. Wireless service is available via entire campus. The **library** has 152,377 books and 25,505 subscriptions.

Campus Life

There are 30 active organizations on campus, including a drama/theater group, newspaper, radio station, and choral group. Point Loma has national **sororities**, local **fraternities**, and local sororities.

   Point Loma is a member of the NAIA. **Intercollegiate sports** (some offering scholarships) include baseball (m), basketball, cross-country running, golf (m), soccer, softball (w), tennis, track and field, volleyball (w).

Campus Safety

Student safety services include late-night transport/escort service, 24-hour patrols by trained security personnel, and student patrols.

Applying

Point Loma requires an essay, SAT or ACT, a high school transcript, 2 recommendations, and a minimum high school GPA of 2.8, and in some cases an interview. It recommends SAT. Application deadline: 3/1; 3/2 priority date for financial aid.

Getting Accepted

1,757 applied
73% were accepted
531 enrolled (41% of accepted)
31% from top tenth of their h.s. class
3.72 average high school GPA
Mean SAT critical reading score: 563
Mean SAT math score: 562
Mean ACT score: 24
37% had SAT critical reading scores over 600
37% had SAT math scores over 600
54% had ACT scores over 24
6% had SAT critical reading scores over 700
4% had SAT math scores over 700
7% had ACT scores over 30
20 valedictorians

Graduation and After

60% graduated in 4 years
9% graduated in 5 years
2% graduated in 6 years
197 organizations recruited on campus

Financial Matters

$24,820 tuition and fees (2008–09)
$8170 room and board
71% average percent of need met
$16,100 average financial aid amount received
   per undergraduate (2006–07 estimated)

POLYTECHNIC UNIVERSITY, BROOKLYN CAMPUS

URBAN SETTING ■ PRIVATE ■ INDEPENDENT ■ COED
BROOKLYN, NEW YORK

Web site: www.poly.edu
Contact: Joy Colelli, Dean of Admissions and New Students, Six Metrotech Center, Brooklyn, NY 11201-2990
Telephone: 718-260-5917 or toll-free 800-POLYTECH
Fax: 718-260-3446
E-mail: uadmit@poly.edu

Getting Accepted

1,482 applied
22% were accepted
331 enrolled (100% of accepted)
31% from top tenth of their h.s. class
3.3 average high school GPA
Mean SAT critical reading score: 545
Mean SAT math score: 630
26% had SAT critical reading scores over 600
58% had SAT math scores over 600
3% had SAT critical reading scores over 700
20% had SAT math scores over 700
25 National Merit Scholars
2 valedictorians

Graduation and After

28% graduated in 4 years
15% graduated in 5 years
4% graduated in 6 years
22% pursued further study
82% had job offers within 6 months
115 organizations recruited on campus

Financial Matters

$30,972 tuition and fees (2007–08)
$8500 room and board
91% average percent of need met
$22,221 average financial aid amount received per undergraduate (2006–07 estimated)

Academics

Polytechnic awards bachelor's, master's, and doctoral **degrees** and post-bachelor's certificates. **Challenging opportunities** include advanced placement credit, accelerated degree programs, an honors program, double majors, and a senior project. Special programs include cooperative education, internships, summer session for credit, and Army and Air Force ROTC.

The most frequently chosen **baccalaureate** fields are engineering, computer and information sciences, and business/marketing. A complete listing of majors at Polytechnic appears in the Majors by College index beginning on page 471.

The **faculty** at Polytechnic has 140 full-time members, 89% with terminal degrees. The student-faculty ratio is 14:1.

Students of Polytechnic

The student body totals 3,317, of whom 1,495 are undergraduates. 19.2% are women and 80.8% are men. Students come from 14 states and territories and 43 other countries. 93% are from New York. 13.1% are international students. 11.7% are African American, 0.2% American Indian, 29.7% Asian American, and 11.7% Hispanic American. 84% returned for their sophomore year.

Facilities and Resources

1,334 **computers/terminals** are available on campus for general student use. Students can access the following: campus intranet, computer help desk, free student e-mail accounts, online (class) grades, online (class) registration, online (class) schedules. Campuswide network is available. Wireless service is available via entire campus. The 2 **libraries** have 150,000 books and 1,621 subscriptions.

Campus Life

There are 39 active organizations on campus, including a newspaper. 6% of eligible men and 4% of eligible women are members of national **fraternities**, national **sororities**, local fraternities, local sororities, and a coed fraternity.

Polytechnic is a member of the NCAA (Division III). **Intercollegiate sports** include baseball (m), basketball, cross-country running, soccer, softball (w), tennis, track and field, volleyball.

Campus Safety

Student safety services include 24-hour patrols by trained security personnel and electronically operated dormitory entrances.

Applying

Polytechnic requires an essay, SAT or ACT, a high school transcript, and 2 recommendations. It recommends SAT Subject Tests and an interview. Application deadline: 2/1. Deferred admission is possible.

POMONA COLLEGE

SUBURBAN SETTING ■ PRIVATE ■ INDEPENDENT ■ COED
CLAREMONT, CALIFORNIA

Web site: www.pomona.edu
Contact: Mr. Bruce Poch, Vice President and Dean of Admissions, 333 North College Way, Claremont, CA 91711
Telephone: 909-621-8134
Fax: 909-621-8952
E-mail: admissions@pomona.edu

Academics

Pomona awards bachelor's **degrees**. **Challenging opportunities** include advanced placement credit, student-designed majors, double majors, independent study, and a senior project. Special programs include internships, off-campus study, study-abroad, and Army and Air Force ROTC. A complete listing of majors at Pomona appears in the Majors by College index beginning on page 471.

The **faculty** at Pomona has 179 full-time members, 99% with terminal degrees. The student-faculty ratio is 8:1.

Students of Pomona

The student body is made up of 1,522 undergraduates. 49.7% are women and 50.3% are men. Students come from 49 states and territories and 31 other countries. 33% are from California. 2.8% are international students. 8.1% are African American, 0.3% American Indian, 14.3% Asian American, and 11.3% Hispanic American. 99% returned for their sophomore year.

Facilities and Resources

180 **computers/terminals** are available on campus for general student use. Students can access the following: computer help desk, free student e-mail accounts, online (class) grades, online (class) schedules. Campuswide network is available. 100% of college-owned or -operated housing units are wired for high-speed Internet access. Wireless service is available via classrooms, computer centers, computer labs, learning centers, libraries, student centers. The 4 **libraries** have 2,500,000 books.

Campus Life

There are 280 active organizations on campus, including a drama/theater group, newspaper, radio station, television station, and choral group. 9% of eligible men are members of local **fraternities**.

Pomona is a member of the NCAA (Division III). **Intercollegiate sports** include baseball (m), basketball, cross-country running, football (m), golf, lacrosse (w), soccer, softball (w), swimming and diving, tennis, track and field, volleyball (w), water polo.

Campus Safety

Student safety services include late-night transport/escort service, 24-hour emergency telephone alarm devices, 24-hour patrols by trained security personnel, and electronically operated dormitory entrances.

Applying

Pomona requires an essay, SAT and SAT Subject Tests or ACT, a high school transcript, and 2 recommendations. It recommends an interview, portfolio or tapes for art and performing arts programs, and a minimum high school GPA of 3.0. Application deadline: 1/2; 2/1 for financial aid. Early and deferred admission are possible.

Getting Accepted

5,907 applied
16% were accepted
375 enrolled (39% of accepted)
87% from top tenth of their h.s. class
Mean SAT critical reading score: 740
Mean SAT math score: 730
Mean SAT writing score: 720
Mean ACT score: 32
96% had SAT critical reading scores over 600
93% had SAT math scores over 600
94% had SAT writing scores over 600
96% had ACT scores over 24
74% had SAT critical reading scores over 700
71% had SAT math scores over 700
65% had SAT writing scores over 700
73% had ACT scores over 30

Graduation and After

86% graduated in 4 years
7% graduated in 5 years
1% graduated in 6 years
33% pursued further study (12% arts and sciences, 9% law, 9% medicine)
150 organizations recruited on campus

Financial Matters

$33,932 tuition and fees (2007–08)
$11,748 room and board
100% average percent of need met
$32,100 average financial aid amount received per undergraduate (2006–07 estimated)

PRESBYTERIAN COLLEGE

SMALL-TOWN SETTING ■ PRIVATE ■ INDEPENDENT RELIGIOUS ■ COED
CLINTON, SOUTH CAROLINA

Web site: www.presby.edu
Contact: Mrs. Leni Patterson, Dean of Admissions and Financial Aid, South
   Broad Street, Clinto, SC 29325
Telephone: 864-833-8229 or toll-free 800-476-7272
Fax: 864-833-8481
E-mail: lpatters@presby.edu

Presbyterian College—with 6 CASE professors of the year—provides an environment that nurtures the best and brightest. Students respect and live by a strong Honor Code, and over half volunteer for community service. Students may also participate in a comprehensive Honors Program or study abroad in locations around the world. Internships and student-faculty research prepare students for graduate school and the job market. A scholarship program for outstanding students is supported by one of the largest per-student endowments in the region.

Getting Accepted
1,138 applied
71% were accepted
290 enrolled (36% of accepted)
32% from top tenth of their h.s. class
3.39 average high school GPA
Mean SAT critical reading score: 560
Mean SAT math score: 580
Mean ACT score: 24
31% had SAT critical reading scores over 600
41% had SAT math scores over 600
63% had ACT scores over 24
5% had SAT critical reading scores over 700
4% had SAT math scores over 700
7% had ACT scores over 30
6 valedictorians

Graduation and After
58% graduated in 4 years
13% graduated in 6 years
25% pursued further study
50% had job offers within 6 months
55 organizations recruited on campus

Financial Matters
$27,902 tuition and fees (2008–09)
$8064 room and board
83% average percent of need met
$19,217 average financial aid amount received
  per undergraduate

Academics

Presbyterian awards bachelor's **degrees**. **Challenging opportunities** include advanced placement credit, accelerated degree programs, an honors program, double majors, independent study, and a senior project. Special programs include internships, summer session for credit, off-campus study, study-abroad, and Army ROTC.

The most frequently chosen **baccalaureate** fields are business/marketing, social sciences, and history. A complete listing of majors at Presbyterian appears in the Majors by College index beginning on page 471.

The **faculty** at Presbyterian has 85 full-time members, 93% with terminal degrees. The student-faculty ratio is 12:1.

Students of Presbyterian

The student body is made up of 1,181 undergraduates. 50.8% are women and 49.2% are men. Students come from 26 states and territories and 10 other countries. 65% are from South Carolina. 7% are African American, 0.3% American Indian, 0.9% Asian American, and 1.1% Hispanic American. 83% returned for their sophomore year.

Facilities and Resources

130 **computers/terminals** and 275 ports are available on campus for general student use. Students can access the following: free student e-mail accounts, online (class) grades, online (class) registration, online (class) schedules. Campuswide network is available. 100% of college-owned or -operated housing units are wired for high-speed Internet access. Wireless service is available via classrooms, computer centers, computer labs, dorm rooms, libraries. The **library** has 135,597 books and 3,113 subscriptions.

Campus Life

There are 60 active organizations on campus, including a drama/theater group, newspaper, radio station, and choral group. 70% of eligible men and 70% of eligible women are members of national **fraternities** and national **sororities**.

Presbyterian is a member of the NCAA (Division I). **Intercollegiate sports** (some offering scholarships) include baseball (m), basketball, cheerleading, cross-country running, football (m), golf, lacrosse, soccer, softball (w), tennis, volleyball (w).

Campus Safety

Student safety services include late-night transport/escort service, 24-hour emergency telephone alarm devices, 24-hour patrols by trained security personnel, and electronically operated dormitory entrances.

Applying

Presbyterian requires an essay, SAT or ACT, a high school transcript, and 1 recommendation. It recommends an interview. Application deadline: 6/1; 3/1 priority date for financial aid. Early and deferred admission are possible.

PRINCETON UNIVERSITY
SUBURBAN SETTING ■ PRIVATE ■ INDEPENDENT ■ COED
PRINCETON, NEW JERSEY

Web site: www.princeton.edu
Contact: Ms. Janet Rapelye, Dean of Admission, PO Box 430, Princeton, NJ 08542-0430
Telephone: 609-258-3060
Fax: 609-258-6743
E-mail: uaoffice@princeton.edu

SPONSOR

> The fourth-oldest college in the country, Princeton was chartered in 1746. Any list of the most frequently cited strengths of Princeton would doubtless include the following: the quality of its academic programs, its relatively small size combined with the resources of one of the world's major research universities, and the emphasis it has always placed on undergraduate education. Distinctive features of Princeton also include its focus on independent work in a student's junior and senior years and the highly participatory nature of the student body.

Academics
Princeton awards bachelor's, master's, and doctoral **degrees**. **Challenging opportunities** include advanced placement credit, student-designed majors, independent study, and a senior project. Special programs include off-campus study, study-abroad, and Army and Air Force ROTC.

The most frequently chosen **baccalaureate** fields are social sciences, engineering, and history. A complete listing of majors at Princeton appears in the Majors by College index beginning on page 471.

The **faculty** at Princeton has 825 full-time members, 93% with terminal degrees. The student-faculty ratio is 8:1.

Students of Princeton
The student body totals 7,334, of whom 4,918 are undergraduates. 46.8% are women and 53.2% are men. Students come from 54 states and territories and 95 other countries. 16% are from New Jersey. 9.3% are international students. 8.6% are African American, 0.7% American Indian, 14.2% Asian American, and 7.5% Hispanic American. 98% returned for their sophomore year.

Facilities and Resources
500 **computers/terminals** are available on campus for general student use. Students can access the following: campus intranet, computer help desk, free student e-mail accounts, online (class) grades, online (class) registration, online (class) schedules, academic applications and courseware. Campuswide network is available. 100% of college-owned or -operated housing units are wired for high-speed Internet access. The 15 **libraries** have 6,495,597 books and 63,987 subscriptions.

Campus Life
There are 250 active organizations on campus, including a drama/theater group, newspaper, radio station, choral group, and marching band. No national or local **fraternities** or **sororities**.

Princeton is a member of the NCAA (Division I). **Intercollegiate sports** include baseball (m), basketball, cheerleading, crew, cross-country running, fencing, field hockey (w), football (m), golf, ice hockey, lacrosse, soccer, softball (w), squash, swimming and diving, tennis, track and field, volleyball, water polo, wrestling (m).

Campus Safety
Student safety services include late-night transport/escort service, 24-hour emergency telephone alarm devices, 24-hour patrols by trained security personnel, student patrols, and electronically operated dormitory entrances.

Applying
Princeton requires an essay, SAT Subject Tests, SAT or ACT, a high school transcript, and 3 recommendations. It recommends an interview. Application deadline: 1/1; 2/1 priority date for financial aid. Early and deferred admission are possible.

Getting Accepted
18,942 applied
10% were accepted
1,242 enrolled (68% of accepted)
96% from top tenth of their h.s. class
3.87 average high school GPA
Mean SAT critical reading score: 718
Mean SAT math score: 724
Mean SAT writing score: 710
97% had SAT critical reading scores over 600
95% had SAT math scores over 600
99% had ACT scores over 24
73% had SAT critical reading scores over 700
72% had SAT math scores over 700
82% had ACT scores over 30

Graduation and After
89% graduated in 4 years
5% graduated in 5 years
1% graduated in 6 years
400 organizations recruited on campus

Financial Matters
$34,290 tuition and fees (2008–09)
$11,405 room and board
100% average percent of need met
$28,792 average financial aid amount received per undergraduate (2005–06)

Getting Accepted
9,802 applied
41% were accepted
988 enrolled (24% of accepted)
45% from top tenth of their h.s. class
3.47 average high school GPA
Mean SAT critical reading score: 588
Mean SAT math score: 592
Mean SAT writing score: 579
Mean ACT score: 25
43% had SAT critical reading scores over 600
51% had SAT math scores over 600
49% had SAT writing scores over 600
71% had ACT scores over 24
7% had SAT critical reading scores over 700
6% had SAT math scores over 700
9% had SAT writing scores over 700
14% had ACT scores over 30
18 National Merit Scholars
51 class presidents
13 valedictorians

Graduation and After
85% graduated in 4 years
2% graduated in 5 years
110 organizations recruited on campus

Financial Matters
$29,499 tuition and fees (2007–08)
$10,335 room and board
86% average percent of need met
$17,906 average financial aid amount received per undergraduate (2005–06)

PROVIDENCE COLLEGE
SUBURBAN SETTING ■ PRIVATE ■ INDEPENDENT RELIGIOUS ■ COED
PROVIDENCE, RHODE ISLAND

Web site: www.providence.edu
Contact: River Avenue and Eaton Street, Providence, RI 02918
Telephone: 401-865-2535 or toll-free 800-721-6444
Fax: 401-865-2826
E-mail: pcadmiss@providence.edu

Academics
PC awards associate, bachelor's, and master's **degrees**. **Challenging opportunities** include advanced placement credit, student-designed majors, an honors program, double majors, independent study, and a senior project. Special programs include cooperative education, internships, summer session for credit, study-abroad, and Army ROTC.

The most frequently chosen **baccalaureate** fields are business/marketing, social sciences, and education. A complete listing of majors at PC appears in the Majors by College index beginning on page 471.

The **faculty** at PC has 291 full-time members, 89% with terminal degrees. The student-faculty ratio is 12:1.

Students of PC
The student body totals 4,759, of whom 3,966 are undergraduates. 55.6% are women and 44.4% are men. Students come from 16 states and territories and 37 other countries. 13% are from Rhode Island. 0.9% are international students. 2% are African American, 0.1% American Indian, 2.3% Asian American, and 2.4% Hispanic American. 92% returned for their sophomore year.

Facilities and Resources
278 **computers/terminals** and 5,000 ports are available on campus for general student use. Students can access the following: campus intranet, computer help desk, free student e-mail accounts, online (class) grades, online (class) registration, online (class) schedules. Campuswide network is available. 100% of college-owned or -operated housing units are wired for high-speed Internet access. Wireless service is available via classrooms, computer centers, computer labs, learning centers, libraries, student centers. The **library** has 567,761 books and 26,766 subscriptions.

Campus Life
There are 109 active organizations on campus, including a drama/theater group, newspaper, radio station, television station, and choral group. No national or local **fraternities** or **sororities**.

PC is a member of the NCAA (Division I). **Intercollegiate sports** (some offering scholarships) include basketball, cross-country running, field hockey (w), ice hockey, lacrosse (m), soccer, softball (w), swimming and diving, tennis (w), track and field, volleyball (w).

Campus Safety
Student safety services include late-night transport/escort service, 24-hour emergency telephone alarm devices, 24-hour patrols by trained security personnel, student patrols, and electronically operated dormitory entrances.

Applying
PC requires an essay, a high school transcript, and 2 recommendations, and in some cases SAT or ACT. Application deadline: 1/15; 2/1 for financial aid. Early and deferred admission are possible.

Purdue University

Suburban setting ■ Public ■ State-supported ■ Coed
West Lafayette, Indiana

Web site: www.purdue.edu
Contact: Ms. Pamela T. Home, Assistant Vice President for Enrollment Management and Dean of Admissions, 475 Stadium Mall Drive, Schleman Hall, West Lafayette, IN 47907-2050
Telephone: 765-494-1776
Fax: 765-494-0544
E-mail: admissions@purdue.edu

Academics

Purdue awards associate, bachelor's, master's, doctoral, and first-professional **degrees**. **Challenging opportunities** include advanced placement credit, accelerated degree programs, freshman honors college, an honors program, double majors, independent study, and a senior project. Special programs include cooperative education, internships, summer session for credit, study-abroad, and Army, Navy, and Air Force ROTC.

The most frequently chosen **baccalaureate** fields are engineering, business/marketing, and engineering technologies. A complete listing of majors at Purdue appears in the Majors by College index beginning on page 471.

The **faculty** at Purdue has 2,097 full-time members, 80% with terminal degrees. The student faculty ratio is 14:1.

Students of Purdue

The student body totals 39,102, of whom 31,186 are undergraduates. 41.9% are women and 58.1% are men. 74% are from Indiana. 6.5% are international students. 3.6% are African American, 0.5% American Indian, 5.5% Asian American, and 2.9% Hispanic American. 85% returned for their sophomore year.

Facilities and Resources

1,986 **computers/terminals** are available on campus for general student use. Students can access the following: free student e-mail accounts, online (class) grades, online (class) schedules. Campuswide network is available. 97% of college-owned or -operated housing units are wired for high-speed Internet access. Wireless service is available via entire campus. The 14 **libraries** have 2,459,943 books and 20,829 subscriptions.

Campus Life

There are 815 active organizations on campus, including a drama/theater group, newspaper, radio station, television station, choral group, and marching band. 16% of eligible men and 17% of eligible women are members of national **fraternities** and national **sororities**.

Purdue is a member of the NCAA (Division I). **Intercollegiate sports** (some offering scholarships) include baseball (m), basketball, cross-country running, football (m), golf, soccer (w), softball (w), swimming and diving, tennis, track and field, volleyball (w), wrestling (m).

Campus Safety

Student safety services include late-night transport/escort service, 24-hour emergency telephone alarm devices, 24-hour patrols by trained security personnel, student patrols, and electronically operated dormitory entrances.

Applying

Purdue requires SAT or ACT and a high school transcript. Application deadline: 3/1; 3/1 priority date for financial aid. Early and deferred admission are possible.

Getting Accepted

25,929 applied
79% were accepted
6,755 enrolled (33% of accepted)
31% from top tenth of their h.s. class
3.5 average high school GPA
30% had SAT critical reading scores over 600
48% had SAT math scores over 600
67% had ACT scores over 24
6% had SAT critical reading scores over 700
13% had SAT math scores over 700
18% had ACT scores over 30
87 National Merit Scholars
245 valedictorians

Graduation and After

37% graduated in 4 years
29% graduated in 5 years
5% graduated in 6 years
71% had job offers within 6 months
629 organizations recruited on campus

Financial Matters

$7750 resident tuition and fees (2008–09)
$23,224 nonresident tuition and fees (2008–09)
$7530 room and board
92% average percent of need met
$12,131 average financial aid amount received per undergraduate (2006–07 estimated)

QUEEN'S UNIVERSITY AT KINGSTON

URBAN SETTING ■ PUBLIC ■ COED
KINGSTON, ONTARIO

Web site: www.queensu.ca
Contact: Ms. Wendy Smith, US Admission Coordinator, Richardson Hall, Kingston, ON K7L 3N6
Telephone: 613-533-2217
Fax: 613-533-6810
E-mail: admission@queensu.ca

Getting Accepted

26,292 applied
44% were accepted
3,205 enrolled (28% of accepted)
52% had SAT critical reading scores over 600
64% had SAT math scores over 600
16% had SAT critical reading scores over 700
22% had SAT math scores over 700

Graduation and After

75% graduated in 4 years
12% graduated in 5 years
2% graduated in 6 years
95% had job offers within 6 months
442 organizations recruited on campus

Financial Matters

$6389 resident tuition and fees (2008–09)
$6389 nonresident tuition and fees (2008–09)
$9867 room and board

Academics

Queen's awards bachelor's, master's, doctoral, and first-professional **degrees**. **Challenging opportunities** include advanced placement credit, accelerated degree programs, student-designed majors, an honors program, and double majors. Special programs include cooperative education, internships, summer session for credit, and study-abroad.

The most frequently chosen **baccalaureate** fields are biological/life sciences, education, and engineering. A complete listing of majors at Queen's appears in the Majors by College index beginning on page 471.

The **faculty** at Queen's has 1,087 full-time members, 96% with terminal degrees. The student-faculty ratio is 15:1.

Students of Queen's

The student body totals 20,716, of whom 15,891 are undergraduates. 59.6% are women and 40.4% are men. Students come from 13 states and territories and 90 other countries. 80% are from Ontario. 95% returned for their sophomore year.

Facilities and Resources

455 **computers/terminals** are available on campus for general student use. Students can access the following: computer help desk, free student e-mail accounts, online (class) grades, online (class) registration, online (class) schedules. Campuswide network is available. 100% of college-owned or -operated housing units are wired for high-speed Internet access. Wireless service is available via computer centers, computer labs, learning centers, libraries, student centers. The 5 **libraries** have 3,509,317 books and 16,109 subscriptions.

Campus Life

There are 270 active organizations on campus, including a drama/theater group, newspaper, radio station, choral group, and marching band. No national or local **fraternities** or **sororities**.

Queen's is a member of the Canadian Interuniversity Athletic Union. **Intercollegiate sports** include basketball, crew, cross-country running, fencing, field hockey (w), football (m), golf (m), ice hockey, lacrosse (w), rugby, skiing (cross-country), soccer, squash, swimming and diving, tennis, track and field, ultimate Frisbee, volleyball, water polo, wrestling.

Campus Safety

Student safety services include late-night transport/escort service, 24-hour emergency telephone alarm devices, 24-hour patrols by trained security personnel, student patrols, and electronically operated dormitory entrances.

Applying

Queen's requires an essay, SAT or ACT, a high school transcript, and a minimum high school GPA of 2.3, and in some cases 1 recommendation. Application deadline: 2/1; 7/1 priority date for financial aid. Deferred admission is possible.

QUINCY UNIVERSITY
SMALL-TOWN SETTING ■ PRIVATE ■ INDEPENDENT RELIGIOUS ■ COED
QUINCY, ILLINOIS

SPONSOR

Web site: www.quincy.edu
Contact: Mrs. Syndi Peck, Director of Admissions, Quincy University,
Admissions Office, Quincy, IL 62301
Telephone: 217-228-5210 or toll-free 800-688-4295
E-mail: admissions@quincy.edu

Academics
Quincy awards associate, bachelor's, and master's **degrees. Challenging opportunities**
include advanced placement credit, accelerated degree programs, student-designed
majors, an honors program, double majors, independent study, and a senior project.
Special programs include internships, summer session for credit, and study-abroad.

The most frequently chosen **baccalaureate** fields are business/marketing, education,
and health professions and related sciences. A complete listing of majors at Quincy appears in the Majors by College index beginning on page 471.

The **faculty** at Quincy has 51 full-time members, 78% with terminal degrees. The
student-faculty ratio is 13:1.

Students of Quincy
The student body totals 1,323, of whom 1,078 are undergraduates. 56.6% are women
and 43.4% are men. Students come from 30 states and territories and 6 other countries.
72% are from Illinois. 0.6% are international students. 6.6% are African American, 0.8%
Asian American, and 2.6% Hispanic American. 72% returned for their sophomore year.

Facilities and Resources
190 **computers/terminals** are available on campus for general student use. Students can
access the following: campus intranet, computer help desk, free student e-mail accounts,
online (class) grades, online (class) registration, online (class) schedules. Campuswide
network is available. 100% of college-owned or -operated housing units are wired for
high-speed Internet access. Wireless service is available via classrooms, computer
centers, computer labs, dorm rooms, learning centers, libraries, student centers. The
library has 204,557 books and 365 subscriptions.

Campus Life
There are 41 active organizations on campus, including a drama/theater group,
newspaper, radio station, and choral group. 15% of eligible men and 28% of eligible
women are members of national **fraternities** and national **sororities**.

Quincy is a member of the NCAA (Division II). **Intercollegiate sports** (some offering scholarships) include baseball (m), basketball, football (m), golf, soccer, softball (w),
tennis, volleyball.

Campus Safety
Student safety services include late-night transport/escort service, 24-hour emergency
telephone alarm devices, 24-hour patrols by trained security personnel, student patrols,
and electronically operated dormitory entrances.

Applying
Quincy requires an essay, SAT or ACT, a high school transcript, ACT or SAT, and a
minimum high school GPA of 2.0, and in some cases recommendations. It recommends
an interview. Application deadline: rolling admissions; 3/15 priority date for financial aid.
Early and deferred admission are possible.

Quincy University (QU) is a dynamic
community located on the scenic
bluffs of the Mississippi River in
Quincy, Illinois. The contemporary
liberal arts-based curriculum and
extensive internship program prepare
students for their chosen fields; the
numerous opportunities for leadership
outside the classroom help prepare
students to take an active role in
society. NCAA Division II sporting
events, more than 40 campus
organizations, and the state-of-the-
art Health and Fitness Center are the
foundation of campus life. QU's
Franciscan heritage of complete
respect for all individuals and their
unique gifts is at the heart of
University life.

Getting Accepted
726 applied
96% were accepted
234 enrolled (34% of accepted)
9% from top tenth of their h.s. class
3.2 average high school GPA
Mean SAT critical reading score: 501
Mean SAT math score: 503
Mean ACT score: 22
14% had SAT critical reading scores over 600
14% had SAT math scores over 600
28% had ACT scores over 24
7% had SAT critical reading scores over 700
2% had ACT scores over 30

Graduation and After
36% graduated in 4 years
10% graduated in 5 years
2% graduated in 6 years
29% pursued further study (8% business, 3%
medicine, 2% education)
61% had job offers within 6 months
45 organizations recruited on campus

Financial Matters
$20,790 tuition and fees (2008–09)
$7900 room and board
80% average percent of need met
$14,145 average financial aid amount received
per undergraduate (2004–05)

Quinnipiac University

Suburban setting ■ Private ■ Independent ■ Coed
Hamden, Connecticut

Web site: www.quinnipiac.edu
Contact: Ms. Joan Isaac Mohr, Vice President and Dean of Admissions, 275 Mount Carmel Avenue, Hamden, CT 06518
Telephone: 203-582-8600 or toll-free 800-462-1944 (out-of-state)
Fax: 203-582-8906
E-mail: admissions@quinnipiac.edu

Getting Accepted

12,060 applied
47% were accepted
1,358 enrolled (24% of accepted)
25% from top tenth of their h.s. class
3.4 average high school GPA
Mean SAT critical reading score: 555
Mean SAT math score: 575
Mean SAT writing score: 590
Mean ACT score: 26
23% had SAT critical reading scores over 600
35% had SAT math scores over 600
78% had ACT scores over 24
2% had SAT critical reading scores over 700
3% had SAT math scores over 700
17% had ACT scores over 30

Graduation and After

67% graduated in 4 years
5% graduated in 5 years
1% graduated in 6 years
31% pursued further study (10% education, 7% business, 3% arts and sciences)
84% had job offers within 6 months
180 organizations recruited on campus

Financial Matters

$30,900 tuition and fees (2008–09)
$11,800 room and board
65% average percent of need met
$15,338 average financial aid amount received per undergraduate (2006–07 estimated)

Academics

Quinnipiac awards bachelor's, master's, doctoral, and first-professional **degrees** and post-bachelor's certificates. **Challenging opportunities** include advanced placement credit, student-designed majors, an honors program, double majors, independent study, and a senior project. Special programs include internships, summer session for credit, study-abroad, and Army and Air Force ROTC.

The most frequently chosen **baccalaureate** fields are business/marketing, health professions and related sciences, and communications/journalism. A complete listing of majors at Quinnipiac appears in the Majors by College index beginning on page 471.

The **faculty** at Quinnipiac has 280 full-time members, 88% with terminal degrees. The student-faculty ratio is 15:1.

Students of Quinnipiac

The student body totals 7,216, of whom 5,765 are undergraduates. 61.8% are women and 38.2% are men. Students come from 28 states and territories and 18 other countries. 30% are from Connecticut. 1.3% are international students. 2.7% are African American, 0.2% American Indian, 2.4% Asian American, and 4.8% Hispanic American. 89% returned for their sophomore year.

Facilities and Resources

600 **computers/terminals** and 2,500 ports are available on campus for general student use. Students can access the following: campus intranet, computer help desk, free student e-mail accounts, online (class) grades, online (class) registration, online (class) schedules, e-commerce 'Q' card for local merchants, food service, dorm card access. Campuswide network is available. 100% of college-owned or -operated housing units are wired for high-speed Internet access. Wireless service is available via entire campus. The 2 **libraries** have 285,000 books and 5,500 subscriptions.

Campus Life

There are 75 active organizations on campus, including a drama/theater group, newspaper, radio station, television station, and choral group. 5% of eligible men and 7% of eligible women are members of national **fraternities**, national **sororities**, and local sororities.

Quinnipiac is a member of the NCAA (Division I). **Intercollegiate sports** (some offering scholarships) include baseball (m), basketball, cross-country running, field hockey (w), golf (m), ice hockey, lacrosse, soccer, softball (w), tennis, track and field, volleyball (w).

Campus Safety

Student safety services include late-night transport/escort service, 24-hour emergency telephone alarm devices, 24-hour patrols by trained security personnel, and electronically operated dormitory entrances.

Applying

Quinnipiac requires an essay, SAT or ACT, a high school transcript, and 1 recommendation, and in some cases a minimum high school GPA of 3.0. It recommends an interview. Application deadline: 2/1, 2/1 for nonresidents; 3/1 priority date for financial aid. Deferred admission is possible.

RANDOLPH COLLEGE

SUBURBAN SETTING ■ PRIVATE ■ INDEPENDENT RELIGIOUS ■ COED
LYNCHBURG, VIRGINIA

Web site: www.randolphcollege.edu
Contact: Mr. Jim Duffy, Senior Associate Director of Admissions, 2500
    Rivermont Avenue, Lynchburg, VA 24503-1526
Telephone: 434-947-8100 or toll-free 800-745-7692
Fax: 434-947-8996
E-mail: admissions@randolphcollege.edu

Academics

Randolph awards bachelor's and master's **degrees**. **Challenging opportunities** include advanced placement credit, accelerated degree programs, student-designed majors, an honors program, double majors, independent study, and a senior project. Special programs include internships, off-campus study, and study-abroad.

The most frequently chosen **baccalaureate** fields are social sciences, visual and performing arts, and biological/life sciences. A complete listing of majors at Randolph appears in the Majors by College index beginning on page 471.

The **faculty** at Randolph has 75 full-time members, 92% with terminal degrees. The student-faculty ratio is 8:1.

Students of Randolph

The student body totals 656, of whom 649 are undergraduates. 88.1% are women and 11.9% are men. Students come from 44 states and territories and 44 other countries. 48% are from Virginia. 12.3% are international students. 8.9% are African American, 0.6% American Indian, 3.2% Asian American, and 5.9% Hispanic American. 78% returned for their sophomore year.

Facilities and Resources

154 **computers/terminals** and 10 ports are available on campus for general student use. Students can access the following: campus intranet, computer help desk, free student e-mail accounts, online (class) grades, online (class) registration, online (class) schedules. Campuswide network is available. 100% of college-owned or -operated housing units are wired for high-speed Internet access. Wireless service is available via classrooms, computer centers, learning centers, libraries, student centers. The **library** has 197,332 books and 618 subscriptions.

Campus Life

There are 41 active organizations on campus, including a drama/theater group, newspaper, radio station, and choral group. No national or local **fraternities** or **sororities**.

Randolph is a member of the NCAA (Division III). **Intercollegiate sports** include basketball, cross-country running, equestrian sports, lacrosse, soccer, softball (w), swimming and diving (w), tennis, volleyball (w).

Campus Safety

Student safety services include late-night transport/escort service, 24-hour emergency telephone alarm devices, and 24-hour patrols by trained security personnel.

Applying

Randolph requires an essay, SAT or ACT, a high school transcript, and 2 recommendations. It recommends an interview. Application deadline: 3/1; 3/1 priority date for financial aid. Early and deferred admission are possible.

At Randolph College, students become world-wise in a community based on honesty, individualized education, intellects, passions, and involvement. Each young woman and man can achieve the skills necessary to live meaningfully in a world that grows more complex and connected every day, through original research conducted with faculty members, leadership positions held in campus organizations, and volunteer work in the Lynchburg community. The class size is small (70 percent of classes have 15 or fewer students), enabling Randolph College students easy access to their professors, which fosters an exciting and engaging atmosphere of academic excellence. Contemporary facilities and advanced technology afford students a competitive edge for career prospects and/or advanced study. Randolph College challenges and empowers each student to engage in the world, take charge of their education throughout their lives, and lead lives of integrity and honor.

Getting Accepted
1,222 applied
83% were accepted
178 enrolled (17% of accepted)
30% from top tenth of their h.s. class
3.4 average high school GPA
Mean SAT critical reading score: 570
Mean SAT math score: 550
Mean ACT score: 24
40% had SAT critical reading scores over 600
29% had SAT math scores over 600
8% had SAT critical reading scores over 700
5% had SAT math scores over 700
2 National Merit Scholars
3 class presidents
10 valedictorians

Graduation and After
65% graduated in 4 years
31% pursued further study (19% arts and sciences, 5% education, 2% law)
60% had job offers within 6 months
12 organizations recruited on campus

Financial Matters
$25,860 tuition and fees (2007–08)
$9000 room and board
89% average percent of need met
$23,411 average financial aid amount received per undergraduate (2006–07 estimated)

REED COLLEGE

URBAN SETTING ■ PRIVATE ■ INDEPENDENT ■ COED
PORTLAND, OREGON

Web site: www.reed.edu
Contact: Mr. Paul Marthers, Dean of Admission, 3203 Southeast Woodstock Boulevard, Portland, OR 97202-8199
Telephone: 503-777-7511 or toll-free 800-547-4750 (out-of-state)
Fax: 503-777-7553
E-mail: admission@reed.edu

Reed's uniqueness lies in the uncompromising rigor of its academic program and the self-discipline and intellectual curiosity of its students. Ranked first among national liberal arts colleges in the percentage of graduates earning Ph.D. degrees and second in the number of Rhodes Scholars, Reed has long been known as a socially progressive and intellectually dynamic school. The Reed campus features Tudor Gothic brick buildings, state-of-the-art research facilities, and plentiful green space—while Portland offers all the advantages of a major city. Reed graduates are leaders in the fields of science and technology, entrepreneurship, social reform, and academia and carry on the school's tradition of scholarship, service, ingenuity, and responsibility.

Getting Accepted
3,365 applied
34% were accepted
346 enrolled (30% of accepted)
61% from top tenth of their h.s. class
3.9 average high school GPA
Mean SAT critical reading score: 717
Mean SAT math score: 668
Mean SAT writing score: 686
Mean ACT score: 30
98% had SAT critical reading scores over 600
87% had SAT math scores over 600
93% had SAT writing scores over 600
100% had ACT scores over 24
67% had SAT critical reading scores over 700
33% had SAT math scores over 700
47% had SAT writing scores over 700
64% had ACT scores over 30
6 National Merit Scholars
7 valedictorians

Graduation and After
58% graduated in 4 years
13% graduated in 5 years
4% graduated in 6 years
53 organizations recruited on campus

Financial Matters
$36,420 tuition and fees (2007–08)
$9460 room and board
100% average percent of need met
$27,257 average financial aid amount received per undergraduate (2006–07 estimated)

Academics

Reed awards bachelor's and master's **degrees**. **Challenging opportunities** include advanced placement credit, double majors, independent study, and a senior project. Special programs include cooperative education, internships, off-campus study, and study-abroad.

The most frequently chosen **baccalaureate** fields are social sciences, biological/life sciences, and physical sciences. A complete listing of majors at Reed appears in the Majors by College index beginning on page 471.

The **faculty** at Reed has 125 full-time members, 91% with terminal degrees. The student-faculty ratio is 10:1.

Students of Reed

The student body totals 1,492, of whom 1,464 are undergraduates. 54.7% are women and 45.3% are men. Students come from 49 states and territories and 43 other countries. 13% are from Oregon. 6.2% are international students. 3% are African American, 1.5% American Indian, 8.4% Asian American, and 6.3% Hispanic American. 91% returned for their sophomore year.

Facilities and Resources

415 **computers/terminals** are available on campus for general student use. Students can access the following: campus intranet, computer help desk, free student e-mail accounts, online (class) registration, online (class) schedules. Campuswide network is available. 100% of college-owned or -operated housing units are wired for high-speed Internet access. Wireless service is available via entire campus. The **library** has 564,598 books and 23,290 subscriptions.

Campus Life

There are 41 active organizations on campus, including a drama/theater group, newspaper, radio station, and choral group. No national or local **fraternities** or **sororities**.

This institution has no intercollegiate sports.

Campus Safety

Student safety services include 24-hour emergency dispatch, late-night transport/escort service, 24-hour emergency telephone alarm devices, 24-hour patrols by trained security personnel, student patrols, and electronically operated dormitory entrances.

Applying

Reed requires an essay, SAT or ACT, a high school transcript, and 2 recommendations. It recommends SAT Subject Tests and an interview. Application deadline: 1/15; 2/1 for financial aid, with a 1/15 priority date. Early and deferred admission are possible.

Regis University

Suburban setting ■ Private ■ Independent Religious ■ Coed
Denver, Colorado

SPONSOR

Web site: www.regis.edu
Contact: Mr. Vic Davolt, Director of Admission, 3333 Regis Boulevard,
Denver, CO 80221-1099
Telephone: 303-458-4905 or toll-free 800-388-2366 Ext. 4900
Fax: 303-964-5534
E-mail: regisadm@regis.edu

Academics

Regis awards bachelor's, master's, and doctoral **degrees**. **Challenging opportunities** include advanced placement credit, accelerated degree programs, student-designed majors, freshman honors college, an honors program, double majors, independent study, and a senior project. Special programs include cooperative education, internships, summer session for credit, off-campus study, study-abroad, and Army and Air Force ROTC.

The most frequently chosen **baccalaureate** fields are business/marketing, interdisciplinary studies, and social sciences. A complete listing of majors at Regis appears in the Majors by College index beginning on page 471.

The **faculty** at Regis has 226 full-time members, 55% with terminal degrees. The student-faculty ratio is 14:1.

Students of Regis

The student body totals 15,740, of whom 7,900 are undergraduates. 62.6% are women and 37.4% are men. Students come from 40 states and territories. 71% are from Colorado. 0.9% are international students. 5.3% are African American, 1% American Indian, 3.6% Asian American, and 9.9% Hispanic American. 84% returned for their sophomore year.

Facilities and Resources

300 **computers/terminals** and 72 ports are available on campus for general student use. Students can access the following: campus intranet, computer help desk, free student e-mail accounts, online (class) grades, online (class) registration, online (class) schedules. Campuswide network is available. 100% of college-owned or -operated housing units are wired for high-speed Internet access. Wireless service is available via entire campus. The **library** has 350,000 books and 20,800 subscriptions.

Campus Life

There are 30 active organizations on campus, including a drama/theater group, newspaper, radio station, and choral group. No national or local **fraternities** or **sororities**.

Regis is a member of the NCAA (Division II). **Intercollegiate sports** (some offering scholarships) include baseball (m), basketball, golf, lacrosse (w), soccer, softball (w), volleyball (w).

Campus Safety

Student safety services include late-night transport/escort service, 24-hour emergency telephone alarm devices, 24-hour patrols by trained security personnel, student patrols, and electronically operated dormitory entrances.

Applying

Regis requires an essay, SAT or ACT, a high school transcript, 1 recommendation, and a minimum high school GPA of 2.5, and in some cases an interview and 2 recommendations. It recommends SAT Subject Tests. Application deadline: rolling admissions, rolling admissions for nonresidents; 3/1 priority date for financial aid.

Getting Accepted
13,912 applied
25% were accepted
549 enrolled (16% of accepted)
25% from top tenth of their h.s. class
3.5 average high school GPA
Mean SAT critical reading score: 544
Mean SAT math score: 542
Mean ACT score: 23
26% had SAT critical reading scores over 600
28% had SAT math scores over 600
42% had ACT scores over 24
4% had SAT critical reading scores over 700
3% had SAT math scores over 700
6% had ACT scores over 30

Graduation and After
45% graduated in 4 years
10% graduated in 5 years
2% graduated in 6 years
15% pursued further study
83 organizations recruited on campus

Financial Matters
$28,700 tuition and fees (2008–09)
$8982 room and board
75% average percent of need met
$17,572 average financial aid amount received per undergraduate (2005–06)

RENSSELAER POLYTECHNIC INSTITUTE

SUBURBAN SETTING ■ PRIVATE ■ INDEPENDENT ■ COED
TROY, NEW YORK

Web site: www.rpi.edu
Contact: Mr. James Nondorf, Vice President for Enrollment, 110 8th Street, Troy, NY 12180
Telephone: 518-276-6216 or toll-free 800-448-6562
Fax: 518-276-4072
E-mail: admissions@rpi.edu

Rensselaer Polytechnic Institute, founded in 1824, is the nation's oldest technological university. The Institute offers bachelor's, master's, and doctoral degrees in engineering, the sciences, information technology, architecture, management, and the humanities and social sciences. Rensselaer faculty members are known for preeminence in research conducted in a wide range of fields, with particular emphasis in biotechnology, nanotechnology, information technology, and the media arts and technology. Prominent graduates include Ed Zander, '68, the chairman of Motorola; Texas Instruments founder J. Erik Jonsson, '22; and Nobel Laureate Ivar Giaever, '64.

Getting Accepted
10,162 applied
49% were accepted
1,288 enrolled (26% of accepted)
64% from top tenth of their h.s. class
Mean SAT critical reading score: 644
Mean SAT math score: 693
Mean SAT writing score: 623
Mean ACT score: 27
77% had SAT critical reading scores over 600
94% had SAT math scores over 600
66% had SAT writing scores over 600
85% had ACT scores over 24
24% had SAT critical reading scores over 700
46% had SAT math scores over 700
15% had SAT writing scores over 700
17% had ACT scores over 30
25 National Merit Scholars
61 valedictorians

Graduation and After
66% graduated in 4 years
14% graduated in 5 years
2% graduated in 6 years
24% pursued further study (10% engineering, 4% arts and sciences, 3% business)
58% had job offers within 6 months
153 organizations recruited on campus

Financial Matters
$37,990 tuition and fees (2008–09)
$10,730 room and board
86% average percent of need met
$26,650 average financial aid amount received per undergraduate (2006–07 estimated)

Academics

Rensselaer awards bachelor's, master's, and doctoral **degrees**. **Challenging opportunities** include advanced placement credit, accelerated degree programs, student-designed majors, an honors program, double majors, independent study, and a senior project. Special programs include cooperative education, internships, summer session for credit, off-campus study, study-abroad, and Army, Navy, and Air Force ROTC.

The most frequently chosen **baccalaureate** fields are engineering, computer and information sciences, and business/marketing. A complete listing of majors at Rensselaer appears in the Majors by College index beginning on page 471.

The **faculty** at Rensselaer has 400 full-time members, 98% with terminal degrees. The student-faculty ratio is 14:1.

Students of Rensselaer

The student body totals 7,299, of whom 5,167 are undergraduates. 26.7% are women and 73.3% are men. Students come from 49 states and territories and 34 other countries. 43% are from New York. 2.2% are international students. 4.1% are African American, 0.4% American Indian, 10.4% Asian American, and 5.7% Hispanic American. 92% returned for their sophomore year.

Facilities and Resources

5,639 **computers/terminals** and 10,000 ports are available on campus for general student use. Students can access the following: campus intranet, computer help desk, free student e-mail accounts, online (class) registration, online (class) schedules, billing. Campuswide network is available. 100% of college-owned or -operated housing units are wired for high-speed Internet access. Wireless service is available via classrooms, computer centers, computer labs, dorm rooms, learning centers, libraries, student centers. The 2 **libraries** have 309,171 books and 10,210 subscriptions.

Campus Life

There are 164 active organizations on campus, including a drama/theater group, newspaper, radio station, television station, and choral group. 25% of eligible men and 18% of eligible women are members of national **fraternities**, national **sororities**, local fraternities, and local sororities.

Rensselaer is a member of the NCAA (Division III). **Intercollegiate sports** (some offering scholarships) include baseball (m), basketball, cross-country running, field hockey (w), football (m), golf (m), ice hockey, lacrosse, soccer, softball (w), swimming and diving, tennis, track and field, volleyball (w).

Campus Safety

Student safety services include campus foot patrols at night, late-night transport/escort service, 24-hour emergency telephone alarm devices, 24-hour patrols by trained security personnel, and electronically operated dormitory entrances.

Applying

Rensselaer requires an essay, SAT or ACT, a high school transcript, and 1 recommendation, and in some cases SAT and SAT Subject Tests or ACT and portfolio for Electronic Arts is required; portfolio for Architecture highly recommended. Application deadline: 1/15; 2/15 priority date for financial aid. Early and deferred admission are possible.

RHODES COLLEGE

SUBURBAN SETTING ■ PRIVATE ■ INDEPENDENT RELIGIOUS ■ COED
MEMPHIS, TENNESSEE

Web site: www.rhodes.edu
Contact: Mr. David J. Wottle, Dean of Admissions and Financial Aid, 2000
  North Parkway, Memphis, TN 38112-1690
Telephone: 901-843-3700 or toll-free 800-844-5969 (out-of-state)
Fax: 901-843-3631
E-mail: adminfo@rhodes.edu

Academics

Rhodes awards bachelor's and master's **degrees** (master's degree in accounting only).
Challenging opportunities include advanced placement credit, student-designed
majors, an honors program, double majors, independent study, and a senior project.
Special programs include internships, off-campus study, study-abroad, and Army and Air
Force ROTC.

The most frequently chosen **baccalaureate** fields are social sciences, biological/life
sciences, and liberal arts/general studies. A complete listing of majors at Rhodes appears
in the Majors by College index beginning on page 471.

The **faculty** at Rhodes has 137 full-time members, 93% with terminal degrees. The
student-faculty ratio is 11:1.

Students of Rhodes

The student body totals 1,698, of whom 1,685 are undergraduates. 58.2% are women
and 41.8% are men. Students come from 44 states and territories and 11 other countries.
27% are from Tennessee. 0.5% are international students. 5.9% are African American,
0.2% American Indian, 5% Asian American, and 1.6% Hispanic American. 88%
returned for their sophomore year.

Facilities and Resources

220 **computers/terminals** are available on campus for general student use. Students can
access the following: online (class) registration. Campuswide network is available. The 4
libraries have 274,886 books and 1,183 subscriptions.

Campus Life

There are 44 active organizations on campus, including a drama/theater group,
newspaper, radio station, television station, and choral group. 45% of eligible men and
51% of eligible women are members of national **fraternities** and national **sororities**.

Rhodes is a member of the NCAA (Division III). **Intercollegiate sports** include
baseball (m), basketball, cross-country running, field hockey (w), football (m), golf, soccer, softball (w), swimming and diving, tennis, track and field, volleyball (w).

Campus Safety

Student safety services include 24-hour monitored security cameras in parking areas,
fenced campus with monitored access at night, late-night transport/escort service, 24-
hour emergency telephone alarm devices, 24-hour patrols by trained security personnel,
and student patrols.

Applying

Rhodes requires an essay, SAT or ACT, a high school transcript, and 2 recommendations. It recommends an interview. Application deadline: rolling admissions; 3/1 for
financial aid, with a 3/1 priority date. Early and deferred admission are possible.

Getting Accepted

3,709 applied
51% were accepted
454 enrolled (24% of accepted)
51% from top tenth of their h.s. class
3.81 average high school GPA
72% had SAT critical reading scores over 600
72% had SAT math scores over 600
96% had ACT scores over 24
21% had SAT critical reading scores over 700
21% had SAT math scores over 700
35% had ACT scores over 30

Graduation and After

70% graduated in 4 years
4% graduated in 5 years
67 organizations recruited on campus

Financial Matters

$30,652 tuition and fees (2007–08)
$7468 room and board
84% average percent of need met
$25,184 average financial aid amount received
  per undergraduate (2006–07 estimated)

Rice University is a comprehensive research university distinguished by its nationally renowned faculty, academic resources, residential college system, and collaborative culture. Rice offers a 5:1 student-faculty ratio, a median class size of 15, and an endowment of $4.6 billion. All undergraduates have access to research, study-abroad, and experiential learning opportunities. Rice is connected to downtown Houston by a light-rail system that is free to Rice students; the excitement of the nation's fourth-largest city adds to the fun and excitement of daily life for all. Rice practices need-blind admission, meets 100 percent of students' demonstrated need, and has eliminated loans from the financial aid packages of its neediest families. Merit scholarships are also available. Rice has a commitment to diversity on multiple levels, from ethnicity (39 percent of its students are members of minority groups) to socioeconomic diversity (20 percent of its students come from families earning under $60,000 per year) to geographic diversity (students come from all fifty states and forty-six other countries).

Getting Accepted
8,968 applied
25% were accepted
742 enrolled (33% of accepted)
83% from top tenth of their h.s. class
88% had SAT critical reading scores over 600
92% had SAT math scores over 600
84% had SAT writing scores over 600
96% had ACT scores over 24
53% had SAT critical reading scores over 700
64% had SAT math scores over 700
48% had SAT writing scores over 700
71% had ACT scores over 30

Graduation and After
78% graduated in 4 years
11% graduated in 5 years
2% graduated in 6 years
41% pursued further study (12% arts and sciences, 11% medicine, 5% engineering)
51% had job offers within 6 months
173 organizations recruited on campus

Financial Matters
$30,479 tuition and fees (2008–09)
$10,750 room and board
99% average percent of need met
$22,048 average financial aid amount received per undergraduate (2006–07 estimated)

RICE UNIVERSITY
URBAN SETTING ■ PRIVATE ■ INDEPENDENT ■ COED
HOUSTON, TEXAS

Web site: www.rice.edu
Contact: Office of Admission, Office of Admission, PO Box 1892, MS 17, Houston, TX 77251-1892
Telephone: 713-348-RICE or toll-free 800-527-OWLS
E-mail: admi@rice.edu

Academics
Rice awards bachelor's, master's, and doctoral **degrees**. **Challenging opportunities** include advanced placement credit, accelerated degree programs, student-designed majors, an honors program, double majors, independent study, and a senior project. Special programs include internships, summer session for credit, off-campus study, study-abroad, and Army, Navy, and Air Force ROTC.

The most frequently chosen **baccalaureate** fields are social sciences, engineering, and biological/life sciences. A complete listing of majors at Rice appears in the Majors by College index beginning on page 471.

The student-faculty ratio is 5:1.

Students of Rice
The student body totals 5,243, of whom 3,051 are undergraduates. 48.3% are women and 51.7% are men. Students come from 57 states and territories and 44 other countries. 55% are from Texas. 5.1% are international students. 6.8% are African American, 0.5% American Indian, 19.2% Asian American, and 12.2% Hispanic American. 97% returned for their sophomore year.

Facilities and Resources
523 **computers/terminals** are available on campus for general student use. Students can access the following: online (class) registration. Campuswide network is available. The **library** has 2,474,352 books and 13,486 subscriptions.

Campus Life
There are 204 active organizations on campus, including a drama/theater group, newspaper, radio station, television station, choral group, and marching band. No national or local **fraternities** or **sororities**.

Rice is a member of the NCAA (Division I). **Intercollegiate sports** (some offering scholarships) include baseball (m), basketball, cross-country running, football (m), golf (m), soccer (w), swimming and diving (w), tennis, track and field, volleyball (w).

Campus Safety
Student safety services include late-night transport/escort service, 24-hour emergency telephone alarm devices, 24-hour patrols by trained security personnel, and electronically operated dormitory entrances.

Applying
Rice requires an essay, SAT and SAT Subject Tests or ACT, a high school transcript, and 2 recommendations, and in some cases portfolio required for architecture students; audition required for music students. It recommends an interview. Application deadline: 1/2; 3/1 priority date for financial aid. Deferred admission is possible.

RIPON COLLEGE

SMALL-TOWN SETTING ■ PRIVATE ■ INDEPENDENT ■ COED
RIPON, WISCONSIN

SPONSOR

Web site: www.ripon.edu
Contact: Office of Admission, 300 Seward Street, PO Box 248, Ripon, WI 54971
Telephone: 920-748-8114 or toll-free 800-947-4766
Fax: 920-748-8335
E-mail: adminfo@ripon.edu

Academics

Ripon awards bachelor's **degrees**. **Challenging opportunities** include advanced placement credit, accelerated degree programs, student-designed majors, double majors, and a senior project. Special programs include internships, off-campus study, study-abroad, and Army ROTC.

The most frequently chosen **baccalaureate** fields are biological/life sciences, business/marketing, and social sciences. A complete listing of majors at Ripon appears in the Majors by College index beginning on page 471.

The **faculty** at Ripon has 52 full-time members, 96% with terminal degrees. The student-faculty ratio is 15:1.

Students of Ripon

The student body is made up of 1,000 undergraduates. 52.5% are women and 47.5% are men. Students come from 31 states and territories and 13 other countries. 76% are from Wisconsin. 1.4% are international students. 2.1% are African American, 0.6% American Indian, 1.3% Asian American, and 2.7% Hispanic American. 86% returned for their sophomore year.

Facilities and Resources

150 **computers/terminals** are available on campus for general student use. Students can access the following: campus intranet, computer help desk, free student e-mail accounts. Campuswide network is available. The **library** has 160,988 books and 939 subscriptions.

Campus Life

There are 45 active organizations on campus, including a drama/theater group, newspaper, radio station, and choral group. 40% of eligible men and 22% of eligible women are members of national **fraternities**, national **sororities**, local fraternities, and local sororities.

Ripon is a member of the NCAA (Division III). **Intercollegiate sports** include baseball (m), basketball, cheerleading (w), cross-country running, football (m), golf, soccer, softball (w), swimming and diving, tennis, track and field, volleyball (w).

Campus Safety

Student safety services include late-night transport/escort service, 24-hour emergency telephone alarm devices, 24-hour patrols by trained security personnel, student patrols, and electronically operated dormitory entrances.

Applying

Ripon requires an essay, SAT or ACT, a high school transcript, 1 recommendation, and a minimum high school GPA of 2.0, and in some cases an interview. It recommends an interview. Application deadline: rolling admissions; 3/1 priority date for financial aid. Deferred admission is possible.

Together with the other members of the College's tight-knit learning community, Ripon students learn more deeply, live more fully, and achieve more success. Students are often surprised to discover that at Ripon they have more opportunities—to be involved, to lead, to speak out, to make a difference, and to explore new interests—than they would at a college ten times Ripon's size. Through collaborative learning, group living, teamwork, and networking, students tap into the power of a community where everyone works together to ensure students' success—at Ripon and beyond.

Getting Accepted
974 applied
80% were accepted
262 enrolled (34% of accepted)
21% from top tenth of their h.s. class
3.38 average high school GPA
Mean SAT critical reading score: 535
Mean SAT math score: 559
Mean ACT score: 24
29% had SAT critical reading scores over 600
35% had SAT math scores over 600
52% had SAT writing scores over 600
52% had ACT scores over 24
14% had SAT math scores over 700
9% had SAT writing scores over 700
9% had ACT scores over 30
1 National Merit Scholar
9 valedictorians

Graduation and After
60% graduated in 4 years
11% graduated in 5 years
2% graduated in 6 years
24% pursued further study (12% arts and sciences, 3% education, 3% medicine)
98% had job offers within 6 months
21 organizations recruited on campus

Financial Matters
$23,298 tuition and fees (2007–08)
$6410 room and board
92% average percent of need met
$19,019 average financial aid amount received per undergraduate (2006–07 estimated)

ROCHESTER INSTITUTE OF TECHNOLOGY

SUBURBAN SETTING ■ PRIVATE ■ INDEPENDENT ■ COED
ROCHESTER, NEW YORK

Web site: www.rit.edu
Contact: Dr. Daniel Shelley, Assistant Vice President, 60 Lomb Memorial
  Drive, Rochester, NY 14623-5604
Telephone: 585-475-6631
Fax: 585-475-7424
E-mail: admissions@rit.edu

RIT is one of the world's leading career-oriented technological universities. RIT's goal is to prepare students for twenty-first-century career success. Students find an incredible array of academic programs and learning opportunities and find diverse, talented, and accessible faculty members and sophisticated facilities to enrich their experience. More than 200 academic programs and eighty minors are offered in business, engineering, engineering technology, art and design, science, mathematics, computing, information sciences, liberal arts, photography, and hospitality, to name a few. Students also find an unusual emphasis on experiential learning through cooperative education, internships, research projects, and study abroad. The RIT campus is a vibrant, connected community that is home to ambitious and creative students from more than ninety-five countries. The result is a unique blend of rigor and imagination, of specialization and perspective, of intellect and practice that defines the RIT experience.

Getting Accepted
11,012 applied
65% were accepted
2,514 enrolled (35% of accepted)
26% from top tenth of their h.s. class
3.7 average high school GPA
42% had SAT critical reading scores over 600
59% had SAT math scores over 600
78% had ACT scores over 24
8% had SAT critical reading scores over 700
13% had SAT math scores over 700
15% had ACT scores over 30
36 valedictorians

Graduation and After
10% pursued further study
93% had job offers within 6 months
700 organizations recruited on campus

Financial Matters
$26,481 tuition and fees (2007–08)
$9054 room and board
88% average percent of need met
$17,100 average financial aid amount received
  per undergraduate (2005–06)

Academics

RIT awards associate, bachelor's, master's, and doctoral **degrees** and post-bachelor's and post-master's certificates. **Challenging opportunities** include advanced placement credit, accelerated degree programs, student-designed majors, an honors program, double majors, independent study, and a senior project. Special programs include cooperative education, internships, summer session for credit, off-campus study, study-abroad, and Army, Navy, and Air Force ROTC.

The most frequently chosen **baccalaureate** fields are engineering, computer and information sciences, and visual and performing arts. A complete listing of majors at RIT appears in the Majors by College index beginning on page 471.

The **faculty** at RIT has 816 full-time members, 70% with terminal degrees. The student-faculty ratio is 14:1.

Students of RIT

The student body totals 15,989, of whom 13,476 are undergraduates. 31.7% are women and 68.3% are men. Students come from 54 states and territories and 95 other countries. 58% are from New York. 11% are international students. 4.1% are African American, 0.4% American Indian, 5.3% Asian American, and 3.6% Hispanic American. 89% returned for their sophomore year.

Facilities and Resources

2,500 **computers/terminals** are available on campus for general student use. Students can access the following: campus intranet, computer help desk, free student e-mail accounts, online (class) grades, online (class) registration, student account information. Campuswide network is available. Wireless service is available via classrooms, computer centers, computer labs, libraries, student centers. The **library** has 408,000 books and 2,800 subscriptions.

Campus Life

There are 175 active organizations on campus, including a drama/theater group, newspaper, radio station, and choral group. 5% of eligible men and 5% of eligible women are members of national **fraternities**, national **sororities**, local fraternities, and local sororities.

RIT is a member of the NCAA (Division III). **Intercollegiate sports** include baseball (m), basketball, crew, cross-country running, ice hockey, lacrosse, soccer, softball (w), swimming and diving, tennis, track and field, volleyball (w), wrestling (m).

Campus Safety

Student safety services include late-night transport/escort service, 24-hour emergency telephone alarm devices, 24-hour patrols by trained security personnel, and student patrols.

Applying

RIT requires an essay, SAT or ACT, and a high school transcript, and in some cases portfolio. It recommends an interview, 1 recommendation, and a minimum high school GPA of 3.0. Application deadline: 2/1; 3/1 priority date for financial aid. Early and deferred admission are possible.

ROLLINS COLLEGE

SUBURBAN SETTING ■ PRIVATE ■ INDEPENDENT ■ COED
WINTER PARK, FLORIDA

Web site: www.rollins.edu
Contact: Mr. David Erdmann, Dean of Admission and Enrollment, 1000 Holt
  Avenue, Box 2720, Winter Park, FL 32789-4499
Telephone: 407-646-2161
Fax: 407-646-1502
E-mail: admission@rollins.edu

Academics

Rollins awards bachelor's and master's **degrees. Challenging opportunities** include
advanced placement credit, accelerated degree programs, student-designed majors, an
honors program, double majors, independent study, and a senior project. Special
programs include internships, off-campus study, and study-abroad.

The most frequently chosen **baccalaureate** fields are social sciences, psychology, and
business/marketing. A complete listing of majors at Rollins appears in the Majors by
College index beginning on page 471.

The **faculty** at Rollins has 193 full-time members, 93% with terminal degrees. The
student-faculty ratio is 10:1.

Students of Rollins

The student body totals 2,532, of whom 1,778 are undergraduates. 58% are women and
42% are men. Students come from 42 states and territories and 34 other countries. 53%
are from Florida. 3.6% are international students. 4.4% are African American, 0.4%
American Indian, 3.8% Asian American, and 10.1% Hispanic American. 84% returned
for their sophomore year.

Facilities and Resources

240 **computers/terminals** and 155 ports are available on campus for general student
use. Students can access the following: campus intranet, computer help desk, free student
e-mail accounts, online (class) grades, online (class) registration, online (class) schedules.
Campuswide network is available. 100% of college-owned or -operated housing units are
wired for high-speed Internet access. Wireless service is available via entire campus. The
library has 303,519 books and 17,874 subscriptions.

Campus Life

There are 112 active organizations on campus, including a drama/theater group,
newspaper, radio station, television station, and choral group. 75% of eligible men and
75% of eligible women are members of national **fraternities**, national **sororities**, local
fraternities, and local sororities.

Rollins is a member of the NCAA (Division II). **Intercollegiate sports** (some offering scholarships) include baseball (m), basketball, crew, cross-country running, golf,
lacrosse, sailing, soccer, softball (w), swimming and diving, tennis, volleyball (w).

Campus Safety

Student safety services include late-night transport/escort service, 24-hour emergency
telephone alarm devices, 24-hour patrols by trained security personnel, and electronically operated dormitory entrances.

Applying

Rollins requires an essay, a high school transcript, and 1 recommendation, and in some
cases SAT or ACT. It recommends an interview and a minimum high school GPA of 2.0.
Application deadline: 2/15; 3/1 for financial aid, with a 3/1 priority date. Early and
deferred admission are possible.

Getting Accepted

2,900 applied
58% were accepted
525 enrolled (31% of accepted)
45% from top tenth of their h.s. class
3.4 average high school GPA
Mean SAT critical reading score: 596
Mean SAT math score: 597
Mean ACT score: 25
49% had SAT critical reading scores over 600
49% had SAT math scores over 600
68% had ACT scores over 24
9% had SAT critical reading scores over 700
10% had SAT math scores over 700
12% had ACT scores over 30

Graduation and After

59% graduated in 4 years
8% graduated in 5 years
1% graduated in 6 years
33% pursued further study (19% arts and
  sciences, 6% business, 6% law)
60% had job offers within 6 months
7 organizations recruited on campus

Financial Matters

$32,640 tuition and fees (2007–08)
$10,200 room and board
93% average percent of need met
$29,865 average financial aid amount received
  per undergraduate (2006–07 estimated)

ROSE-HULMAN INSTITUTE OF TECHNOLOGY

SUBURBAN SETTING ■ PRIVATE ■ INDEPENDENT ■ COED, PRIMARILY MEN
TERRE HAUTE, INDIANA

Web site: www.rose-hulman.edu

Contact: Mr. James Goecker, Dean of Admissions and Financial Aid, 5500 Wabash Avenue, CM 1, Terre Haute, IN 47803-3920

Telephone: 812-877-8894 or toll-free 800-248-7448

Fax: 812-877-8941

E-mail: admissions@rose-hulman.edu

Getting Accepted

3,088 applied
70% were accepted
474 enrolled (22% of accepted)
59% from top tenth of their h.s. class
Mean SAT critical reading score: 617
Mean SAT math score: 670
Mean SAT writing score: 597
Mean ACT score: 29
62% had SAT critical reading scores over 600
86% had SAT math scores over 600
52% had SAT writing scores over 600
96% had ACT scores over 24
16% had SAT critical reading scores over 700
34% had SAT math scores over 700
10% had SAT writing scores over 700
46% had ACT scores over 30
17 National Merit Scholars
50 valedictorians

Graduation and After

73% graduated in 4 years
10% graduated in 5 years
18% pursued further study (14% engineering, 1% arts and sciences, 1% business)
99% had job offers within 6 months
269 organizations recruited on campus

Financial Matters

$30,768 tuition and fees (2007–08)
$8343 room and board
79% average percent of need met
$22,011 average financial aid amount received per undergraduate (2006–07 estimated)

Academics

Rose-Hulman awards bachelor's and master's **degrees**. **Challenging opportunities** include advanced placement credit, accelerated degree programs, double majors, independent study, and a senior project. Special programs include cooperative education, summer session for credit, off-campus study, study-abroad, and Army and Air Force ROTC.

The most frequently chosen **baccalaureate** fields are engineering, computer and information sciences, and mathematics. A complete listing of majors at Rose-Hulman appears in the Majors by College index beginning on page 471.

The **faculty** at Rose-Hulman has 158 full-time members, 99% with terminal degrees. The student-faculty ratio is 12:1.

Students of Rose-Hulman

The student body totals 1,936, of whom 1,829 are undergraduates. 20.6% are women and 79.4% are men. Students come from 51 states and territories and 21 other countries. 42% are from Indiana. 1.5% are international students. 2.1% are African American, 0.2% American Indian, 4.5% Asian American, and 1.7% Hispanic American. 91% returned for their sophomore year.

Facilities and Resources

45 **computers/terminals** and 8,000 ports are available on campus for general student use. Students can access the following: campus intranet, computer help desk, free student e-mail accounts, online (class) grades, online (class) registration, online (class) schedules. Campuswide network is available. 100% of college-owned or -operated housing units are wired for high-speed Internet access. Wireless service is available via classrooms, computer centers, computer labs, learning centers, libraries, student centers. The **library** has 80,094 books and 20,934 subscriptions.

Campus Life

There are 40 active organizations on campus, including a drama/theater group, newspaper, radio station, and choral group. 39% of eligible men and 38% of eligible women are members of national **fraternities** and national **sororities**.

Rose-Hulman is a member of the NCAA (Division III). **Intercollegiate sports** include baseball (m), basketball, cheerleading, cross-country running, football (m), golf, riflery, soccer, softball (w), swimming and diving, tennis, track and field, volleyball (w), wrestling (m).

Campus Safety

Student safety services include late-night transport/escort service, 24-hour emergency telephone alarm devices, 24-hour patrols by trained security personnel, and electronically operated dormitory entrances.

Applying

Rose-Hulman requires SAT or ACT, a high school transcript, 1 recommendation, and curricular. It recommends an essay and an interview. Application deadline: 3/1; 3/1 priority date for financial aid. Deferred admission is possible.

RUTGERS, THE STATE UNIVERSITY OF NEW JERSEY, NEWARK

URBAN SETTING ■ PUBLIC ■ STATE-SUPPORTED ■ COED
NEWARK, NEW JERSEY

Web site: www.newark.rutgers.edu
Contact: Mr. Jason Hand, Director of Admissions, 249 University Avenue, Newark, NJ 07102-1896
Telephone: 973-353-5205
Fax: 973-353-1440
E-mail: admissions@ugadm.rutgers.edu

Academics

Rutgers-Newark awards bachelor's, master's, doctoral, and first-professional **degrees**. **Challenging opportunities** include advanced placement credit, accelerated degree programs, student-designed majors, freshman honors college, an honors program, double majors, independent study, and a senior project. Special programs include cooperative education, summer session for credit, off-campus study, study-abroad, and Army and Air Force ROTC.

The most frequently chosen **baccalaureate** fields are business/marketing, health professions and related sciences, and security and protective services. A complete listing of majors at Rutgers-Newark appears in the Majors by College index beginning on page 471.

The **faculty** at Rutgers-Newark has 401 full-time members, 99% with terminal degrees. The student-faculty ratio is 12:1.

Students of Rutgers-Newark

The student body totals 10,553, of whom 6,685 are undergraduates. 55.3% are women and 44.7% are men. Students come from 25 states and territories and 65 other countries. 97% are from New Jersey. 1.9% are international students. 20.1% are African American, 0.2% American Indian, 23.9% Asian American, and 19.4% Hispanic American.

Facilities and Resources

708 **computers/terminals** are available on campus for general student use. Students can access the following: online grade reports. Campuswide network is available. The 5 **libraries** have 941,103 books and 6,408 subscriptions.

Campus Life

Active organizations on campus include a drama/theater group, newspaper, radio station, and choral group. No national or local **fraternities** or **sororities**.

This institution has no intercollegiate sports.

Applying

Rutgers-Newark requires SAT or ACT and a high school transcript. Application deadline: rolling admissions; 3/15 priority date for financial aid.

Getting Accepted
13,085 applied
49% were accepted
989 enrolled (15% of accepted)
24% from top tenth of their h.s. class
24% had SAT critical reading scores over 600
28% had SAT math scores over 600
4% had SAT critical reading scores over 700
5% had SAT math scores over 700

Graduation and After
26% graduated in 4 years
23% graduated in 5 years
9% graduated in 6 years
395 organizations recruited on campus

Financial Matters
$10,267 resident tuition and fees (2007–08)
$19,435 nonresident tuition and fees (2007–08)
$10,034 room and board
$11,311 average financial aid amount received per undergraduate (2006–07 estimated)

Getting Accepted

28,208 applied
56% were accepted
5,519 enrolled (35% of accepted)
40% from top tenth of their h.s. class
42% had SAT critical reading scores over 600
58% had SAT math scores over 600
9% had SAT critical reading scores over 700
17% had SAT math scores over 700

Graduation and After

47% graduated in 4 years
20% graduated in 5 years
6% graduated in 6 years
80% had job offers within 6 months
500 organizations recruited on campus

Financial Matters

$10,686 resident tuition and fees (2007–08)
$19,854 nonresident tuition and fees (2007–08)
$9762 room and board
70% average percent of need met
$12,536 average financial aid amount received per undergraduate (2006–07 estimated)

RUTGERS, THE STATE UNIVERSITY OF NEW JERSEY, NEW BRUNSWICK

URBAN SETTING ■ PUBLIC ■ STATE-SUPPORTED ■ COED
NEW BRUNSWICK, NEW JERSEY

Web site: www.rutgers.edu
Contact: Ms. Diane Williams Harris, Associate Director of University Undergraduate Admissions, 65 Davidson Road, Room 202, Piscataway, NJ 08854-8097
Telephone: 732-932-4636
Fax: 732-445-0237
E-mail: admissions@ugadm.rutgers.edu

Academics

Rutgers-New Brunswick awards bachelor's, master's, doctoral, and first-professional **degrees** and post-master's certificates. **Challenging opportunities** include advanced placement credit, accelerated degree programs, student-designed majors, an honors program, double majors, independent study, and a senior project. Special programs include cooperative education, study-abroad, and Army and Air Force ROTC.

The most frequently chosen **baccalaureate** fields are social sciences, biological/life sciences, and communications/journalism. A complete listing of majors at Rutgers-New Brunswick appears in the Majors by College index beginning on page 471.

The **faculty** at Rutgers-New Brunswick has 1,533 full-time members, 99% with terminal degrees. The student-faculty ratio is 14:1.

Students of Rutgers-New Brunswick

The student body totals 34,804, of whom 26,829 are undergraduates. 49.1% are women and 50.9% are men. Students come from 48 states and territories and 112 other countries. 93% are from New Jersey. 1.7% are international students. 9.2% are African American, 0.2% American Indian, 24.5% Asian American, and 8.5% Hispanic American.

Facilities and Resources

1,450 **computers/terminals** are available on campus for general student use. Students can access the following: online grade reports. Campuswide network is available. The 15 **libraries** have 4,737,147 books and 17,182 subscriptions.

Campus Life

Active organizations on campus include a drama/theater group, newspaper, radio station, television station, choral group, and marching band. Rutgers-New Brunswick has national **fraternities** and national **sororities**.

Rutgers-New Brunswick is a member of the NCAA (Division I). **Intercollegiate sports** include baseball (m), basketball, crew, cross-country running, fencing, football (m), golf, gymnastics (w), lacrosse, soccer, softball (w), swimming and diving, tennis, track and field, volleyball (w), wrestling (m).

Applying

Rutgers-New Brunswick requires SAT or ACT and a high school transcript. Application deadline: rolling admissions; 3/15 priority date for financial aid.

SAINT FRANCIS UNIVERSITY
RURAL SETTING ■ PRIVATE ■ INDEPENDENT RELIGIOUS ■ COED
LORETTO, PENNSYLVANIA

Web site: www.francis.edu
Contact: Robert Beener, Associate Dean for Enrollment Management, PO
Box 600, 117 Evergreen Drive, Loretto, PA 15940-0600
Telephone: 814-472-3100 or toll-free 800-342-5732
Fax: 814-472-3335
E-mail: rbeener@francis.edu

SPONSOR

Academics
Saint Francis awards associate, bachelor's, and master's **degrees. Challenging opportunities** include advanced placement credit, accelerated degree programs, student-designed majors, freshman honors college, an honors program, double majors, and a senior project. Special programs include internships, summer session for credit, off-campus study, study-abroad, and Army ROTC. A complete listing of majors at Saint Francis appears in the Majors by College index beginning on page 471.

The **faculty** at Saint Francis has 99 full-time members, 73% with terminal degrees. The student-faculty ratio is 16:1.

Students of Saint Francis
The student body totals 2,163, of whom 1,594 are undergraduates. 64.2% are women and 35.8% are men. Students come from 31 states and territories and 5 other countries. 79% are from Pennsylvania. 0.1% are international students. 5% are African American, 0.3% American Indian, 1% Asian American, and 1.1% Hispanic American. 82% returned for their sophomore year.

Facilities and Resources
60 **computers/terminals** are available on campus for general student use. Students can access the following: campus intranet, computer help desk, free student e-mail accounts, online (class) grades, billing, and schedules. Campuswide network is available. 90% of college-owned or -operated housing units are wired for high-speed Internet access. Wireless service is available via entire campus. The **library** has 118,333 books and 7,202 subscriptions.

Campus Life
There are 60 active organizations on campus, including a drama/theater group, newspaper, radio station, television station, and choral group. 12% of eligible men and 10% of eligible women are members of national **fraternities**, national **sororities**, and local sororities.

Saint Francis is a member of the NCAA (Division I). **Intercollegiate sports** (some offering scholarships) include basketball, cross-country running, field hockey (w), football (m), golf, lacrosse (w), soccer, softball (w), swimming and diving, tennis, track and field, volleyball.

Campus Safety
Student safety services include late-night transport/escort service, 24-hour emergency telephone alarm devices, 24-hour patrols by trained security personnel, and electronically operated dormitory entrances.

Applying
Saint Francis requires an essay, SAT or ACT, a high school transcript, and 1 recommendation, and in some cases an interview and 3 recommendations. It recommends an interview. Application deadline: rolling admissions. Deferred admission is possible.

Founded in 1847, Saint Francis is the oldest Franciscan university in the United States. Saint Francis has been helping students to use their minds to reach higher and go farther than they ever dreamed. Graduates have gone on to become teachers, journalists, physical therapists, politicians, engineers, doctors, accountants, chemists, and environmentalists. Nationally ranked programs, a solid and diverse liberal arts curriculum, and a 99-percent placement rate are a few of the outstanding features students experience at Saint Francis. Saint Francis has consistently fostered the ability to be forward thinking, while maintaining the values on which the University is based.

Getting Accepted
1,342 applied
85% were accepted
418 enrolled (36% of accepted)
22% from top tenth of their h.s. class
3.45 average high school GPA
Mean SAT critical reading score: 505
Mean SAT math score: 522
Mean ACT score: 23
14% had SAT critical reading scores over 600
16% had SAT math scores over 600
36% had ACT scores over 24
1% had SAT critical reading scores over 700
3% had SAT math scores over 700
5% had ACT scores over 30
14 class presidents
6 valedictorians

Graduation and After
53% graduated in 4 years
7% graduated in 5 years
1% graduated in 6 years
38% pursued further study (10% medicine, 6% arts and sciences, 4% education)
93% had job offers within 6 months
160 organizations recruited on campus

Financial Matters
$23,494 tuition and fees (2007–08)
$7984 room and board
76% average percent of need met
$17,459 average financial aid amount received per undergraduate (2006–07 estimated)

St. John's College

SMALL-TOWN SETTING ■ PRIVATE ■ INDEPENDENT ■ COED
ANNAPOLIS, MARYLAND

Web site: www.stjohnscollege.edu
Contact: Mr. John Christensen, Director of Admissions, PO Box 2800, 60
   College Avenue, Annapolis, MD 21404
Telephone: 410-626-2522 or toll-free 800-727-9238
Fax: 410-269-7916
E-mail: admissions@sjca.edu

Academics

St. John's awards bachelor's and master's **degrees**. A senior project is a **challenging opportunity**. Special programs include internships and off-campus study.

The most frequently chosen **baccalaureate** field is liberal arts/general studies. A complete listing of majors at St. John's appears in the Majors by College index beginning on page 471.

The **faculty** at St. John's has 76 full-time members, 78% with terminal degrees. The student-faculty ratio is 8:1.

Students of St. John's

The student body totals 563, of whom 481 are undergraduates. 46.8% are women and 53.2% are men. Students come from 45 states and territories and 12 other countries. 17% are from Maryland. 0.4% are international students. 1.5% are African American, 0.2% American Indian, 2.7% Asian American, and 2.9% Hispanic American. 80% returned for their sophomore year.

Facilities and Resources

16 **computers/terminals** are available on campus for general student use. Students can access the following: computer help desk, free student e-mail accounts. Campuswide network is available. 100% of college-owned or -operated housing units are wired for high-speed Internet access. Wireless service is available via computer labs, dorm rooms, libraries. The 2 **libraries** have 124,500 books and 123 subscriptions.

Campus Life

There are 38 active organizations on campus, including a drama/theater group, newspaper, and choral group. No national or local **fraternities** or **sororities**.

This institution has no intercollegiate sports.

Campus Safety

Student safety services include late-night transport/escort service, 24-hour emergency telephone alarm devices, 24-hour patrols by trained security personnel, and electronically operated dormitory entrances.

Applying

St. John's requires an essay, a high school transcript, and 2 recommendations, and in some cases SAT or ACT. It recommends SAT or ACT and an interview. Application deadline: rolling admissions; 2/15 priority date for financial aid. Early and deferred admission are possible.

Great Books Program: St. John's offers an integrated liberal arts and sciences curriculum structured around seminar discussions of major works of Western civilization. These discussions are supported by tutorials in mathematics, music, language, and the physical sciences. Only original sources are read, and all classes are small discussion groups.

Getting Accepted
441 applied
81% were accepted
143 enrolled (40% of accepted)
32% from top tenth of their h.s. class
94% had SAT critical reading scores over 600
65% had SAT math scores over 600
59% had SAT critical reading scores over 700
17% had SAT math scores over 700
7 National Merit Scholars

Graduation and After
63% graduated in 4 years
8% graduated in 5 years
4% graduated in 6 years
13% pursued further study (7% arts and sciences, 3% law, 1% business)
50% had job offers within 6 months
6 organizations recruited on campus

Financial Matters
$36,596 tuition and fees (2007–08)
$8684 room and board
97% average percent of need met
$26,029 average financial aid amount received per undergraduate (2006–07 estimated)

St. John's College

Suburban setting ■ Private ■ Independent ■ Coed
Santa Fe, New Mexico

SPONSOR

Web site: www.stjohnscollege.edu
Contact: Mr. Larry Clendenin, Director of Admissions, 1160 Camino Cruz
Blanca, Santa Fe, NM 87505
Telephone: 505-984-6060 or toll-free 800-331-5232
Fax: 505-984-6162
E-mail: admissions@stjohnscollege.edu

Academics
St. John's awards bachelor's and master's **degrees**. A senior project is a **challenging opportunity.** Special programs include internships, summer session for credit, and off-campus study.

The most frequently chosen **baccalaureate** field is liberal arts/general studies. A complete listing of majors at St. John's appears in the Majors by College index beginning on page 471.

The **faculty** at St. John's has 73 full-time members, 82% with terminal degrees. The student-faculty ratio is 8:1.

Students of St. John's
The student body totals 538, of whom 436 are undergraduates. 39.9% are women and 60.1% are men. Students come from 46 states and territories and 7 other countries. 5% are from New Mexico. 1.8% are international students. 0.7% are African American, 1.4% American Indian, 3.2% Asian American, and 5.5% Hispanic American.

Facilities and Resources
Campuswide network is available. The **library** has 65,000 books and 140 subscriptions.

Campus Life
There are 32 active organizations on campus, including a drama/theater group, newspaper, and choral group. No national or local **fraternities** or **sororities**.

Intercollegiate sports include fencing, soccer.

Campus Safety
Student safety services include late-night transport/escort service, 24-hour emergency telephone alarm devices, 24-hour patrols by trained security personnel, and student patrols.

Applying
St. John's requires an essay, a high school transcript, and 2 recommendations, and in some cases an interview. It recommends an interview and 3 recommendations. Application deadline: rolling admissions; 2/15 for financial aid. Early and deferred admission are possible.

Great works of poetry, philosophy, history, mathematics, natural science and scientific method, religion, theology, and music are the daily study of students and faculty members at St.John's College. The College's pedagogy directs the mind by questions and by practice in the means of answering those questions. The intention is that each individual mind become responsible for its own inquiry, imagination, judgment, and understanding. The means of study include reading, conversation—both formal and informal, mathematical demonstration, writing, translation, direct observation of natural and laboratory appearances, development of hands-on laboratory skills, and practice in the rudimentary skills of music.

Getting Accepted
344 applied
79% were accepted
134 enrolled (49% of accepted)
28% from top tenth of their h.s. class
91% had SAT critical reading scores over 600
70% had SAT math scores over 600
88% had ACT scores over 24
46% had SAT critical reading scores over 700
22% had SAT math scores over 700
29% had ACT scores over 30

Graduation and After
43% graduated in 4 years
11% graduated in 5 years
2% graduated in 6 years
23% pursued further study (9% arts and sciences, 6% education, 3% business)
30% had job offers within 6 months
11 organizations recruited on campus

Financial Matters
$36,596 tuition and fees (2007–08)
$8684 room and board
95% average percent of need met
$24,858 average financial aid amount received per undergraduate (2006–07 estimated)

SPONSOR

Together, the College of Saint Benedict (CSB) and Saint John's University (SJU) form a partnership of two of the nation's top three Catholic liberal arts colleges. Students attend classes and activities on both campuses and have access to twice as many opportunities. Through a commitment to engaged learning, almost all students complete an internship, research project, or other experiential learning activity. An international focus means CSB and SJU enroll nearly 200 international students and are ranked among the top colleges for the number of students studying abroad. The residential campuses are located on 3,300 acres of woods and lakes in central Minnesota.

Getting Accepted
1,527 applied
74% were accepted
515 enrolled (46% of accepted)
23% from top tenth of their h.s. class
3.57 average high school GPA
Mean SAT critical reading score: 568
Mean SAT math score: 597
Mean ACT score: 25
37% had SAT critical reading scores over 600
48% had SAT math scores over 600
72% had ACT scores over 24
11% had SAT critical reading scores over 700
9% had SAT math scores over 700
18% had ACT scores over 30
1 National Merit Scholar

Graduation and After
72% graduated in 4 years
7% graduated in 5 years
2% graduated in 6 years
24% pursued further study (6% arts and sciences, 3% law, 3% medicine)
72% had job offers within 6 months
118 organizations recruited on campus

Financial Matters
$26,530 tuition and fees (2007–08)
$6870 room and board
87% average percent of need met
$18,898 average financial aid amount received per undergraduate (2006–07 estimated)

SAINT JOHN'S UNIVERSITY
COORDINATE WITH COLLEGE OF SAINT BENEDICT
RURAL SETTING ■ PRIVATE ■ INDEPENDENT RELIGIOUS ■ COED, PRIMARILY MEN
COLLEGEVILLE, MINNESOTA

Web site: www.csbsju.edu
Contact: Mr. Matt Beirne, Director of Admission, PO Box 7155, Collegeville, MN 56321-7155
Telephone: 320-363-2196 or toll-free 800-544-1489
Fax: 320-363-2750
E-mail: admissions@csbsju.edu

Academics
St. John's awards bachelor's, master's, and first-professional **degrees** (coordinate with College of Saint Benedict for women). **Challenging opportunities** include advanced placement credit, accelerated degree programs, student-designed majors, an honors program, double majors, independent study, and a senior project. Special programs include internships, off-campus study, study-abroad, and Army ROTC.

The most frequently chosen **baccalaureate** fields are business/marketing, social sciences, and English. A complete listing of majors at St. John's appears in the Majors by College index beginning on page 471.

The **faculty** at St. John's has 148 full-time members, 82% with terminal degrees. The student-faculty ratio is 12:1.

Students of St. John's
The student body totals 2,080, of whom 1,952 are undergraduates. 100% are men. Students come from 32 states and territories and 22 other countries. 83% are from Minnesota. 4.8% are international students. 1% are African American, 0.2% American Indian, 2% Asian American, and 1.1% Hispanic American. 89% returned for their sophomore year.

Facilities and Resources
643 **computers/terminals** and 3,000 ports are available on campus for general student use. Students can access the following: computer help desk, free student e-mail accounts, online (class) grades, online (class) registration, online (class) schedules, online student accounts. Campuswide network is available. 100% of college-owned or -operated housing units are wired for high-speed Internet access. Wireless service is available via classrooms, computer centers, computer labs, dorm rooms, learning centers, libraries, student centers. The 4 **libraries** have 481,338 books and 5,315 subscriptions.

Campus Life
There are 90 active organizations on campus, including a drama/theater group, newspaper, radio station, and choral group. No national or local **fraternities** or **sororities**.

St. John's is a member of the NCAA (Division III). **Intercollegiate sports** include baseball (m), basketball (m), cross-country running (m), football (m), golf (m), ice hockey (m), skiing (cross-country) (m), soccer (m), swimming and diving (m), tennis (m), track and field (m), wrestling (m).

Campus Safety
Student safety services include well-lit pathways, 911 center on campus, closed circuit TV monitors, late-night transport/escort service, 24-hour emergency telephone alarm devices, 24-hour patrols by trained security personnel, and student patrols.

Applying
St. John's requires an essay, SAT or ACT, a high school transcript, and 1 recommendation. It recommends an interview and a minimum high school GPA of 3.0. Application deadline: rolling admissions; 3/15 priority date for financial aid. Deferred admission is possible.

SAINT JOSEPH'S UNIVERSITY

Suburban setting ■ Private ■ Independent Religious ■ Coed
Philadelphia, Pennsylvania

Web site: www.sju.edu
Contact: , 5600 City Avenue, Philadelphia, PA 19131-1395
Telephone: 610-660-1300 or toll-free 888-BEAHAWK (in-state)
Fax: 610-660-1314
E-mail: admit@sju.edu

SPONSOR

Academics
St. Joseph's awards associate, bachelor's, master's, and doctoral **degrees** and post-bachelor's and post-master's certificates. **Challenging opportunities** include advanced placement credit, accelerated degree programs, student-designed majors, an honors program, double majors, independent study, and a senior project. Special programs include cooperative education, internships, summer session for credit, off-campus study, study-abroad, and Army, Navy, and Air Force ROTC.

The most frequently chosen **baccalaureate** fields are business/marketing, social sciences, and education. A complete listing of majors at St. Joseph's appears in the Majors by College index beginning on page 471.

The **faculty** at St. Joseph's has 277 full-time members, 89% with terminal degrees. The student-faculty ratio is 12:1.

Students of St. Joseph's
The student body totals 7,542, of whom 4,998 are undergraduates. 51.5% are women and 48.5% are men. Students come from 37 states and territories and 35 other countries. 51% are from Pennsylvania. 1.6% are international students. 7.5% are African American, 0.2% American Indian, 2.5% Asian American, and 3.1% Hispanic American. 88% returned for their sophomore year.

Facilities and Resources
670 **computers/terminals** are available on campus for general student use. Students can access the following: campus intranet, computer help desk, free student e-mail accounts, online (class) grades, online (class) registration, online (class) schedules. Campuswide network is available. 100% of college-owned or -operated housing units are wired for high-speed Internet access. Wireless service is available via entire campus. The 2 **libraries** have 366,300 books and 11,700 subscriptions.

Campus Life
There are 70 active organizations on campus, including a drama/theater group, newspaper, radio station, and choral group. 8% of eligible men and 14% of eligible women are members of national **fraternities** and national **sororities**.

St. Joseph's is a member of the NCAA (Division I). **Intercollegiate sports** (some offering scholarships) include baseball (m), basketball, cross-country running, field hockey (w), golf (m), lacrosse, soccer, softball (w), tennis, track and field.

Campus Safety
Student safety services include 24-hour shuttle/escort service, bicycle patrols, late-night transport/escort service, 24-hour emergency telephone alarm devices, 24-hour patrols by trained security personnel, and electronically operated dormitory entrances.

Applying
St. Joseph's requires an essay, SAT or ACT, a high school transcript, and 1 recommendation. It recommends a minimum high school GPA of 3.0. Application deadline: 2/1; 5/1 for financial aid, with a 2/15 priority date. Deferred admission is possible.

Getting Accepted
8,779 applied
62% were accepted
1,090 enrolled (20% of accepted)
3.32 average high school GPA
Mean SAT critical reading score: 577
Mean SAT math score: 584
Mean ACT score: 25
39% had SAT critical reading scores over 600
43% had SAT math scores over 600
71% had ACT scores over 24
5% had SAT critical reading scores over 700
5% had SAT math scores over 700
4% had ACT scores over 30

Graduation and After
68% graduated in 4 years
6% graduated in 5 years
1% graduated in 6 years
19% pursued further study (6% arts and sciences, 5% education, 3% business)
94% had job offers within 6 months
430 organizations recruited on campus

Financial Matters
$30,985 tuition and fees (2007–08)
$10,550 room and board
80% average percent of need met
$13,301 average financial aid amount received per undergraduate (2005–06 estimated)

With more than thirty majors and minors from which to choose, St. Lawrence students can sample from a variety of disciplines and specialize in those areas that are most intriguing to them. The diverse options for co-curricular activities, including thirty-two varsity sports, encourage students to further develop their abilities and interests outside the classroom. The University's location provides students with a residential community as well as easy access to the Adirondack Mountains, Ottawa, and Montreal. St.Lawrence alumni successfully pursue careers and graduate study, consistently achieving placement rates higher than 95 percent within one year of graduation.

Getting Accepted
4,645 applied
44% were accepted
627 enrolled (31% of accepted)
35% from top tenth of their h.s. class
3.5 average high school GPA
Mean SAT critical reading score: 600
Mean SAT math score: 605
Mean SAT writing score: 605
Mean ACT score: 26
54% had SAT critical reading scores over 600
63% had SAT math scores over 600
55% had SAT writing scores over 600
91% had ACT scores over 24
5% had SAT critical reading scores over 700
6% had SAT math scores over 700
8% had SAT writing scores over 700
17% had ACT scores over 30
14 valedictorians

Graduation and After
74% graduated in 4 years
3% graduated in 5 years
28% pursued further study (11% education, 7% arts and sciences, 3% medicine)
70.3% had job offers within 6 months
18 organizations recruited on campus

Financial Matters
$35,600 tuition and fees (2007–08)
$9060 room and board
94% average percent of need met
$32,471 average financial aid amount received per undergraduate (2006–07 estimated)

ST. LAWRENCE UNIVERSITY
SMALL-TOWN SETTING ■ PRIVATE ■ INDEPENDENT ■ COED
CANTON, NEW YORK

Web site: www.stlawu.edu
Contact: Ms. Terry Cowdrey, Dean of Admissions and Financial Aid, Payson Hall, Canton, NY 13617-1455
Telephone: 315-229-5261 or toll-free 800-285-1856
Fax: 315-229-5818
E-mail: admissions@stlawu.edu

Academics
St. Lawrence awards bachelor's and master's **degrees** and post-master's certificates. **Challenging opportunities** include advanced placement credit, student-designed majors, double majors, independent study, and a senior project. Special programs include internships, summer session for credit, off-campus study, study-abroad, and Army and Air Force ROTC.

The most frequently chosen **baccalaureate** fields are social sciences, psychology, and visual and performing arts. A complete listing of majors at St. Lawrence appears in the Majors by College index beginning on page 471.

The **faculty** at St. Lawrence has 171 full-time members, 98% with terminal degrees. The student-faculty ratio is 11:1.

Students of St. Lawrence
The student body totals 2,319, of whom 2,198 are undergraduates. 54.5% are women and 45.5% are men. Students come from 43 states and territories and 46 other countries. 52% are from New York. 5.6% are international students. 2.5% are African American, 0.7% American Indian, 2.3% Asian American, and 3.2% Hispanic American. 88% returned for their sophomore year.

Facilities and Resources
569 **computers/terminals** are available on campus for general student use. Students can access the following: computer help desk, free student e-mail accounts, online (class) grades, online (class) registration, online (class) schedules. Campuswide network is available. 100% of college-owned or -operated housing units are wired for high-speed Internet access. Wireless service is available via classrooms, computer centers, computer labs, learning centers, libraries, student centers. The 2 **libraries** have 576,086 books and 1,899 subscriptions.

Campus Life
There are 100 active organizations on campus, including a drama/theater group, newspaper, radio station, television station, and choral group. 3% of eligible men and 19% of eligible women are members of national **fraternities**, national **sororities**, and local sororities.

St. Lawrence is a member of the NCAA (Division III). **Intercollegiate sports** (some offering scholarships) include baseball (m), basketball, crew, cross-country running, equestrian sports, field hockey (w), football (m), golf, ice hockey, lacrosse, skiing (cross-country), skiing (downhill), soccer, softball (w), squash, swimming and diving, tennis, track and field, volleyball (w).

Campus Safety
Student safety services include late-night transport/escort service, 24-hour emergency telephone alarm devices, 24-hour patrols by trained security personnel, student patrols, and electronically operated dormitory entrances.

Applying
St. Lawrence requires an essay, a high school transcript, and 2 recommendations. It recommends an interview and a minimum high school GPA of 2.0. Application deadline: 2/1; 2/15 for financial aid. Early and deferred admission are possible.

St. Louis College of Pharmacy

Urban setting ■ Private ■ Independent ■ Coed
St. Louis, Missouri

Web site: www.stlcop.edu
Contact: Connie Horrall, Administrative Assistant, 4588 Parkview Place, St. Louis, MO 63110-1088
Telephone: 314-446-8328 or toll-free 800-278-5267 (in-state)
Fax: 314-446-8310
E-mail: chorrall@stlcop.edu

Academics

StLCoP awards first-professional **degrees**. Advanced placement credit is a **challenging opportunity.** Special programs include internships, summer session for credit, and Army and Air Force ROTC.

The most frequently chosen **baccalaureate** field is health professions and related sciences. A complete listing of majors at StLCoP appears in the Majors by College index beginning on page 471.

The **faculty** at StLCoP has 64 full-time members, 100% with terminal degrees. The student-faculty ratio is 18:1.

Students of StLCoP

The student body totals 1,156, of whom 648 are undergraduates. 54.8% are women and 45.2% are men. Students come from 19 states and territories and 3 other countries. 50% are from Missouri. 0.5% are international students. 2.3% are African American, 17% Asian American, and 0.8% Hispanic American. 90% returned for their sophomore year.

Facilities and Resources

10 **computers/terminals** are available on campus for general student use. Students can access the following: campus intranet, computer help desk, free student e-mail accounts, online (class) grades, online (class) registration, online (class) schedules. Campuswide network is available. 100% of college-owned or -operated housing units are wired for high-speed Internet access. Wireless service is available via entire campus. The **library** has 73,411 books and 153 subscriptions.

Campus Life

There are 15 active organizations on campus, including a drama/theater group, newspaper, and choral group. 70% of eligible men and 65% of eligible women are members of national **fraternities** and national **sororities**.

StLCoP is a member of the NAIA. **Intercollegiate sports** include basketball, cross-country running, volleyball (w).

Campus Safety

Student safety services include late-night transport/escort service, 24-hour emergency telephone alarm devices, 24-hour patrols by trained security personnel, and electronically operated dormitory entrances.

Applying

StLCoP requires an essay, SAT or ACT, a high school transcript, 2 recommendations, and a minimum high school GPA of 3.0, and in some cases an interview. Application deadline: 2/1; 3/15 priority date for financial aid.

Getting Accepted

565 applied
53% were accepted
241 enrolled (81% of accepted)
34% from top tenth of their h.s. class
3.88 average high school GPA
Mean ACT score: 28
100% had ACT scores over 24
17% had ACT scores over 30
22 valedictorians

Graduation and After

100% had job offers within 6 months

Financial Matters

$20,825 tuition and fees (2008–09)
$8030 room and board
52% average percent of need met
$10,199 average financial aid amount received per undergraduate (2005–06 estimated)

SAINT LOUIS UNIVERSITY

URBAN SETTING ■ PRIVATE ■ INDEPENDENT RELIGIOUS ■ COED
ST. LOUIS, MISSOURI

Web site: www.slu.edu
Contact: Director, 221 North Grand Boulevard, St. Louis, MO 63103-2097
Telephone: 314-977-3415 or toll-free 800-758-3678 (out-of-state)
Fax: 314-977-7136
E-mail: admitme@slu.edu

Getting Accepted
9,169 applied
80% were accepted
1,740 enrolled (24% of accepted)
37% from top tenth of their h.s. class
3.67 average high school GPA
Mean ACT score: 26
52% had SAT critical reading scores over 600
54% had SAT math scores over 600
76% had ACT scores over 24
12% had SAT critical reading scores over 700
14% had SAT math scores over 700
23% had ACT scores over 30

Graduation and After
62% graduated in 4 years
11% graduated in 5 years
1% graduated in 6 years
30% pursued further study
61.3% had job offers within 6 months
271 organizations recruited on campus

Financial Matters
$28,878 tuition and fees (2007–08)
$8550 room and board
60% average percent of need met
$19,034 average financial aid amount received
  per undergraduate (2005–06)

Academics

SLU awards bachelor's, master's, doctoral, and first-professional **degrees** and post-bachelor's and post-master's certificates. **Challenging opportunities** include advanced placement credit, accelerated degree programs, student-designed majors, an honors program, double majors, independent study, and a senior project. Special programs include cooperative education, internships, summer session for credit, off-campus study, study-abroad, and Army and Air Force ROTC.

The most frequently chosen **baccalaureate** fields are business/marketing, health professions and related sciences, and psychology. A complete listing of majors at SLU appears in the Majors by College index beginning on page 471.

The **faculty** at SLU has 614 full-time members, 90% with terminal degrees. The student-faculty ratio is 13:1.

Students of SLU

The student body totals 12,309, of whom 7,556 are undergraduates. 58.3% are women and 41.7% are men. Students come from 53 states and territories and 48 other countries. 43% are from Missouri. 2.9% are international students. 7.3% are African American, 0.3% American Indian, 5.9% Asian American, and 3% Hispanic American. 82% returned for their sophomore year.

Facilities and Resources

750 **computers/terminals** and 4,500 ports are available on campus for general student use. Students can access the following: campus intranet, computer help desk, free student e-mail accounts, online (class) grades, online (class) registration, online (class) schedules. Campuswide network is available. 100% of college-owned or -operated housing units are wired for high-speed Internet access. Wireless service is available via entire campus. The 3 **libraries** have 1,913,018 books and 14,395 subscriptions.

Campus Life

There are 170 active organizations on campus, including a drama/theater group, newspaper, radio station, television station, and choral group. 18% of eligible men and 23% of eligible women are members of national **fraternities** and national **sororities**.

SLU is a member of the NCAA (Division I). **Intercollegiate sports** (some offering scholarships) include baseball (m), basketball, cross-country running, field hockey (w), softball (w), swimming and diving, tennis, track and field, volleyball (w).

Campus Safety

Student safety services include crime prevention program, bicycle patrols, pamphlets, posters, films, late-night transport/escort service, 24-hour emergency telephone alarm devices, 24-hour patrols by trained security personnel, and electronically operated dormitory entrances.

Applying

SLU requires an essay, SAT or ACT, a high school transcript, secondary school report form, and a minimum high school GPA of 2.5. It recommends an interview and 2 recommendations. Application deadline: 8/1, 8/1 for nonresidents; 3/1 priority date for financial aid. Deferred admission is possible.

SAINT MARY'S COLLEGE

SUBURBAN SETTING ■ PRIVATE ■ INDEPENDENT RELIGIOUS ■ WOMEN ONLY
NOTRE DAME, INDIANA

SPONSOR

Web site: www.saintmarys.edu
Contact: Mona Bowe, Director of Admission, Notre Dame, IN 46556
Telephone: 574-284-4587 or toll-free 800-551-7621
Fax: 574-284-4841
E-mail: admission@saintmarys.edu

Academics

Saint Mary's awards bachelor's **degrees**. **Challenging opportunities** include advanced placement credit, accelerated degree programs, student-designed majors, double majors, independent study, and a senior project. Special programs include cooperative education, internships, summer session for credit, off-campus study, study-abroad, and Army, Navy, and Air Force ROTC.

The most frequently chosen **baccalaureate** fields are business/marketing, education, and health professions and related sciences. A complete listing of majors at Saint Mary's appears in the Majors by College index beginning on page 471.

The **faculty** at Saint Mary's has 137 full-time members, 88% with terminal degrees. The student-faculty ratio is 10:1.

Students of Saint Mary's

The student body is made up of 1,604 undergraduates. Students come from 42 states and territories and 5 other countries. 22% are from Indiana. 0.4% are international students. 1.4% are African American, 0.4% American Indian, 1.8% Asian American, and 5.5% Hispanic American. 86% returned for their sophomore year.

Facilities and Resources

209 **computers/terminals** are available on campus for general student use. Students can access the following: computer help desk, free student e-mail accounts, online (class) registration. Campuswide network is available. 100% of college-owned or -operated housing units are wired for high-speed Internet access. Wireless service is available via classrooms, computer centers, computer labs, dorm rooms, learning centers, libraries, student centers. The **library** has 231,713 books and 679 subscriptions.

Campus Life

There are 70 active organizations on campus, including a drama/theater group, newspaper, television station, choral group, and marching band. No national or local **sororities**.

Saint Mary's is a member of the NCAA (Division III). **Intercollegiate sports** include basketball, cross-country running, golf, soccer, softball, swimming and diving, tennis, volleyball.

Campus Safety

Student safety services include late-night transport/escort service, 24-hour emergency telephone alarm devices, 24-hour patrols by trained security personnel, and electronically operated dormitory entrances.

Applying

Saint Mary's requires an essay, SAT or ACT, a high school transcript, and 1 recommendation. It recommends an interview. Application deadline: 2/15; 3/1 priority date for financial aid. Early and deferred admission are possible.

Founded in 1844 and still sponsored by the Congregation of the Sisters of the Holy Cross, Saint Mary's College has preserved the best of its rich heritage as it pioneers new approaches to educating today's women. At Saint Mary's, students obtain a solid liberal arts foundation as well as excellent preparation for career opportunities or graduate and professional programs. Students also enjoy "the best of both worlds" through academic and social co-exchange programs with the University of Notre Dame. With 1,600 students from forty-five states and nine countries, Saint Mary's brings together women from a wide range of geographical areas, social backgrounds, and educational experiences.

Getting Accepted
1,281 applied
81% were accepted
479 enrolled (46% of accepted)
32% from top tenth of their h.s. class
3.72 average high school GPA
Mean SAT critical reading score: 568
Mean SAT math score: 563
Mean SAT writing score: 574
Mean ACT score: 24
34% had SAT critical reading scores over 600
34% had SAT math scores over 600
38% had SAT writing scores over 600
60% had ACT scores over 24
5% had SAT critical reading scores over 700
4% had SAT math scores over 700
5% had SAT writing scores over 700
8% had ACT scores over 30
4 National Merit Scholars
19 class presidents
8 valedictorians

Graduation and After
71% graduated in 4 years
3% graduated in 5 years
22% pursued further study (4% arts and sciences, 3% law, 2% medicine)
67% had job offers within 6 months
58 organizations recruited on campus

Financial Matters
$26,875 tuition and fees (2007–08)
$8675 room and board
81% average percent of need met
$20,191 average financial aid amount received per undergraduate (2005–06)

SAINT MARY'S COLLEGE OF CALIFORNIA

Suburban setting ■ Private ■ Independent Religious ■ Coed
Moraga, California

Getting Accepted
3,929 applied
82% were accepted
611 enrolled (19% of accepted)
3.33 average high school GPA
Mean SAT critical reading score: 530
Mean SAT math score: 540
24% had SAT critical reading scores over 600
22% had SAT math scores over 600
4% had SAT critical reading scores over 700
3% had SAT math scores over 700

Graduation and After
61% graduated in 4 years
6% graduated in 5 years
1% graduated in 6 years
43% pursued further study (19% arts and sciences, 6% law, 3% medicine)
40% had job offers within 6 months
90 organizations recruited on campus

Financial Matters
$31,080 tuition and fees (2007–08)
$11,090 room and board
69% average percent of need met
$21,717 average financial aid amount received per undergraduate (2006–07 estimated)

Web site: www.stmarys-ca.edu
Contact: Ms. Dorothy Jones, Dean of Admissions, PO Box 4800, Moraga, CA 94556-4800
Telephone: 925-631-4224 or toll-free 800-800-4SMC
Fax: 925-376-7193
E-mail: smcadmit@stmarys-ca.edu

Academics
SMC awards bachelor's, master's, and doctoral **degrees**. **Challenging opportunities** include advanced placement credit, student-designed majors, an honors program, double majors, independent study, and a senior project. Special programs include internships, off-campus study, study-abroad, and Army and Air Force ROTC.

The most frequently chosen **baccalaureate** fields are business/marketing, social sciences, and communications/journalism. A complete listing of majors at SMC appears in the Majors by College index beginning on page 471.

The **faculty** at SMC has 196 full-time members, 93% with terminal degrees. The student-faculty ratio is 12:1.

Students of SMC
The student body totals 3,809, of whom 2,685 are undergraduates. 61.7% are women and 38.3% are men. Students come from 40 states and territories and 33 other countries. 88% are from California. 1.9% are international students. 6.1% are African American, 1.1% American Indian, 10% Asian American, and 20.4% Hispanic American. 77% returned for their sophomore year.

Facilities and Resources
325 **computers/terminals** are available on campus for general student use. Students can access the following: campus intranet, computer help desk, free student e-mail accounts, online (class) grades, online (class) registration, online (class) schedules. Campuswide network is available. Wireless service is available via classrooms, computer centers, computer labs, learning centers, libraries, student centers. The **library** has 220,337 books and 15,000 subscriptions.

Campus Life
There are 40 active organizations on campus, including a drama/theater group, newspaper, radio station, television station, and choral group. No national or local **fraternities** or **sororities**.

SMC is a member of the NCAA (Division I). **Intercollegiate sports** (some offering scholarships) include baseball (m), basketball, crew (w), cross-country running, golf (m), lacrosse (w), soccer, softball (w), tennis, volleyball (w).

Campus Safety
Student safety services include late-night transport/escort service, 24-hour emergency telephone alarm devices, and 24-hour patrols by trained security personnel.

Applying
SMC requires an essay, SAT or ACT, a high school transcript, 1 recommendation, and a minimum high school GPA of 2.0, and in some cases an interview and a minimum high school GPA of 3.0. It recommends a minimum high school GPA of 3.0. Application deadline: 2/1; 2/15 priority date for financial aid. Deferred admission is possible.

ST. MARY'S COLLEGE OF MARYLAND

RURAL SETTING ■ PUBLIC ■ STATE-SUPPORTED ■ COED
ST. MARY'S CITY, MARYLAND

Web site: www.smcm.edu
Contact: Mr. Richard Edgar, Director of Admissions, 18952 East Fisher Road,
St. Mary's City, MD 20686-3001
Telephone: 240-895-5000 or toll-free 800-492-7181
Fax: 240-895-5001
E-mail: admissions@smcm.edu

SPONSOR

Academics

St. Mary's awards bachelor's and master's **degrees**. **Challenging opportunities** include advanced placement credit, student-designed majors, freshman honors college, an honors program, double majors, independent study, and a senior project. Special programs include cooperative education, internships, summer session for credit, off-campus study, and study-abroad.

The most frequently chosen **baccalaureate** fields are social sciences, psychology, and English. A complete listing of majors at St. Mary's appears in the Majors by College index beginning on page 471.

The **faculty** at St. Mary's has 138 full-time members, 97% with terminal degrees. The student-faculty ratio is 12:1.

Students of St. Mary's

The student body totals 2,002, of whom 1,980 are undergraduates. 56.5% are women and 43.5% are men. Students come from 34 states and territories and 37 other countries. 84% are from Maryland. 1.7% are international students. 8.1% are African American, 0.6% American Indian, 3.7% Asian American, and 4.6% Hispanic American. 91% returned for their sophomore year.

Facilities and Resources

325 **computers/terminals** and 500 ports are available on campus for general student use. Students can access the following: campus intranet, computer help desk, free student e-mail accounts, online (class) grades, online (class) registration, online (class) schedules, Blackboard. Campuswide network is available. 100% of college-owned or -operated housing units are wired for high-speed Internet access. Wireless service is available via classrooms, computer centers. The **library** has 161,177 books and 1,170 subscriptions.

Campus Life

There are 103 active organizations on campus, including a drama/theater group, newspaper, radio station, television station, and choral group. No national or local **fraternities** or **sororities**.

St. Mary's is a member of the NCAA (Division III). **Intercollegiate sports** include baseball (m), basketball, field hockey (w), lacrosse, sailing, soccer, swimming and diving, tennis, volleyball (w).

Campus Safety

Student safety services include late-night transport/escort service, 24-hour emergency telephone alarm devices, 24-hour patrols by trained security personnel, student patrols, and electronically operated dormitory entrances.

Applying

St. Mary's requires an essay, SAT or ACT, a high school transcript, and a minimum high school GPA of 2.0. It recommends an interview and 2 recommendations. Application deadline: 1/15; 3/1 for financial aid. Early admission is possible.

St. Mary's College of Maryland, with its distinctive identity as Maryland's "Public Honors College," is one of the finest liberal arts and sciences colleges in the country. The lively academic atmosphere and stunning beauty of the riverfront campus create a challenging and memorable college experience. More than 50 percent of the graduates of St. Mary's College of Maryland continue their studies in graduate or professional schools. Suite-style residences were completed in 2007, and the new athletic and recreation center opened in 2005.

Getting Accepted

2,351 applied
55% were accepted
464 enrolled (36% of accepted)
42% from top tenth of their h.s. class
3.5 average high school GPA
Mean SAT critical reading score: 620
Mean SAT math score: 600
Mean SAT writing score: 610
62% had SAT critical reading scores over 600
58% had SAT math scores over 600
57% had SAT writing scores over 600
16% had SAT critical reading scores over 700
10% had SAT math scores over 700
14% had SAT writing scores over 700
11 National Merit Scholars
18 valedictorians

Graduation and After

75% graduated in 4 years
6% graduated in 5 years
1% graduated in 6 years
34% pursued further study (16% arts and sciences, 8% education, 3% law)
59% had job offers within 6 months
80 organizations recruited on campus

Financial Matters

$12,604 resident tuition and fees (2008–09)
$23,454 nonresident tuition and fees (2008–09)
$9225 room and board
62% average percent of need met
$6500 average financial aid amount received per undergraduate (2005–06)

Recognized nationally for its academic program, St. Norbert College provides students with the resources necessary to compete with the nation's finest. With a faculty determined to provide the best instruction and advising possible, the College is committed to helping students achieve their educational goals. The College community, steeped in the values of the Norbertine tradition, encourages students to discover ways in which they can use their talents to enrich their lives, society, and the world. St. Norbert students contribute their talents to twenty-seven on-campus community service organizations.

Getting Accepted
1,789 applied
87% were accepted
543 enrolled (35% of accepted)
27% from top tenth of their h.s. class
3.52 average high school GPA
Mean ACT score: 24
55% had ACT scores over 24
6% had ACT scores over 30
19 valedictorians

Graduation and After
64% graduated in 4 years
5% graduated in 5 years
1% graduated in 6 years
13% pursued further study
70 organizations recruited on campus

Financial Matters
$24,653 tuition and fees (2007–08)
$6579 room and board
90% average percent of need met
$17,303 average financial aid amount received per undergraduate (2006–07 estimated)

ST. NORBERT COLLEGE
SUBURBAN SETTING ■ PRIVATE ■ INDEPENDENT RELIGIOUS ■ COED
DE PERE, WISCONSIN

Web site: www.snc.edu
Contact: Ms. Bridget O'Connor, Interim Vice President for Enrollment Management and Communications, 100 Grant Street, De Pere, WI 54115-2099
Telephone: 920-403-3005 or toll-free 800-236-4878
Fax: 920-403-4072
E-mail: admit@snc.edu

Academics
St. Norbert awards bachelor's and master's **degrees. Challenging opportunities** include advanced placement credit, student-designed majors, an honors program, double majors, independent study, and a senior project. Special programs include internships, summer session for credit, off-campus study, study-abroad, and Army ROTC.

The most frequently chosen **baccalaureate** fields are business/marketing, education, and social sciences. A complete listing of majors at St. Norbert appears in the Majors by College index beginning on page 471.

The **faculty** at St. Norbert has 109 full-time members, 93% with terminal degrees. The student-faculty ratio is 14:1.

Students of St. Norbert
The student body totals 2,169, of whom 2,086 are undergraduates. 57% are women and 43% are men. Students come from 26 states and territories and 29 other countries. 72% are from Wisconsin. 2.8% are international students. 0.9% are African American, 1.1% American Indian, 1.2% Asian American, and 2.7% Hispanic American. 85% returned for their sophomore year.

Facilities and Resources
221 **computers/terminals** are available on campus for general student use. Students can access the following: campus intranet, computer help desk, free student e-mail accounts, online (class) grades, online (class) registration, online (class) schedules. Campuswide network is available. 100% of college-owned or -operated housing units are wired for high-speed Internet access. Wireless service is available via classrooms, libraries. The **library** has 223,096 books and 580 subscriptions.

Campus Life
There are 63 active organizations on campus, including a drama/theater group, newspaper, radio station, television station, and choral group. 7% of eligible men and 7% of eligible women are members of national **fraternities**, national **sororities**, and local sororities.

St. Norbert is a member of the NCAA (Division III). **Intercollegiate sports** include baseball (m), basketball, cross-country running, football (m), golf, ice hockey (m), soccer, softball (w), swimming and diving (w), tennis, track and field, volleyball (w).

Campus Safety
Student safety services include crime prevention programs, late-night transport/escort service, 24-hour emergency telephone alarm devices, 24-hour patrols by trained security personnel, student patrols, and electronically operated dormitory entrances.

Applying
St. Norbert requires SAT or ACT, a high school transcript, and 1 recommendation, and in some cases an interview. It recommends an essay. Application deadline: rolling admissions; 3/1 priority date for financial aid. Early and deferred admission are possible.

St. Olaf College

Small-town setting ■ Private ■ Independent Religious ■ Coed
Northfield, Minnesota

Web site: www.stolaf.edu
Contact: Derek Gueldenzoph, Dean of Admissions, 1520 St. Olaf Avenue,
   Northfield, MN 55057
Telephone: 507-786-3025 or toll-free 800-800-3025
Fax: 507-786-3832
E-mail: admissions@stolaf.edu

Academics

St. Olaf awards bachelor's **degrees**. **Challenging opportunities** include advanced place-ment credit, student-designed majors, double majors, independent study, and a senior project. Special programs include internships, summer session for credit, off-campus study, and study-abroad.

The most frequently chosen **baccalaureate** fields are social sciences, visual and performing arts, and English. A complete listing of majors at St. Olaf appears in the Majors by College index beginning on page 471.

The **faculty** at St. Olaf has 197 full-time members, 91% with terminal degrees. The student-faculty ratio is 13:1.

Students of St. Olaf

The student body is made up of 3,040 undergraduates. 55.4% are women and 44.6% are men. Students come from 45 states and territories and 17 other countries. 57% are from Minnesota. 1.1% are international students. 1.3% are African American, 0.2% American Indian, 4.9% Asian American, and 1.5% Hispanic American. 93% returned for their sophomore year.

Facilities and Resources

969 **computers/terminals** and 2,600 ports are available on campus for general student use. Students can access the following: campus intranet, computer help desk, free student e-mail accounts, online (class) grades, online (class) registration, online (class) schedules. Campuswide network is available. 100% of college-owned or -operated housing units are wired for high-speed Internet access. Wireless service is available via entire campus. The 3 **libraries** have 1,054,284 books and 2,319 subscriptions.

Campus Life

There are 137 active organizations on campus, including a drama/theater group, newspaper, radio station, television station, and choral group. No national or local **fraternities** or **sororities**.

St. Olaf is a member of the NCAA (Division III). **Intercollegiate sports** include baseball (m), basketball, cross-country running, football (m), golf, ice hockey, skiing (cross-country), skiing (downhill), soccer, softball (w), swimming and diving, tennis, track and field, volleyball (w), wrestling (m).

Campus Safety

Student safety services include lighted pathways and sidewalks, first-year only dorms, quiet halls, late-night transport/escort service, 24-hour emergency telephone alarm devices, 24-hour patrols by trained security personnel, and electronically operated dormitory entrances.

Applying

St. Olaf requires an essay, SAT or ACT, a high school transcript, and 2 recommenda-tions. It recommends an interview. Application deadline: rolling admissions; 4/15 for financial aid, with a 1/15 priority date. Deferred admission is possible.

Getting Accepted
4,058 applied
54% were accepted
751 enrolled (34% of accepted)
54% from top tenth of their h.s. class
3.65 average high school GPA
Mean SAT critical reading score: 656
Mean SAT math score: 647
Mean ACT score: 28
76% had SAT critical reading scores over 600
77% had SAT math scores over 600
90% had ACT scores over 24
35% had SAT critical reading scores over 700
25% had SAT math scores over 700
43% had ACT scores over 30
36 National Merit Scholars
9 class presidents
69 valedictorians

Graduation and After
82% graduated in 4 years
3% graduated in 5 years
1% graduated in 6 years
29% pursued further study (14% arts and
   sciences, 4% medicine, 3% law)
64.7% had job offers within 6 months
118 organizations recruited on campus

Financial Matters
$30,600 tuition and fees (2007–08)
$7900 room and board
100% average percent of need met
$15,990 average financial aid amount received
   per undergraduate (2006–07 estimated)

SALEM COLLEGE

URBAN SETTING ■ PRIVATE ■ INDEPENDENT RELIGIOUS
■ UNDERGRADUATE: WOMEN ONLY; GRADUATE: COED
WINSTON-SALEM, NORTH CAROLINA

Web site: www.salem.edu
Contact: Katherine Knapp Watts, Chief Admissions Officer, PO Box 10548,
   Shober House, Winston-Salem, NC 27108
Telephone: 336-721-2621 or toll-free 800-327-2536
Fax: 336-724-7102
E-mail: admissions@salem.edu

Getting Accepted
420 applied
62% were accepted
121 enrolled (47% of accepted)
39% from top tenth of their h.s. class
3.7 average high school GPA
Mean SAT critical reading score: 560
Mean SAT math score: 540
Mean ACT score: 24
35% had SAT critical reading scores over 600
33% had SAT math scores over 600
22% had ACT scores over 24
8% had SAT critical reading scores over 700
2% had SAT math scores over 700
11% had ACT scores over 30
4 valedictorians

Graduation and After
50% graduated in 4 years
2% graduated in 5 years
1% graduated in 6 years
29% pursued further study (13% arts and
   sciences, 8% education, 3% law)
78% had job offers within 6 months

Financial Matters
$19,190 tuition and fees (2007–08)
$10,050 room and board

Academics

Salem awards bachelor's and master's **degrees** (only students age 23 or over are eligible to enroll part-time; men may attend evening program only). **Challenging opportunities** include advanced placement credit, student-designed majors, an honors program, double majors, independent study, and a senior project. Special programs include internships, summer session for credit, off-campus study, and study-abroad.

The most frequently chosen **baccalaureate** fields are social sciences, communications/journalism, and business/marketing. A complete listing of majors at Salem appears in the Majors by College index beginning on page 471.

The **faculty** at Salem has 57 full-time members, 86% with terminal degrees. The student-faculty ratio is 12:1.

Students of Salem

The student body totals 992, of whom 768 are undergraduates. 97.1% are women and 2.9% are men. Students come from 29 states and territories and 18 other countries. 77% are from North Carolina. 12.5% are international students. 18.9% are African American, 0.1% American Indian, 1.2% Asian American, and 3.4% Hispanic American. 76% returned for their sophomore year.

Facilities and Resources

54 **computers/terminals** are available on campus for general student use. Students can access the following: campus intranet, computer help desk, free student e-mail accounts, online (class) grades, online (class) schedules. Campuswide network is available. 100% of college-owned or -operated housing units are wired for high-speed Internet access. Wireless service is available via entire campus. The 2 **libraries** have 151,719 books and 679 subscriptions.

Campus Life

There are 41 active organizations on campus, including a drama/theater group, newspaper, choral group, and marching band. No national or local **sororities**.

Intercollegiate sports include basketball, cross-country running, field hockey, soccer, swimming and diving, tennis, volleyball.

Campus Safety

Student safety services include late-night transport/escort service, 24-hour emergency telephone alarm devices, 24-hour patrols by trained security personnel, and electronically operated dormitory entrances.

Applying

Salem requires an essay, SAT or ACT, a high school transcript, and 2 recommendations. It recommends an interview. Application deadline: rolling admissions; 3/1 priority date for financial aid. Early and deferred admission are possible.

SAMFORD UNIVERSITY

SUBURBAN SETTING ■ PRIVATE ■ INDEPENDENT RELIGIOUS ■ COED
BIRMINGHAM, ALABAMA

SPONSOR

Web site: www.samford.edu
Contact: Dr. Phil Kimrey, Dean of Admissions and Financial Aid, 800
  Lakeshore Drive, Samford Hall, Birmingham, AL 35229-0002
Telephone: 205-726-3673 or toll-free 800-888-7218
Fax: 205-726-2171
E-mail: admiss@samford.edu

Academics

Samford awards associate, bachelor's, master's, doctoral, and first-professional **degrees** and post-master's certificates. **Challenging opportunities** include advanced placement credit, accelerated degree programs, an honors program, double majors, independent study, and a senior project. Special programs include cooperative education, internships, summer session for credit, off-campus study, study-abroad, and Army and Air Force ROTC.

The most frequently chosen **baccalaureate** fields are business/marketing, health professions and related sciences, and communications/journalism. A complete listing of majors at Samford appears in the Majors by College index beginning on page 471.

The **faculty** at Samford has 280 full-time members, 84% with terminal degrees. The student-faculty ratio is 12:1.

Students of Samford

The student body totals 4,485, of whom 2,860 are undergraduates. 63.7% are women and 36.3% are men. Students come from 25 states and territories and 10 other countries. 39% are from Alabama. 6.3% are African American, 0.2% American Indian, 1% Asian American, and 1.3% Hispanic American. 83% returned for their sophomore year.

Facilities and Resources

330 **computers/terminals** are available on campus for general student use. Students can access the following: campus intranet, computer help desk, free student e-mail accounts, online (class) grades, online (class) registration, online (class) schedules. Campuswide network is available. Wireless service is available via computer centers, dorm rooms, learning centers, student centers. The 4 **libraries** have 439,760 books and 3,724 subscriptions.

Campus Life

There are 110 active organizations on campus, including a drama/theater group, newspaper, radio station, choral group, and marching band. 28% of eligible men and 38% of eligible women are members of national **fraternities** and national **sororities**.

Samford is a member of the NCAA (Division I). **Intercollegiate sports** (some offering scholarships) include baseball (m), basketball, cross-country running, football (m), golf, soccer (w), softball (w), tennis, track and field, volleyball (w).

Campus Safety

Student safety services include late-night transport/escort service, 24-hour emergency telephone alarm devices, and 24-hour patrols by trained security personnel.

Applying

Samford requires an essay, SAT or ACT, 1 recommendation, and leadership resumé. It recommends an interview. Application deadline: 12/15; 3/1 priority date for financial aid. Early and deferred admission are possible.

Samford University is the largest private accredited university in Alabama, yet, with more than 4,500 students, it is an ideal size. More than half the undergraduates reside on campus. Students from forty-four states and territories and thirty-three other countries enjoy a beautiful setting characterized by Georgian-Colonial architecture. The institution takes seriously its Christian heritage and is consistently listed in rankings of Southeastern institutions. Faculty members have earned degrees from more than 180 colleges and universities, with more than 80 percent holding the terminal degree in their field. Excellent opportunities to "stretch" academically, socially, physically, and spiritually are provided, as are special opportunities in computer competency, international experiences, and externships.

Getting Accepted
1,810 applied
92% were accepted
713 enrolled (43% of accepted)
32% from top tenth of their h.s. class
3.61 average high school GPA
Mean SAT critical reading score: 560
Mean SAT math score: 560
Mean ACT score: 25
34% had SAT critical reading scores over 600
35% had SAT math scores over 600
58% had ACT scores over 24
10% had SAT critical reading scores over 700
6% had SAT math scores over 700
15% had ACT scores over 30
20 National Merit Scholars
29 class presidents

Graduation and After
150 organizations recruited on campus

Financial Matters
$17,920 tuition and fees (2007–08)
$6320 room and board
70% average percent of need met
$11,977 average financial aid amount received per undergraduate (2005–06)

San Diego State University

URBAN SETTING ■ PUBLIC ■ STATE-SUPPORTED ■ COED
SAN DIEGO, CALIFORNIA

Web site: www.sdsu.edu
Contact: Ms. Beverly Arata, Director of Admissions, 5500 Campanile Drive, San Diego, CA 92182-0771
Telephone: 619-594-6336
E-mail: admissions@sdsu.edu

Getting Accepted
46,718 applied
44% were accepted
5,601 enrolled (27% of accepted)
3.44 average high school GPA
Mean SAT critical reading score: 527
Mean SAT math score: 547
Mean ACT score: 22
16% had SAT critical reading scores over 600
25% had SAT math scores over 600
37% had ACT scores over 24
1% had SAT critical reading scores over 700
2% had SAT math scores over 700
2% had ACT scores over 30

Graduation and After
20% graduated in 4 years
27% graduated in 5 years
9% graduated in 6 years
30% had job offers within 6 months
507 organizations recruited on campus

Financial Matters
$3428 resident tuition and fees (2007–08)
$13,598 nonresident tuition and fees (2007–08)
$10,904 room and board
70% average percent of need met
$7300 average financial aid amount received per undergraduate (2006–07 estimated)

Academics

SDSU awards bachelor's, master's, and doctoral **degrees** and post-bachelor's and post-master's certificates. **Challenging opportunities** include advanced placement credit, student-designed majors, an honors program, double majors, independent study, and a senior project. Special programs include internships, summer session for credit, off-campus study, study-abroad, and Army, Navy, and Air Force ROTC.

The most frequently chosen **baccalaureate** fields are business/marketing, social sciences, and psychology. A complete listing of majors at SDSU appears in the Majors by College index beginning on page 471.

The **faculty** at SDSU has 979 full-time members. The student-faculty ratio is 20:1.

Students of SDSU

The student body totals 36,559, of whom 30,460 are undergraduates. 57.4% are women and 42.6% are men. Students come from 51 states and territories and 64 other countries. 95% are from California. 2.5% are international students. 4.1% are African American, 0.7% American Indian, 15.5% Asian American, and 23.2% Hispanic American. 83% returned for their sophomore year.

Facilities and Resources

506 **computers/terminals** are available on campus for general student use. Students can access the following: online (class) registration. Campuswide network is available. The **library** has 1,342,735 books and 8,245 subscriptions.

Campus Life

There are 253 active organizations on campus, including a drama/theater group, newspaper, radio station, television station, choral group, and marching band. 7% of eligible men and 6% of eligible women are members of national **fraternities**, national **sororities**, local fraternities, and local sororities.

SDSU is a member of the NCAA (Division I). **Intercollegiate sports** (some offering scholarships) include baseball (m), basketball, cross-country running (w), football (m), golf, soccer, softball (w), swimming and diving (w), tennis, track and field (w), volleyball, water polo (w).

Campus Safety

Student safety services include late-night transport/escort service, 24-hour emergency telephone alarm devices, 24-hour patrols by trained security personnel, and student patrols.

Applying

SDSU requires SAT or ACT, a high school transcript, 2.5 GPA for non-California residents, and a minimum high school GPA of 2.0. Application deadline: 11/30; 3/2 for financial aid.

Santa Clara University

Suburban setting ■ Private ■ Independent Religious ■ Coed
Santa Clara, California

Web site: www.scu.edu
Contact: Ms. Sandra Hayes, Dean of Undergraduate Admissions, 500 El Camino Real, Santa Clara, CA 95053
Telephone: 408-554-4700
Fax: 408-554-5255
E-mail: ugadmissions@scu.edu

Academics

Santa Clara awards bachelor's, master's, doctoral, and first-professional **degrees** and post-bachelor's and post-master's certificates. **Challenging opportunities** include advanced placement credit, student-designed majors, an honors program, double majors, independent study, and a senior project. Special programs include cooperative education, internships, summer session for credit, study-abroad, and Army and Air Force ROTC.

The most frequently chosen **baccalaureate** fields are business/marketing, social sciences, and communications/journalism. A complete listing of majors at Santa Clara appears in the Majors by College index beginning on page 471.

The **faculty** at Santa Clara has 511 full-time members, 89% with terminal degrees. The student-faculty ratio is 12:1.

Students of Santa Clara

The student body totals 8,248, of whom 4,824 are undergraduates. 52.7% are women and 47.3% are men. Students come from 39 states and territories and 16 other countries. 65% are from California. 3.5% are international students. 3.4% are African American, 0.5% American Indian, 16.5% Asian American, and 12.7% Hispanic American. 94% returned for their sophomore year.

Facilities and Resources

800 **computers/terminals** and 6,000 ports are available on campus for general student use. Students can access the following: campus intranet, computer help desk, free student e-mail accounts, online (class) grades, online (class) registration, online (class) schedules. Campuswide network is available. 100% of college-owned or -operated housing units are wired for high-speed Internet access. Wireless service is available via entire campus. The 2 **libraries** have 786,360 books and 4,459 subscriptions.

Campus Life

There are 86 active organizations on campus, including a drama/theater group, newspaper, radio station, and choral group. No national or local **fraternities** or **sororities**.

Santa Clara is a member of the NCAA (Division I). **Intercollegiate sports** (some offering scholarships) include baseball (m), basketball, crew, cross-country running, golf, soccer, softball (w), tennis, track and field, volleyball (w), water polo.

Campus Safety

Student safety services include late-night transport/escort service, 24-hour emergency telephone alarm devices, 24-hour patrols by trained security personnel, and electronically operated dormitory entrances.

Applying

Santa Clara requires an essay, SAT or ACT, a high school transcript, and 1 recommendation. Application deadline: 1/7; 2/1 priority date for financial aid. Deferred admission is possible.

Getting Accepted
9,659 applied
60% were accepted
1,204 enrolled (21% of accepted)
36% from top tenth of their h.s. class
3.5 average high school GPA
Mean SAT critical reading score: 597
Mean SAT math score: 618
Mean ACT score: 26
52% had SAT critical reading scores over 600
61% had SAT math scores over 600
82% had ACT scores over 24
9% had SAT critical reading scores over 700
14% had SAT math scores over 700
22% had ACT scores over 30
1 National Merit Scholar

Graduation and After
79% graduated in 4 years
5% graduated in 5 years
1% graduated in 6 years
17% pursued further study (6% arts and sciences, 4% law, 4% engineering)
65% had job offers within 6 months
636 organizations recruited on campus

Financial Matters
$33,000 tuition and fees (2007–08)
$10,644 room and board
68% average percent of need met
$19,689 average financial aid amount received per undergraduate (2006–07 estimated)

Sarah Lawrence, a private, coeducational college of the liberal arts and sciences founded in 1926, is a lively community of students, scholars, and artists just 30 minutes from midtown Manhattan. In its distinctive seminar/conference system, each course consists of two parts: the seminar, limited to 15 students, and the conference, a private biweekly meeting with the seminar professor. In conference, student and teacher create a project that extends the seminar material and connects it to the student's academic goals. To prepare for this rigorous work, all first-year students enroll in a First-Year Studies Seminar. This seminar teacher becomes the student's don, or adviser, throughout his or her Sarah Lawrence years.

Getting Accepted
2,801 applied
44% were accepted
363 enrolled (29% of accepted)
37% from top tenth of their h.s. class
3.6 average high school GPA
6 National Merit Scholars
3 valedictorians

Graduation and After
70% graduated in 4 years
9% graduated in 5 years
1% graduated in 6 years

Financial Matters
$38,090 tuition and fees (2007–08)
$12,720 room and board
91% average percent of need met
$26,435 average financial aid amount received per undergraduate (2006–07 estimated)

SARAH LAWRENCE COLLEGE
SUBURBAN SETTING ■ PRIVATE ■ INDEPENDENT ■ COED
BRONXVILLE, NEW YORK

Web site: www.sarahlawrence.edu
Contact: Mr. Stephen M. Schierloh, Acting Dean of Admission, 1 Mead Way, Bronxville, NY 10708-5999
Telephone: 914-395-2510 or toll-free 800-888-2858
Fax: 914-395-2515
E-mail: slcadmit@sarahlawrence.edu

Academics
Sarah Lawrence awards bachelor's and master's **degrees**. **Challenging opportunities** include advanced placement credit, student-designed majors, double majors, and independent study. Special programs include internships, off-campus study, and study-abroad.

The most frequently chosen **baccalaureate** field is liberal arts/general studies. A complete listing of majors at Sarah Lawrence appears in the Majors by College index beginning on page 471.

The **faculty** at Sarah Lawrence has 195 full-time members. The student-faculty ratio is 6:1.

Students of Sarah Lawrence
The student body totals 1,700, of whom 1,383 are undergraduates. 74.3% are women and 25.7% are men. Students come from 47 states and territories and 34 other countries. 23% are from New York. 2.5% are international students. 3.9% are African American, 0.6% American Indian, 5% Asian American, and 5% Hispanic American. 86% returned for their sophomore year.

Facilities and Resources
110 **computers/terminals** and 30 ports are available on campus for general student use. Students can access the following: campus intranet, computer help desk, free student e-mail accounts. Campuswide network is available. 100% of college-owned or -operated housing units are wired for high-speed Internet access. Wireless service is available via classrooms, computer centers, computer labs, libraries, student centers. The 3 **libraries** have 298,611 books and 917 subscriptions.

Campus Life
There are 30 active organizations on campus, including a drama/theater group, newspaper, radio station, and choral group. No national or local **fraternities** or **sororities**.

Intercollegiate sports include basketball (m), crew, equestrian sports, softball (w), swimming and diving (w), tennis, volleyball (w).

Campus Safety
Student safety services include late-night transport/escort service, 24-hour emergency telephone alarm devices, 24-hour patrols by trained security personnel, and electronically operated dormitory entrances.

Applying
Sarah Lawrence requires an essay, a high school transcript, and 3 recommendations. It recommends an interview and a minimum high school GPA of 3.0. Application deadline: 1/1; 2/1 for financial aid. Early and deferred admission are possible.

Scripps College

Suburban setting ■ Private ■ Independent ■ Women Only
Claremont, California

Web site: www.scrippscollege.edu
Contact: Ms. Patricia F. Goldsmith, Dean of Admission and Financial Aid,
    1030 Columbia Avenue, Claremont, CA 91711
Telephone: 909-621-8149 or toll-free 800-770-1333
Fax: 909-607-7508
E-mail: admission@scrippscollege.edu

Academics

Scripps awards bachelor's **degrees** and post-bachelor's certificates. **Challenging opportunities** include advanced placement credit, accelerated degree programs, student-designed majors, double majors, independent study, and a senior project. Special programs include internships, off-campus study, study-abroad, and Army and Air Force ROTC.

The most frequently chosen **baccalaureate** fields are social sciences, area and ethnic studies, and visual and performing arts. A complete listing of majors at Scripps appears in the Majors by College index beginning on page 471.

The **faculty** at Scripps has 69 full-time members, 100% with terminal degrees. The student-faculty ratio is 11:1.

Students of Scripps

The student body totals 917, of whom 899 are undergraduates. Students come from 44 states and territories and 10 other countries. 42% are from California. 0.6% are international students. 3.6% are African American, 0.7% American Indian, 13.3% Asian American, and 8.1% Hispanic American. 95% returned for their sophomore year.

Facilities and Resources

72 **computers/terminals** are available on campus for general student use. Students can access the following: campus intranet, computer help desk, free student e-mail accounts, online (class) grades, online (class) schedules, 2 ports per dorm room. Campuswide network is available. 100% of college-owned or -operated housing units are wired for high-speed Internet access. Wireless service is available via classrooms, computer centers, computer labs, dorm rooms, libraries, student centers. The 5 **libraries** have 2,540,106 books and 35,033 subscriptions.

Campus Life

There are 200 active organizations on campus, including a drama/theater group, newspaper, radio station, and choral group. No national or local **sororities**.

Scripps is a member of the NCAA (Division III). **Intercollegiate sports** include basketball, cross-country running, golf, lacrosse, soccer, softball, swimming and diving, tennis, track and field, volleyball, water polo.

Campus Safety

Student safety services include late-night transport/escort service, 24-hour emergency telephone alarm devices, 24-hour patrols by trained security personnel, and electronically operated dormitory entrances.

Applying

Scripps requires an essay, SAT or ACT, a high school transcript, 3 recommendations, and graded writing sample. It recommends an interview and a minimum high school GPA of 3.0. Application deadline: 1/1; 2/1 priority date for financial aid. Early and deferred admission are possible.

Getting Accepted

1,969 applied
43% were accepted
227 enrolled (27% of accepted)
72% from top tenth of their h.s. class
4.0 average high school GPA
Mean SAT critical reading score: 692
Mean SAT math score: 660
Mean SAT writing score: 677
Mean ACT score: 29
92% had SAT critical reading scores over 600
87% had SAT math scores over 600
91% had SAT writing scores over 600
97% had ACT scores over 24
48% had SAT critical reading scores over 700
28% had SAT math scores over 700
42% had SAT writing scores over 700
53% had ACT scores over 30
9 National Merit Scholars
17 valedictorians

Graduation and After

74% graduated in 4 years
4% graduated in 5 years
1% graduated in 6 years
21% pursued further study (60% arts and sciences, 13% law, 7% education)
55% had job offers within 6 months
332 organizations recruited on campus

Financial Matters

$35,850 tuition and fees (2007–08)
$10,800 room and board
100% average percent of need met
$29,642 average financial aid amount received per undergraduate (2006–07 estimated)

SEATTLE PACIFIC UNIVERSITY

URBAN SETTING ■ PRIVATE ■ INDEPENDENT RELIGIOUS ■ COED
SEATTLE, WASHINGTON

Web site: www.spu.edu
Contact: Mr. Jobe Nice, Acting Director of Admissions, 3307 3rd Avenue, W, Seattle, WA 98119-1997
Telephone: 206-281-2021 or toll-free 800-366-3344
Fax: 206-281-2669
E-mail: admissions@spu.edu

Getting Accepted
2,055 applied
85% were accepted
716 enrolled (41% of accepted)
3.59 average high school GPA
41% had SAT critical reading scores over 600
34% had SAT math scores over 600
35% had SAT writing scores over 600
60% had ACT scores over 24
11% had SAT critical reading scores over 700
5% had SAT math scores over 700
6% had SAT writing scores over 700
13% had ACT scores over 30

Graduation and After
49% graduated in 4 years
14% graduated in 5 years
3% graduated in 6 years
12% pursued further study
86% had job offers within 6 months
56 organizations recruited on campus

Financial Matters
$25,128 tuition and fees (2007–08)
$8082 room and board
82% average percent of need met
$19,709 average financial aid amount received per undergraduate (2006–07 estimated)

Academics
SPU awards bachelor's, master's, and doctoral **degrees** and post-master's certificates. **Challenging opportunities** include advanced placement credit, student-designed majors, an honors program, double majors, independent study, and a senior project. Special programs include cooperative education, internships, summer session for credit, off-campus study, study-abroad, and Army, Navy, and Air Force ROTC.

The most frequently chosen **baccalaureate** fields are business/marketing, social sciences, and family and consumer sciences. A complete listing of majors at SPU appears in the Majors by College index beginning on page 471.

The **faculty** at SPU has 186 full-time members, 86% with terminal degrees. The student-faculty ratio is 14:1.

Students of SPU
The student body totals 3,842, of whom 3,038 are undergraduates. 67% are women and 33% are men. Students come from 46 states and territories and 24 other countries. 62% are from Washington. 0.7% are international students. 2.2% are African American, 1.1% American Indian, 7.1% Asian American, and 3.1% Hispanic American. 86% returned for their sophomore year.

Facilities and Resources
150 **computers/terminals** are available on campus for general student use. Students can access the following: online (class) registration. Campuswide network is available. The **library** has 191,807 books and 1,230 subscriptions.

Campus Life
There are 50 active organizations on campus, including a drama/theater group, newspaper, radio station, and choral group. No national or local **fraternities** or **sororities**.

SPU is a member of the NCAA (Division II). **Intercollegiate sports** (some offering scholarships) include basketball, crew, cross-country running, gymnastics (w), soccer, track and field, volleyball (w).

Campus Safety
Student safety services include closed-circuit TV monitors, late-night transport/escort service, 24-hour emergency telephone alarm devices, 24-hour patrols by trained security personnel, and student patrols.

Applying
SPU requires an essay, SAT or ACT, a high school transcript, 2 recommendations, and a minimum high school GPA of 2.5. Application deadline: 2/1; 4/1 priority date for financial aid. Early admission is possible.

SEATTLE UNIVERSITY

URBAN SETTING ■ PRIVATE ■ INDEPENDENT RELIGIOUS ■ COED
SEATTLE, WASHINGTON

SPONSOR

Web site: www.seattleu.edu
Contact: Mr. Michael K. McKeon, Dean of Admissions, Broadway and
  Madison, Seattle, WA 98122
Telephone: 206-296-2000 or toll-free 800-542-0833 (in-state), 800-426-7123
  (out-of-state)
Fax: 206-296-5656
E-mail: admissions@seattleu.edu

Academics

Seattle U awards bachelor's, master's, doctoral, and first-professional **degrees** and post-
bachelor's, post-master's, and first-professional certificates. **Challenging opportunities**
include advanced placement credit, accelerated degree programs, student-designed
majors, freshman honors college, an honors program, double majors, independent study,
and a senior project. Special programs include internships, summer session for credit,
off-campus study, study-abroad, and Army and Air Force ROTC.

The most frequently chosen **baccalaureate** fields are business/marketing, health
professions and related sciences, and psychology. A complete listing of majors at Seattle
U appears in the Majors by College index beginning on page 471.

The **faculty** at Seattle U has 401 full-time members, 79% with terminal degrees.
The student-faculty ratio is 13:1.

Students of Seattle U

The student body totals 7,226, of whom 4,160 are undergraduates. 61.2% are women
and 38.8% are men. Students come from 47 states and territories and 76 other countries.
60% are from Washington. 6.4% are international students. 5.6% are African American,
1.6% American Indian, 20.8% Asian American, and 7.2% Hispanic American. 84%
returned for their sophomore year.

Facilities and Resources

401 **computers/terminals** are available on campus for general student use. Students can
access the following: online (class) registration. Campuswide network is available. The 2
libraries have 141,478 books and 2,701 subscriptions.

Campus Life

There are 78 active organizations on campus, including a drama/theater group,
newspaper, radio station, and choral group. No national or local **fraternities** or **sororities**.

Seattle U is a member of the NCAA (Division II) and NAIA. **Intercollegiate sports**
(some offering scholarships) include basketball, cross-country running, soccer, softball
(w), swimming and diving, track and field, volleyball (w).

Campus Safety

Student safety services include bicycle patrols, late-night transport/escort service, 24-
hour emergency telephone alarm devices, 24-hour patrols by trained security personnel,
and electronically operated dormitory entrances.

Applying

Seattle U requires an essay, SAT or ACT, a high school transcript, 2 recommendations,
and a minimum high school GPA of 2.5. Application deadline: rolling admissions; 2/1
priority date for financial aid. Early and deferred admission are possible.

Getting Accepted
4,532 applied
65% were accepted
787 enrolled (27% of accepted)
32% from top tenth of their h.s. class
3.56 average high school GPA
44% had SAT critical reading scores over 600
41% had SAT math scores over 600
65% had ACT scores over 24
10% had SAT critical reading scores over 700
7% had SAT math scores over 700
10% had ACT scores over 30

Graduation and After
43% graduated in 4 years
16% graduated in 5 years
4% graduated in 6 years
220 organizations recruited on campus

Financial Matters
$26,325 tuition and fees (2007–08)
$7860 room and board
74% average percent of need met
$23,740 average financial aid amount received
  per undergraduate (2006–07 estimated)

Sewanee: The University of the South

Small-town setting ■ Private ■ Independent Religious ■ Coed
Sewanee, Tennessee

Getting Accepted
2,424 applied
64% were accepted
402 enrolled (26% of accepted)
47% from top tenth of their h.s. class
3.49 average high school GPA
67% had SAT critical reading scores over 600
57% had SAT math scores over 600
65% had SAT writing scores over 600
86% had ACT scores over 24
21% had SAT critical reading scores over 700
10% had SAT math scores over 700
16% had SAT writing scores over 700
32% had ACT scores over 30
22 National Merit Scholars

Graduation and After
73% graduated in 4 years
3% graduated in 5 years
38% pursued further study (14% arts and sciences, 6% law, 4% business)
74% had job offers within 6 months
17 organizations recruited on campus

Financial Matters
$30,660 tuition and fees (2007–08)
$8780 room and board
97% average percent of need met
$21,439 average financial aid amount received per undergraduate (2006–07 estimated)

Web site: www.sewanee.edu
Contact: Mr. David Lesesne, Dean of Admission, 735 University Avenue, Sewanee, TN 37383-1000
Telephone: 931-598-1238 or toll-free 800-522-2234
Fax: 931-598-3248
E-mail: admiss@sewanee.edu

Academics

Sewanee awards bachelor's, master's, doctoral, and first-professional **degrees** and post-bachelor's, post-master's, and first-professional certificates. **Challenging opportunities** include advanced placement credit, student-designed majors, double majors, independent study, and a senior project. Special programs include internships, summer session for credit, and study-abroad.

The most frequently chosen **baccalaureate** fields are social sciences, English, and visual and performing arts. A complete listing of majors at Sewanee appears in the Majors by College index beginning on page 471.

The **faculty** at Sewanee has 139 full-time members, 94% with terminal degrees. The student-faculty ratio is 11:1.

Students of Sewanee

The student body totals 1,561, of whom 1,475 are undergraduates. 53.1% are women and 46.9% are men. Students come from 41 states and territories and 22 other countries. 22% are from Tennessee. 2.4% are international students. 4.2% are African American, 0.7% American Indian, 2% Asian American, and 2.3% Hispanic American. 87% returned for their sophomore year.

Facilities and Resources

340 **computers/terminals** are available on campus for general student use. Students can access the following: campus intranet, computer help desk, free student e-mail accounts, online (class) grades, online (class) registration, online (class) schedules. Campuswide network is available. 100% of college-owned or -operated housing units are wired for high-speed Internet access. Wireless service is available via entire campus. The **library** has 648,459 books and 3,444 subscriptions.

Campus Life

There are 110 active organizations on campus, including a drama/theater group, newspaper, radio station, and choral group. 65% of eligible men and 55% of eligible women are members of national **fraternities** and local **sororities**.

Sewanee is a member of the NCAA (Division III). **Intercollegiate sports** include baseball (m), basketball, cross-country running, field hockey (w), football (m), golf, soccer, swimming and diving, tennis, track and field, volleyball (w).

Campus Safety

Student safety services include security lighting, late-night transport/escort service, 24-hour emergency telephone alarm devices, 24-hour patrols by trained security personnel, and electronically operated dormitory entrances.

Applying

Sewanee requires an essay, SAT or ACT, a high school transcript, and 2 recommendations. It recommends an interview. Application deadline: 2/1; 3/1 priority date for financial aid. Early and deferred admission are possible.

Siena College

Suburban setting ■ Private ■ Independent Religious ■ Coed
Loudonville, New York

Web site: www.siena.edu
Contact: Ms. Heather Renault, Director of Admissions, 515 Loudon Road,
    Loudonville, NY 12211-1462
Telephone: 518-783-2426 or toll-free 888-AT-SIENA
Fax: 518-783-2436
E-mail: admit@siena.edu

Academics

Siena awards bachelor's **degrees. Challenging opportunities** include advanced placement credit, accelerated degree programs, an honors program, double majors, independent study, and a senior project. Special programs include internships, summer session for credit, off-campus study, study-abroad, and Army and Air Force ROTC.

The most frequently chosen **baccalaureate** fields are business/marketing, psychology, and biological/life sciences. A complete listing of majors at Siena appears in the Majors by College index beginning on page 471.

The **faculty** at Siena has 187 full-time members, 92% with terminal degrees. The student-faculty ratio is 13:1.

Students of Siena

The student body is made up of 3,217 undergraduates. 55.4% are women and 44.6% are men. Students come from 30 states and territories and 6 other countries. 87% are from New York. 0.5% are international students. 2.2% are African American, 0.1% American Indian, 3.7% Asian American, and 3.5% Hispanic American. 87% returned for their sophomore year.

Facilities and Resources

462 **computers/terminals** are available on campus for general student use. Students can access the following: online (class) registration. Campuswide network is available. 100% of college-owned or -operated housing units are wired for high-speed Internet access. Wireless service is available via classrooms, computer labs, dorm rooms, libraries. The **library** has 337,411 books and 6,470 subscriptions.

Campus Life

There are 78 active organizations on campus, including a drama/theater group, newspaper, radio station, and television station. No national or local **fraternities** or **sororities**.

Siena is a member of the NCAA (Division I). **Intercollegiate sports** (some offering scholarships) include baseball (m), basketball, cross-country running, field hockey (w), golf, lacrosse, soccer, softball (w), swimming and diving (w), tennis, volleyball (w), water polo (w).

Campus Safety

Student safety services include call boxes in parking lots and on roadways, late-night transport/escort service, 24-hour emergency telephone alarm devices, 24-hour patrols by trained security personnel, and electronically operated dormitory entrances.

Applying

Siena requires an essay, SAT or ACT, a high school transcript, and 1 recommendation, and in some cases an interview. It recommends an interview. Application deadline: 3/1; 2/1 priority date for financial aid. Early and deferred admission are possible.

Siena develops leaders capable of extraordinary achievement. Students realize their potential through a blending of liberal arts and professional studies that combines challenging academics with real-world experiences. Committed to the development of the whole person, Siena, a private Franciscan and Catholic college, advances the spiritual, intellectual, religious, and ethical growth of its students. The curriculum includes twenty-eight degree programs and forty-six minors and certificate programs in business, liberal arts, and sciences. Siena's 166-acre campus is located in Loudonville, a suburb of Albany, New York, the state capital.

Getting Accepted
5,792 applied
54% were accepted
781 enrolled (25% of accepted)
21% from top tenth of their h.s. class
Mean SAT critical reading score: 552
Mean SAT math score: 573
Mean SAT writing score: 544
Mean ACT score: 25
24% had SAT critical reading scores over 600
40% had SAT math scores over 600
24% had SAT writing scores over 600
38% had ACT scores over 24
2% had SAT critical reading scores over 700
5% had SAT math scores over 700
3% had SAT writing scores over 700
2% had ACT scores over 30

Graduation and After
74% graduated in 4 years
4% graduated in 5 years
1% graduated in 6 years
24% pursued further study (8% arts and sciences, 7% education, 5% medicine)
71% had job offers within 6 months
125 organizations recruited on campus

Financial Matters
$22,685 tuition and fees (2007–08)
$8875 room and board

Simpson College combines the best of a liberal arts education with outstanding career preparation and extracurricular programs. Activities range from an award-winning music program to nationally recognized NCAA Division III teams. Located just 12 miles from Des Moines, Simpson offers the comfort of a small town and the advantages of a metropolitan area. Outstanding facilities have been enhanced with multimillion-dollar expansions and renovations, including the Carver Science Center, named after Simpson's most distinguished alumnus, George Washington Carver. The 4-4-1 academic calendar includes a May Term that provides students with unique learning opportunities. Simpson's beautiful 85-acre, tree-lined campus offers a setting that nurtures creativity, energy, and productivity.

Getting Accepted
1,346 applied
88% were accepted
385 enrolled (33% of accepted)
25% from top tenth of their h.s. class
Mean ACT score: 24
55% had ACT scores over 24
7% had ACT scores over 30
24 valedictorians

Graduation and After
57% graduated in 4 years
7% graduated in 5 years
11% pursued further study
98% had job offers within 6 months
90 organizations recruited on campus

Financial Matters
$24,771 tuition and fees (2008–09)
$6988 room and board
85% average percent of need met
$19,902 average financial aid amount received per undergraduate (2006–07 estimated)

SIMPSON COLLEGE
SMALL-TOWN SETTING ■ PRIVATE ■ INDEPENDENT RELIGIOUS ■ COED
INDIANOLA, IOWA

Web site: www.simpson.edu
Contact: Ms. Deborah Tierney, Vice President for Enrollment, 701 North C Street, Indianola, IA 50125
Telephone: 515-961-1624 or toll-free 800-362-2454 (in-state), 800-362-2454 Ext. 1624 (out-of-state)
Fax: 515-961-1870
E-mail: admiss@simpson.edu

Academics
Simpson awards bachelor's and master's **degrees** and post-bachelor's certificates. **Challenging opportunities** include advanced placement credit, an honors program, double majors, independent study, and a senior project. Special programs include cooperative education, internships, summer session for credit, off-campus study, and study-abroad.

The most frequently chosen **baccalaureate** fields are business/marketing, education, and social sciences. A complete listing of majors at Simpson appears in the Majors by College index beginning on page 471.

The **faculty** at Simpson has 97 full-time members, 88% with terminal degrees. The student-faculty ratio is 16:1.

Students of Simpson
The student body totals 2,039, of whom 2,017 are undergraduates. 58.2% are women and 41.8% are men. Students come from 21 states and territories and 16 other countries. 92% are from Iowa. 0.8% are international students. 1.8% are African American, 0.5% American Indian, 1.4% Asian American, and 1.6% Hispanic American. 82% returned for their sophomore year.

Facilities and Resources
275 **computers/terminals** are available on campus for general student use. Students can access the following: campus intranet, computer help desk, free student e-mail accounts, online (class) grades, online (class) schedules. Campuswide network is available. 100% of college-owned or -operated housing units are wired for high-speed Internet access. Wireless service is available via classrooms, computer centers, computer labs, learning centers, libraries, student centers. The 2 **libraries** have 157,713 books and 558 subscriptions.

Campus Life
There are 81 active organizations on campus, including a drama/theater group, newspaper, radio station, and choral group. 20% of eligible men and 20% of eligible women are members of national **fraternities**, national **sororities**, and local fraternities.

Simpson is a member of the NCAA (Division III). **Intercollegiate sports** include baseball (m), basketball, cheerleading, cross-country running, football (m), golf, soccer, softball (w), swimming and diving (w), tennis, track and field, volleyball (w), wrestling (m).

Campus Safety
Student safety services include late-night transport/escort service, 24-hour emergency telephone alarm devices, 24-hour patrols by trained security personnel, student patrols, and electronically operated dormitory entrances.

Applying
Simpson requires SAT or ACT, a high school transcript, and 1 recommendation. It recommends an interview and rank in upper 50% of high school class. Application deadline: 8/15. Early and deferred admission are possible.

SKIDMORE COLLEGE

SMALL-TOWN SETTING ■ PRIVATE ■ INDEPENDENT ■ COED
SARATOGA SPRINGS, NEW YORK

SPONSOR

Web site: www.skidmore.edu
Contact: Ms. Mary Lou Bates, Dean of Admissions and Financial Aid, 815
   North Broadway, Saratoga Springs, NY 12866-1632
Telephone: 518-580-5570 or toll-free 800-867-6007
Fax: 518-580-5584
E-mail: admissions@skidmore.edu

Academics

Skidmore awards bachelor's and master's **degrees. Challenging opportunities** include advanced placement credit, accelerated degree programs, student-designed majors, an honors program, double majors, independent study, and a senior project. Special programs include internships, summer session for credit, off-campus study, study-abroad, and Army and Air Force ROTC.

The most frequently chosen **baccalaureate** fields are social sciences, visual and performing arts, and business/marketing. A complete listing of majors at Skidmore appears in the Majors by College index beginning on page 471.

The **faculty** at Skidmore has 232 full-time members, 84% with terminal degrees. The student-faculty ratio is 9:1.

Students of Skidmore

The student body totals 2,863, of whom 2,809 are undergraduates. 60.3% are women and 39.7% are men. Students come from 44 states and territories and 41 other countries. 35% are from New York. 2.8% are international students. 3.5% are African American, 0.5% American Indian, 7.5% Asian American, and 4.8% Hispanic American. 94% returned for their sophomore year.

Facilities and Resources

230 **computers/terminals** and 600 ports are available on campus for general student use. Students can access the following: campus intranet, computer help desk, free student e-mail accounts, online (class) grades, online (class) registration, online (class) schedules. Campuswide network is available. 100% of college-owned or -operated housing units are wired for high-speed Internet access. Wireless service is available via classrooms, computer centers, computer labs, learning centers, libraries, student centers. The 2 **libraries** have 376,682 books and 959 subscriptions.

Campus Life

There are 80 active organizations on campus, including a drama/theater group, newspaper, radio station, television station, and choral group. No national or local **fraternities** or **sororities**.

Skidmore is a member of the NCAA (Division III). **Intercollegiate sports** include baseball (m), basketball, crew, equestrian sports (w), field hockey (w), golf (m), ice hockey (m), lacrosse, soccer, softball (w), swimming and diving, tennis, volleyball (w).

Campus Safety

Student safety services include well-lit campus, late-night transport/escort service, 24-hour emergency telephone alarm devices, 24-hour patrols by trained security personnel, and electronically operated dormitory entrances.

Applying

Skidmore requires an essay, SAT or ACT, a high school transcript, and 2 recommendations. It recommends SAT Subject Tests and an interview. Application deadline: 1/15; 1/15 for financial aid. Early and deferred admission are possible.

Skidmore College, located on a beautiful 850-acre campus, is a liberal arts college where creative thought matters. An interdisciplinary liberal studies curriculum challenges students to explore broadly. A rich cocurricular program provides further opportunities for personal growth and leadership. Among the largest majors are business, studio art, English, psychology, government, and biology. Students from forty-four states and territories and twenty-three countries live and learn in Skidmore's lively intellectual climate and beautiful campus surroundings.

Getting Accepted
6,768 applied
37% were accepted
682 enrolled (28% of accepted)
39% from top tenth of their h.s. class
3.33 average high school GPA
Mean SAT critical reading score: 625
Mean SAT math score: 622
Mean SAT writing score: 631
Mean ACT score: 27
68% had SAT critical reading scores over 600
65% had SAT math scores over 600
71% had SAT writing scores over 600
89% had ACT scores over 24
19% had SAT critical reading scores over 700
14% had SAT math scores over 700
21% had SAT writing scores over 700
26% had ACT scores over 30

Graduation and After
78% graduated in 4 years
3% graduated in 5 years
18% pursued further study (10% arts and sciences, 3% education, 2% medicine)
95% had job offers within 6 months
12 organizations recruited on campus

Financial Matters
$36,860 tuition and fees (2007–08)
$9836 room and board
94% average percent of need met
$27,280 average financial aid amount received per undergraduate (2005–06 estimated)

SMITH COLLEGE
SMALL-TOWN SETTING ■ PRIVATE ■ INDEPENDENT
■ UNDERGRADUATE: WOMEN ONLY; GRADUATE: COED
NORTHAMPTON, MASSACHUSETTS

Web site: www.smith.edu
Contact: Ms. Debra Shaver, Director of Admissions, 7 College Lane,
   Northampton, MA 01063
Telephone: 413-585-2500 or toll-free 800-383-3232
Fax: 413-585-2527
E-mail: admission@smith.edu

Students choose Smith because of its outstanding academic reputation. From its founding in 1871, the College has been committed to providing women with countless opportunities for personal and intellectual growth. The open curriculum allows each student, with the assistance of a faculty adviser, to plan an individualized course of study outside the major. Superb facilities, a beautiful New England campus, and a diverse student body complement the rigorous academic schedule. Unique programs include the first engineering science major at a women's college and the guarantee of funding for summer internships that are related to career and academic goals.

Getting Accepted
3,329 applied
52% were accepted
656 enrolled (38% of accepted)
63% from top tenth of their h.s. class
3.85 average high school GPA
75% had SAT critical reading scores over 600
59% had SAT math scores over 600
74% had SAT writing scores over 600
86% had ACT scores over 24
32% had SAT critical reading scores over 700
17% had SAT math scores over 700
27% had SAT writing scores over 700
29% had ACT scores over 30

Graduation and After
83% graduated in 4 years
3% graduated in 5 years
18% pursued further study
63 organizations recruited on campus

Financial Matters
$34,186 tuition and fees (2007–08)
$11,420 room and board
100% average percent of need met
$32,659 average financial aid amount received
   per undergraduate (2006–07 estimated)

Academics
Smith awards bachelor's, master's, and doctoral **degrees** and post-bachelor's and post-master's certificates. **Challenging opportunities** include advanced placement credit, accelerated degree programs, student-designed majors, an honors program, double majors, independent study, and a senior project. Special programs include internships, off-campus study, study-abroad, and Army and Air Force ROTC.

The most frequently chosen **baccalaureate** fields are social sciences, area and ethnic studies, and foreign languages and literature. A complete listing of majors at Smith appears in the Majors by College index beginning on page 471.

The **faculty** at Smith has 281 full-time members, 98% with terminal degrees. The student-faculty ratio is 9:1.

Students of Smith
The student body totals 3,065, of whom 2,596 are undergraduates. 100% are women. Students come from 50 states and territories and 72 other countries. 23% are from Massachusetts. 6.8% are international students. 7.4% are African American, 0.7% American Indian, 12% Asian American, and 6.4% Hispanic American. 90% returned for their sophomore year.

Facilities and Resources
585 **computers/terminals** are available on campus for general student use. Students can access the following: computer help desk, free student e-mail accounts, online (class) registration. Campuswide network is available. 100% of college-owned or -operated housing units are wired for high-speed Internet access. Wireless service is available via classrooms, computer centers, computer labs, dorm rooms, learning centers, libraries, student centers. The 4 **libraries** have 1,408,125 books and 8,741 subscriptions.

Campus Life
There are 112 active organizations on campus, including a drama/theater group, newspaper, radio station, television station, and choral group. No national or local **sororities**.

Smith is a member of the NCAA (Division III). **Intercollegiate sports** include basketball, crew, cross-country running, equestrian sports, field hockey, lacrosse, skiing (downhill), soccer, softball, squash, swimming and diving, tennis, track and field, volleyball.

Campus Safety
Student safety services include self-defense workshops, emergency telephones, programs in crime and sexual assault prevention, late-night transport/escort service, 24-hour emergency telephone alarm devices, and 24-hour patrols by trained security personnel.

Applying
Smith requires an essay, SAT or ACT, a high school transcript, and 3 recommendations. It recommends an interview. Application deadline: 1/15; 2/1 for financial aid. Early and deferred admission are possible.

Southern Methodist University

Suburban setting ■ Private ■ Independent Religious ■ Coed
Dallas, Texas

Web site: www.smu.edu
Contact: Mr. Ron Moss, Director of Admission and Enrollment Management,
PO Box 750181, Dallas, TX 75275-0181
Telephone: 214-768-3417 or toll-free 800-323-0672
Fax: 214-768-0202
E-mail: enrol_serv@smu.edu

SPONSOR

> SMU is a vibrant, diverse academic community in the heart of a dynamic city. Excellence is the standard and success is the goal through nearly eighty majors, access to expert faculty members in relatively small classes, and opportunities to pursue an honors curriculum, research, internships, study abroad, and community service.

Academics

SMU awards bachelor's, master's, doctoral, and first-professional **degrees** and post-bachelor's certificates. **Challenging opportunities** include advanced placement credit, accelerated degree programs, student-designed majors, an honors program, double majors, and independent study. Special programs include cooperative education, internships, summer session for credit, study-abroad, and Army and Air Force ROTC.

The most frequently chosen **baccalaureate** fields are business/marketing, social sciences, and communications/journalism. A complete listing of majors at SMU appears in the Majors by College index beginning on page 471.

The **faculty** at SMU has 633 full-time members, 84% with terminal degrees. The student-faculty ratio is 12:1.

Students of SMU

The student body totals 10,829, of whom 6,176 are undergraduates. 53.9% are women and 46.1% are men. Students come from 50 states and territories and 65 other countries. 58% are from Texas. 4.9% are international students. 4.9% are African American, 0.7% American Indian, 6.1% Asian American, and 7.7% Hispanic American. 89% returned for their sophomore year.

Facilities and Resources

758 **computers/terminals** are available on campus for general student use. Students can access the following: online (class) registration, online billing/payment processing. Campuswide network is available. The 8 **libraries** have 2,848,971 books and 11,701 subscriptions.

Campus Life

There are 180 active organizations on campus, including a drama/theater group, newspaper, radio station, choral group, and marching band. 23% of eligible men and 31% of eligible women are members of national **fraternities** and national **sororities**.

SMU is a member of the NCAA (Division I). **Intercollegiate sports** (some offering scholarships) include basketball, crew (w), cross-country running (w), equestrian sports (w), football (m), golf, soccer, swimming and diving, tennis, track and field (w), volleyball (w).

Campus Safety

Student safety services include late-night transport/escort service, 24-hour emergency telephone alarm devices, 24-hour patrols by trained security personnel, and electronically operated dormitory entrances.

Applying

SMU requires an essay, SAT or ACT, a high school transcript, and 1 recommendation, and in some cases SAT Subject Tests. Application deadline: 1/15; 2/15 priority date for financial aid. Early and deferred admission are possible.

Getting Accepted
8,253 applied
50% were accepted
1,309 enrolled (32% of accepted)
40% from top tenth of their h.s. class
3.55 average high school GPA
Mean SAT critical reading score: 610
Mean SAT math score: 620
Mean SAT writing score: 605
Mean ACT score: 27
58% had SAT critical reading scores over 600
64% had SAT math scores over 600
56% had SAT writing scores over 600
86% had ACT scores over 24
13% had SAT critical reading scores over 700
16% had SAT math scores over 700
10% had SAT writing scores over 700
19% had ACT scores over 30

Graduation and After
56% graduated in 4 years
14% graduated in 5 years
2% graduated in 6 years
Graduates pursuing further study: 5% arts and sciences, 4% engineering, 3% law

Financial Matters
$33,198 tuition and fees (2008–09)
$11,875 room and board
90% average percent of need met
$24,824 average financial aid amount received per undergraduate (2006–07 estimated)

SOUTHWEST BAPTIST UNIVERSITY

SMALL-TOWN SETTING ■ PRIVATE ■ INDEPENDENT RELIGIOUS ■ COED
BOLIVAR, MISSOURI

Web site: www.sbuniv.edu
Contact: Mr. Darren Crowder, Director of Admissions, 1600 University
    Avenue, Bolivar, MO 65613-2597
Telephone: 417-328-1817 or toll-free 800-526-5859
Fax: 417-328-1808
E-mail: dcrowder@sbuniv.edu

Getting Accepted
1,674 applied
65% were accepted
448 enrolled (41% of accepted)
22% from top tenth of their h.s. class
3.39 average high school GPA
Mean SAT critical reading score: 510
Mean SAT math score: 487
Mean ACT score: 23
26% had SAT critical reading scores over 600
18% had SAT math scores over 600
42% had ACT scores over 24
8% had SAT critical reading scores over 700
9% had ACT scores over 30

Graduation and After
36% graduated in 4 years
11% graduated in 5 years
2% graduated in 6 years
20% pursued further study
70% had job offers within 6 months
77 organizations recruited on campus

Financial Matters
$15,870 tuition and fees (2008–09)
$5000 room and board
63% average percent of need met
$10,617 average financial aid amount received
    per undergraduate (2006–07 estimated)

Academics

SBU awards associate, bachelor's, master's, and doctoral **degrees** and post-master's certificates. **Challenging opportunities** include advanced placement credit, student-designed majors, an honors program, double majors, independent study, and a senior project. Special programs include cooperative education, internships, summer session for credit, off-campus study, study-abroad, and Army ROTC.

The most frequently chosen **baccalaureate** fields are education, business/marketing, and psychology. A complete listing of majors at SBU appears in the Majors by College index beginning on page 471.

The **faculty** at SBU has 110 full-time members, 60% with terminal degrees. The student-faculty ratio is 13:1.

Students of SBU

The student body totals 3,539, of whom 2,752 are undergraduates. 65.6% are women and 34.4% are men. Students come from 45 states and territories and 15 other countries. 72% are from Missouri. 1% are international students. 3.7% are African American, 1% American Indian, 0.6% Asian American, and 1.3% Hispanic American. 72% returned for their sophomore year.

Facilities and Resources

261 **computers/terminals** are available on campus for general student use. Students can access the following: computer help desk, free student e-mail accounts, online (class) grades, online (class) registration, online (class) schedules. Campuswide network is available. 90% of college-owned or -operated housing units are wired for high-speed Internet access. Wireless service is available via entire campus. The 4 **libraries** have 180,115 books and 22,080 subscriptions.

Campus Life

There are 27 active organizations on campus, including a drama/theater group, newspaper, and choral group. No national or local **fraternities** or **sororities**.

SBU is a member of the NCAA (Division II). **Intercollegiate sports** (some offering scholarships) include baseball (m), basketball, cheerleading, cross-country running, football (m), golf (m), soccer, softball (w), tennis, track and field, volleyball (w).

Campus Safety

Student safety services include 24-hour emergency telephone alarm devices, 24-hour patrols by trained security personnel, and electronically operated dormitory entrances.

Applying

SBU requires SAT or ACT, a high school transcript, and a minimum high school GPA of 2.5, and in some cases 3 recommendations. It recommends an essay and an interview. Application deadline: rolling admissions; 3/15 priority date for financial aid.

SOUTHWESTERN UNIVERSITY

Suburban setting ■ Private ■ Independent Religious ■ Coed
Georgetown, Texas

Web site: www.southwestern.edu
Contact: Mr. Tom Oliver, Vice President for Enrollment Services, 1001 East University Avenue, Georgetown, TX 78626
Telephone: 512-863-1200 or toll-free 800-252-3166
Fax: 512-863-9601
E-mail: admission@southwestern.edu

Academics

Southwestern awards bachelor's **degrees**. **Challenging opportunities** include advanced placement credit, student-designed majors, double majors, independent study, and a senior project. Special programs include internships, summer session for credit, off-campus study, and study-abroad.

The most frequently chosen **baccalaureate** fields are social sciences, communications/journalism, and biological/life sciences. A complete listing of majors at Southwestern appears in the Majors by College index beginning on page 471.

The **faculty** at Southwestern has 122 full-time members, 98% with terminal degrees. The student-faculty ratio is 10:1.

Students of Southwestern

The student body is made up of 1,294 undergraduates. 60.6% are women and 39.4% are men. Students come from 31 states and territories and 8 other countries. 95% are from Texas. 0.1% are international students. 2.8% are African American, 0.7% American Indian, 4.5% Asian American, and 14% Hispanic American. 87% returned for their sophomore year.

Facilities and Resources

410 **computers/terminals** are available on campus for general student use. Students can access the following: course schedule, course catalog, grades, transcripts. Campuswide network is available. The **library** has 323,000 books and 2,598 subscriptions.

Campus Life

There are 105 active organizations on campus, including a drama/theater group, newspaper, and choral group. 29% of eligible men and 31% of eligible women are members of national **fraternities** and national **sororities**.

Southwestern is a member of the NCAA (Division III). **Intercollegiate sports** include baseball (m), basketball, cross-country running, golf, soccer, swimming and diving, tennis, volleyball (w).

Campus Safety

Student safety services include late-night transport/escort service, 24-hour emergency telephone alarm devices, 24-hour patrols by trained security personnel, student patrols, and electronically operated dormitory entrances.

Applying

Southwestern requires an essay, SAT, a high school transcript, and 1 recommendation, and in some cases SAT and SAT Subject Tests or ACT and an interview. It recommends an interview. Application deadline: 2/15; 3/1 for financial aid, with a 3/1 priority date. Deferred admission is possible.

Southwestern University (SU), a proud member of Colleges That Change Lives, is a selective national liberal arts college recognized for its high-quality undergraduate academic programs, professor-scholars who are dedicated to teaching, superior facilities, and a price that is significantly lower than comparable institutions. Located just north of vibrant Austin, Texas, SU offers its 1,310 students an engaging, values-centered educational experience through a broad-based curriculum, preprofessional programs, and extensive extracurricular opportunities, such as internships, study abroad, collaborative research with faculty members, and NCAA Division III competition. SU recently graduated its second group of Paideia Scholars. The Paideia Program is a distinctive academic option to help students connect their in-classroom and out-of-classroom experiences. SU's facilities are exemplary among schools of its type, and the University offers significant financial assistance to help families with their educational expenses. At Southwestern, minds are engaged and lives transformed.

Getting Accepted
1,916 applied
67% were accepted
371 enrolled (29% of accepted)
50% from top tenth of their h.s. class
61% had SAT critical reading scores over 600
57% had SAT math scores over 600
81% had ACT scores over 24
17% had SAT critical reading scores over 700
13% had SAT math scores over 700
23% had ACT scores over 30

Graduation and After
60% graduated in 4 years
11% graduated in 5 years
1% graduated in 6 years
26% pursued further study (12% arts and sciences, 4% law, 3% medicine)
53% had job offers within 6 months
31 organizations recruited on campus

Financial Matters
$25,740 tuition and fees (2007–08)
$8130 room and board
90% average percent of need met
$20,432 average financial aid amount received per undergraduate (2006–07 estimated)

STANFORD UNIVERSITY

SUBURBAN SETTING ■ PRIVATE ■ INDEPENDENT ■ COED
STANFORD, CALIFORNIA

Web site: www.stanford.edu
Contact: Rick Shaw, Dean of Undergraduate Admission and Financial Aid, Montag Hall, 355 Galvez Street, Stanford, CA 94305-3020
Telephone: 650-723-2091
Fax: 650-725-2846
E-mail: admission@stanford.edu

Getting Accepted
23,958 applied
10% were accepted
1,721 enrolled (70% of accepted)
91% from top tenth of their h.s. class
92% had SAT critical reading scores over 600
95% had SAT math scores over 600
93% had SAT writing scores over 600
98% had ACT scores over 24
61% had SAT critical reading scores over 700
67% had SAT math scores over 700
60% had SAT writing scores over 700
70% had ACT scores over 30

Graduation and After
80% graduated in 4 years
13% graduated in 5 years
3% graduated in 6 years
35% pursued further study
62% had job offers within 6 months
400 organizations recruited on campus

Financial Matters
$34,800 tuition and fees (2007–08)
$10,808 room and board
100% average percent of need met
$29,234 average financial aid amount received per undergraduate (2005–06)

Academics

Stanford awards bachelor's, master's, doctoral, and first-professional **degrees**. **Challenging opportunities** include advanced placement credit, student-designed majors, an honors program, double majors, independent study, and a senior project. Special programs include internships, summer session for credit, off-campus study, study-abroad, and Army, Navy, and Air Force ROTC.

The most frequently chosen **baccalaureate** fields are social sciences, interdisciplinary studies, and engineering. A complete listing of majors at Stanford appears in the Majors by College index beginning on page 471.

The **faculty** at Stanford has 1,028 full-time members, 98% with terminal degrees. The student-faculty ratio is 6:1.

Students of Stanford

The student body totals 19,782, of whom 6,584 are undergraduates. 48.5% are women and 51.5% are men. Students come from 52 states and territories and 68 other countries. 50% are from California. 6.3% are international students. 9.5% are African American, 2.3% American Indian, 24.2% Asian American, and 11.5% Hispanic American. 98% returned for their sophomore year.

Facilities and Resources

1,000 **computers/terminals** and 22,000 ports are available on campus for general student use. Students can access the following: campus intranet, computer help desk, free student e-mail accounts, online (class) grades, online (class) registration, online (class) schedules. Campuswide network is available. 100% of college-owned or -operated housing units are wired for high-speed Internet access. Wireless service is available via entire campus. The 19 **libraries** have 8,200,000 books and 75,000 subscriptions.

Campus Life

There are 600 active organizations on campus, including a drama/theater group, newspaper, radio station, television station, choral group, and marching band. Stanford has national **fraternities** and national **sororities**.

Stanford is a member of the NCAA (Division I) and NAIA. **Intercollegiate sports** (some offering scholarships) include baseball (m), basketball, crew, cross-country running, fencing, field hockey (w), football (m), golf, gymnastics, lacrosse (w), sailing, soccer, softball (w), squash (w), swimming and diving, tennis, track and field, ultimate Frisbee, volleyball, water polo, wrestling (m).

Campus Safety

Student safety services include late-night transport/escort service, 24-hour emergency telephone alarm devices, 24-hour patrols by trained security personnel, and electronically operated dormitory entrances.

Applying

Stanford requires an essay, SAT or ACT, a high school transcript, and 2 recommendations. It recommends SAT Subject Tests. Application deadline: 1/1; 2/15 priority date for financial aid. Deferred admission is possible.

STATE UNIVERSITY OF NEW YORK AT BINGHAMTON

SUBURBAN SETTING ■ PUBLIC ■ STATE-SUPPORTED ■ COED
BINGHAMTON, NEW YORK

Web site: www.binghamton.edu
Contact: Ms. Cheryl S. Brown, Director of Admissions, PO Box 6001, Binghamton, NY 13902-6001
Telephone: 607-777-2171
Fax: 607-777-4445
E-mail: admit@binghamton.edu

Academics

Binghamton awards bachelor's, master's, and doctoral **degrees** and post-master's certificates. **Challenging opportunities** include advanced placement credit, accelerated degree programs, student-designed majors, an honors program, double majors, independent study, and a senior project. Special programs include internships, summer session for credit, off-campus study, study-abroad, and Air Force ROTC.

The most frequently chosen **baccalaureate** fields are social sciences, business/marketing, and psychology. A complete listing of majors at Binghamton appears in the Majors by College index beginning on page 471.

The **faculty** at Binghamton has 575 full-time members, 93% with terminal degrees. The student-faculty ratio is 20:1.

Students of Binghamton

The student body totals 14,435, of whom 11,515 are undergraduates. 47.7% are women and 52.3% are men. Students come from 41 states and territories and 66 other countries. 93% are from New York. 8.5% are international students. 5.3% are African American, 0.2% American Indian, 12.9% Asian American, and 6.6% Hispanic American. 90% returned for their sophomore year.

Facilities and Resources

650 **computers/terminals** are available on campus for general student use. Students can access the following: campus intranet, computer help desk, free student e-mail accounts, online (class) grades, online (class) registration, online (class) schedules, course management system, personal web space. Campuswide network is available. 100% of college-owned or -operated housing units are wired for high-speed Internet access. Wireless service is available via entire campus. The 2 **libraries** have 2,309,457 books and 41,985 subscriptions.

Campus Life

There are 200 active organizations on campus, including a drama/theater group, newspaper, radio station, television station, and choral group. 8% of eligible men and 9% of eligible women are members of national **fraternities**, national **sororities**, local fraternities, and local sororities.

Binghamton is a member of the NCAA (Division I). **Intercollegiate sports** (some offering scholarships) include baseball (m), basketball, cheerleading, cross-country running, golf (m), lacrosse, soccer, softball (w), swimming and diving, tennis, track and field, volleyball (w), wrestling (m).

Campus Safety

Student safety services include safety awareness programs, well-lit campus, self-defense education, secured campus entrance 12 a.m. to 5 a.m. emergency telephones, late-night transport/escort service, 24-hour emergency telephone alarm devices, 24-hour patrols by trained security personnel, student patrols, and electronically operated dormitory entrances.

Applying

Binghamton requires an essay, SAT or ACT, a high school transcript, and recommendations, and in some cases 1 recommendation and portfolio, audition. Application deadline: rolling admissions, rolling admissions for nonresidents; 2/1 priority date for financial aid. Early and deferred admission are possible.

Getting Accepted
25,242 applied
39% were accepted
2,304 enrolled (24% of accepted)
49% from top tenth of their h.s. class
3.7 average high school GPA
Mean SAT critical reading score: 618
Mean SAT math score: 649
Mean ACT score: 28
63% had SAT critical reading scores over 600
80% had SAT math scores over 600
89% had ACT scores over 24
13% had SAT critical reading scores over 700
24% had SAT math scores over 700
23% had ACT scores over 30

Graduation and After
67% graduated in 4 years
10% graduated in 5 years
2% graduated in 6 years
38% pursued further study (9% medicine, 7% education, 7% law)
189 organizations recruited on campus

Financial Matters
$6012 resident tuition and fees (2007–08)
$12,272 nonresident tuition and fees (2007–08)
$9188 room and board
78% average percent of need met
$11,878 average financial aid amount received per undergraduate (2006–07 estimated)

Getting Accepted
10,274 applied
36% were accepted
1,035 enrolled (28% of accepted)
57% from top tenth of their h.s. class
3.8 average high school GPA
Mean SAT critical reading score: 655
Mean SAT math score: 658
Mean ACT score: 29
86% had SAT critical reading scores over 600
89% had SAT math scores over 600
98% had ACT scores over 24
26% had SAT critical reading scores over 700
22% had SAT math scores over 700
31% had ACT scores over 30
44 valedictorians

Graduation and After
42% pursued further study (14% arts and sciences, 4% education, 2% business)
46% had job offers within 6 months
58 organizations recruited on campus

Financial Matters
$5616 resident tuition and fees (2007–08)
$11,876 nonresident tuition and fees (2007–08)
$8550 room and board
86% average percent of need met
$9526 average financial aid amount received per undergraduate (2006–07 estimated)

STATE UNIVERSITY OF NEW YORK COLLEGE AT GENESEO

SMALL-TOWN SETTING ■ PUBLIC ■ STATE-SUPPORTED ■ COED
GENESEO, NEW YORK

Web site: www.geneseo.edu

Contact: Kris Shay, Director of Admissions, 1 College Circle, Geneseo, NY 14454-1401

Telephone: 585-245-5571 or toll-free 866-245-5211

Fax: 585-245-5550

E-mail: admissions@geneseo.edu

Academics
Geneseo awards bachelor's and master's **degrees**. **Challenging opportunities** include advanced placement credit, an honors program, double majors, independent study, and a senior project. Special programs include internships, summer session for credit, off-campus study, study-abroad, and Army and Air Force ROTC.

The most frequently chosen **baccalaureate** fields are education, business/marketing, and social sciences. A complete listing of majors at Geneseo appears in the Majors by College index beginning on page 471.

The **faculty** at Geneseo has 245 full-time members, 83% with terminal degrees. The student-faculty ratio is 19:1.

Students of Geneseo
The student body totals 5,548, of whom 5,395 are undergraduates. 58.3% are women and 41.7% are men. Students come from 24 states and territories and 27 other countries. 99% are from New York. 2.2% are international students. 2% are African American, 0.4% American Indian, 6% Asian American, and 3.2% Hispanic American. 89% returned for their sophomore year.

Facilities and Resources
900 **computers/terminals** are available on campus for general student use. Students can access the following: online (class) registration. Campuswide network is available. 100% of college-owned or -operated housing units are wired for high-speed Internet access. Wireless service is available via entire campus. The **library** has 647,100 books and 25,822 subscriptions.

Campus Life
Active organizations on campus include a drama/theater group, newspaper, radio station, television station, and choral group. 9% of eligible men and 11% of eligible women are members of national **fraternities**, national **sororities**, local fraternities, and local sororities.

Geneseo is a member of the NCAA (Division III). **Intercollegiate sports** include basketball, cross-country running, equestrian sports, field hockey (w), ice hockey (m), lacrosse, soccer, softball (w), swimming and diving, tennis (w), track and field, volleyball (w).

Campus Safety
Student safety services include late-night transport/escort service, 24-hour emergency telephone alarm devices, 24-hour patrols by trained security personnel, student patrols, and electronically operated dormitory entrances.

Applying
Geneseo requires an essay, SAT or ACT, and a high school transcript. It recommends an interview, recommendations, and a minimum high school GPA of 3.5. Application deadline: 1/1; 2/15 for financial aid, with a 2/15 priority date. Early and deferred admission are possible.

STATE UNIVERSITY OF NEW YORK COLLEGE OF ENVIRONMENTAL SCIENCE AND FORESTRY

URBAN SETTING ■ PUBLIC ■ STATE-SUPPORTED ■ COED
SYRACUSE, NEW YORK

SPONSOR

Web site: www.esf.edu
Contact: Ms. Susan Sanford, Director of Admissions, Office of Undergraduate Admissions, 106 Bray Hall, 1 Forestry Lane, Syracuse, NY 13210-2779
Telephone: 315-470-6600 or toll-free 800-777-7373
Fax: 315-470-6933
E-mail: esfinfo@esf.edu

Academics

ESF awards associate, bachelor's, master's, and doctoral **degrees. Challenging opportunities** include advanced placement credit, accelerated degree programs, freshman honors college, an honors program, double majors, independent study, and a senior project. Special programs include cooperative education, internships, off-campus study, study-abroad, and Army and Air Force ROTC.

The most frequently chosen **baccalaureate** fields are natural resources/environmental science, biological/life sciences, and engineering. A complete listing of majors at ESF appears in the Majors by College index beginning on page 471.

The **faculty** at ESF has 128 full-time members, 93% with terminal degrees. The student-faculty ratio is 12:1.

Students of ESF

The student body totals 2,069, of whom 1,544 are undergraduates. 38.3% are women and 61.7% are men. Students come from 22 states and territories and 8 other countries. 89% are from New York. 0.8% are international students. 0.7% are African American, 0.8% American Indian, 2.3% Asian American, and 3.4% Hispanic American. 81% returned for their sophomore year.

Facilities and Resources

150 **computers/terminals** are available on campus for general student use. Students can access the following: online (class) registration. Campuswide network is available. The 2 **libraries** have 135,341 books and 2,000 subscriptions.

Campus Life

There are 300 active organizations on campus, including a drama/theater group, newspaper, radio station, choral group, and marching band. 33% of eligible men and 33% of eligible women are members of national **fraternities** and national **sororities**.

This institution has no intercollegiate sports.

Campus Safety

Student safety services include late-night transport/escort service, 24-hour emergency telephone alarm devices, 24-hour patrols by trained security personnel, and electronically operated dormitory entrances.

Applying

ESF requires an essay, SAT or ACT, a high school transcript, supplemental application, and a minimum high school GPA of 3.3. It recommends an interview and 3 recommendations. Application deadline: 12/1; 3/1 priority date for financial aid. Early and deferred admission are possible.

Getting Accepted
966 applied
64% were accepted
242 enrolled (39% of accepted)
22% from top tenth of their h.s. class
3.6 average high school GPA
Mean SAT critical reading score: 555
Mean SAT math score: 571
Mean ACT score: 24
29% had SAT critical reading scores over 600
36% had SAT math scores over 600
71% had ACT scores over 24
4% had SAT critical reading scores over 700
4% had SAT math scores over 700
3% had ACT scores over 30
1 class president
2 valedictorians

Graduation and After
44% graduated in 4 years
18% graduated in 5 years
2% graduated in 6 years
24% pursued further study (9% arts and sciences, 4% engineering, 4% law)
72% had job offers within 6 months
45 organizations recruited on campus

Financial Matters
$5069 resident tuition and fees (2007–08)
$11,329 nonresident tuition and fees (2007–08)
$10,600 room and board
100% average percent of need met
$12,450 average financial aid amount received per undergraduate (2006–07 estimated)

STETSON UNIVERSITY

SMALL-TOWN SETTING ■ PRIVATE ■ INDEPENDENT ■ COED
DELAND, FLORIDA

Web site: www.stetson.edu

Contact: Ms. Deborah Thompson, Vice President for Enrollment Management and Campus Life, Unit 8378, Griffith Hall, DeLand, FL 32723

Telephone: 386-822-7100 or toll-free 800-688-0101

Fax: 386-822-7112

E-mail: admissions@stetson.edu

Getting Accepted

2,948 applied
64% were accepted
558 enrolled (29% of accepted)
35% from top tenth of their h.s. class
3.70 average high school GPA
Mean SAT critical reading score: 553
Mean SAT math score: 537
Mean SAT writing score: 535
Mean ACT score: 23
30% had SAT critical reading scores over 600
22% had SAT math scores over 600
22% had SAT writing scores over 600
48% had ACT scores over 24
7% had SAT critical reading scores over 700
3% had SAT math scores over 700
2% had SAT writing scores over 700
6% had ACT scores over 30
11 valedictorians

Graduation and After

55% graduated in 4 years
11% graduated in 5 years
2% graduated in 6 years
46% pursued further study (14% arts and sciences, 9% law, 8% business)
150 organizations recruited on campus

Financial Matters

$30,216 tuition and fees (2008–09)
$8436 room and board
83% average percent of need met
$22,727 average financial aid amount received per undergraduate (2006–07 estimated)

Academics

Stetson awards bachelor's, master's, and first-professional **degrees** and post-master's and first-professional certificates. **Challenging opportunities** include advanced placement credit, accelerated degree programs, student-designed majors, an honors program, double majors, independent study, and a senior project. Special programs include internships, summer session for credit, off-campus study, study-abroad, and Army ROTC.

The most frequently chosen **baccalaureate** fields are business/marketing, visual and performing arts, and education. A complete listing of majors at Stetson appears in the Majors by College index beginning on page 471.

The **faculty** at Stetson has 236 full-time members, 93% with terminal degrees. The student-faculty ratio is 11:1.

Students of Stetson

The student body totals 3,721, of whom 2,264 are undergraduates. 58.7% are women and 41.3% are men. Students come from 43 states and territories and 37 other countries. 81% are from Florida. 3.4% are international students. 4.6% are African American, 0.4% American Indian, 2.1% Asian American, and 8.8% Hispanic American. 81% returned for their sophomore year.

Facilities and Resources

450 **computers/terminals** are available on campus for general student use. Students can access the following: campus intranet, computer help desk, free student e-mail accounts, online (class) grades, online (class) registration, online (class) schedules. Campuswide network is available. 100% of college-owned or -operated housing units are wired for high-speed Internet access. Wireless service is available via entire campus. The 2 **libraries** have 395,069 books and 20,000 subscriptions.

Campus Life

There are 103 active organizations on campus, including a drama/theater group, newspaper, radio station, and choral group. 27% of eligible men and 25% of eligible women are members of national **fraternities** and national **sororities**.

Stetson is a member of the NCAA (Division I). **Intercollegiate sports** (some offering scholarships) include baseball (m), basketball, crew, cross-country running, golf, soccer, softball (w), tennis, volleyball (w).

Campus Safety

Student safety services include late-night transport/escort service, 24-hour emergency telephone alarm devices, and 24-hour patrols by trained security personnel.

Applying

Stetson requires an essay, SAT or ACT, a high school transcript, and recommendations. It recommends an interview. Application deadline: 3/15; 3/15 priority date for financial aid. Early and deferred admission are possible.

STEVENS INSTITUTE OF TECHNOLOGY

URBAN SETTING ■ PRIVATE ■ INDEPENDENT ■ COED
HOBOKEN, NEW JERSEY

SPONSOR

Web site: www.stevens.edu
Contact: Mr. Daniel Gallagher, Dean of University Admissions, Castle Point on Hudson, Hoboken, NJ 07030
Telephone: 201-216-5197 or toll-free 800-458-5323
Fax: 201-216-8348
E-mail: admissions@stevens.edu

Academics

Stevens awards bachelor's, master's, and doctoral **degrees** and post-bachelor's certificates. **Challenging opportunities** include advanced placement credit, accelerated degree programs, an honors program, double majors, independent study, and a senior project. Special programs include cooperative education, internships, summer session for credit, off-campus study, study-abroad, and Army and Air Force ROTC.

The most frequently chosen **baccalaureate** fields are engineering, computer and information sciences, and business/marketing. A complete listing of majors at Stevens appears in the Majors by College index beginning on page 471.

The **faculty** at Stevens has 189 full-time members. The student-faculty ratio is 8:1.

Students of Stevens

The student body totals 4,829, of whom 1,853 are undergraduates. 24% are women and 76% are men. Students come from 41 states and territories and 27 other countries. 62% are from New Jersey. 4.7% are international students. 4.2% are African American, 0.3% American Indian, 11.9% Asian American, and 9.4% Hispanic American. 90% returned for their sophomore year.

Facilities and Resources

175 **computers/terminals** are available on campus for general student use. Students can access the following: online (class) registration, online grade and account information. Campuswide network is available. The **library** has 115,234 books and 134 subscriptions.

Campus Life

There are 70 active organizations on campus, including a drama/theater group, newspaper, radio station, television station, and choral group. 34% of eligible men and 31% of eligible women are members of national **fraternities**, national **sororities**, and local sororities.

Stevens is a member of the NCAA (Division III). **Intercollegiate sports** include baseball (m), basketball, cross-country running, equestrian sports (w), fencing, field hockey (w), lacrosse, soccer, swimming and diving, tennis, track and field, volleyball, wrestling (m).

Campus Safety

Student safety services include late-night transport/escort service, 24-hour emergency telephone alarm devices, 24-hour patrols by trained security personnel, and electronically operated dormitory entrances.

Applying

Stevens requires an essay, SAT or ACT, a high school transcript, an interview, and recommendations, and in some cases SAT Subject Tests. Application deadline: 2/15; 2/15 priority date for financial aid. Early and deferred admission are possible.

Getting Accepted

2,278 applied
54% were accepted
483 enrolled (39% of accepted)
53% from top tenth of their h.s. class
3.7 average high school GPA
52% had SAT critical reading scores over 600
85% had SAT math scores over 600
83% had ACT scores over 24
13% had SAT critical reading scores over 700
34% had SAT math scores over 700
22% had ACT scores over 30
11 valedictorians

Graduation and After

31% graduated in 4 years
35% graduated in 5 years
6% graduated in 6 years
18% pursued further study
90% had job offers within 6 months
350 organizations recruited on campus

Financial Matters

$34,620 tuition and fees (2007–08)
$10,750 room and board
85% average percent of need met
$21,139 average financial aid amount received per undergraduate (2005–06 estimated)

STONEHILL COLLEGE

SUBURBAN SETTING ■ PRIVATE ■ INDEPENDENT RELIGIOUS ■ COED
EASTON, MASSACHUSETTS

Web site: www.stonehill.edu
Contact: Mr. Brian P. Murphy, Dean of Admissions and Enrollment, 320 Washington Street, Easton, MA 02357-5610
Telephone: 508-565-1373
Fax: 508-565-1545
E-mail: admissions@stonehill.edu

Getting Accepted
5,704 applied
52% were accepted
659 enrolled (22% of accepted)
49% from top tenth of their h.s. class
3.57 average high school GPA
Mean SAT critical reading score: 590
Mean SAT math score: 590
Mean ACT score: 26
43% had SAT critical reading scores over 600
47% had SAT math scores over 600
79% had ACT scores over 24
8% had SAT critical reading scores over 700
6% had SAT math scores over 700
9% had ACT scores over 30
9 National Merit Scholars
21 class presidents
4 valedictorians

Graduation and After
22% pursued further study (8% arts and sciences, 5% business, 3% medicine)
64% had job offers within 6 months
57 organizations recruited on campus

Financial Matters
$30,150 tuition and fees (2008–09)
$11,830 room and board
81% average percent of need met
$19,235 average financial aid amount received per undergraduate (2006–07 estimated)

Academics

Stonehill awards bachelor's **degrees**. **Challenging opportunities** include advanced placement credit, student-designed majors, an honors program, double majors, independent study, and a senior project. Special programs include internships, summer session for credit, off-campus study, study-abroad, and Army ROTC.

The most frequently chosen **baccalaureate** fields are social sciences, business/marketing, and psychology. A complete listing of majors at Stonehill appears in the Majors by College index beginning on page 471.

The **faculty** at Stonehill has 145 full-time members, 81% with terminal degrees. The student-faculty ratio is 13:1.

Students of Stonehill

The student body totals 2,450, of whom 2,440 are undergraduates. 61.2% are women and 38.8% are men. Students come from 30 states and territories and 8 other countries. 57% are from Massachusetts. 0.4% are international students. 2.3% are African American, 0.2% American Indian, 1.7% Asian American, and 3.6% Hispanic American. 87% returned for their sophomore year.

Facilities and Resources

300 **computers/terminals** and 2,500 ports are available on campus for general student use. Students can access the following: campus intranet, computer help desk, free student e-mail accounts, online (class) grades, online (class) registration, online (class) schedules. Campuswide network is available. 100% of college-owned or -operated housing units are wired for high-speed Internet access. Wireless service is available via classrooms, computer centers, computer labs, learning centers, libraries, student centers. The **library** has 205,400 books and 2,196 subscriptions.

Campus Life

There are 61 active organizations on campus, including a drama/theater group, newspaper, radio station, and choral group. No national or local **fraternities** or **sororities**.

Stonehill is a member of the NCAA (Division II). **Intercollegiate sports** (some offering scholarships) include baseball (m), basketball, cross-country running, equestrian sports (w), field hockey (w), ice hockey (w), lacrosse (w), soccer, softball (w), tennis, track and field, volleyball (w).

Campus Safety

Student safety services include late-night transport/escort service, 24-hour emergency telephone alarm devices, and 24-hour patrols by trained security personnel.

Applying

Stonehill requires an essay, a high school transcript, and 2 recommendations, and in some cases an interview. It recommends SAT or ACT and campus visit. Application deadline: 1/15; 2/1 priority date for financial aid. Early and deferred admission are possible.

STONY BROOK UNIVERSITY, STATE UNIVERSITY OF NEW YORK

SMALL-TOWN SETTING ■ PUBLIC ■ STATE-SUPPORTED ■ COED
STONY BROOK, NEW YORK

Web site: www.sunysb.edu
Contact: Ms. Judith Burke-Berhanan, Nicolls Road, Stony Brook, NY 11794
Telephone: 631-632-6868 or toll-free 800-872-7869 (out-of-state)
Fax: 631-632-9898
E-mail: ugadmissions@notes.cc.sunysb.edu

Academics

Stony Brook awards bachelor's, master's, doctoral, and first-professional **degrees** and post-bachelor's, post-master's, and first-professional certificates. **Challenging opportunities** include advanced placement credit, student-designed majors, freshman honors college, an honors program, double majors, independent study, and a senior project. Special programs include internships, summer session for credit, off-campus study, study-abroad, and Army and Air Force ROTC.

The most frequently chosen **baccalaureate** fields are health professions and related sciences, social sciences, and biological/life sciences. A complete listing of majors at Stony Brook appears in the Majors by College index beginning on page 471.

The **faculty** at Stony Brook has 919 full-time members, 98% with terminal degrees. The student-faculty ratio is 18:1.

Students of Stony Brook

The student body totals 23,347, of whom 15,519 are undergraduates. 50.2% are women and 49.8% are men. Students come from 47 states and territories and 87 other countries. 95% are from New York. 5.8% are international students. 8.6% are African American, 0.2% American Indian, 22.4% Asian American, and 8.5% Hispanic American. 89% returned for their sophomore year.

Facilities and Resources

2,600 **computers/terminals** are available on campus for general student use. Students can access the following: campus intranet, computer help desk, free student e-mail accounts, online (class) grades, online (class) registration, online (class) schedules. Campuswide network is available. Wireless service is available via computer labs, libraries, student centers. The 7 **libraries** have 1,935,212 books and 29,275 subscriptions.

Campus Life

There are 160 active organizations on campus, including a drama/theater group, newspaper, radio station, television station, choral group, and marching band. 2% of eligible men and 3% of eligible women are members of national **fraternities**, national **sororities**, local fraternities, and local sororities.

Stony Brook is a member of the NCAA (Division I) and NAIA. **Intercollegiate sports** (some offering scholarships) include baseball (m), basketball, cross-country running, football (m), lacrosse, soccer, softball (w), swimming and diving, tennis, track and field, volleyball (w).

Campus Safety

Student safety services include late-night transport/escort service, 24-hour emergency telephone alarm devices, 24-hour patrols by trained security personnel, and electronically operated dormitory entrances.

Applying

Stony Brook requires an essay, SAT or ACT, a high school transcript, and a minimum high school GPA of 3.0, and in some cases audition. It recommends SAT Subject Tests, an interview, and 2 recommendations. Application deadline: 3/1; 3/1 priority date for financial aid. Deferred admission is possible.

Getting Accepted
24,060 applied
43% were accepted
2,768 enrolled (27% of accepted)
34% from top tenth of their h.s. class
3.6 average high school GPA
Mean SAT critical reading score: 567
Mean SAT math score: 613
Mean SAT writing score: 556
37% had SAT critical reading scores over 600
59% had SAT math scores over 600
32% had SAT writing scores over 600
6% had SAT critical reading scores over 700
13% had SAT math scores over 700
4% had SAT writing scores over 700
10 National Merit Scholars
23 valedictorians

Graduation and After
39% graduated in 4 years
17% graduated in 5 years
3% graduated in 6 years
47% pursued further study
150 organizations recruited on campus

Financial Matters
$5760 resident tuition and fees (2007–08)
$12,020 nonresident tuition and fees (2007–08)
$8734 room and board
65% average percent of need met
$8200 average financial aid amount received per undergraduate (2005–06)

Susquehanna University

Suburban setting ■ Private ■ Independent Religious ■ Coed
Selinsgrove, Pennsylvania

Web site: www.susqu.edu
Contact: Mr. Chris Markle, Director of Admissions, 514 University Avenue, Selinsgrove, PA 17870-1040
Telephone: 570-372-4260 or toll-free 800-326-9672
Fax: 570-372-2722
E-mail: suadmiss@susqu.edu

Susquehanna University is a national liberal arts college on a beautiful 220-acre campus in Selinsgrove, Pennsylvania. Strong professional programs in areas such as music and business enhance distinctive liberal arts programs, including biology and writing. Faculty members are excellent teachers who are highly engaged in student learning, and many involve students in their research. A vibrant campus enables students to customize their experience with internships, volunteer service, and leadership opportunities. New, award-winning facilities include a high-technology academic center, an athletic complex, and a music and art center. Students gain worldwide connections through a fully wired campus and an array of off-campus programs.

Academics

Susquehanna awards bachelor's **degrees** (also offers evening associate degree program limited to local adult students). **Challenging opportunities** include advanced placement credit, accelerated degree programs, student-designed majors, an honors program, double majors, independent study, and a senior project. Special programs include internships, summer session for credit, off-campus study, study-abroad, and Army ROTC.

The most frequently chosen **baccalaureate** fields are business/marketing, communications/journalism, and education. A complete listing of majors at Susquehanna appears in the Majors by College index beginning on page 471.

The **faculty** at Susquehanna has 121 full-time members, 93% with terminal degrees. The student-faculty ratio is 14:1.

Students of Susquehanna

The student body is made up of 2,039 undergraduates. 53.9% are women and 46.1% are men. Students come from 31 states and territories and 10 other countries. 57% are from Pennsylvania. 1.2% are international students. 3% are African American, 0.1% American Indian, 1.6% Asian American, and 2% Hispanic American. 84% returned for their sophomore year.

Getting Accepted
2,373 applied
86% were accepted
593 enrolled (29% of accepted)
34% from top tenth of their h.s. class
35% had SAT critical reading scores over 600
35% had SAT math scores over 600
4% had SAT critical reading scores over 700
4% had SAT math scores over 700
2 National Merit Scholars
18 class presidents
6 valedictorians

Facilities and Resources

440 **computers/terminals** are available on campus for general student use. Students can access the following: computer help desk, free student e-mail accounts, online (class) grades, online (class) registration, online (class) schedules, class listings and assignments, online voting booth. Campuswide network is available. 100% of college-owned or -operated housing units are wired for high-speed Internet access. Wireless service is available via entire campus. The **library** has 298,458 books and 15,989 subscriptions.

Graduation and After
79% graduated in 4 years
2% graduated in 5 years
1% graduated in 6 years
24% pursued further study (13% arts and sciences, 2% education, 2% law)
74% had job offers within 6 months
61 organizations recruited on campus

Campus Life

There are 129 active organizations on campus, including a drama/theater group, newspaper, radio station, and choral group. 20% of eligible men and 25% of eligible women are members of national **fraternities** and national **sororities**.

Susquehanna is a member of the NCAA (Division III). **Intercollegiate sports** include baseball (m), basketball, cross-country running, field hockey (w), football (m), golf, lacrosse, soccer, softball (w), swimming and diving, tennis, track and field, volleyball (w).

Financial Matters
$31,080 tuition and fees (2008–09)
$8400 room and board
83% average percent of need met
$17,743 average financial aid amount received per undergraduate (2004–05)

Campus Safety

Student safety services include late-night transport/escort service, 24-hour patrols by trained security personnel, and electronically operated dormitory entrances.

Applying

Susquehanna requires an essay, a high school transcript, 1 recommendation, and a minimum high school GPA of 2.5, and in some cases writing portfolio, auditions for music programs. It recommends SAT or ACT, an interview, and a minimum high school GPA of 3.0. Application deadline: 3/1; 3/1 priority date for financial aid. Early and deferred admission are possible.

SWARTHMORE COLLEGE

SUBURBAN SETTING ■ PRIVATE ■ INDEPENDENT ■ COED
SWARTHMORE, PENNSYLVANIA

Web site: www.swarthmore.edu
Contact: Mr. Jim Bock, Dean of Admissions and Financial Aid, 500 College
  Avenue, Swarthmore, PA 19081
Telephone: 610-328-8300 or toll-free 800-667-3110
Fax: 610-328-8580
E-mail: admissions@swarthmore.edu

Academics

Swarthmore awards bachelor's **degrees**. **Challenging opportunities** include advanced
placement credit, student-designed majors, an honors program, double majors,
independent study, and a senior project. Special programs include internships, off-
campus study, study-abroad, and Army and Air Force ROTC.

The most frequently chosen **baccalaureate** fields are social sciences, biological/life
sciences, and foreign languages and literature. A complete listing of majors at
Swarthmore appears in the Majors by College index beginning on page 471.

The **faculty** at Swarthmore has 168 full-time members, 100% with terminal degrees.
The student-faculty ratio is 8:1.

Students of Swarthmore

The student body is made up of 1,491 undergraduates. 52% are women and 48% are
men. Students come from 48 states and territories and 35 other countries. 13% are from
Pennsylvania. 6.6% are international students. 8.4% are African American, 0.9%
American Indian, 17.3% Asian American, and 10.4% Hispanic American. 97% returned
for their sophomore year.

Facilities and Resources

206 **computers/terminals** and 3,300 ports are available on campus for general student
use. Students can access the following: campus intranet, computer help desk, free student
e-mail accounts, online (class) grades, online (class) registration, online (class) schedules.
Campuswide network is available. 100% of college-owned or -operated housing units are
wired for high-speed Internet access. Wireless service is available via entire campus. The
7 **libraries** have 800,667 books and 8,190 subscriptions.

Campus Life

There are 138 active organizations on campus, including a drama/theater group,
newspaper, radio station, and choral group. Swarthmore has national **fraternities** and
local fraternities.

Swarthmore is a member of the NCAA (Division III). **Intercollegiate sports** include
badminton (w), baseball (m), basketball, cross-country running, field hockey (w), golf
(m), lacrosse, soccer, softball (w), swimming and diving, tennis, track and field, volleyball
(w).

Campus Safety

Student safety services include late-night transport/escort service, 24-hour emergency
telephone alarm devices, 24-hour patrols by trained security personnel, and student
patrols.

Applying

Swarthmore requires an essay, SAT and SAT Subject Tests or ACT, a high school
transcript, and 3 recommendations. It recommends an interview. Application deadline:
1/2; 2/15 for financial aid, with a 2/15 priority date. Early and deferred admission are
possible.

Getting Accepted

5,242 applied
18% were accepted
365 enrolled (39% of accepted)
91% from top tenth of their h.s. class
Mean SAT critical reading score: 723
Mean SAT math score: 710
Mean SAT writing score: 711
Mean ACT score: 30
94% had SAT critical reading scores over 600
94% had SAT math scores over 600
91% had SAT writing scores over 600
97% had ACT scores over 24
71% had SAT critical reading scores over 700
64% had SAT math scores over 700
64% had SAT writing scores over 700
62% had ACT scores over 30
14 National Merit Scholars
25 valedictorians

Graduation and After

91% graduated in 4 years
2% graduated in 5 years
1% graduated in 6 years
21% pursued further study (13% arts and
  sciences, 3% law, 3% medicine)
70 organizations recruited on campus

Financial Matters

$34,884 tuition and fees (2007–08)
$5544 room only
100% average percent of need met
$30,369 average financial aid amount received
  per undergraduate (2006–07 estimated)

SWEET BRIAR COLLEGE
RURAL SETTING ■ PRIVATE ■ INDEPENDENT ■ WOMEN ONLY
SWEET BRIAR, VIRGINIA

Web site: www.sbc.edu
Contact: Mr. Ken Huus, Director of Admissions, PO Box B, Sweet Briar, VA 24595
Telephone: 434-381-6142 or toll-free 800-381-6142
Fax: 434-381-6152
E-mail: admissions@sbc.edu

Getting Accepted
619 applied
81% were accepted
202 enrolled (40% of accepted)
22% from top tenth of their h.s. class
3.4 average high school GPA
Mean SAT critical reading score: 560
Mean SAT math score: 525
Mean ACT score: 22
35% had SAT critical reading scores over 600
24% had SAT math scores over 600
39% had ACT scores over 24
9% had SAT critical reading scores over 700
2% had SAT math scores over 700
4% had ACT scores over 30
6 class presidents
2 valedictorians

Graduation and After
69% graduated in 4 years
1% graduated in 5 years
20% pursued further study (8% arts and sciences, 4% education, 2% law)
66% had job offers within 6 months
74 organizations recruited on campus

Financial Matters
$26,995 tuition and fees (2008–09)
$10,160 room and board
83% average percent of need met
$15,150 average financial aid amount received per undergraduate (2006–07 estimated)

Academics
Sweet Briar awards bachelor's and master's **degrees**. **Challenging opportunities** include advanced placement credit, accelerated degree programs, student-designed majors, an honors program, double majors, independent study, and a senior project. Special programs include internships, summer session for credit, off-campus study, and study-abroad.

The most frequently chosen **baccalaureate** fields are social sciences, business/marketing, and visual and performing arts. A complete listing of majors at Sweet Briar appears in the Majors by College index beginning on page 471.

The **faculty** at Sweet Briar has 61 full-time members, 97% with terminal degrees. The student-faculty ratio is 9:1.

Students of Sweet Briar
The student body totals 815, of whom 800 are undergraduates. Students come from 39 states and territories and 4 other countries. 54% are from Virginia. 0.8% are international students. 2.5% are African American, 0.8% American Indian, 1.1% Asian American, and 3.1% Hispanic American. 75% returned for their sophomore year.

Facilities and Resources
123 **computers/terminals** and 3,018 ports are available on campus for general student use. Students can access the following: campus intranet, computer help desk, free student e-mail accounts, online (class) grades, online (class) registration, online (class) schedules. Campuswide network is available. 80% of college-owned or -operated housing units are wired for high-speed Internet access. Wireless service is available via classrooms, dorm rooms, learning centers, libraries, student centers. The 4 **libraries** have 263,066 books and 18,676 subscriptions.

Campus Life
There are 53 active organizations on campus, including a drama/theater group, newspaper, radio station, television station, and choral group. No national or local **sororities**.

Sweet Briar is a member of the NCAA (Division III). **Intercollegiate sports** include field hockey, lacrosse, soccer, softball, swimming and diving, tennis, volleyball.

Campus Safety
Student safety services include front gate security, late-night transport/escort service, 24-hour emergency telephone alarm devices, 24-hour patrols by trained security personnel, and electronically operated dormitory entrances.

Applying
Sweet Briar requires an essay, SAT or ACT, a high school transcript, and 2 recommendations, and in some cases portfolio with courses taken, list of texts covered, essay about homeschooling, campus visit, interview for homeschooled applicants. It recommends an interview. Application deadline: 2/1; 3/1 priority date for financial aid. Early and deferred admission are possible.

Syracuse University

Urban setting ■ Private ■ Independent ■ Coed
Syracuse, New York

SPONSOR

Web site: www.syracuse.edu
Contact: Office of Admissions, 200 Crouse-Hinds Hall, South Crouse Avenue, Syracuse, NY 13244-2130
Telephone: 315-443-3611
E-mail: orange@syr.edu

Academics

Syracuse awards associate, bachelor's, master's, doctoral, and first-professional **degrees** and post-bachelor's and post-master's certificates. **Challenging opportunities** include advanced placement credit, accelerated degree programs, student-designed majors, an honors program, double majors, independent study, and a senior project. Special programs include cooperative education, internships, summer session for credit, off-campus study, study-abroad, and Army and Air Force ROTC.

The most frequently chosen **baccalaureate** fields are business/marketing, social sciences, and visual and performing arts. A complete listing of majors at Syracuse appears in the Majors by College index beginning on page 471.

The **faculty** at Syracuse has 906 full-time members, 88% with terminal degrees. The student-faculty ratio is 15:1.

Students of Syracuse

The student body totals 17,677, of whom 11,796 are undergraduates. 55.1% are women and 44.9% are men. Students come from 50 states and territories and 63 other countries. 44% are from New York. 3.8% are international students. 7.1% are African American, 0.8% American Indian, 8.7% Asian American, and 5.9% Hispanic American. 91% returned for their sophomore year.

Facilities and Resources

2,715 **computers/terminals** and 650 ports are available on campus for general student use. Students can access the following: campus intranet, computer help desk, free student e-mail accounts, online (class) registration, online (class) schedules, online services, networked client and server computing. Campuswide network is available. 100% of college-owned or -operated housing units are wired for high-speed Internet access. Wireless service is available via classrooms, computer centers, computer labs, dorm rooms, libraries, student centers. The 8 **libraries** have 3,161,529 books and 20,637 subscriptions.

Campus Life

There are 340 active organizations on campus, including a drama/theater group, newspaper, radio station, television station, choral group, and marching band. 18% of eligible men and 21% of eligible women are members of national **fraternities** and national **sororities**.

Syracuse is a member of the NCAA (Division I). **Intercollegiate sports** (some offering scholarships) include basketball, cheerleading, crew, cross-country running, field hockey (w), football (m), lacrosse, soccer, softball (w), swimming and diving, tennis (w), track and field, volleyball (w).

Campus Safety

Student safety services include crime prevention and neighborhood outreach programs, late-night transport/escort service, 24-hour emergency telephone alarm devices, 24-hour patrols by trained security personnel, and electronically operated dormitory entrances.

Applying

Syracuse requires an essay, SAT or ACT, a high school transcript, recommendations, and audition for drama and music programs, portfolio for art and architecture programs. It recommends an interview. Application deadline: 1/1; 2/1 for financial aid. Early and deferred admission are possible.

Getting Accepted
21,219 applied
51% were accepted
3,096 enrolled (29% of accepted)
42% from top tenth of their h.s. class
3.6 average high school GPA
43% had SAT critical reading scores over 600
55% had SAT math scores over 600
7% had SAT critical reading scores over 700
12% had SAT math scores over 700

Graduation and After
71% graduated in 4 years
10% graduated in 5 years
1% graduated in 6 years
18% pursued further study (6% arts and sciences, 5% business, 2% education)
74% had job offers within 6 months
300 organizations recruited on campus

Financial Matters
$31,686 tuition and fees (2007–08)
$10,940 room and board
82% average percent of need met
$23,600 average financial aid amount received per undergraduate (2006–07 estimated)

TABOR COLLEGE

SMALL-TOWN SETTING ■ PRIVATE ■ INDEPENDENT RELIGIOUS ■ COED
HILLSBORO, KANSAS

Getting Accepted
241 applied
100% were accepted
120 enrolled (50% of accepted)
18% from top tenth of their h.s. class
3.36 average high school GPA
Mean SAT critical reading score: 506
Mean SAT math score: 518
Mean ACT score: 22
40% had ACT scores over 24
3% had ACT scores over 30
2 National Merit Scholars

Graduation and After
41% graduated in 4 years
3% graduated in 5 years
2% graduated in 6 years
13% pursued further study
79% had job offers within 6 months
105 organizations recruited on campus

Financial Matters
$18,710 tuition and fees (2008–09)
$6750 room and board
89% average percent of need met
$15,751 average financial aid amount received
    per undergraduate (2005–06 estimated)

Web site: www.tabor.edu
Contact: Mr. Rusty Allen, Dean of Enrollment Management, 400 South
    Jefferson, Hillsboro, KS 67063
Telephone: 620-947-3121 or toll-free 800-822-6799
Fax: 620-947-6276
E-mail: rustya@tabor.edu

Academics

Tabor awards associate, bachelor's, and master's **degrees**. **Challenging opportunities**
include advanced placement credit, accelerated degree programs, student-designed
majors, an honors program, double majors, independent study, and a senior project.
Special programs include cooperative education, internships, off-campus study, and
study-abroad.

The most frequently chosen **baccalaureate** fields are business/marketing, health
professions and related sciences, and theology and religious vocations. A complete listing
of majors at Tabor appears in the Majors by College index beginning on page 471.

The **faculty** at Tabor has 33 full-time members, 73% with terminal degrees. The
student-faculty ratio is 10:1.

Students of Tabor

The student body is made up of 574 undergraduates. 50.3% are women and 49.7% are
men. Students come from 27 states and territories and 6 other countries. 59% are from
Kansas. 1% are international students. 6.8% are African American, 0.9% American
Indian, 0.9% Asian American, and 4% Hispanic American. 65% returned for their
sophomore year.

Facilities and Resources

60 **computers/terminals** and 450 ports are available on campus for general student use.
Students can access the following: campus intranet, computer help desk, free student
e-mail accounts, online (class) grades, online (class) registration, online (class) schedules.
Campuswide network is available. 100% of college-owned or -operated housing units are
wired for high-speed Internet access. Wireless service is available via dorm rooms, learning centers, libraries, student centers. The **library** has 80,099 books and 265 subscriptions.

Campus Life

There are 6 active organizations on campus, including a drama/theater group,
newspaper, and choral group. No national or local **fraternities** or **sororities**.

Tabor is a member of the NAIA. **Intercollegiate sports** (some offering scholarships)
include baseball (m), basketball, cheerleading, cross-country running, football (m), golf,
soccer, softball (w), tennis, track and field, volleyball (w).

Applying

Tabor requires an essay, SAT or ACT, a high school transcript, minimum ACT score of
18, and a minimum high school GPA of 2.5. It recommends an interview. Application
deadline: 8/1, 8/1 for nonresidents; 8/15 for financial aid, with a 3/1 priority date. Early
and deferred admission are possible.

Taylor University

RURAL SETTING ■ PRIVATE ■ INDEPENDENT RELIGIOUS ■ COED
UPLAND, INDIANA

Web site: www.taylor.edu
Contact: Mrs. Kathy Thornburgh, Visit Coordinator, 236 West Reade
  Avenue, Upland, IN 46989-1001
Telephone: 765-998-5134 or toll-free 800-882-3456
Fax: 765-998-4925
E-mail: admissions@taylor.edu

Academics

Taylor awards associate, bachelor's, and master's **degrees. Challenging opportunities** include advanced placement credit, student-designed majors, an honors program, double majors, independent study, and a senior project. Special programs include cooperative education, internships, summer session for credit, off-campus study, and study-abroad.

The most frequently chosen **baccalaureate** fields are education, business/marketing, and psychology. A complete listing of majors at Taylor appears in the Majors by College index beginning on page 471.

The **faculty** at Taylor has 122 full-time members, 84% with terminal degrees. The student-faculty ratio is 13:1.

Students of Taylor

The student body is made up of 1,879 undergraduates. 55% are women and 45% are men. Students come from 46 states and territories and 24 other countries. 32% are from Indiana. 1.7% are international students. 2% are African American, 2.3% Asian American, and 1.7% Hispanic American. 87% returned for their sophomore year.

Facilities and Resources

387 **computers/terminals** are available on campus for general student use. Students can access the following: campus intranet, computer help desk, free student e-mail accounts, online (class) grades, online (class) registration, online (class) schedules. Campuswide network is available. 100% of college-owned or -operated housing units are wired for high-speed Internet access. Wireless service is available via entire campus. The **library** has 189,007 books and 12,625 subscriptions.

Campus Life

There are 70 active organizations on campus, including a drama/theater group, newspaper, radio station, television station, and choral group. No national or local **fraternities** or **sororities**.

Taylor is a member of the NAIA. **Intercollegiate sports** (some offering scholarships) include baseball (m), basketball, cross-country running, football (m), golf (m), soccer, softball (w), tennis, track and field, volleyball (w).

Campus Safety

Student safety services include late-night transport/escort service, 24-hour patrols by trained security personnel, and student patrols.

Applying

Taylor requires an essay, SAT or ACT, a high school transcript, an interview, and 2 recommendations. It recommends a minimum high school GPA of 2.8. Application deadline: rolling admissions; 3/10 for financial aid. Deferred admission is possible.

Getting Accepted
1,393 applied
91% were accepted
472 enrolled (37% of accepted)
38% from top tenth of their h.s. class
3.53 average high school GPA
Mean SAT critical reading score: 590
Mean SAT math score: 587
Mean SAT writing score: 564
Mean ACT score: 26
49% had SAT critical reading scores over 600
47% had SAT math scores over 600
71% had ACT scores over 24
18% had SAT critical reading scores over 700
11% had SAT math scores over 700
26% had ACT scores over 30
9 National Merit Scholars
22 valedictorians

Graduation and After
70% graduated in 4 years
5% graduated in 5 years
1% graduated in 6 years
13% pursued further study
71% had job offers within 6 months
90 organizations recruited on campus

Financial Matters
$24,546 tuition and fees (2008–09)
$6352 room and board
75% average percent of need met
$14,752 average financial aid amount received
  per undergraduate (2006–07 estimated)

TENNESSEE TECHNOLOGICAL UNIVERSITY

SMALL-TOWN SETTING ■ PUBLIC ■ STATE-SUPPORTED ■ COED
COOKEVILLE, TENNESSEE

Web site: www.tntech.edu
Contact: Ms. Vanessa Palmer, Interim Director of Admissions, PO Box 5006, Cookeville, TN 38505
Telephone: 931-372-3888 or toll-free 800-255-8881
Fax: 931-372-6250
E-mail: admissions@tntech.edu

Getting Accepted
3,790 applied
88% were accepted
1,661 enrolled (50% of accepted)
26% from top tenth of their h.s. class
3.24 average high school GPA
32% had SAT critical reading scores over 600
36% had SAT math scores over 600
40% had ACT scores over 24
4% had SAT critical reading scores over 700
30% had SAT math scores over 700
6% had ACT scores over 30
4 National Merit Scholars

Graduation and After
10% pursued further study
67% had job offers within 6 months
334 organizations recruited on campus

Financial Matters
$4980 resident tuition and fees (2007–08)
$15,256 nonresident tuition and fees (2007–08)
$6330 room and board
82% average percent of need met
$3156 average financial aid amount received per undergraduate (2006–07)

Academics

Tennessee Tech awards bachelor's, master's, and doctoral **degrees** and post-bachelor's certificates. **Challenging opportunities** include advanced placement credit, accelerated degree programs, an honors program, double majors, independent study, and a senior project. Special programs include cooperative education, internships, summer session for credit, off-campus study, study-abroad, and Army and Air Force ROTC.

The most frequently chosen **baccalaureate** fields are business/marketing, education, and engineering. A complete listing of majors at Tennessee Tech appears in the Majors by College index beginning on page 471.

The **faculty** at Tennessee Tech has 388 full-time members, 80% with terminal degrees. The student-faculty ratio is 18:1.

Students of Tennessee Tech

The student body totals 10,321, of whom 8,060 are undergraduates. 46.5% are women and 53.5% are men. Students come from 40 states and territories and 40 other countries. 96% are from Tennessee. 1.6% are international students. 3.6% are African American, 0.3% American Indian, 1.4% Asian American, and 1.2% Hispanic American. 73% returned for their sophomore year.

Facilities and Resources

800 **computers/terminals** are available on campus for general student use. Students can access the following: online (class) registration. Campuswide network is available. 100% of college-owned or -operated housing units are wired for high-speed Internet access. Wireless service is available via entire campus. The **library** has 640,056 books and 4,847 subscriptions.

Campus Life

There are 178 active organizations on campus, including a drama/theater group, newspaper, radio station, choral group, and marching band. 18% of eligible men and 12% of eligible women are members of national **fraternities** and national **sororities**.

Tennessee Tech is a member of the NCAA (Division I). **Intercollegiate sports** (some offering scholarships) include baseball (m), basketball, cheerleading, cross-country running, football (m), golf, riflery, soccer (w), softball (w), tennis, track and field (w), volleyball (w).

Campus Safety

Student safety services include student safety organization, lighted pathways, late-night transport/escort service, 24-hour emergency telephone alarm devices, and 24-hour patrols by trained security personnel.

Applying

Tennessee Tech requires SAT or ACT, a high school transcript, ACT composite score of 19, and a minimum high school GPA of 2.5. It recommends ACT and an interview. Application deadline: 8/1; 3/15 priority date for financial aid. Early and deferred admission are possible.

Texas A&M University

Suburban setting ■ Public ■ State-supported ■ Coed

College Station, Texas

Web site: www.tamu.edu

Contact: Mr. Scott McDonald, Director of Admissions, 217 John J. Koldus Building, College Station, TX 77843-1265

Telephone: 979-845-3741

Fax: 979-845-8737

E-mail: admissions@tamu.edu

Academics

Texas A&M awards bachelor's, master's, doctoral, and first-professional **degrees** and post-bachelor's certificates. **Challenging opportunities** include advanced placement credit, accelerated degree programs, an honors program, double majors, independent study, and a senior project. Special programs include cooperative education, internships, summer session for credit, off-campus study, study-abroad, and Army, Navy, and Air Force ROTC.

The most frequently chosen **baccalaureate** fields are business/marketing, agriculture, and engineering. A complete listing of majors at Texas A&M appears in the Majors by College index beginning on page 471.

The **faculty** at Texas A&M has 2,188 full-time members, 92% with terminal degrees. The student-faculty ratio is 19:1.

Students of Texas A&M

The student body totals 46,542, of whom 37,357 are undergraduates. 48% are women and 52% are men. Students come from 52 states and territories and 128 other countries. 96% are from Texas. 1.3% are international students. 2.9% are African American, 0.6% American Indian, 4.4% Asian American, and 12.5% Hispanic American. 92% returned for their sophomore year.

Facilities and Resources

1,334 **computers/terminals** and 5,000 ports are available on campus for general student use. Students can access the following: campus intranet, computer help desk, free student e-mail accounts, online (class) grades, online (class) registration, online (class) schedules. Campuswide network is available. 100% of college-owned or -operated housing units are wired for high-speed Internet access. Wireless service is available via classrooms, computer labs, libraries. The 5 **libraries** have 3,575,153 books and 43,949 subscriptions.

Campus Life

There are 700 active organizations on campus, including a drama/theater group, newspaper, radio station, television station, choral group, and marching band. 6% of eligible men and 12% of eligible women are members of national **fraternities**, national **sororities**, local fraternities, and local sororities.

Texas A&M is a member of the NCAA (Division I). **Intercollegiate sports** (some offering scholarships) include archery (w), baseball (m), basketball, cross-country running, equestrian sports (w), football (m), golf, soccer (w), softball (w), swimming and diving, tennis, track and field, volleyball (w).

Campus Safety

Student safety services include student escorts, late-night transport/escort service, 24-hour emergency telephone alarm devices, 24-hour patrols by trained security personnel, and electronically operated dormitory entrances.

Applying

Texas A&M requires an essay, SAT or ACT, and a high school transcript. Application deadline: 2/1.

Getting Accepted

18,817 applied
76% were accepted
8,094 enrolled (56% of accepted)
45% from top tenth of their h.s. class
Mean SAT critical reading score: 580
Mean SAT math score: 613
Mean SAT writing score: 561
Mean ACT score: 26
42% had SAT critical reading scores over 600
59% had SAT math scores over 600
32% had SAT writing scores over 600
70% had ACT scores over 24
9% had SAT critical reading scores over 700
13% had SAT math scores over 700
5% had SAT writing scores over 700
16% had ACT scores over 30
137 National Merit Scholars
216 valedictorians

Graduation and After

38% graduated in 4 years
33% graduated in 5 years
6% graduated in 6 years
17% pursued further study
1063 organizations recruited on campus

Financial Matters

$7335 resident tuition and fees (2007–08)
$15,675 nonresident tuition and fees (2007–08)
$7660 room and board
87% average percent of need met
$10,747 average financial aid amount received per undergraduate (2005–06 estimated)

Texas Christian University
Suburban setting ■ Private ■ Independent Religious ■ Coed
Fort Worth, Texas

Web site: www.tcu.edu
Contact: Mr. Wes Waggoner, Director of Freshman Admissions, TCU Box 297013, Fort Worth, TX 76129-0002
Telephone: 817-257-7490 or toll-free 800-828-3764
Fax: 817-257-7268
E-mail: frogmail@tcu.edu

Getting Accepted
11,888 applied
49% were accepted
1,644 enrolled (28% of accepted)
30% from top tenth of their h.s. class

Graduation and After
390 organizations recruited on campus

Financial Matters
$24,868 tuition and fees (2007–08)
$8200 room and board
73% average percent of need met
$14,771 average financial aid amount received per undergraduate (2005–06)

Academics
TCU awards bachelor's, master's, and doctoral **degrees** and post-bachelor's certificates. **Challenging opportunities** include advanced placement credit, accelerated degree programs, an honors program, double majors, independent study, and a senior project. Special programs include internships, summer session for credit, off-campus study, study-abroad, and Army and Air Force ROTC.

The most frequently chosen **baccalaureate** fields are business/marketing, communications/journalism, and health professions and related sciences. A complete listing of majors at TCU appears in the Majors by College index beginning on page 471.

The **faculty** at TCU has 479 full-time members, 86% with terminal degrees. The student-faculty ratio is 14:1.

Students of TCU
The student body totals 8,668, of whom 7,382 are undergraduates. 58.9% are women and 41.1% are men. Students come from 50 states and territories and 75 other countries. 80% are from Texas. 4.8% are international students. 5% are African American, 0.5% American Indian, 2.6% Asian American, and 7.5% Hispanic American. 86% returned for their sophomore year.

Facilities and Resources
Students can access the following: campus intranet, computer help desk, free student e-mail accounts, online (class) grades, online (class) registration, online (class) schedules. Campuswide network is available. 100% of college-owned or -operated housing units are wired for high-speed Internet access. Wireless service is available via entire campus. The **library** has 1,395,170 books and 32,017 subscriptions.

Campus Life
There are 195 active organizations on campus, including a drama/theater group, newspaper, radio station, television station, choral group, and marching band. 37% of eligible men and 39% of eligible women are members of national **fraternities**, national **sororities**, local fraternities, local sororities, and local coed music fraternities.

TCU is a member of the NCAA (Division I). **Intercollegiate sports** (some offering scholarships) include baseball (m), basketball, cross-country running, football (m), golf, riflery (w), soccer (w), swimming and diving, tennis, track and field, volleyball (w).

Campus Safety
Student safety services include emergency call boxes, video camera surveillance in parking lots, late-night transport/escort service, 24-hour emergency telephone alarm devices, 24-hour patrols by trained security personnel, student patrols, and electronically operated dormitory entrances.

Applying
TCU requires an essay, SAT or ACT, a high school transcript, 2 recommendations, and a minimum high school GPA of 2.0. It recommends an interview and a minimum high school GPA of 3.0. Application deadline: 2/15; 5/1 for financial aid, with a 5/1 priority date. Deferred admission is possible.

Texas Tech University

URBAN SETTING ■ PUBLIC ■ STATE-SUPPORTED ■ COED
LUBBOCK, TEXAS

Web site: www.ttu.edu
Contact: Box 45005, Lubbock, TX 79409-5005
Telephone: 806-742-1480
Fax: 806-742-0062
E-mail: admissions@ttu.edu

Academics

Texas Tech awards bachelor's, master's, doctoral, and first-professional **degrees** and post-bachelor's certificates. **Challenging opportunities** include advanced placement credit, accelerated degree programs, student-designed majors, freshman honors college, an honors program, double majors, independent study, and a senior project. Special programs include cooperative education, internships, summer session for credit, off-campus study, study-abroad, and Army and Air Force ROTC.

The most frequently chosen **baccalaureate** fields are business/marketing, family and consumer sciences, and engineering. A complete listing of majors at Texas Tech appears in the Majors by College index beginning on page 471.

The **faculty** at Texas Tech has 1,078 full-time members, 86% with terminal degrees. The student-faculty ratio is 18:1.

Students of Texas Tech

The student body totals 28,257, of whom 23,018 are undergraduates. 44.2% are women and 55.8% are men. Students come from 49 states and territories and 99 other countries. 96% are from Texas. 1% are international students. 4% are African American, 0.7% American Indian, 2.8% Asian American, and 12.9% Hispanic American. 83% returned for their sophomore year.

Facilities and Resources

3,000 **computers/terminals** are available on campus for general student use. Students can access the following: computer help desk, free student e-mail accounts, online (class) grades, online (class) registration, online (class) schedules, online degree plans, accounts, transcripts, schedules. Campuswide network is available. 100% of college-owned or -operated housing units are wired for high-speed Internet access. Wireless service is available via entire campus. The 4 **libraries** have 2,386,509 books and 30,823 subscriptions.

Campus Life

There are 425 active organizations on campus, including a drama/theater group, newspaper, radio station, choral group, and marching band. 12% of eligible men and 17% of eligible women are members of national **fraternities**, national **sororities**, local fraternities, and local sororities.

Texas Tech is a member of the NCAA (Division I). **Intercollegiate sports** (some offering scholarships) include baseball (m), basketball, cross-country running, football (m), golf, soccer (w), softball (w), tennis, track and field, volleyball (w).

Campus Safety

Student safety services include late-night transport/escort service, 24-hour emergency telephone alarm devices, 24-hour patrols by trained security personnel, and electronically operated dormitory entrances.

Applying

Texas Tech requires SAT or ACT and a high school transcript, and in some cases an essay. Application deadline: 5/1; 4/15 priority date for financial aid. Early admission is possible.

Getting Accepted

12,462 applied
82% were accepted
4,496 enrolled (44% of accepted)
18% from top tenth of their h.s. class
Mean SAT critical reading score: 545
Mean SAT math score: 558
Mean ACT score: 24
23% had SAT critical reading scores over 600
33% had SAT math scores over 600
12% had SAT writing scores over 600
50% had ACT scores over 24
2% had SAT critical reading scores over 700
6% had SAT math scores over 700
1% had SAT writing scores over 700
6% had ACT scores over 30

Graduation and After

28% graduated in 4 years
23% graduated in 5 years
6% graduated in 6 years
80% had job offers within 6 months
525 organizations recruited on campus

Financial Matters

$6783 resident tuition and fees (2007–08)
$15,123 nonresident tuition and fees (2007–08)
$7460 room and board
61% average percent of need met
$7424 average financial aid amount received per undergraduate (2005–06)

Thomas Aquinas College

Rural setting ■ Private ■ Independent Religious ■ Coed
Santa Paula, California

Getting Accepted
222 applied
60% were accepted
102 enrolled (76% of accepted)
75% from top tenth of their h.s. class
3.57 average high school GPA
Mean SAT critical reading score: 680
Mean SAT math score: 620
Mean SAT writing score: 650
Mean ACT score: 27
82% had SAT critical reading scores over 600
60% had SAT math scores over 600
74% had SAT writing scores over 600
80% had ACT scores over 24
42% had SAT critical reading scores over 700
24% had SAT math scores over 700
20% had ACT scores over 30

Graduation and After
68% graduated in 4 years
9% graduated in 5 years
36% pursued further study (9% arts and sciences, 9% law, 9% theology)
75% had job offers within 6 months
8 organizations recruited on campus

Financial Matters
$21,400 tuition and fees (2008–09)
$6950 room and board
100% average percent of need met
$16,202 average financial aid amount received per undergraduate (2006–07 estimated)

Web site: www.thomasaquinas.edu
Contact: Mr. Jonathan P. Daly, Director of Admissions, 10000 North Ojai Road, Santa Paula, CA 93060-9621
Telephone: 805-525-4417 Ext. 5901 or toll-free 800-634-9797
Fax: 805-525-9342
E-mail: admissions@thomasaquinas.edu

Academics
Thomas Aquinas awards bachelor's **degrees**. A senior project is a **challenging opportunity**. Cooperative education is a special program.

The most frequently chosen **baccalaureate** field is liberal arts/general studies. A complete listing of majors at Thomas Aquinas appears in the Majors by College index beginning on page 471.

The **faculty** at Thomas Aquinas has 29 full-time members, 66% with terminal degrees. The student-faculty ratio is 11:1.

Students of Thomas Aquinas
The student body is made up of 360 undergraduates. 49.4% are women and 50.6% are men. Students come from 42 states and territories and 9 other countries. 40% are from California. 5.8% are international students. 0.3% are African American, 0.3% American Indian, 2.8% Asian American, and 5.8% Hispanic American. 92% returned for their sophomore year.

Facilities and Resources
19 **computers/terminals** and 17 ports are available on campus for general student use. Students can access the following: free student e-mail accounts. Campuswide network is available. The **library** has 62,000 books and 85 subscriptions.

Campus Life
There are 5 active organizations on campus, including a drama/theater group and choral group. No national or local **fraternities** or **sororities**.

This institution has no intercollegiate sports.

Campus Safety
Student safety services include daily security daytime patrol and 24-hour emergency telephone alarm devices.

Applying
Thomas Aquinas requires an essay, SAT or ACT, a high school transcript, and 3 recommendations, and in some cases an interview. It recommends a minimum high school GPA of 3.0. Application deadline: rolling admissions; 3/2 for financial aid. Early and deferred admission are possible.

Towson University

Suburban setting ■ Public ■ State-supported ■ Coed
Towson, Maryland

Web site: www.towson.edu
Contact: Ms. Louise Shulack, Director of Admissions, 8000 York Road, Towson, MD 21252
Telephone: 410-704-2113 or toll-free 888-4TOWSON
Fax: 410-704-3030
E-mail: admissions@towson.edu

Academics

Towson awards bachelor's, master's, and doctoral **degrees** and post-bachelor's and post-master's certificates. **Challenging opportunities** include advanced placement credit, accelerated degree programs, student-designed majors, freshman honors college, an honors program, double majors, independent study, and a senior project. Special programs include cooperative education, internships, summer session for credit, off-campus study, study-abroad, and Army and Air Force ROTC.

The most frequently chosen **baccalaureate** fields are business/marketing, education, and public administration and social services. A complete listing of majors at Towson appears in the Majors by College index beginning on page 471.

The **faculty** at Towson has 728 full-time members, 77% with terminal degrees. The student-faculty ratio is 18:1.

Students of Towson

The student body totals 19,758, of whom 16,219 are undergraduates. 60.1% are women and 39.9% are men. Students come from 47 states and territories and 106 other countries. 83% are from Maryland. 2.8% are international students. 11.4% are African American, 0.4% American Indian, 4% Asian American, and 2.4% Hispanic American. 82% returned for their sophomore year.

Facilities and Resources

1,200 **computers/terminals** are available on campus for general student use. Students can access the following: computer help desk, free student e-mail accounts, online (class) grades, online (class) registration, online (class) schedules. Campuswide network is available. 100% of college-owned or -operated housing units are wired for high-speed Internet access. Wireless service is available via entire campus. The **library** has 580,036 books and 4,154 subscriptions.

Campus Life

There are 198 active organizations on campus, including a drama/theater group, newspaper, radio station, television station, choral group, and marching band. 7% of eligible men and 7% of eligible women are members of national **fraternities** and national **sororities**.

Towson is a member of the NCAA (Division I). **Intercollegiate sports** (some offering scholarships) include baseball (m), basketball, cheerleading, cross-country running, field hockey (w), football (m), golf, gymnastics (w), lacrosse, soccer, softball (w), swimming and diving, tennis, track and field, volleyball.

Campus Safety

Student safety services include late-night transport/escort service, 24-hour emergency telephone alarm devices, 24-hour patrols by trained security personnel, and electronically operated dormitory entrances.

Applying

Towson requires SAT or ACT and a high school transcript, and in some cases an essay and an interview. It recommends 2 recommendations and a minimum high school GPA of 3.0. Application deadline: 2/15; 3/1 for financial aid, with a 1/31 priority date. Early and deferred admission are possible.

Getting Accepted

15,464 applied
60% were accepted
2,665 enrolled (29% of accepted)
18% from top tenth of their h.s. class
3.46 average high school GPA
Mean SAT critical reading score: 537
Mean SAT math score: 548
Mean SAT writing score: 538
20% had SAT critical reading scores over 600
25% had SAT math scores over 600
19% had SAT writing scores over 600
29% had ACT scores over 24
2% had SAT critical reading scores over 700
2% had SAT math scores over 700
2% had SAT writing scores over 700
2% had ACT scores over 30

Graduation and After

38% graduated in 4 years
25% graduated in 5 years
4% graduated in 6 years
49 organizations recruited on campus

Financial Matters

$7234 resident tuition and fees (2008–09)
$17,174 nonresident tuition and fees (2008–09)
$7986 room and board
66% average percent of need met
$7887 average financial aid amount received per undergraduate (2006–07 estimated)

TRANSYLVANIA UNIVERSITY

URBAN SETTING ■ PRIVATE ■ INDEPENDENT RELIGIOUS ■ COED
LEXINGTON, KENTUCKY

Web site: www.transy.edu
Contact: Mr. Bradley Goan, Director of Admissions, 300 North Broadway,
    Lexington, KY 40508-1797
Telephone: 859-233-4242 or toll-free 800-872-6798
Fax: 859-233-8797
E-mail: admissions@transy.edu

Founded in 1780 as the nation's sixteenth college, Transylvania consistently ranks among the nation's best liberal arts colleges and is considered an exceptional value in education. Students benefit from an innovative teacher-recognition program, the first in the nation to attract and reward outstanding teaching on a substantial scale. Small classes and individual attention from faculty members prepare students well for highly selective graduate and professional schools as well as for jobs in a highly competitive workforce. Transylvania's location in a historic district near downtown Lexington, Kentucky, provides opportunities for internships, jobs, and cultural activities.

Getting Accepted
1,286 applied
83% were accepted
293 enrolled (27% of accepted)
41% from top tenth of their h.s. class
3.56 average high school GPA
Mean SAT critical reading score: 600
Mean SAT math score: 590
Mean ACT score: 26
58% had SAT critical reading scores over 600
57% had SAT math scores over 600
71% had ACT scores over 24
17% had SAT critical reading scores over 700
16% had SAT math scores over 700
13% had ACT scores over 30
7 National Merit Scholars
31 valedictorians

Graduation and After
61% graduated in 4 years
5% graduated in 5 years
1% graduated in 6 years
32% pursued further study (15% arts and
    sciences, 5% medicine, 4% business)
60% had job offers within 6 months
80 organizations recruited on campus

Financial Matters
$22,300 tuition and fees (2007–08)
$7130 room and board
85% average percent of need met
$17,629 average financial aid amount received
    per undergraduate (2006–07 estimated)

Academics
Transylvania awards bachelor's **degrees**. **Challenging opportunities** include advanced placement credit, student-designed majors, double majors, independent study, and a senior project. Special programs include internships, summer session for credit, off-campus study, study-abroad, and Army and Air Force ROTC.

The most frequently chosen **baccalaureate** fields are business/marketing, social sciences, and biological/life sciences. A complete listing of majors at Transylvania appears in the Majors by College index beginning on page 471.

The **faculty** at Transylvania has 82 full-time members, 91% with terminal degrees. The student-faculty ratio is 13:1.

Students of Transylvania
The student body is made up of 1,117 undergraduates. 58.5% are women and 41.5% are men. Students come from 31 states and territories. 82% are from Kentucky. 2.3% are African American, 0.3% American Indian, 1.7% Asian American, and 1.6% Hispanic American. 70% returned for their sophomore year.

Facilities and Resources
250 **computers/terminals** are available on campus for general student use. Campuswide network is available. The **library** has 125,000 books and 500 subscriptions.

Campus Life
There are 51 active organizations on campus, including a drama/theater group, newspaper, radio station, and choral group. 50% of eligible men and 50% of eligible women are members of national **fraternities** and national **sororities**.

Transylvania is a member of the NCAA (Division III). **Intercollegiate sports** include baseball (m), basketball, cheerleading, cross-country running, field hockey (w), golf, soccer, softball (w), swimming and diving, tennis, volleyball (w).

Campus Safety
Student safety services include late-night transport/escort service, 24-hour emergency telephone alarm devices, 24-hour patrols by trained security personnel, and electronically operated dormitory entrances.

Applying
Transylvania requires an essay, SAT or ACT, a high school transcript, 2 recommendations, and a minimum high school GPA of 2.75, and in some cases an interview. It recommends an interview. Application deadline: 2/1; 3/1 priority date for financial aid. Early and deferred admission are possible.

Trinity College

URBAN SETTING ■ PRIVATE ■ INDEPENDENT ■ COED
HARTFORD, CONNECTICUT

Web site: www.trincoll.edu
Contact: Mr. Larry Dow, Dean of Admissions and Financial Aid, 300 Summit Street, Hartford, CT 06106-3100
Telephone: 860-297-2180
Fax: 860-297-2287
E-mail: admissions.office@trincoll.edu

Academics

Trinity College awards bachelor's and master's **degrees**. **Challenging opportunities** include advanced placement credit, accelerated degree programs, student-designed majors, an honors program, double majors, independent study, and a senior project. Special programs include internships, summer session for credit, off-campus study, study-abroad, and Army ROTC.

The most frequently chosen **baccalaureate** fields are social sciences, area and ethnic studies, and English. A complete listing of majors at Trinity College appears in the Majors by College index beginning on page 471.

The **faculty** at Trinity College has 173 full-time members, 92% with terminal degrees. The student-faculty ratio is 10:1.

Students of Trinity College

The student body totals 2,564, of whom 2,375 are undergraduates. 50.2% are women and 49.8% are men. Students come from 44 states and territories and 31 other countries. 18% are from Connecticut. 3.7% are international students. 6.7% are African American, 0.2% American Indian, 5.3% Asian American, and 6% Hispanic American. 90% returned for their sophomore year.

Facilities and Resources

249 **computers/terminals** and 3,000 ports are available on campus for general student use. Students can access the following: campus intranet, computer help desk, free student e-mail accounts, online (class) grades, online (class) registration, online (class) schedules, Web pages. Campuswide network is available. 100% of college-owned or -operated housing units are wired for high-speed Internet access. Wireless service is available via classrooms, computer centers, computer labs, learning centers, libraries, student centers. The 2 **libraries** have 1,008,701 books and 1,813 subscriptions.

Campus Life

There are 105 active organizations on campus, including a drama/theater group, newspaper, radio station, and choral group. 20% of eligible men and 16% of eligible women are members of national **fraternities**, national **sororities**, local fraternities, local sororities, and coed fraternities.

Trinity College is a member of the NCAA (Division III). **Intercollegiate sports** include baseball (m), basketball, crew, cross-country running, field hockey (w), football (m), golf (m), ice hockey, lacrosse, soccer, softball (w), squash, swimming and diving, tennis, track and field, volleyball (w), wrestling (m).

Campus Safety

Student safety services include late-night transport/escort service, 24-hour emergency telephone alarm devices, 24-hour patrols by trained security personnel, and electronically operated dormitory entrances.

Applying

Trinity College requires an essay, ACT or SAT and SAT Writing Test or three SAT subject tests, a high school transcript, and 3 recommendations. It recommends an interview. Application deadline: 1/1; 3/1 for financial aid, with a 2/1 priority date. Early and deferred admission are possible.

Getting Accepted

5,950 applied
34% were accepted
576 enrolled (28% of accepted)
61% from top tenth of their h.s. class
Mean SAT critical reading score: 643
Mean SAT math score: 645
Mean SAT writing score: 656
Mean ACT score: 28
76% had SAT critical reading scores over 600
79% had SAT math scores over 600
79% had SAT writing scores over 600
94% had ACT scores over 24
24% had SAT critical reading scores over 700
19% had SAT math scores over 700
33% had SAT writing scores over 700
19% had ACT scores over 30

Graduation and After

79% graduated in 4 years
6% graduated in 5 years
1% graduated in 6 years
77% had job offers within 6 months

Financial Matters

$36,870 tuition and fees (2007–08)
$9420 room and board
100% average percent of need met
$25,590 average financial aid amount received per undergraduate (2005–06)

TRINITY UNIVERSITY

URBAN SETTING ■ PRIVATE ■ INDEPENDENT RELIGIOUS ■ COED
SAN ANTONIO, TEXAS

Web site: www.trinity.edu
Contact: Mr. Christopher Ellertson, Dean of Admissions and Financial Aid,
    One Trinity Place, San Antonio, TX 78212-7200
Telephone: 210-999-7207 or toll-free 800-TRINITY
Fax: 210-999-8164
E-mail: admissions@trinity.edu

Getting Accepted
4,511 applied
52% were accepted
631 enrolled (27% of accepted)
53% from top tenth of their h.s. class
3.53 average high school GPA
Mean SAT critical reading score: 646
Mean SAT math score: 648
Mean ACT score: 29
77% had SAT critical reading scores over 600
82% had SAT math scores over 600
99% had ACT scores over 24
23% had SAT critical reading scores over 700
21% had SAT math scores over 700
45% had ACT scores over 30
11 National Merit Scholars

Graduation and After
67% graduated in 4 years
11% graduated in 5 years
1% graduated in 6 years
31% pursued further study

Financial Matters
$27,699 tuition and fees (2008–09)
$8822 room and board
82% average percent of need met
$14,343 average financial aid amount received
    per undergraduate (2004–05 estimated)

Academics
Trinity awards bachelor's and master's **degrees. Challenging opportunities** include advanced placement credit, accelerated degree programs, an honors program, double majors, independent study, and a senior project. Special programs include internships, summer session for credit, study-abroad, and Air Force ROTC.

The most frequently chosen **baccalaureate** fields are health professions and related sciences, social sciences, and foreign languages and literature. A complete listing of majors at Trinity appears in the Majors by College index beginning on page 471.

The **faculty** at Trinity has 221 full-time members, 99% with terminal degrees. The student-faculty ratio is 10:1.

Students of Trinity
The student body totals 2,679, of whom 2,477 are undergraduates. 53.9% are women and 46.1% are men. Students come from 49 states and territories and 38 other countries. 70% are from Texas. 5.1% are international students. 3.6% are African American, 1.1% American Indian, 6.5% Asian American, and 10.9% Hispanic American. 90% returned for their sophomore year.

Facilities and Resources
450 **computers/terminals** are available on campus for general student use. Students can access the following: campus intranet, computer help desk, free student e-mail accounts, online (class) grades, online (class) registration, online (class) schedules. Campuswide network is available. 100% of college-owned or -operated housing units are wired for high-speed Internet access. Wireless service is available via entire campus. The **library** has 937,261 books and 2,118 subscriptions.

Campus Life
Active organizations on campus include a drama/theater group, newspaper, radio station, television station, and choral group. 19% of eligible men and 28% of eligible women are members of local **fraternities** and local **sororities**.

Trinity is a member of the NCAA (Division III). **Intercollegiate sports** include baseball (m), basketball, cross-country running, football (m), golf, soccer, softball (w), swimming and diving, tennis, track and field, volleyball (w).

Campus Safety
Student safety services include late-night transport/escort service, 24-hour emergency telephone alarm devices, 24-hour patrols by trained security personnel, and electronically operated dormitory entrances.

Applying
Trinity requires an essay, SAT or ACT, a high school transcript, and 2 recommendations. It recommends an interview. Application deadline: 2/1; 4/1 for financial aid, with a 2/1 priority date. Deferred admission is possible.

TRUMAN STATE UNIVERSITY

SMALL-TOWN SETTING ■ PUBLIC ■ STATE-SUPPORTED ■ COED
KIRKSVILLE, MISSOURI

Web site: www.truman.edu
Contact: Mr. Brad Chambers, Director of Admissions, 205 McClain Hall, 100
  East Normal Street, Kirksville, MO 63501-4221
Telephone: 660-785-4114 or toll-free 800-892-7792 (in-state)
Fax: 660-785-7456
E-mail: admissions@truman.edu

Academics

Truman State awards bachelor's and master's **degrees**. **Challenging opportunities**
include advanced placement credit, student-designed majors, an honors program, double
majors, and a senior project. Special programs include internships, summer session for
credit, off-campus study, study-abroad, and Army ROTC.

The most frequently chosen **baccalaureate** fields are business/marketing, English,
and parks and recreation. A complete listing of majors at Truman State appears in the
Majors by College index beginning on page 471.

The **faculty** at Truman State has 340 full-time members, 85% with terminal degrees.
The student-faculty ratio is 16:1.

Students of Truman State

The student body totals 5,866, of whom 5,608 are undergraduates. 57.4% are women
and 42.6% are men. Students come from 41 states and territories and 40 other countries.
76% are from Missouri. 4.2% are international students. 4.3% are African American,
0.8% American Indian, 2.4% Asian American, and 2.3% Hispanic American. 88%
returned for their sophomore year.

Facilities and Resources

1,081 **computers/terminals** are available on campus for general student use. Students
can access the following: computer help desk, free student e-mail accounts, online (class)
grades, online (class) registration, online (class) schedules. Campuswide network is available. 100% of college-owned or -operated housing units are wired for high-speed Internet access. Wireless service is available via entire campus. The **library** has 499,536 books
and 3,340 subscriptions.

Campus Life

There are 210 active organizations on campus, including a drama/theater group,
newspaper, radio station, television station, choral group, and marching band. 22% of
eligible men and 18% of eligible women are members of national **fraternities**, national
sororities, and local sororities.

Truman State is a member of the NCAA (Division II). **Intercollegiate sports** (some
offering scholarships) include baseball (m), basketball, cross-country running, football
(m), golf, soccer, softball (w), swimming and diving, tennis, track and field, volleyball (w),
wrestling (m).

Campus Safety

Student safety services include patrols by commissioned officers, late-night transport/
escort service, 24-hour emergency telephone alarm devices, 24-hour patrols by trained
security personnel, and student patrols.

Applying

Truman State requires an essay, SAT or ACT, and a high school transcript. It recommends ACT, an interview, and a minimum high school GPA of 3.0. Application deadline:
3/1; 4/1 priority date for financial aid. Deferred admission is possible.

Getting Accepted

4,076 applied
81% were accepted
1,405 enrolled (43% of accepted)
48% from top tenth of their h.s. class
3.75 average high school GPA
Mean SAT critical reading score: 620
Mean SAT math score: 610
Mean ACT score: 27
65% had SAT critical reading scores over 600
57% had SAT math scores over 600
85% had ACT scores over 24
25% had SAT critical reading scores over 700
17% had SAT math scores over 700
31% had ACT scores over 30
13 National Merit Scholars
161 valedictorians

Graduation and After

46% graduated in 4 years
21% graduated in 5 years
4% graduated in 6 years
54% pursued further study
45.5% had job offers within 6 months
230 organizations recruited on campus

Financial Matters

$6432 resident tuition and fees (2007–08)
$11,042 nonresident tuition and fees (2007–08)
$5815 room and board
83% average percent of need met
$6056 average financial aid amount received
  per undergraduate (2005–06 estimated)

TUFTS UNIVERSITY

SUBURBAN SETTING ■ PRIVATE ■ INDEPENDENT ■ COED
MEDFORD, MASSACHUSETTS

Getting Accepted
15,365 applied
28% were accepted
1,370 enrolled (32% of accepted)
80% from top tenth of their h.s. class
Mean SAT critical reading score: 704
Mean SAT math score: 701
Mean SAT writing score: 701
Mean ACT score: 31
95% had SAT critical reading scores over 600
95% had SAT math scores over 600
43% had SAT writing scores over 600
99% had ACT scores over 24
60% had SAT critical reading scores over 700
57% had SAT math scores over 700
6% had SAT writing scores over 700
76% had ACT scores over 30

Graduation and After
84% graduated in 4 years
4% graduated in 5 years
1% graduated in 6 years
30% pursued further study (11% law, 9% medicine, 8% business)
225 organizations recruited on campus

Financial Matters
$36,700 tuition and fees (2007–08)
$10,160 room and board
100% average percent of need met
$27,064 average financial aid amount received per undergraduate (2006–07 estimated)

Web site: www.tufts.edu
Contact: Mr. Lee Coffin, Office of Undergraduate Admissions, Bendetson Hall, Medford, MA 02155
Telephone: 617-627-3170
Fax: 617-627-3860
E-mail: admissions.inquiry@ase.tufts.edu

Academics
Tufts awards bachelor's, master's, doctoral, and first-professional **degrees** and post-master's certificates. **Challenging opportunities** include advanced placement credit, student-designed majors, an honors program, double majors, independent study, and a senior project. Special programs include internships, summer session for credit, off-campus study, study-abroad, and Army, Navy, and Air Force ROTC.

The most frequently chosen **baccalaureate** fields are social sciences, engineering, and visual and performing arts. A complete listing of majors at Tufts appears in the Majors by College index beginning on page 471.

The **faculty** at Tufts has 664 full-time members, 95% with terminal degrees. The student-faculty ratio is 7:1.

Students of Tufts
The student body totals 9,758, of whom 5,035 are undergraduates. 50.8% are women and 49.2% are men. Students come from 52 states and territories and 93 other countries. 25% are from Massachusetts. 5.7% are international students. 6.5% are African American, 0.2% American Indian, 12.1% Asian American, and 6.2% Hispanic American. 96% returned for their sophomore year.

Facilities and Resources
300 **computers/terminals** are available on campus for general student use. Students can access the following: computer help desk, free student e-mail accounts, online (class) registration, online (class) schedules. Campuswide network is available. 100% of college-owned or -operated housing units are wired for high-speed Internet access. Wireless service is available via classrooms, computer centers, computer labs, learning centers, libraries, student centers. The 2 **libraries** have 1,746,659 books and 4,341 subscriptions.

Campus Life
There are 200 active organizations on campus, including a drama/theater group, newspaper, radio station, television station, choral group, and marching band. 15% of eligible men and 4% of eligible women are members of national **fraternities** and national **sororities**.

Tufts is a member of the NCAA (Division III). **Intercollegiate sports** include baseball (m), basketball, crew, cross-country running, fencing (w), field hockey (w), football (m), golf (m), ice hockey (m), lacrosse, sailing, soccer, softball (w), squash, swimming and diving, tennis, track and field, volleyball (w).

Campus Safety
Student safety services include security lighting, call boxes to campus police, late-night transport/escort service, 24-hour emergency telephone alarm devices, 24-hour patrols by trained security personnel, and electronically operated dormitory entrances.

Applying
Tufts requires an essay, SAT and SAT Subject Tests or ACT, a high school transcript, and 1 recommendation. It recommends an interview. Application deadline: 1/1; 2/15 for financial aid. Early and deferred admission are possible.

Tulane University

Urban setting ■ Private ■ Independent ■ Coed
New Orleans, Louisiana

Web site: www.tulane.edu
Contact: Mr. Earl Retif, Vice President for Enrollment Management and University Registrar, Office of Admissions, 210 Gibson Hall, New Orleans, LA 70118
Telephone: 504-865-5731 or toll-free 800-873-9283
Fax: 504-862-8715
E-mail: undergrad.admission@tulane.edu

Academics

Tulane awards associate, bachelor's, master's, doctoral, and first-professional **degrees** and post-bachelor's certificates. **Challenging opportunities** include advanced placement credit, accelerated degree programs, student-designed majors, freshman honors college, an honors program, double majors, independent study, and a senior project. Special programs include cooperative education, internships, summer session for credit, off-campus study, study-abroad, and Army, Navy, and Air Force ROTC.

The most frequently chosen **baccalaureate** fields are business/marketing, social sciences, and engineering. A complete listing of majors at Tulane appears in the Majors by College index beginning on page 471.

The **faculty** at Tulane has 1,176 full-time members. The student-faculty ratio is 9:1.

Students of Tulane

The student body totals 10,519, of whom 6,449 are undergraduates. 53.5% are women and 46.5% are men. Students come from 53 states and territories and 42 other countries. 33% are from Louisiana. 2.4% are international students. 8.5% are African American, 2.2% American Indian, 5% Asian American, and 4.3% Hispanic American. 87% returned for their sophomore year.

Facilities and Resources

592 **computers/terminals** are available on campus for general student use. Students can access the following: computer help desk, free student e-mail accounts, online (class) grades, online (class) registration, online (class) schedules. Campuswide network is available. 100% of college-owned or -operated housing units are wired for high-speed Internet access. Wireless service is available via entire campus. The 9 **libraries** have 2,500,646 books and 12,607 subscriptions.

Campus Life

There are 250 active organizations on campus, including a drama/theater group, newspaper, radio station, television station, choral group, and marching band. 25% of eligible men and 30% of eligible women are members of national **fraternities** and national **sororities**.

Tulane is a member of the NCAA (Division I). **Intercollegiate sports** (some offering scholarships) include baseball (m), basketball, cross-country running, football (m), golf, soccer (w), swimming and diving (w), tennis, track and field (w), volleyball (w).

Campus Safety

Student safety services include on and off-campus shuttle service, crime prevention programs, lighted pathways, late-night transport/escort service, 24-hour emergency telephone alarm devices, 24-hour patrols by trained security personnel, student patrols, and electronically operated dormitory entrances.

Applying

Tulane requires an essay, SAT or ACT, a high school transcript, and 1 recommendation. Application deadline: 1/15; 2/1 for financial aid, with a 1/15 priority date. Early and deferred admission are possible.

Getting Accepted

16,967 applied
44% were accepted
1,324 enrolled (18% of accepted)
50% from top tenth of their h.s. class
3.39 average high school GPA
Mean SAT critical reading score: 645
Mean SAT math score: 635
Mean SAT writing score: 645
Mean ACT score: 29
80% had SAT critical reading scores over 600
62% had SAT math scores over 600
76% had SAT writing scores over 600
33% had SAT critical reading scores over 700
16% had SAT math scores over 700
22% had SAT writing scores over 700

Financial Matters

$36,610 tuition and fees (2007–08)
$8940 room and board
88% average percent of need met
$25,945 average financial aid amount received per undergraduate (2005–06)

Union College

Suburban setting ■ Private ■ Independent Religious ■ Coed
Lincoln, Nebraska

Web site: www.ucollege.edu
Contact: Huda McClelland, Director of Admissions, 3800 South 48th Street, Lincoln, NE 68506
Telephone: 402-486-2504 or toll-free 800-228-4600 (out-of-state)
Fax: 402-486-2895
E-mail: ucenroll@ucollege.edu

Getting Accepted

903 applied
43% were accepted
164 enrolled (42% of accepted)
6% from top tenth of their h.s. class
3.33 average high school GPA
33% had ACT scores over 24
5% had ACT scores over 30

Graduation and After

Graduates pursuing further study: 4% education, 4% medicine, 2% arts and sciences
89% had job offers within 6 months
96 organizations recruited on campus

Financial Matters

$16,130 tuition and fees (2007–08)
$5270 room and board
71% average percent of need met
$12,234 average financial aid amount received per undergraduate (2005–06)

Academics

Union College awards associate, bachelor's, and master's **degrees**. **Challenging opportunities** include advanced placement credit, accelerated degree programs, student-designed majors, an honors program, double majors, independent study, and a senior project. Special programs include cooperative education, internships, summer session for credit, off-campus study, and study-abroad.

The most frequently chosen **baccalaureate** fields are health professions and related sciences, business/marketing, and education. A complete listing of majors at Union College appears in the Majors by College index beginning on page 471.

The **faculty** at Union College has 59 full-time members, 37% with terminal degrees. The student-faculty ratio is 13:1.

Students of Union College

The student body totals 1,015, of whom 944 are undergraduates. 56% are women and 44% are men. Students come from 48 states and territories and 26 other countries. 18% are from Nebraska. 7.9% are international students. 2.3% are African American, 1.4% American Indian, 2.8% Asian American, and 6.3% Hispanic American. 72% returned for their sophomore year.

Facilities and Resources

520 **computers/terminals** are available on campus for general student use. Campuswide network is available. The **library** has 147,813 books and 1,357 subscriptions.

Campus Life

Active organizations on campus include a drama/theater group, newspaper, and choral group. No national or local **fraternities** or **sororities**.

Intercollegiate sports include basketball, volleyball (w).

Campus Safety

Student safety services include late-night transport/escort service, 24-hour emergency telephone alarm devices, and student patrols.

Applying

Union College requires SAT or ACT, a high school transcript, 3 recommendations, and a minimum high school GPA of 2.5, and in some cases an essay and an interview. Application deadline: rolling admissions.

UNION COLLEGE

URBAN SETTING ■ PRIVATE ■ INDEPENDENT ■ COED
SCHENECTADY, NEW YORK

SPONSOR

Web site: www.union.edu
Contact: Dean of Admissions, Grant Hall, Schenectady, NY 02308
Telephone: 518-388-6112 or toll-free 888-843-6688 (in-state)
Fax: 518-388-6986
E-mail: admissions@union.edu

Academics

Union College awards bachelor's **degrees**. **Challenging opportunities** include advanced placement credit, accelerated degree programs, student-designed majors, an honors program, double majors, independent study, and a senior project. Special programs include internships, summer session for credit, off-campus study, study-abroad, and Army, Navy, and Air Force ROTC.

The most frequently chosen **baccalaureate** fields are social sciences, biological/life sciences, and psychology. A complete listing of majors at Union College appears in the Majors by College index beginning on page 471.

The **faculty** at Union College has 194 full-time members, 95% with terminal degrees. The student-faculty ratio is 10:1.

Students of Union College

The student body is made up of 2,177 undergraduates. 48% are women and 52% are men. Students come from 37 states and territories and 26 other countries. 40% are from New York. 2.2% are international students. 3.4% are African American, 0.2% American Indian, 6% Asian American, and 4.2% Hispanic American. 91% returned for their sophomore year.

Facilities and Resources

482 **computers/terminals** and 3,032 ports are available on campus for general student use. Students can access the following: campus intranet, computer help desk, free student e-mail accounts, online (class) grades, online (class) registration, online (class) schedules, multimedia lab. Campuswide network is available. 100% of college-owned or -operated housing units are wired for high-speed Internet access. Wireless service is available via classrooms, computer centers, computer labs, learning centers, libraries, student centers. The **library** has 604,412 books and 4,453 subscriptions.

Campus Life

There are 105 active organizations on campus, including a drama/theater group, newspaper, radio station, and choral group. 30% of eligible men and 32% of eligible women are members of national **fraternities**, national **sororities**, local fraternities, local sororities, and theme houses.

Union College is a member of the NCAA (Division III). **Intercollegiate sports** include baseball (m), basketball, crew, cross-country running, field hockey (w), football (m), ice hockey, lacrosse, soccer, softball (w), swimming and diving, tennis, track and field, volleyball (w).

Campus Safety

Student safety services include awareness programs, bicycle patrol, shuttle service, late-night transport/escort service, 24-hour emergency telephone alarm devices, 24-hour patrols by trained security personnel, and electronically operated dormitory entrances.

Applying

Union College requires an essay, a high school transcript, and 2 recommendations, and in some cases SAT and SAT Subject Tests or ACT. It recommends an interview. Application deadline: 1/15; 2/1 for financial aid. Early and deferred admission are possible.

Union College, one of the oldest nondenominational colleges in America, is located in the small city of Schenectady, about 3 hours north of New York City. Its distinctive curriculum combines the traditional liberal arts with engineering study. Three basic tenets undergird a Union education: commitments to lifelong learning, the liberal arts, and a close working relationship between students and faculty members. People from many different backgrounds come to Union, attracted by these values and the opportunities they imply: small classes, excellent access to superb facilities, a caring and committed faculty, and an academic program of depth and diversity.

Getting Accepted
4,837 applied
43% were accepted
560 enrolled (27% of accepted)
64% from top tenth of their h.s. class
3.5 average high school GPA
Mean SAT critical reading score: 620
Mean SAT math score: 640
Mean SAT writing score: 620
Mean ACT score: 27
60% had SAT critical reading scores over 600
75% had SAT math scores over 600
63% had SAT writing scores over 600
93% had ACT scores over 24
12% had SAT critical reading scores over 700
15% had SAT math scores over 700
11% had SAT writing scores over 700
23% had ACT scores over 30
8 valedictorians

Graduation and After
79% graduated in 4 years
5% graduated in 5 years
2% graduated in 6 years
33% pursued further study (12% arts and sciences, 6% medicine, 4% law)
286 organizations recruited on campus

Financial Matters
$46,245 comprehensive fee (2007–08)
100% average percent of need met
$26,330 average financial aid amount received per undergraduate (2005–06)

UNION UNIVERSITY

SMALL-TOWN SETTING ■ PRIVATE ■ INDEPENDENT RELIGIOUS ■ COED
JACKSON, TENNESSEE

Web site: www.uu.edu
Contact: Mr. Robbie Graves, Director of Enrollment Services, 1050 Union
    University Drive, Jackson, TN 38305-3697
Telephone: 731-661-5590 or toll-free 800-33-UNION
Fax: 731-661-5017
E-mail: cgraves@uu.edu

Union University enjoys a national reputation for integrating rigorous academics with an authentic Christian commitment. The University's acclaimed faculty members work closely with students, who pursue excellence in more than 100 fields of study. This personal approach is possible because of an 11:1 student-teacher ratio and the faculty's focus on classroom instruction. Union is nationally recognized for its community service programs. It also offers outstanding placement records for employment or graduate study and opportunities to study abroad. Students prepare for the changes, challenges, and opportunities of a competitive world as they strengthen their Christian faith. To find out more about Union University, students should visit http://www.uu.edu.

Getting Accepted
1,140 applied
81% were accepted
467 enrolled (51% of accepted)
35% from top tenth of their h.s. class
3.52 average high school GPA
50% had SAT critical reading scores over 600
41% had SAT math scores over 600
60% had ACT scores over 24
19% had SAT critical reading scores over 700
8% had SAT math scores over 700
16% had ACT scores over 30
4 National Merit Scholars
25 valedictorians

Graduation and After
34% pursued further study (15% arts and sciences, 6% theology, 3% business)
83% had job offers within 6 months
85 organizations recruited on campus

Financial Matters
$18,620 tuition and fees (2007–08)
$6500 room and board
$14,089 average financial aid amount received per undergraduate (2006–07 estimated)

Academics

Union awards associate, bachelor's, master's, and doctoral **degrees** and post-master's certificates. **Challenging opportunities** include advanced placement credit, accelerated degree programs, an honors program, double majors, independent study, and a senior project. Special programs include cooperative education, internships, summer session for credit, off-campus study, and study-abroad.

The most frequently chosen **baccalaureate** fields are health professions and related sciences, interdisciplinary studies, and business/marketing. A complete listing of majors at Union appears in the Majors by College index beginning on page 471.

The **faculty** at Union has 174 full-time members, 82% with terminal degrees. The student-faculty ratio is 12:1.

Students of Union

The student body totals 3,229, of whom 2,310 are undergraduates. 59.8% are women and 40.2% are men. Students come from 44 states and territories and 36 other countries. 70% are from Tennessee. 1.9% are international students. 10.7% are African American, 0.2% American Indian, 1.3% Asian American, and 1.6% Hispanic American. 84% returned for their sophomore year.

Facilities and Resources

236 **computers/terminals** are available on campus for general student use. Students can access the following: campus intranet, computer help desk, free student e-mail accounts, online (class) grades, online (class) registration, online (class) schedules. Campuswide network is available. 100% of college-owned or -operated housing units are wired for high-speed Internet access. Wireless service is available via entire campus. The 2 **libraries** have 149,255 books and 19,919 subscriptions.

Campus Life

There are 52 active organizations on campus, including a drama/theater group, newspaper, and choral group. 8% of eligible men and 12% of eligible women are members of national **fraternities** and national **sororities**.

Union is a member of the NAIA and NCCAA. **Intercollegiate sports** (some offering scholarships) include baseball (m), basketball, cheerleading (w), cross-country running, golf (m), soccer, softball (w), track and field, volleyball (w).

Campus Safety

Student safety services include late-night transport/escort service, 24-hour emergency telephone alarm devices, 24-hour patrols by trained security personnel, and student patrols.

Applying

Union requires SAT or ACT, a high school transcript, and a minimum high school GPA of 2.5, and in some cases recommendations. It recommends an essay, SAT Subject Tests, and an interview. Application deadline: rolling admissions. Early and deferred admission are possible.

UNITED STATES AIR FORCE ACADEMY

SUBURBAN SETTING ■ PUBLIC ■ FEDERALLY SUPPORTED ■ COED, PRIMARILY MEN
USAF ACADEMY, COLORADO

SPONSOR

Web site: www.usafa.edu
Contact: Mr. Rolland Stoneman, Associate Director of Admissions/Selections,
HQ USAFA/RR, 2304 Cadet Drive, Suite 2400, USAF Academy, CO
80840-5025
Telephone: 719-333-2520 or toll-free 800-443-9266
Fax: 719-333-3012
E-mail: rr_webmail@usafa.af.mil

Academics

USAFA awards bachelor's **degrees**. **Challenging opportunities** include advanced placement credit, student-designed majors, double majors, independent study, and a senior project. Special programs include internships, summer session for credit, off-campus study, and study-abroad.

The most frequently chosen **baccalaureate** fields are engineering, social sciences, and business/marketing. A complete listing of majors at USAFA appears in the Majors by College index beginning on page 471.

The **faculty** at USAFA has 563 full-time members, 49% with terminal degrees. The student-faculty ratio is 8:1.

Students of USAFA

The student body is made up of 4,461 undergraduates. 18.6% are women and 81.4% are men. Students come from 52 states and territories and 14 other countries. 6% are from Colorado. 1.2% are international students. 4.7% are African American, 1.9% American Indian, 8.2% Asian American, and 6.7% Hispanic American. 90% returned for their sophomore year.

Facilities and Resources

500 **computers/terminals** are available on campus for general student use. Students can access the following: campus intranet, computer help desk, free student e-mail accounts. Campuswide network is available. Wireless service is available via entire campus. The 3 **libraries** have 490,000 books and 1,600 subscriptions.

Campus Life

There are 87 active organizations on campus, including a drama/theater group, choral group, and marching band. No national or local **fraternities** or **sororities**.

USAFA is a member of the NCAA (Division I). **Intercollegiate sports** include baseball (m), basketball, cheerleading, cross-country running, fencing, football (m), golf (m), gymnastics, ice hockey (m), lacrosse (m), riflery, soccer, swimming and diving, tennis, track and field, volleyball (w), water polo (m), wrestling (m).

Campus Safety

Student safety services include self-defense education, well-lit campus, late-night transport/escort service, 24-hour emergency telephone alarm devices, and 24-hour patrols by trained security personnel.

Applying

USAFA requires an essay, SAT or ACT, a high school transcript, an interview, authorized nomination, and a minimum high school GPA of 2.0. Application deadline: 1/31.

Getting Accepted
9,163 applied
14% were accepted
1,214 enrolled (94% of accepted)
51% from top tenth of their h.s. class
3.85 average high school GPA
Mean SAT critical reading score: 629
Mean SAT math score: 658
Mean SAT writing score: 600
Mean ACT score: 29
73% had SAT critical reading scores over 600
68% had SAT math scores over 600
61% had SAT writing scores over 600
100% had ACT scores over 24
14% had SAT critical reading scores over 700
3% had SAT math scores over 700
12% had SAT writing scores over 700
47% had ACT scores over 30

Graduation and After
69% graduated in 4 years
1% graduated in 5 years
1% graduated in 6 years
8% pursued further study (3% engineering,
2% arts and sciences, 2% medicine)
100% had job offers within 6 months
1 organization recruited on campus

UNITED STATES COAST GUARD ACADEMY

SUBURBAN SETTING ■ PUBLIC ■ FEDERALLY SUPPORTED ■ COED
NEW LONDON, CONNECTICUT

Web site: www.cga.edu
Contact: Capt. Susan Bibeau, Director of Admissions, 31 Mohegan Avenue,
   New London, CT 06320-4195
Telephone: 860-444-8500 or toll-free 800-883-8724
Fax: 860-701-6700
E-mail: admissions@uscga.edu

Founded in 1876, the United States Coast Guard Academy is one of the most selective colleges in America. Unlike the other military service academies, a congressional nomination is not required to apply. There is no tuition at the Academy; cadets receive a full scholarship. The majors offered at the Academy include electrical, naval, and mechanical engineering; marine environmental science; and government. Coast Guard cadets devote themselves to meaningful careers of selfless service to others and graduate to work at sea, on land, in the air, and even in space.

Getting Accepted
1,633 applied
24% were accepted
250 enrolled (63% of accepted)
50% from top tenth of their h.s. class
3.76 average high school GPA
Mean SAT critical reading score: 617
Mean SAT math score: 645
Mean ACT score: 27
64% had SAT critical reading scores over 600
84% had SAT math scores over 600
87% had ACT scores over 24
12% had SAT critical reading scores over 700
20% had SAT math scores over 700
17% had ACT scores over 30
20 class presidents
13 valedictorians

Graduation and After
68% graduated in 4 years
5% graduated in 5 years

Academics

USCGA awards bachelor's **degrees. Challenging opportunities** include an honors program, double majors, independent study, and a senior project. Special programs include internships, summer session for credit, and off-campus study.

The most frequently chosen **baccalaureate** fields are engineering, biological/life sciences, and social sciences. A complete listing of majors at USCGA appears in the Majors by College index beginning on page 471.

The **faculty** at USCGA has 97 full-time members, 44% with terminal degrees. The student-faculty ratio is 9:1.

Students of USCGA

The student body is made up of 996 undergraduates. 28% are women and 72% are men. Students come from 49 states and territories and 7 other countries. 6% are from Connecticut. 1.3% are international students. 3% are African American, 0.5% American Indian, 4.7% Asian American, and 4.8% Hispanic American. 86% returned for their sophomore year.

Facilities and Resources

325 **computers/terminals** are available on campus for general student use. Students can access the following: laptop for each student. Campuswide network is available. The **library** has 155,000 books and 514 subscriptions.

Campus Life

Active organizations on campus include a drama/theater group, choral group, and marching band. No national or local **fraternities** or **sororities**.

USCGA is a member of the NCAA (Division III). **Intercollegiate sports** include baseball (m), basketball, crew, cross-country running, football (m), riflery, sailing, soccer, softball (w), swimming and diving, tennis (m), track and field, volleyball (w), wrestling (m).

Campus Safety

Student safety services include 24-hour patrols by trained security personnel and student patrols.

Applying

USCGA requires an essay, SAT or ACT, a high school transcript, 3 recommendations, and medical exam, physical fitness exam. It recommends an interview. Application deadline: 3/1.

UNITED STATES MERCHANT MARINE ACADEMY

SUBURBAN SETTING ■ PUBLIC ■ FEDERALLY SUPPORTED ■ COED
KINGS POINT, NEW YORK

SPONSOR

Web site: www.usmma.edu
Contact: Capt. Robert E. Johnson, Director of Admissions and Financial Aid,
300 Steamboat Road, Kings Point, NY 11024-1699
Telephone: 516-773-5391 or toll-free 866-546-4778
Fax: 516-773-5390
E-mail: admissions@usmma.edu

Academics
USMMA awards bachelor's and master's **degrees**. **Challenging opportunities** include
an honors program and a senior project. Internships is a special program. A complete
listing of majors at USMMA appears in the Majors by College index beginning on page
471.

The **faculty** at USMMA has 87 full-time members. The student-faculty ratio is 11:1.

Students of USMMA
The student body is made up of 925 undergraduates. 12.9% are women and 87.1% are
men. Students come from 50 states and territories and 5 other countries. 10% are from
New York. 2.3% are international students. 2.1% are African American, 0.6% American
Indian, 4% Asian American, and 3% Hispanic American. 92% returned for their
sophomore year.

Facilities and Resources
1,200 **computers/terminals** are available on campus for general student use. Students
can access the following: campus intranet, computer help desk, free student e-mail accounts, engineering and economics software. Campuswide network is available. The
library has 187,191 books and 961 subscriptions.

Campus Life
There are 45 active organizations on campus, including a drama/theater group,
newspaper, choral group, and marching band. No national or local **fraternities** or
sororities.

USMMA is a member of the NCAA (Division III). **Intercollegiate sports** include
baseball (m), basketball, crew, cross-country running, football (m), golf, lacrosse (m), sailing, soccer (m), softball (w), swimming and diving, tennis, track and field, volleyball (w),
wrestling (m).

Campus Safety
Student safety services include 24-hour patrols by trained security personnel.

Applying
USMMA requires an essay, SAT or ACT, a high school transcript, and 3 recommendations. It recommends an interview. Application deadline: 3/1.

The United States Merchant Marine
Academy is a four-year federal
service academy dedicated to educating and training young men and
women as officers in America's
merchant marine and U.S. Navy
Reserve and as future leaders of the
maritime and transportation
industries. The Academy, in Kings
Point, Long Island, offers accredited
programs in marine transportation
and engineering leading to a B.S.
degree, a U.S. merchant marine officer's license, and a Navy Reserve
commission. Students spend three
trimesters at sea aboard U.S.
merchant ships as part of their training.

Getting Accepted
1,754 applied
16% were accepted
279 enrolled (100% of accepted)
21% from top tenth of their h.s. class
3.6 average high school GPA
Mean SAT critical reading score: 584
Mean SAT math score: 623
Mean ACT score: 28
37% had SAT critical reading scores over 600
68% had SAT math scores over 600
99% had ACT scores over 24
7% had SAT critical reading scores over 700
12% had SAT math scores over 700
10% had ACT scores over 30
17 National Merit Scholars
21 class presidents
11 valedictorians

Graduation and After
2% pursued further study (1% business, 1%
engineering)
95% had job offers within 6 months
70 organizations recruited on campus

UNITED STATES MILITARY ACADEMY
SMALL-TOWN SETTING ■ PUBLIC ■ FEDERALLY SUPPORTED ■ COED, PRIMARILY MEN
WEST POINT, NEW YORK

Web site: www.usma.edu
Contact: Col. Michael Jones, Director of Admissions, Building 606, West Point, NY 10996
Telephone: 845-938-4041
E-mail: 8dad@sunams.usma.army.mil

> West Point is all about leadership. For more than 200 years, West Point has developed many of the nation's finest leaders. The Academy builds leaders of character while developing the foundation for career success. West Point offers a premier undergraduate education, develops strong leadership skills, and provides unique and unforgettable life experiences. West Point's graduates are prepared for a career of professional excellence and service to the nation as an officer in the United States Army. West Point is tough but well worth the challenge. One cadet may have said it best: "The person I have become is so much better than the person who first came here."

Getting Accepted
10,958 applied
14% were accepted
1,194 enrolled (77% of accepted)
50% from top tenth of their h.s. class
Mean SAT critical reading score: 630
Mean SAT math score: 648
Mean ACT score: 29
66% had SAT critical reading scores over 600
77% had SAT math scores over 600
97% had ACT scores over 24
20% had SAT critical reading scores over 700
25% had SAT math scores over 700
34% had ACT scores over 30
226 National Merit Scholars
225 class presidents
85 valedictorians

Graduation and After
2% pursued further study (2% medicine)
100% had job offers within 6 months

Academics
West Point awards bachelor's **degrees. Challenging opportunities** include advanced placement credit and double majors. Special programs include summer session for credit and off-campus study.

The most frequently chosen **baccalaureate** fields are engineering, area and ethnic studies, and computer and information sciences. A complete listing of majors at West Point appears in the Majors by College index beginning on page 471.

The **faculty** at West Point has 604 full-time members, 63% with terminal degrees. The student-faculty ratio is 7:1.

Students of West Point
The student body is made up of 4,231 undergraduates. 14.9% are women and 85.1% are men. Students come from 53 states and territories and 25 other countries. 8% are from New York. 1.3% are international students. 6.1% are African American, 0.9% American Indian, 6.8% Asian American, and 6.6% Hispanic American. 92% returned for their sophomore year.

Facilities and Resources
5,500 **computers/terminals** are available on campus for general student use. Students can access the following: online (class) registration. Campuswide network is available. The 2 **libraries** have 457,340 books and 2,220 subscriptions.

Campus Life
There are 120 active organizations on campus, including a drama/theater group, radio station, and choral group. No national or local **fraternities** or **sororities**.

West Point is a member of the NCAA (Division I). **Intercollegiate sports** include baseball (m), basketball, cross-country running, football (m), golf (m), gymnastics (m), ice hockey (m), lacrosse (m), soccer, softball (w), swimming and diving, tennis, track and field, volleyball (w), wrestling (m).

Campus Safety
Student safety services include late-night transport/escort service, 24-hour emergency telephone alarm devices, 24-hour patrols by trained security personnel, and student patrols.

Applying
West Point requires an essay, SAT or ACT, a high school transcript, 4 recommendations, and medical examination, authorized nomination. It recommends an interview. Application deadline: 2/28.

UNITED STATES NAVAL ACADEMY

SMALL-TOWN SETTING ■ PUBLIC ■ FEDERALLY SUPPORTED ■ COED, PRIMARILY MEN
ANNAPOLIS, MARYLAND

Web site: www.usna.edu
Contact: Dean of Admissions, 117 Decatur Road, United States Naval
    Academy, Annapolis, MD 21402
Telephone: 410-293-4361
Fax: 410-293-4348
E-mail: webmail@usna.edu

Academics

Naval Academy awards bachelor's **degrees**. **Challenging opportunities** include
advanced placement credit, an honors program, double majors, and independent study.
Summer session for credit is a special program.

The most frequently chosen **baccalaureate** fields are engineering, social sciences,
and physical sciences. A complete listing of majors at Naval Academy appears in the
Majors by College index beginning on page 471.

The **faculty** at Naval Academy has 525 full-time members, 64% with terminal
degrees. The student-faculty ratio is 8:1.

Students of Naval Academy

The student body is made up of 4,443 undergraduates. 20.6% are women and 79.4% are
men. Students come from 54 states and territories and 24 other countries. 4% are from
Maryland. 1.1% are international students. 4.4% are African American, 0.8% American
Indian, 2.8% Asian American, and 10% Hispanic American. 96% returned for their
sophomore year.

Facilities and Resources

6,100 **computers/terminals** are available on campus for general student use. Students
can access the following: campus intranet, computer help desk, free student e-mail accounts, online (class) grades, online (class) registration, online (class) schedules.
Campuswide network is available. 100% of college-owned or -operated housing units are
wired for high-speed Internet access. The **library** has 675,000 books and 2,515 subscriptions.

Campus Life

There are 75 active organizations on campus, including a drama/theater group, radio
station, choral group, and marching band. No national or local **fraternities** or **sororities**.

Naval Academy is a member of the NCAA (Division I). **Intercollegiate sports**
include baseball (m), basketball, cheerleading, crew, cross-country running, football (m),
golf (m), gymnastics (m), lacrosse, riflery, sailing, soccer, squash (m), swimming and diving, tennis (m), track and field, volleyball (w), water polo (m), wrestling (m).

Campus Safety

Student safety services include campus gate security, 24-hour emergency telephone
alarm devices, 24-hour patrols by trained security personnel, and student patrols.

Applying

Naval Academy requires an essay, SAT or ACT, a high school transcript, an interview, 2
recommendations, and authorized nomination. Application deadline: 1/31.

Getting Accepted
12,003 applied
10% were accepted
1,161 enrolled (97% of accepted)
56% from top tenth of their h.s. class
Mean SAT critical reading score: 634
Mean SAT math score: 657
61% had SAT critical reading scores over 600
77% had SAT math scores over 600
14% had SAT critical reading scores over 700
24% had SAT math scores over 700

Graduation and After
82% graduated in 4 years
2% pursued further study (1% medicine)
100% had job offers within 6 months
2 organizations recruited on campus

The University at Buffalo (UB) is New York's premier public research university. With the most comprehensive array of degree programs in the State University of New York system, UB has distinguished itself by cultivating a vibrant academic environment where undergraduates work side by side with faculty members who are on the cutting edge of their fields. UB's diverse community of scholars is actively engaged in the pursuit and creation of knowledge, and UB's academic initiatives focused on collaborative and experiential learning encourage students to explore the possibilities offered by UB's extensive resources. From architecture to biophysics to media study, UB students are well-positioned at the forefront of innovation and research.

Getting Accepted
19,831 applied
52% were accepted
3,272 enrolled (32% of accepted)
24% from top tenth of their h.s. class
3.2 average high school GPA
Mean SAT critical reading score: 555
Mean SAT math score: 593
Mean ACT score: 25
30% had SAT critical reading scores over 600
50% had SAT math scores over 600
67% had ACT scores over 24
5% had SAT critical reading scores over 700
9% had SAT math scores over 700
11% had ACT scores over 30
25 valedictorians

Graduation and After
39% graduated in 4 years
18% graduated in 5 years
6% graduated in 6 years
36% pursued further study (35% arts and sciences)
71% had job offers within 6 months
200 organizations recruited on campus

Financial Matters
$6217 resident tuition and fees (2007–08)
$12,477 nonresident tuition and fees (2007–08)
$8620 room and board
69% average percent of need met
$6079 average financial aid amount received per undergraduate (2006–07 estimated)

UNIVERSITY AT BUFFALO, THE STATE UNIVERSITY OF NEW YORK
SUBURBAN SETTING ■ PUBLIC ■ STATE-SUPPORTED ■ COED
BUFFALO, NEW YORK

Web site: www.buffalo.edu
Contact: Ms. Patricia Armstrong, Director of Admissions, 12 Capen Hall, North Campus, Buffalo, NY 14260-1660
Telephone: 716-645-6900 or toll-free 888-UB-ADMIT
Fax: 716-645-6411
E-mail: ub-admissions@buffalo.edu

Academics
UB awards bachelor's, master's, doctoral, and first-professional **degrees** and post-master's and first-professional certificates. **Challenging opportunities** include advanced placement credit, accelerated degree programs, student-designed majors, freshman honors college, an honors program, double majors, independent study, and a senior project. Special programs include cooperative education, internships, summer session for credit, off-campus study, study-abroad, and Army ROTC.

The most frequently chosen **baccalaureate** fields are business/marketing, engineering, and psychology. A complete listing of majors at UB appears in the Majors by College index beginning on page 471.

The **faculty** at UB has 1,193 full-time members, 97% with terminal degrees. The student-faculty ratio is 16:1.

Students of UB
The student body totals 28,054, of whom 18,779 are undergraduates. 46.1% are women and 53.9% are men. Students come from 45 states and territories and 84 other countries. 96% are from New York. 9.8% are international students. 6.7% are African American, 0.4% American Indian, 9.1% Asian American, and 3.5% Hispanic American. 87% returned for their sophomore year.

Facilities and Resources
2,435 **computers/terminals** are available on campus for general student use. Students can access the following: campus intranet, computer help desk, free student e-mail accounts, online (class) grades, online (class) registration, online (class) schedules. Campuswide network is available. 100% of college-owned or -operated housing units are wired for high-speed Internet access. The 8 **libraries** have 3,360,036 books and 34,126 subscriptions.

Campus Life
Active organizations on campus include a drama/theater group, newspaper, radio station, television station, choral group, and marching band. UB has national **fraternities**, national **sororities**, local fraternities, and local sororities.

UB is a member of the NCAA (Division I). **Intercollegiate sports** (some offering scholarships) include baseball (m), basketball, crew (w), cross-country running, football (m), soccer, softball (w), swimming and diving, tennis, track and field, volleyball (w), wrestling (m).

Campus Safety
Student safety services include self-defense and awareness programs, late-night transport/escort service, 24-hour emergency telephone alarm devices, 24-hour patrols by trained security personnel, student patrols, and electronically operated dormitory entrances.

Applying
UB requires SAT or ACT and a high school transcript, and in some cases recommendations and portfolio, audition. It recommends an essay. Application deadline: 3/1 priority date for financial aid. Early admission is possible.

The University of Alabama in Huntsville

Suburban setting ■ Public ■ State-supported ■ Coed
Huntsville, Alabama

Web site: www.uah.edu
Contact: Ms. Sandra Patterson, Director of Admissions, Enrollment Services, 301 Sparkman Drive, Huntsville, AL 35899
Telephone: 256-824-6070 or toll-free 800-UAH-CALL
Fax: 256-824-6073
E-mail: admitme@email.uah.edu

Academics

UAH awards bachelor's, master's, and doctoral **degrees** and post-bachelor's and post-master's certificates. **Challenging opportunities** include advanced placement credit, an honors program, double majors, independent study, and a senior project. Special programs include cooperative education, internships, summer session for credit, off-campus study, study-abroad, and Army ROTC.

The most frequently chosen **baccalaureate** fields are business/marketing, engineering, and health professions and related sciences. A complete listing of majors at UAH appears in the Majors by College index beginning on page 471.

The **faculty** at UAH has 289 full-time members, 91% with terminal degrees. The student-faculty ratio is 16:1.

Students of UAH

The student body totals 7,264, of whom 5,751 are undergraduates. 48.4% are women and 51.6% are men. Students come from 44 states and territories and 61 other countries. 86% are from Alabama. 3.3% are international students. 14.9% are African American, 1.6% American Indian, 3% Asian American, and 2.3% Hispanic American. 77% returned for their sophomore year.

Facilities and Resources

1,153 **computers/terminals** are available on campus for general student use. Students can access the following: campus intranet, computer help desk, free student e-mail accounts, online (class) grades, online (class) registration, online (class) schedules. Campuswide network is available. 100% of college-owned or -operated housing units are wired for high-speed Internet access. Wireless service is available via classrooms, computer centers, computer labs, learning centers, libraries, student centers. The **library** has 334,684 books and 926 subscriptions.

Campus Life

There are 59 active organizations on campus, including a drama/theater group, newspaper, and choral group. 4% of eligible men and 5% of eligible women are members of national **fraternities** and national **sororities**.

UAH is a member of the NCAA (Division II). **Intercollegiate sports** (some offering scholarships) include baseball (m), basketball, cheerleading, cross-country running, ice hockey (m), soccer, softball (w), tennis, track and field, volleyball (w).

Campus Safety

Student safety services include late-night transport/escort service, 24-hour emergency telephone alarm devices, 24-hour patrols by trained security personnel, and electronically operated dormitory entrances.

Applying

UAH requires SAT or ACT and a high school transcript. Application deadline: 8/15; 7/31 for financial aid, with a 4/1 priority date. Deferred admission is possible.

Getting Accepted

1,850 applied
88% were accepted
800 enrolled (49% of accepted)
28% from top tenth of their h.s. class
3.31 average high school GPA
Mean SAT critical reading score: 549
Mean SAT math score: 553
Mean ACT score: 24
27% had SAT critical reading scores over 600
30% had SAT math scores over 600
58% had ACT scores over 24
6% had SAT critical reading scores over 700
3% had SAT math scores over 700
9% had ACT scores over 30
2 National Merit Scholars
1 valedictorian

Graduation and After

14% graduated in 4 years
19% graduated in 5 years
11% graduated in 6 years
302 organizations recruited on campus

Financial Matters

$5216 resident tuition and fees (2007–08)
$11,024 nonresident tuition and fees (2007–08)
$6290 room and board
65% average percent of need met
$6191 average financial aid amount received per undergraduate (2006–07 estimated)

THE UNIVERSITY OF ARIZONA

URBAN SETTING ■ PUBLIC ■ STATE-SUPPORTED ■ COED
TUCSON, ARIZONA

Web site: www.arizona.edu
Contact: Ms. Kasey Urquidez, Director of Recruitment, Admissions, PO Box 210040, Tucson, AZ 85721-0040
Telephone: 520-621-3237
Fax: 520-621-9799
E-mail: appinfo@arizona.edu

Getting Accepted

21,103 applied
80% were accepted
6,569 enrolled (39% of accepted)
10% from top tenth of their h.s. class
3.44 average high school GPA
Mean SAT critical reading score: 540
Mean SAT math score: 555
Mean ACT score: 24
28% had SAT critical reading scores over 600
30% had SAT math scores over 600
50% had ACT scores over 24
5% had SAT critical reading scores over 700
7% had SAT math scores over 700
8% had ACT scores over 30
68 National Merit Scholars

Graduation and After

31% graduated in 4 years
22% graduated in 5 years
6% graduated in 6 years
92% had job offers within 6 months
251 organizations recruited on campus

Financial Matters

$5048 resident tuition and fees (2007–08)
$16,282 nonresident tuition and fees (2007–08)
$7370 room and board
64% average percent of need met
$8078 average financial aid amount received per undergraduate (2005–06)

Academics

Arizona awards bachelor's, master's, doctoral, and first-professional **degrees** and post-bachelor's certificates. **Challenging opportunities** include advanced placement credit, freshman honors college, an honors program, double majors, independent study, and a senior project. Special programs include internships, summer session for credit, study-abroad, and Army, Navy, and Air Force ROTC.

The most frequently chosen **baccalaureate** fields are business/marketing, social sciences, and education. A complete listing of majors at Arizona appears in the Majors by College index beginning on page 471.

The **faculty** at Arizona has 1,408 full-time members, 98% with terminal degrees. The student-faculty ratio is 18:1.

Students of Arizona

The student body totals 37,217, of whom 29,070 are undergraduates. 52.7% are women and 47.3% are men. Students come from 55 states and territories and 124 other countries. 66% are from Arizona. 2.8% are international students. 3.3% are African American, 2.4% American Indian, 6.1% Asian American, and 16.2% Hispanic American. 80% returned for their sophomore year.

Facilities and Resources

2,500 **computers/terminals** are available on campus for general student use. Students can access the following: campus intranet, computer help desk, free student e-mail accounts, online (class) grades, online (class) registration, online (class) schedules. Campuswide network is available. Wireless service is available via computer centers, computer labs, libraries, student centers. The 6 **libraries** have 4,359,195 books and 23,790 subscriptions.

Campus Life

There are 280 active organizations on campus, including a drama/theater group, newspaper, radio station, television station, choral group, and marching band. 15% of eligible men and 15% of eligible women are members of national **fraternities**, national **sororities**, local fraternities, and local sororities.

Arizona is a member of the NCAA (Division I). **Intercollegiate sports** (some offering scholarships) include baseball (m), basketball, cross-country running, football (m), golf, gymnastics (w), soccer (w), softball (w), swimming and diving, tennis, track and field, volleyball (w).

Campus Safety

Student safety services include emergency telephones, late-night transport/escort service, 24-hour patrols by trained security personnel, and student patrols.

Applying

Arizona requires a high school transcript, and in some cases an interview, recommendations, and a minimum high school GPA of 3.0. It recommends SAT or ACT. Application deadline: 4/1. Early admission is possible.

University of Arkansas

SUBURBAN SETTING ■ PUBLIC ■ STATE-SUPPORTED ■ COED
FAYETTEVILLE, ARKANSAS

Web site: www.uark.edu
Contact: Dawn Medley, Director, 232 Silas H. Hunt Hall, Office of
Admissions, Fayetteville, AR 72701-1201
Telephone: 479-575-5346 or toll-free 800-377-5346 (in-state), 800-377-8632
(out-of-state)
Fax: 479-575-7515
E-mail: uofa@uark.edu

Academics

Arkansas awards bachelor's, master's, doctoral, and first-professional **degrees** and post-bachelor's and post-master's certificates. **Challenging opportunities** include advanced placement credit, accelerated degree programs, freshman honors college, an honors program, double majors, independent study, and a senior project. Special programs include cooperative education, internships, summer session for credit, study-abroad, and Army and Air Force ROTC.

The most frequently chosen **baccalaureate** fields are business/marketing, engineering, and education. A complete listing of majors at Arkansas appears in the Majors by College index beginning on page 471.

The **faculty** at Arkansas has 852 full-time members, 88% with terminal degrees. The student-faculty ratio is 17:1.

Students of Arkansas

The student body totals 18,648, of whom 14,948 are undergraduates. 49.2% are women and 50.8% are men. Students come from 47 states and territories and 102 other countries. 76% are from Arkansas. 2.3% are international students. 4.8% are African American, 2% American Indian, 2.8% Asian American, and 3% Hispanic American. 83% returned for their sophomore year.

Facilities and Resources

2,270 **computers/terminals** are available on campus for general student use. Students can access the following: online (class) registration. Campuswide network is available. 100% of college-owned or -operated housing units are wired for high-speed Internet access. Wireless service is available via entire campus. The 6 **libraries** have 1,761,444 books and 18,173 subscriptions.

Campus Life

There are 298 active organizations on campus, including a drama/theater group, newspaper, radio station, television station, choral group, and marching band. 12% of eligible men and 15% of eligible women are members of national **fraternities** and national **sororities**.

Arkansas is a member of the NCAA (Division I). **Intercollegiate sports** (some offering scholarships) include baseball (m), basketball, cross-country running, football (m), golf, gymnastics (w), soccer (w), softball (w), swimming and diving (w), tennis, track and field, volleyball (w).

Campus Safety

Student safety services include RAD (Rape Aggression Defense program), late-night transport/escort service, 24-hour emergency telephone alarm devices, 24-hour patrols by trained security personnel, student patrols, and electronically operated dormitory entrances.

Applying

Arkansas requires SAT or ACT and a high school transcript. It recommends a minimum high school GPA of 3.0. Application deadline: 8/15; 3/15 priority date for financial aid. Early admission is possible.

Getting Accepted
10,132 applied
62% were accepted
2,899 enrolled (46% of accepted)
32% from top tenth of their h.s. class
3.59 average high school GPA
Mean SAT critical reading score: 572
Mean SAT math score: 581
Mean SAT writing score: 571
Mean ACT score: 26
38% had SAT critical reading scores over 600
44% had SAT math scores over 600
10% had SAT critical reading scores over 700
10% had SAT math scores over 700
45 National Merit Scholars

Graduation and After
33% graduated in 4 years
19% graduated in 5 years
6% graduated in 6 years
300 organizations recruited on campus

Financial Matters
$6038 resident tuition and fees (2007–08)
$14,492 nonresident tuition and fees (2007–08)
$7017 room and board
73% average percent of need met
$8068 average financial aid amount received per undergraduate (2006–07 estimated)

University of California, Berkeley

Urban setting ■ Public ■ State-supported ■ Coed
Berkeley, California

Getting Accepted
43,983 applied
23% were accepted
4,225 enrolled (41% of accepted)
98% from top tenth of their h.s. class
3.9 average high school GPA
73% had SAT critical reading scores over 600
82% had SAT math scores over 600
74% had SAT writing scores over 600
32% had SAT critical reading scores over 700
46% had SAT math scores over 700
32% had SAT writing scores over 700

Graduation and After
61% graduated in 4 years
24% graduated in 5 years
300 organizations recruited on campus

Financial Matters
$7164 resident tuition and fees (2007–08)
$26,232 nonresident tuition and fees (2007–08)
$13,848 room and board
89% average percent of need met
$15,710 average financial aid amount received per undergraduate (2006–07 estimated)

Web site: www.berkeley.edu
Contact: Berkeley, CA 94720-1500
Telephone: 510-642-2316
Fax: 510-642-7333
E-mail: ouars@uclink.berkeley.edu

Academics

Berkeley awards bachelor's, master's, doctoral, and first-professional **degrees**. **Challenging opportunities** include advanced placement credit, accelerated degree programs, student-designed majors, an honors program, double majors, independent study, and a senior project. Special programs include internships, summer session for credit, off-campus study, study-abroad, and Army, Navy, and Air Force ROTC.

The most frequently chosen **baccalaureate** fields are social sciences, biological/life sciences, and engineering. A complete listing of majors at Berkeley appears in the Majors by College index beginning on page 471.

The student-faculty ratio is 15:1.

Students of Berkeley

The student body totals 34,953, of whom 24,636 are undergraduates. 53.8% are women and 46.2% are men. Students come from 50 states and territories and 80 other countries. 90% are from California. 3.2% are international students. 3.4% are African American, 0.5% American Indian, 41.7% Asian American, and 11.5% Hispanic American. 97% returned for their sophomore year.

Facilities and Resources

Students can access the following: online (class) registration. Campuswide network is available. The 31 **libraries** have 15,189,997 books and 192,030 subscriptions.

Campus Life

There are 400 active organizations on campus, including a drama/theater group, newspaper, radio station, television station, choral group, and marching band. 11% of eligible men and 10% of eligible women are members of national **fraternities**, national **sororities**, local fraternities, and local sororities.

Berkeley is a member of the NCAA (Division I). **Intercollegiate sports** (some offering scholarships) include baseball (m), basketball, crew, cross-country running, field hockey (w), football (m), golf, gymnastics, lacrosse (w), rugby (m), soccer, softball (w), swimming and diving, tennis, track and field (m), volleyball (w), water polo.

Campus Safety

Student safety services include Office of Emergency Preparedness, late-night transport/escort service, 24-hour emergency telephone alarm devices, 24-hour patrols by trained security personnel, and electronically operated dormitory entrances.

Applying

Berkeley requires an essay, SAT Subject Tests, SAT or ACT, and a high school transcript. Application deadline: 11/30; 3/2 for financial aid, with a 3/2 priority date.

UNIVERSITY OF CALIFORNIA, DAVIS
SUBURBAN SETTING ■ PUBLIC ■ STATE-SUPPORTED ■ COED
DAVIS, CALIFORNIA

Web site: www.ucdavis.edu
Contact: Pamela Burnett, Director of Undergraduate Admissions,
Undergraduate Admission and Outreach Services, 178 Mrak Hall, Davis,
CA 95616
Telephone: 530-752-1011
Fax: 530-752-1280
E-mail: freshmanadmissions@ucdavis.edu

Academics

UC Davis awards bachelor's, master's, doctoral, and first-professional **degrees** and post-bachelor's and post-master's certificates. **Challenging opportunities** include advanced placement credit, student-designed majors, freshman honors college, an honors program, double majors, independent study, and a senior project. Special programs include internships, summer session for credit, study-abroad, and Army, Navy, and Air Force ROTC.

The most frequently chosen **baccalaureate** fields are social sciences, biological/life sciences, and psychology. A complete listing of majors at UC Davis appears in the Majors by College index beginning on page 471.

The **faculty** at UC Davis has 1,595 full-time members, 96% with terminal degrees. The student-faculty ratio is 19:1.

Students of UC Davis

The student body totals 29,796, of whom 23,499 are undergraduates. 56.2% are women and 43.8% are men. Students come from 48 states and territories and 101 other countries. 98% are from California. 1.9% are international students. 3% are African American, 0.7% American Indian, 40.8% Asian American, and 11.9% Hispanic American. 90% returned for their sophomore year.

Facilities and Resources

600 **computers/terminals** are available on campus for general student use. Students can access the following: campus intranet, computer help desk, free student e-mail accounts, online (class) grades, online (class) registration, online (class) schedules, software packages. Campuswide network is available. The 6 **libraries** have 4,447,563 books and 44,020 subscriptions.

Campus Life

There are 320 active organizations on campus, including a drama/theater group, newspaper, radio station, television station, choral group, and marching band. 9% of eligible men and 8% of eligible women are members of national **fraternities**, national **sororities**, and state fraternities and sororities.

UC Davis is a member of the NCAA (Division II). **Intercollegiate sports** include baseball (m), basketball, cross-country running, football (m), golf, gymnastics (w), lacrosse, soccer, softball (w), swimming and diving, tennis, track and field, volleyball, water polo, wrestling (m).

Campus Safety

Student safety services include rape prevention programs, late-night transport/escort service, 24-hour emergency telephone alarm devices, 24-hour patrols by trained security personnel, student patrols, and electronically operated dormitory entrances.

Applying

UC Davis requires an essay, SAT Subject Tests, SAT or ACT, a high school transcript, high school subject requirements, and a minimum high school GPA of 2.8. Application deadline: 11/30; 3/2 priority date for financial aid.

Getting Accepted
35,148 applied
59% were accepted
4,971 enrolled (24% of accepted)
3.7 average high school GPA
Mean SAT critical reading score: 560
Mean SAT math score: 600
Mean ACT score: 24
38% had SAT critical reading scores over 600
54% had SAT math scores over 600
39% had SAT writing scores over 600
57% had ACT scores over 24
7% had SAT critical reading scores over 700
13% had SAT math scores over 700
7% had SAT writing scores over 700
10% had ACT scores over 30

Graduation and After
43% graduated in 4 years
31% graduated in 5 years
6% graduated in 6 years
38% pursued further study (15% arts and sciences, 9% education, 7% medicine)
91% had job offers within 6 months

Financial Matters
$27,744 nonresident tuition and fees (2008–09)
$11,533 room and board
75% average percent of need met
$11,697 average financial aid amount received per undergraduate (2005–06 estimated)

University of California, Irvine

Suburban setting ■ Public ■ State-supported ■ Coed
Irvine, California

Web site: www.uci.edu
Contact: 204 Administration, Irvine, CA 92697-1075
Telephone: 949-824-6703

Getting Accepted
39,956 applied
56% were accepted
4,931 enrolled (22% of accepted)
96% from top tenth of their h.s. class
3.79 average high school GPA
Mean SAT critical reading score: 569
Mean SAT math score: 613
Mean SAT writing score: 575
38% had SAT critical reading scores over 600
60% had SAT math scores over 600
41% had SAT writing scores over 600
8% had SAT critical reading scores over 700
17% had SAT math scores over 700
6% had SAT writing scores over 700

Graduation and After
51% graduated in 4 years
25% graduated in 5 years
3% graduated in 6 years

Financial Matters
$8276 resident tuition and fees (2007–08)
$27,896 nonresident tuition and fees (2007–08)
$10,547 room and board
84% average percent of need met
$13,221 average financial aid amount received per undergraduate (2006–07 estimated)

Academics

UC Irvine awards bachelor's, master's, doctoral, and first-professional **degrees** and post-bachelor's certificates. **Challenging opportunities** include accelerated degree programs, an honors program, double majors, independent study, and a senior project. Special programs include internships, summer session for credit, off-campus study, study-abroad, and Army and Air Force ROTC.

The most frequently chosen **baccalaureate** fields are social sciences, biological/life sciences, and psychology. A complete listing of majors at UC Irvine appears in the Majors by College index beginning on page 471.

The **faculty** at UC Irvine has 1,447 full-time members, 91% with terminal degrees. The student-faculty ratio is 19:1.

Students of UC Irvine

The student body totals 26,483, of whom 21,696 are undergraduates. 51.9% are women and 48.1% are men. 98% are from California. 2.6% are international students. 2.3% are African American, 0.4% American Indian, 51.4% Asian American, and 12.5% Hispanic American. 94% returned for their sophomore year.

Facilities and Resources

1,500 **computers/terminals** are available on campus for general student use. Students can access the following: campus intranet, computer help desk, free student e-mail accounts, online (class) grades, online (class) registration, online (class) schedules. Campuswide network is available. Wireless service is available via entire campus.

Campus Life

There are 401 active organizations on campus, including a drama/theater group, newspaper, radio station, and choral group. 9% of eligible men and 8% of eligible women are members of national **fraternities**, national **sororities**, local fraternities, and local sororities.

UC Irvine is a member of the NCAA (Division I). **Intercollegiate sports** (some offering scholarships) include baseball (m), basketball, crew, cross-country running, fencing, golf, lacrosse, racquetball, rugby (m), sailing, soccer, softball, swimming and diving, table tennis, tennis, track and field, volleyball, water polo, weight lifting.

Applying

UC Irvine requires an essay, SAT and SAT Subject Tests or ACT, a high school transcript, and a minimum high school GPA of 2.8. Application deadline: 11/30; 5/1 for financial aid, with a 3/2 priority date.

University of California, Los Angeles

Urban setting ■ Public ■ State-supported ■ Coed
Los Angeles, California

Web site: www.ucla.edu
Contact: Dr. Vu T. Tran, Director of Undergraduate Admissions, 405 Hilgard Avenue, Box 951436, Los Angeles, CA 90095-1436
Telephone: 310-825-3101
E-mail: ugadm@saonet.ucla.edu

Academics

UCLA awards bachelor's, master's, doctoral, and first-professional **degrees**. **Challenging opportunities** include advanced placement credit, student-designed majors, freshman honors college, an honors program, double majors, independent study, and a senior project. Special programs include internships, summer session for credit, off-campus study, study-abroad, and Army, Navy, and Air Force ROTC.

The most frequently chosen **baccalaureate** fields are social sciences, biological/life sciences, and psychology. A complete listing of majors at UCLA appears in the Majors by College index beginning on page 471.

The **faculty** at UCLA has 1,948 full-time members, 98% with terminal degrees. The student-faculty ratio is 16:1.

Students of UCLA

The student body totals 38,896, of whom 25,928 are undergraduates. 55.3% are women and 44.7% are men. Students come from 49 states and territories and 63 other countries. 96% are from California. 4.1% are international students. 3.3% are African American, 0.4% American Indian, 38.4% Asian American, and 14.7% Hispanic American. 97% returned for their sophomore year.

Facilities and Resources

4,134 **computers/terminals** are available on campus for general student use. Students can access the following: campus intranet, computer help desk, free student e-mail accounts, online (class) grades, online (class) registration, online (class) schedules. Campuswide network is available. 100% of college-owned or -operated housing units are wired for high-speed Internet access. Wireless service is available via entire campus. The 14 **libraries** have 8,157,182 books and 77,509 subscriptions.

Campus Life

Active organizations on campus include a drama/theater group, newspaper, radio station, television station, choral group, and marching band. 13% of eligible men and 13% of eligible women are members of national **fraternities**, national **sororities**, local fraternities, and local sororities.

UCLA is a member of the NCAA (Division I). **Intercollegiate sports** (some offering scholarships) include baseball (m), basketball, crew (w), cross-country running, football (m), golf, gymnastics (w), soccer, softball (w), swimming and diving (w), tennis, track and field, volleyball, water polo.

Campus Safety

Student safety services include late-night transport/escort service, 24-hour emergency telephone alarm devices, 24-hour patrols by trained security personnel, student patrols, and electronically operated dormitory entrances.

Applying

UCLA requires an essay, SAT Subject Tests, and SAT or ACT. Application deadline: 11/30.

Getting Accepted
50,755 applied
24% were accepted
4,564 enrolled (38% of accepted)
97% from top tenth of their h.s. class
4.0 average high school GPA
Mean SAT critical reading score: 621
Mean SAT math score: 659
Mean SAT writing score: 630
Mean ACT score: 27
66% had SAT critical reading scores over 600
76% had SAT math scores over 600
67% had SAT writing scores over 600
79% had ACT scores over 24
20% had SAT critical reading scores over 700
39% had SAT math scores over 700
23% had SAT writing scores over 700
35% had ACT scores over 30

Graduation and After
66% graduated in 4 years
22% graduated in 5 years
1% graduated in 6 years
425 organizations recruited on campus

Financial Matters
$7038 resident tuition and fees (2007–08)
$26,106 nonresident tuition and fees (2007–08)
$12,420 room and board
82% average percent of need met
$14,329 average financial aid amount received per undergraduate (2006–07 estimated)

University of California, Riverside

Urban setting ■ Public ■ State-supported ■ Coed
Riverside, California

Web site: www.ucr.edu
Contact: Emily Engelschall, Director, Undergraduate Recruitment, 1120 Hinderaker Hall, Riverside, CA 92521
Telephone: 951-827-4531
Fax: 951-827-6344
E-mail: discover@ucr.edu

Getting Accepted

20,126 applied
82% were accepted
3,729 enrolled (22% of accepted)
94% from top tenth of their h.s. class
3.4 average high school GPA
Mean SAT critical reading score: 504
Mean SAT math score: 542
Mean SAT writing score: 509
Mean ACT score: 21
15% had SAT critical reading scores over 600
29% had SAT math scores over 600
14% had SAT writing scores over 600
25% had ACT scores over 24
2% had SAT critical reading scores over 700
5% had SAT math scores over 700
1% had SAT writing scores over 700
3% had ACT scores over 30

Graduation and After

36% graduated in 4 years
23% graduated in 5 years
5% graduated in 6 years
26% pursued further study (9% education, 7% arts and sciences, 3% medicine)
52% had job offers within 6 months
459 organizations recruited on campus

Financial Matters

$7355 resident tuition and fees (2007–08)
$26,423 nonresident tuition and fees (2007–08)
$10,800 room and board
83% average percent of need met
$13,933 average financial aid amount received per undergraduate (2006–07 estimated)

Academics

UC Riverside awards bachelor's, master's, and doctoral **degrees** and post-bachelor's certificates. **Challenging opportunities** include advanced placement credit, accelerated degree programs, student-designed majors, an honors program, double majors, independent study, and a senior project. Special programs include cooperative education, internships, summer session for credit, off-campus study, study-abroad, and Army and Air Force ROTC.

The most frequently chosen **baccalaureate** fields are business/marketing, social sciences, and biological/life sciences. A complete listing of majors at UC Riverside appears in the Majors by College index beginning on page 471.

The **faculty** at UC Riverside has 756 full-time members, 98% with terminal degrees. The student-faculty ratio is 19:1.

Students of UC Riverside

The student body totals 17,187, of whom 14,973 are undergraduates. 52.2% are women and 47.8% are men. Students come from 32 states and territories and 31 other countries. 99% are from California. 1.8% are international students. 7.4% are African American, 0.4% American Indian, 41.6% Asian American, and 25.6% Hispanic American. 83% returned for their sophomore year.

Facilities and Resources

793 **computers/terminals** are available on campus for general student use. Students can access the following: campus intranet, computer help desk, free student e-mail accounts, online (class) grades, online (class) registration, online (class) schedules, online viewing of financial information. Campuswide network is available. Wireless service is available via entire campus. The 7 **libraries** have 2,435,296 books and 29,941 subscriptions.

Campus Life

There are 251 active organizations on campus, including a drama/theater group, newspaper, radio station, and choral group. 7% of eligible men and 7% of eligible women are members of national **fraternities**, national **sororities**, local fraternities, local sororities, and coed fraternities.

UC Riverside is a member of the NCAA (Division I). **Intercollegiate sports** (some offering scholarships) include baseball (m), basketball, cross-country running, golf, softball (w), tennis, track and field, volleyball (w).

Campus Safety

Student safety services include late-night transport/escort service, 24-hour emergency telephone alarm devices, 24-hour patrols by trained security personnel, student patrols, and electronically operated dormitory entrances.

Applying

UC Riverside requires an essay, SAT Subject Tests, SAT or ACT, a high school transcript, and a minimum high school GPA of 2.8. Application deadline: 11/30; 3/2 for financial aid, with a 3/2 priority date.

UNIVERSITY OF CALIFORNIA, SAN DIEGO

SUBURBAN SETTING ■ PUBLIC ■ STATE-SUPPORTED ■ COED
LA JOLLA, CALIFORNIA

Web site: www.ucsd.edu
Contact: Ms. Mae Brown, Assistant Vice Chancellor, Admissions and
Relations with Schools, 9500 Gilman Drive, 0021, La Jolla, CA
92093-0021
Telephone: 858-534-4831
E-mail: admissionsinfo@ucsd.edu

Academics

UCSD awards bachelor's, master's, doctoral, and first-professional **degrees**. **Challenging opportunities** include advanced placement credit, accelerated degree programs, student-designed majors, freshman honors college, an honors program, double majors,
independent study, and a senior project. Special programs include cooperative education,
internships, summer session for credit, off-campus study, study-abroad, and Army
ROTC.

The most frequently chosen **baccalaureate** fields are social sciences, biological/life
sciences, and engineering. A complete listing of majors at UCSD appears in the Majors
by College index beginning on page 471.

The **faculty** at UCSD has 1,085 full-time members, 87% with terminal degrees. The
student-faculty ratio is 19:1.

Students of UCSD

The student body totals 27,144, of whom 22,048 are undergraduates. 51.4% are women
and 48.6% are men. 97% are from California. 1% are African American, 44% Asian
American, and 12% Hispanic American. 93% returned for their sophomore year.

Facilities and Resources

1,500 **computers/terminals** are available on campus for general student use. Students
can access the following: computer help desk, free student e-mail accounts, online (class)
registration, online (class) schedules. Campuswide network is available. The 10 **libraries**
have 3,086,871 books and 28,104 subscriptions.

Campus Life

There are 450 active organizations on campus, including a drama/theater group,
newspaper, radio station, television station, and choral group. 10% of eligible men and
10% of eligible women are members of national **fraternities** and national **sororities**.

UCSD is a member of the NCAA (Division II). **Intercollegiate sports** include
baseball (m), basketball, crew, cross-country running, fencing, golf (m), soccer, softball
(w), swimming and diving, tennis, track and field, volleyball, water polo.

Campus Safety

Student safety services include crime prevention programs, late-night transport/escort
service, 24-hour emergency telephone alarm devices, 24-hour patrols by trained security
personnel, and student patrols.

Applying

UCSD requires an essay, ACT Assessment with Writing or SAT Reasoning Test, plus
two SAT Subject Tests, a high school transcript, and a minimum high school GPA of 2.8,
and in some cases a minimum high school GPA of 3.4. Application deadline: 11/30; 3/2
priority date for financial aid.

Getting Accepted

45,072 applied
40% were accepted
4,141 enrolled (23% of accepted)
99% from top tenth of their h.s. class
3.93 average high school GPA
Mean SAT critical reading score: 597
Mean SAT math score: 646
Mean SAT writing score: 608
55% had SAT critical reading scores over 600
76% had SAT math scores over 600
72% had ACT scores over 24
13% had SAT critical reading scores over 700
30% had SAT math scores over 700
19% had ACT scores over 30
49 National Merit Scholars

Graduation and After

40% pursued further study (7% medicine, 6%
education, 6% law)
85% had job offers within 6 months
435 organizations recruited on campus

Financial Matters

$7509 resident tuition and fees (2008–09)
$27,530 nonresident tuition and fees (2008–
09)
$10,237 room and board
83% average percent of need met
$13,745 average financial aid amount received
per undergraduate (2006–07)

UNIVERSITY OF CALIFORNIA, SANTA BARBARA

SUBURBAN SETTING ■ PUBLIC ■ STATE-SUPPORTED ■ COED

SANTA BARBARA, CALIFORNIA

Web site: www.ucsb.edu

Contact: Office of Admissions, 1210 Cheadle Hall, Santa Barbara, CA 93106-2014

Telephone: 805-893-2881

Fax: 805-893-2676

E-mail: admissions@sa.ucsb.edu

Getting Accepted

40,933 applied
54% were accepted
4,335 enrolled (19% of accepted)
96% from top tenth of their h.s. class
3.76 average high school GPA
Mean SAT critical reading score: 592
Mean SAT math score: 601
Mean SAT writing score: 584
Mean ACT score: 26
51% had SAT critical reading scores over 600
56% had SAT math scores over 600
48% had SAT writing scores over 600
74% had ACT scores over 24
11% had SAT critical reading scores over 700
13% had SAT math scores over 700
8% had SAT writing scores over 700
18% had ACT scores over 30

Graduation and After

61% graduated in 4 years
16% graduated in 5 years
3% graduated in 6 years
31% pursued further study (8% arts and sciences, 7% education, 4% law)
91% had job offers within 6 months

Financial Matters

$7896 resident tuition and fees (2007–08)
$27,516 nonresident tuition and fees (2007–08)
$11,604 room and board
82% average percent of need met
$13,437 average financial aid amount received per undergraduate (2005–06)

Academics

UCSB awards bachelor's, master's, and doctoral **degrees** and first-professional certificates. **Challenging opportunities** include advanced placement credit, accelerated degree programs, student-designed majors, an honors program, double majors, and independent study. Special programs include cooperative education, internships, summer session for credit, off-campus study, study-abroad, and Army ROTC.

The most frequently chosen **baccalaureate** fields are social sciences, business/marketing, and biological/life sciences. A complete listing of majors at UCSB appears in the Majors by College index beginning on page 471.

The **faculty** at UCSB has 917 full-time members, 100% with terminal degrees. The student-faculty ratio is 17:1.

Students of UCSB

The student body totals 21,410, of whom 18,415 are undergraduates. 55.2% are women and 44.8% are men. Students come from 51 states and territories and 72 other countries. 96% are from California. 1.2% are international students. 2.7% are African American, 0.7% American Indian, 16.4% Asian American, and 19.4% Hispanic American. 91% returned for their sophomore year.

Facilities and Resources

3,000 **computers/terminals** are available on campus for general student use. Campuswide network is available. The **library** has 3,301,449 books and 36,902 subscriptions.

Campus Life

There are 241 active organizations on campus, including a drama/theater group, newspaper, radio station, television station, and choral group. 4% of eligible men and 4% of eligible women are members of national **fraternities**, national **sororities**, local fraternities, and local sororities.

UCSB is a member of the NCAA (Division I). **Intercollegiate sports** (some offering scholarships) include baseball (m), basketball, cross-country running, golf (m), gymnastics, soccer, softball (w), swimming and diving, tennis, track and field, volleyball, water polo.

Campus Safety

Student safety services include late-night transport/escort service and 24-hour emergency telephone alarm devices.

Applying

UCSB requires an essay, SAT Subject Tests, SAT or ACT, and a high school transcript, and in some cases an interview. Application deadline: 11/30; 3/2 priority date for financial aid.

UNIVERSITY OF CALIFORNIA, SANTA CRUZ

SMALL-TOWN SETTING ■ PUBLIC ■ STATE-SUPPORTED ■ COED
SANTA CRUZ, CALIFORNIA

Web site: www.ucsc.edu
Contact: Admissions Office, Cook House, Santa Cruz, CA 95064
Telephone: 831-459-5779
Fax: 831-459-4452
E-mail: admissions@ucsc.edu

Academics

UCSC awards bachelor's, master's, and doctoral **degrees** and post-bachelor's certificates. **Challenging opportunities** include advanced placement credit, student-designed majors, freshman honors college, double majors, independent study, and a senior project. Special programs include cooperative education, internships, summer session for credit, off-campus study, study-abroad, and Army, Navy, and Air Force ROTC.

The most frequently chosen **baccalaureate** fields are social sciences, biological/life sciences, and visual and performing arts. A complete listing of majors at UCSC appears in the Majors by College index beginning on page 471.

The **faculty** at UCSC has 554 full-time members, 95% with terminal degrees. The student-faculty ratio is 19:1.

Students of UCSC

The student body totals 15,825, of whom 14,403 are undergraduates. 53.6% are women and 46.4% are men. Students come from 43 states and territories and 78 other countries. 98% are from California. 0.7% are international students. 2.6% are African American, 0.9% American Indian, 20.5% Asian American, and 16.4% Hispanic American. 89% returned for their sophomore year.

Facilities and Resources

320 **computers/terminals** are available on campus for general student use. Students can access the following: computer help desk, free student e-mail accounts, online (class) grades, online (class) registration, online (class) schedules. Campuswide network is available. 100% of college-owned or -operated housing units are wired for high-speed Internet access. Wireless service is available via entire campus. The 2 **libraries** have 1,475,344 books and 25,486 subscriptions.

Campus Life

There are 141 active organizations on campus, including a drama/theater group, newspaper, radio station, television station, and choral group. 1% of eligible men and 1% of eligible women are members of national **fraternities**, national **sororities**, local fraternities, and local sororities.

UCSC is a member of the NCAA (Division III). **Intercollegiate sports** include basketball, cross-country running (w), golf (w), soccer, swimming and diving, tennis, volleyball, water polo.

Campus Safety

Student safety services include evening main gate security, campus police force and fire station, late-night transport/escort service, 24-hour emergency telephone alarm devices, 24-hour patrols by trained security personnel, and electronically operated dormitory entrances.

Applying

UCSC requires an essay, SAT or ACT, SAT Subject Tests required in two different areas: history/social science, English literature, mathematics, laboratory science, or language other than English, and a high school transcript. Application deadline: 11/30; 6/1 for financial aid, with a 3/17 priority date.

Getting Accepted

24,453 applied
82% were accepted
3,704 enrolled (18% of accepted)
96% from top tenth of their h.s. class
3.50 average high school GPA
Mean SAT critical reading score: 567
Mean SAT math score: 574
Mean SAT writing score: 563
Mean ACT score: 24
36% had SAT critical reading scores over 600
39% had SAT math scores over 600
36% had SAT writing scores over 600
56% had ACT scores over 24
7% had SAT critical reading scores over 700
6% had SAT math scores over 700
4% had SAT writing scores over 700
10% had ACT scores over 30

Graduation and After

46% graduated in 4 years
19% graduated in 5 years
8500 organizations recruited on campus

Financial Matters

$9534 resident tuition and fees (2008–09)
$30,144 nonresident tuition and fees (2008–09)
$12,831 room and board
87% average percent of need met
$14,422 average financial aid amount received per undergraduate (2006–07 estimated)

University of Central Arkansas
Small-town setting ■ Public ■ State-supported ■ Coed
Conway, Arkansas

Getting Accepted
5,780 applied
49% were accepted
1,793 enrolled (64% of accepted)
3.3 average high school GPA
Mean ACT score: 23
45% had ACT scores over 24
11% had ACT scores over 30

Graduation and After
23% graduated in 4 years
22% graduated in 5 years
9% graduated in 6 years
60 organizations recruited on campus

Financial Matters
$6205 resident tuition and fees (2007–08)
$11,035 nonresident tuition and fees (2007–08)
$4600 room and board

Web site: www.uca.edu
Contact: Ms. Melissa Goff, Director of Institutional Research and Admissions, 201 Donaghey Avenue, Conway, AR 72035
Telephone: 501-450-5371 or toll-free 800-243-8245 (in-state)
Fax: 501-450-5228
E-mail: mgoff@uca.edu

Academics
UCA awards associate, bachelor's, master's, and doctoral **degrees** and post-bachelor's and post-master's certificates. **Challenging opportunities** include advanced placement credit, accelerated degree programs, freshman honors college, an honors program, double majors, independent study, and a senior project. Special programs include cooperative education, internships, summer session for credit, study-abroad, and Army ROTC.

The most frequently chosen **baccalaureate** fields are health professions and related sciences, business/marketing, and education. A complete listing of majors at UCA appears in the Majors by College index beginning on page 471.

The **faculty** at UCA has 510 full-time members, 69% with terminal degrees. The student-faculty ratio is 18:1.

Students of UCA
The student body totals 12,619, of whom 10,675 are undergraduates. 58.1% are women and 41.9% are men. Students come from 44 states and territories and 61 other countries. 94% are from Arkansas. 4% are international students. 14.8% are African American, 0.8% American Indian, 1.4% Asian American, and 1.7% Hispanic American. 71% returned for their sophomore year.

Facilities and Resources
643 **computers/terminals** are available on campus for general student use. Students can access the following: campus intranet, computer help desk, free student e-mail accounts, online (class) grades, online (class) registration, online (class) schedules. Campuswide network is available. 100% of college-owned or -operated housing units are wired for high-speed Internet access. Wireless service is available via entire campus. The **library** has 505,000 books and 2,000 subscriptions.

Campus Life
There are 158 active organizations on campus, including a drama/theater group, newspaper, radio station, television station, choral group, and marching band. 10% of eligible men and 10% of eligible women are members of national **fraternities** and national **sororities**.

UCA is a member of the NCAA (Division I). **Intercollegiate sports** (some offering scholarships) include baseball (m), basketball, cheerleading, cross-country running, football (m), golf, soccer, softball (w), tennis (w), track and field, volleyball (w).

Campus Safety
Student safety services include security personnel at entrances during evening hours, late-night transport/escort service, 24-hour emergency telephone alarm devices, 24-hour patrols by trained security personnel, student patrols, and electronically operated dormitory entrances.

Applying
UCA requires SAT or ACT and a high school transcript. Application deadline: rolling admissions; 2/15 priority date for financial aid. Early and deferred admission are possible.

University of Central Florida

Suburban setting ■ Public ■ State-supported ■ Coed
Orlando, Florida

Web site: www.ucf.edu
Contact: Dr. Gordon Chavis, Assistant Vice President, PO Box 160111, Orlando, FL 32816-0111
Telephone: 407-823-3000
Fax: 407-823-5625
E-mail: admission@mail.ucf.edu

The University of Central Florida (UCF) is a public, multicampus research university dedicated to serving its surrounding communities with their diverse and expanding populations, technological corridors, and international partners. The mission of the University is to offer high-quality undergraduate and graduate education, student development, and continuing education; to conduct research and creative activities; and to provide services that address national and international issues in key areas, contribute to the global community, establish UCF as a major presence, and enhance the intellectual, cultural, environmental, and economic development of the metropolitan region.

Academics

UCF awards associate, bachelor's, master's, and doctoral **degrees** and post-bachelor's certificates. **Challenging opportunities** include advanced placement credit, freshman honors college, an honors program, double majors, and a senior project. Special programs include cooperative education, internships, summer session for credit, off-campus study, study-abroad, and Army and Air Force ROTC.

The most frequently chosen **baccalaureate** fields are business/marketing, education, and health professions and related sciences. A complete listing of majors at UCF appears in the Majors by College index beginning on page 471.

The **faculty** at UCF has 1,193 full-time members, 79% with terminal degrees. The student-faculty ratio is 29:1.

Students of UCF

The student body totals 48,497, of whom 41,320 are undergraduates. 54.4% are women and 45.6% are men. Students come from 51 states and territories and 136 other countries. 95% are from Florida. 1.4% are international students. 8.6% are African American, 0.4% American Indian, 5.2% Asian American, and 13.5% Hispanic American. 84% returned for their sophomore year.

Facilities and Resources

3,276 **computers/terminals** and 200 ports are available on campus for general student use. Students can access the following: campus intranet, computer help desk, free student e-mail accounts, online (class) grades, online (class) registration, online (class) schedules. Campuswide network is available. 100% of college-owned or -operated housing units are wired for high-speed Internet access. Wireless service is available via entire campus. The **library** has 1,368,161 books and 16,368 subscriptions.

Campus Life

There are 329 active organizations on campus, including a drama/theater group, newspaper, radio station, choral group, and marching band. 11% of eligible men and 9% of eligible women are members of national **fraternities**, national **sororities**, local fraternities, and local sororities.

UCF is a member of the NCAA (Division I). **Intercollegiate sports** (some offering scholarships) include baseball (m), basketball, cheerleading, crew (w), cross-country running, football (m), golf, soccer, tennis, track and field (w), volleyball (w).

Campus Safety

Student safety services include late-night transport/escort service, 24-hour emergency telephone alarm devices, 24-hour patrols by trained security personnel, and electronically operated dormitory entrances.

Applying

UCF requires SAT or ACT, a high school transcript, and a minimum high school GPA of 2.0. It recommends an essay. Application deadline: 3/1; 6/30 for financial aid, with a 3/1 priority date. Early admission is possible.

Getting Accepted
26,312 applied
50% were accepted
6,613 enrolled (50% of accepted)
35% from top tenth of their h.s. class
3.63 average high school GPA
Mean SAT critical reading score: 576
Mean SAT math score: 593
Mean SAT writing score: 552
Mean ACT score: 25
37% had SAT critical reading scores over 600
48% had SAT math scores over 600
26% had SAT writing scores over 600
64% had ACT scores over 24
5% had SAT critical reading scores over 700
7% had SAT math scores over 700
3% had SAT writing scores over 700
5% had ACT scores over 30
43 National Merit Scholars
28 valedictorians

Graduation and After
31% graduated in 4 years
22% graduated in 5 years
6% graduated in 6 years
21% pursued further study
95% had job offers within 6 months
3972 organizations recruited on campus

Financial Matters
$3620 resident tuition and fees (2007–08)
$17,821 nonresident tuition and fees (2007–08)
$8164 room and board
54% average percent of need met
$6068 average financial aid amount received per undergraduate (2005–06)

UNIVERSITY OF CHICAGO

URBAN SETTING ■ PRIVATE ■ INDEPENDENT ■ COED
CHICAGO, ILLINOIS

Web site: www.uchicago.edu
Contact: Mr. Theodore O'Neill, Dean of Admissions, Rosenwald Hall, 1101 East 58th Street, Suite 105, Chicago, IL 60637-1513
Telephone: 773-702-8650
Fax: 773-702-4199
E-mail: questions@phoenix.uchicago.edu

Getting Accepted

10,362 applied
35% were accepted
1,300 enrolled (36% of accepted)
83% from top tenth of their h.s. class
Mean SAT critical reading score: 712
Mean SAT math score: 705
Mean ACT score: 30
92% had SAT critical reading scores over 600
92% had SAT math scores over 600
91% had SAT writing scores over 600
87% had ACT scores over 24
64% had SAT critical reading scores over 700
59% had SAT math scores over 700
57% had SAT writing scores over 700
74% had ACT scores over 30
130 National Merit Scholars

Graduation and After

84% graduated in 4 years
5% graduated in 5 years
1% graduated in 6 years

Financial Matters

$35,868 tuition and fees (2007–08)
$11,139 room and board

Academics

Chicago awards bachelor's, master's, doctoral, and first-professional **degrees. Challenging opportunities** include advanced placement credit, accelerated degree programs, student-designed majors, double majors, independent study, and a senior project. Special programs include internships, summer session for credit, off-campus study, study-abroad, and Army and Air Force ROTC.

The most frequently chosen **baccalaureate** fields are social sciences, biological/life sciences, and mathematics. A complete listing of majors at Chicago appears in the Majors by College index beginning on page 471.

The **faculty** at Chicago has 1,084 full-time members, 100% with terminal degrees. The student-faculty ratio is 6:1.

Students of Chicago

The student body totals 12,336, of whom 4,926 are undergraduates. 49.9% are women and 50.1% are men. 22% are from Illinois. 8.2% are international students. 5.2% are African American, 0.3% American Indian, 13.3% Asian American, and 7.6% Hispanic American. 98% returned for their sophomore year.

Facilities and Resources

1,000 **computers/terminals** are available on campus for general student use. Students can access the following: online (class) registration. Campuswide network is available. Wireless service is available via entire campus. The 7 **libraries** have 7,000,000 books and 47,000 subscriptions.

Campus Life

There are 500 active organizations on campus, including a drama/theater group, newspaper, radio station, and choral group. Chicago has national **fraternities** and national **sororities.**

Chicago is a member of the NCAA (Division III). **Intercollegiate sports** include baseball (m), basketball, cross-country running, football (m), soccer, softball (w), swimming and diving, tennis, track and field, volleyball (w), wrestling (m).

Campus Safety

Student safety services include late-night transport/escort service, 24-hour emergency telephone alarm devices, 24-hour patrols by trained security personnel, student patrols, and electronically operated dormitory entrances.

Applying

Chicago requires an essay, SAT or ACT, a high school transcript, and 3 recommendations. It recommends an interview. Application deadline: 1/2; 2/1 priority date for financial aid. Early and deferred admission are possible.

University of Colorado at Boulder

Suburban setting ■ Public ■ State-supported ■ Coed
Boulder, Colorado

Web site: www.colorado.edu
Contact: Admissions Office, Regent Administrative Center 125, 552 UCB, Boulder, CO 80309
Telephone: 303-492-6301
Fax: 303-492-7115
E-mail: apply@colorado.edu

Academics

CU-Boulder awards bachelor's, master's, doctoral, and first-professional **degrees**. **Challenging opportunities** include advanced placement credit, accelerated degree programs, student-designed majors, freshman honors college, an honors program, double majors, independent study, and a senior project. Special programs include cooperative education, internships, summer session for credit, off-campus study, study-abroad, and Army, Navy, and Air Force ROTC.

The most frequently chosen **baccalaureate** fields are business/marketing, social sciences, and biological/life sciences. A complete listing of majors at CU-Boulder appears in the Majors by College index beginning on page 471.

The **faculty** at CU-Boulder has 1,259 full-time members, 91% with terminal degrees. The student-faculty ratio is 16:1.

Students of CU-Boulder

The student body totals 31,470, of whom 26,155 are undergraduates. 47% are women and 53% are men. Students come from 52 states and territories and 101 other countries. 69% are from Colorado. 1.5% are international students. 1.6% are African American, 0.8% American Indian, 6.3% Asian American, and 6.4% Hispanic American. 83% returned for their sophomore year.

Facilities and Resources

1,581 **computers/terminals** are available on campus for general student use. Students can access the following: campus intranet, computer help desk, free student e-mail accounts, online (class) grades, online (class) registration, online (class) schedules, standard and academic software, student government voting. Campuswide network is available. 100% of college-owned or -operated housing units are wired for high-speed Internet access. The 6 **libraries** have 3,554,826 books and 26,152 subscriptions.

Campus Life

There are 200 active organizations on campus, including a drama/theater group, newspaper, radio station, television station, choral group, and marching band. 8% of eligible men and 10% of eligible women are members of national **fraternities**, national **sororities**, and local sororities.

CU-Boulder is a member of the NCAA (Division I). **Intercollegiate sports** (some offering scholarships) include basketball, cross-country running, football (m), golf, skiing (cross-country), skiing (downhill), soccer (w), tennis, track and field, volleyball (w).

Campus Safety

Student safety services include University police department, late-night transport/escort service, 24-hour emergency telephone alarm devices, 24-hour patrols by trained security personnel, student patrols, and electronically operated dormitory entrances.

Applying

CU-Boulder requires SAT or ACT, a high school transcript, and a minimum high school GPA of 2.0, and in some cases audition for music program. It recommends an essay, recommendations, and a minimum high school GPA of 3.0. Application deadline: 1/15; 4/1 priority date for financial aid. Deferred admission is possible.

Getting Accepted

19,857 applied
82% were accepted
5,594 enrolled (35% of accepted)
25% from top tenth of their h.s. class
3.56 average high school GPA
Mean SAT critical reading score: 577
Mean SAT math score: 592
Mean ACT score: 26
41% had SAT critical reading scores over 600
49% had SAT math scores over 600
72% had ACT scores over 24
7% had SAT critical reading scores over 700
9% had SAT math scores over 700
15% had ACT scores over 30
10 National Merit Scholars
200 valedictorians

Graduation and After

41% graduated in 4 years
22% graduated in 5 years
5% graduated in 6 years
38% pursued further study (9% business, 8% arts and sciences, 8% education)
877 organizations recruited on campus

Financial Matters

$6635 resident tuition and fees (2007–08)
$24,797 nonresident tuition and fees (2007–08)
$9088 room and board
92% average percent of need met
$10,362 average financial aid amount received per undergraduate (2006–07 estimated)

UNIVERSITY OF CONNECTICUT

RURAL SETTING ■ PUBLIC ■ STATE-SUPPORTED ■ COED
STORRS, CONNECTICUT

Web site: www.uconn.edu
Contact: Mr. Brian Usher, Associate Director of Admissions, 2131 Hillside Road, U-88, Storrs, CT 06269
Telephone: 860-486-3137
Fax: 860-486-1476
E-mail: beahusky@uconnvm.uconn.edu

Getting Accepted
19,778 applied
51% were accepted
3,241 enrolled (32% of accepted)
38% from top tenth of their h.s. class
Mean SAT critical reading score: 585
Mean SAT math score: 610
45% had SAT critical reading scores over 600
58% had SAT math scores over 600
45% had SAT writing scores over 600
71% had ACT scores over 24
7% had SAT critical reading scores over 700
13% had SAT math scores over 700
7% had SAT writing scores over 700
11% had ACT scores over 30
38 valedictorians

Graduation and After
50% graduated in 4 years
19% graduated in 5 years
3% graduated in 6 years
83% had job offers within 6 months
330 organizations recruited on campus

Financial Matters
$8842 resident tuition and fees (2007–08)
$22,786 nonresident tuition and fees (2007–08)
$8850 room and board
72% average percent of need met
$10,507 average financial aid amount received per undergraduate (2006–07 estimated)

Academics
UConn awards associate, bachelor's, master's, doctoral, and first-professional **degrees** and post-bachelor's and post-master's certificates. **Challenging opportunities** include advanced placement credit, accelerated degree programs, student-designed majors, an honors program, double majors, independent study, and a senior project. Special programs include cooperative education, internships, summer session for credit, off-campus study, study-abroad, and Army and Air Force ROTC.

The most frequently chosen **baccalaureate** fields are social sciences, business/marketing, and liberal arts/general studies. A complete listing of majors at UConn appears in the Majors by College index beginning on page 471.

The **faculty** at UConn has 987 full-time members, 92% with terminal degrees. The student-faculty ratio is 17:1.

Students of UConn
The student body totals 23,557, of whom 16,347 are undergraduates. 51.3% are women and 48.7% are men. Students come from 47 states and territories and 64 other countries. 77% are from Connecticut. 0.8% are international students. 5.3% are African American, 0.4% American Indian, 7.4% Asian American, and 4.5% Hispanic American. 93% returned for their sophomore year.

Facilities and Resources
1,318 **computers/terminals** are available on campus for general student use. Students can access the following: online (class) registration, e-mail. Campuswide network is available. The 4 **libraries** have 2,987,772 books and 17,378 subscriptions.

Campus Life
There are 238 active organizations on campus, including a drama/theater group, newspaper, radio station, television station, choral group, and marching band. 8% of eligible men and 7% of eligible women are members of national **fraternities**, national **sororities**, local fraternities, and local sororities.

UConn is a member of the NCAA (Division I). **Intercollegiate sports** (some offering scholarships) include baseball (m), basketball, crew (w), cross-country running, field hockey (w), football (m), golf (m), ice hockey, lacrosse (w), soccer, softball (w), swimming and diving, tennis, track and field, volleyball (w).

Campus Safety
Student safety services include late-night transport/escort service and 24-hour emergency telephone alarm devices.

Applying
UConn requires an essay, SAT or ACT, and a high school transcript. It recommends 1 recommendation. Application deadline: 2/1; 3/1 priority date for financial aid. Early and deferred admission are possible.

UNIVERSITY OF DALLAS

Suburban setting ■ Private ■ Independent Religious ■ Coed
Irving, Texas

Web site: www.udallas.edu
Contact: Sr. Mary Brian Bole, Assistant Dean of Enrollment Management,
    1845 East Northgate Drive, Irving, TX 75062-4799
Telephone: 972-721-5266 or toll-free 800-628-6999
Fax: 972-721-5017
E-mail: ugadmis@udallas.edu

Academics

Dallas awards bachelor's, master's, and doctoral **degrees** and post-bachelor's and post-master's certificates. **Challenging opportunities** include advanced placement credit, student-designed majors, double majors, independent study, and a senior project. Special programs include internships, summer session for credit, off-campus study, study-abroad, and Army and Air Force ROTC.

The most frequently chosen **baccalaureate** fields are business/marketing, English, and biological/life sciences. A complete listing of majors at Dallas appears in the Majors by College index beginning on page 471.

The **faculty** at Dallas has 125 full-time members, 88% with terminal degrees. The student-faculty ratio is 13:1.

Students of Dallas

The student body totals 2,972, of whom 1,233 are undergraduates. 54.3% are women and 45.7% are men. Students come from 44 states and territories and 11 other countries. 51% are from Texas. 1.3% are international students. 1.2% are African American, 0.4% American Indian, 5.5% Asian American, and 16.1% Hispanic American. 79% returned for their sophomore year.

Facilities and Resources

125 **computers/terminals** are available on campus for general student use. Students can access the following: campus intranet, computer help desk, free student e-mail accounts, online (class) grades, online (class) registration, online (class) schedules. Campuswide network is available. 100% of college-owned or -operated housing units are wired for high-speed Internet access. Wireless service is available via computer centers, computer labs, dorm rooms, learning centers, libraries, student centers. The **library** has 223,350 books and 691 subscriptions.

Campus Life

There are 42 active organizations on campus, including a drama/theater group, newspaper, radio station, and choral group. No national or local **fraternities** or **sororities**.

Dallas is a member of the NCAA (Division III). **Intercollegiate sports** include baseball (m), basketball, cross-country running, golf (m), lacrosse (w), soccer, softball (w), tennis (w), track and field, volleyball (w), wrestling (m).

Campus Safety

Student safety services include late-night transport/escort service, 24-hour emergency telephone alarm devices, 24-hour patrols by trained security personnel, and electronically operated dormitory entrances.

Applying

Dallas requires an essay, SAT or ACT, a high school transcript, and 2 recommendations, and in some cases an interview. It recommends an interview. Application deadline: 8/1; 3/1 priority date for financial aid. Early and deferred admission are possible.

Getting Accepted

1,161 applied
75% were accepted
363 enrolled (42% of accepted)
33% from top tenth of their h.s. class
3.6 average high school GPA
Mean SAT critical reading score: 614
Mean SAT math score: 585
Mean SAT writing score: 596
Mean ACT score: 26
59% had SAT critical reading scores over 600
44% had SAT math scores over 600
52% had SAT writing scores over 600
76% had ACT scores over 24
21% had SAT critical reading scores over 700
10% had SAT math scores over 700
14% had SAT writing scores over 700
21% had ACT scores over 30
6 National Merit Scholars
9 valedictorians

Graduation and After

55% graduated in 4 years
7% graduated in 5 years
1% graduated in 6 years
40% pursued further study (8% arts and sciences, 7% business, 7% medicine)
60% had job offers within 6 months
40 organizations recruited on campus

Financial Matters

$24,770 tuition and fees (2008–09)
$7885 room and board
82% average percent of need met
$17,668 average financial aid amount received per undergraduate (2005–06)

SPONSOR

The University of Dayton (UD) is a top-ten national Catholic university and the largest private university in Ohio. Personal attention, supportive faculty members, a vibrant community, excellent academic programs, and real-world learning opportunities are hallmarks of the UD experience enjoyed by alumni around the world, including four-time Super Bowl winner Chuck Noll, radio-show host and former ESPN anchor Dan Patrick, and the late humorist Erma Bombeck. At the University of Dayton, students engage the world, developing both a critical mind and a compassionate heart. UD students are encouraged to look critically at the world's problems and become part of the solution—from joining service projects in Cameroon and India to boosting literacy and building housing in their own backyard.

Getting Accepted
8,742 applied
82% were accepted
1,762 enrolled (25% of accepted)
23% from top tenth of their h.s. class
3.46 average high school GPA
Mean SAT critical reading score: 570
Mean SAT math score: 590
Mean ACT score: 26
38% had SAT critical reading scores over 600
46% had SAT math scores over 600
68% had ACT scores over 24
6% had SAT critical reading scores over 700
10% had SAT math scores over 700
15% had ACT scores over 30
11 National Merit Scholars
35 valedictorians

Graduation and After
53% graduated in 4 years
21% graduated in 5 years
2% graduated in 6 years
50% had job offers within 6 months
164 organizations recruited on campus

Financial Matters
$25,950 tuition and fees (2007–08)
$7720 room and board
97% average percent of need met
$11,850 average financial aid amount received per undergraduate (2005–06)

UNIVERSITY OF DAYTON

SUBURBAN SETTING ■ PRIVATE ■ INDEPENDENT RELIGIOUS ■ COED
DAYTON, OHIO

Web site: www.udayton.edu
Contact: Mr. Robert Durkle, Director of Admission, 300 College Park, Dayton, OH 45469-1300
Telephone: 937-229-4411 or toll-free 800-837-7433
Fax: 937-229-4729
E-mail: admission@udayton.edu

Academics
UD awards bachelor's, master's, doctoral, and first-professional **degrees** and post-master's certificates. **Challenging opportunities** include advanced placement credit, accelerated degree programs, student-designed majors, an honors program, double majors, independent study, and a senior project. Special programs include cooperative education, internships, summer session for credit, off-campus study, study-abroad, and Army and Air Force ROTC.

The most frequently chosen **baccalaureate** fields are business/marketing, education, and communications/journalism. A complete listing of majors at UD appears in the Majors by College index beginning on page 471.

The **faculty** at UD has 457 full-time members, 91% with terminal degrees. The student-faculty ratio is 16:1.

Students of UD
The student body totals 10,395, of whom 7,434 are undergraduates. 49.6% are women and 50.4% are men. Students come from 51 states and territories and 50 other countries. 65% are from Ohio. 1.3% are international students. 3.4% are African American, 0.3% American Indian, 1.1% Asian American, and 1.9% Hispanic American. 87% returned for their sophomore year.

Facilities and Resources
250 **computers/terminals** and 100 ports are available on campus for general student use. Students can access the following: campus intranet, computer help desk, free student e-mail accounts, online (class) grades, online (class) registration, online (class) schedules, applications, admission/enrollment status, virtual orientation, online digital resources, online courses, assistive technology, learning management system, multimedia labs, payment, cyber cafes, centrally-licensed, downloadable software and training. Campuswide network is available. 100% of college-owned or -operated housing units are wired for high-speed Internet access. Wireless service is available via entire campus. The 3 **libraries** have 973,842 books and 10,481 subscriptions.

Campus Life
There are 200 active organizations on campus, including a drama/theater group, newspaper, radio station, television station, choral group, and marching band. 14% of eligible men and 16% of eligible women are members of national **fraternities**, national **sororities**, local fraternities, and local sororities.

UD is a member of the NCAA (Division I). **Intercollegiate sports** (some offering scholarships) include baseball (m), basketball, cheerleading, crew (w), cross-country running, football (m), golf, soccer, softball (w), tennis, track and field (w), volleyball (w).

Campus Safety
Student safety services include late-night transport/escort service, 24-hour emergency telephone alarm devices, 24-hour patrols by trained security personnel, student patrols, and electronically operated dormitory entrances.

Applying
UD requires an essay, SAT or ACT, a high school transcript, and 1 recommendation, and in some cases audition required for music, music therapy, music education programs. It recommends an interview. Application deadline: rolling admissions; 3/31 priority date for financial aid. Deferred admission is possible.

UNIVERSITY OF DELAWARE

SMALL-TOWN SETTING ■ PUBLIC ■ STATE-RELATED ■ COED
NEWARK, DELAWARE

Web site: www.udel.edu
Contact: Mr. Lou Hirsh, Director of Admissions, 116 Hullihen Hall, Newark, DE 19716
Telephone: 302-831-8123
Fax: 302-831-6905
E-mail: admissions@udel.edu

Academics

Delaware awards associate, bachelor's, master's, and doctoral **degrees**. **Challenging opportunities** include advanced placement credit, accelerated degree programs, student-designed majors, an honors program, double majors, independent study, and a senior project. Special programs include cooperative education, internships, summer session for credit, study-abroad, and Army and Air Force ROTC.

The most frequently chosen **baccalaureate** fields are business/marketing, social sciences, and education. A complete listing of majors at Delaware appears in the Majors by College index beginning on page 471.

The **faculty** at Delaware has 1,167 full-time members, 84% with terminal degrees. The student-faculty ratio is 12:1.

Students of Delaware

The student body totals 19,677, of whom 16,272 are undergraduates. 57.9% are women and 42.1% are men. Students come from 52 states and territories and 100 other countries. 38% are from Delaware. 1% are international students. 5.5% are African American, 0.4% American Indian, 4.2% Asian American, and 5% Hispanic American. 90% returned for their sophomore year.

Facilities and Resources

908 **computers/terminals** are available on campus for general student use. Students can access the following: online (class) registration, e-mail, personal Web page. Campuswide network is available. The 6 **libraries** have 2,704,986 books and 12,532 subscriptions.

Campus Life

There are 200 active organizations on campus, including a drama/theater group, newspaper, radio station, television station, choral group, and marching band. 10% of eligible men and 14% of eligible women are members of national **fraternities**, national **sororities**, local fraternities, and local sororities.

Delaware is a member of the NCAA (Division I). **Intercollegiate sports** (some offering scholarships) include baseball (m), basketball, cheerleading, crew (w), cross-country running, field hockey (w), football (m), golf (m), lacrosse, soccer, softball (w), swimming and diving, tennis, track and field, volleyball (w).

Campus Safety

Student safety services include late-night transport/escort service, 24-hour emergency telephone alarm devices, 24-hour patrols by trained security personnel, student patrols, and electronically operated dormitory entrances.

Applying

Delaware requires an essay, SAT or ACT, a high school transcript, and 1 recommendation. It recommends SAT Subject Tests. Application deadline: 1/15; 3/15 for financial aid, with a 2/1 priority date. Early and deferred admission are possible.

Getting Accepted

20,615 applied
56% were accepted
3,789 enrolled (33% of accepted)
41% from top tenth of their h.s. class
3.6 average high school GPA
44% had SAT critical reading scores over 600
56% had SAT math scores over 600
48% had SAT writing scores over 600
75% had ACT scores over 24
9% had SAT critical reading scores over 700
12% had SAT math scores over 700
8% had SAT writing scores over 700
12% had ACT scores over 30

Graduation and After

64% graduated in 4 years
12% graduated in 5 years
2% graduated in 6 years
12% pursued further study (3% arts and sciences, 3% education, 1% business)
77% had job offers within 6 months
442 organizations recruited on campus

Financial Matters

$8150 resident tuition and fees (2007–08)
$19,400 nonresident tuition and fees (2007–08)
$7948 room and board
79% average percent of need met
$9891 average financial aid amount received per undergraduate (2005–06)

University of Denver (DU) students are bright and energetic leaders committed to personal achievement and community engagement. Although they come from diverse backgrounds and from all fifty states and seventy-eight countries, they share an appreciation for an active and culturally enriched lifestyle. As first-year students, they benefit from a mentoring seminar that immerses them in a rigorous academic culture. As juniors and seniors, many embark on DU-funded research projects and study-abroad experiences that prepare them for life as global citizens. Throughout their years at DU, they work with professors who are committed to empowering greatness through cross-disciplinary learning and innovative curricula.

Getting Accepted
5,072 applied
74% were accepted
1,138 enrolled (30% of accepted)
35% from top tenth of their h.s. class
3.59 average high school GPA
Mean SAT critical reading score: 585
Mean SAT math score: 591
Mean ACT score: 26
44% had SAT critical reading scores over 600
48% had SAT math scores over 600
74% had ACT scores over 24
8% had SAT critical reading scores over 700
7% had SAT math scores over 700
16% had ACT scores over 30

Graduation and After
60% graduated in 4 years
12% graduated in 5 years
2% graduated in 6 years
24% pursued further study
81% had job offers within 6 months
197 organizations recruited on campus

Financial Matters
$32,232 tuition and fees (2007–08)
$9678 room and board
69% average percent of need met
$20,757 average financial aid amount received per undergraduate (2005–06)

UNIVERSITY OF DENVER
SUBURBAN SETTING ■ PRIVATE ■ INDEPENDENT ■ COED
DENVER, COLORADO

Web site: www.du.edu
Contact: Mr. Todd Rinehart, Assistant Vice Chancellor for Enrollment, University Park, Denver, CO 80208
Telephone: 303-871-2036 or toll-free 800-525-9495 (out-of-state)
Fax: 303-871-3301
E-mail: admission@du.edu

Academics
DU awards bachelor's, master's, doctoral, and first-professional **degrees** and post-bachelor's and post-master's certificates. **Challenging opportunities** include advanced placement credit, accelerated degree programs, student-designed majors, freshman honors college, an honors program, double majors, independent study, and a senior project. Special programs include cooperative education, internships, summer session for credit, study-abroad, and Army and Air Force ROTC.

The most frequently chosen **baccalaureate** fields are business/marketing, social sciences, and communications/journalism. A complete listing of majors at DU appears in the Majors by College index beginning on page 471.

The **faculty** at DU has 575 full-time members, 91% with terminal degrees. The student-faculty ratio is 10:1.

Students of DU
The student body totals 11,053, of whom 5,285 are undergraduates. 54.9% are women and 45.1% are men. Students come from 52 states and territories and 50 other countries. 56% are from Colorado. 4.8% are international students. 2.9% are African American, 1.3% American Indian, 5.4% Asian American, and 6.6% Hispanic American. 87% returned for their sophomore year.

Facilities and Resources
300 **computers/terminals** and 30,000 ports are available on campus for general student use. Students can access the following: campus intranet, computer help desk, free student e-mail accounts, online (class) grades, online (class) registration, online (class) schedules. Campuswide network is available. 95% of college-owned or -operated housing units are wired for high-speed Internet access. Wireless service is available via entire campus. The **library** has 1,212,392 books and 6,283 subscriptions.

Campus Life
There are 97 active organizations on campus, including a drama/theater group, newspaper, radio station, television station, and choral group. 20% of eligible men and 11% of eligible women are members of national **fraternities** and national **sororities**.

DU is a member of the NCAA (Division I). **Intercollegiate sports** (some offering scholarships) include basketball, cheerleading (m), golf, gymnastics (w), ice hockey (m), lacrosse, skiing (cross-country), skiing (downhill), soccer, swimming and diving, tennis, volleyball (w).

Campus Safety
Student safety services include 24-hour locked residence hall entrances, late-night transport/escort service, 24-hour emergency telephone alarm devices, 24-hour patrols by trained security personnel, and electronically operated dormitory entrances.

Applying
DU requires an essay, SAT or ACT, a high school transcript, and 2 recommendations, and in some cases a minimum high school GPA of 2.0. It recommends an interview. Application deadline: 1/15; 3/1 priority date for financial aid. Early and deferred admission are possible.

UNIVERSITY OF EVANSVILLE
URBAN SETTING ■ PRIVATE ■ INDEPENDENT RELIGIOUS ■ COED
EVANSVILLE, INDIANA

Web site: www.evansville.edu
Contact: Don Vos, Dean of Admission, 1800 Lincoln Avenue, Evansville, IN 47722
Telephone: 812-488-2468 or toll-free 800-423-8633 Ext. 2468
Fax: 812-488-4076
E-mail: admission@evansville.edu

Academics
Evansville awards associate, bachelor's, master's, and doctoral **degrees** and post-bachelor's certificates. **Challenging opportunities** include advanced placement credit, accelerated degree programs, student-designed majors, an honors program, double majors, independent study, and a senior project. Special programs include cooperative education, internships, summer session for credit, and study-abroad.

The most frequently chosen **baccalaureate** fields are visual and performing arts, education, and health professions and related sciences. A complete listing of majors at Evansville appears in the Majors by College index beginning on page 471.

The **faculty** at Evansville has 177 full-time members, 86% with terminal degrees. The student-faculty ratio is 13:1.

Students of Evansville
The student body totals 2,898, of whom 2,784 are undergraduates. 59.7% are women and 40.3% are men. Students come from 41 states and territories and 47 other countries. 60% are from Indiana. 6.2% are international students. 2.6% are African American, 0.2% American Indian, 0.8% Asian American, and 1.7% Hispanic American. 84% returned for their sophomore year.

Facilities and Resources
300 **computers/terminals** and 3,000 ports are available on campus for general student use. Students can access the following: campus intranet, computer help desk, free student e-mail accounts, online (class) grades, online (class) schedules. Campuswide network is available. 100% of college-owned or -operated housing units are wired for high-speed Internet access. Wireless service is available via entire campus. The 2 **libraries** have 289,593 books and 970 subscriptions.

Campus Life
There are 170 active organizations on campus, including a newspaper, radio station, and choral group. 27% of eligible men and 23% of eligible women are members of national **fraternities**, national **sororities**, and local sororities.

Evansville is a member of the NCAA (Division I). **Intercollegiate sports** (some offering scholarships) include baseball (m), basketball, cross-country running, golf, soccer, softball (w), swimming and diving, tennis (w), volleyball (w).

Campus Safety
Student safety services include late-night transport/escort service, 24-hour emergency telephone alarm devices, 24-hour patrols by trained security personnel, student patrols, and electronically operated dormitory entrances.

Applying
Evansville requires SAT or ACT, a high school transcript, and 1 recommendation, and in some cases an essay and an interview. It recommends an interview and a minimum high school GPA of 3.0. Application deadline: 2/1; 3/10 priority date for financial aid. Deferred admission is possible.

Getting Accepted
2,863 applied
89% were accepted
652 enrolled (26% of accepted)
36% from top tenth of their h.s. class
3.69 average high school GPA
Mean SAT critical reading score: 561
Mean SAT math score: 573
Mean SAT writing score: 551
Mean ACT score: 25
34% had SAT critical reading scores over 600
40% had SAT math scores over 600
29% had SAT writing scores over 600
63% had ACT scores over 24
7% had SAT critical reading scores over 700
6% had SAT math scores over 700
3% had SAT writing scores over 700
12% had ACT scores over 30
4 National Merit Scholars
46 valedictorians

Graduation and After
45% graduated in 4 years
15% graduated in 5 years
2% graduated in 6 years
21% pursued further study
95% had job offers within 6 months
175 organizations recruited on campus

Financial Matters
$24,340 tuition and fees (2007–08)
$7650 room and board
92% average percent of need met
$21,129 average financial aid amount received per undergraduate (2006–07 estimated)

UNIVERSITY OF FLORIDA

SUBURBAN SETTING ■ PUBLIC ■ STATE-SUPPORTED ■ COED
GAINESVILLE, FLORIDA

Web site: www.ufl.edu
Contact: Office of Admissions, PO Box 114000, Gainesville, FL 32611-4000
Telephone: 352-392-1365
E-mail: zevans@ufl.edu

Getting Accepted
24,126 applied
42% were accepted
6,441 enrolled (63% of accepted)
3.8 average high school GPA
63% had SAT critical reading scores over 600
69% had SAT math scores over 600
72% had ACT scores over 24
16% had SAT critical reading scores over 700
21% had SAT math scores over 700
20% had ACT scores over 30
154 National Merit Scholars

Graduation and After
1050 organizations recruited on campus

Financial Matters
$3257 resident tuition and fees (2007–08)
$17,841 nonresident tuition and fees (2007–08)
$7020 room and board
81% average percent of need met
$10,653 average financial aid amount received per undergraduate (2005–06)

Academics
UF awards bachelor's, master's, doctoral, and first-professional **degrees**. **Challenging opportunities** include advanced placement credit, accelerated degree programs, student-designed majors, an honors program, double majors, independent study, and a senior project. Special programs include cooperative education, internships, summer session for credit, off-campus study, study-abroad, and Army and Air Force ROTC.

The most frequently chosen **baccalaureate** fields are business/marketing, social sciences, and engineering. A complete listing of majors at UF appears in the Majors by College index beginning on page 471.

The **faculty** at UF has 2,008 full-time members, 86% with terminal degrees. The student-faculty ratio is 22:1.

Students of UF
The student body totals 51,725, of whom 35,189 are undergraduates. 53.6% are women and 46.4% are men. Students come from 52 states and territories and 139 other countries. 56% are from Florida. 1.2% are international students. 10.1% are African American, 0.3% American Indian, 7.6% Asian American, and 13.5% Hispanic American. 95% returned for their sophomore year.

Facilities and Resources
2,200 **computers/terminals** and 1,000 ports are available on campus for general student use. Students can access the following: campus intranet, computer help desk, free student e-mail accounts, online (class) grades, online (class) registration, online (class) schedules. Campuswide network is available. 100% of college-owned or -operated housing units are wired for high-speed Internet access. Wireless service is available via computer centers, computer labs, learning centers, libraries, student centers. The 9 **libraries** have 5,347,896 books and 25,342 subscriptions.

Campus Life
There are 752 active organizations on campus, including a drama/theater group, newspaper, radio station, television station, choral group, and marching band. 7% of eligible men and 8% of eligible women are members of national **fraternities**, national **sororities**, local fraternities, and local sororities.

UF is a member of the NCAA (Division I). **Intercollegiate sports** (some offering scholarships) include baseball (m), basketball, cross-country running, football (m), golf, gymnastics (w), soccer (w), softball (w), swimming and diving, tennis, track and field, volleyball (w).

Campus Safety
Student safety services include crime and rape prevention programs, late-night transport/escort service, 24-hour emergency telephone alarm devices, 24-hour patrols by trained security personnel, student patrols, and electronically operated dormitory entrances.

Applying
UF requires an essay, SAT or ACT, and a high school transcript. Application deadline: 11/1; 3/15 priority date for financial aid.

UNIVERSITY OF GEORGIA

SUBURBAN SETTING ■ PUBLIC ■ STATE-SUPPORTED ■ COED
ATHENS, GEORGIA

Web site: www.uga.edu
Contact: Mr. Patrick Winter, Associate Director of Admissions, Terrel Hall, Athens, GA 30602
Telephone: 706-542-8776
Fax: 706-542-1466
E-mail: undergrad@admissions.uga.edu

Academics

Georgia awards bachelor's, master's, doctoral, and first-professional **degrees** and post-bachelor's, post-master's, and first-professional certificates. **Challenging opportunities** include advanced placement credit, accelerated degree programs, student-designed majors, an honors program, double majors, independent study, and a senior project. Special programs include cooperative education, internships, summer session for credit, off-campus study, study-abroad, and Army and Air Force ROTC.

The most frequently chosen **baccalaureate** fields are business/marketing, social sciences, and education. A complete listing of majors at Georgia appears in the Majors by College index beginning on page 471.

The **faculty** at Georgia has 1,733 full-time members, 94% with terminal degrees. The student-faculty ratio is 18:1.

Students of Georgia

The student body totals 33,831, of whom 25,335 are undergraduates. 57.6% are women and 42.4% are men. Students come from 54 states and territories and 130 other countries. 84% are from Georgia. 0.7% are international students. 6.2% are African American, 0.3% American Indian, 6.4% Asian American, and 2.2% Hispanic American. 93% returned for their sophomore year.

Facilities and Resources

3,100 **computers/terminals** are available on campus for general student use. Students can access the following: campus intranet, computer help desk, free student e-mail accounts, online (class) grades, online (class) registration, online (class) schedules. Campuswide network is available. 100% of college-owned or -operated housing units are wired for high-speed Internet access. Wireless service is available via classrooms, computer centers, computer labs, dorm rooms, learning centers, libraries, student centers. The 3 **libraries** have 4,028,611 books and 67,268 subscriptions.

Campus Life

There are 430 active organizations on campus, including a drama/theater group, newspaper, radio station, television station, choral group, and marching band. 20% of eligible men and 25% of eligible women are members of national **fraternities**, national **sororities**, local fraternities, and local sororities.

Georgia is a member of the NCAA (Division I). **Intercollegiate sports** (some offering scholarships) include baseball (m), basketball, cheerleading, cross-country running, equestrian sports (w), football (m), golf, gymnastics (w), soccer (w), softball (w), swimming and diving, tennis, track and field, volleyball (w).

Campus Safety

Student safety services include late-night transport/escort service, 24-hour emergency telephone alarm devices, 24-hour patrols by trained security personnel, and electronically operated dormitory entrances.

Applying

Georgia requires SAT or ACT, a high school transcript, and counselor evaluation. It recommends an essay, SAT Subject Tests, and a minimum high school GPA of 2.0. Application deadline: 1/15; 3/1 priority date for financial aid. Early and deferred admission are possible.

Getting Accepted

16,871 applied
55% were accepted
4,675 enrolled (51% of accepted)
51% from top tenth of their h.s. class
3.79 average high school GPA
Mean SAT critical reading score: 611
Mean SAT math score: 617
Mean SAT writing score: 600
Mean ACT score: 27
60% had SAT critical reading scores over 600
62% had SAT math scores over 600
57% had SAT writing scores over 600
87% had ACT scores over 24
15% had SAT critical reading scores over 700
14% had SAT math scores over 700
11% had SAT writing scores over 700
22% had ACT scores over 30

Graduation and After

48% graduated in 4 years
26% graduated in 5 years
4% graduated in 6 years
24% pursued further study
62% had job offers within 6 months
1055 organizations recruited on campus

Financial Matters

$5622 resident tuition and fees (2007–08)
$20,726 nonresident tuition and fees (2007–08)
$7292 room and board
72% average percent of need met
$7767 average financial aid amount received per undergraduate (2006–07 estimated)

UNIVERSITY OF ILLINOIS AT CHICAGO
URBAN SETTING ■ PUBLIC ■ STATE-SUPPORTED ■ COED
CHICAGO, ILLINOIS

Getting Accepted
13,595 applied
64% were accepted
3,291 enrolled (38% of accepted)
23% from top tenth of their h.s. class
Mean ACT score: 24
50% had ACT scores over 24
7% had ACT scores over 30

Graduation and After
22% graduated in 4 years
21% graduated in 5 years
7% graduated in 6 years
23% pursued further study (10% arts and sciences, 5% business, 3% law)
273 organizations recruited on campus

Financial Matters
$10,546 resident tuition and fees (2007–08)
$22,936 nonresident tuition and fees (2007–08)
$7818 room and board
92% average percent of need met
$11,482 average financial aid amount received per undergraduate (2006–07 estimated)

Web site: www.uic.edu
Contact: Mr. Thomas E. Glenn, Executive Director of Admissions, Box 5220, Chicago, IL 60680-5220
Telephone: 312-996-4350
Fax: 312-413-7628
E-mail: uic.admit@uic.edu

Academics
UIC awards bachelor's, master's, doctoral, and first-professional **degrees** and first-professional certificates. **Challenging opportunities** include advanced placement credit, accelerated degree programs, student-designed majors, an honors program, double majors, independent study, and a senior project. Special programs include cooperative education, internships, summer session for credit, off-campus study, study-abroad, and Army, Navy, and Air Force ROTC.

The most frequently chosen **baccalaureate** fields are business/marketing, biological/life sciences, and psychology. A complete listing of majors at UIC appears in the Majors by College index beginning on page 471.

The **faculty** at UIC has 1,163 full-time members, 78% with terminal degrees. The student-faculty ratio is 15:1.

Students of UIC
The student body totals 25,747, of whom 15,672 are undergraduates. 53% are women and 47% are men. Students come from 42 states and territories and 43 other countries. 98% are from Illinois. 1.6% are international students. 8.7% are African American, 0.2% American Indian, 23.2% Asian American, and 16.4% Hispanic American. 79% returned for their sophomore year.

Facilities and Resources
800 **computers/terminals** and 36 ports are available on campus for general student use. Students can access the following: campus intranet, computer help desk, free student e-mail accounts, online (class) grades, online (class) registration, online (class) schedules. Campuswide network is available. 100% of college-owned or -operated housing units are wired for high-speed Internet access. Wireless service is available via entire campus. The 4 **libraries** have 3,047,592 books and 38,392 subscriptions.

Campus Life
There are 233 active organizations on campus, including a drama/theater group, newspaper, radio station, television station, and choral group. 1% of eligible men and 1% of eligible women are members of national **fraternities**, national **sororities**, local fraternities, and local sororities.

UIC is a member of the NCAA (Division I). **Intercollegiate sports** (some offering scholarships) include baseball (m), basketball, cross-country running, gymnastics, soccer (m), softball (w), swimming and diving, tennis, track and field, volleyball (w).

Campus Safety
Student safety services include housing ID stickers, guest escort policy, 24-hour closed circuit videos for exits and entrances, security screen for first floor, late-night transport/escort service, 24-hour emergency telephone alarm devices, 24-hour patrols by trained security personnel, student patrols, and electronically operated dormitory entrances.

Applying
UIC requires SAT or ACT and a high school transcript, and in some cases an interview. It recommends an essay. Application deadline: 1/15; 3/1 priority date for financial aid.

UNIVERSITY OF ILLINOIS AT URBANA–CHAMPAIGN

URBAN SETTING ■ PUBLIC ■ STATE-SUPPORTED ■ COED
CHAMPAIGN, ILLINOIS

Web site: www.uiuc.edu
Contact: Mrs. Stacey Kostell, Director of Admissions, 901 West Illinois, Urbana, IL 61801
Telephone: 217-333-0302
Fax: 217-244-4614
E-mail: ugradadmissions@uiuc.edu

Academics

UIUC awards bachelor's, master's, doctoral, and first-professional **degrees** and post-master's certificates. **Challenging opportunities** include advanced placement credit, accelerated degree programs, student-designed majors, an honors program, double majors, independent study, and a senior project. Special programs include cooperative education, internships, summer session for credit, off-campus study, study-abroad, and Army, Navy, and Air Force ROTC.

The most frequently chosen **baccalaureate** fields are business/marketing, engineering, and social sciences. A complete listing of majors at UIUC appears in the Majors by College index beginning on page 471.

The **faculty** at UIUC has 1,974 full-time members, 92% with terminal degrees. The student-faculty ratio is 17:1.

Students of UIUC

The student body totals 42,326, of whom 30,895 are undergraduates. 47% are women and 53% are men. Students come from 52 states and territories and 69 other countries. 93% are from Illinois. 5.6% are international students. 6.7% are African American, 0.3% American Indian, 12.8% Asian American, and 6.9% Hispanic American. 93% returned for their sophomore year.

Facilities and Resources

3,400 **computers/terminals** and 70,000 ports are available on campus for general student use. Students can access the following: computer help desk, free student e-mail accounts, online (class) grades, online (class) registration, online (class) schedules. Campuswide network is available. 100% of college-owned or -operated housing units are wired for high-speed Internet access. Wireless service is available via classrooms, computer centers, computer labs, dorm rooms, learning centers, libraries, student centers. The 37 **libraries** have 10,371,460 books and 63,413 subscriptions.

Campus Life

There are 981 active organizations on campus, including a drama/theater group, newspaper, radio station, television station, choral group, and marching band. 22% of eligible men and 23% of eligible women are members of national **fraternities**, national **sororities**, local fraternities, and local sororities.

UIUC is a member of the NCAA (Division I). **Intercollegiate sports** (some offering scholarships) include baseball (m), basketball, cheerleading, cross-country running, football (m), golf, gymnastics, soccer (w), softball (w), swimming and diving (w), tennis, track and field, volleyball (w), wrestling (m).

Campus Safety

Student safety services include safety training classes, ID cards with safety numbers, late-night transport/escort service, 24-hour emergency telephone alarm devices, 24-hour patrols by trained security personnel, student patrols, and electronically operated dormitory entrances.

Applying

UIUC requires an essay, SAT or ACT, ACT Writing Component, and a high school transcript, and in some cases an interview, recommendations, and audition, statement of professional interest. Application deadline: 1/2; 3/15 priority date for financial aid. Deferred admission is possible.

Getting Accepted

21,645 applied
71% were accepted
6,940 enrolled (45% of accepted)
55% from top tenth of their h.s. class
Mean SAT critical reading score: 607
Mean SAT math score: 680
Mean ACT score: 27
58% had SAT critical reading scores over 600
85% had SAT math scores over 600
89% had ACT scores over 24
16% had SAT critical reading scores over 700
47% had SAT math scores over 700
36% had ACT scores over 30
57 National Merit Scholars

Graduation and After

63% graduated in 4 years
17% graduated in 5 years
2% graduated in 6 years
26% pursued further study (4% arts and sciences, 3% law, 3% medicine)
50% had job offers within 6 months
6258 organizations recruited on campus

Financial Matters

$11,130 resident tuition and fees (2007–08)
$25,216 nonresident tuition and fees (2007–08)
$8196 room and board
87% average percent of need met
$10,180 average financial aid amount received per undergraduate (2005–06)

The University of Iowa

SMALL-TOWN SETTING ■ PUBLIC ■ STATE-SUPPORTED ■ COED
IOWA CITY, IOWA

Web site: www.uiowa.edu
Contact: Mr. Michael Barron, Assistant Provost for Enrollment Services and Director of Admissions, 107 Calvin Hall, Iowa City, IA 52242
Telephone: 319-335-3847 or toll-free 800-553-4692
Fax: 319-335-1535
E-mail: admissions@uiowa.edu

Getting Accepted
14,678 applied
83% were accepted
4,287 enrolled (35% of accepted)
23% from top tenth of their h.s. class
3.56 average high school GPA
45% had SAT critical reading scores over 600
57% had SAT math scores over 600
66% had ACT scores over 24
14% had SAT critical reading scores over 700
15% had SAT math scores over 700
12% had ACT scores over 30
20 National Merit Scholars
140 valedictorians

Graduation and After
40% graduated in 4 years
22% graduated in 5 years
4% graduated in 6 years
320 organizations recruited on campus

Financial Matters
$6544 resident tuition and fees (2008–09)
$20,658 nonresident tuition and fees (2008–09)
$7673 room and board
97% average percent of need met
$7480 average financial aid amount received per undergraduate (2006–07 estimated)

Academics
Iowa awards bachelor's, master's, doctoral, and first-professional **degrees** and post-master's and first-professional certificates. **Challenging opportunities** include advanced placement credit, accelerated degree programs, student-designed majors, an honors program, double majors, independent study, and a senior project. Special programs include cooperative education, internships, summer session for credit, off-campus study, study-abroad, and Army and Air Force ROTC.

The most frequently chosen **baccalaureate** fields are business/marketing, communications/journalism, and social sciences. A complete listing of majors at Iowa appears in the Majors by College index beginning on page 471.

The **faculty** at Iowa has 1,559 full-time members, 97% with terminal degrees. The student-faculty ratio is 15:1.

Students of Iowa
The student body totals 29,117, of whom 20,907 are undergraduates. 52.7% are women and 47.3% are men. Students come from 54 states and territories and 60 other countries. 66% are from Iowa. 1.4% are international students. 2.2% are African American, 0.5% American Indian, 3.6% Asian American, and 2.7% Hispanic American. 83% returned for their sophomore year.

Facilities and Resources
1,200 **computers/terminals** are available on campus for general student use. Students can access the following: computer help desk, free student e-mail accounts, online (class) grades, online (class) registration, online (class) schedules, online degree process, financial aid summary, bills. Campuswide network is available. Wireless service is available via classrooms, computer labs, dorm rooms, learning centers, libraries, student centers. The 13 **libraries** have 4,027,546 books and 44,644 subscriptions.

Campus Life
There are 425 active organizations on campus, including a drama/theater group, newspaper, radio station, choral group, and marching band. 7% of eligible men and 12% of eligible women are members of national **fraternities** and national **sororities**.

Iowa is a member of the NCAA (Division I). **Intercollegiate sports** (some offering scholarships) include baseball (m), basketball, crew (w), cross-country running, field hockey (w), football (m), golf, gymnastics, soccer (w), softball (w), swimming and diving, tennis, track and field, volleyball (w), wrestling (m).

Campus Safety
Student safety services include late-night transport/escort service, 24-hour emergency telephone alarm devices, 24-hour patrols by trained security personnel, and electronically operated dormitory entrances.

Applying
Iowa requires SAT or ACT, a high school transcript, and must meet Regent Admission Index (RAI) requirement: residents 245 or above; nonresidents 255 or abaove. Application deadline: 4/1. Early and deferred admission are possible.

UNIVERSITY OF KANSAS

SUBURBAN SETTING ■ PUBLIC ■ STATE-SUPPORTED ■ COED
LAWRENCE, KANSAS

Web site: www.ku.edu
Contact: Ms. Lisa Pinamonti Kress, Director of Admissions and Scholarships, KU Visitor Center, 1502 Iowa Street, Lawrence, KS 66045-7576
Telephone: 785-864-3911 or toll-free 888-686-7323 (in-state)
Fax: 785-864-5006
E-mail: adm@ku.edu

Academics

KU awards bachelor's, master's, doctoral, and first-professional **degrees** and post-master's certificates (University of Kansas is a single institution with academic programs and facilities at two primary locations: Lawrence and Kansas City.). **Challenging opportunities** include advanced placement credit, accelerated degree programs, an honors program, double majors, independent study, and a senior project. Special programs include cooperative education, internships, summer session for credit, study-abroad, and Army, Navy, and Air Force ROTC.

The most frequently chosen **baccalaureate** fields are business/marketing, health professions and related sciences, and social sciences. A complete listing of majors at KU appears in the Majors by College index beginning on page 471.

The **faculty** at KU has 1,219 full-time members, 96% with terminal degrees. The student-faculty ratio is 19:1.

Students of KU

The student body totals 28,569, of whom 20,828 are undergraduates. 49.9% are women and 50.1% are men. Students come from 52 states and territories and 81 other countries. 77% are from Kansas. 3% are international students. 3.7% are African American, 1.1% American Indian, 4.3% Asian American, and 3.6% Hispanic American. 79% returned for their sophomore year.

Facilities and Resources

1,500 **computers/terminals** are available on campus for general student use. Students can access the following: campus intranet, computer help desk, free student e-mail accounts, online (class) grades, online (class) registration, online (class) schedules. Campuswide network is available. 100% of college-owned or -operated housing units are wired for high-speed Internet access. Wireless service is available via computer centers, computer labs, libraries, student centers. The 12 **libraries** have 4,853,631 books and 50,992 subscriptions.

Campus Life

There are 508 active organizations on campus, including a drama/theater group, newspaper, radio station, television station, choral group, and marching band. 13% of eligible men and 16% of eligible women are members of national **fraternities** and national **sororities**.

KU is a member of the NCAA (Division I). **Intercollegiate sports** (some offering scholarships) include baseball (m), basketball, crew (w), cross-country running, football (m), golf, soccer (w), softball (w), swimming and diving (w), tennis (w), track and field, volleyball (w).

Campus Safety

Student safety services include University police department, late-night transport/escort service, 24-hour emergency telephone alarm devices, 24-hour patrols by trained security personnel, and electronically operated dormitory entrances.

Applying

KU requires SAT or ACT, a high school transcript, Kansas Board of Regents admissions criteria with GPA of 2.0 resident, 2.5 nonresident; or upper third of high school class; or minimum ACT score 21 resident, 24 nonresident; or minimum SAT score 980 resident, 1090 nonresident, and a minimum high school GPA of 2.0, and in some cases a minimum high school GPA of 2.5. Application deadline: 4/1; 3/1 priority date for financial aid.

Getting Accepted
10,367 applied
92% were accepted
4,084 enrolled (43% of accepted)
28% from top tenth of their h.s. class
3.41 average high school GPA
Mean ACT score: 25
59% had ACT scores over 24
13% had ACT scores over 30
36 National Merit Scholars

Graduation and After
31% graduated in 4 years
23% graduated in 5 years
6% graduated in 6 years
28% pursued further study
45% had job offers within 6 months
500 organizations recruited on campus

Financial Matters
$7146 resident tuition and fees (2007–08)
$17,556 nonresident tuition and fees (2007–08)
$6144 room and board
70% average percent of need met
$7594 average financial aid amount received per undergraduate (2005–06)

UNIVERSITY OF KENTUCKY

URBAN SETTING ■ PUBLIC ■ STATE-SUPPORTED ■ COED
LEXINGTON, KENTUCKY

Web site: www.uky.edu
Contact: Ms. Michelle Nordin, Associate Director of Admissions, 100 W.D. Funkhouser Building, Lexington, KY 40506-0054
Telephone: 859-257-2000 or toll-free 800-432-0967 (in-state)
E-mail: admissio@uky.edu

Getting Accepted
10,024 applied
81% were accepted
4,190 enrolled (52% of accepted)
23% from top tenth of their h.s. class
3.48 average high school GPA
Mean SAT critical reading score: 550
Mean SAT math score: 565
Mean ACT score: 24
33% had SAT critical reading scores over 600
40% had SAT math scores over 600
62% had ACT scores over 24
6% had SAT critical reading scores over 700
9% had SAT math scores over 700
17% had ACT scores over 30
35 National Merit Scholars
157 valedictorians

Graduation and After
29% graduated in 4 years
25% graduated in 5 years
6% graduated in 6 years
574 organizations recruited on campus

Financial Matters
$7096 resident tuition and fees (2007–08)
$14,896 nonresident tuition and fees (2007–08)
$7973 room and board
81% average percent of need met
$7861 average financial aid amount received per undergraduate (2005–06 estimated)

Academics
UK awards bachelor's, master's, doctoral, and first-professional **degrees** and post-master's certificates. **Challenging opportunities** include advanced placement credit, accelerated degree programs, student-designed majors, an honors program, double majors, and independent study. Special programs include cooperative education, internships, summer session for credit, off-campus study, study-abroad, and Army and Air Force ROTC.

The most frequently chosen **baccalaureate** fields are business/marketing, communications/journalism, and social sciences. A complete listing of majors at UK appears in the Majors by College index beginning on page 471.

The **faculty** at UK has 1,211 full-time members, 89% with terminal degrees. The student-faculty ratio is 17:1.

Students of UK
The student body totals 26,382, of whom 19,292 are undergraduates. 51.2% are women and 48.8% are men. Students come from 52 states and territories and 91 other countries. 83% are from Kentucky. 0.8% are international students. 5.5% are African American, 0.1% American Indian, 2.1% Asian American, and 1.1% Hispanic American. 78% returned for their sophomore year.

Facilities and Resources
1,400 **computers/terminals** are available on campus for general student use. Students can access the following: online (class) registration, various software packages. Campuswide network is available. The 16 **libraries** have 3,092,616 books and 29,633 subscriptions.

Campus Life
There are 305 active organizations on campus, including a drama/theater group, newspaper, radio station, choral group, and marching band. 15% of eligible men and 19% of eligible women are members of national **fraternities** and national **sororities**.

UK is a member of the NCAA (Division I). **Intercollegiate sports** (some offering scholarships) include baseball (m), basketball, cross-country running, football (m), golf, gymnastics (w), riflery, soccer, softball (w), swimming and diving, tennis, track and field, volleyball (w).

Campus Safety
Student safety services include late-night transport/escort service, 24-hour emergency telephone alarm devices, 24-hour patrols by trained security personnel, and electronically operated dormitory entrances.

Applying
UK requires SAT or ACT, a high school transcript, and a minimum high school GPA of 2.0. Application deadline: 2/15; 2/15 priority date for financial aid. Early admission is possible.

UNIVERSITY OF MARYLAND, BALTIMORE COUNTY

SUBURBAN SETTING ■ PUBLIC ■ STATE-SUPPORTED ■ COED
BALTIMORE, MARYLAND

Web site: www.umbc.edu
Contact: Mr. Dale Bittinger, Director of Admissions, 1000 Hilltop Circle, Baltimore, MD 21250
Telephone: 410-455-2291 or toll-free 800-UMBC-4U2 (in-state), 800-862-2402 (out-of-state)
Fax: 410-455-1094
E-mail: admissions@umbc.edu

Academics

UMBC awards bachelor's, master's, and doctoral **degrees** and post-bachelor's certificates. **Challenging opportunities** include advanced placement credit, student-designed majors, freshman honors college, an honors program, double majors, independent study, and a senior project. Special programs include cooperative education, internships, summer session for credit, off-campus study, study-abroad, and Army ROTC.

The most frequently chosen **baccalaureate** fields are communication technologies, social sciences, and biological/life sciences. A complete listing of majors at UMBC appears in the Majors by College index beginning on page 471.

The **faculty** at UMBC has 473 full-time members, 88% with terminal degrees. The student-faculty ratio is 18:1.

Students of UMBC

The student body totals 12,041, of whom 9,464 are undergraduates. 45.9% are women and 54.1% are men. Students come from 42 states and territories and 81 other countries. 93% are from Maryland. 3.7% are international students. 16.1% are African American, 0.5% American Indian, 21.4% Asian American, and 3.9% Hispanic American. 85% returned for their sophomore year.

Facilities and Resources

875 **computers/terminals** are available on campus for general student use. Students can access the following: campus intranet, computer help desk, free student e-mail accounts, online (class) grades, online (class) registration, online (class) schedules, student account information. Campuswide network is available. 100% of college-owned or -operated housing units are wired for high-speed Internet access. Wireless service is available via classrooms, computer centers, computer labs, libraries, student centers. The 2 **libraries** have 1,300,994 books and 4,170 subscriptions.

Campus Life

There are 180 active organizations on campus, including a drama/theater group, newspaper, radio station, and choral group. 4% of eligible men and 4% of eligible women are members of national **fraternities** and national **sororities**.

UMBC is a member of the NCAA (Division I). **Intercollegiate sports** (some offering scholarships) include baseball (m), basketball, cross-country running, field hockey (w), lacrosse, soccer, softball (w), swimming and diving, tennis, track and field, volleyball (w).

Campus Safety

Student safety services include late-night transport/escort service, 24-hour emergency telephone alarm devices, and 24-hour patrols by trained security personnel.

Applying

UMBC requires an essay, SAT or ACT, and a high school transcript. It recommends 2 recommendations and a minimum high school GPA of 3.0. Application deadline: 2/1; 2/14 priority date for financial aid. Early and deferred admission are possible.

Getting Accepted
5,836 applied
69% were accepted
1,437 enrolled (36% of accepted)
28% from top tenth of their h.s. class
3.6 average high school GPA
Mean SAT critical reading score: 582
Mean SAT math score: 608
Mean SAT writing score: 576
Mean ACT score: 25
41% had SAT critical reading scores over 600
55% had SAT math scores over 600
38% had SAT writing scores over 600
61% had ACT scores over 24
11% had SAT critical reading scores over 700
13% had SAT math scores over 700
6% had SAT writing scores over 700
11% had ACT scores over 30

Graduation and After
28% graduated in 4 years
20% graduated in 5 years
8% graduated in 6 years
35% pursued further study (25% arts and sciences, 2% business, 2% law)
69% had job offers within 6 months
821 organizations recruited on campus

Financial Matters
$8708 resident tuition and fees (2007–08)
$17,440 nonresident tuition and fees (2007–08)
$8658 room and board
73% average percent of need met
$9876 average financial aid amount received per undergraduate (2005–06)

UNIVERSITY OF MARYLAND, COLLEGE PARK

SUBURBAN SETTING ■ PUBLIC ■ STATE-SUPPORTED ■ COED
COLLEGE PARK, MARYLAND

Web site: www.maryland.edu
Contact: Ms. Barbara Gill, Director of Undergraduate Admissions, Mitchell Building, College Park, MD 20742-5235
Telephone: 301-314-8385 or toll-free 800-422-5867
Fax: 301-314-9693
E-mail: um-admit@uga.umd.edu

Getting Accepted
24,172 applied
47% were accepted
4,236 enrolled (37% of accepted)
56% from top tenth of their h.s. class
3.9 average high school GPA
65% had SAT critical reading scores over 600
76% had SAT math scores over 600
17% had SAT critical reading scores over 700
27% had SAT math scores over 700
142 National Merit Scholars

Graduation and After
58% graduated in 4 years
19% graduated in 5 years
3% graduated in 6 years
42% pursued further study
75% had job offers within 6 months
650 organizations recruited on campus

Financial Matters
$7969 resident tuition and fees (2007–08)
$21,408 nonresident tuition and fees (2007–08)
$8854 room and board
67% average percent of need met
$10,722 average financial aid amount received per undergraduate (2006–07 estimated)

Academics
Maryland, College Park awards bachelor's, master's, doctoral, and first-professional **degrees** and post-bachelor's and post-master's certificates. **Challenging opportunities** include advanced placement credit, accelerated degree programs, student-designed majors, an honors program, double majors, independent study, and a senior project. Special programs include cooperative education, internships, summer session for credit, off-campus study, study-abroad, and Army, Navy, and Air Force ROTC.

The most frequently chosen **baccalaureate** fields are social sciences, business/marketing, and biological/life sciences. A complete listing of majors at Maryland, College Park appears in the Majors by College index beginning on page 471.

The **faculty** at Maryland, College Park has 1,597 full-time members, 92% with terminal degrees. The student-faculty ratio is 18:1.

Students of Maryland, College Park
The student body totals 35,970, of whom 25,813 are undergraduates. 48.4% are women and 51.6% are men. Students come from 54 states and territories and 149 other countries. 77% are from Maryland. 2.2% are international students. 13% are African American, 0.4% American Indian, 14.1% Asian American, and 5.9% Hispanic American. 92% returned for their sophomore year.

Facilities and Resources
11,097 **computers/terminals** are available on campus for general student use. Students can access the following: campus intranet, computer help desk, free student e-mail accounts, online (class) grades, online (class) registration, online (class) schedules, student account information, financial aid summary. Campuswide network is available. 100% of college-owned or -operated housing units are wired for high-speed Internet access. Wireless service is available via classrooms, computer labs, dorm rooms, libraries, student centers. The 7 **libraries** have 3,016,940 books and 34,091 subscriptions.

Campus Life
There are 527 active organizations on campus, including a drama/theater group, newspaper, radio station, television station, choral group, and marching band. 9% of eligible men and 10% of eligible women are members of national **fraternities** and national **sororities**.

Maryland, College Park is a member of the NCAA (Division I). **Intercollegiate sports** (some offering scholarships) include baseball (m), basketball, cheerleading (w), cross-country running, field hockey (w), football (m), golf, gymnastics (w), lacrosse, soccer, softball (w), swimming and diving, tennis, track and field, volleyball (w), water polo (w), wrestling (m).

Campus Safety
Student safety services include campus police, video camera surveillance, late-night transport/escort service, 24-hour emergency telephone alarm devices, 24-hour patrols by trained security personnel, student patrols, and electronically operated dormitory entrances.

Applying
Maryland, College Park requires an essay, SAT or ACT, a high school transcript, and 1 recommendation, and in some cases resume of activities, auditions. It recommends 2 recommendations. Application deadline: 1/20; 2/15 priority date for financial aid. Early and deferred admission are possible.

University of Mary Washington

Small-town setting ■ Public ■ State-supported ■ Coed
Fredericksburg, Virginia

Web site: www.umw.edu
Contact: Dr. Martin Wilder, Vice President for Enrollment and
Communications, 1301 College Avenue, Fredericksburg, VA 22401-5358
Telephone: 540-654-2000 or toll-free 800-468-5614
Fax: 540-654-1857
E-mail: admit@umw.edu

Academics
Mary Washington awards bachelor's and master's **degrees** and post-bachelor's
certificates. **Challenging opportunities** include advanced placement credit, accelerated
degree programs, student-designed majors, double majors, independent study, and a
senior project. Special programs include cooperative education, internships, summer
session for credit, and study-abroad.

The most frequently chosen **baccalaureate** fields are social sciences, business/
marketing, and English. A complete listing of majors at Mary Washington appears in the
Majors by College index beginning on page 471.

The **faculty** at Mary Washington has 251 full-time members, 90% with terminal
degrees. The student-faculty ratio is 15:1.

Students of Mary Washington
The student body totals 5,001, of whom 4,271 are undergraduates. 66.3% are women
and 33.7% are men. Students come from 43 states and territories and 16 other countries.
78% are from Virginia. 0.5% are international students. 3.2% are African American,
0.5% American Indian, 4.2% Asian American, and 3.5% Hispanic American. 87%
returned for their sophomore year.

Facilities and Resources
306 **computers/terminals** are available on campus for general student use. Students can
access the following: computer help desk, free student e-mail accounts, online (class)
registration. Campuswide network is available. The **library** has 355,478 books and 2,419
subscriptions.

Campus Life
There are 99 active organizations on campus, including a drama/theater group,
newspaper, radio station, and choral group. No national or local **fraternities** or **sororities**.

Mary Washington is a member of the NCAA (Division III). **Intercollegiate sports**
include baseball (m), basketball, crew, cross-country running, equestrian sports, field
hockey (w), lacrosse, soccer, softball (w), swimming and diving, tennis, track and field,
volleyball (w).

Campus Safety
Student safety services include self-defense and safety classes, late-night transport/escort
service, 24-hour emergency telephone alarm devices, 24-hour patrols by trained security
personnel, student patrols, and electronically operated dormitory entrances.

Applying
Mary Washington requires an essay, SAT or ACT, and a high school transcript. It recom-
mends SAT Subject Tests. Application deadline: 2/1; 3/1 priority date for financial aid.
Deferred admission is possible.

Getting Accepted
4,475 applied
71% were accepted
966 enrolled (30% of accepted)
30% from top tenth of their h.s. class
3.67 average high school GPA
Mean SAT critical reading score: 608
Mean SAT math score: 584
Mean SAT writing score: 597
Mean ACT score: 25
58% had SAT critical reading scores over 600
43% had SAT math scores over 600
52% had SAT writing scores over 600
13% had SAT critical reading scores over 700
6% had SAT math scores over 700
8% had SAT writing scores over 700
50 class presidents

Graduation and After
68% graduated in 4 years
8% graduated in 5 years
23% pursued further study
70% had job offers within 6 months
64 organizations recruited on campus

Financial Matters
$6494 resident tuition and fees (2007–08)
$16,968 nonresident tuition and fees (2007–08)
$6606 room and board
56% average percent of need met
$5300 average financial aid amount received
per undergraduate (2004–05)

University of Miami

Suburban setting ■ Private ■ Independent ■ Coed
Coral Gables, Florida

Web site: www.miami.edu
Contact: Mr. Edward M. Gillis, Associate Dean of Enrollment and Director of Admission, PO Box 248025, Ashe Building Room 132, Coral Gables, FL 33146-4616
Telephone: 305-284-4472
Fax: 305-284-2507
E-mail: admission@miami.edu

Getting Accepted

19,676 applied
38% were accepted
1,991 enrolled (27% of accepted)
65% from top tenth of their h.s. class
4.0 average high school GPA
Mean SAT critical reading score: 630
Mean SAT math score: 645
Mean SAT writing score: 605
Mean ACT score: 29
70% had SAT critical reading scores over 600
78% had SAT math scores over 600
57% had SAT writing scores over 600
95% had ACT scores over 24
17% had SAT critical reading scores over 700
23% had SAT math scores over 700
10% had SAT writing scores over 700
45% had ACT scores over 30
49 valedictorians

Graduation and After

62% graduated in 4 years
12% graduated in 5 years
1% graduated in 6 years
37% pursued further study (7% law, 6% medicine, 4% business)
435 organizations recruited on campus

Financial Matters

$33,118 tuition and fees (2007–08)
$9606 room and board
79% average percent of need met
$25,088 average financial aid amount received per undergraduate (2006–07 estimated)

Academics

UM awards bachelor's, master's, doctoral, and first-professional **degrees** and post-bachelor's and post-master's certificates. **Challenging opportunities** include advanced placement credit, accelerated degree programs, student-designed majors, an honors program, double majors, independent study, and a senior project. Special programs include internships, summer session for credit, study-abroad, and Army and Air Force ROTC.

The most frequently chosen **baccalaureate** fields are business/marketing, visual and performing arts, and biological/life sciences. A complete listing of majors at UM appears in the Majors by College index beginning on page 471.

The **faculty** at UM has 920 full-time members, 86% with terminal degrees. The student-faculty ratio is 12:1.

Students of UM

The student body totals 15,462, of whom 10,379 are undergraduates. 54.1% are women and 45.9% are men. Students come from 53 states and territories and 114 other countries. 26% are from Florida. 6.1% are international students. 8.5% are African American, 0.3% American Indian, 4.9% Asian American, and 22.7% Hispanic American. 90% returned for their sophomore year.

Facilities and Resources

1,800 **computers/terminals** are available on campus for general student use. Students can access the following: computer help desk, free student e-mail accounts, online (class) grades, online (class) schedules, online student account and grade information. Campuswide network is available. 100% of college-owned or -operated housing units are wired for high-speed Internet access. The 8 **libraries** have 2,992,056 books and 45,953 subscriptions.

Campus Life

There are 275 active organizations on campus, including a drama/theater group, newspaper, radio station, television station, choral group, and marching band. 14% of eligible men and 14% of eligible women are members of national **fraternities** and national **sororities**.

UM is a member of the NCAA (Division I). **Intercollegiate sports** (some offering scholarships) include baseball (m), basketball, cheerleading, crew (w), cross-country running, football (m), golf (w), soccer (w), swimming and diving (w), tennis, track and field, volleyball (w).

Campus Safety

Student safety services include crime prevention and safety workshops, residential college crime watch, late-night transport/escort service, 24-hour emergency telephone alarm devices, 24-hour patrols by trained security personnel, student patrols, and electronically operated dormitory entrances.

Applying

UM requires an essay, SAT or ACT, a high school transcript, recommendations, and counselor evaluation, and in some cases SAT Subject Tests, SAT and SAT Subject Tests or ACT, and an interview. Application deadline: 1/15; 2/1 priority date for financial aid. Early and deferred admission are possible.

UNIVERSITY OF MICHIGAN

SUBURBAN SETTING ■ PUBLIC ■ STATE-SUPPORTED ■ COED
ANN ARBOR, MICHIGAN

Web site: www.umich.edu
Contact: Mr. Ted Spencer, Director of Undergraduate Admissions, 1220
    Student Activities Building, 515 East Jefferson, Ann Arbor, MI 48109-1316
Telephone: 734-764-7433
Fax: 734-936-0740
E-mail: ugadmiss@umich.edu

Academics

Michigan awards bachelor's, master's, doctoral, and first-professional **degrees** and post-bachelor's and post-master's certificates. **Challenging opportunities** include advanced placement credit, accelerated degree programs, student-designed majors, an honors program, double majors, independent study, and a senior project. Special programs include cooperative education, internships, summer session for credit, off-campus study, study-abroad, and Army and Air Force ROTC.

The most frequently chosen **baccalaureate** fields are social sciences, engineering, and psychology. A complete listing of majors at Michigan appears in the Majors by College index beginning on page 471.

The **faculty** at Michigan has 2,367 full-time members, 91% with terminal degrees. The student-faculty ratio is 15:1.

Students of Michigan

The student body totals 41,042, of whom 26,083 are undergraduates. 50.1% are women and 49.9% are men. Students come from 55 states and territories and 82 other countries. 68% are from Michigan. 4.9% are international students. 6.3% are African American, 0.9% American Indian, 12% Asian American, and 4.6% Hispanic American. 96% returned for their sophomore year.

Facilities and Resources

2,600 **computers/terminals** and 2,255 ports are available on campus for general student use. Students can access the following: computer help desk, free student e-mail accounts, online (class) grades, online (class) registration, online (class) schedules, personal websites. Campuswide network is available. 63% of college-owned or -operated housing units are wired for high-speed Internet access. Wireless service is available via classrooms, computer centers, computer labs, libraries, student centers. The 21 **libraries** have 7,958,145 books and 67,554 subscriptions.

Campus Life

There are 1,112 active organizations on campus, including a drama/theater group, newspaper, radio station, television station, choral group, and marching band. 15% of eligible men and 15% of eligible women are members of national **fraternities**, national **sororities**, local fraternities, and local sororities.

Michigan is a member of the NCAA (Division I). **Intercollegiate sports** (some offering scholarships) include baseball (m), basketball, cheerleading, crew (w), cross-country running, field hockey (w), football (m), golf, gymnastics, ice hockey (m), soccer, softball (w), swimming and diving, tennis, track and field, volleyball (w), water polo (w), wrestling (m).

Campus Safety

Student safety services include bicycle patrols, late-night transport/escort service, 24-hour emergency telephone alarm devices, 24-hour patrols by trained security personnel, student patrols, and electronically operated dormitory entrances.

Applying

Michigan requires an essay, SAT or ACT, and a high school transcript, and in some cases SAT Subject Tests and an interview. Application deadline: 2/1; 4/30 for financial aid. Deferred admission is possible.

Getting Accepted

27,474 applied
50% were accepted
5,992 enrolled (43% of accepted)
92% from top tenth of their h.s. class
3.75 average high school GPA
Mean SAT math score: 677
Mean ACT score: 29
73% had SAT critical reading scores over 600
86% had SAT math scores over 600
93% had ACT scores over 24
23% had SAT critical reading scores over 700
43% had SAT math scores over 700
43% had ACT scores over 30

Graduation and After

70% graduated in 4 years
14% graduated in 5 years
2% graduated in 6 years
34% pursued further study
1260 organizations recruited on campus

Financial Matters

$10,447 resident tuition and fees (2007–08)
$31,301 nonresident tuition and fees (2007–08)
$8190 room and board
90% average percent of need met
$11,111 average financial aid amount received per undergraduate (2005–06)

UNIVERSITY OF MICHIGAN–DEARBORN

Suburban setting ■ Public ■ State-supported ■ Coed
Dearborn, Michigan

Web site: www.umd.umich.edu
Contact: Mr. Christopher Tremblay, Director of Admissions and Orientation, 4901 Eveergreen Road, Dearborn, MI 48128-1491
Telephone: 313-593-5100
Fax: 313-436-9167
E-mail: admissions@umd.umich.edu

Getting Accepted

3,438 applied
66% were accepted
893 enrolled (39% of accepted)
25% from top tenth of their h.s. class
3.46 average high school GPA
Mean SAT writing score: 546
54% had ACT scores over 24
9% had ACT scores over 30
5 valedictorians

Graduation and After

14% graduated in 4 years
27% graduated in 5 years
12% graduated in 6 years
23% pursued further study
53% had job offers within 6 months
92 organizations recruited on campus

Financial Matters

$7976 resident tuition and fees (2007–08)
$17,466 nonresident tuition and fees (2007–08)
44% average percent of need met
$4390 average financial aid amount received per undergraduate (2006–07 estimated)

Academics

UM-D awards bachelor's and master's **degrees** and post-bachelor's certificates. **Challenging opportunities** include advanced placement credit, accelerated degree programs, student-designed majors, an honors program, double majors, independent study, and a senior project. Special programs include cooperative education, internships, summer session for credit, off-campus study, study-abroad, and Army, Navy, and Air Force ROTC.

The most frequently chosen **baccalaureate** fields are education, business/marketing, and engineering. A complete listing of majors at UM-D appears in the Majors by College index beginning on page 471.

The **faculty** at UM-D has 292 full-time members, 100% with terminal degrees. The student-faculty ratio is 16:1.

Students of UM-D

The student body totals 8,336, of whom 6,447 are undergraduates. 51.9% are women and 48.1% are men. Students come from 11 states and territories and 28 other countries. 98% are from Michigan. 1.2% are international students. 9.6% are African American, 0.7% American Indian, 5.9% Asian American, and 2.8% Hispanic American. 81% returned for their sophomore year.

Facilities and Resources

350 **computers/terminals** are available on campus for general student use. Campuswide network is available. The **library** has 340,897 books and 1,099 subscriptions.

Campus Life

Active organizations on campus include a drama/theater group, newspaper, radio station, and television station. 25% of eligible men and 25% of eligible women are members of national **fraternities** and national **sororities**.

UM-D is a member of the NAIA. **Intercollegiate sports** (some offering scholarships) include basketball, ice hockey (m), volleyball (w).

Campus Safety

Student safety services include late-night transport/escort service, 24-hour emergency telephone alarm devices, and 24-hour patrols by trained security personnel.

Applying

UM-D requires SAT or ACT, a high school transcript, and a minimum high school GPA of 3.0, and in some cases an interview. Application deadline: rolling admissions; 2/14 priority date for financial aid. Deferred admission is possible.

University of Minnesota, Morris

Small-town setting ■ Public ■ State-supported ■ Coed
Morris, Minnesota

Web site: www.mrs.umn.edu
Contact: Ms. Jaime Moquin, Director of Admissions, 600 East 4th Street,
   Morris, MN 56267-2199
Telephone: 320-539-6035 or toll-free 800-992-8863
Fax: 320-589-1673
E-mail: admissions@morris.umn.edu

Academics

UMM awards bachelor's **degrees**. **Challenging opportunities** include advanced placement credit, accelerated degree programs, student-designed majors, freshman honors college, an honors program, double majors, independent study, and a senior project. Special programs include internships, summer session for credit, off-campus study, and study-abroad.

The most frequently chosen **baccalaureate** fields are social sciences, English, and biological/life sciences. A complete listing of majors at UMM appears in the Majors by College index beginning on page 471.

The **faculty** at UMM has 119 full-time members, 95% with terminal degrees. The student-faculty ratio is 12:1.

Students of UMM

The student body is made up of 1,740 undergraduates. 57.9% are women and 42.1% are men. Students come from 30 states and territories and 11 other countries. 87% are from Minnesota. 1.9% are international students. 2.3% are African American, 11.3% American Indian, 3.5% Asian American, and 1.7% Hispanic American. 86% returned for their sophomore year.

Facilities and Resources

124 **computers/terminals** are available on campus for general student use. Students can access the following: online (class) registration. Campuswide network is available. The 2 **libraries** have 191,469 books and 9,042 subscriptions.

Campus Life

There are 91 active organizations on campus, including a drama/theater group, newspaper, radio station, television station, and choral group. No national or local **fraternities** or **sororities**.

UMM is a member of the NCAA (Division III). **Intercollegiate sports** include baseball (m), basketball, cross-country running (w), football (m), golf, soccer (w), softball (w), swimming and diving (w), tennis, track and field, volleyball (w).

Campus Safety

Student safety services include late-night transport/escort service, 24-hour emergency telephone alarm devices, 24-hour patrols by trained security personnel, and electronically operated dormitory entrances.

Applying

UMM requires an essay, SAT or ACT, and a high school transcript, and in some cases an interview and 1 recommendation. It recommends a minimum high school GPA of 3.0. Application deadline: 3/15. Early and deferred admission are possible.

Getting Accepted
1,216 applied
80% were accepted
377 enrolled (39% of accepted)
28% from top tenth of their h.s. class
Mean SAT critical reading score: 618
Mean SAT math score: 617
Mean SAT writing score: 579
Mean ACT score: 24
66% had SAT critical reading scores over 600
66% had SAT math scores over 600
42% had SAT writing scores over 600
56% had ACT scores over 24
26% had SAT critical reading scores over 700
21% had SAT math scores over 700
19% had SAT writing scores over 700
11% had ACT scores over 30
27 class presidents
36 valedictorians

Graduation and After
40% graduated in 4 years
16% graduated in 5 years
3% graduated in 6 years
30% pursued further study (13% arts and
   sciences, 3% law, 2% education)
80% had job offers within 6 months
90 organizations recruited on campus

Financial Matters
$9112 resident tuition and fees (2007–08)
$9112 nonresident tuition and fees (2007–08)
$6260 room and board
82% average percent of need met
$12,660 average financial aid amount received
   per undergraduate (2005–06 estimated)

UNIVERSITY OF MINNESOTA, TWIN CITIES CAMPUS

URBAN SETTING ■ PUBLIC ■ STATE-SUPPORTED ■ COED
MINNEAPOLIS, MINNESOTA

Web site: www.umn.edu/tc
Contact: Rachelle Hernandez, Associate Director of Admissions, 240 Williamson, Minneapolis, MN 55455-0213
Telephone: 612-625-2008 or toll-free 800-752-1000
Fax: 612-626-1693
E-mail: admissions@tc.umn.edu

Getting Accepted

26,097 applied
57% were accepted
5,280 enrolled (36% of accepted)
44% from top tenth of their h.s. class
58% had SAT critical reading scores over 600
71% had SAT math scores over 600
51% had SAT writing scores over 600
75% had ACT scores over 24
20% had SAT critical reading scores over 700
26% had SAT math scores over 700
14% had SAT writing scores over 700
19% had ACT scores over 30

Graduation and After

32% graduated in 4 years
23% graduated in 5 years
5% graduated in 6 years

Financial Matters

$7950 resident tuition and fees (2007–08)
$19,580 nonresident tuition and fees (2007–08)
$7062 room and board
85% average percent of need met
$11,969 average financial aid amount received per undergraduate (2006–07 estimated)

Academics

U of M-Twin Cities awards bachelor's, master's, doctoral, and first-professional **degrees** and post-bachelor's, post-master's, and first-professional certificates. **Challenging opportunities** include advanced placement credit, accelerated degree programs, student-designed majors, freshman honors college, an honors program, double majors, independent study, and a senior project. Special programs include cooperative education, internships, summer session for credit, off-campus study, study-abroad, and Army, Navy, and Air Force ROTC.

The most frequently chosen **baccalaureate** fields are social sciences, engineering, and business/marketing. A complete listing of majors at U of M-Twin Cities appears in the Majors by College index beginning on page 471.

The **faculty** at U of M-Twin Cities has 1,763 full-time members, 88% with terminal degrees.

Students of U of M-Twin Cities

The student body totals 50,883, of whom 32,294 are undergraduates. 53.2% are women and 46.8% are men. Students come from 51 states and territories and 77 other countries. 73% are from Minnesota. 1.9% are international students. 4.8% are African American, 1% American Indian, 9.7% Asian American, and 2.1% Hispanic American. 88% returned for their sophomore year.

Facilities and Resources

Students can access the following: online (class) registration, e-mail. Campuswide network is available. The 18 **libraries** have 5,700,000 books and 45,000 subscriptions.

Campus Life

There are 350 active organizations on campus, including a drama/theater group, newspaper, radio station, television station, choral group, and marching band. 3% of eligible men and 3% of eligible women are members of national **fraternities**, national **sororities**, and local sororities.

U of M-Twin Cities is a member of the NCAA (Division I). **Intercollegiate sports** (some offering scholarships) include baseball (m), basketball, cross-country running, football (m), golf, gymnastics, ice hockey, soccer (w), softball (w), swimming and diving, tennis, track and field, volleyball (w), wrestling (m).

Campus Safety

Student safety services include safety/security orientation, security lighting, late-night transport/escort service, 24-hour emergency telephone alarm devices, 24-hour patrols by trained security personnel, student patrols, and electronically operated dormitory entrances.

Applying

U of M-Twin Cities requires SAT or ACT and a high school transcript. It recommends a minimum high school GPA of 2.0. Application deadline: rolling admissions. Early and deferred admission are possible.

UNIVERSITY OF MISSOURI–COLUMBIA

SUBURBAN SETTING ■ PUBLIC ■ STATE-SUPPORTED ■ COED
COLUMBIA, MISSOURI

Web site: www.missouri.edu
Contact: Ms. Barbara Rupp, Director of Admissions, 230 Jesse Hall,
Columbia, MO 65211
Telephone: 573-882-7786 or toll-free 800-225-6075 (in-state)
Fax: 573-882-7887
E-mail: mu4u@missouri.edu

Academics

Missouri-Columbia awards bachelor's, master's, doctoral, and first-professional **degrees** and post-master's and first-professional certificates. **Challenging opportunities** include advanced placement credit, accelerated degree programs, student-designed majors, freshman honors college, an honors program, double majors, independent study, and a senior project. Special programs include cooperative education, internships, summer session for credit, off-campus study, study-abroad, and Army, Navy, and Air Force ROTC.

The most frequently chosen **baccalaureate** fields are business/marketing, communications/journalism, and education. A complete listing of majors at Missouri-Columbia appears in the Majors by College index beginning on page 471.

The **faculty** at Missouri-Columbia has 1,266 full-time members, 92% with terminal degrees. The student-faculty ratio is 17:1.

Students of Missouri-Columbia

The student body totals 28,477, of whom 21,654 are undergraduates. 51.9% are women and 48.1% are men. Students come from 53 states and territories and 84 other countries. 86% are from Missouri. 1.4% are international students. 6.2% are African American, 0.6% American Indian, 2.6% Asian American, and 1.8% Hispanic American. 84% returned for their sophomore year.

Facilities and Resources

1,080 **computers/terminals** are available on campus for general student use. Students can access the following: computer help desk, free student e-mail accounts, online (class) registration, online (class) schedules, telephone registration. Campuswide network is available. Wireless service is available via entire campus. The 12 **libraries** have 3,249,783 books and 36,244 subscriptions.

Campus Life

There are 531 active organizations on campus, including a drama/theater group, newspaper, radio station, television station, choral group, and marching band. 20% of eligible men and 25% of eligible women are members of national **fraternities** and national **sororities**.

Missouri-Columbia is a member of the NCAA (Division I). **Intercollegiate sports** (some offering scholarships) include baseball (m), basketball, cross-country running, football (m), golf, gymnastics (w), soccer (w), softball (w), swimming and diving, tennis (w), track and field, volleyball (w), wrestling (m).

Campus Safety

Student safety services include late-night transport/escort service, 24-hour emergency telephone alarm devices, 24-hour patrols by trained security personnel, and electronically operated dormitory entrances.

Applying

Missouri-Columbia requires SAT or ACT, a high school transcript, and specific high school curriculum. It recommends ACT. Application deadline: rolling admissions; 3/1 priority date for financial aid. Deferred admission is possible.

Getting Accepted

12,089 applied
86% were accepted
4,982 enrolled (48% of accepted)
26% from top tenth of their h.s. class
Mean ACT score: 24
49% had SAT critical reading scores over 600
48% had SAT math scores over 600
67% had ACT scores over 24
11% had SAT critical reading scores over 700
10% had SAT math scores over 700
17% had ACT scores over 30
28 National Merit Scholars

Graduation and After

1400 organizations recruited on campus

Financial Matters

$8099 resident tuition and fees (2007–08)
$18,755 nonresident tuition and fees (2007–08)
$7002 room and board
86% average percent of need met
$11,452 average financial aid amount received per undergraduate (2006–07 estimated)

UNIVERSITY OF MISSOURI–KANSAS CITY

URBAN SETTING ■ PUBLIC ■ STATE-SUPPORTED ■ COED
KANSAS CITY, MISSOURI

Web site: www.umkc.edu
Contact: Ms. Jennifer DeHaemers, Director of Admissions, Office of
    Admissions, 5100 Rockhill Road, Kansas City, MO 64110-2499
Telephone: 816-235-1111 or toll-free 800-775-8652 (out-of-state)
Fax: 816-235-5544
E-mail: admit@umkc.edu

Getting Accepted
3,228 applied
71% were accepted
956 enrolled (42% of accepted)
34% from top tenth of their h.s. class
3.31 average high school GPA
Mean SAT critical reading score: 597
Mean SAT math score: 608
Mean ACT score: 24
53% had SAT critical reading scores over 600
62% had SAT math scores over 600
53% had ACT scores over 24
10% had SAT critical reading scores over 700
21% had SAT math scores over 700
13% had ACT scores over 30

Graduation and After
17% graduated in 4 years
13% graduated in 5 years
20% graduated in 6 years
82% had job offers within 6 months
347 organizations recruited on campus

Financial Matters
$7946 resident tuition and fees (2007–08)
$18,642 nonresident tuition and fees (2007–08)
$7047 room and board
51% average percent of need met
$9867 average financial aid amount received per undergraduate (2006–07 estimated)

Academics

UMKC awards bachelor's, master's, doctoral, and first-professional **degrees** and post-master's and first-professional certificates. **Challenging opportunities** include advanced placement credit, accelerated degree programs, student-designed majors, an honors program, double majors, independent study, and a senior project. Special programs include cooperative education, internships, summer session for credit, off-campus study, study-abroad, and Army and Air Force ROTC.

The most frequently chosen **baccalaureate** fields are liberal arts/general studies, business/marketing, and education. A complete listing of majors at UMKC appears in the Majors by College index beginning on page 471.

The **faculty** at UMKC has 664 full-time members, 78% with terminal degrees. The student-faculty ratio is 13:1.

Students of UMKC

The student body totals 14,213, of whom 9,383 are undergraduates. 58.7% are women and 41.3% are men. Students come from 47 states and territories and 63 other countries. 74% are from Missouri. 2.6% are international students. 14.7% are African American, 0.6% American Indian, 5.9% Asian American, and 4.4% Hispanic American. 71% returned for their sophomore year.

Facilities and Resources

671 **computers/terminals** are available on campus for general student use. Students can access the following: online (class) registration. Campuswide network is available. The 4 **libraries** have 1,323,786 books and 25,022 subscriptions.

Campus Life

There are 75 active organizations on campus, including a drama/theater group, newspaper, and choral group. 13% of eligible men and 20% of eligible women are members of national **fraternities**, national **sororities**, and local sororities.

UMKC is a member of the NCAA (Division I). **Intercollegiate sports** (some offering scholarships) include basketball, cheerleading (w), cross-country running, golf, riflery, soccer (m), softball (w), tennis, track and field, volleyball (w).

Campus Safety

Student safety services include late-night transport/escort service, 24-hour emergency telephone alarm devices, 24-hour patrols by trained security personnel, and electronically operated dormitory entrances.

Applying

UMKC requires SAT or ACT and a high school transcript. Application deadline: rolling admissions; 3/1 priority date for financial aid. Deferred admission is possible.

UNIVERSITY OF NEBRASKA–LINCOLN

URBAN SETTING ■ PUBLIC ■ STATE-SUPPORTED ■ COED
LINCOLN, NEBRASKA

Web site: www.unl.edu
Contact: Pat McBride, Director, New Student Enrollment, 1410 Q Street, Lincoln, NE 68588-0256
Telephone: 402-472-2023 or toll-free 800-742-8800
Fax: 402-472-0670
E-mail: admissions@unl.edu

SPONSOR

Academics

UNL awards associate, bachelor's, master's, doctoral, and first-professional **degrees** and post-bachelor's and post-master's certificates. **Challenging opportunities** include advanced placement credit, accelerated degree programs, student-designed majors, an honors program, double majors, and independent study. Special programs include cooperative education, internships, summer session for credit, off-campus study, study-abroad, and Army, Navy, and Air Force ROTC.

The most frequently chosen **baccalaureate** fields are business/marketing, education, and engineering. A complete listing of majors at UNL appears in the Majors by College index beginning on page 471.

The **faculty** at UNL has 1,068 full-time members, 97% with terminal degrees. The student-faculty ratio is 19:1.

Students of UNL

The student body totals 22,973, of whom 18,053 are undergraduates. 46.1% are women and 53.9% are men. Students come from 50 states and territories and 75 other countries. 83% are from Nebraska. 2.8% are international students. 2.4% are African American, 0.7% American Indian, 2.7% Asian American, and 3.3% Hispanic American. 83% returned for their sophomore year.

Facilities and Resources

650 **computers/terminals** are available on campus for general student use. Students can access the following: online (class) registration. Campuswide network is available. The 11 **libraries** have 3,377,546 books and 50,817 subscriptions.

Campus Life

There are 335 active organizations on campus, including a drama/theater group, newspaper, radio station, choral group, and marching band. 15% of eligible men and 18% of eligible women are members of national **fraternities**, national **sororities**, local fraternities, and local sororities.

UNL is a member of the NCAA (Division I). **Intercollegiate sports** (some offering scholarships) include baseball (m), basketball, bowling (m), cross-country running, football (m), golf, gymnastics, riflery (w), soccer (w), softball (w), swimming and diving (w), tennis, track and field, volleyball (w), wrestling (m).

Campus Safety

Student safety services include late-night transport/escort service, 24-hour emergency telephone alarm devices, 24-hour patrols by trained security personnel, student patrols, and electronically operated dormitory entrances.

Applying

UNL requires SAT or ACT and a high school transcript, and in some cases rank in upper 50% of high school class. It recommends ACT. Application deadline: 5/1.

The University of Nebraska–Lincoln offers one of today's most dynamic college experiences. The University has developed a national reputation for its substantial out-of-state scholarship program. As a result, more students nationwide are finding that the University, with its strength in undergraduate education, its tradition of student engagement, its lively campus atmosphere, and its connection to downtown Lincoln, is uniquely suited to provide an exceptional student experience. The University delivers on the promise of the friendliness of a private college with major university resources. It is no wonder alumni stay connected years after graduating and thousands of miles from the campus.

Getting Accepted
9,598 applied
62% were accepted
4,235 enrolled (71% of accepted)
27% from top tenth of their h.s. class
Mean SAT critical reading score: 579
Mean SAT math score: 602
Mean ACT score: 25
47% had SAT critical reading scores over 600
54% had SAT math scores over 600
60% had ACT scores over 24
14% had SAT critical reading scores over 700
17% had SAT math scores over 700
17% had ACT scores over 30
83 National Merit Scholars

Graduation and After
23% graduated in 4 years
33% graduated in 5 years
8% graduated in 6 years
300 organizations recruited on campus

Financial Matters
$6215 resident tuition and fees (2007–08)
$16,235 nonresident tuition and fees (2007–08)
$6523 room and board
85% average percent of need met
$8245 average financial aid amount received per undergraduate (2004–05)

THE UNIVERSITY OF NORTH CAROLINA AT ASHEVILLE

SUBURBAN SETTING ■ PUBLIC ■ STATE-SUPPORTED ■ COED
ASHEVILLE, NORTH CAROLINA

Web site: www.unca.edu
Contact: Ms. Leigh McBride, Associate Director of Admissions, University
Dining Hall, CPO # 1320, Asheville, NC 28804-8510
Telephone: 828-251-6481 or toll-free 800-531-9842
Fax: 828-251-6482
E-mail: admissions@unca.edu

Getting Accepted

2,653 applied
76% were accepted
577 enrolled (29% of accepted)
19% from top tenth of their h.s. class
3.84 average high school GPA
Mean SAT critical reading score: 586
Mean SAT math score: 568
Mean SAT writing score: 565
Mean ACT score: 24
47% had SAT critical reading scores over 600
35% had SAT math scores over 600
36% had SAT writing scores over 600
57% had ACT scores over 24
9% had SAT critical reading scores over 700
5% had SAT math scores over 700
4% had SAT writing scores over 700
4% had ACT scores over 30
3 valedictorians

Graduation and After

33% graduated in 4 years
17% graduated in 5 years
4% graduated in 6 years
21% pursued further study
72% had job offers within 6 months
145 organizations recruited on campus

Financial Matters

$4164 resident tuition and fees (2007–08)
$15,154 nonresident tuition and fees (2007–08)
$6230 room and board
80% average percent of need met
$8231 average financial aid amount received per undergraduate (2006–07 estimated)

Academics

UNC Asheville awards bachelor's and master's **degrees** and post-bachelor's certificates. **Challenging opportunities** include advanced placement credit, student-designed majors, an honors program, double majors, independent study, and a senior project. Special programs include internships, summer session for credit, off-campus study, and study-abroad.

The most frequently chosen **baccalaureate** fields are psychology, business/marketing, and social sciences. A complete listing of majors at UNC Asheville appears in the Majors by College index beginning on page 471.

The **faculty** at UNC Asheville has 206 full-time members, 85% with terminal degrees. The student-faculty ratio is 13:1.

Students of UNC Asheville

The student body totals 3,700, of whom 3,663 are undergraduates. 57.9% are women and 42.1% are men. Students come from 45 states and territories and 16 other countries. 86% are from North Carolina. 0.8% are international students. 2.9% are African American, 0.3% American Indian, 1.3% Asian American, and 2% Hispanic American. 76% returned for their sophomore year.

Facilities and Resources

390 **computers/terminals** are available on campus for general student use. Students can access the following: online (class) registration, online grade reports. Campuswide network is available. 100% of college-owned or -operated housing units are wired for high-speed Internet access. Wireless service is available via classrooms, libraries, student centers. The **library** has 264,248 books and 6,405 subscriptions.

Campus Life

There are 74 active organizations on campus, including a drama/theater group, newspaper, radio station, and choral group. 1% of eligible men and 3% of eligible women are members of national **fraternities** and national **sororities**.

UNC Asheville is a member of the NCAA (Division I). **Intercollegiate sports** (some offering scholarships) include baseball (m), basketball, cheerleading, cross-country running, soccer, tennis, track and field, volleyball (w).

Campus Safety

Student safety services include dorm entrances secured at night, late-night transport/escort service, 24-hour emergency telephone alarm devices, and 24-hour patrols by trained security personnel.

Applying

UNC Asheville requires an essay, SAT or ACT, a high school transcript, recommendations, and Minimum Course Requirement, and in some cases an interview. Application deadline: 2/15; 3/1 priority date for financial aid. Deferred admission is possible.

THE UNIVERSITY OF NORTH CAROLINA AT CHAPEL HILL

SUBURBAN SETTING ■ PUBLIC ■ STATE-SUPPORTED ■ COED
CHAPEL HILL, NORTH CAROLINA

Web site: www.unc.edu

Contact: Stephen Farmer, Assistant Provost and Director of Undergraduate Admissions, Campus Box # 2200, Jackson Hill, Chapel Hill, NC 27599-2200

Telephone: 919-966-3621

Fax: 919-962-3045

E-mail: uadm@email.unc.edu

Academics

UNC Chapel Hill awards bachelor's, master's, doctoral, and first-professional **degrees** and post-bachelor's, post-master's, and first-professional certificates. **Challenging opportunities** include advanced placement credit, student-designed majors, freshman honors college, an honors program, double majors, independent study, and a senior project. Special programs include internships, summer session for credit, off-campus study, study-abroad, and Army, Navy, and Air Force ROTC.

The most frequently chosen **baccalaureate** fields are social sciences, communications/journalism, and psychology. A complete listing of majors at UNC Chapel Hill appears in the Majors by College index beginning on page 471.

The **faculty** at UNC Chapel Hill has 1,514 full-time members, 89% with terminal degrees.

Students of UNC Chapel Hill

The student body totals 28,136, of whom 17,628 are undergraduates. 58.7% are women and 41.3% are men. Students come from 50 states and territories and 103 other countries. 83% are from North Carolina. 1.3% are international students. 10.9% are African American, 0.8% American Indian, 6.9% Asian American, and 4.5% Hispanic American. 97% returned for their sophomore year.

Facilities and Resources

600 **computers/terminals** are available on campus for general student use. Students can access the following: computer help desk, free student e-mail accounts, online (class) grades, online (class) registration, online (class) schedules. Campuswide network is available. 100% of college-owned or -operated housing units are wired for high-speed Internet access. Wireless service is available via entire campus. The 15 **libraries** have 5,712,011 books and 53,444 subscriptions.

Campus Life

There are 557 active organizations on campus, including a drama/theater group, newspaper, radio station, television station, choral group, and marching band. 15% of eligible men and 17% of eligible women are members of national **fraternities** and national **sororities**.

UNC Chapel Hill is a member of the NCAA (Division I). **Intercollegiate sports** (some offering scholarships) include baseball (m), basketball, crew (w), cross-country running, fencing, field hockey (w), football (m), golf, gymnastics (w), lacrosse, soccer, softball (w), swimming and diving, tennis, track and field, volleyball (w), wrestling (m).

Campus Safety

Student safety services include crime prevention programs, late-night transport/escort service, 24-hour emergency telephone alarm devices, 24-hour patrols by trained security personnel, student patrols, and electronically operated dormitory entrances.

Applying

UNC Chapel Hill requires an essay, SAT or ACT, a high school transcript, 1 recommendation, and counselor's statement. Application deadline: 1/15; 3/1 priority date for financial aid. Deferred admission is possible.

Getting Accepted

20,090 applied
35% were accepted
3,893 enrolled (56% of accepted)
76% from top tenth of their h.s. class
Mean SAT critical reading score: 646
Mean SAT math score: 656
Mean SAT writing score: 637
Mean ACT score: 28
75% had SAT critical reading scores over 600
80% had SAT math scores over 600
71% had SAT writing scores over 600
89% had ACT scores over 24
27% had SAT critical reading scores over 700
29% had SAT math scores over 700
22% had SAT writing scores over 700
35% had ACT scores over 30
127 National Merit Scholars

Graduation and After

31% pursued further study (7% arts and sciences, 5% law, 3% education)
61.1% had job offers within 6 months
744 organizations recruited on campus

Financial Matters

$5340 resident tuition and fees (2007–08)
$20,988 nonresident tuition and fees (2007–08)
$7696 room and board
100% average percent of need met
$10,575 average financial aid amount received per undergraduate (2005–06)

The University of North Carolina Wilmington

Urban setting ■ Public ■ State-supported ■ Coed
Wilmington, North Carolina

Web site: www.uncw.edu
Contact: Dr. Terrence M. Curran, Associate Provost, 601 South College Road, Wilmington, NC 28403-3297
Telephone: 910-962-3876 or toll-free 800-228-5571 (out-of-state)
Fax: 910-962-3038
E-mail: admissions@uncw.edu

Getting Accepted
8,740 applied
58% were accepted
1,920 enrolled (38% of accepted)
25% from top tenth of their h.s. class
3.74 average high school GPA
Mean SAT critical reading score: 571
Mean SAT math score: 586
Mean SAT writing score: 557
27% had SAT critical reading scores over 600
37% had SAT math scores over 600
24% had SAT writing scores over 600
49% had ACT scores over 24
2% had SAT critical reading scores over 700
3% had SAT math scores over 700
1% had SAT writing scores over 700
5% had ACT scores over 30

Graduation and After
43% graduated in 4 years
19% graduated in 5 years
4% graduated in 6 years
16% pursued further study (12% arts and sciences, 2% business, 1% law)
145 organizations recruited on campus

Financial Matters
$4398 resident tuition and fees (2007–08)
$14,361 nonresident tuition and fees (2007–08)
$6998 room and board
86% average percent of need met
$6283 average financial aid amount received per undergraduate (2005–06)

Academics
UNCW awards bachelor's, master's, and doctoral **degrees** and post-bachelor's and post-master's certificates. **Challenging opportunities** include advanced placement credit, accelerated degree programs, an honors program, double majors, independent study, and a senior project. Special programs include cooperative education, internships, summer session for credit, and study-abroad.

The most frequently chosen **baccalaureate** fields are history, education, and psychology. A complete listing of majors at UNCW appears in the Majors by College index beginning on page 471.

The **faculty** at UNCW has 544 full-time members, 86% with terminal degrees. The student-faculty ratio is 17:1.

Students of UNCW
The student body totals 11,840, of whom 10,753 are undergraduates. 57.8% are women and 42.2% are men. Students come from 48 states and territories and 41 other countries. 85% are from North Carolina. 0.4% are international students. 5.2% are African American, 0.8% American Indian, 1.8% Asian American, and 3% Hispanic American. 85% returned for their sophomore year.

Facilities and Resources
1,170 **computers/terminals** are available on campus for general student use. Students can access the following: campus intranet, computer help desk, free student e-mail accounts, online (class) grades, online (class) registration, online (class) schedules. Campuswide network is available. 100% of college-owned or -operated housing units are wired for high-speed Internet access. Wireless service is available via entire campus. The **library** has 553,391 books and 22,218 subscriptions.

Campus Life
There are 170 active organizations on campus, including a drama/theater group, newspaper, radio station, television station, and choral group. 7% of eligible men and 9% of eligible women are members of national **fraternities**, national **sororities**, and local sororities.

UNCW is a member of the NCAA (Division I). **Intercollegiate sports** (some offering scholarships) include baseball (m), basketball, cheerleading, cross-country running, golf, soccer, softball (w), swimming and diving, tennis, track and field, volleyball (w).

Campus Safety
Student safety services include escort service, late-night transport/escort service, 24-hour emergency telephone alarm devices, 24-hour patrols by trained security personnel, and electronically operated dormitory entrances.

Applying
UNCW requires an essay, SAT or ACT, and a high school transcript. It recommends recommendations. Application deadline: 2/1. Early and deferred admission are possible.

University of North Florida

Urban setting ■ Public ■ State-supported ■ Coed
Jacksonville, Florida

Web site: www.unf.edu
Contact: Mr. John Yancey, Director of Admissions, 4567 St. Johns Bluff Road South, Jacksonville, FL 32224
Telephone: 904-620-2624
Fax: 904-620-2014
E-mail: admissions@unf.edu

Academics

UNF awards associate, bachelor's, master's, and doctoral **degrees** and post-bachelor's and post-master's certificates (doctoral degree in education only). **Challenging opportunities** include advanced placement credit, accelerated degree programs, student-designed majors, an honors program, double majors, independent study, and a senior project. Special programs include cooperative education, internships, summer session for credit, off-campus study, study-abroad, and Navy ROTC.

The most frequently chosen **baccalaureate** fields are business/marketing, health professions and related sciences, and education. A complete listing of majors at UNF appears in the Majors by College index beginning on page 471.

The **faculty** at UNF has 512 full-time members, 93% with terminal degrees. The student-faculty ratio is 22:1.

Students of UNF

The student body totals 16,406, of whom 14,532 are undergraduates. 56.8% are women and 43.2% are men. Students come from 46 states and territories and 68 other countries. 97% are from Florida. 1.2% are international students. 10.2% are African American, 0.5% American Indian, 5.3% Asian American, and 6.8% Hispanic American. 77% returned for their sophomore year.

Facilities and Resources

750 **computers/terminals** are available on campus for general student use. Students can access the following: campus intranet, computer help desk, free student e-mail accounts, online (class) grades, online (class) registration, online (class) schedules, applications software. Campuswide network is available. 100% of college-owned or -operated housing units are wired for high-speed Internet access. Wireless service is available via entire campus. The **library** has 798,321 books and 3,101 subscriptions.

Campus Life

There are 149 active organizations on campus, including a drama/theater group, newspaper, radio station, television station, and choral group. 8% of eligible men and 6% of eligible women are members of national **fraternities** and national **sororities**.

UNF is a member of the NCAA (Division I). **Intercollegiate sports** (some offering scholarships) include baseball (m), basketball, cheerleading, cross-country running, golf (m), soccer, softball (w), swimming and diving (w), tennis, track and field, volleyball (w).

Campus Safety

Student safety services include electronic parking lot security, late-night transport/escort service, 24-hour emergency telephone alarm devices, 24-hour patrols by trained security personnel, student patrols, and electronically operated dormitory entrances.

Applying

UNF requires SAT or ACT, a high school transcript, and a minimum high school GPA of 2.9, and in some cases an essay, an interview, and recommendations. It recommends a minimum high school GPA of 3.0. Application deadline: 7/2, 7/2 for nonresidents; 4/1 priority date for financial aid. Deferred admission is possible.

Getting Accepted

9,010 applied
66% were accepted
2,283 enrolled (38% of accepted)
18% from top tenth of their h.s. class
3.46 average high school GPA
Mean SAT critical reading score: 563
Mean SAT math score: 560
Mean ACT score: 22
31% had SAT critical reading scores over 600
33% had SAT math scores over 600
23% had ACT scores over 24
4% had SAT critical reading scores over 700
3% had SAT math scores over 700
1% had ACT scores over 30

Graduation and After

20% graduated in 4 years
18% graduated in 5 years
7% graduated in 6 years
324 organizations recruited on campus

Financial Matters

$3491 resident tuition and fees (2007–08)
$15,133 nonresident tuition and fees (2007–08)
$7071 room and board
91% average percent of need met
$1310 average financial aid amount received per undergraduate (2006–07 estimated)

University of Notre Dame

Suburban setting ■ Private ■ Independent Religious ■ Coed

Notre Dame, Indiana

Getting Accepted
14,503 applied
24% were accepted
1,991 enrolled (56% of accepted)
87% from top tenth of their h.s. class
Mean SAT critical reading score: 680
Mean SAT math score: 702
Mean SAT writing score: 674
Mean ACT score: 32
88% had SAT critical reading scores over 600
92% had SAT math scores over 600
85% had SAT writing scores over 600
98% had ACT scores over 24
51% had SAT critical reading scores over 700
58% had SAT math scores over 700
43% had SAT writing scores over 700
83% had ACT scores over 30

Graduation and After
32% pursued further study (11% arts and sciences, 7% medicine, 5% law)
69% had job offers within 6 months
605 organizations recruited on campus

Financial Matters
$35,187 tuition and fees (2007–08)
$9290 room and board
99% average percent of need met
$28,373 average financial aid amount received per undergraduate (2006–07 estimated)

Web site: www.nd.edu
Contact: Office of Undergraduate Admissions, 220 Main Building, Notre Dame, IN 46556-5612
Telephone: 574-631-7505
Fax: 574-631-8865
E-mail: admissions@nd.edu

Academics
Notre Dame awards bachelor's, master's, doctoral, and first-professional **degrees**. **Challenging opportunities** include advanced placement credit, accelerated degree programs, student-designed majors, an honors program, double majors, independent study, and a senior project. Special programs include internships, summer session for credit, off-campus study, study-abroad, and Army, Navy, and Air Force ROTC.

The most frequently chosen **baccalaureate** fields are business/marketing, social sciences, and engineering. A complete listing of majors at Notre Dame appears in the Majors by College index beginning on page 471.

The **faculty** at Notre Dame has 890 full-time members. The student-faculty ratio is 11:1.

Students of Notre Dame
The student body totals 11,733, of whom 8,371 are undergraduates. 46.8% are women and 53.2% are men. Students come from 53 states and territories and 43 other countries. 8% are from Indiana. 2.9% are international students. 4.1% are African American, 0.7% American Indian, 7% Asian American, and 9.3% Hispanic American. 97% returned for their sophomore year.

Facilities and Resources
221 **computers/terminals** are available on campus for general student use. Students can access the following: computer help desk, free student e-mail accounts, online (class) grades, online (class) registration, online (class) schedules. Campuswide network is available. Wireless service is available via entire campus. The 10 **libraries** have 2,914,029 books and 10,553 subscriptions.

Campus Life
There are 263 active organizations on campus, including a drama/theater group, newspaper, radio station, choral group, and marching band. No national or local **fraternities** or **sororities**.

Notre Dame is a member of the NCAA (Division I). **Intercollegiate sports** (some offering scholarships) include baseball (m), basketball, crew (w), cross-country running, fencing, football (m), golf, ice hockey (m), lacrosse, soccer, softball (w), swimming and diving, tennis, track and field, volleyball (w).

Campus Safety
Student safety services include crime prevention and personal safety workshops, full-time trained police investigators, fire sprinklers in all residence halls, late-night transport/escort service, 24-hour emergency telephone alarm devices, 24-hour patrols by trained security personnel, student patrols, and electronically operated dormitory entrances.

Applying
Notre Dame requires an essay, SAT or ACT, a high school transcript, and 1 recommendation, and in some cases SAT Subject Tests. Application deadline: 12/31; 2/15 for financial aid. Deferred admission is possible.

University of Oklahoma

Suburban setting ■ Public ■ State-supported ■ Coed
Norman, Oklahoma

Web site: www.ou.edu
Contact: Mr. Craig Hayes, Executive Director of Recruitment Services, 550 Parrington Oval, L-1, Norman, OK 73019-3032
Telephone: 405-325-2151 or toll-free 800-234-6868
Fax: 405-325-7478
E-mail: ou-pss@ou.edu

Academics

OU awards bachelor's, master's, doctoral, and first-professional **degrees** and post-master's certificates. **Challenging opportunities** include advanced placement credit, accelerated degree programs, student-designed majors, freshman honors college, an honors program, double majors, independent study, and a senior project. Special programs include cooperative education, internships, summer session for credit, off-campus study, study-abroad, and Army, Navy, and Air Force ROTC.

The most frequently chosen **baccalaureate** fields are business/marketing, social sciences, and communications/journalism. A complete listing of majors at OU appears in the Majors by College index beginning on page 471.

The **faculty** at OU has 1,113 full-time members, 86% with terminal degrees. The student-faculty ratio is 19:1.

Students of OU

The student body totals 26,205, of whom 19,693 are undergraduates. 49.1% are women and 50.9% are men. Students come from 52 states and territories and 75 other countries. 75% are from Oklahoma. 1.8% are international students. 5.7% are African American, 7.5% American Indian, 5.7% Asian American, and 4.2% Hispanic American. 84% returned for their sophomore year.

Facilities and Resources

1,200 **computers/terminals** and 500 ports are available on campus for general student use. Students can access the following: campus intranet, computer help desk, free student e-mail accounts, online (class) grades, online (class) registration, online (class) schedules. Campuswide network is available. 100% of college-owned or -operated housing units are wired for high-speed Internet access. Wireless service is available via classrooms, computer centers, computer labs, learning centers, libraries, student centers. The 9 **libraries** have 4,607,559 books and 58,399 subscriptions.

Campus Life

There are 328 active organizations on campus, including a drama/theater group, newspaper, radio station, television station, choral group, and marching band. 20% of eligible men and 27% of eligible women are members of national **fraternities**, national **sororities**, local fraternities, and local sororities.

OU is a member of the NCAA (Division I). **Intercollegiate sports** (some offering scholarships) include baseball (m), basketball, cross-country running, football (m), golf, gymnastics, soccer (w), softball (w), tennis, track and field, volleyball (w), wrestling (m).

Campus Safety

Student safety services include crime prevention programs, police bicycle patrols, self-defense classes, late-night transport/escort service, 24-hour emergency telephone alarm devices, 24-hour patrols by trained security personnel, student patrols, and electronically operated dormitory entrances.

Applying

OU requires SAT or ACT, a high school transcript, 15 specified curricular units, and a minimum high school GPA of 3.0, and in some cases an essay. Application deadline: 4/1.

Getting Accepted

8,767 applied
89% were accepted
3,883 enrolled (50% of accepted)
33% from top tenth of their h.s. class
3.59 average high school GPA
Mean SAT critical reading score: 581
Mean SAT math score: 596
Mean ACT score: 25
41% had SAT critical reading scores over 600
47% had SAT math scores over 600
73% had ACT scores over 24
12% had SAT critical reading scores over 700
12% had SAT math scores over 700
25% had ACT scores over 30
174 National Merit Scholars
289 valedictorians

Graduation and After

26% graduated in 4 years
29% graduated in 5 years
8% graduated in 6 years
1753 organizations recruited on campus

Financial Matters

$4534 resident tuition and fees (2007–08)
$11,825 nonresident tuition and fees (2007–08)
$7058 room and board
87% average percent of need met
$9316 average financial aid amount received per undergraduate (2005–06)

Getting Accepted
22,645 applied
16% were accepted
2,385 enrolled (66% of accepted)
96% from top tenth of their h.s. class
3.83 average high school GPA
Mean SAT critical reading score: 697
Mean SAT math score: 719
Mean SAT writing score: 702
Mean ACT score: 31
93% had SAT critical reading scores over 600
95% had SAT math scores over 600
93% had SAT writing scores over 600
97% had ACT scores over 24
53% had SAT critical reading scores over 700
65% had SAT math scores over 700
57% had SAT writing scores over 700
70% had ACT scores over 30
115 National Merit Scholars
69 class presidents
212 valedictorians

Graduation and After
87% graduated in 4 years
6% graduated in 5 years
2% graduated in 6 years
21% pursued further study (5% arts and sciences, 5% law, 5% medicine)
72% had job offers within 6 months
625 organizations recruited on campus

Financial Matters
$35,916 tuition and fees (2007–08)
$10,208 room and board
100% average percent of need met
$28,633 average financial aid amount received per undergraduate (2005–06)

UNIVERSITY OF PENNSYLVANIA
URBAN SETTING ■ PRIVATE ■ INDEPENDENT ■ COED
PHILADELPHIA, PENNSYLVANIA

Web site: www.upenn.edu
Contact: Eric J. Kaplan, Interim Dean of Admissions, 1 College Hall, Levy Park, Philadelphia, PA 19104
Telephone: 215-898-7507
E-mail: info@admissions.ugao.upenn.edu

Academics
Penn awards associate, bachelor's, master's, doctoral, and first-professional **degrees** and post-bachelor's, post-master's, and first-professional certificates (also offers evening program with significant enrollment not reflected in profile). **Challenging opportunities** include advanced placement credit, accelerated degree programs, student-designed majors, an honors program, double majors, independent study, and a senior project. Special programs include internships, summer session for credit, off-campus study, study-abroad, and Army, Navy, and Air Force ROTC.

The most frequently chosen **baccalaureate** fields are business/marketing, social sciences, and engineering. A complete listing of majors at Penn appears in the Majors by College index beginning on page 471.

The **faculty** at Penn has 1,395 full-time members, 100% with terminal degrees. The student-faculty ratio is 6:1.

Students of Penn
The student body totals 18,916, of whom 9,687 are undergraduates. 49.2% are women and 50.8% are men. Students come from 54 states and territories and 111 other countries. 19% are from Pennsylvania. 10.2% are international students. 7.6% are African American, 0.4% American Indian, 17.4% Asian American, and 5.8% Hispanic American. 98% returned for their sophomore year.

Facilities and Resources
1,295 **computers/terminals** and 1,472 ports are available on campus for general student use. Students can access the following: campus intranet, computer help desk, free student e-mail accounts, online (class) grades, online (class) registration, online (class) schedules, billing information, financial aid application, status, academic records, student services. Campuswide network is available. 100% of college-owned or -operated housing units are wired for high-speed Internet access. Wireless service is available via classrooms, computer centers, computer labs, dorm rooms, learning centers, libraries, student centers. The 16 **libraries** have 5,880,490 books and 47,787 subscriptions.

Campus Life
There are 350 active organizations on campus, including a drama/theater group, newspaper, radio station, television station, choral group, and marching band. 24% of eligible men and 17% of eligible women are members of national **fraternities** and national **sororities**.

Penn is a member of the NCAA (Division I). **Intercollegiate sports** include baseball (m), basketball, crew, cross-country running, fencing, field hockey (w), football (m), golf, gymnastics (w), lacrosse, soccer, softball (w), squash, swimming and diving, tennis, track and field, volleyball (w), wrestling (m).

Campus Safety
Student safety services include late-night transport/escort service, 24-hour emergency telephone alarm devices, 24-hour patrols by trained security personnel, and electronically operated dormitory entrances.

Applying
Penn requires an essay, SAT and SAT Subject Tests or ACT, a high school transcript, and 2 recommendations. Application deadline: 1/1; 2/1 priority date for financial aid. Early and deferred admission are possible.

UNIVERSITY OF PITTSBURGH

URBAN SETTING ■ PUBLIC ■ STATE-RELATED ■ COED
PITTSBURGH, PENNSYLVANIA

Web site: www.pitt.edu
Contact: Dr. Betsy A. Porter, Director of Office of Admissions and Financial Aid, 4227 Fifth Avenue, First Floor, Alumni Hall, Pittsburgh, PA 15260
Telephone: 412-624-7488
Fax: 412-648-8815
E-mail: oafa@pitt.edu

Academics

Pitt awards bachelor's, master's, doctoral, and first-professional **degrees** and post-bachelor's and post-master's certificates. **Challenging opportunities** include advanced placement credit, accelerated degree programs, student-designed majors, freshman honors college, an honors program, double majors, independent study, and a senior project. Special programs include cooperative education, internships, summer session for credit, off-campus study, study-abroad, and Army, Navy, and Air Force ROTC.

The most frequently chosen **baccalaureate** fields are business/marketing, social sciences, and engineering. A complete listing of majors at Pitt appears in the Majors by College index beginning on page 471.

The **faculty** at Pitt has 1,574 full-time members, 92% with terminal degrees. The student-faculty ratio is 16:1.

Students of Pitt

The student body totals 27,020, of whom 17,208 are undergraduates. 51.2% are women and 48.8% are men. Students come from 50 states and territories and 40 other countries. 83% are from Pennsylvania. 0.8% are international students. 8.4% are African American, 0.2% American Indian, 4.7% Asian American, and 1.3% Hispanic American. 90% returned for their sophomore year.

Facilities and Resources

1,150 **computers/terminals** and 1,150 ports are available on campus for general student use. Students can access the following: campus intranet, computer help desk, free student e-mail accounts, online (class) grades, online (class) schedules, online class listings, online tuition payment. Campuswide network is available. 100% of college-owned or -operated housing units are wired for high-speed Internet access. Wireless service is available via entire campus. The 26 **libraries** have 4,640,279 books and 3,767 subscriptions.

Campus Life

There are 300 active organizations on campus, including a drama/theater group, newspaper, radio station, television station, choral group, and marching band. 8% of eligible men and 8% of eligible women are members of national **fraternities** and national **sororities**.

Pitt is a member of the NCAA (Division I). **Intercollegiate sports** (some offering scholarships) include baseball (m), basketball, cross-country running, football (m), gymnastics (w), soccer, softball (w), swimming and diving, tennis (w), track and field, volleyball (w), wrestling (m).

Campus Safety

Student safety services include on-call van transportation, late-night transport/escort service, 24-hour emergency telephone alarm devices, 24-hour patrols by trained security personnel, and electronically operated dormitory entrances.

Applying

Pitt requires SAT or ACT and a high school transcript. It recommends an essay, an interview, and recommendations. Application deadline: rolling admissions; 6/1 for financial aid, with a 3/1 priority date. Early admission is possible.

Getting Accepted

19,056 applied
56% were accepted
3,432 enrolled (32% of accepted)
48% from top tenth of their h.s. class
Mean SAT critical reading score: 619
Mean SAT math score: 629
Mean ACT score: 27
60% had SAT critical reading scores over 600
69% had SAT math scores over 600
83% had ACT scores over 24
18% had SAT critical reading scores over 700
18% had SAT math scores over 700
26% had ACT scores over 30
20 National Merit Scholars
239 valedictorians

Graduation and After

55% graduated in 4 years
18% graduated in 5 years
2% graduated in 6 years
40% pursued further study (8% education, 6% arts and sciences, 5% business)

Financial Matters

$12,876 resident tuition and fees (2007–08)
$22,386 nonresident tuition and fees (2007–08)
$8300 room and board
79% average percent of need met
$9087 average financial aid amount received per undergraduate (2006–07 estimated)

UNIVERSITY OF PORTLAND

URBAN SETTING ■ PRIVATE ■ INDEPENDENT RELIGIOUS ■ COED
PORTLAND, OREGON

Web site: www.up.edu
Contact: Mr. Jason McDonald, Dean of Admissions, 5000 North Willamette
   Boulevard, Portland, OR 97203
Telephone: 503-943-7147 or toll-free 888-627-5601 (out-of-state)
Fax: 503-943-7315
E-mail: admissions@up.edu

Getting Accepted
7,139 applied
59% were accepted
805 enrolled (19% of accepted)
3.66 average high school GPA
Mean SAT critical reading score: 589
Mean SAT math score: 594
45% had SAT critical reading scores over 600
52% had SAT math scores over 600
10% had SAT critical reading scores over 700
9% had SAT math scores over 700

Graduation and After
60% graduated in 4 years
9% graduated in 5 years
1% graduated in 6 years
10% pursued further study
175 organizations recruited on campus

Financial Matters
$28,854 tuition and fees (2007–08)
$8300 room and board
94% average percent of need met
$21,821 average financial aid amount received
   per undergraduate (2005–06 estimated)

Academics

U of P awards bachelor's and master's **degrees** and post-bachelor's and post-master's
certificates. **Challenging opportunities** include advanced placement credit, an honors
program, double majors, independent study, and a senior project. Special programs
include internships, summer session for credit, off-campus study, study-abroad, and
Army and Air Force ROTC.

The most frequently chosen **baccalaureate** fields are health professions and related
sciences, business/marketing, and biological/life sciences. A complete listing of majors at
U of P appears in the Majors by College index beginning on page 471.

The **faculty** at U of P has 199 full-time members, 91% with terminal degrees. The
student-faculty ratio is 13:1.

Students of U of P

The student body totals 3,667, of whom 3,027 are undergraduates. 61.9% are women
and 38.1% are men. Students come from 39 states and territories and 19 other countries.
41% are from Oregon. 1.8% are international students. 1.2% are African American,
0.8% American Indian, 10.3% Asian American, and 3.9% Hispanic American. 85%
returned for their sophomore year.

Facilities and Resources

575 **computers/terminals** and 1,950 ports are available on campus for general student
use. Students can access the following: campus intranet, computer help desk, free student
e-mail accounts, online (class) grades, online (class) registration, online (class) schedules.
Campuswide network is available. 90% of college-owned or -operated housing units are
wired for high-speed Internet access. Wireless service is available via classrooms, dorm
rooms, learning centers, libraries, student centers. The 2 **libraries** have 350,000 books
and 1,400 subscriptions.

Campus Life

There are 40 active organizations on campus, including a drama/theater group,
newspaper, radio station, and choral group. No national or local **fraternities** or **sororities**.

U of P is a member of the NCAA (Division I). **Intercollegiate sports** (some offering
scholarships) include baseball (m), basketball, cross-country running, golf, soccer, tennis,
track and field, volleyball (w).

Campus Safety

Student safety services include late-night transport/escort service, 24-hour patrols by
trained security personnel, student patrols, and electronically operated dormitory
entrances.

Applying

U of P requires an essay, SAT or ACT, a high school transcript, and 1 recommendation.
Application deadline: 6/1; 3/1 priority date for financial aid. Deferred admission is possible.

University of Puget Sound

Suburban setting ■ Private ■ Independent ■ Coed
Tacoma, Washington

Web site: www.ups.edu
Contact: Dr. George Mills, Vice President for Enrollment, 1500 North
　Warner Street, Tacoma, WA 98416-1062
Telephone: 253-879-3211 or toll-free 800-396-7191
Fax: 253-879-3993
E-mail: admission@ups.edu

Academics

Puget Sound awards bachelor's, master's, and first-professional **degrees** and post-master's certificates. **Challenging opportunities** include advanced placement credit, student-designed majors, an honors program, double majors, independent study, and a senior project. Special programs include cooperative education, internships, summer session for credit, study-abroad, and Army ROTC.

The most frequently chosen **baccalaureate** fields are social sciences, business/marketing, and visual and performing arts. A complete listing of majors at Puget Sound appears in the Majors by College index beginning on page 471.

The **faculty** at Puget Sound has 224 full-time members, 88% with terminal degrees. The student-faculty ratio is 11:1.

Students of Puget Sound

The student body totals 2,799, of whom 2,539 are undergraduates. 58.5% are women and 41.5% are men. Students come from 47 states and territories and 19 other countries. 29% are from Washington. 0.3% are international students. 2.7% are African American, 1.3% American Indian, 9.1% Asian American, and 3.9% Hispanic American. 86% returned for their sophomore year.

Facilities and Resources

314 **computers/terminals** and 5,000 ports are available on campus for general student use. Students can access the following: campus intranet, computer help desk, free student e-mail accounts, online (class) grades, online (class) registration, online (class) schedules, financial aid, admission, student employment, library. Campuswide network is available. 100% of college-owned or -operated housing units are wired for high-speed Internet access. Wireless service is available via entire campus. The **library** has 364,662 books and 20,008 subscriptions.

Campus Life

There are 65 active organizations on campus, including a drama/theater group, newspaper, radio station, and choral group. 23% of eligible men and 22% of eligible women are members of national **fraternities** and national **sororities**.

Puget Sound is a member of the NCAA (Division III). **Intercollegiate sports** include baseball (m), basketball, cheerleading, crew, cross-country running, football (m), golf, lacrosse (w), soccer, softball (w), swimming and diving, tennis, track and field, volleyball (w).

Campus Safety

Student safety services include 24-hour locked residence hall entrances, late-night transport/escort service, 24-hour emergency telephone alarm devices, 24-hour patrols by trained security personnel, student patrols, and electronically operated dormitory entrances.

Applying

Puget Sound requires an essay, SAT or ACT, a high school transcript, 2 recommendations, and School Report. It recommends an interview and a minimum high school GPA of 3.0. Application deadline: 2/1; 2/1 priority date for financial aid. Early and deferred admission are possible.

Getting Accepted

5,273 applied
66% were accepted
644 enrolled (18% of accepted)
40% from top tenth of their h.s. class
3.54 average high school GPA
Mean SAT critical reading score: 623
Mean SAT math score: 608
Mean SAT writing score: 607
Mean ACT score: 27
64% had SAT critical reading scores over 600
58% had SAT math scores over 600
58% had SAT writing scores over 600
86% had ACT scores over 24
21% had SAT critical reading scores over 700
11% had SAT math scores over 700
12% had SAT writing scores over 700
25% had ACT scores over 30
48 National Merit Scholars

Graduation and After

68% graduated in 4 years
8% graduated in 5 years
1% graduated in 6 years
36% pursued further study (12% arts and sciences, 7% education, 3% medicine)
63% had job offers within 6 months
68 organizations recruited on campus

Financial Matters

$31,895 tuition and fees (2007–08)
$8265 room and board
82% average percent of need met
$22,740 average financial aid amount received per undergraduate (2006–07 estimated)

At the University of Redlands, students explore connections, blurring the barriers often artificially imposed between academic disciplines, between the classroom and the real world, and between their own views and the way others see things. Academics are combined with a community-based residential life and a range of opportunities to gain firsthand experience through internships, international study, and original faculty-directed research. Students take ownership of their education with the active support of professors who are truly committed to student participation in the learning process; they coax, challenge, captivate, support, nourish, and actively engage students in an exchange of stimulating and provocative ideas.

Getting Accepted
3,607 applied
67% were accepted
31% from top tenth of their h.s. class
3.58 average high school GPA
Mean SAT critical reading score: 590
Mean SAT math score: 586
Mean ACT score: 24
35% had SAT critical reading scores over 600
35% had SAT math scores over 600
56% had ACT scores over 24
7% had SAT critical reading scores over 700
3% had SAT math scores over 700
8% had ACT scores over 30

Graduation and After
54% graduated in 4 years
5% graduated in 5 years
2% graduated in 6 years
45% pursued further study
51% had job offers within 6 months
6 organizations recruited on campus

Financial Matters
$30,626 tuition and fees (2007–08)
$9782 room and board
91% average percent of need met
$25,693 average financial aid amount received
    per undergraduate (2006–07 estimated)

UNIVERSITY OF REDLANDS
SMALL-TOWN SETTING ■ PRIVATE ■ INDEPENDENT ■ COED
REDLANDS, CALIFORNIA

Web site: www.redlands.edu
Contact: Mr. Paul Driscoll, Dean of Admissions, PO Box 3080, Redlands, CA 92373-0999
Telephone: 909-748-8159 or toll-free 800-455-5064
Fax: 909-335-4089
E-mail: admissions@redlands.edu

Academics
Redlands awards bachelor's and master's **degrees** and post-bachelor's and post-master's certificates. **Challenging opportunities** include advanced placement credit, student-designed majors, freshman honors college, an honors program, double majors, independent study, and a senior project. Special programs include internships, off-campus study, study-abroad, and Army and Air Force ROTC.

The most frequently chosen **baccalaureate** fields are liberal arts/general studies, business/marketing, and social sciences. A complete listing of majors at Redlands appears in the Majors by College index beginning on page 471.

The **faculty** at Redlands has 173 full-time members, 87% with terminal degrees.

Students of Redlands
The student body totals 2,445, of whom 2,354 are undergraduates. 57.2% are women and 42.8% are men. Students come from 44 states and territories and 14 other countries. 67% are from California. 1% are international students. 2.6% are African American, 0.3% American Indian, 5.6% Asian American, and 12.1% Hispanic American. 86% returned for their sophomore year.

Facilities and Resources
746 **computers/terminals** and 835 ports are available on campus for general student use. Students can access the following: campus intranet, computer help desk, free student e-mail accounts, online (class) grades, online (class) registration, online (class) schedules. Campuswide network is available. 100% of college-owned or -operated housing units are wired for high-speed Internet access. Wireless service is available via entire campus. The **library** has 268,387 books and 11,800 subscriptions.

Campus Life
There are 105 active organizations on campus, including a drama/theater group, newspaper, radio station, and choral group. 10% of eligible men and 13% of eligible women are members of local **fraternities** and local **sororities**.

Redlands is a member of the NCAA (Division III). **Intercollegiate sports** include baseball (m), basketball, cross-country running, football (m), golf, lacrosse (w), soccer, softball (w), swimming and diving, tennis, track and field, volleyball (w), water polo.

Campus Safety
Student safety services include safety whistles, late-night transport/escort service, 24-hour emergency telephone alarm devices, 24-hour patrols by trained security personnel, student patrols, and electronically operated dormitory entrances.

Applying
Redlands requires an essay, SAT or ACT, a high school transcript, and 2 recommendations. It recommends an interview. Application deadline: 4/1; 2/15 priority date for financial aid. Deferred admission is possible.

University of Rhode Island

Small-town setting ■ Public ■ State-supported ■ Coed
Kingston, Rhode Island

Web site: www.uri.edu
Contact: Ms. Joanne Hood, Assistant Dean of Admissions, Undergrad
   Admission Office, Newman Hall, 14 Upper College Rd., Kingston, RI
   02881
Telephone: 401-874-7110
Fax: 401-874-5523
E-mail: jhood@uri.edu

SPONSOR

Academics

Rhode Island awards bachelor's, master's, doctoral, and first-professional **degrees** and post-bachelor's certificates. **Challenging opportunities** include advanced placement credit, an honors program, double majors, independent study, and a senior project. Special programs include cooperative education, internships, summer session for credit, off-campus study, study-abroad, and Army ROTC.

The most frequently chosen **baccalaureate** fields are business/marketing, communications/journalism, and health professions and related sciences. A complete listing of majors at Rhode Island appears in the Majors by College index beginning on page 471.

The **faculty** at Rhode Island has 704 full-time members, 89% with terminal degrees. The student-faculty ratio is 19:1.

Students of Rhode Island

The student body totals 15,650, of whom 12,516 are undergraduates. 56% are women and 44% are men. Students come from 38 states and territories. 61% are from Rhode Island. 0.3% are international students. 4.9% are African American, 0.5% American Indian, 2.4% Asian American, and 4.8% Hispanic American. 81% returned for their sophomore year.

Facilities and Resources

552 **computers/terminals** are available on campus for general student use. Campuswide network is available. The 2 **libraries** have 1,205,138 books and 7,926 subscriptions.

Campus Life

There are 85 active organizations on campus, including a drama/theater group, newspaper, radio station, television station, choral group, and marching band. 12% of eligible men and 15% of eligible women are members of national **fraternities**, national **sororities**, and local sororities.

Rhode Island is a member of the NCAA (Division I). **Intercollegiate sports** (some offering scholarships) include baseball (m), basketball, crew (w), cross-country running, field hockey (w), football (m), golf (m), gymnastics (w), soccer, softball (w), swimming and diving, tennis, track and field, volleyball (w).

Campus Safety

Student safety services include late-night transport/escort service, 24-hour emergency telephone alarm devices, 24-hour patrols by trained security personnel, student patrols, and electronically operated dormitory entrances.

Applying

Rhode Island requires SAT or ACT and a high school transcript, and in some cases a minimum high school GPA of 3.0. It recommends an interview, recommendations, and a minimum high school GPA of 3.0. Application deadline: 2/1; 3/1 priority date for financial aid. Early admission is possible.

Getting Accepted
14,272 applied
79% were accepted
3,027 enrolled (27% of accepted)
12% from top tenth of their h.s. class
Mean SAT critical reading score: 552
Mean SAT math score: 568
26% had SAT critical reading scores over 600
28% had SAT math scores over 600
2% had SAT critical reading scores over 700
4% had SAT math scores over 700

Graduation and After
38% graduated in 4 years
17% graduated in 5 years
2% graduated in 6 years
155 organizations recruited on campus

Financial Matters
$8184 resident tuition and fees (2007–08)
$23,038 nonresident tuition and fees (2007–08)
$8732 room and board
63% average percent of need met
$12,707 average financial aid amount received per undergraduate (2006–07 estimated)

UNIVERSITY OF RICHMOND

SUBURBAN SETTING ■ PRIVATE ■ INDEPENDENT ■ COED
UNIVERSITY OF RICHMOND, VIRGINIA

Web site: www.richmond.edu
Contact: Ms. Pamela Spence, Dean of Admission, 28 Westhampton Way,
  University of Richmond, VA 23173
Telephone: 804-289-8640 or toll-free 800-700-1662
Fax: 804-287-6003
E-mail: admissions@richmond.edu

Getting Accepted
6,649 applied
40% were accepted
801 enrolled (30% of accepted)
62% from top tenth of their h.s. class
Mean SAT critical reading score: 634
Mean SAT math score: 646
Mean SAT writing score: 639
Mean ACT score: 29
71% had SAT critical reading scores over 600
80% had SAT math scores over 600
75% had SAT writing scores over 600
95% had ACT scores over 24
21% had SAT critical reading scores over 700
24% had SAT math scores over 700
23% had SAT writing scores over 700
52% had ACT scores over 30
9 National Merit Scholars
58 class presidents
22 valedictorians

Graduation and After
81% graduated in 4 years
5% graduated in 5 years
27% pursued further study
264 organizations recruited on campus

Financial Matters
$38,850 tuition and fees (2008–09)
$8200 room and board
100% average percent of need met
$27,205 average financial aid amount received
  per undergraduate (2006–07 estimated)

Academics

Richmond awards associate, bachelor's, master's, and first-professional **degrees** and post-bachelor's certificates. **Challenging opportunities** include advanced placement credit, accelerated degree programs, student-designed majors, an honors program, double majors, independent study, and a senior project. Special programs include cooperative education, internships, summer session for credit, off-campus study, study-abroad, and Army ROTC.

The most frequently chosen **baccalaureate** fields are business/marketing, social sciences, and English. A complete listing of majors at Richmond appears in the Majors by College index beginning on page 471.

The **faculty** at Richmond has 286 full-time members, 92% with terminal degrees. The student-faculty ratio is 9:1.

Students of Richmond

The student body totals 3,448, of whom 2,795 are undergraduates. 49.3% are women and 50.7% are men. Students come from 45 states and territories and 72 other countries. 17% are from Virginia. 6.8% are international students. 5.9% are African American, 0.3% American Indian, 4.1% Asian American, and 3.1% Hispanic American. 91% returned for their sophomore year.

Facilities and Resources

700 **computers/terminals** are available on campus for general student use. Students can access the following: campus intranet, computer help desk, free student e-mail accounts, online (class) registration, online (class) schedules. Campuswide network is available. 100% of college-owned or -operated housing units are wired for high-speed Internet access. Wireless service is available via entire campus. The 3 **libraries** have 1,098,581 books and 43,747 subscriptions.

Campus Life

There are 275 active organizations on campus, including a drama/theater group, newspaper, radio station, and choral group. 28% of eligible men and 43% of eligible women are members of national **fraternities** and national **sororities**.

Richmond is a member of the NCAA (Division I). **Intercollegiate sports** (some offering scholarships) include baseball (m), basketball, cheerleading, cross-country running, field hockey (w), football (m), golf, lacrosse (w), soccer, swimming and diving (w), tennis, track and field.

Campus Safety

Student safety services include campus police, late-night transport/escort service, 24-hour emergency telephone alarm devices, 24-hour patrols by trained security personnel, and electronically operated dormitory entrances.

Applying

Richmond requires an essay, SAT or ACT, a high school transcript, 1 recommendation, signed character statement, and a minimum high school GPA of 2.0. Application deadline: 1/15; 2/25 for financial aid. Early and deferred admission are possible.

University of Rochester

Suburban setting ■ Private ■ Independent ■ Coed
Rochester, New York

SPONSOR

Web site: www.rochester.edu
Contact: Admissions Office, PO Box 270251, 300 Wilson Boulevard,
  Rochester, NY 14627-0251
Telephone: 585-275-3221 or toll-free 888-822-2256
Fax: 585-461-4595
E-mail: admit@admissions.rochester.edu

Academics

Rochester awards bachelor's, master's, doctoral, and first-professional **degrees** and post-bachelor's, post-master's, and first-professional certificates. **Challenging opportunities** include advanced placement credit, accelerated degree programs, student-designed majors, an honors program, double majors, and independent study. Special programs include internships, summer session for credit, off-campus study, study-abroad, and Army, Navy, and Air Force ROTC.

The most frequently chosen **baccalaureate** fields are social sciences, visual and performing arts, and biological/life sciences. A complete listing of majors at Rochester appears in the Majors by College index beginning on page 471.

The **faculty** at Rochester has 515 full-time members, 88% with terminal degrees. The student-faculty ratio is 9:1.

Students of Rochester

The student body totals 9,334, of whom 5,131 are undergraduates. 50.9% are women and 49.1% are men. Students come from 52 states and territories and 52 other countries. 46% are from New York. 5.6% are international students. 4.4% are African American, 0.2% American Indian, 9.9% Asian American, and 3.9% Hispanic American. 93% returned for their sophomore year.

Facilities and Resources

450 **computers/terminals** and 4,000 ports are available on campus for general student use. Students can access the following: computer help desk, free student e-mail accounts, online (class) grades, online (class) registration, online (class) schedules. Campuswide network is available. 100% of college-owned or -operated housing units are wired for high-speed Internet access. Wireless service is available via classrooms, computer centers, computer labs, learning centers, libraries, student centers. The 6 **libraries** have 2,992,204 books and 11,254 subscriptions.

Campus Life

There are 220 active organizations on campus, including a drama/theater group, newspaper, radio station, television station, and choral group. 19% of eligible men and 20% of eligible women are members of national **fraternities** and national **sororities**.

Rochester is a member of the NCAA (Division III). **Intercollegiate sports** include baseball (m), basketball, cross-country running, field hockey (w), football (m), golf (m), lacrosse (w), soccer, softball (w), squash (m), swimming and diving, tennis, track and field, volleyball (w).

Campus Safety

Student safety services include late-night transport/escort service, 24-hour emergency telephone alarm devices, 24-hour patrols by trained security personnel, and electronically operated dormitory entrances.

Applying

Rochester requires an essay, SAT or ACT, a high school transcript, and 1 recommendation, and in some cases SAT and SAT Subject Tests or ACT and audition, portfolio. It recommends SAT Subject Tests, an interview, and 2 recommendations. Application deadline: 1/1, 1/1 for nonresidents; 2/1 priority date for financial aid. Early and deferred admission are possible.

Founded in 1850, the University of Rochester is one of the most innovative private research universities in the country. Rochester offers the diversity of a major university while fostering more individual attention from faculty members. Programs are available in six divisions, including the College (Arts and Sciences and Engineering), Nursing, Education, Business, Medicine, and the Eastman School of Music. The open curriculum eliminates general education courses. Instead, students define a personal course plan based on their own interests, taking advantage of such distinctive opportunities as Take Five (a tuition-free fifth year of study); unique research, study-abroad, and internship options; and guaranteed bachelor's/master's or professional programs, including an eight-year medical program, a six-year business program, and a five-year program in education.

Getting Accepted
11,676 applied
41% were accepted
1,182 enrolled (25% of accepted)
72% from top tenth of their h.s. class
3.72 average high school GPA
Mean SAT critical reading score: 641
Mean SAT math score: 655
Mean ACT score: 29
75% had SAT critical reading scores over 600
84% had SAT math scores over 600
94% had ACT scores over 24
26% had SAT critical reading scores over 700
34% had SAT math scores over 700
45% had ACT scores over 30
32 National Merit Scholars
65 class presidents
46 valedictorians

Graduation and After
71% graduated in 4 years
8% graduated in 5 years
1% graduated in 6 years
47% pursued further study
57% had job offers within 6 months
127 organizations recruited on campus

Financial Matters
$35,190 tuition and fees (2007–08)
$10,640 room and board
86% average percent of need met
$26,667 average financial aid amount received
  per undergraduate (2006–07 estimated)

Getting Accepted
4,652 applied
83% were accepted
1,299 enrolled (34% of accepted)
19% from top tenth of their h.s. class
3.53 average high school GPA
Mean SAT critical reading score: 582
Mean SAT math score: 582
Mean ACT score: 25
42% had SAT critical reading scores over 600
42% had SAT math scores over 600
62% had ACT scores over 24
9% had SAT critical reading scores over 700
9% had SAT math scores over 700
8% had ACT scores over 30
11 National Merit Scholars
34 valedictorians

Graduation and After
62% graduated in 4 years
12% graduated in 5 years
2% graduated in 6 years
85% had job offers within 6 months
60 organizations recruited on campus

Financial Matters
$26,274 tuition and fees (2007–08)
$7312 room and board
78% average percent of need met
$17,223 average financial aid amount received per undergraduate (2006–07 estimated)

UNIVERSITY OF ST. THOMAS
URBAN SETTING ■ PRIVATE ■ INDEPENDENT RELIGIOUS ■ COED
ST. PAUL, MINNESOTA

Web site: www.stthomas.edu
Contact: Ms. Marla Friederichs, Associate Vice President of Enrollment Management, Mail #32F-1, 2115 Summit Avenue, St. Paul, MN 55105-1096
Telephone: 651-962-6150 or toll-free 800-328-6819 Ext. 26150
Fax: 651-962-6160
E-mail: admissions@stthomas.edu

Academics
St. Thomas awards bachelor's, master's, doctoral, and first-professional **degrees** and post-bachelor's and post-master's certificates. **Challenging opportunities** include advanced placement credit, student-designed majors, an honors program, double majors, independent study, and a senior project. Special programs include internships, summer session for credit, off-campus study, study-abroad, and Army, Navy, and Air Force ROTC. A complete listing of majors at St. Thomas appears in the Majors by College index beginning on page 471.

The **faculty** at St. Thomas has 395 full-time members.

Students of St. Thomas
The student body totals 10,712, of whom 5,807 are undergraduates. 50% are women and 50% are men. Students come from 44 states and territories and 7 other countries. 56% are from Minnesota. 1% are international students. 3.3% are African American, 0.6% American Indian, 4.5% Asian American, and 2.1% Hispanic American. 88% returned for their sophomore year.

Facilities and Resources
1,549 **computers/terminals** are available on campus for general student use. Students can access the following: online (class) registration. Campuswide network is available. The 4 **libraries** have 510,355 books and 2,743 subscriptions.

Campus Life
There are 94 active organizations on campus, including a drama/theater group, newspaper, and choral group. No national or local **fraternities** or **sororities**.

St. Thomas is a member of the NCAA (Division III). **Intercollegiate sports** include baseball (m), basketball, cross-country running, football (m), golf, ice hockey, soccer, softball (w), swimming and diving, tennis, track and field, volleyball (w).

Campus Safety
Student safety services include late-night transport/escort service, 24-hour emergency telephone alarm devices, 24-hour patrols by trained security personnel, and electronically operated dormitory entrances.

Applying
St. Thomas requires an essay, SAT or ACT, and a high school transcript. It recommends an interview and recommendations. Application deadline: rolling admissions. Deferred admission is possible.

UNIVERSITY OF ST. THOMAS

URBAN SETTING ■ PRIVATE ■ INDEPENDENT RELIGIOUS ■ COED
HOUSTON, TEXAS

Web site: www.stthom.edu
Contact: 3800 Montrose Boulevard, Houston, TX 77006-4696
Telephone: 713-525-3500 or toll-free 800-856-8565
Fax: 713-525-3558
E-mail: admissions@stthom.edu

Academics

St. Thomas awards bachelor's, master's, doctoral, and first-professional **degrees**. **Challenging opportunities** include advanced placement credit, an honors program, double majors, independent study, and a senior project. Special programs include internships, summer session for credit, off-campus study, study-abroad, and Army ROTC.

The most frequently chosen **baccalaureate** fields are business/marketing, liberal arts/general studies, and social sciences. A complete listing of majors at St. Thomas appears in the Majors by College index beginning on page 471.

The **faculty** at St. Thomas has 131 full-time members, 91% with terminal degrees. The student-faculty ratio is 12:1.

Students of St. Thomas

The student body totals 3,350, of whom 1,708 are undergraduates. 61% are women and 39% are men. Students come from 30 states and territories and 57 other countries. 96% are from Texas. 4.4% are international students. 4.7% are African American, 0.6% American Indian, 11.1% Asian American, and 28.5% Hispanic American. 68% returned for their sophomore year.

Facilities and Resources

Students can access the following: computer help desk, free student e-mail accounts, online (class) grades, online (class) registration, online (class) schedules. Campuswide network is available. Wireless service is available via entire campus. The 2 **libraries** have 223,898 books and 19,351 subscriptions.

Campus Life

There are 69 active organizations on campus, including a drama/theater group, newspaper, and choral group. No national or local **fraternities** or **sororities**.

This institution has no intercollegiate sports.

Campus Safety

Student safety services include late-night transport/escort service, 24-hour emergency telephone alarm devices, 24-hour patrols by trained security personnel, and electronically operated dormitory entrances.

Applying

St. Thomas requires an essay, SAT or ACT, a high school transcript, and a minimum high school GPA of 2.50. Application deadline: rolling admissions; 3/1 priority date for financial aid. Deferred admission is possible.

Getting Accepted
861 applied
84% were accepted
294 enrolled (41% of accepted)
27% from top tenth of their h.s. class
3.41 average high school GPA
Mean SAT critical reading score: 566
Mean SAT math score: 574
Mean SAT writing score: 558
Mean ACT score: 24
37% had SAT critical reading scores over 600
38% had SAT math scores over 600
31% had SAT writing scores over 600
54% had ACT scores over 24
8% had SAT critical reading scores over 700
5% had SAT math scores over 700
6% had SAT writing scores over 700
7% had ACT scores over 30
1 valedictorian

Graduation and After
25% graduated in 4 years
25% graduated in 5 years
5% graduated in 6 years
28 organizations recruited on campus

Financial Matters
$18,900 tuition and fees (2007–08)
$7300 room and board
64% average percent of need met
$13,302 average financial aid amount received
  per undergraduate (2006–07 estimated)

The breadth of programs and depth of facilities at the University of San Diego (USD) mean that students can easily find a course of study that ignites their intellectual fire. In the classroom, course work across disciplines encourages students to develop their critical-thinking skills. Small class size means the instructors know their students and can stimulate curious minds with anything from a spot on a research project to an after-class discussion on topic. In this environment, students begin a lifelong habit of appreciating and cultivating their individual gifts. To complement this instruction, USD's honors program provides a challenging curriculum for USD's uniquely motivated students. Honors students have numerous opportunities for individual counseling and discussions with honors faculty members. USD's 180-acre campus sits atop a mesa overlooking San Diego, Mission Bay, and the Pacific Ocean.

Getting Accepted
10,563 applied
48% were accepted
1,094 enrolled (22% of accepted)
38% from top tenth of their h.s. class
3.76 average high school GPA
Mean SAT critical reading score: 579
Mean SAT math score: 596
Mean SAT writing score: 586
Mean ACT score: 26
44% had SAT critical reading scores over 600
53% had SAT math scores over 600
47% had SAT writing scores over 600
80% had ACT scores over 24
6% had SAT critical reading scores over 700
8% had SAT math scores over 700
6% had SAT writing scores over 700
14% had ACT scores over 30

Graduation and After
63% graduated in 4 years
9% graduated in 5 years
1% graduated in 6 years
85% had job offers within 6 months
109 organizations recruited on campus

Financial Matters
$34,264 tuition and fees (2008–09)
$11,870 room and board
71% average percent of need met
$20,558 average financial aid amount received per undergraduate (2005–06)

UNIVERSITY OF SAN DIEGO
URBAN SETTING ■ PRIVATE ■ INDEPENDENT RELIGIOUS ■ COED
SAN DIEGO, CALIFORNIA

Web site: www.sandiego.edu
Contact: Mr. Stephen Pultz, Director of Admission, 5998 Alcala Park, San Diego, CA 92110
Telephone: 619-260-4506 or toll-free 800-248-4873
Fax: 619-260-6836
E-mail: admissions@sandiego.edu

Academics
USD awards bachelor's, master's, doctoral, and first-professional **degrees** and post-bachelor's, post-master's, and first-professional certificates. **Challenging opportunities** include advanced placement credit, an honors program, double majors, independent study, and a senior project. Special programs include internships, summer session for credit, study-abroad, and Army, Navy, and Air Force ROTC.

The most frequently chosen **baccalaureate** fields are business/marketing, social sciences, and communications/journalism. A complete listing of majors at USD appears in the Majors by College index beginning on page 471.

The **faculty** at USD has 367 full-time members, 95% with terminal degrees. The student-faculty ratio is 15:1.

Students of USD
The student body totals 7,504, of whom 4,932 are undergraduates. 58.1% are women and 41.9% are men. Students come from 50 states and territories. 64% are from California. 2.4% are international students. 2.3% are African American, 1.4% American Indian, 9.5% Asian American, and 14.1% Hispanic American. 85% returned for their sophomore year.

Facilities and Resources
Students can access the following: campus intranet, computer help desk, free student e-mail accounts, online (class) grades, online (class) registration, online (class) schedules. Campuswide network is available. 100% of college-owned or -operated housing units are wired for high-speed Internet access. The 2 **libraries** have 714,082 books and 10,451 subscriptions.

Campus Life
Active organizations on campus include a drama/theater group, newspaper, television station, and choral group. 16% of eligible men and 23% of eligible women are members of national **fraternities** and national **sororities**.

USD is a member of the NCAA (Division I). **Intercollegiate sports** (some offering scholarships) include baseball (m), basketball, crew, cross-country running, football (m), golf (m), soccer, softball (w), swimming and diving (w), tennis, track and field (w), volleyball (w).

Campus Safety
Student safety services include late-night transport/escort service, 24-hour emergency telephone alarm devices, 24-hour patrols by trained security personnel, student patrols, and electronically operated dormitory entrances.

Applying
USD requires an essay, SAT or ACT, a high school transcript, 1 recommendation, and SAT with Written or ACT. Application deadline: 1/15; 2/20 priority date for financial aid. Deferred admission is possible.

THE UNIVERSITY OF SCRANTON
URBAN SETTING ■ PRIVATE ■ INDEPENDENT RELIGIOUS ■ COED
SCRANTON, PENNSYLVANIA

SPONSOR

Web site: www.scranton.edu
Contact: Mr. Joseph Roback, Associate Vice President, Undergraduate
   Admissions and Enrollment, St. Thomas Hall, Room 409, Scranton, PA
   18510-4501
Telephone: 570-941-7540 or toll-free 888-SCRANTON
Fax: 570-941-4370
E-mail: admissions@scranton.edu

Academics
Scranton awards associate, bachelor's, master's, and doctoral **degrees** and post-bachelor's and post-master's certificates. **Challenging opportunities** include advanced placement credit, accelerated degree programs, student-designed majors, an honors program, double majors, independent study, and a senior project. Special programs include internships, summer session for credit, off-campus study, study-abroad, and Army and Air Force ROTC.

The most frequently chosen **baccalaureate** fields are business/marketing, health professions and related sciences, and education. A complete listing of majors at Scranton appears in the Majors by College index beginning on page 471.

The **faculty** at Scranton has 258 full-time members, 84% with terminal degrees. The student-faculty ratio is 11:1.

Students of Scranton
The student body totals 5,612, of whom 4,081 are undergraduates. 57.3% are women and 42.7% are men. Students come from 25 states and territories and 18 other countries. 48% are from Pennsylvania. 0.4% are international students. 1.3% are African American, 0.2% American Indian, 2.2% Asian American, and 4.7% Hispanic American. 90% returned for their sophomore year.

Facilities and Resources
927 **computers/terminals** are available on campus for general student use. Students can access the following: computer help desk, free student e-mail accounts, online (class) grades, online (class) registration, online (class) schedules. Campuswide network is available. 100% of college-owned or -operated housing units are wired for high-speed Internet access. Wireless service is available via classrooms, computer centers, computer labs, dorm rooms, learning centers, libraries, student centers. The 2 **libraries** have 481,542 books and 1,579 subscriptions.

Campus Life
There are 80 active organizations on campus, including a drama/theater group, newspaper, radio station, television station, and choral group. No national or local **fraternities** or **sororities**.

Scranton is a member of the NCAA (Division III). **Intercollegiate sports** include baseball (m), basketball, cross-country running, field hockey (w), golf (m), ice hockey (m), lacrosse (m), soccer, softball (w), swimming and diving, tennis, volleyball (w), wrestling (m).

Campus Safety
Student safety services include late-night transport/escort service, 24-hour emergency telephone alarm devices, 24-hour patrols by trained security personnel, student patrols, and electronically operated dormitory entrances.

Applying
Scranton requires an essay, SAT or ACT, a high school transcript, and recommendations, and in some cases an interview. Application deadline: 3/1; 2/15 priority date for financial aid. Early and deferred admission are possible.

The University of Scranton is known for its outstanding academic programs, well-equipped campus, state-of-the-art technology, and strong sense of community and has been nationally recognized for these qualities. For fourteen consecutive years, *U.S. News & World Report* has ranked Scranton among the ten finest master's universities in the North. For the fourth consecutive year, *U.S. News* has included Scranton among the fifteen colleges listed as "Great Schools at a Great Price" and named Scranton among the five schools in the North with the highest graduation rates. For the past six years, the Princeton Review has included Scranton among its "366 Best Colleges." For the second consecutive year, Scranton's Kania School of Management has been included among the elite colleges listed in the Princeton Review's "Best 282 Business Schools." Other national recognition includes *Kaplan/Newsweek's* 2008 "372 Most Interesting Schools" and inclusion in the latest edition of *Barron's Best Buys in College Education.* Only nineteen schools in Pennsylvania were listed. In addition, Scranton is one of only 100 schools in the nation on Templeton's Honor Roll of Character-Building Colleges.

Getting Accepted
7,609 applied
66% were accepted
1,027 enrolled (20% of accepted)
27% from top tenth of their h.s. class
3.36 average high school GPA
Mean SAT critical reading score: 555
Mean SAT math score: 566
25% had SAT critical reading scores over 600
33% had SAT math scores over 600
4% had SAT critical reading scores over 700
4% had SAT math scores over 700
14 valedictorians

Graduation and After
67% graduated in 4 years
10% graduated in 5 years
87 organizations recruited on campus

Financial Matters
$28,758 tuition and fees (2007–08)
$10,610 room and board
72% average percent of need met
$15,558 average financial aid amount received
   per undergraduate (2004–05 estimated)

SPONSOR

The University of South Carolina (USC) offers a wealth of resources for its high-achieving students. The Honors College provides intensive study, led by the University's top researchers and teachers. Competitive study-abroad grants are available, and assistance is provided for the pursuit of prestigious national awards such as Fulbright grants and Rotary and Truman scholarships. Fall freshman applicants who apply by the University's December 1 priority deadline receive consideration for attractive merit-based scholarships. USC has more than 350 degree programs, and many, such as the number one–ranked undergraduate international business program, receive prominent national accolades. Scholars flourish at USC.

Getting Accepted
14,994 applied
59% were accepted
3,719 enrolled (42% of accepted)
29% from top tenth of their h.s. class
3.87 average high school GPA
Mean SAT critical reading score: 582
Mean SAT math score: 600
Mean ACT score: 26
41% had SAT critical reading scores over 600
53% had SAT math scores over 600
73% had ACT scores over 24
8% had SAT critical reading scores over 700
8% had SAT math scores over 700
14% had ACT scores over 30
50 National Merit Scholars
63 valedictorians

Graduation and After
40% graduated in 4 years
19% graduated in 5 years
3% graduated in 6 years

Financial Matters
$8346 resident tuition and fees (2008–09)
$21,632 nonresident tuition and fees (2008–09)
$6946 room and board
73% average percent of need met
$9840 average financial aid amount received per undergraduate (2006–07 estimated)

UNIVERSITY OF SOUTH CAROLINA
URBAN SETTING ■ PUBLIC ■ STATE-SUPPORTED ■ COED
COLUMBIA, SOUTH CAROLINA

Web site: www.sc.edu
Contact: Mr. Scott Verzyl, Director of Undergraduate Admissions, Columbia, SC 29208
Telephone: 803-777-7700 or toll-free 800-868-5872 (in-state)
Fax: 803-777-0101
E-mail: admissions-ugrad@sc.edu

Academics
South Carolina awards bachelor's, master's, doctoral, and first-professional **degrees** and post-bachelor's and post-master's certificates. **Challenging opportunities** include advanced placement credit, accelerated degree programs, student-designed majors, freshman honors college, an honors program, double majors, independent study, and a senior project. Special programs include cooperative education, internships, summer session for credit, study-abroad, and Army, Navy, and Air Force ROTC.

The most frequently chosen **baccalaureate** fields are business/marketing, social sciences, and communication technologies. A complete listing of majors at South Carolina appears in the Majors by College index beginning on page 471.

The **faculty** at South Carolina has 1,250 full-time members, 84% with terminal degrees. The student-faculty ratio is 16:1.

Students of South Carolina
The student body totals 27,272, of whom 18,827 are undergraduates. 54.5% are women and 45.5% are men. Students come from 56 states and territories and 71 other countries. 76% are from South Carolina. 0.9% are international students. 12.4% are African American, 0.4% American Indian, 2.9% Asian American, and 2% Hispanic American. 87% returned for their sophomore year.

Facilities and Resources
2,800 **computers/terminals** are available on campus for general student use. Students can access the following: computer help desk, free student e-mail accounts, online (class) grades, online (class) registration, online (class) schedules. Campuswide network is available. 100% of college-owned or -operated housing units are wired for high-speed Internet access. Wireless service is available via entire campus. The 8 **libraries** have 3,560,258 books and 53,610 subscriptions.

Campus Life
There are 270 active organizations on campus, including a drama/theater group, newspaper, radio station, choral group, and marching band. 14% of eligible men and 15% of eligible women are members of national **fraternities** and national **sororities**.

South Carolina is a member of the NCAA (Division I). **Intercollegiate sports** (some offering scholarships) include baseball (m), basketball, cross-country running (w), equestrian sports (w), football (m), golf, soccer, softball (w), swimming and diving, tennis, track and field, volleyball (w).

Campus Safety
Student safety services include late-night transport/escort service, 24-hour emergency telephone alarm devices, 24-hour patrols by trained security personnel, student patrols, and electronically operated dormitory entrances.

Applying
South Carolina requires SAT or ACT, a high school transcript, and a minimum high school GPA of 2.00. Application deadline: 12/1; 4/1 priority date for financial aid.

University of Southern California

Urban setting ■ Private ■ Independent ■ Coed
Los Angeles, California

Web site: www.usc.edu
Contact: Katharine L. Harrington, Dean/Director of Admission, University Park Campus, Los Angeles, CA 90089
Telephone: 213-740-1111
Fax: 213-740-6364
E-mail: admitusc@usc.edu

Academics

USC awards bachelor's, master's, doctoral, and first-professional **degrees** and post-bachelor's, post-master's, and first-professional certificates. **Challenging opportunities** include advanced placement credit, accelerated degree programs, student-designed majors, freshman honors college, an honors program, double majors, independent study, and a senior project. Special programs include cooperative education, internships, summer session for credit, off-campus study, study-abroad, and Army, Navy, and Air Force ROTC.

The most frequently chosen **baccalaureate** fields are business/marketing, social sciences, and visual and performing arts. A complete listing of majors at USC appears in the Majors by College index beginning on page 471.

The **faculty** at USC has 1,625 full-time members, 90% with terminal degrees. The student-faculty ratio is 9:1.

Students of USC

The student body totals 33,408, of whom 16,384 are undergraduates. 49.9% are women and 50.1% are men. Students come from 58 states and territories and 115 other countries. 65% are from California. 9% are international students. 5.6% are African American, 0.8% American Indian, 21.7% Asian American, and 13.1% Hispanic American. 96% returned for their sophomore year.

Facilities and Resources

2,700 **computers/terminals** and 6,000 ports are available on campus for general student use. Students can access the following: campus intranet, computer help desk, free student e-mail accounts, online (class) grades, online (class) registration, online (class) schedules, online degree progress, financial aid applications, document sharing, calendars, personal Web space, customizable Web portal, course management systems (including data and video). Campuswide network is available. 100% of college-owned or -operated housing units are wired for high-speed Internet access. Wireless service is available via entire campus. The 20 **libraries** have 3,986,818 books and 60,718 subscriptions.

Campus Life

There are 600 active organizations on campus, including a drama/theater group, newspaper, radio station, television station, choral group, and marching band. 21% of eligible men and 24% of eligible women are members of national **fraternities**, national **sororities**, local fraternities, and local sororities.

USC is a member of the NCAA (Division I). **Intercollegiate sports** (some offering scholarships) include baseball (m), basketball, crew (w), cross-country running (w), football (m), golf, soccer (w), swimming and diving, tennis, track and field, volleyball, water polo.

Campus Safety

Student safety services include late-night transport/escort service, 24-hour emergency telephone alarm devices, 24-hour patrols by trained security personnel, student patrols, and electronically operated dormitory entrances.

Applying

USC requires an essay, SAT or ACT, and a high school transcript, and in some cases recommendations. It recommends an interview and recommendations. Application deadline: 1/10; 1/20 priority date for financial aid.

Getting Accepted

33,760 applied
25% were accepted
2,963 enrolled (35% of accepted)
86% from top tenth of their h.s. class
3.71 average high school GPA
86% had SAT critical reading scores over 600
91% had SAT math scores over 600
90% had SAT writing scores over 600
97% had ACT scores over 24
35% had SAT critical reading scores over 700
46% had SAT math scores over 700
42% had SAT writing scores over 700
58% had ACT scores over 30
236 National Merit Scholars

Graduation and After

66% graduated in 4 years
16% graduated in 5 years
3% graduated in 6 years
716 organizations recruited on campus

Financial Matters

$35,810 tuition and fees (2007–08)
$10,858 room and board
100% average percent of need met
$29,641 average financial aid amount received per undergraduate (2005–06)

THE UNIVERSITY OF TENNESSEE

URBAN SETTING ■ PUBLIC ■ STATE-SUPPORTED ■ COED
KNOXVILLE, TENNESSEE

Web site: www.tennessee.edu
Contact: Mr. Richard Bayer, Dean of Admissions, 305 Student Services
Building, 1331 Circle Park, Knoxville, TN 37996-0230
Telephone: 865-974-2184 or toll-free 800-221-8657 (in-state)
Fax: 865-974-6341
E-mail: admissions@tennessee.edu

Getting Accepted

12,824 applied
71% were accepted
4,351 enrolled (48% of accepted)
39% from top tenth of their h.s. class
3.61 average high school GPA
Mean SAT critical reading score: 572
Mean SAT math score: 580
Mean ACT score: 26
37% had SAT critical reading scores over 600
42% had SAT math scores over 600
75% had ACT scores over 24
6% had SAT critical reading scores over 700
7% had SAT math scores over 700
17% had ACT scores over 30
22 National Merit Scholars
94 valedictorians

Graduation and After

29% graduated in 4 years
24% graduated in 5 years
5% graduated in 6 years
500 organizations recruited on campus

Financial Matters

$6188 resident tuition and fees (2008–09)
$19,028 nonresident tuition and fees (2008–09)
$6676 room and board
71% average percent of need met
$8804 average financial aid amount received per undergraduate (2006–07 estimated)

Academics

Tennessee awards bachelor's, master's, doctoral, and first-professional **degrees** and post-bachelor's, post-master's, and first-professional certificates. **Challenging opportunities** include advanced placement credit, accelerated degree programs, student-designed majors, freshman honors college, an honors program, double majors, independent study, and a senior project. Special programs include cooperative education, internships, summer session for credit, off-campus study, study-abroad, and Army and Air Force ROTC.

The most frequently chosen **baccalaureate** fields are business/marketing, social sciences, and psychology. A complete listing of majors at Tennessee appears in the Majors by College index beginning on page 471.

The **faculty** at Tennessee has 1,550 full-time members, 82% with terminal degrees. The student-faculty ratio is 15:1.

Students of Tennessee

The student body totals 29,937, of whom 21,369 are undergraduates. 50.8% are women and 49.2% are men. Students come from 49 states and territories and 76 other countries. 87% are from Tennessee. 1% are international students. 8.8% are African American, 0.3% American Indian, 2.8% Asian American, and 1.6% Hispanic American. 84% returned for their sophomore year.

Facilities and Resources

600 **computers/terminals** are available on campus for general student use. Students can access the following: campus intranet, computer help desk, free student e-mail accounts, online (class) grades, online (class) registration, online (class) schedules, Black Board Course Management System. Campuswide network is available. 100% of college-owned or -operated housing units are wired for high-speed Internet access. Wireless service is available via entire campus. The 7 **libraries** have 24,437,024 books and 17,628 subscriptions.

Campus Life

There are 350 active organizations on campus, including a drama/theater group, newspaper, radio station, television station, choral group, and marching band. 14% of eligible men and 19% of eligible women are members of national **fraternities** and national **sororities**.

Tennessee is a member of the NCAA (Division I). **Intercollegiate sports** (some offering scholarships) include baseball (m), basketball, cheerleading, crew (w), cross-country running, football (m), golf, soccer (w), softball (w), swimming and diving, tennis, track and field, volleyball (w).

Campus Safety

Student safety services include late-night transport/escort service, 24-hour emergency telephone alarm devices, and 24-hour patrols by trained security personnel.

Applying

Tennessee requires an essay, SAT or ACT, a high school transcript, specific high school units, and a minimum high school GPA of 2.0. Application deadline: 2/1; 3/1 priority date for financial aid. Early and deferred admission are possible.

THE UNIVERSITY OF TENNESSEE AT CHATTANOOGA

URBAN SETTING ■ PUBLIC ■ STATE-SUPPORTED ■ COED
CHATTANOOGA, TENNESSEE

Web site: www.utc.edu
Contact: Mr. Yancy Freeman, Director, Admissions and Recruitment, 615
McCallie Avenue, Guerry Hall, Chattanooga, TN 37403
Telephone: 423-755-4597 or toll-free 800-UTC-MOCS (in-state)
Fax: 423-425-4157
E-mail: yancy-freeman@utc.edu

Academics

UTC awards bachelor's, master's, doctoral, and first-professional **degrees** and post-bachelor's and post-master's certificates. **Challenging opportunities** include advanced placement credit, an honors program, double majors, independent study, and a senior project. Special programs include cooperative education, internships, summer session for credit, off-campus study, and study-abroad.

The most frequently chosen **baccalaureate** fields are business/marketing, family and consumer sciences, and psychology. A complete listing of majors at UTC appears in the Majors by College index beginning on page 471.

The **faculty** at UTC has 400 full-time members, 72% with terminal degrees. The student-faculty ratio is 17:1.

Students of UTC

The student body totals 9,558, of whom 8,194 are undergraduates. 56.2% are women and 43.8% are men. Students come from 43 states and territories and 46 other countries. 76% are from Tennessee. 0.7% are international students. 19% are African American, 0.4% American Indian, 2.2% Asian American, and 1.5% Hispanic American. 64% returned for their sophomore year.

Facilities and Resources

300 **computers/terminals** are available on campus for general student use. Students can access the following: campus intranet, computer help desk, free student e-mail accounts, online (class) grades, online (class) registration, online (class) schedules. Campuswide network is available. Wireless service is available via classrooms, computer labs, libraries. The **library** has 491,179 books and 1,847 subscriptions.

Campus Life

There are 130 active organizations on campus, including a drama/theater group, newspaper, radio station, choral group, and marching band. 6% of eligible men and 5% of eligible women are members of national **fraternities** and national **sororities**.

UTC is a member of the NCAA (Division I). **Intercollegiate sports** (some offering scholarships) include basketball, crew, cross-country running, football (m), golf, soccer, softball (w), tennis, track and field, volleyball (w), wrestling (m).

Campus Safety

Student safety services include late-night transport/escort service, 24-hour emergency telephone alarm devices, 24-hour patrols by trained security personnel, and electronically operated dormitory entrances.

Applying

UTC requires SAT or ACT, a high school transcript, and 1 recommendation. It recommends an essay. Application deadline: 4/1 priority date for financial aid. Deferred admission is possible.

Getting Accepted
5,210 applied
83% were accepted
1,947 enrolled (45% of accepted)
3.18 average high school GPA
Mean ACT score: 22
28% had ACT scores over 24
4% had ACT scores over 30

Graduation and After
25% graduated in 4 years
17% graduated in 5 years
2% graduated in 6 years
73 organizations recruited on campus

Financial Matters
$5062 resident tuition and fees (2007–08)
$11,052 nonresident tuition and fees (2007–08)
$7555 room and board
80% average percent of need met
$8450 average financial aid amount received per undergraduate (2004–05 estimated)

The University of Texas at Austin

Urban setting ■ Public ■ State-supported ■ Coed
Austin, Texas

Web site: www.utexas.edu

Contact: Dr. Bruce Walker, Vice Provost and Director of Admissions, Office of Admissions, Freshman Admissions Center, PO Box 8058, Austin, TX 78713-8058

Telephone: 512-475-7440

Fax: 512-475-7475

Getting Accepted

27,237 applied
51% were accepted
7,478 enrolled (54% of accepted)
69% from top tenth of their h.s. class
Mean SAT critical reading score: 602
Mean SAT math score: 633
Mean SAT writing score: 598
Mean ACT score: 26
55% had SAT critical reading scores over 600
68% had SAT math scores over 600
53% had SAT writing scores over 600
74% had ACT scores over 24
17% had SAT critical reading scores over 700
25% had SAT math scores over 700
14% had SAT writing scores over 700
25% had ACT scores over 30
277 National Merit Scholars

Graduation and After

47% graduated in 4 years
26% graduated in 5 years
5% graduated in 6 years

Financial Matters

$7670 resident tuition and fees (2007–08)
$24,544 nonresident tuition and fees (2007–08)
$8576 room and board
90% average percent of need met
$10,900 average financial aid amount received per undergraduate (2006–07 estimated)

Academics

UT Austin awards bachelor's, master's, doctoral, and first-professional **degrees**. **Challenging opportunities** include advanced placement credit, accelerated degree programs, student-designed majors, an honors program, double majors, independent study, and a senior project. Special programs include cooperative education, internships, summer session for credit, study-abroad, and Army, Navy, and Air Force ROTC.

The most frequently chosen **baccalaureate** fields are social sciences, communications/journalism, and business/marketing. A complete listing of majors at UT Austin appears in the Majors by College index beginning on page 471.

The **faculty** at UT Austin has 2,599 full-time members, 87% with terminal degrees. The student-faculty ratio is 18:1.

Students of UT Austin

The student body totals 50,170, of whom 37,459 are undergraduates. 52% are women and 48% are men. Students come from 54 states and territories and 126 other countries. 96% are from Texas. 4% are international students. 4.6% are African American, 0.4% American Indian, 17.4% Asian American, and 17.8% Hispanic American. 92% returned for their sophomore year.

Facilities and Resources

4,000 **computers/terminals** are available on campus for general student use. Students can access the following: computer help desk, free student e-mail accounts, online (class) grades, online (class) registration, online (class) schedules. Campuswide network is available. 100% of college-owned or -operated housing units are wired for high-speed Internet access. Wireless service is available via computer centers, computer labs, libraries, student centers.

Campus Life

There are 900 active organizations on campus, including a drama/theater group, newspaper, radio station, television station, choral group, and marching band. 9% of eligible men and 14% of eligible women are members of national **fraternities** and national **sororities**.

UT Austin is a member of the NCAA (Division I). **Intercollegiate sports** (some offering scholarships) include baseball (m), basketball, crew (w), cross-country running, football (m), golf, soccer (w), softball (w), swimming and diving, tennis, track and field, volleyball (w).

Campus Safety

Student safety services include late-night transport/escort service, 24-hour emergency telephone alarm devices, 24-hour patrols by trained security personnel, student patrols, and electronically operated dormitory entrances.

Applying

UT Austin requires an essay, SAT or ACT, and a high school transcript, and in some cases SAT Subject Tests. Application deadline: 2/1; 4/1 priority date for financial aid. Deferred admission is possible.

THE UNIVERSITY OF TEXAS AT DALLAS

SUBURBAN SETTING ■ PUBLIC ■ STATE-SUPPORTED ■ COED
RICHARDSON, TEXAS

Web site: www.utdallas.edu
Contact: , Enrollment Services, PO Box 830688, Mail Station HH10,
    Richardson, TX 75083-0688
Telephone: 972-883-2270 or toll-free 800-889-2443
Fax: 972-883-2599
E-mail: interest@utdallas.edu

Academics

UT Dallas awards bachelor's, master's, and doctoral **degrees** and post-bachelor's
certificates. **Challenging opportunities** include advanced placement credit, accelerated
degree programs, student-designed majors, freshman honors college, an honors
program, double majors, independent study, and a senior project. Special programs
include cooperative education, internships, summer session for credit, study-abroad, and
Army and Air Force ROTC.

The most frequently chosen **baccalaureate** fields are business/marketing,
interdisciplinary studies, and psychology. A complete listing of majors at UT Dallas appears in the Majors by College index beginning on page 471.

The **faculty** at UT Dallas has 495 full-time members, 91% with terminal degrees.
The student-faculty ratio is 19:1.

Students of UT Dallas

The student body totals 14,556, of whom 9,266 are undergraduates. 46.1% are women
and 53.9% are men. Students come from 45 states and territories and 123 other
countries. 96% are from Texas. 4% are international students. 7.4% are African
American, 0.6% American Indian, 20.2% Asian American, and 11% Hispanic American.
81% returned for their sophomore year.

Facilities and Resources

630 **computers/terminals** are available on campus for general student use. Students can
access the following: computer help desk, free student e-mail accounts, online (class)
grades, online (class) registration, online (class) schedules. Campuswide network is available. 100% of college-owned or -operated housing units are wired for high-speed Internet access. Wireless service is available via classrooms, computer centers, dorm rooms,
libraries, student centers. The 2 **libraries** have 1,512,831 books and 197,047 subscriptions.

Campus Life

There are 130 active organizations on campus, including a drama/theater group,
newspaper, and radio station. 5% of eligible men and 4% of eligible women are members
of national **fraternities**, national **sororities**, and local sororities.

UT Dallas is a member of the NCAA (Division III). **Intercollegiate sports** include
baseball (m), basketball, cross-country running, golf, soccer, softball (w), tennis, volleyball (w).

Campus Safety

Student safety services include late-night transport/escort service, 24-hour emergency
telephone alarm devices, and 24-hour patrols by trained security personnel.

Applying

UT Dallas requires an essay, SAT or ACT, and a high school transcript, and in some
cases THEA and an interview. It recommends 3 recommendations. Application deadline:
7/1; 4/12 priority date for financial aid. Deferred admission is possible.

Getting Accepted

4,198 applied
56% were accepted
1,057 enrolled (45% of accepted)
43% from top tenth of their h.s. class
3.64 average high school GPA
Mean SAT critical reading score: 603
Mean SAT math score: 637
Mean ACT score: 26
54% had SAT critical reading scores over 600
68% had SAT math scores over 600
45% had SAT writing scores over 600
75% had ACT scores over 24
17% had SAT critical reading scores over 700
24% had SAT math scores over 700
10% had SAT writing scores over 700
24% had ACT scores over 30
34 National Merit Scholars
31 valedictorians

Graduation and After

31% graduated in 4 years
18% graduated in 5 years
7% graduated in 6 years
361 organizations recruited on campus

Financial Matters

$8554 resident tuition and fees (2007–08)
$17,854 nonresident tuition and fees (2007–
    08)
$6671 room and board
75% average percent of need met
$9819 average financial aid amount received
    per undergraduate (2006–07 estimated)

University of the Pacific

Suburban setting ■ Private ■ Independent ■ Coed
Stockton, California

Web site: www.pacific.edu
Contact: Mr. Rich Toledo, Director of Admissions, 3601 Pacific Avenue, Stockton, CA 95211
Telephone: 209-946-2211 or toll-free 800-959-2867
Fax: 209-946-2413
E-mail: admissions@pacific.edu

Getting Accepted
4,976 applied
69% were accepted
766 enrolled (22% of accepted)
41% from top tenth of their h.s. class
3.46 average high school GPA
Mean SAT critical reading score: 570
Mean SAT math score: 657
Mean ACT score: 26
35% had SAT critical reading scores over 600
53% had SAT math scores over 600
35% had SAT writing scores over 600
59% had ACT scores over 24
5% had SAT critical reading scores over 700
16% had SAT math scores over 700
6% had SAT writing scores over 700
12% had ACT scores over 30

Graduation and After
41% graduated in 4 years
22% graduated in 5 years
4% graduated in 6 years
68% had job offers within 6 months
93 organizations recruited on campus

Financial Matters
$28,980 tuition and fees (2007–08)
$9210 room and board
$24,110 average financial aid amount received per undergraduate (2006–07 estimated)

Academics

Pacific awards bachelor's, master's, doctoral, and first-professional **degrees**. **Challenging opportunities** include advanced placement credit, accelerated degree programs, student-designed majors, an honors program, double majors, independent study, and a senior project. Special programs include cooperative education, internships, summer session for credit, study-abroad, and Air Force ROTC.

The most frequently chosen **baccalaureate** fields are business/marketing, biological/life sciences, and social sciences. A complete listing of majors at Pacific appears in the Majors by College index beginning on page 471.

The **faculty** at Pacific has 426 full-time members, 92% with terminal degrees. The student-faculty ratio is 13:1.

Students of Pacific

The student body totals 6,235, of whom 3,470 are undergraduates. 55.2% are women and 44.8% are men. Students come from 36 states and territories and 18 other countries. 87% are from California. 3.1% are international students. 3.1% are African American, 0.6% American Indian, 32.1% Asian American, and 9.7% Hispanic American. 82% returned for their sophomore year.

Facilities and Resources

350 **computers/terminals** are available on campus for general student use. Students can access the following: computer help desk, free student e-mail accounts, online (class) grades, online (class) registration, online (class) schedules. Campuswide network is available. Wireless service is available via entire campus. The 2 **libraries** have 373,759 books and 1,826 subscriptions.

Campus Life

There are 100 active organizations on campus, including a drama/theater group, newspaper, radio station, and choral group. 19% of eligible men and 18% of eligible women are members of national **fraternities**, national **sororities**, and local fraternities.

Pacific is a member of the NCAA (Division I). **Intercollegiate sports** (some offering scholarships) include baseball (m), basketball, cross-country running (w), field hockey (w), golf (m), soccer (w), softball (w), swimming and diving, tennis, volleyball, water polo.

Campus Safety

Student safety services include late-night transport/escort service, 24-hour emergency telephone alarm devices, 24-hour patrols by trained security personnel, and electronically operated dormitory entrances.

Applying

Pacific requires an essay, SAT or ACT, a high school transcript, 1 recommendation, and a minimum high school GPA of 2.5, and in some cases audition for music program. It recommends a minimum high school GPA of 3.0. Application deadline: 1/15; 2/15 priority date for financial aid.

University of the Sciences in Philadelphia

Urban setting ■ Private ■ Independent ■ Coed
Philadelphia, Pennsylvania

Web site: www.usip.edu
Contact: Mr. Louis Hegyes, Director of Admission, 600 South 43rd Street, Philadelphia, PA 19104-4495
Telephone: 215-596-8810 or toll-free 888-996-8747 (in-state)
Fax: 215-596-8821
E-mail: admit@usip.edu

SPONSOR

Academics

USP awards bachelor's, master's, doctoral, and first-professional **degrees** and post-bachelor's certificates. **Challenging opportunities** include advanced placement credit, an honors program, double majors, and a senior project. Special programs include cooperative education, internships, summer session for credit, off-campus study, and Army and Air Force ROTC.

The most frequently chosen **baccalaureate** fields are health professions and related sciences, biological/life sciences, and business/marketing. A complete listing of majors at USP appears in the Majors by College index beginning on page 471.

The **faculty** at USP has 154 full-time members, 79% with terminal degrees. The student-faculty ratio is 13:1.

Students of USP

The student body totals 2,969, of whom 2,128 are undergraduates. 59.1% are women and 40.9% are men. Students come from 32 states and territories and 16 other countries. 52% are from Pennsylvania. 1.4% are international students. 5.3% are African American, 0.4% American Indian, 34.4% Asian American, and 1.8% Hispanic American. 91% returned for their sophomore year.

Facilities and Resources

130 **computers/terminals** are available on campus for general student use. Campuswide network is available. The 2 **libraries** have 87,125 books and 9,817 subscriptions.

Campus Life

There are 65 active organizations on campus, including a drama/theater group, newspaper, and choral group. USP has national **fraternities**, national **sororities**, local fraternities, and local sororities.

USP is a member of the NCAA (Division II) and NAIA. **Intercollegiate sports** (some offering scholarships) include baseball (m), basketball, cross-country running, golf, riflery, softball (w), tennis, volleyball (w).

Campus Safety

Student safety services include late-night transport/escort service, 24-hour emergency telephone alarm devices, 24-hour patrols by trained security personnel, and electronically operated dormitory entrances.

Applying

USP requires SAT or ACT and a high school transcript. It recommends SAT and a minimum high school GPA of 3.0. Application deadline: rolling admissions; 3/15 for financial aid, with a 3/15 priority date. Deferred admission is possible.

A private, coeducational institution of 2,500 students, University of the Sciences in Philadelphia (USP) is located in the University City section of historic Philadelphia—along with its neighbors Drexel University and the University of Pennsylvania. USP offers twenty-one majors in the pharmaceutical sciences, health sciences, and arts and sciences, with pharmacy, physical therapy, occupational therapy, physician assistant studies, biology, and premed being the most popular programs. All programs are direct-entry, whereby candidates are admitted directly into their program of choice. USP also follows a rolling admission policy, and candidates are urged to apply during the fall of their senior year in high school. USP is a member of NCAA Division II.

Getting Accepted
3,963 applied
58% were accepted
557 enrolled (24% of accepted)
41% from top tenth of their h.s. class
3.62 average high school GPA
Mean SAT critical reading score: 566
Mean SAT math score: 608
Mean ACT score: 25
31% had SAT critical reading scores over 600
54% had SAT math scores over 600
71% had ACT scores over 24
3% had SAT critical reading scores over 700
11% had SAT math scores over 700
3% had ACT scores over 30

Graduation and After
54% graduated in 4 years
6% graduated in 5 years
2% graduated in 6 years
30% pursued further study (3% medicine, 2% business, 1% law)
95% had job offers within 6 months
225 organizations recruited on campus

Financial Matters
$26,930 tuition and fees (2007–08)
$10,524 room and board
52% average percent of need met
$11,801 average financial aid amount received per undergraduate (2005–06)

UNIVERSITY OF TULSA

URBAN SETTING ■ PRIVATE ■ INDEPENDENT RELIGIOUS ■ COED
TULSA, OKLAHOMA

Web site: www.utulsa.edu
Contact: Mr. Earl Johnson, Dean of Admission, 600 South College Avenue, Tulsa, OK 74104
Telephone: 918-631-2307 or toll-free 800-331-3050
Fax: 918-631-5003
E-mail: admission@utulsa.edu

Getting Accepted
3,804 applied
51% were accepted
656 enrolled (34% of accepted)
64% from top tenth of their h.s. class
3.8 average high school GPA
Mean SAT critical reading score: 630
Mean SAT math score: 640
Mean ACT score: 27
61% had SAT critical reading scores over 600
68% had SAT math scores over 600
77% had ACT scores over 24
26% had SAT critical reading scores over 700
28% had SAT math scores over 700
28% had ACT scores over 30
68 National Merit Scholars
34 valedictorians

Graduation and After
45% graduated in 4 years
16% graduated in 5 years
2% graduated in 6 years
38% pursued further study (13% arts and sciences, 7% business, 5% law)
85% had job offers within 6 months
196 organizations recruited on campus

Financial Matters
$21,780 tuition and fees (2007–08)
$7404 room and board
87% average percent of need met
$22,586 average financial aid amount received per undergraduate (2005–06)

Academics

TU awards bachelor's, master's, doctoral, and first-professional **degrees** and post-bachelor's and first-professional certificates. **Challenging opportunities** include advanced placement credit, accelerated degree programs, student-designed majors, an honors program, double majors, independent study, and a senior project. Special programs include internships, summer session for credit, study-abroad, and Air Force ROTC.

The most frequently chosen **baccalaureate** fields are business/marketing, engineering, and visual and performing arts. A complete listing of majors at TU appears in the Majors by College index beginning on page 471.

The **faculty** at TU has 309 full-time members, 96% with terminal degrees. The student-faculty ratio is 10:1.

Students of TU

The student body totals 4,165, of whom 2,987 are undergraduates. 48% are women and 52% are men. Students come from 44 states and territories and 46 other countries. 62% are from Oklahoma. 10.9% are international students. 6.3% are African American, 3.5% American Indian, 3% Asian American, and 4% Hispanic American. 88% returned for their sophomore year.

Facilities and Resources

900 **computers/terminals** are available on campus for general student use. Students can access the following: campus intranet, computer help desk, free student e-mail accounts, online (class) grades, online (class) registration, online (class) schedules. Campuswide network is available. 100% of college-owned or -operated housing units are wired for high-speed Internet access. Wireless service is available via entire campus. The 2 **libraries** have 1,190,533 books and 26,228 subscriptions.

Campus Life

There are 272 active organizations on campus, including a drama/theater group, newspaper, radio station, television station, choral group, and marching band. 21% of eligible men and 23% of eligible women are members of national **fraternities** and national **sororities**.

TU is a member of the NCAA (Division I). **Intercollegiate sports** (some offering scholarships) include basketball, crew (w), cross-country running, football (m), golf, soccer, softball (w), tennis, track and field, volleyball (w).

Campus Safety

Student safety services include late-night transport/escort service, 24-hour emergency telephone alarm devices, 24-hour patrols by trained security personnel, and electronically operated dormitory entrances.

Applying

TU requires an essay, SAT or ACT, a high school transcript, an interview, and 1 recommendation. It recommends a minimum high school GPA of 3.0. Application deadline: rolling admissions; 4/1 priority date for financial aid. Early and deferred admission are possible.

UNIVERSITY OF UTAH
URBAN SETTING ■ PUBLIC ■ STATE-SUPPORTED ■ COED
SALT LAKE CITY, UTAH

Web site: www.utah.edu
Contact: Mateo Remsburg, Director of High School Services, 201 Presidents
Circle Room 206, Salt Lake City, UT 84112
Telephone: 801-581-8761 or toll-free 800-444-8638
Fax: 801-585-3257
E-mail: mremsburg@sa.utah.edu

Academics
U of U awards bachelor's, master's, doctoral, and first-professional **degrees** and post-bachelor's and post-master's certificates. **Challenging opportunities** include advanced placement credit, accelerated degree programs, student-designed majors, freshman honors college, an honors program, double majors, independent study, and a senior project. Special programs include cooperative education, internships, summer session for credit, off-campus study, study-abroad, and Army, Navy, and Air Force ROTC.

The most frequently chosen **baccalaureate** fields are social sciences, business/marketing, and communications/journalism. A complete listing of majors at U of U appears in the Majors by College index beginning on page 471.

The **faculty** at U of U has 1,248 full-time members, 84% with terminal degrees. The student-faculty ratio is 13:1.

Students of U of U
The student body totals 28,025, of whom 21,421 are undergraduates. 44.9% are women and 55.1% are men. Students come from 55 states and territories and 104 other countries. 84% are from Utah. 2.6% are international students. 0.9% are African American, 0.7% American Indian, 5.5% Asian American, and 5.1% Hispanic American. 80% returned for their sophomore year.

Facilities and Resources
8,000 **computers/terminals** are available on campus for general student use. Students can access the following: campus intranet, computer help desk, free student e-mail accounts, online (class) grades, online (class) registration, online (class) schedules, online classes. Campuswide network is available. Wireless service is available via entire campus. The 4 **libraries** have 6,199,047 books and 33,517 subscriptions.

Campus Life
There are 170 active organizations on campus, including a drama/theater group, newspaper, radio station, television station, choral group, and marching band. 5% of eligible men and 5% of eligible women are members of national **fraternities**, national **sororities**, local fraternities, and local sororities.

U of U is a member of the NCAA (Division I). **Intercollegiate sports** (some offering scholarships) include baseball (m), basketball (m), cheerleading, cross-country running (w), football (m), golf (m), gymnastics (w), skiing (cross-country), skiing (downhill), soccer (w), softball (w), swimming and diving, tennis, track and field (w), volleyball (w).

Campus Safety
Student safety services include late-night transport/escort service, 24-hour emergency telephone alarm devices, 24-hour patrols by trained security personnel, student patrols, and electronically operated dormitory entrances.

Applying
U of U requires SAT or ACT, a high school transcript, and a minimum high school GPA of 2.6, and in some cases an essay and recommendations. It recommends a minimum high school GPA of 3.0. Application deadline: 4/1; 3/15 priority date for financial aid. Early admission is possible.

Getting Accepted
7,123 applied
82% were accepted
2,743 enrolled (47% of accepted)
25% from top tenth of their h.s. class
3.53 average high school GPA
Mean SAT critical reading score: 560
Mean SAT math score: 560
Mean ACT score: 24
36% had SAT critical reading scores over 600
36% had SAT math scores over 600
52% had ACT scores over 24
8% had SAT critical reading scores over 700
8% had SAT math scores over 700
12% had ACT scores over 30

Graduation and After
21% graduated in 4 years
22% graduated in 5 years
13% graduated in 6 years
80% had job offers within 6 months
190 organizations recruited on campus

Financial Matters
$4986 resident tuition and fees (2007–08)
$15,662 nonresident tuition and fees (2007–08)
$5778 room and board
56% average percent of need met
$8526 average financial aid amount received per undergraduate (2006–07 estimated)

University of Virginia

Suburban setting ■ Public ■ State-supported ■ Coed
Charlottesville, Virginia

Web site: www.virginia.edu
Contact: Mr. John A. Blackburn, Dean of Admission, PO Box 400160,
    Charlottesville, VA 22904-4727
Telephone: 434-982-3200
Fax: 434-954-3587
E-mail: undergrad-admission@virginia.edu

Getting Accepted
17,798 applied
35% were accepted
3,248 enrolled (52% of accepted)
87% from top tenth of their h.s. class
4.0 average high school GPA
Mean SAT critical reading score: 645
Mean SAT math score: 662
75% had SAT critical reading scores over 600
80% had SAT math scores over 600
78% had SAT writing scores over 600
29% had SAT critical reading scores over 700
37% had SAT math scores over 700
30% had SAT writing scores over 700
177 valedictorians

Graduation and After
84% graduated in 4 years
8% graduated in 5 years
1% graduated in 6 years

Financial Matters
$8500 resident tuition and fees (2007–08)
$27,750 nonresident tuition and fees (2007–08)
$7435 room and board
100% average percent of need met
$15,687 average financial aid amount received per undergraduate (2006–07 estimated)

Academics
UVA awards bachelor's, master's, doctoral, and first-professional **degrees** and post-master's certificates. **Challenging opportunities** include advanced placement credit, accelerated degree programs, student-designed majors, an honors program, double majors, independent study, and a senior project. Special programs include cooperative education, internships, summer session for credit, study-abroad, and Army, Navy, and Air Force ROTC.

The most frequently chosen **baccalaureate** fields are social sciences, engineering, and business/marketing. A complete listing of majors at UVA appears in the Majors by College index beginning on page 471.

The **faculty** at UVA has 1,253 full-time members, 92% with terminal degrees. The student-faculty ratio is 15:1.

Students of UVA
The student body totals 24,257, of whom 15,078 are undergraduates. 55.8% are women and 44.2% are men. Students come from 52 states and territories and 113 other countries. 72% are from Virginia. 4.6% are international students. 9% are African American, 0.2% American Indian, 11.2% Asian American, and 4.4% Hispanic American. 97% returned for their sophomore year.

Facilities and Resources
Students can access the following: campus intranet, computer help desk, free student e-mail accounts, online (class) grades, online (class) registration, online (class) schedules, online course management tool. Campuswide network is available. Wireless service is available via classrooms, computer centers, computer labs, dorm rooms, learning centers, libraries, student centers. The 15 **libraries** have 5,397,188 books and 71,832 subscriptions.

Campus Life
There are 300 active organizations on campus, including a drama/theater group, newspaper, radio station, television station, choral group, and marching band. 30% of eligible men and 30% of eligible women are members of national **fraternities**, national **sororities**, and local fraternities.

UVA is a member of the NCAA (Division I). **Intercollegiate sports** (some offering scholarships) include baseball (m), basketball, crew (w), cross-country running, field hockey (w), football (m), golf, lacrosse, soccer, softball (w), swimming and diving, tennis, track and field, volleyball (w), wrestling (m).

Campus Safety
Student safety services include late-night transport/escort service, 24-hour emergency telephone alarm devices, 24-hour patrols by trained security personnel, and electronically operated dormitory entrances.

Applying
UVA requires an essay, SAT, SAT or ACT, a high school transcript, and 1 recommendation. It recommends either SAT or ACT plus optional ACT writing test (ACT alone does not satisfy requirement); two SAT subject tests (student's choice). Application deadline: 1/2; 3/1 priority date for financial aid. Deferred admission is possible.

UNIVERSITY OF WASHINGTON

URBAN SETTING ■ PUBLIC ■ STATE-SUPPORTED ■ COED
SEATTLE, WASHINGTON

Web site: www.washington.edu
Contact: Admissions Office, Office of Admissions, Seattle, WA 98195
Telephone: 206-543-9686
Fax: 206-685-3655

Academics

UW awards bachelor's, master's, doctoral, and first-professional **degrees** and first-professional certificates. **Challenging opportunities** include advanced placement credit, accelerated degree programs, student-designed majors, an honors program, double majors, independent study, and a senior project. Special programs include cooperative education, internships, summer session for credit, study-abroad, and Army, Navy, and Air Force ROTC.

The most frequently chosen **baccalaureate** fields are social sciences, business/marketing, and education. A complete listing of majors at UW appears in the Majors by College index beginning on page 471.

The **faculty** at UW has 2,941 full-time members, 93% with terminal degrees. The student-faculty ratio is 11:1.

Students of UW

The student body totals 39,524, of whom 27,836 are undergraduates. 51.8% are women and 48.2% are men. Students come from 52 states and territories and 59 other countries. 86% are from Washington. 3.6% are international students. 3.2% are African American, 1.3% American Indian, 27.5% Asian American, and 4.8% Hispanic American. 93% returned for their sophomore year.

Facilities and Resources

285 **computers/terminals** are available on campus for general student use. Students can access the following: online (class) registration. Campuswide network is available. The 22 **libraries** have 5,820,229 books and 50,245 subscriptions.

Campus Life

There are 300 active organizations on campus, including a drama/theater group, newspaper, radio station, television station, choral group, and marching band. 12% of eligible men and 11% of eligible women are members of national **fraternities** and national **sororities**.

UW is a member of the NCAA (Division I). **Intercollegiate sports** (some offering scholarships) include baseball (m), basketball, crew, cross-country running, football (m), golf, gymnastics (w), soccer, softball (w), swimming and diving, tennis, track and field, volleyball (w).

Campus Safety

Student safety services include late-night transport/escort service, 24-hour emergency telephone alarm devices, 24-hour patrols by trained security personnel, and electronically operated dormitory entrances.

Applying

UW requires an essay, SAT or ACT, and a minimum high school GPA of 2.0. Application deadline: 1/15; 2/28 priority date for financial aid. Early admission is possible.

Getting Accepted

16,571 applied
68% were accepted
5,475 enrolled (48% of accepted)
84% from top tenth of their h.s. class
3.67 average high school GPA
45% had SAT critical reading scores over 600
59% had SAT math scores over 600
69% had ACT scores over 24
10% had SAT critical reading scores over 700
17% had SAT math scores over 700
17% had ACT scores over 30
37 National Merit Scholars

Graduation and After

46% graduated in 4 years
24% graduated in 5 years
4% graduated in 6 years
450 organizations recruited on campus

Financial Matters

$6385 resident tuition and fees (2007–08)
$22,131 nonresident tuition and fees (2007–08)
$7227 room and board
86% average percent of need met
$12,000 average financial aid amount received per undergraduate (2006–07 estimated)

University of Wisconsin–La Crosse

Suburban setting ■ Public ■ State-supported ■ Coed
La Crosse, Wisconsin

Web site: www.uwlax.edu
Contact: Ms. Kathryn Kiefer, Director of Admissions, 1725 State Street,
  LaCrosse, WI 54601
Telephone: 608-785-8939
Fax: 608-785-8940
E-mail: admissions@uwlax.edu

Getting Accepted
6,777 applied
65% were accepted
1,753 enrolled (40% of accepted)
31% from top tenth of their h.s. class
Mean ACT score: 25
27% had SAT critical reading scores over 600
23% had SAT math scores over 600
66% had ACT scores over 24
8% had SAT critical reading scores over 700
8% had SAT math scores over 700
5% had ACT scores over 30
70 valedictorians

Graduation and After
28% graduated in 4 years
31% graduated in 5 years
8% graduated in 6 years
23% pursued further study
98.3% had job offers within 6 months
78 organizations recruited on campus

Financial Matters
$4876 resident tuition and fees (2007–08)
$12,448 nonresident tuition and fees (2007–08)
$5130 room and board
74% average percent of need met
$5461 average financial aid amount received per undergraduate (2005–06)

Academics
UW-La Crosse awards associate, bachelor's, and master's **degrees** and post-bachelor's certificates. **Challenging opportunities** include advanced placement credit, freshman honors college, an honors program, double majors, and a senior project. Special programs include cooperative education, internships, summer session for credit, off-campus study, study-abroad, and Army ROTC.

The most frequently chosen **baccalaureate** fields are business/marketing, education, and social sciences. A complete listing of majors at UW-La Crosse appears in the Majors by College index beginning on page 471.

The **faculty** at UW-La Crosse has 346 full-time members, 73% with terminal degrees. The student-faculty ratio is 23:1.

Students of UW-La Crosse
The student body totals 9,975, of whom 8,521 are undergraduates. 58.3% are women and 41.7% are men. Students come from 38 states and territories and 37 other countries. 84% are from Wisconsin. 2.4% are international students. 1.1% are African American, 0.7% American Indian, 3.3% Asian American, and 1.5% Hispanic American. 87% returned for their sophomore year.

Facilities and Resources
600 **computers/terminals** and 100 ports are available on campus for general student use. Students can access the following: campus intranet, computer help desk, free student e-mail accounts, online (class) grades, online (class) registration, online (class) schedules. Campuswide network is available. 100% of college-owned or -operated housing units are wired for high-speed Internet access. Wireless service is available via classrooms, computer centers, computer labs, dorm rooms, learning centers, libraries, student centers. The **library** has 687,207 books and 1,181 subscriptions.

Campus Life
There are 180 active organizations on campus, including a drama/theater group, newspaper, radio station, television station, choral group, and marching band. 1% of eligible men and 1% of eligible women are members of national **fraternities** and national **sororities**.

UW-La Crosse is a member of the NCAA (Division III). **Intercollegiate sports** include baseball (m), basketball, cheerleading, cross-country running, football (m), gymnastics (w), soccer (w), softball (w), swimming and diving, tennis, track and field, volleyball (w), weight lifting, wrestling (m).

Campus Safety
Student safety services include late-night transport/escort service, 24-hour emergency telephone alarm devices, 24-hour patrols by trained security personnel, and electronically operated dormitory entrances.

Applying
UW-La Crosse requires SAT or ACT and a high school transcript, and in some cases an interview. It recommends an essay and ACT. Application deadline: rolling admissions, rolling admissions for nonresidents; 3/15 priority date for financial aid. Early admission is possible.

University of Wisconsin–Madison

Urban setting ■ Public ■ State-supported ■ Coed
Madison, Wisconsin

Web site: www.wisc.edu
Contact: Office of Undergraduate Admissions, 716 Langdon Street, Madison, WI 53706-1481
Telephone: 608-262-3961
Fax: 608-262-7706
E-mail: onwisconsin@admissions.wisc.edu

Academics

Wisconsin awards bachelor's, master's, doctoral, and first-professional **degrees** and post-master's and first-professional certificates. **Challenging opportunities** include advanced placement credit, accelerated degree programs, student-designed majors, an honors program, double majors, independent study, and a senior project. Special programs include cooperative education, internships, summer session for credit, study-abroad, and Army, Navy, and Air Force ROTC.

The most frequently chosen **baccalaureate** fields are social sciences, biological/life sciences, and engineering. A complete listing of majors at Wisconsin appears in the Majors by College index beginning on page 471.

The **faculty** at Wisconsin has 2,388 full-time members, 91% with terminal degrees. The student-faculty ratio is 13:1.

Students of Wisconsin

The student body totals 42,041, of whom 30,618 are undergraduates. 53.1% are women and 46.9% are men. Students come from 53 states and territories and 101 other countries. 68% are from Wisconsin. 3.9% are international students. 2.9% are African American, 0.7% American Indian, 5.9% Asian American, and 3.3% Hispanic American. 93% returned for their sophomore year.

Facilities and Resources

Students can access the following: computer help desk, free student e-mail accounts, on-line (class) grades, online (class) registration, online (class) schedules. Campuswide network is available. 100% of college-owned or -operated housing units are wired for high-speed Internet access. Wireless service is available via entire campus.

Campus Life

There are 690 active organizations on campus, including a drama/theater group, newspaper, radio station, choral group, and marching band. 9% of eligible men and 8% of eligible women are members of national **fraternities** and national **sororities**.

Wisconsin is a member of the NCAA (Division I). **Intercollegiate sports** (some offering scholarships) include basketball, cheerleading, cross-country running, football (m), golf, ice hockey, soccer, softball (w), swimming and diving, tennis, track and field, volleyball (w), wrestling (m).

Campus Safety

Student safety services include free cab rides throughout the city, late-night transport/escort service, 24-hour emergency telephone alarm devices, 24-hour patrols by trained security personnel, and electronically operated dormitory entrances.

Applying

Wisconsin requires an essay, SAT or ACT, and a high school transcript. Application deadline: 2/1. Deferred admission is possible.

Getting Accepted

24,870 applied
56% were accepted
5,996 enrolled (43% of accepted)
60% from top tenth of their h.s. class
3.77 average high school GPA
Mean SAT critical reading score: 608
Mean SAT math score: 659
Mean ACT score: 28
59% had SAT critical reading scores over 600
82% had SAT math scores over 600
64% had SAT writing scores over 600
92% had ACT scores over 24
17% had SAT critical reading scores over 700
32% had SAT math scores over 700
16% had SAT writing scores over 700
31% had ACT scores over 30

Graduation and After

47% graduated in 4 years
30% graduated in 5 years
3% graduated in 6 years
69% pursued further study

Financial Matters

$8047 resident tuition and fees (2007–08)
$22,299 nonresident tuition and fees (2007–08)
$11,818 average financial aid amount received per undergraduate (2006–07 estimated)

UNIVERSITY OF WISCONSIN–RIVER FALLS

SUBURBAN SETTING ■ PUBLIC ■ STATE-SUPPORTED ■ COED
RIVER FALLS, WISCONSIN

Getting Accepted
3,183 applied
81% were accepted
1,296 enrolled (50% of accepted)
17% from top tenth of their h.s. class
3.34 average high school GPA
Mean ACT score: 22
28% had ACT scores over 24
1% had ACT scores over 30

Graduation and After
19% pursued further study (5% arts and sciences, 3% veterinary medicine, 2% business)
107 organizations recruited on campus

Financial Matters
$6356 resident tuition and fees (2007–08)
$13,458 nonresident tuition and fees (2007–08)
$5244 room and board
77% average percent of need met
$4429 average financial aid amount received per undergraduate

Web site: www.uwrf.edu
Contact: Dr. Alan Tuchtenhagen, Director of Admissions, 410 South Third Street, 112 South Hall, River Falls, WI 54022-5001
Telephone: 715-425-3500
Fax: 715-425-0676
E-mail: alan.j.tuchtenhagen@uwrf.edu

Academics
UW-River Falls awards bachelor's and master's **degrees** and post-master's certificates. **Challenging opportunities** include advanced placement credit, accelerated degree programs, student-designed majors, an honors program, double majors, independent study, and a senior project. Special programs include cooperative education, internships, summer session for credit, off-campus study, and study-abroad. A complete listing of majors at UW-River Falls appears in the Majors by College index beginning on page 471.

The **faculty** at UW-River Falls has 235 full-time members. The student-faculty ratio is 17:1.

Students of UW-River Falls
The student body totals 5,862, of whom 5,275 are undergraduates. 60.4% are women and 39.6% are men. Students come from 40 states and territories and 18 other countries. 58% are from Wisconsin. 76% returned for their sophomore year.

Facilities and Resources
387 **computers/terminals** are available on campus for general student use. Students can access the following: online (class) registration. Campuswide network is available. The **library** has 448,088 books and 1,660 subscriptions.

Campus Life
There are 120 active organizations on campus, including a drama/theater group, newspaper, radio station, television station, and choral group. 5% of eligible men and 3% of eligible women are members of national **fraternities** and national **sororities**.

UW-River Falls is a member of the NCAA (Division III). **Intercollegiate sports** include basketball, cross-country running, football (m), ice hockey, soccer (w), softball (w), swimming and diving, tennis (w), track and field (w), volleyball (w).

Campus Safety
Student safety services include late-night transport/escort service, 24-hour emergency telephone alarm devices, 24-hour patrols by trained security personnel, student patrols, and electronically operated dormitory entrances.

Applying
UW-River Falls requires ACT and a high school transcript. It recommends rank in upper 40% of high school class. Application deadline: rolling admissions; 3/15 priority date for financial aid. Deferred admission is possible.

Ursinus College

Suburban setting ■ Private ■ Independent ■ Coed
Collegeville, Pennsylvania

Web site: www.ursinus.edu
Contact: Mr. Robert McCullough, Dean of Admissions, Ursinus College, PO
  Box 1000, Main Street, Collegeville, PA 19426
Telephone: 610-409-3200
Fax: 610-409-3662
E-mail: admissions@ursinus.edu

Academics

Ursinus awards bachelor's **degrees. Challenging opportunities** include advanced
placement credit, student-designed majors, an honors program, double majors,
independent study, and a senior project. Special programs include internships, off-
campus study, and study-abroad.

The most frequently chosen **baccalaureate** fields are social sciences, biological/life
sciences, and psychology. A complete listing of majors at Ursinus appears in the Majors
by College index beginning on page 471.

The **faculty** at Ursinus has 119 full-time members, 92% with terminal degrees. The
student-faculty ratio is 12:1.

Students of Ursinus

The student body is made up of 1,583 undergraduates. 51.8% are women and 48.2% are
men. Students come from 28 states and territories and 14 other countries. 62% are from
Pennsylvania. 1.3% are international students. 6.3% are African American, 0.2%
American Indian, 4.9% Asian American, and 2.7% Hispanic American. 88% returned for
their sophomore year.

Facilities and Resources

1,655 **computers/terminals** and 1,100 ports are available on campus for general student
use. Students can access the following: campus intranet, computer help desk, free student
e-mail accounts, online (class) grades, online (class) registration, online (class) schedules.
Campuswide network is available. 100% of college-owned or -operated housing units are
wired for high-speed Internet access. Wireless service is available via classrooms,
computer centers, computer labs, dorm rooms, libraries, student centers. The 3 **libraries**
have 200,000 books and 900 subscriptions.

Campus Life

There are 105 active organizations on campus, including a drama/theater group,
newspaper, radio station, television station, and choral group. 26% of eligible men and
38% of eligible women are members of national **fraternities**, national **sororities**, local
fraternities, and local sororities.

Ursinus is a member of the NCAA (Division III). **Intercollegiate sports** include
baseball (m), basketball, cross-country running, field hockey (w), football (m), golf,
gymnastics (w), lacrosse, soccer, softball (w), swimming and diving, tennis, track and
field, volleyball (w), wrestling (m).

Campus Safety

Student safety services include student EMT Corps for first aid/emergency first
response, late-night transport/escort service, 24-hour emergency telephone alarm
devices, and 24-hour patrols by trained security personnel.

Applying

Ursinus requires an essay, a high school transcript, 2 recommendations, and graded
paper, and in some cases SAT or ACT. It recommends an interview. Application
deadline: 2/15; 2/15 for financial aid. Early and deferred admission are possible.

Getting Accepted
5,141 applied
53% were accepted
468 enrolled (17% of accepted)
40% from top tenth of their h.s. class
Mean SAT critical reading score: 596
Mean SAT math score: 600
Mean ACT score: 23
65% had SAT critical reading scores over 600
57% had SAT math scores over 600
52% had SAT writing scores over 600
57% had ACT scores over 24
18% had SAT critical reading scores over 700
12% had SAT math scores over 700
11% had SAT writing scores over 700
13% had ACT scores over 30
3 National Merit Scholars
13 class presidents
7 valedictorians

Graduation and After
73% graduated in 4 years
2% graduated in 5 years
1% graduated in 6 years
32% pursued further study
60% had job offers within 6 months
50 organizations recruited on campus

Financial Matters
$35,160 tuition and fees (2007–08)
$8000 room and board
80% average percent of need met
$24,109 average financial aid amount received
  per undergraduate (2005–06)

Valparaiso University is home to 4,000 students seeking academic excellence in the Colleges of Arts and Sciences, Business Administration, Engineering, Nursing, and Christ College—The Honors College. Nestled in a safe, residential community of 31,000, the University offers more than seventy areas of study in the liberal arts as well as a law school and extensive graduate programs. Located 1 hour east of Chicago, "Valpo" is consistently ranked by *U.S. News & World Report* as a top regional and best-value university. A low student-faculty ratio encourages mentoring relationships, while the required interdisciplinary freshman curriculum, Valpo Core, fosters a true sense of community. Students who apply before November 1 are considered for Early Action.

Getting Accepted
3,475 applied
90% were accepted
715 enrolled (23% of accepted)
28% from top tenth of their h.s. class
3.36 average high school GPA
Mean SAT critical reading score: 556
Mean SAT math score: 570
Mean SAT writing score: 543
Mean ACT score: 25
34% had SAT critical reading scores over 600
39% had SAT math scores over 600
28% had SAT writing scores over 600
66% had ACT scores over 24
6% had SAT critical reading scores over 700
7% had SAT math scores over 700
3% had SAT writing scores over 700
16% had ACT scores over 30
12 National Merit Scholars
21 valedictorians

Graduation and After
67% graduated in 4 years
10% graduated in 5 years
27% pursued further study (3% law, 2% medicine, 2% theology)
68% had job offers within 6 months
127 organizations recruited on campus

Financial Matters
$25,200 tuition and fees (2007–08)
$7150 room and board
85% average percent of need met
$18,608 average financial aid amount received per undergraduate (2006–07 estimated)

VALPARAISO UNIVERSITY
SMALL-TOWN SETTING ■ PRIVATE ■ INDEPENDENT RELIGIOUS ■ COED
VALPARAISO, INDIANA

Web site: www.valpo.edu
Contact: Office of Admission, Kretzmann Hall, 1700 Chapel Drive, Valparaiso, IN 46383-6493
Telephone: 219-464-5011 or toll-free 888-GO-VALPO
Fax: 219-464-6898
E-mail: undergrad.admissions@valpo.edu

Academics
Valparaiso awards associate, bachelor's, master's, and first-professional **degrees** and post-bachelor's and post-master's certificates. **Challenging opportunities** include advanced placement credit, accelerated degree programs, student-designed majors, freshman honors college, an honors program, double majors, independent study, and a senior project. Special programs include cooperative education, internships, summer session for credit, off-campus study, study-abroad, and Air Force ROTC.

The most frequently chosen **baccalaureate** fields are business/marketing, social sciences, and engineering. A complete listing of majors at Valparaiso appears in the Majors by College index beginning on page 471.

The **faculty** at Valparaiso has 254 full-time members, 91% with terminal degrees. The student-faculty ratio is 12:1.

Students of Valparaiso
The student body totals 3,872, of whom 2,915 are undergraduates. 52.2% are women and 47.8% are men. Students come from 45 states and territories and 41 other countries. 37% are from Indiana. 2.6% are international students. 4.4% are African American, 0.3% American Indian, 1.5% Asian American, and 3.5% Hispanic American. 85% returned for their sophomore year.

Facilities and Resources
901 **computers/terminals** and 5,100 ports are available on campus for general student use. Students can access the following: campus intranet, computer help desk, free student e-mail accounts, online (class) grades, online (class) registration, online (class) schedules, Web academic information, degree audit. Campuswide network is available. 100% of college-owned or -operated housing units are wired for high-speed Internet access. Wireless service is available via classrooms, computer centers, computer labs, dorm rooms, learning centers, libraries, student centers. The 2 **libraries** have 471,645 books and 41,649 subscriptions.

Campus Life
There are 81 active organizations on campus, including a drama/theater group, newspaper, radio station, and choral group. 25% of eligible men and 20% of eligible women are members of national **fraternities** and local **sororities**.

Valparaiso is a member of the NCAA (Division I). **Intercollegiate sports** (some offering scholarships) include baseball (m), basketball, cross-country running, football (m), soccer, softball (w), swimming and diving, tennis, track and field, volleyball (w).

Campus Safety
Student safety services include late-night transport/escort service, 24-hour emergency telephone alarm devices, 24-hour patrols by trained security personnel, and electronically operated dormitory entrances.

Applying
Valparaiso requires an essay, SAT or ACT, and a high school transcript, and in some cases an interview. It recommends an interview and 2 recommendations. Application deadline: 8/15; 3/1 priority date for financial aid. Deferred admission is possible.

VANDERBILT UNIVERSITY

URBAN SETTING ■ PRIVATE ■ INDEPENDENT ■ COED
NASHVILLE, TENNESSEE

Web site: www.vanderbilt.edu
Contact: Mr. Douglas Christiansen, Dean of Undergraduate Admissions, 2305
West End Avenue, Nashville, TN 37203-1700
Telephone: 615-322-2561 or toll-free 800-288-0432
Fax: 615-343-7765
E-mail: admissions@vanderbilt.edu

Academics

Vanderbilt awards bachelor's, master's, doctoral, and first-professional **degrees**. **Challenging opportunities** include advanced placement credit, accelerated degree programs, student-designed majors, an honors program, double majors, independent study, and a senior project. Special programs include cooperative education, internships, summer session for credit, off-campus study, study-abroad, and Army, Navy, and Air Force ROTC.

The most frequently chosen **baccalaureate** fields are social sciences, engineering, and foreign languages and literature. A complete listing of majors at Vanderbilt appears in the Majors by College index beginning on page 471.

Students of Vanderbilt

The student body totals 11,847, of whom 6,532 are undergraduates. 52.6% are women and 47.4% are men. Students come from 54 states and territories and 36 other countries. 17% are from Tennessee. 2.8% are international students. 9.1% are African American, 0.3% American Indian, 6.6% Asian American, and 5.6% Hispanic American. 96% returned for their sophomore year.

Facilities and Resources

400 **computers/terminals** are available on campus for general student use. Students can access the following: productivity and educational software. Campuswide network is available. The 8 **libraries** have 1,812,869 books and 26,885 subscriptions.

Campus Life

There are 264 active organizations on campus, including a drama/theater group, newspaper, radio station, choral group, and marching band. 34% of eligible men and 50% of eligible women are members of national **fraternities** and national **sororities**.

Vanderbilt is a member of the NCAA (Division I). **Intercollegiate sports** (some offering scholarships) include baseball (m), basketball, cross-country running, football (m), golf, lacrosse (w), soccer, tennis, track and field (w).

Campus Safety

Student safety services include late-night transport/escort service, 24-hour emergency telephone alarm devices, 24-hour patrols by trained security personnel, student patrols, and electronically operated dormitory entrances.

Applying

Vanderbilt requires an essay, SAT or ACT, a high school transcript, and 2 recommendations. It recommends SAT Subject Tests. Application deadline: 1/3; 2/1 priority date for financial aid. Deferred admission is possible.

Getting Accepted

12,911 applied
33% were accepted
1,673 enrolled (39% of accepted)
80% from top tenth of their h.s. class
3.67 average high school GPA
91% had SAT critical reading scores over 600
92% had SAT math scores over 600
90% had SAT writing scores over 600
97% had ACT scores over 24
46% had SAT critical reading scores over 700
54% had SAT math scores over 700
43% had SAT writing scores over 700
70% had ACT scores over 30

Graduation and After

85% graduated in 4 years
5% graduated in 5 years
1% graduated in 6 years
32% pursued further study (20% arts and sciences, 7% law, 4% medicine)
63% had job offers within 6 months
250 organizations recruited on campus

Financial Matters

$35,276 tuition and fees (2007–08)
$11,446 room and board
99% average percent of need met
$33,896 average financial aid amount received per undergraduate (2006–07 estimated)

VASSAR COLLEGE

SUBURBAN SETTING ■ PRIVATE ■ INDEPENDENT ■ COED
POUGHKEEPSIE, NEW YORK

Getting Accepted
6,393 applied
29% were accepted
678 enrolled (37% of accepted)
69% from top tenth of their h.s. class
3.7 average high school GPA
Mean SAT critical reading score: 700
Mean SAT math score: 680
Mean ACT score: 30
96% had SAT critical reading scores over 600
93% had SAT math scores over 600
96% had SAT writing scores over 600
58% had SAT critical reading scores over 700
38% had SAT math scores over 700
53% had SAT writing scores over 700
28 class presidents
30 valedictorians

Graduation and After
88% graduated in 4 years
4% graduated in 5 years
1% graduated in 6 years
20% pursued further study (11% arts and
    sciences, 3% medicine, 2% law)
51.8% had job offers within 6 months
29 organizations recruited on campus

Financial Matters
$38,115 tuition and fees (2007–08)
$8570 room and board
100% average percent of need met
$27,982 average financial aid amount received
    per undergraduate (2006–07 estimated)

Web site: www.vassar.edu
Contact: Dr. David M. Borus, Dean of Admission and Financial Aid, 124
    Raymond Avenue, Poughkeepsie, NY 12604
Telephone: 845-437-7300 or toll-free 800-827-7270
Fax: 845-437-7063
E-mail: admissions@vassar.edu

Academics
Vassar awards bachelor's and master's **degrees**. **Challenging opportunities** include
advanced placement credit, student-designed majors, double majors, independent study,
and a senior project. Special programs include cooperative education, internships, off-
campus study, and study-abroad.

The most frequently chosen **baccalaureate** fields are social sciences, English, and
visual and performing arts. A complete listing of majors at Vassar appears in the Majors
by College index beginning on page 471.

The **faculty** at Vassar has 293 full-time members, 88% with terminal degrees. The
student-faculty ratio is 8:1.

Students of Vassar
The student body totals 2,451, of whom 2,450 are undergraduates. 60.6% are women
and 39.4% are men. Students come from 51 states and territories and 50 other countries.
26% are from New York. 5.6% are international students. 4.8% are African American,
0.2% American Indian, 10.2% Asian American, and 6.8% Hispanic American. 96%
returned for their sophomore year.

Facilities and Resources
300 **computers/terminals** are available on campus for general student use. Students can
access the following: campus intranet, computer help desk, free student e-mail accounts,
online (class) grades, online (class) registration, online (class) schedules, Ethernet.
Campuswide network is available. 100% of college-owned or -operated housing units are
wired for high-speed Internet access. Wireless service is available via entire campus. The
2 **libraries** have 886,097 books and 5,302 subscriptions.

Campus Life
There are 120 active organizations on campus, including a drama/theater group,
newspaper, radio station, television station, and choral group. No national or local
fraternities or **sororities**.

Vassar is a member of the NCAA (Division III). **Intercollegiate sports** include
baseball (m), basketball, crew, cross-country running, fencing, field hockey (w), golf (w),
lacrosse, soccer, squash, swimming and diving, tennis, volleyball.

Campus Safety
Student safety services include late-night transport/escort service, 24-hour emergency
telephone alarm devices, 24-hour patrols by trained security personnel, student patrols,
and electronically operated dormitory entrances.

Applying
Vassar requires an essay, SAT and SAT Subject Tests or ACT, a high school transcript,
and 2 recommendations. Application deadline: 1/1; 2/1 for financial aid. Deferred admission is possible.

VILLANOVA UNIVERSITY

SUBURBAN SETTING ■ PRIVATE ■ INDEPENDENT RELIGIOUS ■ COED
VILLANOVA, PENNSYLVANIA

Web site: www.villanova.edu
Contact: Mr. Michael Gaynor, Director of University Admission, 800
  Lancaster Avenue, Villanova, PA 19085-1672
Telephone: 610-519-4000
Fax: 610-519-6450
E-mail: gotovu@villanova.edu

Academics

Villanova awards associate, bachelor's, master's, doctoral, and first-professional **degrees**.
Challenging opportunities include advanced placement credit, accelerated degree
programs, an honors program, double majors, independent study, and a senior project.
Special programs include cooperative education, internships, summer session for credit,
off-campus study, study-abroad, and Army, Navy, and Air Force ROTC.

The most frequently chosen **baccalaureate** fields are business/marketing, social sciences, and engineering. A complete listing of majors at Villanova appears in the Majors
by College index beginning on page 471.

The **faculty** at Villanova has 570 full-time members, 89% with terminal degrees.
The student-faculty ratio is 14:1.

Students of Villanova

The student body totals 10,430, of whom 7,350 are undergraduates. 50.9% are women
and 49.1% are men. Students come from 46 states and territories and 41 other countries.
29% are from Pennsylvania. 2.3% are international students. 4.2% are African
American, 0.2% American Indian, 6.5% Asian American, and 6% Hispanic American.
94% returned for their sophomore year.

Facilities and Resources

6,466 **computers/terminals** and 18,000 ports are available on campus for general
student use. Students can access the following: campus intranet, computer help desk, free
student e-mail accounts, online (class) grades, online (class) registration, online (class)
schedules, learning management system, web-based laundry reservation, electronic
library reserves, electronic portfolios, data vaulting, calendar system, basketball ticket
lottery, printing. Campuswide network is available. 100% of college-owned or -operated
housing units are wired for high-speed Internet access. Wireless service is available via
classrooms, computer centers, computer labs, dorm rooms, learning centers, libraries,
student centers. The 3 **libraries** have 712,000 books and 12,000 subscriptions.

Campus Life

There are 100 active organizations on campus, including a drama/theater group,
newspaper, radio station, television station, choral group, and marching band. 20% of
eligible men and 28% of eligible women are members of national **fraternities** and
national **sororities**.

Villanova is a member of the NCAA (Division I). **Intercollegiate sports** (some offering scholarships) include baseball (m), basketball, cheerleading, crew (w), cross-country
running, field hockey (w), football (m), golf (m), lacrosse, soccer, softball (w), swimming
and diving, tennis, track and field, volleyball (w), water polo (w).

Campus Safety

Student safety services include late-night transport/escort service, 24-hour emergency
telephone alarm devices, 24-hour patrols by trained security personnel, student patrols,
and electronically operated dormitory entrances.

Applying

Villanova requires an essay, SAT or ACT, a high school transcript, recommendations,
and activities resume. Application deadline: 1/7; 2/7 priority date for financial aid. Early
and deferred admission are possible.

Vision and education go hand in hand
at Villanova. The University invests
in students' futures by updating its
facilities and resources. Three of its
newest initiatives include the
construction of the $20-million Center
for Engineering Education and
Research, the completion of $35 mil-
lion in expansion and enhancement of
the Mendel Science Center, and $20
million in renovation of the College of
Commerce and Finance's Bartley Hall.
Overall, in the last ten years,
Villanova has dedicated more than
$212 million to these initiatives and
more, including eight new apartment-
style buildings, the new Student
Health Center, and improvements to
the computing infrastructure.

Getting Accepted
13,760 applied
42% were accepted
1,604 enrolled (28% of accepted)
54% from top tenth of their h.s. class
3.76 average high school GPA
Mean SAT critical reading score: 626
Mean SAT math score: 650
Mean SAT writing score: 631
Mean ACT score: 29
69% had SAT critical reading scores over 600
79% had SAT math scores over 600
92% had ACT scores over 24
15% had SAT critical reading scores over 700
27% had SAT math scores over 700
48% had ACT scores over 30
28 valedictorians

Graduation and After
82% graduated in 4 years
5% graduated in 5 years
1% graduated in 6 years
28% pursued further study (7% arts and sciences, 6% law, 3% business)
67% had job offers within 6 months
315 organizations recruited on campus

Financial Matters
$34,900 tuition and fees (2007–08)
$9810 room and board
78% average percent of need met
$20,503 average financial aid amount received
  per undergraduate (2005–06 estimated)

Virginia Military Institute (VMI) offers a challenging curricular and co-curricular undergraduate experience, with the mission of producing educated and honorable men and women who will be leaders in all walks of life. Its 1,370 cadets pursue B.A. or B.S. degrees in fourteen disciplines in the general fields of engineering, science, and liberal arts. VMI combines a full college curriculum within a framework of military discipline that emphasizes the qualities of honor, integrity, and responsibility. Undergirding all aspects of cadet life is the VMI Honor Code, to which all cadets subscribe.

Getting Accepted
1,704 applied
54% were accepted
410 enrolled (44% of accepted)
14% from top tenth of their h.s. class
3.37 average high school GPA
31% had SAT critical reading scores over 600
31% had SAT math scores over 600
20% had SAT writing scores over 600
42% had ACT scores over 24
3% had SAT critical reading scores over 700
3% had SAT math scores over 700
1% had SAT writing scores over 700
4% had ACT scores over 30

Graduation and After
Graduates pursuing further study: 9% arts and sciences, 7% engineering, 1% dentistry
98% had job offers within 6 months
40 organizations recruited on campus

Financial Matters
$8043 resident tuition and fees (2007–08)
$23,887 nonresident tuition and fees (2007–08)
$6108 room and board
90% average percent of need met
$13,960 average financial aid amount received per undergraduate (2005–06)

VIRGINIA MILITARY INSTITUTE
SMALL-TOWN SETTING ■ PUBLIC ■ STATE-SUPPORTED ■ COED, PRIMARILY MEN
LEXINGTON, VIRGINIA

Web site: www.vmi.edu
Contact: Lt. Col. Tom Mortenson, Associate Director of Admissions, Admissions Office, Lexington, VA 24450
Telephone: 540-464-7211 or toll-free 800-767-4207
Fax: 540-464-7746
E-mail: admissions@vmi.edu

Academics
VMI awards bachelor's **degrees. Challenging opportunities** include advanced placement credit, accelerated degree programs, an honors program, double majors, independent study, and a senior project. Special programs include internships, summer session for credit, study-abroad, and Army, Navy, and Air Force ROTC. A complete listing of majors at VMI appears in the Majors by College index beginning on page 471.

The **faculty** at VMI has 117 full-time members, 98% with terminal degrees. The student-faculty ratio is 10:1.

Students of VMI
The student body is made up of 1,378 undergraduates. 8.1% are women and 91.9% are men. Students come from 45 states and territories and 9 other countries. 58% are from Virginia. 1.6% are international students. 5.5% are African American, 0.4% American Indian, 3.9% Asian American, and 3.4% Hispanic American. 80% returned for their sophomore year.

Facilities and Resources
200 **computers/terminals** are available on campus for general student use. Campuswide network is available. The 2 **libraries** have 162,053 books and 785 subscriptions.

Campus Life
There are 47 active organizations on campus, including a drama/theater group, newspaper, choral group, and marching band. No national or local **fraternities** or **sororities**.

VMI is a member of the NCAA (Division I). **Intercollegiate sports** (some offering scholarships) include baseball (m), basketball (m), cross-country running, football (m), golf (m), lacrosse (m), riflery, soccer (m), swimming and diving, tennis (m), track and field, wrestling (m).

Campus Safety
Student safety services include 24-hour emergency telephone alarm devices, 24-hour patrols by trained security personnel, and student patrols.

Applying
VMI requires SAT or ACT and a high school transcript. It recommends an essay, an interview, and 2 recommendations. Application deadline: 3/1; 3/1 priority date for financial aid. Early admission is possible.

VIRGINIA POLYTECHNIC INSTITUTE AND STATE UNIVERSITY

SMALL-TOWN SETTING ■ PUBLIC ■ STATE-SUPPORTED ■ COED
BLACKSBURG, VIRGINIA

Web site: www.vt.edu
Contact: Ms. Mildred Johnson, Senior Associate Director for Undergraduate Admissions, 201 Burruss Hall, Blacksburg, VA 24061-0202
Telephone: 540-231-6267
Fax: 540-231-3242
E-mail: vtadmiss@vt.edu

Academics

Virginia Tech awards associate, bachelor's, master's, doctoral, and first-professional **degrees**. **Challenging opportunities** include advanced placement credit, accelerated degree programs, an honors program, double majors, independent study, and a senior project. Special programs include cooperative education, internships, summer session for credit, study-abroad, and Army, Navy, and Air Force ROTC.

The most frequently chosen **baccalaureate** fields are business/marketing, engineering, and family and consumer sciences. A complete listing of majors at Virginia Tech appears in the Majors by College index beginning on page 471.

The **faculty** at Virginia Tech has 1,371 full-time members, 89% with terminal degrees. The student-faculty ratio is 17:1.

Students of Virginia Tech

The student body totals 29,898, of whom 23,041 are undergraduates. 41.6% are women and 58.4% are men. Students come from 49 states and territories and 77 other countries. 76% are from Virginia. 1.8% are international students. 4.2% are African American, 0.3% American Indian, 7.2% Asian American, and 2.6% Hispanic American. 89% returned for their sophomore year.

Facilities and Resources

8,000 **computers/terminals** are available on campus for general student use. Students can access the following: campus intranet, computer help desk, free student e-mail accounts, online (class) grades, online (class) registration, online (class) schedules. Campuswide network is available. Wireless service is available via entire campus. The 5 **libraries** have 2,268,619 books and 33,874 subscriptions.

Campus Life

There are 600 active organizations on campus, including a drama/theater group, newspaper, radio station, television station, choral group, and marching band. 13% of eligible men and 20% of eligible women are members of national **fraternities**, national **sororities**, and local fraternities.

Virginia Tech is a member of the NCAA (Division I). **Intercollegiate sports** (some offering scholarships) include baseball (m), basketball (m), cross-country running, football (m), golf (m), lacrosse (w), soccer, swimming and diving, tennis, track and field, ultimate Frisbee, volleyball (w).

Campus Safety

Student safety services include late-night transport/escort service, 24-hour emergency telephone alarm devices, 24-hour patrols by trained security personnel, student patrols, and electronically operated dormitory entrances.

Applying

Virginia Tech requires SAT or ACT and a high school transcript, and in some cases SAT and SAT Subject Tests or ACT. It recommends a minimum high school GPA of 3.0. Application deadline: 1/15; 3/11 priority date for financial aid. Early and deferred admission are possible.

Getting Accepted

19,429 applied
67% were accepted
5,122 enrolled (39% of accepted)
40% from top tenth of their h.s. class
3.76 average high school GPA
Mean SAT critical reading score: 586
Mean SAT math score: 617
Mean SAT writing score: 580
44% had SAT critical reading scores over 600
62% had SAT math scores over 600
43% had SAT writing scores over 600
8% had SAT critical reading scores over 700
13% had SAT math scores over 700
5% had SAT writing scores over 700
73 valedictorians

Graduation and After

52% graduated in 4 years
24% graduated in 5 years
4% graduated in 6 years
18% pursued further study (6% arts and sciences, 3% engineering, 3% medicine)
67% had job offers within 6 months
400 organizations recruited on campus

Financial Matters

$7397 resident tuition and fees (2007–08)
$19,605 nonresident tuition and fees (2007–08)
$5106 room and board
68% average percent of need met
$8171 average financial aid amount received per undergraduate (2005–06)

Wabash College

Small-town setting ■ Private ■ Independent ■ Men Only
Crawfordsville, Indiana

Web site: www.wabash.edu
Contact: Mr. Steve Klein, Dean of Admissions, PO Box 362, Crawfordsville, IN 47933-0352
Telephone: 765-361-6225 or toll-free 800-345-5385
Fax: 765-361-6437
E-mail: admissions@wabash.edu

As a college for men, Wabash helps students achieve their full potential—intellectually, athletically, emotionally, and artistically. Wabash prepares students for leadership in an ever-changing world. The College helps them learn to think clearly and openly and to explore a variety of interests. Independence and responsibility are emphasized and defined by the Gentlemen's Rule, which calls on students to conduct themselves as gentlemen at all times. With the guidance of professors who are accessible, a support staff that cares, and a nationwide network of alumni willing to offer assistance and encouragement, Wabash men frequently surpass even their own expectations.

Academics

Wabash awards bachelor's **degrees**. **Challenging opportunities** include advanced placement credit, double majors, independent study, and a senior project. Special programs include internships, off-campus study, and study-abroad.

The most frequently chosen **baccalaureate** fields are English, social sciences, and psychology. A complete listing of majors at Wabash appears in the Majors by College index beginning on page 471.

The **faculty** at Wabash has 86 full-time members, 98% with terminal degrees. The student-faculty ratio is 10:1.

Students of Wabash

The student body is made up of 917 undergraduates. Students come from 30 states and territories and 19 other countries. 73% are from Indiana. 4.8% are international students. 6% are African American, 0.1% American Indian, 2.2% Asian American, and 5.2% Hispanic American. 88% returned for their sophomore year.

Facilities and Resources

350 **computers/terminals** are available on campus for general student use. Students can access the following: campus intranet, computer help desk, free student e-mail accounts, online (class) grades, online (class) schedules, online course management; degree audit; expenses. Campuswide network is available. 100% of college-owned or -operated housing units are wired for high-speed Internet access. Wireless service is available via entire campus. The **library** has 434,460 books and 5,530 subscriptions.

Campus Life

There are 64 active organizations on campus, including a drama/theater group, newspaper, radio station, and choral group. 60% of eligible undergraduates are members of national **fraternities**.

Wabash is a member of the NCAA (Division III). **Intercollegiate sports** include baseball, basketball, cross-country running, football, golf, soccer, swimming and diving, tennis, track and field, wrestling.

Campus Safety

Student safety services include late-night transport/escort service, 24-hour emergency telephone alarm devices, and 24-hour patrols by trained security personnel.

Applying

Wabash requires SAT or ACT and a high school transcript. It recommends an essay, an interview, and recommendations. Application deadline: rolling admissions; 3/1 for financial aid, with a 2/15 priority date. Early and deferred admission are possible.

Getting Accepted

1,419 applied
47% were accepted
250 enrolled (37% of accepted)
37% from top tenth of their h.s. class
3.6 average high school GPA
Mean SAT critical reading score: 576
Mean SAT math score: 599
Mean SAT writing score: 557
Mean ACT score: 24
38% had SAT critical reading scores over 600
49% had SAT math scores over 600
33% had SAT writing scores over 600
57% had ACT scores over 24
12% had SAT critical reading scores over 700
13% had SAT math scores over 700
6% had SAT writing scores over 700
13% had ACT scores over 30
5 valedictorians

Graduation and After

65% graduated in 4 years
6% graduated in 5 years
37% pursued further study (16% arts and sciences, 10% law, 9% medicine)
60% had job offers within 6 months
90 organizations recruited on campus

Financial Matters

$26,350 tuition and fees (2007–08)
$7700 room and board
100% average percent of need met
$20,607 average financial aid amount received per undergraduate (2006–07 estimated)

WAGNER COLLEGE
URBAN SETTING ■ PRIVATE ■ INDEPENDENT ■ COED
STATEN ISLAND, NEW YORK

Web site: www.wagner.edu

Contact: Ms. Leigh-Ann DePascale, Director of Admissions, One Campus Road, Staten Island, NY 10301

Telephone: 718-390-3411 Ext. 3412 or toll-free 800-221-1010 (out-of-state)

Fax: 718-390-3105

E-mail: adm@wagner.edu

Academics
Wagner awards bachelor's and master's **degrees** and post-master's certificates. **Challenging opportunities** include an honors program, double majors, and a senior project. Special programs include internships, summer session for credit, off-campus study, study-abroad, and Army ROTC.

The most frequently chosen **baccalaureate** fields are business/marketing, visual and performing arts, and health professions and related sciences. A complete listing of majors at Wagner appears in the Majors by College index beginning on page 471.

The **faculty** at Wagner has 98 full-time members, 91% with terminal degrees. The student-faculty ratio is 13:1.

Students of Wagner
The student body totals 2,280, of whom 1,941 are undergraduates. 63.9% are women and 36.1% are men. Students come from 38 states and territories and 14 other countries. 41% are from New York. 0.6% are international students. 5.3% are African American, 0.2% American Indian, 2.3% Asian American, and 5% Hispanic American. 82% returned for their sophomore year.

Facilities and Resources
150 **computers/terminals** are available on campus for general student use. Campuswide network is available. The **library** has 310,000 books and 1,000 subscriptions.

Campus Life
There are 66 active organizations on campus, including a drama/theater group, newspaper, radio station, and choral group. 11% of eligible men and 9% of eligible women are members of national **fraternities**, national **sororities**, local fraternities, and local sororities.

Wagner is a member of the NCAA (Division I). **Intercollegiate sports** (some offering scholarships) include baseball (m), basketball, cross-country running, football (m), golf, lacrosse, soccer (w), softball (w), swimming and diving (w), tennis, track and field, volleyball (w), water polo (w), wrestling (m).

Campus Safety
Student safety services include late-night transport/escort service, 24-hour emergency telephone alarm devices, 24-hour patrols by trained security personnel, and electronically operated dormitory entrances.

Applying
Wagner requires an essay, SAT or ACT, a high school transcript, 2 recommendations, and a minimum high school GPA of 2.7, and in some cases an interview. It recommends an interview and a minimum high school GPA of 3.0. Application deadline: rolling admissions; 2/15 priority date for financial aid. Early and deferred admission are possible.

Getting Accepted
2,862 applied
59% were accepted
529 enrolled (31% of accepted)
17% from top tenth of their h.s. class
3.5 average high school GPA
Mean SAT critical reading score: 565
Mean SAT math score: 560
Mean ACT score: 25
46% had SAT critical reading scores over 600
50% had SAT math scores over 600
45% had SAT writing scores over 600
87% had ACT scores over 24
5% had SAT critical reading scores over 700
8% had SAT math scores over 700
5% had SAT writing scores over 700
6% had ACT scores over 30
24 class presidents
7 valedictorians

Graduation and After
64% graduated in 4 years
5% graduated in 5 years
28% pursued further study
65% had job offers within 6 months
51 organizations recruited on campus

Financial Matters
$29,500 tuition and fees (2007–08)
$8900 room and board
78% average percent of need met
$14,734 average financial aid amount received per undergraduate (2006–07 estimated)

Wake Forest University

Suburban setting ■ Private ■ Independent ■ Coed
Winston-Salem, North Carolina

Web site: www.wfu.edu
Contact: Ms. Martha Allman, Director of Admissions, PO Box 7305,
  Winston-Salem, NC 27109
Telephone: 336-758-5201
Fax: 336-758-5201
E-mail: admissions@wfu.edu

Getting Accepted
7,177 applied
42% were accepted
1,124 enrolled (37% of accepted)
64% from top tenth of their h.s. class
83% had SAT critical reading scores over 600
86% had SAT math scores over 600
26% had SAT critical reading scores over 700
32% had SAT math scores over 700

Graduation and After
79% graduated in 4 years
10% graduated in 5 years
29% pursued further study
58% had job offers within 6 months
435 organizations recruited on campus

Financial Matters
$36,975 tuition and fees (2008–09)
$9867 room and board
86% average percent of need met
$24,745 average financial aid amount received
  per undergraduate (2005–06 estimated)

Academics
Wake Forest awards bachelor's, master's, doctoral, and first-professional **degrees**. **Challenging opportunities** include advanced placement credit, an honors program, double majors, independent study, and a senior project. Special programs include internships, summer session for credit, off-campus study, study-abroad, and Army ROTC.

The most frequently chosen **baccalaureate** fields are social sciences, business/marketing, and foreign languages and literature. A complete listing of majors at Wake Forest appears in the Majors by College index beginning on page 471.

The **faculty** at Wake Forest has 468 full-time members, 90% with terminal degrees. The student-faculty ratio is 10:1.

Students of Wake Forest
The student body totals 6,788, of whom 4,412 are undergraduates. 50.8% are women and 49.2% are men. Students come from 50 states and territories and 25 other countries. 25% are from North Carolina. 1.1% are international students. 6.6% are African American, 0.6% American Indian, 5.1% Asian American, and 2.2% Hispanic American. 94% returned for their sophomore year.

Facilities and Resources
150 **computers/terminals** and 3,500 ports are available on campus for general student use. Students can access the following: campus intranet, computer help desk, free student e-mail accounts, online (class) grades, online (class) registration, online (class) schedules, financial information online, GPA, drop-add, transcript requests. Campuswide network is available. 100% of college-owned or -operated housing units are wired for high-speed Internet access. Wireless service is available via entire campus. The 4 **libraries** have 923,123 books and 16,448 subscriptions.

Campus Life
There are 135 active organizations on campus, including a drama/theater group, newspaper, radio station, television station, choral group, and marching band. 35% of eligible men and 48% of eligible women are members of national **fraternities** and national **sororities**.

Wake Forest is a member of the NCAA (Division I). **Intercollegiate sports** (some offering scholarships) include baseball (m), basketball, cross-country running, field hockey (w), football (m), golf, soccer, tennis, track and field, volleyball (w).

Campus Safety
Student safety services include late-night transport/escort service, 24-hour emergency telephone alarm devices, 24-hour patrols by trained security personnel, and electronically operated dormitory entrances.

Applying
Wake Forest requires an essay, SAT or ACT, a high school transcript, and 1 recommendation. Application deadline: 1/15; 3/1 for financial aid, with a 2/1 priority date. Early and deferred admission are possible.

WARTBURG COLLEGE

SMALL-TOWN SETTING ■ PRIVATE ■ INDEPENDENT RELIGIOUS ■ COED
WAVERLY, IOWA

Web site: www.wartburg.edu
Contact: Mr. Todd Coleman, Assistant Vice President for Admissions, 100
   Wartburg Boulevard, PO Box 1003, Waverly, IA 50677-0903
Telephone: 319-352-8264 or toll-free 800-772-2085
Fax: 319-352-8579
E-mail: admissions@wartburg.edu

Academics

Wartburg awards bachelor's **degrees**. **Challenging opportunities** include advanced placement credit, accelerated degree programs, student-designed majors, an honors program, double majors, independent study, and a senior project. Special programs include internships, summer session for credit, off-campus study, and study-abroad.

The most frequently chosen **baccalaureate** fields are business/marketing, education, and biological/life sciences. A complete listing of majors at Wartburg appears in the Majors by College index beginning on page 471.

The **faculty** at Wartburg has 107 full-time members, 84% with terminal degrees. The student-faculty ratio is 12:1.

Students of Wartburg

The student body is made up of 1,810 undergraduates. 52.3% are women and 47.7% are men. Students come from 24 states and territories and 43 other countries. 77% are from Iowa. 5.6% are international students. 3.1% are African American, 0.4% American Indian, 1.6% Asian American, and 1.5% Hispanic American. 81% returned for their sophomore year.

Facilities and Resources

250 **computers/terminals** are available on campus for general student use. Students can access the following: campus intranet, computer help desk, free student e-mail accounts, online (class) registration. Campuswide network is available. 100% of college-owned or -operated housing units are wired for high-speed Internet access. Wireless service is available via classrooms, libraries, student centers.

Campus Life

There are 96 active organizations on campus, including a drama/theater group, newspaper, radio station, television station, and choral group. No national or local **fraternities** or **sororities**.

Wartburg is a member of the NCAA (Division III). **Intercollegiate sports** include baseball (m), basketball, cheerleading (w), cross-country running, football (m), golf, soccer, softball (w), tennis, track and field, volleyball (w), wrestling (m).

Campus Safety

Student safety services include late-night transport/escort service, 24-hour emergency telephone alarm devices, 24-hour patrols by trained security personnel, and electronically operated dormitory entrances.

Applying

Wartburg requires SAT or ACT, a high school transcript, and a minimum high school GPA of 2.0, and in some cases an interview. It recommends recommendations and secondary school report. Application deadline: rolling admissions; 3/1 priority date for financial aid. Deferred admission is possible.

Getting Accepted

1,982 applied
84% were accepted
545 enrolled (33% of accepted)
31% from top tenth of their h.s. class
3.52 average high school GPA
Mean SAT critical reading score: 549
Mean SAT math score: 580
Mean SAT writing score: 568
Mean ACT score: 24
46% had SAT critical reading scores over 600
36% had SAT math scores over 600
39% had SAT writing scores over 600
50% had ACT scores over 24
7% had SAT critical reading scores over 700
11% had SAT math scores over 700
11% had SAT writing scores over 700
7% had ACT scores over 30

Graduation and After

56% graduated in 4 years
6% graduated in 5 years
20% pursued further study

Financial Matters

$24,300 tuition and fees (2007–08)
$6985 room and board
85% average percent of need met
$17,098 average financial aid amount received
   per undergraduate (2005–06 estimated)

Washington & Jefferson College

SMALL-TOWN SETTING ■ PRIVATE ■ INDEPENDENT ■ COED
WASHINGTON, PENNSYLVANIA

Getting Accepted
7,377 applied
34% were accepted
407 enrolled (16% of accepted)
37% from top tenth of their h.s. class
3.46 average high school GPA
Mean SAT critical reading score: 570
Mean SAT math score: 582
Mean ACT score: 25
42% had SAT critical reading scores over 600
37% had SAT math scores over 600
66% had ACT scores over 24
5% had SAT critical reading scores over 700
4% had SAT math scores over 700
10% had ACT scores over 30
17 valedictorians

Graduation and After
66% graduated in 4 years
4% graduated in 5 years
1% graduated in 6 years
34% pursued further study (7% medicine, 6% arts and sciences, 5% law)
59% had job offers within 6 months
19 organizations recruited on campus

Financial Matters
$29,532 tuition and fees (2007–08)
$8030 room and board
74% average percent of need met
$19,096 average financial aid amount received per undergraduate (2006–07 estimated)

Web site: www.washjeff.edu
Contact: Mr. Alton E. Newell, Vice President for Enrollment Management, 60 South Lincoln Street, Washington, PA 15301
Telephone: 724-223-6025 or toll-free 888-WANDJAY
Fax: 724-223-6534
E-mail: admission@washjeff.edu

Academics
W & J awards associate and bachelor's **degrees. Challenging opportunities** include advanced placement credit, accelerated degree programs, student-designed majors, an honors program, double majors, independent study, and a senior project. Special programs include internships, summer session for credit, off-campus study, study-abroad, and Army and Air Force ROTC.

The most frequently chosen **baccalaureate** fields are business/marketing, biological/life sciences, and psychology. A complete listing of majors at W & J appears in the Majors by College index beginning on page 471.

The **faculty** at W & J has 109 full-time members, 94% with terminal degrees. The student-faculty ratio is 12:1.

Students of W & J
The student body is made up of 1,531 undergraduates. 47.3% are women and 52.7% are men. Students come from 34 states and territories and 6 other countries. 76% are from Pennsylvania. 0.8% are international students. 2.5% are African American, 0.1% American Indian, 1.3% Asian American, and 1% Hispanic American. 84% returned for their sophomore year.

Facilities and Resources
450 **computers/terminals** and 2,000 ports are available on campus for general student use. Students can access the following: campus intranet, computer help desk, free student e-mail accounts, online (class) grades, online (class) registration, online (class) schedules. Campuswide network is available. 100% of college-owned or -operated housing units are wired for high-speed Internet access. Wireless service is available via entire campus. The **library** has 195,059 books and 9,925 subscriptions.

Campus Life
There are 82 active organizations on campus, including a drama/theater group, newspaper, radio station, and choral group. 30% of eligible men and 33% of eligible women are members of national **fraternities** and national **sororities**.

W & J is a member of the NCAA (Division III). **Intercollegiate sports** include baseball (m), basketball, cheerleading, cross-country running, field hockey (w), football (m), golf, lacrosse, soccer, softball (w), swimming and diving, tennis, track and field, volleyball (w), water polo, wrestling (m).

Campus Safety
Student safety services include late-night transport/escort service, 24-hour emergency telephone alarm devices, 24-hour patrols by trained security personnel, and electronically operated dormitory entrances.

Applying
W & J requires an essay, SAT or ACT, a high school transcript, and 1 recommendation, and in some cases an interview. It recommends an interview. Application deadline: 3/1; 3/1 priority date for financial aid. Early and deferred admission are possible.

WASHINGTON AND LEE UNIVERSITY

SMALL-TOWN SETTING ■ PRIVATE ■ INDEPENDENT ■ COED
LEXINGTON, VIRGINIA

Web site: www.wlu.edu
Contact: Mr. William M. Hartog, Dean of Admissions and Financial Aid, 204
   West Washington Street, Lexington, VA 24450-2116
Telephone: 540-458-8710
Fax: 540-458-8062
E-mail: admissions@wlu.edu

Academics

W & L awards bachelor's, master's, and first-professional **degrees. Challenging oppor-tunities** include advanced placement credit, student-designed majors, an honors program, double majors, independent study, and a senior project. Special programs include internships, off-campus study, study-abroad, and Army ROTC.

The most frequently chosen **baccalaureate** fields are business/marketing, social sci-ences, and history. A complete listing of majors at W & L appears in the Majors by Col-lege index beginning on page 471.

The **faculty** at W & L has 212 full-time members, 95% with terminal degrees. The student-faculty ratio is 10:1.

Students of W & L

The student body totals 2,181, of whom 1,778 are undergraduates. 49.7% are women and 50.3% are men. Students come from 49 states and territories and 42 other countries. 15% are from Virginia. 3.9% are international students. 4.3% are African American, 0.3% American Indian, 3.4% Asian American, and 1.5% Hispanic American. 95% returned for their sophomore year.

Facilities and Resources

297 **computers/terminals** are available on campus for general student use. Students can access the following: online (class) registration, e-mail. Campuswide network is available. 100% of college-owned or -operated housing units are wired for high-speed Internet access. Wireless service is available via entire campus. The 3 **libraries** have 936,448 books and 8,621 subscriptions.

Campus Life

There are 127 active organizations on campus, including a drama/theater group, newspaper, radio station, television station, and choral group. 78% of eligible men and 76% of eligible women are members of national **fraternities** and national **sororities**.

W & L is a member of the NCAA (Division III). **Intercollegiate sports** include baseball (m), basketball, cross-country running, equestrian sports, field hockey (w), football (m), golf (m), soccer, swimming and diving, tennis, track and field, volleyball (w), wrestling (m).

Campus Safety

Student safety services include late-night transport/escort service, 24-hour emergency telephone alarm devices, 24-hour patrols by trained security personnel, and electroni-cally operated dormitory entrances.

Applying

W & L requires SAT or ACT, 2 unrelated SAT Subject Tests, a high school transcript, and 3 recommendations. It recommends an essay and an interview. Application deadline: 1/15; 2/1 priority date for financial aid. Deferred admission is possible.

Getting Accepted

4,215 applied
27% were accepted
463 enrolled (40% of accepted)
80% from top tenth of their h.s. class
Mean SAT critical reading score: 693
Mean SAT math score: 693
Mean ACT score: 29
95% had SAT critical reading scores over 600
97% had SAT math scores over 600
100% had ACT scores over 24
47% had SAT critical reading scores over 700
48% had SAT math scores over 700
53% had ACT scores over 30
32 National Merit Scholars
39 valedictorians

Graduation and After

87% graduated in 4 years
1% graduated in 5 years
23% pursued further study (8% arts and sci-ences, 6% law, 5% medicine)
67% had job offers within 6 months
59 organizations recruited on campus

Financial Matters

$35,445 tuition and fees (2007–08)
$8725 room and board
99% average percent of need met
$27,934 average financial aid amount received per undergraduate (2006–07 estimated)

Washington College (WC) has initiated a $40,000 scholarship program expressly for National Honor Society (NHS) members. Washington College NHS Scholarships are $10,000 annual awards renewable through the completion of eight semesters (full-time enrollment and cumulative GPA of 3.0–4.0 required). To be eligible for WC/NHS Scholarship consideration, a student must apply for freshman admission no later than February 1 of the senior year, be admitted to Washington College, and be a member of NHS prior to March 1 of the senior year. For more information, students can contact the Admission Office or visit the Washington College Web site at http://www.washcoll.edu.

Getting Accepted
2,134 applied
60% were accepted
314 enrolled (25% of accepted)
37% from top tenth of their h.s. class
3.48 average high school GPA
Mean SAT critical reading score: 575
Mean SAT math score: 568
Mean ACT score: 23
36% had SAT critical reading scores over 600
32% had SAT math scores over 600
37% had ACT scores over 24
7% had SAT critical reading scores over 700
4% had SAT math scores over 700
2% had ACT scores over 30

Graduation and After
62% graduated in 4 years
6% graduated in 5 years
40% pursued further study
90% had job offers within 6 months
30 organizations recruited on campus

Financial Matters
$32,160 tuition and fees (2007–08)
$6790 room and board
90% average percent of need met
$16,314 average financial aid amount received per undergraduate (2005–06)

WASHINGTON COLLEGE
SMALL-TOWN SETTING ■ PRIVATE ■ INDEPENDENT ■ COED
CHESTERTOWN, MARYLAND

Web site: www.washcoll.edu
Contact: Mr. Kevin Coveney, Vice President for Admissions, 300 Washington Avenue, Chesterton, MD 21620
Telephone: 410-778-7700 or toll-free 800-422-1782
Fax: 410-778-7287
E-mail: admissions_office@washcoll.edu

Academics
WC awards bachelor's and master's **degrees**. **Challenging opportunities** include advanced placement credit, student-designed majors, double majors, independent study, and a senior project. Special programs include internships, off-campus study, and study-abroad.

The most frequently chosen **baccalaureate** fields are social sciences, business/marketing, and English. A complete listing of majors at WC appears in the Majors by College index beginning on page 471.

The **faculty** at WC has 91 full-time members, 88% with terminal degrees. The student-faculty ratio is 12:1.

Students of WC
The student body totals 1,381, of whom 1,307 are undergraduates. 60.1% are women and 39.9% are men. Students come from 36 states and territories and 28 other countries. 50% are from Maryland. 2.8% are international students. 4.3% are African American, 0.3% American Indian, 1.3% Asian American, and 0.9% Hispanic American. 87% returned for their sophomore year.

Facilities and Resources
150 **computers/terminals** are available on campus for general student use. Students can access the following: e-mail. Campuswide network is available. The **library** has 243,030 books and 4,667 subscriptions.

Campus Life
There are 50 active organizations on campus, including a drama/theater group, newspaper, and choral group. 25% of eligible men and 25% of eligible women are members of national **fraternities** and national **sororities**.

WC is a member of the NCAA (Division III). **Intercollegiate sports** include baseball (m), basketball, crew, field hockey (w), lacrosse, sailing, soccer, softball (w), swimming and diving, tennis, volleyball (w).

Campus Safety
Student safety services include late-night transport/escort service, 24-hour emergency telephone alarm devices, 24-hour patrols by trained security personnel, student patrols, and electronically operated dormitory entrances.

Applying
WC requires an essay, SAT or ACT, a high school transcript, and 1 recommendation, and in some cases an interview. It recommends an interview. Application deadline: 3/1, 3/1 for nonresidents; 2/15 priority date for financial aid. Deferred admission is possible.

WASHINGTON UNIVERSITY IN ST. LOUIS

SUBURBAN SETTING ■ PRIVATE ■ INDEPENDENT ■ COED
ST. LOUIS, MISSOURI

Web site: www.wustl.edu
Contact: Ms. Nanette Tarbouni, Director of Admissions, Campus Box 1089, One Brookings Drive, St. Louis, MO 63130-4899
Telephone: 314-935-6000 or toll-free 800-638-0700
Fax: 314-935-4290
E-mail: admissions@wustl.edu

Academics

WUSTL awards bachelor's, master's, doctoral, and first-professional **degrees** and post-bachelor's certificates. **Challenging opportunities** include advanced placement credit, accelerated degree programs, student-designed majors, double majors, and independent study. Special programs include cooperative education, internships, summer session for credit, off-campus study, study-abroad, and Army and Air Force ROTC.

The most frequently chosen **baccalaureate** fields are social sciences, business/marketing, and engineering. A complete listing of majors at WUSTL appears in the Majors by College index beginning on page 471.

The **faculty** at WUSTL has 885 full-time members, 98% with terminal degrees. The student-faculty ratio is 7:1.

Students of WUSTL

The student body totals 13,382, of whom 7,253 are undergraduates. 51.2% are women and 48.8% are men. Students come from 54 states and territories and 57 other countries. 10% are from Missouri. 4% are international students. 9.5% are African American, 0.1% American Indian, 12.8% Asian American, and 2.8% Hispanic American. 97% returned for their sophomore year.

Facilities and Resources

2,500 **computers/terminals** are available on campus for general student use. Students can access the following: campus intranet, computer help desk, free student e-mail accounts, online (class) grades, online (class) registration, online (class) schedules. Campuswide network is available. 90% of college-owned or -operated housing units are wired for high-speed Internet access. Wireless service is available via classrooms, computer centers, computer labs, dorm rooms, learning centers, libraries, student centers. The 14 **libraries** have 1,703,421 books and 44,806 subscriptions.

Campus Life

There are 200 active organizations on campus, including a drama/theater group, newspaper, radio station, television station, and choral group. 25% of eligible men and 25% of eligible women are members of national **fraternities** and national **sororities**.

WUSTL is a member of the NCAA (Division III). **Intercollegiate sports** include baseball (m), basketball, cross-country running, football (m), soccer, softball (w), swimming and diving, tennis, track and field, volleyball (w).

Campus Safety

Student safety services include late-night transport/escort service, 24-hour emergency telephone alarm devices, 24-hour patrols by trained security personnel, student patrols, and electronically operated dormitory entrances.

Applying

WUSTL requires an essay, SAT or ACT, a high school transcript, and 2 recommendations. It recommends portfolio for art and architecture programs and a minimum high school GPA of 3.0. Application deadline: 1/15; 2/15 for financial aid. Early and deferred admission are possible.

Getting Accepted

22,428 applied
17% were accepted
1,338 enrolled (34% of accepted)
95% from top tenth of their h.s. class
97% had SAT critical reading scores over 600
98% had SAT math scores over 600
100% had ACT scores over 24
64% had SAT critical reading scores over 700
74% had SAT math scores over 700
85% had ACT scores over 30

Graduation and After

33% pursued further study (10% arts and sciences, 9% medicine, 7% law)
450 organizations recruited on campus

Financial Matters

$37,248 tuition and fees (2008–09)
$11,636 room and board
100% average percent of need met
$27,310 average financial aid amount received per undergraduate (2006–07 estimated)

Getting Accepted
95 applied
31% were accepted
23 enrolled (79% of accepted)
83% from top tenth of their h.s. class
3.9 average high school GPA
Mean SAT critical reading score: 670
Mean SAT math score: 710
Mean SAT writing score: 650
74% had SAT critical reading scores over 600
100% had SAT math scores over 600
82% had SAT writing scores over 600
35% had SAT critical reading scores over 700
52% had SAT math scores over 700
30% had SAT writing scores over 700
1 valedictorian

Graduation and After
57% graduated in 4 years
5% graduated in 5 years
20% pursued further study (10% engineering, 10% law)
100% had job offers within 6 months
12 organizations recruited on campus

Financial Matters
$0 tuition and fees (2008–09)
$9500 room and board
85% average percent of need met
$2797 average financial aid amount received per undergraduate (2005–06)

WEBB INSTITUTE
SUBURBAN SETTING ■ PRIVATE ■ INDEPENDENT ■ COED
GLEN COVE, NEW YORK

Web site: www.webb-institute.edu
Contact: Crescent Beach Road, Glen Cove, NY 11542-1398
Telephone: 516-671-2213
Fax: 516-674-9838
E-mail: admissions@webb-institute.edu

Academics
Webb awards bachelor's **degrees**. **Challenging opportunities** include double majors, independent study, and a senior project. Special programs include cooperative education, internships, and off-campus study.

The most frequently chosen **baccalaureate** field is engineering. A complete listing of majors at Webb appears in the Majors by College index beginning on page 471.

The **faculty** at Webb has 11 full-time members, 64% with terminal degrees. The student-faculty ratio is 12:1.

Students of Webb
The student body is made up of 91 undergraduates. 22% are women and 78% are men. Students come from 22 states and territories. 22% are from New York. 2.2% are Asian American and 2.2% Hispanic American. 96% returned for their sophomore year.

Facilities and Resources
110 **computers/terminals** are available on campus for general student use. Students can access the following: campus intranet, computer help desk, free student e-mail accounts. Campuswide network is available. 100% of college-owned or -operated housing units are wired for high-speed Internet access. Wireless service is available via entire campus. The **library** has 53,319 books and 270 subscriptions.

Campus Life
Active organizations on campus include a drama/theater group and choral group. Webb has The Webb Women.

Intercollegiate sports include basketball, cross-country running, sailing, soccer, tennis, volleyball.

Campus Safety
Student safety services include 24-hour emergency telephone alarm devices, 24-hour patrols by trained security personnel, and electronically operated dormitory entrances.

Applying
Webb requires SAT, SAT Subject Tests, SAT Subject Tests in math and either physics or chemistry, a high school transcript, an interview, 2 recommendations, proof of US citizenship or permanent residency status, and a minimum high school GPA of 3.5. Application deadline: 2/15; 7/1 priority date for financial aid.

WELLESLEY COLLEGE

SUBURBAN SETTING ■ PRIVATE ■ INDEPENDENT ■ WOMEN ONLY
WELLESLEY, MASSACHUSETTS

Web site: www.wellesley.edu
Contact: Ms. Heather Ayres, Director of Admission, 240 Green Hall,
    Wellesley, MA 02181
Telephone: 781-283-2253
Fax: 781-283-3678
E-mail: admission@wellesley.edu

SPONSOR

Academics

Wellesley awards bachelor's **degrees** (double bachelor's degree with Massachusetts Institute of Technology). **Challenging opportunities** include advanced placement credit, student-designed majors, an honors program, double majors, independent study, and a senior project. Special programs include internships, summer session for credit, off-campus study, study-abroad, and Army and Air Force ROTC.

The most frequently chosen **baccalaureate** fields are social sciences, foreign languages and literature, and psychology. A complete listing of majors at Wellesley appears in the Majors by College index beginning on page 471.

The **faculty** at Wellesley has 225 full-time members, 98% with terminal degrees. The student-faculty ratio is 9:1.

Students of Wellesley

The student body is made up of 2,380 undergraduates. Students come from 53 states and territories and 75 other countries. 17% are from Massachusetts. 8% are international students. 5.7% are African American, 0.5% American Indian, 26.3% Asian American, and 6.8% Hispanic American. 95% returned for their sophomore year.

Facilities and Resources

200 **computers/terminals** and 200 ports are available on campus for general student use. Students can access the following: campus intranet, computer help desk, free student e-mail accounts, online (class) registration, online (class) schedules, electronic bulletin boards. Campuswide network is available. 100% of college-owned or -operated housing units are wired for high-speed Internet access. Wireless service is available via computer labs, learning centers, libraries, student centers. The 4 **libraries** have 864,020 books and 18,180 subscriptions.

Campus Life

There are 160 active organizations on campus, including a drama/theater group, newspaper, radio station, television station, and choral group. No national or local **sororities**.

Wellesley is a member of the NCAA (Division III). **Intercollegiate sports** include basketball, crew, cross-country running, fencing, field hockey, golf, lacrosse, soccer, softball, squash, swimming and diving, tennis, volleyball.

Campus Safety

Student safety services include late-night transport/escort service, 24-hour emergency telephone alarm devices, 24-hour patrols by trained security personnel, and electronically operated dormitory entrances.

Applying

Wellesley requires an essay, SAT and SAT Subject Tests or ACT, a high school transcript, 3 recommendations, and SAT &2 SAT Subject Tests or ACT Writing; Midyear Report, and in some cases an interview. It recommends an interview. Application deadline: 1/15, 1/15 for nonresidents; 1/15 priority date for financial aid. Early and deferred admission are possible.

Wellesley's mission as a liberal arts and sciences college unites three aspirations: to educate women, to strive for academic excellence, and to produce graduates whose lives and careers exemplify an ideal of engagement in the world. With a 9:1 student-faculty ratio, 1,000 course offerings, and more than fifty-three majors, Wellesley provides exceptional opportunities for student-faculty collaboration. The College's outstanding resources enable it to attract talented faculty members and students and remain need-blind in admission. One of the most diverse colleges in the United States, Wellesley is a multicultural community located 12 miles from Boston. Its graduates are leaders in the laboratory, the classroom, the courtroom, the boardroom, and their communities—anywhere they choose.

Getting Accepted
4,017 applied
36% were accepted
590 enrolled (41% of accepted)
78% from top tenth of their h.s. class
Mean SAT critical reading score: 700
Mean SAT math score: 687
Mean SAT writing score: 694
Mean ACT score: 30
92% had SAT critical reading scores over 600
89% had SAT math scores over 600
94% had SAT writing scores over 600
98% had ACT scores over 24
54% had SAT critical reading scores over 700
47% had SAT math scores over 700
52% had SAT writing scores over 700
57% had ACT scores over 30

Graduation and After
85% graduated in 4 years
5% graduated in 5 years
2% graduated in 6 years
22% pursued further study (7% arts and sciences, 4% medicine, 2% law)
67% had job offers within 6 months
179 organizations recruited on campus

Financial Matters
$34,994 tuition and fees (2007–08)
$10,826 room and board
100% average percent of need met
$29,797 average financial aid amount received per undergraduate (2006–07 estimated)

WELLS COLLEGE
RURAL SETTING ■ PRIVATE ■ INDEPENDENT ■ COED, PRIMARILY WOMEN
AURORA, NEW YORK

Web site: www.wells.edu
Contact: Ms. Susan Raith Sloan, 170 Main Street, Aurora, NY 13026
Telephone: 315-364-3264 or toll-free 800-952-9355
Fax: 315-364-3227
E-mail: admissions@wells.edu

Wells College takes a unique approach to higher education that puts experiential learning at the center of all it does. Classroom learning is directly connected to career development through internships, off-campus study, study abroad, research with professors, and community service. This gives students a competitive advantage in gaining entrance to careers as well as top graduate and professional schools. Students work closely with their professors and enjoy small, seminar-style classes—a graduate style of learning that is rarely found in an undergraduate college. At the same time, Wells remains steadfast in its commitment to providing students with a high-quality education at an affordable price.

Getting Accepted
1,148 applied
64% were accepted
174 enrolled (24% of accepted)
25% from top tenth of their h.s. class
3.5 average high school GPA
Mean SAT critical reading score: 577
Mean SAT math score: 541
Mean ACT score: 24
44% had SAT critical reading scores over 600
22% had SAT math scores over 600
62% had ACT scores over 24
10% had SAT critical reading scores over 700
3% had SAT math scores over 700
7% had ACT scores over 30
3 valedictorians

Graduation and After
47% graduated in 4 years
3% graduated in 5 years
1% graduated in 6 years
17% pursued further study (17% arts and sciences, 1% law)
39% had job offers within 6 months
8 organizations recruited on campus

Financial Matters
$19,410 tuition and fees (2008–09)
$8420 room and board
89% average percent of need met
$17,562 average financial aid amount received per undergraduate (2006–07 estimated)

Academics
Wells awards bachelor's **degrees**. **Challenging opportunities** include advanced placement credit, accelerated degree programs, student-designed majors, double majors, independent study, and a senior project. Special programs include internships, off-campus study, study-abroad, and Army and Air Force ROTC.

The most frequently chosen **baccalaureate** fields are social sciences, psychology, and visual and performing arts. A complete listing of majors at Wells appears in the Majors by College index beginning on page 471.

The **faculty** at Wells has 48 full-time members, 98% with terminal degrees. The student-faculty ratio is 9:1.

Students of Wells
The student body is made up of 557 undergraduates. 77% are women and 23% are men. Students come from 31 states and territories and 14 other countries. 70% are from New York. 1.7% are international students. 5.4% are African American, 0.6% American Indian, 2.2% Asian American, and 4.1% Hispanic American. 76% returned for their sophomore year.

Facilities and Resources
96 **computers/terminals** and 1,224 ports are available on campus for general student use. Students can access the following: computer help desk, free student e-mail accounts. Campuswide network is available. 100% of college-owned or -operated housing units are wired for high-speed Internet access. The **library** has 213,221 books and 380 subscriptions.

Campus Life
There are 40 active organizations on campus, including a drama/theater group, newspaper, and choral group. No national or local **fraternities** or **sororities**.

Wells is a member of the NCAA (Division III). **Intercollegiate sports** include cross-country running, field hockey (w), lacrosse, soccer, softball (w), swimming and diving (w), tennis (w).

Campus Safety
Student safety services include late-night transport/escort service, 24-hour emergency telephone alarm devices, 24-hour patrols by trained security personnel, and electronically operated dormitory entrances.

Applying
Wells requires an essay, SAT or ACT, a high school transcript, and 2 recommendations. It recommends an interview. Application deadline: 3/1; 2/15 priority date for financial aid. Early and deferred admission are possible.

WESLEYAN COLLEGE

SUBURBAN SETTING ■ PRIVATE ■ INDEPENDENT RELIGIOUS
■ UNDERGRADUATE: WOMEN ONLY; GRADUATE: COED
MACON, GEORGIA

Web site: www.wesleyancollege.edu
Contact: Ms. Patricia Gibbs, Vice President for Enrollment Services and
   Student Affairs, 4760 Forsyth Road, Macon, GA 31210-4462
Telephone: 478-757-5206 or toll-free 800-447-6610
Fax: 478-757-4030
E-mail: admission@wesleyancollege.edu

Academics

Wesleyan College awards bachelor's and master's **degrees**. **Challenging opportunities**
include advanced placement credit, student-designed majors, an honors program, double
majors, independent study, and a senior project. Special programs include cooperative
education, internships, summer session for credit, off-campus study, and study-abroad.

The most frequently chosen **baccalaureate** fields are business/marketing, education,
and psychology. A complete listing of majors at Wesleyan College appears in the Majors
by College index beginning on page 471.

The **faculty** at Wesleyan College has 50 full-time members, 94% with terminal
degrees. The student-faculty ratio is 7:1.

Students of Wesleyan College

The student body totals 691, of whom 592 are undergraduates. 99.5% are women and
0.5% are men. Students come from 25 states and territories and 16 other countries. 90%
are from Georgia. 29.6% are international students. 22.2% are African American, 0.9%
American Indian, 0.9% Asian American, and 3.7% Hispanic American. 72% returned for
their sophomore year.

Facilities and Resources

24 **computers/terminals** are available on campus for general student use. Students can
access the following: online (class) registration. Campuswide network is available. 100%
of college-owned or -operated housing units are wired for high-speed Internet access.
Wireless service is available via classrooms, libraries. The **library** has 117,547 books and
630 subscriptions.

Campus Life

There are 51 active organizations on campus, including a drama/theater group,
newspaper, and choral group. No national or local **sororities**.

Wesleyan College is a member of the NCAA (Division III). **Intercollegiate sports**
include basketball, equestrian sports, soccer, softball, tennis, volleyball.

Campus Safety

Student safety services include late-night transport/escort service, 24-hour emergency
telephone alarm devices, 24-hour patrols by trained security personnel, and electronically operated dormitory entrances.

Applying

Wesleyan College requires an essay, SAT or ACT, a high school transcript, and a
minimum high school GPA of 2.0. It recommends an interview and 2 recommendations.
Application deadline: 4/1; 4/1 priority date for financial aid. Early and deferred admission are possible.

In 1836, Wesleyan College's founders
dared dream that women could
benefit from a rigorous study of
liberal arts and deserved the same
academic credentials as men, charter-
ing the world's first college specifically for that purpose. History has
proven them right—women achieve
more and learn more effectively at a
women's college. Wesleyan offers a
distinctive and demanding liberal arts
academic program. Students from
across the U.S. and twenty-three
countries value the academic rigor
and close ties offered by a 10:1 student-teacher ratio, crediting both for
their preparation to pursue graduate
studies as well as their postgraduate
successes in law, medicine, and other
fields. Beyond academics, Wesleyan
offers a thriving residence life
program; NCAA Division III athletics,
including a champion IHSA equestrian
program; and volunteer opportunities
through its Lane Center for Community Engagement and Service.

Getting Accepted
617 applied
49% were accepted
110 enrolled (36% of accepted)
34% from top tenth of their h.s. class
3.5 average high school GPA
Mean ACT score: 23
37% had SAT critical reading scores over 600
46% had SAT math scores over 600
36% had ACT scores over 24
6% had SAT critical reading scores over 700
8% had SAT math scores over 700
7% had ACT scores over 30

Graduation and After
24% pursued further study (11% arts and
   sciences, 6% business, 3% medicine)

Financial Matters
$16,500 tuition and fees (2007–08)
$7600 room and board
79% average percent of need met
$10,758 average financial aid amount received
   per undergraduate (2005–06 estimated)

WESLEYAN UNIVERSITY

SMALL-TOWN SETTING ■ PRIVATE ■ INDEPENDENT ■ COED
MIDDLETOWN, CONNECTICUT

Web site: www.wesleyan.edu
Contact: Ms. Nancy Meislahn, Dean of Admission and Financial Aid, Stewart M Reid House, 70 Wyllys Avenue, Middletown, CT 06459-0265
Telephone: 860-685-3000
Fax: 860-685-3001
E-mail: admissions@wesleyan.edu

Wesleyan University is among the largest colleges of liberal arts and sciences, offering a wide range of programs, courses, and resources. Students at Wesleyan make their mark in the wider world through their creativity, intellectual independence, and drive to improve the world. About a third of the undergraduates are self-identified as members of minority groups, while 12 to 15 percent are the first in their families to attend college. Wesleyan is committed to need-blind admission, need-based financial aid, and meeting the full demonstrated financial need of all students.

Getting Accepted
7,750 applied
27% were accepted
733 enrolled (35% of accepted)
71% from top tenth of their h.s. class
3.77 average high school GPA
Mean SAT critical reading score: 700
Mean SAT math score: 700
Mean SAT writing score: 690
Mean ACT score: 30
89% had SAT critical reading scores over 600
89% had SAT math scores over 600
89% had SAT writing scores over 600
98% had ACT scores over 24
56% had SAT critical reading scores over 700
49% had SAT math scores over 700
53% had SAT writing scores over 700
59% had ACT scores over 30

Graduation and After
84% graduated in 4 years
7% graduated in 5 years
1% graduated in 6 years
70% had job offers within 6 months
98 organizations recruited on campus

Financial Matters
$36,806 tuition and fees (2007–08)
$10,130 room and board
100% average percent of need met
$29,465 average financial aid amount received per undergraduate (2005–06)

Academics

Wesleyan awards bachelor's, master's, and doctoral **degrees** and post-master's certificates. **Challenging opportunities** include advanced placement credit, accelerated degree programs, student-designed majors, an honors program, double majors, independent study, and a senior project. Special programs include internships, summer session for credit, off-campus study, study-abroad, and Air Force ROTC.

The most frequently chosen **baccalaureate** fields are social sciences, area and ethnic studies, and visual and performing arts. A complete listing of majors at Wesleyan appears in the Majors by College index beginning on page 471.

The **faculty** at Wesleyan has 325 full-time members, 92% with terminal degrees. The student-faculty ratio is 9:1.

Students of Wesleyan

The student body totals 3,222, of whom 2,817 are undergraduates. 50.4% are women and 49.6% are men. Students come from 52 states and territories and 45 other countries. 8% are from Connecticut. 6.2% are international students. 6.8% are African American, 0.5% American Indian, 10.7% Asian American, and 8.3% Hispanic American. 94% returned for their sophomore year.

Facilities and Resources

190 **computers/terminals** are available on campus for general student use. Students can access the following: campus intranet, computer help desk, free student e-mail accounts, online (class) grades, online (class) registration, online (class) schedules, electronic portfolio, online course drop/add, Blackboard course management system. Campuswide network is available. 100% of college-owned or -operated housing units are wired for high-speed Internet access. Wireless service is available via entire campus. The 4 **libraries** have 1,301,176 books and 6,789 subscriptions.

Campus Life

There are 231 active organizations on campus, including a drama/theater group, newspaper, radio station, and choral group. 4% of eligible men and 3% of eligible women are members of national **fraternities**, national **sororities**, and local fraternities.

Wesleyan is a member of the NCAA (Division III). **Intercollegiate sports** include baseball (m), basketball, crew, cross-country running, field hockey (w), football (m), golf (m), ice hockey, lacrosse, soccer, softball (w), squash, swimming and diving, tennis, track and field, volleyball (w), wrestling (m).

Campus Safety

Student safety services include late-night transport/escort service, 24-hour emergency telephone alarm devices, 24-hour patrols by trained security personnel, student patrols, and electronically operated dormitory entrances.

Applying

Wesleyan requires an essay, SAT and SAT Subject Tests or ACT, a high school transcript, and 2 recommendations, and in some cases an interview. It recommends an interview. Application deadline: 1/1; 2/15 for financial aid. Early and deferred admission are possible.

WESTERN WASHINGTON UNIVERSITY

SMALL-TOWN SETTING ■ PUBLIC ■ STATE-SUPPORTED ■ COED
BELLINGHAM, WASHINGTON

SPONSOR

Web site: www.wwu.edu
Contact: Ms. Karen Copetas, Director of Admissions, 516 High Street, Bellingham, WA 98225-9009
Telephone: 360-650-3440
Fax: 360-650-7369
E-mail: admit@wwu.edu

Academics

Western awards bachelor's and master's **degrees** and post-bachelor's certificates. **Challenging opportunities** include advanced placement credit, accelerated degree programs, student-designed majors, an honors program, double majors, independent study, and a senior project. Special programs include cooperative education, internships, summer session for credit, off-campus study, and study-abroad.

The most frequently chosen **baccalaureate** fields are social sciences, business/marketing, and English. A complete listing of majors at Western appears in the Majors by College index beginning on page 471.

The **faculty** at Western has 505 full-time members, 90% with terminal degrees. The student-faculty ratio is 19:1.

Students of Western

The student body totals 14,276, of whom 13,099 are undergraduates. 55.2% are women and 44.8% are men. Students come from 46 states and territories and 31 other countries. 94% are from Washington. 0.5% are international students. 2.6% are African American, 2.3% American Indian, 8.7% Asian American, and 3.8% Hispanic American. 84% returned for their sophomore year.

Facilities and Resources

2,408 **computers/terminals** are available on campus for general student use. Students can access the following: online (class) registration. Campuswide network is available. 99% of college-owned or -operated housing units are wired for high-speed Internet access. Wireless service is available via classrooms, computer centers, computer labs, dorm rooms, learning centers, libraries, student centers. The 2 **libraries** have 1,341,300 books and 5,236 subscriptions.

Campus Life

There are 140 active organizations on campus, including a drama/theater group, newspaper, radio station, television station, and choral group. No national or local **fraternities** or **sororities**.

Western is a member of the NCAA (Division II). **Intercollegiate sports** (some offering scholarships) include basketball, cheerleading, crew, cross-country running, football (m), golf, soccer, softball (w), track and field, volleyball (w).

Campus Safety

Student safety services include late-night transport/escort service, 24-hour emergency telephone alarm devices, 24-hour patrols by trained security personnel, student patrols, and electronically operated dormitory entrances.

Applying

Western requires SAT or ACT, TOEFL for International Students, and a high school transcript. It recommends an essay. Application deadline: 3/1; 2/15 priority date for financial aid. Deferred admission is possible.

Western Washington University offers students the personal attention one might expect from a small liberal arts college; at the same time, it provides the vast resources and diversity of a university with 13,500 students. Nestled between the North Cascade Mountain Range and the salt waters of the northern Puget Sound, Western's geographic location provides both academic and personal benefits to students, as it provides easy access to fieldwork, internships, recreation, and the arts. Western's focus on undergraduate education gives students unique opportunities to engage in research, work closely with faculty members, and showcase their work regionally and nationally.

Getting Accepted
8,850 applied
73% were accepted
2,586 enrolled (40% of accepted)
26% from top tenth of their h.s. class
3.5 average high school GPA
Mean SAT critical reading score: 559
Mean SAT math score: 558
Mean ACT score: 24
32% had SAT critical reading scores over 600
30% had SAT math scores over 600
52% had ACT scores over 24
6% had SAT critical reading scores over 700
3% had SAT math scores over 700
7% had ACT scores over 30

Graduation and After
14% pursued further study
54 organizations recruited on campus

Financial Matters
$5291 resident tuition and fees (2007–08)
$16,365 nonresident tuition and fees (2007–08)
$7090 room and board
87% average percent of need met
$9310 average financial aid amount received per undergraduate (2006–07 estimated)

Westminster is a nationally recognized, comprehensive liberal arts college. With a broad array of graduate and undergraduate programs, Westminster is distinguished by its unique environment for learning. Westminster prepares students for success through active and engaged learning, real-world experiences, and its vibrant campus community. Westminster's unique location, adjacent to the Rocky Mountains and to dynamic Salt Lake City, further enriches the college experience.

Getting Accepted
1,146 applied
86% were accepted
452 enrolled (46% of accepted)
29% from top tenth of their h.s. class
3.52 average high school GPA
Mean SAT critical reading score: 570
Mean SAT math score: 550
Mean ACT score: 24
38% had SAT critical reading scores over 600
29% had SAT math scores over 600
51% had ACT scores over 24
10% had SAT critical reading scores over 700
4% had SAT math scores over 700
5% had ACT scores over 30
8 National Merit Scholars
8 valedictorians

Graduation and After
37% graduated in 4 years
12% graduated in 5 years
3% graduated in 6 years
25% pursued further study (8% business, 6% arts and sciences, 4% education)
80% had job offers within 6 months
20 organizations recruited on campus

Financial Matters
$22,374 tuition and fees (2007–08)
$6354 room and board
88% average percent of need met
$15,651 average financial aid amount received per undergraduate (2005–06)

WESTMINSTER COLLEGE
SUBURBAN SETTING ■ PRIVATE ■ INDEPENDENT ■ COED
SALT LAKE CITY, UTAH

Web site: www.westminstercollege.edu
Contact: Christina Twelves, Interim Director of Undergraduate Admissions, 1840 South 1300 East, Salt Lake City, UT 84105-3697
Telephone: 801-832-2200 or toll-free 800-748-4753 (out-of-state)
Fax: 801-832-3101
E-mail: admission@westminstercollege.edu

Academics
Westminster College awards bachelor's and master's **degrees** and post-bachelor's certificates. **Challenging opportunities** include advanced placement credit, accelerated degree programs, student-designed majors, an honors program, double majors, independent study, and a senior project. Special programs include cooperative education, internships, summer session for credit, study-abroad, and Army, Navy, and Air Force ROTC.

The most frequently chosen **baccalaureate** fields are business/marketing, health professions and related sciences, and psychology. A complete listing of majors at Westminster College appears in the Majors by College index beginning on page 471.

The **faculty** at Westminster College has 130 full-time members, 94% with terminal degrees. The student-faculty ratio is 10:1.

Students of Westminster College
The student body totals 2,661, of whom 2,048 are undergraduates. 57.7% are women and 42.3% are men. Students come from 41 states and territories and 19 other countries. 82% are from Utah. 1.6% are international students. 0.9% are African American, 0.8% American Indian, 3.4% Asian American, and 6% Hispanic American. 77% returned for their sophomore year.

Facilities and Resources
400 **computers/terminals** and 650 ports are available on campus for general student use. Students can access the following: campus intranet, computer help desk, free student e-mail accounts, online (class) grades, online (class) registration, online (class) schedules. Campuswide network is available. 100% of college-owned or -operated housing units are wired for high-speed Internet access. Wireless service is available via classrooms, computer centers, computer labs, learning centers, libraries, student centers. The 2 **libraries** have 154,069 books and 695 subscriptions.

Campus Life
There are 38 active organizations on campus, including a drama/theater group, newspaper, and choral group. 4% of eligible men and 6% of eligible women are members of local **fraternities** and local **sororities**.

Westminster College is a member of the NAIA. **Intercollegiate sports** (some offering scholarships) include basketball, cross-country running, golf, lacrosse (m), soccer (m), volleyball (w).

Campus Safety
Student safety services include late-night transport/escort service, 24-hour emergency telephone alarm devices, 24-hour patrols by trained security personnel, student patrols, and electronically operated dormitory entrances.

Applying
Westminster College requires an essay, SAT or ACT, a high school transcript, 1 recommendation, and a minimum high school GPA of 2.5. It recommends an interview. Application deadline: rolling admissions, rolling admissions for nonresidents; 4/15 priority date for financial aid. Deferred admission is possible.

WESTMONT COLLEGE

SUBURBAN SETTING ■ PRIVATE ■ INDEPENDENT RELIGIOUS ■ COED
SANTA BARBARA, CALIFORNIA

Web site: www.westmont.edu
Contact: Mrs. Joyce Luy, Dean of Admission, 955 La Paz Road, Santa
    Barbara, CA 93108
Telephone: 805-565-6200 or toll-free 800-777-9011
Fax: 805-565-6234
E-mail: admissions@westmont.edu

Academics

Westmont awards bachelor's **degrees** and post-bachelor's certificates. **Challenging opportunities** include advanced placement credit, accelerated degree programs, student-designed majors, an honors program, double majors, and a senior project. Special programs include internships, summer session for credit, off-campus study, study-abroad, and Army and Air Force ROTC.

The most frequently chosen **baccalaureate** fields are business/marketing, English, and communications/journalism. A complete listing of majors at Westmont appears in the Majors by College index beginning on page 471.

The **faculty** at Westmont has 93 full-time members, 89% with terminal degrees. The student-faculty ratio is 12:1.

Students of Westmont

The student body totals 1,337, of whom 1,336 are undergraduates. 61.3% are women and 38.7% are men. Students come from 41 states and territories and 8 other countries. 69% are from California. 0.7% are international students. 2.3% are African American, 2.3% American Indian, 8.9% Asian American, and 9.9% Hispanic American. 87% returned for their sophomore year.

Facilities and Resources

100 **computers/terminals** are available on campus for general student use. Students can access the following: campus intranet, free student e-mail accounts, online (class) schedules. Campuswide network is available. The **library** has 174,246 books and 380 subscriptions.

Campus Life

Active organizations on campus include a drama/theater group, newspaper, radio station, and choral group. No national or local **fraternities** or **sororities**.

Westmont is a member of the NAIA. **Intercollegiate sports** (some offering scholarships) include baseball (m), basketball, cross-country running, soccer, tennis, track and field, volleyball (w).

Campus Safety

Student safety services include late-night transport/escort service, 24-hour emergency telephone alarm devices, 24-hour patrols by trained security personnel, and electronically operated dormitory entrances.

Applying

Westmont requires an essay, SAT or ACT, a high school transcript, and 1 recommendation, and in some cases TOEFL and an interview. It recommends an interview. Application deadline: 2/20; 3/1 priority date for financial aid.

Getting Accepted

1,651 applied
73% were accepted
389 enrolled (32% of accepted)
45% from top tenth of their h.s. class
3.77 average high school GPA
Mean SAT critical reading score: 600
Mean SAT math score: 600
Mean SAT writing score: 600
Mean ACT score: 26
51% had SAT critical reading scores over 600
52% had SAT math scores over 600
51% had SAT writing scores over 600
78% had ACT scores over 24
12% had SAT critical reading scores over 700
10% had SAT math scores over 700
8% had SAT writing scores over 700
19% had ACT scores over 30

Graduation and After

65% graduated in 4 years
4% graduated in 5 years
1% graduated in 6 years
69% pursued further study
50 organizations recruited on campus

Financial Matters

$31,212 tuition and fees (2007–08)
$9622 room and board
69% average percent of need met
$20,266 average financial aid amount received
    per undergraduate (2006–07 estimated)

WHEATON COLLEGE

SUBURBAN SETTING ■ PRIVATE ■ INDEPENDENT RELIGIOUS ■ COED
WHEATON, ILLINOIS

Web site: www.wheaton.edu
Contact: Ms. Shawn Leftwich, Director of Admissions, 501 College Avenue,
   Wheaton, IL 60187
Telephone: 630-752-5011 or toll-free 800-222-2419 (out-of-state)
Fax: 630-752-5285
E-mail: admissions@wheaton.edu

Getting Accepted

2,160 applied
55% were accepted
582 enrolled (49% of accepted)
56% from top tenth of their h.s. class
3.73 average high school GPA
84% had SAT critical reading scores over 600
80% had SAT math scores over 600
81% had SAT writing scores over 600
95% had ACT scores over 24
39% had SAT critical reading scores over 700
26% had SAT math scores over 700
31% had SAT writing scores over 700
43% had ACT scores over 30

Graduation and After

78% graduated in 4 years
7% graduated in 5 years
1% graduated in 6 years
28% pursued further study (8% arts and sciences, 6% medicine, 5% education)
53% had job offers within 6 months
202 organizations recruited on campus

Financial Matters

$23,730 tuition and fees (2007–08)
$7252 room and board
85% average percent of need met
$19,307 average financial aid amount received per undergraduate (2006–07 estimated)

Academics

Wheaton awards bachelor's, master's, and doctoral **degrees** and post-bachelor's certificates. **Challenging opportunities** include advanced placement credit, student-designed majors, double majors, independent study, and a senior project. Special programs include internships, summer session for credit, off-campus study, study-abroad, and Army ROTC.

The most frequently chosen **baccalaureate** fields are social sciences, theology and religious vocations, and English. A complete listing of majors at Wheaton appears in the Majors by College index beginning on page 471.

The **faculty** at Wheaton has 194 full-time members, 93% with terminal degrees. The student-faculty ratio is 12:1.

Students of Wheaton

The student body totals 2,895, of whom 2,381 are undergraduates. 51% are women and 49% are men. Students come from 52 states and territories and 18 other countries. 23% are from Illinois. 1.3% are international students. 2.8% are African American, 0.3% American Indian, 7.1% Asian American, and 3.8% Hispanic American. 96% returned for their sophomore year.

Facilities and Resources

125 **computers/terminals** and 4,200 ports are available on campus for general student use. Students can access the following: campus intranet, computer help desk, free student e-mail accounts, online (class) grades, online (class) registration, online (class) schedules, financial information, degree requirements evaluation. Campuswide network is available. 100% of college-owned or -operated housing units are wired for high-speed Internet access. Wireless service is available via computer centers, computer labs, dorm rooms, learning centers, libraries, student centers. The **library** has 461,249 books and 4,012 subscriptions.

Campus Life

There are 74 active organizations on campus, including a drama/theater group, newspaper, radio station, television station, and choral group. No national or local **fraternities** or **sororities**.

Wheaton is a member of the NCAA (Division III). **Intercollegiate sports** include baseball (m), basketball, cross-country running, football (m), golf, soccer, softball (w), swimming and diving, tennis, track and field, volleyball (w), water polo (w), wrestling (m).

Campus Safety

Student safety services include late-night transport/escort service, 24-hour emergency telephone alarm devices, 24-hour patrols by trained security personnel, student patrols, and electronically operated dormitory entrances.

Applying

Wheaton requires an essay, SAT or ACT, a high school transcript, and 2 recommendations. It recommends an interview. Application deadline: 1/10; 2/15 priority date for financial aid.

Wheaton College

Small-town setting ■ Private ■ Independent ■ Coed
Norton, Massachusetts

Web site: www.wheatoncollege.edu
Contact: Ms. Gail Berson, Vice President For Enrollment and Dean of Admission and Student Aid, 26 East Main Street, Norton, MA 02766
Telephone: 508-286-8251 or toll-free 800-394-6003
Fax: 508-286-8271
E-mail: admission@wheatoncollege.edu

Academics

Wheaton awards bachelor's **degrees**. **Challenging opportunities** include advanced placement credit, accelerated degree programs, student-designed majors, an honors program, double majors, independent study, and a senior project. Special programs include internships, off-campus study, study-abroad, and Army ROTC.

The most frequently chosen **baccalaureate** fields are social sciences, psychology, and visual and performing arts. A complete listing of majors at Wheaton appears in the Majors by College index beginning on page 471.

The **faculty** at Wheaton has 137 full-time members, 88% with terminal degrees. The student-faculty ratio is 10:1.

Students of Wheaton

The student body is made up of 1,552 undergraduates. 60.2% are women and 39.8% are men. Students come from 45 states and territories and 33 other countries. 35% are from Massachusetts. 2.5% are international students. 4.7% are African American, 0.3% American Indian, 3.4% Asian American, and 2.9% Hispanic American. 88% returned for their sophomore year.

Facilities and Resources

348 **computers/terminals** and 274 ports are available on campus for general student use. Students can access the following: campus intranet, computer help desk, online (class) grades, online (class) registration, online (class) schedules. Campuswide network is available. 100% of college-owned or -operated housing units are wired for high-speed Internet access. Wireless service is available via classrooms, computer centers, computer labs, dorm rooms, learning centers, libraries, student centers. The 2 **libraries** have 397,883 books and 10,923 subscriptions.

Campus Life

There are 60 active organizations on campus, including a drama/theater group, newspaper, radio station, and choral group. No national or local **fraternities** or **sororities**.

Wheaton is a member of the NCAA (Division III). **Intercollegiate sports** include baseball (m), basketball, cross-country running, field hockey (w), lacrosse, soccer, softball (w), swimming and diving, tennis, track and field, volleyball (w).

Campus Safety

Student safety services include late-night transport/escort service, 24-hour emergency telephone alarm devices, 24-hour patrols by trained security personnel, student patrols, and electronically operated dormitory entrances.

Applying

Wheaton requires an essay, a high school transcript, and 2 recommendations. It recommends an interview. Application deadline: 1/15; 2/1 for financial aid. Early and deferred admission are possible.

Getting Accepted
3,833 applied
37% were accepted
418 enrolled (30% of accepted)
44% from top tenth of their h.s. class
3.5 average high school GPA
Mean SAT critical reading score: 630
Mean SAT math score: 620
Mean ACT score: 27

Graduation and After
79% graduated in 4 years
1% graduated in 6 years
22% pursued further study (6% arts and sciences, 3% education, 3% law)
50% had job offers within 6 months
22 organizations recruited on campus

Financial Matters
$36,690 tuition and fees (2007–08)
$8640 room and board
98% average percent of need met
$25,229 average financial aid amount received per undergraduate (2006–07 estimated)

WHITMAN COLLEGE

SMALL-TOWN SETTING ■ PRIVATE ■ INDEPENDENT ■ COED
WALLA WALLA, WASHINGTON

Web site: www.whitman.edu

Contact: Mr. Tony Cabasco, Dean of Admission and Financial Aid, 515 Boyer Avenue, Walla Walla, WA 99362-2083

Telephone: 509-527-5176 or toll-free 877-462-9448

Fax: 509-527-4967

E-mail: admission@whitman.edu

Getting Accepted

2,882 applied
49% were accepted
400 enrolled (29% of accepted)
61% from top tenth of their h.s. class
3.77 average high school GPA
Mean SAT critical reading score: 670
Mean SAT math score: 660
Mean ACT score: 29
86% had SAT critical reading scores over 600
82% had SAT math scores over 600
80% had SAT writing scores over 600
93% had ACT scores over 24
39% had SAT critical reading scores over 700
32% had SAT math scores over 700
28% had SAT writing scores over 700
53% had ACT scores over 30

Graduation and After

80% graduated in 4 years
6% graduated in 5 years
1% graduated in 6 years
50 organizations recruited on campus

Financial Matters

$32,980 tuition and fees (2007–08)
$8310 room and board
91% average percent of need met
$22,300 average financial aid amount received
   per undergraduate (2006–07 estimated)

Academics

Whitman awards bachelor's **degrees**. **Challenging opportunities** include advanced placement credit, accelerated degree programs, student-designed majors, an honors program, double majors, independent study, and a senior project. Special programs include cooperative education, off-campus study, and study-abroad.

The most frequently chosen **baccalaureate** fields are social sciences, biological/life sciences, and visual and performing arts. A complete listing of majors at Whitman appears in the Majors by College index beginning on page 471.

The **faculty** at Whitman has 127 full-time members, 96% with terminal degrees. The student-faculty ratio is 10:1.

Students of Whitman

The student body is made up of 1,489 undergraduates. 56.3% are women and 43.7% are men. Students come from 41 states and territories and 34 other countries. 40% are from Washington. 3.8% are international students. 1.8% are African American, 1.1% American Indian, 10.3% Asian American, and 5% Hispanic American. 94% returned for their sophomore year.

Facilities and Resources

397 **computers/terminals** are available on campus for general student use. Students can access the following: computer help desk, free student e-mail accounts, online (class) grades, online (class) registration, online (class) schedules, course registration information. Campuswide network is available. 100% of college-owned or -operated housing units are wired for high-speed Internet access. Wireless service is available via classrooms, computer centers, computer labs, dorm rooms, learning centers, libraries, student centers. The 2 **libraries** have 395,841 books and 12,843 subscriptions.

Campus Life

There are 60 active organizations on campus, including a drama/theater group, newspaper, radio station, and choral group. 34% of eligible men and 29% of eligible women are members of national **fraternities** and national **sororities**.

Whitman is a member of the NCAA (Division III). **Intercollegiate sports** include baseball (m), basketball, cross-country running, golf, skiing (cross-country), skiing (downhill), soccer, swimming and diving, tennis, volleyball (w).

Campus Safety

Student safety services include late-night transport/escort service, 24-hour emergency telephone alarm devices, 24-hour patrols by trained security personnel, student patrols, and electronically operated dormitory entrances.

Applying

Whitman requires an essay, SAT or ACT, a high school transcript, and 1 recommendation. It recommends an interview. Application deadline: 1/15; 2/1 for financial aid, with a 11/15 priority date. Deferred admission is possible.

WHITWORTH UNIVERSITY
SUBURBAN SETTING ■ PRIVATE ■ INDEPENDENT RELIGIOUS ■ COED
SPOKANE, WASHINGTON

Web site: www.whitworth.edu
Contact: Ms. Marianne Hansen, Director of Admission, 300 West, Hawthorne Road, Spokane, WA 99251
Telephone: 509-777-4348 or toll-free 800-533-4668 (out-of-state)
Fax: 509-777-3758
E-mail: admission@whitworth.edu

Academics
Whitworth awards bachelor's and master's **degrees**. **Challenging opportunities** include advanced placement credit, student-designed majors, double majors, independent study, and a senior project. Special programs include cooperative education, internships, summer session for credit, off-campus study, study-abroad, and Army ROTC.

The most frequently chosen **baccalaureate** fields are business/marketing, education, and social sciences. A complete listing of majors at Whitworth appears in the Majors by College index beginning on page 471.

The **faculty** at Whitworth has 123 full-time members, 77% with terminal degrees. The student-faculty ratio is 13:1.

Students of Whitworth
The student body totals 2,607, of whom 2,331 are undergraduates. 59.1% are women and 40.9% are men. Students come from 30 states and territories and 18 other countries. 64% are from Washington. 1% are international students. 2% are African American, 1.1% American Indian, 3.5% Asian American, and 2.5% Hispanic American. 87% returned for their sophomore year.

Facilities and Resources
300 **computers/terminals** are available on campus for general student use. Students can access the following: campus intranet, computer help desk, free student e-mail accounts, online (class) grades, online (class) registration, online (class) schedules. Campuswide network is available. Wireless service is available via classrooms, computer centers, computer labs, libraries, student centers. The 3 **libraries** have 17,982 books and 773 subscriptions.

Campus Life
There are 80 active organizations on campus, including a drama/theater group, newspaper, radio station, and choral group. No national or local **fraternities** or **sororities**.

Whitworth is a member of the NCAA (Division III). **Intercollegiate sports** include baseball (m), basketball, cross-country running, football (m), golf, soccer, softball (w), swimming and diving, tennis, track and field, volleyball (w).

Campus Safety
Student safety services include late-night transport/escort service, 24-hour emergency telephone alarm devices, and 24-hour patrols by trained security personnel.

Applying
Whitworth requires an essay, a high school transcript, and recommendations, and in some cases SAT or ACT and an interview. Application deadline: 3/1; 3/1 priority date for financial aid. Early and deferred admission are possible.

Getting Accepted
5,062 applied
49% were accepted
533 enrolled (21% of accepted)
3.69 average high school GPA
54% had SAT critical reading scores over 600
57% had SAT math scores over 600
46% had SAT writing scores over 600
84% had ACT scores over 24
12% had SAT critical reading scores over 700
9% had SAT math scores over 700
7% had SAT writing scores over 700
20% had ACT scores over 30

Graduation and After
58% graduated in 4 years
13% graduated in 5 years
3% graduated in 6 years
20% pursued further study
110 organizations recruited on campus

Financial Matters
$25,692 tuition and fees (2007–08)
$7294 room and board
82% average percent of need met
$17,200 average financial aid amount received per undergraduate (2006–07 estimated)

WILLAMETTE UNIVERSITY

URBAN SETTING ■ PRIVATE ■ INDEPENDENT RELIGIOUS ■ COED
SALEM, OREGON

Web site: www.willamette.edu
Contact: Dr. Robin Brown, Vice President for Enrollment, 900 State Street, Salem, OR 97301
Telephone: 877-LIBARTS or toll-free 877-542-2787
Fax: 503-375-5363
E-mail: libarts@willamette.edu

Getting Accepted
2,983 applied
77% were accepted
444 enrolled (19% of accepted)
47% from top tenth of their h.s. class
3.68 average high school GPA
Mean SAT critical reading score: 620
Mean SAT math score: 610
Mean SAT writing score: 610
Mean ACT score: 27
66% had SAT critical reading scores over 600
56% had SAT math scores over 600
56% had SAT writing scores over 600
88% had ACT scores over 24
23% had SAT critical reading scores over 700
12% had SAT math scores over 700
10% had SAT writing scores over 700
24% had ACT scores over 30
18 National Merit Scholars
18 class presidents
34 valedictorians

Graduation and After
73% graduated in 4 years
6% graduated in 5 years
1% graduated in 6 years
25% pursued further study
150 organizations recruited on campus

Financial Matters
$31,968 tuition and fees (2007–08)
$7570 room and board
93% average percent of need met
$26,640 average financial aid amount received per undergraduate (2006–07 estimated)

Academics
Willamette awards bachelor's, master's, and first-professional **degrees** and post-bachelor's and first-professional certificates. **Challenging opportunities** include advanced placement credit, accelerated degree programs, student-designed majors, double majors, independent study, and a senior project. Special programs include cooperative education, internships, off-campus study, study-abroad, and Air Force ROTC.

The most frequently chosen **baccalaureate** fields are social sciences, English, and business/marketing. A complete listing of majors at Willamette appears in the Majors by College index beginning on page 471.

The **faculty** at Willamette has 200 full-time members, 95% with terminal degrees. The student-faculty ratio is 11:1.

Students of Willamette
The student body totals 2,720, of whom 1,932 are undergraduates. 55.2% are women and 44.8% are men. Students come from 43 states and territories and 8 other countries. 38% are from Oregon. 5.2% are international students. 1.2% are African American, 0.5% American Indian, 5.3% Asian American, and 3.5% Hispanic American. 87% returned for their sophomore year.

Facilities and Resources
400 **computers/terminals** are available on campus for general student use. Students can access the following: online (class) registration. Campuswide network is available. The 2 **libraries** have 317,000 books and 1,400 subscriptions.

Campus Life
There are 100 active organizations on campus, including a drama/theater group, newspaper, radio station, and choral group. 35% of eligible men and 29% of eligible women are members of national **fraternities** and national **sororities**.

Willamette is a member of the NCAA (Division III). **Intercollegiate sports** include baseball (m), basketball, crew, cross-country running, football (m), golf, soccer, softball (w), swimming and diving, tennis, track and field, volleyball (w).

Campus Safety
Student safety services include late-night transport/escort service, 24-hour emergency telephone alarm devices, 24-hour patrols by trained security personnel, student patrols, and electronically operated dormitory entrances.

Applying
Willamette requires an essay, SAT or ACT, a high school transcript, 1 recommendation, and a minimum high school GPA of 2.0, and in some cases an interview. It recommends an interview. Application deadline: 2/1; 2/1 priority date for financial aid. Deferred admission is possible.

William Jewell College

SMALL-TOWN SETTING ■ PRIVATE ■ INDEPENDENT RELIGIOUS ■ COED
LIBERTY, MISSOURI

Web site: www.jewell.edu
Contact: Ms. Bridget Gramling, Dean of Admission, 500 College Hill, Liberty, MO 64068
Telephone: 816-415-7511 or toll-free 888-2JEWELL
Fax: 816-415-5040
E-mail: gramblingb@william.jewell.edu

Academics

William Jewell awards bachelor's **degrees** (also offers evening program with significant enrollment not reflected in profile). **Challenging opportunities** include advanced placement credit, student-designed majors, an honors program, double majors, independent study, and a senior project. Special programs include cooperative education, internships, summer session for credit, off-campus study, and study-abroad.

The most frequently chosen **baccalaureate** fields are business/marketing, health professions and related sciences, and psychology. A complete listing of majors at William Jewell appears in the Majors by College index beginning on page 471.

The **faculty** at William Jewell has 78 full-time members, 81% with terminal degrees. The student-faculty ratio is 11:1.

Students of William Jewell

The student body is made up of 1,329 undergraduates. 60.5% are women and 39.5% are men. Students come from 29 states and territories and 2 other countries. 71% are from Missouri. 0.5% are international students. 4.4% are African American, 1.5% American Indian, 1% Asian American, and 3.1% Hispanic American. 81% returned for their sophomore year.

Facilities and Resources

232 **computers/terminals** are available on campus for general student use. Students can access the following: campus intranet, computer help desk, free student e-mail accounts, online (class) grades, online (class) registration, online (class) schedules. Campuswide network is available. 100% of college-owned or -operated housing units are wired for high-speed Internet access. Wireless service is available via classrooms, learning centers, libraries, student centers. The **library** has 255,750 books and 527 subscriptions.

Campus Life

There are 60 active organizations on campus, including a drama/theater group, newspaper, radio station, and choral group. 31% of eligible men and 34% of eligible women are members of national **fraternities** and national **sororities**.

William Jewell is a member of the NAIA. **Intercollegiate sports** (some offering scholarships) include baseball (m), basketball, cheerleading, cross-country running, football (m), golf, soccer, softball (w), tennis, track and field, volleyball (w).

Campus Safety

Student safety services include late-night transport/escort service, 24-hour emergency telephone alarm devices, 24-hour patrols by trained security personnel, and electronically operated dormitory entrances.

Applying

William Jewell requires an essay, SAT or ACT, and a high school transcript, and in some cases an interview. It recommends an interview and recommendations. Application deadline: 8/15; 3/1 priority date for financial aid. Deferred admission is possible.

Getting Accepted

990 applied
92% were accepted
288 enrolled (32% of accepted)
28% from top tenth of their h.s. class
3.62 average high school GPA
Mean ACT score: 25
54% had SAT critical reading scores over 600
43% had SAT math scores over 600
64% had ACT scores over 24
17% had SAT critical reading scores over 700
18% had SAT math scores over 700
16% had ACT scores over 30
11 valedictorians

Graduation and After

56% graduated in 4 years
8% graduated in 5 years
1% graduated in 6 years
27% pursued further study (7% arts and sciences, 6% business, 5% education)
74% had job offers within 6 months
104 organizations recruited on campus

Financial Matters

$23,300 tuition and fees (2008–09)
$6130 room and board
$15,639 average financial aid amount received per undergraduate (2006–07 estimated)

SPONSOR

Williams is a tightly knit residential community with a focus on the direct educational partnership between students and faculty members. The College emphasizes the continuities between academic and extracurricular life while maintaining a firm commitment to excellence in teaching, artistic endeavor, and scholarly research. Williams admits both domestic and international students without regard to financial need and provides financial assistance to meet 100 percent of demonstrated need. The College places a high priority on fostering a multicultural community—to promote an enriched exchange of ideas and to prepare its graduates for a world of increasing diversification.

Getting Accepted
6,478 applied
18% were accepted
540 enrolled (45% of accepted)
89% from top tenth of their h.s. class
94% had SAT critical reading scores over 600
93% had SAT math scores over 600
93% had SAT writing scores over 600
99% had ACT scores over 24
66% had SAT critical reading scores over 700
61% had SAT math scores over 700
61% had SAT writing scores over 700
67% had ACT scores over 30

Graduation and After
91% graduated in 4 years
4% graduated in 5 years
19% pursued further study
65% had job offers within 6 months
100 organizations recruited on campus

Financial Matters
$35,670 tuition and fees (2007–08)
$9470 room and board
100% average percent of need met
$32,979 average financial aid amount received per undergraduate (2006–07 estimated)

WILLIAMS COLLEGE
SMALL-TOWN SETTING ■ PRIVATE ■ INDEPENDENT ■ COED
WILLIAMSTOWN, MASSACHUSETTS

Web site: www.williams.edu
Contact: Mr. Richard L. Nesbitt, Director of Admission, 33 Stetson Court, Williamstown, MA 01267
Telephone: 413-597-2211
Fax: 413-597-4052
E-mail: admission@williams.edu

Academics
Williams awards bachelor's and master's **degrees**. **Challenging opportunities** include advanced placement credit, accelerated degree programs, student-designed majors, an honors program, double majors, independent study, and a senior project. Special programs include internships, off-campus study, and study-abroad.

The most frequently chosen **baccalaureate** fields are social sciences, English, and visual and performing arts. A complete listing of majors at Williams appears in the Majors by College index beginning on page 471.

The **faculty** at Williams has 257 full-time members, 100% with terminal degrees. The student-faculty ratio is 7:1.

Students of Williams
The student body totals 2,046, of whom 1,997 are undergraduates. 50.1% are women and 49.9% are men. Students come from 45 states and territories and 63 other countries. 14% are from Massachusetts. 6.7% are international students. 9.8% are African American, 0.4% American Indian, 10.7% Asian American, and 8.7% Hispanic American. 97% returned for their sophomore year.

Facilities and Resources
252 **computers/terminals** are available on campus for general student use. Students can access the following: online (class) registration, wireless network. Campuswide network is available. The 11 **libraries** have 932,000 books and 12,063 subscriptions.

Campus Life
There are 110 active organizations on campus, including a drama/theater group, newspaper, radio station, and choral group. No national or local **fraternities** or **sororities**.

Williams is a member of the NCAA (Division III). **Intercollegiate sports** include baseball (m), basketball, crew, cross-country running, field hockey (w), football (m), golf (m), ice hockey, lacrosse, skiing (cross-country), skiing (downhill), soccer, softball (w), squash, swimming and diving, tennis, track and field, volleyball (w), wrestling (m).

Campus Safety
Student safety services include late-night transport/escort service, 24-hour emergency telephone alarm devices, 24-hour patrols by trained security personnel, student patrols, and electronically operated dormitory entrances.

Applying
Williams requires an essay, SAT and SAT Subject Tests or ACT, a high school transcript, and 2 recommendations. Application deadline: 1/1; 2/1 for financial aid. Early and deferred admission are possible.

WINONA STATE UNIVERSITY

SMALL-TOWN SETTING ■ PUBLIC ■ STATE-SUPPORTED ■ COED
WINONA, MINNESOTA

Web site: www.winona.edu
Contact: Carl Stange, Director of Admissions, PO Box 5838, Winona, MN
   55987
Telephone: 507-457-5100 or toll-free 800-DIAL WSU
Fax: 507-457-5620
E-mail: admissions@winona.edu

Academics

Winona State awards associate, bachelor's, and master's **degrees** and post-master's certificates. **Challenging opportunities** include advanced placement credit, accelerated degree programs, student-designed majors, an honors program, double majors, independent study, and a senior project. Special programs include internships, summer session for credit, off-campus study, study-abroad, and Army ROTC. A complete listing of majors at Winona State appears in the Majors by College index beginning on page 471.

The **faculty** at Winona State has 322 full-time members, 89% with terminal degrees. The student-faculty ratio is 21:1.

Students of Winona State

The student body totals 8,220, of whom 7,608 are undergraduates. 62% are women and 38% are men. Students come from 21 states and territories and 48 other countries. 66% are from Minnesota. 4% are international students. 1.1% are African American, 0.3% American Indian, 1.8% Asian American, and 0.8% Hispanic American. 75% returned for their sophomore year.

Facilities and Resources

1,400 **computers/terminals** are available on campus for general student use. Students can access the following: online (class) registration. Campuswide network is available. The **library** has 350,000 books and 1,000 subscriptions.

Campus Life

There are 130 active organizations on campus, including a drama/theater group, newspaper, radio station, choral group, and marching band. 3% of eligible men and 3% of eligible women are members of national **fraternities**, national **sororities**, local fraternities, and local sororities.

Winona State is a member of the NCAA (Division II). **Intercollegiate sports** (some offering scholarships) include baseball (m), basketball, cross-country running (w), football (m), golf, gymnastics (w), soccer (w), softball (w), tennis, track and field (w), volleyball (w).

Campus Safety

Student safety services include security cameras, late-night transport/escort service, 24-hour emergency telephone alarm devices, 24-hour patrols by trained security personnel, student patrols, and electronically operated dormitory entrances.

Applying

Winona State requires SAT or ACT, a high school transcript, and class rank, and in some cases an essay, an interview, and recommendations. Application deadline: rolling admissions. Early and deferred admission are possible.

Getting Accepted

5,359 applied
79% were accepted
1,727 enrolled (41% of accepted)
20% from top tenth of their h.s. class
3.3 average high school GPA
59% had ACT scores over 24
3% had ACT scores over 30
2 National Merit Scholars
51 class presidents
28 valedictorians

Graduation and After

27% graduated in 4 years
21% graduated in 5 years
3% graduated in 6 years
25% pursued further study (10% arts and sciences, 6% business, 4% engineering)
80% had job offers within 6 months
240 organizations recruited on campus

Financial Matters

$7320 resident tuition and fees (2007–08)
$11,800 nonresident tuition and fees (2007–08)
$6490 room and board
40% average percent of need met
$6066 average financial aid amount received per undergraduate (2005–06)

Wisconsin Lutheran College, located in Milwaukee, is a traditional liberal arts college for Christian men and women. By offering a strong academic program built on the solid foundation of Jesus Christ, Wisconsin Lutheran has risen to the top tier of comprehensive undergraduate colleges in the Midwest (ranked by *U.S. News & World Report*). Rigorous premedical and unique urban education programs are examples of how Wisconsin Lutheran lives the mission of building strong Christian leaders for the church and the world.

Getting Accepted
581 applied
85% were accepted
198 enrolled (40% of accepted)
20% from top tenth of their h.s. class
3.46 average high school GPA
Mean ACT score: 24
56% had ACT scores over 24
7% had ACT scores over 30
10 valedictorians

Graduation and After
47% graduated in 4 years
19% graduated in 5 years
8% graduated in 6 years
63% had job offers within 6 months
10 organizations recruited on campus

Financial Matters
$19,564 tuition and fees (2007–08)
$6910 room and board
84% average percent of need met
$14,709 average financial aid amount received per undergraduate (2006–07 estimated)

WISCONSIN LUTHERAN COLLEGE
SUBURBAN SETTING ■ PRIVATE ■ INDEPENDENT RELIGIOUS ■ COED
MILWAUKEE, WISCONSIN

Web site: www.wlc.edu
Contact: Ms. Amanda Delaney, 8800 West Bluemound Road, Milwaukee, WI 53226-9942
Telephone: 414-443-8726 or toll-free 888-WIS LUTH
Fax: 414-443-8514
E-mail: amanda.delaney@wlc.edu

Academics
Wisconsin Lutheran awards bachelor's **degrees**. **Challenging opportunities** include advanced placement credit, student-designed majors, double majors, independent study, and a senior project. Special programs include internships, summer session for credit, study-abroad, and Army, Navy, and Air Force ROTC. A complete listing of majors at Wisconsin Lutheran appears in the Majors by College index beginning on page 471.

The **faculty** at Wisconsin Lutheran has 58 full-time members, 67% with terminal degrees. The student-faculty ratio is 10:1.

Students of Wisconsin Lutheran
The student body is made up of 741 undergraduates. 59.1% are women and 40.9% are men. Students come from 28 states and territories and 8 other countries. 81% are from Wisconsin. 1.4% are international students. 1.7% are African American, 0.3% American Indian, 1.1% Asian American, and 1.7% Hispanic American. 79% returned for their sophomore year.

Facilities and Resources
200 **computers/terminals** are available on campus for general student use. Campuswide network is available.

Campus Life
There are 31 active organizations on campus, including a drama/theater group, newspaper, and choral group. No national or local **fraternities** or **sororities**.

Wisconsin Lutheran is a member of the NCAA (Division III). **Intercollegiate sports** include baseball (m), basketball, cross-country running, football (m), golf, soccer, softball (w), tennis (w), track and field, volleyball (w).

Campus Safety
Student safety services include closed-circuit TV monitors, late-night transport/escort service, 24-hour emergency telephone alarm devices, 24-hour patrols by trained security personnel, and electronically operated dormitory entrances.

Applying
Wisconsin Lutheran requires SAT or ACT, a high school transcript, minimum ACT score of 21, and a minimum high school GPA of 2.70, and in some cases an interview. It recommends 1 recommendation. Application deadline: 3/1 priority date for financial aid.

WITTENBERG UNIVERSITY
SUBURBAN SETTING ■ PRIVATE ■ INDEPENDENT RELIGIOUS ■ COED
SPRINGFIELD, OHIO

Web site: www.wittenberg.edu
Contact: Mr. Brad Pochard, Director of Admission, PO Box 720, Springfield, OH 45501-0720
Telephone: 877-206-0332 Ext. 6377 or toll-free 800-677-7558 Ext. 6314
Fax: 937-327-6379
E-mail: admission@wittenberg.edu

Academics
Wittenberg awards bachelor's and master's **degrees**. **Challenging opportunities** include advanced placement credit, student-designed majors, freshman honors college, an honors program, double majors, independent study, and a senior project. Special programs include cooperative education, internships, summer session for credit, off-campus study, study-abroad, and Army and Air Force ROTC.

The most frequently chosen **baccalaureate** fields are biological/life sciences, business/marketing, and social sciences. A complete listing of majors at Wittenberg appears in the Majors by College index beginning on page 471.

The **faculty** at Wittenberg has 142 full-time members, 92% with terminal degrees. The student-faculty ratio is 12:1.

Students of Wittenberg
The student body totals 2,078, of whom 2,066 are undergraduates. 54.8% are women and 45.2% are men. Students come from 36 states and territories and 16 other countries. 76% are from Ohio. 1.7% are international students. 4.9% are African American, 0.2% American Indian, 0.6% Asian American, and 1.2% Hispanic American. 80% returned for their sophomore year.

Facilities and Resources
Students can access the following: computer help desk, free student e-mail accounts, on-line (class) grades, online (class) registration, online (class) schedules. Campuswide network is available. The 3 **libraries** have 407,502 books and 958 subscriptions.

Campus Life
There are 129 active organizations on campus, including a drama/theater group, newspaper, radio station, and choral group. 25% of eligible men and 42% of eligible women are members of national **fraternities** and national **sororities**.

Wittenberg is a member of the NCAA (Division III). **Intercollegiate sports** include baseball (m), basketball, cross-country running, field hockey (w), football (m), golf, lacrosse, soccer, softball (w), swimming and diving, tennis, track and field, volleyball (w).

Campus Safety
Student safety services include crime prevention programs, late-night transport/escort service, 24-hour emergency telephone alarm devices, 24-hour patrols by trained security personnel, student patrols, and electronically operated dormitory entrances.

Applying
Wittenberg requires an essay, a high school transcript, an interview, and recommendations. Application deadline: 3/15 priority date for financial aid. Early and deferred admission are possible.

Getting Accepted
2,887 applied
73% were accepted
551 enrolled (26% of accepted)
29% from top tenth of their h.s. class
3.41 average high school GPA
Mean SAT critical reading score: 554
Mean SAT math score: 559
Mean ACT score: 24
32% had SAT critical reading scores over 600
32% had SAT math scores over 600
58% had ACT scores over 24
5% had SAT critical reading scores over 700
5% had SAT math scores over 700
11% had ACT scores over 30

Graduation and After
57% graduated in 4 years
4% graduated in 5 years
1% graduated in 6 years

Financial Matters
$33,236 tuition and fees (2008–09)
$8314 room and board
83% average percent of need met
$20,155 average financial aid amount received per undergraduate (2005–06)

WOFFORD COLLEGE

URBAN SETTING ■ PRIVATE ■ INDEPENDENT RELIGIOUS ■ COED
SPARTANBURG, SOUTH CAROLINA

Web site: www.wofford.edu
Contact: Jennifer B. Page, Director of Admissions, 429 North Church Street,
    Spartanburg, SC 29303-3663
Telephone: 864-597-4130
Fax: 864-597-4147
E-mail: admission@wofford.edu

Getting Accepted

2,354 applied
53% were accepted
385 enrolled (31% of accepted)
58% from top tenth of their h.s. class
4.0 average high school GPA
Mean SAT critical reading score: 621
Mean SAT math score: 623
Mean ACT score: 25
63% had SAT critical reading scores over 600
63% had SAT math scores over 600
57% had SAT writing scores over 600
63% had ACT scores over 24
19% had SAT critical reading scores over 700
17% had SAT math scores over 700
13% had SAT writing scores over 700
5% had ACT scores over 30
3 National Merit Scholars
9 class presidents
13 valedictorians

Graduation and After

72% graduated in 4 years
4% graduated in 5 years
1% graduated in 6 years
31% pursued further study (9% arts and sciences, 5% medicine, 4% business)

Financial Matters

$27,830 tuition and fees (2007–08)
$7705 room and board
89% average percent of need met
$22,401 average financial aid amount received per undergraduate (2005–06 estimated)

Academics

Wofford awards bachelor's **degrees**. **Challenging opportunities** include advanced placement credit, accelerated degree programs, student-designed majors, double majors, independent study, and a senior project. Special programs include internships, summer session for credit, off-campus study, study-abroad, and Army ROTC.

The most frequently chosen **baccalaureate** fields are business/marketing, biological/life sciences, and social sciences. A complete listing of majors at Wofford appears in the Majors by College index beginning on page 471.

The **faculty** at Wofford has 106 full-time members, 93% with terminal degrees. The student-faculty ratio is 11:1.

Students of Wofford

The student body is made up of 1,327 undergraduates. 47.1% are women and 52.9% are men. Students come from 25 states and territories and 10 other countries. 70% are from South Carolina. 0.8% are international students. 5.6% are African American, 0.3% American Indian, 2.4% Asian American, and 1.8% Hispanic American. 93% returned for their sophomore year.

Facilities and Resources

250 **computers/terminals** are available on campus for general student use. Students can access the following: campus intranet, computer help desk, free student e-mail accounts, online (class) grades, online (class) registration, online (class) schedules. Campuswide network is available. 100% of college-owned or -operated housing units are wired for high-speed Internet access. Wireless service is available via classrooms, computer centers, computer labs, libraries, student centers. The **library** has 208,361 books and 26,971 subscriptions.

Campus Life

There are 80 active organizations on campus, including a drama/theater group, newspaper, and choral group. 43% of eligible men and 60% of eligible women are members of national **fraternities** and national **sororities**.

Wofford is a member of the NCAA (Division I). **Intercollegiate sports** (some offering scholarships) include baseball (m), basketball, cross-country running, football (m), golf, riflery, soccer, tennis, track and field, volleyball (w).

Campus Safety

Student safety services include late-night transport/escort service, 24-hour emergency telephone alarm devices, 24-hour patrols by trained security personnel, and electronically operated dormitory entrances.

Applying

Wofford requires an essay, SAT or ACT, and a high school transcript. It recommends an interview and 2 recommendations. Application deadline: 2/1; 3/15 priority date for financial aid. Early and deferred admission are possible.

WORCESTER POLYTECHNIC INSTITUTE

Suburban setting ■ Private ■ Independent ■ Coed
WORCESTER, MASSACHUSETTS

Web site: www.wpi.edu
Contact: Mr. Edward J. Connor, Director of Admissions, 100 Institute Road,
Worcester, MA 01609-2280
Telephone: 508-831-5286
Fax: 508-831-5875
E-mail: admissions@wpi.edu

SPONSOR

Academics

WPI awards bachelor's, master's, and doctoral **degrees** and post-bachelor's and post-master's certificates. **Challenging opportunities** include advanced placement credit, accelerated degree programs, student-designed majors, double majors, independent study, and a senior project. Special programs include cooperative education, internships, summer session for credit, off-campus study, study-abroad, and Army, Navy, and Air Force ROTC.

The most frequently chosen **baccalaureate** fields are engineering, computer and information sciences, and biological/life sciences. A complete listing of majors at WPI appears in the Majors by College index beginning on page 471.

The **faculty** at WPI has 240 full-time members, 95% with terminal degrees. The student-faculty ratio is 13:1.

Students of WPI

The student body totals 4,157, of whom 3,016 are undergraduates. 25.8% are women and 74.2% are men. Students come from 42 states and territories and 70 other countries. 50% are from Massachusetts. 7.5% are international students. 2.6% are African American, 0.5% American Indian, 6.4% Asian American, and 3.6% Hispanic American. 94% returned for their sophomore year.

Facilities and Resources

500 **computers/terminals** and 745 ports are available on campus for general student use. Students can access the following: campus intranet, computer help desk, free student e-mail accounts, online (class) grades, online (class) registration, online (class) schedules, online course content. Campuswide network is available. 100% of college-owned or -operated housing units are wired for high-speed Internet access. Wireless service is available via entire campus. The **library** has 310,265 books and 23,591 subscriptions.

Campus Life

There are 125 active organizations on campus, including a drama/theater group, newspaper, radio station, choral group, and marching band. 29% of eligible men and 31% of eligible women are members of national **fraternities** and national **sororities**.

WPI is a member of the NCAA (Division III). **Intercollegiate sports** include baseball (m), basketball, crew, cross-country running, field hockey (w), football (m), soccer, softball (w), swimming and diving, track and field, volleyball (w), wrestling (m).

Campus Safety

Student safety services include late-night transport/escort service, 24-hour emergency telephone alarm devices, 24-hour patrols by trained security personnel, student patrols, and electronically operated dormitory entrances.

Applying

WPI requires an essay, a high school transcript, and 2 recommendations, and in some cases SAT or ACT, TOEFL or IELTS, and an interview. Application deadline: 2/1; 2/1 for financial aid, with a 2/1 priority date. Early and deferred admission are possible.

Small classes, a flexible curriculum, hands-on project experience, and one-on-one interaction are hallmarks of the WPI education. Founded more than 140 years ago and located in Worcester, Massachusetts, WPI offers an innovative curriculum that has been widely recognized for its ability to prepare students for success. There are more than thirty-five areas of study in engineering, science, management, and the liberal arts. Exciting new programs are driven by real-world demand, such as robotics engineering (the first undergraduate program in the nation), interactive media and game development, and environmental engineering.

Getting Accepted
5,698 applied
66% were accepted
805 enrolled (22% of accepted)
48% from top tenth of their h.s. class
3.7 average high school GPA
60% had SAT critical reading scores over 600
86% had SAT math scores over 600
54% had SAT writing scores over 600
85% had ACT scores over 24
17% had SAT critical reading scores over 700
35% had SAT math scores over 700
12% had SAT writing scores over 700
26% had ACT scores over 30
11 National Merit Scholars
22 valedictorians

Graduation and After
65% graduated in 4 years
8% graduated in 5 years
2% graduated in 6 years
21% pursued further study

Financial Matters
$34,830 tuition and fees (2007–08)
$10,410 room and board
69% average percent of need met
$24,103 average financial aid amount received
per undergraduate (2006–07 estimated)

XAVIER UNIVERSITY

URBAN SETTING ■ PRIVATE ■ INDEPENDENT RELIGIOUS ■ COED
CINCINNATI, OHIO

Web site: www.xu.edu
Contact: Ms. Marianne Borgmann, Interim Director of Admission, 3800
    Victory Parkway, Cincinnati, OH 45207-5311
Telephone: 513-745-3301 or toll-free 800-344-4698
Fax: 513-745-4319
E-mail: xuadmit@xavier.edu

Getting Accepted

5,649 applied
73% were accepted
858 enrolled (21% of accepted)
29% from top tenth of their h.s. class
3.56 average high school GPA
Mean SAT critical reading score: 563
Mean SAT math score: 579
Mean SAT writing score: 579
Mean ACT score: 26
44% had SAT critical reading scores over 600
45% had SAT math scores over 600
35% had SAT writing scores over 600
68% had ACT scores over 24
8% had SAT critical reading scores over 700
7% had SAT math scores over 700
6% had SAT writing scores over 700
19% had ACT scores over 30
11 National Merit Scholars
18 valedictorians

Graduation and After

28% pursued further study (8% arts and sciences, 5% business, 5% education)
61% had job offers within 6 months
163 organizations recruited on campus

Financial Matters

$26,860 tuition and fees (2008–09)
$9270 room and board
75% average percent of need met
$15,224 average financial aid amount received per undergraduate (2006–07 estimated)

Academics

Xavier awards associate, bachelor's, master's, and doctoral **degrees** and post-bachelor's and post-master's certificates. **Challenging opportunities** include advanced placement credit, an honors program, double majors, independent study, and a senior project. Special programs include cooperative education, internships, summer session for credit, off-campus study, study-abroad, and Army and Air Force ROTC.

The most frequently chosen **baccalaureate** fields are business/marketing, liberal arts/general studies, and communications/journalism. A complete listing of majors at Xavier appears in the Majors by College index beginning on page 471.

The **faculty** at Xavier has 309 full-time members, 78% with terminal degrees. The student-faculty ratio is 12:1.

Students of Xavier

The student body totals 6,646, of whom 3,961 are undergraduates. 56.3% are women and 43.7% are men. Students come from 45 states and territories and 34 other countries. 60% are from Ohio. 2.5% are international students. 10.9% are African American, 0.4% American Indian, 2.5% Asian American, and 3.2% Hispanic American. 88% returned for their sophomore year.

Facilities and Resources

204 **computers/terminals** are available on campus for general student use. Students can access the following: computer help desk, free student e-mail accounts, online (class) grades, online (class) registration, online (class) schedules. Campuswide network is available. 99% of college-owned or -operated housing units are wired for high-speed Internet access. Wireless service is available via entire campus. The 2 **libraries** have 227,200 books and 21,650 subscriptions.

Campus Life

There are 100 active organizations on campus, including a drama/theater group, newspaper, radio station, television station, and choral group. No national or local **fraternities** or **sororities**.

Xavier is a member of the NCAA (Division I). **Intercollegiate sports** (some offering scholarships) include baseball (m), basketball, cross-country running, golf, riflery, soccer, swimming and diving, tennis, volleyball (w).

Campus Safety

Student safety services include campus-wide shuttle service, late-night transport/escort service, 24-hour emergency telephone alarm devices, and 24-hour patrols by trained security personnel.

Applying

Xavier requires an essay, SAT or ACT, a high school transcript, and 1 recommendation. It recommends an interview. Application deadline: 2/1; 2/15 priority date for financial aid. Deferred admission is possible.

Yale University

URBAN SETTING ■ PRIVATE ■ INDEPENDENT ■ COED
NEW HAVEN, CONNECTICUT

Web site: www.yale.edu
Contact: Admissions Director, PO Box 208234, New Haven, CT 06520
Telephone: 203-432-9300
Fax: 203-432-9392
E-mail: undergraduate.admissions@yale.edu

Academics

Yale awards bachelor's, master's, doctoral, and first-professional **degrees** and post-master's certificates. **Challenging opportunities** include advanced placement credit, accelerated degree programs, student-designed majors, an honors program, double majors, independent study, and a senior project. Special programs include internships, summer session for credit, study-abroad, and Army and Air Force ROTC.

The most frequently chosen **baccalaureate** fields are social sciences, history, and interdisciplinary studies. A complete listing of majors at Yale appears in the Majors by College index beginning on page 471.

The **faculty** at Yale has 1,121 full-time members, 90% with terminal degrees. The student-faculty ratio is 6:1.

Students of Yale

The student body totals 11,416, of whom 5,333 are undergraduates. 49.1% are women and 50.9% are men. Students come from 50 states and territories and 74 other countries. 8% are from Connecticut. 8.3% are international students. 8.2% are African American, 0.9% American Indian, 13.5% Asian American, and 7.6% Hispanic American. 99% returned for their sophomore year.

Facilities and Resources

350 **computers/terminals** are available on campus for general student use. Students can access the following: online (class) registration. Campuswide network is available. The 21 **libraries** have 11,100,000 books and 61,649 subscriptions.

Campus Life

There are 300 active organizations on campus, including a drama/theater group, newspaper, radio station, television station, choral group, and marching band. Yale has national **fraternities** and national **sororities**.

Yale is a member of the NCAA (Division I). **Intercollegiate sports** include baseball (m), basketball, crew, cross-country running, fencing, field hockey (w), football (m), golf, gymnastics (w), ice hockey, lacrosse, soccer, softball (w), squash, swimming and diving, tennis, track and field, volleyball (w).

Campus Safety

Student safety services include late-night transport/escort service, 24-hour emergency telephone alarm devices, 24-hour patrols by trained security personnel, and electronically operated dormitory entrances.

Applying

Yale requires an essay, SAT and SAT Subject Tests or ACT, a high school transcript, and 3 recommendations. It recommends an interview. Application deadline: 12/31; 3/1 for financial aid, with a 3/1 priority date. Early and deferred admission are possible.

Getting Accepted

21,101 applied
9% were accepted
1,315 enrolled (70% of accepted)
95% from top tenth of their h.s. class
97% had SAT critical reading scores over 600
98% had SAT math scores over 600
98% had SAT writing scores over 600
76% had SAT critical reading scores over 700
73% had SAT math scores over 700
74% had SAT writing scores over 700

Graduation and After

88% graduated in 4 years
7% graduated in 5 years
1% graduated in 6 years
31% pursued further study (11% arts and sciences, 7% law, 7% medicine)
64% had job offers within 6 months

Financial Matters

$34,530 tuition and fees (2007–08)
$10,470 room and board
100% average percent of need met
$32,533 average financial aid amount received per undergraduate (2006–07 estimated)

INDEXES

SPECIALIZED INDEXES

SINGLE-SEX COLLEGES: MEN ONLY

Morehouse College
Wabash College

SINGLE-SEX COLLEGES: WOMEN ONLY

Agnes Scott College
Barnard College
Bryn Mawr College
College of St. Catherine
Converse College
Mills College
Mount Holyoke College
Saint Mary's College
Salem College
Scripps College
Smith College
Sweet Briar College
Wellesley College
Wesleyan College

COLLEGES WITH RELIGIOUS AFFILIATION

Adventist
Union College (NE)

Baptist
Baylor University
Belmont University
Bethel University
Carson-Newman College
Cedarville University
Georgetown College
Kalamazoo College
Linfield College
Mercer University
Mississippi College
Oklahoma Baptist University
Samford University
Southwest Baptist University
Union University
William Jewell College

Brethren
Elizabethtown College
Juniata College

Christian (Unspecified)
Milligan College

Christian Church (Disciples of Christ)
Chapman University
Hiram College
Texas Christian University
Transylvania University

Church of the Nazarene
Point Loma Nazarene University

Churches of Christ
Harding University
Lipscomb University
Pepperdine University (CA)

Episcopal
Sewanee: The University of the South

Friends
Earlham College
George Fox University

Interdenominational
Berry College
Biola University
Bryan College (TN)
Colorado Christian University
Illinois College
John Brown University
Messiah College
Taylor University

Jewish
List College, The Jewish Theological Seminary

Latter-day Saints (Mormon)
Brigham Young University

Lutheran
Augustana College (IL)
Augustana College (SD)
Concordia College (MN)
Gettysburg College
Gustavus Adolphus College
Luther College
Muhlenberg College
Pacific Lutheran University
St. Olaf College
Susquehanna University
Valparaiso University
Wartburg College
Wisconsin Lutheran College
Wittenberg University

Mennonite
Goshen College
Tabor College

Methodist
Albion College
Albright College
American University
Baldwin-Wallace College
Birmingham-Southern College
Cornell College
DePauw University
Drew University
Duke University
Emory University
Hamline University
Hendrix College
Lebanon Valley College
Lycoming College
McKendree University
Millsaps College
Nebraska Wesleyan University
North Central College
Ohio Northern University
Ohio Wesleyan University
Oklahoma City University
Randolph College
Seattle Pacific University
Simpson College
Southern Methodist University
Southwestern University
University of Evansville
Wesleyan College
Willamette University
Wofford College

Moravian
Moravian College
Salem College

Nondenominational
Asbury College
Azusa Pacific University
Cornerstone University
Gordon College (MA)
LeTourneau University
The Master's College and Seminary (CA)
Northwestern College (MN)
Westmont College
Wheaton College (IL)

Presbyterian
Agnes Scott College
Alma College
Austin College
Carroll College (WI)
Centre College
Coe College
The College of Wooster
Covenant College
Davidson College

Erskine College
Grove City College
Hanover College
Lafayette College
Lyon College
Macalester College
Maryville College
Presbyterian College
Rhodes College
Trinity University
University of Tulsa
Whitworth University

Reformed Churches
Calvin College
Central College
Hope College
Northwestern College (IA)

Roman Catholic
Benedictine University
Boston College
Canisius College
Carroll College (MT)
Christendom College
Christian Brothers University
Clarke College
College of Saint Benedict
College of St. Catherine
The College of St. Scholastica
The College of Saint Thomas More
College of the Holy Cross
Creighton University
Dominican University
Duquesne University
Fairfield University
Fordham University
Franciscan University of Steubenville
Georgetown University
Gonzaga University
John Carroll University
Loyola College in Maryland
Loyola Marymount University
Loyola University Chicago
Loyola University New Orleans
Marquette University
Providence College
Quincy University
Regis University
Saint Francis University
Saint John's University (MN)
Saint Joseph's University
Saint Louis University
Saint Mary's College
Saint Mary's College of California
St. Norbert College
Santa Clara University

Seattle University
Siena College
Stonehill College
Thomas Aquinas College
University of Dallas
University of Dayton
University of Notre Dame
University of Portland
University of St. Thomas (MN)
University of St. Thomas (TX)
University of San Diego
The University of Scranton
Villanova University
Xavier University

United Church of Christ
Elon University

Wesleyan
Houghton College

PUBLIC COLLEGES
Auburn University
Bernard M. Baruch College of the City University of New York
California Polytechnic State University, San Luis Obispo
Clemson University
College of Charleston
The College of New Jersey
The College of William and Mary
Colorado School of Mines
Colorado State University
Florida International University
Florida State University
Georgia Institute of Technology
Georgia State University
Iowa State University of Science and Technology
James Madison University
Louisiana State University and Agricultural and Mechanical College
McGill University
Miami University
Michigan State University
Michigan Technological University
Missouri State University
Missouri University of Science and Technology
Mount Allison University
Mount Saint Vincent University
Murray State University
New College of Florida
New Jersey Institute of Technology
New Mexico Institute of Mining and Technology
North Carolina State University
The Ohio State University
Oklahoma State University
Penn State University Park
Purdue University

Queen's University at Kingston
Rutgers, The State University of New Jersey, Newark
Rutgers, The State University of New Jersey, New Brunswick
St. Mary's College of Maryland
San Diego State University
State University of New York at Binghamton
State University of New York College at Geneseo
State University of New York College of Environmental
    Science and Forestry
Stony Brook University, State University of New York
Tennessee Technological University
Texas A&M University
Texas Tech University
Towson University
Truman State University
United States Air Force Academy
United States Coast Guard Academy
United States Merchant Marine Academy
United States Military Academy
United States Naval Academy
University at Buffalo, the State University of New York
The University of Alabama in Huntsville
The University of Arizona
University of Arkansas
University of California, Berkeley
University of California, Davis
University of California, Irvine
University of California, Los Angeles
University of California, Riverside
University of California, San Diego
University of California, Santa Barbara
University of California, Santa Cruz
University of Central Arkansas
University of Central Florida
University of Colorado at Boulder
University of Connecticut
University of Delaware
University of Florida
University of Georgia
University of Illinois at Chicago

University of Illinois at Urbana–Champaign
The University of Iowa
University of Kansas
University of Kentucky
University of Maryland, Baltimore County
University of Maryland, College Park
University of Mary Washington
University of Michigan
University of Michigan–Dearborn
University of Minnesota, Morris
University of Minnesota, Twin Cities Campus
University of Missouri–Columbia
University of Missouri–Kansas City
University of Nebraska–Lincoln
The University of North Carolina at Asheville
The University of North Carolina at Chapel Hill
The University of North Carolina Wilmington
University of North Florida
University of Oklahoma
University of Pittsburgh
University of Rhode Island
University of South Carolina
The University of Tennessee
The University of Tennessee at Chattanooga
The University of Texas at Austin
The University of Texas at Dallas
University of Utah
University of Virginia
University of Washington
University of Wisconsin–La Crosse
University of Wisconsin–Madison
University of Wisconsin–River Falls
Virginia Military Institute
Virginia Polytechnic Institute and State University
Western Washington University
Winona State University

HISPANIC-SERVING INSTITUTIONS
Florida International University
University of Miami
University of St. Thomas (TX)

Majors by College

Agnes Scott College
African studies; anthropology; art; astrophysics; biochemistry; biology/biological sciences; chemistry; classics and languages, literatures and linguistics; creative writing; dramatic/theater arts; economics; English; French; German; history; interdisciplinary studies; international relations and affairs; literature; mathematics; multi-/interdisciplinary studies related; music; neuroscience; philosophy; physics; political science and government; psychology; religious studies; sociology; Spanish; women's studies.

Albany College of Pharmacy of Union University
Clinical laboratory science/medical technology; cytotechnology; pharmacy, pharmaceutical sciences, and administration related.

Albion College
American studies; anthropology; art; biology/biological sciences; business administration and management; chemistry; computer science; dramatic/theater arts; economics; education; elementary education; English; environmental studies; French; geology/earth science; German; history; human services; international relations and affairs; mass communication/media; mathematics; modern languages; music; philosophy; physical education teaching and coaching; physics; political science and government; pre-law studies; pre-medical studies; pre-veterinary studies; psychology; public policy analysis; religious studies; secondary education; sociology; Spanish; women's studies.

Albright College
Accounting; American studies; apparel and textiles; art; art teacher education; biochemistry; biology/biological sciences; business administration and management; chemistry; communication/speech communication and rhetoric; computer science; criminology; design and visual communications; dramatic/theater arts; economics; elementary education; English; environmental science; finance; forestry; French; history; industrial and organizational psychology; information science/studies; interdisciplinary studies; international business/trade/commerce; kindergarten/preschool education; Latin American studies; marketing/marketing management; mathematics; multi-/interdisciplinary studies related; music; natural resources management and policy; philosophy; physics; physiological psychology/psychobiology; political science and government; pre-law studies; psychology; religious studies; secondary education; sociology; Spanish; special education; women's studies.

Alfred University
Accounting; art; art teacher education; athletic training; biological and physical sciences; biology/biological sciences; biomedical/medical engineering; business administration and management; business teacher education; ceramic arts and ceramics; ceramic sciences and engineering; chemistry; communication/speech communication and rhetoric; criminal justice/law enforcement administration; dramatic/theater arts; economics; electrical, electronics and communications engineering; elementary education; engineering related; English; environmental studies; finance; fine/studio arts; French; general studies; geology/earth science; German; gerontology; history; interdisciplinary studies; international/global studies; literature; marketing/marketing management; materials engineering; mathematics; mechanical engineering; modern languages; philosophy; physics; political science and government; psychology; public administration; science teacher education; secondary education; sociology; Spanish.

Allegheny College
Applied economics; art; art history, criticism and conservation; biochemistry; biology/biological sciences; business/managerial economics; chemistry; communication/speech communication and rhetoric;

computer science; computer software engineering; creative writing; dramatic/theater arts; economics; education; English; environmental science; environmental studies; fine arts related; fine/studio arts; French; geology/earth science; German; health/medical preparatory programs related; history; international relations and affairs; international/global studies; journalism; mass communication/media; mathematics; multi-/interdisciplinary studies related; music; music performance; neuroscience; philosophy; physics; political science and government; pre-dentistry studies; pre-law studies; pre-medical studies; pre-nursing studies; pre-pharmacy studies; pre-veterinary studies; psychology; religious studies; Spanish; technical and business writing; women's studies.

Allen College
Nursing (registered nurse training); radiologic technology/science.

Alma College
Accounting; anthropology; art; art teacher education; biochemistry; biological and physical sciences; biology teacher education; biology/biological sciences; business administration and management; chemistry; chemistry teacher education; communication and media related; computer science; computer teacher education; dance; design and visual communications; dramatic/theater arts; early childhood education; economics; education; elementary education; English; English/language arts teacher education; fine/studio arts; French; French language teacher education; German; German language teacher education; gerontology; graphic design; health science; health teacher education; history; history teacher education; humanities; international business/trade/commerce; kindergarten/preschool teacher education; kinesiology and exercise science; liberal arts and sciences/liberal studies; marketing/marketing management; mathematics; mathematics teacher education; medical illustration; modern languages; music; music performance; music teacher education; philosophy; physical education teaching and coaching; physics; physics teacher education; political science and government; pre-dentistry studies; pre-law studies; pre-medical studies; pre-theology/pre-ministerial studies; pre-veterinary studies; psychology; psychology teacher education; public health; religious studies; science teacher education; secondary education; social science teacher education; social sciences; social studies teacher education; sociology; Spanish; Spanish language teacher education.

American University
American studies; anthropology; applied mathematics; art history, criticism and conservation; audio engineering; biochemistry; biology/biological sciences; business administration and management; chemistry; computer science; design and visual communications; dramatic/theater arts; economics; elementary education; environmental studies; European studies; fine/studio arts; foreign languages and literatures; French; French studies; German; German studies; graphic design; health science; history; interdisciplinary studies; intermedia/multimedia; international relations and affairs; Jewish/Judaic studies; journalism; Latin American studies; legal studies; liberal arts and sciences/liberal studies; literature; marine science/merchant marine officer; mass communication/media; mathematics; music; philosophy; physics; political science and government; psychology; public health education and promotion; public relations/image management; Russian; Russian studies; secondary education; sociology; Spanish; statistics; women's studies.

Amherst College
African American/Black studies; American studies; ancient/classical Greek; anthropology; art; Asian studies; astronomy; biology/biological sciences; chemistry; classics and languages, literatures and linguistics; computer science; dance; dramatic/theater arts; economics; English; European studies; fine/studio arts; French; geology/earth science; Ger-

man; history; interdisciplinary studies; Latin; legal studies; mathematics; music; neuroscience; philosophy; physics; political science and government; psychology; religious studies; Russian; sociology; Spanish; women's studies.

Asbury College

Accounting; ancient Near Eastern and biblical languages; applied mathematics; art teacher education; biblical studies; biochemistry; biology/biological sciences; business/commerce; chemistry; dramatic/theater arts; elementary education; English; equestrian studies; fine/studio arts; French; health and physical education; health/medical preparatory programs related; history; journalism; mathematics; mathematics and statistics related; middle school education; missionary studies and missiology; music; music management and merchandising; music teacher education; physical education teaching and coaching; physical sciences; psychology; psychology related; radio and television broadcasting technology; religious education; social sciences; social work; sociology; Spanish; speech and rhetoric; sport and fitness administration/management; youth ministry.

Auburn University

Accounting; adult and continuing education; aerospace, aeronautical and astronautical engineering; agricultural economics; agricultural teacher education; agricultural/biological engineering and bioengineering; agriculture; agronomy and crop science; airline pilot and flight crew; animal sciences; anthropology; apparel and textiles; applied mathematics; aquaculture; architectural engineering; architecture; audiology and speech-language pathology; aviation/airway management; biochemistry; biology/biological sciences; biomedical sciences; botany/plant biology; broadcast journalism; business administration and management; business teacher education; business/managerial economics; chemical engineering; chemistry; child development; civil engineering; clinical laboratory science/medical technology; clinical/medical laboratory technology; commercial and advertising art; communication and journalism related; computer and information sciences; computer engineering; computer engineering related; computer hardware engineering; computer software engineering; criminology; dairy science; design and visual communications; dramatic/theater arts; early childhood education; economics; electrical, electronics and communications engineering; elementary education; engineering; English; English as a second/foreign language (teaching); English/language arts teacher education; environmental design/architecture; environmental science; environmental studies; family and consumer sciences/human sciences; finance; fine/studio arts; food science; foods, nutrition, and wellness; foreign languages and literatures; forest sciences and biology; French; French language teacher education; geography; geological/geophysical engineering; geology/earth science; German; German language teacher education; graphic design; health teacher education; health/health care administration; history; history teacher education; horticultural science; hospitality administration related; hotel/motel administration; human development and family studies; human resources management; industrial design; industrial engineering; interior architecture; international business/trade/commerce; journalism; kindergarten/preschool education; landscape architecture; logistics and materials management; management information systems; marine biology and biological oceanography; marketing/marketing management; mass communication/media; materials engineering; mathematics; mathematics teacher education; mechanical engineering; medical laboratory technology; medical microbiology and bacteriology; microbiology; molecular biology; music teacher education; nursing (registered nurse training); nutrition sciences; operations management; ornamental horticulture; parks, recreation and leisure; philosophy; physical education teaching and coaching; physics; physics teacher education; plant pathology/phytopathology; plant sciences; plant sciences related; political science and government; poultry science; pre-dentistry studies; pre-law studies; pre-medical studies; pre-pharmacy studies; pre-veterinary studies; psychology; public administration; public relations/image management; radio and television; science teacher education; secondary education; secondary school administration/principalship; social work; sociology; Spanish; Spanish language teacher education; special educa-

tion; special education (vision impaired); special education related; speech and rhetoric; speech therapy; textile sciences and engineering; trade and industrial teacher education; wildlife and wildlands science and management; zoology/animal biology.

Augustana College (IL)

Accounting; anthropology; art; art history, criticism and conservation; art teacher education; Asian studies; biochemistry; biology/biological sciences; business administration and management; chemistry; Chinese; classics and languages, literatures and linguistics; computer science; creative writing; dramatic/theater arts; economics; education; elementary education; engineering physics; engineering related; English; environmental studies; finance; fine/studio arts; French; geography; geology/earth science; German; history; Japanese; jazz/jazz studies; Latin; liberal arts and sciences/liberal studies; literature; marketing/marketing management; mass communication/media; mathematics; mathematics and computer science; music; music performance; music teacher education; occupational therapy; philosophy; physical education teaching and coaching; physics; piano and organ; political science and government; pre-dentistry studies; pre-law studies; pre-medical studies; pre-veterinary studies; psychology; public administration; religious studies; religious/sacred music; Scandinavian languages; science teacher education; secondary education; sociology; Spanish; speech and rhetoric; speech therapy; speech-language pathology; Swedish; violin, viola, guitar and other stringed instruments; voice and opera; wind/percussion instruments; women's studies.

Augustana College (SD)

Accounting; American Sign Language (ASL); art; art teacher education; athletic training; audiology and speech-language pathology; biology/biological sciences; business administration and management; business/corporate communications; chemistry; clinical laboratory science/medical technology; communication/speech communication and rhetoric; computer science; dramatic/theater arts; economics; education (K-12); elementary education; engineering physics; English; foreign languages and literatures; French; German; health/health care administration; history; international relations and affairs; journalism; kinesiology and exercise science; liberal arts and sciences/liberal studies; management information systems; mathematics; music; music teacher education; nursing (registered nurse training); philosophy; physical education teaching and coaching; physics; political science and government; pre-dentistry studies; pre-law studies; pre-medical studies; pre-veterinary studies; psychology; religious studies; secondary education; social studies teacher education; social work; sociology; Spanish; special education; special education (hearing impaired); speech/theater education; sport and fitness administration/management.

Austin College

Art; biochemistry; biology/biological sciences; business administration and management; chemistry; classics and classical languages related; classics and languages, literatures and linguistics; communication/speech communication and rhetoric; computer science; economics; English; French; German; history; international economics; international relations and affairs; Latin; mathematics; multi-/interdisciplinary studies related; music; philosophy; physics; political science and government; psychology; religious studies; sociology; Spanish.

Azusa Pacific University

Accounting; applied art; athletic training; biblical studies; biochemistry; biology/biological sciences; business administration and management; chemistry; communication/speech communication and rhetoric; computer science; cultural studies; divinity/ministry; English; health science; history; international relations and affairs; liberal arts and sciences/liberal studies; management information systems; marketing/marketing management; mathematics; music; natural sciences; nursing (registered nurse training); philosophy; physical education teaching and coaching; physics; political science and government; pre-engineering; pre-law studies; psychology; religious studies; social sciences; social work; sociology; Spanish; theology; web page, digital/multimedia and information resources design.

Babson College

Accounting; accounting and business/management; accounting and finance; auditing; business administration and management; business administration, management and operations related; business/corporate communications; economics; entrepreneurial and small business related; entrepreneurship; finance; finance and financial management services related; international business/trade/commerce; international finance; investments and securities; management information systems; marketing related; marketing/marketing management; office management; operations management; operations research; pre-law studies; sales, distribution and marketing; small business administration.

Baldwin-Wallace College

Accounting; art; art history, criticism and conservation; athletic training; biology/biological sciences; broadcast journalism; business administration and management; chemistry; communication disorders; communication/speech communication and rhetoric; computer science; computer software and media applications related; computer systems analysis; computer systems networking and telecommunications; creative writing; criminal justice/safety; dramatic/theater arts and stagecraft related; early childhood education; econometrics and quantitative economics; economics; English; exercise physiology; film/cinema studies; finance; fine/studio arts; French; German; health and physical education; health professions related; history; human resources management; international/global studies; marketing/marketing management; mass communication/media; mathematics; middle school education; multi-/interdisciplinary studies related; music; music history, literature, and theory; music performance; music teacher education; music theory and composition; music therapy; musicology and ethnomusicology; neuroscience; philosophy; physical sciences related; physics; piano and organ; political science and government; psychology; public relations/image management; religious studies; sociology; Spanish; special education (specific learning disabilities); sport and fitness administration/management; visual and performing arts related.

Bard College

Acting; African studies; American government and politics; American history; American studies; ancient/classical Greek; anthropology; Arabic; archeology; area studies; art; Asian history; Asian studies; biology/biological sciences; chemistry; Chinese; cinematography and film/video production; comparative literature; computer science; creative writing; dance; dramatic/theater arts; economics; English; environmental studies; European history; European studies; film/cinema studies; fine/studio arts; French; German; Hebrew; history; history and philosophy of science and technology; interdisciplinary studies; international relations and affairs; Italian; jazz/jazz studies; Jewish/Judaic studies; Latin; Latin American studies; liberal arts and sciences/liberal studies; literature; mathematics; medieval and Renaissance studies; music; music history, literature, and theory; music performance; music theory and composition; philosophy; photography; physics; playwriting and screenwriting; political science and government; pre-medical studies; psychology; religious studies; Romance languages; Russian; Russian studies; sociology; Spanish; theater literature, history and criticism; voice and opera.

Bard College at Simon's Rock

Acting; African American/Black studies; agricultural business and management; American literature; American native/native American education; American studies; anthropology; applied mathematics; art history, criticism and conservation; Asian studies; biology/biological sciences; ceramic arts and ceramics; chemistry; Chinese; Chinese studies; cognitive psychology and psycholinguistics; computer and information sciences; computer graphics; computer science; creative writing; cultural studies; dance; developmental and child psychology; dramatic/theater arts; drawing; ecology; economics related; English composition; environmental studies; ethnic, cultural minority, and gender studies related; European studies; fine/studio arts; foreign languages and literatures; French; French studies; geography; geology/earth science; German; German studies; interdisciplinary studies; jazz/jazz studies; Latin; Latin American studies; liberal arts and sciences/liberal studies; literature; mathematics; metal and jewelry arts; music; music theory and composition; natural sciences; paint-

ing; philosophy; photography; physics; playwriting and screenwriting; political science and government; pre-law studies; pre-medical studies; printmaking; psychology; religious studies; sculpture; sociology; Spanish; Spanish and Iberian studies; theater design and technology; theater literature, history and criticism; Ukraine studies; visual and performing arts; visual and performing arts related; women's studies.

Barnard College

African studies; American studies; ancient/classical Greek; anthropology; applied mathematics; architectural history and criticism; architecture; art history, criticism and conservation; Asian studies; biochemistry; biology/biological sciences; chemistry; classics; comparative literature; computer and information sciences; dance; dramatic/theater arts; economics; education; English; environmental biology; environmental science; European studies; film/cinema studies; French; French studies; German studies; history; interdisciplinary studies; Italian; Jewish/Judaic studies; Latin; Latin American studies; mathematical statistics and probability; mathematics; medieval and Renaissance studies; music; Near and Middle Eastern studies; neuroscience; philosophy; physics; political science and government; pre-law studies; pre-medical studies; psychology; religious studies; Russian; Russian studies; Slavic studies; sociology; Spanish; Spanish and Iberian studies; statistics; urban studies/affairs; visual and performing arts; women's studies.

Bates College

African American/Black studies; American studies; anthropology; archeology; art; Asian studies (East); biochemistry; biology/biological sciences; chemistry; Chinese; classical, ancient Mediterranean and Near Eastern studies and archaeology; dramatic/theater arts; economics; engineering; English; environmental studies; French; geology/earth science; German; history; Japanese; mathematics; multi-/interdisciplinary studies related; music; Near and Middle Eastern studies; neuroscience; philosophy; physics; political science and government; psychology; religious studies; Russian; sociology; Spanish; speech and rhetoric; women's studies.

Baylor University

Accounting; acting; airline pilot and flight crew; American studies; ancient Near Eastern and biblical languages; ancient/classical Greek; anthropology; applied mathematics; archeology; architecture; art; art history, criticism and conservation; art teacher education; Asian studies; athletic training; biochemistry; bioinformatics; biology teacher education; biology/biological sciences; business administration and management; business statistics; business teacher education; business, management, and marketing related; business/commerce; business/managerial economics; chemistry; chemistry teacher education; classics and languages, literatures and linguistics; clinical laboratory science/medical technology; communication disorders; communication/speech communication and rhetoric; computer science; computer teacher education; digital communication and media/multimedia; drama and dance teacher education; dramatic/theater arts; early childhood education; economics; education; education (specific subject areas) related; electrical, electronics and communications engineering; elementary education; engineering; English; English composition; English/language arts teacher education; entrepreneurship; environmental science; environmental studies; exercise physiology; family and consumer sciences/human sciences; fashion merchandising; fashion/apparel design; finance; financial planning and services; fine/studio arts; foreign language teacher education; forensic science and technology; forestry; French; French language teacher education; geological and earth sciences/geosciences related; geology/earth science; geophysics and seismology; German; German language teacher education; health and physical education; health occupations teacher education; health teacher education; health/medical preparatory programs related; history; human development and family studies; human nutrition; human resources management; humanities; insurance; interior design; international business/trade/commerce; international relations and affairs; journalism; kindergarten/preschool education; Latin; Latin American studies; Latin teacher education; linguistics; logistics and materials management; management information systems; marketing/marketing management; mathematics; mathematics teacher education; mechanical engineering; merchandising, sales, and marketing operations related (specialized); multi-/interdisciplinary studies related; museum studies; music; music history, literature, and theory; music pedagogy; music performance; music teacher education; music theory and composition; neuroscience; nursing (registered nurse training); operations management; philosophy; physical education teaching and coaching; physics; physics teacher education; political science and government; pre-dentistry studies; pre-law studies; pre-medical studies; pre-nursing studies; psychology; public administration; radio and television; reading teacher education; real estate; religious studies; religious/sacred music; Russian; sales, distribution and marketing; science teacher education; secondary education; Slavic studies; social science teacher education; social studies teacher education; social work; sociology; Spanish; Spanish language teacher education; special education; special education (speech or language impaired); speech teacher education; sport and fitness administration/management; statistics; theater design and technology; urban studies/affairs.

Belmont University

Accounting; advertising; ancient Near Eastern and biblical languages; applied mathematics; art; art teacher education; biblical studies; bilingual and multilingual education; biochemistry; biological and physical sciences; biology/biological sciences; broadcast journalism; business administration and management; business teacher education; business/managerial economics; chemistry; clinical laboratory science/medical technology; computer management; computer programming; computer science; consumer merchandising/retailing management; counselor education/school counseling and guidance; developmental and child psychology; divinity/ministry; dramatic/theater arts; economics; education; elementary education; engineering science; English; entrepreneurship; finance; fine/studio arts; health and physical education; health teacher education; health/health care administration; history; information science/studies; international business/trade/commerce; journalism; marketing/marketing management; mass communication/media; mathematics; modern Greek; music; music history, literature, and theory; music management and merchandising; music teacher education; nursing (registered nurse training); parks, recreation and leisure; pastoral studies/counseling; philosophy; physical education teaching and coaching; physics; piano and organ; political science and government; psychology; public relations, advertising, and applied communication related; radio and television; religious/sacred music; social work; sociology; Spanish; special education; speech and rhetoric; voice and opera; western civilization.

Beloit College

Anthropology; art history, criticism and conservation; art teacher education; Asian studies; biochemistry; biology/biological sciences; business administration and management; business/managerial economics; cell biology and histology; chemistry; classics and languages, literatures and linguistics; comparative literature; computer science; creative writing; dramatic/theater arts; economics; education; elementary education; engineering; English; environmental biology; environmental studies; European studies; fine/studio arts; French; geology/earth science; German; history; interdisciplinary studies; international relations and affairs; Latin American studies; literature; mass communication/media; mathematics; modern languages; molecular biology; museum studies; music; music teacher education; philosophy; physics; political science and government; pre-dentistry studies; pre-law studies; pre-medical studies; psychology; religious studies; Romance languages; Russian; Russian studies; science teacher education; secondary education; sociobiology; sociology; Spanish; women's studies.

Benedictine University

Accounting; arts management; biochemistry; biology/biological sciences; business administration and management; business, management, and marketing related; business/commerce; business/managerial economics; chemistry; clinical laboratory science/medical technology; communication/speech communication and rhetoric; comparative literature; computer science; economics; education; elementary education; engineering science; English; environmental studies; finance; fine/studio arts;

health science; health/health care administration; history; information science/studies; international business/trade/commerce; international relations and affairs; marketing/marketing management; mathematics; molecular biology; music; music teacher education; nuclear medical technology; nursing science; nutrition sciences; organizational behavior; philosophy; physics; political science and government; pre-dentistry studies; pre-law studies; pre-medical studies; pre-veterinary studies; psychology; publishing; science teacher education; secondary education; social sciences; sociology; Spanish; special education.

Bennington College

Acting; American government and politics; American history; American literature; American studies; animation, interactive technology, video graphics and special effects; anthropology; architecture; area, ethnic, cultural, and gender studies related; Asian studies; astronomy; biochemistry; biology/biological sciences; botany/plant biology; cell and molecular biology; ceramic arts and ceramics; chemistry; child development; Chinese; cinematography and film/video production; computer and information sciences; computer science; creative writing; dance; design and visual communications; directing and theatrical production; dramatic/theater arts; drawing; early childhood education; ecology; education; elementary education; English; English composition; English literature (British and Commonwealth); environmental biology; environmental studies; European history; European studies; evolutionary biology; evolutionary biology; film/cinema studies; fine/studio arts; foreign languages and literatures; French; gay/lesbian studies; history; humanities; intermedia/multimedia; international relations and affairs; international/global studies; Japanese; jazz/jazz studies; journalism; liberal arts and sciences and humanities related; liberal arts and sciences/liberal studies; mathematics; middle school education; music; music history, literature, and theory; music performance; music theory and composition; musicology and ethnomusicology; painting; peace studies and conflict resolution; philosophy; photography; physical sciences; physics; piano and organ; playwriting and screenwriting; political science and government; pre-law studies; pre-medical studies; printmaking; psychology; sculpture; secondary education; social psychology; social sciences; sociology; Spanish; theater design and technology; theater literature, history and criticism; violin, viola, guitar and other stringed instruments; visual and performing arts; voice and opera; women's studies; zoology/animal biology.

Bentley College

Accounting; business administration and management; business/corporate communications; business/managerial economics; computer and information sciences; finance; interdisciplinary studies; liberal arts and sciences/liberal studies; marketing/marketing management; mathematics; philosophy.

Berea College

Acting/directing; African American/Black studies; agriculture; art; biology/biological sciences; business administration and management; chemistry; economics; education; elementary education; English; French; German; history; human development and family studies; industrial technology; mathematics; middle school education; music; nursing (registered nurse training); philosophy; physics; political science and government; psychology; religious studies; sociology; Spanish; women's studies.

Bernard M. Baruch College of the City University of New York

Accounting; actuarial science; advertising; arts management; business administration and management; business/managerial economics; creative writing; economics; education; English; finance; history; human resources management; information science/studies; interdisciplinary studies; international business/trade/commerce; journalism; literature; management information systems; marketing/marketing management; mathematics; music; natural sciences; operations research; philosophy; political science and government; psychology; public administration; public policy analysis; Romance languages; sociology; Spanish; statistics.

Berry College

Accounting; animal sciences; art; biology/biological sciences; chemistry; communication and journalism related; computer science; early childhood education; economics; engineering technology; English; environmental science; exercise physiology; finance; French; German; history; international relations and affairs; marketing/marketing management; mathematics; mathematics teacher education; middle school education; multi-/interdisciplinary studies related; music; music management and merchandising; music teacher education; nursing (registered nurse training); philosophy and religious studies related; physical education teaching and coaching; physics; political science and government; psychology; social sciences; Spanish; theater/theater arts management.

Bethel University

Area, ethnic, cultural, and gender studies related; art; art teacher education; athletic training; biblical studies; biology teacher education; biology/biological sciences; business administration and management; chemistry; chemistry teacher education; communication/speech communication and rhetoric; community health services counseling; computer and information sciences; dramatic/theater arts; early childhood education; economics; elementary education; engineering science; English; English as a second/foreign language (teaching); English composition; English/language arts teacher education; environmental science; French; French language teacher education; health and physical education; health teacher education; history; international relations and affairs; kinesiology and exercise science; liberal arts and sciences/liberal studies; library science related; mass communication/media; mathematics; mathematics teacher education; molecular biology; multi-/interdisciplinary studies related; music; music performance; music teacher education; nursing (registered nurse training); philosophy; physical education teaching and coaching; physics; physics teacher education; political science and government; psychology; religious/sacred music; science teacher education; social sciences; social studies teacher education; social work; Spanish; Spanish language teacher education; youth ministry.

Biola University

Adult and continuing education; anthropology; biblical studies; bilingual and multilingual education; biochemistry; biology/biological sciences; business administration and management; clinical psychology; commercial and advertising art; communication disorders; computer and information sciences; divinity/ministry; drawing; education; education (K-12); elementary education; English; fine/studio arts; history; humanities; kinesiology and exercise science; mathematics; missionary studies and missiology; music; nursing (registered nurse training); pastoral studies/counseling; philosophy; physical education teaching and coaching; physical sciences; pre-law studies; psychology; radio and television; religious education; religious studies; secondary education; social sciences; sociology; Spanish; theology.

Birmingham-Southern College

Accounting; art; art history, criticism and conservation; art teacher education; Asian studies; biology/biological sciences; business administration and management; chemistry; computer science; dance; dramatic/theater arts; drawing; economics; education; elementary education; English; fine/studio arts; French; German; history; human resources management; interdisciplinary studies; international business/trade/commerce; mathematics; music; music history, literature, and theory; music teacher education; painting; philosophy; physics; piano and organ; political science and government; pre-dentistry studies; pre-law studies; pre-medical studies; printmaking; psychology; religious studies; sculpture; secondary education; sociology; Spanish; voice and opera.

Boston College

Accounting; ancient/classical Greek; art history, criticism and conservation; biochemistry; biology/biological sciences; business administration and management; business/managerial economics; chemistry; classics and languages, literatures and linguistics; communication/speech communication and rhetoric; computer and information sciences; computer science; dramatic/theater arts; economics; elementary education; English; film/

cinema studies; finance; fine/studio arts; French; geology/earth science; geophysics and seismology; German; Hispanic-American, Puerto Rican, and Mexican-American/Chicano studies; history; human development and family studies; human resources management; interdisciplinary studies; Italian; kindergarten/preschool education; Latin; management information systems; marketing/marketing management; mathematics; music; nursing (registered nurse training); operations management; philosophy; physics; political science and government; psychology; Russian; Russian studies; secondary education; Slavic languages; sociology; Spanish; theology.

Boston University

Accounting; acting; aerospace, aeronautical and astronautical engineering; American studies; ancient/classical Greek; animal physiology; anthropology; archeology; area studies related; art history and conservation; art teacher education; Asian studies (East); astronomy; astrophysics; athletic training; bilingual and multilingual education; biochemistry; biological and biomedical sciences related; biology/biological sciences; biomedical/medical engineering; business administration and management; chemistry; chemistry teacher education; cinematography and film/video production; classics and languages, literatures and linguistics; clinical laboratory science/medical technology; commercial and advertising art; communication disorders; communication/speech communication and rhetoric; computer engineering; computer science; dental laboratory technology; drama and dance teacher education; drawing; ecology; economics; education; education (specific levels and methods) related; electrical, electronics and communications engineering; elementary education; engineering; engineering related; English; English/language arts teacher education; environmental studies; ethnic, cultural minority, and gender studies related; finance; foreign language teacher education; foreign languages and literatures; French; geography; geology/earth science; German; health science; history; hospitality administration; hotel/motel administration; industrial engineering; information science/studies; interdisciplinary studies; international business/trade/commerce; international finance; international relations and affairs; Italian; journalism; journalism related; kindergarten/preschool education; kinesiology and exercise science; Latin; Latin American studies; legal assistant/paralegal; linguistics; management information systems; marine biology and biological oceanography; marketing research; marketing/marketing management; mass communication/media; mathematics; mathematics and computer science; mathematics teacher education; mechanical engineering; modern Greek; molecular biology; music history, literature, and theory; music performance; music teacher education; music theory and composition; neuroscience; nutrition sciences; occupational therapy; operations management; organizational behavior; painting; parks, recreation and leisure; philosophy; physical education teaching and coaching; physical therapy; physics; piano and organ; political science and government; pre-dentistry studies; psychology; public relations/image management; radio and television; rehabilitation therapy; religious studies; Russian; Russian studies; science teacher education; sculpture; social sciences related; social studies teacher education; sociology; Spanish; special education; special education (hearing impaired); speech/theater education; theater design and technology; theater literature, history and criticism; urban studies/affairs; voice and opera.

Bowdoin College

African studies; ancient studies; anthropology; archeology; art; art history, criticism and conservation; Asian studies; biochemistry; biology/biological sciences; chemical physics; chemistry; classical, ancient Mediterranean and Near Eastern studies and archaeology; classics and languages, literatures and linguistics; computer science; econometrics and quantitative economics; economics; English; environmental studies; European studies (Central and Eastern); fine/studio arts; French; geochemistry; geology/earth science; geophysics and seismology; German; history; interdisciplinary studies; Latin American studies; mathematics; mathematics and computer science; music; neuroscience; philosophy; physics; political science and government; psychology; religious studies; Romance languages; Russian; sociology; Spanish; theater literature, history and criticism; women's studies.

Bradley University

Accounting; acting; acting/directing; actuarial science; advertising; animation, interactive technology, video graphics and special effects; art; art history, criticism and conservation; biochemistry; biology/biological sciences; broadcast journalism; business administration and management; business/managerial economics; cell and molecular biology; ceramic arts and ceramics; chemistry; civil engineering; clinical laboratory science/medical technology; communication/speech communication and rhetoric; computer engineering; computer science; construction engineering; consumer merchandising/retailing management; creative writing; criminal justice/law enforcement administration; dietetics; dramatic/theater arts; drawing; early childhood education; ecology; economics; education (specific subject areas) related; electrical, electronic and communications engineering technology; electrical, electronics and communications engineering; elementary education; engineering physics; English; entrepreneurship; environmental science; environmental/environmental health engineering; family and consumer sciences/human sciences; family resource management; finance; fine/studio arts; French; German; graphic design; health professions related; health science; history; human resources management; humanities; industrial engineering; information science/studies; insurance; international business/trade/commerce; international relations and affairs; journalism; law and legal studies related; liberal arts and sciences/liberal studies; management information systems; manufacturing engineering; manufacturing technology; marketing/marketing management; mathematics; mechanical engineering; music; music performance; music teacher education; music theory and composition; nursing (registered nurse training); philosophy; photography; photojournalism; physical therapy; physics; political science and government; printmaking; psychology; public relations/image management; radio and television; religious studies; sculpture; selling skills and sales; small business administration; social work; sociology; Spanish; special education (mentally retarded); special education (specific learning disabilities).

Brandeis University

African American/Black studies; American studies; ancient/classical Greek; anthropology; area, ethnic, cultural, and gender studies related; art history, criticism and conservation; Asian studies (East); biochemistry; biology/biological sciences; biophysics; chemistry; comparative literature; computer science; creative writing; dramatic/theater arts; economics; English; European studies; fine/studio arts; French; German; health/health care administration; history; international/global studies; Jewish/Judaic studies; Latin; Latin American studies; linguistics; mathematics; multi-/interdisciplinary studies related; music; Near and Middle Eastern studies; neuroscience; philosophy; physics; political science and government related; psychology; Russian; sociology; Spanish; women's studies.

Brigham Young University

Accounting; accounting related; acting; actuarial science; advertising; agribusiness; agricultural business and management; agricultural economics; American studies; ancient Near Eastern and biblical languages; ancient/classical Greek; animation, interactive technology, video graphics and special effects; anthropology; applied economics; Arabic; art; art history, criticism and conservation; art teacher education; Asian studies; astronomy; athletic training; audiology and speech-language pathology; ballet; biochemistry; bioinformatics; biological and physical sciences; biology/biological sciences; biomedical sciences; biophysics; biostatistics; biotechnology; botany/plant biology; broadcast journalism; business administration and management; business family and consumer sciences/human sciences; business statistics; business/commerce; cartography; ceramic arts and ceramics; chemical engineering; chemistry; chemistry teacher education; child care and support services management; child care provision; child development; Chinese; cinematography and film/video production; civil engineering; classical, ancient Mediterranean and Near Eastern studies and archaeology; classics and languages, literatures and linguistics; clinical laboratory science/medical technology; communication and journalism related; comparative literature; computer engineering; computer science; conservation biology; crafts, folk art and artisanry;

dance; dance related; design and visual communications; dietetics; directing and theatrical production; drama and dance teacher education; dramatic/theater arts; dramatic/theater arts and stagecraft related; drawing; early childhood education; ecology, evolution, systematics and population biology related; economics; education (specific levels and methods) related; education (specific subject areas) related; education related; electrical, electronics and communications engineering; elementary education; engineering technology; English; English as a second/foreign language (teaching); English composition; English/language arts teacher education; entrepreneurship; environmental science; European studies (Central and Eastern); family and consumer economics related; family and consumer sciences/home economics teacher education; family and consumer sciences/human sciences; family and consumer sciences/human sciences business services related; family resource management; family systems; film/cinema studies; film/video and photographic arts related; financial planning and services; fine/studio arts; food science; food technology and processing; foreign language teacher education; French; French language teacher education; geography; geography related; geological and earth sciences/geosciences related; geology/earth science; German; German language teacher education; graphic design; health and physical education; health and physical education related; Hebrew; history; history related; history teacher education; home furnishings and equipment installation; human development and family studies; human resources development; human resources management; humanities; illustration; industrial design; information technology; interior design; international finance; international marketing; international relations and affairs; Italian; Japanese; jazz/jazz studies; journalism; kinesiology and exercise science; Korean; language interpretation and translation; Latin; Latin American studies; Latin teacher education; liberal arts and sciences and humanities related; liberal arts and sciences/liberal studies; linguistic and comparative language studies related; linguistics; logistics and materials management; management information systems; manufacturing engineering; marketing/marketing management; mass communication/media; mass communications; mathematics; mathematics teacher education; mechanical engineering; merchandising, sales, and marketing operations related (general); microbiology; molecular biology; music; music history, literature, and theory; music pedagogy; music performance; music related; music teacher education; music theory and composition; neuroscience; Norwegian; nursing (registered nurse training); nutrition sciences; organizational communication; painting; parks, recreation and leisure; parks, recreation, and leisure related; philosophy; photography; physical education teaching and coaching; physics; physics related; physics teacher education; physiology; piano and organ; plant genetics; playwriting and screenwriting; political science and government; Portuguese; pre-nursing studies; printmaking; psychology; psychology teacher education; public policy analysis; public relations, advertising, and applied communication related; radio, television, and digital communication related; range science and management; retailing; Russian; science teacher education; sculpture; social psychology; social science teacher education; social work; sociology; soil sciences related; Spanish; Spanish language teacher education; special education; speech and rhetoric; speech teacher education; statistics; statistics related; Swedish; technology/industrial arts teacher education; theater design and technology; therapeutic recreation; veterinary/animal health technology; violin, viola, guitar and other stringed instruments; visual and performing arts related; voice and opera; wildlife and wildlands science and management; work and family studies; zoology/animal biology.

Brown University

African American/Black studies; American studies; anthropology; applied mathematics; archeology; architectural history and criticism; art; art history, criticism and conservation; Asian studies (East); Asian studies (South); behavioral sciences; biochemistry; biology/biological sciences; biomedical sciences; biomedical/medical engineering; biophysics; chemical engineering; chemistry; civil engineering; classics and languages, literatures and linguistics; cognitive psychology and psycholinguistics; comparative literature; computer engineering; computer science; creative writing; development economics and international development; dramatic/theater arts; economics; education; electrical, electronics and communications engineering; engineering; engineering physics; English; environmental science; environmental studies; film/cinema studies; fine/studio arts; French; French studies; geochemistry; geology/earth science; geophysics and seismology; German; German studies; Hispanic-American, Puerto Rican, and Mexican-American/Chicano studies; history; international relations and affairs; Italian; Italian studies; Jewish/Judaic studies; Latin American studies; linguistics; marine biology and biological oceanography; materials engineering; mathematics; mathematics and computer science; mechanical engineering; medieval and Renaissance studies; molecular biology; music; music related; musicology and ethnomusicology; Near and Middle Eastern studies; neuroscience; organizational behavior; philosophy; physics; political science and government; psychology; religious studies; Russian studies; sociology; Spanish; urban studies/affairs; visual and performing arts; women's studies.

Bryan College (TN)

Athletic training/sports medicine; biblical studies; biology/biological sciences; business administration and management; business/corporate communications; Christian studies; communication/speech communication and rhetoric; computer science; education; elementary education; English; English/language arts teacher education; health and physical education; history; history teacher education; kindergarten/preschool education; kinesiology and exercise science; liberal arts and sciences/liberal studies; literature; mathematics; mathematics and computer science; mathematics teacher education; middle school education; music; music management and merchandising; music pedagogy; music performance; music teacher education; nursing science; physical education teaching and coaching; piano and organ; political science and government; pre-medical studies; psychology; religious education; religious/sacred music; science teacher education; secondary education; Spanish; voice and opera; wind/percussion instruments; youth ministry.

Bryn Mawr College

Ancient/classical Greek; anthropology; archeology; art; art history, criticism and conservation; Asian studies (East); astronomy; biology/biological sciences; chemistry; classics and classical languages related; classics and languages, literatures and linguistics; comparative literature; economics; English; French; geology/earth science; German; history; Italian; Latin; mathematics; Middle/ Near Eastern and Semitic languages related; music; philosophy; physics; political science and government; psychology; religious studies; Romance languages; Russian; sociology; Spanish; urban studies/affairs.

Bucknell University

Accounting; animal behavior and ethology; anthropology; area studies; art; art history, criticism and conservation; Asian studies (East); biochemistry; biology/biological sciences; biomedical/medical engineering; biopsychology; business administration and management; cell and molecular biology; chemical engineering; chemistry; civil engineering; classics and languages, literatures and linguistics; computer and information sciences; computer engineering; creative writing; dramatic/theater arts; early childhood education; economics; educational statistics and research methods; electrical, electronics and communications engineering; elementary education; English; environmental studies; fine/studio arts; French; geography; geological and earth sciences/geosciences related; geology/earth science; German; history; humanities; interdisciplinary studies; international relations and affairs; kindergarten/preschool education; Latin American studies; mathematics; mechanical engineering; multi-/interdisciplinary studies related; music; music history, literature, and theory; music performance; music teacher education; music theory and composition; philosophy; physics; political science and government; psychology; religious studies; Russian; secondary education; sociology; Spanish; women's studies.

Butler University

Accounting; actuarial science; anthropology; arts management; audiology and speech-language pathology; biology/biological sciences; chemistry; communication disorders; computer and information sciences; criminology; dance; dramatic/theater arts; economics; elementary education;

engineering physics; English; finance; French; German; history; international business/trade/commerce; international relations and affairs; journalism; kindergarten/preschool education; Latin; liberal arts and sciences/liberal studies; management information systems; marketing/marketing management; mathematics; middle school education; modern Greek; music; music history, literature, and theory; music management and merchandising; music performance; music teacher education; music theory and composition; pharmacy; philosophy; philosophy and religious studies related; physician assistant; physics; piano and organ; political science and government; psychology; radio and television; recording arts technology; religious studies; science, technology and society; secondary education; sociology; Spanish; speech and rhetoric; urban studies/affairs; violin, viola, guitar and other stringed instruments; voice and opera; wind/percussion instruments.

California Institute of Technology

Aerospace, aeronautical and astronautical engineering; applied mathematics; astrophysics; biology/biological sciences; business/managerial economics; chemical engineering; chemistry; computational mathematics; computer engineering; computer science; economics; electrical, electronics and communications engineering; English; environmental/environmental health engineering; geochemistry; geology/earth science; geophysics and seismology; history; history of science and technology; materials science; mathematics; mechanical engineering; philosophy; physics; planetary astronomy and science; political science and government.

California Polytechnic State University, San Luis Obispo

Aerospace, aeronautical and astronautical engineering; agricultural business and management; agricultural/biological engineering and bioengineering; agriculture; agronomy and crop science; animal sciences; applied art; architectural engineering; architecture; biochemistry; biology/biological sciences; biomedical/medical engineering; business administration and management; chemistry; child development; city/urban, community and regional planning; civil engineering; commercial and advertising art; computer engineering; computer science; computer software engineering; construction management; cultural studies; dairy science; developmental and child psychology; economics; electrical, electronics and communications engineering; engineering science; English; environmental biology; environmental/environmental health engineering; food science; foods, nutrition, and wellness; forestry; geology/earth science; graphic communications; history; horticultural science; industrial engineering; industrial technology; interdisciplinary studies; journalism; kinesiology and exercise science; landscape architecture; liberal arts and sciences/liberal studies; manufacturing engineering; materials engineering; mathematics; mechanical engineering; mechanical engineering/mechanical technology; medical microbiology and bacteriology; modern languages; music; nutrition science; parks, recreation and leisure; philosophy; physics; political science and government; psychology; social sciences; statistics.

Calvin College

Accounting; art; art history, criticism and conservation; art teacher education; Asian studies; audiology and speech-language pathology; biblical studies; bilingual and multilingual education; biochemistry; biological and physical sciences; biology/biological sciences; biotechnology; business administration and management; business/corporate communications; chemical engineering; chemistry; civil engineering; classics and languages, literatures and linguistics; communication/speech communication and rhetoric; computer science; conducting; development economics and international development; digital communication and media/multimedia; dramatic/theater arts; economics; electrical, electronics and communications engineering; elementary education; engineering; English; English as a second/foreign language (teaching); environmental studies; film/cinema studies; fine/studio arts; French; geography; geology/earth science; German; Germanic languages related; history; interdisciplinary studies; international relations and affairs; kinesiology and exercise science; Latin; management information systems; mass communication/media;

mathematics; mechanical engineering; modern Greek; music; music history, literature, and theory; music performance; music teacher education; music theory and composition; natural sciences; nursing (registered nurse training); occupational therapy; parks, recreation and leisure; philosophy; physical education teaching and coaching; physical sciences; physics; piano and organ; political science and government; pre-dentistry studies; pre-law studies; pre-medical studies; pre-veterinary studies; psychology; public administration; religious studies; religious/sacred music; science teacher education; secondary education; social sciences; social work; sociology; Spanish; special education; speech and rhetoric; sport and fitness administration/management; theology; therapeutic recreation; voice and opera.

Canisius College

Accounting; accounting and finance; accounting technology and bookkeeping; anthropology; art history, criticism and conservation; athletic training; biochemistry; bioinformatics; biological and physical sciences; business administration and management; business administration, management and operations related; chemistry; communication and media related; computer science; creative writing; criminal justice/law enforcement administration; digital communication and media/multimedia; dramatic/theater arts; early childhood education; economics; education; engineering related; English; entrepreneurship; environmental science; European studies; finance; fine/studio arts; forest sciences and biology; French; general studies; German; Germanic languages; history; information technology; international business/trade/commerce; international relations and affairs; marketing related; marketing/marketing management; mathematics and statistics related; neuroscience; philosophy; physical education teaching and coaching; physics; political science and government; psychology; religious studies; science teacher education; secondary education; sociology; Spanish; special education (early childhood); urban studies/affairs; women's studies.

Carleton College

African studies; American studies; ancient/classical Greek; anthropology; art history, criticism and conservation; Asian studies; biology/biological sciences; chemistry; classics and languages, literatures and linguistics; computer science; economics; English; fine/studio arts; French; French studies; geology/earth science; German; history; interdisciplinary studies; international relations and affairs; Latin; Latin American studies; mathematics; music; philosophy; physics; political science and government; psychology; religious studies; Romance languages; Russian; Russian studies; sociology; Spanish; women's studies.

Carnegie Mellon University

Anthropology related; applied mathematics; architectural history and criticism; architectural technology; architecture; architecture related; art; astrophysics; behavioral sciences; biological and biomedical sciences related; biology/biological sciences; biomedical/medical engineering; biophysics; biopsychology; business administration and management; business/managerial economics; chemical engineering; chemical physics; chemistry; chemistry related; Chinese; civil engineering; cognitive science; communication and media related; computational mathematics; computer engineering related; computer science; creative writing; dramatic/theater arts; economics; engineering related; English; English as a second/foreign language (teaching); ethics; ethnic, cultural minority, and gender studies related; European history; European studies; foreign languages and literatures; French; German; history related; industrial design; information science/studies; international relations and affairs; Japanese; Latin American studies; liberal arts and sciences/liberal studies; logic; materials science; mathematical statistics and probability; mathematics and statistics related; mechanical engineering; music performance; music theory and composition; natural resources management and policy; operations research; philosophy; physics; physics related; piano and organ; political science and government; psychology; public policy analysis; science, technology and society; social sciences related; Spanish; statistics; systems science and theory; technical and business writing; violin, viola, guitar and other stringed instruments; voice and opera.

Carroll College (MT)

Accounting; acting; art; biology teacher education; biology/biological sciences; business administration and management; business/managerial economics; chemistry; civil engineering; clinical laboratory science/medical technology; communication/speech communication and rhetoric; computer science; dramatic/theater arts; education; elementary education; engineering; English; English as a second/foreign language (teaching); English/language arts teacher education; environmental studies; finance; French; general studies; health information/medical records administration; history; history teacher education; international relations and affairs; Latin; mathematics; mathematics teacher education; nursing (registered nurse training); philosophy; physical education teaching and coaching; political science and government; pre-dentistry studies; pre-law studies; pre-medical studies; pre-pharmacy studies; pre-veterinary studies; psychology; public administration; public relations/image management; religious education; religious studies; secondary education; social science teacher education; social sciences; social work; sociology; Spanish; Spanish language teacher education; sport and fitness administration/management; technical and business writing; theater design and technology; theology; visual and performing arts.

Carroll College (WI)

Accounting; actuarial science; animal behavior and ethology; applied mathematics; applied mathematics related; art; art teacher education; athletic training; biochemistry; biology teacher education; biology/biological sciences; business administration and management; chemistry; chemistry teacher education; clinical laboratory science/medical technology; commercial and advertising art; communication/speech communication and rhetoric; computer and information sciences; computer software engineering; creative writing; dramatic/theater arts; early childhood education; education; elementary education; engineering physics; English; English/language arts teacher education; environmental science; European studies; finance; fine/studio arts; foreign language teacher education; forensic science and technology; graphic communications; health and physical education; health teacher education; history; history teacher education; human resources management; information science/studies; international relations and affairs; journalism; kinesiology and exercise science; management information systems; marketing/marketing management; mathematics; mathematics teacher education; middle school education; music; music teacher education; natural resources/conservation; nursing (registered nurse training); organizational behavior; organizational communication; photography; physical education teaching and coaching; political science and government; pre-dentistry studies; pre-medical studies; pre-pharmacy studies; pre-veterinary studies; printing management; psychology; psychology teacher education; public relations, advertising, and applied communication related; public relations/image management; religious studies; science teacher education; small business administration; social science teacher education; social studies teacher education; sociology; Spanish; Spanish language teacher education; trade and industrial teacher education.

Carson-Newman College

Accounting; ancient Near Eastern and biblical languages; art; art teacher education; athletic training; biblical studies; biology/biological sciences; broadcast journalism; business administration and management; business teacher education; business/managerial economics; chemistry; child development; clinical laboratory science/medical technology; commercial and advertising art; computer science; consumer services and advocacy; creative writing; developmental and child psychology; dietetics; divinity/ministry; dramatic/theater arts; drawing; economics; education; elementary education; English; family and consumer economics related; family and consumer sciences/home economics teacher education; family and consumer sciences/human sciences; fashion merchandising; film/cinema studies; foods, nutrition, and wellness; French; history; hospital and health care facilities administration; human services; information science/studies; interdisciplinary studies; interior design; international economics; journalism; kindergarten/preschool education; kinesiology and exercise science; liberal arts and sciences/liberal studies; literature;

management information systems; marketing/marketing management; mass communication/media; mathematics; music; music teacher education; music theory and composition; nursing (registered nurse training); parks, recreation and leisure; philosophy; photography; physical education teaching and coaching; physics; physics related; piano and organ; political science and government; psychology; religious studies; secondary education; small business administration; sociology; Spanish; special education; speech and rhetoric; voice and opera.

Case Western Reserve University
Accounting; aerospace, aeronautical and astronautical engineering; American studies; anthropology; applied mathematics; art history, criticism and conservation; art teacher education; Asian studies; astronomy; biochemistry; biology/biological sciences; biomathematics and bioinformatics related; biomedical/medical engineering; business administration and management; chemical engineering; chemistry; civil engineering; classics and languages, literatures and linguistics; cognitive science; communication disorders; comparative literature; computer engineering; computer science; dietetics; dramatic/theater arts; economics; electrical, electronics and communications engineering; engineering; engineering physics; engineering science; English; environmental studies; evolutionary biology; French; French studies; geology/earth science; German; German studies; gerontology; history; history and philosophy of science and technology; human nutrition; international relations and affairs; international/global studies; Japanese studies; materials engineering; materials science; mathematics; mechanical engineering; music; music teacher education; natural sciences; nursing (registered nurse training); nutrition sciences; philosophy; political science and government; polymer/plastics engineering; psychology; religious studies; sociology; Spanish; statistics; systems engineering; women's studies.

Cedarville University
Accounting; administrative assistant and secretarial science; American studies; athletic training; biblical studies; biological and physical sciences; biology teacher education; biology/biological sciences; broadcast journalism; business administration and management; chemistry; clinical laboratory science/medical technology; communication/speech communication and rhetoric; communications technology; computer and information sciences; computer engineering; computer science; criminal justice/law enforcement administration; dramatic/theater arts; early childhood education; electrical, electronics and communications engineering; English; English/language arts teacher education; environmental biology; finance; fine/studio arts; forensic science and technology; graphic design; health and physical education; health teacher education; history; information science/studies; interdisciplinary studies; international business/trade/commerce; international relations and affairs; international/global studies; kinesiology and exercise science; management information systems; marketing/marketing management; mathematics; mathematics teacher education; mechanical engineering; middle school education; missionary studies and missiology; music; music pedagogy; music performance; music teacher education; music theory and composition; nursing (registered nurse training); pastoral counseling and specialized ministries related; pastoral studies/counseling; philosophy; physical education teaching and coaching; physics; physics teacher education; piano and organ; political science and government; pre-dentistry studies; pre-law studies; pre-medical studies; pre-veterinary studies; psychology; public administration; radio and television; religious education; religious studies; religious/sacred music; science teacher education; secondary education; social studies teacher education; social work; sociology; Spanish; Spanish language teacher education; special education; speech and rhetoric; sport and fitness administration/management; technical and business writing; theology; voice and opera; youth ministry.

Central College
Accounting; art; biology/biological sciences; business administration and management; chemistry; communication/speech communication and rhetoric; computer science; dramatic/theater arts; economics; elementary education; English; environmental studies; French; general studies; German studies; history; information science/studies; interdisciplinary studies;

international business/trade/commerce; international/global studies; kinesiology and exercise science; linguistics; mathematics; mathematics and computer science; music; music teacher education; natural sciences; philosophy; physics; political science and government; psychology; religious studies; social sciences; sociology; Spanish.

Centre College
Anthropology; art; art history, criticism and conservation; biochemistry; biology/biological sciences; chemistry; classics and languages, literatures and linguistics; computer science; dramatic/theater arts; economics; elementary education; English; French; German; history; international relations and affairs; mathematics; molecular biology; music; philosophy; physics; physiological psychology/psychobiology; political science and government; psychology; religious studies; secondary education; sociology; Spanish.

Chapman University
Accounting; American history; art; art history, criticism and conservation; athletic training; biology/biological sciences; biopsychology; broadcast journalism; business administration and management; business/managerial economics; chemistry; cinematography and film/video production; communication/speech communication and rhetoric; computer and information sciences; computer science; conducting; creative writing; dance; dramatic/theater arts; English; European history; exercise physiology; film/cinema studies; fine/studio arts; French; graphic design; liberal arts and sciences/liberal studies; mathematics; molecular biology; music; music performance; music teacher education; music theory and composition; music therapy; peace studies and conflict resolution; philosophy; playwriting and screenwriting; political science and government; psychology; public relations/image management; religious studies; social work; sociology; Spanish; voice and opera; wind/percussion instruments.

Christendom College
Classics and languages, literatures and linguistics; history; liberal arts and sciences/liberal studies; literature; philosophy; political science and government; theology.

Christian Brothers University
Biology teacher education; biomedical sciences; business administration and management; chemical engineering; chemistry; chemistry teacher education; civil engineering; computer science; education; electrical, electronics and communications engineering; elementary education; engineering physics; English; English/language arts teacher education; environmental/environmental health engineering; fine/studio arts; history; history teacher education; liberal arts and sciences/liberal studies; mathematics; mathematics teacher education; mechanical engineering; natural sciences; philosophy; physics; physics teacher education; psychology; public relations; religious studies.

Claremont McKenna College
Accounting; African American/Black studies; American government and politics; American studies; anthropology; archeology; area studies related; area, ethnic, cultural, and gender studies related; art; art history, criticism and conservation; Asian studies; Asian-American studies; biochemistry; biology/biological sciences; biophysics; chemistry; Chinese; Chinese studies; classics and languages, literatures and linguistics; computer and information sciences; computer science; dance; dramatic/theater arts; East Asian languages related; economics; economics related; engineering; engineering related; engineering science; engineering/industrial management; English; environmental studies; ethnic, cultural minority, and gender studies related; European studies; European studies (Western); film/cinema studies; fine/studio arts; French; French studies; German; German studies; Germanic languages; Hispanic-American, Puerto Rican, and Mexican-American/Chicano studies; history; international business/trade/commerce; international economics; international relations and affairs; Italian; Japanese; Japanese studies; Korean studies; Latin; Latin American studies; legal studies; literature; mathematics; modern Greek; modern languages; music; music related; Near and Middle Eastern studies; Pacific area/Pacific rim studies; philosophy; philosophy and religious

studies related; philosophy related; physics; physiological psychology/ psychobiology; political science and government; political science and government related; pre-dentistry studies; pre-law studies; pre-medical studies; psychology; religious studies; religious studies related; Russian; Russian studies; sociology; South Asian languages; Spanish; visual and performing arts; visual and performing arts related; women's studies.

Clarke College

Accounting; advertising; art; art history, criticism and conservation; art teacher education; athletic training; biology/biological sciences; business administration and management; chemistry; computer science; dramatic/ theater arts; economics; education; elementary education; English; fine/ studio arts; French; history; information science/studies; international business/trade/commerce; kindergarten/preschool education; liberal arts and sciences/liberal studies; management information systems; marketing/marketing management; mass communication/media; mathematics; middle school education; music; music teacher education; nursing science; philosophy; physical education teaching and coaching; physical therapy; psychology; public relations/image management; religious studies; secondary education; social work; Spanish; special education; sport and fitness administration/management; voice and opera.

Clarkson University

Accounting; aerospace, aeronautical and astronautical engineering; American literature; American studies; applied mathematics; biochemistry; biology/biological sciences; biophysics; biotechnology; business administration and management; cell biology and histology; chemical engineering; chemistry; civil engineering; communication/ speech communication and rhetoric; computer and information sciences; computer engineering; computer science; computer software engineering; construction engineering; digital communication and media/multimedia; e-commerce; ecology; electrical, electronics and communications engineering; engineering; entrepreneurship; environmental health; environmental studies; environmental/environmental health engineering; finance; history; human resources management; humanities; industrial and organizational psychology; information resources management; interdisciplinary studies; international business/trade/commerce; liberal arts and sciences/liberal studies; logistics and materials management; management information systems; manufacturing engineering; marketing/marketing management; materials engineering; materials science; mathematics; mechanical engineering; molecular biology; non-profit management; occupational health and industrial hygiene; operations management; physics; political science and government; pre-dentistry studies; pre-law studies; pre-medical studies; pre-veterinary studies; psychology; social sciences; sociology; statistics; structural engineering; technical and business writing; toxicology.

Clark University

Art history, criticism and conservation; Asian studies; biochemistry; biology/biological sciences; business administration and management; chemistry; classics and languages, literatures and linguistics; commercial and advertising art; comparative literature; computer science; cultural studies; development economics and international development; dramatic/theater arts; ecology; economics; education; elementary education; engineering; English; film/cinema studies; fine/studio arts; French; geography; geology/earth science; history; interdisciplinary studies; international relations and affairs; Jewish/Judaic studies; mass communication/ media; mathematics; middle school education; modern languages; molecular biology; music; natural resources management and policy; neuroscience; peace studies and conflict resolution; philosophy; physics; political science and government; pre-dentistry studies; pre-law studies; pre-medical studies; pre-veterinary studies; psychology; secondary education; sociology; Spanish; women's studies.

Clemson University

Accounting; agricultural business and management; agricultural economics; agricultural mechanization; agricultural teacher education; agricultural/biological engineering and bioengineering; animal sciences; architecture; biochemistry; biology/biological sciences; biomedical/medi-

cal engineering; business administration and management; business, management, and marketing related; ceramic sciences and engineering; chemical engineering; chemistry; civil engineering; communication and journalism related; computer and information sciences; computer engineering; computer programming; computer science; construction management; counselor education/school counseling and guidance; early childhood education; economics; electrical, electronics and communications engineering; elementary education; engineering mechanics; engineering/industrial management; English; finance; fishing and fisheries sciences and management; food science; forest/forest resources management; genetics; geology/earth science; graphic communications; health professions related; health science; history; horticultural science; human resources development; industrial design; industrial engineering; information science/studies; international business/trade/commerce; international public health; landscape architecture; management information systems; marketing/marketing management; mass communications; materials engineering; mathematics; mathematics teacher education; mechanical engineering; microbiology; modern languages; natural resources/conservation; nursing (registered nurse training); parks, recreation and leisure facilities management; philosophy; physics; political science and government; polymer chemistry; psychology; science teacher education; science technologies related; secondary education; sociology; special education; speech and rhetoric; textile sciences and engineering; turf and turfgrass management; visual and performing arts; visual and performing arts related; wildlife biology.

Coe College

Accounting; acting; African American/Black studies; American studies; architecture; area, ethnic, cultural, and gender studies related; art; art teacher education; Asian studies; athletic training; biochemistry; biological and physical sciences; biology/biological sciences; business administration and management; ceramic arts and ceramics; chemistry; classics and languages, literatures and linguistics; computer science; creative writing; directing and theatrical production; dramatic/theater arts; economics; education; elementary education; English; environmental studies; fine/ studio arts; French; French studies; German; German studies; health and physical education related; history; interdisciplinary studies; liberal arts and sciences/liberal studies; literature; mathematics; molecular biology; music; music performance; music teacher education; music theory and composition; nursing (registered nurse training); painting; philosophy; photography; physical education teaching and coaching; physical sciences; physics; political science and government; pre-dentistry studies; pre-law studies; pre-medical studies; pre-veterinary studies; psychology; public relations/image management; religious studies; science teacher education; secondary education; sociology; Spanish; Spanish and Iberian studies; speech and rhetoric; theater design and technology.

Colby College

African American/Black studies; American studies; anthropology; art; art history, criticism and conservation; Asian studies (East); biochemistry; biology/biological sciences; cell biology and histology; chemistry; classics and languages, literatures and linguistics; computer science; creative writing; dramatic/theater arts; economics; English; environmental science; environmental studies; French; geology/earth science; German; history; interdisciplinary studies; international relations and affairs; international/ global studies; Latin American studies; mathematics; molecular biology; music; philosophy; physics; political science and government; psychology; religious studies; Russian studies; science, technology and society; sociology; Spanish; women's studies.

Colgate University

African studies; African American/Black studies; American Indian/Native American studies; anthropology; art; art history, criticism and conservation; Asian studies; Asian studies (East); astronomy; astrophysics; biochemistry; biology/biological sciences; chemistry; Chinese; classics and languages, literatures and linguistics; dramatic/theater arts; economics; education; English; environmental biology; environmental studies; French; geography; geology/earth science; German; history; humanities; international relations and affairs; Japanese; Latin; Latin American studies; mathematics; modern Greek; molecular biology; music; natural sciences; neuroscience; peace studies and conflict resolution; philosophy; physical sciences; physics; political science and government; psychology; religious studies; Romance languages; Russian; Russian studies; social sciences; sociology; Spanish; women's studies.

College of Charleston

Accounting; anthropology; art history, criticism and conservation; arts management; astronomy and astrophysics related; athletic training; biochemistry; biology/biological sciences; business administration and management; chemistry; classics and languages, literatures and linguistics; communication/speech communication and rhetoric; computer and information sciences; dramatic/theater arts; early childhood education; economics; elementary education; English; fine/studio arts; French; geology/earth science; German; historic preservation and conservation; history; hospitality administration; information science/studies; international business/trade/commerce; Latin American studies; marine biology and biological oceanography; mathematics; middle school education; music; philosophy; physical education teaching and coaching; physics; political science and government; pre-dentistry studies; pre-medical studies; psychology; religious studies; sociology; Spanish; special education; urban studies/affairs.

The College of Idaho

Accounting; anthropology; art; biology/biological sciences; business administration and management; chemistry; creative writing; dramatic/theater arts; economics; English; history; international business/trade/commerce; international economics; kinesiology and exercise science; mathematics; music; philosophy; physical education teaching and coaching; physics; political science and government; pre-medical studies; psychology; religious studies; sociology; Spanish; sport and fitness administration/management.

The College of New Jersey

Accounting; art; art teacher education; biology teacher education; biology/biological sciences; biomedical/medical engineering; business administration and management; business/managerial economics; chemistry; chemistry teacher education; commercial and advertising art; computer and information sciences; computer engineering; criminal justice/law enforcement administration; economics; education; electrical, electronics and communications engineering; elementary education; engineering science; English; English/language arts teacher education; finance; fine/studio arts; history; history teacher education; intermedia/multimedia; international business/trade/commerce; international relations and affairs; kindergarten/preschool education; mathematics; mathematics teacher education; mechanical engineering; multi-/interdisciplinary studies related; music; music teacher education; nursing (registered nurse training); philosophy; physical education teaching and coaching; physics; physics teacher education; political science and government; pre-law studies; pre-medical studies; psychology; secondary education; sociology; Spanish; Spanish language teacher education; special education; special education (hearing impaired); speech and rhetoric; statistics; technology/industrial arts teacher education; women's studies.

College of Saint Benedict

Accounting; art; biochemistry; biological and physical sciences; biology/biological sciences; business administration and management; chemistry; classics and languages, literatures and linguistics; clinical/medical laboratory assistant; computer science; dietetics; dramatic/theater arts; economics; education; elementary education; engineering physics; English; environmental studies; fine/studio arts; foods, nutrition, and wellness; forest sciences and biology; forestry; French; German; history; humanities; liberal arts and sciences/liberal studies; mathematics; mathematics and computer science; music; natural sciences; nursing (registered nurse training); nutrition sciences; occupational therapy; peace studies and conflict resolution; philosophy; physical therapy; physics; political science and government; pre-dentistry studies; pre-law studies; pre-medical studies; pre-pharmacy studies; pre-theology/pre-ministerial studies; pre-

veterinary studies; psychology; religious education; secondary education; social sciences; social work; sociology; Spanish; speech and rhetoric; theology; women's studies.

College of St. Catherine

Accounting; art; art history, criticism and conservation; art teacher education; biochemistry; biology teacher education; biology/biological sciences; business administration and management; chemistry; chemistry teacher education; clinical laboratory science/medical technology; computer and information sciences; creative writing; diagnostic medical sonography and ultrasound technology; dietetics; drama and dance teacher education; dramatic/theater arts; economics; education; elementary education; English; English/language arts teacher education; family and consumer sciences/home economics teacher education; family and consumer sciences/human sciences; fashion merchandising; fashion/apparel design; fine/studio arts; foods, nutrition, and wellness; French; French language teacher education; health and physical education; health information/medical records technology; history; intercultural/multicultural and diversity studies; international business/trade/commerce; international economics; international relations and affairs; journalism; kindergarten/preschool education; liberal arts and sciences/liberal studies; literature; management information systems; marketing/marketing management; mass communication/media; mathematics; mathematics teacher education; medical radiologic technology; music; music teacher education; nursing (registered nurse training); occupational therapist assistant; occupational therapy; philosophy; physical education teaching and coaching; physical therapist assistant; physics; political science and government; pre-dentistry studies; pre-law studies; pre-medical studies; pre-veterinary studies; psychology; respiratory care therapy; secondary education; sign language interpretation and translation; social sciences; social studies teacher education; social work; sociology; Spanish; Spanish language teacher education; speech and rhetoric; speech teacher education; substance abuse/addiction counseling; theology; women's studies.

The College of St. Scholastica

Accounting; American native/native American education; applied economics; biochemistry; biology/biological sciences; business administration and management; chemistry; Christian studies; communication/speech communication and rhetoric; computer and information sciences; education (K-12); elementary education; English; exercise physiology; health information/medical records administration; health services/allied health/health sciences; history; humanities; international business/trade/commerce; international/global studies; journalism; liberal arts and sciences/liberal studies; marketing/marketing management; mathematics; music performance; natural sciences; nursing (registered nurse training); organizational behavior; physical sciences related; psychology; public relations, advertising, and applied communication related; religious studies; school librarian/school library media; social sciences; social work.

The College of Saint Thomas More

Liberal arts and sciences/liberal studies.

College of the Atlantic

Art; biological and physical sciences; biology/biological sciences; botany/plant biology; ceramic arts and ceramics; computer graphics; drawing; economics; education; elementary education; English; environmental biology; environmental design/architecture; environmental education; environmental studies; evolutionary biology; human ecology; interdisciplinary studies; landscape architecture; legal studies; liberal arts and sciences/liberal studies; literature; marine biology and biological oceanography; maritime science; middle school education; museum studies; music; natural sciences; oceanography; philosophy; pre-veterinary studies; psychology; public policy analysis; science teacher education; secondary education; wildlife biology; zoology/animal biology.

College of the Holy Cross

Accounting; anthropology; art history, criticism and conservation; Asian studies; biology/biological sciences; chemistry; classics and languages, literatures and linguistics; comparative literature; computer science; dramatic/theater arts; economics; English; environmental studies; fine/studio arts; French; German; German studies; history; Italian; literature; mathematics; medieval and Renaissance studies; music; philosophy; physics; political science and government; pre-medical studies; psychology; religious studies; Russian; Russian studies; sociology; Spanish.

The College of William and Mary

African American/Black studies; American studies; anthropology; art; art history, criticism and conservation; Asian studies (East); biology/biological sciences; biopsychology; business administration and management; chemistry; classics and languages, literatures and linguistics; computer and information sciences; cultural studies; dramatic/theater arts; economics; English; environmental studies; European studies; French; geology/earth science; German; history; interdisciplinary studies; international relations and affairs; Latin; Latin American studies; linguistics; mathematics; medieval and Renaissance studies; modern Greek; modern languages; multi-/interdisciplinary studies related; music; philosophy; physical education teaching and coaching; physics; political science and government; psychology; public policy analysis; religious studies; Russian studies; sociology; Spanish; women's studies.

The College of Wooster

African American/Black studies; archeology; area, ethnic, cultural, and gender studies related; art history, criticism and conservation; biochemistry; biology/biological sciences; business/managerial economics; chemistry; classics and languages, literatures and linguistics; communication/speech communication and rhetoric; comparative literature; computer science; dramatic/theater arts; economics; English; fine/studio arts; French; geology/earth science; German; German studies; history; interdisciplinary studies; international relations and affairs; Latin; mass communication/media; mathematics; molecular biology; multi-/interdisciplinary studies related; music; music history, literature, and theory; music performance; music teacher education; music theory and composition; music therapy; philosophy; physics; physics related; political science and government; psychology; religious studies; Russian studies; sociology; Spanish; urban studies/affairs; women's studies.

Colorado Christian University

Accounting; art; biblical studies; biological and physical sciences; biology/biological sciences; business administration and management; communication/speech communication and rhetoric; computer and information sciences; dramatic/theater arts; English; fine/studio arts; health and physical education; history; international/global studies; liberal arts and sciences/liberal studies; management information systems; management science; mathematics; music; music performance; music related; music teacher education; political science and government; psychology; social sciences; youth ministry.

The Colorado College

Anthropology; art history, criticism and conservation; Asian studies; biochemistry; biology/biological sciences; chemistry; classics and languages, literatures and linguistics; comparative literature; computer and information sciences related; creative writing; dance; dramatic/theater arts; econometrics and quantitative economics; economics; economics related; English; environmental science; ethnic, cultural minority, and gender studies related; film/cinema studies; fine/studio arts; French; French studies; geology/earth science; German; health and physical education; Hispanic-American, Puerto Rican, and Mexican-American/Chicano studies; history; international economics; Italian; liberal arts and sciences and humanities related; mathematics; mathematics and computer science; multi-/interdisciplinary studies related; music; neuroscience; philosophy; physics; political science and government; psychology; regional studies; religious studies; Romance languages related; Russian; Russian studies; social sciences related; sociology; Spanish; women's studies.

Colorado School of Mines

Chemical engineering; chemistry; civil engineering; computer science; economics; electrical, electronics and communications engineering; engineering; engineering physics; engineering science; environmental/environmental health engineering; geological/geophysical engineering; mathematics; mechanical engineering; metallurgical engineering; mining and mineral engineering; petroleum engineering.

Colorado State University

Accounting; agribusiness; agricultural and extension education; agricultural and horticultural plant breeding; agricultural economics; agricultural teacher education; agronomy and crop science; American studies; animal sciences; anthropology; apparel and textile marketing management; apparel and textiles; applied horticulture; applied mathematics; art history, criticism and conservation; art teacher education; Asian studies; Asian-American studies; athletic training; biochemistry; biology teacher education; biology/biological sciences; biomedical sciences; botany/plant biology; business administration and management; business teacher education; ceramic arts and ceramics; chemical engineering; chemistry; chemistry teacher education; civil engineering; commercial and advertising art; communication/speech communication and rhetoric; computer and information sciences; computer engineering; computer science; creative writing; criminal justice/safety; crop production; dance; dietetics; dramatic/theater arts; drawing; economics; electrical, electronics and communications engineering; engineering physics; engineering science; English; English/language arts teacher education; entomology; environmental health; environmental/environmental health engineering; equestrian studies; family and consumer sciences/home economics teacher education; family and consumer sciences/human sciences; fiber, textile and weaving arts; finance; fine/studio arts; fire services administration; fishing and fisheries sciences and management; foods, nutrition, and wellness; foreign languages and literatures; forest sciences and biology; French; French language teacher education; geology/earth science; German; German language teacher education; history; horticultural science; hotel/motel administration; human development and family studies; human nutrition; humanities; information science/studies; interior design; journalism; kinesiology and exercise science; landscape architecture; landscaping and groundskeeping; Latin American studies; liberal arts and sciences/liberal studies; marketing/marketing management; mathematics; mathematics teacher education; mechanical engineering; medical microbiology and bacteriology; metal and jewelry arts; music; music performance; music teacher education; music therapy; natural resources management and policy; natural resources/conservation; painting; parks, recreation and leisure facilities management; philosophy; photography; physical sciences; physics; physics teacher education; plant sciences; political science and government; pre-veterinary studies; printmaking; psychology; public relations/image management; radio and television; range science and management; restaurant/food services management; sales and marketing/marketing and distribution teacher education; science teacher education; sculpture; social sciences; social studies teacher education; social work; sociology; soil science and agronomy; Spanish; Spanish language teacher education; speech and rhetoric; turf and turfgrass management; water, wetlands, and marine resources management; wildlife and wildlands science and management; wildlife biology; zoology/animal biology.

Columbia College (NY)

African American/Black studies; American studies; ancient studies; ancient/classical Greek; anthropology; archeology; architecture; architecture related; art history, criticism and conservation; Asian studies (East); Asian-American studies; astronomy; astrophysics; atomic/molecular physics; biochemistry; biology/biological sciences; biophysics; biopsychology; chemistry; classical, ancient Mediterranean and Near Eastern studies and archaeology; classics and languages, literatures and linguistics; comparative literature; computer science; creative writing; dance; dramatic/theater arts; East Asian languages; economics; education (K-12); English; environmental biology; environmental studies; film/cinema studies; French; French studies; geochemistry; geology/earth science; German; German studies; Hispanic-American, Puerto Rican, and Mexican-American/Chicano studies; history; Italian; Italian studies; Latin American studies; linguistics; mathematics; medieval and Renaissance studies; modern Greek; music; Near and Middle Eastern studies;

philosophy; physics; political science and government; psychology; religious studies; Russian; Russian studies; Slavic languages; sociology; Spanish; statistics; urban studies/affairs; visual and performing arts; women's studies.

Columbia University, The Fu Foundation School of Engineering and Applied Science

Applied mathematics; biomedical/medical engineering; chemical engineering; civil engineering; computer engineering; computer science; electrical, electronics and communications engineering; engineering mechanics; engineering physics; engineering/industrial management; environmental/environmental health engineering; industrial engineering; materials science; mechanical engineering; operations research.

Concordia College (MN)

Accounting; advertising; art; art history, criticism and conservation; art teacher education; biology teacher education; biology/biological sciences; broadcast journalism; business administration and management; business teacher education; business/commerce; chemistry; chemistry teacher education; child development; classics and classical languages related; clinical laboratory science/medical technology; communication/speech communication and rhetoric; computer science; creative writing; dietetics; dramatic/theater arts; economics; education; elementary education; English; English/language arts teacher education; environmental studies; fine/studio arts; foods, nutrition, and wellness; French; French language teacher education; German; German language teacher education; health and physical education; health teacher education; health/health care administration; history; humanities; international business/trade/commerce; international/global studies; journalism; kindergarten/preschool education; kinesiology and exercise science; Latin; mass communication/media; mathematics; mathematics teacher education; music; music performance; music teacher education; music theory and composition; nursing (registered nurse training); philosophy; physical education teaching and coaching; physics; physics teacher education; political science and government; pre-dentistry studies; pre-law studies; pre-medical studies; pre-theology/pre-ministerial studies; pre-veterinary studies; psychology; public relations/image management; radio and television; religious studies; Russian studies; Scandinavian languages; science teacher education; secondary education; social studies teacher education; social work; sociology; Spanish; Spanish language teacher education; speech and rhetoric; voice and opera.

Connecticut College

African studies; American studies; anthropology; architecture; area, ethnic, cultural, and gender studies related; art; art history, criticism and conservation; Asian studies (East); astrophysics; biochemistry; biology/biological sciences; botany/plant biology; cell and molecular biology; chemistry; chemistry related; Chinese; classics and languages, literatures and linguistics; computer science; dance; dramatic/theater arts; ecology; economics; education (multiple levels); elementary education; engineering physics; English; environmental studies; ethnic, cultural minority, and gender studies related; European studies (Central and Eastern); family systems; film/cinema studies; French; German studies; Hispanic-American, Puerto Rican, and Mexican-American/Chicano studies; history; human development and family studies; human ecology; interdisciplinary studies; international relations and affairs; Italian; Italian studies; Japanese; Latin American studies; mathematics; medieval and Renaissance studies; molecular biology; multi-/interdisciplinary studies related; museum studies; music; music related; music teacher education; neuroscience; philosophy; physics teacher education; political science and government; psychology; religious studies; secondary education; Slavic languages; Slavic studies; social sciences related; sociology; Spanish; Spanish language teacher education; urban studies/affairs; women's studies.

Converse College

Accounting; applied art; art; art history, criticism and conservation; art teacher education; art therapy; biochemistry; biology/biological sciences; business administration and management; chemistry; computer science; dramatic/theater arts; economics; education; elementary education;

English; fine/studio arts; French; history; interior design; international business/trade/commerce; kindergarten/preschool education; marketing/marketing management; mathematics; modern languages; music; music history, literature, and theory; music teacher education; music therapy; piano and organ; political science and government; psychology; religious studies; secondary education; sign language interpretation and translation; sociology; Spanish; special education; violin, viola, guitar and other stringed instruments; voice and opera.

Cooper Union for the Advancement of Science and Art

Architecture; chemical engineering; civil engineering; electrical, electronics and communications engineering; engineering; fine/studio arts; mechanical engineering; visual and performing arts.

Cornell College

Anthropology; architecture; art; art history, criticism and conservation; biochemistry; biology/biological sciences; chemistry; classics and languages, literatures and linguistics; computer science; cultural studies; dramatic/theater arts; economics; elementary education; English; environmental studies; ethnic, cultural minority, and gender studies related; French; geology/earth science; German; health and physical education related; history; interdisciplinary studies; international business/trade/commerce; international relations and affairs; Latin; Latin American studies; liberal arts and sciences/liberal studies; mathematics; medieval and Renaissance studies; modern Greek; modern languages; multi-/interdisciplinary studies related; music; music teacher education; philosophy; physical education teaching and coaching; physics; political science and government; psychology; religious studies; Russian; secondary education; sociology; Spanish; speech and rhetoric; women's studies.

Cornell University

African American/Black studies; agribusiness; agricultural and horticultural plant breeding; agricultural business and management; agricultural economics; agricultural teacher education; agricultural/biological engineering and bioengineering; agriculture; agronomy and crop science; American studies; animal genetics; animal physiology; animal sciences; anthropology; archeology; architecture; art history, criticism and conservation; Asian studies; astronomy; atmospheric sciences and meteorology; biochemistry; biological and biomedical sciences related; biology teacher education; biology/biological sciences; biometry/biometrics; chemical engineering; chemistry; chemistry teacher education; city/urban, community and regional planning; civil engineering; classics and languages, literatures and linguistics; communication/speech communication and rhetoric; community organization and advocacy; comparative literature; computer science; consumer economics; dance; dramatic/theater arts; ecology; economics; education; educational psychology; electrical, electronics and communications engineering; engineering; engineering physics; English; entomology; environmental design/architecture; environmental science; environmental/environmental health engineering; family and consumer sciences/home economics teacher education; family and consumer sciences/human sciences; fiber, textile and weaving arts; film/cinema studies; fine/studio arts; food science; foods, nutrition, and wellness; French; gay/lesbian studies; geology/earth science; German; German studies; history; horticultural science; hotel/motel administration; human development and family studies; human services; human services; information technology; interdisciplinary studies; international agriculture; Italian; labor and industrial relations; landscape architecture; liberal arts and sciences/liberal studies; linguistics; materials engineering; mathematics; mathematics teacher education; mechanical engineering; microbiology; multi-/interdisciplinary studies related; music; natural resource economics; natural resources/conservation; Near and Middle Eastern studies; nutrition sciences; operations research; ornamental horticulture; philosophy; physics; physics teacher education; plant pathology/phytopathology; plant sciences; political science and government; pre-medical studies; psychology; public policy analysis; religious studies; restaurant/food services management; Russian; Russian studies; science teacher education; science, technology and society; social sciences; social sciences related; sociology; Spanish; theater design and technology; women's studies.

Cornerstone University

Accounting; airline pilot and flight crew; ancient Near Eastern and biblical languages; biblical studies; biology teacher education; biology/biological sciences; broadcast journalism; business administration and management; business administration, management and operations related; creative writing; early childhood education; education; elementary education; English; English/language arts teacher education; environmental biology; history; history teacher education; information science/studies; interdisciplinary studies; kinesiology and exercise science; management information systems; marketing/marketing management; mass communication/media; mathematics; mathematics teacher education; multi-/interdisciplinary studies related; music; music performance; music teacher education; music theory and composition; pastoral studies/counseling; philosophy; physical education teaching and coaching; political science and government; pre-dentistry studies; pre-law studies; pre-medical studies; pre-theology/pre-ministerial studies; pre-veterinary studies; psychology; religious education; religious studies; science teacher education; secondary education; social science teacher education; social studies teacher education; social work; sociology; Spanish; speech and rhetoric; sport and fitness administration/management.

Covenant College

Biblical studies; biological and physical sciences; biology/biological sciences; business/commerce; chemistry; computer science; dramatic/theater arts; economics; elementary education; English; English/language arts teacher education; fine arts related; foreign languages and literatures; history; history teacher education; interdisciplinary studies; mathematics; mathematics teacher education; music; music history, literature, and theory; music performance; philosophy; philosophy and religious studies related; physical sciences related; physics; psychology; science teacher education; social sciences related; sociology.

Creighton University

Accounting; American Indian/Native American studies; American studies; ancient/classical Greek; anthropology; applied mathematics; art; athletic training; atmospheric sciences and meteorology; biology/biological sciences; chemistry; classical, ancient Mediterranean and Near Eastern studies and archaeology; communication/speech communication and rhetoric; computer science; dramatic/theater arts; economics; elementary education; emergency medical technology (EMT paramedic); English; environmental studies; finance; French; German; graphic design; health/health care administration; history; international business/trade/commerce; international relations and affairs; journalism; kinesiology and exercise science; Latin; management information systems; marketing/marketing management; mathematics; music; nursing (registered nurse training); organizational communication; philosophy; physics; political science and government; pre-law studies; psychology; social work; sociology; Spanish; speech and rhetoric; theological and ministerial studies related; theology.

Dartmouth College

African studies; African American/Black studies; American Indian/Native American studies; ancient/classical Greek; animal genetics; anthropology; Arabic; archeology; art history, criticism and conservation; Asian studies; astronomy; biochemistry; biology/biological sciences; chemistry; chemistry related; Chinese; classics and languages, literatures and linguistics; cognitive psychology and psycholinguistics; comparative literature; computer science; creative writing; dramatic/theater arts; East Asian languages related; ecology; economics; engineering; engineering physics; English; environmental studies; evolutionary biology; film/cinema studies; fine/studio arts; French; geography; geology/earth science; German; Hebrew; Hispanic-American, Puerto Rican, and Mexican-American/Chicano studies; history; Italian; Japanese; Latin; Latin American studies; linguistics; mathematics; molecular biology; multi-/interdisciplinary studies related; music; Near and Middle Eastern studies;

philosophy; physics; political science and government; psychology; religious studies; Romance languages; Russian; Russian studies; sociology; Spanish; women's studies.

Davidson College

Anthropology; art; biology/biological sciences; chemistry; classics and languages, literatures and linguistics; dramatic/theater arts; economics; English; French; German; history; mathematics; multi-/interdisciplinary studies related; music; philosophy; physics; political science and government; psychology; religious studies; sociology; Spanish.

Denison University

African American/Black studies; anthropology; area studies; art; art history, criticism and conservation; Asian studies (East); biochemistry; biology/biological sciences; chemistry; classics and languages, literatures and linguistics; computer science; creative writing; dance; dramatic/theater arts; economics; English; environmental studies; film/cinema studies; fine/studio arts; French; geology/earth science; German; history; international relations and affairs; Latin American studies; mass communication/media; mathematics; music; organizational behavior; philosophy; physical education teaching and coaching; physics; political science and government; psychology; religious studies; sociology; Spanish; speech and rhetoric; women's studies.

DePauw University

African American/Black studies; ancient/classical Greek; anthropology; art history, criticism and conservation; Asian studies (East); athletic training; biochemistry; biology/biological sciences; chemistry; classics and languages, literatures and linguistics; computer science; dramatic/theater arts; economics; elementary education; English; English composition; environmental studies; fine/studio arts; French; geology/earth science; German; history; interdisciplinary studies; kinesiology and exercise science; Latin; mass communication/media; mathematics; multi-/interdisciplinary studies related; music; music management and merchandising; music performance; music teacher education; music theory and composition; peace studies and conflict resolution; philosophy; physical education teaching and coaching; physics; political science and government; psychology; religious studies; Romance languages; Russian studies; sociology; Spanish; women's studies.

Dickinson College

American studies; anthropology; archeology; Asian studies (East); biochemistry; biology/biological sciences; chemistry; classics and languages, literatures and linguistics; computer science; dance; dramatic/theater arts; economics; English; environmental science; environmental studies; fine/studio arts; French; geology/earth science; German; history; international business/trade/commerce; international relations and affairs; Italian; Jewish/Judaic studies; legal studies; mathematics; medieval and Renaissance studies; multi-/interdisciplinary studies related; music; music related; neuroscience; philosophy; physics; political science and government; pre-dentistry studies; pre-medical studies; psychology; public policy analysis; religious studies; Russian; Russian studies; sociology; Spanish; women's studies.

Dominican University

Accounting; American studies; art history, criticism and conservation; biochemistry; biology/biological sciences; business administration and management; chemistry; clinical laboratory science/medical technology; commercial and advertising art; computer engineering; computer science; criminology; dietetics; dramatic/theater arts; economics; education (K-12); electrical, electronics and communications engineering; elementary education; English; environmental studies; fashion merchandising; fashion/apparel design; food science; foods, nutrition, and wellness; foodservice systems administration; French; gerontology; history; information science/studies; international business/trade/commerce; Italian; mass communication/media; mathematics; philosophy; photography; political science and government; pre-dentistry studies; pre-law studies; pre-medical studies; pre-veterinary studies; psychology; religious studies; social sciences; sociology; Spanish; special products marketing.

Drake University

Accounting; accounting and finance; acting; actuarial science; advertising; anthropology; art; art history, criticism and conservation; astronomy; biochemistry; biology/biological sciences; broadcast journalism; business administration and management; business/commerce; chemistry; commercial and advertising art; computer science; directing and theatrical production; dramatic/theater arts; dramatic/theater arts and stagecraft related; drawing; elementary education; English; environmental science; environmental studies; ethics; finance; fine/studio arts; graphic design; history; international business/trade/commerce; international relations and affairs; jazz/jazz studies; journalism; marketing/marketing management; mass communication/media; mathematics; music; music management and merchandising; music performance; music teacher education; neuroscience; painting; pharmacy; pharmacy administration/pharmaceutics; philosophy; physics; piano and organ; political science and government; pre-dentistry studies; pre-engineering; pre-law studies; pre-medical studies; pre-veterinary studies; printmaking; psychology; public relations/image management; radio and television; radio, television, and digital communication related; religious studies; religious/sacred music; sculpture; secondary education; sociology; speech and rhetoric; voice and opera.

Drew University

African studies; anthropology; art; art history, criticism and conservation; behavioral sciences; biochemistry; biology/biological sciences; chemistry; Chinese studies; classics and languages, literatures and linguistics; computer science; dramatic/theater arts; economics; English; French; German; history; mathematics; mathematics and computer science; music; neuroscience; philosophy; physics; political science and government; psychology; religious studies; Russian; sociology; Spanish; women's studies.

Drexel University

Accounting; architectural engineering; architecture; area studies related; biological and physical sciences; biology/biological sciences; biomedical/medical engineering; business, management, and marketing related; business/managerial economics; chemical engineering; chemistry; cinematography and film/video production; civil engineering; civil engineering related; commercial and advertising art; communication and journalism related; computer engineering; computer science; culinary arts; design and applied arts related; education (specific subject areas) related; electrical, electronics and communications engineering; engineering; English language and literature related; environmental studies; environmental/environmental health engineering; fashion/apparel design; finance; general studies; health/health care administration; history; hospitality administration related; human resources management; humanities; industrial engineering; information science/studies; interior design; international business/trade/commerce; management information systems; marketing/marketing management; materials engineering; mathematics; mechanical engineering; music; nutrition sciences; photography; physics related; playwriting and screenwriting; psychology; social sciences; sociology; taxation; technical and business writing; web page, digital/multimedia and information resources design.

Drury University

Accounting; advertising; architecture; art history, criticism and conservation; arts management; biology/biological sciences; business administration and management; chemistry; communication/speech communication and rhetoric; computer and information sciences; computer science; criminology; design and visual communications; dramatic/theater arts; economics; education; elementary education; engineering; English; environmental studies; finance; fine/studio arts; French; German; history; kinesiology and exercise science; marketing/marketing management; mathematics; music; music performance; music teacher education; music theory and composition; occupational therapy; philosophy; physics; political science and government; pre-dentistry studies; pre-law studies; pre-medical studies; pre-pharmacy studies; pre-veterinary studies; psychology; public relations/image management; religious studies; secondary education; sociology; Spanish; sport and fitness administration/management.

Duke University

African American/Black studies; anatomy; ancient/classical Greek; anthropology; art; art history, criticism and conservation; Asian studies; biology/biological sciences; biomedical/medical engineering; Canadian studies; chemistry; civil engineering; classics and languages, literatures and linguistics; computer science; design and visual communications; dramatic/theater arts; economics; electrical, electronics and communications engineering; English; environmental studies; French; geology/earth science; German; history; international relations and affairs; Italian; Latin; linguistics; literature; materials science; mathematics; mechanical engineering; medieval and Renaissance studies; music; philosophy; physics; political science and government; psychology; public policy analysis; religious studies; Russian; Slavic languages; sociology; Spanish; women's studies.

Duquesne University

Accounting; accounting related; ancient/classical Greek; art history, criticism and conservation; athletic training; biochemistry; biology/biological sciences; business administration, management and operations related; business, management, and marketing related; business/commerce; business/corporate communications; business/managerial economics; chemistry; chemistry related; classics and languages, literatures and linguistics; communication/speech communication and rhetoric; computer science; computer software and media applications related; dramatic/theater arts; early childhood education; economics; education; education (multiple levels); elementary education; English; English language and literature related; English/language arts teacher education; entrepreneurship; environmental science; finance; fine/studio arts; foreign languages and literatures; French language teacher education; general studies; health/health care administration; history; international business/trade/commerce; international relations and affairs; investments and securities; journalism; Latin; Latin teacher education; liberal arts and sciences and humanities related; logistics and materials management; management information systems; management science; management sciences and quantitative methods related; marketing related; marketing/marketing management; mathematics; mathematics teacher education; music performance; music related; music teacher education; music therapy; non-profit management; nursing (registered nurse training); occupational therapy; operations management; pharmacy, pharmaceutical sciences, and administration related; philosophy; physical therapy; physician assistant; physics; political science and government; pre-medical studies; psychology; public relations, advertising, and applied communication related; public relations/image management; science teacher education; secondary education; securities services administration; social studies teacher education; sociology; Spanish; Spanish language teacher education; special education; speech and rhetoric; speech-language pathology; theology; web page, digital/multimedia and information resources design; web/multimedia management and webmaster.

Earlham College

African American/Black studies; anthropology; art; biochemistry; biology/biological sciences; business administration and management; business/commerce; chemistry; classics and languages, literatures and linguistics; comparative literature; computer science; dramatic/theater arts; economics; English; environmental studies; French; geological and earth sciences/geosciences related; geology/earth science; German; history; interdisciplinary studies; international relations and affairs; Japanese studies; Latin American studies; mathematics; multi-/interdisciplinary studies related; music; peace studies and conflict resolution; philosophy; physics; physiological psychology/psychobiology; political science and government; pre-medical studies; psychology; religious studies; sociology; Spanish; women's studies.

Elizabethtown College

Accounting; anthropology; art; biochemistry; biology/biological sciences; biotechnology; business administration and management; chemistry; communication/speech communication and rhetoric; computer engineering; computer science; criminal justice/safety; directing and theatrical production; economics; education; elementary education; engineering;

engineering physics; English; environmental studies; French; German; history; industrial engineering; international business/trade/commerce; kindergarten/preschool education; mathematics; modern languages; music; music teacher education; music therapy; occupational therapy; peace studies and conflict resolution; philosophy; physics; political science and government; pre-dentistry studies; pre-law studies; pre-medical studies; pre-veterinary studies; psychology; religious studies; science teacher education; secondary education; social sciences; social work; sociology; Spanish; theater design and technology; theater/theater arts management.

Elmira College

Accounting; American studies; anthropology; art; art teacher education; audiology and speech-language pathology; biochemistry; biology teacher education; biology/biological sciences; business administration and management; business/managerial economics; chemistry; chemistry teacher education; classics and languages, literatures and linguistics; clinical laboratory science/medical technology; criminal justice/law enforcement administration; dramatic/theater arts; economics; education; elementary education; English; English/language arts teacher education; environmental studies; European studies; fine/studio arts; foreign language teacher education; foreign languages and literatures; French; French language teacher education; history; history teacher education; human services; humanities; information science/studies; interdisciplinary studies; international business/trade/commerce; international relations and affairs; liberal arts and sciences/liberal studies; literature; marketing/marketing management; mathematics; mathematics teacher education; mental health/rehabilitation; middle school education; modern languages; music; nursing (registered nurse training); nursing science; philosophy; political science and government; pre-dentistry studies; pre-law studies; pre-medical studies; pre-veterinary studies; psychology; religious studies; Romance languages; science teacher education; secondary education; social science teacher education; social sciences; social studies teacher education; social work; sociology; Spanish; Spanish language teacher education; speech teacher education.

Elon University

Accounting; anthropology; art; art history, criticism and conservation; athletic training; biology/biological sciences; broadcast journalism; business administration and management; business/corporate communications; chemical engineering; chemistry; clinical laboratory science/medical technology; communication/speech communication and rhetoric; computer and information sciences; computer science; dance; dramatic/theater arts; economics; education; elementary education; engineering; English; environmental studies; foreign languages and literatures; French; health teacher education; history; human services; journalism; mathematics; middle school education; music; music performance; music teacher education; parks, recreation and leisure; philosophy; physical education teaching and coaching; physics; political science and government; pre-dentistry studies; pre-law studies; pre-medical studies; pre-veterinary studies; psychology; public administration; religious studies; science teacher education; secondary education; social science teacher education; social studies teacher education; sociology; Spanish; special education; sport and fitness administration/management; theater design and technology.

Embry-Riddle Aeronautical University (AZ)

Aeronautics/aviation/aerospace science and technology; aeronautical and astronautical engineering; airline pilot and flight crew; atmospheric sciences and meteorology; business administration, management and operations related; computer engineering; computer software engineering; electrical, electronics and communications engineering; international relations and affairs; physics related; science, technology and society.

Emerson College

Acting; advertising; audiology and speech-language pathology; broadcast journalism; cinematography and film/video production; communication disorders; communication/speech communication and rhetoric; creative writing; drama and dance teacher education; dramatic/theater arts; film/ cinema studies; interdisciplinary studies; intermedia/multimedia; journalism; marketing/marketing management; mass communication/media; playwriting and screenwriting; political communication; public relations/image management; publishing; radio and television; radio and television broadcasting technology; radio, television, and digital communication related; special education (speech or language impaired); speech and rhetoric; speech therapy; speech-language pathology; theater design and technology; visual and performing arts.

Emory University

Accounting; African studies; African American/Black studies; American studies; anthropology; art history, criticism and conservation; Asian studies; Asian-American studies; banking and financial support services; biology/biological sciences; biomedical sciences; business administration and management; business/managerial economics; chemistry; Chinese; classics and languages, literatures and linguistics; comparative literature; computer science; creative writing; dance; dramatic/theater arts; economics; education; English; film/cinema studies; finance; fine/studio arts; French; German; history; interdisciplinary studies; international relations and affairs; Italian; Japanese; Jewish/Judaic studies; journalism; Latin; Latin American studies; liberal arts and sciences/liberal studies; literature; marketing/marketing management; mathematics; medieval and Renaissance studies; modern Greek; music; neuroscience; nursing (registered nurse training); philosophy; physics; political science and government; psychology; religious studies; Russian; sociology; Spanish; women's studies.

Erskine College

American studies; art; athletic training; behavioral sciences; biblical studies; biological and physical sciences; biology/biological sciences; business administration and management; chemistry; clinical laboratory science/medical technology; elementary education; English; French; history; kindergarten/preschool education; mathematics; music; natural sciences; philosophy; physical education teaching and coaching; physics; psychology; religious education; religious studies; religious/sacred music; social studies teacher education; Spanish; special education; sport and fitness administration/management.

Eugene Lang College The New School for Liberal Arts

Anthropology; communication and media related; creative writing; cultural studies; dance; dramatic/theater arts; economics; education; English; foreign languages and literatures; history; humanities; journalism; liberal arts and sciences/liberal studies; literature; music history, literature, and theory; philosophy; political science and government; psychology; religious studies; social sciences; sociology; urban studies/affairs; women's studies.

Fairfield University

Accounting; American studies; art history, criticism and conservation; biology/biological sciences; business administration and management; chemistry; computer engineering; computer science; computer software engineering; economics; electrical, electronics and communications engineering; English; film/video and photographic arts related; finance; fine/studio arts; French; German; history; information science/studies; international relations and affairs; Italian; management information systems; marketing/marketing management; mass communication/media; mathematics; mechanical engineering; modern languages; music history, literature, and theory; music teacher education; nursing (registered nurse training); philosophy; physics; political science and government; psychology; religious studies; secondary education; sociology; Spanish; visual and performing arts.

Florida Institute of Technology

Accounting; aerospace science; aerospace, aeronautical and astronautical engineering; applied mathematics; aquatic biology/limnology; astrophysics; aviation/airway management; biochemistry; biological and physical sciences; biology teacher education; biology/biological sciences; biomedical sciences; business administration and management; chemical engineering; chemistry; chemistry teacher education; civil engineering; clinical psychology; communication/speech communication and rhetoric; computer engineering; computer science; computer software engineering; construction engineering technology; e-commerce; earth sciences; ecology; electrical, electronics and communications engineering; engineering; environmental science; forensic psychology; general studies; history; humanities; information science/studies; interdisciplinary studies; international business/trade/commerce; management information systems; management science; marine biology and biological oceanography; mathematics teacher education; mechanical engineering; meteorology; military studies; molecular biology; multi-/interdisciplinary studies related; ocean engineering; oceanography; organizational behavior; physics; physics teacher education; pre-medical studies; psychology; science teacher education.

Florida International University
Accounting; applied mathematics; architecture related; art history, criticism and conservation; art teacher education; Asian studies; biology/biological sciences; biomedical/medical engineering; broadcast journalism; business administration and management; chemical engineering; chemistry; civil engineering; communication/speech communication and rhetoric; computer and information sciences; computer engineering; computer science; construction engineering technology; criminal justice/safety; dance; dietetics; dramatic/theater arts; economics; electrical, electronics and communications engineering; elementary education; English; English/language arts teacher education; environmental control technologies related; environmental design/architecture; environmental studies; family and consumer sciences/home economics teacher education; finance; fine/studio arts; foreign language teacher education; French; geography; geology/earth science; German; health information/medical records administration; health science; health services/allied health/health sciences; health teacher education; health/health care administration; history; hospitality administration; human resources management; humanities; information technology; insurance; interior design; international business/trade/commerce; international relations and affairs; Italian; kinesiology and exercise science; liberal arts and sciences/liberal studies; logistics and materials management; management information systems; marine biology and biological oceanography; marketing/marketing management; mathematics; mathematics teacher education; mechanical engineering; music; music teacher education; nursing (registered nurse training); occupational therapy; orthotics/prosthetics; parks, recreation and leisure facilities management; philosophy; physical education teaching and coaching; physics; political science and government; Portuguese; psychology; public administration; real estate; religious studies; science teacher education; social science teacher education; social work; sociology; Spanish; special education (emotionally disturbed); special education (mentally retarded); special education (specific learning disabilities); statistics; systems engineering; tourism and travel services management; trade and industrial teacher education; urban studies/affairs; women's studies.

Florida State University
Accounting; acting; advertising; American studies; anthropology; apparel and textile marketing management; apparel and textiles; applied economics; applied mathematics; art history, criticism and conservation; art teacher education; Asian studies; athletic training; atmospheric sciences and meteorology; bilingual and multilingual education; bilingual, multilingual, and multicultural education related; biochemistry; biology/biological sciences; biomathematics and bioinformatics related; biomedical/medical engineering; business administration and management; business/commerce; Caribbean studies; cell and molecular biology; chemical engineering; chemistry; chemistry related; child development; cinematography and film/video production; civil engineering; classics and languages, literatures and linguistics; commercial and advertising art; communication and media related; communication/speech communication and rhetoric; community health services counseling; computer engineering; computer programming; computer science; computer software and media applications related; computer software engineering; creative writing; criminal justice/safety; criminology; dance; dietetics;

dramatic/theater arts; early childhood education; ecology; economics; electrical, electronics and communications engineering; elementary education; English; English/language arts teacher education; entrepreneurial and small business related; environmental biology; environmental/environmental health engineering; European studies (Central and Eastern); evolutionary biology; family and consumer economics related; family and consumer sciences/home economics teacher education; family and consumer sciences/human sciences; fashion merchandising; fashion/apparel design; film/cinema studies; finance; fine/studio arts; foods, nutrition, and wellness; foreign language teacher education; French; geography; geology/earth science; German; graphic design; health teacher education; history; hospitality administration; hospitality administration related; housing and human environments; human development and family studies; human resources management; humanities; industrial engineering; information science/studies; interior design; international business/trade/commerce; international relations and affairs; Italian; jazz/jazz studies; kindergarten/preschool education; kinesiology and exercise science; Latin; Latin American studies; liberal arts and sciences/liberal studies; literature; marine biology and biological oceanography; mass communication/media; materials engineering; mathematics; mathematics teacher education; mechanical engineering; meteorology; middle school education; modern Greek; multicultural education; music; music history, literature, and theory; music pedagogy; music performance; music teacher education; music theory and composition; music therapy; neurobiology and neurophysiology; nursing (registered nurse training); nutrition sciences; parks, recreation and leisure facilities management; philosophy; physical education teaching and coaching; physical sciences; physical sciences related; physics; piano and organ; plant physiology; political science and government; pre-dentistry studies; pre-law studies; pre-medical studies; pre-pharmacy studies; pre-veterinary studies; psychology; public relations/image management; radio and television; radio, television, and digital communication related; religious studies; Russian; Russian studies; science teacher education; secondary education; social science teacher education; social sciences; social work; sociology; Spanish; special education (emotionally disturbed); special education (mentally retarded); special education (specific learning disabilities); special education (vision impaired); sport and fitness administration/management; statistics; textile science; theater design and technology; violin, viola, guitar and other stringed instruments; vocational rehabilitation counseling; voice and opera; wind/percussion instruments; women's studies; zoology/animal biology.

Fordham University
Accounting; accounting and computer science; African studies; African American/Black studies; American studies; anthropology; art; art history, criticism and conservation; bilingual and multilingual education; biological and physical sciences; biology/biological sciences; broadcast journalism; business administration and management; business/managerial economics; chemistry; classics and languages, literatures and linguistics; commercial and advertising art; comparative literature; computer and information sciences; computer management; computer science; creative writing; criminal justice/law enforcement administration; dance; dramatic/theater arts; economics; education; elementary education; English; entrepreneurship; European studies (Central and Eastern); film/cinema studies; finance; fine/studio arts; French; French studies; German; German studies; health/medical preparatory programs related; Hispanic-American, Puerto Rican, and Mexican-American/Chicano studies; history; human resources management; information science/studies; interdisciplinary studies; international business/trade/commerce; international economics; international relations and affairs; Italian; Italian studies; journalism; Latin; Latin American studies; liberal arts and sciences/liberal studies; literature; management information systems; management information systems and services related; marketing/marketing management; mass communication/media; mathematics; medieval and Renaissance studies; modern Greek; modern languages; music; music history, literature, and theory; natural sciences; Near and Middle Eastern studies; peace studies and conflict resolution; philosophy; photography; physical sciences; physics; playwriting and screenwriting; political science

and government; pre-dentistry studies; pre-law studies; pre-medical studies; pre-pharmacy studies; pre-veterinary studies; psychology; public administration; radio and television; religious studies; Romance languages; Russian; Russian studies; secondary education; social sciences; social work; sociology; Spanish; Spanish and Iberian studies; theology; urban studies/affairs; women's studies.

Franciscan University of Steubenville
Accounting; anthropology; biology/biological sciences; business administration and management; chemistry; child development; classics and languages, literatures and linguistics; communication/speech communication and rhetoric; computer and information sciences; computer science; dramatic/theater arts; economics; elementary education; English; French; general studies; German; history; humanities; legal studies; mathematics; nursing (registered nurse training); philosophy; political science and government; psychiatric/mental health services technology; psychology; religious education; religious/sacred music; social work; sociology; Spanish; theology.

Franklin & Marshall College
African studies; American studies; ancient/classical Greek; animal behavior and ethology; anthropology; art history, criticism and conservation; astronomy; astrophysics; biochemistry; biology/biological sciences; business administration and management; chemistry; classics and languages, literatures and linguistics; creative writing; dance; dramatic/theater arts; economics; English; environmental science; environmental studies; fine/studio arts; French; geology/earth science; German; German studies; history; Latin; mathematics; multi-/interdisciplinary studies related; music; neuroscience; philosophy; physics; political science and government; psychology; religious studies; sociology; Spanish.

Furman University
Accounting; art; art history, criticism and conservation; Asian studies; biochemistry; biology/biological sciences; business administration and management; chemistry; classics; communication/speech communication and rhetoric; computer science; dramatic/theater arts; economics; education; elementary education; English; environmental studies; fine/studio arts; French; geology/earth science; German; history; information technology; kindergarten/preschool education; kinesiology and exercise science; Latin; mathematics; modern Greek; music; music teacher education; neuroscience; philosophy; physics; piano and organ; political science and government; pre-dentistry studies; pre-law studies; pre-medical studies; pre-veterinary studies; psychology; religious studies; religious/sacred music; secondary education; sociology; Spanish; special education; urban studies/affairs; voice and opera.

George Fox University
Acting; art; athletic training; behavioral sciences; biblical studies; biology/biological sciences; broadcast journalism; business administration and management; chemistry; cinematography and film/video production; clinical psychology; cognitive psychology and psycholinguistics; cognitive science; communication/speech communication and rhetoric; computer and information sciences; directing and theatrical production; dramatic/theater arts; economics; electrical, electronics and communications engineering; elementary education; engineering; English; family and consumer sciences/human sciences; fashion merchandising; film/cinema studies; finance; fine/studio arts; foods, nutrition, and wellness; graphic design; health and physical education; health teacher education; history; industrial design; information science/studies; interdisciplinary studies; intermedia/multimedia; international business/trade/commerce; international/global studies; management information systems; marketing/marketing management; mathematics; mechanical engineering; missionary studies and missiology; music; music performance; music teacher education; music theory and composition; nursing (registered nurse training); pastoral studies/counseling; philosophy; physical education teaching and coaching; psychology; public relations/image management; radio and television; religious education; religious studies; social work; sociology; Spanish; sport and fitness administration/management; theater design and technology; youth ministry.

Georgetown College
Accounting; American studies; athletic training; biology/biological sciences; business administration and management; chemistry; communication and media related; computer and information sciences; dramatic/theater arts; ecology; economics; elementary education; English; European studies; fine/studio arts; French; German; history; kinesiology and exercise science; liberal arts and sciences/liberal studies; mathematics; middle school education; multi-/interdisciplinary studies related; music; music teacher education; philosophy; physics; political science and government; psychology; religious studies; sociology; Spanish.

Georgetown University
Accounting; American studies; anthropology; Arabic; art; art history, criticism and conservation; biochemistry; biology/biological sciences; business administration and management; chemistry; Chinese; classics and languages, literatures and linguistics; comparative literature; computer science; economics; English; finance; fine/studio arts; French; German; health science; history; interdisciplinary studies; international business/trade/commerce; international economics; international relations and affairs; Italian; Japanese; liberal arts and sciences/liberal studies; linguistics; marketing/marketing management; mathematics; medieval and Renaissance studies; multi-/interdisciplinary studies related; nursing (registered nurse training); philosophy; physics; political science and government; Portuguese; psychology; Russian; science, technology and society; social sciences related; sociology; Spanish; theology; visual and performing arts; women's studies.

The George Washington University
Accounting; American studies; anthropology; applied mathematics; archeology; art; art history, criticism and conservation; Asian studies; Asian studies (East); audiology and speech-language pathology; biology/biological sciences; business administration and management; business/managerial economics; chemistry; Chinese; civil engineering; classics and languages, literatures and linguistics; clinical laboratory science/medical technology; clinical/medical laboratory technology; computer and information sciences; computer engineering; computer science; criminal justice/law enforcement administration; dance; diagnostic medical sonography and ultrasound technology; dramatic/theater arts; economics; electrical, electronics and communications engineering; emergency medical technology (EMT paramedic); engineering; English; environmental studies; environmental/environmental health engineering; European studies; finance; fine/studio arts; French; genetics related; geography; geology/earth science; German; history; human resources management; human services; humanities; industrial radiologic technology; interdisciplinary studies; international business/trade/commerce; international relations and affairs; Jewish/Judaic studies; journalism; kinesiology and exercise science; Latin American studies; liberal arts and sciences/liberal studies; marketing/marketing management; mass communication/media; mathematics; mechanical engineering; medical laboratory technology; music; Near and Middle Eastern studies; nuclear medical technology; pharmacology and toxicology related; philosophy; physician assistant; physics; political science and government; pre-dentistry studies; pre-law studies; pre-medical studies; psychology; public policy analysis; radio and television; radiologic technology/science; religious studies; Russian; Russian studies; sociology; Spanish; speech and rhetoric; statistics; systems engineering.

Georgia Institute of Technology
Aerospace, aeronautical and astronautical engineering; applied mathematics; applied mathematics related; architecture; architecture related; biochemistry; biology/biological sciences; biomedical/medical engineering; business administration and management; business/managerial economics; chemical engineering; chemistry; civil engineering; computer and information sciences; computer engineering; digital communication and media/multimedia; electrical, electronics and communications engineering; environmental/environmental health engineering; geological and earth sciences/geosciences related; history and philosophy of science and technology; industrial and organizational psychology; industrial design; industrial engineering; international relations and affairs; inter-

national/global studies; materials engineering; mechanical engineering; multi-/interdisciplinary studies related; nuclear engineering; physics; public policy analysis; science, technology and society; textile sciences and engineering.

Georgia State University

Accounting; actuarial science; African American/Black studies; anthropology; art; art teacher education; biology/biological sciences; business administration and management; business/managerial economics; chemistry; computer and information sciences; criminal justice/safety; early childhood education; economics; elementary education; English; facilities planning and management; film/cinema studies; finance; fine/studio arts; foods, nutrition, and wellness; French; geography; geology/earth science; German; health and physical education; history; hotel/motel administration; human resources development; insurance; international business/trade/commerce; journalism; kinesiology and exercise science; marketing/marketing management; mathematics; multi-/interdisciplinary studies related; music management and merchandising; music performance; nursing (registered nurse training); operations management; operations research; philosophy; physics; political science and government; psychology; real estate; religious studies; respiratory care therapy; social work; sociology; Spanish; speech and rhetoric; urban studies/affairs; women's studies.

Gettysburg College

Accounting; African American/Black studies; American history; American studies; ancient/classical Greek; anthropology; area studies; area studies related; area, ethnic, cultural, and gender studies related; art; art history, criticism and conservation; Asian history; Asian studies (East); Asian studies (South); biochemistry; biological and physical sciences; biology/biological sciences; broadcast journalism; business administration and management; business administration, management and operations related; chemistry; classics and languages, literatures and linguistics; computer science; creative writing; dramatic/theater arts; economics; education; elementary education; engineering related; English; English composition; environmental science; environmental studies; European history; fine/studio arts; French; German; health science; Hispanic-American, Puerto Rican, and Mexican-American/Chicano studies; history; interdisciplinary studies; international business/trade/commerce; international economics; international relations and affairs; Italian; Japanese; Japanese studies; journalism; Latin; Latin American studies; liberal arts and sciences/liberal studies; literature; marine biology and biological oceanography; mathematics; middle school education; modern languages; molecular biology; music; music teacher education; non-profit management; peace studies and conflict resolution; philosophy; physical education teaching and coaching; physics; political science and government; pre-dentistry studies; pre-law studies; pre-medical studies; pre-nursing studies; pre-pharmacy studies; pre-veterinary studies; psychology; religious studies; Romance languages; science teacher education; secondary education; social sciences; social sciences related; sociology; Spanish; visual and performing arts; western civilization; women's studies.

Gonzaga University

Accounting; art; Asian studies; biochemistry; biology/biological sciences; broadcast journalism; business administration and management; business/managerial economics; chemistry; civil engineering; computer engineering; computer science; criminal justice/law enforcement administration; dramatic/theater arts; economics; electrical, electronics and communications engineering; elementary education; engineering; English; finance; French; German; history; information science/studies; international business/trade/commerce; international relations and affairs; Italian; journalism; kinesiology and exercise science; liberal arts and sciences/liberal studies; literature; marketing/marketing management; mass communication/media; mathematics; mechanical engineering; music; music teacher education; nursing (registered nurse training); philosophy; physical education teaching and coaching; physics; political science and government; psychology; public relations/image management; religious studies; secondary education; sociology; Spanish; special education; speech and rhetoric; sport and fitness administration/management.

Gordon College (MA)

Accounting; art; biology/biological sciences; business administration and management; chemistry; Christian studies; communication/speech communication and rhetoric; computer science; economics; elementary education; English; foreign languages and literatures; French; German; history; international relations and affairs; kinesiology and exercise science; mathematics; middle school education; music; music performance; music teacher education; parks, recreation and leisure; philosophy; physics; political science and government; psychology; social work; sociology; Spanish; special education; youth ministry.

Goshen College

Accounting; art; art teacher education; art therapy; biblical studies; bilingual and multilingual education; biology/biological sciences; broadcast journalism; business administration and management; business teacher education; chemistry; child development; computer science; dramatic/theater arts; economics; education; elementary education; English; English as a second/foreign language (teaching); environmental studies; family and community services; history; information science/studies; journalism; kindergarten/preschool education; liberal arts and sciences/liberal studies; mass communication/media; mathematics; music; music teacher education; natural sciences; nursing (registered nurse training); peace studies and conflict resolution; physical education teaching and coaching; physical sciences; physics; pre-dentistry studies; pre-law studies; pre-medical studies; pre-veterinary studies; psychology; religious studies; science teacher education; secondary education; sign language interpretation and translation; social work; sociology; Spanish.

Goucher College

American studies; art; biology/biological sciences; business administration and management; chemistry; computer science; dance; dramatic/theater arts; economics; elementary education; English; French; history; interdisciplinary studies; international relations and affairs; mass communication/media; mathematics; music; peace studies and conflict resolution; philosophy; physics; political science and government; psychology; religious studies; Russian; sociology; Spanish; special education; women's studies.

Grinnell College

Anthropology; art; biochemistry; biology/biological sciences; chemistry; Chinese; classics and languages, literatures and linguistics; computer science; dramatic/theater arts; English; French; German; history; interdisciplinary studies; mathematics; music; philosophy; physics; political science and government; psychology; religious studies; Russian; sociology; Spanish.

Grove City College

Accounting; biochemistry; biology/biological sciences; business administration and management; business/managerial economics; chemistry; computer and information sciences; computer management; divinity/ministry; economics; electrical and electronic engineering technologies related; electrical, electronics and communications engineering; elementary education; English; entrepreneurship; finance; French; history; international business/trade/commerce; kindergarten/preschool education; literature; marketing/marketing management; mass communication/media; mathematics; mechanical engineering; mechanical engineering technologies related; modern languages; molecular biology; music; music management and merchandising; music performance; music teacher education; philosophy; physics; political science and government; pre-dentistry studies; pre-law studies; pre-medical studies; pre-veterinary studies; psychology; religious studies; science teacher education; secondary education; sociology; Spanish.

Gustavus Adolphus College

Accounting; anthropology; art; art history, criticism and conservation; art teacher education; athletic training; biochemistry; biology teacher education; biology/biological sciences; business administration and management; business/managerial economics; chemistry; chemistry teacher education; classics and languages, literatures and linguistics; computer science; criminal justice/law enforcement administration; dance; dramatic/theater arts; economics; education; elementary education; English; environmental studies; French; geography; geology/earth science; German; health and physical education related; health teacher education; history; interdisciplinary studies; international business/trade/commerce; Japanese; Japanese studies; Latin American studies; mass communication/media; mathematics; mathematics teacher education; music; music teacher education; nursing (registered nurse training); philosophy; physical education teaching and coaching; physical therapy; physics; physics teacher education; political science and government; pre-dentistry studies; pre-law studies; pre-medical studies; pre-veterinary studies; psychology; religious studies; religious/sacred music; Russian; Russian studies; Scandinavian languages; Scandinavian studies; secondary education; social sciences; social studies teacher education; sociology; Spanish; speech and rhetoric.

Hamilton College (NY)

African studies; American studies; archeology; art; art history, criticism and conservation; Asian studies; Asian studies (East); biochemistry; biology/biological sciences; chemistry; classics and languages, literatures and linguistics; comparative literature; computer science; creative writing; dance; dramatic/theater arts; economics; English; fine/studio arts; French; geology/earth science; German; history; history related; international relations and affairs; Latin; mass communication/media; mathematics; medieval and Renaissance studies; modern Greek; modern languages; molecular biology; music; neuroscience; philosophy; physics; physiological psychology/psychobiology; political science and government; psychology; public policy analysis; religious studies; Russian studies; sociology; Spanish; women's studies.

Hamline University

Anthropology; art; art history, criticism and conservation; Asian studies; Asian studies (East); athletic training; biochemistry; biology/biological sciences; business administration and management; chemistry; criminal justice/law enforcement administration; dramatic/theater arts; economics; education; education (K-12); elementary education; English; environmental studies; European studies; European studies (Central and Eastern); fine/studio arts; French; German; health and physical education; health teacher education; history; international business/trade/commerce; international economics; international relations and affairs; Jewish/Judaic studies; kinesiology and exercise science; Latin American studies; legal assistant/paralegal; legal studies; mass communication/media; mathematics; music; music teacher education; occupational therapy; peace studies and conflict resolution; philosophy; physical education teaching and coaching; physical therapy; physics; political science and government; pre-dentistry studies; pre-law studies; pre-medical studies; pre-veterinary studies; psychology; public administration; religious studies; Russian studies; science teacher education; secondary education; social sciences; sociology; Spanish; speech/theater education; urban studies/affairs; women's studies.

Hampshire College

African American/Black studies; agriculture; American studies; anthropology; applied art; Asian studies; Asian-American studies; biology/biological sciences; chemistry; cognitive science; comparative literature; computer graphics; computer science; dance; demography and population; dramatic/theater arts; economics; education; English; environmental design/architecture; environmental studies; film/video and photographic arts related; fine/studio arts; geology/earth science; Hispanic-American, Puerto Rican, and Mexican-American/Chicano studies; history; international/global studies; Judaic studies; Latin American studies; legal studies; linguistics; mass communication/media; music; nutrition sciences; peace studies and conflict resolution; philosophy; physics; playwriting and screenwriting; political science and government; psychology; public health; religious studies; sociology; urban studies/affairs; women's studies.

Hanover College

Anthropology; art; art history, criticism and conservation; biology/biological sciences; business administration and management; chemistry;

classics and languages, literatures and linguistics; computer science; dramatic/theater arts; economics; English; French; geology/earth science; German; history; international/global studies; Latin American studies; mass communication/media; mathematics; medieval and Renaissance studies; music; philosophy; physical education teaching and coaching; physics; political science and government; psychology; sociology; Spanish; theology.

Harding University

Accounting; advertising; art teacher education; art therapy; athletic training; biblical studies; biochemistry; biology teacher education; biology/biological sciences; broadcast journalism; business administration and management; business/corporate communications; chemistry; Christian studies; clinical laboratory science/medical technology; communication disorders; computer and information sciences; computer engineering; computer science; corrections and criminal justice related; counselor education/school counseling and guidance; design and applied arts related; dietetics; digital communication and media/multimedia; divinity/ministry; dramatic/theater arts; early childhood education; economics; education (multiple levels); educational leadership and administration; electrical, electronics and communications engineering; elementary education; English; English/language arts teacher education; family and consumer sciences/home economics teacher education; family and consumer sciences/human sciences; fashion merchandising; fine/studio arts; French; French language teacher education; general studies; graphic design; health teacher education; health/health care administration; history; human development and family studies related; human resources management; humanities; information technology; interior design; international business/trade/commerce; international/global studies; kinesiology and exercise science; legal studies; marketing/marketing management; marriage and family therapy/counseling; mathematics; mathematics teacher education; mechanical engineering; middle school education; missionary studies and missiology; music; music teacher education; nursing (registered nurse training); painting; pastoral counseling and specialized ministries related; pastoral studies/counseling; photojournalism; physics; political science and government; pre-dentistry studies; pre-medical studies; pre-veterinary studies; psychology; public administration; public relations/image management; reading teacher education; religious education; sales, distribution and marketing; science teacher education; secondary education; social sciences; social studies teacher education; social work; Spanish; Spanish language teacher education; special education (early childhood); special education (specific learning disabilities); special education related; speech teacher education; speech-language pathology; sport and fitness administration/management; theology; youth ministry.

Harvard University

African languages; African studies; African American/Black studies; American studies; ancient Near Eastern and biblical languages; animal genetics; anthropology; applied mathematics; Arabic; archeology; architectural engineering; art; art history, criticism and conservation; artificial intelligence and robotics; Asian studies; Asian studies (East); Asian studies (South); Asian studies (Southeast); astronomy; astrophysics; atmospheric sciences and meteorology; behavioral sciences; biblical studies; biochemistry; biological and physical sciences; biology/biological sciences; biology/biotechnology laboratory technician; biomedical sciences; biomedical/medical engineering; biometry/biometrics; biophysics; cell biology and histology; chemical engineering; chemistry; Chinese; city/urban, community and regional planning; civil engineering; classics and languages, literatures and linguistics; cognitive psychology and psycholinguistics; cognitive science; comparative literature; computer and information sciences; computer engineering; computer engineering technology; computer graphics; computer programming; computer science; creative writing; cultural studies; dramatic/theater arts; ecology; economics; electrical, electronics and communications engineering; engineering; engineering physics; engineering science; English; entomology; environmental biology; environmental design/architecture; environmental studies; environmental/environmental health engineering; European studies; European studies (Central and Eastern); evolutionary biology; film/cinema studies; fine/studio arts; fluid/thermal sciences; folklore; French; geochemistry; geological/geophysical engineering; geology/earth science; geophysics and seismology; German; Hebrew; Hispanic-American, Puerto Rican, and Mexican-American/Chicano studies; history; history and philosophy of science and technology; history of philosophy; human development and family studies; humanities; information science/studies; interdisciplinary studies; international economics; international relations and affairs; Islamic studies; Italian; Japanese; Jewish/Judaic studies; Latin; Latin American studies; liberal arts and sciences/liberal studies; linguistics; literature; marine biology and biological oceanography; materials engineering; materials science; mathematics; mathematics and computer science; mechanical engineering; medical microbiology and bacteriology; medieval and Renaissance studies; metallurgical engineering; modern Greek; modern languages; molecular biology; music; music history, literature, and theory; natural resources/conservation; Near and Middle Eastern studies; neuroscience; nuclear physics; philosophy; physical sciences; physics; physiological psychology/psychobiology; political science and government; polymer chemistry; Portuguese; pre-dentistry studies; pre-law studies; pre-medical studies; pre-veterinary studies; psychology; public policy analysis; religious studies; Romance languages; Russian; Russian studies; Scandinavian languages; Slavic languages; social sciences; sociobiology; sociology; Spanish; statistics; systems engineering; urban studies/affairs; western civilization; women's studies.

Harvey Mudd College

Biology/biological sciences; chemistry; computer science; engineering; mathematics; physics.

Haverford College

African studies; anthropology; archeology; art; art history, criticism and conservation; Asian studies (East); astronomy; biochemistry; biology/biological sciences; biophysics; chemistry; classics and languages, literatures and linguistics; comparative literature; computer science; econometrics and quantitative economics; economics; education; English; French; geology/earth science; German; history; Italian; Latin; Latin American studies; mathematics; modern Greek; music; neuroscience; peace studies and conflict resolution; philosophy; physics; political science and government; pre-law studies; pre-medical studies; pre-veterinary studies; psychology; religious studies; Romance languages; Russian; sociology; Spanish; urban studies/affairs; women's studies.

Hendrix College

Accounting; American studies; anthropology; art; biochemistry/biophysics and molecular biology; biology/biological sciences; business/managerial economics; chemical physics; chemistry; computer science; early childhood education; economics; English; environmental studies; French; German; health services/allied health/health sciences; history; interdisciplinary studies; international relations and affairs; kinesiology and exercise science; mathematics; music; philosophy; philosophy and religious studies related; physics; political science and government; psychology; religious studies; sociology; Spanish.

Hillsdale College

Accounting; American studies; art; biology/biological sciences; business administration and management; chemistry; Christian studies; classics and languages, literatures and linguistics; communication/speech communication and rhetoric; comparative literature; computer science; dramatic/theater arts; early childhood education; economics; education; education (K-12); elementary education; English; European studies; finance; French; German; history; interdisciplinary studies; international relations and affairs; kindergarten/preschool education; marketing/marketing management; mathematics; mathematics related; music; philosophy; physical education teaching and coaching; physics; political science and government; pre-dentistry studies; pre-medical studies; pre-veterinary studies; psychology; religious studies; secondary education; sociology; Spanish.

Hiram College

Accounting and finance; art; art history, criticism and conservation; biological and biomedical sciences related; biology/biological sciences; business administration and management; chemistry; classics and languages, literatures and linguistics; computer science; dramatic/theater arts; economics; elementary education; English; environmental studies; fine/studio arts; French; German; health science; history; interdisciplinary studies; international business/trade/commerce; international economics; mass communication/media; mathematics; music; philosophy; physics; physiological psychology/psychobiology; political science and government; pre-dentistry studies; pre-law studies; pre-medical studies; pre-veterinary studies; psychology; religious studies; secondary education; sociology; Spanish.

Hobart and William Smith Colleges

African studies; African American/Black studies; American studies; ancient/classical Greek; anthropology; architecture; art; art history, criticism and conservation; Asian studies; biochemistry; biology/biological sciences; chemistry; Chinese; classics and languages, literatures and linguistics; comparative literature; computer science; dance; dramatic/theater arts; economics; English; environmental studies; European studies; fine/studio arts; French; gay/lesbian studies; geology/earth science; history; interdisciplinary studies; international relations and affairs; Japanese; Latin; Latin American studies; liberal arts and sciences/liberal studies; mass communication/media; mathematics; medieval and Renaissance studies; modern languages; music; philosophy; physics; political science and government; pre-dentistry studies; pre-law studies; pre-medical studies; pre-veterinary studies; psychology; public policy analysis; religious studies; Russian; Russian studies; sociology; Spanish; urban studies/affairs; women's studies.

Hope College

Accounting; ancient Near Eastern and biblical languages; art history, criticism and conservation; art teacher education; athletic training; biology teacher education; biology/biological sciences; business administration and management; business/managerial economics; chemistry; chemistry teacher education; classics and languages, literatures and linguistics; communication/speech communication and rhetoric; computer science; dance; drama and dance teacher education; dramatic/theater arts; economics; education (specific subject areas) related; elementary education; engineering; engineering physics; English; English/language arts teacher education; environmental studies; fine/studio arts; French; French language teacher education; geology/earth science; geophysics and seismology; German; German language teacher education; history; history teacher education; humanities; interdisciplinary studies; international/global studies; Japanese; jazz/jazz studies; kinesiology and exercise science; Latin; Latin teacher education; mathematics; mathematics teacher education; multi-/interdisciplinary studies related; music; music performance; music teacher education; music theory and composition; nursing (registered nurse training); philosophy; physical education teaching and coaching; physics; physics teacher education; piano and organ; political science and government; psychology; religious studies; science teacher education; secondary education; social sciences; social studies teacher education; social work; sociology; Spanish; Spanish language teacher education; special education (emotionally disturbed); special education (specific learning disabilities); theology and religious vocations related; violin, viola, guitar and other stringed instruments; voice and opera.

Houghton College

Accounting; art; biblical studies; biochemistry; biological and physical sciences; biology/biological sciences; business administration and management; chemistry; clinical laboratory science/medical technology; computer science; creative writing; cultural studies; elementary education; English; English as a second/foreign language (teaching); environmental biology; French; health and physical education; history; humanities; information technology; international relations and affairs; liberal arts and sciences/liberal studies; literature; mathematics; music; music performance; music teacher education; music theory and composition;

natural sciences; parks, recreation and leisure; pastoral studies/counseling; philosophy; physical education teaching and coaching; physics; piano and organ; political science and government; pre-dentistry studies; pre-law studies; pre-medical studies; pre-veterinary studies; psychology; religious education; religious studies; secondary education; sociology; Spanish; special education; theology; violin, viola, guitar and other stringed instruments; voice and opera; wind/percussion instruments.

Illinois College

Accounting; art; biology/biological sciences; business administration and management; business/managerial economics; chemistry; clinical laboratory science/medical technology; computer science; cytotechnology; dramatic/theater arts; early childhood education; economics; education; education (K-12); elementary education; English; environmental studies; finance; French; German; history; information science/studies; interdisciplinary studies; international relations and affairs; liberal arts and sciences/liberal studies; management information systems; mass communication/media; mathematics; music; occupational therapy; philosophy; physical education teaching and coaching; physics; political science and government; pre-dentistry studies; pre-law studies; pre-medical studies; pre-veterinary studies; psychology; religious studies; secondary education; sociology; Spanish; speech and rhetoric.

Illinois Institute of Technology

Aerospace, aeronautical and astronautical engineering; applied mathematics; architectural engineering; architecture; biochemistry/biophysics and molecular biology; biology/biological sciences; biomedical/medical engineering; biophysics; business/commerce; chemical engineering; chemistry; civil engineering; communication and journalism related; computer engineering; computer science; design and visual communications; electrical, electronics and communications engineering; engineering/industrial management; environmental/environmental health engineering; industrial technology; information science/studies; information technology; manufacturing technology; materials engineering; mechanical engineering; metallurgical engineering; multi-/interdisciplinary studies related; physics; political science and government; psychology; technical and business writing.

Illinois Wesleyan University

Accounting; acting; African studies; American studies; anthropology; area studies related; art; Asian studies; biology/biological sciences; business administration and management; chemistry; classics and languages, literatures and linguistics; computer science; dramatic/theater arts; economics; education; elementary education; environmental studies; European studies (Western); French; German; history; insurance; insurance/risk management; international business/trade/commerce; international relations and affairs; Latin American studies; liberal arts and sciences/liberal studies; mathematics; music; music performance; music related; music teacher education; music theory and composition; nursing (registered nurse training); philosophy; physics; piano and organ; political science and government; psychology; religious studies; sociology; Spanish; theater design and technology; voice and opera; women's studies.

Iowa State University of Science and Technology

Accounting; advertising; aerospace, aeronautical and astronautical engineering; agricultural business and management; agricultural mechanization; agricultural teacher education; agricultural/biological engineering and bioengineering; agriculture; agronomy and crop science; animal sciences; anthropology; apparel and textiles; applied horticulture; architecture; art; atmospheric sciences and meteorology; biochemistry; biology/biological sciences; biophysics; botany/plant biology; business administration and management; business, management, and marketing related; chemical engineering; chemistry; city/urban, community and regional planning; civil engineering; commercial and advertising art; computer and information sciences; computer engineering; dairy science; design and visual communications; dietetics; dramatic/theater arts; early childhood education; ecology; economics; education; electrical, electronics and communications engineering; elementary education; engineering; engineering related; engineering science; English; entomology;

entrepreneurship; environmental science; environmental studies; family and community services; family and consumer economics related; family and consumer sciences/home economics teacher education; family and consumer sciences/human sciences; family resource management; farm and ranch management; fashion/apparel design; finance; fish/game management; food services technology; foods, nutrition, and wellness; forestry; French; genetics; geology/earth science; German; graphic design; health and physical education; health teacher education; history; horticultural science; hotel/motel administration; industrial engineering; interdisciplinary studies; interior design; international agriculture; international business/trade/commerce; international relations and affairs; journalism; landscape architecture; liberal arts and sciences/liberal studies; linguistics; logistics and materials management; management information systems; marketing/marketing management; mass communication/media; materials engineering; mathematics; mechanical engineering; medical illustration; microbiology; multi-/interdisciplinary studies related; music; music teacher education; natural resources management and policy; operations management; ornamental horticulture; philosophy; physics; plant protection and integrated pest management; political science and government; pre-dentistry studies; pre-law studies; pre-medical studies; pre-veterinary studies; psychology; public administration; religious studies; Russian studies; secondary education; sociology; Spanish; special products marketing; speech and rhetoric; statistics; technical and business writing; trade and industrial teacher education; visual and performing arts; women's studies.

Ithaca College

Accounting; acting; anthropology; applied economics; applied mathematics; art; art history, criticism and conservation; art teacher education; arts management; athletic training; audiology and speech-language pathology; biochemistry; biology teacher education; biology/biological sciences; broadcast journalism; business administration and management; business/commerce; business/managerial economics; chemistry; chemistry teacher education; cinematography and film/video production; communication and journalism related; computer and information sciences; computer science; creative writing; dance; dramatic/theater arts; economics; education (K-12); education (multiple levels); educational/instructional media design; English; English/language arts teacher education; environmental studies; film/cinema studies; finance; fine/studio arts; foods, nutrition, and wellness; French; French language teacher education; German; German language teacher education; German studies; gerontology; health and physical education; health and physical education related; health teacher education; health/health care administration; health/medical preparatory programs related; history; history teacher education; hospital and health care facilities administration; industrial and organizational psychology; interdisciplinary studies; international business/trade/commerce; jazz/jazz studies; journalism; kinesiology and exercise science; labor and industrial relations; liberal arts and sciences/liberal studies; marketing research; marketing/marketing management; mass communication/media; mathematics; mathematics and computer science; mathematics teacher education; middle school education; multi-/interdisciplinary studies related; music; music performance; music teacher education; music theory and composition; occupational therapy; parks, recreation and leisure; philosophy; photography; physical education teaching and coaching; physical therapy; physics; physics teacher education; piano and organ; political science and government; pre-law studies; pre-medical studies; psychology; public health education and promotion; public relations/image management; radio and television; recording arts technology; rehabilitation therapy; science teacher education; secondary education; social sciences; social studies teacher education; sociology; Spanish; Spanish language teacher education; special education (speech or language impaired); speech and rhetoric; sport and fitness administration/management; telecommunications; theater design and technology; therapeutic recreation; visual and performing arts; voice and opera.

James Madison University

Accounting; anthropology; art; art history, criticism and conservation; athletic training; biology/biological sciences; business administration and management; business/managerial economics; chemistry; community health services counseling; computer and information sciences; dramatic/theater arts; economics; engineering; English; finance; finance and financial management services related; foods, nutrition, and wellness; foreign languages and literatures; geography; geology/earth science; health and physical education; health/health care administration; history; hospitality administration; information science/studies; international business/trade/commerce; international relations and affairs; liberal arts and sciences/liberal studies; marketing/marketing management; mathematics; music performance; nursing (registered nurse training); philosophy and religious studies related; physics; political science and government; psychology; public administration; science, technology and society; social sciences; social work; sociology; speech-language pathology; systems science and theory; technical and business writing.

John Brown University
Accounting; athletic training; biblical studies; biochemistry; biology teacher education; biology/biological sciences; broadcast journalism; business administration and management; business teacher education; chemistry; chemistry teacher education; computer graphics; construction engineering; construction management; divinity/ministry; early childhood education; education; electrical, electronics and communications engineering; elementary education; engineering; engineering technology; engineering/industrial management; English; English as a second/foreign language (teaching); English/language arts teacher education; environmental science; environmental studies; health teacher education; history; interdisciplinary studies; international business/trade/commerce; international relations and affairs; journalism; kindergarten/preschool education; kinesiology and exercise science; liberal arts and sciences/liberal studies; marketing/marketing management; mass communication/media; mathematics; mechanical engineering; middle school education; missionary studies and missiology; music; music teacher education; pastoral studies/counseling; psychology; public relations, advertising, and applied communication related; public relations/image management; radio and television; radio, television, and digital communication related; religious education; religious studies; secondary education; social sciences; social studies teacher education; Spanish; special education; theology; youth ministry.

John Carroll University
Accounting; art history, criticism and conservation; Asian studies; Asian studies (East); biological and physical sciences; biology/biological sciences; business administration and management; chemistry; classics and languages, literatures and linguistics; computer science; economics; education; education (K-12); elementary education; engineering physics; English; environmental studies; finance; French; German; gerontology; history; humanities; interdisciplinary studies; international economics; international relations and affairs; kindergarten/preschool education; Latin; literature; marketing/marketing management; mass communication/media; mathematics; modern Greek; neuroscience; philosophy; physical education teaching and coaching; physics; political science and government; pre-dentistry studies; pre-law studies; pre-medical studies; pre-veterinary studies; psychology; public administration; religious education; religious studies; secondary education; sociology; Spanish; special education.

The Johns Hopkins University
Anthropology; applied mathematics; art history, criticism and conservation; Asian studies (East); behavioral sciences; biological and physical sciences; biology/biological sciences; biomedical/medical engineering; biophysics; business/commerce; chemical engineering; chemistry; civil engineering; classics and languages, literatures and linguistics; cognitive psychology and psycholinguistics; computer and information sciences; computer engineering; creative writing; economics; electrical, electronics and communications engineering; electroneurodiagnostic/electroencephalographic technology; engineering; engineering mechanics; English; environmental studies; environmental/environmental health engineering; film/cinema studies; French; geography; geology/earth science; German; history; history and philosophy of science and technology; industrial engineering; interdisciplinary studies; international relations

and affairs; Italian; Latin American studies; liberal arts and sciences and humanities related; liberal arts and sciences/liberal studies; literature; materials engineering; materials science; mathematics; mechanical engineering; music; natural sciences; Near and Middle Eastern studies; neuroscience; nursing (registered nurse training); philosophy; physics; physiological psychology/psychobiology; political science and government; psychology; public health; social sciences; sociology; Spanish.

Juniata College
Accounting; anthropology; art history, criticism and conservation; biochemistry; biology teacher education; biology/biological sciences; botany/plant biology; business administration and management; business/commerce; cell biology and histology; chemistry; chemistry teacher education; communication and journalism related; communication/speech communication and rhetoric; computer and information sciences; criminal justice/safety; criminology; early childhood education; ecology; economics; education; education (multiple levels); elementary education; engineering; engineering physics; English; English/language arts teacher education; environmental science; environmental studies; finance; fine/studio arts; foreign language teacher education; foreign languages and literatures; French; French language teacher education; geology/earth science; German; German language teacher education; health communication; health/medical preparatory programs related; history; human resources management; humanities; information resources management; information technology; international business/trade/commerce; international relations and affairs; kindergarten/preschool education; liberal arts and sciences/liberal studies; marine biology and biological oceanography; marketing/marketing management; mathematics; mathematics teacher education; microbiology; molecular biology; museum studies; natural sciences; peace studies and conflict resolution; philosophy; philosophy and religious studies related; physical sciences; physics; physics teacher education; political science and government; pre-dentistry studies; pre-law studies; pre-medical studies; pre-nursing studies; pre-pharmacy studies; pre-theology/pre-ministerial studies; pre-veterinary studies; psychology; public administration; religious studies; Russian; science teacher education; secondary education; social sciences; social studies teacher education; social work; sociology; Spanish; Spanish language teacher education; special education (early childhood); special education related; theater/theater arts management; zoology/animal biology.

Kalamazoo College
Anthropology; art; art history, criticism and conservation; biology/biological sciences; business/managerial economics; chemistry; classics and languages, literatures and linguistics; computer science; dramatic/theater arts; English; French; German; health science; history; interdisciplinary studies; mathematics; music; philosophy; physics; political science and government; psychology; religious studies; sociology; Spanish.

Kenyon College
African studies; African American/Black studies; American studies; ancient/classical Greek; anthropology; art; art history, criticism and conservation; Asian studies; biochemistry; biology/biological sciences; chemistry; classics and languages, literatures and linguistics; creative writing; dance; dramatic/theater arts; economics; English; environmental studies; ethnic, cultural minority, and gender studies related; fine/studio arts; foreign languages and literatures; French; German; history; humanities; interdisciplinary studies; international relations and affairs; international/global studies; Latin; legal studies; literature; mathematics; modern Greek; modern languages; molecular biology; multi-/interdisciplinary studies related; music; natural sciences; neuroscience; philosophy; physics; political science and government; pre-dentistry studies; pre-law studies; pre-medical studies; pre-veterinary studies; psychology; public policy analysis; religious studies; Romance languages; sociology; Spanish; statistics; women's studies.

Kettering University
Applied mathematics; biochemistry; business administration, management and operations related; chemistry; chemistry related; computer

engineering; computer science; electrical, electronics and communications engineering; engineering physics; industrial engineering; mechanical engineering; physics.

Knox College

African American/Black studies; American studies; anthropology; art; art history, criticism and conservation; Asian studies; biochemistry; biology/biological sciences; chemistry; classics and languages, literatures and linguistics; computer and information sciences; creative writing; dramatic/theater arts; economics; education; English; environmental studies; foreign languages and literatures; French; German; history; international relations and affairs; mathematics; multi-/interdisciplinary studies related; music; philosophy; physics; political science and government; psychology; Russian; Russian studies; sociology; Spanish; women's studies.

Lafayette College

American studies; anthropology; art; art history, criticism and conservation; biochemistry; biology/biological sciences; business/managerial economics; chemical engineering; chemistry; civil engineering; computer science; economics; electrical, electronics and communications engineering; engineering; English; environmental/environmental health engineering; fine/studio arts; French; geology/earth science; German; history; international relations and affairs; mathematics; mechanical engineering; music; music history, literature, and theory; philosophy; physics; political science and government; psychology; religious studies; Russian studies; sociology; Spanish.

Lake Forest College

American studies; anthropology; art history, criticism and conservation; Asian studies; biology/biological sciences; business/managerial economics; chemistry; communication/speech communication and rhetoric; computer science; dramatic/theater arts; economics; education; elementary education; English; environmental studies; fine/studio arts; French; history; international relations and affairs; Latin American studies; mathematics; music; philosophy; physics; political science and government; psychology; secondary education; sociology; Spanish; theology.

Lawrence Technological University

Architecture; biochemistry; biomedical/medical engineering; business administration and management; chemical technology; chemistry; chemistry related; civil engineering; communications technology; computer engineering; computer science; construction engineering technology; construction management; electrical and electronic engineering technologies related; electrical, electronic and communications engineering technology; electrical, electronics and communications engineering; engineering technology; engineering/industrial management; environmental design/architecture; general studies; humanities; illustration; industrial technology; information technology; interior architecture; manufacturing technology; mathematics; mathematics and computer science; mechanical engineering; mechanical engineering/mechanical technology; physics; physics related; psychology; radio and television.

Lawrence University

Ancient/classical Greek; anthropology; archeology; art history, criticism and conservation; art teacher education; Asian studies (East); biochemistry; biology/biological sciences; chemistry; Chinese; classics and classical languages related; classics and languages, literatures and linguistics; cognitive psychology and psycholinguistics; cognitive science; computer science; dramatic/theater arts; ecology; economics; English; environmental studies; ethnic, cultural minority, and gender studies related; fine/studio arts; French; geology/earth science; German; history; international economics; international relations and affairs; Japanese; Latin; linguistics; mathematics; mathematics and computer science; music; music pedagogy; music performance; music teacher education; music theory and composition; neuroscience; philosophy; physics; piano and organ; political science and government; pre-dentistry studies; pre-law studies; pre-medical studies; pre-veterinary studies; psychology; religious studies; Russian; Russian studies; secondary education; Slavic

studies; social psychology; Spanish; violin, viola, guitar and other stringed instruments; voice and opera; wind/percussion instruments.

Lebanon Valley College

Accounting; actuarial science; American studies; art history, criticism and conservation; biochemistry; biochemistry/biophysics and molecular biology; biology/biological sciences; business administration and management; chemistry; clinical/medical laboratory science and allied professions related; computer science; criminology; digital communication and media/multimedia; economics; elementary education; English; fine/studio arts; French; general studies; German; health services/allied health/health sciences; health/health care administration; history; liberal arts and sciences/liberal studies; mathematics; multi-/interdisciplinary studies related; music management and merchandising; music performance; music teacher education; philosophy; physics; physiological psychology/psychobiology; political science and government; psychology; recording arts technology; religious studies; sociology; Spanish.

Lehigh University

Accounting; African American/Black studies; American studies; anthropology; architecture; art; art history, criticism and conservation; Asian studies; astronomy; astrophysics; biochemistry; biological and biomedical sciences related; biological and physical sciences; biology/biological sciences; biomedical/medical engineering; biopsychology; business administration and management; business/commerce; business/managerial economics; chemical engineering; chemistry; chemistry related; civil engineering; classics and languages, literatures and linguistics; communication and journalism related; computer and information sciences and support services related; computer engineering; computer science; design and applied arts related; design and visual communications; dramatic/theater arts; dramatic/theater arts and stagecraft related; ecology; education; electrical, electronics and communications engineering; engineering mechanics; engineering physics; engineering related; English; environmental science; environmental studies; environmental/environmental health engineering; finance; French; geological and earth sciences/geosciences related; German; history; industrial engineering; information science/studies; international relations and affairs; journalism; logistics and materials management; management information systems; marketing/marketing management; materials engineering; mathematics; mechanical engineering; molecular biology; music; music theory and composition; neuroscience; philosophy; physical and theoretical chemistry; physics; political science and government; pre-dentistry studies; pre-medical studies; psychology; religious studies; Russian studies; science technologies related; social sciences; social sciences related; sociology; Spanish; statistics; structural engineering; urban studies/affairs; women's studies.

LeTourneau University

Accounting; airframe mechanics and aircraft maintenance technology; airline pilot and flight crew; avionics maintenance technology; biblical studies; biology/biological sciences; biomedical/medical engineering; business administration and management; chemistry; computer engineering; computer engineering technology; computer science; drafting and design technology; electrical, electronic and communications engineering technology; electrical, electronics and communications engineering; elementary education; engineering; engineering technology; English; finance; history; information science/studies; interdisciplinary studies; international business/trade/commerce; management information systems; marketing/marketing management; mathematics; mechanical engineering; mechanical engineering/mechanical technology; missionary studies and missiology; natural sciences; physical education teaching and coaching; pre-dentistry studies; pre-law studies; pre-medical studies; pre-veterinary studies; psychology; religious studies; secondary education; sport and fitness administration/management; welding technology.

Lewis & Clark College

Anthropology; art; Asian studies (East); biochemistry; biology/biological sciences; chemistry; communication/speech communication and rhetoric; computer science; dramatic/theater arts; economics; English; environmental studies; foreign languages and literatures; French; German; Hispanic-American, Puerto Rican, and Mexican-American/Chicano studies; history; international relations and affairs; mathematics; modern languages; music; philosophy; physics; political science and government; pre-engineering; psychology; religious studies; sociology; Spanish.

Lincoln Memorial University

Accounting; art; art teacher education; athletic training; biology teacher education; biology/biological sciences; business administration and management; business/managerial economics; chemistry; chemistry teacher education; clinical laboratory science/medical technology; computer and information sciences; criminal justice/law enforcement administration; economics; education; elementary education; English; environmental studies; finance; health and physical education; health teacher education; history; history teacher education; humanities; kindergarten/preschool education; kinesiology and exercise science; liberal arts and sciences/liberal studies; marketing/marketing management; mass communication/media; mathematics; mathematics teacher education; nursing (registered nurse training); physical education teaching and coaching; pre-law studies; pre-medical studies; pre-veterinary studies; psychology; science teacher education; secondary education; social work; veterinary sciences; veterinary technology; wildlife and wildlands science and management.

Linfield College

Accounting; anthropology; area, ethnic, cultural, and gender studies related; art; athletic training; biology/biological sciences; business/commerce; chemistry; communication/speech communication and rhetoric; computer science; creative writing; design and visual communications; dramatic/theater arts; economics; elementary education; English; environmental studies; finance; fine/studio arts; French; German; health and physical education; history; international business/trade/commerce; Japanese; kinesiology and exercise science; mass communication/media; mathematics; music; music performance; music theory and composition; nursing (registered nurse training); philosophy; physical sciences; physics; physics related; political science and government; psychology; religious studies; sociology; Spanish.

Lipscomb University

Accounting; American studies; apparel and textiles; architecture related; art teacher education; athletic training; biblical languages/literatures; biblical studies; biochemistry; biology teacher education; biology/biological sciences; business administration and management; business/managerial economics; chemistry; chemistry teacher education; commercial and advertising art; computer engineering; computer science; dietetics; drama and dance teacher education; dramatic/theater arts; education; elementary education; engineering mechanics; engineering related; engineering science; English; English as a second/foreign language (teaching); English/language arts teacher education; environmental studies; family and consumer sciences/human sciences; family systems; fashion merchandising; fine/studio arts; foodservice systems administration; French; French language teacher education; general studies; German; health/medical preparatory programs related; history; history teacher education; human resources management; information science/studies; information technology; international business/trade/commerce; journalism; kinesiology and exercise science; legal studies; management information systems; marketing/marketing management; mass communication/media; mathematics; mathematics teacher education; mechanical engineering; missionary studies and missiology; music performance; music teacher education; music theory and composition; nursing (registered nurse training); organizational communication; pastoral counseling and specialized ministries related; pharmacy; philosophy; physical education teaching and coaching; physics; physics teacher education; piano and organ; political science and government; pre-dentistry studies; pre-law studies; pre-medical studies; pre-nursing studies; pre-pharmacy studies; pre-veterinary studies; psychology; public administration; public relations/image management; social work; Spanish; Spanish language teacher education; speech and rhetoric; urban studies/affairs; voice and opera; youth ministry.

List College, The Jewish Theological Seminary

Ancient Near Eastern and biblical languages; biblical studies; Hebrew; history; Jewish/Judaic studies; literature; music; philosophy; religious education; religious studies; talmudic studies; women's studies.

Louisiana State University and Agricultural and Mechanical College

Accounting; adult and continuing education; agricultural business and management; animal sciences; anthropology; architecture; audiology and speech-language pathology; biochemistry; biology/biological sciences; biomedical/medical engineering; business administration and management; business/managerial economics; chemical engineering; chemistry; civil engineering; computer engineering; computer science; construction management; dietetics; dramatic/theater arts; early childhood education; economics; electrical, electronics and communications engineering; elementary education; English; environmental science; environmental/environmental health engineering; family and consumer sciences/human sciences; fashion merchandising; finance; fine/studio arts; food science; forest/forest resources management; French; general studies; geography; geology/earth science; German; history; industrial engineering; interior architecture; international business/trade/commerce; international/global studies; landscape architecture; Latin; liberal arts and sciences/liberal studies; management science; marketing/marketing management; mass communication/media; mathematics; mechanical engineering; microbiology; music; music performance; music teacher education; natural resources management and policy; petroleum engineering; philosophy; physical education teaching and coaching; physics; plant sciences; political science and government; psychology; secondary education; sociology; Spanish; speech and rhetoric; women's studies.

Loyola College in Maryland

Accounting; applied mathematics; art; biology/biological sciences; business/commerce; chemistry; classics and languages, literatures and linguistics; communication/speech communication and rhetoric; computer and information sciences; creative writing; economics; education; electrical, electronics and communications engineering; elementary education; engineering; English; finance; French; German; history; interdisciplinary studies; international business/trade/commerce; mathematics; philosophy; physics; political science and government; psychology; religious studies; sociology; Spanish; special education; speech-language pathology.

Loyola Marymount University

Accounting; African American/Black studies; art history, criticism and conservation; Asian-American studies; biochemistry; biology/biological sciences; business administration and management; chemistry; cinematography and film/video production; civil engineering; classics and languages, literatures and linguistics; computer engineering; computer science; conducting; dance; dramatic/theater arts; economics; electrical, electronics and communications engineering; engineering physics; English; European studies; fine/studio arts; French; Hispanic-American, Puerto Rican, and Mexican-American/Chicano studies; history; humanities; international economics; Latin; liberal arts and sciences/liberal studies; mass communication/media; mathematics; mechanical engineering; modern Greek; music; music history, literature, and theory; music theory and composition; musicology and ethnomusicology; natural sciences; philosophy; physics; playwriting and screenwriting; political science and government; psychology; sociology; Spanish; theology; urban studies/affairs; voice and opera.

Loyola University Chicago

Accounting; advertising; ancient/classical Greek; anthropology; bilingual and multilingual education; bioinformatics; biology/biological sciences; business administration and management; business, management, and marketing related; business/managerial economics; chemistry; classics and languages, literatures and linguistics; clinical nutrition; communication and media related; communication/speech communication and rhetoric; computer and information sciences; computer and information systems security; computer science; criminal justice/safety; dramatic/theater arts;

elementary education; English; environmental studies; finance; fine/studio arts; forensic science and technology; French; general studies; German; health/health care administration; history; human resources management; human services; international business/trade/commerce; international relations and affairs; Italian; journalism; Latin; management information systems; marketing/marketing management; mass communication/media; mathematics; mathematics and computer science; mathematics teacher education; music; nursing (registered nurse training); operations management; organizational behavior; philosophy; physics; political science and government; psychology; psychology related; religious education; secondary education; social work; sociology; Spanish; special education; statistics; theology; women's studies.

Loyola University New Orleans

Accounting; art; behavioral sciences; biology/biological sciences; business administration and management; business/managerial economics; chemistry; classics and languages, literatures and linguistics; commercial and advertising art; communication/speech communication and rhetoric; computer and information sciences; creative writing; criminal justice/safety; dramatic/theater arts; economics; education; elementary education; English; finance; forensic science and technology; French; general studies; German; history; humanities; information science/studies; international business/trade/commerce; jazz/jazz studies; marketing/marketing management; mathematics; music; music management and merchandising; music performance; music teacher education; music theory and composition; nursing (registered nurse training); philosophy; physics; piano and organ; political science and government; psychology; religious education; religious studies; religious/sacred music; Russian; social sciences; sociology; Spanish; visual and performing arts.

Luther College

Accounting; African American/Black studies; ancient Near Eastern and biblical languages; anthropology; art; athletic training; biology/biological sciences; business administration and management; chemistry; communication/speech communication and rhetoric; computer science; dramatic/theater arts; economics; elementary education; English; environmental studies; French; German; health and physical education; history; interdisciplinary studies; international relations and affairs; management information systems; mathematics; music; nursing (registered nurse training); philosophy; physical education teaching and coaching; physics; political science and government; psychology; religious studies; Scandinavian studies; social work; sociology; Spanish; statistics; women's studies.

Lycoming College

Accounting; actuarial science; American studies; anthropology; applied mathematics related; archeology; area studies related; art; art history, criticism and conservation; astronomy; biology/biological sciences; business administration and management; chemistry; classical, ancient Mediterranean and Near Eastern studies and archaeology; commercial and advertising art; communication/speech communication and rhetoric; computer and information sciences; creative writing; dramatic/theater arts; economics; English; finance; fine/studio arts; foreign languages and literatures; French; German; history; international business/trade/commerce; international relations and affairs; literature; marketing/marketing management; mathematics; multi-/interdisciplinary studies related; music; philosophy; physics; political science and government; pre-dentistry studies; pre-law studies; pre-medical studies; pre-veterinary studies; psychology; religious studies; social sciences; sociology.

Lyon College

Accounting; art; biochemistry; biology/biological sciences; business administration and management; chemistry; computer science; dramatic/theater arts; early childhood education; economics; English; environmental studies; history; mathematics; music; philosophy and religious studies related; political science and government; psychology; Spanish.

Macalester College

Anthropology; art history, criticism and conservation; Asian studies; biology/biological sciences; chemistry; classics and languages, literatures and linguistics; communication/speech communication and rhetoric; computer science; dramatic/theater arts; economics; English; environmental studies; fine/studio arts; French; geography; geology/earth science; history; humanities; Latin American studies; linguistics; mathematics; music; neuroscience; philosophy; physics; political science and government; psychology; religious studies; Russian studies; sociology; Spanish; women's studies.

Maharishi University of Management

Ayurvedic medicine; business administration and management; cinematography and film/video production; computer science; elementary education; English; environmental studies; fine/studio arts; mathematics; secondary education.

Marietta College

Accounting; art; athletic training; biochemistry; biology/biological sciences; business administration and management; business/corporate communications; chemistry; commercial and advertising art; communication/speech communication and rhetoric; computer science; dramatic/theater arts; economics; education; elementary education; English; environmental science; environmental studies; fine/studio arts; geology/earth science; graphic design; history; human resources management; information science/studies; international business/trade/commerce; journalism; liberal arts and sciences/liberal studies; marketing/marketing management; mathematics; music; petroleum engineering; philosophy; physics; political science and government; psychology; public relations, advertising, and applied communication related; radio and television; secondary education; Spanish; speech and rhetoric.

Marist College

Accounting; advertising; American studies; applied mathematics; art; art history, criticism and conservation; athletic training; biochemistry; biology teacher education; biology/biological sciences; biomedical sciences; business administration and management; chemistry; chemistry teacher education; clinical laboratory science/medical technology; computational mathematics; computer programming; computer programming (vendor/product certification); computer science; criminal justice/law enforcement administration; digital communication and media/multimedia; dramatic/theater arts; economics; English; English/language arts teacher education; environmental studies; fashion merchandising; fashion/apparel design; fine/studio arts; French; French language teacher education; general studies; history; information science/studies; information technology; journalism; mathematics; mathematics teacher education; organizational communication; philosophy; political science and government; psychology; public relations/image management; radio and television; secondary education; social studies teacher education; social work; Spanish; Spanish language teacher education; special education.

Marlboro College

African studies; American studies; anthropology; applied mathematics; art; art history, criticism and conservation; Asian studies; Asian studies (East); astronomy; astrophysics; behavioral sciences; biblical studies; biochemistry; biology/biological sciences; botany/plant biology; cell biology and histology; ceramic arts and ceramics; chemistry; classics and languages, literatures and linguistics; comparative literature; computer science; creative writing; cultural studies; dance; developmental and child psychology; dramatic/theater arts; drawing; ecology; economics; English; environmental biology; environmental studies; European studies; European studies (Central and Eastern); experimental psychology; film/cinema studies; fine/studio arts; folklore; French; German; history; history of philosophy; humanities; interdisciplinary studies; international economics; international relations and affairs; Italian; Latin; Latin American studies; linguistics; literature; mathematics; medieval and Renaissance studies; modern Greek; modern languages; molecular biology; music; music history, literature, and theory; natural resources/conservation; natural sciences; philosophy; photography; physics; political science and government; Portuguese; pre-law studies; pre-medical studies;

pre-veterinary studies; psychology; religious studies; Romance languages; Russian studies; sculpture; social sciences; sociology; Spanish; women's studies.

Marquette University
Accounting; advertising; African American/Black studies; anthropology; athletic training; audiology and speech-language pathology; biochemistry; biology/biological sciences; biomedical sciences; biomedical/medical engineering; broadcast journalism; business administration and management; business/managerial economics; chemistry; civil engineering; classics and languages, literatures and linguistics; clinical/medical laboratory technology; communication and journalism related; communication/speech communication and rhetoric; computational mathematics; computer engineering; computer science; creative writing; criminology; dental hygiene; dramatic/theater arts; economics; education; education (specific subject areas) related; electrical, electronics and communications engineering; elementary education; engineering; engineering related; English; English/language arts teacher education; environmental/environmental health engineering; finance; foreign language teacher education; foreign languages related; French; German; history; history of philosophy; history related; human resources management; industrial engineering; information science/studies; intercultural/multicultural and diversity studies; interdisciplinary studies; international business/trade/commerce; international relations and affairs; international/global studies; journalism; kinesiology and exercise science; management information systems; marketing/marketing management; mass communication/media; mathematics; mathematics teacher education; mechanical engineering; middle school education; molecular biology; multi-/interdisciplinary studies related; nursing (registered nurse training); philosophy; physical therapy; physician assistant; physics; political science and government; pre-dentistry studies; pre-law studies; pre-medical studies; psychology; public relations/image management; religious studies; science teacher education; secondary education; social science teacher education; social studies teacher education; social work; sociology; Spanish; speech and rhetoric; statistics; women's studies.

Maryville College
American Sign Language (ASL); art history, criticism and conservation; art teacher education; atomic/molecular physics; biochemistry; biology teacher education; biology/biological sciences; business administration and management; chemistry; chemistry teacher education; computer and information sciences related; computer science; developmental and child psychology; dramatic/theater arts; economics; education; engineering; English; English as a second/foreign language (teaching); English/language arts teacher education; environmental studies; fine/studio arts; health and physical education; health teacher education; history; history teacher education; international business/trade/commerce; international relations and affairs; mathematics; mathematics and computer science; mathematics teacher education; multi-/interdisciplinary studies related; music performance; music teacher education; nursing (registered nurse training); parks, recreation and leisure; physical education teaching and coaching; physics teacher education; piano and organ; political science and government; psychology; religious studies; sign language interpretation and translation; social studies teacher education; sociology; Spanish; Spanish language teacher education; technical and business writing; voice and opera; wind/percussion instruments.

Maryville University of Saint Louis
Accounting; accounting related; actuarial science; applied mathematics; art teacher education; biological and physical sciences; biology teacher education; biology/biological sciences; biomedical sciences; business administration and management; business/commerce; chemistry; chemistry teacher education; clinical laboratory science/medical technology; computer science; criminology; e-commerce; elementary education; English; English/language arts teacher education; environmental science; environmental studies; fine/studio arts; graphic design; health science; health/medical preparatory programs related; history; history teacher education; industrial and organizational psychology; interdisciplinary studies; interior design; kindergarten/preschool education; legal assistant/

paralegal; liberal arts and sciences/liberal studies; management information systems; marketing/marketing management; mass communication/media; mathematics; mathematics teacher education; middle school education; music therapy; nursing (registered nurse training); psychology; public health; secondary education; social psychology; sociology; sport and fitness administration/management; vocational rehabilitation counseling.

Massachusetts Institute of Technology
Aerospace, aeronautical and astronautical engineering; anthropology; architecture; biology/biological sciences; biomedical/medical engineering; business/commerce; chemical engineering; chemistry; city/urban, community and regional planning; civil engineering; cognitive psychology and psycholinguistics; computer science; creative writing; economics; electrical, electronics and communications engineering; English; environmental/environmental health engineering; foreign languages and literatures; geology/earth science; history; liberal arts and sciences/liberal studies; linguistics; mass communication/media; materials engineering; mathematics; mathematics and computer science; mechanical engineering; music; neuroscience; nuclear engineering; ocean engineering; philosophy; physics; political science and government; science, technology and society.

The Master's College and Seminary (CA)
Accounting; actuarial science; American government and politics; ancient Near Eastern and biblical languages; applied mathematics; biblical studies; biological and physical sciences; biology/biological sciences; business administration and management; computer and information sciences; divinity/ministry; education; elementary education; English; environmental biology; family and consumer sciences/human sciences; finance; foods, nutrition, and wellness; health and physical education; history; kinesiology and exercise science; liberal arts and sciences/liberal studies; management information systems; mass communication/media; mathematics; middle school education; music; music management and merchandising; music teacher education; natural sciences; pastoral studies/counseling; physical education teaching and coaching; physical sciences; piano and organ; political science and government; pre-law studies; pre-medical studies; public relations/image management; radio and television; religious education; religious studies; religious/sacred music; science teacher education; secondary education; speech and rhetoric; theology; voice and opera.

McDaniel College
Art; art history, criticism and conservation; biochemistry; biology/biological sciences; business administration and management; chemistry; communication/speech communication and rhetoric; computer and information sciences; dramatic/theater arts; economics; English; environmental science; French; German; history; kinesiology and exercise science; mathematics; multi-/interdisciplinary studies related; music; philosophy; physical education teaching and coaching; physics; political science and government; psychology; religious studies; social work; sociology; Spanish.

McGill University
Accounting; accounting and finance; African studies; agricultural business and management; agricultural economics; agricultural/biological engineering and bioengineering; agriculture; agronomy and crop science; analytical chemistry; anatomy; animal behavior and ethology; animal sciences; anthropology; applied horticulture; applied mathematics; aquatic biology/limnology; architecture; art history, criticism and conservation; Asian history; Asian studies (East); atmospheric physics and dynamics; atmospheric sciences and meteorology; auditing; bilingual and multilingual education; biochemistry; biological and physical sciences; biology teacher education; biology/biological sciences; biomedical sciences; botany/plant biology; business/commerce; business/managerial economics; Canadian history; Canadian studies; Caribbean studies; cell biology and anatomy; cell biology and histology; chemical engineering; chemistry; chemistry teacher education; civil engineering; classics and languages, literatures and linguistics; cognitive science; computer and

information sciences; computer engineering; computer science; computer software engineering; development economics and international development; dramatic/theater arts; e-commerce; early childhood education; East Asian languages; ecology; economics; education; electrical, electronics and communications engineering; elementary education; English; English as a second/foreign language (teaching); English/language arts teacher education; entrepreneurship; environmental biology; environmental science; environmental studies; European history; finance; food science; foods, nutrition, and wellness; French; French as a second/foreign language (teaching); French language teacher education; genetics; geography; geography teacher education; geology/earth science; geophysics and seismology; German; German studies; health and physical education; health teacher education; Hispanic-American, Puerto Rican, and Mexican-American/Chicano studies; history; history teacher education; human nutrition; human resources management; humanities; hydrology and water resources science; inorganic chemistry; insurance; international business/trade/commerce; international finance; Italian; Italian studies; jazz/jazz studies; Jewish/Judaic studies; kinesiology and exercise science; labor and industrial relations; language interpretation and translation; Latin American studies; legal studies; linguistics; management science; marine biology and biological oceanography; marketing/marketing management; materials engineering; mathematical statistics and probability; mathematics; mathematics and computer science; mathematics teacher education; mechanical engineering; medical microbiology and bacteriology; metallurgical engineering; microbiology; mining and mineral engineering; molecular biology; music; music history, literature, and theory; music pedagogy; music performance; music teacher education; music theory and composition; natural resources management and policy; natural resources/conservation; natural sciences; Near and Middle Eastern studies; neuroanatomy; nursing (registered nurse training); nutrition sciences; operations management; organic chemistry; organizational behavior; philosophy; physical education teaching and coaching; physics; physics teacher education; physiology; piano and organ; planetary astronomy and science; plant sciences; political science and government; psychology; regional studies; religious education; religious studies; religious/sacred music; Russian; Russian studies; science teacher education; secondary education; social science teacher education; social studies teacher education; social work; sociology; soil science and agronomy; Spanish; Spanish and Iberian studies; statistics; taxation; theology; transportation management; urban studies/affairs; violin, viola, guitar and other stringed instruments; voice and opera; wildlife and wildlands science and management; wildlife biology; women's studies; zoology/animal biology.

McKendree University

Accounting; art; art teacher education; athletic training; biology teacher education; biology/biological sciences; business administration and management; business teacher education; chemistry; clinical laboratory science/medical technology; computer science; criminal justice/law enforcement administration; economics; education (K-12); elementary education; English; English/language arts teacher education; finance; history; history teacher education; information science/studies; international relations and affairs; marketing/marketing management; mass communication/media; mathematics; mathematics teacher education; middle school education; music; music teacher education; nursing (registered nurse training); occupational therapy; organizational communication; philosophy; physical education teaching and coaching; political science and government; pre-dentistry studies; pre-law studies; pre-medical studies; pre-veterinary studies; psychology; public relations/image management; religious studies; sales, distribution and marketing; secondary education; social science teacher education; social sciences; social work; sociology; speech and rhetoric; speech/theater education.

Mercer University

African American/Black studies; art; biochemistry; biology/biological sciences; business administration, management and operations related; business/commerce; chemistry; Christian studies; classics and languages, literatures and linguistics; communication and journalism related; community organization and advocacy; computer science; criminal justice/

safety; dramatic/theater arts; economics; education related; elementary education; engineering; English; environmental science; environmental studies; French; German; health/medical preparatory programs related; history; human services; information science/studies; international relations and affairs; journalism; Latin; liberal arts and sciences/liberal studies; mass communication/media; mathematics; middle school education; multi-/interdisciplinary studies related; music; music performance; music related; music teacher education; nursing (registered nurse training); philosophy; physics; political science and government; pre-dentistry studies; pre-medical studies; psychology; regional studies; sociology; Spanish.

Messiah College

Accounting; art history, criticism and conservation; art teacher education; athletic training; biblical studies; biochemistry; biology teacher education; biology/biological sciences; biopsychology; business administration and management; business, management, and marketing related; business/managerial economics; chemistry; chemistry teacher education; civil engineering; clinical nutrition; communication/speech communication and rhetoric; computer science; criminal justice/safety; dramatic/theater arts; e-commerce; early childhood education; economics; elementary education; engineering; English; English/language arts teacher education; entrepreneurship; environmental science; environmental studies; family and community services; fine/studio arts; French; French language teacher education; German; German language teacher education; history; human resources management; humanities; information science/studies; international business/trade/commerce; journalism; kinesiology and exercise science; marketing/marketing management; mathematics; mathematics teacher education; multi-/interdisciplinary studies related; music; music teacher education; nursing (registered nurse training); parks, recreation and leisure; philosophy; physical education teaching and coaching; physics; political science and government; psychology; radio and television; religious education; religious studies; social studies teacher education; social work; sociology; Spanish; Spanish language teacher education; sport and fitness administration/management.

Miami University

Accounting; accounting technology and bookkeeping; administrative assistant and secretarial science; aerospace, aeronautical and astronautical engineering; African American/Black studies; American studies; ancient/classical Greek; anthropology; architecture; art; art history, criticism and conservation; art teacher education; Asian studies (East); athletic training; audiology and speech-language pathology; biochemistry; biology teacher education; biology/biological sciences; botany/plant biology; business administration and management; business/commerce; business/managerial economics; chemical engineering; chemical technology; chemistry; child development; city/urban, community and regional planning; classics and languages, literatures and linguistics; clinical laboratory science/medical technology; computer and information sciences; computer engineering; computer systems analysis; creative writing; data processing and data processing technology; dietetics; dramatic/theater arts; early childhood education; economics; electrical, electronic and communications engineering technology; electrical, electronics and communications engineering; elementary education; engineering physics; engineering technology; engineering/industrial management; English; English/language arts teacher education; environmental design/architecture; family and consumer economics related; family and consumer sciences/home economics teacher education; family and consumer sciences/human sciences; finance; fine/studio arts; French; geography; geology/earth science; German; graphic design; health and physical education; health teacher education; history; human development and family studies; human resources management; industrial engineering; interdisciplinary studies; interior design; international relations and affairs; Italian studies; journalism; kindergarten/preschool education; kinesiology and exercise science; Latin; liberal arts and sciences/liberal studies; linguistics; management information systems; management science; marketing/marketing management; mass communication/media; mathematics; mechanical engineering; mechanical engineering/mechanical technology; medical microbiology and bacteriology; middle school education; modern Greek; multi-/interdisciplinary studies related; music; music performance; music teacher education; nursing (registered nurse training); office management; operations management; operations research; organizational behavior; philosophy; physical education teaching and coaching; physics; political science and government; pre-dentistry studies; pre-law studies; pre-medical studies; pre-veterinary studies; psychology; public administration; purchasing, procurement/acquisitions and contracts management; religious studies; Russian; science teacher education; secondary education; social studies teacher education; social work; sociology; Spanish; special education; speech and rhetoric; speech-language pathology; sport and fitness administration/management; statistics; systems science and theory; technical and business writing; women's studies; wood science and wood products/pulp and paper technology; zoology/animal biology.

Michigan State University

Accounting; advertising; agricultural business and management; agricultural communication/journalism; agricultural economics; agricultural/biological engineering and bioengineering; agriculture and agriculture operations related; American studies; ancient studies; animal sciences; anthropology; apparel and textiles; applied economics; applied mathematics; art; art history, criticism and conservation; art teacher education; astrophysics; audiology and speech-language pathology; biochemistry; biochemistry/biophysics and molecular biology; biological and physical sciences; biology/biological sciences; biomedical/medical engineering; botany/plant biology; business administration and management; chemical engineering; chemical physics; chemistry; chemistry teacher education; child development; city/urban, community and regional planning; civil engineering; clinical laboratory science/medical technology; communication/speech communication and rhetoric; computational mathematics; computer and information science; computer engineering; construction management; criminal justice/law enforcement administration; criminal justice/safety; dietetics; dramatic/theater arts; East Asian languages related; economics; education; electrical, electronics and communications engineering; elementary education; engineering; English; entomology; environmental biology; environmental science; environmental studies; family and community services; family and consumer sciences/home economics teacher education; family and consumer sciences/human sciences; fashion/apparel design; finance; food science; forestry; French; geography; geology/earth science; geophysics and seismology; German; history; horticultural science; hospitality administration; hotel/motel administration; human resources management; humanities; interior design; international relations and affairs; international/global studies; jazz/jazz studies; journalism; kinesiology and exercise science; landscape architecture; logistics and materials management; marketing/marketing management; mass communication/media; materials science; mathematics; mechanical engineering; merchandising; microbiology; music; music pedagogy; music performance; music teacher education; music theory and composition; music therapy; natural resource economics; nursing (registered nurse training); nutrition sciences; operations management; parks, recreation and leisure facilities management; philosophy; physical and theoretical chemistry; physical education teaching and coaching; physical sciences; physics; physiology; plant pathology/phytopathology; political science and government; pre-law studies; pre-medical studies; pre-veterinary studies; psychology; public administration; radio and television; religious studies; Russian; science, technology and society; social science teacher education; social sciences; social work; sociology; soil science and agronomy; Spanish; special education; special education (hearing impaired); special education (specific learning disabilities); statistics; technical and business writing; telecommunications; veterinary technology; veterinary/animal health technology; zoology/animal biology.

Michigan Technological University

Accounting; actuarial science; applied mathematics; audio engineering; biochemistry; bioinformatics; biology teacher education; biology/biological sciences; biology/biotechnology laboratory technician; biomedical/medical engineering; business administration and management; business teacher education; business/managerial economics; chemical engineering; chemical physics; chemistry; civil engineering; civil engineering technology; clinical laboratory science/medical technology; communication/

speech communication and rhetoric; computational mathematics; computer engineering; computer programming; computer science; computer software engineering; computer systems networking and telecommunications; computer teacher education; construction engineering; cytotechnology; digital communication and media/multimedia; ecology; economics; electrical, electronic and communications engineering technology; electrical, electronics and communications engineering; electromechanical technology; engineering; engineering mechanics; engineering physics; engineering technology; English; English/language arts teacher education; environmental science; environmental/environmental health engineering; finance; forestry; forestry technology; general studies; geological/geophysical engineering; geology/earth science; geophysics and seismology; histologic technology/histotechnologist; history; humanities; industrial engineering; information science/studies; liberal arts and sciences/liberal studies; management information systems; marine biology; marketing/marketing management; materials engineering; mathematics; mathematics teacher education; mechanical engineering; mechanical engineering/mechanical technology; medical microbiology and bacteriology; medicinal/pharmaceutical chemistry; metallurgical engineering; microbiology; molecular biochemistry; operations management; physical sciences; physics; pre-dentistry studies; pre-law studies; pre-medical studies; pre-pharmacy studies; pre-veterinary studies; psychology; science teacher education; secondary education; social sciences; statistics; survey technology; system administration; technical and business writing; technology/industrial arts teacher education; theater design and technology; wildlife and wildlands science and management.

Middlebury College

American literature; American studies; art history, criticism and conservation; Asian studies (East); biochemistry; biology/biological sciences; chemistry; Chinese; cinematography and film/video production; classics and languages, literatures and linguistics; computer science; dance; dramatic/theater arts; economics; English; environmental studies; European studies; European studies (Central and Eastern); fine/studio arts; French; geography; geology/earth science; German; history; international relations and affairs; Italian; Japanese; Latin American studies; liberal arts and sciences/liberal studies; mathematics; modern languages; molecular biology; music; neuroscience; philosophy; physics; political science and government; psychology; religious studies; Russian; Russian studies; sociology; Spanish; women's studies.

Milligan College

Accounting; biblical studies; biology/biological sciences; business administration and management; chemistry; communication and media related; computer and information sciences; computer science; early childhood education; education; English; English language and literature related; fine/studio arts; health and physical education; health science; history; humanities; mathematics; music; music teacher education; nursing (registered nurse training); pastoral studies/counseling; psychology; public administration and social service professions related; sociology.

Millsaps College

Accounting; anthropology; art history, criticism and conservation; biology/biological sciences; business administration and management; chemistry; classics and languages, literatures and linguistics; computer science; dramatic/theater arts; economics; education; English; European studies; fine/studio arts; French; geology/earth science; German; history; mathematics; multi-/interdisciplinary studies related; music; philosophy; philosophy and religious studies related; physics; political science and government; psychology; public administration; religious studies; sociology; Spanish.

Mills College

American studies; anthropology; art; art history, criticism and conservation; biochemistry; biology/biological sciences; business/managerial economics; chemistry; comparative literature; computer science; creative writing; cultural studies; dance; developmental and child psychology;

economics; engineering; English; environmental science; environmental studies; fine/studio arts; French; French studies; Hispanic-American, Puerto Rican, and Mexican-American/Chicano studies; history; interdisciplinary studies; intermedia/multimedia; international relations and affairs; liberal arts and sciences/liberal studies; mathematics; music; philosophy; physiological psychology/psychobiology; political science and government; psychology; public policy analysis; sociology; Spanish; women's studies.

Milwaukee School of Engineering

Architectural engineering; biomedical/medical engineering; business administration and management; business/commerce; communication and journalism related; computer engineering; computer software engineering; construction management; electrical, electronic and communications engineering technology; electrical, electronics and communications engineering; engineering; industrial engineering; international business/trade/commerce; management information systems; mechanical engineering; mechanical engineering/mechanical technology; nursing (registered nurse training).

Mississippi College

Accounting; art; art history, criticism and conservation; art teacher education; biochemistry; biology/biological sciences; business administration and management; business teacher education; chemistry; Christian studies; communication and journalism related; communication/speech communication and rhetoric; computer and information sciences; computer science; criminal justice/law enforcement administration; education; elementary education; English; foreign languages and literatures; foreign languages related; French; graphic design; health and physical education; history; interior design; kinesiology and exercise science; language interpretation and translation; legal assistant/paralegal; liberal arts and sciences/liberal studies; marketing/marketing management; mass communication/media; mathematics; music; music performance; music teacher education; music theory and composition; nursing (registered nurse training); physics; piano and organ; political science and government; pre-dentistry studies; pre-law studies; pre-medical studies; pre-pharmacy studies; pre-veterinary studies; psychology; public relations/image management; religious/sacred music; science teacher education; secondary education; social science teacher education; social sciences; social sciences related; social studies teacher education; social work; sociology; Spanish; special education; sport and fitness administration/management; voice and opera.

Missouri State University

Accounting; agribusiness; agricultural teacher education; agriculture; agronomy and crop science; ancient studies; animal sciences; anthropology; apparel and textiles; art; art history, criticism and conservation; art teacher education; athletic training; audiology and speech-language pathology; biology teacher education; biology/biological sciences; business administration and management; business administration, management and operations related; business teacher education; business/commerce; cartography; cell and molecular biology; chemistry; chemistry teacher education; city/urban, community and regional planning; clinical laboratory science/medical technology; communication/speech communication and rhetoric; computer science; construction management; dance; design and visual communications; dietetics; dramatic/theater arts; early childhood education; economics; education (specific subject areas) related; elementary education; engineering/industrial management; English; English/language arts teacher education; entrepreneurship; family and consumer sciences/home economics teacher education; finance; fine/studio arts; French; French language teacher education; geography; geology/earth science; German; German language teacher education; gerontology; history; history teacher education; horticultural science; hospitality administration; housing and human environments; human development and family studies; insurance; intermedia/multimedia; journalism; Latin; logistics and materials management; management information systems; marketing/marketing management; mass communication/media; mathematics; mathematics teacher education; middle school education; molecular biology; music; music performance; music

teacher education; nursing (registered nurse training); parks, recreation and leisure; philosophy; physical education teaching and coaching; physical science technologies related; physics; physics teacher education; political science and government; psychology; public administration; radiologic technology/science; religious studies; respiratory care therapy; science teacher education; social work; sociology; Spanish; Spanish language teacher education; special education; technical and business writing; visual and performing arts; wildlife and wildlands science and management.

Missouri University of Science and Technology

Aerospace, aeronautical and astronautical engineering; agricultural/biological engineering and bioengineering; applied mathematics; architectural engineering; biology/biological sciences; business administration and management; business/commerce; ceramic sciences and engineering; chemical engineering; chemistry; civil engineering; computer and information sciences and support services related; computer engineering; computer science; economics; electrical, electronics and communications engineering; engineering/industrial management; English; environmental/environmental health engineering; geological/geophysical engineering; geology/earth science; geophysics and seismology; history; industrial engineering; information science/studies; manufacturing engineering; materials engineering; mechanical engineering; metallurgical engineering; mining and mineral engineering; nuclear engineering; petroleum engineering; philosophy; physics; pre-dentistry studies; pre-law studies; pre-medical studies; psychology; secondary education; systems engineering.

Moravian College

Accounting; art; art history, criticism and conservation; art teacher education; biochemistry; biology teacher education; biology/biological sciences; business administration and management; chemistry; chemistry teacher education; classics and languages, literatures and linguistics; clinical laboratory science/medical technology; clinical psychology; computer science; creative writing; criminal justice/law enforcement administration; dramatic/theater arts; economics; education; elementary education; English; English language and literature related; environmental studies; experimental psychology; fine/studio arts; foreign language teacher education; French; French language teacher education; geology/earth science; German; German language teacher education; German studies; graphic design; history; history teacher education; industrial and organizational psychology; international business/trade/commerce; mathematics; mathematics teacher education; music; music performance; music teacher education; music theory and composition; natural resources management; nursing (registered nurse training); philosophy; physics; physics teacher education; political science and government; psychology; religious studies; religious/sacred music; science teacher education; secondary education; social psychology; social sciences; social studies teacher education; sociology; Spanish; Spanish language teacher education; theater literature, history and criticism.

Morehouse College

African American/Black studies; art; biology/biological sciences; business administration and management; chemistry; computer and information sciences; dramatic/theater arts; economics; education; engineering; English; French; general studies; health and physical education; history; international relations and affairs; mathematics; music; philosophy; physics; political science and government; psychology; religious studies; sociology; Spanish; urban studies/affairs.

Mount Allison University

Accounting; American studies; ancient/classical Greek; anthropology; applied mathematics; art history, criticism and conservation; biochemistry; biological and physical sciences; biology/biological sciences; biopsychology; business administration and management; business/commerce; business/managerial economics; Canadian studies; chemistry; classics and languages, literatures and linguistics; computer science; dramatic/theater arts; drawing; economics; English; environmental studies; fine/studio arts; French; geography; geology/earth science; German; history; humanities; interdisciplinary studies; international business/trade/

commerce; international relations and affairs; Latin; liberal arts and sciences/liberal studies; literature; mathematics; mathematics and computer science; medieval and Renaissance studies; modern languages; music; music history, literature, and theory; music performance; natural sciences; philosophy; photography; physics; physiological psychology/psychobiology; piano and organ; political science and government; pre-dentistry studies; pre-law studies; pre-medical studies; pre-pharmacy studies; pre-theology/pre-ministerial studies; pre-veterinary studies; printmaking; psychology; religious studies; Romance languages; sculpture; sociology; Spanish; violin, viola, guitar and other stringed instruments; voice and opera; wind/percussion instruments.

Mount Holyoke College
African American/Black studies; American studies; ancient studies; ancient/classical Greek; anthropology; architecture related; area, ethnic, cultural, and gender studies related; art history, criticism and conservation; Asian studies; astronomy; biochemistry; biology/biological sciences; chemistry; classics and languages, literatures and linguistics; computer science; dance; dramatic/theater arts; economics; education; education related; engineering; English; environmental studies; European studies; film/cinema studies; fine/studio arts; French; geography; geology/earth science; German; history; interdisciplinary studies; international relations and affairs; Italian; Jewish/Judaic studies; Latin; Latin American studies; mathematics; medieval and Renaissance studies; modern Greek; music; neuroscience; philosophy; physics; political science and government; psychology; psychology related; religious studies; Romance languages; Russian studies; social sciences related; sociology; Spanish; statistics; women's studies.

Mount Saint Vincent University
Accounting; adult development and aging; anthropology; applied mathematics; art teacher education; biological and physical sciences; biology/biological sciences; business administration and management; chemistry; child development; computer and information sciences; computer systems analysis; developmental and child psychology; dietetics; economics; education; elementary education; English; family and consumer economics related; fine/studio arts; foods, nutrition, and wellness; French; German; gerontology; history; hospitality administration; hotel/motel administration; human ecology; humanities; information science/studies; interdisciplinary studies; kindergarten/preschool education; liberal arts and sciences/liberal studies; linguistics; literature; management information systems; marketing research; marketing/marketing management; mathematics; mathematics and computer science; modern languages; nutrition sciences; peace studies and conflict resolution; philosophy; political science and government; psychology; public relations/image management; reading teacher education; religious studies; secondary education; social sciences; sociology; Spanish; special products marketing; statistics; tourism and travel services management; tourism and travel services marketing; women's studies.

Muhlenberg College
Accounting; American studies; anthropology; art; biochemistry; biology/biological sciences; business administration and management; chemistry; dance; dramatic/theater arts; economics; economics related; English; environmental science; French; German; history; international relations and affairs; mathematics; music; natural sciences; neuroscience; philosophy; physical sciences; physics; political science and government; political science and government related; psychology; religious studies; Russian studies; social sciences; sociology; Spanish.

Murray State University
Accounting; administrative assistant and secretarial science; agricultural business and management; agricultural teacher education; agriculture; apparel and textiles; art teacher education; audiology and speech-language pathology; biology teacher education; biology/biological sciences; business administration and management; business teacher education; business/commerce; chemical engineering; chemical technology; chemistry; chemistry teacher education; child care provision; civil engineering technology; clinical laboratory science/medical technology; computer and

information sciences; computer engineering technology; criminal justice/safety; drafting and design technology; dramatic/theater arts; early childhood education; economics; electromechanical technology; elementary education; engineering; engineering technology; English; English as a second/foreign language (teaching); English/language arts teacher education; environmental engineering technology; executive assistant/executive secretary; family and consumer economics related; family and consumer sciences/home economics teacher education; finance; fine/studio arts; fishing and fisheries sciences and management; foods, nutrition, and wellness; foodservice systems administration; foreign language teacher education; French; French language teacher education; general studies; geography; geology/earth science; German; German language teacher education; graphic and printing equipment operation/production; health teacher education; history; history teacher education; human development and family studies; industrial technology; information science/studies; international business/trade/commerce; international relations and affairs; journalism; kinesiology and exercise science; liberal arts and sciences/liberal studies; library science; management information systems; manufacturing technology; marketing/marketing management; mass communication/media; mathematics; mathematics teacher education; mechanical drafting and CAD/CADD; mechanical engineering; mechanical engineering/mechanical technology; middle school education; military technologies; music; music teacher education; nursing (registered nurse training); occupational safety and health technology; office management; parks, recreation and leisure facilities management; perioperative/operating room and surgical nursing; philosophy; physical education teaching and coaching; physics; physics teacher education; political science and government; psychology; public administration; public relations, advertising, and applied communication related; public relations/image management; radio and television; reading teacher education; science teacher education; secondary education; social science teacher education; social studies teacher education; social work; sociology; Spanish; Spanish language teacher education; special education; speech and rhetoric; speech teacher education; speech therapy; technical and business writing; technology/industrial arts teacher education; telecommunications; trade and industrial teacher education; veterinary/animal health technology; water quality and wastewater treatment management and recycling technology; wildlife and wildlands science and management.

Nebraska Wesleyan University
Accounting; art; athletic training; biochemistry; biochemistry/biophysics and molecular biology; biology/biological sciences; biopsychology; business administration and management; business, management, and marketing related; chemistry; communication/speech communication and rhetoric; computer science; dramatic/theater arts; dramatic/theater arts and stagecraft related; economics; elementary education; English; English/language arts teacher education; French; German; health and physical education; history; industrial and organizational psychology; information science/studies; interdisciplinary studies; international business/trade/commerce; international/global studies; kinesiology and exercise science; mathematics; middle school education; music; music performance; music teacher education; nursing administration; philosophy; physical education teaching and coaching; physics; political communication; political science and government; psychology; religious studies; science teacher education; social science teacher education; social work; sociology; Spanish; special education; speech and rhetoric; sport and fitness administration/management; women's studies.

New College of Florida
Anthropology; art history, criticism and conservation; biology/biological sciences; chemistry; classics and classical languages related; comparative literature; economics; English; environmental studies; fine/studio arts; foreign languages and literatures; French; French studies; general studies; German; Germanic languages; history; humanities; international/global studies; liberal arts and sciences/liberal studies; marine biology and biological oceanography; mathematics; medieval and Renaissance studies; music; music history, literature, and theory; natural sciences; neurobiology and neurophysiology; philosophy; physics; political science and

government; psychology; public policy analysis; religious studies; Russian; social sciences; sociology; Spanish; urban studies/affairs.

New Jersey Institute of Technology

Actuarial science; applied mathematics; architecture; biology/biological sciences; biomedical/medical engineering; business administration and management; chemical engineering; chemistry; civil engineering; computer and information sciences; computer and information sciences and support services related; computer engineering; electrical, electronics and communications engineering; engineering science; engineering technologies related; engineering technology; environmental/environmental health engineering; geological/geophysical engineering; history; industrial engineering; information science/studies; manufacturing engineering; mechanical engineering; natural resources/conservation; nursing (registered nurse training); nursing science; physics related; science, technology and society; technical and business writing.

New Mexico Institute of Mining and Technology

Biology/biological sciences; business administration and management; chemical engineering; chemistry; civil engineering; computer science; electrical, electronics and communications engineering; engineering mechanics; environmental studies; environmental/environmental health engineering; general studies; geology/earth science; geophysics and seismology; information technology; materials engineering; mathematics; mechanical engineering; mining and mineral engineering; petroleum engineering; physical sciences; physical sciences related; physics; psychology; technical and business writing.

New York School of Interior Design

Interior design.

New York University

Accounting; actuarial science; African American/Black studies; anthropology; archeology; area, ethnic, cultural, and gender studies related; art; art history, criticism and conservation; Asian studies (East); biochemistry; biology teacher education; biology/biological sciences; business administration and management; business, management, and marketing related; business/managerial economics; chemistry; chemistry teacher education; cinematography and film/video production; city/urban, community and regional planning; classics and languages, literatures and linguistics; communication/speech communication and rhetoric; comparative literature; computer and information sciences; computer programming; computer science; dance; dental hygiene; diagnostic medical sonography and ultrasound technology; digital communication and media/multimedia; dramatic/theater arts; economics; education; elementary education; engineering related; English; English/language arts teacher education; European studies; film/cinema studies; finance; fine/studio arts; foods, nutrition, and wellness; foreign language teacher education; French; French language teacher education; general studies; German; graphic communications; health information/medical records technology; health/health care administration; Hebrew; history; hospitality administration; hotel/motel administration; human services; humanities; information science/studies; interdisciplinary studies; international business/trade/commerce; international relations and affairs; Italian; Jewish/Judaic studies; journalism; kindergarten/preschool education; Latin; Latin American studies; liberal arts and sciences/liberal studies; linguistics; management information systems; marketing/marketing management; mass communication/media; mathematics; mathematics and statistics related; mathematics teacher education; medieval and Renaissance studies; middle school education; modern Greek; music; music management and merchandising; music performance; music teacher education; music theory and composition; Near and Middle Eastern studies; neuroscience; nursing (registered nurse training); operations research; philosophy; photography; physical therapist assistant; physics; physics teacher education; piano and organ; playwriting and screenwriting; political science and government; Portuguese; pre-dentistry studies; pre-medical studies; psychology; radio and television; real estate; religious studies; Romance languages; Russian; secondary education; social sciences; social studies teacher education; social work;

sociology; Spanish; special education; special education (speech or language impaired); sport and fitness administration/management; statistics; theater literature, history and criticism; tourism and travel services management; urban studies/affairs; voice and opera.

North Carolina State University

Accounting; aerospace, aeronautical and astronautical engineering; agribusiness; agricultural and extension education; agricultural and food products processing; agricultural business and management; agricultural economics; agricultural teacher education; agricultural/biological engineering and bioengineering; agriculture; agronomy and crop science; American government and politics; animal sciences; anthropology; apparel and textile manufacturing; apparel and textile marketing management; applied mathematics; architecture; arts management; biochemistry; biology teacher education; biology/biological sciences; biomedical/medical engineering; botany/plant biology; business administration and management; chemical engineering; chemistry; chemistry teacher education; civil engineering; communication/speech communication and rhetoric; computer engineering; computer science; construction engineering; construction management; creative writing; criminology; design and applied arts related; design and visual communications; ecology; economics; education; electrical, electronics and communications engineering; engineering; English; English/language arts teacher education; environmental design/architecture; environmental science; environmental studies; environmental/environmental health engineering; film/cinema studies; finance; fishing and fisheries sciences and management; food science; foreign language teacher education; forest/forest resources management; French; French language teacher education; geology/earth science; graphic design; health occupations teacher education; history; history teacher education; horticultural science; human resources management; hydrology and water resources science; industrial design; industrial engineering; information technology; landscape architecture; landscaping and groundskeeping; liberal arts and sciences/liberal studies; marketing/marketing management; mass communication/media; materials engineering; materials science; mathematics; mathematics teacher education; mechanical engineering; meteorology; microbiology; middle school education; natural resources management and policy; natural resources/conservation; nuclear engineering; oceanography (chemical and physical); paleontology; parks, recreation and leisure facilities management; parks, recreation, and leisure related; philosophy; physics; physics related; physics teacher education; plant protection and integrated pest management; political science and government; political science and government related; poultry science; psychology; psychology related; public policy analysis; public relations/image management; religious studies; sales and marketing/marketing and distribution teacher education; science teacher education; science, technology and society; secondary education; social studies teacher education; social work; sociology; soil science and agronomy; Spanish; Spanish language teacher education; sport and fitness administration/management; statistics; technology/industrial arts teacher education; textile science; textile sciences and engineering; tourism and travel services management; turf and turfgrass management; wildlife and wildlands science and management; wood science and wood products/pulp and paper technology; zoology/animal biology.

North Central College

Accounting; actuarial science; applied mathematics; art; art teacher education; Asian studies (East); athletic training; biochemistry; biological and physical sciences; biology/biological sciences; business administration and management; chemistry; classics and languages, literatures and linguistics; creative writing; dramatic/theater arts; dramatic/theater arts and stagecraft related; economics; education; elementary education; English; finance; French; German; graphic design; history; human resources management; humanities; international business/trade/commerce; Japanese; jazz/jazz studies; journalism; kinesiology and exercise science; liberal arts and sciences/liberal studies; management information systems; marketing/marketing management; mathematics; medical radiologic technology; multi-/interdisciplinary studies related; music; music teacher education; nuclear medical technology; organizational communication; philosophy; physical education teaching and coaching; physics; political science and government; pre-dentistry studies; pre-law studies; pre-medical studies; pre-veterinary studies; psychology; radio and television; religious studies; secondary education; small business administration; social sciences; sociology; Spanish; speech and rhetoric; sport and fitness administration/management.

Northwestern College (IA)

Accounting; actuarial science; art; art teacher education; athletic training; biology teacher education; biology/biological sciences; business administration and management; business teacher education; chemistry; cinematography and film/video production; clinical laboratory science/medical technology; computer science; dramatic/theater arts; economics; education (K-12); elementary education; English; environmental biology; graphic design; history; humanities; journalism; kinesiology and exercise science; mathematics; music; music teacher education; nursing (registered nurse training); philosophy; physical education teaching and coaching; political science and government; psychology; religious education; religious studies; secondary education; social work; sociology; Spanish; speech and rhetoric; speech/theater education.

Northwestern College (MN)

Accounting; animation, interactive technology, video graphics and special effects; art teacher education; biblical studies; biology/biological sciences; business administration and management; communication/speech communication and rhetoric; creative writing; criminal justice/safety; dramatic/theater arts; early childhood education; elementary education; engineering; English; English as a second/foreign language (teaching); English/language arts teacher education; finance; fine/studio arts; graphic design; health and physical education; history; international business/trade/commerce; journalism; kinesiology and exercise science; liberal arts and sciences/liberal studies; management information systems; marketing/marketing management; mathematics; mathematics teacher education; missionary studies and missiology; multi-/interdisciplinary studies related; music; music performance; music teacher education; music theory and composition; pastoral counseling and specialized ministries related; physical education teaching and coaching; piano and organ; pre-theology/pre-ministerial studies; psychology; public relations/image management; radio and television; social studies teacher education; technical and business writing; theological and ministerial studies related; violin, viola, guitar and other stringed instruments; voice and opera; youth ministry.

Northwestern University

African studies; African American/Black studies; American studies; anthropology; applied mathematics; area studies related; art; art history, criticism and conservation; Asian studies; astronomy; audiology and hearing sciences; audiology and speech-language pathology; biochemistry; biological and physical sciences; biology/biological sciences; biomedical/medical engineering; Caribbean studies; cell biology and histology; chemical engineering; chemistry; civil engineering; classics and languages, literatures and linguistics; cognitive psychology and psycholinguistics; communication and media related; communication disorders; communication/speech communication and rhetoric; community organization and advocacy; community psychology; comparative literature; computer and information sciences; computer engineering; computer science; counseling psychology; dance; dramatic/theater arts; East Asian languages related; ecology; economics; education; electrical, electronics and communications engineering; engineering; engineering related; engineering science; English; environmental science; environmental studies; environmental/environmental health engineering; film/cinema studies; French; general studies; geography; geology/earth science; German; history; humanities; industrial engineering; information science/studies; interdisciplinary studies; international relations and affairs; Italian; jazz/jazz studies; journalism; legal studies; liberal arts and sciences/liberal studies; linguistics; manufacturing engineering; materials engineering; materials science; mathematics; mathematics teacher education; mechanical engineering; molecular biology; multi-/interdisciplinary studies related; music; music history, literature, and theory; music performance; music related; music teacher education; music theory and composition; musicology and ethnomusicology; neuroscience; organizational behavior;

philosophy; physics; piano and organ; political science and government; pre-medical studies; psychology; public policy analysis; radio and television; religious studies; science, technology and society; secondary education; Slavic languages; Slavic studies; social and philosophical foundations of education; social sciences related; sociology; South Asian languages; Spanish; special education (specific learning disabilities); speech and rhetoric; speech therapy; speech-language pathology; statistics; theater literature, history and criticism; urban studies/affairs; violin, viola, guitar and other stringed instruments; visual and performing arts; voice and opera; wind/percussion instruments; women's studies.

Oberlin College

African American/Black studies; anthropology; archeology; art; art history, criticism and conservation; Asian studies (East); biochemistry; biology/biological sciences; chemistry; classics and languages, literatures and linguistics; comparative literature; computer science; creative writing; dance; dramatic/theater arts; ecology; economics; English; environmental studies; fine/studio arts; French; geology/earth science; German; history; interdisciplinary studies; jazz/jazz studies; Jewish/Judaic studies; Latin; Latin American studies; legal studies; mathematics; modern Greek; music; music history, literature, and theory; music teacher education; music theory and composition; Near and Middle Eastern studies; neuroscience; philosophy; physics; physiological psychology/psychobiology; piano and organ; political science and government; psychology; religious studies; Romance languages; Russian; Russian studies; sociology; Spanish; violin, viola, guitar and other stringed instruments; voice and opera; wind/percussion instruments; women's studies.

Occidental College

American studies; anthropology; art history, criticism and conservation; Asian studies; biochemistry; biology/biological sciences; business/managerial economics; chemistry; cognitive psychology and psycholinguistics; cognitive science; comparative literature; dramatic/theater arts; economics; English; fine/studio arts; French; geology/earth science; geophysics and seismology; history; international relations and affairs; kinesiology and exercise science; mathematics; music; philosophy; physics; physiological psychology/psychobiology; political science and government; psychology; public policy analysis; religious studies; sociology; Spanish; women's studies.

Oglethorpe University

Accounting; American studies; art; art history, criticism and conservation; biology/biological sciences; biopsychology; business administration and management; business/managerial economics; chemistry; communication/speech communication and rhetoric; economics; engineering; English; French; history; interdisciplinary studies; international relations and affairs; mass communication/media; mathematics; philosophy; physics; political science and government; pre-dentistry studies; pre-law studies; pre-medical studies; pre-veterinary studies; psychology; social work; sociology; Spanish; theater/theater arts management; urban studies/affairs.

Ohio Northern University

Accounting; art; art teacher education; athletic training; biochemistry; biology teacher education; biology/biological sciences; business administration and management; business/commerce; ceramic arts and ceramics; chemistry; chemistry related; chemistry teacher education; civil engineering; civil engineering related; clinical laboratory science/medical technology; commercial and advertising art; communication and journalism related; communication/speech communication and rhetoric; computer engineering; computer engineering related; computer science; creative writing; criminal justice/law enforcement administration; criminal justice/police science; criminal justice/safety; design and visual communications; dramatic/theater arts; early childhood education; education (multiple levels); education related; electrical, electronics and communications engineering; elementary education; engineering; engineering related; English; English/language arts teacher education; environmental studies; fine/studio arts; foreign language teacher education; French; French language teacher education; general studies; German language teacher education; Germanic languages related; graphic design; health and physical education; health and physical education related; health teacher education; history; history teacher education; industrial arts; industrial technology; international business/trade/commerce; international relations and affairs; journalism; kindergarten/preschool education; kinesiology and exercise science; management science; management sciences and quantitative methods related; mass communication/media; mathematics; mathematics related; mathematics teacher education; mechanical engineering; medicinal and pharmaceutical chemistry; middle school education; molecular biology; music; music management and merchandising; music performance; music related; music teacher education; organizational communication; painting; pharmacy; pharmacy, pharmaceutical sciences, and administration related; philosophy; philosophy related; physical education teaching and coaching; physics; physics related; physics teacher education; political science and government; pre-dentistry studies; pre-law studies; pre-medical studies; pre-theology/pre-ministerial studies; pre-veterinary studies; printmaking; psychology; psychology related; public relations/image management; radio and television; religious studies; religious studies related; science teacher education; sculpture; secondary education; social studies teacher education; sociology; Spanish; Spanish language teacher education; sport and fitness administration/management; statistics; statistics related; technical and business writing; theater/theater arts management; visual and performing arts; visual and performing arts related.

The Ohio State University

Accounting; actuarial science; aerospace, aeronautical and astronautical engineering; African studies; African American/Black studies; agricultural and food products processing; agricultural business and management; agricultural economics; agricultural teacher education; agricultural/biological engineering and bioengineering; agronomy and crop science; animal genetics; animal sciences; anthropology; apparel and textiles; Arabic; architecture; art; art history, criticism and conservation; art teacher education; Asian studies (East); Asian-American studies; astronomy; athletic training; audiology and speech-language pathology; aviation/airway management; avionics maintenance technology; biochemistry; biology/biological sciences; biotechnology; botany/plant biology; business administration and management; business family and consumer sciences/human sciences; business/managerial economics; ceramic arts and ceramics; ceramic sciences and engineering; chemical engineering; chemistry; Chinese; city/urban, community and regional planning; civil engineering; classics and languages, literatures and linguistics; clinical laboratory science/medical technology; clothing/textiles; commercial and advertising art; communication and journalism related; communication/speech communication and rhetoric; comparative literature; computer and information sciences; computer engineering; computer science; creative writing; criminal justice/safety; criminology; cultural studies; dance; dental hygiene; design and visual communications; development economics and international development; dietetics; drama and dance teacher education; dramatic/theater arts; drawing; economics; electrical, electronics and communications engineering; engineering physics; English; entomology; environmental education; environmental studies; chemistry; European studies (Western); family resource management; finance; fine/studio arts; fishing and fisheries sciences and management; folklore; food science; foods, nutrition, and wellness; forestry; French; geography; geology/earth science; German; health information/medical records administration; health professions related; Hebrew; history; history related; horticultural science; hospitality administration; human development and family studies; human resources management; humanities; industrial design; industrial engineering; information science/studies; insurance; interior design; international business/trade/commerce; international relations and affairs; Islamic studies; Italian; Japanese; jazz/jazz studies; Jewish/Judaic studies; journalism; kinesiology and exercise science; landscape architecture; Latin American studies; linguistics; logistics and materials management; management information systems; marketing/marketing management; materials engineering; materials science; mathematics; mathematics and statistics related; mechanical engineering; medical microbiology and bacteriology; medical radiologic technology; metallurgical engineering; modern Greek; music; music history, literature,

and theory; music performance; music teacher education; music theory and composition; natural resources management; natural resources management and policy; Near and Middle Eastern studies; nursing (registered nurse training); nursing science; occupational therapy; operations management; painting; peace studies and conflict resolution; pharmacy; philosophy; physical education teaching and coaching; physical therapy; physics; piano and organ; plant pathology/phytopathology; plant sciences; political science and government; Portuguese; printmaking; psychology; radiologic technology/science; real estate; religious studies; respiratory care therapy; Russian; Russian studies; sculpture; social sciences; social work; sociology; soil conservation; Spanish; special education; survey technology; systems engineering; technical teacher education; technology/industrial arts teacher education; turf and turfgrass management; voice and opera; wildlife and wildlands science and management; women's studies; zoology/animal biology.

Ohio Wesleyan University

Accounting; African American/Black studies; ancient studies; animal genetics; anthropology; art history, criticism and conservation; art teacher education; art therapy; Asian studies (East); astronomy; astrophysics; biology teacher education; biology/biological sciences; botany/plant biology; broadcast journalism; business administration and management; business teacher education; business/managerial economics; chemistry; chemistry teacher education; classics and languages, literatures and linguistics; computer science; creative writing; cultural studies; drama and dance teacher education; dramatic/theater arts; early childhood education; economics; education; education (K-12); education (multiple levels); elementary education; engineering related; engineering science; English; environmental studies; fine/studio arts; foreign language teacher education; French; French language teacher education; general studies; genetics; geography; geology/earth science; German; German language teacher education; health teacher education; history; history teacher education; humanities; international business/trade/commerce; international relations and affairs; journalism; kindergarten/preschool education; Latin American studies; Latin teacher education; literature; mathematics; mathematics teacher education; medical microbiology and bacteriology; medieval and Renaissance studies; middle school education; multi-/interdisciplinary studies related; music; music performance; music teacher education; neuroscience; philosophy; physical education teaching and coaching; physics; physics teacher education; political science and government; pre-dentistry studies; pre-law studies; pre-medical studies; pre-theology/pre-ministerial studies; pre-veterinary studies; psychology; psychology teacher education; public administration; religious studies; secondary education; social studies teacher education; sociology; Spanish; Spanish language teacher education; statistics; urban studies/affairs; women's studies; zoology/animal biology.

Oklahoma Baptist University

Accounting; advertising; ancient Near Eastern and biblical languages; applied art; art; art teacher education; athletic training; biblical studies; biological and physical sciences; biology teacher education; biology/biological sciences; broadcast journalism; business administration and management; chemistry; chemistry teacher education; child development; child guidance; computer and information sciences; computer management; computer programming (specific applications); computer science; computer systems analysis; developmental and child psychology; divinity/ministry; drama and dance teacher education; dramatic/theater arts; education; elementary education; English; English composition; English/language arts teacher education; finance; fine/studio arts; French; French language teacher education; German; German language teacher education; health and physical education; history; history teacher education; human resources management; humanities; information science/studies; interdisciplinary studies; international business/trade/commerce; international marketing; journalism; kindergarten/preschool education; kinesiology and exercise science; management information systems; marketing/marketing management; marriage and family therapy/counseling; mass communication/media; mathematics; mathematics teacher education; missionary studies and missiology; museum studies; music; music teacher education; music theory and composition; natural sciences;

nursing (registered nurse training); parks, recreation and leisure; pastoral studies/counseling; philosophy; physical education teaching and coaching; physical sciences; physics; piano and organ; political science and government; pre-dentistry studies; pre-law studies; pre-medical studies; pre-pharmacy studies; pre-veterinary studies; psychology; public relations/image management; radio and television; religious education; religious studies; religious/sacred music; science teacher education; secondary education; social science teacher education; social sciences; social studies teacher education; social work; sociology; Spanish; Spanish language teacher education; special education; special education (emotionally disturbed); special education (mentally retarded); special education (specific learning disabilities); speech and rhetoric; speech teacher education; telecommunications; theology; voice and opera; wind/percussion instruments.

Oklahoma City University

Accounting; advertising; American studies; art history, criticism and conservation; art teacher education; arts management; biochemistry; biological and physical sciences; biology/biological sciences; biophysics; broadcast journalism; business administration and management; business/commerce; business/managerial economics; chemistry; cinematography and film/video production; commercial and advertising art; computer science; corrections; criminal justice/law enforcement administration; criminal justice/police science; dance; dramatic/theater arts; education; elementary education; English; finance; fine/studio arts; French; German; history; humanities; international business/trade/commerce; journalism; kindergarten/preschool education; kinesiology and exercise science; liberal arts and sciences/liberal studies; management information systems; marketing/marketing management; mass communication/media; mathematics; Montessori teacher education; music; music management and merchandising; music teacher education; music theory and composition; nursing (registered nurse training); philosophy; physical education teaching and coaching; physics; piano and organ; political science and government; pre-dentistry studies; pre-law studies; pre-medical studies; pre-nursing studies; pre-pharmacy studies; pre-veterinary studies; psychology; public relations/image management; radio and television; religious education; religious studies; religious/sacred music; science teacher education; secondary education; sociology; Spanish; speech and rhetoric; speech/theater education; theater design and technology; violin, viola, guitar and other stringed instruments; voice and opera; wind/percussion instruments.

Oklahoma State University

Accounting; aeronautics/aviation/aerospace science and technology; aerospace, aeronautical and astronautical engineering; agricultural business and management; agricultural communication/journalism; agricultural economics; agricultural teacher education; agriculture; American studies; animal sciences; architectural engineering; architecture; art; athletic training; biochemistry; biochemistry, biophysics and molecular biology related; biology/biological sciences; biomedical/medical engineering; botany/plant biology; broadcast journalism; business/commerce; business/managerial economics; cell and molecular biology; chemical engineering; chemistry; civil engineering; communication disorders; computer management; computer science; construction management; dramatic/theater arts; ecology; economics; education; electrical, electronic and communications engineering technology; electrical, electronics and communications engineering; elementary education; engineering; engineering technology; English; entomology; environmental science; environmental studies; finance; fire protection and safety technology; food science; forestry; French; general studies; geography; geology/earth science; German; health science; history; horticultural science; hotel/motel administration; human development and family studies; industrial engineering; interior design; international business/trade/commerce; journalism; landscape architecture; liberal arts and sciences/liberal studies; management information systems; management science; marketing/marketing management; mathematics; mechanical engineering/mechanical technology; microbiology; music; music teacher education; nutritional sciences; philosophy; physical education teaching and coaching; physics; physiol-

ogy; plant sciences; political science and government; pre-veterinary studies; psychology; public health education and promotion; Russian; secondary education; sociology; Spanish; speech and rhetoric; statistics; technical teacher education; zoology/animal biology.

Pacific Lutheran University

Anthropology; art; biology/biological sciences; business administration and management; chemistry; Chinese; Chinese studies; classics and languages, literatures and linguistics; computer science; economics; education; engineering; English; environmental studies; fine/studio arts; French; geological and earth sciences/geosciences related; geology/earth science; German; history; international/global studies; mathematics; military studies; movement therapy and movement education; music; music teacher education; Norwegian; nursing (registered nurse training); philosophy; physics; political science and government; pre-law; pre-medical studies; psychology; religious studies; Scandinavian studies; social work; sociology; Spanish; theology; women's studies.

Pacific University

Accounting; art; art teacher education; athletic training; biology/biological sciences; broadcast journalism; business administration and management; chemistry; Chinese; computer science; creative writing; dramatic/theater arts; economics; education; elementary education; English; environmental studies; finance; French; German; health science; history; humanities; international relations and affairs; Japanese; journalism; kindergarten/preschool education; kinesiology and exercise science; liberal arts and sciences/liberal studies; literature; marketing/marketing management; mass communication/media; mathematics; modern languages; music; music performance; music teacher education; philosophy; physics; political science and government; pre-dentistry studies; pre-medical studies; pre-veterinary studies; psychology; radio and television; secondary education; social work; sociology; Spanish; telecommunications.

Peabody Conservatory of Music of The Johns Hopkins University

Audio engineering; jazz/jazz studies; music; music teacher education; piano and organ; violin, viola, guitar and other stringed instruments; voice and opera; wind/percussion instruments.

Penn State University Park

Accounting; acting; actuarial science; adult and continuing education administration; advertising; aerospace, aeronautical and astronautical engineering; African American/Black studies; agribusiness; agricultural and extension education; agricultural business and management related; agricultural mechanization; agricultural/biological engineering and bioengineering; agriculture; agronomy and crop science; animal sciences; animal sciences related; anthropology; applied economics; archeology; architectural engineering; architecture; art; art history, criticism and conservation; art teacher education; Asian studies (East); astronomy; atmospheric sciences and meteorology; biochemistry; biological and biomedical sciences related; biological and physical sciences; biology/biological sciences; biology/biotechnology laboratory technician; biomedical/medical engineering; business/commerce; business/managerial economics; chemical engineering; chemistry; civil engineering; classics and languages, literatures and linguistics; communication and journalism related; communication disorders; communication/speech communication and rhetoric; comparative literature; computer and information sciences; computer engineering; criminal justice/law enforcement administration; dietitian assistant; economics; electrical, electronics and communications engineering; elementary education; engineering science; English; environmental/environmental health engineering; film/cinema studies; finance; food science; foreign language teacher education; forest sciences and biology; forestry technology; French; geography; geological and earth sciences/geosciences related; geology/earth science; German; graphic design; health/health care administration; history; horticultural science; hospitality administration related; human development and family studies; human nutrition; industrial engineering; information science/studies; international business/trade/commerce;

international relations and affairs; Italian; Japanese; Jewish/Judaic studies; journalism; kinesiology and exercise science; labor and industrial relations; landscape architecture; landscaping and groundskeeping; Latin American studies; liberal arts and sciences/liberal studies; management information systems; management sciences and quantitative methods related; marketing/marketing management; materials science; mathematics; mechanical engineering; medical microbiology and bacteriology; medieval and Renaissance studies; mining and mineral engineering; music; music performance; music teacher education; natural resources and conservation related; natural resources/conservation; nuclear engineering; nursing (registered nurse training); organizational behavior; parks, recreation and leisure facilities management; petroleum engineering; philosophy; physics; political science and government; pre-medical studies; psychology; rehabilitation and therapeutic professions related; religious studies; Russian; secondary education; sociology; soil science and agronomy; Spanish; special education; statistics; theater design and technology; toxicology; turf and turfgrass management; visual and performing arts; women's studies.

Pepperdine University (CA)
Accounting; advertising; art; art history, criticism and conservation; athletic training; biology/biological sciences; business administration and management; chemistry; communication/speech communication and rhetoric; computer science; dramatic/theater arts; dramatic/theater arts and stagecraft related; economics; education; elementary education; English; foods, nutrition, and wellness; French; German; history; humanities; interdisciplinary studies; international business/trade/commerce; international relations and affairs; journalism; kinesiology and exercise science; liberal arts and sciences/liberal studies; mathematics; mathematics teacher education; music; music teacher education; natural sciences; philosophy; physical education teaching and coaching; political science and government; pre-dentistry studies; pre-law studies; pre-medical studies; psychology; public relations/image management; religious education; religious studies; secondary education; sociology; Spanish; speech and rhetoric; telecommunications.

Pitzer College
African American/Black studies; American studies; anthropology; art; art history, criticism and conservation; Asian studies; Asian-American studies; biochemistry; biology/biological sciences; chemistry; classics; classics and languages, literatures and linguistics; creative writing; dance; dramatic/theater arts; ecology; economics; engineering; English; environmental science; environmental studies; European studies; film/cinema studies; fine/studio arts; foreign languages and literatures; French; German; Hispanic-American, Puerto Rican, and Mexican-American/Chicano studies; history; interdisciplinary studies; international relations and affairs; international/global studies; Latin American studies; linguistics; literature; mathematics; molecular biology; music; neuroscience; organizational behavior; philosophy; physics; political science and government; pre-medical studies; psychology; regional studies; religious studies; Romance languages; Russian; science, technology and society; sociology; Spanish; women's studies.

Point Loma Nazarene University
Accounting; art; art teacher education; athletic training; biblical studies; biochemistry; biology/biological sciences; broadcast journalism; business administration and management; business/corporate communications; chemistry; child development; communication/speech communication and rhetoric; computer science; development economics and international development; dietetics; dramatic/theater arts; engineering physics; English language and literature related; family and community services; family and consumer sciences/human sciences; fine arts related; foods, nutrition, and wellness; graphic communications; graphic design; health and physical education; history; industrial and organizational psychology; international/global studies; journalism; kinesiology and exercise science; liberal arts and sciences/liberal studies; management information systems; mass communication/media; mathematics; music; music performance; music teacher education; music theory and composition; nursing (registered nurse training); philosophy; philosophy and religious studies

related; physics; political science and government; pre-theology/pre-ministerial studies; psychology; religious studies related; religious/sacred music; Romance languages; social sciences; social work; sociology; Spanish; theological and ministerial studies related; youth ministry.

Polytechnic University, Brooklyn Campus
Agricultural/biological engineering and bioengineering; bioinformatics; chemistry; civil engineering; computer engineering; computer science; construction management; electrical, electronics and communications engineering; journalism; liberal arts and sciences/liberal studies; management information systems; mathematics; mechanical engineering; molecular biochemistry; physics.

Pomona College
African American/Black studies; American studies; anthropology; art; art history, criticism and conservation; Asian studies; Asian studies (East); Asian-American studies; astronomy; biochemistry; biology/biological sciences; chemistry; Chinese; classics and languages, literatures and linguistics; cognitive science; computer science; dance; dramatic/theater arts; ecology; economics; English; environmental studies; film/cinema studies; fine/studio arts; French; geology/earth science; German; Hispanic-American, Puerto Rican, and Mexican-American/Chicano studies; history; humanities; interdisciplinary studies; international relations and affairs; Japanese; Latin American studies; liberal arts and sciences/liberal studies; linguistics; mathematics; medical microbiology and bacteriology; modern languages; molecular biology; music; neuroscience; philosophy; physics; political science and government; pre-medical studies; psychology; public policy analysis; religious studies; Romance languages; Russian; sociology; Spanish; women's studies.

Presbyterian College
Accounting and business/management; art; art history, criticism and conservation; biology/biological sciences; business administration and management; business/managerial economics; chemistry; computer science; dramatic/theater arts; early childhood education; economics; education; English; fine arts related; fine/studio arts; foreign languages and literatures; French; German; history; mathematics; middle school education; modern languages; music; music performance; music teacher education; philosophy; physics; physics related; political science and government; psychology; religious studies; religious/sacred music; sociology; Spanish; special education.

Princeton University
Anthropology; architecture; art history, criticism and conservation; Asian studies (East); astrophysics; chemical engineering; chemistry; civil engineering; classics and languages, literatures and linguistics; comparative literature; computer engineering; ecology; economics; electrical, electronics and communications engineering; English; French; geological and earth sciences/geosciences related; German; history; mathematics; mechanical engineering; molecular biology; multi-/interdisciplinary studies related; music; Near and Middle Eastern studies; operations research; philosophy; physics; political science and government; psychology; public policy analysis; religious studies; Slavic languages; sociology; Spanish.

Providence College
Accounting; American studies; art history, criticism and conservation; banking and financial support services; biochemistry; biology/biological sciences; business administration and management; ceramic arts and ceramics; chemistry; community organization and advocacy; computer science; divinity/ministry; drawing; economics; engineering physics; English; finance; fine/studio arts; fire science; French; general studies; health/health care administration; history; humanities; international/global studies; Italian; liberal arts and sciences/liberal studies; marketing/marketing management; mathematics; multi-/interdisciplinary studies related; music; music teacher education; painting; philosophy; political science and government; psychology; secondary education; social sciences; social work; sociology; Spanish; special education; systems engineering; theology; visual and performing arts; visual and performing arts related.

Purdue University

Accounting; accounting and business/management; accounting and finance; acting; actuarial science; advertising; aeronautical/aerospace engineering technology; aeronautics/aviation/aerospace science and technology; aerospace, aeronautical and astronautical engineering; African American/Black studies; agricultural and food products processing; agricultural communication/journalism; agricultural economics; agricultural mechanization; agricultural production; agricultural teacher education; agricultural/biological engineering and bioengineering; agriculture; agronomy and crop science; air traffic control; airline pilot and flight crew; animal sciences; anthropology; apparel and textiles; applied horticulture; applied mathematics; architectural engineering technology; art; art history, criticism and conservation; art teacher education; Asian studies; athletic training; atmospheric sciences and meteorology; audiology and hearing sciences; audiology and speech-language pathology; aviation/airway management; biochemistry; biochemistry/biophysics and molecular biology; biological and physical sciences; biology teacher education; biology/biological sciences; biomedical/medical engineering; botany/plant biology; broadcast journalism; business administration and management; business/commerce; cell and molecular biology; chemical engineering; chemistry; chemistry teacher education; civil engineering; classics and languages, literatures and linguistics; clinical laboratory science/medical technology; communication/speech communication and rhetoric; computer and information sciences; computer and information sciences and support services related; computer engineering; computer engineering technology; computer graphics; computer science; computer systems networking and telecommunications; construction engineering; construction engineering technology; creative writing; criminal justice/law enforcement administration; design and visual communications; dietetic technician; dramatic/theater arts; early childhood education; education; electrical, electronic and communications engineering technology; electrical, electronics and communications engineering; elementary education; engineering related; engineering/industrial management; English; entomology; environmental science; family and community services; family and consumer sciences/home economics teacher education; family and consumer sciences/human sciences; farm and ranch management; fashion merchandising; fashion/apparel design; film/cinema studies; financial planning and services; fine/studio arts; fishing and fisheries sciences and management; food science; foods, nutrition, and wellness; foreign language teacher education; foreign languages and literatures; forestry; French language teacher education; French studies; geology/earth science; German language teacher education; German studies; health and physical education; health professions related; health services/allied health/health sciences; health teacher education; history; horticultural science; hospitality administration related; hotel/motel administration; human development and family studies; human resources management; humanities; industrial engineering; industrial technology; interdisciplinary studies; interior design; Japanese; Japanese studies; journalism; kindergarten/preschool education; kinesiology and exercise science; landscape architecture; liberal arts and sciences/liberal studies; management information systems and services related; manufacturing technology; marketing/marketing management; materials engineering; mathematics; mathematics teacher education; mechanical drafting and CAD/CADD; mechanical engineering; mechanical engineering technologies related; mechanical engineering/mechanical technology; meteorology; microbiology; molecular biology; music; natural resources/conservation; nuclear engineering; nursing (registered nurse training); nutrition sciences; occupational health and industrial hygiene; operations management; pharmacy; philosophy; photography; physical education teaching and coaching; physics; physics teacher education; plant genetics; political science and government; pre-dentistry studies; pre-medical studies; psychology; public relations/image management; religious studies; robotics technology; Russian; science teacher education; secondary education; social sciences; social studies teacher education; social work; sociology; Spanish; Spanish language teacher education; special education (early childhood); speech-language pathology; statistics; survey technology; surveying engineering; technology/industrial arts teacher education; tourism and travel services management; trade and industrial teacher educa-

tion; veterinary/animal health technology; visual and performing arts; wildlife and wildlands science and management; women's studies; zoology/animal biology.

Queen's University at Kingston

American native/native American education; art history, criticism and conservation; biochemistry; biology/biological sciences; business/commerce; Canadian studies; cartography; chemical engineering; chemistry; civil engineering; cognitive science; computer engineering; computer science; dramatic/theater arts; economics; education; education (multiple levels); electrical, electronics and communications engineering; elementary education; engineering; engineering physics; engineering related; English; environmental science; film/cinema studies; French; geography; geological/geophysical engineering; geology/earth science; German; German studies; health and physical education; history; linguistics; mathematics; mechanical engineering; mining and mineral engineering; music; nursing (registered nurse training); occupational therapy; philosophy; physical education teaching and coaching; physical therapy; physics; political science and government; psychology; religious studies; science teacher education; sociology; Spanish; statistics; technical teacher education; theology; women's studies.

Quincy University

Accounting; airline pilot and flight crew; arts management; aviation/airway management; biology/biological sciences; business administration and management; chemistry; clinical laboratory science/medical technology; communication/speech communication and rhetoric; computer and information sciences; computer science; criminal justice/safety; elementary education; English; finance; graphic design; history; human services; humanities; information science/studies; journalism; language interpretation and translation; marketing/marketing management; mathematics; music; music teacher education; nursing (registered nurse training); philosophy; physical education teaching and coaching; political science and government; pre-dentistry studies; pre-medical studies; pre-veterinary studies; psychology; public administration and social service professions related; public relations/image management; radio and television; social work; special education; sport and fitness administration/management; theological and ministerial studies related; theology.

Quinnipiac University

Accounting; actuarial science; advertising; applied mathematics; athletic training; biochemistry; biological and physical sciences; biology/biological sciences; broadcast journalism; business administration and management; business/managerial economics; chemistry; child development; cinematography and film/video production; communication and journalism related; computer science; criminal justice/safety; developmental and child psychology; dramatic/theater arts; economics; education; English; entrepreneurship; film/cinema studies; finance; gerontology; history; human resources management; human services; information science/studies; international business/trade/commerce; international relations and affairs; journalism; legal assistant/paralegal; legal studies; liberal arts and sciences/liberal studies; literature; marketing/marketing management; mass communication/media; mathematics; medical laboratory technology; medical microbiology and bacteriology; nursing (registered nurse training); occupational therapy; physical therapy; physician assistant; physiological psychology/psychobiology; political science and government; pre-dentistry studies; pre-law studies; pre-medical studies; pre-veterinary studies; psychology; public relations/image management; radiologic technology/science; sales, distribution and marketing; social sciences; sociology; Spanish; veterinary technology; web page, digital/multimedia and information resources design.

Randolph College

Ancient/classical Greek; art; art history, criticism and conservation; biology/biological sciences; business/commerce; chemistry; classics and languages, literatures and linguistics; communication/speech communication and rhetoric; creative writing; dance; dramatic/theater arts; economics; elementary education; engineering physics; English; environmental studies; fine/studio arts; French; German; health professions related; history; international relations and affairs; Latin; liberal arts and sciences/liberal studies; mathematics; museum studies; music history, literature, and theory; music performance; music theory and composition; philosophy; physics; political science and government; psychology; religious studies; sociology; Spanish.

Reed College
American studies; anthropology; art; biochemistry; biology/biological sciences; chemistry; Chinese; classics and languages, literatures and linguistics; dance; dramatic/theater arts; economics; English; fine/studio arts; French; German; history; international relations and affairs; linguistics; literature; mathematics; music; philosophy; physics; political science and government; psychology; religious studies; Russian; sociology; Spanish.

Regis University
Accounting; biochemistry; biology/biological sciences; business administration and management; chemistry; communication/speech communication and rhetoric; computer science; criminal justice/law enforcement administration; economics; education; elementary education; English; environmental studies; French; health information/medical records administration; history; human ecology; humanities; liberal arts and sciences/liberal studies; mathematics; neuroscience; nursing (registered nurse training); philosophy; political science and government; pre-dentistry studies; pre-law studies; pre-medical studies; pre-veterinary studies; psychology; religious studies; sociology; Spanish; visual and performing arts.

Rensselaer Polytechnic Institute
Aerospace, aeronautical and astronautical engineering; Air Force R.O.T.C./air science; applied mathematics; architecture; architecture related; Army R.O.T.C./military science; biochemistry; bioinformatics; biological and biomedical sciences related; biological and physical sciences; biology/biological sciences; biomedical/medical engineering; biophysics; building/construction finishing, management, and inspection related; business administration and management; chemical engineering; chemistry; civil engineering; communication/speech communication and rhetoric; computer and information sciences; computer engineering; computer science; economics; electrical, electronics and communications engineering; engineering; engineering physics; engineering science; environmental/environmental health engineering; finance; geology/earth science; hydrology and water resources science; industrial engineering; information technology; interdisciplinary studies; management information systems; management information systems and services related; manufacturing engineering; marketing/marketing management; materials engineering; mathematics; mechanical engineering; Navy/Marine Corps R.O.T.C./naval science; nuclear engineering; philosophy; pre-law studies; pre-medical studies; psychology; science, technology and society; social sciences; systems engineering; visual and performing arts related.

Rhodes College
Anthropology; art; art history, criticism and conservation; biochemistry; biology/biological sciences; business administration and management; chemistry; classics and languages, literatures and linguistics; computer science; dramatic/theater arts; economics; English; fine/studio arts; French; German; history; interdisciplinary studies; international business/trade/commerce; international economics; international relations and affairs; Latin; mathematics; modern Greek; music; philosophy; physics; political science and government; psychology; religious studies; Russian studies; sociology; Spanish; urban studies/affairs.

Rice University
Ancient/classical Greek; anthropology; applied mathematics; architecture; art; art history, criticism and conservation; Asian studies; astronomy; astrophysics; biochemistry; biology/biological sciences; biomedical/medical engineering; business administration and management; chemical engineering; chemistry; civil engineering; classics and languages, literatures and linguistics; computer and information sciences; computer engineering; ecology; economics; electrical, electronics and communica-

tions engineering; English; environmental/environmental health engineering; evolutionary biology; fine/studio arts; French; geology/earth science; geophysics and seismology; German; history; kinesiology and exercise science; Latin; Latin American studies; linguistics; materials engineering; materials science; mathematics; mechanical engineering; multi-/interdisciplinary studies related; music; music history, literature, and theory; music performance; music theory and composition; neuroscience; philosophy; physical and theoretical chemistry; physics; political science and government; psychology; public policy analysis; religious studies; Russian; Russian studies; sociology; Spanish; statistics; visual and performing arts related; women's studies.

Ripon College
Anthropology; art; biochemistry; biology/biological sciences; business administration and management; chemistry; communication/speech communication and rhetoric; computer science; dramatic/theater arts; early childhood education; economics; education; elementary education; English; environmental studies; French; German; history; interdisciplinary studies; Latin American studies; mathematics; music; music teacher education; philosophy; physical education teaching and coaching; physical sciences; physiological psychology/psychobiology; political science and government; pre-dentistry studies; pre-law studies; pre-medical studies; pre-veterinary studies; psychology; religious studies; Romance languages; secondary education; sociology; Spanish.

Rochester Institute of Technology
Accounting; advertising; aerospace, aeronautical and astronautical engineering; animation, interactive technology, video graphics and special effects; biochemistry; bioinformatics; biological and biomedical sciences related; biomedical/medical engineering; biopsychology; biotechnology; cardiovascular technology; civil engineering technology; clinical laboratory science/medical technology; commercial photography; communication and media related; computer and information sciences; computer and information systems security; computer engineering; computer engineering technology; computer graphics; computer software engineering; computer systems analysis; computer systems networking and telecommunications; crafts, folk art and artisanry; criminal justice/law enforcement administration; criminal justice/safety; data modeling/warehousing and database administration; design and visual communications; economics; electrical and electronic engineering technologies related; electrical, electronics and communications engineering; electromechanical technology; engineering; engineering related; engineering science; engineering-related technologies; environmental science; finance; foodservice systems administration; graphic communications; hazardous materials management and waste technology; hospitality administration; hospitality and recreation marketing; human nutrition; illustration; industrial engineering; industrial safety technology; information technology; interdisciplinary studies; international business/trade/commerce; international relations and affairs; management information systems; manufacturing technology; marketing/marketing management; mathematics; mathematics and computer science; mechanical engineering; medical illustration; natural resources management and policy; occupational safety and health technology; ophthalmic laboratory technology; photographic and film/video technology; photojournalism; physician assistant; polymer chemistry; pre-dentistry studies; pre-law studies; pre-medical studies; pre-veterinary studies; psychology; public policy analysis; public relations, advertising, and applied communication related; public relations/image management; publishing; quality control and safety technologies related; sculpture; special products marketing; statistics; system administration; system, networking, and LAN/WAN management; systems engineering; telecommunications; telecommunications technology; tourism and travel services marketing; web page, digital/multimedia and information resources design; web/multimedia management and webmaster.

Rollins College
Anthropology; art history, criticism and conservation; biochemistry; biology/biological sciences; chemistry; classics and languages, literatures and linguistics; computer science; dramatic/theater arts; economics; educa-

tion; English; environmental studies; European studies; fine/studio arts; French; history; international business/trade/commerce; international relations and affairs; Latin American studies; marine biology; mathematics; music; philosophy; physics; political science and government; pre-dentistry studies; pre-law studies; pre-medical studies; psychology; religious studies; sociology; Spanish.

Rose-Hulman Institute of Technology

Biology/biological sciences; biomedical/medical engineering; chemical engineering; chemistry; civil engineering; computer engineering; computer science; computer software engineering; economics; electrical, electronics and communications engineering; engineering physics; engineering related; mathematics; mechanical engineering; physics; systems engineering.

Rutgers, The State University of New Jersey, Newark

Accounting; African American/Black studies; allied health diagnostic, intervention, and treatment professions related; American studies; anthropology; applied mathematics; art; biological and biomedical sciences related; biology/biological sciences; botany/plant biology; business administration and management; chemistry; classics and classical languages related; classics and languages, literatures and linguistics; clinical laboratory science/medical technology; computer and information sciences; criminal justice/safety; cultural studies; dramatic/theater arts; economics; engineering; English; environmental studies; finance; fine arts related; French; geological/geophysical engineering; geology/earth science; German; Hispanic-American, Puerto Rican, and Mexican-American/Chicano studies; history; information science/studies; journalism; marketing/marketing management; mathematics; multi-/interdisciplinary studies related; music; nursing (registered nurse training); philosophy; physics; physics related; political science and government; psychology; science, technology and society; Slavic, Baltic, and Albanian languages related; social work; sociology; Spanish; women's studies; zoology/animal biology.

Rutgers, The State University of New Jersey, New Brunswick

Accounting; African studies; agricultural/biological engineering and bioengineering; agriculture; American studies; ancient/classical Greek; animal genetics; animal physiology; animal sciences; animal/livestock husbandry and production; anthropology; art; art history, criticism and conservation; Asian studies (East); astrophysics; atmospheric sciences and meteorology; biochemistry; biology/biological sciences; biomedical sciences; biomedical/medical engineering; biometry/biometrics; biotechnology; business administration and management; cell biology and anatomical sciences related; cell biology and histology; ceramic arts and ceramics; ceramic sciences and engineering; chemical engineering; chemistry; Chinese; civil engineering; classics and languages, literatures and linguistics; clinical laboratory science/medical technology; commercial and advertising art; communication/speech communication and rhetoric; comparative literature; computer engineering; computer science; criminal justice/law enforcement administration; cultural studies; dance; dramatic/theater arts; drawing; ecology; economics; electrical, electronics and communications engineering; engineering science; English; environmental design/architecture; environmental studies; equestrian studies; European studies (Central and Eastern); evolutionary biology; film/cinema studies; finance; food science; foreign languages and literatures; French; geography; geology/earth science; German; Hispanic-American, Puerto Rican, and Mexican-American/Chicano studies; history; human ecology; industrial engineering; information science/studies; interdisciplinary studies; Italian; jazz/jazz studies; Jewish/Judaic studies; journalism; kinesiology and exercise science; labor and industrial relations; Latin; Latin American studies; liberal arts and sciences/liberal studies; linguistics; management science; management sciences and quantitative methods related; marine biology and biological oceanography; marketing/marketing management; mass communication/media; mathematics; mechanical engineering; medical microbiology and bacteriology; medieval and Renaissance studies; molecular biology; music; music teacher education; natural resources management; natural resources/

conservation; Near and Middle Eastern studies; nursing (registered nurse training); nutrition sciences; painting; pharmacy; philosophy; photography; physics; plant sciences; political science and government; Portuguese; pre-dentistry studies; pre-law studies; pre-medical studies; printmaking; psychology; public health; religious studies; Russian; Russian studies; sculpture; social sciences related; social work; sociology; Spanish; statistics; turf and turfgrass management; urban studies/affairs; veterinary sciences; visual and performing arts; women's studies.

Saint Francis University

Accounting; accounting and finance; American studies; anthropology; biology teacher education; biology/biological sciences; business administration and management; chemistry; chemistry teacher education; clinical laboratory science/medical technology; computer programming; computer science; criminal justice/law enforcement administration; criminology; economics; education; elementary education; engineering; English; English/language arts teacher education; environmental science; environmental studies; exercise physiology; finance; fine arts related; foreign language teacher education; forensic science and technology; French; French language teacher education; history; history teacher education; human resources management; international business/trade/commerce; international relations and affairs; journalism; labor and industrial relations; literature; management information systems; marine biology and biological oceanography; marketing/marketing management; mass communication/media; mathematics; mathematics and computer science; mathematics teacher education; modern languages; nursing (registered nurse training); occupational therapy; pastoral studies/counseling; philosophy; physical therapy; physician assistant; political science and government; pre-dentistry studies; pre-law studies; pre-medical studies; pre-veterinary studies; psychology; public administration; public relations/image management; real estate; religious studies; science teacher education; secondary education; social studies teacher education; social work; sociology; Spanish; special education.

St. John's College (MD)

Interdisciplinary studies; liberal arts and sciences/liberal studies; western civilization.

St. John's College (NM)

Ancient/classical Greek; classics and languages, literatures and linguistics; English; ethics; foreign languages and literatures; French; general studies; history; history of philosophy; humanities; liberal arts and sciences and humanities related; liberal arts and sciences/liberal studies; literature; mathematics; philosophy; philosophy and religious studies related; philosophy related; physical sciences; physics; pre-medical studies; religious studies; western civilization.

Saint John's University (MN)

Accounting; art; biochemistry; biology/biological sciences; business administration and management; chemistry; classics and languages, literatures and linguistics; computer science; dietetics; dramatic/theater arts; economics; education; elementary education; engineering physics; English; environmental studies; fine/studio arts; foods, nutrition, and wellness; forest sciences and biology; French; German; history; humanities; mathematics; mathematics and computer science; music; natural sciences; nursing (registered nurse training); occupational therapy; peace studies and conflict resolution; philosophy; physical therapy; physics; political science and government; pre-dentistry studies; pre-law studies; pre-medical studies; pre-pharmacy studies; pre-theology/pre-ministerial studies; pre-veterinary studies; psychology; religious education; secondary education; social sciences; social work; sociology; Spanish; speech and rhetoric; theology.

Saint Joseph's University

Accounting; actuarial science; biochemistry; biology/biological sciences; business administration and management; chemistry; communication/speech communication and rhetoric; computer and information sciences; criminology; economics; elementary education; English; English/language arts teacher education; environmental studies; European studies;

finance; foreign language teacher education; French; French studies; German; health services/allied health/health sciences; history; hospital and health care facilities administration; humanities; information science/studies; international business/trade/commerce; international marketing; international relations and affairs; Italian; Latin; legal studies; liberal arts and sciences/liberal studies; management information systems; marketing/marketing management; mathematics; mathematics teacher education; philosophy; physics; political science and government; psychology; public administration; purchasing, procurement/acquisitions and contracts management; religious studies; science teacher education; secondary education; social sciences; social studies teacher education; sociology; Spanish; special education; special products marketing; visual and performing arts.

St. Lawrence University

African studies; American literature; anthropology; art; art history, criticism and conservation; Asian studies; biochemistry; biology/biological sciences; biophysics; Canadian studies; chemistry; computer science; creative writing; dramatic/theater arts; economics; English; English literature (British and Commonwealth); environmental studies; fine/studio arts; foreign languages and literatures; French; geology/earth science; geophysics and seismology; German; history; international/global studies; mathematics; mathematics and computer science; modern languages; music; neurobiology and neurophysiology; neuroscience; philosophy; physics; political science and government; psychology; religious studies; sociology; Spanish.

St. Louis College of Pharmacy

Pharmacy.

Saint Louis University

Aeronautical/aerospace engineering technology; aerospace, aeronautical and astronautical engineering; airline pilot and flight crew; American studies; art history, criticism and conservation; atmospheric sciences and meteorology; audiology and speech-language pathology; aviation/airway management; biochemistry; biology/biological sciences; biomedical/medical engineering; business administration and management; chemistry; city/urban, community and regional planning; classics and classical languages related; clinical laboratory science/medical technology; clinical/medical laboratory science and allied professions related; communication/speech communication and rhetoric; computer and information sciences; computer engineering; corrections; criminal justice/law enforcement administration; cytotechnology; dramatic/theater arts; economics; education (multiple levels); electrical, electronics and communications engineering; engineering physics; engineering/industrial management; English; environmental science; fine/studio arts; foods, nutrition, and wellness; foreign languages and literatures; French; geology/earth science; geophysics and seismology; German; health information/medical records administration; health/health care administration; history; human resources management; humanities; international business/trade/commerce; international relations and affairs; kinesiology and exercise science; management information systems; management science; marketing/marketing management; mathematics; mechanical engineering; meteorology; modern Greek; music; nuclear medical technology; nursing (registered nurse training); occupational therapy; organizational behavior; philosophy; physical therapy; physics; political science and government; psychology; purchasing, procurement/acquisitions and contracts management; religious studies related; Russian; social work; sociology; Spanish; theology; urban studies/affairs; women's studies.

Saint Mary's College

Accounting; applied mathematics related; art; art teacher education; biology/biological sciences; business administration and management; business teacher education; chemistry; clinical laboratory science/medical technology; communication/speech communication and rhetoric; creative writing; cytotechnology; dramatic/theater arts; economics; education; elementary education; English literature (British and Commonwealth); finance; French; history; humanities; interdisciplinary studies; inter-

national business/trade/commerce; Italian; management information systems; marketing/marketing management; mathematics; mathematics and computer science; music; music teacher education; nursing (registered nurse training); philosophy; political science and government; psychology; religious studies; social work; sociology; Spanish.

Saint Mary's College of California

Accounting; accounting related; American studies; anthropology; archeology; area, ethnic, cultural, and gender studies related; art; art history, criticism and conservation; biochemistry; biological and biomedical sciences related; biology/biological sciences; business administration and management; business/commerce; chemistry; chemistry related; communication and journalism related; communication/speech communication and rhetoric; dance; dramatic/theater arts; economics; engineering; English; English language and literature related; European studies; finance and financial management services related; foreign languages related; French; German; health and physical education; health and physical education related; health professions related; historic preservation and conservation; history; industrial and organizational psychology; interdisciplinary studies; international business/trade/commerce; international relations and affairs; Italian; kinesiology and exercise science; Latin; Latin American studies; liberal arts and sciences and humanities related; liberal arts and sciences/liberal studies; literature; mathematics; mathematics and computer science; mathematics and statistics related; modern Greek; modern languages; multi-/interdisciplinary studies related; music; nursing (registered nurse training); philosophy; physics; physiological psychology/psychobiology; political science and government; political science and government related; psychology; psychology related; religious studies; social sciences; social sciences related; sociology; Spanish; sport and fitness administration/management; theater literature, history and criticism; theology; visual and performing arts related; women's studies.

St. Mary's College of Maryland

Anthropology; art; biochemistry; biological and physical sciences; biology/biological sciences; business administration and management; business/commerce; chemistry; communication disorders; communication/speech communication and rhetoric; computer and information sciences; dramatic/theater arts; economics; elementary education; engineering physics; English; fine arts related; foreign languages and literatures; history; journalism; liberal arts and sciences/liberal studies; mass communication/media; mathematics; multi-/interdisciplinary studies related; music; music pedagogy; music performance; music related; music theory and composition; philosophy; physics; political science and government; psychology; psychology related; public policy analysis; religious studies; religious/sacred music; sociology; theology and religious vocations related.

St. Norbert College

Accounting; art; biological and physical sciences; biology/biological sciences; business administration and management; chemistry; commercial and advertising art; communication/speech communication and rhetoric; computer and information sciences; economics; elementary education; English; environmental science; environmental studies; French; geology/earth science; German; history; humanities; international business/trade/commerce; international relations and affairs; mathematics; music; music teacher education; philosophy; physics; political science and government; psychology; religious studies; sociology; Spanish.

St. Olaf College

American studies; ancient studies; ancient/classical Greek; art; art history, criticism and conservation; Asian studies; biology/biological sciences; chemistry; classics and languages, literatures and linguistics; computer science; dance; dramatic/theater arts; economics; English; environmental studies; ethnic, cultural minority, and gender studies related; French; German; history; kinesiology and exercise science; Latin; Latin American studies; liberal arts and sciences/liberal studies; mathematics; multi-/interdisciplinary studies related; music; music performance; music related; music teacher education; music theory and composition; Norwegian; nursing (registered nurse training); philosophy; physics; political science and government; psychology; religious studies; Russian; Russian studies; social studies teacher education; social work; sociology; Spanish; women's studies.

Salem College

Accounting; American studies; art history, criticism and conservation; arts management; biology/biological sciences; business administration and management; chemistry; clinical laboratory science/medical technology; creative writing; economics; education; English; fine/studio arts; French; German; history; interdisciplinary studies; interior design; international business/trade/commerce; international relations and affairs; mass communication/media; mathematics; music; music performance; non-profit management; philosophy; physician assistant; psychology; religious studies; sociology; Spanish.

Samford University

Accounting; Asian studies; athletic training; biochemistry; biology teacher education; biology/biological sciences; business administration and management; cartography; chemistry; classical, ancient Mediterranean and Near Eastern studies and archaeology; classics and languages, literatures and linguistics; commercial and advertising art; community organization and advocacy; computer science; counseling psychology; criminal justice/law enforcement administration; dramatic/theater arts; engineering physics; engineering related; English; English/language arts teacher education; environmental studies; environmental studies; family and community services; foreign languages and literatures; French; general studies; geography; German; health and physical education; history; history teacher education; human development and family studies; human nutrition; human resources management; interior design; international business/trade/commerce; international relations and affairs; journalism; kinesiology and exercise science; Latin; Latin American studies; marine biology and biological oceanography; mathematics; music performance; music teacher education; music theory and composition; nursing (registered nurse training); philosophy; philosophy and religious studies related; physical education teaching and coaching; physics; piano and organ; political science and government; pre-medical studies; psychology; public administration; religious studies; religious/sacred music; science teacher education; science, technology and society; social science teacher education; social sciences; sociology; Spanish; speech and rhetoric; speech teacher education; visual and performing arts related; voice and opera.

San Diego State University

Accounting; advertising; advertising; aerospace, aeronautical and astronautical engineering; African American/Black studies; agricultural business and management; American Indian/Native American studies; American studies; anthropology; applied mathematics; art history, criticism and conservation; Asian studies; astronomy; atomic/molecular physics; biology/biological sciences; business/commerce; chemistry; child development; civil engineering; classics and classical languages related; classics and languages, literatures and linguistics; communication and journalism related; communication disorders; comparative literature; computer engineering; computer science; construction engineering technology; creative writing; criminal justice/law enforcement administration; dance; design and visual communications; dietetics; dramatic/theater arts; early childhood education; early childhood education; economics; electrical, electronics and communications engineering; engineering; English; environmental science; environmental studies; environmental/environmental health engineering; European studies; European studies (Central and Eastern); finance; fine/studio arts; French; geography; geology/earth science; German; gerontology; graphic design; health and physical education; health professions related; health services/allied health/health sciences; Hispanic-American, Puerto Rican, and Mexican-American/Chicano studies; history; hospitality administration; human resources management; humanities; information science/studies; information technology; interior design; international business/trade/commerce; international relations and affairs; Japanese; Jewish/Judaic studies; journalism; Judaic studies; Latin American studies; liberal arts and sciences/liberal studies; linguistics; marketing/marketing management; mass

communication/media; mathematics; mechanical engineering; microbiology; multi-/interdisciplinary studies related; music related; music teacher education; nursing (registered nurse training); nursing related; operations management; parks, recreation and leisure; philosophy; physical sciences; physics; political science and government; psychology; public administration; public relations; public relations/image management; radio and television; real estate; religious studies; Russian; Russian studies; social sciences; social work; sociology; Spanish; speech and rhetoric; statistics; trade and industrial teacher education; urban studies/affairs; women's studies.

Santa Clara University

Accounting; accounting and business/management; ancient studies; ancient/classical Greek; anthropology; art history, criticism and conservation; biochemistry; biological and physical sciences; biology/biological sciences; business/managerial economics; chemistry; civil engineering; classics and languages, literatures and linguistics; communication/speech communication and rhetoric; computer engineering; computer science; dramatic/theater arts; economics; electrical, electronics and communications engineering; engineering; engineering physics; English; environmental science; finance; fine/studio arts; French; French studies; German studies; history; interdisciplinary studies; Italian; Italian studies; Latin; liberal arts and sciences/liberal studies; management information systems; marketing/marketing management; mathematics; mechanical engineering; music; organizational behavior; philosophy; physics; political science and government; psychology; religious studies; sociology; Spanish; Spanish and Iberian studies.

Sarah Lawrence College

Acting; African studies; African American/Black studies; American history; American literature; American studies; animal genetics; anthropology; archeology; architectural history and criticism; art; art history, criticism and conservation; Asian history; Asian studies; Asian studies (East); Asian studies (South); astronomy; biological and physical sciences; biology/biological sciences; chemistry; Chinese studies; cinematography and film/video production; classics and languages, literatures and linguistics; comparative literature; computer science; creative writing; dance; dance related; developmental and child psychology; directing and theatrical production; dramatic/theater arts; drawing; early childhood education; ecology; economics; education; elementary education; English; English language and literature related; English language and literature (British and Commonwealth); environmental studies; European history; European studies; European studies (Central and Eastern); film/cinema studies; fine/studio arts; foreign languages and literatures; French; gay/lesbian studies; geology/earth science; German; history; history and philosophy of science and technology; history related; human development and family studies; human/medical genetics; humanities; interdisciplinary studies; international relations and affairs; Italian; Japanese; jazz/jazz studies; kindergarten/preschool education; Latin; Latin American studies; liberal arts and sciences and humanities related; liberal arts and sciences/liberal studies; literature; marine biology and biological oceanography; mathematics; Middle/ Near Eastern and Semitic languages related; modern languages; molecular biology; music; music history, literature, and theory; music performance; music theory and composition; natural sciences; Near and Middle Eastern studies; organic chemistry; painting; philosophy; philosophy and religious studies related; photography; physics; piano and organ; playwriting and screenwriting; political science and government; pre-dentistry studies; pre-law studies; pre-medical studies; pre-veterinary studies; printmaking; psychology; public policy analysis; religious studies; religious studies related; Romance languages; Russian; sculpture; social sciences; social sciences related; sociology; Spanish; urban studies/affairs; violin, viola, guitar and other stringed instruments; visual and performing arts; visual and performing arts related; voice and opera; western civilization; wind/percussion instruments; women's studies.

Scripps College

African American/Black studies; American studies; anthropology; art; art history, criticism and conservation; Asian studies; Asian studies (East); Asian-American studies; biochemistry; biology/biological sciences;

chemistry; Chinese; classics and languages, literatures and linguistics; computer science; dance; dramatic/theater arts; economics; English; environmental science; environmental studies; European studies; film/video and photographic arts related; fine/studio arts; foreign languages and literatures; French; geology/earth science; German; Hispanic-American, Puerto Rican, and Mexican-American/Chicano studies; history; international relations and affairs; Italian; Japanese; Jewish/Judaic studies; Latin; Latin American studies; legal studies; linguistics; mass communication/media; mathematics; modern languages; molecular biology; multi-/interdisciplinary studies related; music; neuroscience; organizational behavior; philosophy; physics; physiological psychology/psychobiology; political science and government; pre-engineering; pre-medical studies; psychology; religious studies; Russian; science, technology and society; sociology; Spanish; visual and performing arts related; women's studies.

Seattle Pacific University

Accounting; apparel and textiles; art; art teacher education; biochemistry; biology teacher education; biology/biological sciences; business administration and management; chemistry; classics and languages, literatures and linguistics; communication/speech communication and rhetoric; computer science; computer systems analysis; computer/information technology services administration related; dramatic/theater arts; economics; electrical, electronics and communications engineering; engineering science; English; English/language arts teacher education; European studies; family and consumer economics related; family and consumer sciences/home economics teacher education; foods, nutrition, and wellness; French; general studies; German; history; kinesiology and exercise science; Latin; Latin American studies; liberal arts and sciences/liberal studies; mathematics; mathematics and statistics related; mathematics teacher education; music; music teacher education; nursing (registered nurse training); philosophy; physical education teaching and coaching; physics; political science and government; pre-dentistry studies; pre-law studies; pre-medical studies; psychology; religious education; Russian; science teacher education; social science teacher education; sociology; Spanish; special education; theology.

Seattle University

Accounting; applied mathematics; art; art history, criticism and conservation; Asian studies (East); biochemistry; biological and physical sciences; biology/biological sciences; business administration and management; business/managerial economics; chemistry; civil engineering; clinical laboratory science/medical technology; computer science; creative writing; criminal justice/law enforcement administration; diagnostic medical sonography and ultrasound technology; dramatic/theater arts; economics; electrical, electronics and communications engineering; English; environmental studies; environmental/environmental health engineering; European studies (Western); finance; fine/studio arts; forensic science and technology; French; German; history; humanities; industrial engineering; insurance; international business/trade/commerce; international economics; international relations and affairs; journalism; liberal arts and sciences/liberal studies; management information systems; marketing/marketing management; mass communication/media; mathematics; mechanical engineering; nursing (registered nurse training); operations management; philosophy; photography; physics; political science and government; psychology; public administration; public relations/image management; religious studies; social work; sociology; Spanish.

Sewanee: The University of the South

American studies; anthropology; applied art; art; art history, criticism and conservation; Asian studies; biology/biological sciences; chemistry; classics and languages, literatures and linguistics; comparative literature; computer science; dramatic/theater arts; drawing; economics; English; environmental studies; European studies; fine/studio arts; forestry; French; geology/earth science; German; history; international relations and affairs; Latin; literature; mathematics; medieval and Renaissance studies; modern Greek; music; music history, literature, and theory; natural

resources management and policy; philosophy; physics; political science and government; psychology; religious studies; Russian; Russian studies; social sciences; Spanish.

Siena College

Accounting; American studies; biology/biological sciences; chemistry; classics and languages, literatures and linguistics; computer and information sciences; ecology; economics; English; finance; fine/studio arts; French; history; marketing/marketing management; mathematics; philosophy; physics; political science and government; pre-dentistry studies; pre-law studies; pre-medical studies; psychology; religious studies; secondary education; social work; sociology; Spanish.

Simpson College

Accounting; advertising; art; art teacher education; athletic training; biochemistry; biological and physical sciences; biology/biological sciences; business administration and management; business/corporate communications; chemistry; clinical laboratory science/medical technology; computer science; criminal justice/law enforcement administration; dramatic/theater arts; economics; elementary education; English; environmental biology; forensic science and technology; French; German; history; information science/studies; international business/trade/commerce; international relations and affairs; kindergarten/preschool education; mass communication/media; mathematics; music; music performance; music teacher education; philosophy; physical education teaching and coaching; political science and government; pre-dentistry studies; pre-law studies; pre-medical studies; pre-veterinary studies; psychology; religious studies; secondary education; social sciences; sociology; Spanish; sport and fitness administration/management.

Skidmore College

American studies; anthropology; area, ethnic, cultural, and gender studies related; art; art history, criticism and conservation; Asian studies; biology/biological sciences; business, management, and marketing related; business/commerce; chemistry; classics and languages, literatures and linguistics; computer and information sciences; dance; dramatic/theater arts; economics; elementary education; English; English language and literature related; environmental studies; fine arts related; French; French studies; geology/earth science; German; history; international relations and affairs; kinesiology and exercise science; Latin American studies; law and legal studies related; liberal arts and sciences/liberal studies; mathematics; music history, literature, and theory; neuroscience; philosophy; physics; political science and government; psychology; religious studies; social sciences related; social work; sociology; Spanish; women's studies.

Smith College

African American/Black studies; American studies; ancient/classical Greek; anthropology; architecture; art; art history, criticism and conservation; Asian studies (East); astronomy; biochemistry; biology/biological sciences; chemistry; classics and languages, literatures and linguistics; comparative literature; computer science; dance; dramatic/theater arts; East Asian languages; economics; education; engineering science; English; fine/studio arts; French; French studies; geology/earth science; German; German studies; history; interdisciplinary studies; Italian; Latin; Latin American studies; mathematics; medieval and Renaissance studies; music; Near and Middle Eastern studies; neuroscience; philosophy; physics; political science and government; Portuguese; pre-law studies; pre-medical studies; psychology; religious studies; Russian; Russian studies; sociology; Spanish; women's studies.

Southern Methodist University

Accounting; advertising; African American/Black studies; anthropology; applied economics; art history, criticism and conservation; biochemistry; biology/biological sciences; business administration and management; business/commerce; chemistry; civil engineering; computer engineering; computer science; creative writing; dance; dramatic/theater arts; econometrics and quantitative economics; economics; electrical, electronics and communications engineering; English; environmental studies;

environmental/environmental health engineering; European studies; film/cinema studies; finance; finance and financial management services related; financial planning and services; fine/studio arts; French; geology/earth science; geophysics and seismology; German; Hispanic-American, Puerto Rican, and Mexican-American/Chicano studies; history; humanities; information science/studies; international relations and affairs; Italian; journalism; Latin American studies; liberal arts and sciences and humanities related; management science; marketing/marketing management; mathematics; mechanical engineering; medieval and Renaissance studies; multi-/interdisciplinary studies related; music; music performance; music teacher education; music theory and composition; music therapy; philosophy; physics; piano and organ; political science and government; psychology; public policy analysis; public relations; public relations/image management; religious studies; social sciences; sociology; Spanish; statistics; voice and opera.

Southwest Baptist University
Accounting; art; art teacher education; athletic training; biblical studies; biology teacher education; biology/biological sciences; business administration and management; business/commerce; chemistry; chemistry teacher education; clinical laboratory science/medical technology; commercial and advertising art; communication/speech communication and rhetoric; computer and information sciences; computer science; criminal justice/law enforcement administration; customer service management; dramatic/theater arts; early childhood education; elementary education; emergency medical technology (EMT paramedic); English; English/language arts teacher education; finance; general studies; health and physical education; health teacher education; history; human services; human services; marketing/marketing management; mathematics; mathematics teacher education; middle school education; missionary studies and missiology; music; music teacher education; nursing (registered nurse training); occupational safety and health technology; office management; parks, recreation and leisure; pastoral studies/counseling; physical education teaching and coaching; political science and government; psychology; religious education; religious studies; science teacher education; social science teacher education; sociology; Spanish; speech teacher education; sport and fitness administration/management; theology.

Southwestern University
Accounting; American studies; animal behavior and ethology; anthropology; art; art history, criticism and conservation; biochemistry; biology/biological sciences; business/commerce; chemistry; Chinese; classics and languages, literatures and linguistics; communication/speech communication and rhetoric; computer and information sciences; dramatic/theater arts; economics; education; elementary education; English; environmental studies; French; German; history; international relations and affairs; Latin; Latin American studies; liberal arts and sciences and humanities related; mass communication/media; mathematics; music; music history, literature, and theory; music performance; music teacher education; music theory and composition; musicology and ethnomusicology; philosophy; physical education teaching and coaching; physical sciences; physics; political science and government; psychology; religious studies; science teacher education; social studies teacher education; sociology; Spanish; visual and performing arts related; women's studies.

Stanford University
Aerospace, aeronautical and astronautical engineering; African studies; African American/Black studies; American Indian/Native American studies; American studies; ancient studies; ancient/classical Greek; anthropology; archeology; art; art history, criticism and conservation; Asian studies; Asian studies (East); biology/biological sciences; biomedical/medical engineering; chemical engineering; chemistry; Chinese; civil engineering; classics and languages, literatures and linguistics; communication/speech communication and rhetoric; comparative literature; computer engineering; computer science; cultural studies; dramatic/theater arts; earth sciences; economics; electrical, electronics and communications engineering; engineering; English; environmental design/architecture; environmental studies; environmental/environmental health engineering; film/cinema

studies; fine/studio arts; French; geological and earth sciences/geosciences related; geology/earth science; geophysics and seismology; German; German studies; Hispanic-American, Puerto Rican, and Mexican-American/Chicano studies; history; humanities; industrial design; interdisciplinary studies; international relations and affairs; Italian; Japanese; Latin; linguistics; materials science; mathematics; mathematics and computer science; mechanical engineering; medical biomathematics/biometrics; music; petroleum engineering; philosophy; physics; political science and government; Portuguese; psychology; public policy analysis; religious studies; science, technology and society; Slavic languages; sociology; Spanish; statistics; systems science and theory; urban studies/affairs; women's studies.

State University of New York at Binghamton
Accounting; African American/Black studies; ancient/classical Greek; anthropology; Arabic; art; art history, criticism and conservation; Asian-American studies; biochemistry; biology/biological sciences; biomedical/medical engineering; business administration and management; business/commerce; cell and molecular biology; chemistry; cinematography and film/video production; classics and classical languages related; classics and languages, literatures and linguistics; comparative literature; computer and information sciences; computer engineering; computer science; creative writing; dance; design and visual communications; directing and theatrical production; dramatic/theater arts; ecology; economics; electrical, electronics and communications engineering; engineering; English; environmental studies; evolutionary biology; fine/studio arts; French; geography; geology/earth science; geophysics and seismology; German; Hebrew; history; human development and family studies related; industrial engineering; information science/studies; international business/trade/commerce; international relations and affairs; international/global studies; Italian; Jewish/Judaic studies; Latin; Latin American studies; linguistics; management information systems; management science; marketing/marketing management; mathematics; mechanical engineering; medieval and Renaissance studies; multi-/interdisciplinary studies related; music; music history, literature, and theory; music performance; nursing (registered nurse training); philosophy; philosophy related; physics; physics related; physiological psychology/psychobiology; political science and government; pre-law studies; pre-medical studies; psychology; sculpture; social sciences; sociology; Spanish; systems engineering; theater design and technology; visual and performing arts.

State University of New York College at Geneseo
Accounting; African American/Black studies; American studies; anthropology; art; art history, criticism and conservation; biochemistry; biology/biological sciences; biophysics; business administration and management; chemistry; communication/speech communication and rhetoric; comparative literature; computer science; dramatic/theater arts; early childhood education; economics; education; elementary education; English; fine/studio arts; French; geochemistry; geography; geology/earth science; geophysics and seismology; history; international relations and affairs; mathematics; music; natural sciences; philosophy; physics; political science and government; pre-dentistry studies; pre-law studies; pre-medical studies; pre-veterinary studies; psychology; sociology; Spanish; special education; special education (early childhood); speech therapy; visual and performing arts related.

State University of New York College of Environmental Science and Forestry
Agricultural/biological engineering and bioengineering; biochemistry; biological and physical sciences; biology teacher education; biology/biological sciences; biotechnology; botany/plant biology; chemical engineering; chemistry; chemistry teacher education; city/urban, community and regional planning; construction engineering; construction management; ecology; entomology; environmental biology; environmental design/architecture; environmental education; environmental studies; environmental/environmental health engineering; fish/game management; fishing and fisheries sciences and management; forest engineering; forest sciences and biology; forest/forest resources management; forestry; hydrology and water resources science; land use planning

and management; landscape architecture; natural resources management and policy; natural resources/conservation; parks, recreation and leisure; physical therapy; plant pathology/phytopathology; plant physiology; plant protection and integrated pest management; plant sciences; polymer chemistry; pre-dentistry studies; pre-law studies; pre-medical studies; pre-veterinary studies; science teacher education; water resources engineering; wildlife and wildlands science and management; wildlife biology; wood science and wood products/pulp and paper technology; zoology/animal biology.

Stetson University
Accounting; American studies; aquatic biology/limnology; art; biochemistry; biology/biological sciences; business administration and management; business/managerial economics; chemistry; clinical laboratory science/medical technology; communication/speech communication and rhetoric; computer science; dramatic/theater arts; e-commerce; economics; education; elementary education; English; entrepreneurial and small business related; environmental science; finance; French; geography; German; health services/allied health/health sciences; history; humanities; international business/trade/commerce; international relations and affairs; kinesiology and exercise science; Latin American studies; management information systems; management science; marketing/marketing management; mathematics; molecular biology; music; music performance; music teacher education; music theory and composition; philosophy; physics; piano and organ; political science and government; pre-dentistry studies; pre-law studies; pre-medical studies; pre-veterinary studies; psychology; religious studies; Russian studies; secondary education; social science teacher education; social sciences; sociology; Spanish; sport and fitness administration/management; violin, viola, guitar and other stringed instruments; visual and performing arts related; voice and opera; web page, digital/multimedia and information resources design.

Stevens Institute of Technology
Biochemistry; biomedical/medical engineering; business administration and management; chemical engineering; chemistry; civil engineering; computational mathematics; computer engineering; computer science; electrical, electronics and communications engineering; engineering physics; engineering/industrial management; English; environmental/environmental health engineering; history; history and philosophy of science and technology; humanities; mathematics; mechanical engineering; Near and Middle Eastern studies; philosophy; physics; pre-dentistry studies; pre-law studies; pre-medical studies; systems engineering.

Stonehill College
Accounting; American studies; biochemistry; biology/biological sciences; business administration and management; chemistry; communication/speech communication and rhetoric; computer engineering; computer science; criminology; early childhood education; economics; elementary education; English; environmental studies; ethnic, cultural minority, and gender studies related; finance; fine/studio arts; foreign languages and literatures; health/health care administration; history; international relations and affairs; marketing/marketing management; mathematics; multi-/interdisciplinary studies related; neuroscience; philosophy; political science and government; psychology; public administration; religious studies; sociology.

Stony Brook University, State University of New York
African American/Black studies; American studies; anthropology; applied mathematics; art history, criticism and conservation; Asian-American studies; astronomy; athletic training; atmospheric sciences and meteorology; biochemistry; biology/biological sciences; biomedical/medical engineering; business administration and management; chemistry; chemistry related; clinical laboratory science/medical technology; comparative literature; computer hardware engineering; computer science; cytotechnology; dramatic/theater arts; economics; electrical, electronics and communications engineering; engineering; English; environmental studies; European studies; fine/studio arts; French; geology/earth science; German; health professions related; history; humanities; information science/studies; Italian; journalism; linguistics; marine

biology; mathematics; mechanical engineering; multi-/interdisciplinary studies related; music; nursing (registered nurse training); pharmacology; philosophy; physical sciences related; physics; political science and government; psychology; religious studies; respiratory care therapy; Russian; social sciences; social work; sociology; Spanish; women's studies.

Susquehanna University
Accounting; art; art history, criticism and conservation; biochemistry; biology/biological sciences; broadcast journalism; business administration and management; business/managerial economics; chemistry; communication/speech communication and rhetoric; computer science; creative writing; dramatic/theater arts; ecology; economics; elementary education; English; entrepreneurship; finance; French; geology/earth science; German; graphic design; history; human resources management; information science/studies; international relations and affairs; journalism; kindergarten/preschool education; marketing/marketing management; mass communication/media; mathematics; music; music teacher education; philosophy; physics; piano and organ; political science and government; pre-dentistry studies; pre-law studies; pre-medical studies; pre-veterinary studies; psychology; public relations/image management; radio and television; religious studies; religious/sacred music; secondary education; sociology; Spanish; speech and rhetoric; violin, viola, guitar and other stringed instruments; voice and opera; wind/percussion instruments.

Swarthmore College
Ancient studies; ancient/classical Greek; anthropology; art history, criticism and conservation; Asian studies; astronomy; astrophysics; biochemistry; biology/biological sciences; chemical physics; chemistry; Chinese; classics and languages, literatures and linguistics; comparative literature; computer and information sciences; dance; dramatic/theater arts; economics; education related; engineering; English; film/video and photographic arts related; fine/studio arts; French; German; German studies; history; Latin; linguistics; mathematics; medieval and Renaissance studies; music; philosophy; physics; physiological psychology/psychobiology; political science and government; psychology; religious studies; Russian; social sciences related; sociology; Spanish.

Sweet Briar College
Anthropology; archeology; art history, criticism and conservation; biochemistry, biophysics and molecular biology related; biology/biological sciences; business, management, and marketing related; chemistry; classics and languages, literatures and linguistics; computer science; creative writing; dance; dramatic/theater arts; economics; engineering science; English; environmental science; environmental studies; fine/studio arts; foreign languages and literatures; French; German; German studies; history; interdisciplinary studies; international relations and affairs; Italian; Italian studies; liberal arts and sciences/liberal studies; mathematics; music; philosophy; physics; political science and government; psychology; religious studies; sociology; Spanish; theoretical and mathematical physics.

Syracuse University
Accounting; advertising; aerospace, aeronautical and astronautical engineering; African American/Black studies; American studies; anthropology; apparel and textiles; architecture; area, ethnic, cultural, and gender studies related; art; art history, criticism and conservation; art teacher education; audiology and speech-language pathology; biochemistry; biological and biomedical sciences related; biology/biological sciences; biomedical/medical engineering; business administration and management; business, management, and marketing related; chemical engineering; chemistry; chemistry teacher education; cinematography and film/video production; civil engineering; classics and languages, literatures and linguistics; commercial and advertising art; communication and journalism related; communication/speech communication and rhetoric; computer and information sciences; computer and information sciences and support services related; computer engineering; creative writing; dramatic/theater arts; economics; education (specific subject areas) related; education related; electrical, electronics and communications

engineering; engineering physics; English literature (British and Commonwealth); English/language arts teacher education; entrepreneurship; environmental/environmental health engineering; family and consumer sciences/home economics teacher education; finance; fine arts related; fine/studio arts; foods, nutrition, and wellness; foodservice systems administration; foreign languages and literatures; French; geography; geology/earth science; German; health professions related; history; human development and family studies; information science/studies; interior architecture; international relations and affairs; Italian; journalism; Latin American studies; legal professions and studies related; liberal arts and sciences/liberal studies; library science; linguistics; marketing/marketing management; mathematics; mathematics teacher education; mechanical engineering; mechanical engineering/mechanical technology; music; music history, literature, and theory; music performance; music teacher education; music theory and composition; operations research; philosophy; philosophy and religious studies related; photography; physical education teaching and coaching; physics; physics teacher education; political science and government; psychology; public administration; radio and television; religious studies; Russian; Russian studies; sales, distribution and marketing; social sciences; social studies teacher education; social work; sociology; Spanish; special education; special education (hearing impaired); speech and rhetoric; transportation and materials moving related; visual and performing arts related; women's studies.

Tabor College

Accounting; actuarial science; administrative assistant and secretarial science; adult and continuing education; agricultural business and management; art teacher education; athletic training; biblical studies; biological and physical sciences; biology/biological sciences; business administration and management; business teacher education; chemistry; clinical laboratory science/medical technology; communication/speech communication and rhetoric; computer science; divinity/ministry; education; education (K-12); elementary education; English; environmental biology; health teacher education; history; humanities; interdisciplinary studies; international relations and affairs; journalism; kindergarten/preschool education; legal administrative assistant/secretary; marketing/marketing management; mass communication/media; mathematics; medical administrative assistant and medical secretary; music; music management and merchandising; music teacher education; natural sciences; pastoral studies/counseling; philosophy; physical education teaching and coaching; piano and organ; pre-dentistry studies; pre-medical studies; psychology; public relations/image management; religious studies; science teacher education; secondary education; social sciences; sociology; special education; voice and opera.

Taylor University

Accounting; ancient Near Eastern and biblical languages; art; art teacher education; athletic training; biblical studies; biology teacher education; biology/biological sciences; business administration and management; chemistry; chemistry teacher education; clinical laboratory science/medical technology; commercial and advertising art; communication/speech communication and rhetoric; computer engineering; computer graphics; computer programming; computer science; creative writing; dramatic/theater arts; economics; education; elementary education; engineering physics; English; environmental biology; environmental studies; finance; French; history; history teacher education; human resources management; information science/studies; international business/trade/commerce; international economics; international relations and affairs; kindergarten/preschool education; literature; management information systems; marketing/marketing management; mass communication/media; mathematics; middle school education; music; music management and merchandising; music performance; music teacher education; natural sciences; philosophy; physical education teaching and coaching; physical sciences; physics; piano and organ; political science and government; pre-dentistry studies; pre-law studies; pre-medical studies; pre-veterinary studies; psychology; religious education; religious studies; religious/sacred music; science teacher education; secondary education; social science teacher education; social sciences; social work; sociology; Spanish; Span-

ish language teacher education; speech teacher education; sport and fitness administration/management; theology; voice and opera.

Tennessee Technological University

Accounting; agricultural business and management; agricultural teacher education; agricultural/biological engineering and bioengineering; agronomy and crop science; animal sciences; art; art teacher education; biochemistry; biology/biological sciences; business administration and management; chemical engineering; chemistry; child development; civil engineering; clothing/textiles; computer engineering; computer science; dietetics; economics; education; electrical, electronics and communications engineering; elementary education; English; family and consumer sciences/home economics teacher education; family and consumer sciences/human sciences; fashion merchandising; finance; foods, nutrition, and wellness; French; geology/earth science; German; health teacher education; history; horticultural science; industrial engineering; industrial technology; information science/studies; international business/trade/commerce; journalism; kindergarten/preschool education; labor and industrial relations; landscaping and groundskeeping; marketing/marketing management; mathematics; mechanical engineering; music; music teacher education; nursing (registered nurse training); operations management; physical education teaching and coaching; physics; political science and government; pre-dentistry studies; pre-law studies; pre-medical studies; pre-veterinary studies; psychology; secondary education; social work; sociology; Spanish; special education; technical and business writing; turf and turfgrass management; web page, digital/multimedia and information resources design; wildlife and wildlands science and management.

Texas A&M University

Accounting; aerospace, aeronautical and astronautical engineering; agribusiness; agricultural and food products processing; agricultural animal breeding; agricultural business and management; agricultural economics; agricultural production; agricultural/biological engineering and bioengineering; agriculture; agronomy and crop science; American studies; animal sciences; animal/livestock husbandry and production; anthropology; applied horticulture; applied mathematics; aquaculture; architecture; atmospheric sciences and meteorology; biochemistry; biology/biological sciences; biomedical sciences; biomedical/medical engineering; botany/plant biology; business administration and management; cartography; cell and molecular biology; chemical engineering; chemistry; civil engineering; community health services counseling; computer engineering; computer science; construction engineering technology; curriculum and instruction; dairy science; digital communication and media/multimedia; dramatic/theater arts; ecology; economics; electrical, electronic and communications engineering technology; electrical, electronics and communications engineering; engineering technology; English; entomology; environmental design/architecture; environmental science; environmental studies; farm and ranch management; finance; fishing and fisheries sciences and management; food science; foods, nutrition, and wellness; forest/forest resources management; forestry; French; geography; geological and earth sciences/geosciences related; geology/earth science; geophysics and seismology; German; health and physical education; history; horticultural science; industrial engineering; interdisciplinary studies; international/global studies; journalism; landscape architecture; management science; manufacturing technology; marketing/marketing management; mathematics; mechanical engineering; mechanical engineering/mechanical technology; microbiology; molecular genetics; multi-/interdisciplinary studies related; museum studies; music; natural resources/conservation; nuclear engineering; ocean engineering; ornamental horticulture; parks, recreation and leisure; parks, recreation and leisure facilities management; petroleum engineering; philosophy; physics; plant protection and integrated pest management; political science and government; poultry science; pre-veterinary studies; psychology; public relations, advertising, and applied communication related; range science and management; Russian; sales, distribution and marketing; sociology; Spanish; speech and rhetoric; tourism and travel services management; urban forestry; wildlife and wildlands science and management; zoology/animal biology.

Texas Christian University

Accounting; advertising; anthropology; art history, criticism and conservation; art teacher education; astronomy and astrophysics related; athletic training; ballet; bilingual and multilingual education; biochemistry; biology/biological sciences; broadcast journalism; business administration, management and operations related; chemistry; communication/speech communication and rhetoric; computer and information sciences; computer and information sciences related; counselor education/school counseling and guidance; creative writing; criminal justice/safety; dietetics; dietetics and clinical nutrition services related; dramatic/theater arts; e-commerce; early childhood education; economics; educational leadership and administration; elementary education; engineering; English; English/language arts teacher education; environmental science; farm and ranch management; fashion merchandising; finance; fine/studio arts; French; general studies; geography; geology/earth science; health and physical education; health and physical education related; health science; history; interior design; international business/trade/commerce; international economics; international finance; international marketing; international relations and affairs; journalism; Latin American studies; liberal arts and sciences/liberal studies; management science; marketing/marketing management; mass communication/media; mathematics; mathematics teacher education; military studies; movement therapy and movement education; music; music performance; music teacher education; music theory and composition; neuroscience; nursing (registered nurse training); painting; philosophy; photography; physical education teaching and coaching; physics; piano and organ; political science and government; printmaking; psychology; radio and television; real estate; religious studies; science teacher education; sculpture; secondary education; social studies teacher education; social work; sociology; Spanish; special education; special education (gifted and talented); special education (hearing impaired); speech-language pathology; technical teacher education; theater literature, history and criticism.

Texas Tech University

Accounting; acting; advertising; agricultural business and management; agricultural communication/journalism; agricultural economics; agriculture; agronomy and crop science; animal sciences; anthropology; apparel and textiles; applied horticulture; architectural engineering technology; architecture; art; art history, criticism and conservation; biochemistry; biological and physical sciences; biology/biological sciences; business administration and management; business administration, management and operations related; business/commerce; cell and molecular biology; chemical engineering; chemistry; child development; civil engineering; classics and languages, literatures and linguistics; computer and information sciences; computer engineering; dance; dietetics; dramatic/theater arts; economics; electrical, electronic and communications engineering technology; electrical, electronics and communications engineering; engineering; engineering physics; engineering technology; English; environmental/environmental health engineering; family and community services; family and consumer sciences/human sciences; family systems; fashion merchandising; fashion/apparel design; finance; fine/studio arts; fishing and fisheries sciences and management; food science; foods, nutrition, and wellness; French; general studies; geography; geology/earth science; geophysics and seismology; German; graphic design; health and physical education; health services/allied health/health sciences; history; hotel/motel administration; human development and family studies; industrial engineering; interdisciplinary studies; interior architecture; international business/trade/commerce; journalism; landscape architecture; Latin American studies; liberal arts and sciences/liberal studies; management information systems; marketing/marketing management; mathematics; mechanical engineering; mechanical engineering/mechanical technology; microbiology; multi-/interdisciplinary studies related; music; music performance; music theory and composition; natural resources/conservation; petroleum engineering; philosophy; photojournalism; physics; plant protection and integrated pest management; political science and government; psychology; public relations/image management; radio and television; range science and management; Russian studies; social work; sociology; Spanish; speech and rhetoric; theater design and technology; wildlife and wildlands science and management; work and family studies; zoology/animal biology.

Thomas Aquinas College

Interdisciplinary studies; liberal arts and sciences/liberal studies; multi-/interdisciplinary studies related; western civilization.

Towson University

Accounting; art; art history, criticism and conservation; art teacher education; athletic training; biochemistry, biophysics and molecular biology related; biology/biological sciences; business administration and management; business administration, management and operations related; chemistry; chemistry related; communication/speech communication and rhetoric; computer and information sciences; dance; dramatic/theater arts; early childhood education; ecology; economics; education related; elementary education; English; family systems; forensic science and technology; French; geography; geology/earth science; German; gerontology; health and physical education related; health professions related; health/health care administration; history; information science/studies; interdisciplinary studies; international relations and affairs; kinesiology and exercise science; mass communication/media; mathematics; music; music teacher education; nursing (registered nurse training); occupational therapy; philosophy; photographic and film/video technology; physical education teaching and coaching; physics; political science and government; psychology; psychology related; religious studies; social sciences; social sciences related; Spanish; special education; speech-language pathology; sport and fitness administration/management; urban studies/affairs; women's studies.

Transylvania University

Accounting; anthropology; art; art history, criticism and conservation; art teacher education; biology/biological sciences; business administration and management; chemistry; computer science; dramatic/theater arts; economics; elementary education; English; fine/studio arts; French; history; kinesiology and exercise science; mathematics; middle school education; music performance; music related; music teacher education; philosophy; physical education teaching and coaching; physics; political science and government; psychology; religious studies; social sciences related; sociology; Spanish.

Trinity College

American studies; anthropology; art; art history, criticism and conservation; biochemistry; biology/biological sciences; biomedical/medical engineering; chemistry; Chinese; classics and languages, literatures and linguistics; comparative literature; computer engineering; computer science; creative writing; dance; dramatic/theater arts; economics; education; electrical, electronics and communications engineering; engineering; English; environmental science; fine/studio arts; French; gay/lesbian studies; German; history; interdisciplinary studies; international relations and affairs; Italian; Japanese; Jewish/Judaic studies; mathematics; mechanical engineering; modern languages; music; neuroscience; philosophy; physics; political science and government; psychology; public policy analysis; religious studies; Russian; sociology; Spanish; women's studies.

Trinity University

Accounting; acting; anthropology; art; art history, criticism and conservation; Asian studies; biochemistry; biology/biological sciences; business administration and management; chemistry; Chinese; classics and languages, literatures and linguistics; communication/speech communication and rhetoric; computer and information sciences; dramatic/theater arts; economics; engineering science; English; European studies; finance; French; geology/earth science; German; history; humanities; international business/trade/commerce; Latin American studies; management science; marketing/marketing management; mathematics; music; music performance; music theory and composition; neuroscience; philosophy; physics; political science and government; pre-dentistry studies; pre-law studies; pre-medical studies; pre-veterinary studies; psychology; religious studies; Russian; sociology; Spanish; speech and rhetoric; theater design and technology; urban studies/affairs; voice and opera.

Truman State University
Accounting; agricultural business and management; agriculture; agronomy and crop science; animal sciences; applied art; art; art history, criticism and conservation; athletic training; biology/biological sciences; business administration and management; chemistry; classics and languages, literatures and linguistics; commercial and advertising art; communication disorders; communication/speech communication and rhetoric; computer and information sciences; criminal justice/police science; criminal justice/safety; design and visual communications; dramatic/theater arts; economics; English; equestrian studies; exercise physiology; finance; fine/studio arts; French; German; health science; health services/allied health/health sciences; history; horticultural science; journalism; kinesiology and exercise science; linguistics; management information systems; marketing/marketing management; mass communication/media; mathematics; multi-/interdisciplinary studies related; music; music performance; nursing (registered nurse training); philosophy; physics; piano and organ; political science and government; pre-dentistry studies; pre-law studies; pre-medical studies; pre-pharmacy studies; pre-veterinary studies; psychology; public health; religious studies; Romance languages; Russian; sociology; Spanish; speech and rhetoric; visual and performing arts; voice and opera.

Tufts University
African American/Black studies; American studies; anthropology; archeology; architectural engineering; art history, criticism and conservation; Asian studies; Asian studies (Southeast); astronomy; behavioral sciences; biology/biological sciences; chemical engineering; chemistry; child development; Chinese; civil engineering; classics and languages, literatures and linguistics; community health and preventive medicine; computer engineering; computer science; developmental and child psychology; dramatic/theater arts; ecology; economics; electrical, electronics and communications engineering; elementary education; engineering; engineering physics; engineering related; engineering science; English; environmental studies; environmental/environmental health engineering; experimental psychology; French; geological/geophysical engineering; geology/earth science; German; history; industrial engineering; international relations and affairs; Jewish/Judaic studies; kindergarten/preschool education; Latin; mathematics; mechanical engineering; mental health/rehabilitation; modern Greek; music; philosophy; physics; political science and government; psychology; public health; Romance languages; Russian; Russian studies; secondary education; sociobiology; sociology; Spanish; special education; urban studies/affairs; women's studies.

Tulane University
Accounting; African studies; American studies; anatomy; anthropology; architecture; art; art history, criticism and conservation; Asian studies; biochemistry; biology/biological sciences; biomedical/medical engineering; biostatistics; business administration and management; business/commerce; cell biology and anatomical sciences related; cell biology and histology; chemical engineering; chemistry; civil engineering; classics and classical languages related; classics and languages, literatures and linguistics; cognitive psychology and psycholinguistics; communication and journalism related; communication/speech communication and rhetoric; computer and information sciences; computer engineering; computer science; corrections; criminal justice/safety; dramatic/theater arts; ecology; economics; electrical, electronics and communications engineering; engineering science; English; environmental biology; environmental studies; environmental/environmental health engineering; evolutionary biology; finance; fine/studio arts; foreign languages and literatures; French; geology/earth science; German; Hispanic-American, Puerto Rican, and Mexican-American/Chicano studies; history; information science/studies; international relations and affairs; Italian; Jewish/Judaic studies; kinesiology and exercise science; Latin; Latin American studies; legal assistant/paralegal; legal professions and studies related; liberal arts and sciences and humanities related; liberal arts and sciences/liberal studies; linguistics; marketing/marketing management; mass communication/media; mathematics; mathematics and statistics related;

mechanical engineering; medieval and Renaissance studies; modern Greek; molecular biology; multi-/interdisciplinary studies related; music; neuroscience; philosophy; physics; political science and government; Portuguese; psychology; religious studies; Russian; Russian studies; sociology; Spanish; women's studies.

Union College (NE)
Accounting; art; art teacher education; biochemistry; biology teacher education; biology/biological sciences; business administration and management; business teacher education; chemistry; chemistry teacher education; clinical laboratory science/medical technology; commercial and advertising art; computer science; computer teacher education; education; elementary education; engineering; English; English/language arts teacher education; entrepreneurship; fine/studio arts; French; German; graphic design; health science; health/medical preparatory programs related; history; history teacher education; information science/studies; international relations and affairs; journalism; kinesiology and exercise science; mathematics; mathematics teacher education; music; music performance; music teacher education; nursing (registered nurse training); pastoral studies/counseling; physical education teaching and coaching; physician assistant; physics; physics teacher education; psychology; public relations/image management; religious education; religious studies; secondary education; social science teacher education; social sciences; social work; Spanish; sport and fitness administration/management; theology.

Union College (NY)
American studies; anthropology; astronomy; biochemistry; biological and biomedical sciences related; biological and physical sciences; biology/biological sciences; chemistry; classics and languages, literatures and linguistics; computer and information sciences; economics; electrical, electronics and communications engineering; English; fine/studio arts; foreign languages and literatures; geology/earth science; history; humanities; liberal arts and sciences/liberal studies; mathematics; mechanical engineering; neuroscience; philosophy; physics; political science and government; psychology; social sciences; sociology.

Union University
Accounting; advertising; ancient Near Eastern and biblical languages; art; art teacher education; athletic training; biblical studies; biological and physical sciences; biology/biological sciences; broadcast journalism; business administration and management; business/managerial economics; chemistry; clinical laboratory science/medical technology; computer science; dramatic/theater arts; economics; education; elementary education; English; English as a second/foreign language (teaching); family and community services; finance; foreign languages and literatures; French; history; information science/studies; journalism; kindergarten/preschool education; kinesiology and exercise science; marketing/marketing management; mass communication/media; mathematics; music; music management and merchandising; music performance; music teacher education; nursing (registered nurse training); parks, recreation and leisure facilities management; philosophy; philosophy and religious studies related; physical education teaching and coaching; physics; piano and organ; political science and government; pre-dentistry studies; pre-law studies; pre-medical studies; pre-pharmacy studies; psychology; public relations/image management; radio and television; religious studies; religious/sacred music; science teacher education; secondary education; social work; sociology; Spanish; special education; speech and rhetoric; sport and fitness administration/management; theology; theology and religious vocations related; voice and opera.

United States Air Force Academy
Aerospace, aeronautical and astronautical engineering; area studies; atmospheric sciences and meteorology; behavioral sciences; biochemistry; biological and physical sciences; biology/biological sciences; business administration and management; chemistry; civil engineering; computer science; economics; electrical, electronics and communications engineering; engineering; engineering mechanics; engineering science; English; environmental/environmental health engineering; geography; history;

humanities; interdisciplinary studies; legal studies; materials science; mathematics; mechanical engineering; military studies; operations research; physics; political science and government; social sciences.

United States Coast Guard Academy
Civil engineering; electrical, electronics and communications engineering; management science; mechanical engineering; naval architecture and marine engineering; oceanography (chemical and physical); operations research; political science and government.

United States Merchant Marine Academy
Engineering-related technologies; engineering/industrial management; marine science/merchant marine officer; marine transportation related; maritime science; naval architecture and marine engineering; nuclear engineering technology; transportation and materials moving related.

United States Military Academy
Aerospace, aeronautical and astronautical engineering; American studies; applied mathematics; Arabic; Army R.O.T.C./military science; Asian studies (East); behavioral sciences; biological and physical sciences; biology/biological sciences; business administration and management; chemical engineering; chemistry; Chinese; civil engineering; computer engineering; computer science; economics; electrical, electronics and communications engineering; engineering; engineering physics; engineering/industrial management; environmental studies; environmental/environmental health engineering; European studies; European studies (Central and Eastern); French; geography; German; history; humanities; information science/studies; interdisciplinary studies; Latin American studies; literature; mathematics; mechanical engineering; modern languages; Near and Middle Eastern studies; nuclear engineering; operations research; philosophy; physics; political science and government; Portuguese; pre-law studies; pre-medical studies; psychology; public policy analysis; Russian; Spanish; systems engineering.

United States Naval Academy
Aerospace, aeronautical and astronautical engineering; Arabic; chemistry; computer and information sciences; computer hardware engineering; computer science; econometrics and quantitative economics; economics; electrical, electronics and communications engineering; engineering; English; French; history; mathematics; mechanical engineering; naval architecture and marine engineering; ocean engineering; oceanography (chemical and physical); physical sciences; physics; political science and government; systems engineering.

University at Buffalo, the State University of New York
Aerospace, aeronautical and astronautical engineering; African American/Black studies; American studies; anthropology; architecture; art; art history, criticism and conservation; Asian studies; audiology and speech-language pathology; biochemistry; bioinformatics; biological and biomedical sciences related; biology/biological sciences; biophysics; biostatistics; biotechnology; business administration and management; chemical engineering; chemistry; chemistry related; civil engineering; classics and languages, literatures and linguistics; clinical laboratory science/medical technology; communication/speech communication and rhetoric; computer engineering; computer science; dance; dramatic/theater arts; dramatic/theater arts and stagecraft related; economics; electrical, electronics and communications engineering; engineering; engineering physics; engineering science; English; environmental design/architecture; environmental/environmental health engineering; film/cinema studies; fine/studio arts; French; geography; geology/earth science; German; history; humanities; industrial engineering; information science/studies; Italian; kinesiology and exercise science; liberal arts and sciences/liberal studies; linguistics; mass communication/media; maternal/child health and neonatal nursing; mathematics; mathematics related; mechanical engineering; multi-/interdisciplinary studies related; music; music performance; nuclear medical technology; nursing (registered nurse training); nursing related; nutrition sciences; occupational therapy; pediatric nursing; pharmacology; pharmacology and toxicology; pharmacy

administration/pharmaceutics; pharmacy, pharmaceutical sciences, and administration related; philosophy; physics; physics related; political science and government; psychology; sociology; Spanish; structural engineering; theoretical and mathematical physics; women's studies.

The University of Alabama in Huntsville
Accounting; art; biology/biological sciences; business administration and management; chemical engineering; chemistry; civil engineering; computer and information sciences; computer engineering; electrical, electronics and communications engineering; elementary education; engineering related; English; finance; foreign languages and literatures; history; industrial engineering; management information systems; marketing/marketing management; mathematics; mechanical engineering; music; nursing (registered nurse training); philosophy; physics; political science and government; psychology; sociology; speech and rhetoric.

The University of Arizona
Accounting; aerospace, aeronautical and astronautical engineering; agricultural economics; agricultural teacher education; agricultural/biological engineering and bioengineering; agriculture; animal sciences; anthropology; architecture; art history, criticism and conservation; art teacher education; Asian studies (East); astronomy; atmospheric sciences and meteorology; biochemistry; biology teacher education; biology/biological sciences; business/commerce; business/managerial economics; cell biology and histology; chemical engineering; chemistry; chemistry teacher education; city/urban, community and regional planning; civil engineering; classics; clinical laboratory science/medical technology; communication disorders; communication/speech communication and rhetoric; computer and information sciences; computer engineering; consumer economics; creative writing; criminal justice/law enforcement administration; dance; drama and dance teacher education; dramatic/theater arts; early childhood education; economics; education (specific subject areas) related; electrical, electronics and communications engineering; elementary education; engineering; engineering physics; engineering related; engineering/industrial management; English; English as a second/foreign language (teaching); English/language arts teacher education; entrepreneurship; environmental science; environmental studies; family and consumer sciences/home economics teacher education; finance; fine/studio arts; foreign language teacher education; French; French language teacher education; geography; geological engineering; geology/earth science; German; German language teacher education; health teacher education; health/health care administration; Hispanic-American, Puerto Rican, and Mexican-American/Chicano studies; history; history teacher education; human development and family studies; human resources management; industrial/manufacturing engineering; Italian; Jewish/Judaic studies; journalism; Judaic studies; kindergarten/preschool education; landscape architecture; Latin American studies; liberal arts and sciences/liberal studies; linguistics; management information systems; marketing/marketing management; materials science; mathematics; mathematics teacher education; mechanical engineering; mining and mineral engineering; multi-/interdisciplinary studies related; music; music performance; music related; music teacher education; Near and Middle Eastern studies; nuclear engineering; nursing (registered nurse training); nutrition sciences; operations management; optical sciences; philosophy; physical education teaching and coaching; physics; physics teacher education; physiology; plant sciences; political science and government; pre-veterinary studies; psychology; public administration; radio and television; religious studies; Russian; science teacher education; science technologies related; secondary education; social science teacher education; social studies teacher education; sociology; soil sciences; Spanish; Spanish language teacher education; special education; speech teacher education; systems engineering; theater design and technology; visual and performing arts; water resources engineering; wildlife and wildlands science and management; women's studies.

University of Arkansas
Accounting; agribusiness; agricultural communication/journalism; agricultural teacher education; agricultural/biological engineering and bioengineering; American studies; animal sciences; anthropology; apparel

and textiles; architecture; art; biology/biological sciences; business administration and management; business/commerce; business/managerial economics; cell biology and anatomical sciences related; chemical engineering; chemistry; civil engineering; classics and languages, literatures and linguistics; communication/speech communication and rhetoric; computer and information sciences; computer engineering; criminal justice/safety; crop production; dramatic/theater arts; early childhood education; earth sciences; economics; electrical, electronics and communications engineering; elementary education; English; environmental science; finance; food science; foods, nutrition, and wellness; French; geological and earth sciences/geosciences related; geology/earth science; German; health and physical education; health science; history; horticultural science; hospitality administration; human development and family studies; industrial engineering; information technology; interior design; international business/trade/commerce; international relations and affairs; journalism; kinesiology and exercise science; landscape architecture; logistics and materials management; marketing/marketing management; mathematics; mechanical engineering; middle school education; music; nursing (registered nurse training); philosophy; physics; political science and government; poultry science; psychology; public administration; recreation products/services marketing operations; social work; sociology; Spanish; transportation and highway engineering.

University of California, Berkeley
African American/Black studies; American Indian/Native American studies; American studies; ancient/classical Greek; anthropology; applied mathematics; architecture; art; art history, criticism and conservation; Asian studies; Asian studies (Southeast); Asian-American studies; astrophysics; atmospheric sciences and meteorology; biology/biological sciences; biomedical/medical engineering; botany/plant biology; business administration and management; cell and molecular biology; Celtic languages; chemical engineering; chemistry; chemistry related; Chinese; civil engineering; classical, ancient Mediterranean and Near Eastern studies and archaeology; classics and languages, literatures and linguistics; cognitive science; comparative literature; computer science; dance; dramatic/theater arts; Dutch/Flemish; economics; electrical, electronics and communications engineering; engineering physics; engineering science; English; environmental science; environmental studies; environmental/environmental health engineering; ethnic, cultural minority, and gender studies related; film/cinema studies; foreign languages related; forest/forest resources management; forestry; French; geography; geological/geophysical engineering; geology/earth science; German; Hispanic-American, Puerto Rican, and Mexican-American/Chicano studies; history; Italian; Japanese; landscape architecture; Latin; Latin American studies; legal studies; linguistics; manufacturing engineering; mass communication/media; materials science; mathematics; mechanical engineering; microbiology; multi-/interdisciplinary studies related; music; natural resources management and policy; natural resources/conservation; Near and Middle Eastern studies; nuclear engineering; nutrition sciences; operations research; peace studies and conflict resolution; philosophy; physical sciences; physics; political science and government; psychology; public health related; religious studies; Scandinavian languages; Slavic languages; social sciences related; social work; sociology; Spanish; speech and rhetoric; statistics; toxicology; urban studies/affairs; women's studies.

University of California, Davis
Aerospace, aeronautical and astronautical engineering; African American/Black studies; agricultural business and management related; agriculture and agriculture operations related; American Indian/Native American studies; American studies; animal sciences; animal sciences related; anthropology; apparel and textiles; applied mathematics; art history, criticism and conservation; Asian studies (East); Asian-American studies; atmospheric sciences and meteorology; biology/biological sciences; biomedical/medical engineering; biotechnology; botany/plant biology; cell biology and histology; chemical engineering; chemistry; Chinese; city/urban, community and regional planning; civil engineering; classical, ancient Mediterranean and Near Eastern studies and archaeology; communication/speech communication and rhetoric; comparative literature; computational mathematics; ecology, evolution, systematics and popula-

tion biology related; economics; electrical, electronics and communications engineering; engineering related; English; entomology; environmental studies; environmental toxicology; exercise physiology; film/cinema studies; fine/studio arts; food science; French; genetics; geology/earth science; German; Hispanic-American, Puerto Rican, and Mexican-American/Chicano studies; history; human development and family studies; hydrology and water resources science; international agriculture; international relations and affairs; Italian; Japanese; landscape architecture; linguistics; materials engineering; mathematics; mechanical engineering; microbiology; molecular biochemistry; multi-/interdisciplinary studies related; music; natural resources and conservation related; natural resources/conservation; neurobiology and neurophysiology; nutrition sciences; philosophy; physical sciences related; physics; physics related; political science and government; political science and government related; psychology; religious studies; international science and agronomy; Spanish; statistics; urban forestry; visual and performing arts related; women's studies; zoology/animal biology.

University of California, Irvine
Aerospace, aeronautical and astronautical engineering; African American/Black studies; anthropology; area, ethnic, cultural, and gender studies related; art history, criticism and conservation; Asian studies (East); Asian-American studies; biochemistry/biophysics and molecular biology; biology/biological sciences; biomedical/medical engineering; business/managerial economics; cell biology and histology; chemical engineering; chemistry; Chinese; civil engineering; classical, ancient Mediterranean and Near Eastern studies and archaeology; classics and languages, literatures and linguistics; comparative literature; computer and information sciences; computer and information sciences and support services related; computer engineering; computer science; criminology; dance; dramatic/theater arts; ecology; ecology, evolution, systematics and population biology related; econometrics and quantitative economics; economics; electrical, electronics and communications engineering; English; environmental design/architecture; environmental/environmental health engineering; European studies; film/cinema studies; fine/studio arts; French; geology/earth science; German; German studies; Hispanic-American, Puerto Rican, and Mexican-American/Chicano studies; history; human ecology; humanities; information science/studies; international/global studies; Japanese; journalism; linguistics; literature; materials engineering; mathematics; mechanical engineering; microbiological sciences and immunology related; microbiology; multi-/interdisciplinary studies related; music; music performance; neuroscience; nursing related; pharmacy, pharmaceutical sciences, and administration related; philosophy; physics; political science and government; psychology; public health related; religious studies; Russian; social psychology; social sciences; sociology; Spanish; women's studies.

University of California, Los Angeles
Aerospace, aeronautical and astronautical engineering; African languages; African American/Black studies; agricultural/biological engineering and bioengineering; American Indian/Native American studies; American literature; ancient/classical Greek; anthropology; applied mathematics; Arabic; architecture; area studies related; area, ethnic, cultural, and gender studies related; art; art history, criticism and conservation; Asian studies; Asian studies (East); Asian studies (Southeast); Asian-American studies; astrophysics; atmospheric sciences and meteorology; atmospheric sciences and meteorology related; biochemistry; biology/biological sciences; biomathematics and bioinformatics related; biophysics; biotechnology; botany/plant biology; business/managerial economics; cell and molecular biology; chemical engineering; chemistry; Chinese; civil engineering; classical, ancient Mediterranean and Near Eastern studies and archaeology; classics and classical languages related; cognitive science; communication/speech communication and rhetoric; comparative literature; computational mathematics; computer and information sciences; computer engineering; design and applied arts related; development economics and international development; dramatic/theater arts; East Asian languages related; ecology; economics; electrical, electronics and communications engineering; English; environmental science; European studies; film/cinema studies; fine arts related; foreign languages related;

French; geography; geography related; geological and earth sciences/geosciences related; geological/geophysical engineering; geology/earth science; geophysics and seismology; German; Hebrew; Hispanic-American, Puerto Rican, and Mexican-American/Chicano studies; history; international economics; international/global studies; Italian; Japanese; Korean; Latin; Latin American studies; liberal arts and sciences and humanities related; linguistic and comparative language studies related; linguistics; marine biology and biological oceanography; materials engineering; materials science; mathematics; mathematics related; mechanical engineering; microbiological sciences and immunology related; multi-/interdisciplinary studies related; music; music history, literature, and theory; musicology and ethnomusicology; neuroscience; nursing related; philosophy; physics; physiological psychology/psychobiology; physiology; political science and government; Portuguese; psychology; religious studies; Russian; Russian studies; Scandinavian languages; Slavic languages; sociology; Spanish; statistics; women's studies.

University of California, Riverside

African American/Black studies; American Indian/Native American studies; anthropology; anthropology related; art; art history, criticism and conservation; Asian studies; Asian-American studies; biochemistry; biology/biological sciences; biomedical sciences; biomedical/medical engineering; botany/plant biology; business administration and management; business/managerial economics; chemical engineering; chemistry; Chinese; classics and languages, literatures and linguistics; comparative literature; computer engineering; computer science; creative writing; cultural studies; dance; dramatic/theater arts; economics; economics related; electrical, electronics and communications engineering; English; entomology; environmental studies; environmental/environmental health engineering; ethnic, cultural minority, and gender studies related; fine/studio arts; foreign languages and literatures; foreign languages related; French; geology/earth science; geophysics and seismology; German; Hispanic-American, Puerto Rican, and Mexican-American/Chicano studies; history; history related; human development and family studies; humanities; information science/studies; international relations and affairs; international/global studies; Latin American studies; legal studies; liberal arts and sciences/liberal studies; linguistics; materials science; mathematics; mechanical engineering; multi-/interdisciplinary studies related; music; music related; neuroscience; philosophy; philosophy related; physical sciences; physics; physiological psychology/psychobiology; political science and government; political science and government related; pre-law studies; psychology; psychology related; public administration; public policy analysis; religious studies; Russian; Russian studies; social sciences; social sciences related; sociology; Spanish; statistics; women's studies.

University of California, San Diego

Aerospace, aeronautical and astronautical engineering; animal physiology; anthropology; applied mathematics; archeology; art; art history, criticism and conservation; atomic/molecular physics; biochemistry; biology/biological sciences; biomedical/medical engineering; biophysics; biotechnology; cell biology and histology; chemical engineering; chemistry; chemistry teacher education; Chinese; classics and languages, literatures and linguistics; cognitive psychology and psycholinguistics; computer engineering; computer science; creative writing; cultural studies; dance; dramatic/theater arts; ecology; econometrics and quantitative economics; economics; electrical, electronics and communications engineering; engineering; engineering physics; engineering science; English; environmental studies; film/cinema studies; fine/studio arts; foreign languages and literatures; French; geology/earth science; German; history; human ecology; interdisciplinary studies; intermedia/multimedia; Italian; Japanese; Jewish/Judaic studies; Latin American studies; linguistics; literature; management science; mass communication/media; mathematics; mathematics teacher education; mechanical engineering; medical microbiology and bacteriology; medicinal and pharmaceutical chemistry; molecular biology; music; music history, literature, and theory; natural resources management and policy; philosophy; physics; physics teacher education; political science and government; psychology; religious studies;

Russian; Russian studies; sociology; Spanish; structural engineering; systems engineering; urban studies/affairs; women's studies.

University of California, Santa Barbara

African American/Black studies; anthropology; applied mathematics related; aquatic biology/limnology; area studies related; art history, criticism and conservation; Asian studies; Asian-American studies; biochemistry; biochemistry, biophysics and molecular biology related; biology/biological sciences; biopsychology; business/managerial economics; cell biology and histology; chemical engineering; chemistry; chemistry related; Chinese; classics and languages, literatures and linguistics; communication/speech communication and rhetoric; comparative literature; computer engineering; computer science; dance; dramatic/theater arts; ecology, evolution, systematics and population biology related; econometrics and quantitative economics; economics; electrical, electronics and communications engineering; English; environmental studies; film/cinema studies; fine/studio arts; French; geography; geology/earth science; geophysics and seismology; German; Hispanic-American, Puerto Rican, and Mexican-American/Chicano studies; history; hydrology and water resources science; interdisciplinary studies; international/global studies; Italian; Japanese; legal studies; liberal arts and sciences and humanities related; liberal arts and sciences/liberal studies; linguistics; marine biology and biological oceanography; mathematics; mechanical engineering; medical microbiology and bacteriology; medieval and Renaissance studies; microbiology; molecular biology; multi-/interdisciplinary studies related; music; Near and Middle Eastern studies; pharmacology; philosophy; physics; physiology; political science and government; Portuguese; pre-law studies; psychology; public/applied history and archival administration; religious studies; Slavic languages; sociology; Spanish; statistics; women's studies; zoology/animal biology.

University of California, Santa Cruz

Agricultural/biological engineering and bioengineering; American studies; anthropology; art; art history, criticism and conservation; biochemistry; bioinformatics; biology/biological sciences; business/managerial economics; cell biology and histology; chemistry; classics and languages, literatures and linguistics; cognitive psychology and psycholinguistics; computer engineering; computer graphics; computer science; creative writing; developmental and child psychology; dramatic/theater arts; ecology; economics; education; electrical, electronics and communications engineering; environmental studies; family and community services; family/community studies; film/cinema studies; foreign languages and literatures; geology/earth science; German; health science; Hispanic-American, Puerto Rican, and Mexican-American/Chicano studies; history; information science/studies; international economics; Italian studies; Latin American studies; legal studies; linguistics; literature; marine biology and biological oceanography; mathematics; molecular biology; music; neuroscience; philosophy; physics; plant sciences; political science and government; pre-law; pre-medical studies; psychology; Russian studies; sociology; women's studies.

University of Central Arkansas

Accounting; African American/Black studies; art; athletic training; audiology and speech-language pathology; biological and physical sciences; biology/biological sciences; business administration and management; business teacher education; business/commerce; cardiovascular technology; chemistry; cinematography and film/video production; clinical laboratory science/medical technology; community health services counseling; computer and information sciences; dramatic/theater arts; economics; English composition; English/language arts teacher education; environmental studies; family and consumer sciences/home economics teacher education; family and consumer sciences/human sciences; finance; French; general studies; geography; health professions related; history; insurance; international/global studies; journalism; kindergarten/preschool education; kinesiology and exercise science; management information systems; marketing/marketing management; mathematics; mathematics teacher education; middle school education; multi-/interdisciplinary studies related; music; music performance; nuclear medical technology; nursing (registered nurse training); philosophy; physical education teaching and coaching; physics; political science and government; psychology; public administration; public relations, advertising, and applied communication related; religious studies; science teacher education; social studies teacher education; sociology; Spanish; speech and rhetoric; substance abuse/addiction counseling.

University of Central Florida

Accounting; actuarial science; advertising; aerospace, aeronautical and astronautical engineering; anthropology; art; art teacher education; audiology and speech-language pathology; biology/biological sciences; business administration and management; business teacher education; business/commerce; business/managerial economics; chemistry; cinematography and film/video production; civil engineering; clinical laboratory science/medical technology; computer and information sciences; computer engineering; computer technology/computer systems technology; criminal justice/safety; dramatic/theater arts; early childhood education; economics; electrical, electronic and communications engineering technology; electrical, electronics and communications engineering; elementary education; engineering technology; English; English/language arts teacher education; environmental/environmental health engineering; finance; fine/studio arts; foreign language teacher education; foreign languages and literatures; forensic science and technology; French; health information/medical records administration; health science; health services/allied health health sciences; health/health care administration; history; hospitality administration; humanities; industrial engineering; information technology; intermedia/multimedia; journalism; legal assistant/paralegal; liberal arts and sciences/liberal studies; management information systems; marketing/marketing management; mass communication/media; mathematics; mathematics teacher education; mechanical engineering; mechanical engineering technologies related; medical microbiology and bacteriology; medical radiologic technology; music performance; music teacher education; nursing (registered nurse training); philosophy; photography; physical education teaching and coaching; physics; political science and government; psychology; public administration; radio and television; respiratory care therapy; science teacher education; social science teacher education; social sciences; social work; sociology; Spanish; special education; speech and rhetoric; statistics; trade and industrial teacher education.

University of Chicago

African studies; African American/Black studies; American studies; ancient Near Eastern and biblical languages; ancient/classical Greek; anthropology; applied mathematics; Arabic; area, ethnic, cultural, and gender studies related; art; art history, criticism and conservation; Asian studies; Asian studies (East); Asian studies (South); Asian studies (Southeast); behavioral sciences; Bengali; biochemistry; biology/biological sciences; chemistry; Chinese; classics and languages, literatures and linguistics; comparative literature; computer science; creative writing; economics; English; English language and literature related; environmental studies; European studies (Central and Eastern); film/cinema studies; fine/studio arts; French; geography; geophysics and seismology; German; Hindi; history; human development and family studies; humanities; interdisciplinary studies; international/global studies; Italian; Japanese; Jewish/Judaic studies; Latin; Latin American studies; liberal arts and sciences/liberal studies; linguistics; mathematics; medieval and Renaissance studies; modern languages; music; music history, literature, and theory; Near and Middle Eastern studies; philosophy; physics; political science and government; psychology; public policy analysis; religious studies; Romance languages; Russian; Russian studies; Sanskrit and classical Indian languages; Slavic languages; social sciences; sociology; South Asian languages; Spanish; statistics; Tamil; Tibetan; Turkish; Urdu.

University of Colorado at Boulder

Accounting; advertising; aerospace, aeronautical and astronautical engineering; anthropology; applied mathematics; architectural engineering; Asian studies; astronomy; audiology and hearing sciences; biochemistry; broadcast journalism; cell and molecular biology; chemical engineering; chemistry; Chinese; civil engineering; classics and languages, literatures and linguistics; communication and media related; communica-

tion/speech communication and rhetoric; computer engineering; computer science; cultural studies; dance; dramatic/theater arts; ecology, evolution, systematics and population biology related; economics; electrical, electronics and communications engineering; engineering physics; English; environmental design/architecture; environmental studies; environmental/environmental health engineering; ethnic, cultural minority, and gender studies related; film/cinema studies; finance; fine/studio arts; French; geography; geology/earth science; Germanic languages; history; humanities; international/global studies; Italian; Japanese; journalism; linguistics; marketing/marketing management; mathematics; mechanical engineering; music; music performance; music teacher education; philosophy; physics; physiology; political science and government; psychology; religious studies; Russian studies; sociology; Spanish; women's studies.

University of Connecticut

Accounting; acting; actuarial science; agricultural economics; agricultural teacher education; agriculture; agronomy and crop science; allied health diagnostic, intervention, and treatment professions related; American studies; animal physiology; animal sciences; animal/livestock husbandry and production; anthropology; applied horticulture; applied mathematics; art history, criticism and conservation; biology/biological sciences; biomedical/medical engineering; biophysics; business/commerce; cell biology and anatomical sciences related; chemical engineering; chemistry; civil engineering; classics and languages, literatures and linguistics; clinical laboratory science/medical technology; cognitive science; communication/speech communication and rhetoric; computer engineering; computer science; cytotechnology; dietetics; dramatic/theater arts; dramatic/theater arts and stagecraft related; ecology; economics; electrical, electronics and communications engineering; elementary education; engineering physics; engineering related; English; environmental studies; environmental/environmental health engineering; finance; fine/studio arts; French; general studies; geography; geology/earth science; German; health/health care administration; history; horticultural science; human development and family studies; industrial engineering; insurance; Italian; journalism; landscape architecture; Latin American studies; linguistics; management information systems; management science; manufacturing engineering; marine biology and biological oceanography; marketing/marketing management; materials engineering; mathematics; mechanical engineering; multi-/interdisciplinary studies related; music; music teacher education; natural resources/conservation; nursing (registered nurse training); nutrition sciences; parks, recreation and leisure facilities management; pathology/experimental pathology; pharmacy; pharmacy, pharmaceutical sciences, and administration related; philosophy; physical education teaching and coaching; physical therapy; physics; political science and government; pre-pharmacy studies; psychology; real estate; sociology; Spanish; special education; statistics; structural biology; theater design and technology; theater literature, history and criticism; urban studies/affairs; women's studies.

University of Dallas

Art; art history, criticism and conservation; biochemistry; biology/biological sciences; business administration and management; ceramic arts and ceramics; chemistry; classics and languages, literatures and linguistics; dramatic/theater arts; economics; education; elementary education; English; fine/studio arts; French; German; history; mathematics; painting; philosophy; physics; political science and government; pre-dentistry studies; pre-law studies; pre-medical studies; pre-theology/pre-ministerial studies; printmaking; psychology; sculpture; secondary education; Spanish; theology.

University of Dayton

Accounting; American studies; applied art; applied mathematics related; art history, criticism and conservation; art teacher education; biochemistry; biology/biological sciences; broadcast journalism; business administration and management; business/managerial economics; chemical engineering; chemistry; civil engineering; commercial and advertising art; computer engineering; computer engineering technology; computer science; criminal justice/law enforcement administration; dietetics;

dramatic/theater arts; economics; education; electrical, electronic and communications engineering technology; electrical, electronics and communications engineering; elementary education; English; environmental biology; environmental studies; finance; fine/studio arts; foods, nutrition, and wellness; French; general studies; geology/earth science; German; health teacher education; history; industrial technology; information science/studies; international business/trade/commerce; international relations and affairs; journalism; kindergarten/preschool education; kinesiology and exercise science; management information systems; marketing/marketing management; mass communication/media; mathematics; mechanical engineering; mechanical engineering/mechanical technology; music; music teacher education; music therapy; philosophy; photography; physical education teaching and coaching; physical sciences; physics; political science and government; pre-dentistry studies; pre-law studies; pre-medical studies; psychology; public relations/image management; radio and television; religious education; religious studies; science teacher education; secondary education; sociology; Spanish; special education; sport and fitness administration/management.

University of Delaware
Accounting; agribusiness; agricultural business and management; agricultural economics; agricultural teacher education; agricultural/biological engineering and bioengineering; agriculture; agronomy and crop science; animal sciences; anthropology; art; art history, criticism and conservation; Asian studies (East); athletic training; bilingual and multilingual education; biochemistry; biology teacher education; biology/biological sciences; biology/biotechnology laboratory technician; biotechnology; botany/plant biology; business administration and management; business/managerial economics; chemical engineering; chemistry; chemistry teacher education; civil engineering; clinical laboratory science/medical technology; commercial and advertising art; communication/speech communication and rhetoric; community organization and advocacy; comparative literature; computer and information sciences; computer engineering; computer science; consumer economics; criminal justice/law enforcement administration; developmental and child psychology; dietetics; ecology; economics; education; electrical, electronics and communications engineering; elementary education; engineering; English; English as a second/foreign language (teaching); English/language arts teacher education; entomology; environmental engineering technology; environmental studies; environmental/environmental health engineering; family and community services; family and consumer economics related; fashion merchandising; fashion/apparel design; finance; food science; foods, nutrition, and wellness; foreign language teacher education; foreign languages and literatures; French; geography; geology/earth science; geophysics and seismology; German; health and physical education; health teacher education; history; history teacher education; horticultural science; hospitality and recreation marketing; hotel/motel administration; human development and family studies; international relations and affairs; Italian; journalism; kindergarten/preschool education; kinesiology and exercise science; Latin; Latin American studies; liberal arts and sciences/liberal studies; linguistics; management information systems; marketing/marketing management; mass communication/media; mathematics; mathematics teacher education; mechanical engineering; music; music pedagogy; music teacher education; music theory and composition; natural resources management and policy; neuroscience; nursing (registered nurse training); nursing science; nutrition sciences; operations management; ornamental horticulture; philosophy; physical education teaching and coaching; physics; physics teacher education; piano and organ; plant protection and integrated pest management; political science and government; psychology; public relations/image management; sociology; soil conservation; soil science and agronomy; Spanish; sport and fitness administration/management; theater design and technology; wildlife and wildlands science and management; women's studies.

University of Denver
Accounting; animal sciences; anthropology; area, ethnic, cultural, and gender studies related; art; art history, criticism and conservation; art teacher education; Asian-American studies; biochemistry; bioinformatics;

biological and physical sciences; biology/biological sciences; business administration and management; business statistics; business/commerce; business/managerial economics; chemistry; chemistry related; commercial and advertising art; communication/speech communication and rhetoric; computer engineering; computer science; computer software and media applications related; computer systems analysis; construction management; creative writing; criminology; digital communication and media/multimedia; dramatic/theater arts; ecology; economics; electrical, electronics and communications engineering; engineering; English; environmental science; ethnic, cultural minority, and gender studies related; finance; fine arts related; French; geography; German; graphic design; history; hospitality administration; hotel/motel administration; information technology; international business/trade/commerce; international relations and affairs; Italian; journalism; Latin American studies; management information systems; marketing/marketing management; mathematics; mechanical engineering; molecular biology; multi-/interdisciplinary studies related; music; music performance; music related; musicology and ethnomusicology; philosophy; physics; political science and government; psychology; public policy analysis; real estate; religious studies; Russian; social sciences; social sciences related; sociology; Spanish.

University of Evansville
Accounting; archeology; art; art history, criticism and conservation; art teacher education; athletic training; biblical studies; biochemistry; biology teacher education; biology/biological sciences; business administration and management; business/managerial economics; chemistry; chemistry teacher education; civil engineering; classics and languages, literatures and linguistics; clinical laboratory science/medical technology; cognitive science; communication and journalism related; communication and media related; computer and information sciences; computer and information sciences and support services related; computer engineering; creative writing; design and visual communications; drama and dance teacher education; dramatic/theater arts; economics; education; electrical, electronics and communications engineering; elementary education; English; English composition; English/language arts teacher education; environmental science; environmental studies; finance; French; French language teacher education; German; German language teacher education; graphic design; health/health care administration; health/medical preparatory programs related; history; international business/trade/commerce; international relations and affairs; kinesiology and exercise science; legal professions and studies related; liberal arts and sciences/liberal studies; management information systems; marketing/marketing management; mathematics; mathematics teacher education; mechanical engineering; multi-/interdisciplinary studies related; music; music management and merchandising; music performance; music teacher education; music therapy; neuroscience; nursing (registered nurse training); philosophy; physical education teaching and coaching; physical therapist assistant; physics; physics teacher education; political science and government; pre-dentistry studies; pre-medical studies; pre-pharmacy studies; pre-veterinary studies; psychology; science teacher education; social science teacher education; social studies teacher education; sociology; Spanish; Spanish language teacher education; special education; sport and fitness administration/management; theater/theater arts management.

University of Florida
Accounting; advertising; aerospace, aeronautical and astronautical engineering; agricultural and food products processing; agricultural economics; agricultural teacher education; agricultural/biological engineering and bioengineering; agronomy and crop science; American studies; animal sciences; anthropology; architecture; art history, criticism and conservation; art teacher education; Asian studies; astronomy; athletic training; audiology and speech-language pathology; biology/biological sciences; botany/plant biology; business administration and management; chemical engineering; chemistry; civil engineering; classics and languages, literatures and linguistics; community health services counseling; computer and information sciences; computer engineering; construction engineering technology; criminology; dairy science; dance; dramatic/

theater arts; East Asian languages related; economics; electrical, electronics and communications engineering; elementary education; engineering science; English; entomology; environmental science; environmental/environmental health engineering; family and community services; finance; fine/studio arts; fire science; food science; forestry; French; geography; geology/earth science; German; graphic design; health services/allied health/health sciences; health teacher education; history; horticultural science; industrial engineering; insurance; interior design; intermedia/multimedia; Jewish/Judaic studies; journalism; kinesiology and exercise science; landscape architecture; linguistics; management science; marketing/marketing management; materials engineering; mathematics; mechanical engineering; medical microbiology and bacteriology; middle school education; multi-/interdisciplinary studies related; music; music teacher education; nuclear engineering; nursing (registered nurse training); ornamental horticulture; parks, recreation and leisure facilities management; philosophy; physical education teaching and coaching; physics; plant pathology/phytopathology; plant sciences; plant sciences related; political science and government; Portuguese; poultry science; psychology; public relations/image management; radio and television; real estate; religious studies; Russian; sociology; soil science and agronomy; Spanish; special education; sport and fitness administration/management; statistics; survey technology; systems engineering; wildlife and wildlands science and management; women's studies; zoology/animal biology.

University of Georgia
Accounting; advertising; African American/Black studies; agricultural business and management; agricultural communication/journalism; agricultural economics; agricultural sciences; agricultural sciences related; agricultural teacher education; agricultural/biological engineering and bioengineering; ancient/classical Greek; animal health; animal sciences; anthropology; apparel and textiles; applied horticulture; art; art history, criticism and conservation; art teacher education; athletic training/sports medicine; biochemistry; biological and physical sciences; biology/biological sciences; botany/plant biology; broadcast journalism; business, management, and marketing related; cell biology and histology; ceramic sciences and engineering; chemistry; child development; classics and languages, literatures and linguistics; cognitive psychology and psycholinguistics; communication disorders; comparative literature; computer and information sciences; consumer economics; criminal justice/safety; dairy science; dance; dietetics; digital communication and media/multimedia; drama and dance teacher education; dramatic/theater arts; drawing; early childhood education; ecology; economics; English; English/language arts teacher education; entomology; environmental health; environmental science; family and consumer sciences/home economics teacher education; fashion and fabric consulting; fashion merchandising; film/cinema studies; finance; fishing and fisheries sciences and management; food science; foreign language teacher education; foreign languages and literatures; forest sciences and biology; forestry; French; genetics; geography; geology/earth science; German; Germanic languages related; graphic design; health and physical education; health and physical education related; health occupations teacher education; health teacher education; history; horticulture science; housing and human environments; human development and family studies; insurance/risk management; interdisciplinary studies; interior design; interior environments; international business/trade/commerce; international relations and affairs; Italian; Japanese; journalism; landscape architecture; landscaping and groundskeeping; Latin; linguistics; management information systems; marketing/marketing management; mass communication/media; mathematics; mathematics teacher education; medical microbiology and bacteriology; metal and jewelry arts; microbiology; middle school education; modern Greek; music; music performance; music teacher education; music theory and composition; music therapy; nutrition sciences; painting; philosophy; physical education teaching and coaching; physics; plant protection and integrated pest management; plant sciences; political science and government; poultry science; pre-engineering; pre-medical studies; pre-veterinary studies; printmaking; psychology; public relations/image management; reading teacher education; real estate; religious studies; Romance languages related; Russian; sales and marketing/marketing and distribution teacher education; sales, distribution and marketing;

science teacher education; sculpture; Slavic languages; social science teacher education; social work; sociology; Spanish; speech and rhetoric; sport and fitness administration/management; statistics; technology/industrial arts teacher education; telecommunications; turf and turfgrass management; water, wetlands, and marine resources management; wildlife and wildlands science and management; women's studies.

University of Illinois at Chicago
Accounting; African American/Black studies; anthropology; architecture; art history, criticism and conservation; art teacher education; biochemistry; biology teacher education; biology/biological sciences; biomedical/medical engineering; business administration and management; chemical engineering; chemistry; chemistry teacher education; cinematography and film/video production; civil engineering; classics and languages, literatures and linguistics; commercial and advertising art; computer and information sciences; computer engineering; criminal justice/safety; dietetics; dramatic/theater arts; economics; electrical, electronics and communications engineering; elementary education; engineering physics; engineering/industrial management; English; English/language arts teacher education; entrepreneurship; finance; fine/studio arts; foreign language teacher education; French; French language teacher education; geology/earth science; German; German language teacher education; graphic design; health information/medical records administration; history; history teacher education; industrial design; industrial engineering; Italian; kinesiology and exercise science; Latin American studies; management information systems; marketing/marketing management; mathematics; mathematics and computer science; mathematics teacher education; mechanical engineering; music; nursing (registered nurse training); philosophy; photography; physics; physics teacher education; Polish; political science and government; pre-dentistry studies; pre-law studies; psychology; Russian; science teacher education; secondary education; Slavic languages; social science teacher education; social work; sociology; Spanish; Spanish language teacher education; speech and rhetoric; statistics.

University of Illinois at Urbana–Champaign
Accounting; accounting and business/management; actuarial science; advertising; aerospace, aeronautical and astronautical engineering; agricultural and extension education; agricultural business and management; agricultural communication/journalism; agricultural economics; agricultural mechanization; agricultural public services related; agricultural teacher education; agricultural/biological engineering and bioengineering; agronomy and crop science; airline pilot and flight crew; animal sciences; animal sciences related; animal/livestock husbandry and production; anthropology; applied horticulture; architecture; architecture related; area studies related; art history, criticism and conservation; art teacher education; Asian studies (East); astronomy; athletic training; atmospheric sciences and meteorology; audiology and hearing sciences; audiology and speech-language pathology; aviation/airway management; banking and financial support services; biochemistry; biological and biomedical sciences related; biology/biological sciences; biomedical/medical engineering; biophysics; biotechnology; botany/plant biology; broadcast journalism; business administration and management; business teacher education; business/commerce; cell and molecular biology; cell biology and histology; ceramic sciences and engineering; chemical engineering; chemistry; chemistry teacher education; child development; city/urban, community and regional planning; civil engineering; classics and languages, literatures and linguistics; communication and journalism related; communication/speech communication and rhetoric; community health and preventive medicine; comparative literature; computational mathematics; computer and information sciences; computer and information systems security; computer engineering; computer programming; computer science; computer software engineering; construction engineering; consumer economics; crafts, folk art and artisanry; dance; dietetics; directing and theatrical production; dramatic/theater arts; early childhood education; East Asian languages; ecology; economics; economics related; education (multiple levels); electrical, electronics and communications engineering; elementary education; engineering; engineering mechanics; engineering

physics; English; English composition; English/language arts teacher education; entomology; entrepreneurship; entrepreneurship; environmental health; environmental science; environmental/environmental health engineering; family and consumer sciences/human sciences business services related; farm and ranch management; fashion merchandising; film/cinema studies; finance; financial planning and services; food science; food science and technology related; food technology and processing; foreign language teacher education; forest sciences and biology; forestry; French; French language teacher education; general studies; geography; geological and earth sciences/geosciences related; geology/earth science; geotechnical engineering; German; German language teacher education; graphic design; health services administration; Hebrew; history; history teacher education; horticultural science; hospitality administration; human development and family studies; human nutrition; human resources management; humanities; industrial and organizational psychology; industrial design; industrial engineering; insurance; international agriculture; international/global studies; Italian; jazz/jazz studies; journalism; kindergarten/preschool education; kinesiology and exercise science; landscape architecture; Latin American studies; Latin teacher education; liberal arts and sciences and humanities related; liberal arts and sciences/liberal studies; linguistics; logistics and materials management; management information systems; management science; manufacturing engineering; marketing research; marketing/marketing management; mass communication/media; materials engineering; materials science; mathematics; mathematics and computer science; mathematics teacher education; mechanical engineering; metallurgical engineering; microbiology; music; music history, literature, and theory; music performance; music teacher education; music theory and composition; natural resources management; natural resources management and policy; natural resources/conservation; natural resources/conservation related; nuclear engineering; operations management; operations research; organizational behavior; organizational communication; ornamental horticulture; painting; parks, recreation and leisure; philosophy; photography; physical education teaching and coaching; physics; physics teacher education; physiology; plant molecular biology; plant protection and integrated pest management; political science and government; polymer/plastics engineering; Portuguese; pre-law studies; pre-veterinary studies; psychology; public health related; purchasing, procurement/acquisitions and contracts management; real estate; religious studies; restaurant, culinary, and catering management; Russian; Russian studies; sales, distribution and marketing; science teacher education; sculpture; secondary education; Slavic languages; social science teacher education; social studies teacher education; sociology; Spanish; Spanish language teacher education; special education; special education (early childhood); special education (multiply disabled); speech and rhetoric; sport and fitness administration/management; statistics; structural engineering; technical teacher education; theater literature, history and criticism; urban forestry; vocational rehabilitation counseling; voice and opera; water resources engineering; wildlife and wildlands science and management; women's studies.

The University of Iowa
Accounting; actuarial science; African studies; African American/Black studies; Air Force R.O.T.C./air science; American Indian/Native American studies; American Sign Language related; American studies; ancient studies; ancient/classical Greek; anthropology; applied mathematics related; Army R.O.T.C./military science; art; art history, criticism and conservation; art teacher education; arts management; Asian studies; astronomy; athletic training; audiology and hearing sciences; audiology and speech-language pathology; biochemistry; biology teacher education; biology/biological sciences; biomedical/medical engineering; business administration and management; business/managerial economics; ceramic arts and ceramics; chemical engineering; chemistry; chemistry teacher education; Chinese; cinematography and film/video production; civil engineering; classics and languages, literatures and linguistics; clinical laboratory science/medical technology; communication/speech communication and rhetoric; comparative literature; computer and information sciences; computer science; dance; drama and dance teacher education; dramatic/theater arts; drawing; economics; electrical, electron-

ics and communications engineering; elementary education; engineering; English; English as a second/foreign language (teaching); English language and literature related; entrepreneurship; environmental science; environmental studies; film/cinema studies; film/video and photographic arts related; finance; fine/studio arts; French; French language teacher education; geography; geography teacher education; geology/earth science; German; German language teacher education; history; history teacher education; human resources management; industrial engineering; interdisciplinary studies; international/global studies; Italian; Japanese; jazz/jazz studies; journalism; kinesiology and exercise science; labor and industrial relations; Latin; Latin American studies; Latin teacher education; liberal arts and sciences/liberal studies; linguistics; literature; management information systems; management sciences and quantitative methods related; marketing related; marketing/marketing management; mass communication/media; mathematics; mathematics teacher education; mechanical engineering; medieval and Renaissance studies; metal and jewelry arts; microbiology; modern Greek; museum studies; music; music management and merchandising; music teacher education; music theory and composition; music therapy; nuclear medical technology; nursing (registered nurse training); painting; parks, recreation and leisure; pharmacy; philosophy; photography; physics teacher education; piano and organ; political science and government; Portuguese; pre-dentistry studies; pre-law studies; pre-medical studies; pre-pharmacy studies; pre-veterinary studies; printmaking; psychology; radiologic technology/science; religious studies; Russian; Russian studies; science teacher education; sculpture; secondary education; social studies teacher education; social work; sociology; Spanish; Spanish language teacher education; speech and rhetoric; speech teacher education; sport and fitness administration/management; statistics; theater/theater arts management; therapeutic recreation; violin, viola, guitar and other stringed instruments; voice and opera; wind/percussion instruments; women's studies.

University of Kansas
Accounting; aerospace, aeronautical and astronautical engineering; African studies; African American/Black studies; American studies; ancient studies; anthropology; architectural engineering; architectural history and criticism; architecture; art history, criticism and conservation; art teacher education; astronomy; atmospheric sciences and meteorology; behavioral sciences; biochemistry/biophysics and molecular biology; biological and biomedical sciences related; biology/biological sciences; business/commerce; ceramic arts and ceramics; chemical engineering; chemistry; civil engineering; classics and languages, literatures and linguistics; clinical laboratory science/medical technology; cognitive psychology and psycholinguistics; communication disorders; community health services counseling; computer and information sciences; computer engineering; cytotechnology; dance; design and visual communications; dramatic/theater arts; East Asian languages; economics; electrical, electronics and communications engineering; elementary education; engineering physics; English; environmental studies; European studies; fiber, textile and weaving arts; finance; fine/studio arts; French; geography; geology/earth science; Germanic languages; graphic design; health and physical education; health information/medical records administration; history; humanities; illustration; industrial design; interior design; international relations and affairs; journalism; Latin American studies; liberal arts and sciences/liberal studies; linguistics; logistics and materials management; management information systems; marketing/marketing management; mathematics; mechanical engineering; metal and jewelry arts; microbiology; middle school education; molecular biology; music; music performance; music teacher education; music theory and composition; music therapy; musicology and ethnomusicology; nursing science; occupational therapy; painting; petroleum engineering; pharmacy; philosophy; physical education teaching and coaching; physics; piano and organ; political science and government; printmaking; psychology; public administration; religious studies; respiratory care therapy; Russian studies; sculpture; secondary education; Slavic languages; social work; sociology; Spanish; speech and rhetoric; stringed instruments;

theater design and technology; violin, viola, guitar and other stringed instruments; voice and opera; wind/percussion instruments; women's studies.

University of Kentucky

Accounting; advertising; agricultural economics; agricultural/biological engineering and bioengineering; agriculture and agriculture operations related; agronomy and crop science; animal sciences; anthropology; apparel and textiles; architecture; art history, criticism and conservation; art teacher education; arts management; audiology and speech-language pathology; biology/biological sciences; business/commerce; business/managerial economics; cell biology and anatomical sciences related; chemical engineering; chemistry; civil engineering; classics and languages, literatures and linguistics; clinical laboratory science/medical technology; communication/speech communication and rhetoric; computer and information sciences; dramatic/theater arts; economics; education (specific subject areas) related; electrical, electronics and communications engineering; elementary education; English; family and consumer sciences/human sciences; finance; fine/studio arts; food science; foods, nutrition, and wellness; forest sciences and biology; French; geography; geology/earth science; German; health teacher education; health/health care administration; history; hospitality administration; interdisciplinary studies; interior design; journalism; kindergarten/preschool education; landscape architecture; Latin American studies; linguistics; management science; marketing/marketing management; materials engineering; mathematics; mechanical engineering; middle school education; mining and mineral engineering; multi-/interdisciplinary studies related; music history, literature, and theory; music performance; music teacher education; natural resources/conservation; nursing (registered nurse training); nursing related; philosophy; physical education teaching and coaching; physical therapy; physics; political science and government; psychology; radio and television; Russian; science teacher education; social sciences; social work; sociology; Spanish; special education.

University of Maryland, Baltimore County

African studies; African American/Black studies; American studies; ancient studies; anthropology; area, ethnic, cultural, and gender studies related; art; art history, criticism and conservation; biochemistry/biophysics and molecular biology; bioinformatics; biology/biological sciences; business administration and management; business administration, management and operations related; chemical engineering; chemistry; computer engineering; computer science; computer/information technology services administration related; dance; dramatic/theater arts; economics; emergency medical technology (EMT paramedic); engineering; English; environmental science; environmental studies; film/cinema studies; geography; health professions related; health science; health/health care administration; history; information science/studies; interdisciplinary studies; linguistics; mass communication/media; mathematics; mechanical engineering; modern languages; music; philosophy; photography; physical therapy; physics; physics teacher education; political science and government; pre-dentistry studies; pre-medical studies; pre-nursing studies; pre-pharmacy studies; psychology; social work; sociology; statistics; visual and performing arts; women's studies.

University of Maryland, College Park

Accounting; aerospace, aeronautical and astronautical engineering; African American/Black studies; agricultural economics; agricultural/biological engineering and bioengineering; agriculture; agriculture and agriculture operations related; agronomy and crop science; American studies; animal sciences; anthropology; architecture; art history, criticism and conservation; art teacher education; astronomy; biochemistry; biology/biological sciences; business administration and management; business, management, and marketing related; business/commerce; chemical engineering; chemistry; Chinese; civil engineering; classics and languages, literatures and linguistics; communication/speech communication and rhetoric; computer and information sciences; computer engineering; criminology; dance; dietetics; dramatic/theater arts; ecology; economics; education; electrical, electronics and communications engineering; elementary education; engineering; engineering related; English; English/

language arts teacher education; family and community services; finance; fine/studio arts; food science; foods, nutrition, and wellness; foreign language teacher education; foreign languages and literatures; French; geography; geology/earth science; German; health teacher education; history; horticultural science; human resources management; information science/studies; international business/trade/commerce; Italian; Japanese; Jewish/Judaic studies; journalism; kindergarten/preschool education; landscape architecture; Latin; linguistics; logistics and materials management; management science; marketing/marketing management; materials engineering; mathematics; mathematics teacher education; mechanical engineering; medical microbiology and bacteriology; multi-/interdisciplinary studies related; music; music performance; music teacher education; natural resources/conservation; philosophy; physical education teaching and coaching; physical sciences; physics; plant sciences; political science and government; pre-dentistry studies; pre-law studies; psychology; Romance languages; Russian; Russian studies; science teacher education; secondary education; social studies teacher education; sociology; Spanish; special education; speech-language pathology; visual and performing arts; women's studies.

University of Mary Washington

American studies; art; art history, criticism and conservation; biology/biological sciences; business administration and management; chemistry; classics and languages, literatures and linguistics; computer science; dramatic/theater arts; economics; elementary education; English; environmental studies; fine/studio arts; French; geography; geology/earth science; German; historic preservation and conservation; history; interdisciplinary studies; international relations and affairs; Latin; liberal arts and sciences/liberal studies; mathematics; modern languages; music; music teacher education; philosophy; physics; political science and government; pre-dentistry studies; pre-law studies; pre-medical studies; pre-veterinary studies; psychology; religious studies; secondary education; sociology; Spanish.

University of Miami

Accounting; acting; advertising; aerospace, aeronautical and astronautical engineering; African American/Black studies; American studies; anthropology; applied mathematics; architectural engineering; architecture; art; art history, criticism and conservation; athletic training; biochemistry; biology/biological sciences; biomedical/medical engineering; biophysics; broadcast journalism; business administration and management; business administration, management and operations related; business/managerial economics; ceramic arts and ceramics; chemistry; chemistry related; cinematography and film/video production; civil engineering; classics and languages, literatures and linguistics; communication/speech communication and rhetoric; computer and information systems security; computer engineering; computer graphics; computer science; conducting; creative writing; criminology; design and visual communications; dramatic/theater arts; dramatic/theater arts and stagecraft related; economics; education; electrical, electronics and communications engineering; elementary education; engineering science; English; entrepreneurship; environmental/environmental health engineering; film/cinema studies; finance; fine/studio arts; French; general studies; geography; geology/earth science; German; graphic design; health and medical administrative services related; health services/allied health/health sciences; history; human resources management; illustration; industrial engineering; information science/studies; international business/trade/commerce; international relations and affairs; jazz/jazz studies; Jewish/Judaic studies; journalism; kinesiology and exercise science; legal studies; marine biology and biological oceanography; marketing/marketing management; mass communication/media; mathematical statistics and probability; mathematics; mathematics and statistics related; mathematics related; mechanical engineering; medical microbiology and bacteriology; meteorology; music; music performance; music related; music teacher education; music theory and composition; music therapy; musicology and ethnomusicology; natural resources management and policy; neuroscience; nursing (registered nurse training); oceanography (chemical and physical); painting; parks, recreation and leisure facilities management; philosophy; photography;

photojournalism; physics; piano and organ; political science and government; printmaking; psychology; public relations/image management; radio and television; religious studies; sculpture; secondary education; sociology; Spanish; special education; sport and fitness administration/management; theater design and technology; theater/theater arts management; voice and opera; women's studies.

University of Michigan

Actuarial science; aerospace, aeronautical and astronautical engineering; African American/Black studies; American studies; anthropology; applied mathematics; Arabic; architecture; art history, criticism and conservation; art teacher education; Asian studies; Asian studies (South); Asian studies (Southeast); astronomy; athletic training; atmospheric sciences and meteorology; biochemistry; biology/biological sciences; biomedical sciences; biophysics; biopsychology; botany/plant biology; business administration and management; ceramic arts and ceramics; chemical engineering; chemistry; Chinese; civil engineering; classics and languages, literatures and linguistics; clinical laboratory science/medical technology; commercial and advertising art; comparative literature; computer engineering; computer science; creative writing; dance; dental hygiene; design and visual communications; dramatic/theater arts; drawing; economics; education; electrical, electronics and communications engineering; elementary education; engineering; engineering physics; engineering science; English; environmental studies; environmental/environmental health engineering; European studies; fiber, textile and weaving arts; film/cinema studies; French; general studies; geology/earth science; German; Hebrew; history; humanities; industrial design; industrial engineering; interdisciplinary studies; intermedia/multimedia; international relations and affairs; Islamic studies; Italian; Japanese; jazz/jazz studies; Jewish/Judaic studies; kinesiology and exercise science; landscape architecture; Latin; Latin American studies; linguistics; mass communication/media; materials engineering; materials science; mathematics; mathematics teacher education; mechanical engineering; medieval and Renaissance studies; metal and jewelry arts; modern Greek; molecular biology; music; music history, literature, and theory; music teacher education; music theory and composition; natural resources management and policy; naval architecture and marine engineering; Near and Middle Eastern studies; nuclear engineering; nursing (registered nurse training); painting; philosophy; photography; physical education teaching and coaching; piano and organ; political science and government; printmaking; psychology; religious studies; Romance languages; Russian; Russian studies; Scandinavian studies; sculpture; secondary education; social sciences; sociology; Spanish; speech and rhetoric; sport and fitness administration/management; statistics; theater design and technology; Turkic, Ural-Altaic, Caucasian, and Central Asian languages related; violin, viola, guitar and other stringed instruments; visual and performing arts; voice and opera; wildlife biology; wind/percussion instruments; women's studies; zoology/animal biology.

University of Michigan–Dearborn

Accounting; American studies; anthropology; area studies related; art history, criticism and conservation; biochemistry; biology/biological sciences; business administration and management; business administration, management and operations related; chemistry; chemistry teacher education; communication/speech communication and rhetoric; computer and information sciences; computer programming; criminal justice/safety; early childhood education; economics; education; electrical, electronics and communications engineering; elementary education; engineering related; English; environmental science; environmental studies; finance; French; general studies; geology/earth science; health/health care administration; history; human resources management; humanities; industrial engineering; liberal arts and sciences/liberal studies; management information systems; manufacturing engineering; marketing/marketing management; mathematics; mathematics teacher education; mechanical engineering; microbiology; multi-/interdisciplinary studies related; philosophy; physics; political science and government; psychology; science teacher education; secondary education; social sciences; social studies teacher education; sociology; Spanish; women's studies.

University of Minnesota, Morris

Anthropology; art history, criticism and conservation; biology/biological sciences; business administration and management; chemistry; computer science; dramatic/theater arts; economics; education; education (K-12); elementary education; English; European studies; fine/studio arts; French; geology/earth science; German; history; human services; Latin American studies; liberal arts and sciences/liberal studies; management science; mathematics; music; philosophy; physical therapy; physics; political science and government; pre-dentistry studies; pre-law studies; pre-medical studies; pre-pharmacy studies; pre-veterinary studies; psychology; secondary education; social sciences; sociology; Spanish; speech and rhetoric; speech/theater education; statistics; women's studies.

University of Minnesota, Twin Cities Campus

Accounting; actuarial science; aerospace, aeronautical and astronautical engineering; African studies; African American/Black studies; agricultural business and management; agricultural teacher education; agricultural/biological engineering and bioengineering; agriculture; agronomy and crop science; American Indian/Native American studies; American studies; animal genetics; animal physiology; animal sciences; anthropology; architecture; art; art history, criticism and conservation; art teacher education; Asian studies (East); Asian studies (South); astronomy; astrophysics; audiology and speech-language pathology; biochemistry; biology/biological sciences; botany/plant biology; business teacher education; cell biology and histology; chemical engineering; chemistry; Chinese; civil engineering; clinical laboratory science/medical technology; clothing/textiles; commercial and advertising art; comparative literature; computer science; construction management; dance; dental hygiene; developmental and child psychology; dramatic/theater arts; ecology; economics; education; electrical, electronics and communications engineering; elementary education; emergency medical technology (EMT paramedic); English; English/language arts teacher education; environmental studies; European studies; family and community services; family and consumer sciences/home economics teacher education; film/cinema studies; finance; fish/game management; foods, nutrition, and wellness; foreign language teacher education; forest/forest resources management; forestry; French; funeral service and mortuary science; geography; geological/geophysical engineering; geology/earth science; geophysics and seismology; German; health and physical education related; Hebrew; Hispanic-American, Puerto Rican, and Mexican-American/Chicano studies; history; industrial engineering; insurance; interior design; international business/trade/commerce; international relations and affairs; Italian; Japanese; Jewish/Judaic studies; journalism; kindergarten/preschool education; landscape architecture; Latin; Latin American studies; linguistics; management information systems; marketing/marketing management; mass communication/media; materials engineering; materials science; mathematics; mathematics teacher education; mechanical engineering; medical microbiology and bacteriology; modern Greek; music; music teacher education; music therapy; natural resources management and policy; Near and Middle Eastern studies; neuroscience; nursing (registered nurse training); occupational therapy; parks, recreation and leisure facilities management; philosophy; physical education teaching and coaching; physical therapy; physics; plant sciences; political science and government; Portuguese; pre-dentistry studies; pre-law studies; pre-medical studies; pre-veterinary studies; psychology; public health; religious studies; Russian; Russian studies; Scandinavian languages; science teacher education; social science teacher education; sociology; soil science and agronomy; Spanish; urban studies/affairs; women's studies; wood science and wood products/pulp and paper technology.

University of Missouri–Columbia

Accounting; advertising; agricultural business and management; agricultural communication/journalism; agricultural economics; agricultural mechanization; agricultural teacher education; agriculture; animal sciences; anthropology; apparel and textiles; archeology; art; art history, criticism and conservation; art teacher education; Asian studies (East); Asian studies (South); atmospheric sciences and meteorology; behavioral sciences; biochemistry; biology teacher education; biology/

biological sciences; broadcast journalism; business administration and management; business teacher education; business/managerial economics; chemical engineering; chemistry; chemistry teacher education; civil engineering; classics and languages, literatures and linguistics; communication disorders sciences and services related; communication/speech communication and rhetoric; computer and information sciences; computer engineering; computer science; diagnostic medical sonography and ultrasound technology; dietetics; dramatic/theater arts; early childhood education; economics; education; education related; electrical, electronics and communications engineering; elementary education; English; environmental studies; European studies; European studies (Central and Eastern); family and consumer economics related; finance; fish/game management; fishing and fisheries sciences and management; food science; foods, nutrition, and wellness; forestry; French; general studies; geography; geology/earth science; German; health/medical preparatory programs related; history; hotel/motel administration; housing and human environments; human development and family studies; human nutrition; industrial engineering; interdisciplinary studies; interior architecture; international agriculture; international business/trade/commerce; international economics; journalism; kindergarten/preschool education; Latin; Latin American studies; linguistics; management information systems; marketing/marketing management; mass communication/media; mathematics; mathematics teacher education; mechanical engineering; medical radiologic technology; microbiology; middle school education; modern Greek; music; music teacher education; natural resources/conservation; nuclear medical technology; nursing (registered nurse training); nutrition sciences; occupational therapy; parks, recreation and leisure; peace studies and conflict resolution; philosophy; photojournalism; physics; physics teacher education; plant sciences; political science and government; psychology; publishing; radio and television; radiologic technology/science; real estate; religious studies; respiratory care therapy; restaurant/food services management; Russian; Russian studies; science teacher education; secondary education; social studies teacher education; social work; sociology; Spanish; special education related; statistics; technical teacher education; tourism and travel services marketing; wildlife and wildlands science and management.

University of Missouri–Kansas City
Accounting; American studies; art; art history, criticism and conservation; biology/biological sciences; business administration and management; chemistry; civil engineering; clinical/medical laboratory technology; communication/speech communication and rhetoric; computer science; criminal justice/law enforcement administration; criminology; dance; dental hygiene; dramatic/theater arts; early childhood education; economics; electrical, electronics and communications engineering; elementary education; English; fine/studio arts; French; geography; geology/earth science; German; history; information technology; interdisciplinary studies; liberal arts and sciences/liberal studies; mass communication/media; mathematics; mechanical engineering; middle school education; music; music performance; music teacher education; music theory and composition; nursing (registered nurse training); pharmacy; philosophy; physics; political science and government; psychology; secondary education; sociology; Spanish; statistics; urban education and leadership; urban studies/affairs.

University of Nebraska–Lincoln
Accounting; actuarial science; advertising; agricultural and food products processing; agricultural business and management; agricultural communication/journalism; agricultural economics; agricultural mechanization; agricultural teacher education; agricultural/biological engineering and bioengineering; agriculture; agronomy and crop science; ancient studies; ancient/classical Greek; animal sciences; anthropology; apparel and textiles; architectural engineering; architecture; art history, criticism and conservation; art teacher education; athletic training; atmospheric sciences and meteorology; audiology and hearing sciences; biochemistry; biology teacher education; biology/biological sciences; biomedical/medical engineering; botany/plant biology; broadcast journalism; business administration and management; business teacher education; business/managerial economics; chemical engineering; chemistry; chemistry

teacher education; civil engineering; classics and languages, literatures and linguistics; communication/speech communication and rhetoric; community health services counseling; computer and information sciences; computer engineering; computer teacher education; construction engineering technology; dance; dramatic/theater arts; economics; education (multiple levels); education (specific subject areas) related; electrical, electronics and communications engineering; elementary education; engineering related; English; English as a second/foreign language (teaching); English/language arts teacher education; entomology; environmental studies; European studies (Western); family and consumer economics related; film/cinema studies; finance; fine/studio arts; fire protection and safety technology; food science; foods, nutrition, and wellness; foreign language teacher education; forensic science and technology; French; French language teacher education; geography; geology/earth science; German; German language teacher education; health teacher education; history; history teacher education; horticultural science; hospitality administration; industrial engineering; industrial production technologies related; interior architecture; international business/trade/commerce; international relations and affairs; journalism related; landscape architecture; landscaping and groundskeeping; Latin; Latin American studies; law and legal studies related; legal professions and studies related; liberal arts and sciences/liberal studies; management science; marketing/marketing management; mathematics; mathematics teacher education; mechanical engineering; medieval and Renaissance studies; middle school education; music; natural resources management and policy; natural resources/conservation; philosophy; physical education teaching and coaching; physics; physics teacher education; plant protection and integrated pest management; political science and government; pre-dentistry studies; pre-medical studies; pre-pharmacy studies; pre-veterinary studies; psychology; range science and management; reading teacher education; Russian; sales and marketing/marketing and distribution teacher education; science teacher education; social science teacher education; sociology; soil science and agronomy; Spanish; Spanish language teacher education; special education (hearing impaired); special education related; speech-language pathology; technology/industrial arts teacher education; trade and industrial teacher education; veterinary/animal health technology; women's studies.

The University of North Carolina at Asheville
Accounting; art; atmospheric sciences and meteorology; biology/biological sciences; business administration and management; chemistry; classics and languages, literatures and linguistics; computer science; dramatic/theater arts; economics; engineering; English; environmental studies; fine/studio arts; French; German; history; liberal arts and sciences/liberal studies; mass communication/media; mathematics; music; music related; operations management; philosophy; physics; political science and government; psychology; religious studies; sociology; Spanish; web page, digital/multimedia and information resources design; women's studies.

The University of North Carolina at Chapel Hill
African American/Black studies; American studies; anthropology; applied mathematics; area, ethnic, cultural, and gender studies related; art history, criticism and conservation; Asian studies; astronomy; biology/biological sciences; biostatistics; business administration and management; chemistry; classics and languages, literatures and linguistics; clinical laboratory science/medical technology; communication/speech communication and rhetoric; comparative literature; computer science; dental hygiene; dramatic/theater arts; early childhood education; economics; elementary education; English; environmental health; environmental science; environmental studies; fine/studio arts; foods, nutrition, and wellness; geography; geology/earth science; German; health and physical education; health/health care administration; history; human resources management; information science/studies; Latin American studies; liberal arts and sciences/liberal studies; mass communication/media; mathematics; medical radiologic technology; middle school education; music; music performance; nursing (registered nurse training); parks, recreation and leisure facilities management; pathology/experimental pathology; peace studies and conflict resolution; pharmacy, pharmaceutical sciences, and administration related; philosophy; physical sciences related; physics;

political science and government; psychology; public policy analysis; religious studies; Romance languages; Romance languages related; Russian studies; Slavic, Baltic, and Albanian languages related; sociology; women's studies.

The University of North Carolina Wilmington

Accounting; anthropology; art history, criticism and conservation; athletic training; biology teacher education; biology/biological sciences; business administration and management; business/managerial economics; chemistry; chemistry teacher education; cinematography and film/video production; communication/speech communication and rhetoric; computer science; creative writing; criminal justice/safety; dramatic/ theater arts; economics; education (specific subject areas) related; elementary education; English; English/language arts teacher education; environmental science; environmental studies; finance; fine/studio arts; French; French language teacher education; geography; geology/earth science; German; health and physical education; health professions related; history; history teacher education; kindergarten/preschool education; management information systems; marine biology and biological oceanography; marketing/marketing management; mathematics; mathematics teacher education; middle school education; music; music performance; music teacher education; nursing (registered nurse training); parks, recreation and leisure facilities management; philosophy and religious studies related; physical education teaching and coaching; physics; political science and government; psychology; social work; sociology; Spanish; Spanish language teacher education; special education; special education (emotionally disturbed); special education (mentally retarded); special education (multiply disabled); special education (specific learning disabilities); statistics; therapeutic recreation.

University of North Florida

Accounting; anthropology; art; art teacher education; athletic training; banking and financial support services; biology/biological sciences; business administration and management; business/managerial economics; chemistry; civil engineering; computer and information sciences; construction engineering technology; criminal justice/safety; early childhood education; economics; electrical, electronics and communications engineering; elementary education; English; finance; fine/studio arts; general studies; health services/allied health/health sciences; health/health care administration; history; international business/trade/commerce; international relations and affairs; international/global studies; jazz/jazz studies; liberal arts and sciences/liberal studies; marketing/marketing management; mass communication/media; mathematics; mathematics teacher education; mechanical engineering; middle school education; music; music performance; music teacher education; nursing (registered nurse training); philosophy; physical education teaching and coaching; physics; political science and government; psychology; science teacher education; secondary education; sign language interpretation and translation; sociology; Spanish; special education; sport and fitness administration/management; statistics; trade and industrial teacher education; transportation management.

University of Notre Dame

Accounting; aerospace, aeronautical and astronautical engineering; African American/Black studies; American studies; ancient/classical Greek; anthropology; Arabic; architecture; art history, criticism and conservation; biochemistry; biological and physical sciences; biology/ biological sciences; business administration, management and operations related; business/commerce; chemical engineering; chemistry; chemistry related; Chinese; civil engineering; classics and languages, literatures and linguistics; computer and information sciences; computer and information sciences and support services related; computer engineering; design and visual communications; dramatic/theater arts; economics; electrical, electronics and communications engineering; English; environmental science; environmental/environmental health engineering; film/ studio arts; French; German; history; Italian; Japanese; liberal arts and sciences/liberal studies; management information systems; marketing/ marketing management; mathematics; mechanical engineering; medieval and Renaissance studies; music; philosophy; philosophy and religious

studies related; physics; physics related; political science and government; pre-medical studies; psychology; Romance languages; Russian; science teacher education; sociology; Spanish; theology.

University of Oklahoma

Accounting; advertising; aeronautics/aviation/aerospace science and technology; aerospace, aeronautical and astronautical engineering; African American/Black studies; American Indian/Native American studies; anthropology; architecture; architecture related; area studies; area studies related; art; art history, criticism and conservation; astronomy; astrophysics; atmospheric sciences and meteorology; biomedical/medical engineering; botany/plant biology; broadcast journalism; business administration and management; business/managerial economics; chemical engineering; chemistry; Chinese; cinematography and film/video production; civil engineering; classics and languages, literatures and linguistics; clinical/medical laboratory technology; communication and journalism related; communication/speech communication and rhetoric; computer and information sciences; computer engineering; criminology; dance; design and visual communications; dramatic/theater arts; early childhood education; economics; education (specific subject areas) related; electrical, electronics and communications engineering; elementary education; engineering; engineering physics; English; English language and literature related; English/language arts teacher education; entrepreneurship; environmental design/architecture; environmental science; environmental/environmental health engineering; finance; fine/ studio arts; foreign language teacher education; French; geography; geological and earth sciences/geosciences related; geology/earth science; geophysics and seismology; German; health and physical education; history; human resources management and services related; industrial engineering; interior design; international business/trade/commerce; journalism; liberal arts and sciences/liberal studies; library science; linguistics; management information systems; marketing/marketing management; mathematics; mathematics teacher education; mechanical engineering; medical laboratory technology; microbiology; multi-/ interdisciplinary studies related; music; music performance; music theory and composition; petroleum engineering; philosophy; photography; physics; piano and organ; political science and government; professional studies; psychology; public administration; public relations/image management; religious studies; Russian; science teacher education; social studies teacher education; social work; sociology; Spanish; special education; violin, viola, guitar and other stringed instruments; visual and performing arts related; voice and opera; wind/percussion instruments; women's studies; zoology/animal biology.

University of Pennsylvania

Accounting; actuarial science; African studies; African American/Black studies; American studies; anthropology; architecture; art history, criticism and conservation; Asian studies (East); Asian studies (South); biochemistry; bioinformatics; biology/biological sciences; biomedical sciences; biomedical/medical engineering; biophysics; business administration and management; business administration, management and operations related; chemical engineering; chemistry; classics and languages, literatures and linguistics; cognitive science; communication/ speech communication and rhetoric; community health services counseling; comparative literature; computer engineering; computer graphics; computer systems networking and telecommunications; dramatic/theater arts; e-commerce; East Asian languages; economics; electrical, electronics and communications engineering; elementary education; engineering related; English; English language and literature related; environmental design/architecture; environmental studies; environmental/environmental health engineering; film/cinema studies; finance; fine/studio arts; French; geology/earth science; German; health professions related; health/health care administration; history; history and philosophy of science and technology; human resources management; humanities; insurance; international business/trade/commerce; international relations and affairs; international/global studies; Italian; Jewish/Judaic studies; Latin American studies; legal professions and studies related; liberal arts and sciences/ liberal studies; linguistics; logic; management information systems; management sciences and quantitative methods related; marketing/

marketing management; materials engineering; materials science; mathematics; mechanical engineering; music; natural sciences; neuroscience; nursing (registered nurse training); nursing related; operations management; philosophy; philosophy related; physics; political science and government; psychology; public policy analysis; real estate; religious studies; Romance languages related; Russian; sales, distribution and marketing; Semitic languages; social sciences; sociology; Spanish; statistics; systems engineering; transportation management; urban studies/affairs; visual and performing arts; women's studies.

University of Pittsburgh

Accounting; African American/Black studies; anthropology; applied mathematics; art history, criticism and conservation; audiology and speech-language pathology; biological and physical sciences; biology/biological sciences; biomedical/medical engineering; business/commerce; chemical engineering; chemistry; Chinese; civil engineering; classics and languages, literatures and linguistics; computer and information sciences and support services related; computer engineering; computer science; corrections; creative writing; dental hygiene; dietetics; dramatic/theater arts; ecology; economics; educational psychology; electrical, electronics and communications engineering; engineering; engineering physics; English; English literature (British and Commonwealth); ethnic, cultural minority, and gender studies related; film/cinema studies; finance; fine/studio arts; French; geological and earth sciences/geosciences related; geology/earth science; German; health information/medical records administration; health professions related; history; history and philosophy of science and technology; humanities; industrial engineering; information science/studies; interdisciplinary studies; Italian; Japanese; legal studies; liberal arts and sciences/liberal studies; linguistics; marketing/marketing management; materials engineering; mathematics; mathematics and statistics related; mathematics related; mechanical engineering; metallurgical engineering; microbiology; molecular biology; multi-/interdisciplinary studies related; music; neuroscience; nursing (registered nurse training); occupational therapy; pharmacy; philosophy; physical education teaching and coaching; physical sciences; physics; political science and government; psychology; public administration; rehabilitation and therapeutic professions related; religious studies; Russian; Slavic languages; social sciences; social work; sociology; Spanish; speech and rhetoric; statistics; urban studies/affairs.

University of Portland

Accounting; arts management; biology/biological sciences; business administration and management; chemistry; civil engineering; computer engineering; computer science; criminal justice/safety; dramatic/theater arts; education; electrical, electronics and communications engineering; elementary education; engineering; engineering science; engineering/industrial management; English; environmental studies; finance; history; interdisciplinary studies; international business/trade/commerce; journalism; marketing/marketing management; mass communication/media; mathematics; mechanical engineering; music; music teacher education; nursing (registered nurse training); philosophy; physics; political science and government; pre-dentistry studies; pre-law studies; pre-medical studies; psychology; secondary education; social work; sociology; Spanish; theology.

University of Puget Sound

Art; Asian studies; biochemistry; biology/biological sciences; business/commerce; chemistry; classics and languages, literatures and linguistics; communication/speech communication and rhetoric; computer programming (specific applications); computer science; creative writing; developmental biology and embryology; dramatic/theater arts; economics; English; French; geology/earth science; German; history; interdisciplinary studies; international business/trade/commerce; international economics; international relations and affairs; kinesiology and exercise science; mathematics; molecular biology; music; music management and merchandising; music performance; music teacher education; natural sciences; philosophy; physics; political science and government;

pre-dentistry studies; pre-law studies; pre-medical studies; pre-veterinary studies; psychology; religious studies; science, technology and society; sociology; Spanish.

University of Redlands

Accounting; anthropology; art history, criticism and conservation; Asian studies; audiology and speech-language pathology; biology/biological sciences; business administration and management; business/commerce; chemistry; computer science; creative writing; economics; education; elementary education; English; environmental studies; fine/studio arts; French; German; history; interdisciplinary studies; international relations and affairs; liberal arts and sciences/liberal studies; literature; management information systems; mathematics; music; music history, literature, and theory; music performance; music teacher education; music theory and composition; philosophy; physics; piano and organ; political science and government; psychology; religious studies; secondary education; sociology; Spanish; speech therapy; voice and opera.

University of Rhode Island

Accounting; animal sciences; anthropology; apparel and accessories marketing; apparel and textiles; applied economics; art; art history, criticism and conservation; biology/biological sciences; biomedical/medical engineering; business administration and management; chemical engineering; chemistry; civil engineering; classics and languages, literatures and linguistics; clinical laboratory science/medical technology; communication disorders; communication/speech communication and rhetoric; comparative literature; computer and information sciences; computer engineering; consumer economics; dental hygiene; dietetics; econometrics and quantitative economics; economics; electrical, electronics and communications engineering; elementary education; English; environmental studies; finance; fishing and fisheries sciences and management; foods, nutrition, and wellness; French; geology/earth science; German; health/health care administration; history; human development and family studies; human services; industrial engineering; interdisciplinary studies; international business/trade/commerce; Italian; journalism; landscape architecture; Latin American studies; liberal arts and sciences/liberal studies; management information systems; marine biology and biological oceanography; marketing/marketing management; mathematics; mechanical engineering; medical microbiology and bacteriology; music; music performance; music teacher education; music theory and composition; natural resources management and policy; natural resources/conservation; nursing (registered nurse training); ocean engineering; pharmacy; philosophy; physical education teaching and coaching; physics; political science and government; psychology; public policy analysis; secondary education; sociology; Spanish; turf and turfgrass management; wildlife and wildlands science and management; women's studies; zoology/animal biology.

University of Richmond

Accounting; American studies; art; art history, criticism and conservation; art teacher education; biology/biological sciences; business administration and management; business/managerial economics; chemistry; classics and languages, literatures and linguistics; computer science; criminal justice/law enforcement administration; dramatic/theater arts; economics; English; environmental studies; European studies; European studies (Central and Eastern); finance; fine/studio arts; French; German; health teacher education; history; human resources management; interdisciplinary studies; international business/trade/commerce; international economics; international relations and affairs; journalism; Latin; Latin American studies; legal administrative assistant/secretary; management information systems; marketing/marketing management; mathematics; middle school education; modern Greek; molecular biology; music; music history, literature, and theory; philosophy; physical education teaching and coaching; physics; political science and government; psychology; religious studies; secondary education; sociology; Spanish; speech and rhetoric; urban studies/affairs; women's studies.

University of Rochester

African American/Black studies; American Sign Language (ASL); anthropology; applied mathematics; art history, criticism and conservation; biological and physical sciences; biology/biological sciences; biomedical/medical engineering; chemical engineering; chemistry; classics and languages, literatures and linguistics; cognitive science; comparative literature; computer science; economics; electrical, electronics and communications engineering; engineering science; English; environmental science; environmental studies; film/cinema studies; fine/studio arts; French; geological/geophysical engineering; geology/earth science; German; history; Japanese; jazz/jazz studies; linguistics; mathematics; mathematics and statistics related; mechanical engineering; music; music teacher education; music theory and composition; nursing (registered nurse training); optical sciences; philosophy; physics; physics related; political science and government; psychology; religious studies; Russian; Russian studies; social sciences related; Spanish; statistics; women's studies.

University of St. Thomas (MN)

Accounting; actuarial science; ancient/classical Greek; art history, criticism and conservation; Asian studies (East); biochemistry; biology teacher education; biology/biological sciences; broadcast journalism; business administration and management; business administration, management and operations related; business/corporate communications; chemistry; chemistry teacher education; classics and classical languages related; classics and languages, literatures and linguistics; clinical/medical social work; communication/speech communication and rhetoric; computer and information sciences; creative writing; criminology; drama and dance teacher education; dramatic/theater arts; econometrics and quantitative economics; economics; education (K-12); education (specific subject areas) related; electrical, electronics and communications engineering; elementary education; English; English/language arts teacher education; entrepreneurship; finance; foreign language teacher education; foreign languages related; French; geography; geology/earth science; German; health and physical education; health science; health teacher education; history; human resources management; interdisciplinary studies; international business/trade/commerce; international economics; international relations and affairs; Japanese; journalism; journalism related; Latin; marketing/marketing management; mathematics; mathematics teacher education; mechanical engineering; middle school education; multi-/interdisciplinary studies related; music; music teacher education; operations management; peace studies and conflict resolution; philosophy; physical education teaching and coaching; physics; physics teacher education; political science and government; psychology; psychology related; public administration; public health education and promotion; real estate; religious studies; Russian; Russian studies; science teacher education; social sciences; social studies teacher education; social work; sociology; Spanish; speech/theater education; women's studies.

University of St. Thomas (TX)

Accounting; biology/biological sciences; business administration and management; chemistry; communication/speech communication and rhetoric; dramatic/theater arts; economics; education; elementary education; English; environmental studies; finance; fine/studio arts; French; general studies; history; international relations and affairs; liberal arts and sciences/liberal studies; management information systems; marketing/marketing management; mathematics; music; music teacher education; pastoral studies/counseling; philosophy; political science and government; pre-dentistry studies; pre-law studies; pre-medical studies; pre-pharmacy studies; pre-veterinary studies; psychology; secondary education; Spanish; theology; theology and religious vocations related.

University of San Diego

Accounting; anthropology; art; art history, criticism and conservation; biochemistry; biology/biological sciences; business administration and management; business/managerial economics; chemistry; communication/speech communication and rhetoric; computer science; dramatic/theater arts; economics; electrical, electronics and communications engineering; English; finance; French; history; humanities; industrial engineering; intercultural/multicultural and diversity studies; international relations and affairs; liberal arts and sciences/liberal studies; marine biology and biological oceanography; marketing/marketing

management; mathematics; mechanical engineering; music; nursing (registered nurse training); philosophy; physics; political science and government; psychology; religious studies; sociology; Spanish.

The University of Scranton

Accounting; ancient/classical Greek; biology/biological sciences; biomathematics and bioinformatics related; biophysics; business administration and management; business administration, management and operations related; chemistry; chemistry related; clinical laboratory science/medical technology; communication/speech communication and rhetoric; communications technologies and support services related; computer and information sciences and support services related; computer engineering; computer science; criminal justice/safety; dramatic/theater arts; early childhood education; economics; electrical, electronics and communications engineering; elementary education; English; entrepreneurship; finance; foreign languages and literatures; French; German; gerontology; health/health care administration; history; human resources management; human services; information science/studies; international business/trade/commerce; international relations and affairs; Italian; kindergarten/preschool education; kinesiology and exercise science; Latin; management science; marketing/marketing management; mathematics; mathematics and statistics related; neuroscience; nursing (registered nurse training); operations management; philosophy; physics; political science and government; psychology; religious studies; secondary education; sociology; Spanish; special education.

University of South Carolina

Accounting; advertising; African American/Black studies; anthropology; aquatic biology/limnology; art history, criticism and conservation; art teacher education; biology/biological sciences; broadcast journalism; business administration and management; business/managerial economics; chemical engineering; chemistry; civil engineering; classics and languages, literatures and linguistics; computer and information sciences; computer engineering; criminal justice/law enforcement administration; dramatic/theater arts; economics; electrical, electronics and communications engineering; English; European studies; experimental psychology; finance; fine/studio arts; French; general retailing/wholesaling; geography; geology/earth science; geophysics and seismology; German; history; hospitality administration; insurance; international relations and affairs; Italian; journalism; kinesiology and exercise science; Latin American studies; liberal arts and sciences/liberal studies; management science; marine biology; marine biology and biological oceanography; marine science/merchant marine officer; marketing/marketing management; mathematics; mechanical engineering; music; music teacher education; nursing (registered nurse training); oceanography; office management; philosophy; physical education teaching and coaching; physics; political science and government; public relations/image management; real estate; religious studies; sociology; Spanish; sport and fitness administration/management; statistics; women's studies.

University of Southern California

Accounting; acting; aerospace, aeronautical and astronautical engineering; African American/Black studies; American literature; American studies; anthropology; anthropology related; architecture; art; art history, criticism and conservation; Asian studies (East); Asian-American studies; astronomy; biochemistry; biology/biological sciences; biomedical/medical engineering; biophysics; broadcast journalism; business administration and management; business administration, management and operations related; business, management, and marketing related; chemical engineering; chemistry; cinematography and film/video production; city/urban, community and regional planning; civil engineering; classics and languages, literatures and linguistics; cognitive psychology and psycholinguistics; communication/speech communication and rhetoric; comparative literature; computer and information sciences; computer engineering; computer engineering related; computer science; construction engineering; creative writing; cultural studies; dental hygiene; directing and theatrical production; dramatic/theater arts; East Asian languages; economics; electrical, electronics and communications engineering; engineering; English; English literature (British and Commonwealth);

environmental studies; environmental/environmental health engineering; ethics; film/cinema studies; fine/studio arts; French; general studies; geography; geology/earth science; German; gerontology; health science; Hispanic-American, Puerto Rican, and Mexican-American/Chicano studies; history; interdisciplinary studies; international business/trade/commerce; international relations and affairs; Italian; jazz/jazz studies; Jewish/Judaic studies; journalism; kinesiology and exercise science; landscape architecture; linguistics; mass communication/media; mathematics; mechanical engineering; music; music management and merchandising; music performance; music related; music teacher education; music theory and composition; neuroscience; occupational therapy; petroleum engineering; philosophy; physical sciences; physics; playwriting and screenwriting; political science and government; polymer/plastics engineering; Portuguese; psychology; public administration; public health education and promotion; public policy analysis; public relations/image management; radio and television; religious studies; Russian; Slavic languages; social sciences; sociology; Spanish; structural engineering; systems engineering; theater design and technology; theater/theater arts management; urban studies/affairs; violin, viola, guitar and other stringed instruments; water resources engineering.

The University of Tennessee
Accounting; advertising; aerospace, aeronautical and astronautical engineering; agricultural business and management related; agricultural economics; agricultural teacher education; agricultural/biological engineering and bioengineering; animal sciences; anthropology; architecture; area, ethnic, cultural, and gender studies related; art history, criticism and conservation; art teacher education; audiology and hearing sciences; biochemistry; biology/biological sciences; botany/plant biology; business administration and management; business teacher education; business/commerce; business/managerial economics; chemical engineering; chemistry; civil engineering; classics and languages, literatures and linguistics; clinical laboratory science/medical technology; commercial and advertising art; computer engineering; computer science; consumer economics; cultural studies; dramatic/theater arts; ecology; economics; electrical, electronics and communications engineering; engineering physics; engineering science; English; family and consumer sciences/home economics teacher education; family systems; finance; fine/studio arts; food science; foods, nutrition, and wellness; forestry; French; geography; geology/earth science; German; health teacher education; history; hotel/motel administration; human development and family studies; industrial engineering; interior design; Italian; journalism; kinesiology and exercise science; logistics and materials management; marketing/marketing management; materials engineering; mathematics; mechanical engineering; medical microbiology and bacteriology; multi-/interdisciplinary studies related; music; music teacher education; nuclear engineering; nursing (registered nurse training); ornamental horticulture; parks, recreation and leisure facilities management; philosophy; physics; plant protection and integrated pest management; plant sciences; political science and government; psychology; public administration; radio and television; religious studies; Russian; social work; sociology; Spanish; special education; speech and rhetoric; speech-language pathology; sport and fitness administration/management; statistics; technical teacher education; wildlife and wildlands science and management; zoology/animal biology.

The University of Tennessee at Chattanooga
Applied mathematics; art; art teacher education; biology/biological sciences; business administration and management; chemistry; clinical laboratory science/medical technology; computer science; criminal justice/law enforcement administration; criminal justice/police science; dramatic/theater arts; economics; engineering; engineering/industrial management; English; environmental studies; fine/studio arts; French; geology/earth science; history; human ecology; human services; humanities; kinesiology and exercise science; Latin; legal assistant/paralegal; mass communication/media; mathematics; middle school education; modern Greek; music; nursing (registered nurse training); parks, recreation and leisure; philosophy and religious studies related; physical therapy; physics;

political science and government; psychology; science teacher education; secondary education; social work; sociology; Spanish; special education.

The University of Texas at Austin
Accounting; advertising; aerospace, aeronautical and astronautical engineering; American studies; ancient studies; ancient/classical Greek; anthropology; apparel and textiles; Arabic; archeology; architectural engineering; architecture; art; art history, criticism and conservation; Asian studies; astronomy; athletic training; biochemistry; biological and physical sciences; biology/biological sciences; biomedical/medical engineering; botany/plant biology; business administration and management; business administration, management and operations related; business/commerce; chemical engineering; chemistry; civil engineering; classics and languages, literatures and linguistics; clinical laboratory science/medical technology; communication disorders; communication/speech communication and rhetoric; computer and information sciences; Czech; dance; design and visual communications; dramatic/theater arts; East Asian languages; ecology; economics; electrical, electronics and communications engineering; English; English composition; ethnic, cultural minority, and gender studies related; European studies; family and consumer sciences/human sciences; finance; fine/studio arts; foods, nutrition, and wellness; foreign languages and literatures; French; geography; geological and earth sciences/geosciences related; geology/earth science; geophysics and seismology; German; health and physical education; health services/allied health/health sciences; Hebrew; history; human development and family studies; humanities; hydrology and water resources science; interior design; Iranian/Persian languages; Islamic studies; Italian; Jewish/Judaic studies; journalism; Latin; Latin American studies; liberal arts and sciences/liberal studies; linguistics; logistics and materials management; management information systems; marketing/marketing management; mathematics; mathematics and computer science; mechanical engineering; multi-/interdisciplinary studies related; music; music performance; music theory and composition; Near and Middle Eastern studies; nursing (registered nurse training); petroleum engineering; philosophy; physics; political science and government; Portuguese; psychology; public administration; radio and television; religious studies; Russian; Russian studies; Scandinavian languages; Semitic languages; social work; sociology; Spanish; sport and fitness administration/management; Turkish; urban studies/affairs; visual and performing arts; women's studies.

The University of Texas at Dallas
Accounting; American studies; applied mathematics; audiology and speech-language pathology; biochemistry; biology/biological sciences; business/commerce; chemistry; cognitive psychology and psycholinguistics; computer and information sciences; computer engineering; computer science; computer software engineering; criminology; economics; electrical, electronics and communications engineering; ethnic, cultural minority, and gender studies related; finance; geography; geology/earth science; history; humanities; interdisciplinary studies; international business/trade/commerce; literature; mathematics; molecular biology; neuroscience; physics; political science and government; psychology; public administration; sociology; statistics; visual and performing arts.

University of the Pacific
Art; art history, criticism and conservation; audiology and speech-language pathology; biochemistry; biology/biological sciences; biomedical/medical engineering; business administration and management; chemistry; chemistry related; civil engineering; classics and languages, literatures and linguistics; commercial and advertising art; communication/speech communication and rhetoric; computer engineering; computer science; dramatic/theater arts; economics; education; electrical, electronics and communications engineering; engineering physics; engineering/industrial management; English; environmental studies; fine/studio arts; French; geology/earth science; German; history; information science/studies; interdisciplinary studies; international relations and affairs; Japanese; kinesiology and exercise science; mathematics; mechanical engineering; music; music history, literature, and theory; music manage-

ment and merchandising; music teacher education; music theory and composition; music therapy; pharmacy; philosophy; physical sciences; physics; piano and organ; political science and government; psychology; religious studies; social sciences; sociology; Spanish; special education; voice and opera.

University of the Sciences in Philadelphia

Biochemistry; bioinformatics; biology/biological sciences; chemistry; clinical laboratory science/medical technology; computer science; environmental science; health services/allied health/health sciences; health/medical psychology; marketing/marketing management; medical pharmacology and pharmaceutical sciences; medicinal and pharmaceutical chemistry; microbiology; pharmacology and toxicology; pharmacy; pharmaceutical sciences, and administration related; psychology.

University of Tulsa

Accounting; anthropology; applied mathematics; art history, criticism and conservation; arts management; athletic training; audiology and speech-language pathology; biochemistry; biology/biological sciences; business administration and management; business/commerce; chemical engineering; chemistry; communication/speech communication and rhetoric; computer science; dramatic/theater arts; early childhood education; economics; education; electrical, electronics and communications engineering; elementary education; engineering physics; English; environmental studies; film/cinema studies; finance; fine/studio arts; French; geology/earth science; geophysics and seismology; German; history; information science/studies; information technology; international business/trade/commerce; kinesiology and exercise science; legal professions and studies related; liberal arts and sciences/liberal studies; management information systems; marketing/marketing management; mathematics; mathematics teacher education; mechanical engineering; music; music performance; music related; music teacher education; music theory and composition; nursing (registered nurse training); organizational behavior; petroleum engineering; philosophy; physics; piano and organ; political science and government; psychology; religious studies; Russian studies; sociology; Spanish; special education (hearing impaired); sport and fitness administration/management; voice and opera.

University of Utah

Accounting; anthropology; Arabic; architecture; architecture related; art; art history, criticism and conservation; Asian studies; audiology and speech-language pathology; ballet; biology/biological sciences; biomedical/medical engineering; business administration and management; business, management, and marketing related; business/commerce; cell biology and histology; chemical engineering; chemistry; Chinese; civil engineering; classics and languages, literatures and linguistics; communication/speech communication and rhetoric; computer engineering; computer science; dance; developmental and child psychology; dramatic/theater arts; economics; education; electrical, electronics and communications engineering; elementary education; engineering; English; environmental studies; family and consumer economics related; family resource management; film/cinema studies; finance; French; geography; geological and earth sciences/geosciences related; geological/geophysical engineering; geology/earth science; geophysics and seismology; German; health and physical education; health services/allied health/health sciences; history; human development and family studies; humanities; international/global studies; Japanese; kinesiology and exercise science; linguistics; management information systems; marketing/marketing management; mass communication/media; materials engineering; mathematics; mechanical engineering; metallurgical engineering; meteorology; mining and mineral engineering; music; Near and Middle Eastern studies; nursing (registered nurse training); occupational therapy; parks, recreation and leisure; pharmacy; philosophy; physical sciences; physical therapy; physics; political science and government; pre-pharmacy studies; psychology; public relations/image management; radio and television; Russian; secondary education; social sciences; social work; sociology; Spanish; special education; speech and rhetoric; urban studies/affairs; visual and performing arts; women's studies.

University of Virginia

Aerospace, aeronautical and astronautical engineering; African American/Black studies; anthropology; architectural history and criticism; architecture; area studies related; art; astronomy; audiology and speech-language pathology; biology/biological sciences; biomedical/medical engineering; business/commerce; chemical engineering; chemistry; city/urban, community and regional planning; civil engineering; classics and languages, literatures and linguistics; comparative literature; computer and information sciences; computer engineering; cultural studies; dramatic/theater arts; economics; electrical, electronics and communications engineering; engineering; English; environmental science; French; German; history; international relations and affairs; Italian; liberal arts and sciences/liberal studies; mathematics; mechanical engineering; multi-/interdisciplinary studies related; music; nursing (registered nurse training); philosophy; physical education teaching and coaching; physics; political science and government; psychology; religious studies; Slavic languages; sociology; Spanish; systems engineering.

University of Washington

Accounting; aerospace, aeronautical and astronautical engineering; African American/Black studies; Air Force R.O.T.C./air science; American Indian/Native American studies; ancient/classical Greek; anthropology; applied mathematics; architecture; Army R.O.T.C./military science; art; art history, criticism and conservation; Asian studies; Asian studies (East); Asian studies (South); Asian studies (Southeast); astronomy; atmospheric sciences and meteorology; audiology and speech-language pathology; bilingual and multilingual education; biochemistry; biology teacher education; biology/biological sciences; biostatistics; botany/plant biology; business administration and management; business/commerce; Canadian studies; cell biology and histology; ceramic arts and ceramics; ceramic sciences and engineering; chemical engineering; chemistry; Chinese; city/urban, community and regional planning; civil engineering; classics and languages, literatures and linguistics; clinical laboratory science/medical technology; commercial and advertising art; communication/speech communication and rhetoric; comparative literature; computer and information sciences; computer engineering; computer science; construction management; construction management; creative writing; criminal justice/law enforcement administration; cultural studies; dance; data processing and data processing technology; dental hygiene; dramatic/theater arts; economics; education; education (multiple levels); electrical, electronics and communications engineering; elementary education; engineering; English; English as a second/foreign language (teaching); environmental health; environmental studies; European studies; fiber, textile and weaving arts; fishing and fisheries sciences and management; forest engineering; forest sciences and biology; forest/forest resources management; forestry; French; general studies; geography; geology/earth science; geophysics and seismology; German; Hispanic-American, Puerto Rican, and Mexican-American/Chicano studies; history and philosophy of science and technology; humanities; industrial design; industrial engineering; information science/studies; interdisciplinary studies; interior architecture; international business/trade/commerce; international relations and affairs; Italian; Japanese; Jewish/Judaic studies; landscape architecture; Latin; Latin American studies; liberal arts and sciences/liberal studies; linguistics; management information systems; management science; materials engineering; maternal/child health and neonatal nursing; mathematics; mechanical engineering; medical microbiology and bacteriology; metal and jewelry arts; metallurgical engineering; molecular biology; music; music history, literature, and theory; music performance; music teacher education; music theory and composition; musical instrument fabrication and repair; musicology and ethnomusicology; natural resources management and policy; Navy/Marine Corps R.O.T.C./naval science; Near and Middle Eastern studies; nursing (registered nurse training); occupational therapy; oceanography (chemical and physical); orthotics/prosthetics; painting; pharmacy; philosophy; photography; physical therapy; physician assistant; physics; piano and organ; political science and government; printmaking; psychology; public administration; public health; public health/community nursing; religious studies; Romance languages; Russian; Russian studies; Scandinavian languages; Scandinavian studies; science teacher education;

sculpture; secondary education; Slavic languages; social sciences; social work; sociology; Spanish; speech and rhetoric; statistics; technical and business writing; violin, viola, guitar and other stringed instruments; voice and opera; wildlife and wildlands science and management; women's studies; wood science and wood products/pulp and paper technology; zoology/animal biology.

University of Wisconsin–La Crosse

Accounting; archeology; art; athletic training; biology/biological sciences; business administration and management; chemistry; clinical laboratory science/medical technology; communication/speech communication and rhetoric; computer and information sciences; dramatic/theater arts; economics; elementary education; English; finance; French; general studies; geography; German; health teacher education; history; international business/trade/commerce; kinesiology and exercise science; management information systems; marketing/marketing management; mathematics; microbiology; music; nuclear medical technology; parks, recreation and leisure facilities management; philosophy; physical therapy; physician assistant; physics; political science and government; psychology; rehabilitation and therapeutic professions related; science teacher education; social studies teacher education; sociology; Spanish; therapeutic recreation.

University of Wisconsin–Madison

Accounting; actuarial science; advertising; African languages; African studies; African American/Black studies; agricultural business and management; agricultural economics; agricultural teacher education; agricultural/biological engineering and bioengineering; agriculture; agronomy and crop science; American studies; animal genetics; animal sciences; anthropology; applied art; applied mathematics; art; art history, criticism and conservation; art teacher education; Asian studies; Asian studies (Southeast); astronomy; biochemistry; biology/biological sciences; biomedical/medical engineering; botany/plant biology; broadcast journalism; business administration and management; cartography; cell biology and histology; chemical engineering; chemistry; child development; Chinese; civil engineering; classics and languages, literatures and linguistics; clinical laboratory science/medical technology; clothing/textiles; comparative literature; computer engineering; computer science; construction management; consumer services and advocacy; dairy science; developmental and child psychology; dietetics; dramatic/theater arts; electrical, electronics and communications engineering; elementary education; engineering; engineering mechanics; engineering physics; English; entomology; environmental/environmental health engineering; experimental psychology; family and consumer economics related; family and consumer sciences/home economics teacher education; family and consumer sciences/human sciences; farm and ranch management; fashion merchandising; finance; food science; foods, nutrition, and wellness; forestry; French; geography; geology/earth science; geophysics and seismology; German; Hebrew; Hispanic-American, Puerto Rican, and Mexican-American/Chicano studies; history; history and philosophy of science and technology; horticultural science; hydrology and water resources science; industrial engineering; insurance; interior design; international relations and affairs; Italian; Japanese; journalism; kindergarten/preschool education; labor and industrial relations; landscape architecture; Latin; Latin American studies; linguistics; mass communication/media; mathematics; mechanical engineering; medical microbiology and bacteriology; metallurgical engineering; mining and mineral engineering; modern Greek; molecular biology; music; music teacher education; natural resources management and policy; nuclear engineering; nursing (registered nurse training); occupational therapy; parks, recreation and leisure; pharmacology; pharmacy; philosophy; physical education teaching and coaching; physician assistant; political science and government; Portuguese; poultry science; psychology; public relations/image management; radio and television; real estate; Russian; Scandinavian languages; science teacher education; secondary education; Slavic languages; social sciences; social work; sociology; Spanish; special education; speech therapy; statistics; survey technology; toxicology; urban studies/affairs; wildlife and wildlands science and management; women's studies; zoology/animal biology.

University of Wisconsin–River Falls

Accounting; agricultural business and management; agricultural teacher education; agricultural/biological engineering and bioengineering; agriculture; agronomy and crop science; animal sciences; art; art teacher education; biochemistry; biology teacher education; biology/biological sciences; biotechnology; broadcast journalism; business administration and management; chemistry; chemistry teacher education; communication disorders; computer and information sciences; computer science; computer teacher education; dairy science; dramatic/theater arts; economics; education; elementary education; engineering technology; English; English as a second/foreign language (teaching); English/language arts teacher education; environmental studies; equestrian studies; finance; food science; French; French language teacher education; geography; geology/earth science; German; German language teacher education; history; history teacher education; horticultural science; information science/studies; journalism; land use planning and management; liberal arts and sciences/liberal studies; management information systems; marketing/marketing management; mathematics; mathematics teacher education; music; music teacher education; natural resources/conservation; natural sciences; physical education teaching and coaching; physical sciences; physics; physics teacher education; political science and government; pre-dentistry studies; pre-law studies; pre-medical studies; pre-pharmacy studies; pre-veterinary studies; psychology; public relations/image management; radio and television; science teacher education; secondary education; social science teacher education; social sciences; social studies teacher education; social work; sociology; soil science and agronomy; Spanish; Spanish language teacher education; speech and rhetoric; speech therapy.

Ursinus College

American studies; anthropology; art; Asian studies (East); biological and physical sciences; biology/biological sciences; business administration and management; chemistry; civil engineering; classics; classics and languages, literatures and linguistics; computer science; economics; electrical, electronics and communications engineering; English; environmental studies; fine arts related; French; German; health and physical education; history; international relations and affairs; mass communication/media; mathematics; mechanical engineering; metallurgical engineering; multi-/interdisciplinary studies related; neuroscience; philosophy; physics; political science and government; psychology; social sciences related; sociology; Spanish.

Valparaiso University

Accounting; actuarial science; American studies; art; art teacher education; Asian studies (East); atmospheric sciences and meteorology; biochemistry; biological and physical sciences; biology teacher education; biology/biological sciences; chemistry; chemistry teacher education; civil engineering; classics and languages, literatures and linguistics; communication and journalism related; computer engineering; computer science; criminology; drama and dance teacher education; dramatic/theater arts; economics; economics related; electrical, electronics and communications engineering; elementary education; English; English/language arts teacher education; environmental science; finance; fine/studio arts; foreign language teacher education; French; French language teacher education; geography; geography teacher education; geology/earth science; German; German language teacher education; health and physical education; history; history teacher education; humanities; international business/trade/commerce; international economics; international relations and affairs; journalism; kinesiology and exercise science; management science; management sciences and quantitative methods related; marketing/marketing management; mass communication/media; mathematics; mathematics teacher education; mechanical engineering; middle school education; multi-/interdisciplinary studies related; music; music management and merchandising; music performance; music teacher education; music theory and composition; nursing (registered nurse training); organizational communication; philosophy; physical education teaching and coaching; physics; physics teacher education; piano and organ; political science and government; psychology; psychology teacher education; public relations/image management; radio and television; religious/sacred music; science teacher education; secondary education; social science teacher education; social sciences; social work; sociology; Spanish; Spanish language teacher education; sport and fitness administration/management; teacher assistant/aide; technical and business writing; theology; voice and opera.

Vanderbilt University
African studies; African American/Black studies; American studies; anthropology; art; Asian studies (East); astronomy; biology/biological sciences; biomedical/medical engineering; chemical engineering; chemistry; civil engineering; classics and languages, literatures and linguistics; cognitive psychology and psycholinguistics; computer engineering; computer science; dramatic/theater arts; ecology; economics; education; electrical, electronics and communications engineering; elementary education; engineering; engineering science; English; European studies; French; geology/earth science; German; history; human development and family studies; human resources management; interdisciplinary studies; kindergarten/preschool education; Latin American studies; mass communication/media; mathematics; mechanical engineering; molecular biology; music; philosophy; physics; piano and organ; political science and government; Portuguese; psychology; religious studies; Russian; secondary education; sociology; Spanish; special education; urban studies/affairs; violin, viola, guitar and other stringed instruments; voice and opera; wind/percussion instruments.

Vassar College
African studies; American studies; ancient/classical Greek; anthropology; art history, criticism and conservation; Asian studies; astronomy; biochemistry; biology/biological sciences; chemistry; Chinese; classics and languages, literatures and linguistics; cognitive psychology and psycholinguistics; computer and information sciences; dramatic/theater arts; economics; English; environmental science; environmental studies; film/cinema studies; fine/studio arts; French; geography; geology/earth science; German; history; interdisciplinary studies; international relations and affairs; Italian; Japanese; Jewish/Judaic studies; Latin; Latin American studies; liberal arts and sciences and humanities related; mass communication/media; mathematics; medieval and Renaissance studies; multi-/interdisciplinary studies related; music; philosophy; physics; physiological psychology/psychobiology; political science and government; psychology; religious studies; Russian; science, technology and society; sociology; Spanish; urban studies/affairs; visual and performing arts; women's studies.

Villanova University
Accounting; art history, criticism and conservation; astronomy; astrophysics; biology/biological sciences; business administration and management; business/managerial economics; chemical engineering; chemistry; civil engineering; classics and languages, literatures and linguistics; computer engineering; computer science; criminal justice/law enforcement administration; economics; education; electrical, electronics and communications engineering; elementary education; English; finance; French; geography; German; history; human services; information science/studies; international business/trade/commerce; Italian; liberal arts and sciences/liberal studies; management information systems; marketing/marketing management; mass communication/media; mathematics; mechanical engineering; nursing (registered nurse training); philosophy; physics; political science and government; psychology; religious studies; secondary education; sociology; Spanish.

Virginia Military Institute
Biology/biological sciences; chemistry; civil engineering; computer science; economics; electrical, electronics and communications engineering; English; history; international relations and affairs; mathematics; mechanical engineering; modern languages; physics; psychology.

Virginia Polytechnic Institute and State University
Accounting; aerospace, aeronautical and astronautical engineering; agricultural economics; agronomy and crop science; animal sciences; architecture; art; biochemistry; biology/biological sciences; business administration and management; business family and consumer sciences/human sciences; business/managerial economics; chemical engineering; chemistry; civil engineering; clothing/textiles; communication/speech communication and rhetoric; computer and information sciences; computer engineering; computer science; construction management; consumer/homemaking education; dairy science; dramatic/theater arts; economics; electrical, electronics and communications engineering; engineering mechanics; English; environmental studies; finance; food science; foods, nutrition, and wellness; forestry; French; geography; geology/earth science; German; history; horticultural science; hotel/motel administration; human development and family studies; industrial design; industrial engineering; information science/studies; interdisciplinary studies; interior design; international relations and affairs; landscape architecture; management science; marketing/marketing management; materials engineering; mathematics; mechanical engineering; mining and mineral engineering; music; ocean engineering; philosophy; physics; political science and government; poultry science; psychology; public policy analysis; secondary education; sociology; Spanish; statistics.

Wabash College
Art; biology/biological sciences; chemistry; classics and languages, literatures and linguistics; dramatic/theater arts; economics; English; French; German; history; Latin; mathematics; modern Greek; music; philosophy; physics; political science and government; pre-law studies; pre-medical studies; pre-veterinary studies; psychology; religious studies; Spanish; speech and rhetoric.

Wagner College
Accounting; anthropology; art; arts management; biology/biological sciences; business administration and management; chemistry; computer and information sciences related; computer science; dramatic/theater arts; economics; education; elementary education; English; finance; history; international relations and affairs; kindergarten/preschool education; mathematics; medical microbiology and bacteriology; music; nursing (registered nurse training); physician assistant; physics; political science and government; pre-dentistry studies; pre-engineering; pre-law studies; pre-medical studies; pre-theology/pre-ministerial studies; psychology; public administration; secondary education; sociology; Spanish.

Wake Forest University
Accounting; ancient/classical Greek; anthropology; art history, criticism and conservation; biology/biological sciences; business/commerce; chemistry; Chinese; classics and languages, literatures and linguistics; clinical laboratory science/medical technology; communication/speech communication and rhetoric; computer and information sciences; dramatic/theater arts; econometrics and quantitative economics; economics; education (multiple levels); engineering; English; finance; fine/studio arts; French; German; history; Japanese; kinesiology and exercise science; Latin; management information systems; management science; mathematics; music; philosophy; physician assistant; physics; political science and government; psychology; religious studies; Russian; sociology; Spanish.

Wartburg College
Accounting; art; art teacher education; arts management; biochemistry; biology/biological sciences; broadcast journalism; business administration and management; chemistry; clinical laboratory science/medical technology; commercial and advertising art; computer science; economics; elementary education; engineering; English; English composition; finance; French; German; history; history teacher education; information science/studies; international business/trade/commerce; international relations and affairs; journalism; kindergarten/preschool education; marketing/marketing management; mass communication/media; mathematics; mathematics teacher education; music; music performance; music teacher education; music theory and composition; music therapy; occupational therapy; philosophy; physical education teaching and coaching; physics; political science and government; psychology; public relations/image management; religious studies; religious/sacred music;

secondary education; social science teacher education; social work; sociology; Spanish; speech/theater education; sport and fitness administration/management.

Washington & Jefferson College

Accounting; art; art teacher education; biochemistry; biology/biological sciences; biophysics; business/commerce; cell biology and anatomical sciences related; chemistry; chemistry related; economics; education; English; environmental studies; French; German; history; information technology; international business/trade/commerce; international/global studies; mathematics; multi-/interdisciplinary studies related; music; philosophy; physics; political science and government; psychology; sociology; Spanish; theater literature, history and criticism.

Washington and Lee University

Accounting; anthropology; archeology; art history, criticism and conservation; Asian studies (East); biochemistry; biology/biological sciences; business administration and management; chemical engineering; chemistry; classics; computer and information sciences; computer science; dramatic/theater arts; economics; engineering physics; English; fine/studio arts; foreign languages and literatures; French; geological and earth sciences/geosciences related; geology/earth science; German; history; journalism; mathematics; medieval and Renaissance studies; multi-/interdisciplinary studies related; music; neuroscience; philosophy; physics; political science and government; psychology; public policy analysis; religious studies; Russian studies; sociology; Spanish.

Washington College

American studies; anthropology; art; biology/biological sciences; business administration and management; chemistry; computer science; dramatic/theater arts; ecology; economics; English; environmental studies; foreign languages and literatures; French; German; history; humanities; international relations and affairs; Latin American studies; liberal arts and sciences/liberal studies; mathematics; multi-/interdisciplinary studies related; music; philosophy; physics; physiological psychology/psychobiology; political science and government; pre-dentistry studies; pre-law studies; pre-medical studies; pre-veterinary studies; psychology; sociology; Spanish.

Washington University in St. Louis

Accounting; advertising; African studies; African American/Black studies; American literature; American studies; ancient studies; ancient/classical Greek; anthropology; applied art; applied mathematics; Arabic; archeology; architectural engineering technology; architectural technology; architecture; architecture related; area studies; area studies related; area, ethnic, cultural, and gender studies related; art; art history, criticism and conservation; art teacher education; Asian studies; Asian studies (East); biochemistry; biological and biomedical sciences related; biological and physical sciences; biology teacher education; biology/biological sciences; biomedical/medical engineering; biophysics; biopsychology; business administration and management; business administration, management and operations related; business/commerce; business/managerial economics; ceramic arts and ceramics; chemical engineering; chemistry; chemistry related; chemistry teacher education; Chinese; civil engineering; classics and languages, literatures and linguistics; cognitive psychology and psycholinguistics; commercial and advertising art; communication and journalism related; communication/speech communication and rhetoric; comparative literature; computer and information sciences; computer and information sciences and support services related; computer engineering; computer science; computer/information technology services administration related; creative writing; cultural studies; dance; design and visual communications; drama and dance teacher education; dramatic/theater arts; drawing; East Asian languages related; economics; education; education (K-12); education (specific levels and methods) related; electrical, electronics and communications engineering; elementary education; engineering; English; English language and literature related; English literature (British and Commonwealth); English/language arts teacher education; entrepreneurship; environmental studies; ethnic, cultural minority, and gender studies related; European studies; fashion/apparel

design; film/cinema studies; finance; fine/studio arts; French; French language teacher education; geology/earth science; German; German language teacher education; Germanic languages; graphic design; health professions related; Hebrew; history; history teacher education; human resources management; humanities; illustration; industrial and organizational psychology; information science/studies; international business/trade/commerce; international economics; international finance; international relations and affairs; Islamic studies; Italian; Japanese; Jewish/Judaic studies; Latin; Latin American studies; liberal arts and sciences/liberal studies; literature; marketing related; marketing/marketing management; mathematics; mathematics and computer science; mathematics teacher education; mechanical engineering; medieval and Renaissance studies; merchandising, sales, and marketing operations related (general); middle school education; modern languages; multi-/interdisciplinary studies related; music; music history, literature, and theory; music theory and composition; natural resources/conservation; natural sciences; Near and Middle Eastern studies; neuroscience; operations management; painting; philosophy; philosophy and religious studies related; photography; physics; physics teacher education; political science and government; pre-dentistry studies; pre-medical studies; pre-pharmacy studies; pre-veterinary studies; printmaking; psychology; regional studies; religious studies; Romance languages; Russian; Russian studies; science teacher education; science, technology and society; sculpture; secondary education; social and philosophical foundations of education; social science teacher education; social sciences; social sciences related; social studies teacher education; Spanish; Spanish language teacher education; statistics; systems engineering; systems science and theory; theater literature, history and criticism; urban studies/affairs; voice and opera; women's studies.

Webb Institute

Naval architecture and marine engineering.

Wellesley College

African studies; African American/Black studies; American studies; ancient/classical Greek; anthropology; archeology; architecture; art history, criticism and conservation; Asian studies (East); astronomy; astrophysics; biochemistry; biology/biological sciences; chemistry; Chinese; classics and languages, literatures and linguistics; cognitive psychology and psycholinguistics; comparative literature; computer science; digital communication and media/multimedia; dramatic/theater arts; economics; English; environmental studies; ethnic, cultural minority, and gender studies related; film/cinema studies; fine/studio arts; French; geology/earth science; German; German studies; history; international relations and affairs; Islamic studies; Italian; Italian studies; Japanese; Jewish/Judaic studies; Latin; Latin American studies; linguistics; mathematics; medieval and Renaissance studies; music; Near and Middle Eastern studies; neuroscience; peace studies and conflict resolution; philosophy; physics; political science and government; psychology; religious studies; Russian; Russian studies; sociology; Spanish; women's studies.

Wells College

African American/Black studies; American studies; anthropology; art; art history, criticism and conservation; biochemistry; biology/biological sciences; business administration and management; chemistry; computer science; creative writing; dance; dramatic/theater arts; economics; education; elementary education; engineering; English; environmental studies; fine/studio arts; French; history; international relations and affairs; mathematics; molecular biology; music; philosophy; physics; political science and government; pre-dentistry studies; pre-law studies; pre-medical studies; pre-veterinary studies; psychology; public policy analysis; religious studies; secondary education; sociology; Spanish; women's studies.

Wesleyan College

Advertising; American studies; art history, criticism and conservation; biology/biological sciences; business administration and management; chemistry; communication/speech communication and rhetoric; computer and information sciences; early childhood education; economics; education; English; environmental science; fine/studio arts; French; history; humanities; interdisciplinary studies; international business/trade/commerce; international relations and affairs; mathematics; middle school education; music; philosophy; physical sciences; physics; political science and government; psychology; religious studies; social sciences; Spanish.

Wesleyan University
African American/Black studies; American studies; anthropology; archeology; art; art history, criticism and conservation; Asian studies (East); astronomy; biochemistry; biology/biological sciences; chemistry; classics and languages, literatures and linguistics; computer science; dance; dramatic/theater arts; economics; English; environmental studies; European studies (Central and Eastern); film/cinema studies; fine/studio arts; French; geology/earth science; German; health and physical education; history; humanities; interdisciplinary studies; Italian; Latin American studies; mathematics; medieval and Renaissance studies; molecular biology; music; philosophy; physics; political science and government; psychology; religious studies; Romance languages; Russian; Russian studies; science, technology and society; social sciences; sociology; Spanish; women's studies.

Western Washington University
Accounting; accounting and computer science; American studies; anthropology; archeology; art; art history, criticism and conservation; art teacher education; Asian studies; Asian studies (East); audiology and speech-language pathology; biochemistry; biological and physical sciences; biology/biological sciences; business administration and management; Canadian studies; cell and molecular biology; cell biology and histology; ceramic arts and ceramics; chemistry; chemistry teacher education; classics and languages, literatures and linguistics; communication/speech communication and rhetoric; community health services counseling; computer science; counselor education/school counseling and guidance; creative writing; cultural studies; design and visual communications; developmental and child psychology; dramatic/theater arts; drawing; economics; education; education (multiple levels); educational leadership and administration; electrical, electronic and communications engineering technology; elementary education; engineering related; engineering technology; English; environmental biology; environmental education; environmental science; environmental studies; fiber, textile and weaving arts; finance; fine/studio arts; French; general studies; geography; geology/earth science; geophysics and seismology; German; graphic design; health teacher education; history; human resources management; human services; humanities; industrial design; industrial technology; interdisciplinary studies; intermedia/multimedia; international business/trade/commerce; jazz/jazz studies; journalism; kindergarten/preschool education; kinesiology and exercise science; Latin American studies; liberal arts and sciences/liberal studies; linguistics; literature; management information systems; manufacturing technology; marine biology and biological oceanography; marketing/marketing management; mathematics; music; music history, literature, and theory; music teacher education; operations management; painting; parks, recreation and leisure; philosophy; physical education teaching and coaching; physics; plastics engineering technology; political science and government; printmaking; psychology; science teacher education; sculpture; secondary education; sociology; Spanish; special education; visual and performing arts; women's studies.

Westminster College (UT)
Accounting; airline pilot and flight crew; art; arts management; aviation/airway management; biology teacher education; biology/biological sciences; business administration and management; business/commerce; business/managerial economics; chemistry; chemistry teacher education; communication/speech communication and rhetoric; computer science; economics; elementary education; English; environmental studies; finance; financial planning and services; history; international business/trade/commerce; management information systems and services related; marketing/marketing management; mathematics; neuroscience; nursing

(registered nurse training); philosophy; physics; political science and government; psychology; social science teacher education; social sciences; sociology.

Westmont College
Anthropology; art; art teacher education; biology/biological sciences; business/commerce; business/managerial economics; chemistry; communication/speech communication and rhetoric; computer science; dance; dramatic/theater arts; economics; education; elementary education; engineering physics; English; English/language arts teacher education; French; history; kinesiology and exercise science; liberal arts and sciences/liberal studies; mathematics; mathematics teacher education; modern languages; music; neuroscience; philosophy; physical education teaching and coaching; physics; political science and government; pre-dentistry studies; pre-law studies; pre-medical studies; pre-pharmacy studies; pre-theology/pre-ministerial studies; pre-veterinary studies; psychology; religious studies; secondary education; social science teacher education; social sciences; sociology; Spanish.

Wheaton College (IL)
Anthropology; archeology; art; biblical studies; biology/biological sciences; business/managerial economics; chemistry; classics and classical languages related; communication/speech communication and rhetoric; computer science; economics; elementary education; engineering related; English; environmental studies; French; geology/earth science; German; health services/allied health/health sciences; history; international relations and affairs; mathematics; multi-/interdisciplinary studies related; music; music history, literature, and theory; music performance; music related; music teacher education; music theory and composition; nursing related; philosophy; physics; political science and government; psychology; religious education; religious studies; science teacher education; secondary education; social studies teacher education; sociology; Spanish.

Wheaton College (MA)
African studies; American studies; ancient studies; ancient/classical Greek; anthropology; art history, criticism and conservation; Asian studies; astronomy; biochemistry; bioinformatics; biology/biological sciences; chemistry; classics and languages, literatures and linguistics; computer science; dance; dramatic/theater arts; economics; English; fine/studio arts; French studies; German; German studies; Hispanic-American, Puerto Rican, and Mexican-American/Chicano studies; history; international relations and affairs; Italian studies; Latin; mathematics; music; philosophy; physics; physiological psychology/psychobiology; political science and government; psychology; religious studies; Russian; Russian studies; sociology; women's studies.

Whitman College
Anthropology; art; art history, criticism and conservation; Asian studies; astronomy; astrophysics; biochemistry; biochemistry/biophysics and molecular biology; biology/biological sciences; biophysics; chemistry; chemistry related; classics and languages, literatures and linguistics; communication/speech communication and rhetoric; dramatic/theater arts; economics; English; ethnic, cultural minority, and gender studies related; film/cinema studies; French; geological and earth sciences/geosciences related; geology/earth science; German; history; mathematics; mathematics and computer science; molecular biology; music; music history, literature, and theory; music performance; music theory and composition; philosophy; physics; physics related; political science and government; political science and government related; psychology; religious studies; social sciences related; sociology; Spanish.

Whitworth University
Accounting; American studies; art; art teacher education; arts management; athletic training; biology/biological sciences; business administration and management; chemistry; computer science; dramatic/theater arts; economics; elementary education; English; fine/studio arts; French; history; international business/trade/commerce; international relations and affairs; journalism; mass communication/media; mathematics; music; music teacher education; nursing (registered nurse training); peace studies

and conflict resolution; philosophy; physical education teaching and coaching; physics; piano and organ; political science and government; pre-dentistry studies; pre-law studies; pre-medical studies; pre-veterinary studies; psychology; religious studies; secondary education; sociology; Spanish; special education; speech and rhetoric; voice and opera.

Willamette University
American studies; anthropology; art; art history, criticism and conservation; Asian studies; biology/biological sciences; chemistry; classics and languages, literatures and linguistics; comparative literature; computer science; dramatic/theater arts; economics; English; environmental science; fine/studio arts; French; German; history; humanities; international/global studies; Japanese studies; kinesiology and exercise science; Latin American studies; mathematics; music; music performance; music theory and composition; philosophy; physics; piano and organ; political science and government; psychology; religious studies; science technologies related; sociology; Spanish; speech and rhetoric; violin, viola, guitar and other stringed instruments; voice and opera; women's studies.

William Jewell College
Accounting; art; art teacher education; biochemistry; biology/biological sciences; business administration and management; business/managerial economics; cell biology and histology; chemistry; chemistry teacher education; clinical laboratory science/medical technology; computer science; drama and dance teacher education; dramatic/theater arts; economics; elementary education; English; English/language arts teacher education; foreign language teacher education; French; French language teacher education; history; information science/studies; international business/trade/commerce; international relations and affairs; mathematics; middle school education; molecular biology; music; music performance; music teacher education; music theory and composition; nursing (registered nurse training); parks, recreation and leisure; philosophy; physical education teaching and coaching; physics; physics teacher education; political science and government; psychology; religious studies; religious/sacred music; secondary education; Spanish; Spanish language teacher education; speech and rhetoric; speech teacher education.

Williams College
American studies; anthropology; art history, criticism and conservation; Asian studies; astronomy; astrophysics; biology/biological sciences; chemistry; Chinese; classics and languages, literatures and linguistics; computer science; dramatic/theater arts; economics; English; ethnic, cultural minority, and gender studies related; fine/studio arts; French; geology/earth science; German; history; Japanese; literature; mathematics; music; philosophy; physics; political science and government; psychology; religious studies; Russian; sociology; Spanish; women's studies.

Winona State University
Accounting; advertising; applied art; applied mathematics; art; art teacher education; athletic training; aviation/airway management; biological and physical sciences; biology/biological sciences; broadcast journalism; business administration and management; business teacher education; business/managerial economics; chemical engineering; chemistry; clinical laboratory science/medical technology; clinical/medical laboratory technology; commercial and advertising art; computer and information sciences; computer programming; computer science; consumer merchandising/retailing management; corrections; criminal justice/law enforcement administration; criminal justice/police science; cytotechnology; dramatic/theater arts; drawing; ecology; economics; education; elementary education; engineering; English; environmental biology; finance; fine/studio arts; French; geology/earth science; German; health science; health teacher education; health/health care administration; history; human resources management; information science/studies; international relations and affairs; journalism; kindergarten/preschool education; kinesiology and exercise science; labor and industrial relations; legal assistant/paralegal; legal studies; liberal arts and sciences/liberal studies; management information systems; marketing/marketing management; mass communication/media; materials engineering; mathematics;

mechanical engineering; middle school education; music; music management and merchandising; music teacher education; natural resources/conservation; natural sciences; nursing (registered nurse training); parks, recreation and leisure; parks, recreation and leisure facilities management; physical education teaching and coaching; physical sciences; physical therapy; physics; political science and government; polymer chemistry; polymer/plastics engineering; pre-dentistry studies; pre-law studies; pre-medical studies; pre-veterinary studies; psychology; public administration; public health; public relations/image management; quality control technology; radio and television; reading teacher education; science teacher education; secondary education; social sciences; social work; sociology; Spanish; special education; speech and rhetoric; sport and fitness administration/management; statistics; telecommunications; therapeutic recreation; voice and opera; wildlife and wildlands science and management; wildlife biology; zoology/animal biology.

Wisconsin Lutheran College
Art; biochemistry; biology/biological sciences; business/managerial economics; chemistry; communication and journalism related; communication/speech communication and rhetoric; dramatic/theater arts; elementary education; English; history; interdisciplinary studies; mathematics; multi-/interdisciplinary studies related; music; political science and government; psychology; social sciences; Spanish; theology.

Wittenberg University
American studies; art; Asian studies (East); biochemistry/biophysics and molecular biology; biology/biological sciences; business administration and management; chemistry; communication/speech communication and rhetoric; computer science; dramatic/theater arts; economics; education; English; French; geography; geological and earth sciences/geosciences related; geology/earth science; German; history; liberal arts and sciences/liberal studies; mathematics; music; philosophy; physics; political science and government; psychology; religious studies; religious/sacred music; Russian studies; sociology; Spanish.

Wofford College
Accounting; art history, criticism and conservation; biology/biological sciences; business/managerial economics; chemistry; Chinese; computer science; creative writing; dramatic/theater arts; economics; English; finance; French; German; history; humanities; international business/trade/commerce; international relations and affairs; mathematics; neuroscience; philosophy; physics; political science and government; pre-dentistry studies; pre-law studies; pre-medical studies; pre-veterinary studies; psychology; religious studies; sociology; Spanish.

Worcester Polytechnic Institute
Actuarial science; aerospace, aeronautical and astronautical engineering; animal genetics; applied mathematics; biochemistry; biology/biological sciences; biology/biotechnology laboratory technician; biomedical sciences; biomedical/medical engineering; business administration and management; cell biology and histology; chemical engineering; chemistry; civil engineering; computer and information sciences; computer engineering; computer science; economics; electrical, electronics and communications engineering; engineering mechanics; engineering physics; engineering related; engineering/industrial management; environmental studies; environmental/environmental health engineering; fluid/thermal sciences; history; history and philosophy of science and technology; humanities; industrial engineering; information science/studies; interdisciplinary studies; intermedia/multimedia; management information systems; materials engineering; materials science; mathematics; mechanical engineering; medical microbiology and bacteriology; medicinal and pharmaceutical chemistry; molecular biology; music; nuclear engineering; philosophy; physical sciences related; physics; robotics; science, technology and society; social sciences; technical and business writing.

Xavier University
Accounting; advertising; art; athletic training; biological and physical sciences; biology teacher education; biology/biological sciences; business

administration and management; business/managerial economics; chemical engineering; chemistry; chemistry teacher education; classics and languages, literatures and linguistics; clinical laboratory science/medical technology; computer science; corrections; criminal justice/safety; economics; education; education (specific levels and methods) related; elementary education; English; entrepreneurship; finance; fine/studio arts; French; German; history; human resources management; international business/trade/commerce; international relations and affairs; liberal arts and sciences/liberal studies; management information systems; marketing/marketing management; mathematics; middle school education; Montessori teacher education; music; music teacher education; natural sciences; nursing science; occupational therapy; philosophy; physics; physics teacher education; political science and government; psychology; public relations/image management; radio and television; science teacher education; social work; sociology; Spanish; special education; sport and fitness administration/management; theology.

Yale University

African studies; African American/Black studies; American studies; ancient/classical Greek; anthropology; applied mathematics; archeology; architecture; art; art history, criticism and conservation; Asian studies (East); astronomy; astrophysics; biology/biological sciences; biomedical/medical engineering; cell biology and anatomical sciences related; chemical engineering; chemistry; Chinese; classics and languages, literatures and linguistics; cognitive psychology and psycholinguistics; computer and information sciences; cultural studies; dramatic/theater arts; ecology; economics; electrical, electronics and communications engineering; engineering physics; engineering science; English; environmental studies; environmental/environmental health engineering; ethnic, cultural minority, and gender studies related; evolutionary biology; film/cinema studies; foreign languages related; French; geological and earth sciences/geosciences related; German; history; humanities; Italian; Japanese; Jewish/Judaic studies; Latin; Latin American studies; linguistics; literature; mathematics; mathematics and computer science; mechanical engineering; molecular biology; multi-/interdisciplinary studies related; music; philosophy; physics; political science and government; Portuguese; psychology; religious studies; Russian; Russian studies; sociology; South Asian languages; Spanish; systems science and theory; women's studies.

GEOGRAPHICAL LISTING OF COLLEGES

NOTES

NOTES

NOTES

NOTES

NOTES

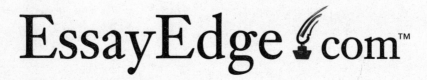

Peterson's
Book Satisfaction Survey

Give Us Your Feedback

Thank you for choosing Peterson's as your source for personalized solutions for your education and career achievement. Please take a few minutes to answer the following questions. Your answers will go a long way in helping us to produce the most user-friendly and comprehensive resources to meet your individual needs.

When completed, please tear out this page and mail it to us at:

Publishing Department
Peterson's, a Nelnet company
2000 Lenox Drive
Lawrenceville, NJ 08648

You can also complete this survey online at **www.petersons.com/booksurvey.**

1. **What is the ISBN of the book you have purchased? (The ISBN can be found on the book's back cover in the lower right-hand corner.)** _____

2. **Where did you purchase this book?**
   ❑ Retailer, such as Barnes & Noble
   ❑ Online reseller, such as Amazon.com
   ❑ Petersons.com
   ❑ Other (please specify) _____

3. **If you purchased this book on Petersons.com, please rate the following aspects of your online purchasing experience on a scale of 4 to 1 (4 = Excellent and 1 = Poor).**

	4	3	2	1
Comprehensiveness of Peterson's Online Bookstore page	❑	❑	❑	❑
Overall online customer experience	❑	❑	❑	❑

4. **Which category best describes you?**
   ❑ High school student
   ❑ Parent of high school student
   ❑ College student
   ❑ Graduate/professional student
   ❑ Returning adult student
   ❑ Teacher
   ❑ Counselor
   ❑ Working professional/military
   ❑ Other (please specify) _____

5. **Rate your overall satisfaction with this book.**

Extremely Satisfied	Satisfied	Not Satisfied
❑	❑	❑

6. **Rate each of the following aspects of this book on a scale of 4 to 1 (4 = Excellent and 1 = Poor).**

	4	3	2	1
Comprehensiveness of the information	❏	❏	❏	❏
Accuracy of the information	❏	❏	❏	❏
Usability	❏	❏	❏	❏
Cover design	❏	❏	❏	❏
Book layout	❏	❏	❏	❏
Special features (e.g., CD, flashcards, charts, etc.)	❏	❏	❏	❏
Value for the money	❏	❏	❏	❏

7. **This book was recommended by:**
   - ❏ Guidance counselor
   - ❏ Parent/guardian
   - ❏ Family member/relative
   - ❏ Friend
   - ❏ Teacher
   - ❏ Not recommended by anyone—I found the book on my own
   - ❏ Other (please specify) _____

8. **Would you recommend this book to others?**

Yes	Not Sure	No
❏	❏	❏

9. **Please provide any additional comments.**

   _____

   _____

   _____

   _____

   _____

Remember, you can tear out this page and mail it to us at:

> Publishing Department
> Peterson's, a Nelnet company
> 2000 Lenox Drive
> Lawrenceville, NJ 08648

or you can complete the survey online at **www.petersons.com/booksurvey**.

Your feedback is important to us at Peterson's, and we thank you for your time!

If you would like us to keep in touch with you about new products and services, please include your e-mail address here: _____